Bioethics and the Law

ASPEN CASEBOOK SERIES

Bioethics and the Law

Third Edition

Janet L. Dolgin

*Jack and Freda Dicker
Distinguished Professor of Health Care Law
Maurice A. Deane School of Law at Hofstra University
Professor of Science Education
Hofstra North Shore–LIJ School of Medicine*

Lois L. Shepherd

*Professor of Public Health Sciences
Center for Biomedical Ethics and Humanities
University of Virginia School of Medicine
Professor of Law
University of Virginia School of Law*

Wolters Kluwer
Law & Business

Published by Wolters Kluwer Law & Business in New York.

Wolters Kluwer Law & Business serves customers worldwide with CCH, Aspen Publishers, and Kluwer Law International products. (www.wolterskluwerlb.com)

To contact Customer Service, e-mail customer.service@wolterskluwer.com, call 1-800-234-1660, fax 1-800-901-9075, or mail correspondence to:

Wolters Kluwer Law & Business
Attn: Order Department
PO Box 990
Frederick, MD 21705

Printed in the United States of America.

1 2 3 4 5 6 7 8 9 0

ISBN 978-1-4548-1076-6

Library of Congress Cataloging-in-Publication Data

Dolgin, Janet L., 1947-
    Bioethics and the law / Janet L. Dolgin, Jack and Freda Dicker Distinguished Professor of Health Care Law, Hofstra University School of Law, Lois L. Shepherd, Center for Biomedical Ethics and Humanities, Professor of Law, Associate Professor, Public Health Sciences, University of Virginia.—Third edition.
        pages cm.—(Aspen casebook series)
    Includes index.
    ISBN 978-1-4548-1076-6 (alk. paper)
    1. Medical laws and legislation—United States. 2. Medical care—Law and legislation—United States. 3. Bioethics—United States. I. Shepherd, Lois L., 1962- II. Title.

    KF3821.D65 2013
    344.7304'1—dc23

                                                                          2012044369

About Wolters Kluwer Law & Business

Wolters Kluwer Law & Business is a leading global provider of intelligent information and digital solutions for legal and business professionals in key specialty areas, and respected educational resources for professors and law students. Wolters Kluwer Law & Business connects legal and business professionals as well as those in the education market with timely, specialized authoritative content and information-enabled solutions to support success through productivity, accuracy and mobility.

Serving customers worldwide, Wolters Kluwer Law & Business products include those under the Aspen Publishers, CCH, Kluwer Law International, Loislaw, Best Case, ftwilliam. com and MediRegs family of products.

CCH products have been a trusted resource since 1913, and are highly regarded resources for legal, securities, antitrust and trade regulation, government contracting, banking, pension, payroll, employment and labor, and healthcare reimbursement and compliance professionals.

Aspen Publishers products provide essential information to attorneys, business professionals and law students. Written by preeminent authorities, the product line offers analytical and practical information in a range of specialty practice areas from securities law and intellectual property to mergers and acquisitions and pension/benefits. Aspen's trusted legal education resources provide professors and students with high-quality, up-to-date and effective resources for successful instruction and study in all areas of the law.

Kluwer Law International products provide the global business community with reliable international legal information in English. Legal practitioners, corporate counsel and business executives around the world rely on Kluwer Law journals, looseleafs, books, and electronic products for comprehensive information in many areas of international legal practice.

Loislaw is a comprehensive online legal research product providing legal content to law firm practitioners of various specializations. Loislaw provides attorneys with the ability to quickly and efficiently find the necessary legal information they need, when and where they need it, by facilitating access to primary law as well as state-specific law, records, forms and treatises.

Best Case Solutions is the leading bankruptcy software product to the bankruptcy industry. It provides software and workflow tools to flawlessly streamline petition preparation and the electronic filing process, while timely incorporating ever-changing court requirements.

ftwilliam.com offers employee benefits professionals the highest quality plan documents (retirement, welfare and non-qualified) and government forms (5500/PBGC, 1099 and IRS) software at highly competitive prices.

MediRegs products provide integrated health care compliance content and software solutions for professionals in healthcare, higher education and life sciences, including professionals in accounting, law and consulting.

Wolters Kluwer Law & Business, a division of Wolters Kluwer, is headquartered in New York. Wolters Kluwer is a market-leading global information services company focused on professionals.

Summary of Contents

Contents

—2—

|| *Autonomy and Bodily Integrity* || *45*

—3—
|| *Personhood* || *121*

---4---

Privacy, Essentialism, and Enhancements 181

PART II   BIOETHICS AND THE INDIVIDUAL

—5—

Avoiding Reproduction: Sterilization, Contraception, and Abortion   *249*

—6—

|| *Assisting and Monitoring Reproduction* || *321*

—8—

‖ *Death* ‖   *513*

—9—

Medical Decision Making for Others

—10—

Discrimination in Health Care

PART III   BIOETHICS AND THE COMMUNITY

—11—

Human Subject Research and Experimental Health Care — 677

—12—
‖ *Public Health* ‖ *753*

—13—

The Business of Health Care   *815*

—14—

Social Justice: Access to Care, Distribution of Care, and the Social Determinants of Health   *901*

Preface

Many topics of concern to bioethicists have occasioned passionate debate and have resulted in widely divergent responses from both professional bioethicists and from the wider society. Bioethics brings scholars and practitioners into the center of a number of pervasive, often emotional, social and moral debates, debates about such issues as abortion, stem-cell research, and assisted suicide. Many such debates involve questions about the meaning of personhood and the ways in which persons should be respected or cared for as they seek health for themselves and others and as they make decisions about reproduction and death. At the same time, debates about access to health care, the just distribution of care, and the appropriate aims and limits of public health initiatives have intensified in the United States. Such debates implicate people's deepest concerns about how to live and about how to understand and relate to other people within intimate settings, within larger communities, and within a national or global context.

In light of this, it should not be surprising that the study and practice of bioethics often require an interdisciplinary approach. For lawyers working in the field, bioethical questions are often located in a space between law and some other profession or discipline (e.g., medicine, nursing, public health, philosophy, economics, psychology). This book provides students with articles and references that will assist them in exploring the interdisciplinary context of bioethical debate. At the same time, the book, constructed primarily to teach bioethics to law students, frames each issue in light of judicial, legislative, and regulatory rules that may, as a practical matter, channel or limit options available to those attempting to resolve bioethical conundrums.

We have not shied away from the excitement, at times even volatility, that divergent viewpoints bring to the field. At the same time, we have aimed to provide a "balanced" presentation of bioethics. We have worked to achieve that balance by including a variety of controversial perspectives. We have not, in short, included many "neutral" readings in this book. Rather we have included provocative readings and have aimed to achieve balance by challenging each reading with another, contrasting perspective, or with a series of questions placed after the reading. We hope this approach will stimulate classroom discussion and help students shape their own responses to the dilemmas that bioethicists ponder and to the disputes that lawyers involved with bioethical questions may be asked to help resolve.

We organized materials in the first and second editions of this book around the development of the human "lifespan." This edition resembles earlier editions in presenting bioethical issues as they develop from birth, through childhood, adulthood, and old age, through dying and death. But in this edition, we have encompassed the lifespan approach within a larger frame that distinguishes between issues that primarily implicate individual concerns and issues that primarily implicate communal concerns. We believe that this frame provides for the presentation of lifespan issues and also brings pressing new questions about public health, population health, and social justice into focus.

As in the first and second editions of the book, Part I of the third edition presents concepts basic to bioethical inquiry. This Part includes updated versions of the three chapters in the first part of earlier editions. It also includes a new chapter ("Privacy, Essentialism, and Enhancements") that considers questions posed by developments related to genetics, genomics, and neuroimaging, as well as questions about a variety of enhancements. This chapter consolidates material that was scattered throughout earlier editions, and it presents issues that have developed since the second edition appeared.

Part II (Bioethics and the Individual) focuses on bioethical conundrums that primarily affect individuals. These include questions about abortion, reproduction, dying, death, medical decision making, and discrimination in the provision of health care. The chapters on medical decision making and discrimination are new to this edition. Each of these chapters includes materials that were distributed in several chapters of the book's earlier editions, as well as some new material. Many of the materials in Part II of this edition implicate relationships as well as personhood, but issues that affect the community more than individuals (and their relationships with specific others) are addressed in Part III.

Part III (Bioethics and the Community) includes materials about bioethical issues that directly affect communities larger than families and friendship groups. This Part includes two updated versions of chapters in the second edition ("Human Subject Research" and "Public Health") and two new chapters, focusing respectively on the business parameters of health care and on social justice in the delivery and coverage of health care. Some of the topics in this Part (e.g., human subject research) are generally covered in bioethics courses. Others, however, are not (e.g., financial conflicts of interest and social justice in the delivery of health care).

In sum, the bipartite division of topics into those that primarily affect individuals (along with the people closest to them) and those that primarily affect communities provides a useful framework that should encourage readers to consider the complicated interconnections within bioethical inquiry among social assumptions, individual options, and society's choices about how to distribute resources affecting health within populations and what may be properly asked of individuals and communities. Finally, we believe that the result of the decision to include provocative viewpoints is a collection of fascinating, often colorful readings that together permit an in-depth, piercing, and critical look at the assumptions, traditions, and alternative approaches that constitute bioethical inquiry. Reading this book and studying the topics it presents are likely to be challenging. But the process will, we hope, never be boring.

We are grateful for the help of many in the creation and production of this book. We thank Peter Skagestad of Wolters Kluwer for his help and guidance in completing this third edition and Kenny Chumbley for his assistance with the third edition's production process, as well as our previous editors at Aspen, Richard Mixter, Eric Holt, Troy Froebe, Fran Anderson, and Taylor Kearns. We also thank the several anonymous reviewers of all three editions who offered many helpful and insightful comments to guide our process. Particularly significant research assistance was provided by Katherine Dieterich, Maggie Emma, James Koffler, Alex Lo, Roshni Persaud, Amie Rice, Rick Savage, Reema Sultan, Jessica Smith, and Henry Sire. We are grateful to Toni Aiello, Reference Librarian at the Maurice A. Dean School of Law at Hofstra University, for her generous and intelligent assistance, and Margaret Foster Riley of the University of Virginia School of Law for her review of and helpful comments on the chapter on the business of health care. We are also appreciative of the secretarial and administrative assistance of Frances Avnet (Hofstra law), Carrie Gumm (University of Virginia Center for Biomedical Ethics and Humanities), Megan Hensley (Florida State University College of Law), and Craig Hartman (Florida State University College of Law). We both also thank our respective schools for their continuing support of our scholarly and teaching endeavors.

Janet L. Dolgin
Lois L. Shepherd

January 2013

Acknowledgments

Excerpts from the following books and articles appear with the kind permission of the copyright holders:

American Medical Association, AMA Principles of Medical Ethics (2001). Reprinted by permission.

Annas, G., Faith (Healing), Hope, and Charity at the FDA: The Politics of AIDS Drug Trials, 34 Villanova Law Review 771 (1989). Reprinted by permission.

Annas, G., Mapping the Human Genome and the Meaning of Monster Mythology, 39 Emory Law Journal 629 (1990). Reprinted by permission.

Arras, J., Principles and Particularity: The Role of Cases in Bioethics, 69 Indiana Law Journal 983 (1994). Reprinted by permission.

Bagley, M., Patent First, Ask Questions Later: Morality and Biotechnology in Patent Law, 45 William and Mary Law Review 469, 490-491, 517-519 (2003). Reprinted by permission.

Baldwin, D.C., Jr., The Role of the Physician in End-of-Life Care: What More Can We Do?, 2 Journal of Health Care Law and Policy 258 (1999). Reprinted by permission.

Beh, H.G., The Role of Institutional Review Boards in Protecting Human Subjects: Are We Really Ready to Fix a Broken System?, 26 Law and Psychology Review 1 (2002). Reprinted by permission.

Blitz, J., Freedom of Thought for the Extended Mind: Cognitive Enhancement and the Constitution, 2010 Wisconsin Law Review 1049, 1058-1061 (2010). Reprinted by permission.

Bobinski, M.A., Symposium: Inequities in Healthcare—Article: Health Disparities and the Law: Wrongs in Search of a Right, 29 American Journal of Law and Medicine 363, 373-374 (2003). Reprinted by permission.

Botkin, J.R., Prenatal Diagnosis and the Selection of Children, 30 Florida State University Law Review 265, 273-276 (2002).

Bowman, J., The Plight of Poor African-Americans: Public Policy on Sickle Hemoglobin and AIDS, in African-American Perspectives on Biomedical Ethics (Harley E. Flack & Edmund d. Pellegrino, eds.), Georgetown University Press (1992), 173-192. Reprinted by permission.

Brown, T., and Murphy, E., Through a Scanner Darkly: Functional Neuroima-
    ging as Evidence of a Criminal Defendant's Past Mental States, 62 Stanford
    Law Review 1119, 1127, 1136-1139 (2010). Reprinted by permission.

Burris, S., From Health Care Law to the Social Determinants of Health: A Public
    Health Law Research Perspective, 159 University of Pennsylvania Law
    Review 1649, 1649, 1651, 1653-1654 (2011). Reprinted by permission.

Burris, S., Strathdee, S., and Vernick, J.S., Lethal Injections: The Law, Science,
    and Politics of Syringe Access for Injection Drug Users, 37 University of San
    Francisco Law Review 813 (2003). Reprinted by permission.

Calabresi, G., Reflections on Medical Experimentation in Humans, 98(2) Dae-
    dalus 387-405 (1969). Reprinted by permission of MIT Press Journals.

Cantor, N., The Permanently Unconscious Patient, Non-Feeding and Euthana-
    sia, 15 American Journal of Law and Medicine, 381, 403-405, 411-412, 414-
    415, 419-421 (1989). Reprinted by permission.

Cherry, A., Symposium Remarks: Maternal-Fetal Conflicts, The Social Construc-
    tion of Maternal Deviance and Some Thoughts About Love and Justice, 8
    Texas Journal of Women and the Law 245, 247-255 (1999). Reprinted by
    permission.

Coale, D.S., Note, Norplant Bonuses and the Unconstitutional Conditions Doc-
    trine, 71 Texas Law Review 189, 204-208 (1992). Reprinted by permission.

Cohen, B., The Controversy Over Hospital Charges to the Uninsured - No Vil-
    lains, No Heroes, 51 Villanova Law Review 95 (2006). Reprinted by
    permission.

Conley, J., Doerr, A., and Vorhaus, D., Enabling Responsible Public Genomics,
    20 Health Matrix 325, 330-335 (2010). Reprinted by permission.

Crossley, M., Of Diagnoses and Discrimination: Discriminatory Nontreatment of
    Infants with HIV Infection, 91 Columbia Law Review 1581, 1615, 1618,
    1624-1627 (1993). Reprinted by permission.

Crossley, M., Retrospective: Becoming Visible the ADA's Impact on Health Care
    for Persons with Disabilities, 52 Alabama Law Review, 51, 52, 57-60 (2000).
    Reprinted by permission.

Daniels, N., The Ethics of Health Reform: Why We Should Care About Who is
    Missing Coverage, 44 Connecticut Law Review, 1057, 1062-1064 (2012).
    Reprinted by permission.

Dolgin, J., The Constitution as Family Arbiter: A Moral in the Mess?, 102 Colum-
    bia Law Review 337, 347-352 (2002). Reprinted by permission.

Dolgin, J., The Family in Transition: From Griswold to Eisenstadt and Beyond, 82
    Georgetown Law Journal 1519, 1556-1558 (1994). Reprinted with
    permission.

Dolgin, J., and Dieterich, K., When Others Get Too Close: Immigrants, Class and
    the Health Care Debate, 19 Cornell Journal of Law and Public Policy 283
    (2010). Reprinted by permission.

Dresser, R., Precommitment: A Misguided Strategy for Securing Death with
    Dignity, 81 Texas Law Review 1823 (2003). Reprinted by permission.

Dubler, N.N., See You Out of Court? The Role of ADR in Health Care: A 'Prin-
    cipled Resolution': The Fulcrum of Bioethics Mediation, 74 Law and Con-
    temporary Problems 177, 185-187 (2011). Reprinted by permission.

Elhauge, E., Allocating Health Care Morally, 82 California Law Review 1449,
    1451-1453 (1994). Reprinted by permission.

Ely, J., The Wages of Crying Wolf: A Comment on Roe v. Wade, 82 Yale Law Journal, 920, 923-926 (1973). Reprinted by permission.

Farmer, P., and Campos, N.G., Rethinking Medical Ethics: A View from Below, 4 Developing Word Bioethics 17 (2004). Blackwell Publishing. Reprinted by permission.

Feldman, H., Pushing Drugs: Genomics and Genetics, The Pharmaceutical Industry and the Law of Negligence, 42 Washburn Law Journal 575, 575-576, 581-582, 587-589 (2003). Reprinted by permission.

Field, M.A., Killing "The Handicapped"—Before and After Birth, 16 Harvard Women's Law Journal 79, 81-83, 96-97, 103, 104, 137 (1993). Reprinted by permission.

Fine, D.K., Physician Liability and Managed Care: A Philosophical Perspective, 19 Georgia State University Law Review 641, 647-649, 663, 665-666 (2003). Reprinted by permission.

Finkler, K., Experiencing the New Genetics: Family, Kinship on the Medical Frontier, University of Pennsylvania Press 177-178 (2000). Reprinted by permission.

Gill, C., Health Professionals, Disability, and Assisted Suicide: An Examination of Relevant Empirical Evidence and Reply to Batavia, 6 Psychology, Public Policy and Law Journal, 526, 528-529, 533-534 (2000). Copyright © 2000 by the American Psychological Association. Reproduced by permission. The use of APA information does not imply endorsement by APA.

Glenn, L.M., Case Study: Ethical and Legal Issues in Human Machine Mergers (Or the Cyborgs Cometh), 21 Annals of Health Law, 175, 177-178 (2012). Reprinted by permission.

Goldner, J.A., Dealing with Conflicts of Interest in Biomedical Research, 28 Journal of Law, Medicine & Ethics, 379 (2000). American Society of Law, Medicine & Ethics. Reprinted by permission.

Goodwin, M., Empire: Empires of the Flesh: Tissue and Organ Taboos, 60 Ala. L. Rev. 1219, 1242-1245 (2009).

Gordijn, B., Converging NBIC Technologies for Improving Human Performance: A Critical Assessment of the Novelty and the Prospects of the Project, 34 Journal of Law, Medicine and Ethics 726, 728-731 (2006). American Society of Law, Medicine & Ethics. Reprinted with permission.

Gostin, L.O., The Model State Emergency Health Powers Act: Public Health and Civil Liberties in a Time of Terrorism, 13 Health Matrix 3 (Winter, 2003). Reprinted by permission.

Hall, M., A Corporate Ethics of "Care" in Health Care, 3 Seattle Journal for Social Justice 417 (2004). Reprinted by permission.

Hartman, R.G., Coming of Age, 28 American Journal of Law & Medicine 409, 422-426 (2002). Reprinted by permission.

Hector, C., and Podgurski, A., Nudging Towards Nutrition? Soft Paternalism and Obesity-Related Reform, 67 Food and Drug Law Journal 103 (2012). Reprinted by permission.

Hiller, J., et al., Privacy and Security in the Implementation of Health Information Technology (Electronic Health Records): U.S. and EU Compared, 17 Boston University Journal of Science and Technology 1, 6-8 (2011). Reprinted by permission.

Hoffman, S., and Podgurski, A. In Sickness, Health, and Cyberspace: Protecting the Security of Electronic Private Health Information, 48 Boston College Law Review 331, 332-335 (2007). Reprinted by permission.

Institute for Bioethics, Health Policy and Law, University of Louisville School of Medicine, Quarantine and Isolation: Lessons Learned from SARS 14, 17, 19-21. (2003). Reprinted by permission.

Joh, E., DNA Theft: Recognizing the Crime of Nonconsensual Genetic Testing, 91 Boston University Law Review 665, 666-667, 670 (2011). Reprinted by permission.

Katz, J., Human Sacrifice and Human Experimentation: Reflections at Nuremberg, 22 Yale Journal of International Law 401 (1997). Reprinted by permission.

Katz, K.D., Parenthood from the Grave: Protocols for Retrieving and Utilizing Gametes from the Dead or Dying, 2006 University of Chicago Legal Forum 289 (2006). Reprinted by permission.

Klein, D., When Coercion Lacks Care: Competency to Make Medical Treatment Decisions and Parens Patriae Civil Commitments, 45 University of Michigan Journal of Law Reform 561, 586-588 (2012). Reprinted by permission.

Kronebusch, K., Schlesinger, M., and Thomas, T., Managed Care Regulation in the States: The Impact on Physicians' Practices and Clinical Autonomy, 34 Journal of Health Politics Policy and Law, 219 (2009). Reprinted by permission.

Latham, S.R., Living Wills and Alzheimer's Disease, 23 Quinnipiac Probate Law Journal, 425, 430-431 (2010). Reprinted by permission.

Lemmens, T., and Miller, P. B., The Human Subjects Trade: Ethical and Legal Issues Surrounding Recruitment Incentives, 31 Journal of Law, Medicine & Ethics, 398-418 (2003). American Society of Law, Medicine & Ethics. Reprinted by permission.

Libreria Editrice Vaticana, Evangelium Vitae (The Gospel of Life) (1995). Reprinted by permission.

Lombardo, P., Taking Eugenics Seriously: Three Generations of ??? Are Enough?, 30 Florida State University Law Review 191, 202-205, 208-211, 214 (2003). Reprinted by permission.

Longmore, P.K., Elizabeth Bouvia, Assisted Suicide and Social Prejudice, 3 Issues in Law and Medicine, 141-170 (1987). Reprinted by permission.

Lynn, J., Why I Don't Have a Living Will, 19 Law, Medicine & Health Care 101, 101-104 (1991). Reprinted by permission.

Mahowald, M., Aren't We All Eugenicists?: Commentary on Paul Lombardo's "Taking Eugenics Seriously," 30 Florida State University Law Review 219 (2003). Reprinted by permission.

McCartney, J.J., Embryonic Stem Cell Research and Respect for Human Life: Philosophical and Legal Reflections, 65 Albany Law Review, 597 (2002). Reprinted by permission.

McGill, M., The Human Right to Health Care in the State of Vermont, 37 Vermont Bar Journal and Law Digest 28, 28-29 (2011). Reprinted by permission.

Morreim, E.H., Playing Doctor: Corporate Medical Practice and Medical Malpractice, 32 University of Michigan Journal of Law Reform 939, 944-951 (1999). Reprinted by permission.

Moulton, B. and King, J., Aligning Ethics with Medical Decision-Making: The Quest for Informed Patient Choice, 38 Journal of Law, Medicine, and Ethics 85, 85, 89-90 (2012). American Society of Law, Medicine, and Ethics. Reprinted by permission.

Noah, L., Too High a Price for Some Drugs? The FDA Burdens Reproductive Choice, 44 San Diego Law Review 231, 233-236 (2007). Reprinted by permission.

Orentlicher, D., The Influence of a Professional Organization on Physician Behavior, 57 Albany Law Review 583 (1994). Reprinted by permission.

Ouellette, A., Shaping Parental Authority Over Children's Bodies, 85 Indiana Law Journal 955, 960-964 (2010). Reprinted by permission.

Parasidis, E., Patients Over Politics: Addressing Legislative Failure in the Regulation of Medical Products, 2011 Wisconsin Law Review, 929, 966-967 (2011). Reprinted by permission.

Pendo, E.A., Images of Health Insurance in Popular Film: The Dissolving Critique, 37 Journal of Health Law 267 (2004). Reprinted by permission.

Perry, J.E., Physician-Owned Specialty Hospitals and the Patient Protection and Affordable Care Act: Health Care Reform at the Intersection of Law and Ethics, 49 American Business Law Journal 369 (2012). Reprinted by permission.

Phelps, T.G., The Sound of Silence Breaking: Catholic Women, Abortion, and the Law, 59 Tennessee Law Review 547, 565-569 (1992). Reprinted by permission.

Podgurski, A., In Sickness, Health, and Cyberspace: Protecting the Security of Electronic Private Health Information, 48 Boston College Law Review, 331, 332-335 (2007). Reprinted by permission.

Pope, T.M., Medical Futility Statutes: No Safe Harbor to Unilaterally Refuse Life-Sustaining Treatment, 75 Tennessee Law Review 1, 13-20, 66, 68-69, 79, 80 (2007). Reprinted with permission.

Pope, T.M., Health Law and Bioethics: Pressing Issues and Changing Times: Surrogate Selection: An Increasingly Viable, But Limited, Solution to Intractable Futility Disputes, 35 St. Louis University Journal of Health Law and Policy 183, 206-208 (2010). Reprinted by permission.

Quill, T., Death and Dignity—A Case of Individualized Decision Making, 324 New England Journal of Medicine 691 (1991). Copyright ©1991 Massachusetts Medical Society. All rights reserved. Reprinted by permission.

Rao, R., Law and Equality: Constitutional Misconceptions, 93 Michigan Law Review 1473, 1473-1474, 1477-1478 (1995). Reprinted by permission.

Roberts, D., The Genetic Tie, 62 University of Chicago Law Review 209, 244-246 (1995). Reprinted by permission.

Rosenbaum, S., Realigning the Social Order: The Patient Protection and Affordable Care Act and the U.S. Health Insurance System, 7 Journal of Health and Biomedical Law 1, 11-16 (2011). Reprinted by permission.

Ross, L.F., Children as Research Subjects: A Proposal to Revise the Current Federal Regulations Using a Moral Framework, 8 Stanford Law & Policy Review 159, 159-160, 165-167 (1997). Reprinted by permission.

Rothenberg, K.H., Gender Matters: Implications for Clinical Research and Women's Health Care, 32 Houston Law Review 1201, 1206, 1208-1209, 1211, 1213 (1996). Reprinted by permission.

Schuck, P., Rethinking Informed Consent, 103 Yale Law Journal 899, 902-905 (1994). Reprinted by permission of the Yale Law Journal Company and William S. Hein Company.

Scott, C., Why Law Pervades Medicine: An Essay on Ethics in Health Care, 14 Notre Dame Journal of Law, Ethics, and Public Policy 245 (2000). Reprinted by permission.

Shepherd, L., Dignity and Autonomy After Washington v. Glucksberg, 7 Cornell Journal of Law and Public Policy 431 (1998). Reprinted by permission.

Siegel, R., Reasoning from the Body: A Historical Perspective on Abortion Regulation and Questions of Equal Protection, 44 Stanford Law Review 261, 379-380 (1992). Reprinted by permission.

Silver, L.M., Popular Cloning Versus Scientific Cloning in Ethical Debates, 4 NYU Journal of Legislation and Public Policy 47, 49-54 (2000/2001). Reprinted by permission.

Silvers, A., and Francis, L.P., Playing God with Baby Doe: Quality of Life and Unpredictable Life Standards at the Start of Life, 25 Georgia State University Law Review, 1061 (2009). Reprinted by permission.

Smith, A.H., and Rother, J., Older Americans and the Rationing of Health Care, 140 University of Pennsylvania Law Review 1847, 1852-1855 (1992). Reprinted by permission.

Smith, C.B., et al., Are There Characteristics of Infectious Diseases That Raise Special Ethical Issues?, 4 Developing World Bioethics 1, 2-3, 12-16 (2004). Blackwell Publishing. Reprinted by permission.

Smith, G.P., II, Distributive Justice and Health Care, 18 Journal of Contemporary Health Law and Policy 421, 427-428 (2002). Reprinted by permission.

Stalcup, C., Reviewing the Review Boards: Why Institutional Review Board Liability Does Not Make Good Business Sense, 82 Washington University Law Quarterly 1593, 1596-1600 (2004). Reprinted by permission.

Stempsey, W. E., Religion, Philosophy, and the Commodification of Human Body Parts, 55 DePaul Law Review 875, 883-885, 887-888 (2006). Reprinted with permission.

Storrow, R., Therapeutic Reproduction and Human Dignity, 21 Law and Literature 257, 261-263 (2009). Reprinted by permission.

Strasser, M., Wrongful Life, Wrongful Birth, Wrongful Death, and the Right to Refuse Treatment: Can Reasonable Jurisdictions Recognize All But One? 64 Missouri Law Review 29, 64-67 (1999).

Suter, S.M., The Allure and Peril of Genetics Exceptionalism: Do We Need Special Genetics Legislation? 79 Washington University Law Quarterly 669 (2001). Reprinted by permission.

Teitelbaum, J., and Rosenbaum, S., Symposium: Inequities in Healthcare—Article: Medical Care as a Public Accommodation: Moving the Discussion to Race, 29 American Journal of Law and Medicine, 381, 382-383, 394 (2003). Reprinted by permission.

Tenenbaum, E., Sexual Expression and Intimacy Between Nursing Home Residents with Dementia: Balancing the Current Interests and Prior Values of Heterosexual and LGBT Residents, 21 Temple Political and Civil Rights Law Review 459 (2012). Reprinted by permission.

Tong, R., Feminist Approaches to Bioethics, in Feminism and Bioethics: Beyond Reproduction (Susan M. Wolf, ed.), Oxford University Press 67, 76-82 (1996). Reprinted by permission.

Volokh, E., Medical Self-Defense, Prohibited Experimental Therapies, and Payment for Organs, 120 Harvard Law Review 1813, 1832-1835, 1843-1844 (2007). Reprinted with permission.

Wales, S., The Stark Law: Boon or Boondoggle? An Analysis of the Prohibition on Physician Self-Referrals, 27 Law and Psychology Review 1, 5-7 (2003). Reprinted by permission.

Warren, M.A., On the Moral and Legal Status of Abortion, 57 The Monist 1 (1973). Reprinted by permission.

Watson, S.D., Health Law Symposium: Foreword, 48 St. Louis University Law Journal 1, 4-5, 7 (2003). Reprinted by permission.

Watson, S.D., Section 1557 of the Affordable Care Act: Civil Rights, Health Reform, Race, and Equity, 55 Howard Law Journal 855 (2012). Reprinted by permission.

Wesley, P., Dying Safely, 8 Issues in Law & Medicine, 467-485 (1993). Reprinted by permission.

Whitton, L.S., Ageism: Paternalism and Prejudice, 46 DePaul Law Review 453, 453-455 (1997). Reprinted by permission.

Wing, K., Policy Choices and Model Acts: Preparing for the Next Public Health Emergency, 13 Health Matrix 71, 74-75, 81 (2003). Reprinted by permission.

Wise, S., Dismantling the Barriers to Legal Rights for Nonhuman Animals, 7 Animal Law 9 (2001). Reprinted by permission.

Wolf, S., Kahn, J., and Wagner, J., Using Preimplantation Genetic Diagnosis to Create a Stem Cell Donor: Issues, Guidelines and Limits, The Journal of Law, Medicine & Ethics 327, 328-329 (2003). American Society of Law, Medicine, and Ethics. Reprinted by permission.

Woodhouse, B.B., Hatching the Egg: A Child-Centered Perspective on Parents' Rights, 14 Cardozo Law Review 1747, 1748-1753, 1767-1768 (1993). Reprinted by permission.

Yearby, R., Breaking the Cycle of "Unequal Treatment" with Health Care Reform: Acknowledging and Addressing the Continuation of Racial Bias, 44 Connecticut Law Review 1281 (2012). Reprinted by permission.

Zumpano-Canto, J., Nonconsensual Sterilization of the Mentally Disabled in North Carolina: An Ethics Critique of the Statutory Standard and Its Judicial Interpretation, 13 Journal of Contemporary Health Law and Policy 79, 80-84 (1996). Reprinted by permission.

= PART I =

BIOETHICS: BASIC CONCEPTS

= 1 =

|| *Law, Medicine,* ||
|| *and Philosophy* ||

What, exactly, is *bioethics*? This casebook presents problems and materials on bioethics and law, but many students probably are a bit unsure about what bioethics is—although perhaps fairly certain that issues such as abortion, cloning, and end-of-life decision making will be covered. An exact definition of bioethics is elusive. The field of bioethics is relatively new, as the brief history later in this chapter explains, and furthermore is continuing to evolve. How an individual scholar of bioethics might define the field can also reflect that scholar's ideological bent or merely her scholarly agenda. The "spillover" phenomenon of bioethics can be seen almost daily in one internet discussion list of bioethics scholars, whose members are constantly reminding, and sometimes chiding, one another to limit postings to bioethics. Thus, when discussions about the role of U.S. military doctors in the medical treatment of prisoners abused during the Iraq war were followed by postings debating the war more generally, some members of the discussion list basically said, "Wait a minute, this is not bioethics." Others, however, disagreed, taking the more expansive view that if life and justice are involved, bioethicists have particular expertise, analytical training, interest, and perhaps even passion, to bring to bear on the subject.

In this book we treat the boundaries of bioethical inquiry somewhat more narrowly than the latter view, but also more broadly than the field's original focus on medical and research ethics. The relationship of patient to health care provider is certainly a central component, even the core, of bioethics. Thus, Part II ("Bioethics and the Individual") focuses on ethical and related legal issues that arise in the individual patient–provider relationship; for example, issues about informed consent, treatment refusals, and confidentiality. Like many scholars in the field, however, we include within bioethics issues of health and the human body that lie outside the individual patient–provider relationship. Part III ("Bioethics and the Community") raises questions that involve communal relationships and concentrates on public health and social justice.

3

Thus, our definition of bioethics includes ethical inquiry related to biological interventions of the human body or body material or to other interventions of the human body or body material aimed primarily at creating, sustaining, or improving human life, as well as ethical inquiry about the just distribution of resources related to the provision of health care. More specifically, we recognize the significance of individual autonomy as well as the significance of protecting the health of the public and ensuring social justice in the promotion of health care. These goals sometimes conflict and must therefore be balanced.

The definition of bioethics included in the Encyclopedia of Bioethics (1995) is similar but less inclusive than our definition: the "systematic study of the moral dimensions—including moral vision, decisions, conduct, and policies—of the life sciences and health care, employing a variety of ethical methodologies in an interdisciplinary setting." The inclusion of "health care" in this definition emphasizes the medical treatment aspect of many questions of bioethics, and signals that the following are appropriate areas of inquiry: Who does and does not receive health care services and why? Who does and who should make decisions about an individual's health care? Are there any limitations on the choices that an individual should be allowed to make that affect that person's health? The inclusion of the "life sciences" in the definition of bioethics provided by the Encyclopedia of Bioethics emphasizes to the existing or future scientific ability to alter biological processes of the human body or its materials, and points to somewhat different questions, such as whether individuals should be permitted to engage in human cloning, whether research should be permitted on embryos, and the like.

The Encyclopedia definition, however, would not appear to include ethical issues that arise in the context of public health policies, which we believe belong within the field. Moreover, the Encyclopedia's definition does not encourage one to focus on the challenge of affecting social justice in the implementation and distribution of health care. While a public health policy to isolate a contagious individual would not necessarily involve health care or an application of the life sciences, we believe that a study of the ethical dimensions of such a policy properly lies in the domain of bioethics, as the practice naturally evokes some of the same kinds of questions raised by forced vaccination or organ procurement policies, issues more traditionally understood as within the field of bioethics. Similarly, we include within bioethics attention to the social determinants of health. That bioethicists are beginning to turn their attention to public health issues and issues of social justice suggests that the definition of bioethics is still undergoing refinement.

The study of bioethics is truly interdisciplinary, encompassing philosophy, sociology, economics, psychology, and, of especial importance for our purposes, law. It requires some understanding of ethics and of moral philosophy. In addition, the more practice-oriented the problems of bioethics are, the more an understanding is needed of the shifting structure and economics of health care practice (including the relationships among health care providers and between them and patients), of culturally molded assumptions about human bodies as well as about health and disease, and of the intersection between health care and law. Virtually every chapter of this casebook includes analyses dependent on each of these areas of study. This introductory chapter provides some preliminary material about each area.

A. HISTORY OF BIOETHICS AND "BIOLAW"

Bioethics developed as a separate field of discourse in the late twentieth century. Yet, the roots of the field's central questions and its responses to those questions extend far back into medical and philosophical history. The fourth century B.C. Greek healer Hippocrates, often associated with the effort to separate medicine from religion and philosophy, is credited with composition of the Hippocratic Oath. (For the text of the Oath, see section D, below.) Some of the central concepts that inform contemporary bioethics can be derived from that Oath and the Hippocratic corpus (most of which probably was not actually written by Hippocrates). Among those concepts are the obligation to benefit patients (*beneficence*) and the obligation to avoid harming them (*nonmaleficence*). Yet, not all aspects of the Hippocratic tradition survived the creation of modern medical ethics. In particular, the paternalism of the Hippocratic tradition, which assumed that health care decisions resided with the physician, not the patient, has been widely and successfully challenged in the last several decades.

During the first half of the twentieth century, medicine was largely a cottage industry; doctors took the Hippocratic Oath upon graduation from medical school and mostly remembered that their first duty was to heal and not to harm patients. Not all doctors were ethical, but in the early decades of the twentieth century, they were widely esteemed as caring healers. One of the most salient aspects of this earlier period of American medicine is the discretion doctors enjoyed to make medical decisions outside the scrutiny of others and sometimes without even consulting their patients. Historian David J. Rothman, in his well-known book on the history of bioethics, describes the earlier deference accorded doctors as follows:

> Well into the post-World War II period, decisions at the bedside were the almost exclusive concern of the individual physician, even when they raised fundamental ethical and social issues. It was mainly doctors who wrote and read about the morality of withholding a course of antibiotics and letting pneumonia serve as the old man's best friend, of considering a newborn with grave birth defects a "stillbirth" and sparing the parents the agony of choice and the burden of care, of experimenting on the institutionalized retarded to learn more about hepatitis, or of giving one patient and not another access to the iron lung when the machine was in short supply. Moreover, it was usually the individual physician who decided these matters at the bedside or in the privacy of the hospital room, without formal discussions with patients, their families, or even with colleagues, and certainly without drawing the attention of journalists, judges, or professional philosophers. And they made their decisions on a case-by-case basis, responding to the particular circumstances as they saw fit, reluctant by both training and practice to formulate or adhere to guidelines or rules.

David J. Rothman, Strangers at the Bedside: A History of How Law and Bioethics Transformed Medical Decision Making 1–2 (1991).

In the 1960s, the practice of medicine underwent swift and remarkable changes as patients began to expect and demand more decision-making authority over their own bodies and health care choices that affected them. By the mid-1970s, Rothman writes, medical decision making was no longer the exclusive province of doctors, but was shared with their patients. In addition, when the decisions contained clear ethical dimensions, the doctor's prerogative might also be circumscribed by hospital ethics committees, courts, and legal regulation—"outsiders" were now at the bedside. Id.

In tandem with the dramatic changes that were taking place in the 1960s and 1970s in the doctor–patient relationship, biomedical research practices also came under increased scrutiny from those outside the medical research community. After World War II, with revelations about the horrors of Nazi experimentation, jurists, doctors, and researchers focused on the ethics of research involving human subjects, resulting in a number of ethical codes. (These responses are discussed in Chapter 11.) Yet, researchers in the United States did not all immediately abandon what most people would agree was clearly unethical research on human subjects. A 1966 article published in the New England Journal of Medicine summarized a wide set of such studies that had been undertaken by medical researchers in the United States. One subjected normal newborn babies to catheterization and multiple x-rays to study their bladders. In a second experiment, children residing in a state institution for "mentally defective" children were purposely given hepatitis to study the period of the disease's infectivity. In another, military servicemen were denied the best known treatment for streptococcal respiratory infections so that researchers could compare the incidence of the development of rheumatic fever in this group with its development in a group of control subjects. Perhaps the most remarkable aspect of the many studies described was that none was kept secret; the results of all were published in reputable journals. Henry K. Beecher, Ethics and Clinical Research, 274 New Eng. J. Med. 1354 (1966).

In the 1970s Congress passed the National Research Act of 1974, promulgated in response to a variety of factors, including concerns presented by the public revelation of a number of continuing unethical research projects (especially what is known as the Tuskegee Syphilis Study, a federally funded project at the Tuskegee Institute on a group of poor, African-American males with syphilis), questions among some about research on fetuses, and the developing potential of medical technology to alter the character of health care and ultimately, perhaps, of the species. The National Research Act of 1974 established a National Commission for the Protection of Human Subjects of Biomedical and Behavioral Research. Among other things, the law directed the commission to provide guidance to the Secretary of Health, Education, and Welfare in the construction of regulations geared toward protecting humans involved in research. That guidance was provided in what has become known as the Belmont Report. The principles of ethical conduct in research delineated by the commission have had an important influence on the development of bioethics in the United States. Moreover, the model of government relying on appointed commissions to entertain bioethical questions and to provide advice has proved powerful. From 1995 to 2001, the National Bioethics Advisory Commission (NBAC), established by executive order of the President, issued a number of influential reports on current issues such as human subject research (within the United States and developing countries) and cloning. NBAC's commission expired in 2001, but a new presidential commission was then established, known as the President's Council on Bioethics. Much of its work has focused on the ethics of research on embryos and cloning (see Chapter 3).

The last several decades have witnessed the institutionalization of bioethics as a profession, replete with professors, conferences, journals, centers, "experts," and calls for licensing or certification of those working in the field. The first reference to bioethics in the catalog of the Library of Congress was in 1973 in reference to an article by Daniel Callahan (Bioethics as a Discipline), published in the first volume of the Hastings Center Studies. Some attribute the first important contemporary use of the word to the Kennedy Institute in Washington, DC. The Institute was founded in 1971; its full name is The Joseph and Rose Kennedy Institute for the Study of Human Reproduction and Bioethics.

These last several decades have also witnessed the increasing legal oversight of medicine and of bioethics issues more generally. Such oversight is piecemeal, uncoordinated, and somewhat haphazard, issuing from various federal and state courts applying constitutional and common law and from federal and state legislatures and regulatory bodies creating statutory and regulatory schemes. By the very nature of how courts work—that is, accepting those cases brought before them by litigants—courts have responded issue by issue, and jurisdiction by jurisdiction, so that the law of one state on a particular bioethics issue might be opposite that of another, whereas a third has not yet considered the issue at all. Legislatures, in theory at least, have more freedom to set their own agendas and create comprehensive statutory schemes, but they have also tended to react on an issue-by-issue basis, especially in response to news events or public interest in an issue.

How much "biolaw" exists in the United States, how much will and should exist in the future, and with what purpose and effect? How, indeed, do ethics and law relate to one another? These are questions that pervade any study of bioethics and law and are raised repeatedly by the materials in this book, but here is what one commentator has had to say on the subject.

Charity Scott, Why Law Pervades Medicine:
An Essay on Ethics in Health Care
14 Notre Dame J.L. Ethics &
Pub. Pol'y 245 (2000)

Law pervades medicine because ethics pervades medicine, and in America, we use the law to resolve ethical dilemmas in health care.

Law deals with ethics? Many people react with surprise, amusement, or cynicism when they see those two words—law and ethics—together in the same sentence. To many people, the two concepts seem wholly distinct, like the proverbial apples and oranges, or even radically opposed, as different as night and day. In medical circles, one senses an antagonism to law, not just to lawyers. On hospital ethics committees, talk of law as well as lawyers may be banned from the ethical discussions. On medical rounds, I may be asked to help the residents and medical students keep a bright line between law and ethics so that, I am told, they'll know when they're dealing with one and not the other.

A central thesis of this essay is that there is no such bright line between law and ethics in America, at least not in medicine. During the second half of the twentieth century, most difficult issues in health care which have raised profound ethical dilemmas have been addressed by law. For better or for worse, law and ethics have been evolving in health care together; hand in glove is perhaps the more apt simile. . . .

1.   Law as a Consensus Statement of Ethics

While lawyers may suffer some unpopularity, the law still reflects society's idealism. Immanuel Kant believed that: "The greatest problem for the human species, the solution of which nature compels him to seek, is that of attaining a civil society which can administer justice universally." Justice is an ethical concept of universal fairness for and among individuals; law is the vehicle by which society attempts to achieve this lofty ideal. Oliver Wendell Holmes observed that: "The law is the witness and external deposit of our moral life. Its history is the history of the moral development of the race." Thus the law reflects what, at any given point in time, society views as acceptable, ethically appropriate behavior.

We often enact our moral views in our laws; in effect, we legislate morality. Looking at our laws is like looking at a snapshot in time of our society's moral views about how people ought to behave towards each other. Over time we may change our views as to which behaviors are right or wrong, and we reflect that change by changing our laws. For example, for some considerable time in our nation's history we regarded it as morally appropriate for individuals of different color or gender to be treated differently. We reflected those views in our laws governing who could vote, who could own property, who could be educated in which schools, who could marry whom, who could eat or work or live where, and so forth. Today, our anti-discrimination laws reflect the moral view that it is wrong to perpetuate those distinctions among individuals in our society.

In health care, our society has used the law to ask (and answer) questions about what are ethically appropriate behaviors among those who provide, or receive, or pay for health care services. Frequently, the law is a reaction to perceived ethical wrong-doing in health care. As discussed below, federal laws over the past three decades illustrate how American society has reacted to perceived or potential ethical abuses in health care by calling for laws to resolve the ethical conflicts. The legal resolution in effect becomes a societal consensus statement on ethics, at least for the time being and until the laws are changed.

a.   The 1970s and 1980s: Patient Care and Medical Ethics

Federal law was used to address an ethical dilemma caused by the shortage in the 1960s of hemodialysis machines to treat patients with kidney disease. To allocate those scarce resources in Washington, a group (later dubbed the "Seattle God Committee") was given authority to decide, according to various "social worth" criteria, which patients would or would not be given this treatment. Patients were evaluated according to, among other things: age, gender, income and net worth, marital status, number of dependents, educational and employment background, and their "past performance and future potential." Societal unease about the ethics of this form of health care rationing found expression in the enactment of the Social Security Amendments of 1972, allowing Medicare reimbursement for most patients with end-stage renal disease.

Federal law was enacted in the 1970s to address the ethical issues raised by the decades-long decision by the U.S. Department of Public Health to deprive hundreds of African-American men in rural Alabama of available antibiotics to treat syphilis. Government officials who authorized the Tuskegee Syphilis Study viewed it as an opportunity to benefit both scientific research and the Southern black community. After the public revelations and congressional hearings, however, society reacted to what it judged to have been unethical behavior by enacting national laws to develop ethical standards for the protection of human research subjects.

In the 1980s, conflicting ethical views about what was appropriate medical care for critically ill newborns were socially expressed by the legal controversy over the so-called Baby Doe regulations. Promulgated by the Reagan administration, these regulations prohibited hospitals from withholding life-sustaining treatment from very ill infants solely by reason of their handicaps, and allowed the federal government to monitor medical treatment decisions as potential violations of federal anti-discrimination laws through twenty-four-hour hot lines and warning notices posted in hospitals. These regulations have since been invalidated by the Supreme Court. Alternative legislation was subsequently enacted which represented a compromise between the ethical positions held by those (primarily doctors' groups) who believed such treatment decisions should be largely left to the discretion of parents and physicians, and those (primarily advocates for the disabled) who believed that the treatment decisions should not be based on predictions about an infant's future "quality of life."

That a health care law can represent society's views on ethics was also illustrated by the 1980s controversy over so-called "patient dumping," or the practice by many private hospitals of transferring poor or uninsured emergency patients to public hospitals. Prior to the 1980s, hospitals generally had no obligation under state and federal law to give life-saving treatment to emergency patients, or to provide obstetrical care to women in labor, if these patients could not pay for these services. Congressional hearings on the nationwide problem of patient-dumping resulted in the Emergency Medical Treatment and Active Labor Act. Prompted by societal concern over individual patient horror stories, the Act reflected emerging societal agreement that it was wrong for hospitals to refuse to treat women in labor or patients in a potentially life-threatening emergency based on their inability to pay.

In each of these four examples, the activities that gave rise to the public controversies and subsequent legislation posed important and debatable ethical questions in health care. Many of the actors at the time did not regard their actions as ethically problematic, even if others later did. The members of the Seattle God Committee and those who authorized the Tuskegee Syphilis Study believed their activities to be ethical promotions of the public good. The hospitals who transferred poor patients to public hospitals rather than treat them did not view it as ethically wrong to decline to give service to someone who could not pay for it. Certainly there remain sharply divergent views about what constitutes the ethical treatment of critically ill newborns. The point is that in each case, the law was called upon to weigh the merits of the differing ethical positions, to adopt some and reject others (implicitly if not expressly), and to provide guidelines for what society agreed (by proxy, through the democratic vote on the legislation) would be considered unethical behavior in the future. As a consensus statement on ethics, the law reflected society's views, at least for the time being, of where the ethical balance should be struck.

b.   The 1990s: Managed Care and Business Ethics

Many of the legal controversies involving medical ethics in the 1970s and 1980s tended to focus on perceived ethical problems arising out of the provider–patient relationship. In other words, these ethical questions frequently focused on how those who provide health care services (the hospitals, doctors, or researchers) should treat those who receive the services (the patients). By contrast, many of the ethical conflicts in health care in the 1990s involve the business practices of payers (those who pay for health care services, such as managed care and insurance companies), which raise ethical questions about how the payers should treat both patients and providers (particularly doctors and hospitals). Throughout the 1990s, providers and patients alike have vociferously expressed their sense of ethical wrong-doing by insurers and managed care companies who, for example, attempt to insert so-called "gag clauses" in their contracts with physicians; who may try to cut costs by limiting hospital stays down to the point of paying only for so-called "drive-through" deliveries and "drive-through" mastectomies; who may create financial incentives for doctors to deny or limit care or otherwise interfere with the doctor–patient relationship by denying payment for care that the patient needs and the doctor wants to provide; who impose restrictions on patients' choice of provider; who appear to lack protections for the confidentiality of patients' records; or who will not pay for emergency services without a lot of pre-authorization red tape.

The HMOs and insurance companies who engage in these behaviors do not view them as wrong or unethical: on the contrary, it is just good business to try to contain costs and allocate health care rationally. But others in our society view these behaviors as ethically wrong, unfair, or abusive. And where do they go when their sense of moral outrage gets strong enough? To the law, of course. Each of these asserted unethical behaviors has generated calls for social resolution, principally by legal ban at federal and state levels.

2.   *Law as Enforcer of Socially Agreed-Upon Values: Law Packs Ethics with a Punch*

While law and ethics both focus on questions of right and wrong in human relationships, they differ starkly in their ability to enforce ethical behavior. Ethics is aspirational only: it posits ethical ideals for human behavior. If we say "ought," we mean ethics. By contrast, law provides penalties for failure to abide by socially agreed upon ethical norms. If we say "must," we mean law. The old adage that "virtue is its own reward" is only partially true: sometimes the threat of jail time or heavy monetary penalties can provide a more compelling incentive for virtuous behavior than simple knowledge that one is "doing the right thing." Law packs ethics with the "punch" of potential sanctions.

2. *Clarification About the Consensus*

While law often serves these two primary roles—expressing social agreement on what is ethically inappropriate behavior between individuals, and backing that agreement up with penalties for violation—two further points are needed to clarify the nature of this social agreement.

a. Consensus Reflects General Agreement, Not Unanimity

First, by societal "consensus" or social "agreement" this essay does not mean to suggest that everyone in society agrees that the ethically correct resolution has been expressed by the law in every case. Plenty of people obviously will disagree. We live, after all, in a pluralistic society where uniformity of opinion is virtually impossible. What is meant by "consensus" is less than unanimity and more a sense of general agreement. Whether a bare majority or a substantial majority, "consensus" in this essay means a democratic resolution we have agreed to abide by in our social contract, even if individually some (or even many) of us believe a particular resolution is wrong.

b. Law Sets Ethical Minimums, Not Maximums

Second, through the law, our society does not attempt to agree upon all conduct which is ethical, and all conduct which is unethical. Law performs a much narrower function. In the universe of ethics, right and wrong behaviors lie along a spectrum, with ethically good or even ideal conduct at one end (perhaps we could agree to put honesty, loyalty, generosity, altruism, and respect for others at this end) and ethically bad behavior at the other end (most of us might place murder, lying, cheating, and stealing, for example, at this end). Much of human behavior lies somewhere in the middle, where there is significant division of social opinion as to whether or to what extent it may be right or wrong, good or bad, acceptable or unacceptable. Society often uses law to identify those behaviors primarily at one end of the spectrum: those behaviors about which there is general agreement that they are unethical, wrong, or unacceptable. In our society, we often express our consensus about behavior being ethically wrong by making it illegal. But that leaves much conduct—perhaps most human conduct—simply not addressed by law, and over which there may be significant differences of opinion.

By addressing what we have generally agreed is wrong behavior or bad actions, the law sets the legal minimums for behavior; it does not address the ethical maximums. The law provides sanctions for wrongdoing; it does not tend to provide rewards for doing good or even sanctions for failing to do good. The law will punish you if you hit a person and leave him bleeding in the street; but if you are walking down the street and happen to see someone lying and bleeding in the gutter, the law will not penalize you if you walk on by and fail to help him out. American law does not require you to be the "Good Samaritan," nor reward you if you are. That is the province of ethics—it goes beyond the law.

. . . The very power of the law can create pitfalls for real ethical reflection in other ways. Paradoxically, more law can result in less ethical debate. When we focus on the law, we tend to lose sight of the ethical underpinnings for it. In trying to focus on the "letter of the law," we often lose sight of its "spirit." When law becomes pervasive, we often forget about the original ethical questions that prompted the legal resolutions. We also tend to forget that generally, the law sets only the floor for ethical behavior, and that we have come to societal consensus only on these behaviors which fall below that ethical level. We get so focused on making sure that our behavior does not fall below that floor—that we cannot be held legally liable for something—that we do not examine whether our behavior is reaching far enough toward the ethical high ground. We worry only about avoiding legal accountability, not about promoting ethical responsibility. Our obsession with the law—or more particularly, with avoiding law's punch—means that we tend to substitute our conformity with the legal minimums for our need to reflect on the ethical maximums. We are too quickly satisfied that our compliance with these legal minimums was all that ethics required us to do.

NOTES AND QUESTIONS

1. *Relationship of law and ethics.*   What is the relationship of law and ethics, according to Charity Scott? How do law and ethics differ? Are there costs to legislating morality? What are they?

Scott's article appeared in the first year of the twenty-first century. Her description of the relationship between law and ethics has continued to raise challenging questions even as law and ethics have responded to recent developments. These include innovations in science and information technology; the last decade of the twentieth century and the first years of this century witnessed the advent of cloning, the production of new, powerful psychopharmaceutical drugs, and significant developments in embryonic stem cell research, genomics, and neuroimaging. Further, within clinical medicine, the triumph of autonomy as a central bioethical principle in the last quarter of the twentieth century has been challenged by attention to the negative consequences of limiting beneficence in the name of autonomy. Clinicians, anxious to provide for the well-being of their patients, have been frustrated by the power of the appeal to patient autonomy. Further, in thinking about the health of populations, twenty-first century bioethics has been strongly influenced by innovative work on the social determinants of health and has focused on facilitating fair access to health care and social justice in the provision of health care. Questions raised by Scott's description of the relationship between legal and ethical responses to medicine and health care have been occasioned by each of these developments.

2. *International development of biolaw.*   Countries in Europe and elsewhere have moved somewhat more rapidly from "bioethics" to "biolaw" (at least if law is viewed as legislative and regulatory rules) than has the United States. See generally Sev S. Fluss, An International Overview of Developments in Certain Areas, 1984–1994 11, 12–13 in A Legal Framework for Bioethics (Cosimo Marco Mazzoni ed. 1998). In both France and Britain, 1984 was a crucial year in the legalization of bioethical principles. In that year, the Warnock Report (on human fertilization and embryology) was presented in the United Kingdom,

and in France, the National Ethical Consultative Committee for the Life and Health Sciences (established in 1983) presented its "Recommendation for Legislation on Human Experimentation." Four years later, the French Parliament passed the Law on Human Experimentation. Id. at 25–26. Such legislative efforts represent the fledgling institutionalization of consensus. Yet, as Linda Nielsen of the University of Copenhagen has noted, "the interaction between bioethics and biolaw can be expected to be on the agenda nationally and internationally in the years to come." Linda Nielsen, From Bioethics to Biolaw 39, 39 in Mazzoni, supra.

In 2005, the UNESCO General Conference adopted the Universal Declaration on Bioethics and Human Rights. Article 2(a) declares that the document aims to offer a "universal framework of principles and procedures to guide States in the formulation of their legislation, policies or other instruments in the field of bioethics," http://portal.unesco.org/en/ev.php-URL_ID=31058&URL_DO=DO_TOPIC&URL_SECTION=201.html.

If there are costs to legislating morality, as Charity Scott suggests, are there special or different costs to regulating new applications of biotechnology? If there are, what might they be? Much of the biolaw in Europe and elsewhere has focused on biotechnology, in particular, assisted reproductive technologies and the creation or manipulation of embryos. By comparison, the United States has little regulation of these subject matters. What are the costs of regulating such matters? The costs of not regulating them?

One scholar considering this issue has written that supporters of biotechnology believe that the biotechnology industry will affirm the values of personal autonomy, self-determination, liberty, and equality and will "channel potentially life-saving biotechnological innovations in directions harmless to all but the human embryo." Such supporters favor a self-regulated industry. "In contrast, opponents of biotechnology fear the natural inclination of the market is to lead us toward 'the dehumanized hell of Brave New World.'" Nathan A. Adams, Creating Clones, Kids & Chimera: Liberal Democratic Compromise at the Crossroads, 20 Issues L. & Med. 3, 4 (2004). Do you fall into one of these two camps? Some place in the middle?

3. Charity Scott, supra, explores the presumptive divide between law and ethics and asserts that in medical contexts, there is no "bright line" distinguishing one from the other. Yet, broadly, she suggests that law sets a floor for behavior, not an "ethical maximum." Law is only one field that helps frame and respond to bioethical issues. Daniel Sulmasy and Jeremy Sugarman describe "medical ethics" as one of the "few academic fields in which truly interdisciplinary study is flourishing." Daniel P. Sulmasy & Jeremy Sugarman, The Many Methods of Medical Ethics (Or, Thirteen Ways of Looking at a Blackbird) in Methods in Medical Ethics 17 (Daniel P. Sulmasy & Jeremy Sugarman, eds., 2d ed. 2010).

It is worth further exploration of Sulmasy and Sugarman's understanding of medical ethics as a "truly interdisciplinary field." As a preliminary matter, note that Sulmasy and Sugarman distinguish medical ethics from bioethics. They view bioethics as a broader field. That notwithstanding, Sulmasy and Sugarman's understanding of medical ethics as a "field," not a "discipline" would seem to apply as well to bioethics. They write:

> We take the view that medical ethics is a single field of inquiry of great interest to many disciplines rather than a discipline in its own right. What medical ethicists

share is a common subject matter, not a common disciplinary mode of investigating that subject. Their common subject matter is the normative aspect of health care. This is the medical ethicists' blackbird. It is their field. However, they view it through the eyes of a view variety of disciplines. These disciplines employ a wide variety of methods, some shared by several disciplines and some unique to a particular discipline. Medical ethics is one field that embraces a variety of disciplines and methods.

Id. at 5–6.

4. *Bibliographic note.*   The history of bioethics in the United States is described in Albert R. Jonsen, *The Birth of Bioethics* (1998) and *The Encyclopedia of Bioethics* (Warren Reich ed. 1995) (see entry for "medical ethics, history of"). Other useful sources include Daniel P. Sulmasy, Dignity and Bioethics: History, Theory, and Selected Applications in Human Dignity and Bioethics: Essays Commissioned by the President's Council on Bioethics 469 (2008); Nancy C. Jecker, Albert R. Jonsen, & Robert A. Pearlman eds., Bioethics: An Introduction to the History, Methods, and Practice (2007); Onora O'Neill, Autonomy and Trust in Bioethics (2002); Robert Baker et al., The American Medical Ethics Revolution (1998); and William Rothstein, American Physicians in the Nineteenth Century: From Sects to Science (1973).

B.   PHILOSOPHICAL PRINCIPLES INFORMING BIOETHICS

Many of the most important philosophical theories that inform contemporary bioethics were developed in earlier centuries by moral philosophers in Europe and the United States. This section summarizes some of the more salient approaches within Western moral philosophy that have been brought to bear on bioethical inquiry. It is, by necessity, brief and therefore a bit dense. For those who have had little previous exposure to moral philosophy, the most successful way to approach the following material will likely be to focus on broad themes rather than to attempt to master either the intricacies of any particular theory or its historical development. If some of the material seems elusive in application, take heart in reading a leading bioethicist's opinion about what he describes as the fragile link between moral philosophy and contemporary bioethics. Tom Beauchamp writes:

> Many individuals in law, theological ethics, political theory, the social and behavioral sciences, and the health professions carefully address mainstream issues of bioethics without finding ethical theory essential or breathtakingly attractive. This is not surprising. Moral philosophers have traditionally formulated theories of the right, the good, and the virtuous in the most general terms. A practical price is paid for theoretical generality. It is often unclear whether and, if so, how theory is to be brought to bear on dilemmatic problems, public policy, moral controversies, and moral conflict—which I will here refer to as problems of practice. By "problems of practice" I mean the actual moral difficulties and issues presented in health policy and the health professions when decisions must be made about a proper action or policy.

Tom L. Beauchamp, Does Ethical Theory Have a Future in Bioethics? 32 J.L. Med. & Ethics 209, 209 (2004).

Notwithstanding Beauchamp's questioning of the relevance of moral philosophy to applied bioethics, we plunge ahead, for any study of bioethics in the United States must recognize the ever-present appeal to, search for, and argument about fundamental ethical principles.

1. Philosophical Ethical Theory

Those who founded the United States as a modern nation were heavily influenced by the works of both classical and contemporary philosophers. The "founders" looked for direction from John Locke, Charles-Louis Montesquieu, Hugo Grotius, Jean-Jacques Rousseau, and Bernard Mandeville, among others. The works of such thinkers assisted the founders in developing a useful understanding of politics that predicated government "[n]ot on man as he ought to be but on man as he often is: ignoble, self-interested, and ignorant." Daniel A. Farber & Suzanna Sherry, A History of the American Constitution 17 (1990).

Developments in European philosophy in the decades before 1776 were central to the thinking of the founders of the American nation. As a group, Americans of the late eighteenth century accepted the essential presumption of Lockean sensationalism that all people were born *equal* and were then altered by the consequences of environmental forces affecting their senses. But they modulated this position with the belief that people were inherently social and were equipped with basic moral categories that allowed them to make order out of the chaos of sensation. (This aspect of American philosophical history is described in Gordon Wood, The Radicalism of the American Revolution 229–243 (1992).)

Moral philosophy was prized as a subject of study in the early years of the Republic. Yet, as American philosophy developed, new, native voices replaced those of European thinkers. These new philosophical voices included those of William James and John Dewey. James, himself a doctor, spurned the notion of a final truth in ethics. Dewey, committed to science as the preferred model for rational thinking, saw science as a tool for arriving at ethical solutions to life's problems.

A variety of moral theories that continue to inform bioethics study developed from the work of these European and American moral philosophers. Tom Beauchamp and James Childress present five discrete moral theories or approaches constructed within the European-American tradition: utilitarianism, Kantianism, liberal individualism, communitarianism, and the ethics of care. Their book, Principles of Biomedical Ethics, (5th ed. 2001), is a useful reference for anyone seeking to pursue the study of moral philosophy as a foundation for contemporary bioethics. The remainder of this section summarizes each of the traditions of moral thought that Beauchamp and Childress have identified. It then considers several other approaches to bioethics that have been influential in the development of the field.

2. Utilitarianism

Utilitarianism, associated with two British philosophers, Jeremy Bentham (1748–1832) and John Stuart Mill (1806–1873), is referred to as a consequentialist or teleological approach to morals because actions are judged by their results (and not, for instance, by the character of the actor or the principles by which he chooses to act).

There are many different variations of utilitarianism but these early authors are associated with what is known as "hedonistic" and "act" utilitarianism. Results are judged by a hedonistic measure—by the pleasure and pain produced or avoided. Moreover, the morality of each act is viewed on a case-by-case basis, separately from the consequences of a potential aggregation of similar types of acts. Thus, an act is morally right if it causes greater net utility/happiness/pleasure than other potential acts, and one needn't consider what would happen if other people chose to follow a similar course of action. ("Rule" utilitarianism asks instead what general rules (rather than what specific act) would lead to the greatest happiness and then determines whether that rule applies to a specific situation.)

One rather obvious problem with utilitarianism is the difficulty of defining utility (pleasure) and disutility (pain). Bentham is known for an indiscriminate view toward pleasure, so that if a simple game creates more pleasure than poetry, then it is valued on that ground alone. John Stuart Mill amended Bentham's theory by proposing that some forms of pleasure are more noble than others. When compelled to explain how one decides which pleasures are the most noble, Mill concluded that the highest pleasures can be identified through reference to the rankings of the most impressive judges. In a well-known passage Mill explained:

> It is better to be a human being dissatisfied than a pig satisfied; better to be Socrates dissatisfied than a fool satisfied. And if the fool, or the pig, are of a different opinion, it is because they only know their own side of the question. The other party to the comparison knows both sides.

Mill, Utilitarianism (quoted in Basil Wiley, Nineteenth Century Studies: Coleridge to Matthew Arnold 171 (1949)). Nevertheless, this more discriminate or "qualitative" hedonism has been subject to its own criticisms—for example, as ultimately reflective of values other than mere pleasure—and thus not hedonistic at all. A more contemporary approach to defining utility is to consider individuals' preferences. Utility is considered achieved when preferences are fulfilled. This variation of utilitarianism provides an emphasis on individuals defining for themselves what they want, and is aligned with the law and economics movement of the past few decades.

Criticisms: There are many criticisms of utilitarianism beyond the difficulty of defining utility. Some common criticisms are (1) that utilitarianism provides no means of weighing different utilities against one another, a problem compounded when it is the happiness of one individual weighed against the suffering of another, and (2) utilitarianism can justify practices that are contrary to our considered moral judgments, to our notions of justice and fairness (one example often given is that utilitarianism would appear able to justify, under the right circumstances, the sacrifice of a few for the happiness of many). John D. Arras et al., Moral Reasoning in the Medical Context in Ethical Issues in Modern Medicine 1, 9–14 (John D. Arras & Bonnie Steinbock eds., 5th ed. 1999).

As a practical matter, utilitarianism is probably more important to American decision making than any other tradition from Western philosophy. Often explicitly, but much more often implicitly, Americans resolve apparent social dilemmas with reference to the comparative good and bad that they think will follow from a set of options, or the "cost–benefit" ratio as this sometimes translates to in economic realms. But that is not always the case. The moral philosophy of eighteenth-century philosopher Immanuel Kant has also retained a central place in contemporary bioethical theory. Arras et al., supra, at 14, suggest that Kantian ethics provides at least one response to a concern that utilitarianism could permit "hurting innocent people" if the majority is made happy.

3.   Kantianism

Basic to Kant's moral philosophy is the notion that one should follow a general principle of moral action. Kant rejected the teleological position of utilitarianism. For Kant, people's acts were not to be found right or wrong through reference to their consequences. Rather, in Kant's moral philosophy, general rules matter, and the principle on which a person acts is more important than the act's consequences. For this reason, Kant's perspective is labeled deontological. In Kant's Groundwork of the Metaphysics of Morals (H. J. Paton trans., Harper & Row, 1785, 1964), he formulated the essential principle (the so-called categorical imperative) as follows: "I ought never to act except in such a way that my maxim shall become a universal law." Id. at 70. This principle is often explained as something equivalent to the golden rule, "Do unto others as you would have them do unto you."

Kant constructed a second version of the categorical imperative. In this second version, Kant proposed that one should never treat any person (including oneself) as a means only; rather all people should always be treated as ends. This second formulation has been of great significance in bioethics as the foundation for focusing on autonomy as a basic bioethical principle. Kant's second formulation of the categorical imperative was grounded on an understanding of the person as something of absolute worth—"an end in itself," what Kant refers to as an "objective end." Arras et al., supra, at 14–17.

Acts were deemed good by Kant not because their results were good, not even because they were done out of love or affection, but because they harmonized with *duty*. Duties (obligations) follow from universal principles. A person performs his or her duty by acting in harmony with general moral principles. One of the basic conundrums that Kantian morality presents to bioethicists is that in which various apparent duties seem to conflict with each other. One might, for instance, find that Kantian ethics suggests a duty to tell the truth, but one might discover as well a duty to keep confidences. Yet, it might be impossible to do both at once.

For Kant, moral autonomy was of essential importance but he did not mean by this what contemporary bioethicists usually mean. Kant did not consider all chosen acts to be autonomous. For him, a person could be described as acting autonomously only if that person chose to act in accord with universally valid rules. Kant labeled acts driven by passion, intuition, ambition, and all other motivations as heteronomous. In this, Kant's view of moral autonomy differed widely from what present-day bioethicists and lawmakers intend when they discuss the significance of protecting autonomy. In short, unlike much of Western thought today, Kant's view of moral autonomy did not presume unlimited choice. Rather, for Kant, moral autonomy presumed a commitment to the a priori rules of practical reason. Francis Fukuyama describes those rules as having "forced us often to do things at cross-purposes with our natural individual desires and inclinations." Francis Fukuyama, Our Posthuman Future 124 (2002). In contrast, explains Fukuyama, "[c]ontemporary understandings of individual autonomy . . . seldom provide a way to distinguish between genuine moral choices and choices that amount to the pursuit of individual inclinations, preferences, desires, and gratifications." In effect, contemporary culture has swallowed Kant's notion of moral autonomy with a utilitarian endgame. Id.

The more recent work of philosopher John Rawls embodies the classical Kantian approach with its emphasis on autonomy, equality, and reason (Beauchamp & Childress, supra, at 352), but it also provides new insights into thinking about moral problems. Rawls argues in his famous work, A Theory of Justice (1971), that we can discern principles of justice by imagining an initial situation in which all members of the community have an equal voice in choosing the principles by which society shall be governed, but in making such choices they are under a "veil of ignorance," so that they do not know their own social and economic status, or any other characteristics about themselves that would influence their views of the principles considered. This hypothetical "social contract" should, according to Rawls, yield principles that are fair to all. See Arras et al., supra, at 17–19.

4.   Liberal Individualism

By "liberal individualism" authors Beauchamp and Childress refer to the notion that individuals in society have various rights that protect them from intrusion (especially by the state) with regard to a wide set of personal choices and acts. The roots of this liberal individualism go back to the seventeenth century. This perspective is deeply embedded within the American legal system and in its constitutional protection of individual liberties, and at least some version of liberal individualism has been internalized by most Americans who routinely discuss or assert their own right to be free from various potential intrusions by others, including the state.

Despite the widespread internalization of a rights perspective in the United States today, liberal individualism has its critics. Liberal individualism tends to focus on negative rights (e.g., the right to be free from some governmental intrusion) over positive rights (e.g., the right to receive aid from the government) and thus favors liberty over welfare, arguably without adequate regard to the consequences for individual or societal well-being. Another criticism of liberal individualism is the lack of a comprehensive justification (a "meta-theory") for determining what rights individuals should be viewed as possessing and why. Finally, as the Charity Scott reading above suggests with respect to law, the "rights" espoused by liberal individualism do not readily answer what should be done in many situations—just because someone has a right to do something, doesn't mean that she should do it. See Beauchamp & Childress, supra, at 360–361. Some of the limitations of liberal individualism are especially relevant in the context of bioethics and medical ethics. Among other things, public health and medical research sometimes demand that individuals' rights be displaced or at least limited for the sake of some larger community.

Defending a rights-based approach from various critics, Beauchamp and Childress summarize their own view of rights-based theory by concluding:

> No part of the moral vocabulary has done more to protect the legitimate interests of citizens in political states than the language of rights. Predictably, injustice and inhumane treatment occur most frequently in states that fail to recognize human rights in their political rhetoric and documents.

Id. at 362.

5.   Communitarianism

Both what has been called the "communitarian ethic" and what has been called the "ethic of care" present explicit alternatives to a moral perspective that places greatest value on the individual and his or her rights.

Communitarianism focuses on the good of the community rather than of specific individuals composing the community and generally values communal traditions and cooperation. Liberal individualism, by contrast, arguably precludes the sort of wisdom that stems from comprehending the person's place within the larger community. Alasdair MacIntyre, After Virtue (2d ed. 1984). Ezekiel Emanuel has applied one version of a communitarian approach to health care in suggesting that communal traditions and shared understandings of virtue have helped form the universe of health care. Emanuel explains his understanding of the advantages of focusing on communal practice and belief in place of the liberal position that visions of the good life should be left to the individual to choose:

> Liberalism espouses the ideal of neutrality, namely that public institutions, laws, and policies should not promote any particular view of what is worthy or good. But, absent judgments about what is worthy or good, we cannot decide whether a medical intervention promotes a patient's well-being or is deemed harmful.
>   . . . It is not just that different people will have different views on what is worthy or good and that in practice achieving consensus on these judgments will be difficult; it is that by prohibiting the polity from espousing particular views of the good life, liberal political philosophy excludes, even in theory, a shared framework for resolving such medical ethical questions.

Ezekiel J. Emanuel, The Ends of Human Life: Medical Ethics in a Liberal Polity 7 (1991).

6.   Ethics of Care

The ethics of care resembles communitarianism in rejecting the centrality of individualism to moral practice, but unlike communitarianism it focuses intently on the space between particular actors. The creation, sustenance, and transformation of relationships become a primary concern for one committed to an ethics of care. This perspective, which developed in large part from the work of psychologist Carol Gilligan, can offer guidance in thinking about consequences of various actions for relationships between those participating in the health care system. In her path-breaking book, In a Different Voice (1982), Gilligan differentiated an "ethic of justice [which] proceeds from the premise of equality" (an ethic more often voiced by men than by women) from "an ethic of care," which presumes that "no one should be hurt" (more often voiced by women than by men). Id. at 174. Gilligan differentiated the moral reasoning of two young children (aged 11), one a girl whom Gilligan calls Amy and the other a boy, called Jake. Whereas Amy analyzed a moral dilemma by presuming a world "comprised of relationships rather than of people standing alone, a world that coheres through human connection rather than through systems of rules," Jake saw the world through the lens of "systems of logic and law." Id. at 28. Gilligan's description of Amy's moral system has become a prototype of sorts for an approach that focuses on how various responses are likely to affect relationships.

The reading from feminist philosopher Rosemarie Tong, which follows this summary of ethical theory, provides more information about the ethics of care as applied to the practice of medicine and the provision of health care.

7. Bioethics Principles

Although each of the five ethical theories described above have had considerable influence in the literature and general construction of bioethical inquiry, there are some approaches in bioethics that deliberately reject "metatheory" as unworkable. The most prominent of these has become known as *Principlism,* which has "virtually corner[ed] the methodological market in bioethics." John Arras, Principles and Particularity: The Role of Cases in Bioethics, 69 Ind. L.J. 983 (1994). Principlism, espoused by Tom Beauchamp and James Childress, posits that dilemmas in biomedical ethics should be resolved by application of the midlevel principles of autonomy, nonmaleficence, beneficence, and justice (with none of these principles given priority). Arras explains some of the appeal to this approach by contrasting it with more traditional philosophical theories, which have elusive practical applicability for those who actually confront ethical dilemmas. He writes that the "theory-driven" ethicist

> could offer advice in the vein of a "Consumer Reports" Service: "Well, in this situation a Kantian would do 'X,' a utilitarian would promote 'Y,' and a natural rights theorist would advocate 'Z.'" Needless to say, such "advice" might not prove enormously helpful to those doctors, nurses, and social workers who haven't quite figured out where they stand in the ongoing debate between the partisans of Kant, Mill, and Locke.

Id. at 989. Although the Principlism framework has been highly influential, of course it is not without its own critics, Arras among them, who urges less of a "top-down" approach from principles to facts and more attention to the particularity of a given situation (a more casuistic (case-based) or narrative approach). Others criticize Principlism for not being "theoretical enough" (where do the principles come from, they ask) and for not providing guidance when the principles appear to collide in a given situation (how should conflicts between the principles be resolved?).

Throughout this book you will find many opportunities to discuss the midlevel principles that are often appealed to in consideration of bioethical dilemmas, and to consider their adequacy in resolving those problems. In addition, you will be pressed, often in the notes and questions following the readings, to consider the particularities of a given situation and their import in resolving bioethics questions. Chapter 11 also includes a reading by John Arras specifically aimed at exploring the importance of detail—the example given is one of a public health challenge.

8. *"Critical" Perspectives*

Bioethics has also been influenced by what are often considered "critical" perspectives, perspectives in which central recognition is given to the reality of existing inequalities along gender, race, ethnicity, class, and other lines. Such perspectives challenge the power structures that have created and perpetuated those inequalities. Among such critical approaches are feminist perspectives other than that constructed directly as a result of Gilligan's work (these are discussed in the next reading) and perspectives developed out of critical race theory. Susan Sherwin summarizes the concerns of many feminists and critical race theorists about bioethical issues:

> North American society is characteristically sexist, racist, classist, homophobic, and frightened of physical or mental imperfections; we can anticipate, then, that those who are oppressed by virtue of their gender, race, class, sexual orientation, or disabilities—and especially, those who are oppressed in a number of different ways—will experience a disproportional share of illness and will often suffer reduced access to resources. . . . Ethical analyses of the distribution of health and health care must take into consideration the role that oppression plays in a person's prospects for health and well-being.

Susan Sherwin, Gender, Race, and Class in the Delivery of Health Care 392, 393 in Bioethics: An Introduction to the History, Methods, and Practice (Nancy S. Jecker et al. eds. 1997).

In the 1980s, a group of African-American scholars created the African-American Perspectives on Biomedical Ethics Project to encourage thought and discussion of whether there is a unique African-American perspective in bioethics and, if so, how it might be described. These questions produced a number of different and sometimes opposing answers, some of which are published in African-American Perspectives on Biomedical Ethics (Harley E. Flack & Edmund D. Pellegrino eds. 1992). Annett Dula argued in one paper published in this volume that yes, African Americans do have a unique perspective on bioethics that follows from their experiences in unequal power relationships in the health care system and society in general. Those experiences justify a general and pervasive skepticism about informed consent within such unequal relationships as well as attention to broad questions of distributive justice. She writes compellingly about the disparate attention certain bioethical issues receive: "[T]wice as many black babies die as white babies. We should perhaps give special attention to this problem. For surely it is an ethical issue at least as important as a custody fight for frozen embryos." Annette Dula, Yes, There Are African-American Perspectives in Bioethics, in African-American Perspectives on Biomedical Ethics, supra, at 193, 201. Cheryl Sanders answers the central question posed by the project somewhat differently. She writes that "[u]ltimately the ethical question is not that of an African-American perspective but of African-American partic-ipation and inclusion." Cheryl J. Sanders, Problems and Limitations of an African-American Perspective in Biomedical Ethics: A Theological View, in African-American Perspectives on Biomedical Ethics, supra, at 165, 171.

In summary, bioethical inquiry often draws from many different traditions and sources, from classical philosophical theories that have general applicability to ethical problems, to approaches more closely tailored to the perceived real-ities of applied bioethics, to more modern critical approaches, and finally, as discussed in section C, from various religious or theological traditions.

The following reading by philosophy professor Rosemarie Tong explains some of the distinctions between the at times radically different perspectives that are identified generally under "feminism," distinctions that might be unfamiliar to many readers. Moreover and perhaps more important, Tong's approach to the case of Armando Dimas illustrates that much of what the study of bioethics attempts to do is to frame the relevant questions rather than provide the clear answers to a situation encountered or policy choice to be made.

Rosemarie Tong, *Feminist Approaches to Bioethics*
In Feminism and Bioethics, Beyond Reproduction 67, 76–82 (Susan M. Wolf ed. 1996)

Clearly when it comes to moral concerns about women and reproduction, liberal, radical, and cultural feminists offer traditional bioethics some new per-spectives. Yet these same perspectives may also be applied to cases beyond women and reproduction, because issues of choice, control, and caring are omnipresent in bioethical decision making. Moreover, I believe that these (and other) feminist perspectives not only can but should be brought to tradi-tional bioethics, because what feminists see about human relationships, espe-cially male–female relationships, others cannot easily see. This claim is a large one, and although I cannot thoroughly defend it here, I will try to illustrate it by interpreting a case voluntarily reported to Lisa Belkin by the involved parties and subsequently published in the New York Times Magazine. Entitled "The High Cost of Living," Belkin's case shows how male as well as female patients can lose their powers of choice, control, and caring before the power of authority, and suggests why a feminist analysis may be better suited than a traditional one to explore such issues of domination and subordination.

The Armando Dimas Case: Moving Beyond Women and Reproduction

As told by Belkin, the night that twenty-four-year-old Armando Dimas was shot, the emergency room of Houston's Hermann Hospital was crowded to capacity, a fact that caused some of the hospital staff to speculate that Dimas was admitted largely because hospital authorities viewed him as a potential organ donor. After a preliminary examination of Dimas, David MacDougall, the neurosurgeon on call, concluded that "This guy should be dead." But he was not dead. The patient had been resuscitated, returned to consciousness, and put on a ventilator for life support. Gathered around his bed were his immediate family: a fourteen-member group of illegal Mexican immigrants who had recently applied for residency in the United States under a new amnesty law. Although most of the hospital staff believed that Dimas would want to die if he knew his actual condition, his mother, Victoria Dimas, refused to let anyone tell her son that he would never walk again. MacDougall finally broke the gridlock. He asked social worker Cindy Walker to convene a meeting between Dimas's major hospital care givers and his family. Directing his attention primarily to Mrs. Dimas, and speaking through an interpreter, MacDougall told her that it was time to face reality: no one was going to perform a miracle on her son. Mrs. Dimas responded angrily to MacDougall, exploding in Spanish that it was wrong to lie to her son: "He can walk, he will walk. He can breathe; he will not need that machine." The meeting, to which the patient had not been invited, ended as abruptly as it had been convened.

Informed about the unsuccessful confrontation, hospital authorities decided it was best to tell Dimas about his condition, his mother's protests notwithstanding. They selected nurse Norma McNair to tell him the awful truth. To everyone's surprise, Dimas did not opt for a do-not-resuscitate order. Using two blinks of his eyes for "yes" and one for "no," he communicated a desire for full treatment. He wanted it all—cardiopulmonary resuscitation, antibiotics, ventilators, feeding tubes. The staff was speechless. Since patients in Dimas's condition should not want to live, they did not know what to do.

As Dimas's drama unfolded, he became a problem for the hospital's cost controller, former nurse Hazel Mitchell. Because Dimas lacked insurance and his family was too poor to pay even a fraction of his bill, the hospital had to absorb the total cost. Dimas also became a major challenge for occupational therapist Mary Coffey. She soon realized that besides teaching Dimas how to speak and eat, she could accomplish little else for him until he had a custom made wheelchair to support his back and head, thereby enabling him to use a "mouthstick." With this device, Dimas would have an opportunity to learn the kind of skills that could secure him future employment. Although Mitchell initially refused to pour more hospital resources in Dimas, she later relented and ordered the special chair (which turned out not to fit him). However, she also decided to move Dimas to Hermina Bartkowski's Total Life Care Center ("Bart's," for short). There the bills would be $300 a day instead of $890, largely because the staff consisted of Polish immigrant physicians plus nurses willing to work as nurses' aides for very low salaries.

Dimas liked Bart's, where the standard of care was amazingly high due to the efforts of director Bartkowski, widely revered as a saint. Compared to the rough-and-tumble life in the streets Dimas once walked, Bart's was a safe and comfortable haven: "I see my family . . . my sister brings me food. . . . If I hadn't been shot, I would have died." However, after four and one-half years and approximately $750,000 worth of treatment, Hermann Hospital was tired of paying Dimas's bills at Bart's and gave his family one month to learn how to care for him at home. Although the Dimas family objected to this turn of events, Dimas was sent home at the end of the thirty days, still without an adequate wheelchair. There he remains, with round-the-clock care provided by his family, but primarily by his ailing mother. Dimas seems to be happy, however, spending much time with his elementary-school-aged, illegitimate son, who visits frequently. He no longer complains that he was sent home, stating matter-of-factly, "Things changed. This is the way it is. That's all."

But is that all? Is this the way it should be? Why did things change? Focusing on issues of choice, liberal feminists might initially be persuaded that Dimas's case was handled in an ethically appropriate manner. The principle of autonomy (liberalism's major playing card) seemed to appropriately trump the principle of beneficence. After all, the hospital staff honored Dimas's decision to go on living, despite their overall belief that he would be better off dead. . . .

Liberal:

On further reflection, however, liberal feminists might wonder just how autonomous Dimas's choices had really been. Communication gaps were numerous in his case, and since any lack of communication tends to empty the meaning of informed consent, it is more than conceivable that Dimas did not always understand his treatment options. To be sure, the staff eventually gave him the information he needed to decide to refuse a do-not-resuscitate order, but they may not have also given him enough information to decide to participate (or not participate) in his own rehabilitation program. The fact that Dimas never protested his not learning the mouthstick skills Coffey regarded as essential to his rehabilitation might signal to liberal feminists that he either did not want to learn these skills, deeming them a paternalistic intrusion into his life, or that he did not understand how limited his life opportunities would be without them.

Similarly, liberal feminists might come to doubt that hospital authorities really treated Dimas as fairly as they should have. Had Dimas been insured, a properly-fitting wheelchair would probably have been found for him quickly, and every effort would have been made to teach him any learnable skills he wanted to acquire. Negative rights—the right to refuse unwanted treatment—are only half the story. Positive rights—the right to demand wanted treatment—may be the other. If the only choice poor patients have is the choice to say "no," their range of treatment options is limited indeed.

Radical:

Instead of focusing on what they perceive as beside-the-point issues of choice, most radical feminists would examine issues of control. They would emphasize how powerless patients are relative to the physicians, other health care professionals, and hospital administrators in charge of their treatment. Specifically, they might view as inappropriate the hospital staff's eagerness to get Dimas's consent to a do-not-resuscitate order. In comparison to most of the people in charge of his fate—that is, the socially and economically privileged hospital physicians and administrators—Dimas, a poor, uneducated, Mexican American day laborer, was always relatively powerless. His powerlessness became nearly absolute when MacDougall pronounced him "a head in a bed," a thing to run from as quickly as possible.

Articulating a variation on this same theme, radical feminists might also note that, like Dimas, his relatives were relatively powerless within the health care system and its structures. The Dimas family panicked when hospital authorities gave them one month to learn how to care for Dimas at home (home being a five-room trailer with an on-again, off-again electrical system, a dysfunctional heating system, and three times as many occupants as rooms). . . . In the end, the Dimas family adjusted to the rigors of home care for a quadriplegic. They had no other option, not if they wanted Dimas to go on living. . . . Made under conditions of severe constraint, such "choices" are not, in the view of radical feminists, true expressions of one's will. Rather they are coping mechanisms: strategies to make the best out of situations one has little or no power to change.

Interested in all the uses, misuses, and abuses of power in Dimas's case, most radical feminists would be particularly interested in gender inequities. They might be quick to observe that the people with the least power in Dimas's case (the nurses, nurses' aides, occupational therapists, and social workers) occupy traditionally female-dominated positions. Indeed, almost all of the people doing the hard work in Dimas's case—cleaning his body, sticking him with needles, teaching him how to eat and talk, bearing the brunt of his home care—are women.

In their concern that women sometimes care too much for others and not enough for themselves, radical feminists might even dare to ask some troubling questions about Dimas. He may be powerless relative to white men, educated men, propertied men, men who are United States citizens, able bodied men, and even "exceptional women" such as Mitchell, the former nurse turned cost controller who succeeds in a male-dominated occupation. Yet Dimas is not powerless relative to most women, especially the women in his family who, like him, belong to an ethnic group in which the man rules the roost. Radical feminists might wonder how caring Dimas would be if his mother had been the injured one. They might also wonder whether Mrs. Dimas, knowing how difficult it is to care for a severely disabled person at home, would either expect or want her family to devote themselves totally to her care. . . .

[R]adical feminists would probably speculate that an injured Mrs. Dimas, not wishing to be a burden on her family, especially her daughters, would willingly refuse further medical treatment for herself.

In contrast to radical feminists, cultural feminists would focus on issues of ***Cultural:*** caring and connection rather than control and occupation. They would probably comment on the kind of relationships established between Dimas and the health care professions assigned to his case. They might speculate that Mitchell and Walker, for example, really wanted to do more for Dimas, but could not. When Mitchell refers to an ancient Chinese saying—"if you save a life, you are responsible for it"—cultural feminists might hear Mitchell expressing a desire to do everything possible for Dimas, a desire frustrated by the nature of her job which requires her to view Dimas and all the patients at Hermann as statistics and costs. Similarly, in Walker's words, "We can't just buy him a custom-made wheelchair. . . . We have to face the fact that we can't afford him as it is," cultural feminists might hear not the voice of a hardened social worker, fixed on the financial bottom line, but of a caring social worker, painfully aware of the scarce nature of medical resources. An ethics of justice was the only morality Walker's and Mitchell's jobs really permitted them, and within its constraints, they cared for Dimas and their other patients as best they could.

In addition to interpreting Mitchell's and Walker's actions sympathetically, cultural feminists would probably single out Mary Coffey, Hermina Bartkowski, and Victoria Dimas for special praise, emphasizing their apparent decisions to move beyond the impartiality of an ethics of justice to the partiality of an ethics of care. They might note that Coffey fought to get Dimas connected to the world beyond his family, realizing full well that unless he could learn how to use a mouthstick, he would always remain the one cared for. Since he had no chance to acquire this skill without a properly-fitted wheelchair, Coffey made securing that wheelchair her main priority.

Similarly, cultural feminists might observe that for Bartkowski each one of her patients was a unique individual, deserving of special attention. She viewed none of them as just a body. On the contrary, Bartkowski spoke to each of her patients, even the unresponsive ones, as if they understood her every word. Offensive phrases such as "head-in-a-bed" never crossed her consciousness.

Finally, cultural feminists might note that while the bulk of the hospital staff worried about getting a do-not-resuscitate order from Dimas and closing the "case," Mrs. Dimas felt what her son probably felt: fear and anger. Indeed, when MacDougall informed her "that this is all there will ever be" for a "head in a bed," Mrs. Dimas reacted with rage against what she probably perceived as an arrogant universalization. How could MacDougall possibly know the things she knew about her son—his singular strengths as well as hidden weaknesses? Indeed, how could anyone on the hospital staff know better than she what her son really needed? The whole time the staff was preoccupied with getting Dimas to consent to a do-not-resuscitate order, it never occurred to Mrs. Dimas or, for that matter, to anyone else in the Dimas family, to think that they could disconnect from Armando at will. Instead of viewing Mrs. Dimas as an irrational woman who made excessive demands on the health care system, cultural feminists would probably see her as a caring mother who in seeking treatment for her son relied on her "feelings, needs, impressions, and . . . sense of personal ideal" rather than on some set of moral axioms, theorems, or principles.

NOTES AND QUESTIONS

1. *Feminist perspectives.*   According to Rosemarie Tong, what are the questions that liberal, radical, and cultural feminists would ask regarding the care of Armando Dimas? Do you find one of these approaches more helpful than the others? What makes these approaches feminist? What additional questions would you have to ask about the Dimas case?

2. *Other ethical perspectives.*   How might a utilitarian approach the facts of the Dimas case? A Kantian? Someone who finds liberal individualism a compelling perspective?

C.   RELIGION AND BIOETHICS

Although many bioethical quandaries might find resolution within one or another religious tradition, in the American context, constitutional provisions preclude the perspective of any one religion displacing others. Thus, although different religious organizations have sought to weigh in on bioethical debates, and some scholars write from an explicitly religious viewpoint, as a matter of policy making, religious views tend to be considered more out of respect for religion in general and as proof of attention to morality than as a path toward the concrete resolution of bioethical issues. In short, the multiplicity of religious traditions in the United States and the constitutional protection afforded to each of them precludes lawmakers from resolving bioethics dilemmas through express resort to the beliefs and rules of any particular religious tradition. At the same time, religious perspectives often rely on a "natural law" perspective, which embodies common intuitions about what is right and good and offers some counterweight to a purely utilitarian calculus. Whereas among bioethics scholars, utilitarian arguments might be countered with a Kantian or Rawlsian approach, among the general public and policymakers in general, a "natural law" approach, often grounded in religious tradition, provides a more easily understood basis for objecting to or questioning a utilitarian conclusion.

The 1999 Report of the National Bioethics Advisory Commission on cloning illustrates both the value and the limitations of relying on religious traditions to create public policy and law. The commission, asked by President Clinton to make recommendations about human cloning soon after the birth of the first cloned mammal in 1997, reviewed a variety of religious perspectives but relied on none of them. Report and Recommendations of the National Bioethics Advisory Commission, Cloning Human Beings I (1997). In Chapter 3 of the report (situated between a chapter about the science of cloning and a chapter about "ethical considerations"), the commission summarized the relevance of several "Western" religious traditions to deliberations about human cloning. The commission identified several themes common to those traditions, including "responsible human dominion over nature, human dignity and destiny, procreation, and family life." Id. at 106. What follows are portions of the report's discussion concerning various religious traditions' understanding of "responsible human dominion over nature" as it relates to cloning.

Report and Recommendations of the National Bioethics Advisory Commission, Cloning Human Beings
(1997)

The question of personhood or human distinctiveness is commonly described and explained in Judaism and Christianity with reference to the theological theme of creation in the image of God. Interpretations of the moral meaning of the image of God depend on prior convictions about the nature of God and the characteristics of God that human beings are believed to reflect. The biblical story of creation is most commonly used for interpreting the image of God. Particularly significant is the language of Genesis, chapter 1, verses 27–28: "So God created man in his own image, in the image of God he created him, male and female he created them. And God blessed them, and God said to them, 'Be fruitful and multiply, and fill the earth and subdue it; and have dominion over the fish of the sea and over the birds of the air and over every living thing that moves upon the earth'" (Revised Standard Version).

. . . Religious traditions variously interpret the biblical mandate of human dominion over nature. Three different interpretations are particularly significant in debates about cloning humans. One common model is an ethic of stewardship, which holds that humans are entrusted with administrative responsibility for creation. Human stewardship involves caring for and cultivating creation after the manner of a gardener. This stewardship ethic, one version of which is prominent in Roman Catholicism, accepts nature as a good to be maintained and preserved.

A second model suggests a "partnership" between human beings and God in caring for and improving upon creation. Rabbi Dorff notes that "we are God's 'partners in the ongoing act of creation' when we improve the human lot in life." The Jewish tradition emphasizes that God has given humans a "positive commandment" to "master the world," and some Jewish thinkers explicate human mastery over nature by reference to the two directions for Adam and Eve in the Garden: They were "to work it [the garden] and to preserve it" (Genesis 2:15). To "work" nature is to improve it to meet human needs, and this activity is both right and obligatory "as long as we preserve nature." It also includes efforts to heal. Human responsibility, in the final analysis, involves "balancing" human and divine actions in this partnership.

This second model also appears in some Islamic thought. One Islamic scholar stresses that "as participants in the act of creating with God, human beings can actively engage in furthering the overall well-being of humanity by intervening in the works of nature, including the early stages of embryonic development, to improve human health." The natural world on this second model is inherently malleable and can be shaped in several different ways in service of valuable human and divine goals. Proponents of this model could view cloning research, and perhaps even cloning humans in some circumstances, as using human creative potential for good.

A third perspective, which some Protestants defend, is potentially even more receptive to the prospect of cloning humans. It understands human beings as "created co-creators." On the one hand, human beings are created, dependent on God, and finite and fallible. On the other hand, they assume the role of co-creator to acquire and implement knowledge to improve humanity and the world. Human beings are called to "play human" through their freedom and responsibility in creating an essentially open human future. Reproductive and genetic technologies, along with technologies to create a child through cloning, can express responsible created co-creatorship.

Although Genesis notes that creation is "good" and humanity "very good," humans have displayed, according to some traditions, an irremediable propensity to use their divinely authorized dominion for unauthorized domination, to violate their covenant of partnership with God, and to create after their own image rather than the divine image. The person created in the image of God is thus also marked by a tendency to transgress limits, to commit what some traditions call sin. As a consequence, all human activities are pervasively imperfect. The narratives in Genesis of Adam and Eve in the Garden of Eden, their eating of the fruit of the Tree of the Knowledge of Good and Evil, and the later Tower of Babel often appear in religious discussions of human temptations and tendencies to transgress appropriate limits.

The prospect that humans can and will choose evil rather than good dictates caution as a moral necessity. Even though human imperfection does not necessarily justify halting technological advances, it should, according to many religious thinkers, evoke modesty about human aspirations and achievements.

NOTES AND QUESTIONS

1. *The role of religion in bioethical inquiry.*   The commission explained that it was interested in religious perspectives on human cloning because "religious traditions influence and guide many citizens' responses to various issues in biomedicine, including such novel developments as human cloning." Id. at 39. If a particular policy would engender widespread opposition on religious grounds, it might not be feasible. Id. at 40. In addition, the commission was interested in determining whether there might be common ground between religious and secular positions because some religious positions rest on basic premises that are appealing to individuals outside the religious traditions— premises that ascribe importance to "nature," "basic human values," or the like. Id. at 39. Do you agree that these are good reasons to include a consider- ation of religious views in debates that could influence law or policy? Should the commission have excluded this discussion?

2. *Religious pluralism.*   What does the report conclude with respect to the position of various religious traditions on the issue of cloning? Although you have only a small excerpt here, what does the common religious theme of "responsible dominion over nature" suggest for the ethical propriety of human cloning?

The commission's report discusses other religious themes as well, but its ultimate conclusion with regard to religious matters can be foreseen in this brief discussion of "responsible dominion": American culture is exceedingly plural- istic, and in keeping with that pluralism, "there is no single 'religious' view on cloning humans." Id. at 57. Thus, despite the commission's attention to religious thought, the commission's most essential conclusion elided all of the religious perspectives. It ultimately concluded that no one should attempt to clone a human because "current scientific information indicates that this technique is not safe to use in humans at this time." Id. at 108. According to law professor Janet Dolgin,

> By invoking a wide assortment of theological voices (all within the Western tradition), the Report establishes that no one such voice can be allowed to speak exclusively and definitively within the public arena. Yet, by invoking sacred tradition, the Report situates its efforts within a greater American civil religion that demands mention of divine direction in all important endeavors.

Janet L. Dolgin, *In a Pod*, 38 Jurimetrics J. 47, 51 (1997).

3. *Science and religion.*   The commission's report fell back to science to answer the question about the current ethical propriety of cloning (i.e., it's not safe, so let's not do it . . . yet). Some might question, then, whether its dis- cussion of religious traditions was even necessary or appropriate, if in the end it was the science that mattered.

An opposite concern has been described by law professor Steven Goldberg and others. Their concern is not that religion might be invoked to answer sci- entific questions, but that science might be invoked to answer religious ques- tions. Goldberg worries that religious leaders are giving too much credence to "science," that they are defining the "good" and the "right" in light of the latest study reported by the media rather than in light of theological conclusions and philosophical debate. Steven Goldberg, Religious Contributions to the Bioethics Debate: Utilizing Legal Rights While Avoiding Scientific Temptations, 30 Fordham Urb. L.J. 35 (2002):

> Part of the problem with giving science an unduly large role in our thinking is that we then tend to believe that only those things that are quantifiable are worthy of our attention. This perspective is quite widespread in our society. As Gertrude Himmelfarb has pointed out, we now see "the attempt of political philosophy to transform itself into political science, history into social science, literary criticism into semiotics. . . ." Religious organizations should stand against this tendency; they should not exemplify it.

Science can tell us about what is, but not about what ought to be. Id. at 42. See also Dominic J. Balestra, Toward Epistemic Justice: A Response to Professor Goldberg, 30 Fordham Urb. L.J. 47, 48 (2002) (arguing for an "intellectually acceptable space for a religious perspective in our attempts to arrive at the 'right' course of action in response to the challenges presented by today's sciences and technologies").

4. *Religion and clinical care.*   Differing religious perspectives, as between a patient and his or her clinician, can create biases that affect both parties. Mark Carr suggests that on a "faith–science continuum," clinicians are likely to sit at the "science end," but patients and their families might sit at the "faith" end. In such cases, communication could be limited and creation of a "healing relationship" might be stymied. Mark F. Carr, The Spectrum of Religion and Science in Clinical Encounters, 19 J. Clinical Ethics 360 (2008). Carr suggests the best response for both sides (although he seems to place the essential responsibility on clinicians) is to become aware of their biases and the implications that those biases hold for creation of the clinician–patient relationship.

5. *Do all ethics theories begin in myth?*   Is a religious point of view really different from other ethical viewpoints? Philosophy professor (and Franciscan friar and MD) Daniel P. Sulmasy argues that every ethical theory, and not just religious theory, relies on an underlying myth—a "narrative" mostly, which explains "the origins of a given condition and the model for further developments." Daniel P. Sulmasy, Every *Ethos* Implies a *Mythos*: Bioethics and Faith, in Notes from a Narrow Ridge: Religion and Bioethics (Dena Davis & Laurie Zoloth eds. 1997). Although ethics uses reason, the "reason begins in myth." As one among several examples he offers, Sulmasy explains the ethical system of bioethics scholar H. Tristram Engelhardt, Jr., as being fundamentally about individual freedom (and little about equality) and based on "the myth of the American frontier," in which "life is a great frontier to be tamed by powerful individuals." Although the normative ethics that derive from Engelhardt's bioethical system contrast dramatically with the ethics promoted by bioethics scholars such as Laurie Zoloth and Edmund Pellegrino, who often explicitly write from Jewish and Christian traditions, respectively, each of these systems of ethics is similarly reliant on myth. The central myth defining morality in the Jewish and Christian traditions, writes Sulmasy, is the care given to the stranger and the

powerless, "the myth of the patient as stranger." Why, Sulmasy asks, give preference to one of these myths over the other?

CHALLENGING ISSUES: APPLYING ETHICAL THEORY

Consider the following bioethical issues and identify the kinds of questions that should frame a discussion of the issue from the standpoint of several of the ethical theories or approaches described in this chapter (e.g., Kantianism, utilitarianism, ethic of care, principlism). Try to choose theories that bring very different questions to bear on resolution of the issues.

1. *The case of conjoined twins.*   Suppose twin girls were joined at birth in such a way that if they were not separated, both would die within a year. If they were separated, the weaker one would die but the stronger one would have a good chance of survival. The surgical separation of the twins would itself cause the death of the weaker twin. The parents do not want the children separated. It is against their religious beliefs to make a choice between the two infants. They are also concerned that if the twins are separated, the surviving twin will need very expensive and extraordinary care that they cannot provide because they have little money and live in a relatively undeveloped country. Although they have traveled to a more industrialized country with advanced medical resources to consult about the twins' case, they will be returning to their country of origin soon. The physicians for the twins have petitioned the court for an order requiring the parents to consent to the surgery. (This problem is based on the English case of In re A, excerpted and discussed in Chapter 3.)

2. *Clinical trials in Africa.*   A U.S. pharmaceutical company is conducting clinical trials of a new investigational drug believed to reduce the risk of transmission of HIV infection from a pregnant woman to her fetus. A different drug already exists that is used in the United States with very good results of reducing perinatal transmission. The company is trying to develop a less expensive drug with the same effect. Is it ethically permissible for the company to run blind control studies in African populations to test the effectiveness of the drug? In other words, half of the women with HIV infection who will be enrolled in the study will not receive any drug to reduce perinatal transmission and the other half will receive the new investigational drug. (This protocol is discussed in Chapter 11.)

3. *Medical training on anesthetized patients.*   An attending physician is performing a pelvic examination of an anesthetized woman to determine the presence of fibroid tumors. He tells the three medical students in attendance with him that they should also conduct a pelvic examination for the purposes of their training, which they do. On entering the research and training hospital, the woman was informed that medical students and residents might participate in her care under the supervision of an attending physician. (This scenario is based on a problem presented in One More Pelvic Exam, Hastings Ctr. Rpt., Nov.–Dec. 1993.) For further information relating to this practice, see Robin Fretwell Wilson, Unauthorized Practice: Teaching Pelvic Examination on Women Under Anesthesia, Commentary, 58 J. Am. Med. Women's Assoc. 217 (Fall 2003).

D. ETHICS OF THE MEDICAL PROFESSION AND THE "BIOETHICS OF BIOETHICS"

1. *Formalized Medical Ethics*

Although the field known as bioethics may be marked by the inclusion of "outsiders"—people and institutions other than patients and physicians—in questioning and determining the ethical dimensions of medical decision making, the "insiders," in particular, physicians, have long adopted, formally and informally, various principles for ethical medical practice. The Hippocratic Oath, at least 2,000 years old, has been a traditional source of ethical direction for doctors for many years. Its popularity might have peaked in the United States in the mid-nineteenth century, but an oath of some sort, commonly called Hippocratic, is still taken at many U.S. medical schools, and oath-taking appears to be on the rise. At the start of the twenty-first century, one American medical school still used a classic rendition of the Hippocratic Oath, but at other schools, graduating students recited a modified version of the oath or another oath such as the Declaration of Geneva. Kevin B. O'Reilly, Only 1 Medical School Uses Classic Version of Hippocratic Oath, American Medical News, Feb. 20, 2006, http://www.ama-assn.org/amednews/2006/02/20/prsb0220.htm. One scholar writes that "[I]t is doubtful that Hippocrates would recognize most of the pledges that are anachronistically ascribed to him. . . . [T]he tinkering with Hippocrates' Oath began soon after its first utterance and generally reflected the changing values, customs, and beliefs associated with the ethical practice of medicine." Howard Markel, "I Swear by Apollo"—On Taking the Hippocratic Oath, 350 New Eng. J. Med. 2026 (May 13, 2004), at 2026. See also Steven Miles, The Hippocratic Oath and the Ethics of Medicine (2004). Here the oath is reprinted in its historical form, as translated from the Greek by Dr. Ludwig Edelstein.

‖ *Hippocratic Oath* ‖

I swear by Apollo Physician and Asclepius and Hygieia and Panacea and all the gods and goddesses, making them my witness, that I will fulfill according to my ability and judgment this oath and this covenant:

To hold him who has taught me this art as equal to my parents and to live my life in partnership with him, and if he is in need of money to give him a share of mine, and to regard his offspring as equal to my brothers in male lineage and to teach them this art—if they desire to learn it—without fee and covenant; to give a share of precepts and oral instruction and all the other learning to my sons and to the sons of him who has instructed me and to pupils who have signed the covenant and have taken an oath according to the medical law, but to no one else.

I will apply dietetic measures for the benefit of the sick according to my ability and judgment; I will keep them from harm and injustice.

I will neither give a deadly drug to anybody if asked for it, nor will I make a suggestion to this effect. Similarly I will not give to a woman an abortive remedy. In purity and holiness I will guard my life and my art.

I will not use the knife, nor even on sufferers from stone, but will withdraw in favor of such men as are engaged in this work.

Whatever house I may visit, I will come for the benefit of the sick, remaining free of all intentional injustice, of all mischief and in particular sexual relations with both female and male persons, be they free or slaves.

Whatever I may see or hear in the course of the treatment in regard to the life of men, which on no account one must spread abroad, I will keep to myself holding such things shameful to be spoken about.

If I fulfill this oath and do not violate it, may it be granted to me to enjoy life and art, being honored with fame among all men for all time to come; if I transgress it and swear falsely, may the opposite of all this be my lot.

NOTES AND QUESTIONS

1. *Oath taking.*   What is the significance of an oath? Do you think doctors should take one? What about lawyers? Consider how one physician has described his experience of taking the oath:

> To most of us . . . the solemn and moving high spot of the doctor's career was the moment when the class stood up; and with grim or beaming faces, intoned the Oath of Hippocrates. The Oath symbolized crossing the bridge into a kind of priesthood. . . . No matter if some of the wording of the Oath seemed archaic. It had style and it told the public that, like the priest, we were sworn to solemn vows.

Lisa R. Hasday, The Hippocratic Oath as Literary Text: A Dialogue between Law and Medicine, 2 Yale J. Health Pol'y L. & Ethics 299, 302 (2002). Do you think an experience such as the one described by this physician when taking the oath is more likely to lead to patient welfare, patient harm, or neither?

2. *Abortion and euthanasia.*   A study of the content of oaths administered by U.S. medical schools at the end of the twentieth century revealed that only about 14 percent included a prohibition against euthanasia and only 8 percent prohibited abortion. Orr et al., supra. Robert D. Orr et al., Use of the Hippocratic Oath: A Review of Twentieth Century Practice and a Content Analysis of Oaths Administered in the U.S. and Canada in 1993, 9 J. Clin. Ethics 374 (1997). Is the early Oath's prohibition against these practices relevant to modern-day discussions about their wisdom? What about their constitutional status? Should courts or advocates make reference to the Hippocratic Oath in evaluating or arguing whether there is a constitutional right to abortion or physician-assisted suicide?

3. *Comparing the Hippocratic Oath to the current AMA Principles of Medical Ethics.* In what ways does the Hippocratic Oath, in its historical form, differ from the current principles of ethics adopted by American Medical Association (reprinted below)?

The American Medical Association, at its first official meeting in 1847, set about establishing a code of ethics to govern members of the profession. Since then, the principles of the ethics code have undergone several revisions and have been supplemented by lengthier opinions adopted by the AMA's Council on Ethical and Judicial Affairs. The current principles are reprinted here, followed by an assessment by David Orentlicher (both an MD and a JD) of the efficacy of self-regulation.

American Medical Association, Principles of Medical Ethics

Preamble:

The medical profession has long subscribed to a body of ethical statements developed primarily for the benefit of the patient. As a member of this profession, a physician must recognize responsibility not only to patients, but also to society, to other health professionals, and to self. The following Principles adopted by the American Medical Association are not laws, but standards of conduct which define the essentials of honorable behavior for the physician.

I. A physician shall be dedicated to providing competent medical service with compassion and respect for human dignity.

II. A physician shall uphold the standards of professionalism, be honest in all professional interactions, and strive to report physicians deficient in character or competence, or engaging in fraud or deception, to appropriate entities.

III. A physician shall respect the law and also recognize a responsibility to seek changes in those requirements which are contrary to the best interests of the patient.

IV. A physician shall respect the rights of patients, of colleagues, and of other health professionals, and shall safeguard patient confidences within the constraints of the law.

V. A physician shall continue to study, apply and advance scientific knowledge, make relevant information available to patients, colleagues, and the public, obtain consultation, and use the talents of other health professionals when indicated.

VI. A physician shall, in the provision of appropriate patient care, except in emergencies, be free to choose whom to serve, with whom to associate, and the environment in which to provide medical services.

VII. A physician shall recognize a responsibility to participate in activities contributing to the community and the betterment of public health.

VIII. A physician shall, while caring for a patient, regard responsibility to the patient as paramount.

IX. A physician shall support access to medical care for all people.

David Orentlicher, The Influence of a Professional Organization on Physician Behavior
57 Alb. L. Rev. 583 (1994)

The AMA's Council on Ethical and Judicial Affairs issues a Code of Ethics for physicians that is analogous to the ABA's Model Code of Professional Responsibility. Physicians who violate the AMA's code are subject to discipline by the AMA, and by their county and state medical societies. A number of specialty societies, including the American Academy of Family Physicians and the American Psychiatric Association, have adopted the AMA's code and hold their members accountable for violations. In some states, the medical licensing statute expressly considers violations of the AMA's code as grounds for discipline. Apparently, state licensing boards generally view the AMA's code as probative, though not dispositive, evidence of the expected standard of conduct when deciding whether a physician has committed professional misconduct.

From my five years as Secretary to the Council on Ethical and Judicial Affairs, I will discuss an example of successful self-regulation and an example of unsuccessful self-regulation and suggest why the two efforts had different results.

1.   GIFTS TO PHYSICIANS FROM INDUSTRY

During the 1980's, there was increasing concern in the medical profession about gifts to physicians from pharmaceutical and other companies. Commentators were troubled both by the magnitude and kinds of industry gift-giving. Data on magnitude was developed by the Senate Labor and Human Resources Committee, which tracked expenditures by eighteen large pharmaceutical companies on gifts to physicians between 1975 and 1988. Over that period, after taking inflation into account, gift expenditures nearly quintupled. There also appeared to be a greater tendency for companies to give gifts particularly likely to influence the treatment decisions of physicians. Gift-giving extended well beyond pens, mugs, and grants for educational programs to all-expense paid weekend trips at lavish resorts for physicians and their spouses, frequent prescriber programs offering free airline tickets for every fifty prescriptions, and "studies" which paid physicians hundreds of dollars if they prescribed expensive antibiotics and collected data that was essentially demographic in nature.

By 1990, guidelines on gift-giving had been issued by a number of professional societies, including England's Royal College of Physicians, the American College of Physicians, and the American College of Cardiology. However, there was little evidence of change in industry gift-giving practices. While praiseworthy, the guidelines lacked specificity. For example, physicians were admonished to decline gifts that they were not willing to have "generally known" to others. This vagueness made it difficult to charge anyone with violations of these guidelines.

Following nearly a year of deliberations, the AMA issued its own guidelines on gift-giving in December 1990. The guidelines explicitly prohibit cash payments, subsidies for the travel expenses of physicians attending conferences, gifts tied to prescribing practices, and any gift not related to patient care. In addition, the guidelines limit the magnitude of individual gifts and require that grants to defray registration fees for educational conferences be given directly to conference sponsors and not to physicians.

Ordinarily, it is difficult to measure the impact of ethical guidelines. It is not always certain whether ethical guidelines result in behavioral changes. Even when changes are detected, it is often not clear whether the changes reflect the ethical guideline or other contemporaneous influences. For example, if there is an increase in services provided to the poor after the issuance of a guideline calling on physicians to care for the indigent, the increase may be the result of the ethical guideline or perhaps, the result of a coincidental rise in Medicaid reimbursement rates.

With the AMA gift-giving guidelines, however, the impact was immediate and substantial. Companies canceled educational and promotional conferences that were not strong enough to attract physicians willing to pay their own travel expenses, and promotional dinners where physicians received a free meal and a $100 payment were also abandoned. At the Council on Ethical and Judicial Affairs, we received calls from travel agencies complaining about the impact of the gift-giving guidelines on their businesses, and physicians reported that lavish evening receptions were disappearing at major medical meetings. In this case, the ethical guidelines changed physician behavior dramatically and meaningfully.

Why were these guidelines so successful? First, the pharmaceutical industry incorporated the guidelines into its ethics code for marketing practices. As a result, the success of the guidelines was not solely dependent on the willingness of physicians to adhere to their ethical responsibilities. After implementation, drug companies generally stopped offering inappropriate gifts; thus physicians were not in a position to accept them. In fact, the industry probably did not fight the guidelines too vigorously because in some ways, companies welcomed the restrictions.

. . . Second, while there are more than one hundred drug companies, a small number of large companies dominate the market. Consequently, in order to ensure that the guidelines achieved their purpose, it was necessary to achieve compliance from only a few major companies. Moreover, with the focus on just the dominant players in the industry, policing the guidelines became much easier as well.

Third, detection of violations is relatively easy. Gift-giving occurs openly, and companies usually offer the same gift to hundreds, if not thousands of physicians. . . .

Fourth, concern about government regulation gave both physicians and industry a strong incentive to follow the AMA's guidelines. Immediately following the issuance of the guidelines, Senator Edward Kennedy convened hearings on the pharmaceutical industry's gift-giving practices. After the hearings, he indicated that he would refrain from taking any legislative or regulatory efforts if the AMA's guidelines eliminated abusive gift-giving practices. . . .

Fifth, the guidelines draw a number of "bright line" rules, establishing clear distinctions between permissible and impermissible conduct. The pharmaceutical industry had previously adopted the American College of Physician's guidelines on gift-giving practices, but, because those guidelines essentially enunciated general principles, industry had a good deal of freedom in interpreting them.

In short, the AMA gift-giving guidelines probably succeeded because the rules were clear, because they actually served the interests of one of the parties [a]ffected,[1] because there was a credible threat of enforcement in the form of greater government oversight, and because violations could be detected with relative ease.

---

1. The principles were redrafted in 2001. Provisions VIII and IX were added and provision II was changed. The 1980 version of provision II read: "A physician shall deal honestly with patients and colleagues, and strive to expose those physicians deficient in character or competence, or who engage in fraud or deception." American Medical Association, Principles of Medical Ethics (June 1980), *http://www.ama-assn.org/resources/doc/ethics/1980_principles.pdf*.–EDS.

2.   TREATMENT OF HIV-INFECTED PATIENTS

There has apparently been less success with the AMA's ethical guideline on the duty of physicians to treat patients with HIV infection. In December 1987, the Council on Ethical and Judicial Affairs issued a guideline stating that physicians may not refuse to treat patients on account of their HIV infection. Since then, however, studies suggest that a substantial number of physicians have not followed the guideline. In an August 1990 random national sample of primary care physicians, 50% of the physicians surveyed stated that, if given a choice, they would not work with AIDS patients, and 48% stated that they preferred to refer patients with HIV infection. Since these surveys report attitudes rather than actual practices, it is possible that the surveyed physicians overcame their unwillingness to treat patients with HIV infection and hewed to their ethical responsibilities. Indeed, a 1986 survey of orthopedic surgeons suggested that while more than two-thirds of orthopedists believed that a surgeon could ethically refuse to operate on a patient with HIV infection, 90% of the orthopedists who had an opportunity to operate on infected patients had done so on at least one patient with HIV infection.

Several other studies, however, indicate that actual practices deviate from the ethical duty to treat. In a survey of Los Angeles County primary care physicians in late 1990, researchers found that 48% of the physicians surveyed had either refused or would refuse to accept HIV infected patients into their practice. Similarly, in a June 1990 survey of North Carolina physicians, 40% reported that they either refused to treat HIV-infected patients or referred the patients elsewhere. . . .

Why has there been less success with the guideline on the duty to treat patients with HIV infection than with the guideline on gifts from industry? A number of possible explanations come to mind. First, there are strong personal incentives to ignore the obligation to provide treatment. Physicians, particularly surgeons, are concerned that they will become infected from HIV patients while treating them. While the perceived risk may be greater than the actual risk, it is perceptions that drive behavior. Physicians may also be discouraged from treating HIV-infected patients because of the psychological burdens of providing care. That is, because of the difficult clinical course, caring for HIV-infected patients is often time-consuming and emotionally draining.

Second, it is easy to camouflage violations of the obligation to treat. Physicians who do not want to treat a patient with HIV infection can simply tell the patient that they are not taking any new patients, or that they accept patients only through a referral. Moreover, even when violations are detected, there may not be a credible threat of enforcement. Currently, the Americans with Disabilities Act ("ADA") prohibits physicians from denying care to patients on account of their HIV infection. However, until the ADA went into effect in July of 1992, state anti-discrimination laws provided weak protection for patients with HIV infection.

From these two examples of ethics guidelines, we can take away two important points. First, the medical profession is perfectly capable of devising meaningful and responsible guidelines on ethical matters, even when guidelines require conduct that might not be in the physician's own personal interest. Second, the profession is less successful when it comes to ensuring that guidelines are followed. Consequently, guidelines will probably not be adopted in practice unless there is some credible method of enforcement from outside the profession.

. . . Self-enforcement is . . . weak because it is poorly funded. Physicians who serve on the disciplinary boards of their professional bodies do so without compensation. In addition, there is little money available for staff, and the boards have no subpoena authority. Consequently, few cases can be pursued, and rigorous investigations are not possible. Moreover, even when cases are prosecuted, there are substantial financial risks to the professional society. Physicians who are disciplined often challenge their sanction through time-consuming and costly litigation. Indeed, the legal fees for defending a case can deplete much of a small medical society's annual budget. Antitrust liability is of particular concern with its potential for treble damage and attorneys' fee awards. As the U.S. Congress found when it enacted the Health Care Quality Improvement Act of 1986 to provide physicians some protection against retaliatory lawsuits, the threat of liability "unreasonably discourages physicians from participating in effective professional peer review."

CONCLUSION

As policymakers consider how to regulate the use of medical innovations by physicians, they should recognize the important differences between establishing and enforcing professional guidelines. The medical profession's experience with ethics guidelines and practice guidelines indicates that society can rely on the profession to develop responsible standards. In addition, principles of change theory suggest that physicians will be more receptive to restrictions on their autonomy if they are involved in the process of developing the restrictions. However, on the issue of enforcement, reliable mechanisms have come from outside the profession, generally in the form of regulatory mandates or reimbursement policies.

NOTES AND QUESTIONS

1. *The efficacy of self-regulation.*   What, according to Professor Orentlicher, distinguishes between those physician behaviors that are more and those that are less likely to be adequately addressed by self-regulation? This is a question you might want to return to throughout the course as you encounter practices that you think merit change. Any medical practice in need of reform might be subject to a number of responses—from governmental regulation, to the recognition of a private right of action on behalf of individuals or institutions, to self-regulation through the profession itself. In considering the latter solution, it is helpful to know how past self-regulation has or has not been effective.

2. *Self-serving regulation?*   Would it surprise you that some professional statements of ethics are self-serving rather than, or at least in addition to being, protective of the interests of those whom the profession is to serve? At one time the AMA ethics code prohibited physicians from referring patients to chiropractors, a prohibition the federal courts ultimately found to be an illegal restraint of trade and a violation of federal antitrust laws. See Wilk v. American Medical Ass'n, 895 F.2d 352 (7th Cir. 1990). What do you think of principle VI? Self-serving or appropriate statement of ethics?

At the AMA's annual meeting in the summer of 2004, an AMA delegate introduced a proposal that urged the AMA to inform physicians that, except in emergencies, it is not unethical to refuse care to plaintiffs' attorneys and their spouses. Although the sponsor of the proposal asked that it be withdrawn prior to consideration, the proposal still drew passionate speeches denouncing it. Internal Medicine News, 37:14 (July 15, 2004) at 5; Don Babwin, Refusing Treatment Makes Malpractice Debate Even Uglier, Charlotte Observer, June 19, 2004. Putting aside the proposal's implicit encouragement for physicians to refuse to treat attorneys, didn't the proposal merely state the essential meaning of principle VI?

3. *The ethics of research.* The Hippocratic Oath and the Principles of Medical Ethics speak primarily to the physician treating patients. You might wonder about the ethical duties of the physician engaged purely in medical research, studying and manipulating human tissue or DNA. Do any of the ethical precepts found in the Oath or the Principles translate to these endeavors? What do you think the duties of a researcher should be toward the sources (people) from whom samples come? This complex subject, which is receiving more attention as genetic research proliferates, is discussed more fully in Chapter 11.

2.   The Ethics of Bioethicists

If, as some maintain, bioethicists (a term open to some defining itself) provide a necessary or at least desirable check on the actions of health care professionals, or might be seen as needed or appropriate advisors in the realm of health policy making, shouldn't their own practices be subject to scrutiny? To the extent the advice of such individuals or groups is heeded, shouldn't their practices be regulated as well to ensure adequate qualification or, at a minimum, lack of improper bias? Recently, the practices of bioethicists have been subject to examination under the lens of bioethics, a "bioethics of bioethics" if you will. In this regard, a variety of commentators have noted the involvement of many bioethicists in the companies whose work they assess. Bioethicists are now employed by pharmaceutical and biotechnology companies and by professional organizations. Some commentators have urged bioethicists to disclose sources of funding and potential conflicts of interest that they face in evaluating practices in science and in health care.

Sally Satel and Christine Stolba, harsh critics of the contemporary bioethics enterprise, locate the origins of the discipline in the "campus upheavals of the 1960s" which, they contend, encouraged philosophers to focus on "applied philosophy." Satel and Stolba are especially critical of bioethicists who offer "bedside" guidance to health care providers. In their view, there are "few meaningful standards" guiding this work. Even worse, they contend, bioethicists' "expanding role in American healthcare directly impinges on the traditional duties of physicians." They conclude that hospital patients need "ethical doctors" far more than they need "self-styled professional ethicists." Sally Satel & Christine Stolba, Who Needs Medical Ethics?, 1111 Commentary 37 (Feb. 1, 2001).

Others have argued, however, that doctors generally are not trained to focus on bioethical dilemmas. Physician training takes longer than training for other health care specialties, and physicians tend to set the tone of the health care institutions within which they work. Thus, the moral perspective that doctors bring to their work is especially important. In 1999, Albert Gunn, Associate

Dean for Admissions at a Texas medical school, argued that the "medical school educational process should focus on producing doctors who have a set of values and who can think for themselves." But for the most part, Gunn concluded, that is not what happens. He attributed part of the problem to the medical school admission process that rewards students who do whatever they are told to do and who often are woefully uneducated outside the fields of science. Gunn also notes that most of those working directly in the field of bioethics are not doctors but social scientists and philosophers: "Thoughtful, well-educated physicians with notions differing from the accepted wisdom are . . . a hindrance to the ethics apparatchik currently in control, or at least to those who wish to use that apparatus to implement their agenda." Albert E. Gunn, The Healing Profession Needs Healers: The Crisis in Medical Education, 15 Issues L. & Med. 125, 133 (1999).

NOTES

1. *Role of bioethicists?* As you read the material in this book consider what (if any) dimensions of the bioethicists' work could be done as well, or better, by health care practitioners.

2. *Professionalizing bioethics.* Not surprisingly, perhaps, as bioethics becomes an institutionalized profession with nondegree certificate programs, graduate programs, and talk about some sort of "licensing" or "certification," a few members of the profession challenge the presumption that bioethicists follow bioethics' central dictates. In late 2011, the work of one bioethicist, the founder and editor-in-chief of an important journal (the American Journal of Bioethics), occasioned concern and dismay when it was learned that he had become "president for ethics" at CellTex Therapeutics in Texas. CellTex promotes the use of stem-cell therapies developed by a Korean company; CellTex's stem-cell treatments have not been approved in the United States or in South Korea. David Cyranowki, Editor's Move Sparks Backlash, 482 Nature (Feb. 21, 2012, updated Mar. 1, 2012), available at http://www.nature.com/news/editor-s-move-sparks-backlash-1.10068. At least four editors of the journal resigned because of discomfort with the journal's conflict-of-interest policies. Id.

3. *Bibliographic note.* A wide set of essays about the "ethics of bioethics" can be found in Lisa A. Eckenwiler & Felicia G. Cohn, eds., The Ethics of Bioethics: Mapping the Moral Landscape (2007).

E.   THE HUMAN BODY, HEALTH, AND DISEASE

In many—perhaps most—cultures, understandings of personhood and community are reflected in understandings of the human body. (See Chapter 3 for a discussion of notions of personhood.) British anthropologist Mary Douglas described the body as a "highly restricted medium of expression." Even more, Douglas argues, the forms the body takes in moving and in resting differ from culture to culture and among different groups within a culture. Those forms "express social pressures":

The care that is given to [the body], in grooming, feeding and therapy, the theories about what it needs in the way of sleep and exercise, about the stages it should go through, the pains it can stand, its span of life, all the cultural categories in which it is perceived, must correlate closely with the categories in which society is seen in so far as these also draw upon the same culturally processed idea of the body.

Mary Douglas, Natural Symbols: Explorations in Cosmology 65 (1970).

Any broad presentation of bioethical issues demands some understanding of the importance of cultural assumptions about bodies, health, disease, and "human nature."

For the most part, people do not think much about the precise definition of disease or sickness or illness, and they do not wonder whether the three terms imply different conditions. The meanings and referents of these common terms are generally taken to be self-evident. Moreover, it is frequently assumed that the condition of being "sick," "ill," or "diseased" is the consequence either of some natural (even if unpleasant) process such as aging and stress or of some foreign matter (commonly referred to as "germs") having invaded the body.

In only a few contexts is the precise meaning of disease (or sickness, illness, and a few other terms such as bodily disorder) framed as significant. In those contexts the meaning of the terms could become the subject of dispute. This might occur, for instance, in the effort to discern the extent of health insurance coverage (described contractually through terms such as disease, sickness, and illness). See, for example, Katskee v. Blue Cross/Blue Shield of Nebraska, 515 N.W.2d 645 (1994) (interpreting use of terms "bodily disorder or disease" in insurance policy to include "breast-ovarian carcinoma syndrome" and thus requiring insurance company to pay for prophylactic surgery).

In the main, most people simply assume that those who are ill (or sick or suffering from a disease) do not feel well—that they have certain unpleasant symptoms of the health condition. Yet, that is not always the case; everyone has heard of diseases that remain asymptomatic for long periods. A series of public-media advertisements warning people to seek periodic monitoring for high blood pressure stressed that the condition is especially worrisome because it can exist in the absence of symptoms and might thus go untreated. Most people also know that the development and proliferation of cancer cells might not be accompanied by symptoms and that various sorts of periodic screening are recommended so that the disease can be "caught early."

Although disease can be and has been romanticized, and many people have found some solace in the "sick role," people generally view disease as a bad thing. What they do not often consider is the extent to which understandings of disease do not simply reflect natural processes. Many diseases and many interpretations of disease are culturally constructed, sometimes even self-consciously.

Carl Elliott, a philosopher at the University of Minnesota, suggests that categories of illness are constructed for a variety of social, cultural, psychological, and economic reasons. The history of depression-as-illness and of antidepressants as treatment provides a startling illustration. Carl Elliott, American Bioscience Meets the American Dream, The American Prospect 39 (June 2003), at 39 (available on Lexis). Clinical depression was considered rare before the second half of the twentieth century. In fact, few pharmaceutical companies focused on creating antidepressants because they were not thought to be profitable. In the early

1960s, Merck produced a new antidepressant, amitriptyline, and, according to Elliott, succeeded in selling the drug by selling the notion of depression as a pervasive condition. Elliott reports that the company bought 50,000 copies of Frank Ayd's Recognizing the Depressed Patient and distributed them to physicians. The strategy worked. "Yet," explains Elliott, "it would be a mistake to think this is merely a matter of the market creating an illness. It is also a matter of a technology creating an illness." By this he means that once a treatment is proffered, existential states are reconceptualized as medical problems. Infertility provides a second example of this process. "[O]nce new reproductive technologies—such as in vitro fertilization and sperm donation—came on the scene, that fact of nature [infertility] was reconceptualized as a medical problem." Id.

Similarly, the shape of people's bodies has also been medicalized in recent years. In an earlier age, for instance, bodies that would now be categorized as overweight were instead viewed as evidence of economic status. During the twentieth century, obesity was redefined as a precursor of various diseases and is now viewed as a disease itself as well as a precursor of other diseases. Increasingly, Americans have idealized thinness, especially for women, while they have, in fact, become heavier. Between 1970 and 2009, the percentage of people categorized in the United States as obese increased from about 15 percent of the population to about 33 percent. Richard Wilkinson & Kate Pickett, The Spirit Level: Why Greater Equality Makes Societies Stronger 89 (2010). At the same time, the last half-century has witnessed a dramatic increase in Americans—especially young girls (ages 15–24)—suffering from eating disorders, including anorexia nervosa and bulimia nervosa. Cassandra A. Soltis, Dying to be a Supermodel: Can Requiring a Healthy BMI be Fashionable?, 26 J. Contemp. Health L. & Pol'y 49, 53–54 (2009).

In a remarkable historic twist, obesity—especially that manifest as central body adiposity—has come to reflect lower-class status. Even more, social responses to those who are obese resemble responses to poor people. Society stigmatizes poor people and fat people, and both groups are viewed as responsible for their condition. These issues are considered in detail in Janet L. Dolgin & Katherine R. Dieterich, Weighing Status: Obesity, Class and Health Reform, 898 Oregon L. Rev. 1113 (2011).

The new genetics and genomics, heralded as both the cause and potential cure of most disease and many social ills, carries unique risks of medicalization. As anthropologist Kaja Finkler explains in the following reading, not only is genetic variation labeled as abnormality, defect, or disease, but the knowledge of this variation restructures the reality of both the individual learning of the genetic variation and her kin.

Kaja Finkler, Experiencing the New Genetics: Family and Kinship on the Medical Frontier
177–178 (2000)

Medicalization restructures reality by intruding on the world people take for granted, on their tacit understanding of what is normal, by transforming the taken-for-granted state into an abnormal, disconcerting state, separating the individual from the larger whole. Contemporarily, the view is that human beings are constituted of myriad genes that describe the whole organism, and the genetic system in all humans is the same; variation is normal. Deviations among people are expressed chiefly in anomalies or defects. If people differ from their kin, or from what is construed to be the ideal in their kin map, they are considered abnormal.

Consider three examples from Mexico that are especially instructive of the ways in which the medicalization process changes one's view of oneself and reality. In the first instance, we see a person resisting medicalization. A peasant woman gave birth to two Down's syndrome children in succession. She was counseled to avoid having any more children; however, she refused to regard these children as suffering from an affliction. In fact, she claimed that she preferred such children because they were more docile and more manageable than her other children. The Down's syndrome children were also better field hands than the rest. For this peasant woman, her Down's syndrome children were an asset and unproblematic. By medicalizing their beings, the woman began to perceive her children adversely rather than as positive contributions to the household welfare.

The second example is of three sisters diagnosed with oculopharyngeal muscular dystrophy. Two of the sisters, on referral by their physicians, had surgery performed to correct the condition, even though they failed to comprehend why their situation was considered a disease, since their mother, sister, and several other family members experienced the same condition. These women unwittingly became patients and viewed themselves as abnormal only after their physicians referred them to the hospital.

The last example is of a woman who, having been diagnosed with neurofibromatosis Type 1, failed to comprehend that she had a disease. Although she regarded the brown spots on her body as aesthetically unattractive, even repulsive, and she feared that it might make her less attractive to her husband when he returned from the United States, where he had been working for several years, she attributed the ugly spots to witchcraft and not to disease. When this 37-year-old woman learned that she was suffering from a hereditary disorder, her one concern was that her only child, a ten-year-old girl, would blame her for transmitting the condition. In this case, the woman's aesthetic reality was transformed into a medical actuality that provoked terror in her life.

As with all human actions, medicalization can be a double-edged sword. On the one hand, it standardizes aspects of human life to fit into a medical norm so that anyone who fails to fit that norm is considered to suffer from a disease. While medicalizing a set of problems may relieve afflicted individuals of one set of devaluing labels, they become burdened with another. Thus, in all three Mexican cases, the normal and taken-for-granted became transformed into the abnormal and the evil, for which the family became culpable.

NOTES AND QUESTIONS

1. *Conditions that have been "medicalized."* The above materials have referred to obesity and infertility as conditions that have been "medicalized," meaning generally that the conditions are now seen as ones for which the

medical profession has an essential role in care and treatment. Can you think of other conditions that have been medicalized?

Who benefits from medicalization? Certainly, the medicalization of body size (e.g., obesity) has produced astonishing financial opportunities. Obesity, alone, has spawned a panoply of special (often costly) diets, pills, teas, organizations that promise to help in the effort to lose weight, injections, and weight-loss surgery.

2. *Consequences of medicalization.*   What appear to be the consequences of the medicalization of a particular condition? Does medicalizing a condition increase or decrease one's responsibility for it?

3. *Medicalization and the goals of medicine.*   Does increasing medicalization of various conditions mean that the goals of medicine are changing? Is the role of the physician in improving one's life or body becoming more all-encompassing and is this an appropriate expansion? To be more specific, if a number of physicians perform a certain procedure, does this mean that there is a medical need for the procedure, or do physicians no longer respond (if they ever did) only to medical need? For example, the media has reported that some female, high school seniors receive money for breast implants as a graduation gift, and that surgical breast augmentation is becoming popular with this segment of the population. What does the availability of this procedure by physicians tell us about the role of medicine in the United States today? Feminist bioethics scholars such as Susan Sherwin have long criticized the medicalization of certain normal female processes, such as pregnancy and menopause, as unnecessarily placing women under the power of patriarchal medicine. See Susan Sherwin, *No Longer Patient* (1993). What are the forces behind this new trend? How should physicians respond?

4. *Demedicalizing disability.*   Whereas some conditions have become medicalized, others are becoming demedicalized—or at least there are concerted efforts to make this happen. The prime example is disability. Advocates for persons with disabilities have tried in recent decades to replace a medical model of disability with a social or minority group model of disability. See Mary Crossley, The Disability Kaleidoscope, 74 Notre Dame L. Rev. 621 (1999). Crossley explains that under the medical model of disability, "[t]he individual is the locale of the disability and, thus, the individual is properly understood as needing aid and assistance in remediating that disability. . . . [W]hile the cause of impairments may vary, the disabled individual is viewed as innately, biologically different and inferior." Id. at 649–650. By contrast, the social model of disability views the "disadvantaged status of persons with disabilities [as] the product of a hostile (or at least inhospitable) social environment, not simply the product of bodily defects." Id. at 172. The minority group model of disability is a civil rights model. It not only considers persons with disabilities as being unfairly defined and disadvantaged by society's inhospitality, but transforms that understanding "into a political call to action." Id. at 658.

= 2 =

‖ *Autonomy and Bodily Integrity* ‖

The notion of autonomous individuality is central to contemporary Western culture. The word *autonomy* is a combination of two Greek words, *autos,* meaning self, and *nomos,* meaning rule. In ancient Greece, autonomy was used in reference only to the city-state. An autonomous city-state ruled itself.

In moral philosophy, the importance of the notion of autonomous individuality is comparatively recent.[1] It is attributed to Immanuel Kant (late eighteenth century) and to John Stuart Mill (nineteenth century). In Kant's view, autonomy was at the heart of moral acts. Mill prized the development and protection of "persons of individuality and character" and posited liberty from state interference as essential to those goals. Mill defined liberty as "the only unfailing and permanent source of improvement" for individuals and for society. John Stuart Mill, On Liberty (1863), in Utilitarianism, On Liberty and Other Essays (Mary Warnock ed. 1962).

A related, although somewhat different emphasis on autonomy, and one with major consequences for later social developments, emerged from the nineteenth-century marketplace. There, individual autonomy was posited as essential to "individual agents" rather than to morality. Onora O'Neill, Autonomy and Trust in Bioethics 29 (2002). The Industrial Revolution depended on and fostered the notion that people are autonomous agents, free to negotiate their own bargains and the terms for rescinding those bargains.

After World War II the notion that protecting individual autonomy is essential to moral interactions was generalized within Western society. That process was essential to the transformation of the American family, the development of feminism, and the reconceptualization of the doctor–patient relationship. Gerald Dworkin, a moral philosopher, sums up that reconceptualization with regard to health care as a shift from the notion that "doctor knows best" to the notion that health care decisions should be defined by the patient's insistence that "it's my body." Gerald Dworkin, Can You Trust Autonomy? 33 Hastings Ctr. Rpt. 42 (2003).

---

1. See Chapter 1 for a fuller discussion of the philosophical roots of contemporary bioethics.

The following questions outline the issues considered in this chapter:

1. What assumptions about people are central to the law's regulation of the relationship between patients and health care providers?
2. When, if ever, should people be given health care without their having consented?
3. When, if ever, should people be given health care against their express wishes?
4. Should health care information always be private? Sometimes? Never?
5. When, if ever, should health care workers be obliged to reveal otherwise confidential information about patients?
6. Should people have a proprietary interest in their body parts and information (e.g., genetic information) about their bodies?

A.   INFORMED CONSENT[2]

1.   Bioethical and Social Perspectives

The development of the informed consent doctrine in American law reflects the increasing emphasis on individual autonomy in American thought generally. The doctrine developed out of an earlier requirement that patients *consent* before being provided with health care. In the second half of the twentieth century lawmakers expanded the "consent" requirement and began to demand that consent be premised on information provided to a patient about his or her health or ill health and about diagnostic and treatment options. Ever since, bioethicists, legislators, judges, health care providers, and others have debated the type and extent of information a patient must be given and the practical usefulness of that information to the patient in making health care choices.

	Peter H. Schuck,	
	Rethinking Informed Consent	
	103 Yale L.J. 899, 902–905 (1994)	

The doctrine of informed consent in health care shared in the more general expansion of American tort liability that proceeded well into the 1980s and that now appears to have stabilized. Everyone, it seems, favors the principle of informed consent; it is "only" the specific details and applications of the doctrine that arouse serious debate. In order to map and enlarge this debate, it is useful to distinguish three different versions of informed consent doctrine. The first is the letter and spirit of the doctrine as developed primarily by courts—the law "in books." The second is the doctrine as imagined, feared, and often caricatured by some physicians—the law "in the mind." The third version, a

---

2. Additional materials relating to informed consent can be found in Chapter 7 (with regard to dying patients not competent to grant informed consent) and Chapter 11 (with regard to human subject research).

consequence both of the gap between the first two and of other situational constraints, is the doctrine as actually practiced by clinicians—the law "in action." (Of course, there are almost as many laws-in-action as there are distinct physician–patient relationships.)

Most commentators on informed consent deploy one or more of these versions of the law. Generally (and crudely) speaking, these commentators fall into two camps: idealists and realists. Informed consent idealists—primarily some judges and medical ethicists—advocate a relatively expansive conception of the physician's obligation to disclose and elicit information about risks and alternatives. More specifically, the idealists tend to define informed consent law's pivotal concepts—materiality of risk, disclosure, alternatives, and causation—broadly and subjectively from the perspective of the individual patient rather than that of the professional, while defining the law's exceptions to the duty narrowly. Perhaps most important, idealists emphasize the qualitative dimension of physician–patient interactions concerning treatment decisions. They insist that these interactions be dialogic rather than authoritative, tailored to the individual patient's emotional needs and cognitive capacities rather than formulaic, aimed at maximizing patient autonomy and comprehension rather than mere information flow, and sensitive to the distortions that can be created by power differentials between physician and patient.

The idealists employ a distinctive rhetorical strategy. Capitalizing on the universal support for the principles and goals of informed consent, they point to the often striking difference between the law in books and the law in action—a difference that I call the "informed consent gap." The existence of this gap, they argue, shows that the law in action falls far short of the law in books. Since the law that they think should be in the books is often even more demanding, the true gap is wider still. The problem, then, is not so much the law in books, which tends to demand too little of physicians; rather, it is the laws in action and in the mind. For the idealist, therefore, the goal of reform must be to close the informed consent gap by conforming the law in action, at the very least, to the law now in books.

The realists—primarily practicing physicians—harbor a different vision of informed consent. Although they emphatically do not contest the principle and goals of informed consent, they do question whether most patients really desire the kind of dialogue that the idealists propose. They also question whether, whatever patients desire, the gains in patient autonomy and improved outcomes produced by the dialogue are worth the additional time, money, and needless patient anxiety and confusion that informed consent may entail. Like the idealists, many realists employ a characteristic rhetoric. Rather than master the doctrinal details of the informed consent law in books, they point instead to the law in their minds, which they can easily caricature in order to demonstrate the law's folly. Although some realists do not concede that the law in action actually deviates from the law in their minds, many others readily admit that a gap does in fact exist. To them, however, this gap simply demonstrates how impractical the idealists' vision is and why it cannot be implemented in the demanding world of contemporary clinical practice.

In a real sense, then, informed consent idealists and realists argue past one another, producing a debate that is oblique and inconclusive rather than pointed and fruitful. . . .

... [T]he informed consent gap is essentially structural—that is, it reflects the constraints imposed by human psychology, the physician–patient relationship, the tort law system, and an increasingly cost-conscious health care delivery system—and ... these constraints are largely intractable. I therefore doubt that the idealists' most ambitious goals are desirable, since they cannot likely be attained at any socially acceptable cost. I am doubtful because, although I find reasons to think that the idealists are wrong, I am not yet as convinced of their error as some realists appear to be. The truth is that no one has yet undertaken the kind of research and analysis, much of it empirical and perhaps comparative, that would be necessary to resolve these doubts conclusively. ...

Benjamin Moulton & Jaime S. King, Aligning Ethics with Medical Decision Making: The Quest for Informed Patient Choice
38 J.L. Med. & Ethics 85, 85, 89–90 (2012)

... [O]ver the last three decades, medical ethicists have shifted from guiding physicians to focus on beneficence and improving patient health as emphasized in the Hippocratic oath toward a more subjective and "patient-centered" practice, which also prioritizes patient autonomy in medical decision making. While this shift toward autonomy is well represented in the literature and ethical guidelines, health services research demonstrates that in clinical practice many physicians have yet to strike the ideal balance between absolute patient autonomy and beneficence. Recent studies have found that most physicians still undervalue disclosure and underestimate the variability in patient preferences. Alternatively, in an effort to promote a more "patient-centered" model of decision making, we have received anecdotal reports that other physicians have altered their disclosure practices to provide patients with information on the risks and benefits of the treatment options, but then require the patient to make the treatment decision without the benefit of the physician's medical opinion. In these infrequent instances, the pendulum has swung too far. The unmitigated rise of autonomy can result in the decline of beneficence. In today's medical practice, patients frequently receive either too little medical information to make an informed treatment decision or too little physician opinion to feel confident in their choice. To satisfy their ethical obligations to patients, health care providers should implement a system of medical decision making that balances the importance of both ethical principles. ...

For purposes of this article, we define shared medical decision making as a process of communication in which the physician and patient use unbiased and complete information on the risks and benefits associated with all viable treatment alternatives and information from the patient on personal factors that might make one treatment alternative more preferable than the others to come to a treatment decision. While this definition encompasses the traditional disclosure essential for legal informed consent to treatment, it goes beyond the mere recitation of facts, risks and alternatives. Shared decision making involves a more robust discussion, which engages both the patient and the physician in evaluating the patient's medical goals and lifestyle preferences to come to an informed choice.

As a result, shared decision making promotes both autonomy and benef-icence. While valuable for any medical decision, its methods prove most effective for use with preference sensitive conditions. In this instance, the provider and patient share information to better understand the full scope of the options the patient faces, and to think about the patient's personal values as they relate to the risks and benefits of each option. While the physician and patient jointly participate in the treatment decision, shared decision making prioritizes patient autonomy over beneficence, but only enough to tip an otherwise even balance. In instances of disagreement after discussion, the patient's preference should determine the treatment. By protecting patient autonomy and acknowledging the importance of provider opinion and analysis, shared decision making pro-vides the most effective method of enabling physicians to satisfy their ethical obligations to patients.

NOTES AND QUESTIONS

1. *Research on informed consent.* Peter Schuck suggests that research is needed to assess different approaches to informed consent. What kind of research would you plan if you were about to undertake the project that Schuck recommends? Would you rely primarily on observational studies, interviews, or questionnaires, or would you use all these approaches? What sorts of questions would you ask and of whom?

2. According to Moulton and King, supra, the "pendulum has swung too far" in the direction of autonomy. This involves the prototypic scenario in which a physician adequately informs a patient about risks and benefits of treatment options, and then asks the patient to make an independent decision (i.e., without physician input). Do you agree with Moulton and King's quest to balance patient autonomy with beneficence? How would you balance autonomy and beneficence or, as an ethical matter, would you conclude that one should be significantly more important than the other in medical decision making?

3. One study of factors inhibiting patient autonomy reported four themes identified by patients as relevant to the success of clinical encounters. Dominick L. Frosch et al., Authoritarian Physicians and Patients' Fear of Being Labeled 'Difficult' Among Key Obstacles to Shared Decision Making, 31 Health Affairs 1030 (May 2012). Researchers organized focus groups that included 48 people, distributed among several groups. Participants were asked about their interest in participating in medical decision making and their ability, in fact, to do so. Four themes emerged. These themes suggest a variety of restraints on shared decision making. First, participants noted a need to be a "good" patient, which meant limiting questions about physicians' recommendations so as to avoid annoying the physician. Participants feared that annoyed physicians might treat patients with less concern. Second, participants reported facing "authoritarian," rather than "authoritative," doctors. Third, some participants felt they were compelled to seek information on their own because their physicians had limited time for them and did not provide them with sufficient information. One participant wondered whether the inadequacy of the information she had received from her physician was a product of her own reticence or of the physician's not giving the time necessary for a proper informed consent conversation. Id. at 1034. And

fourth, participants believed it useful to bring relatives or friends to conversations with clinicians. Id. at 1034. The third and fourth themes are not an obstacle to patient autonomy, and they may be useful as responses to the social and time pressures common in clinical interactions.

Frosch and colleagues suggest a few changes that could mitigate obstacles to patient autonomy in clinical decision making. Physicians should be compensated for the time they spend discussing patients' conditions and options. Health care teams should be organized so that team members share tasks and use medical technology to facilitate conversations with patients about care. Physicians should be educated about patients' anxieties and expectations and about how to construct a "safe environment" in which patients feel comfortable questioning their physicians about their care. And those running health care systems must demonstrate, in a concrete manner, that they value physician–patient discourse about patient care.

The authors noted that participants in their study were from a comparatively affluent area in California and for the most part, were highly educated; about 98 percent had had some college education, and almost 50 percent had completed graduate school. The authors suggested that the study results might not be generalizable to other economic and social groups but opined that less well-off groups would probably not feel more comfortable than the people in the study at engaging in shared medical decision making with clinicians. Id. at 1031.

4. *Importance of patient and physician cultural experiences.* Patients in different cultural and subcultural settings may interpret information differently; they may vary in the importance they attach to autonomy in the patient or subject role; and they may approach physicians, scientists, and health care institutions with different degrees of deference, anxiety, or respect. Patients who share their physicians' broad view of disease, treatment, relationships, and personhood are more likely to be given the sort of information needed to reach an informed consent to health care. This follows from the physician's likely responses to the patient and from the patient's likely responses to the physician and to the physician's style of presenting information.

5. *Consent in Japan.* Not every culture supports the sort of attention to patient autonomy and informed consent that has become common in the United States. In some places, it is often assumed that doctors know better than patients how best to serve patients' interests. Professor Norio Higuchi, a law professor at the University of Tokyo, reported in 1992 that in Japan 40 percent of people surveyed concluded that doctors should not inform a patient about a cancer diagnosis. Norio Higuchi, The Patient's Right to Know of a Cancer Diagnosis: A Comparison of Japanese Paternalism and American Self-Determination, 31 Washburn L. Rev. 455, 455 (1992).

Higuchi describes a case brought in Japan by surviving family members against the hospital that treated their dead wife and mother, Kazuko Makino. Makino had been examined for stomach pains. The doctors concluded that she probably was ill with cholecystic cancer. The doctors wanted to do exploratory surgery to be certain of the diagnosis. They did not, however, inform the patient about their suspicion. Rather, they told her that she had a "rather bad gall bladder" and that she should make an appointment to have an operation. Instead, Makino took a trip overseas. She did not return to the hospital after the trip, and two months later she collapsed at work.

Makino's husband and children claimed that she did not return to the hospital in a timely fashion for further examination and possible treatment because she did not know that cancer was suspected. She believed the doctors' explanation of her stomach pains to have been the result of a gall bladder condition. Makino v. The Red Cross Hosp., Nagoya Dist. Ct. Judgment, May 29, 1989, 1325 HANJI 103 (cited in Higuchi, supra).

The district court acknowledged that doctors have a general duty to inform patients and their families about a patient's condition, and then belied that proposition, according to Higuchi, by concluding that "it would never be the general view of the medical profession in our country to inform the patient of this type of cancer, which is virtually incurable in most cases." Makino, 1325 HANJI 103 (quoted in Higuchi, supra at 460).

The district court explained further that in general a doctor is obliged at least to inform a patient's family, if not the patient, that the patient suffers from a serious disease. That obligation was excused in the Makino case only because the doctor who explained to Makino that she had a "rather bad gall bladder" had not yet met her family. From a contemporary American perspective, this obligation is startling. It reflects the values of a society that places great emphasis on family as a social unit. Informed consent practices in Japan are discussed in Robert B. Leflar, Informed Consent and Patients' Rights in Japan, 33 Hous. L. Rev. 1, 25 (1996).

6. *Bibliographic note.* There is a large literature on the development of informed consent doctrine. Jay Katz's The Silent World of Doctor and Patient (1984) is a classic. Kathleen Boozang, Carl H. Coleman, & Kate Greenwood, An Argument Against Embedding Conflicts of Interest Disclosures in Informed Consent, 4 J. Health & Life Sci. L. 230 (2011); Marc D. Ginsberg, Informed Consent: NO Longer Just What the Doctor Ordered? The "Contributions" of Medical Associations and Courts to a More Patient Friendly Doctrine, 15 Mich. St. J. Med. & Law 17 (2011); David E. Winickoff, Governing Population Genomics: Law, Bioethics, and Biopolitics in Three Case Studies, 43 Jurimetrics J. 187 (2003) (considering informed consent in context of studies of human genomics); Sheldon F. Kurtz, The Law of Informed Consent: From "Doctor Is Right" to "Patient Has Rights," 50 Syracuse L. Rev. 1243 (2000); Susan M. Wolf, Quality Assessment of Ethics in Health Care: The Accountability Revolution, 20 Am. J.L. & Med. 105 (1994). A useful survey of informed consent issues (largely in research contexts) can be found in Kenneth Getz & Deborah Borfitz, Informed Consent: The Consumer's Guide to the Risks and Benefits of Volunteering for Clinical Trials (2002); the publisher's website, http://www.centerwatch.com, is a useful source for information about informed consent rules that relate to research.

2. Legal Approaches

States divide almost evenly between those that assess the legal adequacy of informed consent through reference to a patient-based standard and those that look to a physician-based standard. Jaime Staples King & Benjamin W. Moulton, Rethinking Informed Consent: The Case for Shared Medical Decision Making, 32 Am. J.L. & Med. 429 (2006). A patient-based standard focuses on the risks, benefits, and options that a reasonable patient would want to know in reaching a treatment decision. The physician-based standard, in contrast, focuses on the practice of a "reasonably prudent" physician (or other, relevant health care provider). The first case below relies on a patient-based standard and the second on a physician-based standard.

Miller-McGee v. Washington Hosp. Center
920 A.2d 430 (D.C. App. 2007)

Opinion by Judge THOMPSON.

[Angel Miller-McGee sued after suffering a large vaginal tear as the result of the forceps delivery of her daughter. The tear developed into a rectovaginal fistula. Repair of the fistula required two operations. The patient sued for malpractice and for negligent infliction of emotional distress. The trial court held for defendants. On appeal, the court agreed with the plaintiff that she should have been afforded the opportunity to amend her complaint to allege that the defendants failed to obtain her informed consent. The court then considered the parameters of her informed consent claim.]

PP:

Our case law on lack of informed consent recognizes the "duty of a physician to inform the patient of the consequences of a proposed treatment," a duty that "stems from the right of every competent adult human being to determine what shall be done with his own body." "In order to prevail in an action based on a theory of informed consent, the plaintiff must prove that if he had been informed of the material risk, he would not have consented to the procedure and that he had been injured as a result of submitting to the procedure." Adhering to the rationale of Canterbury [v. Spence, 464 F.2d 772 (1972)], we have said that:

Rule:

> The test for mandatory disclosure of information on treatment of the patient's condition is whether a reasonable person in what the physician knows or should know to be the patient's position would consider the information material to his decision. The information is material if the reasonable person in what the physician knows or should know to be the patient's position would be likely to attach significance to the risks in deciding to accept or forego the proposed treatment. . . . [A]t a minimum, a physician must disclose the nature of the condition, the nature of the proposed treatment, any alternate treatment procedures, and the nature and degree of risks and benefits inherent in undergoing and in abstaining from the proposed treatment.

Crain [v. Allison], 443 A.2d [558,] 562 [D.C. Ct. App. 1982]. "[N]ot all risks need be disclosed; only material risks must be disclosed."[7] Thus, to recover on a claim of lack of informed consent, a plaintiff must prove that there was an undisclosed risk that was material; that the risk materialized, injuring plaintiff; and that plaintiff would not have consented to the procedure if she had been

P must prove:

---

7. "A physician is relieved of his duty to inform his patient (1) in an emergency situation when the patient is incapable of consent, no relative or guardian can be obtained to give the necessary consent to the treatment, and imminent harm from non-treatment outweighs any harm threatened by the proposed treatment; and (2) when the physician reasonably believes that the patient's reaction to the risk information will pose a threat to the patient's well being." *Crain,* 443 A.2d at 562–563.

informed of the risk. A material risk is a risk "which a reasonable person would consider significant in deciding whether to undergo a particular medical treatment."

There must be expert testimony to establish some of the elements of proof. In general, expert testimony is "required to establish the nature of the risks inherent in a particular treatment, the probabilities of therapeutic success, the frequency of the occurrence of particular risks, the nature of available alternatives to treatment and whether or not disclosure would be detrimental to a patient." But a plaintiff "can establish a prima facie case of lack of informed consent through the expert testimony of defendant physicians and defense witnesses without calling independent experts." Issues "not requiring expert testimony typically ask a jury to determine whether an unrevealed risk materialized, whether the physician told the patient about that risk, and whether the physician should have known that knowledge of that risk might affect the patient's decision."

. . . .

[Appellee, defendant Dr. Muangman "maintains that he told [the plaintiff] Miller-McGee about the 'possibility of a perineal tear.' She asserted that '[a]t no time did anyone discuss a vaginally assisted birth with me, and at no time did anyone discuss with me the possibility of a recto-vaginal tear that could result from a vaginally assisted birth,' and that she 'did not have any discussion with Dr. Muangman regarding risks, benefits and alternatives of a vaginal delivery.' Whether Dr. Muangman disclosed the risks attendant to an assisted vaginal delivery and did so adequately is a jury question." The court then explained that "whether the risk of an extensive vaginal tear was material" "is an issue for the fact-finder." It is the jury's role] to say whether the known risks of vaginal laceration and of a rectovaginal fistula were sufficiently material that there was a duty to disclose them to appellant."[21]

Finally, appellees argue that Miller-McGee cannot prove that she would have withheld consent to an assisted vaginal delivery if she had been informed of the risk of sustaining an extensive vaginal laceration. They imply that appellant would have had no choice but to consent, because appellees' own experts would "not testify that a caesarian was a viable alternative." In the trial court, appellees relied on [a physician's] affidavit [which] stated that "a caesarian section was not medically indicated in Plaintiff's case"; that a c-section "is not offered to a patient as an alternative to vaginal delivery or assisted vaginal delivery unless for some reason surgery is medically necessary"; and that "[o]nly when a caesarian is medically indicated, is it considered to be an alternative." However, the record before us also includes Dr. Muangman's deposition testimony that "[i]t was my opinion that, given the station of the

---

21. In *Canterbury*, the court found that when it was established "that paralysis can be expected in one percent of laminectomies," the evidence that the doctor "did not reveal the risk of paralysis from the laminectomy made out a prima facie case of violation of the physician's duty to disclose," and it became "the jury's responsibility to decide whether that peril was of sufficient magnitude to bring the disclosure duty into play." 464 F.2d at 779, 794; see also id. at 464 F.2d at 788 n.86, and accompanying text (noting that a "very small chance of death or serious disablement may well be significant," and collecting cases referencing percentage chances of injury and determining whether disclosure of the risk was required).

baby's head and *the different delivery options, that the option that would have gotten the baby delivered the most expeditiously was the assisted vaginal delivery, which the patient did agree to*" (italics added). Thus, on this factual record, we cannot say that appellant could not prove that had she known of the risk of a rectovaginal fistula, she could have and would have opted for some method of delivery other than a forceps-assisted vaginal delivery.

. . . .

We cannot tell from the record here whether a cesarean section would have been one of the options for Miller-McGee given the specific complications that developed with her delivery and the time pressures that surrounded it. Among other things, it is not clear to us whether Dr. Muangman's testimony that a cesarean section was "not medically indicated" means that a cesarean section would not have been feasible or viable for whatever reason, or that Dr. Muang-man would not have been willing to perform one, or that a cesarean section was not necessary, or something else. We conclude only that, on the record as it stands before us, it is not a foregone conclusion that Miller-McGee would not have been able to prove, without an expert of her own, that there was an alternative to a forceps-assisted vaginal delivery, and that a reasonable person in her place would have chosen that alternative if informed of the risks that an assisted delivery presents.

Holding:

Accordingly, for the foregoing reasons, we reverse the dismissal of the lack of informed consent cause of action and remand the case for further proceedings consistent with this opinion.

So ordered.

Culbertson v. Mernitz
602 N.E.2d 98 (Ind. 1992)

Opinion by KRAHULIK, J.

Roland B. Mernitz, M.D., (Appellee-Defendant) seeks transfer from the Court of Appeals' reversal of a summary judgment entered in his favor. The issue squarely presented in this petition is whether expert medical testimony is required to establish the standard of care of health care providers on the issue of informed consent.

Issue:

The facts of the case are as follows. Dr. Mernitz first saw Patty Jo Culbertson on March 28, 1988. Her chief complaint was that of uncontrollable leakage of urine and discharge from the vagina. [Dr. Mernitz recommended an operation to] suspend the bladder and either a hysterectomy or cryosurgery to freeze the infected tip of the cervix. . . . [He advised her of certain risks. But [b]oth parties . . . agree that Dr. Mernitz did not advise her of a risk that the cervix could become adhered to the wall of the vagina.]

[Culbertson decided to have the surgery.]

Following this office visit, Mrs. Culbertson decided to proceed with the bladder suspension and cryosurgery. She was admitted to the hospital and underwent these procedures. Post-surgically, Mrs. Culbertson's cervix adhered to the wall of her vagina. . . . [Under the care of a second physician, Culbertson eventually underwent] a total abdominal hysterectomy, bilateral salpingo-oophorectomy which involves the removal of both ovaries, and another bladder suspension.

Following this surgery, Mr. and Mrs. Culbertson filed a proposed complaint against Dr. Mernitz. . . . [They alleged medical malpractice and failure to] inform Mrs. Culbertson of the alternatives to surgery and the inherent risks and complications of surgery. . . .

[The Culberstons] argued to the trial court that the "prudent patient" standard should be utilized in evaluating informed consent claims. The trial court entered summary judgment on all . . . counts. The Culbertsons appealed to the Court of Appeals on the informed consent issue and argued that expert medical testimony is not necessary to make a prima facie case of lack of informed consent because the "prudent patient" standard is the law in this State and such standard does not contemplate the necessity of expert medical testimony.

The Court of Appeals agreed with the Culbertsons that the trial court had erroneously entered summary judgment . . . [on the informed consent count]. . . .

In order for a lay jury to know whether a physician complied with the legally prescribed standard of care, expert testimony has generally been held to be required. This requirement was premised on the logical belief that a non-physician could not know what a reasonably prudent physician would or would not have done under the circumstances of any given case. Therefore, an expert familiar with the practice of medicine needed to establish what a reasonably prudent physician would or would not have done in treating a patient in order to set before the jury a depiction of the reasonably prudent physician against which to judge the actions of the defendant physician. . . . This was the settled law of most American jurisdictions, including Indiana, prior to the early 1970s when two cases on the opposite coasts carved out an additional exception to the requirement of expert medical testimony in the area of "informed consent."

In Cobbs v. Grant (1972), 502 P.2d 1, the California Supreme Court held that expert testimony is not required to establish a physician's duty to disclose risks of a proposed treatment. The premise of this opinion was that placing unlimited discretion in the medical community to determine what risks to disclose was irreconcilable with the basic right of a patient to make the ultimate informed decision regarding a course of treatment. The court reasoned that a physician is in the best position to appreciate the risks inherent in the proposed procedure, the risks inherent in deciding not to undergo the proposed procedure, as well as the chances of a successful outcome. The court held that once this information had been disclosed, however, the expert function of the physician had been performed, and the decisional task of weighing the positive benefits of the proposed procedure against the negative possibilities inherent in the procedure passed solely and exclusively to the patient. Finally, the court opined that a jury is in the best position to determine whether the physician gave the patient the information needed by the patient to weigh the alternatives and make the ultimate decision of whether to proceed with the proposed treatment.

In the same year, the Court of Appeals for the District of Columbia decided Canterbury v. Spence (1972), 464 F.2d 772, cert. den. 409 U.S. 1064. In *Canterbury,* the court also held that expert testimony was not required to establish a physician's duty to disclose risks of a proposed treatment. It reasoned that while an expert may be required to identify for the jury the risks of the proposed treatment and the risks of non-treatment, a jury did not need expert guidance on whether a particular risk was material to a patient's ultimate decision. The court held that "a risk is thus material when a reasonable person, in what the physician knows or should know to be the patient's position, would be likely to attach significance to the risk or cluster of risks in deciding whether or not to forego the proposed therapy." With that as the standard of care in informed consent cases, the court concluded that a lay jury was in as good a position as a physician to determine whether the physician had informed the patient of the facts such a patient would "need to know" in order to arrive at a decision.

. . . .

Ind. Rule

The general rule [in Indiana] is that expert medical opinion testimony is required to establish the content of "reasonable disclosure" unless the situation is clearly within the realm of laymen's comprehension, as where disclosure is so obvious that laymen could recognize the necessity of such disclosure.

. . . .

Resolution of the issue of the necessity of expert medical testimony in informed consent cases depends on whether the issue is viewed through the eyes of the physician or the patient. When viewed through the eyes of the physician, it is easy to see that a physician should not be required to guess or speculate as to what a hypothetical "reasonably prudent patient" would "need to know" in order to make a determination. A physician should only be required to do that which he is trained to do, namely, conduct himself as a reasonably prudent physician in taking a history, performing a physical examination, ordering appropriate tests, reaching a diagnosis, prescribing a course of treatment, and discussing with the patient the medical facts of the proposed procedure, including the risks inherent in either accepting or rejecting the proposed course of treatment. From a physician's viewpoint, he should not be called upon to be a "mind reader" with the ability to peer into the brain of a prudent patient to determine what such patient "needs to know" but should simply be called upon to discuss medical facts and recommendations with the patient as a reasonably prudent physician would.

On the other hand, from the patient's viewpoint, the physician should be required to give the patient sufficient information to enable the patient to reasonably exercise the patient's right of self-decision in a knowledgeable manner. Viewed from this vantage point, the patient does not want the medical profession to determine in a paternalistic manner what the patient should or should not be told concerning the course of treatment. Thus, such a patient would view the reasonably prudent physician standard as destroying the patient's right of self-decision and, impliedly, placing such decision under the exclusive domain of the medical profession. While this viewpoint may or may not have been justified in 1972 when *Canterbury,* supra, and *Cobbs,* supra, were decided, a review of medical ethics standards of care in 1992 should assuage this fear.

The 1992 Code of Medical Ethics, as prepared by the Council on Ethical and Judicial Affairs of the American Medical Association, sets forth the medical profession's standard on informed consent. It reads as follows:

> The patient's right of self-decision can be effectively exercised only if the patient possesses enough information to enable an intelligent choice. The patient should make his own determination on treatment. The physician's obligation is to present the medical facts accurately to the patient or to the individual responsible for his care and to make recommendations for management in accordance with good medical practice. The physician has an ethical obligation to help the patient make choices from among the therapeutic alternatives consistent with good medical practice. Informed consent is a basic social policy for which exceptions are permitted (1) where the patient is unconscious or

otherwise incapable of consenting and harm from failure to treat is imminent; or (2) when risk-disclosure poses such a serious psychological threat of detriment to the patient as to be medically contraindicated. Social policy does not accept the paternalistic view that the physician may remain silent because divulgence might prompt the patient to forego needed therapy. Rational, informed patients should not be expected to act uniformly, even under similar circumstances, in agreeing to or refusing treatment.

We recognize this statement as a reasonable statement on the issue of informed consent. There is no need to change Indiana law on this issue. We therefore hold that, except in those cases where deviation from the standard of care is a matter commonly known by lay persons, expert medical testimony is necessary to establish whether a physician has or has not complied with the standard of a reasonably prudent physician.

Holding:

In the present case we cannot say that the risk of the adherence of the cervix to the vaginal wall is a matter commonly known to lay persons. Therefore, the Culbertsons needed to provide expert medical testimony to refute the unanimous opinion issued by the medical review panel in order to present a material issue of fact as to what a reasonably prudent physician would have discussed concerning this proposed surgery. Without the presentation of such expert medical opinion, the trial court could only conclude that there was no genuine issue of material fact and that summary judgment should be entered for Dr. Mernitz.

For D:

We affirm the entry of summary judgment in this case.

NOTES AND QUESTIONS

1. *Earlier cases.* Harbingers of the informed consent doctrine can be found in a few legal cases entertained decades before the doctrine was named. In Schloendorff v. The Society of the New York Hospital, 105 N.E. 92 (N.Y. 1914), then-Judge Cardozo forged a doctrine protecting patients from treatment in the absence of consent. The case involved a woman who came to New York Hospital in 1908, suffering from stomach troubles. Her doctor suggested an "ether examination." She agreed to be examined but did not agree to surgery. Nonetheless, surgery was performed. After the operation, the patient suffered from gangrene in her arm and eventually lost some fingers. Judge Cardozo wrote:

> In the case at hand, the wrong complained of is not merely negligence. It is trespass. Every human being of adult years and sound mind has a right to determine what shall be done with his own body; and a surgeon who performs an operation without his patient's consent, commits an assault, for which he is liable in damages. This is true except in cases of emergency where the patient is unconscious and where it is necessary to operate before consent can be obtained. The fact that the wrong complained of here is trespass rather than negligence, distinguishes this case from most of the cases that have preceded it. . . . [The plaintiff] had never consented to become a patient for any purpose other than an examination under ether. She had never waived the right to recover damages for any wrong resulting from this operation, for she had forbidden the operation. . . .

105 N.E. at 93–94.

Salgo v. Leland Stanford Junior University Board of Trustees, 317 P.2d 170 (Cal. App. 1957), identified as the first case to use the term *informed consent,* proclaimed that although patients have a right to informed consent, that right must be abridged by the physician's decision to withhold alarming information from a patient. Jessica W. Berg et al., Informed Consent: Legal Theory and Clinical Practice 44–45 (2001).

Canterbury v. Spence, 464 F.2d 772 (D.C. Cir. 1972) and Cobbs v. Grant, 502 P.2d 1 (Cal. 1972) were decided almost a half-century after *Schloendorff* and a decade and a half after *Salgo*. In *Canterbury* the court explains that a physician has a duty to the patient "beyond those associated with arm's-length transactions" because the patient relies heavily on the physician for information that may have important implications for the patient's life and health.

2. *Elaboration of the informed consent doctrine.*   Rena Truman was under the care of family physician Dr. Claude R. Thomas from the time of her second pregnancy in 1963 until a little over a year before her death from cervical cancer in 1970 at the age of 30, Truman v. Thomas, 611 P.2d 902 (Cal. 2980). During this period Dr. Thomas did not do a Pap smear on Mrs. Truman. In 1969, after complaining of a urinary tract infection (which Dr. Thomas had previously treated), Mrs. Truman sought help from another doctor. She was diagnosed with advanced cervical cancer. Mrs. Truman's young children sued Dr. Thomas. They argued that had he performed a Pap smear between 1964 and 1969, the cancer might well have been discovered in time for their mother to be cured. Dr. Thomas explained that he had suggested to Mrs. Truman that a Pap smear be done. But apparently Mrs. Truman had said the test was too costly or that "she just didn't feel like it." The court rejected Dr. Thomas's argument that the state's informed consent doctrine applied only to cases in which a patient was treated:

> The duty to disclose was imposed in *Cobbs* [*v. Grant*] so that patients might meaningfully exercise their right to make decisions about their own bodies. The importance of this right should not be diminished by the manner in which it is exercised. Further, the need for disclosure is not lessened because patients reject a recommended procedure. Such a decision does not alter "what has been termed the 'fiducial qualities' of the physician–patient relationship," since patients who reject a procedure are as unskilled in the medical sciences as those who consent. To now hold that patients who reject their physician's advice have the burden of inquiring as to the potential consequences of their decisions would be to contradict *Cobbs*. It must be remembered that Dr. Thomas was not engaged in an arms-length transaction with Mrs. Truman. . . .

The dissent in *Truman* argued that the court's decision would necessitate doctors' spending inordinate amounts of time and energy educating patients about a vast set of medical tests and procedures:

> Carried to its logical end, the majority decision requires physicians to explain to patients who have not had a recent general examination the intricacies of chest examinations, blood analyses, X-ray examinations, electrocardiograms, urine analyses and innumerable other procedures. In short, today's ruling mandates doctors to provide each such patient with a summary course covering most of his or her medical education.

Assuming the accuracy of testimony offered at trial indicating that Dr. Thomas had suggested that Rena Truman have a Pap smear, what more should Thomas have done? Even in the 1960s, how likely was it that Mrs. Truman was unaware of the purpose of the Pap smear? If she was in fact aware of what the test might indicate and of the possible consequences should the test be refused, should Dr. Thomas have continued to pressure her to have the test performed? How might he have done this? If Mrs. Truman was not aware of the test's uses, what should Dr. Thomas have told her?

Might one respond to the dissent's argument by asserting that Pap smears are different from many of the other tests the dissent delineated because they are comparatively cheap and easy to perform, and because cervical cancer, if caught early, is treatable? If you believe that a doctor should educate his or her patients about a wide variety of medical procedures, might this be done through the distribution of written materials or must the doctor speak individually to each patient?

3. *Further elaboration of the informed consent doctrine.* Contemporary informed consent rules are premised on the right of the patient to autonomous decision making. Perhaps inevitably, rules requiring health care providers to inform patients about treatment and diagnostic options decrease the disparity in knowledge, and thus in decision making capacity, between patients and health care providers.

A somewhat different sort of informed consent rule further levels the relationship between providers and patients by focusing attention on a provider's own illnesses or inadequacies. This second sort of rule, exemplified by Johnson v. Kokemoor, 545 N.W.2d 495 (Wis. 1996), requires health care workers to inform patients about the health care worker's own infirmities and limitations. The case arose after Dr. Richard Kokemoor operated on an enlarging aneurysm at the back of Donna Johnson's brain, leaving her with multiple disabilities including an inability to walk and to control her bladder and bowel movements. Kokemoor told Johnson before the surgery that there was a 2 percent risk of death or "serious impairment" and that the surgery was comparable in its risk to "routine procedures such as tonsillectomies, appendectomies and gall bladder surgeries."

Johnson sued Kokemoor, claiming, among other things, that he had failed to inform her that he was inexperienced with the particular sort of surgery he performed on her and that he had understated morbidity and mortality statistics associated with the surgery, even in cases in which that surgery was performed by surgeons far more experienced in clipping the sort of aneurysm from which Johnson suffered than was Kokemoor himself. Johnson also claimed that Dr. Kokemoor was obliged to inform her of the availability of more experienced surgeons and to have referred her to one of them. The court explained:

> [E]ven the most accomplished posterior circulation aneurysm surgeons reported morbidity and mortality rates of fifteen percent for basilar bifurcation aneurysms. Furthermore, the plaintiff introduced expert testimony indicating that the estimated morbidity and mortality rate one might expect when a physician with the defendant's relatively limited experience performed the surgery would be close to thirty percent.

Relevant Wisconsin statutory law required that a physician disclose "the availability of all alternative, viable medical modes of treatment" as well as "the benefits and risks of those treatments." In light of this law, the court concluded:

> [W]hile there may be a general risk of ten percent that a particular surgical procedure will result in paralysis or death, that risk may climb to forty percent when the particular procedure is performed by a relatively inexperienced surgeon. It defies logic to interpret this statute as requiring that the first, almost meaningless statistic be divulged to a patient while the second, far more relevant statistic should not be. . . .

Johnson dropped her negligent treatment claim against Kokemoor before trial. Thus, she did not argue that Dr. Kokemoor's negligence related to the surgery per se but rather to his failure to inform her about the specific risks of the surgery in light, in particular, of his own inexperience.

Do you think *Kokemoor* establishes a sound principle of law? Should physicians and other health care providers be required to inform patients that they did not do well in school; that they take antidepressants; that they once suffered from an alcohol or drug addiction; that they had too much to drink the night before? Should other groups of professionals, such as lawyers, accountants, and architects, be required to inform clients about similar facts?

The principle laid down in *Kokemoor* is regarded as an extension of the informed consent doctrine developed in *Canterbury* and subsequent cases. Perhaps the social or psychological motivation behind the two kinds of informed consent laws differs. Might one argue, for example, that *Canterbury* is basically premised on the notion of patient autonomy but that a rule (such as that announced in *Kokemoor*) requiring health care providers to divulge their own limitations flows from a diminution of trust that patients have in physicians and other providers?

As a practical matter, most physicians do not provide the sort of information to patients that *Kokemoor* requires. Moreover, all experienced surgeons were once inexperienced. In his book about the varied "complications" of practicing surgery, Atul Gawande describes the need for surgeons to practice new techniques to become proficient at doing them. Patients "eventually benefit" from new techniques, but the first few patients on whom the techniques are tried "may even be harmed." Yet, suggests Gawande, surgeons do not tell patients, "I'm still learning," or "other surgeons have more experience than I do." "Given the stakes," Gawande explains, "who in their right mind would agree to be practiced upon?" Atul Gawande, Complications: A Surgeon's Notes on an Imperfect Science 27, 30 (2002).

4. *Questioning physicians' previous experience.* Duttry v. Patterson, 771 A.2d 1255 (2001), contrasts with Johnson v. Kokemoor, supra. In *Duttry,* the Supreme Court of Pennsylvania refused to recognize an informed consent claim by a plaintiff alleging that her physician did not accurately answer her question about how many times he had previously performed the type of surgery he proposed performing on her as treatment for esophageal cancer. Pennsylvania relies on a battery cause of action in informed consent cases. This was not, however, of direct relevance to the state supreme court's analysis. The state intermediate appellate court had held for the plaintiff, Cloma Duttry. The intermediate court distinguished its own decision in a previous case, Kaskie v. Wright,

589 A.2d 213 (Pa. Super. Ct. 1991), on the grounds that in *Kaskie* the plaintiff had not specifically asked the physician for information about his own competency, but Cloma Duttry had expressly asked her physician (Dr. Patterson) about his experience with the surgery he proposed. The state's highest court reversed, explaining:

> We are unpersuaded by the Superior Court's reasoning. The expansive approach taken by the Superior Court below is in opposition to this commonwealth's traditional view that the doctrine of informed consent is a limited one. We have historically demanded that a physician acquaint the patient only with "the nature of the operation to be performed, the seriousness of it, the organs of the body involved, the disease or incapacity sought to be cured, and the possible results." . . .
>
> Furthermore, we note that this holding does not shift depending upon whether a patient inquires as to the physician's experience. We find the Superior Court's rationale that evidence of the physician's personal characteristics is relevant to an informed consent claim whenever the particular patient requests such information to be highly problematic. The Superior Court's reasoning on this point is divorced from the fundamental principle of the informed consent doctrine that information is material to the procedure at hand, and therefore must be divulged in order to obtain the patient's informed consent, if a reasonable person would wish to know it. . . .

Id. at 1259.

Similarly, Duffy v. Flagg, 905 A.2d 15 (2006), contrasts with *Kokemoor*. In *Duffy*, the Supreme Court of Connecticut limited the sort of information about prior medical experiences that a physician must reveal as part of the informed consent process. The case was brought by Kathleen Duffy, whose baby died during an attempted vaginal delivery following a cesarean (VBAC). The defendants had informed Duffy that the risks of a VBAC included uterine rupture and the consequent death of the infant and the mother. On another occasion, Duffy asked Dr. Flagg about her prior experiences performing the procedure. The physician noted that one of her patients suffered a uterine rupture during a VBAC; the doctor did not mention that the baby had died. The plaintiff contended that had she known of the infant's death, she would not have attempted a vaginal delivery. The court, holding for the defendants, explained:

> We . . . strive to establish a rule of general applicability based on the reasonable patient standard. Although physicians should answer each patient's questions accurately and candidly, we must be mindful not to expand unduly the contours of the informed consent doctrine such that physicians would lack a clear understanding of the scope of the disclosure that they must make, and patients thereby would be burdened with immaterial information that many might find confusing.

Id. at 22.

5. *Lack of informed consent can merge with malpractice.* Informed consent cases are tort cases. Often informed consent claims blur into malpractice claims. A New York court entertained a claim about a doctor's failure to provide informed consent to a patient with an aortic aneurysm. Enright v. Mount Sinai Hospital, N.Y.L.J. (S.C.N.Y. July 16, 2003), at 19. William Enright decided to undergo an experimental procedure—a stent-graft repair—at Mount Sinai

Hospital. The court noted that Enright's doctors had indisputably informed him about three treatment options, one of which was the procedure Enright chose. Enright was told about the risks of each procedure. Enright's expert argued, however, that Enright was not an appropriate candidate for the procedure he selected. Enright argued that he should have been told this. The court did not find this to constitute an informed consent problem. Justice Sklar, for New York's Supreme Court, wrote:

> That Enright's preexisting medical conditions [e.g., cardiac arrhythmia and emphysema] allegedly did not, according to plaintiff's expert, make him an appropriate candidate for the stent-graft procedure [see Motion, exh J, p 34, which recites that "[o]nly patients who are at a particularly high risk for standard surgical therapy because of severe comorbid medical illnesses will be candidates for cardiovascular stent grafts"], an assertion which is disputed by the defendant physicians consent [see e.g., Hollier EBT pp. 23, 25; Marin EBT pp. 16–17], does not state a valid lack of informed consent cause of action. Rather, it constitutes an alleged departure from good and accepted medical practice in performing a surgical procedure which was allegedly unwarranted. Even plaintiff's expert labels the performance of the stent-graft procedure as a departure from standards of good and accepted medical practice. A physician as part of obtaining a patient's informed consent to a procedure does not have to tell that patient that such physician is negligently recommending that procedure to that patient. Accordingly, the lack of informed consent cause of action is dismissed as to each of the defendants.

Could one analyze the issue in Johnson v. Kokemoor similarly? Was it negligent of Dr. Kokemoor to recommend that he operate on Donna Johnson insofar as he was ill-prepared to do the sort of surgery involved? Might the informed consent claim in *Kokemoor* have been dealt with as the New York court dealt with the informed consent claim in *Enright*?

Greenberg v. Miami Children's Hospital Research Institute[3]
264 F. Supp. 2d 1064 (S.D. Fla. 2003)

. . . The Complaint alleges a tale of a successful research collaboration gone sour. In 1987, Canavan disease [a fatal genetic disease] still remained a mystery—there was no way to identify who was a carrier of the disease, nor was there a way to identify a fetus with Canavan disease. Plaintiff Greenberg approached Dr. Matalon, a research physician who was then affiliated with the University of Illinois at Chicago for assistance. Greenberg requested Matalon's involvement in discovering the genes that were ostensibly responsible for this fatal disease, so that tests could be administered to determine carriers and allow for prenatal testing for the disease.

At the outset of the collaboration, Greenberg and the Chicago Chapter of the National Tay-Sachs and Allied Disease Association, Inc. ("NTSAD") located other Canavan families and convinced them to provide tissue (such as blood, urine, and autopsy samples), financial support, and aid in identifying the

---

3. Other portions of this opinion can be found in Chapter 13 and additional discussion of the case in Chapter 11.

location of Canavan families internationally. The other individual Plaintiffs began supplying Matalon with the same types of information and samples beginning in the late 1980s. Greenberg and NTSAD also created a confidential database and compilation—the Canavan registry—with epidemiological, medical, and other information about the families.

Defendant Matalon became associated in 1990 with Defendants Miami Children's Hospital Research Institute, Inc. [MCHRI] and Variety Children's Hospital d/b/a Miami Children's Hospital [MCH]. Defendant Matalon continued his relationship with the Plaintiffs after his move, accepting more tissue and blood samples as well as financial support.

The individual Plaintiffs allege that they provided Matalon with these samples and confidential information "with the understanding and expectations that such samples and information would be used for the specific purpose of researching Canavan disease and identifying mutations in the Canavan disease which could lead to carrier detection within their families and benefit the population at large." Plaintiffs further allege that it was their "understanding that any carrier and prenatal testing developed in connection with the research for which they were providing essential support would be provided on an affordable and accessible basis, and that Matalon's research would remain in the public domain to promote the discovery of more effective prevention techniques and treatments and, eventually, to effectuate a cure for Canavan disease." . . .

There was a breakthrough in the research in 1993. Using Plaintiffs' blood and tissue samples, familial pedigree information, contacts, and financial support, Matalon and his research team successfully isolated the gene responsible for Canavan disease. After this key advancement, Plaintiffs allege that they continued to provide Matalon with more tissue and blood in order to learn more about the disease and its precursor gene.

In September 1994, unbeknownst to Plaintiffs, a patent application was submitted for the genetic sequence that Defendants had identified. This application was granted in October 1997, and Dr. Matalon was listed as an inventor on the gene patent and related applications for the Canavan disease. Through patenting, Defendants acquired the ability to restrict any activity related to the Canavan disease gene, including without limitation: carrier and prenatal testing, gene therapy and other treatments for Canavan disease and research involving the gene and its mutations.

Although the Patent was issued in October 1997, Plaintiffs allege that they did not learn of it until November 1998, when MCH revealed their intention to limit Canavan disease testing through a campaign of restrictive licensing of the Patent. Specifically, on November 12, 1998, Plaintiffs allege that Defendants MCH and MCHRI began to "threaten" the centers that offered Canavan testing with possible enforcement actions regarding the recently-issued patent. Defendant MCH also began restricting public accessibility through negotiating exclusive licensing agreements and charging royalty fees. . . .

In Count I of the Complaint, the individual Plaintiffs, who served as research subjects, and the corporate plaintiff Dor Yeshorim claim that Defendants owed a duty of informed consent. The Complaint alleges a continuing duty of informed consent to disclose any information that might influence their decision to participate or decline to participate in his research. Defendants breached this duty, Plaintiffs claim, when they did not disclose the intent to patent and enforce for their own economic benefit the Canavan disease gene.

P
argument:

The duty was also breached by the misrepresentation of the research purpose that Matalon had included on the written consent forms. Finally, the Plaintiffs allege that if they had known that the Defendants would "commercialize" the results of their contributions, they would not have made the contributions.

1. DUTY TO OBTAIN AN INFORMED CONSENT FOR MEDICAL RESEARCH

D argument:

Defendants first assert that the Complaint fails to state a claim because the duty of informed consent is only owed to patients receiving medical treatment. Furthermore, they claim that even if the duty extends to nontherapeutic research, it does not extend beyond the actual research to research results.

The doctrine of informed consent grew out of a treating physician's fiduciary duty to disclose to the patient all facts which might affect the patient's decision to allow medical treatment. The basic principle of informed consent has been embraced by tort law in order to guard a patient's control over decisions affecting his or her own health. The state common law of informed consent is often fortified by statute. Florida's medical consent law, for example, applies to the patient/treating doctor relationship.

The question of informed consent in the context of medical research, however, is a relatively novel one in Florida. Medical consent law does not apply to medical researchers. . . . Florida [statutory law] does require, however, that a person's informed consent must be obtained when any genetic analysis is undertaken on his or her tissue.

Defendants argue that this statute is inapplicable to the case at bar because the statute does not apply to medical research, only test results. Moreover, none of the individual Plaintiffs have alleged that they were personally tested, just that they donated their genetic material. Furthermore, although Federal regulations do mandate that consent must be obtained from the subjects of medical research, the informed consent does not cover more than the research itself. Other courts in New York and Pennsylvania have dismissed attempts by patient plaintiffs to stretch the informed consent doctrine to cover medical research. . . . Plaintiffs contend these cases are distinguishable because they do not address informed consent in the research setting or the related issue of commercialization.

With Florida statutory law at best unclear on the duty of informed consent relating to medical research, Plaintiffs refer to cases in other jurisdictions where courts have found that researchers face a duty to obtain informed consent from their research subjects. See Grimes v. Kennedy Krieger Inst. [This case is reproduced in part in Chapter 11—EDS.] . . . Defendants counter that these cases are inapposite because Plaintiffs miss the crucial distinction between the use of medical research and human experimentation. Each of the cases cited by Plaintiffs as providing a duty of informed consent regarding medical research was based on some egregious practice, which Defendants argue is absent here. Additionally, there was no actual human experimentation as part of an ongoing relationship alleged in the Complaint.

Since the law regarding a duty of informed consent for research subjects is unsettled and fact-specific and further, Defendants conceded at oral argument that a duty does attach at some point in the relationship, the Court finds that in certain circumstances a medical researcher does have a duty of informed consent. Nevertheless, without clear guidance from Florida jurisprudence, the Court must consider whether this duty of informed consent in medical research can be extended to disclosure of a researcher's economic interests.

2. EXTENSION OF DUTY OF INFORMED CONSENT TO THE RESEARCHER'S ECONOMIC INTERESTS

Defendants assert that extending a possible informed consent duty to disclosing economic interests has no support in established law, and more ominously, this requirement would have pernicious effects over medical research, as it would give each donor complete control over how medical research is used and who benefits from that research. The Court agrees and declines to extend the duty of informed consent to cover a researcher's economic interests in this case. *Holding:*

Plaintiffs cite a variety of authorities in support of their contention that the duty of informed consent mandates that research subjects must be informed of the financial interests of the researcher. They first rely on Moore v. Regents of the University of California, where the court held that a physician/researcher had a duty of informed consent to disclose that he was both undertaking research and commercializing it. Plaintiffs also reference a Florida law that requires health care providers to provide written disclosures to patients of potential financial conflicts of interest. . . . Finally, in *Grimes,* the Maryland Court of Appeals found that researchers must provide "all material information" to their subjects.

These authorities do not control the outcome here, however, and the Court is not persuaded that they can be synthesized into a viable extension of the duty of informed consent. Moreover, Defendants correctly contest Plaintiffs' interpretation of *Moore,* the case that is most analogous to the situation at hand. *Moore* involved a physician breaching his duty when he asked his patient to return for follow-up tests after the removal of the patient's spleen because he had research and economic interests. The doctors did not inform their patient that they were using his blood and tissue for medical research. The allegations in the Complaint are clearly distinguishable as Defendants here are solely medical researchers and there was no therapeutic relationship as in *Moore.*

In declining to extend the duty of informed consent to cover economic interests, the Court takes note of the practical implications of retroactively imposing a duty of this nature. First, imposing a duty of the character that Plaintiffs seek would be unworkable and would chill medical research as it would mandate that researchers constantly evaluate whether a discloseable event has occurred. Second, this extra duty would give rise to a type of dead-hand control that research subjects could hold because they would be able to dictate how medical research progresses. Finally, these Plaintiffs are more accurately portrayed as donors rather than objects of human experimentation, and thus the voluntary nature of their submissions warrants different treatment. Accordingly, the Court finds that Plaintiffs have failed to state a claim upon which relief may be granted, and this count is DISMISSED. *Rationale:*

NOTES AND QUESTIONS

1. *Settlement agreement.*   Soon after the district court decision in *Greenberg,* the parties entered into a confidential settlement agreement. The Canavan Foundation announced that under the terms of the agreement, tests for the genetic alteration associated with the condition would continue to bring royalties to license holders, but those undertaking research using the Canavan gene would not be required to pay royalties. http://www.canavanfoundation.org/news/09-03_miami.php (last visited June 5, 2008).

2. *AMA provision.*   In *Greenberg,* the court referred in a footnote (not printed supra) to the Code of Ethics of the American Medical Association provision that doctors with an interest in using human tissue for commercial ends should obtain the patient's informed consent before using the patients' "organs or tissues in clinical research." 264 F. Supp. 2d 1064, 1070 n.2. Further, the rule provides that patients should be informed of possible commercial uses of "biological material" before profits accrue; patients' informed consent must precede the commercial use of human tissue and the products of such tissue. E-2.08. Other provisions of the rule are not directly relevant to informed consent. American Medical Association, Council on Ethical and Judicial Affairs, Code of Medical Ethics: Current Opinions with Annotations, E-2.08 (2002–2003 ed.). The district court decision in *Greenberg* dismissed the rule as inapplicable, explaining: "[T]hese regulations were only promulgated in 1994 and there is no evidence that they bind the parties in this case," because they entered the research effort prior to that time.

3. *Access to results of genetic testing.*   The Greenbergs and other plaintiffs presumed their rights to lie in the researchers' use of their and their children's body tissue. What sort of moral and/or legal right of access to testing for the genetic alteration associated with Canavan disease (if any) do you think should belong to Canavan disease carriers who did not participate in the research that resulted in identification of the relevant genetic alteration? What right to access (practical and financial) should people in general have to genetic testing?

4. *Between clinical practice and research.*   As the district court framed *Greenberg,* neither informed consent laws dealing with doctors and patients nor those dealing with researchers and research subjects were precisely applicable. In fact, even cases more clearly involving human research subjects might not be covered by laws that require researchers to obtain subjects' informed consent. For instance, studies based on retrospective chart review by physicians in private practice might escape legal regulation. See Roni Rabin, The Consent Gap, Newsday, Aug. 26, 2003, at A31.

5. *Between clinical practice and research.*   Difficult informed consent questions arise in cases in which patients contemplate innovative procedures or treatments that carry startling potential benefits and equally startling potential burdens. Face transplants present a paradigmatic case. The surgery involves removing a patient's face and replacing it with that of a cadaver. The first such operation was performed in 2005 in France on a woman whose face had been mauled by a dog.

In the same year, the Cleveland Clinic gave Dr. Maria Siemionow approval to perform a face transplant. Marilynn Marchione, Cleveland Doc Wants to Try Face Transplant, Sept. 17, 2005, http://www.newsday.com/news/health/. At the time, Dr. Siemionow sought a patient who was badly disfigured by burns or some other accident and who had enough healthy skin so that grafts could be done if the transplant failed. In fact, the first near-total face transplant was done at Cleveland Clinic in 2008. Gunshots had seriously damaged the face of the patient. By 2012, 22 face transplants had been performed globally. Meredith Cohn, Hopkins to Begin Performing Face Transplants, Baltimore Sun, Aug. 15, 2012, http://articles.baltimoresun.com/2012–08–15/health/bal-poh-hopkins-to-perform-face-transplants_1_face-transplants-facial-transplants-reconstructive-surgery; CNN, Face Transplant Patient Likes the Results, News (CNN), Chicagoland, Dec. 28, 2010, available in Lexis/Nexis.

A truly informed consent may not be possible for a patient contemplating a face transplant. In addition to the physical risks (including infection, the need for additional surgery, and the likelihood of having to take lifetime medication that itself increases a patient's risk of cancer and kidney trouble), face transplant surgery poses extraordinary questions about identity and personhood.

Rhonda Gay Hartman has suggested that "any concept of informed decision making in this context [of a face transplant] seems counterintuitive." Yet, she has also suggested that it may be "equally plausible to think that the values of autonomy and well-being underlying informed consent are not necessarily opposed in this context."

> Altruistic willingness to forge ahead despite unknown risks in pursuit of meaning in suffering, which includes participation in a procedure for the long-term betterment of others similarly afflicted, along with meaning derived from being a part of something beyond oneself, cannot be devalued as contributing to personal welfare. Nor should contributing to the collective welfare be dismissed in relation to personal well-being. . . .

Rhonda Gay Hartman, Face Value: Challenges of Transplant Technology, 31 Am. J.L. & Med. 7, 14–15 (2005). A number of articles about the bioethical dimensions of face transplantation appear in the American Journal of Bioethics, summer 2004.

Similar challenges arise in the context of infertility care. Patients are often anxious to try any treatment that comes with the promise of progeny. Yet, many treatments carry significant risks. For instance, multiple gestations resulting from the implantation of three or more embryos can result in premature births and significant health risks to the fetuses. Informed consent in the context of reproductive choices is considered in Pamela Laufer-Ukeles, Reproductive Choices and Informed Consent: Fetal Interests, Women's Identity, and Relational Autonomy, 37 Am. J.L. & Med. 567 (2011).

6. *Genomic information.*   The revolution in the study of genomics, represented and symbolized by the successful mapping of the human genome, has stretched the limits of the informed consent system constructed between the late 1940s and the 1970s.[4] The study and revelation of genomic information about people and groups of people creates psychological and social risks rather than physical risks. Often it is not possible to provide a potential subject with adequate information about future uses of genetic information. In addition,

---

4. See infra, section D (Anatomical Gifts) for further consideration of issues raised in this note.

genetic information may be different from other medical information in that it is often *viewed* as revealing the secrets of an individual's past and future more completely than other sorts of medical information. The National Bioethics Advisory Commission (NBAC) responded to some of these concerns with suggestions that preclude the need for informed consent if tissue samples being studied have been coded to protect privacy. National Bioethics Advisory Commission, Research Involving Human Biological Materials: Ethical Issues and Policy Guidance 66–70 (1999). See David E. Winickoff, Governing Population Genomics: Law, Bioethics, and Biopolitics in Three Case Studies, 43 Jurimetrics J. 187, 207–214 (2003) (considering the inadequacy of informed consent forms in several large-scale projects involved in the study of genetic information). See Chapter 11, Section D(2), for discussion of the NIH Genome-Wide Association Studies data repository.

7. *Informed consent.* The rapid development of an industry providing "personal genetic testing" to customers (often available for purchase online) raises profound questions about informed consent, as well as about many other matters. Through companies such as 23 and Me, consumers can obtain genealogical information, information about the risk of a variety of illnesses, and information about one's own or some other's character traits, www.23andme.com. Some companies are now conducting research using genetic information from online participants. Such projects occasion significant challenges to informed consent doctrine and to those concerned with the ethics of human subject research more generally. For instance, they are not typically reviewed by institutional review boards (IRBs). (IRBs are considered in Chapter 11.) Many of the issues at stake are considered in Valerie Gutmann Koch, PGTandMe: Social Networking-based Genetic Testing and the Evolving Research Model, 22 Health Matrix 33 (2012).

8. *Who owns donated tissue?* In Wash. Univ. v. Catalona, 490 F.3d 667 (8th Cir. 2007), *cert. denied,* sub nom. Catalona v. Wash. Univ., 2008 U.S. Lexis 1203 (2008), the Eighth Circuit affirmed a decision of a Missouri federal district court that had held that biological materials donated by research subjects and stored at Washington University (WU) belonged to WU rather than to Dr. Catalona, a physician-researcher, who had wanted the materials transferred to him at Northwestern University, his new place of employment. Research subjects had signed various informed consent forms, depending on the particular study for which the tissue of each was sought. Before leaving WU for Northwestern, Dr. Catalona sent a letter to his patients, and to some other research participants who had donated tissue, requesting their permission to transfer their stored tissue. About 6,000 of the research subjects signed and returned the release forms to Catalona. The release read:

> I have donated a tissue and/or blood sample for Dr. William J. Catalona's research studies. Please release all of my samples to Dr. Catalona at Northwestern University upon his request. I have entrusted these samples to Dr. Catalona to be used only at his direction and with his express consent for research projects.

Holding for WU, the district court found that the research subjects had donated their tissue to the University as inter vivos gifts. The Circuit Court agreed in light of the fact that the donors had intended to make a gift of their biological material to the donee University; they had delivered the property in question to the donee University; and the University had accepted the gift. The court noted, with regard to its conclusion about the donees' intent, that the consent forms bore the University's logo, and the forms referred to the subjects' participation "as a 'donation.'" Moreover, some of the forms named Dr. Catalona as the principal investigator, but others named other researchers, and even those that named Dr. Catalona noted that the study was to be "conducted by Dr. William J. Catalona and/or colleagues." The Circuit Court concluded that:

> The district court properly concluded the [research participants] made informed and voluntary decisions to participate in genetic cancer research, and thereby donated their biological materials to WU as valid inter vivos gifts. This voluntary transfer of tissue and blood samples to WU—without any consideration or compensation as an incentive for doing so—demonstrates WU owns the biological samples currently housed in the Biorepository. Whatever rights or interests the RPs retained following their donation of biological materials, the right to direct or authorize the transfer of their biological materials from WU to another entity was not one of them. Thus, the release forms authored by Dr. Catalona and signed by approximately 6,000 RPs are ineffective to transfer possession of biological samples housed in the Biorepository to another entity. Given WU's ownership of the biological materials, the district court neither abused its discretion in denying Dr. Catalona's motion for injunctive relief, nor erred in granting summary judgment in WU's favor.

Id. at 676–677.

CHALLENGING ISSUES: INFORMED CONSENT AND AUTONOMY

1. One day last year, Craig, a 21-year-old artist, was celebrating with Alice, his girlfriend. It was Alice's birthday. Both of them decided to take a short drive. Both Craig and Alice had been drinking and smoking marijuana. The two left in Alice's car with Alice driving. Alice collided with another vehicle. Her car rolled over. Alice was only minimally hurt, but Craig's right hand—the one he used for his art work—was crushed between Alice's automobile and a tree. He was taken to a local hospital's emergency room. The emergency room doctor called a surgeon because of the injuries to Craig's hand. Craig was still under the influence of alcohol and marijuana when he was asked to sign a preprinted consent form. He was told the surgeon would discuss his injuries with him when the surgeon, Dr. P., arrived at the hospital. Craig remembers having signed the form with his left hand. He does not remember that anyone ever explained what sort of treatment Dr. P. was likely to provide.

Dr. P. arrived at the hospital after Craig signed the hospital's consent form. Dr. P's written orders indicate that he asked the nurse to add the following language to the consent form that Craig had signed: "possible amputation of fingers right hand." There is no evidence that Craig was told that the surgeon was contemplating amputation. Craig does remember saying to Dr. P: "I'm an artist. You need to save my fingers."

Dr. P. operated on Craig within the hour. He amputated the fingers on Craig's right hand. In the year since, Craig has tried to learn to write and do some simple drawing with his left hand. He is improving, but has not been able to return to serious art work and may never be able to do so.

Craig is thinking about bringing a suit against Dr. P. It does not seem that Dr. P. was negligent. However, Craig is beginning to gather evidence suggesting that there might have been a few options in addition to amputation. The options were more risky, but Craig says he would have done anything that might have avoided the amputation.

Do you think Craig has an "informed consent" case against Dr. P.? If you were drafting a complaint for Craig, what would you include?

2. Dr. Rachel Jones recently learned from a colleague about the case of a patient named Harvey Strong. Mr. Strong was dying of cancer when his doctor, Dr. Mill, learned of a new medicine (Drug X) that was thought to be an effective treatment for the condition from which Harvey suffered. Harvey learned of the medicine and, gasping for air, he begged Dr. Mill to treat him with Drug X. The drug worked miraculously. Two days later Harvey was walking around the hospital, breathing easily, and joking with the staff. The tumors that were killing Harvey diminished by more than half within a few days. A few months later, Harvey read reports that Drug X was possibly less effective than had at first been thought. The tumors reappeared. Dr. Mill then told Harvey he had gotten a new, stronger, more effective version of Drug X and would inject Harvey with it. In fact, Dr. Mill injected water. Once again, Harvey improved markedly in a very short period of time. A couple of months after this, Harvey read a definitive report describing Drug X as "useless." He died two days later.

Dr. Jones is impressed by the power of the placebo effect, as illustrated by Harvey's case as well as by some others about which she has recently read. She wonders whether she should consider telling one of her sickest patients, Gertrude Winter, that there is a drug that might cure her. Dr. Jones thinks Gertrude would be susceptible to the placebo effect; Dr. Jones knows that Gertrude is very anxious to live for at least six months because her only daughter plans to get married at that time. Do you think Dr. Jones would be justified in trying to treat Gertrude with a placebo without informing her of that fact?

The story of Harvey Strong (a pseudonym) is based on Bernie S. Siegel, Love, Medicine, and Miracles 33 (1986); W. John Thomas, Informed Consent, the Placebo Effect, and the Revenge of Thomas Percival, 22 J. Legal Med. 313 (2001).

B.   THE ABSENCE OF INFORMED CONSENT: COERCED TREATMENT AND TREATMENT OF PEOPLE UNABLE TO CONSENT[5]

Respect for autonomous individuality assumes a person is capable of reviewing options and choosing among them. Historically, the law deemed various groups of people incapacitated for a variety of legal purposes. Many of these groups (including women, African Americans, poor people, and children) were—or in the case of children still are—identified as incapable of

---

5. Additional materials involving health care decision making for people deemed incapable of making their own decisions are found in Chapter 7 (regarding dying patients) and Chapter 9 (regarding medical decision making for others).

participating in various legal tasks as a result of a status grounded in biological distinctions (of gender, "race," or age); others have, more or less explicitly, been excluded from exercising autonomy in various legal settings as a result of class discrimination. Today children below a certain age continue to be identified as unable to provide informed consent for their own medical care.

Gender and "race" are no longer considered legitimate grounds for denying people the right to define their own health care options. However, treatment is still sometimes forced on pregnant women. In addition, individual health care providers may consciously or less consciously presume that certain individuals, identified on the basis of gender, race, ethnicity, or class, are less autonomous than others or simply may not understand how to communicate to a variety of people with backgrounds different from their own. As a consequence, health care providers may present people whom they view as different from themselves with less information than they present to other patients, or may forcefully pressure people whom they view as different from themselves into accepting professional conclusions, resulting in a subtle form of coercion.

This section considers the law's responses to three sorts of patients often considered incapable, or less than fully capable, of engaging in medical decision making: those who are clearly incompetent because, for instance, they are in coma; those who seem competent in certain respects but incompetent in other respects (e.g., certain people with psychiatric illnesses); and those who are competent but whose health care decisions are deemed unacceptable for a variety of reasons.

Most adults openly identified as incapable of providing informed consent are judged incapable as a consequence of medical assessments. Some conclusions about a patient's incapacity are comparatively straightforward. These include conclusions about people in a coma or in a persistent vegetative state or people with extremely low mental functioning. Other decisions are harder. For patients in need of health care, but presumed unable to provide consent, the law has devised a number of alternative approaches. One approach applies only to people who were once competent. If such a person left some clear statement, while competent, about medical choices should they become incompetent, the law will look to those previously expressed wishes. That is to say, the law may look to what the person once wanted to presumptively determine what the now incompetent person "would want" were he or she competent. This approach raises difficult philosophical questions about whether anyone can really know what the competent self would want if rendered incompetent. In addition, it does not provide for many incompetent people, including those who were never competent and those who never spoke to the issue.

The most common approaches to medical decision making for incompetent patients involve seeking a substituted judgment or assessing a patient's best interests. Both approaches, as well as an approach that relies on referring to the previously expressed wishes of a now incompetent, but once competent, patient, are considered in Norman Cantor's article (below). In addition, Cantor describes an approach based on the effort to preserve human dignity.

A different, although related, set of questions involves individuals who are arguably or even probably competent but whose medical choices are unacceptable to their health care providers, their families, or the state. Patients suffering from certain psychiatric illnesses and patients in prison may fall within this category. The case of Dr. Sell, infra, involves a patient whose health care choices differed from those of the state. Other cases involving patients with health care choices that the state or family members challenge include patients refusing blood transfusions on religious grounds, and patients, not diagnosed as terminally ill, refusing life-sustaining medical treatment and nutrition and hydration.

1. Patients Incapable of Giving Consent[6]

> ### Norman L. Cantor, The Permanently Unconscious Patient, Non-Feeding and Euthanasia
> 15 Am. J.L. & Med. 381, 403–405, 411–412, 414–415, 419–421 (1989)

Some authorities question whether it makes sense to invoke rights involving autonomy, privacy, and bodily integrity when the patient is unconscious. The patient by definition will not realize whether his or her previously expressed preferences are being honored, and he or she will not sense any bodily invasion that accompanies continued medical treatment. Nonetheless, it does make sense to talk about the unconscious patient's "rights." If the patient's will has been clearly expressed, then self-determination is indeed being respected even if the patient cannot sense its fulfillment. Self-determination means imposition of personal value choices. This is precisely what is done when a person defines the circumstances under which he or she wants life-support machinery to be withdrawn. Probate of a will disposing of real or personal property honors self-determination even though the testator cannot appreciate the will's implementation. Likewise, implementation of a person's prior instructions regarding life support honors patient autonomy even if the patient is unconscious. In addition, persons who have left prior instructions benefit while still competent from the peace of mind flowing from knowledge that their wishes will subsequently be followed. . . .

[T]he patient's interest in bodily integrity remains, even if the patient can no longer sense a bodily invasion. If a photographer snuck into the room of a vegetative patient, snapped pictures, and published them, most people would agree that an invasion of the patient's privacy rights had taken place, even if the patient could not sense the actual invasion. A similar reaction would flow from any effort to perform non-therapeutic medical experiments on the unconscious patient, or to harvest organs from that patient. A right to privacy may also be infringed (for example, by hidden recording devices) regardless of whether the subject of surveillance was aware of the physical intrusion. For all these reasons, courts have extended their recognition of both the autonomy and privacy interests of previously competent patients to the context of the permanently unconscious patient. Where such a patient, while competent, clearly expressed a desire to have life-support systems removed in the event of permanent

---

6. See also Chapters 7 and 9.

unconsciousness, that wish has been honored. Again, the long potential duration of existence has not mattered. . . .

What about the incompetent patient who never clearly expressed preferences about life-preserving medical intervention? Considerations of self-determination and autonomy are absent in these cases. What permits a decisionmaker other than the patient to make a determination that the incompetent patient should be allowed to die in the face of the state's contention that a sanctity of life interest warrants continuation of all preservable life? One answer is that every patient can and should be deemed to possess a "right" to be treated in a humane and dignified fashion, even if self-determination is not implicated because of the absence of prior articulated instructions. . . .

Medical decisionmakers acting on behalf of a permanently incompetent patient might employ the "best interests" of the patient standard. This standard is consistent with traditional notions of guardians' responsibility toward helpless wards, and with the state's parens patriae relation to incompetent persons. The problem is application of the standard to the stable, permanently vegetative individual. . . .

Another approach to the permanently unconscious patient employs substituted judgment. This standard involves reaching the decision which the patient would have reached if he or she were miraculously made competent and aware of the current situation. However, most commentators agree that this is a quixotic enterprise in the absence of clearcut prior expressions by the patient. Neither the prior lifestyle of the now incompetent patient, nor his or her religion provide a sufficient foundation for discerning the patient's actual preferences on the complex issue of terminal care. Consequently, absent clearcut prior expressions by the patient, the courts have tended to resort to the best interests standard. . . .

The real reason why most people would prefer death over permanent unconsciousness, and why courts are willing to allow guardians to make such determinations on behalf of vegetative patients, is that an indefinite insensate limbo constitutes a demeaning and degraded status devoid of human dignity. The total helplessness, dependence, dysfunction and exposure of every aspect of privacy to others—all without any prospect of regaining consciousness—make permanent unconsciousness distasteful and undignified. This "dignity factor" has been acknowledged by several courts in upholding terminal decisions involving permanently unconscious patients. In addition, many sources have suggested that the dignity factor should be included within the criteria of best interests of any incompetent patient. Such an approach is particularly appealing where the now permanently vegetative patient was previously a vibrant and vigorous person. In such instances, the demeaning nature of the comatose status is particularly stark and glaring.

The question arises whether the element of human dignity—commonly tied to notions of embarrassment, humiliation, and frustration—has any place in the context of insentient beings. The patient is unaware and uncomprehending. What difference does it make whether such a patient's status is demeaning?

One answer is that a basic societal norm impels treatment of all helpless humans with dignity, whether or not they can appreciate the benefits. The rationale is probably two-fold. First, by respecting the helpless person's dignity, society perhaps sets a tone which promotes the general welfare in the form of more sensitive human interaction. Second, it is reassuring and useful for every citizen to know that, in the event he or she becomes permanently unconscious, human dignity will be respected. People care now about the prospect of future maintenance in a debilitated, helpless state. People care now about how they will be remembered by survivors. . . .

A standard which focuses on human dignity is most useful where the customary "best interests" approach cannot function. A best interests analysis dictates assessment of the "burdens" (generally physical and emotional suffering) versus the benefits for the patient flowing from life-sustaining medical intervention. The problem is that many seriously incompetent patients are essentially noncommunicative and perhaps even insensate. Accurately assessing the painful or pleasurable feeling of these patients is impossible. We do not know how much suffering is reflected in the groans and sighs of a semiconscious patient. Nor do we know how much pleasure is reflected in the occasional smile elicited from the demented, inarticulate being. . . .

Some preliminary steps can be taken toward development of a dignity-based approach. It is possible to list the elements which most persons regard as impinging on dignity in the context of patient care. Helplessness is one factor. A previously vigorous person may well think inability to feed or dress or bathe oneself is a frustrating and demeaning condition. Immobility may be a source of frustration and degradation for a previously active person. Incontinence and the corollary subjection of bodily processes to public exposure may be a source of embarrassment and potential degradation. Extreme mental dysfunction, for example an inability to recognize relatives or friends, may constitute an element of embarrassment and indignity. Disfigurement may be offensive and degrading. Prolonged physical or chemical restraints—such as tying the patient, or drugging the patient into stupor to prevent tampering with his or her medical equipment—might be an important factor. What remains to be developed is an understanding of what combination or combinations of such factors would prompt a clear majority of competent persons to label the patient's status as demeaning and so devoid of human dignity that these competent persons would choose death.

NOTES AND QUESTIONS

1. *Privacy and dignity owed incompetent people.*   Do you agree with Professor Cantor's suggestion that an incompetent patient's privacy would be invaded by a photographer who took photographs of the person and published them? If so, why? What does it mean to say that the right to privacy survives the loss of competency? Does society owe respect to the person that is, the person that once was, the person that might have been, or to all of them? Is respect owed to the patient's loved ones? Why does Cantor assert that insentient beings should be treated with dignity? What does Cantor's article suggest about proper responses to a patient such as Sheila Pouliot (discussed in Blouin v. Spitzer, infra). (Chapter 9 discusses decision making for people with limited capacity, and Chapter 7 considers in much greater detail the debate about the dignity owed incompetent, dying people. Also, Chapter 8 considers the respect owed to dead bodies.)

CHALLENGING ISSUES: INFORMED CONSENT FOR DENTAL CARE

Freida D. was a patient at a state developmental center for persons with "mental retardation and developmental disabilities." Later she became a voluntary resident at a community residence center. Now she lives at the Danston Individualized Residential Alternative, licensed by the state and operated by the Five Lakes Developmental Disabilities Service Office. The medical director of that office petitioned to have comprehensive dental care under general anesthesia done on Ms. D. The court was informed that Ms. D. has "fairly poor oral hygiene with at least six teeth with restorative needs" and that she has "only fair ability to cooperate with treatment." The medical director asserted in the petition that Ms. D. is "totally disabled because of mental retardation and is not capable of giving consent." Her IQ has been assessed as 36. Yet, Ms. D. is capable of responding to simple questions and of making her basic needs and wishes known. She has no living parent and no guardian.

The Mental Hygiene Legal Service represents Ms. D. The lawyer asserts that Ms. D. objects to the dental treatment plan and should not be forced to have care that she chooses not to have.

State regulations (passed pursuant to statutory law) provide that informed consent may be obtained from residents of facilities such as the one in which Ms. D. resides. How do you think the court should respond to Ms. D.'s case? What more might you want to know about Ms. D. and her situation if you were the judge? What would you want to know about relevant laws?

2. Patients Who May or May Not Be Capable of Medical Decision Making

a. Bioethical and Social Perspectives

> ### Stephen R. Latham, Living Wills and Alzheimer's Disease
> **23 Quinn. Prob. L.J. 425, 430–431 (2010)**

. . . [T]here is a serious philosophical argument that it simply does not make sense that the previous desires of someone who is essentially not here anymore should rule in our present context. It is precisely the autonomous part of the person who wrote the advance directive that is absent when the directive is invoked. Why should we listen now to what it once had to say? The current self, after all, has interests; the relatives and caregivers have interests, too. Why allow an essentially dead hand to trump those live interests? The thread of life is already broken. Perhaps conflicting interests of caregivers and survivors ought to be counted when the original drafter of the living will is gone.

I'm going to close with a personal example. My dad has Alzheimer's. He does not know me anymore. He cannot recall my mother's name. He cannot read anymore. He has lost a lot of vocabulary. He does not recognize his own back yard—one day, recently, he looked around and remarked, "They keep this pretty nice." It was he who had been doing the keeping.

So, he has many of the cognitive disabilities in the list I quoted above. Worse than that, though, he has acquired, for the first time in his life, a temper. He has, several times, lashed out physically against his family members.

On the other hand, he can still go clamming. He can walk around the local cranberry bog. He can make and eat a nice sandwich. He can play catch with my son, although he does not know who my son is. He enjoys light social chat. And my mom wants him around even in his cognitively diminished state.

It is pretty plain to all of us that my dad of, say, six years ago would not have wanted to live like this. But subjectively, as he is now, he is perfectly happy. And there was never an appropriate moment for an intervention, never a time at which to stop his evolution from being the guy who would not have wanted to live like this to becoming the guy who's perfectly happy in this diminished state. Neither a living will nor a durable power of attorney are yet even relevant to his condition, but already all of his former self's interests have been defeated. The preservation of our pristine memories of the person that he once was, his sense of dignity, the thread of his life: all of that is already gone. And all we can do now is wait for it to get worse.

Dora W. Klein, When Coercion Lacks Care: Competency to Make Medical Treatment Decisions and Parens Patriae Civil Commitments
45 U. Mich. J.L. Reform 561, 586–588 (2012)

Involuntary treatment compromises the autonomy of people who are competent to make medical treatment decisions for themselves. As many commentators have explained, administering medical treatment to someone who has made an autonomous choice to refuse treatment is paternalistic. What is also clear, although stated much less frequently, is that overriding a non-autonomous decision is not paternalistic.

In the context of medical treatment decisions, autonomy is defined in terms of competence: a decision is autonomous if the decisionmaker is competent to make the decision. Thus, the critical question is, what is necessary for a decision to be competent, and thereby autonomous? Current definitions of competence to make medical treatment decisions focus on capacity. . . . So long as the patient can recite back what he has been told about the treatment's risks and benefits, he is competent to decide whether to accept or refuse the treatment. . . .

Requiring rational understanding promotes autonomy because autonomy is a good not only in and of itself, but also as a means of achieving other goods. To some extent, the making of a choice is a good regardless of what is chosen. But what of choices that are contrary to the decision maker's own goals for himself—what of choices to limit future autonomy, for example? John Stuart Mill, well known for his fierce denunciation of government paternalism, suggested that the choice to become a slave should not be respected. Mill recognized that autonomy is not only the making of choices but more fully is the making of choices that help us become the selves that we want to be.

That overriding some decisions can promote autonomy does not mean that all decisions causing harm should be overridden. Many decisions to refuse medical treatment, though likely to cause future harm, are autonomous and should be respected. But when someone who is experiencing active psychotic symptoms—and who has been found to be unable to care for herself because of those symptoms—decides to refuse antipsychotic medication, it is worth taking care to find out whether that decision is indeed autonomous, not only in the sense of making a choice but also in the sense of promoting the decision maker's own goals and values. Consider, for example, a college student, diagnosed with schizophrenia, who is besieged by voices telling her that she is worthless and deserves to suffer, so she refuses to eat or drink. She has been committed because her behavior threatens her survival. But she also wants to leave the hospital and return to college. If she does not understand that without medication the voices are likely to remain, while medication offers the best chance of abating these symptoms and enabling her to achieve her own goal of continuing her education, then perhaps she is not competent to decide to refuse antipsychotic medication.

. . . .

Like questions of autonomy and mental illness, questions of stigma and mental illness are confounding: untreated mental illness compromises autonomy and stigmatizes, yet involuntary treatment also compromises autonomy and stigmatizes. Some critics of civil commitment and involuntary medication argue that special rules for people who are mentally ill are stigmatizing. In general, we do not confine or insist upon providing treatment to people who are dangerous and physically ill; therefore, it is degrading to confine or insist upon providing treatment to people who are dangerous and mentally ill.

This argument is highly, although not entirely, persuasive. The problem is that to fail to treat people with mental illnesses differently than people with physical illnesses is to accept other, perhaps more harmful consequences than stigmatization. Involuntary treatment is harmful. But untreated psychosis is harmful too. When people are competent to decide, we leave the choice to them whether psychosis is more harmful than antipsychotic medication. But when people are not competent to decide, the government must provide some way for a choice to be made. In defining the standard for competency to decide, the government should not regard people with mental illnesses differently than people with physical illnesses unless the benefit of different regard is greater than the harm. Requiring that people whose mental illnesses have made them unable to care for themselves have a rational understanding of the consequences of refusing antipsychotic medication before they are considered competent to refuse this treatment does regard some people with mental illnesses differently than people with physical illnesses, but arguably the benefits of this different regard outweigh the harms.

NOTE AND QUESTIONS

1. *The price of autonomy.* Dora Klein, supra, suggests that the price of protecting the right to make autonomous decisions about one's health care may be protecting some decisions that, on deep examination, are not in fact autonomous. Is it worth allowing people to bear the burdens (whatever they may be) of

nonautonomous decisions in medical contexts firmly to safeguard the *right* to make autonomous decisions? Are there other reasonable options?

b.   Legal Approaches

In 1997, a dentist named Charles Sell was charged, along with his wife, under 18 U.S.C. §1035(a)(5), with having submitted false claims to Medicaid and other insurers for dental services not provided. United States v. Sell, 383 F.3d 360 (8th Cir. 2002). Sell was released on bond, but in 1998 the government claimed that Sell had tried to intimidate a witness and petitioned to revoke Sell's bond. Sell was brought before a magistrate judge. A psychiatrist testified that Sell was a danger to himself and to others.

A federal district court found that Sell was not competent to stand trial. Government doctors concluded that Sell would become competent to stand trial only if he took antipsychotic medication. Sell, however, did not want to take medication.

In August 2000, a magistrate judge authorized that Sell be forcibly medicated. United States v. Sell, No. 4:98CR177 (E.D. Mo. Aug. 9, 2000). The district court affirmed that order even though it reversed the magistrate's determination that Sell presented a danger to himself and to others. United States v. Sell, 2000 U.S. Dist. LEXIS 22425 (E.D. Mo. Aug. 23, 2000). The Eighth Circuit affirmed the district court's determination that Sell should be medicated against his will. United States v. Sell, 282 F.3d 560 (2002). Sell claimed that he had a "God-given right not to have [my brain] altered by the government's antipsychotic, psychotropic medication." Warren Richey, Forced Medication, The Christian Science Monitor, March 3, 2003, at 1.

‖ ***Sell v. United States*** ‖
‖ **539 U.S. 166 (2003)** ‖

Opinion by Justice BREYER.

The question presented is whether the Constitution permits the Government to administer antipsychotic drugs involuntarily to a mentally ill criminal defendant—in order to render that defendant competent to stand trial for serious, but nonviolent, crimes. We conclude that the Constitution allows the Government to administer those drugs, even against the defendant's will, in limited circumstances, i.e., upon satisfaction of conditions that we shall describe. Because the Court of Appeals did not find that the requisite circumstances existed in this case, we vacate its judgment. . . .

[I]n March 2002, a divided panel of the Court of Appeals affirmed the District Court's . . . determination that Sell was not dangerous. The majority noted that, according to the District Court, Sell's behavior at the Medical Center "amounted at most to an 'inappropriate familiarity and even infatuation' with a nurse." The Court of Appeals agreed, "upon review," that "the evidence does not support a finding that Sell posed a danger to himself or others at the Medical Center."

The Court of Appeals also affirmed the District Court's order requiring medication in order to render Sell competent to stand trial. Focusing solely on the serious fraud charges, the panel majority concluded that the "government has an essential interest in bringing a defendant to trial." . . .

We turn now to the basic question presented: Does forced administration of antipsychotic drugs to render Sell competent to stand trial unconstitutionally deprive him of his "liberty" to reject medical treatment? U.S. Const., Amdt. 5 (Federal Government may not "deprive" any person of "liberty . . . without due process of law"). Two prior precedents, *Harper*[7] and *Riggins*,[8] set forth the framework for determining the legal answer. . . .

[In *Harper*,] [t]he Court found that the State's interest in administering medication was "legitimate" and "important," and it held that "the Due Process Clause permits the State to treat a prison inmate who has a serious mental illness with antipsychotic drugs against his will, if the inmate is dangerous to himself or others and the treatment is in the inmate's medical interest." The Court concluded that, in the circumstances, the state law authorizing involuntary treatment amounted to a constitutionally permissible "accommodation between an inmate's liberty interest in avoiding the forced administration of antipsychotic drugs and the State's interests in providing appropriate medical treatment to reduce the danger that an inmate suffering from a serious mental disorder represents to himself or others."

In *Riggins,* the Court repeated that an individual has a constitutionally protected liberty "interest in avoiding involuntary administration of antipsychotic drugs"—an interest that only an "essential" or "overriding" state interest might overcome. The Court suggested that, in principle, forced medication in order to render a defendant competent to stand trial for murder was constitutionally permissible. . . .

These two cases, *Harper* and *Riggins,* indicate that the Constitution permits the Government involuntarily to administer antipsychotic drugs to a mentally ill defendant facing serious criminal charges in order to render that defendant competent to stand trial, but only if the treatment is medically appropriate, is substantially unlikely to have side effects that may undermine the fairness of the trial, and, taking account of less intrusive alternatives, is necessary significantly to further important governmental trial-related interests.

This standard will permit involuntary administration of drugs solely for trial competence purposes in certain instances. But those instances may be rare. That is because the standard says or fairly implies the following:

First, a court must find that important governmental interests are at stake. The Government's interest in bringing to trial an individual accused of a serious crime is important. That is so whether the offense is a serious crime against the person or a serious crime against property. In both instances the Government seeks to protect through application of the criminal law the basic human need for security. See *Riggins,* supra, at 135-136 ("[P]ower to bring an accused to trial is fundamental to a scheme of "ordered liberty" and prerequisite to social justice and peace" (quoting Illinois v. Allen, 397 U.S. 337, 347 (1970) (Brennan, J., concurring))).

Courts, however, must consider the facts of the individual case in evaluating the Government's interest in prosecution. . . .

---

7. Washington v. Harper, 494 U.S. 210 (1990)—Eds.
8. Riggins v. Nevada, 504 U.S. 127 (1992)—Eds.

[T]he court must conclude that involuntary medication will significantly further . . . concomitant state interests. It must find that administration of the drugs is substantially likely to render the defendant competent to stand trial. At the same time, it must find that administration of the drugs is substantially unlikely to have side effects that will interfere significantly with the defendant's ability to assist counsel in conducting a trial defense, thereby rendering the trial unfair. . . .

Third, the court must conclude that involuntary medication is necessary to further those interests. The court must find that any alternative, less intrusive treatments are unlikely to achieve substantially the same results. . . .

Fourth, as we have said, the court must conclude that administration of the drugs is medically appropriate, i.e., in the patient's best medical interest in light of his medical condition. . . . We shall assume that the Court of Appeals' conclusion about Sell's dangerousness was correct. But we make that assumption only because the Government did not contest, and the parties have not argued, that particular matter. If anything, the record before us . . . suggests the contrary. . . .

[W]e must assume that Sell was not dangerous. And on that hypothetical assumption, we find that the Court of Appeals was wrong to approve forced medication solely to render Sell competent to stand trial. For one thing, the Magistrate's opinion makes clear that he did not find forced medication legally justified on trial competence grounds alone. Rather, the Magistrate concluded that Sell was dangerous, and he wrote that forced medication was "the only way to render the defendant not dangerous and competent to stand trial."

Moreover, the record of the hearing before the Magistrate shows that the experts themselves focused mainly upon the dangerousness issue. Consequently the experts did not pose important questions—questions, for example, about trial-related side effects and risks—the answers to which could have helped determine whether forced medication was warranted on trial competence grounds alone. Rather, the Medical Center's experts conceded that their proposed medications had "significant" side effects and that "there has to be a cost benefit analysis." . . . And in making their "cost benefit" judgments, they primarily took into account Sell's dangerousness, not the need to bring him to trial.

The failure to focus upon trial competence could well have mattered. Whether a particular drug will tend to sedate a defendant, interfere with communication with counsel, prevent rapid reaction to trial developments, or diminish the ability to express emotions are matters important in determining the permissibility of medication to restore competence, but not necessarily relevant when dangerousness is primarily at issue. We cannot tell whether the side effects of antipsychotic medication were likely to undermine the fairness of a trial in Sell's case. . . .

For these reasons, we believe that the present orders authorizing forced administration of antipsychotic drugs cannot stand. The Government may pursue its request for forced medication on the grounds discussed in this opinion, including grounds related to the danger Sell poses to himself or others. Since Sell's medical condition may have changed over time, the Government should do so on the basis of current circumstances.

The judgment of the Eighth Circuit is vacated, and the case is remanded for further proceedings consistent with this opinion.

Holding:

NOTES AND QUESTIONS

1. *Eighth Circuit decision.*   The Supreme Court reversed the Eighth Circuit's decision in *Sell.* The circuit court had concluded:

> The district court did not err in applying the wrong standard of review. As required, the court found that the government has an essential interest in adjudicating the serious charges against Sell. The court found that involuntary medication is the only way for the government to achieve its interest in fairly trying Sell and found that the medication is medically appropriate for him. The government proved these elements by clear and convincing evidence. Therefore, we find no reversible error in the standard of review employed by the district court.

United States v. Sell, 282 F.3d 560, 571 (2002).

The Eighth Circuit's approval of forced medication of Sell galvanized discussions about "dehumanization, domination, and force exerted by man on man, man on woman, and doctor on patient." Review (Mental Illness) of Roland Littlewood, Pathologies of the West, 290 JAMA 536 (2003). The review, not entirely favorable toward a book characterized as "unreadable," ends by describing the circuit court's decision that Sell could be medicated "so that he might be rendered sufficiently sane to appreciate the corrective of [punishment]" as some evidence that the despair of the book's author might be justified. Id.

2. *United States v. Loughner.*   Jared Lee Loughner was accused of the murder of six people, one a federal judge, and of the attempted murder of 13 others, including U.S. Congresswoman Gabrielle Giffords. United States v. Loughner (9th Cir. 2012). Loughner appealed a federal district court decision that ordered his commitment to a federal prison medical facility where an assessment would be made about his competency to stand trial. The facility held hearings that supported the conclusion that Loughner was a danger to himself or others and medicated him against his wishes. Loughner was diagnosed as having schizophrenia. The Ninth Circuit upheld both the decision to confine Loughner in the prison medical facility and the decision to allow involuntary medication. Id. Loughner's attorney contested her client's forced medication because the decision that Loughner posed a danger to himself or others was reached during an administrative hearing by officials of the prison, not by a judge. In reviewing *Sell* (supra), Judge Bybee's opinion for the Ninth Circuit focused on "an important caveat": "'A court need not consider whether to allow forced medication for [trial competency purposes], if forced medication is warranted for a different purpose, such as [one] . . . related to the individual's dangerousness.'" Id. at 2381 (quoting *Sell* at 539 U.S. at 181–182). Further, explained Judge Bybee: "So long as Loughner is a pretrial detainee, and lawfully held, his rights are limited by the facility's legitimate goals and policies, and his dangerousness to himself or to others (while a pretrial detainee) may be judged by the same standard applied to convicted detainees. Judge Berzon dissented. She explained that the court was being asked to determine

> whether a district court may rely on a prior administrative authorization to medicate involuntarily a pretrial detainee based on dangerousness to self, issued while the detainee was under an earlier commitment order, to justify a new commitment for the express purpose of restoration of competency

pursuant to 18 U.S.C. Sec. 4241(d)(2)(A). The question is a difficult one, for it requires us to weight the interests and values at stake in two separate, but related proceedings, conducted for different reasons. Reviewing those interests, together with the principles gleaned from *Sell* and our post-*Sell* cases, I conclude that a court may not commit a pretrial detainee for the purpose of restoring his trial competency through involuntary medication without itself deciding that involuntary medication is both justified on some properly applicable ground and unlikely to infringe the detainee's fair trial rights.

In effect, Judge Berzon suggested in *Loughner* that a decision about involuntary medication as a response to "dangerousness" is essentially medical and can be fairly entertained by an administrative hearing, but a decision about involuntary medication with the goal of "restoring . . . trial competency" should be handled as a legal matter and is for a court to determine. Do you agree? Why or why not?

3. *Claims about newer antipsychotic drugs.*   Before the Supreme Court rendered its decision in *Sell* but after the Eighth Circuit decided the case, Dr. Douglas Mossman suggested that the appearance of a new generation of antipsychotic drugs, with apparently less harsh side effects than older antipsychotics, might influence judicial positions about administering antipsychotics to patients committed under civil law, to incompetent patients with guardians, and to condemned prisoners found incompetent to be executed. Douglas Mossman, Unbuckling the "Chemical Straightjacket": The Legal Significance of Recent Advances in the Pharmacological Treatment of Psychosis, 39 San Diego L. Rev. 1033 (2002). Mossman argued that in light of the lower rate of negative side effects of newer antipsychotics as well as the lower risk of neurological harm, and "possibly better outcomes," it was time to "reconsider the legal significance of antipsychotic medication." Id. at 1043.

In a case involving nonviolent crimes, how much weight do you think should be given to a defendant's concern that antipsychotic medications can alter a person's unique view of reality in light of the claim, voiced by Dr. Mossman, that newer antipsychotics are less likely to cause serious side effects (including neurological damage) than was the case a few years ago?

4. *Involuntarily committed psychiatric patients.*   Despite the general absence of a duty in U.S. law to take action to protect another (absent special circumstances), several courts have held psychiatrists liable for harmful acts committed after the release of involuntarily committed psychiatric patients. For instance, in Perreira v. State, 768 P.2d 1198 (Colo. 1989), Colorado's highest court found a "special relationship" between Victor Perreira and Dr. Anders. Perreira shot a police officer after he was released from involuntary commitment in a state mental health facility. The officer's widow brought suit, alleging that the state hospital and its staff psychiatrist were liable for her husband's death. The court decided that

when, as here, a staff psychiatrist of a state mental health facility is considering whether to release an involuntarily committed mental patient, the psychiatrist has a legal duty to exercise due care, consistent with the knowledge and skill ordinarily possessed by psychiatric practitioners under similar circumstances, to determine whether the patient has a propensity for violence and would thereby present an unreasonable risk of serious bodily harm to others if released from the involuntary commitment, and, further, that in discharging this legal duty the psychiatrist may be required to take reasonable precautions to protect the public from the danger created by the release of the involuntarily committed patient, including the giving of due consideration to extending the term of the patient's commitment or to placing appropriate conditions and restrictions on the patient's release. We accordingly reverse the judgment of the court of appeals. Because the standard of duty herein adopted had not been formulated as the controlling law when this case was tried, we believe the interests of fairness require a remand of the case for a new trial.

Id. at 1201.

5. *Coerced treatment of people diagnosed with mental illnesses.* A varied set of questions about coerced treatment relates to people in mental hospitals. Judging the capacity of people diagnosed as mentally ill can be extremely difficult. As a result, questions about the morality and legality of coercive treatment are especially troubling in the context of mental illness. Psychiatric diagnoses are rarely issued with certainty, and the likelihood that psychiatric patients will recover is often unknown. Questions about treatment decisions can plague family members and loved ones and can pose hard questions for state actors, including those operating state psychiatric facilities. Within psychiatric facilities, the right of those committed involuntarily to refuse treatment can conflict with the right to be given treatment that will help them recover.

Involuntary commitment that lasts only as long as a patient is deemed dangerous to self or others may end with the release of the patient on medication. That can pose a serious problem for family members and others if the patient stops taking the medication and becomes disruptive or dangerous again. In such cases, relatives are sometimes faced with terrible choices.

6. *Bibliographic note.* Elyn R. Saks, Refusing Care: Forced Treatment and the Rights of the Mentally Ill (2002); Daniel R. H. Mendelsohn, The Right to Refuse: Should Prison Inmates Be Allowed to Discontinue Treatment for Incurable, Noncommunicable Medical Conditions, 71 Md. L. Rev. 295 (2011); Devin M. Cremin et al., Ensuring a Fair Hearing for Litigants with Mental Illnesses: The Law and Psychology of Capacity, Admissibility, and Credibility Assessments in Civil Proceedings, 17 J.L. & Pol'y 455 (2009); Maurice S. Fisher, Jr., Psychiatric Advance Directives and the Right to Be Presumed Competent, 25 J. Contemp. Health L. & Pol'y 386 (2009); Erin Talati, When a Spoonful of Sugar Doesn't Help the Medicine Go Down: Informed Consent, Mental Illness, and Moral Agency, 6 Ind. Health L. Rev. 171 (2009); Vera Bergelson, The Right to Be Hurt: Testing the Boundaries of Consent, 75 Geo. Wash. L. Rev. 165 (2007).

CHALLENGING ISSUES: NATIONAL TRACKING SYSTEM

Lisa Suhay, whose mentally ill brother made "terroristic threats" to harm Suhay's children, describes her decision to inform the police about her brother:

I helped put my bipolar younger brother in prison. Knowing that breaks my heart, but it keeps my family safe. When he's stable, he's a shy man and he plays guitar like Segovia. It never lasts. For 15 years he's danced all over the cracks in the foundation of our medical and legal systems. He's often been homeless, surviving through luck and cunning. He is over age 18; that means by law, hospitals, police, and treatment programs can tell us nothing. We have no right to know where he is or how he is, no right to help. We can't protect ourselves or our community.

He was sentenced to four years probation in a halfway house with no family contact after I testified before a grand jury that he made terroristic threats to harm my children and others. In the dead of night he repeatedly called me saying, "I'm going to take away everything important to you starting with your kids so you'll know how it feels to be me."

And in January he destabilized. He smashed up his rooms in the halfway house and took off. Nobody notified us he was rampaging. . . .

This time I called and faxed everyone from police to state senators. I begged for help until New York and New Jersey prosecutors, police, and the hospital agreed to have him picked up upon release. He was transferred from the hospital to prison in February where he waits resentencing. Even if the judge rules that he belongs in a treatment facility, I worry that the shortage of state psychiatric facilities in New Jersey will force him to remain in prison.

Lisa Suhay, Incarcerating Bipolar Sibling, Morning Edition, National Public Radio (Bob Edwards, anchor), May 22, 2003. Suhay suggests that a "national tracking system" be established to protect violent psychiatric patients, their families, and third parties. Without such a system, Suhay says, "I'm afraid someday I'll face the family of a person he has hurt or killed as they ask, 'Why didn't you stop him?'"

Do you think such a system is a good idea? What form might it take? Can you construct other effective, yet moral and constitutional, responses to the dilemma Suhay describes?

3.   Competent Patients Whose Health Care Choices Are Questioned

a.   Bioethical and Social Perspectives[9]

> ## Carol J. Gill, Health Professionals, Disability, and Assisted Suicide: An Examination of Relevant Empirical Evidence and Reply to Batavia
> ### 6 Psychol. Pub. Pol'y & L. 526, 526–527, 528–529, 533–534 (2000)

This article examines a challenge raised by disability rights advocates regarding the fitness of health care professionals, particularly physicians, to referee requests for assisted suicide from persons with disabilities. Although some prominent individuals with disabilities have lobbied in favor of legalizing assisted suicide, most major disability rights organizations in the United States—including the National Council on Disability, American Disabled for Attendant Programs Today (known as ADAPT), the National Council on Independent

---

9. Additional materials relevant to this section can be found in Chapter 9 (about medical decision making for others).

Living, the World Association of Persons with Disabilities, Justice for All, the Association for Persons with Severe Handicaps (TASH), the National Spinal Cord Injury Association, and World Institute on Disability—have adopted positions in opposition. In contrast, no major disability rights organization has endorsed legalization. In 1996, a national group of disability rights activists, calling themselves Not Dead Yet, organized for the sole purpose of countering efforts to legalize assisted suicide and euthanasia. Several hundred members captured media attention by demonstrating outside the U.S. Supreme Court in January 1997 as the justices considered the constitutionality of state bans on assisted suicide. Among the primary targets of these activists' written critiques, testimony, and political actions have been health care professionals and medical ethicists who endorse legalized assisted suicide. . . .

THE CRITICAL QUESTION: IS DISABILITY A BASIS FOR ASSISTED SUICIDE?

Disability rights opponents of legalized assisted suicide argue that requests to die from persons with disabilities should elicit the same protective interventions afforded suicidal nondisabled individuals. On the other hand, health professionals who support legalized assisted suicide for persons with disabilities have argued that severe functional loss, intractable discomfort, and unremitting psychological distress associated with disability in some individuals can substantially impair if not negate quality of life and are, therefore, sufficient grounds for physician-assisted suicide. These conflicting views raise a critical question: Is there evidence that disability reduces quality of life to a degree that justifies an exceptional response—that compels medical and mental health professionals, when confronted by disabled persons requesting suicide assistance, to deviate from the conventional standard of suicide prevention applied to physically unimpaired suicidal individuals?

DISABILITY AND QUALITY OF LIFE ASSESSMENTS OF PEOPLE WITH DISABILITIES

A review of recent research on quality of life and life satisfaction of persons with disabilities yields little support for a differential response to suicidal feelings based on disability status. Researchers find that people with disabilities generally say they are glad to be alive, the majority rating the quality of their lives as good to excellent. Although some studies indicate that quality-of-life ratings are somewhat lower for persons with disabilities than for nondisabled control participants, other studies reveal no significant difference, and some suggest that many persons perceive their lives as better after disability onset than before it. In cases where the ratings are lower for disability samples, social correlates of disability (such as inadequate social support, economic insecurity, and lack of meaningful activity or control over life choices) rather than physical factors may account for the difference.

Negative Health Treatment Experiences of People with Disabilities

Consistent with the empirical evidence linking health professionals' negative disability judgments to their clinical actions is a body of research documenting the health services experiences of people with disabilities. Distressing encounters with physicians and other health professionals has been a recurring theme in the verbal and written accounts of persons with disabilities, covering such experiences as privacy violations, unexplained and forced treatments, patronizing conversation, uninformed medical advice, incorrect predictions of early mortality, rough handling, and dismissive attitudes toward sexuality and gender. Only in the last decade, however, have researchers systematically studied these reports. For example, Lonsdale (1990)[10] examined the life experiences of women with physical and sensory disabilities. Regarding their encounters with health care providers, she concludes:

> The women in this study regularly reported bad experiences (with) health professionals, in particular doctors, describing them as punitive, patronizing, dismissive and unhelpful. . . . Every now and then a woman might have come across a general practitioner or a consultant who was helpful and acted in partnership with them. The gratitude, enthusiasm and warmth with which these women described such contacts suggest that they are rare encounters.

Similarly, in her study of women with physical disabilities, Nosek[11] reports that a majority reported having experienced "frightening, frustrating, and psychologically damaging interactions with medical professionals" leaving them "unable to perceive control of their health status and care." These experiences echo repeatedly throughout in-depth interviews and focus group discussions with men and women with disabilities I conducted over the last 4 years. With notable exceptions, respondents describe physicians and mental health providers as unaware of disability issues, patronizing, and disrespectful. A common concern, expressed in the words of one wheelchair user, is, "Doctors need to realize that I have a real life and it's a valuable life."

NOTE

There is a significant support for the assessment made by the patient whom Gill quotes as having said that doctors often do not understand that patients have "a real life and . . . a valuable life." Relevant sources include Daniel Gilbert, Stumbling on Happiness (2006); R. Amundson, Quality of Life, Disability, and Hedonic Psychology, 40 J. Theory Soc. Beh. 374 (2010); and P. Brickman et al., Lottery Winners and Accident Victims, 36 J. Personality & Soc. Psych. 917 (1978).

---

10. Susan Lonsdale, Women and Disability: The Experience of Physical Disability Among Women 52, 52 (1990)–Eds.

11. M. A. Nosek, Sexual Abuse of Women with Physical Disabilities in Physical Medicine and Rehabilitation State of the Art Reviews: Sexuality and Disability 487, 498 (T. N. Monga ed. 1995)–Eds.

b. Legal Approaches

|| *Bouvia v. Superior Court* ||
225 Cal. Rptr. 297 (Cal. Ct. App. 1986)

This case is found in Chapter 7, pp. 457–460.

NOTES AND QUESTIONS

1. *Proposed standards for assessing competence.* The California court described Elizabeth Bouvia as "intelligent, very mentally competent." Jessica Wilen Berg et al. summarize four "components of competence standards." Jessica Wilen Berg, Paul S. Appelbaum, & Thomas Grisso, Constructing Competence: Formulating Standards of Legal Competence to Make Medical Decisions, 48 Rutgers L. Rev. 345, 348–358 (1996). These components are (1) the "ability to communicate a choice," (2) "to understand relevant information," (3) "to appreciate the nature of the situation and its likely consequences," and (4) "to manipulate information rationally." There would not seem to be a question about Bouvia's competence in light of these four components of competence.

Several commentators have suggested that had Bouvia not been disabled, medical and legal professionals might have focused more centrally on her state of mind. They might, for instance, have diagnosed and treated her for depression. Bouvia's life experiences, apart from her physical problems, would have depressed many, if not most, people. Among other things, she had married, become pregnant, lost the pregnancy, and divorced. In addition, her father had decided that he could not deal with her living at home, she had financial worries, and she had to drop out of graduate school. Why do you think the court focused on Bouvia's physical problems rather than on her other problems?

Although the court characterized Bouvia as living a helpless, undignified life, other characterizations are possible. In the view of Joseph Shapiro (at the time, a senior writer at U.S. News & World Report, speaking at a 1997 conference at Northwestern University), Bouvia was "far from being this helpless woman that is described by the court." Shapiro continued:

> Bouvia was "a woman who operated a power wheelchair and was on her way to a master's degree and a career in social work. This [was] a woman who married, made love with her husband and planned to become a mother." This was a woman who still could and might do all those things if she had been given appropriate psychiatric and medical treatment. Instead she was given a right to die.

Conference, Socially-Assisted Dying, Session III, 7 Cornell J.L. & Pub. Pol'y 267 (1998).

Diane Coleman, founder and president of Not Dead Yet, described the *Bouvia* decision as "one of many cases in which courts discuss disability with the same degree of ignorance and prejudice that prevails in the majority of society." Prepared Testimony of Diane Coleman before the House Judiciary Committee, Constitution Subcommittee, In Support of H.R. 4006, The Lethal Drug Abuse

Prevention Act of 1998, July 14, 1998. Not Dead Yet was founded to oppose the legalization of assisted suicide and euthanasia because of the dangers those options pose for people with disabilities.

2. *Bouvia's view after the court's decision.*   After the court granted Elizabeth Bouvia the right to die, she changed her mind. In a 1997 interview with Mike Wallace that aired on *60 Minutes,* Bouvia explained that she tried several times to starve herself to death but that it became too hard physically for her to do so. Elizabeth: Quadriplegic with Cerebral Palsy Decides to Live After Winning Court Case to Remove Food-Induced Food Supply So That She May Starve Herself to Death, 60 Minutes, CBS News Transcripts, Sept. 7, 1997. At that time Wallace asked Bouvia if she wanted to live. She replied: "Not really. I—you know, no, I don't." And then she added, when asked if she continued to think about taking her life, "But the thing is, physically, I can't."

3. *Coerced treatment of pregnant women.*   A somewhat different sort of coercive treatment case with competent patients has involved pregnant women. In these cases, nonconsensual treatment has generally been predicated on the interests of the fetus. Many of these cases have involved women who have refused care on religious grounds. For instance, Jehovah's Witnesses are forbidden from consenting to blood transfusions. Other pregnant women have refused doctors' recommendations for cesarean sections. Some of these women have often based their refusals on religious beliefs, but they come from a variety of religious backgrounds. A few cases have involved pregnant women with uncertain capacity to make their own health care decisions. The best known of these cases is that of Angela Carder. In re A.C., 573 A.2d 1235 (D.C. Cir. 1990). Carder was about 25 weeks pregnant when a cancer that had been in remission since she was an adolescent reappeared. Carder was hospitalized and agreed to palliative care that would keep her alive until at least the 28th week of pregnancy when the prognosis for the baby would have been much improved. Carder's condition worsened quickly, however. Less than a week after the cancer was discovered, the hospital sought a declaratory judgment allowing it to carry out cesarean surgery. The trial court convened a hearing at the hospital, heard testimony from family members, doctors, and counsel, and ordered that a cesarean be performed. The court heard no evidence suggesting that Carder would have opted for a cesarean before the 28th week.

The baby died within hours of the cesarean, and Carder died two days later. The District of Columbia Court of Appeals concluded that the case was not moot for a variety of reasons. That court explained that the trial court should have expressly determined Carder's competency. In such cases, if the patient is found incapable of medical decision making, the court should make a "substituted judgment." The court explained:

> It is improper to presume that a patient is incompetent. We have no reason to believe that, if competent, A.C. would or would not have refused consent to a caesarean. We hold, however, that without a finding through substituted judgment that A.C. would not have consented to the surgery, it was error for the trial court to proceed to a balancing analysis, weighing the rights of A.C. against the interests of the state.

The *Carder* court left open the possibility that a cesarean might be ordered in a different case. The court explained that if a patient is found competent, her wishes should control the course of treatment except in "extremely rare and truly exceptional" cases. Carder, the court declared, was not such a rare and exceptional case.

A number of commentators have suggested, largely on the basis of anecdotal evidence, that women who have refused doctor-recommended cesareans have delivered healthy babies despite their doctors' having predicted that a good outcome was virtually impossible without a section. In Jefferson v. Griffin Spalding County Hospital Authority, 274 S.E.2d 457 (Ga. 1981), for instance, the trial court had assessed the likelihood that the fetus would die if born vaginally at 99 percent. It further surmised that the mother had only a 50 percent chance of surviving a vaginal delivery. In fact, the baby, born vaginally, survived, as did the mother. Law professor Michelle Oberman explains that "[a]lthough it is impossible to design a retrospective study evaluating how many of doctor-recommended cesarean sections actually were necessary to maternal or fetal well-being, a surprising number of cases in which women refused treatment have ended favorably for mother and baby alike." Michelle Oberman, Mothers and Doctors' Orders: Unmasking the Doctor's Fiduciary Role in Maternal-Fetal Conflicts, 94 Nw. U. L. Rev. 451 (2000). See also Veronika E. B. Kolder et al., Court-Ordered Obstetrical Interventions, 316 New Eng. J. Med. 1192, 1193 (1987).

Further consideration of nonconsensual health care treatment of pregnant women can be found in April L. Cherry, The Free Exercise Rights of Pregnant Women Who Refuse Medical Treatment, 69 Tenn. L. Rev. 563 (2002); Nancy K. Rhoden, The Judge in the Delivery Room: The Emergence of Court-Ordered Cesareans, 74 Cal. L. Rev. 1951 (1986).

4. *Elective cesareans.*   A contrary challenge to that presented by nonconsensual health care of pregnant women involves women seeking elective cesareans (for nonmedical reasons). (Elective cesareans for medical reasons are almost universally approved.) In Britain, the phenomenon has been dubbed "too posh to push." Marcia Cheng, AP, Too Posh to Push? More C-Section on Demand in UK, Nov. 4, 2011, www.cnsnews.com. The label followed the publicized, elective cesarean births by a number of celebrity women. However, guidelines issued by the British National Institute for Health and Clinical Excellence (NICE) recommended allowing women cared for under the British national healthcare system to seek elective cesareans for nonmedical reasons. NICE did recommend that women seeking nonmedical cesareans be required first to discuss the choice with mental health professionals.

The rate of births by cesarean varies fairly widely throughout the world. In Britain about 25 percent of births are cesareans. The majority of these cesareans occur in response to medical emergencies. In Italy the rate is about 40 percent, and in the United States, it is about 30 percent.

5. *Refusing mandated vaccinations.*   Another type of case involving competent decision makers precluded from effecting their own decisions is that of parents challenging laws mandating vaccination as a prerequisite for admission to school.[12] Because school attendance is mandatory, parents whose children are barred from school because the parents refuse to have them vaccinated are subject to fines, and sometimes to imprisonment. At least one state court ordered that an unvaccinated child be removed from parental custody. Cude v. State, 377

---

12. Mandatory vaccination is considered further in Chapter 12.

S.W.2d 816 (Ark. 1964). Three of Archie Cude's and Mary Frances's eight children were not attending school because the parents refused to have them vaccinated on religious grounds. The court noted that the father had previously been fined for refusing to vaccinate his children and thereby precluding their attendance at school. The court then explained:

> This action was not instituted for the purpose of punishing Cude, but to enable the children to obtain a reasonable education. The fact that Cude has been fined for violation of the law in not sending his children to school in no way benefitted the children. It did not bring about the desired result of the children being sent to school.

Id. at 821.

The wisdom of mandating vaccination (or not) against certain diseases is discussed in Lea Ann Fracasso, Developing Immunity: The Challenges in Mandating Vaccinations in the Wake of a Biological Terrorist Attack, 13 DePaul J. Health Care L. 1 (2010) and in Allan J. Jacobs, Needles and Notebooks: The Limits of Requiring Immunization for School Attendance, 33 Hamline L. Rev. 171 (2010).

CHALLENGING ISSUES: MEDICAL DECISION MAKING

1. Life was never easy for Rachel Raines. She is intelligent, but as a young girl, she struggled more with schoolwork than did most of the other students in her class. She now wonders if her difficulties in school were related to her parents' divorce when she was still a young child. During her girlhood and adolescence, Rachel lived with her father for a time, but after she graduated from college, he suggested that she should move out.

Several years ago, Rachel married Ed Tonson. Rachel and Ed were married for a short time and have now experienced a difficult divorce. During the marriage, Rachel became pregnant, but the pregnancy ended in a miscarriage. Rachel was deeply saddened by the loss of the pregnancy and sometimes wonders whether that event had anything to do with the disintegration of her marriage.

Now Rachel has decided that life is too difficult to be worth it all and is considering suicide. She has recently mentioned this to her internist, Dr. Anna Janes. Rachel has asked Dr. Janes whether it's painful to die by starvation and how long it would likely take. She has also asked Dr. Janes for advice about other methods of committing suicide. Among other things, she wanted assurance that she would not be force-fed should she be hospitalized during the period of her self-enforced starvation. How do you think Dr. Janes would or should respond to Rachel?

2. Sue Sandor is 35 weeks pregnant with her first child. Her obstetrician, Dr. Mankin, has informed her that the fetus is not receiving enough oxygen, probably the result of a problem with the placenta. Dr. Mankin has recommended that Sue have a cesarean section as soon as possible. Sue rejects this option on personal religious grounds. She believes that her fetus is fine, and that God's healing powers will protect her and the fetus. Her husband agrees with her. No one questions Sue's capacity.

Yet, Dr. Mankin and South General, the hospital where Dr. Mankin works, have petitioned the state's attorney for wardship of the fetus. A hearing was convened. The state's attorney asked the judge to order a cesarean section immediately. Dr. Mankin testified at the hearing that there was hardly more than a 0 percent chance that the fetus would survive "natural labor," but that if the baby did survive, it would likely suffer mental impairment. The chance of the baby's surviving a cesarean birth was rated very high—close to 100 percent. Testimony was also introduced to the effect that the danger of death from the cesarean to the mother was about 1 in 10,000; the danger of the mother's dying in natural childbirth was 1 in 20,000 to 1 in 50,000. How should the court think about this case? Is there any ground on which the court should allow the hospital to proceed with the surgery despite Sue's refusing to consent?

C.   PRIVACY AND CONFIDENTIALITY[13]

A patient's right to privacy and to confidentiality is linked with the right not to be treated absent informed consent. An informed patient may consent to forgo privacy and to permit the revelation of otherwise confidential information. So, for instance, cases of "coerced treatment," considered supra, fall into a larger set of cases that includes those in which a patient's privacy has been inappropriately invaded.

In the United States, the right to privacy originally was understood as a right to be "let alone." Legal application of the notion broadened in the late twentieth century, largely as a result of the U.S. Supreme Court's identifying a constitutional right to privacy. For the most part, the Court applied that right to the protection of individuals' reproductive and sexual lives. The right has also been successfully invoked in other—mostly familial—settings, including various rights of parents vis-à-vis their children. Moreover, health care workers have long been required, as part of their common law fiduciary duty, to protect confidential information about a patient.

1.   Bioethical and Social Perspectives

> *Sharona Hoffman & Andy Podgurski,*
> *In Sickness, Health, and Cyberspace:*
> *Protecting the Security of Electronic Private*
> *Health Information*
> **48 B.C.L. Rev. 331, 332–335 (2007)**

The risks associated with the electronic storage and transmission of personal information in general and health data in particular are indeed

---

13. Safeguarding privacy and confidentiality are discussed in greater detail in Chapter 4.

grave. A New Year's Day 2006 article in the New York Times included the following statement:

> Every week seems to bring reports of a new breach of the computer networks that contain our most intimate personal information. Scores of companies—including Bank of America, MasterCard, ChoicePoint, and Marriott International—have admitted to security lapses that exposed millions of people's financial information to potential abuse by identity thieves.[5]

Another article reported that between February and June of 2005 alone, "businesses, universities, and government agencies lost . . . ten million records" and that, according to a Gallup poll conducted in August of 2005, nearly one out of five Americans experienced identity theft. In May of 2006, a burglary at the home of a Department of Veterans Affairs employee resulted in the well-publicized theft of discs containing names, birthdates, and Social Security numbers of as many as 26.5 million military veterans. Even private cell phone use is vulnerable to public disclosure. Reportedly, dozens of internet-based companies sell information concerning calls made and received by cell phone users, which they obtain by posing as customers and asking for copies of bills.

The confidentiality of personal health information appears to be compromised with disturbing frequency. A report that focused on discarded hard drives and disk sanitization practices disclosed that in August of 2002, the U.S. Veterans Administration Medical Center in Indianapolis sold or donated 139 of its old computers without removing confidential information contained on their hard drives, including the names of veterans who had AIDS and mental illnesses. An earlier paper published by the British Medical Association reported numerous instances of private health information abuse, including the case of a banker who served on a state health commission and obtained a list of all cancer patients in his state, which he used to single out these individuals and call in their loans. On April 26, 2006, Aetna announced that a laptop computer containing personal information concerning 38,000 consumers had been stolen, and on May 12, 2006, a newspaper article reported that a computer breach may have led to the theft of personal information relating to 60,000 patients who visited Ohio University's health center. Other reported incidents include an inadvertent internet posting of identifying information and details of the sex lives of ninety psychotherapy patients, an inadvertent posting of sixty children's psychological records on the University of Montana's website, a hacker's illegal downloading of thousands of patients' medical files from a university medical center, and the stealing of health information belonging to military personnel and their families from a contractor's database.

Why would anyone want to obtain the health information of others? The reasons are numerous. Private health information can be useful to employers who wish to hire and retain the healthiest employees, lenders and other businesses with a stake in individuals' financial futures and thus in their health statuses, drug companies that wish to influence doctors' prescribing decisions, advertisers and marketers who wish to tailor their material for particular audiences, health insurers making eligibility and premium rate decisions concerning individual insurance policies, and even educational institutions that might wish

---

5. John Schwartz, The Nation: Spy Game; What Are You Lookin' At? N.Y. TIMES, Jan. 1, 2006, §4, at 1.

to recruit and accept students with the greatest potential for success and longevity. In a world in which electronic health information can be easily stolen or accessed, it could also become increasingly appealing to blackmailers and other criminals. For example, after a computer was stolen from a general medical practice, two prominent women received letters from blackmailers who threatened to publicize the fact that the women had undergone abortions. Even potential romantic partners looking for a low-risk mate might try to obtain personal health information if it were easily accessible.

Trafficking in personal health information poses a significant risk to the public. Once the data is dispersed on the internet, it becomes available to anyone who is willing to pay for it, and it cannot be expunged. Consequently, the harm to an individual from illicit or accidental disclosure of health information is potentially unlimited. It is quite possible for the affected individual to remain unaware of the disclosure and its consequences, and it may be difficult or impossible to establish how the disclosure actually occurred. Loss or corruption of health data can also require the duplication of painful medical tests or even cause serious and life-threatening medical errors.

> ## Efthimios Parasidis, Patients over Politics: Addressing Legislative Failure in the Regulation of Medical Products
> ### Wis. L. Rev. 929, 966–967 (2011)

The Health Information Technology for Economic and Clinical Health Act ("HITECH Act"), which is part of ARRA (the American Recovery and Reinvestment Act of 2009, Pub. L. 111-5), allocates over $2 billion to help providers become meaningful users of EMRs [electronic medical records] and establishes the groundwork for an advanced health information network. As scholars and commentators have properly observed, these investments not only are investments in health IT, but also represent "efforts to improve the health of Americans and the performance of their health care system."

It is widely understood that installation of EMR systems alone will accomplish little. The HITECH Act recognizes these limits and clearly states that mere adoption of EMR systems is insufficient. Rather, providers must meaningfully use EMRs to achieve health and efficiency goals. To achieve these ends, the HITECH Act allocates $643 million to establish up to seventy regional extension centers, which support providers to adopt and meaningfully use health IT technologies, and $564 million to fund state initiatives to create health information exchanges. Health information exchanges integrate health care stakeholders—including physicians, labs, and hospitals—in order to set up an infrastructure for the electronic exchange of medical information.

The HITECH Act further allocates tens of millions of dollars to support comparative effectiveness research and research that focuses on secondary use analysis of EMR data. Along with these initiatives, the HITECH Act supports the creation of a Nationwide Health Information Network (NHIN). NHIN will focus on a nationwide electronic exchange of health information, and may serve as a national data source that may be leveraged for secondary use analysis related to health outcomes measurements. The vision for a national exchange relies on the emergence of local and regional health information exchanges. In this respect, NHIN essentially creates a "network of networks."

Robust information transfer has long been an integral component of medical care. At the individual level, it is clear that the sharing of health information is an important aspect of health care. Sharing information allows providers to coordinate the provision of care for an individual and assists in avoiding contraindicated medications and duplicate tests. Health information exchanges facilitate these important goals, and also play a significant role in population-level quality-of-care management. In terms of active post-market surveillance, medical information aggregated by health information exchanges will provide an important data access point for monitoring and evaluating adverse health events, and for conducting health outcomes and comparative effectiveness research.

> ### Janine Hiller et al., Privacy and Security in the Implementation of Health Information Technology (Electronic Health Records): U.S. and EU Compared
> **17 B.U. J. Sci. & Tech. L. 1, 6–8 (2011)**

Despite the benefits of widespread EHR adoption, its acceptance and implementation will not be achieved unless its risks are mitigated. Perhaps the most complex set of risks is to patient privacy and security. In fact, a significant obstacle to public acceptance of EHRs is the concern over the privacy and security of personal health information. In a 2006 survey, 62% of the public said "the use of electronic medical records makes it more difficult to ensure patients' privacy," however "similar proportions recognized the potential for EHRs in cost and error reductions and increased patient safety." Asked about a "network to provide people with access to personal health information online," respondents said they were "very concerned" about the following: 80% about medical identity theft, 77% about marketing firm access, 56% about employer access, and 53% about insurance company access to the information. Additional concerns expressed by the public include the loss of sensitive health information, increased sharing of information without patients' knowledge, inadequate data security, and the possibility that medical errors could increase.

The disparity between patient desires for privacy and what is provided by some electronic health record systems, is illustrated by the results of a 2007 study commissioned by HHS, which found that the privacy policies of Personal Health Record (PHR) vendors, a type of health record controlled by the patient, generally "lacked the standard components of privacy notices." Revealing a lack of attention to individual privacy, "only two of thirty PHR vendors described what would happen to consumer's data if the vendor were sold or went out of business, and only one had a policy with respect to accounts terminated by the consumer."

. . . .

Medical identity theft (MIT) is generally defined as the theft of personally identifiable health information in order to gain access to health treatment or to fraudulently file for reimbursements for false medical treatment. The consequences of MIT are similar across stakeholder groups; with the common themes of both diminished healthcare quality and financial loss as the primary risks. Based upon self-reported cases to the Federal Trade Commission (FTC), it is estimated that MIT comprises 3% of all reported identity theft cases. However, the FTC figure is likely low since the U.S. Department of Health and Human Services, the most likely agency to which complaints of health care theft are reported, had not previously kept specific records on MIT.

There are two common types of MIT: when an internal employee steals a patient's information (often sold to another party), or an individual uses another's identity to receive medical services or goods. Traditionally, when MIT occurred via the theft of paper records, the physical nature of paper records limited the extent of the theft. The transition to EHRs and the storage of information in electronic databases will exponentially increase the number of patient records obtainable by MIT thieves, also making notification to victims more difficult. It is also clear that MIT can result in life threatening damage if the medical records of an individual are changed, absent, or erroneous as a result of the theft. In a well-known case, a medical office worker stole the electronic records of over 1,000 patients, selling them to a relative who made nearly three million dollars by filing false medical claims. As a result of these types of incidents, some medical offices require their patients to provide photo ID. This identification procedure is not universally implemented.

NOTES

1. *Medical privacy and federal law.*   The use of electronic media to store and transmit medical information has greatly increased the risk that medical information will be inappropriately disseminated. The federal government responded to those concerns with the Health Insurance Portability and Accountability Act of 1996 (HIPAA), Pub. L. No. 104-191, 110 Stat. 1936 (1996). Ironically, the privacy rules were originally a by-product of an effort by insurance companies to obtain medical information about payer claims through electronic transmission in order to eliminate the need to work with paper. Concern was immediately expressed about the implications of putting that much private information about people's mental and physical condition in electronic form. The HIPAA privacy rules, 45 C.F.R. §164.500–164.534 (2001), aimed to safeguard the privacy of health information in electronic, paper, or any other form by requiring hospitals and professionals (including physicians, dentists, pharmacists, and others) to get patient consent before communicating information about a patient to almost anyone. HIPAA gave responsibility for enforcement to the Department of Health and Human Services. But enforcement, contingent on patient complaints to the Department of Health and Human Services, was weak for many years. Between the implementation of the provisions and 2006, the Department received almost 20,000 grievances. In almost three-quarters of these cases, the government found no violation or it requested the entity involved to remedy the problem. At that time, the remainder of the grievances that had been brought remained open. Rob Stein, Medical Privacy Law Nets No Fines, Wash. Post, June 5, 2006, www.washingtonpost.com. In the last few years, however, HHS has become more active in enforcing HIPAA's provisions. In 2011, HHS imposed a civil monetary penalty

(the first imposed pursuant to HIPAA) of $4.3 million against Cignet Health of Prince George's County, Maryland. U.S. Dept HHS, Civil Money Penalty, http://www.hhs.gov/ocr/privacy/hipaa/news/cignetnews.html (last visited July 9, 2012). Cignet was penalized for its failure to provide a group of patients with access to their "protected health information" and for failing to cooperate with the government's investigation. Notice of Proposed Determination, HHS, http://www.hhs.gov/ocr/privacy/hipaa/enforcement/examples/cignetpenaltynotice.pdf. Information about filing complaints can be found at http://www.hhs.gov/ocr/privacy/hipaa/complaints/ (last visited July 9, 2012). The penalty that HHS imposed against Cignet reflected passage of the Health Information Technology for Economic and Clinical Health (HITECH) Act in 2009 (described, supra, by Efthimios Parasidis; also see United States v. Zhou, infra).

2. *Patient privacy.* Efthimios Parasidis, supra, describes some of the aims of HITECH. However, for those concerned about the privacy of patient information, the Act presents a major challenge. Janine Hiller and her colleagues, supra, present some of these concerns. HITECH modified HIPAA in response to such concerns. Among other things, HITECH expanded the entities and individuals to which HIPAA privacy rules apply. HITECH now subjects those doing legal work that involves discovering identifiable health information to HIPAA's privacy rules. 45 CFR Sec. 160.103. Further, HITECH requires health plans and providers (aware of a breach of privacy) to notify anyone whose health information may have been breached.

3. *Genetic Information Nondiscrimination Act (GINA).* In 2008 Congress passed the Genetic Information Nondiscrimination Act of 2008 (Pub. L. No. 110-233). The Act, which adds "genetic information" to the characteristics protected under Title VII of the Civil Rights Act of 1964, prohibits employers from discriminating against employees (in hiring, firing, setting compensation, and other matters) on the basis of genetic information. It further prohibits health care insurers and group health plans from requiring genetic tests and from discriminating against people on the basis of genetic information. The Act's provisions are enforceable in the same manner as other claims under Title VII. (GINA is further considered in Chapter 4.)

4. *Social media.* The growing use of social media by almost everyone— including patients, clinicians, and others in the health care professions—raises a host of challenges about the protection of patient privacy. Do you think it is ethical, for instance, for a physician or nurse to "friend" a patient on Facebook? Why or why not? An interesting review of the topic can be found in Nicolas P. Terry, Physicians and Patients Who 'Friend' or 'Tweet': Constructing a Legal Framework for Social Networking in a Highly Regulated Domain, 43 Ind. L. Rev. 285, 319 (2011).

CHALLENGING ISSUES: PATIENT PRIVACY AND HEALTH CARE PROXIES

Jane Rider is the health care proxy for her mother, Anna James. Anna is now hospitalized and is not capable of making her own health care decisions. Jane knows she has authority to make medical decisions for her mother. Therefore, Jane would like access to her mother's medical records.

Anna's health proxy form provided many details about how Jane should make health care decisions should Anna become incompetent. However, Jane believes that she cannot adequately fulfill her obligation to her mother unless she knows everything her mother, if she were competent, would have a right to know about her own prognosis and her health care. The hospital believes that state and federal law preclude its releasing information about Anna to Anna's daughter. Why might a hospital be concerned about protecting a patient's private medical information from a surrogate decision maker such as Jane?

2.   *Legal Approaches*

Horne v. Patton
287 So. 2d 824 (Ala. 1973)

Opinion by Bloodworth, J.

Plaintiff Larry Horne comes here on a voluntary nonsuit assigning as error the trial court's ruling in sustaining defendant's demurrer to his complaint.

This case is alleged to have arisen out of the disclosure by Dr. Patton, defendant herein, to plaintiff's employer of certain information acquired in the course of a doctor–patient relationship between plaintiff Horne and defendant doctor, contrary to the expressed instructions of patient Horne. Plaintiff Horne's original complaint asserted that the alleged conduct constituted a breach of fiduciary duty and an invasion of the plaintiff's right of privacy. . . .

Count I

Whether or not there is a confidential relationship between doctor and patient which imposes a duty on the doctor not to freely disclose information obtained from his patients in the course of treatment is a question of first impression in this state. The question has received only a limited consideration in other jurisdictions, and its resolution has been varied. Those states which have enacted a doctor–patient testimonial privilege statute have been almost uniform in allowing a cause of action for unauthorized disclosure.

Alabama, however, has not enacted such a privilege statute. In reviewing cases from other states which also do not have a doctor–patient testimonial privilege, the jurisdictions are split about evenly on this issue. After a careful consideration of this issue, it appears that the sounder legal position recognizes at least a qualified duty on the part of a doctor not to reveal confidences obtained through the doctor–patient relationship. . . .

It should be noted that Alabama has a . . . statute which gives the state licensing board for the healing arts the power and imposes on it the duty of suspending or revoking a doctor's license who willfully betrays a professional secret. [This statute] reads as follows:

> The state licensing board for the healing arts shall have the power and it is its duty to suspend for a specified time, to be determined in the discretion of the

board, or revoke any license to practice the healing arts or any branch thereof in the state of Alabama whenever the licensee shall be found guilty of any of the following acts or offenses; . . . (14) Willful betrayal of a professional secret;

Moreover, the established ethical code of the medical profession itself unequivocally recognizes the confidential nature of the doctor–patient relationship. Each physician upon entering the profession takes the Hippocratic Oath. One portion of that required pledge reads as follows:

Whatever in connection with my professional practice, or not in connection with it, I see or hear, in the life of men, which ought not be spoken of abroad, I will not divulge, as reckoning that all such should be kept secret.

This pledge has been reaffirmed in the Principles of Medical Ethics promulgated by the American Medical Association in Principle 9, viz:

A physician may not reveal the confidences entrusted to him in the course of medical attendance, or the deficiencies he may observe in the character of patients, unless he is required to do so by law or unless it becomes necessary in order to protect the welfare of the individual or of the community.

American Medical Association, Principles of Medical Ethics, 1957, §9 (Published by AMA).

When the wording of Alabama's state licensing statute is considered alongside the accepted precepts of the medical profession itself, it would seem to establish clearly that public policy in Alabama requires that information obtained by a physician in the course of a doctor–patient relationship be maintained in confidence, unless public interest or the private interest of the patient demands otherwise. Is it not important that patients seeking medical attention be able to freely divulge information about themselves to their attending physician without fear that the information so revealed will be frivolously disclosed? . . .

The trial court erred in sustaining the demurrer to Count I.

COUNT II

The gravamen of Count II is that defendant's release to plaintiff's employer of information concerning plaintiff's health constituted an invasion of plaintiff's privacy.

This court has recognized the right of a person to be free from unwarranted publicity or unwarranted appropriation or exploitation of one's personality, publicization of one's private affairs with which the public has no legitimate concern, or the wrongful intrusion of one's private activities in such manner as to outrage or cause mental suffering, shame or humiliation to a person of ordinary sensibilities.

Whether or not unauthorized disclosure of a person's medical record constitutes an invasion of this right of privacy is likewise a question of first impression in Alabama. Looking to other jurisdictions which have considered this question, those courts have almost uniformly recognized such disclosure as a violation of the patient's right of privacy. . . .

Unauthorized disclosure of intimate details of a patient's health may amount to unwarranted publicization of one's private affairs with which the public has no legitimate concern such as to cause outrage, mental suffering, shame or humiliation to a person of ordinary sensibilities. Nor can it be said that an employer is necessarily a person who has a legitimate interest in knowing each and every detail of an employee's health. Certainly, there are many ailments about which a patient might consult his private physician which have no bearing or effect on one's employment. If the defendant doctor in the instant case had a legitimate reason for making this disclosure under the particular facts of this case, then this is a matter of defense.

The trial court erred in sustaining the demurrer to Count II.

COUNT III

The gravamen of Count III is that the alleged disclosure breached an implied contract to keep confidential all personal information given to defendant doctor by his patient. This count alleges that defendant doctor entered into a physician–patient contractual relationship wherein the plaintiff agreed to disclose to defendant all facts which would help him in his diagnosis and treatment of the plaintiff, that defendant agreed to treat the plaintiff to the best of his medical ability, and to keep confidential all personal information given to him by the plaintiff. It is alleged that this agreement is implied from the facts through common custom and practice. . . .

The trial court erred in sustaining demurrer to Count III.

The judgment of the trial court is therefore due to be reversed and remanded. Dissent by: McCALL, J. . . .

In my opinion the overriding competing interest and responsibility of an employer for the welfare of all of his employees, to the public who come to his establishment and who buy his merchandise, and to the furtherance of his own business venture, should entitle him to be free from the shackles of secrecy that would prevent a physician from disclosing to the employer critical information concerning the physical or mental condition of his employees.

United States v. Zhou
678 F.3d 1110 (9th Cir. 2012)

Opinion M. SMITH, Circuit Judge

Defendant-Appellant Huping Zhou, a former research assistant at the University of California at Los Angeles Health System (UHS), accessed patient records without authorization after his employment was terminated. In an information, the government charged him with violating the Health Insurance Portability and Accountability Act of 1996 (HIPAA), which imposes a misdemeanor penalty on "[a] person who knowingly and in violation of this . . . obtains individually identifiable health information relating to an individual[.]" Zhou moved to dismiss the information because it did not allege that Zhou knew that the statute prohibited him from obtaining the health information. The district court denied the motion to dismiss. Zhou entered a conditional guilty plea, reserving the right to appeal the denial of his motion to dismiss.

. . . .

Zhou was hired as a research assistant in rheumatology at UHS on February 2, 2003. On October 29, 2003, UHS issued Zhou a notice of intent to dismiss due to "continued serious job deficiencies and poor judgment." On November 12, 2003, after a formal internal grievance hearing, Zhou received a dismissal letter effective November 14, 2003.

After his termination on November 14, 2003, there were at least four instances, on November 17 and 19, in which Zhou accessed patient records without authorization. The information charged Zhou with crimes only for accessing patients' medical information after he was terminated and no longer treating patients at the hospital.

HIPAA provides that: "[a] person who knowingly and in violation of this part—(1) uses or causes to be used a unique health identifier; (2) obtains individually identifiable health information relating to an individual; or (3) discloses individually identifiable health information to another person, shall be punished as provided in subsection (b)." 42 U.S.C. §1320d-6(a).

On November 17, 2008, Zhou was charged by information under subsection 2 of that HIPAA provision. The four misdemeanor counts in the information stated that Zhou "knowingly and for reasons other than permitted by Title 42 United States Code Chapter 7, Subchapter XI, Part C, obtained and caused to be obtained individually identifiable health information relating to an individual. . . ." Each count alleged access to a patient record after Zhou's termination.

On October 19, 2009, Zhou moved to dismiss the information, arguing that the information did not allege that he knew that it was illegal to obtain the health information. On November 12, 2009, the magistrate judge denied the motion in a ruling from the bench.

. . . .

Zhou contends that the information failed to meet these requirements because it did not explicitly state that Zhou knew that obtaining the health information was illegal. He argues that "knowingly," as used in 42 U.S.C. §1320d-6(a), modifies "in violation of this part." Under Zhou's interpretation of the statute, a defendant is guilty only if he knew that obtaining the personal healthcare information was illegal.

We reject Zhou's argument because it contradicts the plain language of HIPAA. The statute's misdemeanor criminal penalty applies to an individual who "knowingly and in violation of this part . . . obtains individually identifiable health information relating to an individual." The word "and" unambiguously indicates that there are two elements of a . . . violation: 1) knowingly obtaining individually identifiable health information relating to an individual; and 2) obtaining that information in violation of Title 42 United States Code Chapter 7, Subchapter XI, Part C. Thus, the term "knowingly" applies only to the act of obtaining the health information.

. . . Section 1320d-6's title indicates a broad scope. See Christensen v. Comm'r of Internal Revenue, 523 F.3d 957, 960 (9th Cir. 2008) ("[O]ur first indication of the statute's scope is set forth in the title."). The section is titled "Wrongful disclosure of individually identifiable health information." 42 U.S.C. §1320d-6. Had Congress intended to confine this penalty to people who knew that the disclosure was illegal, the title likely would have limited the scope to knowingly illegal conduct.

. . . .

In sum, we hold that 42 U.S.C. §1320d-6(a)(2) is not limited to defendants who knew that their actions were illegal. Rather, the defendant need only know that he obtained individually identifiable health information relating to an individual. Therefore, the information satisfies the requirements of both the Due Process Clause and Federal Rule of Criminal Procedure 7.2.

. . . .

For the foregoing reasons, the district court's denial of the motion to dismiss the information is affirmed.

NOTES AND QUESTIONS

1. *Exceptions.*   In Horne v. Patton, supra, the Alabama Supreme Court noted the possibility of "exceptions prompted by the supervening interests of society." In Mull v. String, 448 So. 2d 952 (1984), the Alabama court recognized such an exception. Rased Mull sued a hospital where he had been a patient in connection with a burn he suffered from a heating pad. In the context of that litigation, Mull asked Dr. String to detail Mull's injuries in a letter. String, without receiving Mull's consent, sent the letter to the hospital and to its lawyer.

The court held for String because, among other things, the doctor's letter was legally discoverable by the hospital and because the "absence of a statutory physician–patient testimonial privilege in Alabama . . . evidences a legislative intent to uphold the public's interest in full disclosure to obtain a just determination of the controversy." Id. at 954. However, the court also decided that the allegation in Mull's complaint which stated that Dr. String verbally disclosed to others his medical opinion on the cause of Mull's injuries, when viewed most strongly in Mull's favor, does state a claim on which relief could be granted, because Mull could possibly establish that these recipients of Dr. String's unauthorized disclosures were in fact persons other than the defendant hospital and its attorney. It was therefore error to dismiss this portion of Mull's complaint for failure to state a claim.

The law has recognized several other sorts of exceptions to the broad rule that protects confidentiality within health care contexts. Many of the exceptions relate to public health concerns. So, for instance, physicians are mandated to report certain contagious diseases to health authorities. Other exceptions involve situations in which a patient's condition poses risks other than contagion to some other person or people.

In Tarasoff v. Regents of the University of California, 551 P.2d 334 (Cal. 1976), the Supreme Court of California determined that a psychotherapist's obligation to preserve patient confidentiality "must yield to the extent to which disclosure is essential to avert danger to others. The protective privilege ends where the public peril begins." The case involved two university students. One of them, Prosenjit Poddar, an exchange student from India, murdered the other, Tatiana Tarasoff, an undergraduate student at the University of California at Berkeley. (Poddar's own history is described in the criminal case brought against him, People v. Poddar, 518 P.2d 342 (Cal. 1974).) After the murder, Tatiana's parents sued Poddar's psychologist, the psychologist's superior and the University of California hospital where both worked, alleging that defendants knew Poddar posed a danger to Tatiana but failed to warn either her or her parents. The California court concluded that in light of the defendants' special relationship to Poddar, they were responsible to issue a warning about the danger he posed to Tarasoff. Justice Trobiner wrote for the Supreme Court of California:

> [O]nce a therapist does in fact determine, or under applicable professional standards reasonably should have determined, that a patient poses a serious danger of violence to others, he bears a duty to exercise reasonable care to protect the foreseeable victim of that danger. . . .
>
> We recognize the public interest in supporting effective treatment of mental illness and in protecting the rights of patients to privacy, and the consequent public importance of safeguarding the confidential character of psychotherapeutic communication. Against this interest, however, we must weigh the public interest in safety from violent assault. . . .
>
> We realize that the open and confidential character of psychotherapeutic dialogue encourages patients to express threats of violence, few of which are ever executed. Certainly a therapist should not be encouraged routinely to reveal such threats; such disclosures could seriously disrupt the patient's relationship with his therapist and with the persons threatened. To the contrary, the therapist's obligations to his patient require that he not disclose a confidence unless such disclosure is necessary to avert danger to others, and even then that he do so discretely, and in a fashion that would preserve the privacy of his patient to the fullest extent compatible with the prevention of the threatened danger.

Justice Clark, who dissented in *Tarasoff*, argued that the duty imposed on psychotherapists by the majority would "frustrate psychiatric treatment, invade fundamental patient rights and increase violence," and that the duty offered "virtually no benefit to society." Despite such concerns and despite predictions that *Tarasoff* would not be followed widely, *Tarasoff* has become the rule in many, although not in all, states. Fillmore Buckner & Marvin Firestone, "Where the Public Peril Begins": 25 Years After Tarasoff, 21 J. Legal Med. 187 (2000).

In United States v. Hayes, 227 F.3d 578 (6th Cir. 2000), the Sixth Circuit distinguished a psychotherapist's privilege in a criminal trial from the *Tarasoff* exception to confidentiality rules. The court held that there is no "'dangerous patient' exception to the federal psychotherapist–patient testimonial privilege under Fed. R. Evid. 501." Id. at 579. The court explained that in the context of criminal trials, recognition of a "dangerous patient" exception surely would have a deleterious effect on the "atmosphere of confidence and trust" in the psychotherapist–patient relationship. Although early advice to the patient that, in the event of the disclosure of a serious threat of harm to an identifiable victim, the therapist will have a duty to protect the intended victim, might have a marginal effect on a patient's candor in therapy sessions, an additional warning that the patient's statements may be used against him in a subsequent criminal prosecution would certainly chill and very likely terminate open dialogue. Id. at 585. *Hayes* is considered in Recent Cases, 114 Harv. L. Rev. 2194 (2001).

2. *Limitation on* Tarasoff. The California state legislature limited *Tarasoff*'s reach by providing that a psychotherapist's duty to warn about a patient's violence applies only if the "patient has communicated to the psychotherapist a serious threat of physical violence against a reasonably identifiable victim or

victims." In addition, California law now provides that it is sufficient for a psychotherapist facing the situation in which warning is required to make "reasonable efforts to communicate the threat to the victim or victims and to a law enforcement agency." Cal. Civ. Code Sec. 43.92 (2012).

3. *Should knowledge of rule be required?* One commentator on United States v. Zhou expressed dismay that the Ninth Circuit premised liability on knowledge of HIPAA's prohibition against revealing patient information (information that Zhou claimed not to have had). The commentator noted the possibility that a home health care worker or an employee in a small mental health practice might be liable for illegitimately accessing protected health information (or presumably otherwise violating HIPAA) despite ignorance of HIPAA's existence. HIPAA Applies to Those Who Don't Know About It, Newstex Web Blogs, EMR and HIPAA, May 17, 2012 (available in Lexis/Nexis, News Library). Do you think this is a compelling concern?

4. *Warning at-risk relatives.* The obligation on health care providers to warn relatives of patients with contagious illnesses was extended in Bradshaw v. Daniel, 854 S.W.2d 865 (Tenn. 1993) to require a physician to warn an ill patient's relative that the relative was also at risk of developing the noncontagious condition from which the patient suffered. Elmer Jones was diagnosed with Rocky Mountain spotted fever by Dr. Daniel. The condition is communicated by ticks. Elmer died a few days after he was diagnosed. His wife, Genevieve, was at risk because she and Elmer had been in the same tick-infested area. Dr. Daniel did not explain this risk to Genevieve, who later developed the condition and died. Suit was brought by Genevieve's son, John Bradshaw. The Tennessee Supreme Court concluded that Dr. Daniel was obliged to have warned Genevieve of the risk. The court wrote:

> [T]he existence of the physician–patient relationship is sufficient to impose upon a physician an affirmative duty to warn identifiable third persons in the patient's immediate family against foreseeable risks emanating from a patient's illness. Accordingly, we hold that under the factual circumstances of this case, viewing the evidence in a light most favorable to the plaintiff, the defendant physician had a duty to warn his patient's wife of the risk to her of contracting Rocky Mountain Spotted Fever, when he knew, or in the exercise of reasonable care, should have known, that his patient was suffering from the disease.

Id. at 872.

A remarkable case, decided in New Jersey in 1996, Safer v. Pack, 677 A.2d 1188 (N.J. Super. 1996), involved a suit against a physician by a deceased patient's child. Donna Safer sued Dr. George Pack, who had treated Robert Batkin, Safer's father, during the years that Batkin suffered with a hereditary form of colon cancer. Safer, diagnosed with the same illness at age 36 (26 years after her father's death) argued that Pack was obliged to have informed Safer that she was at risk for developing the condition that killed her father. The court, holding for Safer, explained:

> We see no impediment, legal or otherwise, to recognizing a physician's duty to warn those known to be at risk of avoidable harm from a genetically transmissible condition. In terms of foreseeability especially, there is no essential difference between the type of genetic threat at issue here and the menace

of infection, contagion or a threat of physical harm. . . . The individual or group at risk is easily identified, and substantial future harm may be averted or minimized by a timely and effective warning. . . .

Although an overly broad and general application of the physician's duty to warn might lead to confusion, conflict or unfairness in many types of circumstances, we are confident that the duty to warn of avertable risk from genetic causes, by definition a matter of familial concern, is sufficiently narrow to serve the interests of justice. Further, it is appropriate . . . that the duty be seen as owed not only to the patient himself but that it also "extends beyond the interests of a patient to members of the immediate family of the patient who may be adversely affected by a breach of that duty." . . . We need not decide, in the present posture of this case, how, precisely, that duty is to be discharged, especially with respect to young children who may be at risk, except to require that reasonable steps be taken to assure that the information reaches those likely to be affected or is made available for their benefit. We are aware of no direct evidence that has been developed concerning the nature of the communications between physician and patient regarding Mr. Batkin's disease: what Dr. Pack did or did not disclose; the advice he gave to Mr. Batkin, if any, concerning genetic factors and what ought to have been done in respect of those at risk; and the conduct or expressed preferences of Mr. Batkin in response thereto. There may be enough from Mrs. Batkin's testimony and other evidence for inferences to be drawn, however.

We decline to hold as the Florida Supreme Court did in Pate v. Threlkel, that, in all circumstances, the duty to warn will be satisfied by informing the patient. It may be necessary, at some stage, to resolve a conflict between the physician's broader duty to warn and his fidelity to an expressed preference of the patient that nothing be said to family members about the details of the disease. We cannot know presently, however, whether there is any likelihood that such a conflict may be shown to have existed in this matter or, if it did, what its qualities might have been. As the matter is currently constituted, it is as likely as not that no such conflict will be shown to have existed and that the only evidence on the issue will be Mrs. Batkin's testimony, including that she received no information, despite specific inquiry, that her children were at risk. We note, in addition, the possible existence of some offsetting evidence that Donna was rectally examined as a young child, suggesting that the risk to her had been disclosed.

. . . [I]f evidence is produced that will permit the . . . jury to find that Dr. Pack received instructions from his patient not to disclose details of the illness or the fact of genetic risk, the court will be required to determine whether, as a matter of law, there are or ought to be any limits on physician–patient confidentiality, especially after the patient's death where a risk of harm survives the patient, as in the case of genetic consequences. . . .

After the decision in *Safer,* the New Jersey legislature promulgated a statute aimed at protecting genetic privacy. Under the statute, health care providers may only communicate information about a patient's genetic condition to relatives of the patient if the patient has consented to the disclosure or if the patient has died. Genetic Privacy Act, N.J. Stat. Ann. §17B:30-12 (West 2012).

5. *Privacy, informed consent, and genomic information. Safer* suggests many questions about privacy and informed consent that emerge in the context of genetic information. A person's genome may provide information about diseases that that person is likely to suffer from or die from. In addition, information about one's genome is information about one's parents' genomes as well as the genomes of one's siblings, one's children, and even more distantly related

people. Therefore, some commentators argue that the impact of revealing genetic information might be more troubling than the impact of revealing similar information obtained through a family's medical history.

Some of the implications of genetic information can be explored by considering the case of identical twins. If a health care provider cares for two patients, each of whom is the other's identical twin, how should the provider respond if one twin wants to be given information about his or her genome and the other does not? In practice, giving the information to one twin may be tantamount to giving it to the other insofar as the two share a genome. The health care provider will, for instance, be privy to genomic information about the twin who does not want to know that information. Can the health care provider take the genomic information into account in caring for the twin who does not want the information? What might be the consequences of not taking the information into account? Might the health care provider be obliged not to treat one of the twins? If so, which one?

Genetic counselors are faced daily with decisions about how to provide genetic information to people, what information to provide, and to whom. Dorothy C. Wertz and John C. Fletcher conducted two surveys (the first in 1984 and the second in 1994) about the ethical perspectives of professionals dealing with genetic information about patients. Dorothy C. Wertz, Society and the Not-So-New Genetics: What Are We Afraid Of? Some Future Predictions from a Social Scientist, 13 J. Contemp. Health L. & Pol'y 299 (1997). Wertz reports that geneticists throughout the world had particular difficulty deciding whether to inform patients' relatives that the relatives could be at a genetic risk. In the United States, 53 percent of the geneticists (and 34 percent outside of the United States) responded that they would preserve patient confidentiality and not inform relatives.

Wertz focuses on cultural dimensions of privacy and confidentiality:

> In many parts of the world, the family, rather than the individual, is considered the unit of confidentiality. In these locations, genetic information belongs to the family, who not only share genes, but will be responsible for the care of children or other family members should they fall ill. If family members ask about genetic risk, the prevailing thought is that they "ought to know" or "deserve to know." The term "right to know" appears less often outside of North America or Europe. Sometimes family members may even have a "duty to know" and to use the information to prevent harm.

Id. at 313. Do you think, in general, that rules about medical privacy and confidentiality in the United States should take subcultural differences into account?

6. *Does genetic information differ from other sorts of medical information?*   Commentators and lawmakers disagree about whether genetic information should be treated differently than other kinds of medical information. Arguments supporting the proposition that genetic information differs from other information about people's bodies and health focus on the powerful predictive value of genetic information, its association with people's essential identity, and its implications for family members. On the other side, it can be argued that genetic information is essential to research, that harsh restrictions on its use could

preclude or slow important developments in health care, that the dangers of genetic information's being revealed are less draconian than some imagine, and that whatever dangers do exist can be handled in other ways. For instance, discrimination in the workplace and by insurers can be prohibited even if employers and insurance companies are given access to genetic information. The Genetic Information Nondiscrimination Act of 2008 (Pub. L. No. 110-233) prohibits discrimination on the basis of genetic information by employers, health insurers, and group health plans. In effect, the Act treats information about a person's genome as comparable to information about a person's race, color, religion, sex, or national origin. Civil Rights Act of 1964, §702(a), 42 U.S.C. §2000e-2.

7. *Confidentiality and HIV/AIDS.*   Although many states have carved out exceptions to rules of confidentiality with regard to patients with contagious diseases, lawmakers have limited the right of health care workers to reveal information about patients who are HIV-positive or have AIDS. Within a decade of the first AIDS cases in the 1980s, over three-fifths of the states had laws that prohibited HIV/AIDS testing without the patient's informed consent, and almost all the states safeguarded the confidentiality of patients diagnosed with HIV/AIDS. Lauren E. Palmer, New York Legislation: Note: Solving the HIV Testing Problem: An Analysis of New York's New Legislation, 4 Alb. Gov't L. Rev. 758 (2011); Elizabeth B. Cooper, Social Risk and the Transformation of Public Health Law: Lessons from the Plague Years, 86 Iowa L. Rev. 869, 930 n.278 (2001).

Since the recognition of HIV infection, a variety of public health efforts have raised questions about the right of an HIV-positive or AIDS patient "not to know" the diagnosis. In 1988, in an effort to limit the spread of AIDS, Illinois required HIV testing for anyone seeking a marriage license. Couples were not precluded from marrying if one member was HIV-positive; however, both were informed of a positive result. The program proved to be unduly expensive and led to many state residents' seeking marriage licenses outside Illinois. (See Chapter 4 for consideration of prenatal testing for HIV/AIDS.)

8. *Medical privacy under Convention for Protection of Human Rights and Fundamental Freedoms.*   In I. v. Finland, the European Court of Human Rights (ECHR) (Fourth Section), Application No. 20511/03, June 2008, agreed with the applicant (referred to as "I.") that her right to medical privacy under Article 8 of the Convention for Protection of Human Rights and Fundamental Freedoms was violated by Finland's failure to protect the confidentiality of information about her in a patient registry. I., the applicant, was HIV-positive. She worked as a nurse at a public eye hospital at which she was also a patient and believed that colleagues had learned about her HIV-positive status through the hospital's patient registry to which they had free access. The ECHR explained:

> The protection of personal data, in particular medical data, is of fundamental importance to a person's enjoyment of his or her right to respect for private and family life as guaranteed by Article 8 of the Convention. Respecting the confidentiality of health data is a vital principle in the legal systems of all the Contracting Parties to the Convention. It is crucial not only to respect the sense of

privacy of a patient but also to preserve his or her confidence in the medical profession and in the health services in general. The above considerations are especially valid as regards protection of the confidentiality of information about a person's HIV infection, given the sensitive issues surrounding this disease. The domestic law must afford appropriate safeguards to prevent any such communication or disclosure of personal health data as may be inconsistent with the guarantees in Article 8 of the Convention.

Id. at Para. 38, p. 9. The case is available at http://cmiskp.echr.coe.int////tkp197/viewhbkm.asp?action=open&table=F69A27FD8FB86142BF01C1166DEA398649&key=71800&sessionId=11881439&skin=hudoc-en&attachment=true.

9. *Patient's right to medical information.*   Related questions have arisen with regard to a patient's right to see his or her own medical records, including test results. In Cornelio v. Stamford Hospital, 717 A.2d 140 (1998), Angela Cornelio sued Stamford Hospital, arguing among other things that she had a property right to five pathology slides containing Pap smear specimens that had been taken from her. Cornelio wanted the slides in connection with a malpractice action against the hospital. The hospital agreed to allow Cornelio's experts to examine the slides but was unwilling to surrender them to her. The court denied Cornelio's right to the slides in light of rules pertaining to patients' access to their hospital records. Connecticut law gave patients a right to examine and obtain copies of their hospital medical records but allowed the hospital to retain the original "to ensure . . . that such records are available to the hospital in the event of a malpractice action." Id. at 147. The court concluded that the slides in question, even though they could not be duplicated, were part of Cornelio's medical records and could be retained by the hospital.

A dissenting justice noted the importance of respecting people's control over their bodies:

> In this case, the patient sought to regain control of cells taken from her for medical treatment. This decision now severely restricts the patient's control over her own cells at a time when the advance of genetic science should raise very wide privacy implications. Because she sought these cells for litigation-related purposes, the majority now holds that the patient has no right to immediate possession to parts of her own body. . . .
>
> [T]he majority relies on legislation concerning medical records to ascertain a legislative intent to restrict a patient's right to her tissue samples. The majority, however, fails to consider legislation explicitly covering this case. The legislature recently enacted . . . "An Act Concerning Patient Access to Tissue Slides in Health Records." The act provides that institutions are required to send a patient's tissue slides to the institution, laboratory or physician that the patient designates without restrictions as to the patient's purpose. I, therefore, disagree that the patient may not direct that her tissue slides be sent to her designated physician for litigation-related purposes.

Id. at 149.

Under HHS regulations, Standards for Privacy of Individually Identifiable Health Information (promulgated pursuant to the Health Insurance Accountability and Portability Act of 1996, Pub. L. No. 104-91, 110 Stat. 1936 (1996)), patients have a right of access to most medical records. 42 C.F.R. §164.524(a). However, exceptions include health information covered by (or exempt from) the Clinical Laboratory Improvements Amendments of 1988. Id. A summary is found in Arthur S. Di Dio, The Hype About HIPAA: Standards for Privacy of Individually Identifiable Health Information 47–48, Nat'l Leg. Cent. for the Pub. Interest (2002).

10. *Bibliographic note.*   Useful references include Joi T. Montiel, The Psychotherapist–Patient Privilege as an "Occasional Instrument of Injustice:" An Argument for a Criminal Threat Exception, 36 S. Ill. U.L.J. 445 (2012); David Orentlicher, The Effects of Health Information Technology on the Physician–Patient Relationship: Prescription Data Mining and the Protection of Patients' Interests, 38 J.L. Med. & Ethics 74 (2010); Marc A. Rodwin, Patient Data: Property, Privacy & the Public Interest, 36 Am. J.L. & Med. 586 (2010); Mark A. Rothstein, Legal Conceptions of Equality in the Genomic Act, 25 Law & Ineq. J. 429 (2007); Peter A. Winn, Confidentiality in Cyberspace: The HIPAA Privacy Rules and the Common Law, 33 Rutgers L.J. 617 (2002); Graeme Laurie, Genetic Privacy: A Challenge to Medico-Legal Norms (2001); Comment, Andrea Sudell, To Tell or Not to Tell: The Scope of Physician-Patient Confidentiality When Relatives Are at Risk of Genetic Disease, 18 J. Contemp. Health L. & Pol'y 273 (2001); Jeffrey Rosen, The Unwanted Gaze: The Destruction of Privacy in America (2000); Roger C. Cramton & Lori P. Knowles, Professional Secrecy and Its Exceptions: Spaulding v. Zimmerman Revisited, 83 Minn. L. Rev. 63 (1998); Caryn Lerman et al., Family Disclosure in Genetic Testing for Cancer Susceptibility: Determinants and Consequences, 1 J. Health Care L. & Pol'y 353 (1998); Lawrence O. Gostin, Health Information Privacy, 80 Cornell L. Rev. 451 (1995).

CHALLENGING ISSUES: CONFIDENTIALITY AND POTENTIAL TISSUE/ORGAN DONORS

Jack Long has been diagnosed with leukemia. His doctors believe that his greatest chance for improvement lies with a bone marrow transplantation. However, it will be very difficult to locate a compatible donor. Long made a call to the bone marrow transplant unit at the hospital where he is being treated and learned that one woman, listed on the hospital's registry, might be a possible donor for him. The woman's tissue had been typed to discover whether she might be a suitable platelet donor for a relative. This woman, known as Ms. X, did not know the hospital had placed her name in the bone marrow registry when it set up its bone marrow transplant unit. In fact, Ms. X had expressly declined to have her name included on the list of possible bone marrow donors. She had explained that she would consider such a donation only for a family member, not for a stranger.

Jack has asked the hospital either to contact Ms. X to learn whether she might be willing to consider donating to him or to give him Ms. X's name and allow him to contact her. The hospital has refused to do either thing.

Do you think the law protects Ms. X's confidentiality? Should she be provided with the information that a particular, sick patient could benefit from her bone marrow—a fact she of course did not know when she refused to be included in the list of potential bone marrow donors?

D. ANATOMICAL GIFTS[14]

1. Bioethical and Social Perspectives

> ## William E. Stempsey, Religion, Philosophy, and the Commodification of Human Body Parts
> ### DePaul L. Rev. 875, 883–885, 887–888 (2006)

. . . .

Proponents of an overt market in human organs usually assert that people have a property right to their organs. Classifying human bodies and body parts as "quasi-property" has a long legal tradition. This might be the best legal strategy we have for protecting important interests, but we should note that this strategy arose from the interest of individuals in disposing of their remains and directing their families to look after the task after their death. These property rights view the body not as property to be traded, but rather as a cherished former person's remains, which must be properly interred so as not to turn into a horror. If the body is property, it is far different from property such as land, houses, and furniture.

Thomas Murray rightly pointed out that money and markets are the dominant way of distributing goods in America, but he argued that "there are many goods that money should not be able to buy"—legal verdicts, Pulitzer Prizes, and children are a few that he named. Murray argued that tyranny, in Pascal's sense of desiring powers outside one's own sphere, reigns when human organs are converted into money. Properly placing the line between one's own sphere and what lies outside is admittedly difficult, yet we do draw such lines. We admire those who are paid for using their bodies for a hard day's work, but we frown on those who are paid for using their bodies in prostitution. It takes wisdom to draw such lines.

My philosophical concerns, though, take us even deeper into a shadowy and contentious place—the philosophy of mind. I believe that seeing organs as property is rooted in an unquestioned presupposition of a problematic philosophical position on the relation of body and mind. The problem, going back at least to Plato but definitively set up in the first part of the seventeenth century by Rene Descartes, is that of mind–body dualism. When you claim a property right to your kidneys, just exactly who is the "you" that owns the kidneys? Descartes famously claimed that the essence of the human being is the res cogitans: the mind, or soul—the thing that thinks. The body is surely connected to this thinking substance but is not essential to the person. . . . Descartes [was the] first [to] conceptualize[] the body as a machine, a substance wholly unlike the mental substance that constitutes the true essence of the person. This view has become so ingrained in most of us that it is hardly questioned. The idea of body as a machine has enabled contemporary technical medicine to flourish with unprecedented empirical success.

. . . .

---

14. Organ donation is considered in Chapter 9. The focus there is on the scarcity of, and access to, organs for transplantation.

[The philosopher] Maurice Merleau-Ponty may have given us the best expression of a phenomenology of the body. Merleau-Ponty's phenomenology rejected the Cartesian dichotomy between body and soul. For Merleau-Ponty, the body is not just an object that can be known by a subject; rather, it is "the experience of our own body" that "reveals to us an ambiguous mode of existing." He made an argument using the example of the phantom limb, when a person who has lost an arm or leg continues to feel its presence. Merleau-Ponty argued that neither physiological nor psychological explanations adequately elucidate this phenomenon. Physiological factors alone cannot explain the phenomenon, for anesthesia does not eliminate the sensation. Likewise, psychological factors cannot furnish the sole explanation because severing the nerves to the brain does abolish the phenomenon, indicating that physiological factors play some part in the explanation.

Merleau-Ponty's solution to this problem is to reject the root cause of the dilemma—the underlying mind–body dualism—and to adopt the perspective of the lived body. The phenomenon can only be understood in the perspective of "being-in-the-world," and the body is the "vehicle" for being-in-the-world. He wrote: "To have a phantom arm is to remain open to all the actions of which the arm alone is capable; it is to retain the practical field which one enjoyed before mutilation."

Ruth Richardson found a "fearful symmetry" between an organ market and the practice of grave robbing in the eighteenth and nineteenth centuries: "In the grave-robbing era, [corpses were] quarried for teeth, hair, skeletons, and so on," and sold to dentists, wigmakers, and those who made specimens for medical study. This is a practice that most of us would take to be repugnant. Yet Richardson argued that several key factors that led to the practice are the same as those that confront organ transplantation today: (1) "increasing demand for human tissue," (2) "shortage of donors and public resistance," (3) "competition among users/consumers," and (4) "money values attached to human tissue." Richardson rightly pointed out that fear is at the heart of the resistance to organ donation, and that the "semantic massage" in euphemisms such as "donor," "procurement," "harvesting," and "cadaver" seek to conceal unpalatable truths about the realities of organ transplantation. There even seems to be ongoing semantic massage—non-heart-beating cadavers have now become non-heart-beating donors.

. . . .

We would do well to reconsider the ways we have swept some of the realities of organ transplantation below the surface in order to promote it. If we are honest, we will find some repulsion in cutting a kidney out of one person and sewing it into another. This is not to say that the practice ought to be stopped. Sometimes we must learn to suppress some feelings in order to carry out necessary tasks; the work of surgeons, for instance, requires this. Yet such suppression always carries the danger of routinization and the loss of reverence for what ought to be revered. A phenomenological appreciation of the body ought to cause us to reflect on what we are doing when we turn warm, living human parts into commodities redeemable for cold cash.

> *Eugene Volokh, Medical Self-Defense,*
> *Prohibited Experimental Therapies,*
> *and Payment for Organs*
> 120 Harv. L. Rev. 1813, 1832–1835,
> 1843–1844 (2007)

To live, Olivia needs a kidney transplant. Though kidney dialysis is keeping her alive for now, each year on dialysis she faces a 6% risk of death. If Olivia is in her twenties and not diabetic, her expected lifespan on dialysis is thirty years less than her expected lifespan with a transplant.

But Olivia is one of the approximately 70,000 people on the American kidney transplant waiting list. (Roughly 25,000 more wait for other organs.) The median wait for adult recipients added to the list in 2001–02 was over four years. Each year, only about 6500 living Americans donate kidneys, and only 45% of the 26,000 usable cadaveric kidneys—kidneys gathered from the bodies of people who die from accidents or other causes that leave their organs young and healthy—are donated.

This shortage is not surprising: Since 1984, "receiving or . . . transferring any human organ for valuable consideration for use in human transplantation" has been a federal felony. Price controls diminish supply. Setting the price at zero diminishes supply dramatically.

Lack of compensation naturally makes living donors less likely to incur the pain, lost time, and (slight) risk that accompany organ extraction. The relatives of the recently dead have less to lose (at least tangibly) from authorizing use of the decedent's organs; but even they may be put off by what strikes many as a macabre idea, may refuse consent if they are not sure what the decedent wanted, and may not want to discuss the matter in their time of grief. The prospect of (say) $100,000 for their children's education might lead them to overcome these barriers.

While living organ donations are almost always for the benefit of relatives, friends, or other known recipients, a few living donors (less than 1.5% of the total 99) and many next-of-kin of the recently dead donate to strangers. Yet kindness to strangers is generally not as strong a motivation as the desire for financial reward, or as a combined desire to help strangers while putting money aside for the education of one's children.

We pay hospitals and surgeons well for their roles in transplants. If we didn't, there would likely not be nearly enough transplant services provided, though many hospitals are charitable institutions and many doctors routinely donate their time to provide free medical care. Why should we expect organ suppliers to provide enough organs based solely on charity to strangers? We would likely get far better results if we offered organ providers compensation—or, more precisely, offered them the choice of keeping the compensation, forgoing it, donating it to a familiar cause of their choice (for instance, their church) rather than to a stranger, or spending it on their children.

. . . .

What about the argument that compensation for organs is just inherently wrong? "The human body and its parts cannot be the subject of commercial transactions," the argument goes. . . . In the words of leading conservative bioethicist Leon Kass, three-year chair of the President's Council on Bioethics, "the human body especially belongs in that category of things that defy or resist commensuration—like love or friendship or life itself":

> . . . We surpass all defensible limits of such conventional commodification when we contemplate making the convention-maker—the human being—just another one of the commensurables. . . . Selling our bodies, we come perilously close to selling out our souls. . . .

Yet, once we look past the figures of speech to see what is really being asserted, this analysis is unpersuasive. Love, friendship, and prizes can't properly be gotten for money because paid-for love, friendship, and prizes are not "love," "friendship," and "prizes" as we define the terms. But a paid-for kidney is a kidney, just as a paid-for transplant operation is a transplant operation. It has the same meaning and worth regardless of whether it is paid for: it can save a human life.

> . . . .

[R]ecognizing a constitutional and moral right to self-defense ought to resolve this impasse. Something more demonstrably compelling than Professor Kass's conclusory assertions must be present to justify substantially burdening such a right.

NOTES AND QUESTIONS

1. *Characterizing donations of body parts.* Stempsey and Volokh frame the implications of organ sale (and even of organ donation) differently.

Thomas Murray, referred to by Stempsey, supra, writes about impersonal gifts in large Western societies. He mentions charitable giving. And he mentions blood donations. Do you think the motivation to "give charity" differs generally from the motivation to give blood? How are the two acts different or similar? Is the act of giving money likely to create a different sort of bond between giver and receiver than the act of giving blood?

The question would seem to be answered one way by a man, a captain in the Air Force, Kirk Folk, who voluntarily donated a kidney to the wife of his former office superintendent. Folk denied any claim that his donation was a "big deal." He explained: "I've always been involved in my church. I've done the community and volunteerism things. . . . I try to help my troops as far as I can." Eric M. Grill, The Life Giver: Airman at Eglin Donates Kidney to "Help Troops," 46 Airman, July 2002, at 38(6). Folk's assertion conflates personal and professional obligations. It suggests a vision of the Air Force more consistent with traditional understandings of "home" than with traditional understandings of "work." Do you think voluntary donations to nonrelatives, such as Folk's, are more likely to occur in "work" contexts openly defined through metaphors of loyalty or community (such as the Air Force) than in other work contexts?

CHALLENGING ISSUES: ALTRUISTIC DONATIONS

The following narrative is based on a story reported in The New Yorker by Ian Parker, Annals of Philanthropy: The Gift, Aug. 2, 2004, at 54.

In 2003 a man who, for purposes of this narrative, will be called Rick T., gave away almost all of a large fortune that he had acquired through a series of brilliant investments. In all, he gave over $40 million to charity.

Soon thereafter, Rick decided that he hadn't given enough. He read a newspaper article about nondirected kidney donations. He learned that 1 in 4,000 people who donate kidneys die as a result of the surgery. Some time after reading this article, Rick decided to give a kidney to an unknown, needy recipient—to make a nondirected donation of a kidney. He justified his decision by referring to the certainty that the donee (of his kidney) would die without a transplant. He thus concluded: "I'd be valuing my life at four thousand times hers if I let consideration of mortality sway me." Parker, supra, at 59.

Rick has four young children and a wife. He expected his wife, a doctor, to applaud his decision to give a kidney to an as-yet unknown, needy recipient. She did not.

Rick proceeded with his plans despite his wife's opposition. In fact, on the morning of the surgery, he "snuck out" of the house so that his wife would not know where he was going.

The surgery was successful. Rick's right kidney was implanted in a young woman who soon would have died without a kidney transplant.

Do you think Rick's decision was moral? If so, is it immoral for others not to follow Rick's example? Does it matter that Rick's wife opposed the kidney donation? Should a spouse have a say in such matters? Would Rick's wife be responsible for caring for him if he became ill as a result of the surgery? Should the best interests of Rick's children have been taken into account? If so, in what way?

2. Legal Approaches

Wilson v. Adkins
941 S.W.2d 440 (Ark. Ct. App. 1997)

TERRY CRABTREE, Judge.

Appellant Alta Wilson, a resident of Florida, sued her nephew, Ronnie Adkins, in chancery court for detrimental reliance, breach of contract, and fraud stemming from an alleged agreement in which the appellant agreed to donate bone marrow to her ailing sister in exchange for $101,500.00 as compensation for risk in the procedure. . . . We affirm the chancellor's dismissal based on the blatantly illegal nature of the alleged contract. . . .

Here, the complaint states in paragraph II:

> That on or about the 1st day of April 1992, the Plaintiff, Alta Wilson and the Defendant Ronnie Adkins and the Defendant Georgia Adkins, now deceased, entered into an agreement whereby the Plaintiff would elect and act as a bone marrow donor for the benefit of the Defendant, Georgia Adkins.

The complaint artfully characterizes the agreement as an exchange of $101,500.00 for the risk, difficulties, and insurance consequences of appellant's marrow donation. While appellants' attorney goes to great lengths to disguise the nature of the contract, it is, as the trial court noted, "so intertwined and commingled that [it] cannot be separated," and clearly falls under the rubric of federal law on the sale of human organs. Here, the complaint essentially admits that the parties contracted for an illegal sale of organs. No matter how the appellants' attorney characterizes the transaction, the dollar amount and the consideration are telling signs that the contract is one for the sale of an organ in violation of federal law.

> Title 42 of the United States Code section 274(e) provides the following:
>   (a) Prohibition
>   It shall be unlawful for any person to knowingly acquire, receive, or otherwise transfer any human organ for valuable consideration for use in human transplantation if the transfer affects interstate commerce. . . .

While this statute does allow "reasonable payments" for the cost of the procedure and incidental expenses, it is clear that $101,500.00 is not payment for reasonable incidental expenses incurred in the organ donation, but is an illegal sale of an organ specifically prohibited by federal law.

Since the contract's subject matter is so plainly illegal, long standing Arkansas precedent supports the trial court's [dismissal]. . . .

[T]he act of selling one's organs is . . . offensive, and . . . clearly illegal. . . . While the statute regarding organ sales is relatively modern (1986), its genesis is in a clear public policy based on long standing attitudes about transplantation of organs. "Laws regarding the removal of human tissues for transplantation implicate moral, ethical, theological, philosophical, and economic concerns which do not readily lend themselves to analysis within a traditional legal framework." State v. Powell, 497 So. 2d 1188, 1194 (Fla. 1986). In commenting on *Powell,* another court noted:

> For that reason, the courts should look instead to the particular statutes that were written on those subjects in an effort to balance the peculiar interests involved. Recently, the California Supreme Court said that courts should not look to conversion law but to the specialized statutes dealing "with human biological materials as objects sui generis, regulating their disposition to achieve policy goals rather than abandoning them to the general law of personal property." Moore v. Regents of the University of California. The same could be said for resorting strictly to contract law when there is an alleged agreement for the transfer of human remains.

Perry v. Saint Francis Hosp. & Medical Ctr., 886 F. Supp. 1551, 1563 n.7 (D. Kan. 1995).

In *Perry,* the court addressed the issue of an alleged contract between a hospital nurse and a grieving family for the donation of tissues from a deceased patient. While the family did recover on other grounds for the hospital's overreaching organ harvesting, the court rejected a contract approach to the communication between the family and the hospital, stating, "A contract approach is not reconcilable with societal beliefs and values on this subject." In support of this contention, the *Perry* court cited the Uniform Anatomical Gift Act (1987), 8A U.L.A. 25 at §10(a), and the federal law, discussed above, at 42 U.S.C. 274(e). Further, the court cited commentary on both the uniform law and the federal act that these laws "embody a commitment to the belief that organs should be given as a gift, either to a specific individual or to society at large." . . .

Here, it is clear on the face of appellants' complaint that the activity amounted to a sale of organs in violation of federal law. Accordingly, the trial court's dismissal was appropriate.

Affirmed.

Flynn v. Holder
665 F.3d 1048 (9th Cir. 2011, amended 2012)

Opinion By: Andrew J. KLEINFELD, Sr. Cir. J.

The district court dismissed the complaint for failure to state a claim upon which relief could be granted. We take the facts from the allegations in the complaint to determine whether, if proved, they would state an actionable claim.

The complaint challenges the constitutionality of the ban on compensation for human organs in the National Organ Transplant Act, as applied to bone marrow transplants. Plaintiffs seek declaratory and injunctive relief to allow harvesting of "hematopoietic stem cells." The complaint is not crystal clear on whether plaintiffs claim that compensation for all bone marrow transplantation is constitutionally protected, but the focus of the arguments is on cells extracted by "peripheral blood stem cell apheresis." This is a relatively new method of bone marrow transplant that avoids the need to invade the bone for marrow.

Some plaintiffs are parents of sick children who have diseases such as leukemia and a rare type of anemia, which can be fatal without bone marrow transplants. Another plaintiff is a physician and medical school professor, and an expert in bone marrow transplantation. He says that at least one out of five of his patients dies because no matching bone marrow donor can be found, and many others have complications when scarcity of matching donors compels him to use imperfectly matched donors. One plaintiff is a parent of mixed race children, for whom sufficiently matched donors are especially scarce, because mixed race persons typically have the rarest marrow cell types. One plaintiff is an African-American man suffering from leukemia who received a bone marrow transplant from his sister. She was an imperfect match and, though the transplant saved his life, he continues to suffer from life-threatening and disabling complications on account of the slight genetic mismatch.

Another plaintiff is a California nonprofit corporation that seeks to operate a program incentivizing bone marrow donations. . . .

Until about twenty years ago, bone marrow was extracted from donors' bones by "aspiration." Long needles, thick enough to suck out the soft, fatty marrow, were inserted into the cavities of the anesthetized donor's hip bones. These are large bones with big central cavities full of marrow. Aspiration is a painful, unpleasant procedure for the donor. It requires hospitalization and general or local anesthesia, and involves commensurate risks.

The complaint explains that a new technology [referred to as "peripheral blood stem cell apheresis"] has superseded this technique during the last twenty years, after enactment of the National Organ Transplant Act. With this new technique, now used for at least two-thirds of bone marrow transplants, none of the soft, fatty marrow is actually donated. Patients who need bone marrow transplants do not need everything that the soft, fatty substance from bone cavities contains, just some of the marrow's "hematopoietic stem cells." These stem cells are seeds from which white blood cells, red blood cells, and platelets grow.

. . . .

The main difference between an ordinary blood donation and apheresis is that instead of just filling up a plastic bag with whole blood, the donor sits for some hours in a recliner while the blood passes through the apheresis machine. . . .

Though the new process makes bone marrow donations much like ordinary blood donations, the matching problem remains. Deep genetic compatibility is critical in bone marrow transplants, because our bodies are xenophobic: white blood cells produced from a donor's imperfectly matched blood stem cells treat the recipient patient's body as foreign, attacking it. This is graft-versus-host disease, which can be fatal or can result in lifelong medical problems for the transplant recipient. . . . The more diverse the patient's genetic heritage, the rarer the match. For example, African-Americans have especially great difficulty finding a compatible unrelated donor, as they tend to have a mix of African, Caucasian, and Native-American genes, and fewer potential donors are registered in the national civilian registry.

The establishment of this registry, the National Marrow Donor Program, which is funded by the federal government to assist in finding matches, was an important aspect of the statute at issue here. But even with this registry, good matches often cannot be found. And even when a good match is found in the registry, tracking down the potential donor from what may be an outdated address may be impossible to accomplish in time to save the patient's life—assuming the potential donor is willing to go through with the process when found.

The plaintiff nonprofit proposes to mitigate this matching problem by using a financial incentive. The idea is that the financial incentive will induce more potential donors to sign up, stay in touch so that they can be located when necessary, and go through with the donations. The nonprofit plans to focus its attention initially on minority and mixed race donors, because their marrow cell types are rarer. The financial incentives would be $3,000 in scholarships, housing allowances, or gifts to charities of the donor's choice, which the nonprofit acknowledges would be "valuable consideration" under the statutory prohibition.

. . . .

The core of plaintiffs' argument is that there is no rational basis for allowing compensation for blood, sperm, and egg donations, while disallowing compensation for bone marrow donations, because bone marrow donations can now be accomplished through apheresis without removing marrow, and the donor's body quickly regenerates the donated stem cells. Since the distinction, they argue, is without a rational basis, it violates the Equal Protection Clause, despite highly deferential "rational basis" review.

The Attorney General responds that the statute plainly classifies "bone marrow" as an organ for which compensation is prohibited, and that the congressional determination is indeed rational. The statute makes it a felony "to knowingly acquire, receive, or otherwise transfer any human organ for valuable consideration for use in human transplantation." And it defines the term "human organ" to include "bone marrow." . . .

Plaintiffs address their arguments largely to the peripheral blood stem cell apheresis method of extracting hematopoietic stem cells, but their complaint appears to challenge the prohibition on bone marrow transplants regardless of method. They do not, in their complaint or their brief, confine their challenge to transplants by means of apheresis. They apparently propose to give compensated donors the choice between aspiration and apheresis. To the extent that plaintiffs challenge the constitutionality of the compensation ban on bone marrow donation by the old aspiration method—where a long needle is inserted into the cavity of the hip bone to extract the soft, fatty marrow—the challenge must fail.

The statute says that the term "human organ" includes "bone marrow." The soft, fatty stuff that the needle extracts is bone marrow. . . .

Congress may have had philosophical as well as policy reasons for prohibiting compensation. People tend to have an instinctive revulsion at denial of bodily integrity, particularly removal of flesh from a human being for use by another, and most particularly "commodification" of such conduct, that is, the sale of one's bodily tissue. While there is reportedly a large international market for the buying and selling of human organs, in the United States, such a market is criminal and the commerce is generally seen as revolting. . . .

Here, Congress made a distinction between body material that is compensable and body material that is not. The distinction has a rational basis, so the prohibition on compensation for bone marrow donations by the aspiration method does not violate the Equal Protection Clause.

The focus, though, of plaintiffs' arguments is compensation for "bone marrow donations" by the peripheral blood stem cell apheresis method. For this, we need not answer any constitutional question, because the statute contains no prohibition. Such donations of cells drawn from blood flowing through the veins may sometimes anachronistically be called "bone marrow donations," but none of the soft, fatty marrow is donated, just cells found outside the marrow, outside the bones, flowing through the veins.

Congress could not have had an intent to address the apheresis method when it passed the statute, because the method did not exist at that time. We must construe the words of the statute to see what they imply about extraction of hematopoietic stem cells by this method. This issue has not been addressed by any of our sister circuits.

. . . .

The government concedes that the common practice of compensating blood donors is not prohibited by the statute.

. . . .

[E]very blood draw includes some hematopoietic stem cells. All that differentiates the blood drawn in peripheral blood stem cell apheresis from the blood drawn from a compensated blood donor, other than the filtration process, is the medicine given to donors in the days before the blood draw to increase hematopoietic stem cell secretion. Once the stem cells are in the bloodstream, they are a "subpart" of the blood, not the bone marrow.

. . . .

We construe "bone marrow" to mean the soft, fatty substance in bone cavities, as opposed to blood, which means the red liquid that flows through the blood vessels. The statute does not prohibit compensation for donations of blood and the substances in it, which include peripheral blood stem cells. The Secretary of Health and Human Services has not exercised regulatory authority to define blood or peripheral blood stem cells as organs. We therefore need not decide whether prohibiting compensation for such donations would be unconstitutional.

REVERSED. The judgment is VACATED and the case REMANDED for such additional proceedings as may be appropriate. . . .

NOTES AND QUESTIONS

1. *Nonintact body parts and parts of dead bodies.*   An interesting legal distinction has developed between one's relation to one's intact body parts and one's relation to body parts that have been severed from the body. The Constitution protects a person's intact body as part of the right to privacy. In Rochin v. California, 342 U.S. 165 (1952), the Supreme Court concluded that the state's forcibly pumping the stomach of an accused man to obtain evidence (in the form of morphine that the accused had swallowed) violated the man's Fourteenth Amendment due process rights. In *Rochin,* the Court announced the "conduct that shocks the conscience" test. Id. at 172–173. In contrast, body parts no longer part of a person's body are usually dealt with by the law through rules developed to regulate property. Radhika Rao, Property, Privacy, and the Human Body, 80 B.U. L. Rev. 359, 453–454 (2000). Rao refers to Green v. Commissioner, 74 T.C. 1229, 1232 (T.C. 1880) as illustrative. Margaret Green had a rare type of blood that she routinely sold for profit. The Tax Court treated blood as a taxable commodity and concluded that income earned from the sale of Green's blood was taxable. Rao contrasts this case with one in which the state might want to extract someone's rare blood to use it to help others in need. This second sort of case, Rao notes, would not be understood through the rules that govern commodities. Rather, a court would examine a potential donor's Fourteenth Amendment rights.

Do you think the same set of rules applies (or should apply) to body parts of dead people? Mississippi expressly provides for the sale of posthumous body parts. Miss. Code Ann. §41-39-9 (West). The Mississippi statute provides that it is "lawful for any person eighteen (18) years of age and over, having a sound and disposing mind, to enter into a written contract with a qualified hospital or medical school to donate his eyes, heart, kidney or other transplantable part of a human body to medical science or for medical purposes. Any contract entered into under the terms of this section is hereby declared to be binding upon the surviving spouse or other heirs of the deceased who have the right under general law to claim his body." Id.

2. *Prohibiting sale of body organs.*   Federal law makes it illegal to "knowingly acquire, receive, or otherwise transfer any human organ for valuable consideration for use in human transplantation if the transfer affects interstate

commerce." National Organ Transplant Act, 42 U.S.C. §274e(a) (2004).[15] In 2007 Congress provided an exception for "human organ paired donation." 42 U.S.C. §247e(a). The exception allows an individual (the "first donor"), anxious to make a living donation of an organ to a specific patient (the "first patient") with whom he or she is not biologically compatible, to pair up with another donor–patient set (including a "second donor" and a "second patient"). The donor–patient pairs may include more than two of each. The 2007 amendment provides for "all donors and patients in the group of donor–patient pairs (whether 2 pairs or more than 2 pairs) [to] enter into a single agreement to donate and receive such human organs, respectively, according to such biological compatibility in the group." 42 U.S.C. §274e (c)(4)(E).

3. *Could* Flynn *facilitate payment for whole body organs?* *Flynn* does not pave a clear legal path toward allowing compensation for whole body organs. Yet, as a psychological matter, the case could make it easier to accept the sale of body organs for transplantation. Might another court, for instance, agree that compensation for parts of livers should be permitted because liver cells regenerate? Dr. Sally Satel, herself a kidney recipient, has hailed *Flynn* for offering an opportunity to rethink the prohibition on compensating organ donors. Sally Satel, An Organ 'Donor' Revolution, Wall St. J., July 9, 2012, available at http://online.wsj .com/article/SB10001424052702304467704577513371992426352.html.

---

15. The statute defines "human organ" as "the human (including fetal) kidney, liver, heart, lung, pancreas, bone marrow, cornea, eye, bone, and skin or any subpart thereof and any other human organ (or any subpart thereof, including that derived from a fetus) specified by the Secretary of Health and Human Services by regulation." 42 U.S.C. §274e(c)(1).

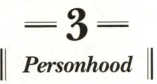

=3=
‖ *Personhood* ‖

The study of bioethics, and in particular the intersection of law and bioethics, often entails exploration of the rights of individual persons. Who is a rightsholder, whether in regard to medically related issues or otherwise, is a question that has received much attention and debate over the centuries in both philosophical and legal quarters. The issue has traditionally rested on the question of who qualifies as a *person*, or who is a *human being*. These terms are often used interchangeably. They denote more than biological fact; they identify who is entitled to be treated with a certain respect due equally to all in that category, who has rights—the right to life, for example. Another way that philosophers (most notably, Immanuel Kant) have described the special moral status of human beings, or persons, is to say that they are "ends-in-themselves," and unlike things and perhaps nonhuman animals, cannot ethically be used as a mere means to another's ends.

What distinguishes persons from things or nonhuman animals that justifies this preferred status? Aristotle, writing in the fourth century B.C.E., distinguished human beings from other animals by their possession of a rational soul. For him, the category of human beings did not therefore include "natural slaves," whom he believed lacked rational capacity, with the result that such people could be used as instruments for other's purposes (i.e., as slaves). See Encyclopedia of Ethics (2d ed. 2001), at 1294. Over time, of course, unequal treatment on the basis of race, ethnicity, or gender has lost any legitimacy. Debate continues, however, about other qualities that might be considered to distinguish persons from things, as we will see in this chapter's readings exploring the status of fetuses, embryos, and other forms of life. Moreover, the idea that there are only two categories (persons with full and equal rights and things with no rights), or even three (persons, things, and nonhuman animals) is very much open to debate among scholars and policymakers as they wrestle with questions arising out of the applications of biotechnology. Indeed, such simple categorization seems inadequate to describe a world in which embryos can be created and sustained outside the womb and in which the potential exists to combine human and animal genes to create entirely new forms of life. If there are only these two or three categories, where do frozen embryos fit? Where, if they are ever developed, will human–animal hybrids fit? Some believe that rather than recognizing different forms of life as having either the full panoply of rights or no rights at all, it may be appropriate to recognize some entities or beings as having *some* rights, or being entitled to *some* respect, although the difficult question then follows as to what that might mean.

A different approach altogether is advocated by some scholars. They argue that it is time to abandon a *status*-oriented approach, and look instead at the *interests* that any form of life might have—such as an interest in avoiding suffering, or an interest in continued life—and to respect those interests irrespective of the type of life—whether born or unborn, human or animal, natural or unnatural.

This chapter is divided into three sections. The first section includes readings related to the status of fetuses and embryos, raising questions about how, why, and whether "personhood" status should be considered to attach to the early stages of human life. The second section presents readings about severely impaired human individuals, animals, and human–animal hybrids, raising important questions about the relevance of distinctions between those who are fully human beings as a biological matter and other intelligent and sentient beings. Both of these sections also address overarching questions about the concept of personhood—what it might properly include and whether the concept as a whole has merit.

The third section concerns the unique legal claim known as "wrongful life" and the related claim of "wrongful birth." These cases involve allegations that health care providers negligently failed to provide appropriate information to prospective parents about the risks that their child might be born ill or with disabilities. In the wrongful life cause of action, a child (on whose behalf the claim is brought) essentially claims that he would have been better off had he not been born. Courts have generally rejected the claim because of the difficulty—some courts say the impossibility—of comparing life with disabilities to nonexistence.

Some of the recurring questions posed by the materials in this chapter include the following:

1. How important are biological facts (including genetics) in determining how different living beings are considered (as persons or otherwise)?
2. Do relationships matter? What if "clearly persons" care dearly about the life in question, or, alternatively, see it as a threat to their own personhood?
3. Should and do utilitarian concerns ever weigh in on questions of personhood status—for example, how much "good" might be done for others by denying personhood status to a particular life form?
4. Can being brought into existence ever be considered a harm? And if so, what are the damages?

A. FETUSES AND EMBRYOS

1. Theories of Personhood

> **Mary Ann Warren, On the Moral**
> **and Legal Status of Abortion**
> **57 The Monist 43–61 (1973)***

Imagine a space traveler who lands on an unknown planet and encounters a race of beings utterly unlike any he has ever seen or heard of. If he wants to be sure of behaving morally toward these beings, he has to somehow decide whether they are people, and hence have full moral rights, or whether they are the sort of thing which he need not feel guilty about treating as, for example, a source of food.

. . . I suggest that the traits which are most central to the concept of personhood, or humanity in the moral sense, are, very roughly, the following:

1. Consciousness (of objects and events external and/or internal to the being), and in particular the capacity to feel pain;
2. Reasoning (the *developed* capacity to solve new and relatively complex problems);
3. Self-motivated activity (activity which is relatively independent of either genetic or direct external control);
4. The capacity to communicate, by whatever means, messages of an indefinite variety of types, that is, not just with an indefinite number of possible contents, but on indefinitely many possible topics;
5. The presence of self-concepts, and self-awareness, either individual or racial, or both.

Admittedly, there are apt to be a great many problems involved in formulating precise definitions of these criteria, let alone in developing universally valid behavioral criteria for deciding when they apply. But I will assume that both we and our explorer know approximately what (1)-(5) mean, and that he is also able to determine whether or not they apply. How, then, should he use his findings to decide whether or not the alien beings are people? We needn't suppose that an entity must have *all* of these attributes to be properly considered a person; (1) and (2) alone may well be sufficient for personhood, and quite probably (1)-(3) are sufficient. Neither do we need to insist that any one of these criteria is *necessary* for personhood, although once again (1) and (2) look like fairly good candidates for necessary conditions, as does (3), if "activity" is construed so as to include the activity of reasoning.

All we need to claim, to demonstrate that a fetus is not a person, is that any being that satisfies *none* of (1)-(5) is certainly not a person. I consider this claim to be so obvious that I think anyone who denied it, and claimed that a being which satisfied none of (1)-(5) was a person all the same, would thereby demonstrate that he had no notion at all of what a person is—perhaps because he had confused the concept of a person with that of genetic human-ity. If the opponents of abortion were to deny the appropriateness of these five criteria, I do not know what further arguments would convince them. We would probably have to admit that our conceptual schemes were indeed irreconcilably different, and that our dispute could not be settled objectively.

I do not expect this to happen, however, since I think that the concept of a person is one which is very nearly universal (to people), and that it is common to both proabortionists and antiabortionists, even though neither group has fully realized the relevance of this concept to the resolution of their dispute. Further-more, I think that on reflection even the antiabortionists ought to agree not only that (1)-(5) are central to the concept of personhood, but also that it is a part of this concept that all and only people have full moral rights. The concept of a person is in part a moral concept; once we have admitted that *x* is a person we have recognized, even if we have not agreed to respect, *x*'s right to be treated as a member of the moral community. . . .

Now if (1)-(5) are indeed the primary criteria of personhood, then it is clear that genetic humanity is neither necessary nor sufficient for establish-ing that an entity is a person. Some human beings are not people, and there may well be people who are not human beings. A man or woman whose consciousness has been permanently obliterated but who remains alive is a human being which is no longer a person; defective human beings, with no appreciable mental capacity, are not and presumably never will be people; and a fetus is a human being which is not yet a person, and which therefore cannot coherently be said to have full moral rights. Citizens of the next cen-tury should be prepared to recognize highly advanced, self-aware robots or computers, should such be developed, and intelligent inhabitants of other worlds, should such be found, as people in the fullest sense, and to respect their moral rights. But to ascribe full moral rights to an entity which is not a person is as absurd as to ascribe moral obligations and responsibilities to such an entity.

At the time philosopher Mary Ann Warren wrote this famous essay, the status of early human life was important primarily to the debate over the morality of abortion. Since then, and as reflected in the following excerpt on the science and morality of embryonic stem cell research, the ability to create embryos outside the womb and to use those embryos for purposes other than reproduc-tion have added new dimensions to the inquiry of the proper treatment of early human life. (A fuller description of the science of embryonic development is provided in Appendix A of this book.)

> ## James J. McCartney, Embryonic Stem Cell Research and Respect for Human Life: Philosophical and Legal Reflections
> ### 65 Alb. L. Rev. 597 (2002)

II. STEM CELLS AND CLONING

Stem cells can briefly be described as unspecialized cells that give rise to various types of specialized cells. In more scientific terms, stem cells are described as pluripotent cells, which means that they have the ability to develop into many kinds of tissues and organs of the body. These pluripotent cells have the capacity for prolonged self-renewal, and can be induced by chemical and electric means to form different types of specialized somatic cells and tissues. Stem cells are retrieved from the body by simple removal or extraction. When stem cells are derived from the umbilical cord, which is saved after birth and then frozen, they can eventually produce bone marrow. "[Adult] stem cells—found . . . in various locations in the adult body—can form a number of different tissues and so could in theory[,] be used to treat a vast array of diseases." Embryonic stem cells, on the other hand, are derived from embryos in the following way: "At the point at which dividing cells develop into a hollow ball, the embryo is called a blastocyst. [Human embryonic stem] cells are derived by destroying the outer shell of the blastocyst, which would normally become the placenta, and culturing cells from the inner cell mass." These cells, which are grown in tissue culture and can actually develop into organs, are now referred to as pluripotent rather than totipotent since they are no longer able to develop into embryos.

. . . For background purposes, two other phenomena should be mentioned at this point: twinning and chimera formation. Up until the formation of the primitive streak, which will develop into the spinal cord, and cell differentiation, which occurs about fourteen days after fertilization, the developing embryo can cleave naturally or artificially, resulting in the production of identical siblings. Therefore, embryonic cells that are still part of the inner cell mass are described as totipotent because they can give rise to new organisms, i.e., twins. Another possibility during this stage is that two developing embryonic cell masses with different genotypes will fuse to form what is called a chimera. "A chimera is an organism whose cells derive from two or more distinct zygote lineages." After the cells have begun to differentiate and the primitive streak has formed, twinning and chimera formation are no longer possible.

III. RESPECT FOR HUMAN LIFE

Since the Supreme Court's legalization of abortion in 1973, many philosophical and theological battles have been fought over the concept of "personhood." Personhood has been identified at the formation of the zygote, and is sometimes considered the equivalent of an entity that is animated with a rational soul. Some have proffered conditions for personhood, such as the concept of "social personhood," which has been suggested for situations where conditions for personhood have not been met, but individuals within society wish to endow that "person" with human rights. All of these approaches seem to consider "personhood" as a metaphysical problem to be solved. The fact that a consensus on the attributes of personhood has yet to be developed after twenty-five years of discussion resembles a situation analogous to the Derridean quest for justice—a "passion for the impossible." This quest must nonetheless continue, despite the fact that our conceptual frameworks are inadequate to the task at hand and will continually require further discussion.

My reflections here are not intended to be metaphysical, since it has been proven difficult, if not impossible, to develop a philosophical theory of personhood. Rather, I begin with the assertion—perhaps an intuition—that a person, in a non-metaphysical sense, is an individual of a living species, some of whose members demonstrate the capacities to think, choose, reason, and possess inalienable rights. Individuation within the human species is a necessary and sufficient condition for personhood, which alone is sufficient to claim fundamental human rights. The question of human rights, including the right to life, should therefore focus on human individuation—when does human biological life become an individual? My reflections on personhood below will assume this "rights bearing" approach rather than a metaphysical concept of personhood.

Anicius Manlius Severinus Boethius, a fifth century philosopher, describes personhood as "the individual substance of a rational nature." His use of the words "individual substance" is similar to Aristotle's use of "primary" or "first" substance, meaning a singular and concrete person, and was not intended to mean an essence, a metaphysical personhood. He believes that to be a person one must be an individual, which means that until an entity can become an individual, it cannot be a person. For Boethius, a person is an existential "who," not an essential "what." The "who" for Boethius comes from the fact that this individual entity has a rational nature. The person is always a substantial individual with a rational nature. In this context, the word "nature" signifies that the thrust or goal of members of this species is towards the attainment of rationality. It does not mean that humans, or other rational species, as individuals, must possess rationality in order to be persons, or bearers of rights. While others may disagree with me, I interpret Boethius to mean that this individual belongs to a species, some of whose members experience freedom, thought, and the capacity to reason. Thus, for Boethius, human individuation is a necessary as well as a sufficient condition for personhood and its accompanying rights.

This description of personhood implies that Boethius would count as bearers of rights those humans who are incapable of rational thought due to genetic or developmental anomalies, or as a result of injury or disease. The very fact that they are individuals of a species, some of whose members are rational, would suffice to count them as persons. The same holds true for fetuses, children, and those sleeping. I would argue, however, that an individual developing into a member of the human species is not a human individual until such time as the embryo cannot potentially become more than one individual of the human species through twinning or less than one through chimera formation.

. . . As stated previously, during the first fourteen days of the developmental process, the totipotentiality of the cells of the inner mass of the very early embryo can split spontaneously to form identical twins or be cleaved chemically at an earlier stage to form what are referred to as blastomeres. In addition, already cleaved totipotential cells can be fused to form a single developing cell mass that will eventually become one human being, referred to as a chimera. Chimeras can also be formed by two developing cell masses of totipotent cells of different genotypes that fuse and form one developing cell mass. At the blastocyst stage, a few days after fertilization, the embryonic cells in the inner cell mass can be changed by researchers from totipotent (able to form new individuals) to pluripotent (able to form many different tissue types). Taking into consideration all of these possibilities, [Saint Thomas] Aquinas would seem to suggest that if "being x" can potentially be part of "being y," then "being x" cannot possibly be a person because "x" as part of "y" is not yet a unique individual of the species until such time as the possibility of its being part of something else is closed off. Thus, from fertilization until the formation of the primitive streak, a developing individual life with a new human genotype exists, but it is not a life with a rational nature—a human individual, a person.

The following letter of Pope John Paul II addresses the issue of the moral status of both fetuses and embryos. Although obviously there are many different religious perspectives on this issue, the question of the status of nascent human life is one matter on which the Catholic Church has been outspoken and influential in contemporary ethical debates about reproductive matters. In fact, in 2001, when President George W. Bush was considering what his administration's policy should be regarding federal support of embryonic research (see section 2(b), infra), the President met with the Pope at the Vatican and discussed the ethical issues involved. Aline Kalbian, Stem Cells and the Catholic Church, in The Stem Cell Controversy (Michael Ruse & Christopher A. Pynes eds. 2003).

‖ *Evangelium Vitae (The Gospel of Life),* ‖ *Encyclical Letter of John Paul II* (March 25, 1995)[1]

58. . . . The moral gravity of procured abortion is apparent in all its truth if we recognize that we are dealing with murder and, in particular, when we consider the specific elements involved. The one eliminated is a human being at the very beginning of life. No one more absolutely *innocent* could be imagined. In no way could this human being ever be considered an aggressor, much less an unjust aggressor! He or she is *weak,* defenseless, even to the point of lacking that minimal form of defence consisting in the poignant power of a newborn baby's cries and tears. The unborn child is *totally entrusted* to the protection and care of the woman carrying him or her in the womb. And yet sometimes it is

---

1. Quotations to text within the letter are to related church documents–Eds.

precisely the mother herself who makes the decision and asks for the child to be eliminated, and who then goes about having it done. . . .

60. Some people try to justify abortion by claiming that the result of conception, at least up to a certain number of days, cannot yet be considered a personal human life. But in fact, "from the time that the ovum is fertilized, a life is begun which is neither that of the father nor the mother; it is rather the life of a new human being with his own growth. It would never be made human if it were not human already. This has always been clear, and . . . modern genetic science offers clear confirmation. It has demonstrated that from the first instance there is established the program of what this living being will be: a person, this individual person with his characteristic aspects already well determined. Right from fertilization the adventure of a human life begins, and each of its capacities requires time—a rather lengthy time—to find its place and to be in a position to act." Even if the presence of a spiritual soul cannot be ascertained by empirical data, the results themselves of scientific research on the human embryo provide "a valuable indication for discerning by the use of reason a personal presence at the moment of the first appearance of a human life: how could a human individual not be a human person?"

Furthermore, what is at stake is so important that, from the standpoint of moral obligation, the mere probability that a human person is involved would suffice to justify an absolutely clear prohibition of any intervention aimed at killing a human embryo. Precisely for this reason, over and above all scientific debates, and those philosophical affirmations to which the Magisterium has not expressly committed itself, the Church has always taught and continues to teach that the result of human procreation, from the first moment of its existence, must be guaranteed that unconditional respect which is morally due to the human being in his or her totality and unity as body and spirit: "*The human being is to be respected and treated as a person from the moment of conception;* and therefore from that same moment his rights as a person must be recognized, among which in the first place is the inviolable right of every innocent human being to life." . . .

63. This evaluation of the morality of abortion is to be applied also to the recent forms of *intervention on human embryos* which, although carried out for purposes legitimate in themselves, inevitably involve the killing of those embryos. This is the case with *experimentation on embryos,* which is becoming increasingly widespread in the field of biomedical research and is legally permitted in some countries. Although "one must uphold as licit procedures carried out on the human embryo which respect the life and integrity of the embryo and do not involve disproportionate risks for it, but rather are directed to its healing, the improvement of its condition of health, or its individual survival," it must nonetheless be stated that the use of human embryos or fetuses as an object of experimentation constitutes a crime against their dignity as human beings who have a right to the same respect owed to a child once born, just as to every person.

This moral condemnation also regards procedures that exploit living human embryos and fetuses—sometimes specifically "produced" for this purpose by in vitro fertilization—either to be used as "biological material" or as *providers of organs or tissue for transplants* in the treatment of certain diseases. The killing of innocent human creatures, even if carried out to help others, constitutes an absolutely unacceptable act.

NOTES AND QUESTIONS

1. *Traits of personhood.*   Philosopher Mary Ann Warren does not begin her consideration of the concept of personhood with the genetic or biological beginnings of an individual human being. Rather, she lists certain traits that she suggests are central to personhood. What do you think of her approach? Of the list of traits she provides?

In later papers, Warren acknowledges that her argument for why a fetus is not a person and therefore may be aborted can also lead to the conclusion that infants are not people and therefore that infanticide is morally acceptable. Are there ways in which abortion and infanticide can be distinguished while accepting Warren's criteria for personhood? For a well-known defense of infanticide, on the grounds that an organism has a right to life only if it possesses a consciousness of itself as a continuing subject of experiences, see Michael Tooley, Abortion and Infanticide, 2 Philosophy & Public Affairs 37 (1972).

2. *Individuality.*   At what point in human development does the encyclical letter of Pope John Paul II claim that a person exists? On what basis does he make this claim? Professor James McCartney also considers individuality to be a central characteristic of personhood. But he argues that early embryos should be distinguished from later-stage embryos because any consideration of the moral status of embryos should take into account two developmental possibilities that might occur within the first 14 days following creation of the embryos. What are these developments and why does he consider them relevant? Do you agree? (Note that viewing the embryo as a person only after 14 days permits the embryo's stem cells to be harvested for research and potential therapeutic uses.)

3. *The "personhood" of pregnant women.*   In a well-known essay published in 1998, philosopher and law professor Robin West opened with the question, "What is a human being?" Robin West, Jurisprudence and Gender, 55 U. Chi. L. Rev. 1 (1998). She answered, provocatively, that for many legal theorists, "women are not human beings." Her argument is that current U.S. legal theory revolves around an understanding of human beings as "distinct from one another," "physically individuated from every other," a claim that is untrue for women in at least four ways: pregnancy, heterosexual penetration, menstruation, and breast-feeding. And while women value the intimacy these experiences entail, they "long for individuation and independence." Laws prohibiting abortion, by failing to recognize the threat of fetal invasion to the personhood of women, construct women as something other than human beings. West writes:

> [F]etal invasion is not understood to be harmful, and therefore the claim that I ought to be able to protect myself against it is heard as nonsensical. The argument that the right to abortion mirrors the right of self defense falls on deaf ears for a reason: the analogy is indeed flawed. The right of self defense is the right to protect the body's security against annihilation liberally understood, not invasion. But the danger an unwanted fetus poses is not to the body's security at all, but rather to the body's integrity. Similarly, the woman's fear is not that she will die, but that she will cease to be or never become a self. The danger of unwanted pregnancy is the danger of invasion by the other, not of annihilation by the other.

Id. at 59, 68. Mary Ann Warren has written, somewhat similarly, "There is room for only one person with full and equal rights inside a single human skin." Mary

Ann Warren, The Moral Significance of Birth, 4 Hypatia 46 (1989), reprinted in *Feminist Perspectives in Medical Ethics* (H. B. Holmes & L. Purdy, eds., Indiana University Press, 1992), at 213. Do you agree?

4. *Self-defense?*   Both Robin West and Pope John Paul II reject the analogy of abortion to self-defense. Why? How does the Pope's letter characterize the woman who seeks an abortion? Who is the aggressor and who is the aggrieved?

5. *More on self-defense: Does "personhood" matter in the abortion debate?*   How much does it or should it matter to the question of the morality of abortion that a fetus is or is not considered to be a "person"? The argument against permitting abortion is often made as follows: A fetus is a person (from some point, perhaps the moment of conception, perhaps later), every person has a right to life, the fetus's right to life outweighs the mother's right to decide what happens to her body, thus abortion is impermissible. In a famous essay from 1971, philosopher Judith Jarvis Thomson defended abortion under some circumstances even if the fetus *is* a person. Thomson asks her readers to imagine the following:

> You wake up in the morning and find yourself back to back in bed with an unconscious violinist. A famous unconscious violinist. He has been found to have a fatal kidney ailment, and the Society of Music Lovers has canvassed all the available medical records and found that you alone have the right blood type to help. They have therefore kidnapped you, and last night the violinist's circulatory system was plugged into yours, so that your kidneys can be used to extract poisons from his blood as well as your own. The director of the hospital now tells you, "Look, we're sorry the Society of Music Lovers did this to you—we would never have permitted it if we had known. But still, they did it, and the violinist now is plugged in to you. To unplug you would be to kill him. But never mind, it's only for nine months. By then he will have recovered from his ailment, and can safely be unplugged from you." Is it morally incumbent on you to accede to this situation? No doubt it would be very nice of you if you did, a great kindness. But do you *have* to accede to it?

Thomson assumes that the reader will agree that unplugging yourself from the violinist would not be acting unjustly toward him, even though he has a right to life. The right to life "consists not in the right not to be killed, but rather in the right not to be killed unjustly." Accepting that the fetus is a person, like the violinist, and has a right to life like every living person, Thomson concludes nonetheless that not all abortion is unjust killing and therefore abortion is sometimes permissible.

Because Thomson's argument that abortion is sometimes permissible relies on the bodily sacrifice of the pregnant woman, as the person attached to the violinist, she emphasizes that she is not arguing for the right of the woman to "secure the death of the unborn child":

> It is easy to confuse these two things in that up to a certain point in the life of the fetus it is not able to survive outside the mother's body; hence removing it from her body guarantees its death. But they are importantly different. I have argued that you are not morally required to spend nine months in bed, sustaining the life of that violinist; but to say this is by no means to say that if, when you unplug yourself, there is a miracle and he survives, you then have a right to turn round and slit his throat. You may detach yourself even if this costs him his life; you have no right to be guaranteed his death, by some other means, if unplugging yourself does not kill him. There are some people who will feel dissatisfied by

this feature of my argument. A woman may be utterly devastated by the thought of a child, a bit of herself, put out for adoption and never seen or heard of again. She may therefore want not merely that the child be detached from her, but more, that it die. Some opponents of abortion are inclined to regard this as beneath contempt—thereby showing insensitivity to what is surely a powerful source of despair. All the same, I agree that the desire for the child's death is not one which anybody may gratify, should it turn out to be possible to detach the child alive.

Judith Jarvis Thomson, A Defense of Abortion, 1 Philosophy & Public Affairs 47 (1971).

In 1971, when Thomson wrote this essay, today's reality of custody disputes over frozen embryos was remote. If embryos and fetuses are to be equated (an important, unanswered question), how do you think Thomson's argument would play out in a custody dispute that considers a man's right to have frozen embryos destroyed following divorce as against his ex-wife's right to donate them to another couple? See Davis v. Davis, infra.

2. Fetuses

Although the embryonic stage precedes the fetal stage of human development, the legal cases regarding the fetus came before and served as precedent for the more recent legal decisions surrounding the embryo. For this reason, readings on the legal status of the fetus are set out first below.

‖   Roe v. Wade   ‖
410 U.S. 113 (1973)

Opinion of the Court by Justice BLACKMUN.

[In *Roe,* the Court defined a limited right to abortion as part of a right to privacy. The case developed out of a challenge to a Texas anti-abortion law. Selections from the decision in this chapter relate to the Court's discussion of fetal and embryonic status. *Roe* is considered more fully in Chapter 5.]

IX

A. The appellee [Texas] and certain *amici* argue that the fetus is a "person" within the language and meaning of the Fourteenth Amendment. In support of this, they outline at length and in detail the well-known facts of fetal development. If this suggestion of personhood is established, the appellant's case, of course, collapses, for the fetus' right to life would then be guaranteed specifically by the Amendment. . . .

The Constitution does not define "person" in so many words. Section 1 of the Fourteenth Amendment contains three references to "person." The first, in defining "citizens," speaks of "persons born or naturalized in the United States." The word also appears both in the Due Process Clause and in the Equal Protection Clause. "Person" is used in other places in the Constitution. . . . But in nearly all these instances, the use of the word is such that it has application only postnatally. None indicates, with any assurance, that it has any possible prenatal application.[54]

All this, together with our observation that throughout the major portion of the 19th century prevailing legal abortion practices were far freer than they are today, persuades us that the word "person," as used in the Fourteenth Amendment, does not include the unborn. This is in accord with the results reached in those few cases where the issue has been squarely presented. . . .

This conclusion, however, does not of itself fully answer the contentions raised by Texas, and we pass on to other considerations.

B. The pregnant woman cannot be isolated in her privacy. She carries an embryo and, later, a fetus, if one accepts the medical definitions of the developing young in the human uterus. See Dorland's Illustrated Medical Dictionary (24th ed. 1965), at 478–479, 547. The situation therefore is inherently different from marital intimacy, or bedroom possession of obscene material, or marriage, or procreation, or education, with which Eisenstadt and Griswold, Stanley, Loving, Skinner, and Pierce and Meyer were respectively concerned. As we have intimated above, it is reasonable and appropriate for a State to decide that at some point in time another interest, that of health of the mother or that of potential human life, becomes significantly involved. The woman's privacy is no longer sole and any right of privacy she possesses must be measured accordingly.

Texas urges that, apart from the Fourteenth Amendment, life begins at conception and is present throughout pregnancy, and that, therefore, the State has a compelling interest in protecting that life from and after conception. We need not resolve the difficult question of when life begins. When those trained in the respective disciplines of medicine, philosophy, and theology are unable to arrive at any consensus, the judiciary, at this point in the development of man's knowledge, is not in a position to speculate as to the answer.

It should be sufficient to note briefly the wide divergence of thinking on this most sensitive and difficult question. There has always been strong support for the view that life does not begin until live birth. This was the belief of the Stoics. It appears to be the predominant, though not the unanimous, attitude of the Jewish faith. It may be taken to represent also the position of a large segment of the Protestant community, insofar as that can be ascertained; organized groups that have taken a formal position on the abortion issue have generally regarded abortion as a matter for the conscience of the individual and her family. As we have noted, the common law found greater significance in quickening. Physicians and their scientific colleagues have regarded that event with less interest and have tended to focus either upon conception, upon live birth, or upon the interim point at which the fetus becomes "viable," that is, potentially able to live outside the mother's womb, albeit with artificial aid. Viability is usually placed at about seven months (28 weeks) but may occur earlier, even at 24 weeks. The Aristotelian theory of "mediate animation," that held sway

---

54. When Texas urges that a fetus is entitled to Fourteenth Amendment protection as a person, it faces a dilemma. Neither in Texas nor in any other State are all abortions prohibited. Despite broad proscription, an exception always exists. The exception . . . for an abortion procured or attempted by medical advice for the purpose of saving the life of the mother, is typical. But if the fetus is a person who is not to be deprived of life without due process of law, and if the mother's condition is the sole determinant, does not the Texas exception appear to be out of line with the Amendment's command? . . .

throughout the Middle Ages and the Renaissance in Europe, continued to be official Roman Catholic dogma until the 19th century, despite opposition to this "ensoulment" theory from those in the Church who would recognize the existence of life from the moment of conception. The latter is now, of course, the official belief of the Catholic Church. As one brief *amicus* discloses, this is a view strongly held by many non-Catholics as well, and by many physicians. Substantial problems for precise definition of this view are posed, however, by new embryological data that purport to indicate that conception is a "process" over time, rather than an event, and by new medical techniques such as menstrual extraction, the "morning-after" pill, implantation of embryos, artificial insemination, and even artificial wombs.

In areas other than criminal abortion, the law has been reluctant to endorse any theory that life, as we recognize it, begins before live birth or to accord legal rights to the unborn except in narrowly defined situations and except when the rights are contingent upon live birth. For example, the traditional rule of tort law denied recovery for prenatal injuries even though the child was born alive. That rule has been changed in almost every jurisdiction. In most States, recovery is said to be permitted only if the fetus was viable, or at least quick, when the injuries were sustained, though few courts have squarely so held. In a recent development, generally opposed by the commentators, some States permit the parents of a stillborn child to maintain an action for wrongful death because of prenatal injuries. Such an action, however, would appear to be one to vindicate the parents' interest and is thus consistent with the view that the fetus, at most, represents only the potentiality of life. Similarly, unborn children have been recognized as acquiring rights or interests by way of inheritance or other devolution of property, and have been represented by guardians *ad litem*. Perfection of the interests involved, again, has generally been contingent upon live birth. In short, the unborn have never been recognized in the law as persons in the whole sense.

‖ *Vernon's Annotated Missouri Statutes* ‖

1.205. Life begins at conception—unborn child, defined—failure to provide prenatal care, no cause of action for

1. The general assembly of this state finds that:

(1) The life of each human being begins at conception;

(2) Unborn children have protectable interests in life, health, and well-being;

(3) The natural parents of unborn children have protectable interests in the life, health, and well-being of their unborn child.

2. Effective January 1, 1988, the laws of this state shall be interpreted and construed to acknowledge on behalf of the unborn child at every stage of development, all the rights, privileges, and immunities available to other persons, citizens, and residents of this state, subject only to the Constitution of the United States, and decisional interpretations

thereof by the United States Supreme Court and specific provisions to the contrary in the statutes and constitution of this state.

3.   As used in this section, the term "unborn children" or "unborn child" shall include all unborn child or children or the offspring of human beings from the moment of conception until birth at every stage of biological development.

4.   Nothing in this section shall be interpreted as creating a cause of action against a woman for indirectly harming her unborn child by failing to properly care for herself or by failing to follow any particular program of prenatal care.

NOTES AND QUESTIONS

1. *When "life" begins.*   The court states that it "need not resolve the difficult question of when life begins." But can it avoid the question when "personhood" begins, and are these the same question for the court's purposes? And doesn't it resolve that question at live birth? On what basis does it do so?

2. *Fetal development.*   In *Roe,* the Court dismissed efforts to prove fetal personhood through reference to the "well-known facts of fetal development." Does it make sense after doing so for the Court to begin its own discussion of the state's interest in the fetus by citing a medical dictionary? Moreover, in *Roe* the Court relies heavily on a medical view of fetal development in concluding that the right to abortion shifts as a pregnancy progresses through each trimester of gestation, so that in the third trimester the state has an interest in protecting the fetus that is compelling enough to prohibit abortion. When is it appropriate to make moral and legal conclusions on the basis of biological facts, and when is it inappropriate?

3. *Privacy rights precedent.*   *Roe* contrasts the situation of the pregnant woman with that found in previous privacy cases: Griswold v. Connecticut, 381 U.S. 479 (1965) (invalidating state law prohibiting use of contraceptives as violative of right of privacy); Eisenstadt v. Baird, 405 U.S. 438 (1972) (extending the right to use contraceptives to unmarried couples); Stanley v. Georgia, 394 U.S. 557 (1969) (state's power to regulate obscenity does not extend to mere possession by individual in privacy of home); Loving v. Virginia, 388 U.S. 1 (1967) (striking down state antimiscegenation statute as violative of right to marry); Skinner v. Oklahoma, 316 U.S. 535, 541 (1942) (invalidating on equal protection grounds state law requiring sterilization of certain repeat criminal offenders; recognizing right to procreate as "one of the basic civil rights of man"); Pierce v. Society of Sisters, 268 U.S. 510 (1925) (holding that compulsory public education denied parents the right to direct their children's upbringing and education); Meyer v. Nebraska, 262 U.S. 390 (1923) (invalidating state law prohibiting teaching in modern foreign languages). How does the court distinguish the abortion context? In what ways is that distinction problematic? How does it affect the privacy rights of pregnant women?

4. *"Personhood" statutes.*   As of early 2012, only Missouri had what is now referred to as a "personhood" statute, supra, although other states (through

legislative bodies or constitutional amendment initiatives) have considered or are considering them (Oklahoma, Mississippi). Oklahoma, Weighing "Personhood" Law, May Be Next Abortion Flashpoint, Reuters, April 9, 2012. The Missouri statute requires that it be interpreted in accordance with the U.S. Constitution and Supreme Court precedent. The "personhood" bills more recently proposed have not always contained that caveat, potentially setting up a direct challenge to the constitutionally recognized right to an abortion. Id.

In Webster v. Reproductive Health Services, 492 U.S. 490 (1989), the U.S. Supreme Court declined to pass on the constitutionality of the preamble to Missouri's statute, supra, regulating abortion. In declining to pass on the constitutionality of the preamble, the Supreme Court explained that it could be read simply to express a value judgment favoring childbirth over abortion, which states are permitted to do. Do you agree? How important is the language used to describe a fetus? To describe the woman carrying the fetus (pregnant woman, mother) and the doctor performing an abortion (physician, abortionist)? (Note the language used in the excerpt from Stenberg v. Carhart, reprinted below.)

5. *Emerging "fetal rights" in tort and criminal law?* At the time of the *Roe* decision, and as reflected in that opinion, most states did not allow recovery for the wrongful death of a fetus or "unborn child." Part of the rationale for denying recovery in such instances was that an unborn child was considered a part of the mother and not a separate individual. The weight of more modern authority is to allow such actions, at least where the fetus was viable at the time of the tortious injury. Annotation, Right to Maintain Action or to Recover Damages for Death of Unborn Child, 84 A.L.R.3d 411 (1978). Some states even allow wrongful death actions if the fetus was not viable at the time of injury. See, e.g., Fryover v. Forbes, 433 Mich. 878 (1989) (vehicular accident involving 16-week-old fetus).

Criminal law punishing harm done to fetuses is also changing in ways that bolster a view of the fetus as a person. Over half the states have passed legislation punishing feticide (fetal homicide), although, as with tort law, the state laws vary regarding the required age of the fetus. In some states, the fetus must be "viable" or "quick" (when the fetus's movement in the womb can be felt), but a few states include fetuses at any stage of development. Texas's Prenatal Protection Act of 2003 covers "an unborn child at every stage of gestation from fertilization until birth." Tex. Civ. Prac. & Rem. Code Ann. §71.001(3) (Vernon 2004). Punishments vary from a sentence of a number of years to life in prison. Kathleen Murphy, Conn. L. Trib. (June 2, 2003), at 5; see also Lori K. Mans, Note, Liability for the Death of a Fetus: Fetal Rights or Women's Rights? 15 U. Fla. J.L. & Pub. Pol'y 295 (2004) (surveying state law on feticide legislation and fetal wrongful death actions).

The federal Unborn Victims of Violence Act, enacted in 2004, adds a separate offense to the federal criminal code for harm caused to a fetus during the commission of certain federal crimes. It applies to a "member of the species homo sapiens, at any stage of development, who is carried in the womb." 18 U.S.C.A. §1841. Punishment for the offense is the same as that provided for the conduct if it had caused injury to the mother of the "unborn child." Id.

What do such developments suggest, if anything, about the future of abortion rights? Generally, those who oppose abortion rights support such laws, whereas those in favor of abortion rights oppose them. Although the latter might favor stiffer penalties for those who harm a pregnant woman and cause the loss of her pregnancy, they fear the implications of equating harm to a fetus with harm to a person, especially as it is done in those statutes that explicitly refer to a fetus as a person or unborn child. Ronald Reagan made use of California's feticide law in the presidential election debate of 1984, asking, "Isn't it strange that that same woman could have taken the life of her unborn child and it was abortion, not murder, but if somebody else does it, that's murder?" Murphy, supra. Such use of the fetal homicide laws is exactly what opponents of these laws fear. What do you think? Are fetal homicide laws and abortion rights compatible?

6. *Research and legislation on fetal pain.*   As of early 2008, bills requiring that women having abortions be warned about fetal pain have been introduced in 25 states and passed in 5—Arkansas, Georgia, Louisiana, Minnesota, and Oklahoma. Annie Murphy Paul, The First Ache, New York Times Magazine, Feb. 10, 2008. Similar federal legislation, introduced by Senator Sam Brownback, Republican of Kansas, in 2004 and every year since as the "Unborn Child Pain Awareness Act," requires doctors to read a script on fetal pain to women seeking abortions of a "pain-capable unborn child" (defined as "an unborn child who has reached a probable stage of development of twenty weeks after fertilization") and offering to deliver anesthesia directly to the fetus. The script states, "The Congress of the United States has determined that at this stage of development, an unborn child has the physical structures necessary to experience pain." Fetal pain statutes are supported by many anti-abortion groups. Advocates for abortion rights say the real purpose of the measures is to discourage women from seeking abortions. In 2005, a review of "several hundred scientific papers" concluded that fetuses likely do not feel pain prior to 29 weeks' gestation. Susan J. Lee, Henry J. Peter Ralston, Eleanor A. Drey, John Colin Partridge, & Mark A. Rosen, Fetal Pain: A Systematic Multidisciplinary Review of the Evidence, 294 JAMA 947 (2005).

7. *Ultrasound legislation.*   A number of states have recently considered legislation requiring doctors to offer ultrasounds to pregnant women prior to an abortion, and several bills have passed. Oklahoma's ultrasound law of 2010 was ruled unconstitutional in March 2012 by a federal district court of the 10th Circuit because "it addresses only patients, physicians and sonographers dealing with abortions and does not address them concerning other medical care." Judge Strikes Down Ultrasound Law, CBS News, Mar. 28, 2012, http://www.cbsnews.com/8301–250_162–57406036/judge-strikes-down-oklahoma-ultrasound-law/. The law requires providers to place the ultrasound image in front of the women and describe the image. However, Texas's mandatory ultrasound law was recently upheld by a three-panel federal circuit court of appeals of the 5th Circuit. Christy Hoppe & Sommer Ingram, Texas Sonogram Law Can Go Forward, Federal Appeals Court Says, The Dallas Morning News, Jan. 10, 2012, http://www.dallasnews.com/news/politics/texas-legislature/headlines/20120110-texas-sonogram-law-can-go-forward-federal-appeals-court-says.ece. For a state-by-state description of ultrasound legislation, see Guttmacher Institute, State Policies in Brief: Requirements for Ultrasound, as of October 1, 2012, http://www.guttmacher.org/statecenter/spibs/spib_RFU.pdf.

8. *Experimenting with fetal tissue.* Research and experimental therapy using fetal tissue from spontaneous or induced abortions has been a controversial issue for many years. According to many medical researchers, such tissue is useful for both basic and preclinical research on biological processes and also offers potentially helpful transplantation therapies for diseases and disorders such as Alzheimer's disease, Parkinson's disease, diabetes, spinal cord injuries, muscular dystrophy, and others. Fetal tissue research is not new; early transplantation experiments took place in the late 1920s, and in the 1950s, fetal tissue was used in developing the polio vaccine. Mary Carrington Coutts, Fetal Tissue Research, Kennedy Institute of Ethics Journal, March 1993, 81.

Antiabortion groups generally oppose the use of fetal tissue because they consider the fetus to be a person whose body should not be harvested following abortion. Ronald Reagan banned federal funding for fetal tissue research in the 1980s, a ban that was continued by the first President George Bush. In 1993, President Bill Clinton, on his second day in office, removed the ban. Later in the year, Congress passed the National Institutes of Health (NIH) Revitalization Act, 42 U.S.C. §§289g-1 and 289g-2, which specifically permits federal funding for fetal tissue transplantation research for "therapeutic purposes" and limits the power of the executive branch to unilaterally deny such funding in the future. The 1993 law places some restrictions on the retrieval of fetal tissue, requiring women who donate tissue to give written informed consent and to be informed of their physicians' interests, if any, in the research to be conducted. In addition, because of concerns that a woman might get pregnant for the sole purpose of aborting and providing fetal tissue for therapeutic transplantation for herself or a family member, the law prohibits a donor from knowing or restricting the identity of the recipient. Both the NIH Revitalization Act and the National Organ Transplant Act, 42 U.S.C.A. §273, further prohibit the donor of fetal tissue from receiving any compensation for it, including the payment of expenses for the abortion. State law also addresses the issue, with many states' Uniform Anatomical Gift Act expressly permitting transplantation of fetal tissue. Some states, however, prohibit such use. See, e.g., Arizona's law, Ariz. Rev. Stat. §36-2302 (prohibiting experimentation or medical investigation of human fetus or embryo).

As we discuss in Chapter 5, in 1992, in the case of Planned Parenthood v. Casey, the Supreme Court affirmed but limited a woman's constitutional right to an abortion. At the time of the decision, changes in membership on the Court since the 1973 *Roe* opinion had led many supporters of the abortion right to fear that the Court would abandon *Roe*'s central ruling. Although it did not do so at that time, continued constitutional protection of abortion rights is far from certain. In 2003, Congress passed the Partial-Birth Abortion Ban Act, reprinted in part below. Although the federal law was very similar to a Nebraska statute struck down in 2000 by a 5–4 vote in Stenberg v. Carhart (*Carhart I*), 530 U.S. 914 (2000), the Supreme Court upheld the federal law in Gonzales v. Carhart (*Carhart II*), 127 S. Ct. 1610 (2007). The more recent case is excerpted and discussed extensively in Chapter 5; reprinted below are some passages from the Court's majority opinion (written by Justice Kennedy) and the dissent of Justice Ginsburg that go to the issue of the physical development of the aborted fetuses and the state's interest vis-à-vis that development.

Partial-Birth Abortion Ban Act of 2003
18 U.S.C. §1531(a) & (b) (2003)

Sec. 1531. Partial-birth abortions prohibited:

(a) Any physician who, in or affecting interstate or foreign commerce, knowingly performs a partial-birth abortion, and thereby kills a human fetus shall be fined under this title or imprisoned not more than 2 years, or both. This subsection does not apply to a partial-birth abortion that is necessary to save the life of a mother whose life is endangered by a physical disorder, physical illness, or physical injury, including a life-endangering physical condition caused by or arising from the pregnancy itself. . . .

(b) As used in this section—

(1) the term "partial-birth abortion" means an abortion in which the person performing the abortion—

(A) deliberately and intentionally vaginally delivers a living fetus until, in the case of a head-first presentation, the entire fetal head is outside the body of the mother, or, in the case of breech presentation, any part of the fetal trunk past the navel is outside the body of the mother, for the purpose of performing an overt act that the person knows will kill the partially delivered living fetus; and

(B) performs the overt act, other than completion of delivery, that kills the partially delivered living fetus.

Gonzales v. Carhart (Carhart II)
127 S. Ct. 1610 (2007)

Opinion by Mr. Justice KENNEDY.

. . . A description of the prohibited abortion procedure demonstrates the rationale for the congressional enactment. The Act proscribes a method of abortion in which a fetus is killed just inches before completion of the birth process. Congress stated as follows: "Implicitly approving such a brutal and inhumane procedure by choosing not to prohibit it will further coarsen society to the humanity of not only newborns, but all vulnerable and innocent human life, making it increasingly difficult to protect such life." Congressional Findings (14)(N). The Act expresses respect for the dignity of human life.

Congress was concerned, furthermore, with the effects on the medical community and on its reputation caused by the practice of partial-birth abortion. The findings in the Act explain:

> "Partial-birth abortion . . . confuses the medical, legal, and ethical duties of physicians to preserve and promote life, as the physician acts directly against the physical life of a child, whom he or she had just delivered, all but the head, out of the womb, in order to end that life." Congressional Findings (14)(J).
>
> There can be no doubt the government "has an interest in protecting the integrity and ethics of the medical profession." Washington v. Glucksberg, 521 U.S. 702, 731 (1997); see also Barsky v. Board of Regents of Univ. of N.Y., 347 U.S. 442, 451 (1954) (indicating the State has "legitimate concern for maintaining high standards of professional conduct" in the practice of medicine).

Under our precedents it is clear the State has a significant role to play in regulating the medical profession.

. . . The Act's ban on abortions that involve partial delivery of a living fetus furthers the Government's objectives. . . . Congress determined that the abortion methods it proscribed had a "disturbing similarity to the killing of a newborn infant," Congressional Findings (14)(L), and thus it was concerned with "draw[ing] a bright line that clearly distinguishes abortion and infanticide." Congressional Findings (14)(G).

Justice GINSBURG, with whom Justice STEVENS, Justice SOUTER, and Justice BREYER join, dissenting.

. . . Delivery of an intact, albeit nonviable, fetus warrants special condemnation, the Court maintains, because a fetus that is not dismembered resembles an infant. But so, too, does a fetus delivered intact after it is terminated by injection a day or two before the surgical evacuation, or a fetus delivered through medical induction or cesarean. Yet, the availability of those procedures—along with D & E by dismemberment—the Court says, saves the ban on intact D & E from a declaration of unconstitutionality. Never mind that the procedures deemed acceptable might put a woman's health at greater risk.

NOTES AND QUESTIONS

1. *D&E vs. intact D&E abortion procedures.* The abortion procedure banned by the statute at issue in *Carhart II* was the "intact D&E" (dilation and evacuation) procedure, sometimes also known as D&X (dilation and extraction). In other portions of the opinion (reprinted in Chapter 5), Justice Kennedy explains that "[t]he main difference between the two procedures is that in intact D&E a doctor extracts the fetus intact or largely intact with only a few passes [into the woman's uterus with the forceps]. . . . In an intact D&E procedure the doctor extracts the fetus in a way conducive to pulling out its entire body, instead of ripping it apart. . . ." In *Carhart I* the Court struck down a Nebraska statute similar to (but also different from) the federal statute because it lacked an exception for the health of the pregnant woman and because the statute's language could be read to prohibit the regular "D&E" procedure, the most common and safest method of abortion for second trimester pregnancies. The Supreme Court in *Carhart II* concluded that the language in the federal statute sufficiently distinguished between the two procedures. With respect to the lack of a health exception, the Court concluded that the federal statute could survive facial attack in the face of medical uncertainty about whether prohibiting the procedure would ever impose significant health risks on women. Another important change helps explain the seeming incongruity between the Court's 5–4 decision in 2007 upholding the federal statute and its 2000 decision invalidating the Nebraska statute: the appointment of Justice Samuel Alito to replace Justice Sandra Day O'Connor.

2. *State interests.* The federal statute's ban of the intact D&E procedure is not for the purpose of saving fetal life because abortion using other methods is still available. What, then, are the state's interests here? How strong do you think they are? Are these interests tied to the stage of development of the fetus? To the fetus's beginning physical "separation" from the pregnant woman?

CHALLENGING ISSUES: GUARDIAN FOR A FETUS?

A mentally incompetent 22-year-old woman, S. J., who had been under the care of a state department of children and family services (DCF) from the time she was three years old until she was 18, has recently been found to have been raped and impregnated in a state-licensed group home. S. J. has not had a guardian or any active or coordinated state protection since she was 18. Now that S. J.'s story has made the news, the DCF intends to ask the appropriate court to declare that S. J. is incompetent and to appoint a guardian for her and for her child, if and when she gives birth. The governor of the state, who is against abortion, has told the newspapers that he intends to ask that the state department of children and family services seek a guardian for the fetus as well.

If you were the attorney working for DCF assigned to this case, what approach would you take? In deciding your course of action, consider the arguments that might be made by the attorney whom the governor sends to discuss this issue with DCF. Organizations protective of a woman's right to an abortion have also requested an opportunity to speak with you about the issue. What do you expect they will say? How will you respond?

3.   Embryos

The developmental stage preceding that of the fetus is the embryo, understood generally to encompass the period between fertilization until the end of the eighth week of gestation, when the developing organism becomes known as a fetus. Sometimes, as in the *Davis* case below, the term *preembryo* is used to refer to a fertilized egg that has not been implanted in a uterus; in a naturally occurring pregnancy, implantation in the uterine wall occurs at about 14 days. Most often, general reference is made simply to embryos or, to denote those cryogenically preserved, "frozen embryos." For an explanation of the development of embryos and the process of cloning (discussed infra), see Appendix A.

The question of the moral status of embryos has primarily arisen in two different contexts. The first is that of the disposition of "leftover" embryos from assisted reproductive efforts, which often involves the question who gets to control their disposition, as seen in the following subsection highlighting the case of Davis v. Davis. The second is the use of embryos or stem cells derived from embryos in research or transplantation therapies, the subject of the materials in subsections b (Therapeutic Cloning) and c (Funding of Research on Human Embryos).

a.   Custody Disputes

|| ***Davis v. Davis*** ||
842 S.W.2d 588 (Tenn. 1992)

[This case involved divorcing spouses who were unable to resolve a dispute about seven fertilized ova (embryos) that had been frozen during infertility treatment. Mary Sue Davis sought "custody" of the embryos for implantation purposes; Junior Davis sought possession to avoid implantation. This excerpt focuses on the status of the embryos; other aspects of the decision are considered in Chapter 6.]

IV.   THE "PERSON" VS. "PROPERTY" DICHOTOMY

One of the fundamental issues the inquiry poses is whether the preembryos in this case should be considered "persons" or "property" in the contemplation of the law. The Court of Appeals held, correctly, that they cannot be considered "persons" under Tennessee law:

> The policy of the state on the subject matter before us may be gleaned from the state's treatment of fetuses in the womb. . . . The state's Wrongful Death Statute does not allow a wrongful death for a viable fetus that is not first born alive. Without live birth, the Supreme Court has said, a fetus is not a "person" within the meaning of the statute. Other enactments by the legislature demonstrate even more explicitly that viable fetuses in the womb are not entitled to the same protection as "persons." Tenn. Code Ann. §39-15-201 incorporates the trimester approach to abortion outlined in Roe v. Wade. [The case was written shortly before the Court decided Planned Parenthood of Southeastern Pennsylvania v. Casey, 505 U.S. 833 (1992); see Chapter 6.] . . .

Left undisturbed, the trial court's ruling [which categorized the fertilized ova as "children, in vitro"] would have afforded preembryos the legal status of "persons" and vested them with legally cognizable interests separate from those of their progenitors. Such a decision would doubtless have had the effect of outlawing IVF programs in the state of Tennessee. But in setting aside the trial court's judgment, the Court of Appeals, at least by implication, may have swung too far in the opposite direction.

The intermediate court, without explicitly holding that the preembryos in this case were "property," nevertheless awarded "joint custody" of them to Mary Sue Davis [the wife] and Junior Davis [the husband] for the proposition that "the parties share an interest in the seven fertilized ova." The intermediate court did not otherwise define this interest.

The intermediate court's reliance on York v. Jones, is even more troublesome. That case involved a dispute between a married couple undergoing IVF procedures at the Jones Institute for Reproductive Medicine in Virginia. When the Yorks decided to move to California, they asked the Institute to transfer the one remaining "frozen embryo" that they had produced to a fertility clinic in San Diego for later implantation. The Institute refused and the Yorks sued. The federal district court assumed without deciding that the subject matter of the dispute was "property." The York court held that the "cryopreservation agreement" between the Yorks and the Institute created a bailment relationship, obligating the Institute to return the subject of the bailment to the Yorks once the purpose of the bailment had terminated. [717 F. Supp. 421 (E.D. Va. 1989).]

In this case, by citing to York v. Jones but failing to define precisely the "interest" that Mary Sue Davis and Junior Davis have in the preembryos, the Court of Appeals has left the implication that it is in the nature of a property interest. For purposes of clarity in future cases, we conclude that this point must be further addressed.

To our way of thinking, the most helpful discussion on this point is found not in the minuscule number of legal opinions that have involved "frozen embryos," but in the ethical standards set by The American Fertility Society, as follows:

> Three major ethical positions have been articulated in the debate over preembryo status. At one extreme is the view of the preembryo as a human subject after fertilization, which requires that it be accorded the rights of a person. This position entails an obligation to provide an opportunity for implantation to occur and tends to ban any action before transfer that might harm the preembryo or that is not immediately therapeutic, such as freezing and some preembryo research.
>
> At the opposite extreme is the view that the preembryo has a status no different from any other human tissue. With the consent of those who have decision making authority over the preembryo, no limits should be imposed on actions taken with preembryos.
>
> A third view—one that is most widely held—takes an intermediate position between the other two. It holds that the preembryo deserves respect greater than that accorded to human tissue but not the respect accorded to actual persons. The preembryo is due greater respect than other human tissue because of its potential to become a person and because of its symbolic meaning for many people. Yet, it should not be treated as a person, because it has not yet developed the feature of personhood, is not yet established as developmentally individual, and may never realize its biologic potential.

Although the report alludes to the role of "special respect" in the context of research on preembryos not intended for transfer, it is clear that the Ethics Committee's principal concern was with the treatment accorded the transferred embryo. Thus, the Ethics Committee concludes that "special respect is necessary to protect the welfare of potential offspring . . . [and] creates obligations not to hurt or injure the offspring who might be born after transfer [by research or intervention with a preembryo]."

In its report, the Ethics Committee then calls upon those in charge of IVF programs to establish policies in keeping with the "special respect" due preembryos and suggests:

> Within the limits set by institutional policies, decision making authority regarding preembryos should reside with the persons who have provided the gametes. . . . As a matter of law, it is reasonable to assume that the gamete providers have primary decision making authority regarding preembryos in the absence of specific legislation on the subject. A person's liberty to procreate or to avoid procreation is directly involved in most decisions involving preembryos.

We conclude that preembryos are not, strictly speaking, either "persons" or "property," but occupy an interim category that entitles them to special respect because of their potential for human life. It follows that any interest that Mary Sue Davis and Junior Davis have in the preembryos in this case is not a true property interest. However, they do have an interest in the nature of ownership, to the extent that they have decision making authority concerning disposition of the preembryos, within the scope of policy set by law.

NOTES AND QUESTIONS

1. *Interim category.*   Why, according to the *Davis* court, is it inappropriate to view embryos as persons? As property? The "interim category" chosen by the court entitles embryos to "special respect." Why? What does it mean by "special respect" if disposition of the embryos can be awarded to an individual (in this case, Junior Davis) who intends to have them thawed and thus destroyed?

2. *Relationship of genetic information to personhood.*   In concluding that the preembryos were "persons," the trial court relied heavily on the testimony of one of five expert witnesses, Dr. Jerome Lejeune, a French professor of genetics. Lejeune, known in the world of science for having discovered the chromosome responsible for Down syndrome, had worked actively to have abortion made illegal. He testified for Mary Sue Davis at the *Davis* trial. Lejeune's explanations were premised on the notion that fertilization in vitro is not significantly different from fertilization in vivo (inside a woman's body), and that therefore the status of embryos in vitro is the same as the status of embryos in vivo. Lejeune further explained:

> It is not at all the inseminator who makes fertilization, he just puts on the right medium, a ripe ovum, active sperm, and it is the sperm who make the fertilization. Man would be unable to make a fertilization. It has to be done directly by the cells. And it's because they were normally floating in the fluid that this extracorporeal technique is at all possible.
>
>   Now, the reproduction process is a very impressive phenomenon in the sense that what is reproduced is never the matter, but it is information.

Transcript of Proceedings, Davis v. Davis, No. E-14496 (Tenn. Cir. Ct., Aug. 10, 1989), vol. III, at 23. With this testimony, Dr. Lejeune aimed to establish the presumptions necessary for proving that eight-cell embryos are humans. In Dr. Lejeune's view, eight-cell embryos, whether created in vitro or in vivo, contain the information necessary to produce a human. Therefore, concluded Lejeune, those embryos enjoy the moral status of human beings. Relying on Lejeune's testimony, the trial court explained that

> it is to the manifest best interest of the children, *in vitro,* that they be made available for implantation to assure their opportunity for live birth; implantation is their sole and only hope for survival. The Court respectfully finds and concludes that it further serves the best interest of these children for Mrs. Davis to be permitted the opportunity to bring these children to term through implantation.

Davis, 1989 Tenn. App. LEXIS 641, at *37.

For a criticism of approaches such as Lejeune's that tie the moral status of human beings to the genetic information contained in gametes, see Barbara Katz Rothman, Daddy Plants a Seed: Personhood Under Patriarchy, 47 Hastings L.J. 1241 (1996). Rothman maintains that such emphasis on the genetic "seed" is patriarchal and dismissive of the significance of nurturance:

> In a mother-based system, a person is what mothers grow. People are made of the care and nurturance that bring a baby forth into the world and turn that baby into a member of society. In a patriarchal system, a person is what grows

out of a seed; originally a man's seed, but now expanded to the sex-neutral language of "gametes." The essence of what a person is, in patriarchal thinking, is there when the seed is planted. Motherhood becomes, in such thinking, a place. Providing the place becomes a service.

Id. at 1245.

3. *Other custody disputes.*   Although the issue of the status—property, living human being, potential human being, or something else—of the embryo received considerable attention in Davis v. Davis, it has generally played less of a role in resolving other disputes concerning who shall control the disposition of embryos. For consideration of the analysis employed in such cases, see Chapter 4. See also Kass v. Kass, 91 N.Y.2d 554 (1998) (agreeing with the *Davis* court that embryos, or "pre-zygotes," are not recognized as "persons" for constitutional purposes and thus determining that the relevant inquiry was limited to who has dispositional authority over them in a divorce action; because neither party challenged the validity of the agreement on grounds of a violation of public policy, the court found no reason to decide whether the pre-zygotes were entitled to "special respect"). See also In re Marriage of Dahl and Angle, 194 P.3d 834 (Or. App. 2008), where the Oregon Court of Appeals described its decision as following "the general framework set forth by the courts in *Davis* and *Kass,* in which courts give effect to the progenitors' intent by enforcing the progenitors' advance directive regarding the embryos." Before reaching the conclusion to follow the advance agreement of the parties, the court first determined that the contractual right to possess or dispose of the frozen embryos was "personal property" subject to distribution in a dissolution proceeding. Cf. A.Z. v. B.Z., 725 N.E. 2d 1051 (Mass. 2001) (declaring the court "would not enforce an agreement that would compel one donor to become a parent against his or her will" while avoiding discussion of status of the embryos).

4. *Actions for wrongful destruction of embryos.*   In a few cases progenitors of embryos have sued infertility clinics for failure to properly cryopreserve and store embryos. Use of wrongful death statutes for this purpose has been unsuccessful to date. See Miller v. American Infertility Group, 897 N.E.2d 837, 2008 WL 4722566 (Ill. App. 2008) (reversing trial court decision holding that a pre-embryo is a "human being" within meaning of state wrongful death statute); Jeter v. Mayo Clinic Arizona, 211 Ariz. 386 (Ct. App. Div. 1 2005) (three-day-old eight-cell preembryo not a "person" under wrongful death statute). What other legal claims might be asserted in situations like these?

CHALLENGING ISSUES: EMBRYO ADOPTION

You are a state legislator in a state that, like most states, has no current statutory law regulating the creation, status, or use of human embryos. A group of fellow legislators has called for legislation that would encourage as well as regulate what they are referring to as the "adoption" of extra cryopreserved (frozen) embryos from couples who created them for reproductive purposes but do not wish to implant them. Most of the infertility clinics in the state currently allow patients to choose the option of donating their leftover embryos to other couples, but this is generally done through a contractual provision that cedes dispositional control of the extra embryos to the clinic. Recently, however, a religiously based organization has sprung up to promote the "adoption" of embryos, seeking to match infertile couples who wish to "adopt" an embryo with couples who have extra embryos cryopreserved and stored at fertility clinics in the state. In its literature advertising and explaining its services, the organization states that every embryo is a baby waiting to be born. Some of the issues that have already arisen in the initial debate about state regulation are as follows:

1. Is the language of "adoption" appropriate in this context? Would you wish to use this language or alternative language to describe the transfer of embryos from one couple to another?

2. Should there be any restrictions on the receipt of embryos from another couple? For example, should couples wishing to "adopt" an embryo be required to meet the same or similar requirements that apply to the adoption of children within the state, such as meeting certain age requirements or character and fitness criteria, or passing a home visit?

3. What kind of fees might appropriately be charged by the organization arranging the transfer of embryos? By the couple donating the embryos?

4. Should the transfer of embryos be limited to those that are left over from infertility treatment efforts, or should fertility clinics be able to create embryos "made to order" for adoption purposes?

5. Should the "adopting" couple or individual be required to implant the embryos or should they be free to dispose of them as they wish?

6. Should embryo transfers of this sort be encouraged by public awareness campaigns? By grants to organizations facilitating such transfers? What effect might public endorsement of "embryo adoption" have on traditional adoption, on the donation and use of embryos for stem cell research, or on the legalization of abortion?

7. Are there any constitutional issues that must be considered?

As you consider these issues, take a look at Louisiana's unique and controversial statute. Do you think it is constitutional?

‖ *La. Rev. Stat. Ann. 9:121–9:133* ‖

§121. Human embryo; definition

A "human embryo" for the purposes of this Chapter is an in vitro fertilized human ovum, with certain rights granted by law, composed of one or more living human cells and human genetic material so unified and organized that it will develop in utero into an unborn child.

§122. Uses of human embryo in vitro

The use of a human ovum fertilized in vitro is solely for the support and contribution of the complete development of human in utero implantation. No in vitro fertilized human ovum will be farmed or cultured solely for research purposes or any other purposes. The sale of a human ovum, fertilized human ovum, or human embryo is expressly prohibited.

§123. Capacity

An in vitro fertilized human ovum exists as a juridical person until such time as the in vitro fertilized ovum is implanted in the womb; or at any other time when rights attach to an unborn child in accordance with law.

§124. Legal status

As a juridical person, the in vitro fertilized human ovum shall be given an identification by the medical facility for use within the medical facility which entitles such ovum to sue or be sued. The confidentiality of the in vitro fertilization patient shall be maintained.

§126. Ownership

An in vitro fertilized human ovum is a biological human being which is not the property of the physician which acts as an agent of fertilization, or the facility which employs him or the donors of the sperm and ovum. If the in vitro fertilization patients express their identity, then their rights as parents as provided under the Louisiana Civil Code will be preserved. If the in vitro fertilization patients fail to express their identity, then the physician shall be deemed to be temporary guardian of the in vitro fertilized human ovum until adoptive implantation can occur. A court in the parish where the in vitro fertilized ovum is located may appoint a curator, upon motion of the in vitro fertilization patients, their heirs, or physicians who caused in vitro fertilization to be performed, to protect the in vitro fertilized human ovum's rights.

§129. Destruction

A viable in vitro fertilized human ovum is a juridical person which shall not be intentionally destroyed by any natural or other juridical person or through the actions of any other such person. An in vitro fertilized human ovum that fails to develop further over a thirty-six hour period except when the embryo is in a state of cryopreservation, is considered non-viable and is not considered a juridical person.

§130. Duties of donors

An in vitro fertilized human ovum is a juridical person which cannot be owned by the in vitro fertilization patients who owe it a high duty of care and prudent administration. If the in vitro fertilization patients renounce, by notarial act, their parental rights for in utero implantation, then the in vitro fertilized human ovum shall be available for adoptive implantation in accordance with written procedures of the facility where it is housed or stored. The in vitro fertilization patients may renounce their parental rights in favor of another married couple, but only if the other couple is willing and able to receive the in vitro fertilized ovum. No compensation shall be paid or received by either couple to renounce parental rights. Constructive fulfillment of the statutory provisions for adoption in this state shall occur when a married couple executes a notarial act of adoption of the in vitro fertilized ovum and birth occurs.

§131. Judicial standard

In disputes arising between any parties regarding the in vitro fertilized ovum, the judicial standard for resolving such disputes is to be in the best interest of the in vitro fertilized ovum.

See also 10 Okla. Stat. Ann. §556. Oklahoma's statute expressly authorizes embryo transfer, but provides little regulation of the practice. It requires the transfer to be made only by a licensed physician and that the written consent of the donating and receiving "husband and wife" be obtained prior to transfer and submitted to a court "having adoption jurisdiction," but that such consents will not be open to the public. Finally, the statute establishes the parentage of the resulting child to be that of the receiving couple.

b. Therapeutic Cloning

The debate about embryonic and fetal status in the United States took on new dimensions by the end of the twentieth century as a result of the advent of mammalian cloning (somatic cell nuclear transfer) in 1997 and the isolation of embryonic stem cells in 1998. The standard techniques used to derive stem cells from human embryos have resulted in the destruction of the embryo, although new techniques being developed in animals may allow stem cells to be removed and the embryo to continue to develop. Both of these techniques may be seen as problematic for different reasons. For those who believe that the embryo is a person, or entitled to some moral status similar to personhood, destruction of the embryo for these purposes appears unethical. On the other hand, a technique that allows an embryo to develop after removing one or more of its very limited number of cells appears to be experimentation on the embryo with neither benefit to the person who may develop from that embryo nor the person-to-be's consent (although the progenitors' consent might be obtained). More than experimentation even, the technique appears to involve an actual removal or taking of the person's body preimplantation.

A number of medical researchers believe that the potential benefits of stem cell research and therapy will be greater if stem cells are produced from a cloned human embryo that would be a genetic match of the stem cell transplant recipient. Creating embryos through cloning is variously called *nonreproductive cloning, therapeutic cloning,* or, more recently, *cloning for biomedical research.* The latter term has been adopted by the President's Council on Bioethics, which issued a report on human cloning in July 2001. That report defines "human cloning" as "the asexual production of a new human organism that is, at all stages of development, genetically virtually identical to a currently existing or previously existing human being." Typically the process envisioned for human cloning would be the removal or inactivation of an egg's nucleus, into which the nuclear material of a donor somatic cell is inserted (also sometimes called *somatic cell nuclear transfer*). Electric stimulation of the egg, rather than fertilization, would spur the process of cell division to develop an embryo.

The production of cloned human embryos for the purpose of harvesting stem cells raises some of the same but also many different ethical issues than reproductive cloning (cloning to produce children). Although the President's Council on Bioethics agreed that cloning to produce children is unsafe and morally unacceptable, it was unable to reach similar agreement about the ethics of cloning for biomedical purposes. Reprinted below is a portion of the executive summary of its report showing this division of opinion. (For more on the science of cloning and a glossary of terms related to cloning, see Appendix A.) It provides a range of approaches to questions about the status and use of human embryos in research, whether cloning is involved or not.

> ## President's Council on Bioethics, Human Cloning and Human Dignity: An Ethical Inquiry
> ### (July 2002)

THE ETHICS OF CLONING-FOR-BIOMEDICAL RESEARCH

Ethical assessment of cloning-for-biomedical-research is far more vexing [than assessment of cloning-to-produce-children]. On the one hand, such research could lead to important knowledge about human embryological development and gene action, both normal and abnormal, ultimately resulting in treatments and cures for many dreaded illnesses and disabilities. On the other hand, the research is morally controversial because it involves the deliberate production, use, and ultimate destruction of cloned human embryos, and because the cloned embryos produced for research are no different from those that could be implanted in attempts to produce cloned children. The difficulty is compounded by what are, for now, unanswerable questions as to whether the research will in fact yield the benefits hoped for, and whether other promising and morally nonproblematic approaches might yield comparable benefits. The Council, reflecting the differences of opinion in American society, is divided regarding the ethics of research involving (cloned) embryos. *Yet we agree that all parties to the debate have concerns vital to defend, vital not only to themselves but to all of us. No human being and no society can afford to be callous to the needs of suffering humanity, or cavalier about the treatment of nascent human life, or indifferent to the social effects of adopting one course of action rather than another.*

To make clear to all what is at stake in the decision, Council Members have presented, as strongly as possible, the competing ethical cases for and against cloning-for-biomedical research in the form of first-person attempts at moral suasion. Each case has tried to address what is owed to suffering humanity, to the human embryo, and to the broader society. Within each case, supporters of the position in question speak only for themselves, and not for the Council as a whole.

A.   The Moral Case for Cloning-for-Biomedical Research

The moral case for cloning-for-biomedical research rests on our obligation to try to relieve human suffering, an obligation that falls most powerfully on medical practitioners and biomedical researchers. We who support cloning-for-biomedical research all agree that it may offer uniquely useful ways of investigating and possibly treating many chronic debilitating diseases and disabilities, providing aid and relief to millions. We also believe that the moral objections to this research are outweighed by the great good that may come from it. Up to this point, we who support this research all agree. But we differ among ourselves regarding the weight of the moral objections, owing to differences about the moral status of the cloned embryo. These differences of opinion are sufficient to warrant distinguishing two different moral positions within the moral case for cloning-for-biomedical research:

Position Number One. Most Council Members who favor cloning-for-biomedical research do so with serious moral concerns. Speaking only for ourselves, we acknowledge the following difficulties, but think that they can be addressed by setting proper boundaries.

- *Intermediate moral status.* While we take seriously concerns about the treatment of nascent human life, we believe there are sound moral reasons for not regarding the embryo in its earlier stages as the moral equivalent of a human person. We believe the embryo has a developing and intermediate moral worth that commands our special respect, but that it is morally permissible to use early-stage cloned human embryos in important research under strict regulation.

- *Deliberate creation for use.* We acknowledge the concern that some researchers might seek to develop cloned embryos beyond the blastocyst stage, and for those of us who believe that the cloned embryo has a developing and intermediate moral status, this is a very real worry. We approve, therefore, only of research on cloned embryos that is strictly limited to the first fourteen days of development—a point near when the primitive streak is formed and before organ differentiation occurs.

- *Other moral hazards.* We believe that concerns about the exploitation of women and about the risk that cloning-for-biomedical research could lead to cloning-to-produce children can be adequately addressed by appropriate rules and regulations. These concerns need not frighten us into abandoning an important avenue of research.

Position Number Two. A few Council Members who favor cloning-for-biomedical research do not share all the ethical qualms expressed above. Speaking only for ourselves, we hold that this research, at least for the purposes presently contemplated, presents no special moral problems, and therefore should be endorsed with enthusiasm as a potential new means of gaining knowledge to serve humankind. Because we accord no special moral status to the early-stage cloned embryo and believe it should be treated essentially like all other human cells, we believe that the moral issues involved in this research are no different from those that accompany any biomedical research. What is required is the usual commitment to high standards for the quality of research, scientific integrity, and the need to obtain informed consent from donors of the eggs and somatic cells used in nuclear transfer.

B.   The Moral Case Against Cloning-for-Biomedical Research

The moral case against cloning-for-biomedical research acknowledges the possibility—though purely speculative at the moment—that medical benefits might come from this particular avenue of experimentation. But we believe it is morally wrong to exploit and destroy developing human life, even for good reasons, and that it is unwise to open the door to the many undesirable consequences that are likely to result from this research. We find it disquieting, even somewhat ignoble, to treat what are in fact seeds of the next generation as mere raw material for satisfying the needs of our own. Only for very serious reasons should progress toward increased knowledge and medical advances be slowed. But we believe that in this case such reasons are apparent.

- *Moral status of the cloned embryo.* We hold that the case for treating the early-stage embryo as simply the moral equivalent of all other human cells (Position Number Two, above) is simply mistaken: it denies the continuous history of human individuals from the embryonic to fetal to infant stages of existence; it misunderstands the meaning of potentiality; and it ignores the hazardous moral precedent that the routinized creation, use, and destruction of nascent human life would establish. We hold that the case for according the human embryo "intermediate and developing moral status" (Position Number One, above) is also unconvincing, for reasons both biological and moral. Attempts to ground the limited measure of respect owed to a maturing embryo in certain of its developmental features do not succeed, and the invoking of a "special respect" owed to nascent human life seems to have little or no operative meaning if cloned embryos may be created in bulk and used routinely with impunity. If from one perspective the view that the embryo seems to amount to little may invite a weakening of our respect, from another perspective its seeming insignificance should awaken in us a sense of shared humanity and a special obligation to protect it.
- *The exploitation of developing human life.* To engage in cloning-for-biomedical research requires the irreversible crossing of a very significant moral boundary: the creation of human life expressly and exclusively for the purpose of its use in research, research that necessarily involves its deliberate destruction. If we permit this research to proceed, we will effectively be endorsing the complete transformation of nascent human life into nothing more than a resource or a tool. Doing so would coarsen our moral sensibilities and make us a different society: one less humble toward that which we cannot fully understand, less willing to extend the boundaries of human respect ever outward, and more willing to transgress moral boundaries once it appears to be in our own interests to do so.

- *Moral harm to society.* Even those who are uncertain about the precise moral status of the human embryo have sound ethical-prudential reasons to oppose cloning-for-biomedical research. Giving moral approval to such research risks significant moral harm to our society by (1) crossing the boundary from sexual to asexual reproduction, thus approving in principle the genetic manipulation and control of nascent human life; (2) opening the door to other moral hazards, such as cloning-to-produce children or research on later-stage human embryos and fetuses; and (3) potentially putting the federal government in the novel and unsavory position of mandating the destruction of nascent human life. Because we are concerned not only with the fate of the cloned embryos but also with where this research will lead our society, we think prudence requires us not to engage in this research.

- *What we owe the suffering.* We are certainly not deaf to the voices of suffering patients; after all, each of us already shares or will share in the hardships of mortal life. We and our loved ones are all patients or potential patients. But we are not only patients, and easing suffering is not our only moral obligation. As much as we wish to alleviate suffering now and to leave our children a world where suffering can be more effectively relieved, we also want to leave them a world in which we and they want to live—a world that honors moral limits, that respects all life whether strong or weak, and that refuses to secure the good of some human beings by sacrificing the lives of others.

NOTES AND QUESTIONS

1. *The moral status of human embryos.* The case made in the council's report for approving cloning-for-biomedical research is premised on the view that the early cloned human embryo is deserving of either "intermediate" moral status (Position Number One) or that it is equivalent to any other human cells (Position Number Two). How does the case made for disapproving such research define the moral status of the human embryo—or does it avoid defining it? Does one have to view the embryo as a "person" to consider it unethical to engage in cloning-for-biomedical research? Is it possible to reconcile an ethical opposition to cloning-for-biomedical research and a pro-choice position on abortion rights?

2. *Council policy recommendations.* Because the council could not agree on the ethics of cloning-for-biomedical research, it was unable to adopt a joint policy recommendation on the issue. Instead, the council produced a majority recommendation, supported by ten members and a minority recommendation, supported by seven members. The majority recommendation was for a four-year moratorium on cloning-for-biomedical research and a federal review of current and projected practices related to human embryo research. The minority recommendation was for regulation of the use of cloned embryos for biomedical research, which might include rules regarding "the secure handling of embryos, licensing and prior review of research projects, the protection of egg donors, and the provision of equal access to benefits." Both the majority and minority

recommendations supported a complete and permanent ban on cloning-to-produce children.

3. *Human Embryo Research Panel.*   An earlier panel assembled to advise the National Institutes of Health on the propriety of federal financing of human embryo research similarly could not reach agreement on the moral status of the embryo. Law professor Alta Charo describes the efforts of the Human Embryo Research Panel (the Panel), of which she was a member, in The Hunting of the Snark: The Moral Status of Embryos, Right-to-Lifers, and Third World Women, 6 Stan. L. & Pol'y Rev. 1, 11 (1995). Charo describes the panel's recommendations as a "generally reasonable political compromise." It provided for federal financing of research using human embryos only if research on animals was not a good option. Such research could use embryos up to the fourteenth day of development. It further provided that such embryos be obtained without compensation from among those embryos created for reproductive purposes but no longer needed for that purpose by the gamete donors, and only with the consent of those donors. Id. at 11–12. See National Institutes of Health, Report of the Human Embryo Research Panel, Sept. 27, 1994. Charo explains that the report's conclusions are not connected to any philosophical vision or to any discussion about which view of embryonic status is the correct one. The Panel's own view of embryonic status was that reflected in the Tennessee Supreme Court decision in *Davis*—that embryos are not persons or property but that they are owed "special respect" because of their developmental potential to become human. It is, however, hard to discern the parameters or implications of that respect. Charo quotes Daniel Callahan's take on the notion that embryos are somehow special but can be used in research or discarded. "An odd form of esteem," declared Callahan, "at once high-minded and altogether lethal." "What in the world," he continued, "can that kind of respect mean?" Daniel Callahan, The Puzzle of Profound Respect, 25 Hastings Ctr. Rpt. 39, 39 (1995).

4. *Religious views.*   If embryonic status cannot be effectively delineated by governmental commissions and panels, should religious views be entertained? Alta Charo, among others, recognizes that theological analyses may be able to define the scope of embryonic status but concludes that such analyses are out of place in a country such as the United States, in which religious diversity is protected by the Constitution. Charo, supra, at 12. Do you agree?

5. *Legislation related to cloning.*   A number of bills to prohibit human cloning (some of which would include a prohibition on cloning-for-biomedical research) have been debated in the U.S. legislature, but no federal legislation has yet been passed. A number of states, however, have already adopted statutes that prohibit all or some forms of human cloning. See, e.g., Arkansas, Ark. Code Ann. §20-16-1003 (prohibiting reproductive and therapeutic cloning); Louisiana, La. Rev. Stat. §40:1299.36.2 (prohibiting only reproductive cloning).

Nine of the countries within the European Union had banned embryonic stem cell research by late 2003. Other countries, in Europe and elsewhere, permit such research. Stem Cell Research Around the World, http://www.cnn.worldnews (visited September 22, 2003). According to the International Society for Stem Cell Research, "The policies on human embryonic stem cell (hESC) research used by different countries vary tremendously and change frequently." The Society's website, http://www.isscr.org/public/regions/index.cfm, contains databases on the policies of countries throughout the world.

c.   Funding of Research on Human Embryos

Although some states prohibit by law embryonic stem cell research, others, like California, not only permit it, but finance it. State funding of embryonic stem cell research was designed to fill a gap in funding of basic science research that would normally be supplied by the federal government. The following case provides some background of the controversy over federal funding in this area, which continues.

|| *Sherley v. Sebelius* ||
|| 689 F.3d 776 (2012) ||

Appellants are researchers in the field of adult stem cells who oppose the use of federal funding for the development of embryonic stem-cell research. In district court they filed a complaint seeking declaratory and injunctive relief against appellee Secretary of Health and Human Services' implementation of regulations allowing federal funding of such research. They appeal from a district court order entering summary judgment in favor of the defendant. Because we conclude that the district court committed no error, we affirm the order and judgment under review.

. . . Beginning in 1996, Congress has regularly included in appropriation bills a rider called the Dickey–Wicker Amendment. The Dickey–Wicker Amendment prohibits NIH from funding "(1) the creation of a human embryo or embryos for research purposes; or (2) research in which a human embryo or embryos are destroyed, discarded, or knowingly subjected to risk of injury or death greater than that allowed for research on fetuses in utero under 45 C.F.R. 46.204(b) and [42 U.S.C. §289g(b)]." Id.

At the time of the adoption of the first Dickey–Wicker rider, scientists had not yet isolated embryonic stem cells (ESC), and the original enactment was apparently directed at another type of research performed on human embryos in the field of in vitro fertilization. By 1998, researchers had generated a stable line of ESCs available for further research. Although more mature stem cells were and remain available, many researchers consider the ESCs far more valuable because they are pluripotent—that is, they can be developed into any of nearly 200 different types of human cells for use in a broad range of medical research.

Isolating ESCs for research requires that the cells be removed from a human embryo, cultured, and stabilized into a "stem cell line." This process of "derivation" destroys the embryo. The cells from this line may then be used for years by researchers, who differentiate the cells into whatever kinds of cells they need for a particular research project. Thus, the initial derivation process requires the destruction of a human embryo. The particular research projects using the earlier derived stem cells, however, do not involve the destruction of any further embryos.

It is this distinction between funding research projects directly involving the destruction of a human embryo and projects using embryonic stem cells derived from an earlier destruction that underlies the controversy giving rise to the present litigation. In 2001, President George W. Bush, for ethical reasons, declared that federal funds would be used in research on embryonic stem cells only if such cells were drawn from one of the sixty or so stem cell lines already existing at the time of President Bush's declaration. President Bush later formalized this policy in an Executive Order.

So matters stood until 2009, when President Obama issued an Executive Order revoking [the previous Executive Order.] The Order stated that NIH "may support and conduct responsible, scientifically worthy human stem cell research, including human embryonic stem cell research, to the extent permitted by law."

As required by the Executive Order and after notice and comment, NIH issued new "Guidelines for Human Stem Cell Research," 74 Fed. Reg. 32,170 (July 7, 2009) (Guidelines). . . . Under the Guidelines, an ESC research project may receive NIH funding as long as it utilizes cells from lines (1) created by *in vitro* fertilization for reproductive purposes, (2) no longer needed for that purpose, and (3) voluntarily donated by the individuals who owned them— even if that line was derived after 2001. . . .

1.   DICKEY–WICKER

Appellants' first and principal argument is that the NIH guidelines violate the Dickey–Wicker ban on federal funding of "research in which a human embryo or embryos are destroyed." On this issue, the law of the case is established against them.

The purpose of the law-of-the-case doctrine is to ensure that "the *same* issue presented a second time in the *same case* in the *same court* should lead to the *same result*." . . . Briefly put, appellants contend that all ESC research is "research" in which a human embryo or embryos are destroyed and, therefore, NIH's guidelines violate Dickey–Wicker by authorizing federal funding of such research. This is precisely the same argument we rejected in our review of the preliminary injunction order.

Applying *Chevron* analysis, we held that NIH had reasonably interpreted Dickey–Wicker's ban on funding "research in which . . . embryos are destroyed" to allow federal funding of ESC research. We explained that "research" as used in Dickey–Wicker was a "flexible" (*i.e.,* ambiguous) term. It could be understood as the plaintiffs construed the term—an "extended process" that would include the initial derivation of stem cells. Or "research" could take on NIH's narrow interpretation as a "discrete project" separate from derivation. Given that ambiguity, we deferred under *Chevron* to NIH's permissible construction of Dickey–Wicker: "research" as used in Dickey–Wicker may reasonably be understood to mean a "discrete endeavor" that excludes the initial derivation of ESCs. Under that interpretation, Dickey–Wicker permits federal funding of research projects that utilize already-derived ESCs—which are not themselves embryos— because no "human embryo or embryos *are* destroyed" in such projects. . . .

2. Subjected to Risk

Appellants make a second argument that is intertwined with their first. They note that Dickey–Wicker also bans "research in which a human embryo or embryos are . . . knowingly subjected to risk of injury or death." §508(a)(2). . . . They theorize that conducting a federally funded ESC research project increases the demand for more ESC lines, which in turn incentivizes the destruction of more embryos to create those lines, thus subjecting those embryos to risk. NIH responds that no embryos are subjected to risk of injury or death in any ESC research project using already derived ESCs and not otherwise involving the use of embryos.

. . . Appellants' theory shifts focus from the embryo destroyed in the past to embryos for which an ESC research project "incentivizes" future destruction. But none of those embryos are "destroyed" or "subjected to risk" *in* an ESC research project. The language of Dickey–Wicker does not ban funding for, *e.g.,* "research which provides an incentive to harm, destroy, or place at risk human embryos." As we have held before, the NIH interpretation of the statute's actual language is reasonable.

NOTES AND QUESTIONS

1. *Embryos created for research vs. "leftover" embryos.* The current guidelines for federal funding on research involving human embryos are described briefly in *Sherley.* Among other things, the guidelines restrict funding to research on embryos "left over" from in vitro fertilization. This distinction appears to be based on a perceived moral difference between intentionally creating embryos for purposes of research in which the embryo would be destined at the outset for use and destruction, and using embryos that were created for reproductive purposes but were not, for one reason or another, implanted in a woman's uterus for development. (Estimates of the number of frozen embryos in 2004 were 400,000, but how many are, in effect, "leftover" is unknown. Cathy Kightlinger, Couples Fight Over Custody of Embryos, Indianapolis News, July 11, 2004, at A1.) Do you find this moral distinction persuasive?

Compare the views of Michael Sandel (who served on the President's Council on Bioethics and whose personal statement is included within the Council's report, supra) and William Fitzpatrick, whose views are expressed in Surplus Embryos, Nonreproductive Cloning, and the Intend/Foresee Distinction, 33 Hastings Ctr. Rpt. 29 (2003). Sandel argues that if cloning for research violates the respect owed the embryo, so do in vitro fertilization procedures that create and then discard excess embryos; "the moral arguments for research cloning and for research on leftover embryos stand or fall together." Fitzpatrick disagrees:

> [W]hile IVF doctors foresee that probably not all of the embryos they create for reproduction will wind up being needed, leaving some to be discarded or donated for research, they do not create embryos with the intention of destructively using them; nor do the researchers who derive stem cells from surplus IVF embryos. Only in the case of research cloning are we creating embryos with such an intention, exhibiting the distinctively exploitative and opportunistic attitude bound up with such a practice.

Do you find one of these positions more persuasive than the other?

B.   CAPABILITIES AND INTERESTS OF LIVING BEINGS

Although the moral status of human life in embryonic and fetal stages has captured the recent attention of policymakers, the public, the media, and bioethicists, there are other questions of personhood that remain just as vexing and have been in the past, and continue to be, the subject of heated debate. This section presents materials about a number of other forms of life (some clearly human, such as severely disabled newborns; others clearly not, such as animals) and considers their status as "persons" from the perspective of their capabilities (rather than their stage of development) and, separate from whether they should be recognized as persons, with all the attendant rights, considers how their interests stack up against other moral claims.

Recall philosopher Mary Ann Warren's list of traits that suggest when personhood status is appropriate. She writes, "Some human beings are not people, and there may well be people who are not human beings." She includes within the former category "defective human beings, with no appreciable mental capacity," and includes within the latter category, "self-aware robots or computers, should such be developed." Warren, supra.

Thus far, the law of our society has resolutely held fast to the idea that no matter how severely disabled a human being may be, he or she is nonetheless a person and entitled to be treated equally with other persons. Yet debate still continues about the ethical propriety of this view, especially when (1) other persons may benefit from the termination of the life of a human being whose own ability to experience life is severely limited or nonexistent, and (2) other living beings (such as certain animals) with greater capacities to think, feel, and otherwise experience life are treated much more poorly than humans with no such capacities.

The significance of capabilities to personhood status is considered first with respect to severely disabled individuals and then, by way of comparison, with respect to our society's treatment of animals. The possibilities of new forms of life are then considered: radically "enhanced" human beings, human–animal hybrids and "self-aware" robots.

In the following case the English court considered whether conjoined twins must be separated, when doing so would save the life of one, but cause the death of the other.

1.   Severely Disabled Individuals

In re A
(2000) 4 All E.R. 961

Opinion by Lord Justice WARD.

. . . In a nutshell the problem is this. Jodie and Mary are conjoined twins. They each have their own brain, heart and lungs and other vital organs and they each have arms and legs. They are joined at the lower abdomen. Whilst not underplaying the surgical complexities, they can be successfully separated.

But the operation will kill the weaker twin, Mary. That is because her lungs and heart are too deficient to oxygenate and pump blood through her body. Had she been born a singleton, she would not have been viable and resuscitation would have been abandoned. She would have died shortly after her birth. She is alive only because a common artery enables her sister, who is stronger, to circulate life-sustaining oxygenated blood for both of them. Separation would require the clamping and then the severing of that common artery. Within minutes of doing so Mary will die. Yet if the operation does not take place, both will die within three to six months, or perhaps a little longer, because Jodie's heart will eventually fail. The parents cannot bring themselves to consent to the operation. The twins are equal in their eyes and they cannot agree to kill one even to save the other. As devout Roman Catholics they sincerely believe that it is God's will that their children are afflicted as they are and they must be left in God's hands. The doctors are convinced they can carry out the operation so as to give Jodie a life which will be worthwhile. . . .

[A] preliminary issue: is this a fused body of two separate persons, each having a life in being?

. . . There was total unanimity [among the medical personnel involved in the case] about their individuality. The neonatologist said: "The twins are considered to be separate individuals. There are two heads, two brains and at different times of the day and night they exhibit different states of wakefulness/alertness and clearly their feeding abilities and patterns are very different."

The cardiologist said: "Although the twins share some common tissue, they each have separate hearts, brains, etc., and thus medically I feel are separate individuals."

In the face of that evidence it would be contrary to common-sense and to everyone's sensibilities to say that Mary is not alive or that there are not two separate persons. It is, therefore, unnecessary to examine the law in any depth at all. . . .

Here Mary has been born in the sense that she has an existence quite independent from her mother. The fact that Mary is dependent upon Jodie, or the fact that twins may be interdependent if they share heart and lungs, should not lead the law to fly in the face of the clinical judgment that each child is alive and that each child is separate both for the purposes of the civil law and the criminal law. . . .

I would not wish to leave this topic without saying firmly that the notions expressed in earlier times that Siamese twins were "monsters" is totally unacceptable, indeed repugnant and offensive to the dignity of these children in the light of current medical knowledge and social sensibility. I deprecate any idea of "monstrous birth."

NOTES AND QUESTIONS

1. *"Individuality."*   Rather than basing its decision that Mary is a person on whether she could have been born alive separate from Jodie (a test somewhat like the viability of a fetus), the court turns instead to the opinion of medical professionals on the "individuality" of the twins. How is this a different test than physical separation? What would be the implications of a legal test of individuality on determining the personhood of embryos or fetuses?

2. *Utilitarianism and personhood analysis.*   The court in the case In re A ultimately held that the conjoined twins could be separated even though it would inevitably cause Mary's death. In so deciding, the court emphasized the unique circumstances involved in the case—if Mary were not separated from Jodie, both Jodie and Mary would die; only separation would enable Jodie to live. Mary would ultimately have died within the year anyway. Is this simply a utilitarian calculus? How do utilitarianism and personhood theory mesh—or do they mesh? Do you think the court properly respected Mary's rights as a person?

CHALLENGING ISSUES: INFANTS WITH ANENCEPHALY AND PERSONS IN A PERSISTENT VEGETATIVE STATE

Certainly the case of Mary and Jodie is unique, but there are many possibilities for hastening the death of someone "about to die" or someone who will forever lack consciousness to save the life of another human being. In particular, the possibility of taking the organs of still living anencephalic infants for the benefit of other infants in desperate need of a transplant has been debated for years. Anencephaly "is a birth defect invariably fatal, in which the child typically is born with only a 'brain stem' but otherwise lacks a human brain." In re T.A.C.P., 609 So. 2d 588 (Fla. 1992). If it were permissible to remove the vital organs of such infants while they were still breathing, those organs would remain healthy and transplantable because of continued oxygenation. If it were necessary to wait until the infant's death to harvest the organs, they would suffer a deterioration that would likely make the organs useless for transplantation.

In the case of T.A.C.P., the Florida Supreme Court considered whether the parents of an anencephalic infant could donate her organs; because such a donation would violate the rule against taking the vital organs of a still-living person (the "dead donor rule"), the court considered (and rejected) the proposition that the infant might be dead. (The case is reprinted in Chapter 13.) This ruling appears to have been part of the impetus for the revision, in 1994, of the opinion of the Council on Ethical and Judicial Affairs of the American Medical Association regarding the propriety of harvesting the organs of anencephalic newborns for transplant purposes. Whereas a previous opinion had expressed disapproval of the idea, this new opinion stated that it "is ethically acceptable to transplant the organs of anencephalic neonates even before the neonates die, as long as there is parental consent and certain other safeguards are followed." The report of the AMA's ethics council supported the taking of organs from anencephalic infants without claiming that such infants were not persons or were not alive. Instead, the report stated that the dead donor rule protected the *fundamental interest in life* of the persons from whom the organs might be taken. The purpose of the rule was not furthered by prohibiting the taking from anencephalic infants because they had *no interest in life.* The report reads:

> Because they have never experienced consciousness and will never experience consciousness, anencephalic neonates cannot have interests of any kind. They cannot experience any pleasure or pain; they have no thoughts, memories, or sensations, and they have no ability to communicate. If their lives are shortened, they lose days of life, but they have no awareness of that loss. If there is a loss, it is a

loss for others, whether for their parents or society generally. Similarly, the value in the life of an anencephalic neonate is a value only for others. The neonate feels no better or worse by living longer or by not living at all. Accordingly, prohibiting parental donation or organs from anencephalic neonates cannot be justified in terms of protecting the interests of the neonates themselves.

Council on Ethical and Judicial Affairs, American Medical Association, The Use of Anencephalic Neonates as Organ Donors, 273 JAMA 1614 (1995).

The report further stated that according to a survey of leading medical experts in anencephaly and leading experts in ethics, two-thirds of those surveyed considered the use of organs from anencephalic infants "intrinsically moral," and over half supported legal changes that would permit the use of such organs in transplant. Despite this support from experts, the reaction of the general medical community to issuance of the report was negative and it was withdrawn.

Whereas the controversial report of the AMA ethics council approved the use of anencephalic infants as organ donors because they had no cognizable interests, other commentators have argued that they should be considered and treated as "nonpersons" or as dead. The fact that such infants permanently lack consciousness seems to be the most compelling argument to regard them as nonpersons.

The issue of taking organs from anencephalic infants appears to have receded in recent years, perhaps for a variety of reasons. Proponents of using such infants' organs have been unable to achieve broad support for the idea in the face of substantial ethical and legal obstacles. In addition, the availability of prenatal testing for the condition followed by abortion has reduced the number of infants born with anencephaly, so that the potential supply of organs has been significantly reduced.

Nevertheless, the debate about the personhood status of such infants or the interests they possess remains important because of its potential application, by analogy, to persons living in a permanent vegetative state, who also permanently lack consciousness.

1.   What do you think of the argument that infants with anencephaly are not persons and therefore their organs might be harvested while they are still living to save the lives of other newborns?
2.   Even if infants with anencephaly are persons, might their organs still be harvested because they have no interest in living (the suggestion of the AMA ethics council report)? How do you assess the utilitarian claims of using the infants as organ donors? How analogous is this situation to the case of In re A?
3.   What similarities and differences can you identify between infants with anencephaly and persons in a permanent vegetative state as suitable sources of transplantable organs?
4.   How should such individuals be treated in comparison to higher functioning nonhuman animals? (See the reading by Steven Wise below.)[2]

_____

2. In Chapter 8, the question of the moral and legal status of infants with anencephaly and persons in a permanent vegetative state is revisited. There we consider the argument that such individuals might be considered a suitable source of organs because they are "dead."–EDS.

2.   *Nonhuman Animals*

Steven Wise, Dismantling the Barriers to Legal Rights for Nonhuman Animals
7 Animal L. 9 (2001)*

JEROM'S STORY

Jerom died on February 13, 1996, ten days shy of his fourteenth birthday. The teenager was dull, bloated, depressed, sapped, anemic, and plagued by diarrhea. He had not played in fresh air for eleven years. As a thirty-month-old infant, he had been intentionally infected with HIV virus SF2. At the age of four, he had been infected with another HIV strain, LAV-1. A month short of five, he was infected with yet a third strain, NDK. Throughout the Iran-Contra hearings, almost to the brink of the Gulf War, he sat in the small, windowless, cinder-block Infectious Disease Building. Then he was moved a short distance to a large, windowless, gray concrete box, one of eleven bleak steel-and-concrete cells 9 feet by 11 feet by 8.5 feet. Throughout the war and into Bill Clinton's campaign for a second term as president, he languished in his cell. This was the Chimpanzee Infectious Disease Building. It stood in the Yerkes Regional Primate Research Center near grassy tree-lined Emory University, minutes from the bustle of downtown Atlanta, Georgia. . . .

The Ancient Greeks denied reason, intellect, thought and belief to every nonhuman animal, and sometimes even the ability to perceive, remember, or experience. Nonhuman animals were nothing but robots. They were wrong. Certainly bonobos (pygmy chimpanzees) and chimpanzees, such as Jerom, are conscious, probably self-conscious, are aware of their surroundings, feel pain and suffer. They act intentionally. They solve problems insightfully. They understand cause and effect. They use and make tools. They live in diverse cultures. They imitate, cooperate, and flourish in rough and tumble societies so political that they are routinely dubbed "Machiavellian." Given the appropriate opportunity and motivation, they can teach, deceive, self-medicate, and empathize. They can learn symbols, words, and numbers. They can count, perhaps to ten. They can add simple numbers and even fractions. They can mentally share the world with humans and others of their own species. They symbolically play.

They absorb words like sponges and three-year-old children. Enculturated by humans, they can understand spoken English at the level of a three-year-old, without being taught. The bonobo, Kanzi, has shown, for example, that when one ball lies before his eyes and another sits in the bedroom, he can differentiate one request to "go get the ball that's in the bedroom" from another to "take the ball to the bedroom." They produce human language like a two-year-old, and the language they produce appears marked by a proto-grammar. . . . That humans, bonobos, and chimpanzees share so many advanced cognitive abilities is hardly remarkable when you consider that we share about 99.5% of our

---

* Remarks from an address at The Great Hall, Faneuil Hall, Boston, Mass. (Feb. 8, 2000).

working DNA and that a mere fifty genes may account for our mental differences.

"All law," said one Roman jurist, "was established for men's sake." And why not? Everything else was. The Ancient Greeks claimed that plants were made for animals and animals made for us and that men were by nature superior to women and that slaves lived for their masters. Horses existed to labor for us and the pig was created for slaughter. . . . When Shakespeare was alive, it was claimed that apes and parrots had been put on earth to make us laugh. The year that Washington was born, we were informed that the tides had been created to move ships in and out of ports. Half a decade before the American Civil War, the California Supreme Court barred Chinese witnesses from testifying against whites in court because they were a race "whom nature has marked as inferior and who are incapable of progress or intellectual development beyond a certain point." Two years later, the United States Supreme Court wrote in the infamous Dred Scott case that, at the time of the American Revolution, blacks were thought to exist so far below whites in the scale of created beings that they had no rights that whites were bound to respect. In 1965, a Virginia judge upheld a statute that forbade marriages between people of different races because "Almighty God created the races white, black, yellow, malay, and red, and he placed them on separate continents. . . . The fact that He separated the races shows that he did not intend for the races to mix."

These beliefs about the purposes of horses and oxen, women and races, ocean tides and pigs, parrots, slaves, and apes may appear to be unconnected, but they are not. These believers heard the universe whisper that it had been divinely designed for a single end—themselves. It was not just that we were different from every other animal, but that our value was radically incommensurable with the value of anything else. We humans like to hear that.

. . . Yet these hoary ideas play a critical role in perpetuating the "legal thinghood" of nonhuman animals. They were the death of Jerom! For the teaching that all law was made for humans, implicit throughout ancient Western law, was incorporated by Justinian into his immensely influential legal codes. Eventually it was absorbed into the legal writings of the great lawyers, judges, and commentators of the English common law and received nearly whole by their American descendants. While philosophers and scientists have recanted, the law has not. The belief that Jerom was somehow placed on this earth for us was what allowed us to torture and kill him.

. . . Basic rights protect basic interests. Most fundamentally, autonomy generates the dignity that produces the basic legal rights to bodily integrity and bodily liberty. These "dignity-rights" form the core of liberty. But the autonomy that judges respect need not be complex. We need to be conscious, have the capacity to desire, act intentionally, and have a sense of self that allows us to experience our lives as being lived by us. Jerom had it. We need not have advanced mental abilities such a moral sense or a sense of justice. If we did, hundreds of millions of humans would be ineligible.

. . . Some have argued that the issue is actually one of kind. Many humans lack such advanced mental abilities as a sense of justice or morality. But, this argument goes, the abilities of the advanced should be imputed to every human, regardless of actual abilities. But this assumes that we should determine how an individual is to be treated, not on the basis of her qualities but on the basis of the qualities of others. . . .

Some humans—infants, very young children, babies born without major parts of their brains, the severely mentally retarded, and those in persistent vegetative states—are awarded basic legal rights even though they lack autonomy. I applaud this. But if judges recognize the basic rights of these humans, then reject the same rights of chimpanzees and bonobos with much greater autonomy, they act perversely and their decisions cannot be defended except as acts of naked prejudice. At some point the disparity between the "legal thinghood" of a mentally complex chimpanzee or bonobo and the legal personhood of profoundly retarded humans or babies born without brains becomes completely indefensible.

NOTES AND QUESTIONS

1. *Distinguishing between legal persons and legal things.*   What are the qualities that Wise identifies as sufficient to qualify bonobos and chimpanzees as "persons"? Does he suggest that human beings lacking these qualities (such as infants with anencephaly) should not be considered persons?

2. *The capacity to suffer and equating like interests.*   Other animal liberationists, such as philosopher Peter Singer, have argued against the use of animals in biomedical experimentation on other grounds. Rather than pointing to the cognitive abilities of higher animals as the reason they must be treated with more respect and care, he points to the capacity of animals to suffer like humans. In this respect, he takes a more utilitarian than rights-based approach, arguing that the interests of all beings who have the capacity to experience pleasure and pain should be taken into account on the principle of equal consideration of interests. Singer has written,

> If a being suffers there can be no moral justification for refusing to take that suffering into consideration. No matter what the nature of the being, the principle of equality requires that its suffering be counted equally with the like suffering—insofar as rough comparisons can be made—of any other being. If a being is not capable of suffering, or of experiencing enjoyment or happiness, there is nothing to be taken into account. So the limit of sentience (using the term as a convenient if not strictly accurate shorthand for the capacity to suffer and/or experience enjoyment) is the only defensible boundary of concern for the interests of others. To mark this boundary by some other characteristic like intelligence or rationality would be to mark it in an arbitrary manner. Why not choose some other characteristic, like skin color?
>
> Racists violate the principle of equality by giving greater weight to the interests of members of their own race when there is a clash between their interests and the interests of those of another race. Sexists violate the principle of equality by favoring the interests of their own sex. Similarly, speciesists allow the interests of their own species to override the greater interests of members of other species. The pattern is identical in each case.

Peter Singer, Animal Liberation (2d ed. 1990).

Singer would rather we abolished categories such as "person" or "thing" and treat all similar interests with equal concern. What do you think of this approach? What would it mean for research use of embryos as compared to research use of animals?

3. *"Speciesism."*   Carl Cohen has vigorously supported the use of animals in biomedical research and in doing so has countered both the idea that animals have rights, in the form of personhood rights (as Wise argues), and that their interests must be taken into equal consideration with human interests (Singer's approach). "I am a speciesist," he firmly announces and adds that everyone else should be one, too, if they are to engage in morally right conduct, which requires distinguishing between species. Against the rights approach, Cohen argues that the holders of rights must be "beings of a kind capable [of] exercising or responding to moral claims"—in other words, they must have the capacity to understand moral claims and make moral judgments. Humans have this capacity, and animals do not. See Carl Cohen, The Case for the Use of Animals in Biomedical Research, 315 New Eng. J. Med. 865 (1986). Under this view, humans may still have an obligation to treat animals with decency and care, but that does not mean that animals have rights.

Cohen further dismisses the "interests" approach on the grounds that it makes two errors: the first being that it counts the pains of all animate beings equally, when there are morally relevant distinctions between them; the second being that the true utilitarian calculus must take into account the benefits of the biomedical research in which animals are used. "The elimination of horrible disease, the increase of longevity, the avoidance of great pain, the saving of lives, and the improvement of the quality of lives (for humans and for animals) achieved through research using animals is so incalculably great that the argument of these critics, systematically pursued, establishes not their conclusion but its reverse: to refrain from using animals in biomedical research is, in utilitarian grounds, morally wrong." Id. What do you think of Cohen's approach?

3.   Future Prospects: Radically "Enhanced" Humans, Human–Animal Chimera, and Robots

Although the scientific ability to produce new life forms with human qualities does not yet exist, the possibility of such future creation has fascinated writers for hundreds of years. In the following excerpt, law professor George J. Annas explores how the classic story of Frankenstein embodies some of the themes that continue to mark the discussion about whether such endeavors should be permitted and to what end they might lead.

> ## George J. Annas, Mapping the Human Genome and the Meaning of Monster Mythology
> ### 39 Emory L.J. 629 (1990)

Mary Shelley's masterpiece, Frankenstein, has become the metaphor for all scientific attempts to create life. In her gothic novel, Victor Frankenstein is obsessed with creating life from a construction of dead body parts. Shelley does not explain how Victor was able to "infuse a spark of being into the lifeless thing," but she does describe Victor's emotions upon seeing "the dull yellow eye of the creature open":

> His limbs were in proportion, and I had selected his features as beautiful. Beautiful! Great God! His yellow skin scarcely covered the work of muscles and arteries beneath; his hair was of a lustrous black, and flowing; his teeth of a pearly whiteness.

But Victor's burst of emotion at achieving his goal quickly changes to horror as he gazes at the creature's "watery eyes . . . his shrivelled complexion and straight black lips": "now that I had finished, the beauty of the dream vanished, and breathless horror and disgust filled my heart."

Victor leaves his laboratory to sleep, and the creature escapes. The remainder of the novel deals with the creature, which is never given a name but is simply referred to as "the monster," and its relationship to Victor. Indeed, it seems most reasonable to consider the monster either as Victor's alter ego, or as a projection of his inner thoughts made flesh. Perhaps this is why we often think of the monster, instead of its creator, as Frankenstein. Victor's creation eventually kills his young nephew William, his friend Clerval, his wife Elizabeth, and, indirectly, Victor himself.

At one point in the story, the monster convinces Victor to create a wife for him. In this scene, Victor is seen as God the creator, and the monster as his Adam, or alternatively, as Lucifer, the fallen angel. But having constructed the monster's would-be mate on a remote island, Victor decides he cannot give her life for fear that she and the monster might propagate a "race of devils" that would "make the very existence of the species of man a condition precarious and full of terror." Victor consequently tears the female's body apart while the monster looks on, letting out a "howl of devilish despair and revenge. . . ." This scene, as much as any other, focuses the theme of the novel: the scientist's simultaneous capacity for creation and destruction.

The President's Commission for the Study of Ethical Problems in Medicine and Biomedical and Behavioral Research was established by Congress in 1978 and operated until 1983 as an ethical advisory body to the President and Congress. The commission prepared the report, "Splicing Life," from which the following excerpt was taken, in response to a letter received by President Carter in July 1980 from Jewish, Catholic, and Protestant church associations expressing concern that no governmental body "was exercising adequate oversight or control, nor addressing the fundamental ethical questions" of genetic engineering techniques, particularly as applied to human beings. Understanding its contribution primarily as "stimulating thoughtful, long-term discussion," the commission raised and discussed various viewpoints regarding a number of ethical and social concerns related to human genetic engineering. Its conclusions were limited, but included a general endorsement of continued research into and use of genetic engineering techniques to improve human health, albeit with greater regulatory oversight.

*President's Commission for the Study of Problems in
Medicine and Biomedical and Behavioral Research,
Splicing Life: A Report on the Social and Ethical
Issues of Engineering with Human Beings*
56–59 (1982)

CREATING NEW LIFE FORMS

If "creating new life forms" is simply producing organisms with novel characteristics, then human beings create new life forms frequently and have done so since they first learned to cultivate new characteristics in plants and breed new traits in animals. Presumably the idea is that gene splicing creates new life forms, rather than merely modifying old ones, because it "breaches species barriers" by combining DNA from different species—groups of organisms that cannot mate to produce fertile offspring.

Genetic engineering is not the first exercise of humanity's ability to create new life forms through nonsexual reproduction. The creation of hybrid plants seems no more or no less natural than the development of a new strain of *E. coli* bacteria through gene splicing. Further, genetic engineering cannot accurately be called unique in that it involves the creation of new life forms through processes that do not occur in nature without human intervention. . . . [S]cientists have found that the transfer of DNA between organisms of different species occurs in nature without human intervention. Yet, as one eminent scientist in the field has pointed out, it would be unwarranted to assume that a dramatic increase in the frequency of such transfers through human intervention is not problematic simply because DNA transfer sometimes occurs naturally.

In the absence of specific religious prohibitions, either revealed or derived by rational argument from religious premises, it is difficult to see why "breaching species barriers" as such is irreligious or otherwise objectionable. In fact, the very notion that there are barriers that must be breached prejudges the issue. The question is simply whether there is something intrinsically wrong with intentionally crossing species lines. Once the question is posed in this way the answer must be negative—unless one is willing to condemn the production of tangelos by hybridizing tangerines and grapefruits or the production of mules by the mating of asses with horses.

There may nonetheless be two distinct sources of concern about crossing species lines that deserve serious consideration. First, gene splicing affords the possibility of creating hybrids that can reproduce themselves (unlike mules, which are sterile). So the possibility of self-perpetuating "mistakes" adds a new dimension of concern, although here again, the point is not that crossing species lines is inherently wrong, but that it may have undesirable consequences and that these consequences may multiply beyond human control. . . .

Second, there is the issue of whether particular crossings of species— especially the mixing of human and nonhuman genes—might not be illicit. The moral revulsion at the creation of human–animal hybrids may be traced in part to the prohibition against sexual relations between human beings and lower animals. Sexual relations with lower animals are thought to degrade human beings and insult their God-given dignity as the highest of God's creatures. But unease at the prospect of human–animal hybrids goes beyond sexual prohibitions.

The possibility of creating such hybrids calls into question basic assumptions about the relationship of human beings to other living things. For example, those who believe that the current treatment of animals—in experimentation, food production, and sport—is morally suspect would not be alone in being troubled by the prospect of exploitive or insensitive treatment of creatures that possess even more human-like qualities than chimpanzees or porpoises do. Could genetic engineering be used to develop a group of virtual slaves—partly human, partly lower animal—to do people's bidding? Paradoxically, the very characteristics that would make such creatures more valuable than any existing animals (that is, their heightened cognitive powers and sensibilities) would also make the moral propriety of their subservient role more problematic. Dispassionate appraisal of the long history of gratuitous destruction and suffering that humanity has visited upon the other inhabitants of the earth indicates that such concerns should not be dismissed as fanciful.

Accordingly, the objection to the creation of new life forms by crossing species lines (whether through gene splicing or otherwise) reflects the concern that human beings lack the God-like knowledge and wisdom required for the exercise of these God-like powers. Specifically, people worry that inter-specific hybrids that are partially human in their genetic makeup will be like Dr. Frankenstein's monster. A striking lesson of the Frankenstein story is the uncontrollability and uncertainty of the consequences of human interferences with the natural order. Like the tale of the Sorcerer's apprentice or the myth of the golem created from lifeless dust by the 16th century rabbi, Loew of Prague, the story of Dr. Frankenstein's monster serves as a reminder of the difficulty of restoring order if a creation intended to be helpful proves harmful instead. Indeed, each of these tales conveys a painful irony: in seeking to extend their control over the world, people may lessen it. The artifices they create to do their bidding may rebound destructively against them—the slave may become the master.

Suggesting that someone lacks sufficient knowledge or wisdom to engage in an activity the person knows how to perform thus means that the individual has insufficient knowledge of the consequences of that activity or insufficient wisdom to cope with those consequences. But if this is the rational kernel of the admonition against playing God, then the use of gene splicing technology is not claimed to be wrong as such but wrong because of its potential consequences. Understood in this way, the slogan that crossing species barriers is playing God does not end the debate, but does make a point of fundamental importance. It emphasizes that any realistic assessment of the potential consequences of the new technology must be founded upon a sober recognition of human fallibility and ignorance. At bottom, the warning not to play God is closely related to the Socratic injunction "know thyself": in this case, acknowledge the limits of understanding and prediction, rather than assuming that people can foresee all the consequences of their actions or plan adequately for every eventuality.

Any further examination of the notion that the hybridization of species, at least when one of the species is human, is intrinsically wrong (and not merely wrong as a consequence of what is done with the hybrids) involves elaboration of two points. First, what characteristics are uniquely human, setting humanity apart from all other species? And second, does the wrong lie in bestowing some but not all of these characteristics on the new creation or does it stem from depriving the being that might otherwise have arisen from the human genetic material of the opportunity to have a totally human makeup?

> ## *Bert Gordijn, Converging NBIC Technologies for Improving Human Performance: A Critical Assessment of the Novelty and the Prospects of the Project*
> ### 34 J. L. Med. & Ethics 726 (2006)

In recent times, optimistic views have been advanced about the convergence of nanotechnology, biotechnology, information technology, and cognitive science and the way in which this so-called "NBIC convergence" could and should be used to enhance human performance, such as to improve our sensory, motorial and/or cognitive abilities, as well as our moods and physical appearance.

. . . Up to now we have been improving our performance through education, study and exercise. Furthermore, we have developed houses, clothes, and technological instruments like telephones, telescopes, cars and computers—thus technologically transforming our natural surroundings to serve the improvement of our performance.

In addition to these traditional ways of improving performance, the proponents of NBIC convergence now advocate that we start technologically transforming our own blueprint. Of course, we have already taken the first cautious steps to technologically reshape ourselves, for example by means of cosmetic surgery and dentistry, "smart drugs," mood enhancers, sports doping, and growth hormones. Yet, the outlook of the proponents of NBIC convergence fundamentally diverges from past practice and experience. In the dominant view of the current medical establishment, enhancement by means of technological transformation is still seen as relatively peripheral and highly ambivalent. In the NBIC convergence program, on the other hand, it is esteemed as something pivotal and highly positive. Moreover, the kind of medico-technological autotransformation that is advocated by the proponents of NBIC convergence has a more drastic dimension. It involves radically transforming ourselves in order to improve our sensory, motorial and cognitive skills and abilities.

After all, proponents propose the use of brain-to-brain interaction and brain–machine interfaces (using direct connections to our neural system). Furthermore, we are to have new organs, new skills and new genes. With an information-gulping sixth sense, for example, we might be able to instantaneously gulp down the information of an entire book, making it a structural part of our wetware "ready for inferencing, reference, etc., with some residual sense of the whole, as part of the gulp experience." If these future prospects of NBIC convergence become reality, we will be entering a genuinely new age which will bear witness to pervasive use of NBIC sciences and technologies to transform our biological design for the purpose of enhancing performance.

SHOULD WE BE OPTIMISTIC?

At this early stage it is not easy to say just where the project of improving human performance by means of NBIC technologies will lead. However, let us suppose—for the sake of the discussion—that future developments in NBIC sciences and technologies will indeed enable us to reshape our biological design, just as the advocates of NBIC convergence envision.

It is incontestable that some enhancements of our design might turn out to have genuinely valuable effects. At first sight, it is not difficult to imagine a plethora of positive aspects attached to having better sensory, motorial and cognitive skills and abilities. Yet it seems likely that there also may be negative consequences that emerge in proportion to the magnitude of the adjustments and modifications that are introduced through NBIC. . . .

Personal Identity

When a human being thinks about his own person, he particularly examines issues such as: What am I good at? How do I perform? Do I act responsibly? What is my particular character? What makes me unique? What can I remember? What is my life-history? If a human being were regularly subjected to new NBIC-enabled technological interventions to improve his sensory, motorial or cognitive abilities, it could become increasingly difficult to answer such questions. Improving the cognitive abilities of an individual, for example, could mean that certain mental efforts almost cease, and one could become extremely dependent on high-performance implants. As a result, that individual might find it increasingly difficult to say which of his thoughts and actions still constitute a *personal* achievement. Thus, it is difficult to foretell whether our satisfaction with our NBIC-enabled higher achievements will be increased, or whether our expectations will merely shift to the right.

If emotional, as well as cognitive, enhancement systems were to become available for implantation, it might become increasingly difficult to determine the characteristics specific to an individual. If, in addition, many different people were to share the possibility of being permanently connected to databases, the exclusiveness of possessing particular information would become relative, which in turn would reduce the uniqueness of those people. Implantation of brain-to-brain communication systems—which would "wire up" different individuals to enable them to instantaneously exchange their conscious thoughts and experiences—could blur the borderline between the self and the cyberthink community. In the face of such mental wiring, how are one's own thoughts and experiences and life-history to be kept separate from those of others? And the borders between the real world and the virtual world would become increasingly blurred. As a result, it would become more and more difficult to determine one's own personal identity.

Blurred Self-Perception as a Human Being

Widespread and frequent use of NBIC technologies to enhance our biological design will make the symbiosis between man and technology increasingly narrower. We would not only become more and more embedded in all manner of technological systems and networks, but our bodies themselves would increasingly become products of technology. This process can be referred to as "artifactualization" of human beings.

This process of artifactualization will probably be accompanied by a second process that is likely to be stimulated by future NBIC progress: technological systems will increasingly be developed along the lines of organic systems. This is already happening in the fields of artificial intelligence, artificial life, robotics and neural computing networks, to name just a few examples. In the long term it is hoped that certain technological systems will be able to imitate various human traits or skills. This process can be termed an "anthropomorphization" of technology.

The combination of these two processes, the artifactualization of human beings and the anthropomorphization of technology, could, long term, lead to the following problem: pairs of opposites which have been around for hundreds of years, like "nature/nurture," "organic/inorganic," "conscious/unconscious," and "living/nonliving" could become fundamentally nebulous. And yet for a very long time such pairs of opposites have represented essential elements within human self-perception. Their growing fuzziness or even disappearance would necessitate fundamental changes in human self-perception to fit the new situation. All in all, the increasing confusion and the fundamental changes in connection with human self-perception might give rise to feelings of uneasiness, creeping disorientation and even existential panic. The very foundations of our image of mankind would be shaken.

NOTES AND QUESTIONS

1. *The Frankenstein metaphor.*   When people evoke the Frankenstein metaphor to explain their opposition to genetic engineering, what concerns are they expressing? How legitimate do you think these concerns are?

2. *Problematic because of consequences or intrinsically wrong?*   In the reprinted portion of the commission's report, we see an attempt to distinguish between those objections to creating new life forms that are based on undesirable consequences and those that are based on the idea that it is intrinsically wrong to do so. Do you find one line of argument more persuasive than the other? What undesirable consequences from the hybridization of species are of concern? What troubling consequences from radically altering human beings through NBIC technologies does Gordijn identify?

3. *Science and uses of human–animal chimera.*   Human–animal chimeras or hybrids might be formed in a number of ways. One method that has been successful in producing a "geep," a combination of a sheep and a goat, combined and manipulated portions of embryos from the two different species to produce a single embryo that was implanted in a surrogate sheep. The resulting "chimera" consists of some cells from one species and other cells from the other species, rather than an actual genetic mix within any single cell. For this reason, chimera, although they can reproduce, will produce an animal that is of one or the other species; in the case of the "geep," either a sheep or a goat. A human–animal chimera could theoretically be formed in the same way. Possible uses for

a human–animal chimera would be research on human disease and the development of organs for human transplantation. See Nathan A. Adams, IV, Creating Clones, Kids & Chimera: Liberal Democratic Compromise at the Crossroads, 17 Notre Dame J.L. Ethics & Pub. Pol'y 71 (2003); Thomas Magnani, The Patentability of Human–Animal Chimeras, 14 Berkeley Tech. L.J. 443 (1999); Michael D. Rivard, Comment, Toward a General Theory of Constitutional Personhood: A Theory of Constitutional Personhood for Transgenic Humanoid Species, 39 UCLA L. Rev. 1425 (1992). Do you think such development should be permitted?

4. *Patenting human–animal chimeras.*   In 1980, the United States Supreme Court in the closely decided (5–4) and controversial case Diamond v. Chakrabarty, 447 U.S. 303 (1980), upheld the patentability of a living organism—a genetically altered bacterium that can digest oil and therefore be used in cleaning up oil spills. Since then, patents have been permitted on a number of genetically altered animals, including mammals, some of which have incorporated human genes, although decisions are made on a case-by-case basis without clear guidelines. See Ryan M.T. Iwasaka, Note, Chakrabarty to Chimeras: The Growing Need for Evolutionary Biology in Patent Law, 109 Yale L.J. 1505 (2000).

Although a human–animal chimera has yet to be developed, a patent application for one was filed in 1998 by biologist Stuart Newman and social critic Jeremy Rifkin for the purpose of blocking the use of such technology. In the event a patent had been issued, the applicants' stated plan was to prevent others from developing such a chimera for the 20-year statutory patent period, during which time social awareness of the moral problems associated with the creation of such beings would be heightened. A denial of the patent application would also serve their intended purpose of highlighting these unresolved moral concerns and focus attention on the current law regarding patentable organisms.

Newman and Rifkin's patent application was denied, the letter of disallowance stating that the claimed invention was not patentable subject matter because under a broad interpretation it "embraces" a human being. In an interview at the time of the Newman and Rifkin application, the PTO Commissioner further said that "there will be no patents on monsters, at least not while I'm commissioner."

The letter of disallowance's reference to the human nature of the proposed invention would appear to relate to a statement issued by the United States Patent and Trademark Office in 1987 that human beings were not patentable subject matter, because "the grant of a limited, but exclusive property right in a human being is prohibited by the Constitution." The constitutional reference is presumably to the Thirteenth Amendment, which prohibits human slavery. See Patents: PTO Disallows Bio-Patent Application as Crossing Line to "Embrace" Humans, BNA Patent, Trademark & Copyright Law Daily News, June 21, 1999. Critics of the current law (or lack thereof) on the patentability of human–animal hybrids maintain that the PTO's reference to the Thirteenth Amendment is inadequate because although the amendment prohibits ownership of other human beings, it does not define what a human being is. Moreover, a patent does not actually grant ownership rights in the being created, but only grants rights to prevent others from making, owning, or selling the invention, so the issue is not properly understood as one of slavery. See Rachel Fishman, Patenting Human Beings: Do Sub-Human Creatures Deserve Constitutional Protection?, 15 Am. J.L. & Med. 461 (1989).

More critical than the question of whether a human–animal chimera is patentable is the question whether it would have a right to treatment, under the Constitution and otherwise, as a human being or person. Even if not recognized as such, would it be entitled to a certain "special respect" in the manner in which it would be treated, as the *Davis* court suggested of human embryos? Although these latter questions are the more critical, the patent issue has received more attention to date, probably because its immediacy is more apparent—first, a human–animal chimera does not yet exist whose rights or treatment are in question, and second, the Newman–Rifkin patent application and the patenting of other living organisms places the patentability issue in the forefront. Moreover, if patents are ever permitted in human–animal hybrids, such that valuable property rights are recognized as belonging to their creators, it will be more difficult to unseat those vested property rights by claims to the inherent rights belonging to the creation.

5. *Bibliographic note.* For an excellent collection of articles on the ethics of crossing species boundaries, see 3 American Journal of Bioethics (August 2003).

CHALLENGING ISSUES: "SELF-AWARE" ROBOTS

Could a robot or computer be developed in the future that could ever be considered a person, and thus entitled to the rights of persons? What qualities, in your view, would such a robot or computer have to possess to qualify for consideration as a person?

C.   WRONGFUL LIFE, WRONGFUL BIRTH

1.   Bioethical and Social Perspectives

Wrongful birth suits generally are understood as claims brought by parents arguing that they would have terminated a pregnancy that resulted in the birth of an ill or disabled child had proper testing been performed and/or had the results been adequately communicated to them. In contrast, wrongful life suits generally refer to suits brought by a child born ill or disabled. The child's suit claims that the child would not have been born had the defendant advised the child's parents of the risk of disability or illness before the child's birth. Many more courts recognize wrongful birth claims than recognize wrongful life claims. See, e.g., Harbeson v. Parke-Davis, Inc., 656 P.2d 483 (1983); Turpin v. Sortini, 643 P.2d 954 (Cal. 1982); Rosen v. Katz, No. 93-394A, 1996 Mass. Super. LEXIS 618 (Mass. Super. Ct. 1996); Procanik v. Cillo, 478 A.2d 755 (N.J. 1984).

Courts have often refused to recognize the wrongful life claim because it is difficult—and perhaps presumptuous—to compare a particular life with non-life. See Smith v. Cote, 513 A.2d 341 (N.H. 1986) (rejecting wrongful life cause of action). (See Chapter 4 for discussion of disability rights critique of embryo selection and abortion to avoid disabled or ill children.) Some commentators, however, argue that wrongful life claims should be entertained more widely. Mark Strasser, whose article appears below, argues that in light of courts' readiness to entertain wrongful birth and wrongful death cases, they should also recognize wrongful life claims. (Wrongful death cases in the context of this section involve claims against someone—often a health care professional—whose acts allegedly contributed to the death of a fetus in utero.) Strasser further argues that wrongful life claims should be entertained in light of the respect paid for "subjective quality of life preferences in refusal of treatment jurisprudence." Mark Strasser, Wrongful Life, Wrongful Birth, Wrongful Death, and the Right to Refuse Treatment: Can Reasonable Jurisdictions Recognize All But One?, 64 Mo. L. Rev. 29, 73 (1999).

Both wrongful birth and wrongful life claims are increasingly likely to make allegations about preconception and prenatal genetic tests that should have been performed but were not, or about genetic tests that were misinterpreted or the results of which were not communicated to the prospective parent or parents. Other wrongful birth and wrongful life suits involve claims about other forms of testing and diagnosis during pregnancy, including rubella titre testing, amniocentesis, chorionic villus sampling of fetal cells, and ultrasound. These suits raise important questions about the kinds of tests that should be offered, which is related to the "kind of child" they expect or desire, and about the willingness of the law to entertain such expectations and desires.

> ## Jeffrey R. Botkin, Prenatal Diagnosis and the Selection of Children
> ### 30 Fla. St. U. L. Rev. 265, 273-276 (2002)

[Several authors] argue from a "right to life" perspective that one of the very foundations of modern law and civilized society is that life has enormous intrinsic value.

> [W]rongful birth/life claims . . . require a new legal theory, in that life itself is considered a wrong, and death is preferred over life with disabilities. By deviating from the general principle, historically found in civilized law, that life, even with disabilities, is valuable and that only wrongful death is compensable, wrongful birth/life actions are a radical departure from fundamental legal philosophy.[29]

Similarly, authors writing from a disabilities rights perspective assert that it is simply wrong that those with disabilities lead lives of hopeless despair. The greatest difficulties for those with impairments, it is claimed, are often not due to the condition per se, but to the discriminatory attitudes and barriers in society. Wrongful life (and wrongful birth) suits are seen by many of these authors as reflective of an inaccurate and inappropriate attitude in society toward life with a disability.

Finally, some bioethicists claim that the assertion that life with impairments is worse than non-existence is only justifiable for a few extremely severe

---

29. James Bopp et al., The "Rights" and "Wrongs" of Wrongful Birth and Wrongful Life: A Jurisprudential Analysis of Birth Related Torts, 27 Duq. L. Rev. 461, 514 (1989).

conditions. From the perspective of the child, even the most rudimentary awareness and existence might be sufficient to experience a life of value. According to these authors, the kinds of conditions for which wrongful life suits have been brought, such as Down syndrome or congenital rubella syndrome, would not be justified from the perspective of the child.

The limited success of the wrongful life suits is not likely to change in the next decade or two. The primary challenge to these claims is the philosophical conundrum they pose. Some courts have been willing to overlook this problem in search of support for a disabled plaintiff when adequate support for medical expenses is not otherwise available. We might expect this pattern to continue in the future, at least until we have a more comprehensive health care financing system. But the other reason wrongful life suits are recognized or pursued is the existence of the wrongful birth claims that usually speak to the same set of events. The wrongful birth claims have been considerably more successful in the courts. . . .

While there is prevalent support for the wrongful birth claim in the judicial system, there remains a debate over the appropriate calculation of damages in courts recognizing the tort. Courts have considered several options that attempt to balance the benefits and costs of having and raising an impaired child. One method of calculation is to award the parents a monetary sum equal to the costs of the continued pregnancy, the delivery, and the medical costs incurred by the child's impairment. These are seen as the additional costs directly incurred because of the claimed negligence of the physician. An additional award might be added to compensate for the emotional pain and suffering of bearing and raising a child with a disability. A third element that courts have variously considered is an offset to either of these damages for the benefits that a child brings to a family. Therefore, the damages for emotional pain might be reduced by the jury's estimate of the child's positive value to the family.

> ## Mark Strasser, Wrongful Life, Wrongful Birth, Wrongful Death, and the Right to Refuse Treatment: Can Reasonable Jurisdictions Recognize All But One?
> ### 64 Mo. L. Rev. 29, 64-67 (1999)

Some courts have refused to recognize wrongful life claims because they claimed not to know (and that a jury could not know) the appropriate value to assign to nonexistence. The Florida Supreme Court asked rhetorically, "How do we assign a 'value' to nonexistence, to nothingness?"[196] The Colorado Supreme Court explained that because the court could not assign a value to the child's nonexistence,[197] the court could not calculate the damages.

Yet, it is not immediately clear why a "value" could not be assigned to nonexistence, e.g., a value of zero. Presumably, the real issue for these courts was the appropriate value to assign to existence rather than to nonexistence. Even that, however, may be a misleading way to look at the relevant issue since the positive value of existence per se is not questioned by the wrongful life

---

196. Kush v. Lloyd, 616 So. 2d 415, 423 (Fla. 1992).
197. Lininger By and Through Lininger v. Eisenbaum, 764 P.2d 1202, 1210 (Colo. 1988).

plaintiff. Rather, the positive value of existence with a terrible affliction is what is at issue. Just as individuals who refuse life-saving treatment need not question the value of life and indeed "may fervently wish to live, but to do so free of unwanted medical technology, surgery, or drugs, and without protracted suffering," the wrongful life plaintiff need not be questioning the value of life but merely asserting that life with a terrible affliction can be worse than not having lived at all.

The Florida and Colorado Supreme Courts might have been making either of two different claims: (1) it is impossible to fix a particular value on never having existed rather than on having lived a pain-filled life, and thus it would be impossible to say just how preferable the former option might be in a particular case, or (2) it is impossible to make any value assignments whatsoever in these kinds of cases and therefore impossible to say whether it would have been better not to have existed at all than to have lived a pain-filled life. The latter is a much stronger claim than the former.

In Harbeson v. Parke-Davis, Inc., the Washington Supreme Court argued that "measuring the value of an impaired life as compared to nonexistence is a task that is beyond mortals, whether judges or jurors," concluding therefore that general damages were "beyond computation." However, the court pointed out that "one of the consequences of the birth of the child who claims wrongful life is the incurring of extraordinary expenses for medical care and special training." The court suggested that these expenses were calculable and that special damages could be awarded in wrongful life cases.

Other courts have considered whether special damages may be awarded in wrongful life actions but have concluded that such damages should be awarded in wrongful birth actions instead. However, that position has certain drawbacks. Wrongful birth actions are designed to compensate parents for their losses. If the parents are only responsible for the child until she reaches majority, then the special expenses required for her care after majority would fall onto the child or the state. . . .

[I]f it is impossible to say whether it would be better to be alive than not to exist, then it would seem that wrongful death actions should not be recognized, since it would be impossible to establish that the individual had been harmed by having had her life end prematurely. After all, the person might have been benefitted by having received her "just" rewards earlier rather than later.

The claim here is not that courts or legislatures should deny recovery for wrongful death in those instances in which it seemed "reasonable" to believe that the person had not been harmed because she had gone to heaven. Nor is the claim that an evil individual should receive more compensation for wrongful death because it seemed "reasonable" to believe that he had been forced to go to hell prematurely. Rather, it is merely that considerations of whether there is an afterlife and what such a life would be like do not affect or preclude recovery in other areas of tort and there is no reason that analogous considerations should have such a role in the wrongful life context. . . .

NOTE AND QUESTIONS

1. *Questioning effects of wrongful life suit on child.* Once wrongful birth and wrongful life claims are recognized, complicated questions arise about the

potential long-term, negative effects of these suits on the parties involved. For instance, what is the likely emotional effect on a child of having won a wrongful life suit? Or of the child's parents having won a wrongful birth suit? The child will likely benefit from whatever money is received as a result of these suits. But will a child with capacity feel stigmatized and degraded by the character of the suit? Might a parent try to prevent a child from ever knowing that such a suit was brought? Is that practical? Even if one wins such a suit, will it have been "worth it"? Will the child be harmed by learning that a court (and his or her parents) characterized his or her life (or birth or conception) as "wrongful"? If the answer is "yes," or "it seems likely," should such suits be reserved for children with devastating problems or for children who will presumably never have the capacity to understand that a court or their parents described their lives or births as wrongful? Carl Coleman asserts that "some situations involve such unqualified suffering that, given a choice, it might be better not to have been born at all." Carl Coleman, Conceiving Harm: Disability Discrimination in Assisted Reproductive Technologies, 50 UCLA L. Rev. 17, 46 (2002). What sort of "suffering" does Coleman refer to? Is Down syndrome within that category? What about deafness? What about cystic fibrosis? What about Tay-Sachs disease?

2. Legal Approaches

Kassama v. Magat
792 A.2d 1102 (Ct. App. Md. 2002)

Opinion by WILNER, J.

This is a medical malpractice action brought by petitioner, Millicent Kassama, for herself and for her young daughter, Ibrion, against Aaron Magat, the obstetrician who treated her during her pregnancy. The action arises from the unfortunate fact that Ibrion was born with Down's Syndrome. Dr. Magat is not charged with having caused that disorder but rather with causing Ibrion to be born, with negligently having precluded petitioner from exercising her option to abort the pregnancy.

The gravamen of the complaint, as it has evolved during the course of the litigation, is that Dr. Magat failed to advise petitioner of the result of an alpha-fetoprotein (AFP) blood test that indicated a heightened possibility that Ibrion might be afflicted with Down's Syndrome. Had she received that information, petitioner now contends, she would have undergone an amniocentesis, which would have confirmed that prospect, and, had that occurred, she would have chosen to terminate the pregnancy through an abortion. . . .

The claim asserted . . . falls within a cluster of tort actions that arise from the allegation that the negligence of some third person has caused a child to be born, either at all or with some defect or impairment. These kinds of claims take many forms. The earlier and more traditional of them, brought either by the parents or on behalf of the child, were to recover damages for a prenatal injury actually caused to the child by the negligence of the defendant. The gravamen of the action is the injury so caused. . . .

The actions now before us are of a type that were not and, as a practical matter, could not have been, brought before the last half of the Twentieth Century. At their core, they rest to a large extent on the more recent advances in medical and scientific knowledge that made contraception more practical and reliable and made potential fetal injuries and defects detectable prior to birth, and even prior to conception, coupled with the loosening of the fetters on abortions triggered in 1973 by Roe v. Wade.

. . . [T]his newer variety of claims tends to fall into three general categories. The first, sometimes labeled "wrongful conception" or "wrongful pregnancy," are brought by "parents of a normal but unplanned child [seeking] damages either from a physician who allegedly was negligent in performing a sterilization procedure or abortion, or from a pharmacist or pharmaceutical manufacturer who allegedly was negligent in dispensing or manufacturing a contraceptive prescription or device." *Walker,* 790 P.2d at 737. The second, sometimes denoted as "wrongful birth," consists of cases in which parents of a child born with birth defects allege that the negligence of prenatal health care providers or genetic counselors deprived them of the ability to abort the pregnancy because of the likelihood that the child would be born in an injured or impaired state. Id. Those actions are by the parents to recover the damages and expenses accruing to them from having to endure and raise such a child.

The third category, sometimes called "wrongful life," comprises actions brought by, or on behalf of, the child. At least two types of claims fall within this category—claims by "normal but unwanted children who seek damages either from [their] parents [or from others] negligently responsible for their conception or birth," and, as here, claims by impaired children asserting that, as a result of the defendant's negligence, their parents were precluded from making a decision to abort the pregnancy. Although there is often some similarity or overlapping in the allegations of negligence that underlie these various kinds of claims, virtually every court has recognized some critical distinctions between the third category, of actions on behalf of the children, and the others. . . .

Here, the alleged injury is to the child, for her own disability and the expenses she will have to bear, but . . . the disability itself, from which the expenses will flow, was not caused by the defendant. The injury sued upon, that was allegedly caused by the defendant, is the fact that she was born; she bears the disability and will bear the expenses only because, but for the alleged negligence of Dr. Magat, her mother was unable to terminate the pregnancy and avert her birth. The issue is whether Maryland law is prepared to recognize that kind of injury—the injury of life itself.

It appears, at this point, that 28 States deny recovery for this kind of action—18 by case law, 10 by statute[13]—but that three, California, New Jersey, and Washington, provide for a limited recovery. The issue has generated a great deal of commentary. The States that, by case law, have refused to recognize this kind of action have given a variety of reasons—that the damage determination is too complex, the philosophical conundrum posed in determining whether a

---

13. See Idaho Code §5-334 (2000); Ind. Code Ann. §34-12-1-1 (Michie 2001); Me. Rev. Stat. Ann. tit. 24, §2931 (West 2000) (refusing to recognize wrongful life cause of action when healthy child is born); Mich. Comp. Laws Ann. §600.2971 (West 2001); Minn. Stat. Ann. §145.424 (West 2000); Mo. Rev. Stat. §188.130 (2000); N.D. Cent. Code §32-03-43 (2001); 42 Pa. Cons. Stat. Ann. §8305 (B) (West 2001); S.D. Codified Laws §21-55-1 (Michie 2001); Utah Code Ann. §78-11-24 (2001).

disabled existence is worse than non-existence, whether life, itself, can ever be regarded as an injury, and whether recognition of such an action would (1) be inconsistent with more fundamental principles that sanctify life, (2) denigrate the rights and dignity of disabled persons, and (3) because of the nearly theological nature of the underlying premise, create unacceptably disparate results if placed into the hands of judges and juries.

One of the earliest cases to address the issue and set out a framework for denying recognition of such a claim was Gleitman v. Cosgrove, 227 A.2d 689 (N.J. 1967). . . . The claim in *Gleitman* on behalf of the child, was that the mother, during the early part of her pregnancy, had contracted German measles, that she so informed her obstetrician but that he negligently assured her that there was no problem, that, as a result of that assurance, she did not abort the pregnancy, and that the child was born with substantial defects arising from his mother's exposure. Although *Gleitman* was decided before Roe v. Wade, the court assumed that, in light of the possible birth defects that predictably could arise from the exposure, Mrs. Gleitman would have been able to have a lawful abortion. The court rejected the claim, however, on the ground that it was impossible to measure damages. Noting that damages in tort actions are compensatory in nature and are measured by "comparing the condition plaintiff would have been in, had the defendants not been negligent, with plaintiff's impaired condition as a result of the negligence," the court viewed the child's claim as measuring "the difference between his life with defects against the utter void of non-existence," and it concluded that "it is impossible to make such a determination." The court explained:

> This Court cannot weigh the value of life with impairments against the nonexistence of life itself. By asserting that he should not have been born, the infant plaintiff makes it logically impossible for a court to measure his alleged damages because of the impossibility of making the comparison required by compensatory remedies. . . .

Three States have reached the conclusion that a child born with some impairment does have a limited cause of action where, because of the defendant's negligence, the child's parents were effectively deprived of the informed opportunity either not to conceive the plaintiff child or to abort the pregnancy and thus prevent the child's birth. Those States do not allow the child to recover "general" damages but permit a recovery for the extraordinary expenses of dealing with the impairment. [See Procanik by Procanik v. Cillo, 97 N.J. 339, 478 A.2d 755 (N.J. 1984); Harbeson v. Parke- Davis, Inc., 98 Wash. 2d 460, 656 P.2d 483 (Wash. 1983); Turpin v. Sortini, 31 Cal. 3d 220, 643 P.2d 954, 182 Cal. Rptr. 337 (Cal. 1982).] . . . These three cases are now 18 to 20 years old. No other appellate court has agreed with them. Some have noted but simply declined to follow them. Others have been outright critical of their reasoning. . . .

We align ourselves with the majority view and hold that, for purposes of tort law, an impaired life is not worse than non-life, and, for that reason, life is not, and cannot be, an injury. This case, indeed, illustrates why that is so. Ibrion has Down's Syndrome and the disabilities and impairments that proceed from that abnormality. There was no evidence that she is not deeply loved and cared for by her parents or that she does not return that love. Every recent study shows that people afflicted with Down's Syndrome can lead useful, productive, and meaningful lives—that they can be educated, that they are employable, that they can form friendships and relationships and can get along in society. . . .

In our view, the crucial question, value judgment about life itself, is too deeply immersed in each person's own individual philosophy or theology to be subject to a reasoned and consistent community response, in the form of a jury verdict. Allowing a recovery of extraordinary life expenses on some theory of fairness—that the doctor or his or her insurance company should pay not because the doctor caused the injury or impairment but because the child was born—ignores this fundamental issue and strikes us as simply a hard, sympathetic case making bad law. We shall affirm.

NOTES AND QUESTIONS

1. *Damages.*   As the court in Kassama v. Magat, supra, explained, wrongful conception (or wrongful pregnancy) claims are related to wrongful birth and wrongful life claims. A wrongful conception claim is brought by a parent, claiming that a health care provider's negligence resulted in an unwanted pregnancy. The most common sort of wrongful conception case involves the claim that sterilization was performed negligently.

Wrongful conception claims are generally recognized. But they often involve debate about how to assess damages. For the most part, courts have limited damages in such cases to the expenses incurred by the pregnancy and birth. A few courts have, however, allowed parents to recover for the cost of raising the child. Some have balanced the costs of raising the child by the benefit to the parents of having the child. The Wisconsin Supreme Court rejected the so-called benefit rule. The court explained its decision to award the parents damages for the costs of raising their healthy child, conceived after an allegedly negligent sterilization.

> The parents made a decision not to have a child. It was precisely to avoid that "benefit" that the parents went to the physician in the first place. Any "benefits" that were conferred upon them as a result of having a new child in their lives were not asked for and were sought to be avoided. With respect to emotional benefits, potential parents in this situation are presumably well aware of the emotional benefits that might accrue to them as the result of a new child in their lives. When parents make the decision to forego this opportunity for emotional enrichment, it hardly seems equitable to not only force this benefit upon them but to tell them they must pay for it as well by offsetting it against their proven emotional damages. With respect to economic benefits, the same argument prevails. In addition, any economic advantages the child might confer upon the parents are ordinarily insignificant. Accordingly, we conclude that the costs of raising the child to the age of majority may not be offset by the benefits conferred upon the parents by virtue of the presence of the child in their lives.

Marciniak v. Lundborg, 450 N.W.2d 243, 249 (Wis. 1990).

2. *Reluctance to recognize wrongful life claims.*   Many judges and commentators have agreed with the *Kassama* court in concluding that it is not possible to balance having been born "even with gross deficiencies" against "never having been born at all." Becker v. Schwartz, 386 N.E.2d 807 (N.Y. 1978). This

conclusion is important in explaining the reluctance of most courts to recognize wrongful life claims.

From the perspective of the disability rights critique, embryo selection and abortion intended to preclude the birth or conception of people with disabilities is harmful to existing disabled people. Adrienne Asch has described prenatal testing and embryo screening and selection as "justified by mistaken assumptions about the quality of life of people with disabilities." She finds those assumptions mistaken because, among other things, "[t]hey fail to recognize the extent to which the disadvantages associated with impairments result from discriminatory attitudes and practices rather than anything intrinsic to the impairment." Adrienne Asch, Disability Equality and Prenatal Testing: Contradictory or Compatible?, 30 Fla. St. U. L. Rev. 315, 318 (2003).

3. *States' recognition of wrongful birth and wrongful life claims.*   As of 2006, one state (Maine) had passed a law recognizing wrongful birth claims. Twenty-two other states recognized the claim as the result of judicial decisions. And three states (California, New Jersey, and Washington), as noted in Kassama, supra, recognized claims for wrongful life. Darpana M. Sheth, Better Off Unborn? An Analysis of Wrongful Birth and Wrongful Life Claims Under the Americans with Disabilities Act, 73 Tenn. L. Rev. 641, 650-51 (2006).

CHALLENGING ISSUES: CLAIMS OF SIBLINGS

Matt was born a year ago. At birth, he was diagnosed with Down syndrome. He is more significantly affected by the condition than many people born with it. Among other things, Matt is unlikely to progress beyond a developmental stage of the average $2\frac{1}{2}$-year-old. In addition, he has a congenital heart condition related to Down's.

During Matt's gestation, his mother, Jill, was under the care of Dr. Ralph. Dr. Ralph did not inform Jill about the availability of prenatal testing even though Jill was thirty-nine during the pregnancy, an age at which women have a higher chance of having a child with Down syndrome. Jill and her husband, Ed, have two other children, Harriet and Henry, ages eight and five. Jill and Ed claim that if they had been told about amniocentesis, Jill would have had the test done. They also say that when the test revealed the presence of a fetus with Down syndrome, they would have terminated the pregnancy. Jill and Ed say that, among other things, they would not have thought it "fair" to continue with a pregnancy that would result in Harriet and Henry having a sibling with Down syndrome.

Jill and Ed have sought damages for wrongful birth, and Matt seeks damages for wrongful life. In addition, Harriet and Henry are seeking damages. They claim that Matt's birth and life are causing them to suffer financial and emotional difficulties and that they are being deprived of the attention their parents would be able to give them if Jill and Ed were not required to devote so much time and energy as well as money to the care of Matt.

Do you think as an ethical matter that Harriet and Henry should proceed with their suit? Do you think as a legal matter that they will be allowed to go forward with their claim?

=4=

‖ *Privacy, Essentialism, and Enhancements* ‖

This chapter continues the discussion of personhood introduced in the last chapter and addresses challenges to understandings of personhood created by innovative medical and technological developments. It also explores some of the implications of those challenges for efforts to safeguard privacy. More specifically, this chapter focuses on new developments in genetics, genomics,[1] neuroscience, psychopharmaceuticals, and other methods that promise to "enhance" or otherwise alter personhood, that offer predictions about future health risks, or that are taken to suggest something essential about a person's physiological or emotional constitution.

Until recently, society assumed that a person's private thoughts were protected from public revelation unless the person chose to make them public. That might no longer be the case.

> The government could not manipulate our minds from the inside; its only way of restricting mental activity was to target the communication or other expression that embodies such activity. Those who wished to recruit resources from the outside world to reshape their framework of internal beliefs would do so by seeking religious or other cultural resources in the world around them.
>
> The development of neuroscience, psychiatry, and cognitive enhancement, however, has changed this state of affairs. Studies of the brain have in recent years generated a flood of discoveries about the biology that underlies our thinking.

Marc Jonathan Blitz, Freedom of Thought for the Extended Mind: Cognitive Enhancement and the Constitution, 2010 Wis. L. Rev. 1049, 1052 (2010).

---

1. The World Health Organization differentiates between genetics and genomics: "The main difference between genomics and genetics is that genetics scrutinizes the functioning and composition of the single gene whereas genomics addresses all genes and their interrelationships in order to identify their combined influence on the growth and development of the organism. World Health Organization, WHO Definitions of Genetics and Genomics, http://www.who.int/genomics/geneticsVSgenomics/en/ (last visited July 30, 2012).

Similarly, Jeffrey Rosen, referring to the work of law professor Henry Greeley, asks whether the use of brain scans to reveal people's thought processes might successfully challenge the deeply ingrained principle in U.S. law that people can be held responsible for their actions but not for their thoughts. Jeffrey Rosen, The Brain on the Stand, N.Y. Times, Mar. 11, 2007, www.nytimes.com.

Similarly, stunning and discomforting challenges are raised by increasingly rapid and inexpensive gene sequencing techniques, functional neuroimaging, drugs that ward off fatigue or that increase intelligence or physical prowess. These challenges present many difficult questions to bioethicists, to health care professionals, and to society broadly. As you read this chapter think about how you would respond to some of the questions below. Even more, construct your own questions. This chapter covers developments that call for a search for the relevant questions as much as they ask for answers to questions that have already been formulated.

1. Is privacy an outmoded notion that carried significant value during the nineteenth and twentieth centuries, but that is no longer worth its price?
2. What *is* the price of safeguarding privacy in general and, more specifically, in the context of medical information?
3. Is it more important to protect people against the revelation of certain sorts of medical information (e.g., genomic information or information obtained through neuroimaging) than against the revelation of medical information more generally? Why or why not?
4. Can the law adequately protect against the risks created by the dissemination of private information? Can it protect those whose medical information has been made public from discrimination and other untoward consequences?
5. Do you think a person's deepest self can be discerned through some combination of genomic and neurological information?
6. Are there moral or practical limits to the "enhancements" that people should be able to obtain for themselves or their children? What are the class implications of creating increasingly broad markets in enhancements?

A.   GENETICS AND GENOMICS

The Human Genome Project commenced work in 1990. At the start of this century, scientists completed a map (referred to as a "working draft" in an NIH guide to human genetics) of the human genome. Then, in 2003—two years before schedule and at a lower cost than originally projected—the National Human Genome Research Institute (part of the National Institutes of Health) announced that the International Human Genome Sequencing Consortium had completed "a high-quality sequence of essentially the entire human genome." Genetics Home Reference, NIH, http://ghr.nlm.nih.gov/handbook/hgp/accomplishments. More specifically, the Human Genome Project mapped the sequence of amino acids on the genes found on human DNA. That map is of great use to science and medicine, but it did not—and still has not—resulted in full knowledge about the implications of genetic alterations for health, illness, and personhood.

Medicine now relies on genetic testing for diagnosing and predicting an expanding set of illnesses and conditions. Moreover, genetic testing kits are available to the public online and even at some chain drugstores. Although genetic tests are now available for thousands of diseases or conditions, interpretation of many of these tests is uncertain. They might not offer valid information, and they are easily misinterpreted. Centers for Disease Control and Prevention (CDC), Public Health Genomics, http://www.cdc.gov/genomics/gtesting/. Further, preimplantation and prenatal uses of genetic testing have become almost routine in American medicine. Yet, the misuses and possible abuses of these forms of genetic testing are numerous and worrisome.

Genetic testing occasions concern at different levels. Some are social, some are individual, and some are both. Genetic testing can result in discrimination against individuals as well as against their families and ethnic groups. It can facilitate stigma. And it can lead to years of worry and anxiety, even in cases in which a particular disease or condition for which an individual is at risk might never become manifest.

Most genetic alterations associated with disease or disability for which an individual tests positive mean only that the person has a risk somewhat greater than the average risk of developing the condition in question. Only in a few cases—such as Huntington disease—does a positive test result indicate that the tested individual will certainly develop the condition (assuming that he or she lives until a certain age—generally the 40s or 50s, in the case of Huntington disease). Additional concerns are occasioned by the use of prenatal genetic testing and preimplantation genetic diagnosis. In particular, such testing could become part of a new form of eugenics, allowing people to select for children with certain talents or physical traits or against children who might not reflect parental dreams and ambitions.

For years, Congress attempted, but failed, to pass legislation aimed at protecting people against genetic discrimination in employment and insurance contexts. Finally, in 2008 the Genetic Information and Nondiscrimination Act of 2008 (GINA) became law. Congress introduced the Act with five findings. Pub. L. 110-233, Sec. 2. (Section A(1)(a)(iii) of this chapter describes protections against discrimination afforded by the Act.) These findings delineate benefits of revealing genetic information as well as many concerns about harmful uses of genetic information. The first finding describes the benefits of genetic testing.

> (1) Deciphering the sequence of the human genome and other advances in genetics open major new opportunities for medical progress. New knowledge about the genetic basis of illness will allow for earlier detection of illnesses, often before symptoms have begun. Genetic testing can allow individuals to take steps to reduce the likelihood that they will contract a particular disorder. New knowledge about genetics may allow for the development of better therapies that are more effective against disease or have fewer side effects than current treatments. These advances give rise to the potential misuse of genetic information to discriminate in health insurance and employment.

The section finding briefly notes a history of discriminatory eugenics.

(2) The early science of genetics became the basis of State laws that provided for the sterilization of persons having presumed genetic "defects" such as mental retardation, mental disease, epilepsy, blindness, and hearing loss, among other conditions. The first sterilization law was enacted in the State of Indiana in 1907. By 1981, a majority of States adopted sterilization laws to "correct" apparent genetic traits or tendencies. Many of these State laws have since been repealed, and many have been modified to include essential constitutional requirements of due process and equal protection. However, the current explosion in the science of genetics, and the history of sterilization laws by the States based on early genetic science, compels Congressional action in this area.

The third finding set out by Congress notes the link between "genetic conditions and disorders" and particular groups described through reference to their physicality.

(3) Although genes are facially neutral markers, many genetic conditions and disorders are associated with particular racial and ethnic groups and gender. Because some genetic traits are most prevalent in particular groups, members of a particular group may be stigmatized or discriminated against as a result of that genetic information. This form of discrimination was evident in the 1970s, which saw the advent of programs to screen and identify carriers of sickle cell anemia, a disease which afflicts African Americans. Once again, State legislatures began to enact discriminatory laws in the area, and in the early 1970s began mandating genetic screening of all African Americans for sickle cell anemia, leading to discrimination and unnecessary fear. To alleviate some of this stigma, Congress in 1972 passed the National Sickle Cell Anemia Control Act, which withholds Federal funding from States unless sickle cell testing is voluntary.

Finding number four reports on discriminatory practices based on genetic tests in the workplace.

(4) Congress has been informed of examples of genetic discrimination in the workplace. These include the use of pre-employment genetic screening at Lawrence Berkeley Laboratory, which led to a court decision in favor of the employees in that case Norman-Bloodsaw v. Lawrence Berkeley Laboratory (135 F.3d 1260, 1269 (9th Cir. 1998)). Congress clearly has a compelling public interest in relieving the fear of discrimination and in prohibiting its actual practice in employment and health insurance.

The fifth finding describes the limits of federal law (as it existed before GINA) for protecting people from genetic discrimination in health insurance and in employment settings.

(5) Federal law addressing genetic discrimination in health insurance and employment is incomplete in both the scope and depth of its protections. Moreover, while many States have enacted some type of genetic non-discrimination law, these laws vary widely with respect to their approach, application, and level of protection. Congress has collected substantial evidence that the American public and the medical community find the existing patchwork of State and Federal laws to be confusing and inadequate to protect them from discrimination. Therefore Federal legislation establishing a national and uniform basic standard is necessary to fully protect the public from discrimination and allay

their concerns about the potential for discrimination, thereby allowing individuals to take advantage of genetic testing, technologies, research, and new therapies.

Pub. L. 110-233, Sec. 2. Such concerns have occasioned great challenges for society and the law.

1.   Uses and Misuses of Genetic and Genomic Tests

a.   Bioethical and Social Perspectives

i.   Developments in Genetics and Genomics

Within about a decade, human genomics emerged from the laboratory to enter clinical medicine as well as the commercial marketplace. The article by Conley, Doerr, and Vorhaus, infra, describes some of these developments.

> *John M. Conley, Adam K. Doerr, and
> Daniel B. Vorhaus Enabling Responsible
> Public Genomics*
> **20 Health Matrix 325, 330–335 (2010)**

The path to public genomics began even before the official launch of the Human Genome Project in 1990, an extraordinarily ambitious and publicly funded attempt to develop and publish a complete roadmap of the human genome. The widely publicized—and, at the time, widely criticized—venture saw an international consortium of government agencies and research centers produce a "rough draft" of the consensus human genome in 2000, followed by a "final draft" in 2003. This historic achievement—the genomics moonshot—is well chronicled, and the sheer magnitude of the undertaking is often conveyed by reference to the tremendous time and budget of the project: more than a decade and nearly three billion dollars.

The pace of technological and scientific innovation has significantly accelerated since the Human Genome Project's completion, enabling the construction of several large-scale human genomic databases designed to build upon the Human Genome Project's work. International efforts, including the International HapMap Project and the 1000 Genomes Project, continue to dramatically increase the level of detail and sensitivity of available human genome reference data, expanding upon the limited consensus genome produced by the Human Genome Project. Other projects, such as the UK Biobank, are attempting to categorize genomic variation within geographically delimited populations. Still others aggregate the results from targeted genome-wide association studies that seek the genetic bases of specific diseases and other complex human traits. A host of new large-scale genomic research projects recently established or under consideration indicates that the rapid pace of development will continue.

The proliferation of large-scale genomic databases exhibits the characteristics of a simple supply and demand relationship: researchers demand ever-richer datasets to solve genomic puzzles while a burgeoning industry of genomic sequencing hardware and service providers compete to supply the tools and technologies needed to generate those datasets.

For genomic researchers, the identification of the genetic bases for certain traits was underway prior to the Human Genome Project's completion, particularly for those traits, like Huntington disease, where family histories demonstrated a high degree of heritability and strongly suggested a single gene–trait relationship. These monogenic traits—traits defined by a single gene—were the first to have their genetic underpinnings clearly identified. It is now widely believed that the majority of this "low-hanging fruit" has already been plucked.

Although public resources including the Human Genome Project, the International HapMap Project, and the 1000 Genomes Project continue to produce increasingly refined maps of human genomic variation, there is a growing recognition that a host of factors beyond common genetic variation, including rare genetic variants, copy number variation (CNV) and other rearrangements of the genome and epigenetic or environmental factors, are key contributors to many complex traits, demonstrating the need for richer datasets that include whole-genome sequence data. The challenge now is to characterize and understand the genomic underpinnings of more complex phenotypes, such as height or heart disease. Although some progress has been made in this area, the reality is that the genotype–phenotype associations identified to date account for only a very small portion of the exhibited population variance for nearly every complex trait.

For example, although genomic research has identified more than fifty regions of the genome that contribute to height, a recent study found that those genetic loci were able to predict only four to six percent of the variance in individual height, while a much less sophisticated (and substantially less expensive) predictive model developed by Sir Francis Galton in 1886, which relies solely on knowing the heights of an individual's parents, was able to predict forty percent of that same variance. Accordingly, to identify the genomic factors that meaningfully contribute to complex phenotypes such as height, researchers require datasets that allow them to peer deeply into individual genomes in search of rare genetic modifications and other sources of variation and test their hypotheses against large cohorts of both similar and dissimilar populations.

NOTE AND QUESTION

1. *Personal genomes.* The Human Genome Project developed the so-called "human genome" map from the DNA of a few people. Since then, scientists have called for sequencing personal genomes. A 2005 editorial in Molecular Systems Biology described the use of "the first personal genome" as akin to the "first fax machine, web page, or computer." The editorial describes the "early" participants as "heroes and human guinea pigs." Editorial: The Personal Genome Project, Molecular Systems Biol., Dec. 13, 2005, http://www.nature.com/msb/journal/v1/n1/pdf/msb4100040.pdf. What do you think the journal editorial meant by referring to the first group of people to agree to personal genomic sequencing as heroes and as guinea pigs?

ii.   Identity

> ### Elizabeth Joh, DNA Theft: Recognizing
> ### the Crime of Nonconsensual Genetic Testing
> ### 91 B.U.L. Rev. 665, 666–667, 670 (2011)

The fact that you leave genetic information behind on discarded tissues, used coffee cups, and smoked cigarettes everywhere you go is generally of little consequence. Trouble arises, however, when third parties retrieve this detritus of everyday life for the genetic information you have left behind. These third parties may be the police, and the regulation over their ability to collect this evidence is unclear.

The police are not the only ones who are interested in other people's genetic information. Consider:

- The political party that is interested in discovering and publicizing any predispositions to disease that might render a presidential candidate of the opposing party unsuitable for office.

- An historian who wishes to put to rest rumors about those who claim to be the illegitimate descendants of a former president but refuse to submit to genetic testing.

- A professional sports team that wants to analyze the genetic information of a prospective player, despite his protests, to screen for risks of fatal health conditions before offering him a multi-million dollar contract.

- An individual's personal enemy who would be thrilled to analyze the genetic information of his target and post information on the internet about the target's likelihood of becoming an alcoholic, a criminal, or obese.

- A wealthy grandparent who suspects that a grandchild is not genetically related to her and plans to disinherit him if that is the case

- A person involved in a romantic relationship who wants to find out whether his partner carries the gene for male pattern baldness or persistent miscarriage.

- A couple who would like to know if their prospective adoptive child has any potential health issues before they make a final decision.

- Fans who would pay a high price to buy the genetic information of their favorite celebrity.

. . . .

[T]he nonconsensual collection and analysis of another person's DNA merits serious consideration as a distinct criminal offense. The existing laws on DNA analysis in the United States, with a few exceptions, fail to address the problem. While strong similarities exist between DNA theft and traditional theft offenses, the issues surrounding DNA collection and analysis are sufficiently complex that American jurisdictions should recognize a distinct crime of DNA theft rather than try to subsume DNA theft within traditional theft law. Without such a law, potential victims of DNA theft have little protection. And unlike with financial records, internet data, and conventional private property, there are few if any private precautions that can prevent DNA theft.

NOTES AND QUESTIONS

1. *A right not to know?* Elizabeth Joh, supra, asserts that part of the right to control one's genetic information is the right *not* to know about a deleterious genetic alteration. Why might someone not want to know such information?

2. *DNA theft.* Although there is not yet a U.S. law identifying DNA theft as a crime, in Britain, the Human Tissue Act of 2004 criminalizes taking organs or tissues from others without their consent. Joh, supra. The Act was promulgated in response to the discovery that organs and tissue had been taken from children who had died at hospitals in Britain. Explanatory Notes, Human Tissue Act 2004, http://legislation.data.gov.uk/ukpga/2004/30/notes/data.pdf. The Act prohibits (with some exceptions) a person's having "human material with a view to analyzing its DNA without consent." Id.

iii.   Direct-to-Consumer Genetic Testing

Genetic tests are available directly to consumers through companies selling them online. Companies are recommending the tests to assess the risk of disease, to get information about character and personality, to trace ancestry, or to identify paternity. Andrew S. Robertson, Regulations and Protections in Direct-to-Consumer Genetic Testing, 24 Berkeley Tech. L.J. 213, 217 (2009). One website offers genetic testing with the promise that it can provide information about the likely success of romantic relationships. Id. The website claims that those who are "genetically highly compatible" will experience a "perfect chemistry." GenePartner, http://www.genepartner.com/index.php/aboutgenepartner (last visited Jan. 25, 2012).

Statement of Gregory Kutz (Managing Director, Forensic Audits and Special Investigations), Direct-to-Consumer Genetic Tests: Misleading Test Results Are Further Complicated by Deceptive Marketing and Other Questionable Practices
Testimony before the Subcommittee on Oversight and Investigations, Committee on Energy and Commerce, House of Representatives, July 22, 2010

Thank you for the opportunity to discuss our follow-up investigation of genetic tests sold directly to consumers via the Internet. Using kits at home, consumers simply swab their cheeks or collect saliva and send these DNA samples back to a company for analysis and a report of the results. While the importance of genetics in individual medical care shows promise for the future, the usefulness of the tests these companies offer is much debated.

. . . .

Despite [earlier warnings, based on investigations undertaken in 2006] several new DTC [direct-to-consumer] genetic test companies have been touted as being more reputable and medically accurate than those we tested previously; in 2008, Time magazine named one new company's test the "invention of the year." More recently, another company's plan to sell tests at retail pharmacies has drawn significant attention from the media and scientists. However, given the scientific evidence currently available, many experts remain concerned that the medical predictions contained in the results mislead consumers. In this context, you requested that we proactively test DTC genetic products currently on the market and the advertising methods used to sell these products to consumers.

To investigate DTC genetic products currently on the market, we purchased tests, for $299 to $999, from a nonrepresentative selection of four of the dozens of genetic testing companies selling kits to consumers on the internet. Using online search terms likely to be used by actual consumers, we identified and selected these companies because they were frequently cited as being credible by the media and in scientific publications and because they all provided consumers with risk predictions, accessible through secure Web sites, for a range of diseases and conditions. Although their tests are not identical, all four companies' Web sites contain a variation of the statement that their tests help consumers and their physicians detect disease risks early so that they can take preventive steps to reduce these risks. They also note that their tests are not intended to provide medical advice or to treat or diagnose disease. We purchased 10 tests from each company (40 tests in total) to compare risk predictions for a variety of serious illnesses and determine whether the companies were consistent in their predictions. We selected for comparison 15 common diseases and conditions that were tested by at least three of the four companies: Alzheimer disease, atrial fibrillation (a type of irregular heart beat), breast cancer, celiac disease (a chronic digestive problem caused by an inability to process gluten), colon cancer, heart attack, hypertension, leukemia, multiple sclerosis, obesity, prostate cancer, restless leg syndrome, rheumatoid arthritis, type 1 diabetes, and type 2 diabetes.

. . . [W]e then selected five DNA donors and created two profiles for each donor, one using factual information about the donor and one using fictitious information, including age, race or ethnicity, and medical history.

For each donor, we sent two DNA samples (saliva or a cheek swab) to each company—one sample using the factual profile and one using the fictitious—to determine whether altering the donors' backgrounds had any effect on the companies' DNA analysis. Three of the four companies asked for age and race or ethnicity prior to purchase; only one asked for medical history information. We also made undercover telephone calls to the companies seeking additional medical advice for both our factual and fictitious donors. We then documented our observations on the test results and advice we received. It is important to emphasize that we did not conduct a rigorous scientific study; our observations are those that could be made by any consumer. To assess whether we received any scientifically based or medically useful information, we consulted with external experts in the field of genetics and incorporated their comments as appropriate. . . .

To investigate the advertising methods used to sell DTC genetic products, we reviewed the Web sites of a nonrepresentative selection of 15 genetic testing companies, including the 4 from which we purchased tests. We identified the companies by again using online search terms likely to be used by actual consumers. Posing as fictitious consumers, we made contact with these companies, both by phone and in person, seeking additional information about genetic testing. During these contacts, we asked a series of questions about the reliability and usefulness of test results, privacy policies regarding consumers' genetic information, and the sale of supplements or other products. To assess the accuracy and reasonableness of the marketing claims, we again consulted with external experts in the field of genetics. We also purchased supplements sold by one of the companies.

Our findings are limited to the individual DTC genetic test companies we investigated and cannot be projected to any other companies. We performed our work from June 2009 to June 2010 in accordance with standards prescribed by the Council of Inspectors General for Integrity and Efficiency.

The test results we received are misleading and of little or no practical use to consumers. Comparing results for 15 diseases, we made the following observations: (1) each donor's factual profile received disease risk predictions that varied across all four companies, indicating that identical DNA can yield contradictory results depending solely on the company it was sent to for analysis; (2) these risk predictions often conflicted with the donors' factual illnesses and family medical histories; (3) none of the companies could provide the donors who submitted fictitious African American and Asian profiles with complete test results for their ethnicity but did not explicitly disclose this limitation prior to purchase; (4) one company provided donors with reports that showed conflicting predictions for the same DNA and profile, but did not explain how to interpret these different results; and (5) follow-up consultations offered by three of the companies provided only general information and not the expert advice the companies promised to provide. The experts we spoke with agreed that the companies' claims and test results are both ambiguous and misleading. Further, they felt that consumers who are concerned about their health should consult directly with their physicians instead of purchasing these kinds of DTC genetic tests. . . .

Different companies often provide different results for identical DNA: Each donor received risk predictions for the 15 diseases that varied from company to company, demonstrating that identical DNA samples produced contradictory results.

. . . .

When we asked genetics experts if any of the companies' markers and disease predictions were actually more accurate than the others, they told us that there are too many uncertainties and ambiguities in this type of testing to rely on any of the results. Unlike well-established genetic testing for diseases like cystic fibrosis, the experts feel that these tests are "promising for research, but the application is premature." In other words, "each company's results could be internally consistent, but not tell the full story . . . [because] the science of risk prediction based on genetic markers is not fully worked out, and that the limitations inherent in this sort of risk prediction have not been adequately disclosed." As one expert further noted, "the fact that different companies, using the same samples, predict different . . . directions of risk is telling and is important. It shows that we are nowhere near really being able to interpret [such tests]." We also asked our experts if any of our donors should be concerned if the companies all agreed on a risk prediction; for example, all four companies told Donor 1 she was at increased risk for Alzheimer disease. The experts told us this consensus means very little because there are so many demographic, environmental, and lifestyle factors that contribute to the occurrence of the types of diseases tested by the four companies.

NOTES AND QUESTIONS

1. *Genetic tests available through the internet.* At the start of the twenty-first century, most genetic testing was recommended by physicians for purposes of diagnosis or prognostication of illness, or it was sought for legal purposes (e.g., paternity testing). Now, people access internet sites that offer tests for discovering one's ancestry, finding a mate, or discerning one's intelligence. Jessica D. Gabel, Redeeming the Genetic Groupon: Efficacy, Ethics, and Exploitation in Marketing DNA to the Masses, 81 Miss. L.J. 363 (2012). Do you think it is advisable—and if it is advisable, is it possible—to monitor genetic tests sold on the internet?

2. *Analyzing students' genes.* The University of California, Berkeley, asked freshmen entering the undergraduate college in 2010 to submit DNA samples. Three sets of genes were to be analyzed—those implicated in the metabolism of alcohol, lactose, and folates. The University, which did not intend to compel participation, explained that it hoped the genetic information would help students learn about personalized medicine. Tamar Lewin, College Bound, DNA Swab in Hand, N.Y. Times, May 18, 2010. Would you agree to participate in such a program if it were organized at your university?

By August, the University abandoned plans to inform individual students of genetic information obtained from their cheek swabs. The University shifted its position in response to a ruling of the state's Public Health Department that required pretesting approval from students' physicians and that required that any testing be done by clinical laboratories with special licenses, not by University personnel. Larry Gordon, UC Berkeley Adjusts Freshman Orientation's Gen-testing Program, L.A. Times, Aug. 13, 2010, www.latimes.com.

b. Legal Approaches

Genetic Information Nondiscrimination Act of 2008. Congress constructed the Genetic Information Nondiscrimination Act of 2008 (GINA) as a civil rights law. Pub. L. 110-233, 122 Stat. 881. It prohibits genetic discrimination by employers of more than 15 employees and by health insurers. The statute follows the civil rights model of Title VII of the Civil Rights Act of 1964.

> [GINA] makes it unlawful for employers to "fail to hire or refuse to hire, or to discharge, any employee, or otherwise discriminate against any employee with respect to compensation, terms, conditions, or privileges of employment, because of genetic information with respect to the employee; or to limit, segregate, or classify the employees of the employer in any way that would deprive or tend to deprive any employee of employment opportunities or otherwise adversely affect the status of the employee because of genetic information with respect to the employee.

Furthermore, GINA says that an employer cannot "request, require, or purchase genetic information with respect to an employee or family member of the employee." Employers are also prohibited from retaliating against someone for exercising his/her rights under GINA."

Patricia Nemeth & Terry W. Bonnette, Don't Be Blind-Sided by GINA: The Surprisingly Wide Reach of the Genetic Information Nondiscrimination Act, Nienhouse Media, Inc., Oct.-Nov. 2011, at 24.

One scholar, while concluding that a civil rights frame was appropriate to GINA's aims, noted certain important differences between the sort of discrimination GINA prohibits and that prohibited by most civil rights legislation.

GINA differs from all previous antidiscrimination statutes. First and foremost, genetic information is fundamentally unlike other antidiscrimination categories. It does not, at present, form the basis of a widely recognized social group, nor does it currently have an associated identity. Moreover, genetic-information discrimination is not yet occurring on a large scale. Thus, instead of reacting to existing discrimination in the past and present, GINA anticipates discrimination in the future, making it the first predominantly forward-looking antidiscrimination statute.

Jessica L. Roberts, The Genetic Information Nondiscrimination Act as an Antidiscrimination Law, 86 Notre Dame L. Rev. 597, 600 (2011) (footnotes omitted).

GINA defines genetic information as information about an individual's genetic tests, genetic tests of a person's family members, and "the manifestation of a disease or disorder in family members of such individual." Sec. 201(4)(A). It expressly excludes information about a person's age or gender and information about the manifestation of a disease or disorder in the individual, himself or herself as well as genetic information about a woman's fetus. Sec. 210.

Title I of the law focuses on prohibiting genetic discrimination by health insurers. Title II focuses on limiting genetic discrimination by employers. More specifically, the statute prohibits health insurers from requiring or requesting genetic information and from setting rates on the basis of genetic information about an individual or an individual's family members. Secs. 101–106. It further prohibits employers from failing to hire or from discharging an employee and from "otherwise discriminate[ing] against any employee with respect to the compensation, terms, conditions, or privileges of employment . . . because of genetic information with respect to the employee" or classifying an employee in a discriminatory fashion based on genetic information. Section 202(a)(1) and (2).

Remedies for violations of GINA include corrective action and monetary penalties. The Department of Labor, the Department of the Treasury, and the Department of Health and Human Services are responsible for enforcing Title I of GINA, and the Equal Employment Opportunity Commission (EEOC) is responsible for enforcing Title II of GINA. Individuals may also have the right to pursue private litigation under Title II.

GINA's protections against discrimination are significant but not comprehensive. It does not protect against discrimination by life insurers, disability insurers, or long-term care insurers. And it does not protect certain categories of people, including those covered by the Indian Health Service, those in the military, and federal employees insured by Federal Employees Health Benefit

Plans. Those anxious to buy life insurance, disability insurance, or long-term care insurance can of course avoid genetic testing. But the price for that decision for one's health—depending on the condition or disease at issue—may be high.

NOTES AND QUESTIONS

1. *Limitations of GINA's protections.* As noted, supra, GINA does not prohibit life insurers, disability insurers, or long-term care insurers from basing insurance decisions on genetic information. It also fails to offer protection from the discriminatory use of genetic information by adoption agencies, prisons, and schools. Should clinicians take these factors into account in advising particular patients to undergo genetic testing for a genetic alteration linked to breast cancer? For a genetic alteration indicating that a person will or will not develop Huntington disease? For a genetic alteration suggesting a risk of Alzheimer disease?

2. *Fears of genetic discrimination.* Before the passage of GINA, there was widespread concern that genetic test results could be used to exclude people from employment, health insurance protection, and other benefits. Jessica Roberts reported that before GINA's passage, 90 percent of the public feared genetic discrimination. Jessica L. Roberts, The Genetic Information Nondiscrimination Act as an Antidiscrimination Law, 86 Notre Dame L. Rev. 597, 603 (2011). Does GINA respond adequately to those concerns?

3. *The Equal Employment Opportunity Commission (EEOC) final GINA regulations.* The EEOC issued final regulations under GINA in early 2011. A year later, only a very small number of complaints had been lodged with the EEOC for violation of GINA. However, employers were advised to develop plans to comply with some of the statute's technical parts, such as recordkeeping. Brett Coburn & Wes R. McCart, Assessing GINA's Impact on Employers After Two Years: Review of Litigation, EEOC Activity, Liability Risks, and Compliance Tips, BNA's Privacy and Security Law Reporter, 11 PVLR 11 (Jan. 2, 2012). Commission statistics for 2010 (the year before publication of EEOC's final regulations) show that of almost 100,000 charges filed with the Commission, only about 0.2 percent involved charges pursuant to GINA. U.S. Equal Employment Opportunity Commission, Charging Statistics FY 1997 Through FY 2010, http://www.eeoc.gov/eeoc/statistics/enforcement/charges.cfm. The EEOC's final rule about recordkeeping pursuant to GINA, 29 CFR Part 1602 ("Recordkeeping and Reporting Requirements Under Title VII, the ADA, and GINA") added title II of GINA to the rules already covering recordkeeping under title VII of the Civil Rights Act of 1964 and the Americans with Disabilities Act. Title II of GINA, just as does Title VII, covers employers with at least 15 employees.

Does it make sense to classify discrimination against people with genetic alterations that predict an increased risk for disease or disability with civil rights laws? What are the implications of this classification?

4. *State genetic nondiscrimination laws.* About 30 states have laws prohibiting certain types of genetic discrimination. Many of these laws predated GINA. Brett Coburn & Wes R. McCart, Assessing GINA's Impact on Employers After Two Years: Review of Litigation, EEOC Activity, Liability Risks, and Compliance Tips,

BNA's Privacy and Security Law Reporter, 11 PVLR 11 (Jan. 2, 2012). In general, protections afforded by these statutes are narrower than GINA's protections. However, in 2011 California passed a genetic nondiscrimination law that offers broader protections against genetic discrimination than does GINA. The California law added genetic information to the bases on which discrimination was already prohibited under the Unruh Civil Rights Act. Sen. Bill No. 559, signed by Gov. Sept. 6, 2011, available at http://op.bna.com/pl.nsf/id/dapn-81hsgq/ $File/sb_559_bill_20110906_chaptered.pdf. Thus, in California, genetic discrimination is prohibited in health insurance and employment contexts and in others, including housing, education, and public accommodations. California Enacts New Genetic Discrimination Law, BNA Privacy & Security L. Rep., 10 PVLR 1312 (2011).

5. *Regulating direct-to-consumer genetic tests.* Two federal agencies (the Centers for Medicaid and Medicare Services (CMS) and the Food and Drug Administration (FDA)) and state agencies have some authority to regulate direct-to-consumer genetic testing. However, there is, in fact, little regulation. CMS certifies laboratories pursuant to the Clinical Laboratories Improvements Amendments "Act of 1988, 42 U.S.C. §263a. However, CMS has not claimed oversight over the validity or use of the results of genetic tests. Moreover, the FDA has approved only about 10 percent of the thousands of genetic tests now available. The FDA regulates genetic tests if they are sold as "in vitro diagnostic devices" (IVDs, also called "test kits"), but, in fact, most genetic tests are developed within clinical laboratories and are therefore not defined as IVDs; they are therefore outside the domain of FDA regulation. Andrew S. Robertson, Regulations and Protections in Direct-to-Consumer Genetic Testing, 24 Berkeley Tech. L.J. 213, 221–225 (2009). Do you think that regulations should be crafted? Is it more harmful than beneficial to allow members of the public to receive genetic test results and to rely on their own interpretations of those results?

6. *Privacy and electronic health records.* In significant part, privacy concerns about genomic information resemble privacy concerns about other forms of medical information. For instance, debate about the risks and benefits of electronic medical records (EMRs) often resembles debate about the privacy of genetic information. Patient Privacy Rights, founded by Dr. Deborah Peel, a psychiatrist, acknowledges that EMRs have benefits but also describes a much darker side to them. Patient Privacy Rights suggests that the astonishing expansion of access to sensitive health information resulting from EMRs also facilitates the "misuse, abuse and discrimination by employers, insurers, creditors, government and others" of health information. The Coalition for Patient Privacy (the "Coalition"), http://patientprivacyrights.org/wp-content/uploads/2010/11/Coalition-Need-for-Privacy-in-HIT.pdf (last visited Sept. 9, 2012). The data presented by the Coalition is worrisome. Over one-third of Fortune 500 companies have acknowledged reviewing potential employees' medical data before making job offers or promotion decisions. Id. (citing 65 Fed. Reg. 82, 467). The Coalition further suggests that as people increasingly become aware of the extent to which EMRs make private information public, they will respond by withholding information from clinicians, refusing tests, and even using false names when seeking health care. Each of these responses risks undermining the success of health care.

Dr. Peel has compared the risk of making private medical information public to the risks presented by many smart phone apps. She writes: "Imagine the reactions smart phone users will have when they discover the vast, hidden industry that collects, uses, and sells personal health data—from prescription records to DNA to diagnoses." http://patientprivacyrights.org/2012/09/consumers-say-no-to-mobile-apps-that-grab-too-much-data/ (last visited Sept. 9, 2012). Increasingly, reports Peel, people are declining to install apps that collect personal information. She then queries:

> If Americans can figure out and ACT to prevent cell phone apps from grabbing their contacts and location information—what will they do when they find out that electronic health systems collect, use, and sell mountains of detailed, intimate information about their minds and bodies—and they can't turn these "apps" off?
>
> People CAN choose to live without Angry Birds (or whatever app they decide against) but they really CAN'T choose to go without healthcare—at least not without possibly serious health repercussions. People can choose what personal info to share online (to some degree), but really can't choose what health info is shared.
>
> Health technology systems that eliminate patient control over who can see and use sensitive health data are causing the nation's greatest hidden privacy disaster. It can only be fixed when the public finds out.

Deborah C. Peel, Consumers Say No to Mobile Apps That Grab Too Much Data, Sept. 5, 2012, http://patientprivacyrights.org/2012/09/consumers-say-no-to-mobile-apps-that-grab-too-much-data/ (last visited Sept. 9, 2012).

How do you think lawmakers should best respond to the concerns that Dr. Peel, along with many others, has raised about the risks attendant on society's rapid expansion of the use of electronic medical records?

7. *Hidden data mining.*   Deborah Peel, the psychiatrist and advocate for the protection of privacy quoted in Note 6, supra, has commented as well on a "hidden data mining industry." Acxiom Corporation, a marketing technology company that collects a great deal of data about people and uses it, among other things, to help marketers reach consumers and predict their future "needs," poses a significant threat to those concerned with safeguarding privacy. CNN has referred to Acxiom as "the world's largest processor of consumer data." Richard Behar, Never Heard of Acxiom?, CNN Money, Feb. 23, 2004, http://money.cnn.com/magazines/fortune/fortune_archive/2004/02/23/362182/index.htm. Natasha Singer described the company as "peer[ing] deeper into American life than the F.B.I. or the I.R.S." Natasha Singer, You for Sale: Mapping, and Sharing, the Consumer Genome, N.Y. Times, June 16, 2012, www.nytimes.com. (A few years ago, at least two groups were hacking Acxiom's data, additionally fueling concern about the protection of privacy.) Behar, supra.

Peel describes Singer's story as necessary reading for anyone interested in understanding

> how the use of personal data threatens people's jobs, reputations, and future opportunities. The information is analyzed and sold to those who want detailed real-time profiles of who we are, including the health of our minds and bodies. Data analytics enable Acxiom to create and sell far more intimate, detailed personality and behavioral portraits than our own mothers or analysts might know about us (and would never share).

Comment/Blog, http://patientprivacyrights.org (last visited June 17, 2012). Peel continues:

> Even though the hidden data mining industry began by using personal information to improve marketing and advertising, Acxiom proves that the kind and amounts amount of identifiable data being collected are simply unacceptable. As for the collection of health information, the data mining industry is clearly violating Americans' very strong legal, Constitutional, and ethical rights to control and keep personal health data private. To the public, this is theft of personal health information.
>
> . . . .
>
> Health data has long been used to discriminate against people for jobs, insurance, and credit. This fact is so well known that every year tens of millions of us refuse to get early diagnoses and treatment for cancer, depression, and sexually transmitted diseases. Hidden data flow causes bad health outcomes; treatment delays can be deadly. We need the same kind of control/consent over the use of electronic health data that we have always had for paper medical records.
>
> . . . .
>
> Unless we know where trillions of bytes of our personal data flow, who uses it and why, we cannot weigh the benefits and risks of using the Internet, electronic systems, or cell phones. It's time for Congress to end the massive hidden flows of personal data.

Id.

8. *DNA in court.* It is possible that courts will increasingly admit DNA evidence in civil cases involving disagreements about medical causation, about damage from workplace injuries, and other similar matters. Jon Lichtenstein reports, for instance that an NIH study has pointed to a gene linked to disc degeneration. He suggests that if a "plaintiff has a genetic marker for early onset arthritis, arguably the arthritis was not traumatically induced, and knee replacement surgery was inevitable." Jon D. Lichtenstein, Beyond Paternity: Future of Genetic Testing in Personal Injury Litigation, NYLJ, July 31, 2012. Does court-ordered DNA testing in a personal injury case unfairly expose the tested party to the revelation of private information?

9. *Bibliographic note.* The following articles consider the regulation of genetic testing: Valerie Gutmann Koch, PGTandMe: Social Networking-based Genetic Testing and the Evolving Research Model, 22 Health Matrix 33 (2012); Serra J. Schlanger, Putting Together the Pieces: Recent Proposals to Fill in the Genetic Testing Regulatory Puzzle, 21 Ann. Health L. 383 (2012); Jessica L. Roberts, The Genetic Information Nondiscrimination Act as an Antidiscrimination Law, 86 Notre Dame L. Rev. 597 (2011); Timothy J. Aspinwall, Imperfect Remedies: Legislative Efforts to Prevent Genetic Discrimination, 19 Ann. Health L. 121 (2010); Gaia Bernstein, Direct-to-Consumer Genetic Testing: Gatekeeping the Production of Genetic Information, 79 UMKC L. Rev. 283 (2010); Morse Hyun-Myung Tan, Advancing Civil Rights, The Next Generation: The Genetic Information Nondiscrimination Act of 2008 and Beyond, 19 Health Matrix 63 (2009); Perry W. Payne, Jr., Genetic Information Nondiscrimination Act of 2008: The Federal Answer for Genetic Discrimination, 5 J. Health & Biomed. L. 33 (2009); Recent Legislation: Health Law—Genetics—Congress Restricts Use of Genetic Information by Insurers and Employers, 122 Harv. L. Rev. 1038 (2009).

2. Genetics, Genomics, and Public Health

Often, the study of public health has concentrated on responding to the threat of infectious diseases. However, public health concerns also include challenges presented by inherited characteristics. (Chapter 12 considers public health issues more generally.)

The overarching question in this section asks if it is appropriate for government to favor policies that require or even merely encourage testing for certain genetic traits. If it is appropriate, when is it appropriate, and what goals should governmental policies that favor genetic testing aim to serve?

> ## James E. Bowman, The Plight of Poor African-Americans: Public Policy on Sickle Hemoglobin and AIDS
> **In African-American Perspectives on Biomedical Ethics (Harley E. Flack & Edmund D. Pellegrino, eds. 1992), at 173, 173–192**

Sickle-cell disease is an inherited disorder of hemoglobin (the oxygen-carrying protein of blood) in which, under conditions of reduced oxygen tension, the red cells assume the form of a sickle. This results in the plugging of blood vessels with subsequent damage to tissue or organs. The most common sites affected are the lungs, liver, kidneys, brain, heart, and hips. The life expectancy is quite variable and unpredictable, unlike that of Tay-Sachs disease. Some individuals with sickle cell disease die at an early age; some are intermittently ill throughout a short or long life; others reach adulthood without knowing that they have the disorder; a few live late into the seventh decade of life.

The carrier state is termed "sickle cell trait" (hemoglobin AS). Medical reports often associate sickle cell trait with sudden death. A study of Armed Forces recruits showed an increased incident of death during or following vigorous exercise associated with dehydration. Yet some of our best football and track athletes have sickle cell trait and perform in the high altitudes of Denver (over 5,000 feet) and Mexico City (7,500) without difficulty.

Occasionally a person with sickle cell trait may have rare episodes of blood in the urine, but an overwhelming majority does not. In the early days of sickle hemoglobin testing, many physicians, community groups, and publications from the National Institutes of Health did not delineate sickle cell trait from sickle cell disease. The confusion of sickle cell trait with sickle cell disease was undoubtedly the principal basis for the flood of early mandatory state sickle cell hemoglobin legislation.

Sickle hemoglobin is found in high frequency in peoples of African origin, in Southern Italians (particularly Sicilians), Greeks, Eti-Turks, Arabs, Egyptians, Eastern Jews, Southern Iranians, and Asiatic Indians. In the United States about 8 percent of African-Americans have sickle cell trait; about one in 500 black newborns have sickle cell disease, and approximately 45,000 African-Americans have sickle cell disease.

. . . Sickle cell programs were prompted by the making of a commercial test for the presence of sickle hemoglobin produced by Ortho-Pharmaceutical Corporation and later altered by many other companies. This test was advertised as a test for sickle hemoglobin, but it did not differentiate sickle cell trait from sickle cell disease. Community and other lay groups and even physicians began mass genetic screening programs using only the solubility tests. Some groups counseled that sickle cell trait was a mild form of sickle cell disease. Unknowledgeable physicians asserted that patients who had sickle cell anemia would not live past early childhood or would be dead by the age of twenty. Spurious and reputable sickle cell anemia organizations were created nationwide. Thousands of dollars were raised for mass screening with inappropriate tests; individuals were often improperly counseled by physicians and lay persons who were swayed by the propaganda. Consequently, legislators were pressed to pass mandatory sickle hemoglobin screening laws by persons who erroneously believed that one in twelve black Americans had a disease that would kill them before age twenty. Unfortunately, the stigma and misinformation about sickle cell trait and sickle cell disease is almost as prevalent today as it was in the early 1970s.

. . . There are lessons to be learned from misguided sickle hemoglobin programs that were instituted in the early 1970s. These programs led to: (1) stigmatization of potentially two million African-Americans with sickle cell trait; (2) mandatory sickle hemoglobin screening laws in twelve states (including the District of Columbia); some were quite subtle, others were not . . . ; (3) increased insurance rates for persons with sickle cell trait, even though morbidity and mortality in this group is not significantly different from those who do not have sickle cell trait; (4) the firing of flight attendants with sickle cell trait; (5) rejection of persons with sickle cell trait from flight and other hazardous service in the Armed Forces; (6) the banning of persons with sickle cell trait from athletics, even though some of the best football, basketball, and track athletes have sickle cell trait and compete effectively at high altitudes; and (7) sterilization of carriers of sickle hemoglobin.

Mary B. Mahowald, Aren't We All Eugenicists?: Commentary on Paul Lombardo's "Taking Eugenics Seriously"
30 Fla. St. U. L. Rev. 219 (2003)

Etymologically, the term eugenics comes from the Greek eugenes, which means "well born." In light of this derivation, its meaning is as difficult as it has ever been to answer the perennial philosophical question, what is "the good"? Still, by its literal definition, eugenics does mean something good, not bad: well born, not ill born. Presumably, this meaning is what led some eugenicists of the past to think that the practice they advocated was good, even when others recognized it as good in name but not in fact. Francis Galton, who coined the term in 1883, probably thought he was doing "good" by championing eugenics as the "science of improving the stock." Of course, thinking something is good does not make it so.

To the extent that eugenics is construed as morally objectionable, it is generally associated with coercion. . . . [W]hat people object to in eugenics is not the goal, such as improving the health of the population, but the means employed to achieve it. From this standpoint, in the absence of coercion (as reflected in law or obvious forms of social pressure), policies designed with the good of the population in mind are not properly labeled "eugenic." Note, however, that coercion is not an element in the etymology of the term; neither is it included in scientific and dictionary definitions of eugenics as a science by which the human race is improved. Even if the concept or term were mentioned, what constitutes "coercion" is arguable in its own right. For some, coercion implies the presence of formal, legal barriers to choice; to others, practical impediments such as economic costs and social pressures function coercively. The Holmes decision [in Buck v. Bell] was coercive in the first sense; in an age in which reproductive freedom is supported by law, women may nonetheless experience coercion in the second sense. Although I am no more able to define "the good" definitively than philosophers throughout history have been, I believe it is possible to arrive at an approximate understanding of what constitutes good or bad eugenics by approaching the issue indirectly, starting from the extreme ends of a spectrum of practices that most people consider ethically reprehensible or ethically praiseworthy. Popular approval and prevalent practice do not confer moral validity, which is why the mere fact that prenatal testing and termination after positive diagnosis is widely accepted does not make the practice morally justifiable. Nonetheless, the extreme ends of the spectrum are not just widely endorsed, but universally upheld by reasonable people. This makes the argument for moral validity much more compelling than it would be if controversy prevailed regarding their moral or legal status.

Let us consider, therefore, some examples of activities undertaken or omitted in the name of eugenics that seem manifestly wrong, and some that seem manifestly right or good. On one side, put the genocide committed by the Nazis or other groups who kill classes of people whom they consider undesirable; on the other side, put the health promoting behavior of the great majority of pregnant women. Between these opposite ends of the spectrum are a range of behaviors that may be construed as eugenic—sometimes separately, and sometimes in combination; they all fulfill in some way the literal meaning of eugenic as well-born. Many decisions about fertility, whether it is curtailment through contraception, sterilization, or abortion, or it is enhancement through various reproductive technologies, fall within the spectrum of eugenics; so do social policies, laws and cultural norms that affect such decisions. Perinatal decisions may also be eugenic—if their goal is to promote well-bornness. Prenatal testing and selective abortion are at neither end of the spectrum between good and bad eugenics. By broad social agreement, the Buck v. Bell decision belongs closer to the bad end. However, determination of where a particular behavior belongs on the spectrum depends on multiple variables, some of which are identifiable through examination of the practices that are clearly locatable at either end of the spectrum. The following characteristics distinguish between the two extremes:

Nazi Genocide	Health-Promoting Behavior During Pregnancy
Coercive intervention by state or government	Autonomous decisions by potential parents
Directed to born persons as a group	Directed to potential children as individuals
Terminating their lives	Supporting their lives
To avoid a specific trait or traits	To promote health or other conditions
Judged by state to be undesirable	Judged by potential parents to be desirable

Notice that one side opposes and the other respects the autonomy of those who are directly affected. Note too that one side involves people already born, while the other involves individuals that have not been born and may not even have been conceived. One side is eugenic practice through termination, not just prevention, of already-born individuals who are considered undesirable; on the other side is the avoidance of harms and promotion of benefits to intended offspring. On one side, the practice is driven by the state or government and directed towards an entire group of people who are defined by a single trait or set of traits. On the other side, the practice is driven by individual women or couples and directed towards potential children as individuals. As Aristotle observed long ago, the good of society generally outweighs the good of the individual as such. Based on that priority, the implicit emphasis on social welfare in the left column is a good, but other characteristics in that column are not. In contrast, the characteristics on the right are generally understood in a positive moral light. Coercion, for example, carries a moral onus that respect for autonomy does not—even though both are sometimes justifiable and sometimes not. And decisions to terminate lives are obviously tougher (and for pacifists, impossible) to justify than decisions to extend life—because life is a prima facie good. Terminating lives is even tougher to justify when the individuals to be killed are already born, and the sole criteria for termination are single traits or sets of traits found in whole groups of people who may also be killed by those criteria. In contrast, the lives to be supported on the right are seen wholistically, as individual potential children whose worth and right to life are not definable solely on grounds of any single trait or sets of traits.

The Buck v. Bell decision is on the left side of the eugenics spectrum because it fulfills all but one of the characteristics listed under Nazi genocide. The Supreme Court's ruling in *Buck* authorized the forced sterilization, but not the killing, of "imbeciles." Nonetheless, it constituted government endorsement of coercive intervention to avoid a specific trait deemed socially undesirable by state legislators. Worse, the Holmes decision purported to effect its eugenic goal by preventing individuals from exercising a right that is central to many people's lives, i.e., the right to have a child. Admittedly, some people with disabilities may be incapable of raising a child or, at least, raising one by themselves. Many are, nonetheless, capable of biological and social parenthood. So the Holmes decision is only as much removed from the far left as sterilization is from homicide. . . .

Prenatal testing is of course separable from termination of affected fetuses. When it is considered separately, prenatal testing may be not only close to but at the right end of the spectrum of eugenics. Some women seek testing with no intention of terminating their pregnancies if the fetus is found to have an anomaly. They may request tests solely to identify a condition that is potentially and effectively treatable in utero, to determine a mode of delivery that is likely to optimize the outcome for the child, or simply to prepare themselves or other family members for the birth of an affected child. In such cases, the testing is either eugenically neutral or "good eugenics."

When prenatal testing is undertaken to identify anomalies and terminate affected fetuses, it belongs closer to the left side of the spectrum. Two factors distinguish this from forced sterilization: the eugenic decision is made autonomously by the pregnant woman rather than by government imposition; and the life of the fetus, rather than the capacity for reproduction, is thereby ended. Governmental coercion puts sterilization closer to the far left, but direct killing of the fetus may be just as bad or worse if the fetus is imputed to have moral status. This brings us to the charge leveled by some people with disabilities against those who support prenatal testing and termination of affected fetuses. To them, these routine practices clearly constitute bad eugenics. . . .

NOTES AND QUESTIONS

1. *The role of the state and institutions.* A recurring question in response to challenges presented by genetic information is whether there is any role for the state to play in the promotion of genetic health. Clearly one of the main concerns here is coercion in reproductive practices—more specifically, whether state policies that encourage, even though they do not mandate, prenatal or carrier screening will cause prospective parents to feel compelled to avoid having a child whose genetic health is "subpar." There are other concerns as well, such as unequal treatment, as demonstrated by the poor history of sickle cell programs that led to wide-scale discrimination directed against members of a minority group who were already subject to discrimination because of race. There are further huge and unresolved, perhaps, irresolvable, issues of what subpar health means (i.e., which conditions should be tested for and with what expected consequences) and who decides.

2. *What is genetic health?* Should we (the state, individuals, society) defer to medical professionals about what conditions should be avoided? Should physicians speak with one voice on these matters—for instance, through statements made by professional medical groups?

The highly controversial issue of line-drawing in reproductive medical practice might be stated as follows: Given that it is possible to test for certain genetic conditions for the purposes of aborting affected fetuses or selecting against certain embryos in the context of in vitro fertilization, is it appropriate for health care professionals to offer and society to support tests for only certain conditions and not for others? Are some genetic conditions clearly so undesirable that testing should always be offered (and perhaps encouraged) and some genetic conditions clearly so trivial that selection on the basis of them is inappropriate and should be discouraged or even unavailable? Testing for some conditions but not others, in particular, testing only for disabling conditions, risks harm to people currently living with disabilities by further stigmatizing impairment. It also potentially intrudes on reproductive choice to the extent that the mere existence of certain tests and not others suggests that a parent should want to avoid giving birth to a child with the disabling condition tested for. On the other hand, allowing parents to test and select for any trait, such as perfect musical pitch, risks commodifying children and weakening the parent–child relationship. Unrestricted choice in testing might also feed discriminatory attitudes toward people with certain behavioral traits, such as homosexuality, if parents in the future are able to test to avoid those traits. See Mary Crossley & Lois Shepherd, Genes and Disability: Questions at the Crossroads, 30 Fla. St. U. L. Rev. xi (2003); and see, generally, volume 30, issue 2 of the Florida State University Law Review (symposium issue on Genes and Disability). What do you think about drawing lines between certain conditions and others for testing purposes?

3. *Good or bad eugenics?*   What does philosopher Mary Mahowald identify as the characteristics of "good" and "bad" eugenics? Do you agree? Interestingly, Mahowald concludes in the remainder of the article, not printed here, that the widespread practice of aborting fetuses diagnosed as having Down syndrome is "bad eugenics." Why do you think she might so conclude?

4. *Birth prevalence of Down syndrome.*   Recent studies about the incidence of Down syndrome, detection through prenatal screening, and termination through abortion are fairly scarce. However, those studies that have taken place show, across various countries, an increase in the incidence of Down syndrome (linked to the increased age of women at pregnancy, which is associated with a higher chance of an affected fetus) but also a very high termination rate. Veronica R. Collins et al., Is Down Syndrome a Disappearing Birth Defect?, J. Pediatr. 152(1) (2008): 20–24. In one study of Victoria, Australia, only 5 percent of pregnancies in which the fetus was diagnosed with Down syndrome resulted in a live birth. Id. The authors of this study concluded: "The data presented in this article, together with the greater life expectancy now experienced by people with DS, underline the need for continual monitoring to ensure appropriate provision of services for individuals born with DS and their families." Id. at 23. An editorial accompanying the study's publication, however, drew a different conclusion: "There is every reason to believe that increasing the proportion of cases diagnosed prenatally (among younger or older mothers) will result in an increase in selective pregnancy terminations and reduced birth prevalence, a desirable and attainable goal." David A. Savits, How Far Can Prenatal Screening Go in Preventing Birth Defects, J. Pediatr. 152(1) (2008): 4. Discussing the decrease in birth prevalence for both Down syndrome and cystic fibrosis, Savitz concluded, "There are few situations in which investment in health services has such a clear public health impact." Id. What do you think of these differing conclusions?

5. *When practices become routine.*   If certain practices become "routine" without governmental coercion or perhaps even governmental support, is it nonetheless possible to think of individuals' decisions in conformity with those "routines" as being somewhat "coerced"? What conditions in society

would make that decision (e.g., the decision to abort a fetus with Down syndrome) seem more or less voluntary, more or less coerced?

6. *The association of public health with undesirable eugenics.*   Some scholars reject the idea that clear distinctions can be made between bad and good eugenics—with public health initiatives more clearly falling within the first category, and individual reproductive choices falling within the latter. While individuals making reproductive choices for themselves are not thinking of the health of the population, nevertheless the aggregate effect of a number of similar choices can have effects on the population as a whole. According to one set of author-philosophers, the concerns for the individual prospective child and society are not neatly distinguished. They write,

> Consider these statements:
>
> Ia. I favour a genetic intervention because I want my child to have the "best" (healthiest, etc.) genes.
> Ib. We favor genetic interventions (on behalf of each of us) because we want our children to have the "best" (healthiest, etc.) genes.
> Ic. I favor genetic interventions (for each person in our group) because I want our children to have the "best" (healthiest, etc.) genes.
>
> If Ia is morally acceptable, it doesn't become wrong when voiced by several people (in the form of Ib.) And how can one person be faulted for endorsing that group's hope (Ic)? Ib and Ic are merely the aggregate of many instances of Ia. One might expect to hear Ic uttered by, say, a health official or a legislator who sponsors a measure that would provide genetic services to large numbers of people. Concern for the welfare of large numbers of people is part of their job descriptions.

Allen Buchanan, Dan W. Brock, Norman Daniels & Daniel Wikler, From Chance to Choice 53 (2000). Do you agree with this analysis?

CHALLENGING ISSUES: SETTING PUBLIC POLICY FOR PRENATAL TESTING

Suppose you are a state legislator and a proposal has come before your committee on health affairs that the state investigate the benefits of a program to ensure that all pregnant women receive, as a matter of routine prenatal care, the opportunity to submit to a blood test that would determine with a fairly high degree of accuracy that the fetus they are carrying has Down syndrome. You know that in 1974 a U.S. government analyst calculated that a $5 billion investment by the federal government over 20 years to encourage voluntary testing would (assuming a reduction in the births of children with Down syndrome of 50 percent) result in savings of more than $18 billion. (Buchanan, supra, at 55.) You imagine state savings could also be significant if fewer children with Down syndrome were born in the state, especially because the proposal imposes very little cost to the state. The state would not pay for the tests, but would simply require physicians in the provision of prenatal care to inform women of the availability of the test and to obtain their signature on a form documenting their decision to accept or refuse the test. Would you be in favor of pursuing the proposal? Would it affect your opinion if the proposal were being sponsored by a fellow legislator who had just given birth to a child with Down syndrome and argues that she should have been told by her doctor of the possibility of learning about her child's condition in utero in time to abort?

Note: You should know that such a simple blood test is not available at this time for a reasonable cost, but it might soon be. It is, however, the standard of care in many jurisdictions to offer pregnant women the alpha-fetoprotein screen, conducted by a blood test in early pregnancy, to detect neural tube anomalies, such as spina bifida. An elevated AFP test result can also be a first sign of an increased chance that the fetus has Down syndrome, but more testing in the form of chorionic villus sampling or amniocentesis is then required. The state of California has a law similar to the one described in this problem, although it is for the AFP screen and not to test specifically for Down syndrome. See Cal. Code Regs. Tit. 17 §6527 (2002). Arthur Caplan pointed out that California's mandate that physicians offer alpha-fetoprotein screening to all pregnant woman is done "in the hope that some of those who are found to have children with neural tube defects will choose not to bring them to term; thereby, preventing the state from having to bear the burden of their care." Arthur L. Caplan, Neutrality Is Not Morality: The Ethics of Genetic Counseling, in Prescribing Our Future: Ethical Challenges in Genetic Counseling 158–159 (Dianne M. Bartels et al. eds. 1993). See also Sonia Mateu Suter, The Routinization of Prenatal Testing, 28 Am. J.L. & Med. 233 (2002) (describing how the mandate caused physicians to overreach in persuading their patients to have the test, "the clearest evidence of compliance" that it was offered). Id. at 253.

3.   Special Issues Involving Preimplantation and Prenatal Genetic Testing and Genetic Testing of Children

a.   Preimplantation and Prenatal Genetic Testing

This section revisits some of issues raised in the excerpt from Mary Mahowald's article, Aren't We All Eugenists, 31 Fla. St. U.L. Rev. 219 (2003) (printed earlier in this chapter). It focuses on genetic testing before or during pregnancy (preimplantation genetic diagnosis and prenatal testing, respectively).

A diverse group of people have opposed preimplantation genetic diagnosis. Andrew B. Coan, Is There a Constitutional Right to Select the Genes of One's Offspring?, 63 Hastings L.J. 233, 236 (2011). Coan includes among this group some feminists, concerned that women could be compelled by physicians or male partners to undergo procedures that do not serve them; some religious conservatives, concerned about a variety of matters including the destruction of embryos; some "leftist communitarians," concerned about the commodification of babies; and some disability rights advocates, worried about the consequences of prospective parents' selecting against embryos likely to be born or to become disabled. Id.

> ### *Report for President's Council on Bioethics, Reproduction and Responsibility: The Regulation of New Biotechnologies*
> ### March 2004, Part I, Chapter 3

... [I]nnovations in assisted reproduction and molecular genetics have yielded new ways to test early-stage embryos in vitro for genetic markers and characteristics. After such testing only those embryos with the desired genetic characteristics are transferred to initiate a pregnancy. By comparison with the older form of screening [e.g., amniocentesis and chorionic villus sampling], this approach is more "positively" selective; it amounts more to "choosing in" rather than merely to "weeding out." ...

I. USES AND TECHNIQUES

A. *Preimplantation Genetic Diagnosis of Embryos*

PGD is a technique that permits clinicians to analyze embryos in vitro for certain genetic (or chromosomal) traits or markers and to select accordingly for purposes of transfer. The early embryo (six to eight cells) is biopsied by removal of one or two cells, and the sample cell(s) is then examined for the presence or absence of the markers of interest. ... PGD was first used in 1989 as an adjunct to in vitro fertilization (IVF) for treating infertility. Official statistics do not tell us how many children have been conceived following PGD. Estimates vary widely. ...

At present, PGD can identify genetic markers that correlate with (or suggest a predisposition for) [many] diseases, including illnesses that become manifest much later in life, such as early-onset Alzheimer disease. As genomic knowledge increases and more genes that correlate with diseases are identified, the applications for PGD will likely increase. ... Many couples with family histories of diseases [linked to genetic alterations] may be drawn to PGD, even in the absence of infertility. Moreover, if genetic associations with other, non-medical conditions are identified, PGD might one day be used to screen for positive traits and characteristics such as height, leanness, or temperament. ...

II. ETHICAL CONSIDERATIONS

PGD, when effective, enables parents to avoid the deep grief and hardship that accompany the birth of a child with dreaded and incurable diseases such as cystic fibrosis and Tay-Sachs. And by screening out embryos with genetic abnormalities before a pregnancy begins, it prevents many women from having to decide whether to abort an abnormal fetus. Yet PGD also raises a number of ethical concerns, similar to but extending beyond the concerns attached to assisted reproduction itself. ...

C.   Increased Control Over the Characteristics of Children

PGD gives prospective parents the capacity to screen and select for specific genetic traits in their children. For now, that capacity is limited. Technical limitations on the number of embryos that can be produced in a single PGD cycle and on the number of tests that can be performed on a single blastomere severely restrict the number of characteristics for which practitioners can now test. Similarly, the complexity of the relationship between identifiable single genes and phenotypic characteristics will complicate the development of genetic tests for many traits and characteristics of interest (for example, where traits have polygenic contributions or result from complex gene–environmental interactions). Moreover, one cannot select for genes that are not brought to the embryos by their genetic progenitors; efforts at positive selection will be limited. Thus, the capacity to use PGD to select for a "superior genotype"—a "designer baby"—is in our estimation not on the horizon.

The present, more modest, applications of PGD—screening for severe medical conditions, screening for genetic predispositions or risk factors for a given disease, elective sex selection, and selection with an eye to creating a matching tissue donor—do give rise to ethical concerns about possible impacts on children and families. PGD used for these purposes might in some cases treat the resulting child as a means to the parents' ends. This concern would be amplified should the reasons for embryo screening move from "medical" purposes to nonmedical or enhancement purposes, from preventing the birth of a diseased child to trying to "maximize" a child's genotype for desired characteristics. (This line is, admittedly, hard to draw.) Because the prospective child is deliberately selected on qualitative, genetic grounds out of a pool of possible embryonic siblings, PGD risks normalizing the idea that a child's particular genetic make-up is quite properly a province of parental reproductive choice, or the idea that entrance into the world depends on meeting certain genetic criteria. Even if the prospective parents are guided by their own sense of what would be a good or healthy baby, their selection may in some cases serve their own interests more than the child's (as in the case, for example, of a deaf couple using PGD in an effort to produce a deaf child). . . .

D.   PGD for Late-Onset Disease

PGD can be used not only to identify abnormalities that would lead to certain and immediate diseases (like Tay-Sachs or Down syndrome), but can also be used to identify an increased susceptibility to particular diseases later in life. Is PGD justified to avoid the birth of a child who will be likely to live "only" thirty years? Is it justified to avoid the birth of a child who is especially susceptible to a late-onset disease like breast cancer or Alzheimer disease? Questions like these will need to be confronted as the ability to make biological and genetic predictions about unimplanted embryos continues to grow.

E. Eugenics and Inequality

For some critics, PGD calls to mind the specter of "eugenics"; it is seen as a technology that facilitates the selection of "better" children. Some worry that as PGD becomes more widespread, it will serve to further stigmatize the disabled and promote the notion that some lives are not worth living or are better off prevented in the first place. This is in a sense nothing new—amniocentesis and prenatal diagnosis are common and have already raised similar concerns. What is novel about PGD, though, is that it can be used to select "for" desirable traits, not just "against" markers for disease.

Other commentators worry that widespread use of PGD (so long as it is not covered by insurance or subsidized by taxpayers) could widen and worsen the gap between the "haves" and the "have-nots" in society, as access to PGD, like access to IVF itself, is restricted to those who can afford it. . . .

NOTES AND QUESTIONS

1. *High-speed DNA sequencing.* In 2012, scientists from the University of Washington reported that, relying on high-speed DNA sequencing, they had developed a method to reconstruct a fetus's genome. Andrew Pollack, DNA Blueprint for Fetus Built Using Tests of Parents, N.Y. Times, June 6, 2012, www. nytimes.com. The method, which relies only on blood from the pregnant woman and a saliva swab from the biological father, is about 98 percent accurate and is still extremely expensive. At a cost of between $20,000 and $50,000 for each genome studied, the method is not ready for general use. But it might soon be.

The method raises questions not unlike those raised by amniocentesis or preimplantation genetic diagnosis. However, the ethical challenges are magnified with the new technique because it will be possible for prospective parents to learn easily about thousands of genetic conditions that might affect their child. Id. Commentators have suggested that the ethical challenges created by the technique include parents' choosing to abort a fetus that does not fit their image of the child they should have. In addition to facilitating prospective parents' selecting against fetuses with deleterious genetic alteration, the method might encourage "positive selection" for children with specified traits. Id.

2. *Attitudes about genetic technology.* A national survey involving 1,211 respondents (18 and older), taken by the Genetics and Public Policy Center with Princeton Survey Research Associates soon after a draft of the human genome was published (between October 15 and October 29, 2002), indicated that most Americans favored using genetic technology to improve health but did not favor relying on this technology for enhancing traits considered desirable, such as strength and intelligence. Public Awareness and Attitudes About Reproductive Genetic Technology, The Genetics and Public Policy Center with Princeton Survey Research Associates, Dec. 9, 2002, http://www.dnapolicy.org/index. The survey found that evangelical Christians were less likely to favor using genetic technology than others, that men favored use of the technology more than women, and that people between 18 and 29 were more positive about using genetic technology than were people over 30. The survey found no statistically significant differences based on ethnicity or race with

regard to support for genetic technology. Id. at 11–12. Follow-up surveys revealed that about 40 percent of the respondents were unaware of PGD; a bit more than two-thirds of the respondents favored genetic testing to select against fatal illnesses; and a large proportion of the respondents (84 percent) favored greater regulation of reproductive technology. Reproductive Genetic Testing: What America Thinks, Genetics and Public Policy Center (2004), http://www.pewtrusts.org/uploadedFiles/wwwpewtrustsorg/Reports/Genetics _and_Public_Policy/GPPC_RGT_Opinion_0205.pdf.

A later study of attitudes about prenatal genetic testing among people with a familial history of a common form of hereditary colorectal cancer found that about two-thirds of the study population (161 people at risk for or diagnosed with colon cancer) agreed with the assertion that prenatal testing for the condition was ethical. Only 9 percent of those questioned concluded that such testing was "unethical." A. Dewanwata et al., Attitudes Toward Childbearing and Prenatal Testing in Individuals Undergoing Genetic Testing for Lynch Syndrome, 10 Fam. Cancer 549 (2011). Another study reported that 75 percent of a group of 201 parents of children with intellectual disabilities would not terminate a pregnancy if prenatal testing suggested their child's disability. A third of the group said that they would refuse prenatal testing altogether. M. Kuppermann et al., Attitudes Toward Prenatal Testing and Pregnancy Termination Among a Diverse Population of Parents of Children with Intellectual Disabilities, 13 Prenat. Diagn. 1251 (2011).

3. *Views of disability rights critique.*   PGD has been strongly condemned by the disability rights critique. The critique opposes PGD followed by abortion as "morally problematic" and "driven by misinformation." Erik Parens & Adrienne Asch, The Disability Rights Critique of Prenatal Genetic Testing: Reflections and Recommendations, in Prenatal Testing and Disability Rights 3, 13 (Erik Parens & Adrienne Asch eds. 2000). Parens and Asch describe the critique's essential assertions as follows: first, that discrimination is the central problem for disabled people and for their families; second, that those who abort a "desired child" because of a disability diagnosed through prenatal testing "suggest that they are unwilling to accept any significant departure from the parental dreams that a child's characteristics might occasion"; and third, that selective abortion constitutes an "unfortunate, often misinformed decision that a disabled child will not fulfill what most people seek in child rearing." Id. at 12–13.

Some prospective parents have relied on assisted reproductive technology to have a child bearing a disability. One deaf lesbian couple, reproducing with donated sperm, selected a deaf donor to produce a deaf child who, the couple hoped, would participate fully in the parents' deaf community. Christine Stolba, Overcoming Motherhood: Pushing the Limits of Reproductive Choice, Policy Rev., December 1, 2002, at 31.

In Genetic Dilemmas: Reproductive Technology, Parental Choices, and Children's Futures (2001), Dena Davis argues strongly against selecting for a deaf child before the child's conception or birth. This sort of prenatal decision, argues Davis, "that confines [a child] forever to a narrow group of people and a limited choice of careers so violates the child's right to an open future that no genetic counselor should acquiesce to it." Id. at 65.

Prenatal genetic testing is considered further in Brigham A. Fordham, Disability and Designer Babies, 45 Val. U.L. Rev. 1473 (2011); Marsha Saxton,

Disability Rights and Selective Abortion, in Abortion Wars: A Half Century of Struggle, 1950–2000 374 (Rickie Solinger ed. 1998). Stacy Klein, Note, Prenatal Genetic Testing and Its Impact on Incidence of Abortion, 7 Cardozo J. Int'l & Comp. L. 73 (1999). The Florida State University Law Review has printed the proceedings of a 2002 symposium at the University's College of Law on Genes and Disability: Defining Health and the Goals of Medicine, 30 Fla. St. U. L. Rev. (Winter 2003).

4. *Role of genetic counselors.*   Some of those associated with the disability rights critique have focused on the role of genetic counselors in advising people undergoing prenatal testing. Genetic counseling is widely recognized as an area of health care specialization. Genetic counselors are expected to provide people with information so that they will understand the implications of genetic testing before they agree to undergo testing. Among other things, genetic counselors typically discuss medical facts about diseases for which tests are being done, statistics about the likelihood of a disease appearing if a genetic alteration is found, and information about potential psychological consequences of learning about the presence (in an embryo or a fetus, or in oneself or one's spouse) of a deleterious genetic alteration.

Some believe that genetic counselors should provide direction. Others, including proponents of the disability rights critique, suggest that counselors should be nondirective, simply providing clients with adequate information to reach their own conclusions about whether to proceed with testing and about how to handle disappointing results. Lynn A. Jansen, Role of the Nurse in Clinical Genetics 133, 135 in Genetics in the Clinic: Clinical, Ethical, and Social Implications for Primary Care (Mary B. Mahowald et al. eds. 2001). Other useful references include Kevin Costello, The Limitations of Wrongful Life Claims and Genetic Diagnosis, L.A. Lawyer (April 2007) (considering genetic counseling and wrongful life claims); Larry I. Palmer, Genes and Disability: Defining Health and the Goals of Medicine: Genetic Health and Eugenics Precedents: A Voice of Caution, 30 Fla. St. U. L. Rev. 237 (2003) (considering implications of notion of "genetic health" for individuals and for society).

A more general concern about genetic counselors concerns those working in hospitals and physicians' offices who are employed by commercial enterprises. Andrew Pollack, The Ethics of Advice, N.Y. Times, July 14, 2012, www.nytimes.com. Questions have been raised about the possibility that such counselors (whose jobs depend on their employers' success) will be too ready to suggest tests offered by their employers and slow to suggest tests offered only by rival companies.

5. *Gender selection.*   Prenatal testing, including preimplantation genetic diagnosis, is also being used for gender selection. Other methods used for gender selection include diagnosis during pregnancy through ultrasound or through chromosomal analysis using amniocentesis or chorionic villus sampling. Gender selection using these techniques involves readiness to abort a fetus of the "wrong" gender. Several techniques can be used before the start of a pregnancy. One of these involves sperm sorting. The Genetics and IVF Institute in Fairfax, Virginia, claims the technique (called MicroSort) is successful in over 90 percent of cases in which a girl is desired and in 73 percent of cases in which a boy is desired. The institute has an exclusive license to use MicroSort. The institute offers sperm sorting for nonmedical reasons but only for family

balancing. Thus, the institute does not allow its use to select the gender of a first child in the absence of medical reasons.

The standard gender ratio at birth is 105 boys to every 100 girls. The use of gender selection is presumed wherever that ratio differs significantly from the standard. In the United States, some women use gender selection to produce daughters. Christine Stolba, Overcoming Motherhood: Pushing the Limits of Reproductive Choice, Policy Rev., Dec. 1, 2002, at 31. In other places such as India and China, the preference is generally to select for male fetuses. In 2003, the ratio in Delhi, India and in China was 117 boys to 100 girls, and in Cuba it was 118 to 100. These figures, as well as a broad review of the issues raised by gender selection, are reported in a 2003 staff working paper prepared for the President's Council on Bioethics. Ethical Aspects of Sex Control, http://www.bioethics.gov/material/sex_control.html.

In India, where sons have long been preferred to daughters and where young married women could be under strong pressure from their husbands and other relatives to give birth to sons, a sex determination clinic was set up in Amritsar in 1979. Within a short time, pregnant women throughout the country were learning the gender of their fetuses through ultrasound. Many women aborted female fetuses. Beginning in the late 1980s, Indian states began to pass laws prohibiting prenatal diagnosis for gender selection. Then in 1991, after a census showed the extent to which gender selection was being practiced, the central Indian government passed legislation prohibiting prenatal gender selection. This history is described in Kenan Farrell, Where Have All the Young Girls Gone?: Preconception Gender Selection in India and the United States, 13 Ind. Int'l & Comp. L. Rev. 253 (2002). One small-scale study found that some PGD providers and patients in the United States expressed concern about using the technique to select a child's gender but others asserted that they did not think that the risk was significant because of the comparative absence of a "cultural gender bias in the US," at least as compared with other countries. Andrea L. Kalfoglou, PGD Patients' and Providers' Attitudes to the Use and Regulation of Preimplantation Genetic Diagnosis, 11 Reproductive BioMed. Online, Aug. 2, 2005, available at http://www.umbc.edu/happ/AK/Kalfoglou%2010-05%20final.pdf (last visited July 30, 2012).

British law prohibits gender selection for nonmedical reasons. As a result, well-off prospective parents from Britain now travel to the United States to "balance" their families. One Manhattan clinic, the Fertility Institutes, claims to provide preimplantation genetic diagnosis to about 40 couples from Britain each year for the purpose of "family balancing" at a cost of ¢30,000 (more than $47,600 in September 2012) per IVF cycle. Ayesha Ahmad, Wealthy Couples Flock to USA to Avoid UK Sex Selection Ban, IVF Medic Claims, Sept. 3, 2012, BioNews, available at http://www.bionews.org.uk/page_170956.asp?dinfo=fLg8CfFCr9VovEQq9KIjA3zi&PPID=170565 (last visited Sept. 3, 2012).

Do you think people should be permitted to select the gender of their children, especially in the absence of medical concerns? What will be the consequences for society of altered gender ratios? Will use of these techniques alter society's understanding of gender? Should gender selection be illegal? Would that interfere unfairly with reproductive choice? What arguments might support gender control? Does it make sense to argue that offering people the chance to choose their baby's gender might help limit population growth because people will not continue to have children in the hope that they will conceive a child of the desired gender?

6. *Concerns beyond eugenics.*   Not all concerns about genetic enhancement involve concern about eugenics. For instance, some have worried about the effect of PGD followed by embryo selection or prenatal testing followed by abortion on evolution, and others have worried about the hubris on which such practices are grounded.

> Some have speculated that genetic enhancement might affect human evolution. Geneticists have countered that the power to control human evolution is unlikely, as the evolution of the human species is a nonrandom change in allelic frequencies resulting from selective pressure. The change progresses over generations because individuals with specific patterns of alleles are favored reproductively. If new alleles were introduced by gene transfer, the impact on the species would be negligible. Moreover, there is no certainty that genetically enhanced individuals would have greater biological fitness, as measured by reproductive success.

National Human Genome Research Institute, National Institutes of Health, http://www.genome.gov/10004767 (prepared by Kathi E. Hanna) (2006).

7. *Bibliographic note.* Additional useful references include Karen H. Rothenberg, From Eugenics to the 'New' Genetics: 'The Play's the Thing,' 79 Fordham L. Rev. 407 (2010) (exploring eugenic notions in the form of a play); Mary B. Mahowald et al. eds., Genetics in the Clinic: Clinical, Ethical and Social Implications for Primary Care (2003). This edited volume contains articles that discuss the biology, application, risks, and ethics of genetic testing. See also David M. Smolin, The Missing Girls of China: Population, Policy, Culture, Gender, Abortion, Abandonment, and Adoption in East-Asian Perspective, 41 Cumb. L. Rev. 1 (2010–2011); Sagit Ziskind, The Genetic Information Nondiscrimination Act: A New Look at an Old Problem, 35 Rutgers Computer & Tech. L.J. 163 (2009); Francy E. Foral, Note, Necessity's Sharp Pinch: Parental and States' Rights in Conflict in an Era of Newborn Genetic Screening, 2 J. Health & Biomed. L. 109 (2006) (considers newborn genetic screening, informed consent, child's best interests, and potential for genetic discrimination); Lori B. Andrews, A Conceptual Framework for Genetic Policy: Comparing the Medical, Public Health, and Fundamental Rights Models, 79 Wash. U. L.Q. 221 (2001) (considering sociolegal implications of genetic testing and delineating legal framework for regulating genetic information); Jeri E. Reutenauer, Note, Medical Malpractice Liability in the Era of Genetic Susceptibility Testing, 19 Quinnipiac L. Rev. 539 (2000); Mark A. Rothstein & Sharona Hoffman, Genetic Testing, Genetic Medicine, and Managed Care, 34 Wake Forest L. Rev. 849 (1999) (providing recommendations for practice of genetic medicine in context of managed care).

b.   Having a Baby to Cure a Sick Child

A number of diseases—some the result of a genetic alteration, some not—that affect children can be treated with a bone marrow transplantation. Bone marrow can only be successfully transplanted if it is taken from a donor with matching human leukocyte antigens (HLA). Moreover, since the mid-1990s, it has become clear that use of cord blood cells taken at birth from a matched sibling is likely to be even more successful than transplantation of bone marrow from an older sibling. Cord blood can be obtained from a placenta or from an umbilical cord. Some couples with children in need of transplants and no available donors have sought to have another child in the hope that that child would be a compatible donor for the sick sibling.

There are two risks. First, if the condition from which the first child suffers is the result of a genetic alteration, a second child could suffer from the same condition. Second, even if the second child is healthy, he or she might not be a compatible donor.

Preimplantation genetic diagnosis can allow potential parents to select an embryo that does not carry the feared genetic alteration. The technique can also ensure that the resulting child will be a compatible donor to his or her sick sibling. Public controversy has surrounded the use of preimplantation genetic diagnosis for this purpose.

> ### Susan M. Wolf, Jeffrey P. Kahn, & John E. Wagner, Using Preimplantation Genetic Diagnosis to Create a Stem Cell Donor: Issues, Guidelines, and Limits
> **31 J.L. Med. & Ethics 327, 328–329 (2003)**

The index case is that of a 6-year-old female child with rapidly progressive bone marrow failure and myelodysplastic syndrome secondary to FA [Fanconi anemia]. The Nash case was publicized with identifiers with the parents' permission. After four unsuccessful attempts to use IVF and PGD to create a healthy and HLA-matched donor, the Nashes were the first couple to succeed. The HealthONE Institutional Review Board (IRB) in Denver approved the IVF and PGD protocols, the Illinois Masonic Medical Center IRB in Chicago approved the PGD protocol as well, and the University of Minnesota IRB approved the transplant protocol. A child was born in August of 2000. He is HLA-identical to his sister. He carries one FANCC IVS4 A>T mutation, like each of his parents, and therefore is not at risk for FA. Three weeks after his birth, the family came to Minneapolis where the child with FA was treated with high dose chemoradiotherapy followed by the infusion of blood collected from her brother's placenta and umbilical cord after his birth. She showed bone marrow recovery at four weeks. Three years later, her hematopoietic and immune systems are normal.

The Nash case illustrates the successful combination of three technologies: IVF, PGD, and stem cell transplant. However, because of the success so far of the cord blood transplant, the Nash case does not illustrate the reality that children conceived to be HLA-matched face the possibility of donation throughout their lives. The initial cord blood donation could fail for any of several reasons: inadequate cord blood cell dose, graft failure after cord blood transplant, or the recipient child experiencing a recurrence of leukemia after transplant. If cord blood transplant fails, the next step is bone marrow harvest and transplant. This, too, might not engraft or leukemia may recur, requiring yet another bone marrow transplant. Further, once an HLA-matched donor is created, the need for tissues beyond bone marrow may arise. Indeed, after bone marrow transplant, toxicities related to chemotherapy and irradiation or immunosuppressive drugs could produce organ failure involving the kidneys, liver, or other organs. Then the question would arise whether to harvest a solid organ from the donor child. The HLA-matched child created in the Nash case has thus far escaped further need for tissue or organs by his sister. However, he is quite young. He and all children created as donors face the potential of requests for donation throughout their lives.

|| **Richard F. Storrow, Therapeutic Reproduction and Human Dignity** 21 Law and Literature 257, 261–263 (2009) ||

[The European Society for Human Reproduction and Embryology,] ESHRE articulates both ethical and legal justifications in favor of [the] creation [of savior siblings]. ESHRE's legal opinion draws support from the presumption that parents will act in the best interests of their children. ESHRE believes that the presumption encompasses the determination of fully informed and counseled parents to impose a detriment upon their child for the benefit of his sibling, at least where they judge that the "risks are outweighed by the benefits for the receiving sibling." From this reasoning, ESHRE fashions a "postnatal test" for savior siblings: "If the parents have the authority to 'volunteer' an existing child as a bone marrow donor for a sibling, it is also acceptable that they create a child as a bone marrow donor for a sibling." The condition embodied in the postnatal test reflects the fact that the law sets a higher standard for parental decision making when the medical procedure is of no direct medical benefit to the donor child. ESHRE and commentators have suggested that this higher standard can be met through the psychological benefits the donor receives from helping the sick sibling, benefits that range from contributing to the family's stability and survival to the boost in self-esteem gained from having a power to heal that others lack. ESHRE's second legal argument in support of the creation of savior siblings is that a court may substitute its judgment for that of the unconceived donor in the same way it does when considering whether medical procedures should be performed upon persons too incapacitated to give informed consent. In the context of savior siblings, ESHRE anticipates that a court will conclude that "the future sibling on whose behalf the decision to donate is made will agree with the present decision when he/she becomes autonomous." Despite its generally favorable attitude toward the creation of savior siblings, ESHRE cautions that creating a child to donate nonregenerating organs is unacceptable "in view of the risks involved for the donor child."

As an ethical response to fears that savior siblings will not enjoy "full respect for their personal uniqueness and dignity," ESHRE believes using PGD for HLA matching is not instrumentalizing if obtaining tissue is not the only motive for the parents to have the child. As long as the parents intend to love and care for the donor child to the same extent as they love and care for the affected child, they can clear this "single-motive" hurdle and avert psychological and emotional harm to the donor offspring. This ethical analysis is similar to [the position of the American Society for Reproductive Medicine (ASRM)] that preconception gender selection is acceptable where parents are counseled against unrealistic expectations and "affirm that they will fully accept children of the opposite sex if the preconception gender selection fails."

Commentators on the single-motive test emphasize how extremely difficult it would be to show that parents harbor a single motive for creating a savior sibling. Indeed, especially when parents undertake Herculean efforts to save their sick child, it perhaps is highly unlikely that they will treat their carefully chosen donor child with any less devotion, especially if the donations successfully treat the sick child. In that case, the donor may actually receive an emotional boost from having been of such great assistance. The thrust of these perspectives is that without red flags to warn us that parents will abuse, neglect, or abandon their donor children, we lack justification for assuming anything other than that a parental project to create a child to save another falls well within the sphere of deference parents have traditionally enjoyed.

Of course, not every ethical analysis proceeds in the direction of general permissiveness. Convened by former President Bush in 2001, the President's Council on Bioethics took a very firm stance against sex selection for nonmedical reasons and expressed a number of concerns about the creation of savior siblings. The Council was particularly concerned that when technology removes the "genetic lottery" from human reproduction, parental expectations become fixed in ways that deprive the resulting children of an "open future." In the case of nonmedical sex selection, the Council adopted reasoning from its earlier work opposing human reproductive cloning and stated: "[W]e should be reluctant to see ourselves as people who may appropriately dictate such a crucial part of the identity of our child [lest we turn human reproduction] into a form of manufacture and open the door to a new eugenics." The Council disagreed that counseling and a parental affirmation that a child of the undesired gender will be fully accepted pull the poison from sex selection. Similarly, the President's Council did not dispute that savior siblings are probably loved by their parents but nonetheless queried whether assigning the role of savior to a child as a condition for its existence is an appropriate exercise of human reproductive potential. In essence, the President's Council viewed the creation of savior siblings as a genetic trait selection technology that goes beyond therapy. Unlike ESHRE and ASRM, then, the President's Council believed these technologies to threaten important understandings of human reproduction and even of human dignity.

NOTES AND QUESTIONS

1. *Donor siblings.*   Do you think it is ethical to use PGD to create a "donor sibling"? Wolf, Kahn, and Wagner, supra, conclude that the technique should be used only under limited conditions because of the risk that the donor child will be required (or urged) to donate tissue to the sick sibling for many years or throughout life. They suggest that, at present, PGD should only be used to create a "donor sibling" in the context of a research protocol subject to review by an institutional review board. Id. at 331.

The authors conclude:

> The most fundamental protections we recommend are: (1) to combine these three technologies [IVF, PGD, and HLA matching] only in the context of research at present, with the attendant human subject protections and need for oversight, and (2) to safeguard the future interests of the donor child-to-be, and later the interests of the donor child. Both protections are essential to ethical conduct in the use of these technologies.

Id. at 336.

Yet, the European Society for Human Reproduction and Embryology concluded that parents should be permitted to create savior siblings to donate bone marrow (but not nonregenerative organs). On what assumption does ESHRE ground that conclusion?

2. *British law.* Until 2004, the British Human Fertilisation and Embryology Authority (HFEA) permitted IVF and preimplantation genetic diagnosis to create a sibling donor only in cases in which the sick sibling suffers from a genetic condition. The HFEA reasoned that in such cases the donor sibling benefits from the procedure in that he or she is protected through genetic diagnosis and embryo selection from inheriting the genetic alteration that would or might result in serious illness. In cases in which the sick sibling suffers from a nongenetic condition, PGD is used in Britain only to choose an embryo that will be a fit donor for the sick sibling.

In 2004, the HFEA announced its willingness to allow preimplantation genetic diagnosis in cases in which the process is used only to enable the birth of a "matched" donor sibling but in which there is no need to rely on genetic testing to prevent a matched sibling from carrying a deleterious genetic alteration. Suzi Leather, chair of the HFEA, explained that use of preimplantation genetic diagnosis for purposes of tissue typing only did not appear to harm babies that result. She noted that the risks of stem cell donations between siblings were low. HFEA Allow PGD for HLA Tissue Typing, 268 BioNews, July 26, 2004, http://www.bionews.org. Permission to perform the procedure for tissue typing only would be premised on the doctors of the sick child having tried other alternatives (e.g., use of cells from histocompatible family members) without success.

c. Special Issues Involving Genetic Testing of Children

The mapping of the human genome and society's increasing readiness to attribute behavioral and physical traits to "a gene" have shifted assessments of the comparative roles of nature and nurture in child rearing. With this shift, the notion of parental responsibility has taken on new dimensions. Parents, once considered responsible for protecting, educating, and guiding their children, can now be considered "responsible" for transmitting advantageous and disadvantageous genes to their children.

This new genetic responsibility, however, lacks the moral dimensions of traditional parental responsibility. Indeed, "responsibility" is in significant part a misnomer in connection with genetic inheritance. DNA is amoral. And so, relationships defined largely through genetic inheritance rather than through shared history and interaction might themselves be defined as amoral. The implications of genetic inheritance among kinship groups is considered by Kaja Finkler in Experiencing the New Genetics (2000). Finkler, an anthropologist, analyzed an "ideology of genetic inheritance." Her research involved interviews with three groups of people: women not suffering from cancer but from families with a history of breast, colon, or ovarian cancer; women who had experienced breast cancer; and adoptees who had sought or were seeking their birth mothers. Finkler concluded that biomedicine, through the notion of genetic inheritance, "pins down and defines the family in precise terms by uniting, wittingly or unwittingly, individuals with their families and kin." Id. at 206.

As the range of tests for genetic conditions broadens, a host of new questions arises about testing children for genetic alterations associated with illness or disability. Arguably, genetic testing raises difficult issues that are unlike those raised by other sorts of medical testing.

First, genetic testing of parents might reveal likely or certain information about a child's genome. If one person in a "genetic family" tests positive for a deleterious genetic alteration, others are at risk of carrying the same alteration. Thus genetic information about a parent or a child might also be information about the other, and similarly with regard to siblings and even cousins and less closely related genetic kin.

Second, a child might internalize a negative conception of self as a result of learning about genetic test results or could suffer serious anxiety about developing an illness that might or might not ever become manifest.

Third, despite the passage of the Genetic Information Nondiscrimination Act (see supra), U.S. law does not uniformly and comprehensively protect people against all forms of genetic discrimination. Thus, a child known to carry a deleterious genetic alteration could be treated unfairly during childhood or later in life by a variety of groups and institutions including schools, health care providers or, even prospective spouses or domestic partners.

Decisions about genetic testing are additionally complicated because interpreting genetic test results for patients is an art as well as a science. Positive results could reveal the presence of conditions that will become manifest during childhood, of conditions that will develop later in life, or of conditions that might or might not ever develop. That is, some genetically based conditions develop early in life. Others might not appear until middle age or old age. Moreover, some genetic conditions are almost certain to appear if the carrier survives to a certain age. Others might not ever appear despite a genetic predisposition. The term *penetrance* is used to assess the statistical likelihood that a condition associated with a particular genetic alteration will become manifest during a person's life span. Furthermore, some genetic conditions can be treated and others cannot be treated. Thus, depending on the character of the genetic alteration at issue, the wisdom and practical consequences of testing children (or adults) varies.

The least controversial genetic testing of children is that done for diagnostic purposes on children exhibiting symptoms of illness. In general, presymptomatic testing is more controversial, especially if the suspected condition cannot be lessened in severity or precluded by treatment should the test result be positive. Genetic testing on minors is harder to sanction if the condition in question cannot be treated or prevented, especially if the condition is unlikely to become manifest for many years. Testing a child for the genetic alteration associated with Huntington disease illustrates this latter sort of case. The condition cannot be prevented, and it cannot be treated once it becomes symptomatic. Moreover, a positive test result predicts with almost absolute certainly that the child tested will develop the condition (assuming, of course, that he or she survives to middle age). Lainie Friedman Ross & Margaret R. Moon, Ethical Issues in Pediatric Genetics in Genetics in the Clinic: Clinical, Ethical, and Social Implications for Primary Care 153 (Mary B. Mahowald et al. eds. 2001).

Other specific questions emerge about testing children for carrier status. Someone with a recessive genetic alteration will not suffer the consequences of the associated condition, but could pass the condition on to a child if the other gamete donor carries the same genetic alteration. In such cases, obtaining genetic information will not directly affect the health of the tested child but could determine the child's later reproductive decisions. Information about recessive traits can be obtained through prenatal testing. Sometimes, however, it is obtained outside the context of reproductive decision making. Carrier status can be ascertained, for example, as a result of routine screening of newborns.

Screening of newborns for hemoglobin S is illustrative. Those with a certain level are retested. Children who are heterozygous (carrying one rather than two relevant genetic alterations) for the trait associated with sickle cell anemia can pass it on to their offspring but will not develop the condition. Friedman and Moon, supra, recommend that parents be informed that a child is a carrier but that parents receive counseling so that they will understand the implications of the test results.

Friedman Ross and Moon, supra, delineate arguments that favor elective testing of a child for carrier status and other arguments that disfavor such testing. Among arguments favoring such testing are that it might be easier for a child to adjust to genetic information in childhood than later in life; that it might serve other members of the family; and that parents are in a better position than the state to know what will serve their child. Among arguments disfavoring such testing are that testing might "frustrate the child's right not to know as an adult"; it interferes with the child's "right to confidential reproductive knowledge"; it might diminish the child's sense of self; and it could lead to genetic discrimination. Friedman Ross & Moon, supra, at 161.

NOTES AND QUESTIONS

1. *Genetic families?*   In Safer v. Pack, 677 A.2d 1188 (Super. Ct. N.J. 1996), a New Jersey court extended a physician's "duty to warn" to include providing information about the risks (for family members) of a patient's genetic condition to the patient's child. The case (introduced in Chapter 2, Part C) suggests that for certain purposes families should be understood through reference to genetics. The "genetic family" (assumed in *Safer*) is an ideological construct. From the perspective of the genetic family, family members are understood through reference to DNA. From this perspective, each family member is substitutable for each other family member. For some commentators, the notion is unnerving; within the genetic family (as suggested by *Safer*), the genetic whole replaces the individual as the unit of essential social value. The notion of a genetic family suggests that family members have no right to privacy vis-à-vis one another. If each family member is seen as substitutable for each other, there is

no need to protect the privacy of any one from any other. This form of family is discussed in more depth in Kaja Finkler, Experiencing the New Genetics (2000) and in Janet L. Dolgin, Personhood, Discrimination and the New Genetics, 66 Brook. L. Rev. 755 (2000).

At least one professional society, the American Society of Human Genetics (ASHG), has endorsed *Safer's* view of the genetic family to some extent. American Society of Human Genetics Social Issues Subcommittee on Familial Disclosure, The ASHG Statement: Professional Disclosure of Familial Genetic Information, 62 Am. J. Hum. Genet. 474 (1998). The society's proposal recommends that health care providers be given the "discretionary right" to contravene normal rules of confidentiality in some cases involving genetic information. The society described two sets of "exceptional" cases:

> [First, are cases] where attempts to encourage disclosure on the part of the patient have failed; where the harm is highly likely to occur and is serious and foreseeable; where the at-risk relative(s) is identifiable; and where either the disease is preventable/treatable or medically accepted standards indicate that early monitoring will reduce the genetic risk.

Id. at 474. The second set of cases described by the ASHG includes those in which "the harm that may result from failure to disclose should outweigh the harm that may result from disclosure." Id. The ASHG defined "at-risk relatives" to include a patient's children, siblings, parents, cousins, aunts, and uncles. This proposal, much as the decision of the New Jersey court in *Safer*, assumes a genetic family understood through reference to shared DNA. Indeed, the ASHG proposal refers approvingly to the possibility that a health care provider's "patient" might not be an individual, but might be a genetic family (understood not as a social unit but as a group with shared DNA).

As noted in Chapter 2, following the decision in *Safer*, the New Jersey legislature promulgated a statute providing that health care providers may only communicate information about a patient's genetic condition to relatives of the patient if the patient has consented to the disclosure or if the patient has died. Genetic Privacy Act, N.J. Stat. Ann. §17B:30-12 (West 2012).

2. *Consequences of genetic information for children.*   In addition to the notion that fate is a product of genes, scientists suggest that health and well-being are products of environmental factors. Some of these factors could be present during the gestational period. The Child Is Father to the Patient, Economist.com, June 12, 2003, available at http://www.economist.com. In June 2003, some scientists at a conference in Brighton, England that focused on the fetal origins of adult diseases suggested that "[h]eart disease, obesity and late-onset diabetes frequently seem to trace their origins back to conditions in the womb or in the first few weeks of infancy. So," they suggest, "do cognitive ability, earning power, and even greed and sloth." Id. Should such findings be used to encourage or compel pregnant women to eat more or less food during pregnancy or to select their prospective child's genes to balance their own culinary habits during pregnancy? If it were possible to test for an "obesity" gene, should children be tested? If so, at what age? And should it be possible to learn that a child carries a gene for obesity, will parents likely respond by restricting the child's food intake or by allowing the child to eat anything because he or she is "fated" for obesity?

3. *Genetic and metabolic screening of newborns and consent.* Screening newborn babies for genetic and metabolic conditions could raise particularly difficult questions about parental consent. Since the early 1970s, states have required hospitals to screen all newborns for phenylketonuria (PKU). PKU is a rare metabolic disorder that can result in retardation if left untreated. At present, all states screen for PKU and for congenital hypothyroidism. In addition, most states screen newborns for sickle cell disease and galactosemia, and many screen newborns for a variety of other conditions including HIV status and hearing loss. Serving the Family from Birth to the Medical Home: A Report from the Newborn Screening Task Force Convened in Washington DC, May 10-11, 1999, 106 Pediatrics (2 Pt 2) 383, 391 (Aug. 2000). See also 2008 Mini-Symposium: Important Medical Issues in the Near Future (Transcription), 13 Mich. St. J. Med. & Law 487 (2009). Most of the screening programs provide for at least a limited right of parental refusal. Many states allow parental refusal only for religious reasons; most of the remaining states allow parental refusal on religious and/or personal grounds. E. Hiller et al., Public Participation in Medical Policy-Making and the Status of Consumer Autonomy: The Example of Newborn-Screening Programs in the United States, 87 Am. J. Pub. Health 1280, 1281 (1997).

Increasingly, states have provided for wider screening programs involving newborns. This becomes especially controversial in the context of genetic conditions for which no cure is available. This sort of screening could increase the risk that the children involved will suffer discrimination or even social marginalization if the test results become public.

A related question concerns storage of test results. A group of parents sued the Texas Department of State Health Service as well as others, claiming the department "'seized' blood samples taken from babies in Texas at the time of birth . . . and continue to unlawfully store those samples or 'spots' indefinitely for undisclosed purposes unrelated to the purposes for which the blood was originally drawn without knowledge or consent of the infants' parents." Beleno v. Lakey, Civil Action No. SA-09-CA-188-FB (USDC W.D. Tex. Sept. 17, 2009), http://www.genomicslawreport.com/wp-content/uploads/2010/01/Beleno-order.pdf. The court found the plaintiffs' claims that their Fourth Amendment rights had been violated were cognizable. *Beleno* was settled in late 2009:

> The parties settled the *Beleno* case in November 2009. Pursuant to the settlement agreement, the Department agreed to destroy all blood specimens that were taken as part of the newborn screening program and received by the Department before May 27, 2009 in its or Texas A&M Health Science Center's possession (Texas A&M facilities were used to store the specimens) for which it did not have written consent for continued retention and use. The Department further agreed to post on the newborn screening program website a list of all research projects for which the defendants had provided blood specimens, and also agreed to post a comprehensive list of categories of quality assurance and quality control uses for which defendants provided the blood specimens. Last, the Department agreed to inform the named plaintiffs in writing of the uses to which their children's blood specimens had been put, as well as any financial transactions regarding those specimens.

Higgins v. Tex. Dep't of Health Servs., 801 F. Supp. 2d 541, 545–546 (USDC W.D. Tex. 2011).

Moreover, during the pendency of the case, the state legislature amended relevant state statutory law, 801 F. Supp. 2d at 544–545 (citing Act of May 27, 2009, 81st Leg., R.S., ch. 179, §33.0111 ("Disclosure"), §33.0112 ("Statement Prohibiting Retention of Genetic Material"), and §33.017 ("confidentiality"). The amendments require the Department to provide information about genetic screening to a parent or guardian of newborns and to give the parents or guardian the right to limit the "use of genetic material; they allow a parent or guardian to prohibit the department or a laboratory from keeping genetic material obtained from newborn screening tests; and they impose a confidentiality requirement that aims to safeguard information obtained from newborn genetic screening from becoming public." *Higgins*, 801 F. Supp. 2d at 544–545.

The advantages and disadvantages of newborn screening and questions about the need for parental consent are discussed in Lainie Friedman Ross & Margaret R. Moon, Ethical Issues in Pediatric Genetics in Genetics in the Clinic: Clinical, Ethical, and Social Implications for Primary Care 153 (Mary B. Mahowald et al. eds. 2001). Other useful references include Sheila Wildeman & Jocelyn Downie, Genetic and Metabolic Screening of Newborns: Must Health Care Providers Seek Explicit Parental Consent?, 9 Health L.J. 61 (2001) (comparing relevant laws in the United States and in Canada).

4. *Genes for sporting talent?*   Britain's Progress Education Trust found that 62 percent of people polled about genetic testing to reveal a talent at sports would not take such a test and 38 percent would take it. (The question was hypothetical because such a test does not exist.) Sandy Starr, What Is the Role of Genetics in Sports?, 66 BioNews, July 30, 2012, available at http://www.bionews.org.uk/page_163170.asp?dinfo=fLg8CfFCr9VovEQq9KIjA3zi&PPID=162026 (last visited July 30, 2012). Testing children for similar traits raises additional issues. Children might be pressured to "live up to" their sporting potential or might even feel like abysmal failures if their "genetic promise" did not in fact become manifest despite their trying to succeed at sports.

5. *Bibliographic note.*   Useful bibliographic materials about children and genetic information include Kaja Finkler, Experiencing the New Genetics (2000) (presenting an anthropological analysis of the ideology of genetic inheritance through study of adoptees and women with familial breast cancer); Ellen Wright Clayton, Current in Contemporary Ethics, 38 J.L. Med. & Ethics 697 (2010); Ken M. Gatter, Genetic Information and the Importance of Context: Implications for the Social Meaning of Genetic Information and Individual Identity, 47 St. Louis L.J. 423 (2003); John Balint, Issues of Privacy and Confidentiality in the New Genetics, 9 Alb. L.J. Sci. & Tech. 27 (1998); Ellen Wright Clayton, What Should the Law Say About Disclosure of Genetic Information to Relatives?, 1 J. Health Care L. & Pol'y 373 (1998).

CHALLENGING ISSUES: QUESTIONS ABOUT GENETIC TESTING OF CHILDREN

At present, parents are likely to consider genetic testing of their children if members of the family have exhibited a genetic condition or if a diagnosis is sought for a child who shows symptoms of a condition that might be linked with a genetic alteration. Routine genetic testing of children is still not recommended by health care professionals or sought by parents or children. In cases in which genetic testing might be indicated, difficult questions emerge. Some scenarios in which genetic testing of children might be undertaken are presented by the questions that follow:

1. Would you recommend genetic testing of a three-year-old whose grandfather developed Alzheimer disease at the age of 44 and whose mother (now age 38) has recently been diagnosed with the condition? Despite some hopeful research, Alzheimer cannot definitively be prevented or treated. If the genetic alteration is present, the child will be at increased risk of developing early-onset Alzheimer.

2. Would you recommend genetic testing of a six-year-old whose mother and father are both known to carry the genetic alteration associated with Tay-Sachs disease? It is clear that the child does not have the condition, but he or she may be a carrier.

3. Would you recommend genetic testing of an 11-year-old girl whose mother's sister and mother's mother both died of breast cancer and whose father's sister has recently been diagnosed with the disease? If the child tests positive for one of the genetic alterations associated with breast cancer, she has a markedly increased risk of developing the condition, but she could live into old age and die without ever developing it. If she tests positive, early screening for breast cancer can be started during the child's adolescent years.

For one set of responses to similar questions, see AMA Council on Ethical and Judicial Affairs, Code of Medical Ethics, Sec. 2.138 (2012–2013).

B. NEUROIMAGING

1. Bioethical and Social Perspectives

Neuroimaging technology is being used to diagnose disorders of consciousness, to assess capacity, to evaluate assertions of pain, to identify lies, and to discern the guilt or innocence of a criminal defendant. Each of these applications can raise ethical questions for clinicians, lawyers, and society generally. Many of these questions resemble questions being asked about the uses and abuses of genetic testing and genomic information. Many responses to both genomic information and information gained from neuroimaging are grounded on the assumption that such information offers a key to the human soul or at least to understanding and predicting individuals' health, propensities, and character.

In 2007, the MacArthur Foundation committed $10 million to launch the Law and Neuroscience Project, an interdisciplinary project focused on "the intersection of neuroscience and criminal justice," http://www.lawneuro. org/. Two years later, the National Institutes of Health initiated the Human Connectome Project. This project aims to construct a map of networks in the human brain and to amass data that may be useful in exploring various neurological disorders, http://www.nih.gov/news/health/jul2009/ninds-15.htm (last visited July 16, 2012).

> ## Teneille Brown & Emily Murphy, Through a Scanner Darkly: Functional Neuroimaging as Evidence of a Criminal Defendant's Past Mental States
> ### 62 Stan. L. Rev. 1119, 1127, 1136–1139 (2010)

Functional neuroimaging (or functional brain imaging) refers to a class of nonsurgical devices and methodologies that allow measurement of living brain activity. This category is distinct from structural imaging, such as a CT scan or MRI. Structural imaging provides images of gross anatomical features, but not of underlying neuronal or metabolic activity.

There are a few different types of functional neuroimaging devices. fMRI is the most popular functional brain imaging device in cognitive neuroscience research. . . . Tremendous excitement abounds regarding the research and clinical applications of fMRI. . . .

Several functional neuroimaging techniques predate fMRI in development and in the courtroom, and we briefly review them here. Positron Emission Tomography (PET) and Single Photon Emission Computed Tomography (SPECT) rely on the injection of a radioactive tracer into the subject's bloodstream. The tracer emits pairs of gamma rays, which are detected and interpreted by a computer, and eventually result in a 3-D image of the brain. PET's temporal resolution is on the order of seconds or minutes. PET and SPECT have been quite useful clinically to diagnose many types of cancers, heart disease, and brain abnormalities. PET and SPECT share some commonalities with fMRI, including some of the basic methodologies for constructing the image from the data.

Electroencephalography (EEG) measures electrical activity produced by the brain as recorded from electrodes placed on the scalp. Relative to PET or SPECT, EEG has poor spatial resolution and is limited to assessing neural activity close to the scalp, but its temporal resolution is much better—on the order of milliseconds. Beyond its clinical uses, various forms of EEG-based investigation or interrogation techniques have received considerable media attention. One methodology was recently relied upon by an Indian court to convict a woman based on her "experiential knowledge" of the murder. Another method dubbed "brain fingerprinting" is hailed by its developers as the next generation of biologically-based deception detection, despite strong academic criticism and official rejection. The lack of peer-reviewed data on the various methodologies of both forensic EEG-based technologies makes us similarly skeptical of the scientific validity of their use. . . .

Most of the reported court cases that cite to neuroimaging refer to PET or SPECT. However, these methodologies are largely being replaced by fMRI in research and in practice. Unlike PET or SPECT, fMRI does not require the injection of a radioactive tracer. fMRI's temporal and spatial resolution are also superior to PET's. The temporal resolution and signal-to-noise ratio of fMRI is not as good as that of EEG. Though it is too early in the technology's history for many appellate opinions to have discussed fMRI, experts agree that it will dominate older methods as courtroom evidence. This is due in part to the increased availability of fMRI devices and the reduction in their cost. . . .

fMRI is a relatively safe and noninvasive technique that indirectly measures the brain's activity. The fact that fMRI is an indirect measurement cannot be stressed enough. fMRI does not directly measure neuronal activity or firing. What follows is the rationale for nonetheless using fMRI to measure brain activity in studies of cognition and behavior.

Perceiving, thinking, acting, feeling, and even resting have associated neuronal firing. A growing body of evidence suggests that mental states—such as thoughts and emotions—are represented by patterns of neuronal activation in specific regions or networks of the brain. For many such cognitive or emotional tasks, an increase in neural firing in a particular region or network is interpreted as the brain doing "more" of that particular cognitive or emotional task.

Because neurons do not have internal reserves of energy, when they fire in response to some activity, oxygen-carrying blood must be transported to the neurons. This is called the "hemodynamic response."

Blood that is carrying oxygen behaves differently in magnetic fields than deoxygenated blood does. The difference in the magnetic properties of oxygenated blood allows fMRI to detect changes in blood flow related to activity. This is called the Blood Oxygen Level Dependent (BOLD) response.

In simple terms, when a region of the brain is "activated" in response to a perception or to enable a behavior, that region receives more oxygenated blood. Because oxygenated blood behaves differently in a magnetic field, the large magnet in the fMRI device can measure this influx. If the local oxygen use is more than adequately supplied by the influx of blood, then a positive BOLD response will result. If the local demand for oxygen exceeds that provided by the regional blood flow, then a negative BOLD response will result. Because the change in the blood oxygenation level in a spatial volume (called a voxel, like a three-dimensional pixel) does not directly capture the activity of neurons, fMRI does not yet provide detailed physiological information about the neural mechanisms underlying the mental state.

NOTES AND QUESTIONS

1. *Reductionism.* Neuroimaging has encouraged some observers to equate the human condition to "brain wiring," as reflected on neuroscans. Such observations represent a form of reductionism that displaces efforts to understand the human condition and human relationships through art, music, psychology, literature, or poetry. One commentator analogized reductionist responses to neuroimaging to a much older set of efforts to understand consciousness—the so-called "homunculus fallacy." This fallacy depends on positing some inner "real me inside"—an "inner homunculus." Roger Scruton, Neuroscience Wants to BE the Answer to Everything. It Isn't, Spectator.co.uk, Mar. 12, 2012, http://www.spectator.co.uk/essays/all/7714533/brain-drain.thtml. Scruton contended that one should consider carefully the implications of a science of consciousness that seems, mostly, to "read[] back into the explanation the feature that needs to be explained." Even more, he suggested that the deepest questions about people and their acts in the world are best analyzed through interpretations that flow

from questions about meaning. He noted the particular dangers of "neurolaw," which, in his view, is virtually certain to undermine freedom and responsibility because neither freedom nor responsibility will appear in a neuroimage. Id.

2.   *Legal Approaches*

a.   Decisions by U.S. Courts

In a dissenting opinion in Brown v. Entertainment Merchants Association, Justice Breyer explained that "[c]utting-edge neuroscience" offered scientific evidence that exposure to virtual violence leads to "neural patterns" associated with "aggressive cognition and behavior." 131 S. Ct. 2729, 2768 (2010) (Breyer, J., dissenting). The case involved a First Amendment challenge to a California statute that prohibited the sale or rental of "violent video games" to minors. The Court invalidated the statute.

In general, courtroom uses of neuroimaging in the United States remain limited. Yet, attorneys are starting to present evidence from neuroscience in court. At the same time, scholars, jurists, and others are considering the legal and ethical implications of relying on neuroimaging to assess states of mind, truthfulness, levels of pain, future dangerousness, morality, and a host of other matters. Arkansas Judge Looney notes some of the legal questions that relying on neuroimaging for such purposes may raise:

> First, there is the basic issue of whether the present state of the science can meet the standards for admissibility in judicial proceedings. Second, Fifth Amendment, self-incrimination issues might be raised if prosecutors use these techniques in a criminal proceeding. Third, questions as to whether a reasonable search was conducted may arise if these techniques are deemed to constitute a Fourth Amendment search. Beyond these basic legal considerations, there are right-to-privacy issues that arise when an individual is held responsible for thoughts instead of actions.

J. W. Looney, Neuroscience's New Techniques for Evaluating Future Dangerousness: Are We Returning to Lombroso's Biological Criminality?, 32 U. Ark. Little Rock L. Rev. 301, 308 (2010).

In the United States, brain scans are increasingly being offered (although generally without success) in both criminal and civil cases as evidence of what people were or might have been thinking. Francis X. Shen & Owen D. Jones, Brain Scans as Evidence: Truths, Proofs, Lies, and Lessons, 62 Mercer 861, 861 (2010). Shen and Jones explain the potential usefulness of such evidence:

> In criminal law, for example, the same act can yield anything from mere probation to decades in prison, depending on what the legal fact finders believe a defendant was probably thinking. In the civil context, the beliefs held by a defendant about a particular risk are often central to a plaintiff's recovery. The unavoidable consequence is this: what a brain was actually doing at the time of an act, and indeed what a brain in court recollects about past acts, often matters a great deal to the administration of justice. And in all such cases, judges and jurors have it hard. It is simply not easy to read the mind of a stranger or to assess with complete confidence either the subjective belief or objective accuracy of expressed recollections.

Id. at 862.

Courts have been slow to admit such evidence. Shen and Jones report that for the first time in 2010, a federal court entertained the admissibility of brain scan data as evidence of lying or truthfulness in a criminal trial. The case involved Lorne Semrau, a Tennessee psychologist, indicted for defrauding Medicaid, Medicare, and other health benefit programs. U.S. v. Semrau, 2010 U.S. Dist. Lexis 143402 (2010), aff'd, 2012 U.S. App. Lexis 18824 (6th Cir. 2012). Cephos Corporation, described by a Tennessee magistrate as one of two U.S. companies that provided lie detection services using fMRIs, carried out the fMRI assessment of Semrau's truthfulness. Steven Laken, the CEO of Cephos, reported that "Dr. Semrau's brain indicates he is telling the truth in regards to not cheating or defrauding the government." 2010 U.S. Dist. Lexis 143402 at 24.

At the request of the federal government, the Tennessee district court held a *Daubert* hearing to determine the admissibility of fMRI images provided by Cephos Corporation. (In Daubert v. Merrill Dow Pharmaceuticals, Inc., 509 U.S. 579 (1993), the U.S. Supreme Court held that to be admissible in court, scientific evidence had to meet a set of scientific standards to be interpreted flexibly by the trial court judge.) The Sixth Circuit affirmed the opinion of the Tennessee district court. This decision is reprinted below, followed by a New York state court opinion applying the older *Frye* text of "general acceptance."

U.S. v. Semrau
2012 U.S. App. LEXIS 18824 (6th Cir. 2012)

Opinion by Jane B. STRANCH

[Dr. Lorne Semrau, a psychologist, owned two companies that offered follow-up psychiatric care to patients in nursing homes in Tennessee and Mississippi. Dr. Semrau was found guilty of Medicare fraud by the U.S.D.C. W.D. Tenn. in violation of 18 USCS §1347. In particular, the companies were found to have billed under the wrong Medicare code—one that resulted in higher payments than should have been received.]

II. DISCUSSION
A. Admissibility of fMRI Tests

Dr. Semrau argues that the district court erred in excluding opinion testimony from Dr. Steven Laken, who would have testified that fMRI testing indicated that Dr. Semrau was generally truthful when he said he attempted to follow proper billing practices in good faith. The admissibility of fMRI lie detection testing in a criminal case is an issue of first impression for any jurisdiction in the country, state and federal. After carefully reviewing the scientific and factual evidence, we conclude that the district court did not abuse its discretion in excluding the fMRI evidence under Federal Rule of Evidence 702 because the technology had not been fully examined in "real world" settings and the testing administered to Dr. Semrau was not consistent with tests done in research studies. We also hold that the testimony was independently inadmissible under Rule 403 because the prosecution did not know about the test before it was conducted, constitutional concerns caution against admitting lie detection tests to bolster witness credibility, and the test results do not purport to indicate whether Dr. Semrau was truthful about any single statement.

1. Background

a. fMRI Science

Dr. Steven J. Laken, Ph.D., is the President and CEO of Cephos Corporation, a company he founded in Tyngsboro, Massachusetts in 2004. Cephos markets itself as a company that provides a variety of investigative services, including DNA forensic analysis, private detective services, and lie detection/truth verification using fMRI. Regarding its fMRI-based lie detection service, Cephos claims that it uses "state-of-the-art technology that is unbiased and scientifically validated. We have offered expert testimony and have presented fMRI evidence in court." . . .

At the heart of Dr. Laken's lie detection method is fMRI imaging. An fMRI enables researchers to assess brain function "in a rapid, non-invasive manner with a high degree of both spatial and temporal accuracy." When undergoing an fMRI scan, a subject lies down on a bed that slides into the center of a donut-shaped magnet core. As the subject remains still, he or she is asked to perform a task while magnetic coils in the scanner receive electric current and the device gathers information about the subject's Blood Oxygen Level Dependent ("BOLD") response. By comparing the subject's BOLD response signals with the control state, small changes in signal intensity are detectable and can provide information about brain activity.

Dr. Laken began working closely with a small group of researchers in this field in or around 2003 and conducted a series of laboratory studies to determine whether fMRI could be used to detect deception. Generally, these studies involved a test subject performing a task, such as "stealing" a ring or watch, and then scanning the subject while he or she answered questions about the task. The subjects were usually offered a modest monetary incentive if their lie was not detected. Dr. Laken agreed during cross-examination that he had only conducted studies on such "mock scenarios" and was not aware of any research in a "real-life setting" in which people are accused of "real crimes." . . .

Based on these studies, as well as studies conducted by other researchers, Dr. Laken and his colleagues determined the regions of the brain most consistently activated by deception and claimed in several peer-reviewed articles that by analyzing a subject's brain activity, they were able to identify deception with a high level of accuracy. During direct examination at the *Daubert* hearing, Dr. Laken reported these studies found accuracy rates between eighty-six percent and ninety-seven percent. During cross-examination, however, Dr. Laken conceded that his 2009 "Mock Sabotage Crime" study produced an "unexpected" accuracy decrease to a rate of seventy-one percent.

Dr. Laken testified that fMRI lie detection has "a huge false positive problem" in which people who are telling the truth are deemed to be lying around sixty to seventy percent of the time. One 2009 study was able to identify a "truth teller as a truth teller" just six percent of the time, meaning that about "nineteen out of twenty people that were telling the truth we would call liars." Another study expressed concern that "accuracy rates drop by almost twenty-five percentage points when a person starts becoming fatigued." Dr. Laken also explained that a person can become sufficiently fatigued during testing such that results are impacted after about two "scans" because "[t]heir brain starts kind of going to sleep." Similarly, inadequate sleep the night before a test could cause such fatigue.

b.   Testing Conducted on Dr. Semrau

In late 2009, Dr. Semrau's attorney, J. Houston Gordon, contacted Dr. Laken to inquire about having an fMRI-based lie detection test conducted on Dr. Semrau in hopes of bolstering the defenses that Dr. Semrau lacked intent to defraud and undertook actions to ensure proper billing compliance. Dr. Laken agreed to test Dr. Semrau and testify about his results at no cost. Dr. Laken decided to conduct two separate fMRI scans on Dr. Semrau, one involving questions regarding the healthcare fraud charges discussed above and the other involving questions regarding charges that he improperly billed for Abnormal Movement Scale ("AIMS") tests.

. . . .

[Three scans were performed on Dr. Semrau.] Each scan took around sixteen minutes. . . . From the first scan, . . . the results showed that Dr. Semrau was "not deceptive." However, from the second scan, . . . the results showed that Dr. Semrau was "being deceptive." Dr. Laken's report noted, however, that "testing indicates that a positive test result in a person reporting to tell the truth is only accurate 6 percent of the time and may be affected by fatigue." Based on his findings for the second test, Dr. Laken suggested that Dr. Semrau be administered another fMRI test . . . , but with shorter questions and conducted later in the day to reduce the effects of fatigue. . . .

[Laken reviewed the third scan] and concluded that Dr. Semrau's brain activity showed he was "not deceptive" in his answers. He further testified that, based on his prior studies, the third test was "more valid" because Dr. Semrau "didn't have fatigue" and the data produced "has a very high probability of being correct." In fact, Dr. Laken's report stated that "a finding such as this is 100% accurate in determining truthfulness from a truthful person."

During cross-examination at the *Daubert* hearing, Dr. Laken agreed that the test results do not indicate whether Dr. Semrau responded truthfully as to any specific question but rather show only whether he was generally truthful as to all of his answers collectively. Accordingly, Dr. Laken conceded that it is "certainly possible" that Dr. Semrau was lying on some of the particularly significant questions. Dr. Laken was unable to state the percentage of questions on which Dr. Semrau could have lied while still producing the same result. He also acknowledged that the scan results only show whether someone believes what he is saying at the time of the test rather than what his mental state was at the time of the events discussed, and that there is no research on the effect of a "long-term lie."

. . . .

3.   Admissibility Under Rule 702

a.   Applicable Law

Federal Rule of Evidence 702, which contains the standard for admissibility of expert testimony, provides as follows:

> A witness who is qualified as an expert by knowledge, skill, experience, training, or education may testify in the form of an opinion or otherwise if:
>
> (a)   the expert's scientific, technical, or other specialized knowledge will help the trier of fact to understand the evidence or to determine a fact in issue;
> (b)   the testimony is based on sufficient facts or data;
> (c)   the testimony is the product of reliable principles and methods; and
> (d)   the expert has reliably applied the principles and methods to the facts of the case.

. . . .

b.   Analysis

The magistrate judge's R&R, which was adopted by the district court, weighed several factors in Dr. Semrau's favor: "[T]he underlying theories behind fMRI-based lie detection are capable of being tested, and at least in the laboratory setting, have been subjected to some level of testing. It also appears that the theories have been subjected to some peer review and publication." *Semrau,* 2010 U.S. Dist. Lexis 143402, 2010 WL 6845092, at *10. The Government does not appear to challenge these findings, although it does point out that the bulk of the research supporting fMRI research has come from Dr. Laken himself.

The magistrate judge determined that Dr. Semrau could not satisfy the rate of error and controlling standards factor: "While it is unclear from the testimony what the error rates are or how valid they may be in the laboratory setting, there are no known error rates for fMRI-based lie detection outside the laboratory setting, i.e., in the 'real-world' or 'real-life' setting." 2010 U.S. Dist. Lexis 143402, [WL] at *11. . . . Dr. Peter Imrey, a statistician, testified: "There are no quantifiable error rates that are usable in this context. The error rates [Dr. Laken] proposed are based on almost no data, and under circumstances [that] do not apply to the real world [or] to the examinations of Dr. Semrau." Dr. Imrey also stated that the false positive accuracy data reported by Dr. Laken does not "justify the claim that somebody giving a positive test result . . . [h]as a six percent chance of being a true liar. That simply is mathematically, statistically and scientifically incorrect."

Based on Dr. Imrey's testimony, there was a reasonable and objective basis for the magistrate judge to reject Dr. Laken's stated error rates. Moreover, the magistrate judge qualified his conclusion by specifying such rates are unknown specifically for fMRI-based lie detection in the "real world" as opposed to the "laboratory." *Semrau,* 2010 U.S. Dist. Lexis 143402, 2010 WL 6845092, at *11. . . .

. . . .

Although Dr. Laken offered various plausible sounding explanations and theories for [differences between the tests done on Semrau and earlier studies which Laken described and, specifically, among the three scans done on Semrau], the record reveals uncertainty from the relevant scientific community as to whether and to what extent the distinctions may, in fact, matter. It is likely that jurors, most of whom lack advanced scientific degrees and training, would be poorly suited for resolving these disputes and thus more likely to be confused rather than assisted by Dr. Laken's testimony. See Fed. R. Evid. 702(a) (requiring expert testimony "will help the trier of fact to understand the evidence or to determine a fact in issue"). Accordingly, we conclude that the district court did not abuse its discretion in excluding Dr. Laken's testimony about Dr. Semrau's fMRI lie detection results under Rule 702.

4. Admissibility Under Rule 403

The magistrate judge's R&R, as adopted by the district court, also excluded Dr. Laken's testimony under Federal Rule of Evidence 403, which permits a court to exclude relevant evidence if its probative value is substantially outweighed by a danger of confusing the issues or misleading the jury, among other things.

. . . .

We hold that the district court did not abuse its discretion in excluding the fMRI evidence pursuant to Rule 403 in light of (1) the questions surrounding the reliability of fMRI lie detection tests in general and as performed on Dr. Semrau, (2) the failure to give the prosecution an opportunity to participate in the testing, and (3) the test result's inability to corroborate Dr. Semrau's answers as to the particular offenses for which he was charged.[12]

|| *Wilson v. Medina* ||
|| **900 N.Y.S.2d 639 (SCNY, Kings County 2010)** ||

Opinion by Robert J. MILLER, J.

In this pretrial motion in limine, the defendants Corestaff Services L.P. and Edwin Medina (Defendants) move to preclude plaintiff's expert witness from testifying regarding plaintiff's witness Ronald Armstrong's (Armstrong) submission to and the results of a Functional Magnetic Resonance Imaging (fMRI) test.

Plaintiff Cynette Wilson (Wilson) opposes the motion and cross moves to "be allowed a Frye Hearing concerning the results of functional Magnetic

---

12. The prospect of introducing fMRI lie detection results into criminal trials is undoubtedly intriguing and, perhaps, a little scary. See Daniel S. Goldberg, Against Reductionism in Law & Neuroscience, 11 Hous. J. Health L. & Pol'y 321, 324 n.6 (2012) (reviewing literature that "challenges the very idea that fMRI or other novel neuroimaging techniques either can or should be used as evidence in criminal proceedings"). There may well come a time when the capabilities, reliability, and acceptance of fMRI lie detection—or even a technology not yet envisioned—advances to the point that a trial judge will conclude, as did Dr. Laken in this case: "I would subject myself to this over a jury any day." Though we are not at that point today, we recognize that as science moves forward the balancing of Rule 403 may well lean toward finding that the probative value for some advancing technology is sufficient.

Resonance Imaging testing which indicate that the witness Ronald K. Armstrong is being truthful when he states that defendant Edwin Medina told him not to place plaintiff Cynette Wilson in temporary work assignments because she complained of sexual harassment." Wilson disclosed pursuant to [N.Y. law] her intent to call an expert, Steven Laken, Ph.D. (Laken) President and CEO of Cephos Corporation. The intention is to use Laken as an expert to testify that Armstrong was not lying because the fMRI could show "that to a very high probability" Armstrong "is being truthful when he testifies."

Essentially, plaintiff seeks to utilize the fMRI test to bolster the credibility of a key witness in this case. Plaintiff Wilson asserts a claim under New York City and State Human Rights Law that she was retaliated against by the defendants after she reported an inappropriate action by a fellow employee at the work site. The defendant Corestaff is a temporary employment agency that placed Wilson at an investment banking firm (the Bank). While on assignment, an employee of the Bank faxed an offensive nude photo to the plaintiff's work station. Wilson reported the incident to both Corestaff and the Bank. Armstrong is the only witness who will testify as to an alleged retaliatory statement made by Corestaff employee Medina. As such, his credibility is a key issue in the case.

. . . .

New York courts have restated and followed the principles of *Frye* [Frye v. United States, 293 F. 1013 (DC 1923)] and set forth a test as to the admissibility of the expert testimony relating to scientific theory. New York courts permit expert testimony if it is based on scientific principles, procedures or theory only after the principles, procedures or theories have gained general acceptance in the relevant scientific field, proffered by a qualified expert and on a topic beyond the ken of the average juror.

Apparently, there is no reported case in New York or in the rest of the country which deals with the admissibility of the results of fMRI test. The Court inquired of counsel for both parties if they were aware of any reported cases and both advised that this is a case of apparent first impression. However, long established precedent under *Frye* as well as long established principles of jurisprudence provide the Court with ample precedent and guidelines.

. . . .

As the *Williams* court observed, our common law tradition provides that credibility is a matter solely for the jury. Anything that impinges on the province of the jury on issues of credibility should be treated with a great deal of skepticism.

It is for this reason that courts have advised that the threshold question under *Frye* in passing on the admissibility of expert's testimony is whether the testimony is "within the ken of the typical juror." Furthermore, it is well established that unless the jurors are unable or incompetent to evaluate the evidence and draw inferences and conclusions, the opinion of an expert, which intrudes on the province of the jury, is both unnecessary and improper. Expert testimony is proper only when it would help to clarify an issue calling for professional or technical knowledge possessed by the expert and is beyond the ken of the typical juror. The proffered fMRI test is akin to a polygraph test which has been widely rejected by New York State courts.

Here the opinion to be offered by Laken is of a collateral matter, i.e. the credibility of a fact witness. Since credibility is a matter solely for the jury and is clearly within the ken of the jury, plaintiff has failed to meet this key prong of the *Frye* test and no other inquiry is required. However, even a cursory review of the scientific literature demonstrates that the plaintiff is unable to establish that the use of the fMRI test to determine truthfulness or deceit is accepted as reliable in the relevant scientific community. The scientific literature raises serious issues about the lack of acceptance of the fMRI test in the scientific community to show a person's past mental state or to gauge credibility.

Accordingly, defendants' motion in limine to exclude the testimony of the fMRI expert is granted and plaintiff's motion for a *Frye* hearing is denied.

b.   Decision by Indian Court

Outside the United States, some courts have accepted evidence from brain scans. In India courts have relied on neuroimaging in criminal cases. In 2008, a Mumbai judge concluded that a 24-year-old woman was guilty of using arsenic to murder her ex-fiancé (Udit Bharati). The judge relied on the defendant's responses to a brain scan. The defendant, Aditi Sharma, agreed to be tested with the so-called brain electrical oscillation signature (BEOS). About 30 electrodes were connected to Sharma's head; then an electro-encephalogram (EEG) was performed. A tape-recorded voice uttered a series of statements about the alleged murder, as investigators had constructed it. The EEG registered brightly colored responses when Sharma heard a series of incriminating statements (e.g., "I got arsenic . . . I called Udit . . . The sweets killed Udit."). Angela Saini, The Brain Police: Judging Murder with an MRI, Wired.co.uk, http://www.wired.co.uk/magazine/archive/2009/06/features/guilty?page=all (May 27, 2009). An Indian psychologist, Champadi Raman Mukundan, developed the BEOS system. One of his assistants explained that the system indicates activation in that part of the brain in which memories are stored. Larry Dossey, Are the Thought Police Knocking on Our Door, Ions: Institute of Noetic Sciences, June 29, 2010, http://www.noetic.org/blog/are-thought-police-knocking-our-door/; Anand Giridharadas, India's Novel Use of Brain Scans in Courts Is Debated, N.Y. Times, Sept. 14, 2008, www.nytimes.com. The evidence convinced Judge Shalini Phansalkar-Joshi of Sharma's guilt. He sentenced her to life in prison.

Yet, soon serious questions emerged about the science underlying BEOS. In 2009 Sharma was released on bail. Her case is being appealed, but appeals in India can take many, many years. In the meantime, after Sharma's conviction, at least two other people in India were convicted of murder on the basis of evidence obtained from Mukundan's BEOS system. Id.

In 2010, the Indian Supreme Court banned compulsory neuroimaging as well as lie detector tests and narco-analysis (the use of so-called "truth drugs") as an unconstitutional infringement on individual rights. Rakesh Bhatnagar, Supreme Court Makes Narco, Lie Detector, Brain Mapping Tests Illegal, BNA, May 5, 2010, http://www.dnaindia.com. The court concluded that the tests being contested could be administered only with the consent of the person to be tested and only in accordance with ethical guidelines. Id.

Relevant parts of the Indian case, Maharashtra v. Sharma, follow.

|| **State of Maharashtra v. Sharma** ||
No. 508/07 (Court of Sessions, June 12, 2008)

This case presents a tragic scenario as the budding and flourishing love relationship between accused No. 1 Aditi and deceased Aditi Bharati, which was on the threshold of marriage and sailing smoothly with consent and approval of the parents on both sides, got swerved to the wrong side and sank into tragedy when . . . Aditi came in to contact with . . . Pravin, got enamoured by him, fell in love with him and left the deceased to settle with Pravin and ultimately, as per prosecution case, eliminated deceased from this world, in conspiracy with Pravin, for which both of them are indicted and charge sheeted by the police for the offence.

. . . .

EVIDENCE OF POLYGRAPH AND BEOS TEST

One . . . link in the circumstantial evidence is the evidence of two Psycho Logical Evaluation Tests conducted on accused No. 1 Aditi. Witness No. 29, Sunny Joseph who is working as Assistant Chemical Analyser in Forensic Science Laboratory, Mumbai, has conducted the said Tests. In all he has conducted 2 Tests, one Polygraph Test and the other Brain Electrical Oscillation Signature Profiling [BEOS] Test on Aditi.

. . . .

Sunny has in his report and also in his evidence given the details of how the BEOS Test is conducted. According to it, BEOS is a Test which is an application of the EEG [Electro Encephalogram]. It is commonly used in a medical set up for diagnostic purposes. In medical field EEG is done for the purpose of detecting any abnormality in the brain. In this process electrodes are attached to different parts of the brain to detect electrical activation of different parts in the brain. The subject is asked to wear a cap with 32 electrodes. Out of these 32 electrodes 2 electrodes are on two ear lobes and remaining 30 are on different parts of the brain. These electrodes are arranged in a universally accepted manner touching the scalp to detect electrical activation inside the brain. It is not an invasive procedure. By this method, different aspects of the memory are studied, such as: conceptual knowledge and experiential knowledge. Conceptual memory is related to semantic processing. Semantic means the use of words, vocabulary knowledge of language, etc. This aspect of memory is restricted to the information that we receive from various sources, such as reading newspaper, watching TV, etc. Experiential knowledge is acquired only through participation in an activity or event leading the person to have an experience of that event. According to him, this BEOS system is programmed in such a way that it detects and differentiates between the electrical activation related to conceptual and experiential knowledge. Based on the information of the case . . . , they prepare number of probes—meaning short sentences or phrases. These probes are arranged in a sequential order to depict different scenarios. The probes are of three different categories: viz. neutral, which are presented to prepare base line for cognitive process; second, control probes. Those are related to personal information of that subject. Third: relevant probes. Those are related directly to the case. These probes were recorded in a computer and presented to the subject. The subject is asked to sit with his eyes closed and listen to probes. The subject is asked not to give any answers verbally. After the Test is completed, the system analyses the electrical activation for relevant probes in comparison to the baseline for each individual probe. After analysis the system generates a report that tells us what kind of cognitive processing that took place when each probe was presented. There is no manual analysis involved in this system. As per his evidence the report prepared by the system shows the experiential knowledge against a probe only when electrical activation suggestive of memory related to processing related to an event is present.

In his evidence he has proved on record the list of probes which was presented to Aditi along with her responses. . . . These probes are qualified into 8 categories relating to different cognitive processes in the brain when probes are presented. Those cognitive processes are attention, primary processing, encoding, familiarity, experiential knowledge, negative response, activation suppression, and emotional response. . . .

His report discloses that findings of the BEOS conducted on Aditi showed Experiential Knowledge on a number of target probes presented to her, indicating her involvement in the murder of Udit Bharati. Experiential Knowledge was found to be present on probes depicting her having an affair with Udit taking admission along with him in Pune and her having some interpersonal conflict with Udit and, therefore, both of them not talking much to each other. It is also revealed in BEOS, that Aditi knew that Udit was not really happy about her affair with Pravin and about her getting married to Pravin. Aditi was found to have Experiential Knowledge for having a plan to murder Udit by giving him Arsenic. Experiential Knowledge was also found for her having gone to a temple and collected Prasad, buying Arsenic from a shop, and keeping some 'Prasad' aside for Udit. She was also found to have Experiential Knowledge for her having called Udit up and given him the 'Prasad' that was mixed with Arsenic. Experiential Knowledge for the emotional experience of getting relieved and scared in relation to giving Udit the 'Prasad' was also found present on BEOS Test. Thus, these findings clearly indicate Aditi's involvement in the murder of Udit.

Therefore, in conclusion he has stated that Psychological Evaluation including Psychological Profiling, Polygraph Testing and BEOS of the subject Aditi Sharma clearly indicated her involvement in the murder of Udit. The Psychological Evaluation tests of Aditi thus, clearly proves her involvement in Udit's murder as indicated by Deceptive responses on the relevant questions in Polygraph Test and by the presence of Experiential Knowledge on the target probes in BEOS in terms of having a plan to murder him, collecting 'Prasad' and Arsenic, meeting Udit and giving him the Prasad.

NOTES AND QUESTIONS

1. *Neuroimaging for sale.*   Two U.S. companies, Cephos Corp. and No Lie MRI, market functional MRIs and sell "deception detection" services. Saini, supra. No Lie MRI's website, www.noliemri.com, promotes its services to businesses, for screening employees and potential employees; to lawyers, for validating a witness's statement in court; to the government, to aid with security

clearance; and to individuals to test dates for truthfulness and to develop "trust" in "interpersonal relationships." (Cephos Corp. provided the services that were at issue in *Semrau*.)

2. *Jury response in Semrau case.*   A jury convicted Dr. Lorne Semrau of three counts of health care fraud. United States v. Semrau, 2011 U.S. Dist. Lexis 246 (W.D. Tenn. 2011). On sentencing, the court concluded that Semrau had submitted more than 5,000 fraudulent claims to Medicare. Id. at 22. The circuit court affirmed Dr. Semrau's conviction. 2012 U.S. App. LEXIS 18824 (6th Cir. 2012).

3. *Merging genetic information with information from neuroimaging.*   Daniel Buchman and Judy Iles suggest some possible consequences of merging genetic information with information derived from neuroimaging. Daniel Z. Buchman & Judy Iles, Neuroscience: Imaging Genetics for Our Neurogenetic Future, 11 Minn. J.L. Sci. & Tech. 79 (2010). Buchman and Iles consider potential uses of combining these two sources of information in the effort to diagnose and predict mental illness. This process—which they refer to as "genetic imaging"—raises at least as many challenges to privacy and confidentiality as are raised by genetic tests or neuroimaging alone. And it requires even more complicated modes of interpretation by those doing the testing so that those being tested, or relying on such testing, can understand the implications of test results.

4. *Effects of violence in video games?*   In Brown v. Entertainment Merchants Association, 131 S. Ct. 2729 (2011), the Supreme Court dismissed the conclusion that studies supported a California law restricting the sale or rental of violent video games to children on the ground that the games encouraged violent behavior. Justice Scalia noted that the studies showed a correlation but did not show causation. The Court invalidated the state statute on First Amendment grounds. Yet, as noted in the introduction to this section, in a dissenting opinion, Justice Breyer asserted that "[c]utting-edge neuroscience has shown that 'virtual violence in video game playing results in those neural patterns that are considered characteristic for aggressive cognition and behavior.'" 131 S. Ct. at 2768.

5. *Is legislation needed?*   Would you favor the development of legislation that protects people from discriminatory uses of neurological information such as the information that can be obtained from an fMRI? Should there be a statute comparable to the Genetic Information Nondiscrimination Act of 2008 (GINA) that focuses on uses of information derived from neuroscans?

6. *Bibliographic note.*   Nina A. Farahany, Incriminating Thoughts, 64 Stan. L. Rev. 351 (2012) (reviewing self-incrimination doctrine in light of "neuroscience revolution"); Theodore Y. Blumoff, The Brain Sciences and Criminal Law Norms, 62 Mercer L. Rev. 705 (2011) (reviewing "possibilities" and "dreams" presented by neuroscience and serving as foreword to symposium issue on "Brain Sciences in the Courtroom"); Teneille Brown & Emily Murphy, Through a Scanner Darkly: Functional Neuroimaging as Evidence of a Criminal Defendant's Past Mental States, 62 Stan. L. Rev. 1119 (2010) (suggesting that at present, functional brain images should not be accepted as evidence in criminal cases); Carl E. Fisher & Paul S. Appelbaum, Law, Science, and Innovation: The Embryonic Stem Cell Controversy: Diagnosing Consciousness: Neuroimaging,

Law, and the Vegetative State, 38 J.L. Med. & Ethics 374 (2010) (considering disorders of consciousness and the significance of neuroimaging techniques in diagnosing such disorders); J. R. H. Law, Cherry-Picking Memories: Why Neuroimaging-based Lie Detection Requires a New Framework for the Admissibility of Scientific Evidence Under FRE 702 and *Daubert*, 14 Yale J.L. & Tech 1 (2011) (calling for new approach to admission of scientific evidence in cases in which brain scan evidence is offered as evidence); Francis X. Shen, The Law and Neuroscience Bibliography: Navigating the Emerging Field of Neurolaw, 38 Int'l J. Legal Info. 352 (2010) (discussing and offering bibliography, updated at http://www.lawneuro.org); Joelle Anne Moreno, The Future of Neuroimaged Lie Detection and the Law, 42 Akron L. Rev. 717 (2009) (addressing how to shape legal responses to neuroscience); Stacey A. Tovino, Neuroimaging Research into Disorders of Consciousness: Moral Imperative or Ethical and Legal Failure?, 13 Va. J.L. & Tech 2 (2008) (suggesting standards to apply in cases in which neuroimaging is conducted for research purposes on people with disorders of consciousness); Jeffrey Rosen, The Brain on the Stand, N.Y. Times, Mar. 11, 2007, www.nytimes.com.

C. ALTERING IDENTITY AND PERSONHOOD WITH PSYCHOPHARMACEUTICALS AND DEVICES THAT ENHANCE

1. *Psychopharmaceuticals*

For millennia, people in many cultures have used chemical substances that alter mental states. These have included wine, beer, peyote, kava, and cocaine, among many others. Such substances have been taken to dull pain, to relieve depression, to produce energy, to foster religious visions, to celebrate joy, to drown sorrow, or just to get through the day. The effects of such substances have long raised questions about whether the behavior and language of a person under their influence should be taken as the person's "own" language and behavior.

Mental illnesses have raised similar questions, as have the drugs used to treat mental illnesses. Both the illnesses and the cures have led to serious questions for those affected, for their friends, family, clinicians, and employers, and for lawmakers about the authenticity of the affected person's responses. A 2011 issue of the Hastings Center Report features an article that reports on 29 interviews with women diagnosed with anorexia nervosa, a serious eating disorder. The article (reflecting questions raised by the interviewees themselves) asks whether "respecting other people" implies that one should respect their "authentic—but not their inauthentic—choices." Tony Hope et al., Anorexia Nervosa and the Language of Authenticity, 41 Hastings Cent. Rep. 19, 19 (2011). The question is particularly troubling insofar as it is difficult—often impossible—to distinguish one from the other. Yet, it holds serious implications for medical decision making and law enforcement as well as for personal identity.

> ## Jonathan Blitz, Freedom of Thought for the Extended Mind: Cognitive Enhancement and the Constitution
> 2010 Wis. L. Rev. 1049, 1058–1061 (2010)

[Peter] Kramer observed that Prozac seemed to do more than treat [his patients'] underlying depression; it markedly changed their personalities. In one patient, it was not only a deep and abiding feeling of sadness and hopelessness that disappeared, but the shyness, uncertainty, and caution that had characterized her as a person. Another reported that Prozac not only made him feel better after years of depression, but "better than well." Indeed, Kramer was stunned by how "global" the drug's effects were. The drug did not merely banish the patient's illness, but "reshaped [her] identity."

As Kramer noticed, these personality modification powers might well be of interest not only to those who want to banish illness, but to those who want to change their personalities for other reasons. . . .

Prozac is only the most well-known of a growing number of cognitive-enhancement drugs. Most of these were developed (and are still used primarily) to treat psychological illnesses. . . . [H]ealthy individuals have also found these substances helpful aids to increase their calmness or happiness, sharpen their focus and attention, improve their memory, and maintain alertness when they would normally be overwhelmed by fatigue.

. . . .

The rise of these new cognitive-enhancement tools has sparked a vigorous debate among scientists, policymakers, and public intellectuals about whether such use is wise or ethical and whether it is acceptable for psychiatrists to prescribe these drugs to individuals who are not mentally ill. Recently, a group of prominent neuroscientists and neuroethicists added energy to this debate by proposing, in Nature, that healthy people should generally be allowed to take advantage of enhancement-technology, where it is safe to do so, calling for "a presumption that mentally competent adults should be able to engage in cognitive enhancement using drugs." By contrast, other prominent commentators have urged extreme caution—if not outright opposition—regarding the use of such drugs to enhance mental function rather than to treat mental illnesses. Carl Elliott worries that cognitive-enhancement may make our lives or identities less authentic. Even if SSRI drugs afford someone a better personality, he writes, "it isn't [his] personality." Francis Fukuyama warns that far from enhancing our freedom, drugs like Prozac may lead us to seek a quick dose of "self-esteem in a bottle" where we have previously sought it in human achievement and development of character. President George W. Bush's Council on Bioethics likewise warns, in a 2003 report on enhancement technologies, that "mood brighteners" might produce "feelings of contentment severed from action in the world or from relationships with other people."

NOTES AND QUESTIONS

1. *The ethics of cognitive enhancement.*   In a part of Blitz's article not included above, he describes a number of "key issues" at the center of the debate about

using cognitive enhancements. What do you think some of the ethical issues might be?

2. *"Cosmetic neurology."*   College students, seeking cognitive enhancers, are looking to drugs developed to treat a variety of medical conditions such as Attention Deficit Hyperactivity Disorder (ADHD) and narcolepsy. Some healthy university students are also using Aricept (donepezil), developed for the treatment of people diagnosed with Alzheimer disease, as a memory-enhancing drug. On some U.S. campuses as many as a quarter of students in any year use drugs for cognitive enhancement. Commentary: Towards Responsible Use of Cognitive-Enhancing Drugs by the Healthy, 456 Nature 702 (Dec. 2008) (hereinafter Commentary, Nature). One neurologist referred to this use of drugs as "cosmetic neurology" and has predicted a future in which some neurologists will function as "quality-of-life consultants." Margaret Margaret Talbot, Can a Pill a Day Really Boost Your Brain Power?, The Observer Magazine, Sept. 9, 2009, at 18, available at http://www.guardian.co.uk/science/2009/sep/20/neuroenhancers-us-brain-power-drugs (quoting Anjan Chatterjee, a neurologist). Talbot reported that a student newspaper columnist asked whether a person can "take credit" for work done while using drugs such as Adderall (mixed amphetamine salts) and Ritalin (methyphenidate), both used to treat ADHD, or Provigil (modafinil), used to treat narcolepsy. Talbot suggested that the question might be no different than asking whether one can take credit for work done while drinking coffee or smoking nicotine. Id. Do you see any differences between using Adderall, Ritalin, or Provigil and using caffeine or nicotine?

A commentary, published in Nature in 2008, goes further, suggesting that cognitive enhancing drugs (assuming that they are "safe and effective" for enhancement in healthy people) should be welcomed for the attractive benefits they offer to students, academics, and those studying for licensure exams, among others. The piece argues that cognitive enhancing drugs "along with newer technologies such as brain stimulation and prosthetic brain chips, should be viewed in the same general category as education, good health habits, and information technology—ways that our uniquely innovative species tries to improve itself." Henry Greely et al., Commentary, Nature, supra, at 702. The commentary does acknowledge that different forms of cognitive enhancement may raise different moral questions. What do you think the authors mean by this?

3. *Compelled use of cognitive enhancers.*   Some commentators, discussing drugs aimed at cognitive enhancement, have wondered whether such drugs will be, or ever should be, compelled by governments, schools, or other institutions. Commentary, Nature, supra. And even if ingestion of such drugs is not forced, how irresistible, at least to some, might be the example of peers and classmates succeeding through use of such drugs? In the United States, those in the military must take drugs that are ordered for them. Soldiers have long been offered drugs intended to enhance alertness. Id. at 703. The use of psychopharmaceuticals in military contexts and for security purposes raises especially provocative and troubling ethical questions. Cognitive enchancers that curtail the need for sleep could be of use in combat situations. Do you think that the military should have the authority to compel soldiers to take such medications, particularly insofar as their long-term risks are not yet known? See The Royal

Society, Brain Waves Module 3: Neuroscience, Conflict and Security, RS Policy document 06/11 (Feb. 2012), www.royalsociety.org.

4. *Cognitive enhancers for children.* Giving cognitive enhancing drugs to children raises particularly difficult questions. First, and most important, the effects of such drugs on children could be significantly different than the effects on adults. Second, children, especially young children, are not able to understand informed consent conversations and thus are not able to consent on their own to use of cognitive enhancers (as well, of course, to the use of other drugs). How acceptable would it be for a parent to suggest (or compel) a child to take cognitive enhancers so that the child might have a better chance of doing well academically or of getting accepted to a school of (the parent's) choice or of achieving success in school sporting events?

5. *A "morality pill."* Instances of immoral behavior, such as passer-bys ignoring a dying child in the street to get to a meeting on time, have been contrasted with instances of great heroism aimed at saving a stranger's life. Peter Singer and Agata Sagan wonder about the continuum of morality within populations and suggest that differences might be "rooted in our genes." Peter Singer & Agata Sagan, Are We Ready for a "Morality Pill"?, N.Y. Times, Jan. 28, 2012, www.opinionator.blogs.nytimes.com. Even more, they suggest that if a propensity to act to save others correlates with biochemical patterns in the brains of those who do so as compared with those who do not do so, it might be possible to develop a "morality pill." If such a pill were ever developed, could governments compel people to take it? Would it be ethical to offer it as an alternative to prison?

6. *Drugs and racial prejudice.* Can drugs reduce or increase prejudice? Researchers in Britain found that in a laboratory context, propranolol (a beta-blocker generally used to treat coronary disease) reduced subconscious (although not explicit) racial prejudice. The authors noted that their results were tentative and that further research is in order. Researchers attributed the observed effect to propranolol's role in blocking autonomic nervous system activation and in decreasing responses of the amygdala to certain stimuli linked with anger and fear. Sylvia Terbeck et al., Propranolol Reduces Implicit Negative Racial Bias, Psychopharmacology (published online Feb. 28, 2012), http://www.springerlink.com/content/63v2561264075373/fulltext.html; see also Michael Cook, Towards a Cure for Racism? Bioedge (Mar. 10, 2012), www.bioedge.org.

CHALLENGING ISSUES: MANDATING NEUROPHARMACEUTICALS

It is 2022, and the military as well as private individuals—students, ambitious business executives, and others—have been using neuropharmaceuticals (often legally, sometimes not quite legally in the context of private use) for many years. Now, a new generation of drugs that wards off sleepiness and increases energy and cognitive acuity is being distributed widely by three pharmaceutical companies. Each of the companies contends that the new generation of neuropharmaceuticals has largely eliminated the side effects that once restricted people's interest in such drugs. Among other things, a new class of neuropharmaceuticals that seem to carry little potential for addiction is in wide use.

As a result, ten large companies (collectively called the Ten) have joined together to create what they call Project Employee Effectiveness (PEE). As a group, the Ten has decided that employees in all ten of the companies supporting PEE who serve in mid- to high-level positions must take a set of neuropharmaceuticals every day or forfeit their positions.

The ten companies backing PEE plan to pay for the drugs they will require employees to ingest. Drugs will be distributed at the start of each working day. Employees must submit to neuroimaging every six months. Neuroimaging results will be used to monitor the effects of the drugs on the brains of those who use them (referred to as a "safety" precaution), and results will be used as research data for PEE scientists who are continually working on the development of even more effective neuropharmaceuticals. One group of PEE researchers is about to announce early results suggesting that a new drug (called drug PX) will allow adults to work continuously for 96 hours without need for sleep or rest. Do you think the companies should be allowed to proceed with their plans? As a moral matter? As a legal matter?

2.   Devices That "Enhance"

As is the case with psychopharmaceuticals, people use some enhancement devices to expand their skills, others to develop one or more of their senses, and still others to prolong life. Enhancement devices range from familiar items long used by many people in many societies such as eyeglasses and hearing aids, to more complicated devices used to prolong life and increase health, such as heart valves and hip joints.

> ## Linda MacDonald Glenn, Case Study: Ethical and Legal Issues in Human Machine Mergers (or the Cyborgs Cometh)
> ### 21 Ann. Health L. 175, 177-178 (2012)

[The following analysis is based around a legal case for which the author was an attorney of record. Her client, a man named Mr. Collins, was wounded while serving in the military. He lost the use of both legs and one arm. The Department of Veterans Affairs supplied him with a "powered mobility assistance device (MAD)." Mr. Collins is unable to rely on a manual wheelchair because he is at risk of slipping into a position that could interfere with his breathing. In October 2009, Mr. Collins flew to Puerto Rico on Allways Airlines. His MAD was damaged by Allways. The airline admitted responsibility for rendering the MAD dysfunctional, but, in part because of their failure to understand the differences between the MAD and a manual wheelchair, bureaucracy moved slowly. The VA replaced Mr. Collins's MAD but not for 11 months. During the period in which he did not have a MAD, Mr. Collins was "essentially bedridden."]

These interactive prosthetics, along with other emerging technologies, are blurring our bodily boundaries. Distinctions between "natural" and "artificial," between "alive" and "not alive" or "animate" and "inanimate" are ones that are becoming increasingly difficult to determine. Similarly, the stark dichotomy between "property" and "person" is changing. The notion of what a "person" is has changed and shifted under the law. Legal (or juridical) "persons" also include ships and corporations, and the law is currently evolving to recognize that the dichotomy does not always work, that there may be a need to create a continuum rather than a dichotomy.

As these boundaries are challenged through technological developments, the case at hand brought to mind the philosophical thought experiment that has been termed the "Ship of Theseus." A classic philosophical puzzle about identity, ancient historian Plutarch recounts the story of the famous ship of Theseus, which was displayed in Athens for many centuries. Plutarch asked, over time as the ship's planks wore down and were gradually replaced, whether the ship became a new ship by replacing all its wooden parts or did it remain the same ship?

In the current case study, Mr. Collins' MAD replaced many of his bodily parts. And while today, the MAD and Mr. Collins could be distinguished or separated for short periods of time, with advancing technology, one could easily envision replacement parts that are not easily distinguishable or separable. In terms of individuals with disabilities, the miniaturization and ease of wear and use of these technologies would present a boom, and a chance to end discrimination against those with disabilities. The rapid adaptation and accelerating use of these technologies could lead us to a variation of the Ship of Theseus puzzle: How many parts of Mr. Collins could be replaced until he was no longer legally Mr. Collins? Or could that point never be reached?

NOTES AND QUESTIONS

1. *Merging with one's devices.*   At the end of the article by Linda MacDonald Glenn, excerpted above, MacDonald Glenn reports that she and her co-counsel explained to Allways Airlines that they were looking forward to bringing a "test" case in which they planned to argue that Mr. Collins and the MAD had essentially merged, becoming one and thus, for Mr. Collins, loss of the MAD was tantamount to a loss of part of himself. With that, the adjuster for Allways, who had previously offered Mr. Collins $1,500, increased the airline's offer to $20,000 in compensation. Mr. Collins accepted that offer.

2. *"Ordinary human capacities" as impairments.* A 2010 law review note queries whether developments in cybernetic-enhancement technology could lead to "ordinary human capacities" being defined as "impairments." Even more, the note asserts that the Americans with Disabilities Act, 42 U.S.C. §§12101–12213, does not safeguard people without enhancements from discrimination in favor of those with enhancements. The note suggests amending the ADA so that it defines "impairment" to include "an ordinary human capacity." Collin R. Bockman, Note, Cybernetic-Enhancement Technology and the Future of Disability Law, 95 Iowa L. Rev. 1315 (2010). Do you agree with this note's conclusion?

3. *An "eyeborg," an "earborg," and a "noseborg."*   A hospital in Barcelona, Spain has agreed to do surgery sought by a local artist named Neil Harbisson. Harbisson, born colorblind, "sees" color through a device that he now wears on his head that converts color into sound. Jennifer S. Lee, A Surgical Implant for

Seeing Colors Through Sounds, N.Y. Times Blogs, July 2, 2012, available in Lexis/Nexis, News Library. Harbisson, who calls the device he now wears an "eyeborg," was asked to speak with the hospital's ethics committee before permission for the surgery was granted. Harbisson expressed hope that the device could soon be developed to allow people without sight to read. He and a friend created the Cyborg Foundation. The Foundation is now supporting work on the further development of "earborgs." An "earborg" is described as "cybernetic ears to allow humans [to] perceive sound through color, shapes and light." Further, the Foundation is working on "noseborgs," described as "cybernetic noses to allow humans [to] perceive smell through electromagnetic signals," and on the development of prosthetic fingers that will allow users to take pictures with their fingers. http://www.harbisson.com/Cyborg_Foundation/About_us.html (last visited July 4, 2012).

4. *The risks of warnings.* Medical devices do not always function as those who use them expect. Sometimes new risks faced by those wearing implanted devices become known. Physicians must warn patients of such risks, even if they are rare. One commentator provides an example: a patient with a cardioverter defibrillator (implanted beneath the skin) seems to face a rare risk that the device will short-circuit. If that were to happen, the device, which serves to maintain a normal heart rhythm and thus prevent sudden cardiac death, would become nonfunctional. A patient, told about the risk of a short circuit in the device, has a few choices. Doing nothing until the battery needs to be replaced in any event might make sense, given that the risk is very small, but the patient might worry nonetheless. The patient might instead opt for immediate surgery to replace the device. This poses new risks for the patient—from the surgery and from the possibility that the new device will also entail risks. Lisa V. von Biela, A Disclosure Dilemma: What You Don't Know Can Kill You, But So Can What You Do Know, 65 Food Drug L.J. 317, 317 (2010). (Similar issues can develop in the wake of new vaccines and medications.) Assuming the maker of cardioverter defibrillators informed physicians of the risk that the device might short-circuit, how do you think a physician should advise a patient in whom one of the devices had been implanted?

3. The Case For and Against Aging

Especially as the baby boomer generation faces old age, interest has surged in pharmaceuticals and devices that promise to postpone or mask aging. Some bioethicists oppose the development of biotechnology aimed at extending life beyond what is considered a natural life span.

Should replacement parts and new genetic and pharmaceutical therapies allow the extension of life well beyond the present norm, it is not yet clear whether those added years will be healthy years or years of poor health and increased dependence. Some commentators have suggested that the specter of a very long old age marked by dependence and ill health displaces an ancient fear of death with a more modern fear of life—including the fear that one's assets will not stretch to cover requisite long-term care needs during old age. See Nathalie D. Martin, Funding Long-Term Care: Some Risk Spreaders Create More Risks Than They Cure, 16 J. Contemp. Health L. & Pol'y 355, 355

(2000). The specter of long life without health and without money terrifies many people. Others counter, however, that prolonged life does not necessarily mean life without health, and new modes of financing health care and long-term care might dissipate financial fears. Moreover, for many people the extension of life is valuable even if the consequence is ill health and greater dependence.

> ## The President's Council on Bioethics,
> ## Beyond Therapy: Biotechnology and the
> ## Pursuit of Happiness
> ### (October 2003)

[The full Report can be found at http://www.bioethics.gov.]

CHAPTER FOUR: AGELESS BODIES

. . . [I]f there is merit in the suggestion that too long a life, with its end out of sight and mind, might diminish its worth, one might wonder whether we have already gone too far in increasing longevity. If so, one might further suggest that we should, if we could, roll back at least some of the increases made in the average human lifespan over the past century.

These remarks prompt some large questions: Is there an optimal human lifespan and an ideal contour of a human life? If so, does it resemble our historical lifespan (as framed and constrained by natural limits)? Or does the optimal human lifespan lie in the future, to be achieved by some yet-to-be-developed life-extending technology? Whatever the answers to these intriguing and important questions, nothing in our inquiry ought to suggest that the present average lifespan is itself ideal. We do not take the present (or any specific time past) to be "the best of all possible worlds," and we would not favor rolling back the average lifespan even if it were doable. Although we suggest some possible problems with substantially longer lifespans, we have not expressed, and would not express, a wish for shorter lifespans than are now the norm. To the contrary, all of us surely want more people to be able to enjoy the increased longevity that the last century produced. Those previous efforts that have increased average lifespans have done so by reducing the risks and removing the causes of premature death, allowing many more people to live out their biblical three-score (today, four-score) and ten. Yet during that time, there has been relatively little increase in the maximum human life span, and not many people are living longer than the longest-lived people ever did. Although we may learn about the future by studying somewhat similar changes in the past, the effects of changes of the past are not an adequate guide for the radically new possibilities that age-retardation may bring into being. Thus, to be committed, as we are, to trying to help everyone make it through the natural human lifespan (surely a better world than the present) does not require our being committed to altering or increasing that lifespan. Conversely, to be concerned about the implications of departing from a three-to-four-generational lifespan does not necessitate a reactionary embrace of any putative virtues of premature death.

   The past century's advances in average lifespan, now approaching eighty years for the majority of our fellow citizens, have come about through largely intelligible operations within a natural world shaped by human understanding and human powers. It is a conceptually manageable lifespan, with individuals living not only through childhood and parenthood but long enough to see their own grandchildren, and permitted a taste of each sort of relationship. It is a world in which one's direct family lineage is connected by both genetics and personal experience, not so attenuated by time that relatives feel unrelated. Generation and nurture, dependency and reciprocated generosity, are in some harmony of proportion, and there is a pace of journey, a coordinated coherence of meter and rhyme within the repeating cycles of birth, ascendancy, and decline—a balance and beauty of love and renewal giving answer to death that, however poignant, bespeaks the possibility of meaning and goodness in the human experience. All this might be overthrown or forgotten in the rush to fashion a technological project only along the gradient of our open-ended desires and ambitions.

   Contemplating the speculative prospect of altering the human life cycle brings us to the crucial question: Is there a goodness and meaning in life so fundamental that it is too wide to be grasped by our scientific vision and too deep to be plumbed by the imperious exigencies of our natural desire? If we go with the grain of our desires and pursue indefinite prolongation and ageless bodies for ourselves, will we improve the parts and heighten the present, but only at the cost of losing the coherence of an ordered and integrated whole? Might we be cheating ourselves by departing from the contour and constraint of natural life (our frailty and finitude), which serve as a lens for a larger vision that might give all of life coherence and sustaining significance? Conversely, in affirming the unfolding of birth and growth, aging and death, might we not find access to something permanent, something beyond this "drama of time," something that at once transcends and gives purpose to the processes of the earth, lifting us to a dignity beyond all disorder, decay, and death? To raise these questions is not to answer them, but simply to indicate the enormous matters that are at stake.

   . . . In Aldous Huxley's Brave New World, Bernard and Lenina are hovering in a helicopter over the city, wondering how to best spend their evening together. Lenina (typically jejune) suggests a game of electromagnetic golf. Bernard demurs and replies, "No, that would be a waste of time." Lenina answers back, "What's time for?" Only aging and death remind us that time is of the essence. They invite us to notice that the evolution of life on earth has produced souls with longings for the eternal and, if recognized, a chance to participate in matters of enduring significance that ultimately could transcend time itself.

   The broader issue has to do with the meaning of certain elements of our human experience that medical science may now allow us to alter and manipulate. The ability to retard aging puts into question the meaning of aging in our lives, and the way we ought best to regard it: Is aging a disease? Is it a condition to be treated or cured? Does that mean that all the generations that have come before us have lived a life of suffering, either waiting for a cure that never came or foolishly convincing themselves that their curse was just a blessing in disguise? Is the finitude of human life, as our ancestors experienced it and as our faiths and our philosophies have taught us to understand it, really just a problem waiting to be solved? The anti-aging medicine of the not-so-distant future would treat what we have usually thought of as the whole, the healthy, human life as a condition to be healed. It therefore presents us with a questionable notion both of full humanity and of the proper ends of medicine. . . .

Some foreseeable biotechnologies, like those of effective age-retardation, hold out the prospect of perfecting some among our imperfections, and must lead us to ask just what sort of project this is that we have set upon. Is the purpose of medicine and biotechnology, in principle, to let us live endless, painless lives of perfect bliss? Or is its purpose rather to let us live out the humanly full span of life within the edifying limits and constraints of humanity's grasp and power? As that grasp expands, and that power increases, these fundamental questions of human purposes and ends become more and more important, and finding the proper ways to think about them becomes more vital but more difficult. The techniques themselves will not answer these questions for us, and ignoring the questions will not make them go away, even if we lived forever.

NOTES AND QUESTIONS

1. *Moral consequences of expanding the life span.* Do you agree with the suggestion in the Report of the President's Council, supra, that the spirit of humanity—"the possibility of meaning and goodness in the human experience"—might be sacrificed with the success of the effort to expand the average life span significantly through biotechnological enhancements? Does this project threaten some larger "natural" order? If the answer is yes, does it make sense to prohibit research that will produce "biotechnologies, like those of effective age-retardation"; to proceed with research while working simultaneously to preserve existing understandings of what the council refers to as "full humanity"; or to let research proceed, understanding that every age reconstructs its view of life and of what it means to be a person? In short, do you think the council is right in suggesting that cultural and social changes likely to develop as consequences of biotechnologies that retard aging will be fundamentally different from earlier cultural and social changes; and, if so, do you think that if these biotechnological developments are not halted or closely monitored, they threaten to transform the human species unalterably?

2. *Anti-aging medical care.* Membership of the American Academy of Anti-Aging grew by almost 50 percent between 2001 and 2003 (from 8,500 to 12,000 members). But the results of anti-aging medicine do not all seem good. Some researchers caution that even some apparently benign anti-aging drugs, available over the counter, could have serious negative consequences. Andrea Petersen, Doctors Begin to Treat Aging as a Preventable Disease, Increasing Your "Health Span," Wall St. Journal, May 20, 2003, at D1.

Moreover, the line between enhancement and treatment for illness and disability is not distinct. Certainly, treatment for conditions such as arteriosclerosis or high blood pressure will, if successful, enhance the recipient's quality of life and will quite likely prolong that life. Moreover, existing anti-aging treatments range from mainstream responses and over-the-counter drugs to highly controversial drugs; and from vitamins and exercise programs to human growth hormones.

Hormone replacement therapy for women, touted (in large part mistakenly) as a tool for warding off heart disease and bone thinning, has also been used by women to diminish menopausal symptoms and signs associated with physical aging. Now, use of testosterone therapy by men is becoming increasingly popular. The therapy, much like comparable hormone therapies used by women, is being described as a panacea for those anxious to defy aging. However, the Institute of Medicine of the National Academies has cautioned that the effects of testosterone therapy have not yet been adequately studied. Sara Schaefer Munoz, Men Shouldn't Use Testosterone to Ward off Aging, Panel Warns, Wall St. Journal, Nov. 13, 2003, at D3. In 1999, doctors wrote 650,000 prescriptions for testosterone. In 2002, the number had increased to over 1.75 million. Eli Chester Ridgway, president of the Endocrine Society and a supporter of the Institute of Medicine's conclusions, explained: "There is this cult out there among men that think their testosterone levels are slipping so their vigor for life in all categories is going down." Id.

3. *Extending life/extending health.*   Several commentators have noted the difference between biotechnologies that extend life and those that extend health. David Gems, writing in the Hastings Center Report in 2003, suggested reason to be concerned even about biotechnologies that extend health as well as life. David Gems, Is More Life Always Better?: The New Biology of Aging and the Meaning of Life, 33 Hastings Ctr. Rpt. 31 (July-Aug. 2003). Among the concerns Gems outlines is overpopulation and with it increased demand for limited resources (including health care). Moreover, if extended longevity can only be achieved at great expense, a serious form of distributive injustice is built into the pursuit of a longer and longer life span. Id. at 34. Gems also wonders whether a significantly longer life span will end in a "state of terminal boredom." Do you think people of 50 are generally more "bored" than people of 30? Are people of 75 more bored than people of 50? If so, what is responsible for the difference? Might people find new life paths at 65 or 75 (ages of retirement today) if they knew they were likely to live another half-century? Or would most people fear decades of boredom or loneliness?

4. *Regeneration.*   A few biotechnology companies are working to develop regenerative medicine. One of the aims is to make it feasible to use stem cells to generate new organs and tissues. Andrew Pollack, Forget Botox: Anti-Aging Pills May Be Next, N.Y. Times, Sept. 21, 2003, www.nytimes.com. Another approach has emerged from research suggesting that extremely low-calorie diets extend life 30 to 50 percent in rats and mice; however, the animals subjected to such diets have suffered from weakened immune systems and low sexual drive. A few biotechnology companies are trying to develop drugs that will provide the sort of life-extending effects that extreme calorie restriction might provide. Francis Fukuyama imagined a "national nursing home scenario" in which people live until 150 but spend a half-century of their lives in institutional care. Francis Fukuyama, Our Posthuman Future 690 (2002). Fukuyama suggested that

> If there is no molecular shortcut to postponing death because aging is the result of the gradual accumulation of damage to a wide range of different biological systems, then there is no reason to think that future medical advances will proceed with a neat simultaneity, any more than they have in the past. . . . In the future, biotechnology is likely to offer us bargains that trade off length of life span for quality of life.

= PART II =

BIOETHICS AND THE INDIVIDUAL

5

Avoiding Reproduction: Sterilization, Contraception, and Abortion

This chapter considers ethical questions that attend coercive or consensual acts intended to preclude reproduction. The first section of the chapter considers coerced sterilization and coerced use of contraception. The second section considers consensual acts aimed at avoiding reproduction, focusing first on contraception and then turning to the complicated debate about abortion as it developed, largely in legal settings, in the second half of the twentieth century up to the present.

The following questions suggest the variety of issues raised by sterilization, contraception, and abortion:

1. How important is the ability to reproduce? Is there a culture-neutral approach to the question or are assessments of the significance of reproduction inevitably the product of particular socio-religious traditions?

2. Is reproduction more or less important for women than for men? Again, to what extent is one's answer to this question a product of the cultural frame within which one contemplates the question?

3. Is the right to *avoid* reproduction more or less important for women than for men? Does your answer reflect an understanding of biological, social, religious, or economic facts?

4. Do you think coercive sterilization or contraception is more or less objectionable if it affects everyone in a society (e.g., a one-child policy) or if it affects only certain categories of people (e.g., disabled people)?

5. In what way, if at all, can the debate about avoiding reproduction in the United States be understood as part of a wider debate about the meaning and scope of family life?

A.   NONCONSENSUAL AVOIDANCE OF REPRODUCTION[1]

1.   Coerced Sterilization

Some cases of coerced sterilization have been justified by those responsible (the state, parents, guardians) as serving the best interests of the sterilized individual. These cases may involve pubescent children or young adults with limited mental capacity. Other cases of coerced sterilization are justified as serving the best interests of society. Many of these involve eugenic justifications.

Before World War II, sterilization was encouraged to rid society of those considered genetically deficient. The eugenics movement was successful in much of Western Europe and in the United States from the 1920s until World War II. In the United States about 30 states had provided for the involuntary sterilization of people diagnosed with various conditions, including uncontrollable epilepsy, mental deficiency, or insanity. California sterilized more than 7,500 institutionalized dependents in those years. Ellen Chesler, Woman of Valor: Margaret Sanger and the Birth Control Movement in America 215–217 (1992). In the country as a whole, more than 60,000 people were sterilized during the twentieth century. Of the states in which these sterilizations occurred, one, Virginia, has officially condemned its history of coerced sterilization and apologized for it. Paul A. Lombardo, Taking Eugenics Seriously: Three Generations of ??? Are Enough?, 30 Fla. St. U. L. Rev. 191, 202 (2003). In the 1920s, Harry Laughlin, superintendent of the Eugenics Record Office (where the American eugenics movement stored data relevant to its programs) proposed a model law aimed at what Laughlin referred to as the "submerged tenth"—"the most worthless one-tenth of the present population." His model law would have provided for the sterilization of "potential parents carrying degenerate hereditary qualities." Stephen Jay Gould, Carrie Buck's Daughter, 111 Natural History 12 (2002).

After World War II, the eugenics movement in the United States was discredited and quickly fell apart. The horrific use of eugenic policies in Nazi Germany had rendered the movement's potential for evil undeniable. Matthew Lippman described the origin and use of Nazi eugenics laws:

> The Nazi government passed the Law for the Prevention of Genetically Diseased Offspring on July 14, 1933. This permitted the sterilization of those suffering from various allegedly hereditary diseases. . . .
>
> The Fuhrer next took steps to eliminate the mentally and physically challenged. . . . The utilization of doctors was crucial for portraying these murders as medical treatment. . . .
>
> The sterilization and euthanasia programs set the stage for the extermination of the Jews. Those subjected to sterilization and euthanasia had been selected due to their disability or disease. The entire Jewish race, however, was portrayed as pestilent and was pictured as a threat to the public health.

Matthew Lippman, War Crimes Prosecutions of Nazi Health Professionals and the Contemporary Protection of Human Rights, 21 T. Marshall L. Rev. 11, 17–19

---

1. Sections (B)(1) (Medical Intervention During Pregnancy) and (B)(2) (Substance Abuse During Pregnancy) in Chapter 6 raise questions related to those raised in this section.

(1995). Nazi eugenics policies and their consequences are described in much greater detail in Lippman's article.

a. Buck v. Bell and Its Cultural Context

i. Bioethical and Social Perspectives

> ## Paul A. Lombardo, Taking Eugenics Seriously: Three Generations of ??? Are Enough?
> ### 30 Fla. St. U. L. Rev. 191, 202–205, 208–211, 214 (2003)

The *Buck* case and related laws to permit state-sponsored sterilization provide a touchstone for discussions of the eugenics movement. While the word itself had many meanings to the variety of people who used it early in the twentieth century, it is employed almost exclusively today as a pejorative term to signal coercive state measures. Connections between eugenic ideology and the Nazi Holocaust, along with the sterilization history . . . , explain much of the contemporary negative reaction to the term "eugenics." The racist focus of much of the eugenics movement provides even more reason for the negative connotations of the term. An instructive view of the dark side of the science concerned with "better breeding" can begin with a look at the careers of some U.S. eugenicists. Prominent among them was Charles B. Davenport.

Davenport represented the public face of eugenics in America from 1910 until his death in 1944. He was the Resident Director of the Long Island based Eugenics Record Office (ERO). The ERO was the best-funded and most successful of the organizations that emerged to promote the ideas of the eugenics movement in the first quarter of the twentieth century. Later it would also be associated with some of the most malignant members of the movement, described by today's publications of the Cold Spring Harbor Laboratory (now a center of genomic research) as "self-righteously bigoted." . . .

[Davenport] proposed a system that would survey family traits. Such a plan would "identify those lines which supply our families of great men." But

> [w]e [should] also learn whence come our 300,000 insane and feeble-minded, our 160,000 blind or deaf, the 2,000,000 that are annually cared for by our hospitals and Homes, our 80,000 prisoners and the thousands of criminals that are not in prison, and our 100,000 paupers in almshouses and out.
>
> This three or four per cent of our population is a fearful drag on our civilization. Shall we as an intelligent people, proud of our control of nature in other respects, do nothing but vote more taxes or be satisfied with the great gifts and bequests that philanthropists have made for the support of the delinquent, defective and dependent classes? Shall we not rather take the steps that scientific study dictates as necessary to dry up the springs that feed the torrent of defective and degenerate protoplasm?

. . . The agenda of the Eugenics Record Office embraced government coercion as the proper means to enforce a eugenically sanitized population and further stigmatized people with disabilities and their families. While Davenport and his ilk railed against the "socially inadequate," others within the eugenics movement debated the proper uses of the law as a means of addressing disabling conditions. . . .

Francis Galton, the man who coined the term "eugenics" defined it as "hereditarily endowed with noble qualities" or more simply "well-born." Galton's elaborated definition included "all influences that tend in however remote a degree to give the more suitable races or strains of blood a better chance of prevailing speedily over the less suitable than they otherwise would have had." Within a generation, adherents to Galton's scientific credo would include statesmen and Presidents, as well as a Who's Who of scientists and physicians who eventually embraced eugenics. Nobel Laureates, such as Theodore Roosevelt (1906), Elihu Root (1912), Woodrow Wilson (1919) and Winston Churchill (1953), joined more than a dozen Nobel Prize winners from the sciences who openly supported some form of eugenics at one time during their careers. They included such noteworthy scientists and social scientists as Alexis Carrel (1912), Thomas Hunt Morgan (1933), Jane Addams (1931), H. J. Muller (1946), William Shockley (1956), Linus Pauling (1962), Joshua Lederberg (1958), Francis Crick (1962), Konrad Lorenz (1973), and Gunnar Myrdal (1974).

The popular face of eugenics was often a happy one, with the winners of "better babies" contests pledged to future "eugenic" marriages and county fairs rewarded the fittest families. Never too far behind a popular movement, even politicians jumped on the eugenics bandwagon. One Chicago politico is reported to have even invoked the new field on his own behalf, claiming a spot on the Chicago City Council as "[the] eugenic candidate." . . .

Representatives of the government health establishment concurred in endorsing the validity of eugenics. The U.S. Public Health Service Surgeon General supervised eugenic examinations and issued eugenic marriage certificates. Dr. W. C. Rucker, the assistant surgeon general, said "Eugenics is a science. It is a fact, not a fad." Social work leader and later Nobel Laureate Jane Addams applauded "the new science of eugenics with its recently appointed university professors. Its organized societies publish an ever-increasing mass of information as to that which constitutes the inheritance of well-born children." Even disability rights icon Helen Keller agreed that some "defective" children should not be saved from a premature death because of their propensity to criminality.

The rush to endorse new ideas seemingly anchored in scientific truth was hardly unusual, and one should not make too much of the early popularity of disparate ideas labeled "eugenic." However, the extraordinary success of proponents of some variety of eugenics in capturing the public's moral imagination cannot be ignored. Despite the disfavor into which the "dark side" of eugenics has fallen, the seductive message of the eugenics movement is worthy of analysis. Early followers rallied to a fundamental eugenic premise: that science could be used to alleviate suffering and improve the human condition. The attraction to eugenics for many was that it promised, if not a medical Utopia, free of diseases, at least a future in which some debilitating conditions could be relegated to the dustbin of history. . . .

To enable doctors to understand the importance of the workings of heredity in daily practice, [Harvey Earnest] Jordan [Chair of the American Association for the Study and Prevention of Infant Mortality and a faculty member and then Dean at the University of Virginia School of Medicine] argued that eugenics should be part of the curriculum of every medical school. The doctor of the future would not be merely a "dispenser of medicines" but a eugenic advisor who could point the way toward the "elimination of as much of the physical, mental and moral sickness and weakness as can be prevented." Jordan urged that health enhancing practices must be promoted toward an "ultimate ideal" of a "perfect society constituted of perfect individuals." But because Jordan was aware of the expense of "social therapy" and environmental interventions to cure problems thought traceable to heredity, he favored a preventive strategy.

Eugenics provided the means to realize his prophylactic goal. "Medicine is fast becoming a science of the prevention of weakness and morbidity; their permanent not temporary cure, their racial eradication rather than their personal palliation. . . . Eugenics, embracing genetics, is thus one of the important disciplines among the future medical sciences."

NOTES AND QUESTIONS

1. *Are "eugenic" policies (circa 1912) still being voiced?*   Do Harvey Jordan's words (in the last paragraph of the excerpt from Lombardo, supra), uttered in 1912, seem relevant today or are they of historic interest only? Were a contemporary "Harvey Jordan" to pronounce similar beliefs today, would the language likely change from that uttered in 1912?

Paul Lombardo's description of the eugenics movement in the United States before World War II suggests that the movement was defined by a complicated set of motives and perspectives. Despite broad differences within the movement, many of those who favored various forms of eugenic practice at that time were united by a deep faith in science and in the value of scientific "truth" to improve social reality. Americans abandoned the eugenics movement forged in the first half of the twentieth century. Yet, support for contemporary work in genetics sometimes echoes themes found in the statements of the early twentieth-century eugenicists. Even as scientific "facts" have changed and reproductive options have shifted, people continue to justify their goals and delineate their options in light of a persistent faith in the power of science to illuminate the "truth."

2. *Eugenics or genetic choice?*   In short, even as individual control has replaced state control as the locus of eugenic choice, see Mary B. Mahowald, Chapter 4, Section A(2), there are significant similarities between the eugenics movement of the early twentieth century and the contemporary interest in genetic choice. One commentator expresses "unease" about various instances of genetic choice now being entertained. Dov Fox, Silver Spoons and Golden Genes, 33 Am. J.L. & Med. 567, 620 (2007). In particular, Fox suggests that the growing popularity of genetic control threatens both an egalitarian ethos and the development of compassion. Section A(2) of Chapter 4 elaborates on this discussion.

3. *Bibliographic note.*   For a summary of the history of eugenics policies in the United States, see Paul A. Lombardo, Disability, Eugenics, and the Cultural Wars, 2 St. Louis U.J. Health L. & Pol'y 57 (2008).

ii. Legal Approaches

One of the most infamous nonconsensual sterilization cases in U.S. legal history is that of Carrie Buck. Carrie was 17 and had been committed to a state institution in Virginia "for Epileptics and Feeble Minded." The institution decided to have Carrie sterilized.

Buck v. Bell
274 U.S. 200 (1927)

Opinion by Mr. Justice HOLMES . . .

This is a writ of error to review a judgment of the Supreme Court of Appeals of the State of Virginia, affirming a judgment of the Circuit Court of Amherst County, by which the defendant in error, the superintendent of the State Colony for Epileptics and Feeble Minded, was ordered to perform the operation of salpingectomy upon Carrie Buck, the plaintiff in error, for the purpose of making her sterile. 143 Va. 310. The case comes here upon the contention that the statute authorizing the judgment is void under the Fourteenth Amendment as denying to the plaintiff in error due process of law and the equal protection of the laws.

Carrie Buck is a feeble minded white woman who was committed to the State Colony above mentioned in due form. She is the daughter of a feeble minded mother in the same institution, and the mother of an illegitimate feeble minded child. She was eighteen years old at the time of the trial of her case in the Circuit Court, in the latter part of 1924. Virginia, approved March 20, 1924, recites that the health of the patient and the welfare of society may be promoted in certain cases by the sterilization of mental defectives, under careful safeguard, &c.; that the sterilization may be effected in males by vasectomy and in females by salpingectomy, without serious pain or substantial danger to life; that the Commonwealth is supporting in various institutions many defective persons who if now discharged would become a menace but if incapable of procreating might be discharged with safety and become self-supporting with benefit to themselves and to society; and that experience has shown that heredity plays an important part in the transmission of insanity, imbecility, etc. . . .

We have seen more than once that note. The public welfare may call upon the best citizens for their lives. It would be strange if it could not call upon those who already sap the strength of the State for these lesser sacrifices, often not felt to be such by those concerned, in order to prevent our being swamped with incompetence. It is better for all the world, if instead of waiting to execute degenerate offspring for crime, or to let them starve for their imbecility, society can prevent those who are manifestly unfit from continuing their kind. The principle that sustains compulsory vaccination is broad enough to cover cutting the Fallopian tubes. Jacobson v. Massachusetts, 197 U.S. 11. Three generations of imbeciles are enough.

[Affirmed.]

NOTES AND QUESTIONS

1. *Eugenics and the assessment of people.*   Buck v. Bell raises questions about eugenics and, specifically, about the rights of people defined as socially or mentally marginal—and thus perhaps viewed as undesirable. The case raises questions about the criteria scientists use to assess people as socially or mentally inferior.

Americans became much less willing to sanction eugenic policies after World War II in light of revelations about Nazi programs aimed at exterminating groups identified as inferior and impure.

In the United States, laws that provide for limiting the reproductive capacity of people identified as mentally disabled may be challenged under the Constitution as state interference with individual autonomy. Assessing people's mental or emotional states may be harder than society and the law believe. In this regard, the case of Carrie Buck is telling. The intelligence tests that were used by the state facility in which Carrie resided are now considered of little use. And Carrie's daughter, Vivian, whom the Court identified as a third-generation imbecile, was described as bright by her teachers. See Owen D. Jones, Behavioral Genetics and Crime, 69 Law & Contemp. Prob. 81 (2006); Marcia Johnson, Genetic Technology and Its Impact on Culpability for Criminal Actions, 46 Clev. St. L. Rev. 443 (1998); Robert J. Cynkar, Buck v. Bell, 81 Colum. L. Rev. 1418 (1981). Stephen Jay Gould offers a different explanation of the state's interest in sterilizing Carrie Buck:

> When we understand why Carrie Buck was committed in January 1924, we can finally comprehend the hidden meaning of her case and its message for us today. The silent key, again and as always, is her daughter Vivian, born on March 28, 1924, and then but an evident bump on her belly. Carrie Buck was one of several illegitimate children borne by her mother, Emma. She grew up with foster parents, J.T. and Alice Dobbs, and continued to live with them, helping out with chores around the house. She was apparently raped by a relative of her foster parents, then blamed for her resultant pregnancy. Almost surely, she was (as they used to say) committed to hide her shame (and her rapist's identity), not because enlightened science had just discovered her true mental status. In short, she was sent away to have her baby. Her case never was about mental deficiency; it was always a matter of sexual morality and social deviance. The annals of her trial and hearing reek with the contempt of the well-off and well-bred for poor people of "loose morals." Who really cared whether Vivian was a baby of normal intelligence; she was the illegitimate child of an illegitimate woman. Two generations of bastards are enough. Harry Laughlin [superintendent of the Eugenics Record Office] began his "family history" of the Bucks by writing: "These people belong to the shiftless, ignorant and worthless class of anti-social whites of the South."

Stephen Jay Gould, Carrie Buck's Daughter, 111 Natural History 12 (2002). Gould suggests that eugenics laws created state control over people viewed as socially undesirable through a moral lens developed within a class system. Eugenics laws clearly reflected class and race prejudices. Virginia's eugenics law, for instance, was also aimed expressly at precluding "racial mixing." The law, passed in 1924 and repealed in 1979, prohibited intermarriage between whites and nonwhites.

2. *Discrediting Buck v. Bell.*   Buck v. Bell has never been overruled. However, it has been widely discredited. In 2001, the Virginia legislature apologized for the state's having sterilized almost 7,500 Virginians under its 1924 eugenics law. The

law provided for forced sterilization of people believed to suffer from mental illness, mental retardation, epilepsy, criminal tendencies, alcoholism, and immorality. The apology expressed "profound regret" for the state's support and use of eugenics laws in sterilizing thousands of people involuntarily. National News Briefs; Virginia Expresses Regret for Past Sterilization, N.Y. Times, Feb. 15, 2001, at A22.

b.   After Buck v. Bell

i.   Bioethical and Social Perspectives

> ## Joe Zumpano-Canto, Nonconsensual Sterilization of the Mentally Disabled in North Carolina: An Ethics Critique of the Statutory Standard and Its Judicial Interpretation
> 13 J. Contemp. Health L. & Pol'y 79,
> 80–84 (1996)

When analyzing the ethical issues involved in sterilization of the mentally disabled, the autonomy interests of the mentally disabled individual should receive primary consideration. Subordination of sexual autonomy to alleged social interests is incompatible with educational efforts providing the mentally disabled with an environment that stresses autonomy. Current educational programs pursue "normalization," a process by which mentally disabled individuals learn to develop skills that enable them to live independent and self-sufficient lives. "Normalization" programs have placed an emphasis on sexual autonomy because sexual activity is viewed as an integral part of an independent and self-sufficient life. Philosophical approaches toward sterilization that subordinate sexual autonomy to society's alleged interests run counter to the process of "normalization." These approaches constitute an unacceptable return to the distancing and isolation from "mainstream" society previously experienced by the mentally disabled. Two approaches that often subordinate the sexual autonomy of the mentally disabled to society's alleged interests include the eugenics based rationales and the "best interests" rationales. A eugenics approach to sterilization of the mentally disabled would subordinate sexual autonomy for the sake of preventing genetic transmission of mental deficiencies. The first reason for rejecting eugenics based rationales for sterilization of the mentally disabled is that the underlying scientific basis for such rationales has been discredited. The following excerpt explains: "Most of the profoundly retarded are incapable of reproduction because of physical or genetic disabilities, and others remain in protected environments that make sterilization unnecessary. Thus, the number of retarded who lack the ability to consent and who may need involuntary sterilization is small." In addition, data shows that in most instances children born to mentally retarded individuals will not have genetic defects. Science has established that less than five percent of mental retardation is hereditary. Thus, one can conclude that the decision to allow sterilization of the mentally disabled, when made without precise knowledge that a defective gene will be transmitted, sacrifices autonomy and, in the majority of cases provides no "benefit" to society's gene pool. A second reason for rejecting the eugenics rationale is that the decision to allow sterilization in the small number of cases where transmission of a genetic defect is scientifically predictable is ethically flawed. Ninety percent of the mentally disabled are born to non-mentally disabled parents. To target the mentally disabled solely on eugenic grounds, without targeting normal parents who will genetically transmit mental disability, would constitute groundless discrimination. Because society places the "sexual autonomy" of non-mentally disabled parents above eugenics concerns, such concerns should not infringe upon the sexual autonomy of the mentally disabled. Although eugenic principles underlie provisions in some state statutes, most states have adopted statutes and judicial standards espousing a "best interests" analysis. This approach generally professes to consider the "best interests" of the patient, but also usually considers the best interests of society. The "best interests" approach, as the eugenics approach, often subordinates the sexual autonomy of the mentally disabled to the interests of society. In so doing, the "best interests" approach provides a return to the unacceptable distancing and isolation of the mentally disabled from "mainstream" society, which they experienced prior to the "normalization" trend.

NOTES AND QUESTIONS

1. *Repealed North Carolina sterilization law.*   In parts of his article not printed supra, Zumpano-Canto criticized a North Carolina law that allowed a parent, guardian, or public official responsible for "a mentally retarded person" to petition the relevant state court "for the sterilization operation of any mentally ill or retarded resident or patient thereof as may be considered in the best interest of the mental, moral, or physical improvement of the resident or patient, or for the public good." N.C. Gen. Stat. §§35–36. In April 2003, North Carolina Governor Mike Easley signed into law a bill that repealed most of the provisions providing for compelled sterilization. Under the new law, coerced sterilizations of "mentally ill or mentally retarded wards" of the state are permitted only in the case of "medical necessity." 2003 N.C. H.B. 36, S. 617 (signed by Governor, April 17, 2003). Do you think that the term "*medical necessity*" in this context is likely to give too much or too little discretion to those ordering sterilization and to courts reviewing cases that might arise? Should "medical necessity" here be interpreted to include psychological as well as physical needs?

At the same time, Governor Easley created a state board to consider compensation for those sterilized pursuant to the state's compulsory sterilization law. The board recommended providing the people involved with various educational and health care benefits. Governor Easley approved these recommendations. North Carolina Governor Approves Compensation Recommendations for Forced Sterilization Program Survivors, http://www.kaisernetwork.org/healthpolicyreport.

The Los Angeles Times reported in 2012 that North Carolina was supposed to pay $50,000 to victims of a state eugenics program that forcibly sterilized almost 7,600 people between 1929 and 1974. David Zucchino, Sterilized by North Carolina, She Felt Raped Once More, L.A. Times, Jan. 25, 2012. The vast majority of the victims were women or girls. One victim of the program— sterilized in 1968 after becoming pregnant as the result of a rape—told the

Times that she would reject the compensation, which she described as completely inadequate to make up for the humiliation and pain that she has endured, including the pain of infertility. Id. However, the state budget, announced in June 2012, did not in fact include any compensation for victims of the state's compelled sterilization program. North Carolina Budget Drops Payment to Forced Sterilization Victims, June 20, 2012, http://usnews.msnbc.msn.com/_news/2012/06/20/12321330-north-carolina-budget-drops-payment-to-forced-sterilization-victims?lite.

2. *"Global review" of literature about women's reproductive health and mental health.*   Jill Astbury and Susie Allanson note that mentally ill women or women who abuse alcohol may be unable to consent to sex and "are less likely to use contraception effectively" than other women (citing L. Hankoff & P. Darney, Contraceptive Choices for Behaviorally Disordered Women, 168 Am. J. Ob. & Gyn. 1986 (1993)). Jill Astbury & Susie Allanson, Psychosocial Aspects of Fertility Regulation in Jane Fisher et al., Mental Health Aspects of Women's Reproductive Health: A Global Review of the Literature (WHO) (2009), http://whqlibdoc.who.int/publications/2009/9789241563567_eng.pdf. In particular, the review notes that mentally ill women are less likely to comply with birth-control methods "that require regular self-administration." The report concludes:

> Women's decision-making latitude, including their control over participation in family planning programmes and use of contraception, is critically linked to their emotional well-being and their status in the family. Support from health professionals for autonomous decision-making is associated with fewer psychosomatic complaints and depressive symptoms.

Id. at 51.

ii.   Legal Approaches

> ### Skinner v. Oklahoma
> #### 316 U.S. 535 (1942)

Opinion by Mr. Justice DOUGLAS.

This case touches a sensitive and important area of human rights. Oklahoma deprives certain individuals of a right which is basic to the perpetuation of a race—the right to have offspring. . . .

The statute involved is Oklahoma's Habitual Criminal Sterilization Act. That Act defines an "habitual criminal" as a person who, having been convicted two or more times [in any state] for crimes "amounting to felonies involving moral turpitude," is thereafter convicted of such a felony in Oklahoma and is sentenced to a term of imprisonment in an Oklahoma penal institution. Machinery is provided for the institution by the Attorney General of a proceeding against such a person in the Oklahoma courts for a judgment that such person shall be rendered sexually sterile. Notice, an opportunity to be heard, and the right to a jury trial are provided. The issues triable in such a proceeding are narrow and confined. If the court or jury finds that the defendant is an "habitual criminal" and that he "may be rendered sexually sterile without detriment to his or her general health," then the court "shall render judgment to the effect that said defendant be rendered sexually sterile" by the operation of vasectomy in case of a male, and of salpingectomy in case of a female. Only one other provision of the Act is material here, and that is [a section] which provides that "offenses arising out of the violation of the prohibitory laws, revenue acts, embezzlement, or political offenses, shall not come or be considered within the terms of this Act."

Petitioner was convicted in 1926 of the crime of stealing chickens, and was sentenced to the Oklahoma State Reformatory. In 1929 he was convicted of the crime of robbery with firearms, and was sentenced to the reformatory. In 1934 he was convicted again of robbery with firearms, and was sentenced to the penitentiary. He was confined there in 1935 when the Act was passed. In 1936 the Attorney General instituted proceedings against him. Petitioner in his answer challenged the Act as unconstitutional by reason of the Fourteenth Amendment. A jury trial was had. The court instructed the jury that the crimes of which petitioner had been convicted were felonies involving moral turpitude, and that the only question for the jury was whether the operation of vasectomy could be performed on petitioner without detriment to his general health. The jury found that it could be. A judgment directing that the operation of vasectomy be performed on petitioner was affirmed by the Supreme Court of Oklahoma by a five to four decision. . . .

[T]here is a feature of the Act which clearly condemns it. That is, its failure to meet the requirements of the equal protection clause of the Fourteenth Amendment. . . .

A few examples will suffice. In Oklahoma, grand larceny is a felony. Larceny is grand larceny when the property taken exceeds $20 in value. Id. Embezzlement is punishable "in the manner prescribed for feloniously stealing property of the value of that embezzled." Hence, he who embezzles property worth more than $20 is guilty of a felony. A clerk who appropriates over $20 from his employer's till and a stranger who steals the same amount are thus both guilty of felonies. If the latter repeats his act and is convicted three times, he may be sterilized. But the clerk is not subject to the pains and penalties of the Act no matter how large his embezzlements nor how frequent his convictions. A person who enters a chicken coop and steals chickens commits a felony and he may be sterilized if he is thrice convicted. If, however, he is a bailee of the property and fraudulently appropriates it, he is an embezzler. Hence, no matter how habitual his proclivities for embezzlement are and no matter how often his conviction, he may not be sterilized. Thus, the nature of the two crimes is intrinsically the same and they are punishable in the same manner. . . .

[T]he instant legislation runs afoul of the equal protection clause, though we give Oklahoma that large deference which the rule of the foregoing cases requires. We are dealing here with legislation which involves one of the basic civil rights of man. Marriage and procreation are fundamental to the very existence and survival of the race. The power to sterilize, if exercised, may have subtle, far-reaching and devastating effects. In evil or reckless hands it can cause races or types which are inimical to the dominant group to wither and disappear. There is no redemption for the individual whom the law touches. Any experiment which the State conducts is to his irreparable injury. He is forever deprived of a basic liberty.

[Reversed.]

NOTES AND QUESTIONS

1. *The waning of eugenics.* The *Skinner* Court did not overrule Buck v. Bell. However, the Court's categorization of procreation as a fundamental right and its later application of the most stringent review to statutes that interfered with that right left little room for future courts to invoke Justices Holmes's 1927 decision in Buck v. Bell as precedent for the state's right to compulsorily sterilize members of social groups deemed marginal by the state. Erwin Chemerinsky, a constitutional law scholar, suggests that *Skinner* may be a product of the "waning of the eugenics movement that had inspired the laws challenged" in both *Skinner* and *Buck*. He further suggests that exposure to Nazi eugenics, which placed the notion of a "master race" at its core, may have convinced Americans to eschew laws reflecting eugenic polices. Erwin Chemerinsky, Constitutional Law: Principles and Policies 784 (2002).

2. *Mother arranges sterilization of daughter.* In 1971, Ora Spitler McFarlin petitioned in court to have a tubal ligation performed on her 15-year-old daughter. McFarlin claimed that the girl was "somewhat retarded," that she was spending time with "older youth or young men," and that she had stayed out overnight with such men. The mother's petition explained:

> Affiant [mother] states that her daughter's mentality is such that she is considered to be somewhat retarded although she is attending or has attended the public schools in DeKalb Central School System and has been passed along with other children in her age level even though she does not have what is considered normal mental capabilities and intelligence. Further, that said affiant has had problems in the home of said child as a result of said daughter leaving the home on several occasions to associate with older youth or young men and as a matter of fact having stayed overnight with said youth or men and about which incidents said affiant did not become aware of until after such incidents occurred. As a result of this behavior and the mental capabilities of said daughter, affiant believes that it is to the best interest of said child that a Tubal Ligation be performed on said minor daughter to prevent unfortunate circumstances to occur and since it is impossible for the affiant as mother of said minor child to maintain and control a continuous observation of the activities of said daughter each and every day.

Stump v. Sparkman, 435 U.S. 349, 351 (1978). Judge Harold Stump approved the mother's petition. Linda, the adolescent daughter, was told that she was entering the hospital for an appendectomy. Instead, a tubal ligation was performed.

Two years later, Linda married Leo Sparkman. She did not become pregnant. The couple then learned about the sterilization. Linda and Leo sued a number of people, including Linda's mother, the doctors who performed the surgery, the hospital where it was performed, and Judge Stump (who approved the mother's petition). The court dismissed the claims against all of the defendants (except Judge Stump) because of an absence of state action. The Supreme Court (reversing the circuit court) held that the judge did have jurisdiction over the petition to sterilize Linda. The Court noted that Judge Stump might have treated Linda unfairly but concluded nonetheless that he was protected by judicial immunity.

When Ora McFarlin petitioned to have her daughter sterilized in Indiana, the state had a statute that provided for sterilizing certain institutionalized people. No statute provided for involuntary sterilization of a girl such as Linda, and no statute expressly prohibited such a sterilization procedure. 435 U.S. 349, 366 (Stewart, J., dissenting).

At present, a number of state statutes limit the right of a parent or guardian to have a mentally retarded charge sterilized. In Colorado, for instance, a mentally retarded minor cannot be sterilized unless the presiding judge attempts to elicit the wishes of the individual to be sterilized. If the individual does not want to be sterilized that will "weigh heavily against authorizing the procedure." Colo. Rev. Stat. §27-10.5-128 (2004).

3. *Invalidation of state sterilization law.* In 1985, the California Supreme Court invalidated a state law that precluded sterilization of state wards and conservatees. Conservatorship of Valerie N., 707 P.2d 760 (Cal. 1985). The case arose when Mildred and Eugene G., Valerie N.'s mother and stepfather and her co-conservators, petitioned for authorization to have a tubal ligation performed on Valerie, then in her 20s. Valerie, born with Down syndrome, had an IQ of about 30 and was, in the court's view, unable to make her own reproductive choices. The court wrote:

> The question is whether she has a constitutional right to have these decisions made for her, in this case by her parents as conservators, in order to protect her interests in living the fullest and most rewarding life of which she is capable. At present her conservators may, on Valerie's behalf, elect that she not bear or rear children. As means of avoiding the severe psychological harm which assertedly would result from pregnancy, they may choose abortion should she become pregnant; they may arrange for any child Valerie might bear to be removed from her custody; and they may impose on her other methods of contraception, including isolation from members of the opposite sex. They are precluded from making, and Valerie from obtaining the advantage of, the one choice that may be best for her, and which is available to all women competent to choose—contraception through sterilization. We conclude that the present legislative scheme, which absolutely precludes the sterilization option, impermissibly deprives developmentally disabled persons of privacy and liberty interests protected by the Fourteenth Amendment to the United States Constitution, and article I, section 1 of the California Constitution.

Id. at 771–772. Justice Byrd, in dissent, focused on Valerie's right to procreate rather than on her right to choose:

> The majority's failure to engage in a meaningful weighing of these interests is indicative of a basic problem with their analysis. In their effort to protect Valerie's rights of liberty and procreative "choice," they fail to seriously acknowledge her right to procreate. The majority make several unsupported assumptions which suggest that they recognize Valerie's right to procreate for purposes of conceptual symmetry only. They do not regard it as a real right, entitled to meaningful protection.
>
> For example, the majority assert without citation to any authority that Valerie's conservators may legally compel her to undergo an abortion or to surrender custody over any child she might bear. . . . Indeed, having incorrectly cast Valerie's fundamental right to procreate as a right of procreative choice, the majority summarily conclude that she will never have the right to bear children because she will never be competent. "That right has been taken from her both by nature which has rendered her incapable of making a

voluntary choice, and by the state through the powers already conferred upon the conservator."

I strongly disagree. As explained above, the roots of the fundamental right to procreate go deeper. A woman should not be stripped of that right by conditioning its recognition on her capacity to make informed choices.

In sum, the majority's constitutional analysis fails to give proper weight to the fundamental right to procreate. It also fails to acknowledge that the right to procreate has independent roots which, in contrast to the right to sterilization, are not linked to a capacity for decision and choice. . . .

Id. at 487–488. Do you think there is merit to Justice Byrd's notion that the right to procreate must be understood apart from a right to choose because the fundamental right to procreate, in her view, has roots "not linked to a capacity for decision and choice"? What are those roots?

4. Ideological undercurrents to Skinner. Law professor Ariella Dubler offered a novel interpretation of ideological undercurrents that buttressed the Court's decision in *Skinner*. She suggested that sterilization began to seem problematic not only because it was coercive, "but also because of its potential to uncouple sex from the traditional, procreative family." Ariella Dubler, Sexing Skinner: History and the Politics of the Right to Marry, 110 Colum L. Rev. 1348, 1367 (2010). In short, even as the Court sided with an interest in curtailing eugenics practices, it also buttressed a more conservative interest in protecting traditional understandings of family. Id. at 1348. Dubler suggests several understandings of Jack Skinner himself in the context of the Supreme Court case:

> Seen through the lens of proponents of eugenics, a sterilized Jack Skinner would have seemed like an unthreatening member of society—no longer a danger to long-term social stability. Seen through the lens of those concerned about excessive state power, a sterilized Jack Skinner might have been constructed as the victim of an unjust and potentially draconian legal regime. An entirely different picture emerges, however, when Jack Skinner is viewed through the prism of debates about birth control and sexual promiscuity: Suddenly, a sterilized Skinner might seem to be a potential sexual threat to others and, more generally, to the sexual norms thought to undergird an orderly society.
>
> Indeed, Skinner—sterilized and, thus, liberated to engage in sex free from anxieties about pregnancy—might begin to look more like a possible sexual predator than either a reformed criminal or a deprived potential parent. A cautious judiciary, then, might be concerned not only with the harm inflicted upon Skinner by the State's decision to sterilize him, but also with the potential ramifications of creating a class of sterilized criminals, free to pursue their sexual desires unchecked by the deterrent of accidental pregnancy and, potentially, emboldened by the heightened pleasure of post-vasectomy sexual prowess (whether physical or psychological). In their brief, Skinner's lawyers certainly tried to create this more complicated picture of the unintended social consequences of forced sterilization.

Id. at 1366.

5. Psychological factors relevant to court-ordered sterilization. In V.H. v. K.E.J. (In re Estate of K.E.J.), 2008 Ill. App. LEXIS 357, an Illinois appellate court reviewed some of the psychological factors relevant to guardian V.H.'s request that her niece and ward, K.E.J., be involuntarily sterilized. K.E.J., who had suffered a head injury in a car accident at age 8, was not mentally competent. At age 29, K.E.J., who apparently understood the meaning of the proposed surgery and its consequences, opposed the sterilization. She explained: "I want to have children because they are—I will love taking care of them, I will love, you know, to see how they grow and stuff, you know, just—just all the things that, you know, any person would want to have a child." Id. at 6. In denying the guardian's petition to sterilize K.E.J., the trial court took K.E.J.'s wishes into consideration. Yet, the court concluded that K.E.J. did not have the capacity to consent to or to refuse the sterilization. The appellate court affirmed the trial court's denial of the guardian's petition for a tubal ligation. In reaching its decision, the court reviewed a number of psychological factors it found relevant. Both courts relied on a "best interest" standard because, in the appellate court's phrase, reliance on a substituted judgment standard would have been "little more than wild speculation."

Among other things, the appellate court took into account K.E.J.'s "dreams of having children" and the possibility that a tubal ligation would have caused her to become seriously depressed. On the other hand, the court explained, were K.E.J. to become pregnant, she would not have been able successfully to raise a child. Were it thus to become necessary to take a child from K.E.J., she would likely have suffered terribly. This, however, the court balanced against the promise of K.E.J.'s father that he would care for any child K.E.J. might have. The court further noted the possibility that K.E.J. might marry someone with the capacity to care for a child. K.E.J. understood that unprotected sex relations could result in pregnancy. Nevertheless, the court was concerned that K.E.J.'s inadequate "impulse control" might result in her engaging in unprotected sex. Is K.E.J.'s situation significantly different from that of many women considered capable of reproductive decision making? How much weight should the court have paid to K.E.J.'s opinion?

Finally, the court concluded that ordering "less intrusive and less psychologically harmful alternatives to a tubal ligation" would be adequate to protect K.E.J.

6. *Redefining legal "incompetence."*   Martha Field has asserted that in general far too many people are defined as "incompetent" and that many more of these people should be treated as autonomous with regard to medical decision making. Martha A. Field, Pregnancy and AIDS, 52 Md. L. Rev. 402, 423 n.79 (1993). Field notes that in the case of an individual clearly incapable of participating in his or her medical decision making, there is widespread debate about whether medical decisions should be left to the state or to a substitute decision maker. Id.

7. *Federal law.*   Federal regulations prohibit federally assisted family planning programs from performing sterilizations without informed consent. 42 C.F.R. 50.204 (2012). The regulations provide that informed consent cannot be obtained "while the individual to be sterilized is: (1) In labor or childbirth; (2) Seeking to obtain or obtaining an abortion; or (3) Under the influence of alcohol or other substances that affect the individual's state of awareness." Id. at 50.204(e). Why do you think the first two limitations were included in the federal regulation? Was it assumed that a woman in labor or a woman seeking an abortion resembles someone under the influence of alcohol or drugs in that she is incapable of providing informed consent? Do you agree with that? What other sort of explanation can you provide?

8. *Physicians' conditioning care on sterilization.*   In Walker v. Pierce, 560 F.2d 609 (4th Cir. 1977), two African-American women brought suit against an

obstetrician and a number of other defendants for violation of their civil rights. The plaintiffs, recipients of Medicaid, alleged that Dr. Pierce required them to undergo tubal ligation after the birth of a third child. In testimony, Dr. Pierce explained:

> My policy was with people who were unable to financially support themselves, whether they be on Medicaid or just unable to pay their own bills, if they were having a third child, to request they voluntarily submit to sterilization following the delivery of the third child. If they did not wish this as a condition for my care, then I requested that they seek another physician other than myself.

Holding for Dr. Pierce, the Fourth Circuit explained:

> We perceive no reason why Dr. Pierce could not establish and pursue the policy he has publicly and freely announced. Nor are we cited to judicial precedent or statute inhibiting this personal economic philosophy. Particularly is this so when all persons coming to him as patients are seasonably made fully aware of his professional attitude toward the increase in offspring and his determination to see it prevail. At no time is he shown to have forced his view upon any mother. Indeed, quite the opposite appears. In the single occasion in this case of a sterilization by this doctor, not just one but three formal written consents were obtained—the first before delivery of the fourth child and two afterwards.
>   But if his conduct is nevertheless to be judged by the factors of section 1983, Dr. Pierce was not a violator. He was not acting under color of State law when treating the only successful plaintiff, Brown. His fee for her delivery was paid by her and her employer's insurance plan; there was no use of Medicaid money. Incidentally, he did not sterilize her; the tort charged to him is his discharge and release of her from the Hospital, an accepted procedure there. . . .

The dissenting judge described one witness to have testified as follows:

> He came in and he hadn't examined me or anything. I was laying on the table. And, he said, "Listen here young lady." He said, "This is my tax money paying for something like this." He said, "I am tired of people going around here having babies and my tax money paying for it." He said, "So, if you don't want this done, you go and find yourself another doctor."

In the dissent's view, Dr. Pierce's acts constituted state action:

> In this case, the state's involvement is readily apparent. The questioned activity is the grant or denial of Medicaid benefits for fiscal reasons unrelated to a patient's health. Under the Medicaid statute, the state is responsible for ascertaining which women are entitled to receive Medicaid benefits for the delivery of their children. Because the state is involved in the activity under scrutiny, one criterion for applying §1983 is satisfied. . . .
>   The nexus between the state and Dr. Pierce was sufficient to establish that his sterilization of Medicaid patients for economic reasons not related to their health can be fairly treated as the action of the state. In fact, Dr. Pierce was his patientss' most important contact with the state program. Therefore, I would affirm the district judge's ruling that Dr. Pierce was acting under color of law within the meaning of 42 U.S.C. §1983.

The plaintiffss' case against Dr. Pierce depended on the presence of state action. The case shows that, absent state action, a doctor has broad freedom to dismiss patients who do not do things as the doctor prefers them to be done. Correlatively, doctors have broad power to coerce patients to undergo (or not undergo) various procedures for reasons unrelated to the patient's health by threatening to dismiss recalcitrant patients. That threat may be especially powerful in geographic areas with few doctors accepting additional Medicaid patients.

9. *Involuntary sterilization of HIV-positive women.*   Janine Kossen reports that some countries (including Namibia, Chile, and Venezuela, among others) have sterilized HIV-positive women against their wishes. Kossen describes this as especially troubling because new medicines have dramatically curtailed mother-to-child transmission of HIV. Janine Kossen, Rights, Respect, Responsibility: Advancing the Sexual and Reproductive Health and Rights of Young People Through International Human Rights Law, 15 U. Pa. J.L. & Soc. Change 143, 160 (2012). In Namibia, two groups, the International Community of Women Living with HIV/AIDS and the Legal Assistance Center, filed suit on behalf of a number of HIV-positive women who had been involuntarily sterilized. Defendants included the nation's Ministry of Health and Social Services and a number of hospitals. Id. In 2012, a judge found that three of the women involved in the suit were sterilized involuntarily, but did not find adequate evidence to prove that the sterilizations were done because of the women's HIV status. Nkepile Mabuse, Namibian Women Were Sterilized Without Consent, Judge Rules, CNN, July 31, 2012, http://www.cnn.com/2012/07/30/world/africa/namibia-forced-sterilization/index.html

10. *Sterilization, abortion, and foreign relations.*   The Seventh Circuit decided in 2006 that Junshao Zhang, a native of China, was eligible for asylum in the United States as the spouse of a woman forced to have an abortion under China's population control laws. Zhang v. Gonzales, 434 F.3d 993 (7th Cir. 2006). The court looked to §601(a)(1) of the Illegal Immigration Reform and Immigrant Responsibility Act of 1996, 110 Stat. 3009, which amended the Act's definition of "refugee." Under the section a "refugee" includes one who

> has been forced to abort a pregnancy or to undergo involuntary sterilization, or who has been persecuted for failure or refusal to undergo such a procedure or for other resistance to a coercive population control program . . . and a person who has a well-founded fear that he or she will be forced to undergo such a procedure or subject to persecution for such failure, refusal, or resistance.

The circuits have split on whether asylum under §601(a) should be offered to fiancés and boyfriends of victims.

11. *Bibliographic note.*   Other relevant readings include Mary Ziegler, Reinventing Eugenics: Reproductive Choice and Law Reform After World War II, 4 Cardozo J.L. & Gender 319 (2008) (reviewing responses to eugenics after World War II); Note, Maura McIntyre, Buck v. Bell and Beyond: A Revised Standard to Evaluate the Best Interests of the Mentally Disabled in the Sterilization Context, 2007 U. Ill. L. Rev. 1303; Vanessa Volz, A Matter of Choice: Women with Disabilities, Sterilization, and Reproductive Autonomy in the Twenty-First Century, 27 Women's Rts. L. Rep. 203 (2006) (considering reproductive rights of women with disabilities); Jana Leslie-Miller, From Bell to Bell: Responsible Reproduction in the Twentieth Century, 8 Md. J. Contemp. Legal Issues 123 (1997); Sheldon Gelman, The Biological Alteration Cases, 36 Wm. & Mary L. Rev. 1203 (1995) (analyzing constitutional issues that arise from state efforts to alter people

biologically; examples discussed include sterilization, drugs that alter brain chemistry, and forced vaccination); Elizabeth S. Scott, Sterilization of Mentally Retarded Persons: Reproductive Rights and Family Privacy, 1986 Duke L.J. 806.

2. *Coerced Contraception*

In the early 1990s, the Food and Drug Administration (FDA) approved Norplant (1990) and Depo-Provera (1992) as contraceptives. Both offer long-term, reversible contraception. Norplant, usually implanted in capsule form in a woman's upper arm, provides effective contraception for up to five years.[2] Depo-Provera, administered through injection, is effective for several months. Some commentators describe the consequence of such drugs as sterilization, albeit temporary, rather than contraception. In 2006, the FDA approved Implanon, manufactured by Organon USA. It is a single-rod implantable contraceptive that resembles Norplant in that it can be implanted for several years. Implanon's effects are reversible when the implantation is removed. It cannot safely remain implanted for more than three years. See Daily Med, http://daily med.nlm.nih.gov/dailymed/drugInfo.cfm?id=64479#section-4.

Norplant and other related drugs became controversial because of their potential use as mechanisms of state control. Soon after Norplant's appearance, an editorial in the Philadelphia Inquirer suggested that it could be used to "reduce[] the underclass" and recommended that women on welfare be paid to stop reproducing. The editorial was widely condemned as racist, and the paper printed an apology and retraction. Faye Wattleton, Opinion, Using Birth Control as Coercion, Los Angeles Times, Jan. 13, 1991, at M7. However, since that time, courts and legislatures have conditioned probation on a woman's agreeing to temporary sterilization, and have proposed that welfare payments be similarly conditioned, or that poor mothers be given "bonuses" not to have additional children. See, e.g., Stacey L. Arthur, The Norplant Prescription: Birth Control, Woman Control or Crime Control?, 40 UCLA L. Rev. 1 (1992).

Fears about the coercive use of Norplant intensified in 1991 when Judge Howard Broadman in Tulare County, California, conditioned the parole of a mother convicted of child abuse on the woman's use of Norplant for three years. People v. Johnson (Cal. Super. Ct., Tulare County 1991) (No. 29390). Darlene Johnson, a young African-American mother on welfare, initially agreed to the condition. But after reconsidering it, she moved to have the Norplant condition modified. Johnson claimed that she had not understood enough about Norplant to make an informed decision, that she was pressured to agree to use Norplant because she did not want to go to prison, and that the Norplant condition violated her constitutional right to privacy. The trial judge disagreed. Johnson appealed, but her appeal was dismissed as moot after her probation was revoked by a different judge. The facts of the *Johnson* case are described in Broadman v. Commission on Judicial Performance, 959 P.2d 715 (1998) (affirming decision of the Commission on Judicial Performance that Judge Broadman be censured for three instances of prejudicial conduct and one of willful misconduct). See also Arthur, supra.

---

2. See p. 352, infra (reporting discontinuance of Norplant by its manufacturer in 2002).

Other judicial decisions, rendered before Norplant was available, provided models for Judge Broadman's decision in *Johnson*. Some of these conditioned probation on the use of contraception or on sterilization. Others conditioned reduction of a criminal sentence on a similar agreement to limit or preclude reproduction. See Arthur, supra, at 1, 6 n.19 (noting that in at least 20 cases between 1966 and 1991, trial courts in ten states ordered criminal defendants to limit reproduction or to undergo sterilization and thus preclude future reproduction completely). Before Norplant was available, however, it was harder to monitor a woman's agreement to use contraception, and trial courts' orders to condition probation or a reduced sentence on sterilization were subject to reversal, especially in the absence of a state statute that authorized such orders. See, e.g., Smith v. Superior Court, 725 P.2d 1101 (Ariz. 1986) (holding trial judge exceeded court's jurisdiction in ordering sterilization as condition of lesser sentence).

Both Kansas and Louisiana proposed, but did not pass, legislation extending extra benefits to welfare recipients agreeing to use Norplant. Other states, including South Carolina and Mississippi, proposed legislation making welfare benefits contingent on Norplant use. Moreover, a few states require that women on welfare be given information about Norplant. Laurie Madziar, Comment, State v. Oakley: How Much Further Will the Courts Go in Trying to Enforce Child Support?, 24 Women's Rights L. Rep. 65 (2002); Note, Eugenics and Equality: Does the Constitution Allow Policies Designed to Discourage Reproduction among Disfavored Groups?, 20 Yale L. & Pol'y Rev. 481 (2002).

In July 2002, Wyeth Pharmaceuticals, Norplant's manufacturer, removed it from the market. Leslie Berger, After Long Hiatus, New Contraceptives Emerge, N.Y. Times, Dec. 10, 2002, at F5. Its removal followed concern both about its being used as a condition of probation and its effects on health. Among other things, it caused unpredictable bleeding and was often difficult to remove because the Norplant rods embedded themselves in scar tissue. Two years earlier, Norplant had been subject to recall because certain lots were apparently ineffective. Id. At that time, Wyeth advised women with implanted Norplant to use alternative contraceptives.

In his book, Children of Choice, law professor John A. Robertson argues that public assistance may be conditioned on a recipient's agreeing to use Norplant or some other long-term contraceptive. The following excerpt is from a review of Robertson's book. (Page references are to that book.)

Radhika Rao, Law and Equality: Constitutional Misconceptions (Reviewing John A. Robertson, Children of Choice)
93 Mich. L. Rev. 1473, 1473–1474, 1477–1478 (1995)

... Professor John A. Robertson proposes a unifying principle—the presumptive primacy of procreative liberty—that is elegant in its simplicity. Applying this principle, he methodically canvasses each [reproductive] technology and concludes that almost every practice necessary to procreate should receive constitutional protection. He finds a constitutional right to reproduce technologically, to purchase sperm, eggs, and gestational services, and even to enforce preconception agreements to rear offspring. . . .

Robertson . . . applies his principle of procreative liberty to proposed legislation to restrict irresponsible reproduction by means of new contraceptive technology. Such proposals focus upon the drug Norplant,[3] a surgically-implanted contraceptive approved by the FDA in 1990, which Robertson believes to be safe, convenient, and effective at preventing pregnancy for up to five years. The author concludes that programs that encourage the voluntary use of Norplant, either by paying women on welfare a "bonus" to accept Norplant or by requiring them to use Norplant as a condition to receive welfare, do not infringe upon procreative liberty. Although a Norplant bonus "may be attractive enough to get a woman's attention and even influence her decision, it does not deny her something that she would otherwise receive, and thus should not be considered coercive" (pp. 87–88). Similarly, conditioning the receipt of welfare on Norplant use does not offend the Constitution because "a state has no constitutional obligation to provide welfare at all, [so] it would be free to provide it only if certain conditions rationally related to the program are met" (p. 89). Programs that make the use of Norplant compulsory, however, rather than tying it to the distribution of public funds, are unconstitutional because even convicted child-abusers, HIV-positive women, and teenagers possess "interests in procreation or bodily integrity which mandatory use of Norplant violates" (p. 93). Only severely retarded women, who are "so mentally impaired that the concept of reproduction and parenthood has no meaning" (p. 90), may be forced to use Norplant because they lack the capacity to exercise procreative choice. For such women, Robertson believes, "the notion of reproductive choice is no more meaningful . . . than is electoral choice" (p. 90).

David S. Coale, Note, Norplant Bonuses and the Unconstitutional Conditions Doctrine
71 Tex. L. Rev. 189, 204–208 (1992)

The unconstitutional conditions doctrine prohibits a government policy from affecting a constitutional right in a way that government would not be allowed to do directly. Two bodies of constitutional law prevent the state from directly forcing Norplant upon women.

1. The Right to Privacy.—The first body of law that prevents the state from directly forcing women to take Norplant is the broad right of privacy in sexual matters established in Griswold v. Connecticut.[4] Griswold held that a government could not prohibit the use of contraceptives by married persons. . . .

The Supreme Court expanded the right of privacy beyond married couples in Eisenstadt v. Baird. Eisenstadt struck down a ban on contraceptive sales to

---

3. As noted, supra, Norplant has been withdrawn from the market. However, the issues it raised remain relevant. Implanon, a similar drug, soon is likely to become available in the United States.–EDS.

4. Griswold v. Connecticut and Eisenstadt v. Baird are found in section B(1)(b), infra.

minors, holding that "[i]f the right of privacy means anything, it is the right of the individual, married or single, to be free from unwarranted governmental intrusion into matters so fundamentally affecting a person as the decision whether to bear or beget a child." This language, together with *Griswold*'s, strongly suggests that the Constitution protects a woman's ability to freely decide whether or not to use contraception.

While *Griswold* and *Eisenstadt* only directly addressed government denials of access to contraception, two other cases strongly suggest that the Constitution's protection of privacy covers government efforts to force contraceptive use as well. First, in Skinner v. Oklahoma, the Court struck down an Oklahoma law that required the sterilization of two-time felons. . . .

Second, in the 1990 case Cruzan v. Director, Missouri Department of Health the Supreme Court assumed that the Constitution granted a competent person the right to refuse lifesaving medical treatment. That assumption was based on a long line of cases recognizing constitutionally protected liberty interests in avoiding nonconsensual medical treatment. That right can be read to protect women from forced contraceptive use, since none of the factors that allowed the Court to balance away the liberty interest in earlier cases are present. When a medical procedure is long-term, has direct physical effects, and the recipients have no disabilities justifying state paternalism, the recipients should have a right to reject it under *Cruzan* and its predecessors.

2. The Free Exercise Clause.—The First Amendment Free Exercise Clause may also keep the state from forcing women to take Norplant. State and federal cases interpreting that clause have recognized the importance of religious objections to some medicines and treatments. Religious opposition to contraceptive use means that those cases could be read to proscribe an effort to force women to take contraceptives. . . .

The interests affected by forced Norplant use are best balanced by reading the First Amendment to prevent it. Most of the decisions allowing nonconsensual medical treatment are based on the state's compelling interest in life under severe time constraints. They either involved situations where the recipients were in imminent danger of death or epidemics where a failure to inoculate an entire population would quickly result in widespread sickness and death. None of the rationales for a Norplant bonus program involve such an imminent harm. And none of the programs sustained by the Court involved a violation as intrusive and long-lasting. . . .

The right to bodily integrity is at the heart of personal liberty. The Constitution gives strong protection to that right through the *Griswold* line of cases and through its interpretation of the First Amendment's Free Exercise Clause. That protection is enough to satisfy the first element of an unconstitutional conditions challenge to a Norplant bonus program.

|| **Lars Noah, *Too High a Price for Some Drugs?***
The FDA Burdens Reproductive Choice
44 San Diego L. Rev. 231, 233–236 (2007) ||

In 1982, the FDA approved Hoffmann-La Roche's application to market isotretinoin (Accutane®) for use in patients with severe recalcitrant nodular acne. Although no one doubts its efficacy in treating this disfiguring (though otherwise nonserious) condition, the drug is a potent teratogen: it carries a significant (more than 25%) risk of miscarriage and major birth defects such as facial deformities, severe mental retardation, and lethal cardiac abnormalities. As further details about the teratogenic potential of isotretinoin have emerged over the course of the last quarter of a century, the FDA and the manufacturer adopted increasingly aggressive mechanisms designed to prevent its use by pregnant women.

. . . .

In 2000, after receiving reports of gestational exposures caused by failures in using hormonal contraceptives, the manufacturer revised the labeling to recommend the use of two different forms of contraception. In 2001, when the FDA realized that these additional warnings and related voluntary measures had still not prevented all use by pregnant women, the agency approved SMART® (System to Manage Accutane-Related Teratogenicity), a still more aggressive risk management program developed by Hoffmann-La Roche. SMART attempted to require (through physician registration with the manufacturer and use of special qualification stickers as a prerequisite for dispensing by pharmacists) a negative pregnancy test before prescribing a nonrefillable one month supply in addition to an agreement by patients to use two methods of contraception or abstain from sexual activity. The agency modeled this program on a similar effort undertaken by the manufacturer of Thalomid® (thalidomide), which the FDA had approved for the treatment of Hansen's disease (leprosy): STEPS® (System for Thalidomide Education and Prescribing Safety) sought to ensure that this infamous teratogen stay out of the hands of persons who might become pregnant. Because semen could carry residues of thalidomide, male patients also had to agree to use contraceptives.

In 2005, because SMART had not entirely lived up to expectations, the FDA approved the iPLEDGE® risk management program established by the manufacturers of isotretinoin, which required prescribers, distributors, and patients to register (on-line or by using a toll-free number) and attest to their understanding of the risks and commitment to abide by the pregnancy testing and contraception requirements. Physicians and patients have expressed frustration about the sometimes cumbersome barriers to access erected by iPLEDGE, but at least initially the program has succeeded where its predecessors had failed—namely, in preventing pregnancies among users of the drug. In contrast with the gradual adoption of ever tighter access requirements for isotretinoin in this country, British regulators long ago imposed even more stringent distribution restrictions, including a requirement that patients agree to undergo an immediate abortion in case they become pregnant while using the drug.

NOTES AND QUESTIONS

1. *Conditioning welfare benefits on use of contraception.*   Robertson and Coale present contrary positions on the constitutionality of offering bonuses to mothers on welfare who agree to use Norplant. Which position seems more compelling? Do you think a state welfare system should be allowed to condition extra benefits on a woman's agreeing to use some form of contraception? Additional discussion of the issue, reflecting a variety of viewpoints beyond those

contained in this section, can be found in Kimberly A. Smith, Conceivable Sterilization: A Constitutional Analysis of a Norplant/Depo-Provera Welfare Condition, 77 Ind. L.J. 389, 389–390 (2002); Dorothy E. Roberts, The Only Good Poor Woman: Unconstitutional Conditions and Welfare, 72 Denv. U. L. Rev. 931, 931–932 (1995); Laurence C. Nolan, The Unconstitutional Conditions Doctrine and Mandating Norplant for Women on Welfare Discourse, 3 Am. U. J. Gender & L. 15, 33–37 (1994).

2. *"Penalizing" constitutional rights.*   In a part of his essay not reprinted supra, David Coale considers the implications of the abortion funding cases for state policies that coerce women to use Norplant. In Maher v. Roe, 432 U.S. 464 (1977), the Court upheld a state Medicaid regulation that did not pay for therapeutic abortions but that did pay for childbirth expenses, and in Harris v. McRae, 448 U.S. 297 (1980), the Court upheld a federal law that precluded the use of federal Medicaid funds to pay for abortions unless necessary to save the life of the mother. In these cases, the Court concluded that the funding limits did not preclude women from exercising their constitutional right to abortion. If that right was restricted, the Court opined, it was a result of poverty and health care costs, not state action. These cases indicate, explains Coale, that the state "has some power to make value judgments about what its money supports. Accordingly, the state can decide not to subsidize constitutionally protected activity. However, the government cannot actively assert its power to penalize the exercise of constitutional rights." Coale, supra, at 200. Coale thus suggests that it is not constitutional to premise benefits on the use of Norplant or other similar drugs. That sort of condition fits into the category of penalizing the exercise of constitutional rights to which Coale refers because the condition is aimed at depriving women of money they would receive but for their refusal to use long-term contraception.

3. *Abortion counseling by family planning programs receiving federal money.*   On a related note, the Supreme Court decided in 1991 that programs that received federal money for family planning activities could be prohibited from counseling their patients regarding the option of abortion or referring them to an abortion provider. Rust v. Sullivan, 500 U.S. 173 (1991). Federal regulations that barred such activities did not violate the First Amendment free speech rights of the fund recipients (e.g., doctors and clinics) because, rather than discriminating on the basis of viewpoint, "the Government has merely chosen to fund one activity to the exclusion of the other." Doctors could still engage in abortion advocacy and counseling, just not within the context of the federally funded program. The Court also rejected the claim that the regulations violated a woman's right to abortion. Relying on *McRae*, discussed in the previous note, the Court stated that even if clients of the federally funded programs were precluded by their poverty from seeing a health care provider who would provide abortion-related services, they were in no worse position than if Congress had never funded these programs to begin with. The Court concluded that their poverty, not the government, restricted their ability to enjoy the full range of their constitutional freedoms.

Justice Blackmun, in dissent, argued that even given the *McRae* precedent (with which he disagreed), the restriction on speech contained in the regulations at issue in *Rust* were a very different matter than the refusal to fund abortions because the speech regulations involved an element of government coercion.

Both the purpose and result of the challenged regulations are to deny women the ability voluntarily to decide their procreative destiny. For these women, the Government will have obliterated the freedom to choose as surely as if it had banned abortions outright. The denial of this freedom is not a consequence of poverty but of the Government's ill-intentioned distortion of information it has chosen to provide.

Blackmun took particular exception to the intrusion of the government in the doctor-patient relationship.

The Supreme Court upheld the regulations. But they were ultimately repealed prior to their implementation by newly elected President Clinton in 1993. For a discussion of the effect such regulations or ones like them potentially would have on African-American women in particular, see Dorothy E. Roberts, Rust v. Sullivan and the Control of Knowledge, 61 Geo. Wash. L. Rev. 587 (1993) (arguing that the *Rust* decision "failed to recognize that the government's control of knowledge available to poor Black women not only suppresses an idea, it also represses a people"). See also Paula Berg, Toward a First Amendment Theory of Doctor-Patient Discourse and the Right to Receive Unbiased Medical Advice, 74 B.U. L. Rev. 201 (1994) (regulation of doctor–patient discourse may be constitutional if it promotes autonomous, rational choices, but not if it imposes "official dogma").

To what extent should the dialogue between doctor and patient be protected from government regulation? Is there a difference between state laws requiring that doctors give certain information to pregnant women who are considering an abortion (e.g., information about the option of adoption, as discussed in the *Casey* decision, infra) and laws restricting doctors from providing certain information, such as information about the availability of abortion providers? What if the doctor is providing information about something that is illegal—such as marijuana use?[5]

4. *Offering money for sterilization or use of contraception.*   Private as well as governmental interests have spearheaded efforts to limit the reproductive capacity of drug- or alcohol-addicted men and women by offering them money if they agree to be sterilized or to use long-term contraception. One group, Children Requiring a Caring Kommunity (called "Crack"), was started in Orange County, California, in 1997, by Barbara Harris after she adopted four children from a mother addicted to drugs. Harris's group began by offering $200 to those who agreed to use contraception or be sterilized. Crack's stated goal is to preclude the birth of babies born with addictions. Lynn Paltrow, Executive Director of National Advocates for Pregnant Women, describes Crack as suggesting that the people to whom it provides money for agreeing to undergo sterilization or use contraception "are not worthy of reproducing. It is very much like the eugenics history in America." The story of Crack is told in Cecilia M. Vega, Sterilization Offer to Addicts Reopens Ethics Issue, N.Y. Times, Jan. 6, 2003, at B1, and in

---

5. In 2002, the Ninth Circuit Court of Appeals ruled that the federal government could not revoke the licenses of physicians who recommended medical marijuana to ease the suffering of their patients. Punishing doctors in this manner would constitute an improper intrusion into the doctor–patient relationship and violate the First Amendment. Conant v. Walters, 309 F.3d 629 (9th Cir. 2002). In 2003, the Supreme Court, without comment, rejected the Bush Administration's challenge to this ruling. 540 U.S. 946 (2003) (denying certiorari).

Janet Simmonds, Coercion in California: Eugenics Reconstituted in Welfare Reform, the Contracting of Reproductive Capacity, and Terms of Probation, 17 Hastings Women's L.J. 269, 282-288 (2006).

The Crack program relies on a contract between the organization and the person agreeing to be sterilized or use contraception. Is this contract unconscionable? Is Crack's offer of cash for contraception comparable to the offer of cash for human organs? Is it comparable to the offer of cash for sex?

5. *Restricting reproduction among women taking teratogens.*   The article by Lars Noah, supra, describes the efforts of the FDA and drug manufacturers to limit reproduction among women taking a teratogen. The FDA and the manufacturer of isotretinoin (Accutane®) recommended a series of responses—among them, that women submit a negative pregnancy test before receiving the drug from a pharmacy or that women with prescriptions for the drug register online and agree to pregnancy testing and the use of contraception before the drug could be dispensed to them. Do you think that such a drug should be available? If so, should the government, the manufacturer, or both, attempt to prevent users of the medication from becoming pregnant? And how best to do that?

6. *ART and eugenics.*   Some commentators have suggested that infertility can be understood as coerced contraception—coerced, of course by physiology, not the state. However, laws that limit infertility care can be viewed as tantamount to compelled contraception. A more nuanced form of this argument has been offered by Kerry Macintosh:

> Legal academics and federal policymakers argue that children conceived with the aid of ART face higher rates of birth defects, low birth weight, and other health problems. Their recommendations include undertaking massive new studies of child health, creating new regulatory agencies, and limiting access to problematic technologies, all in the name of public health.
>
> However, the debate over the regulation of ART is incomplete in two significant ways. First, regulators and academics have only skimmed the surface of a complex body of medical literature. ART may not be to blame for health problems observed in children. In fact, there are good reasons to believe these problems stem from underlying characteristics of infertility patients.
>
> Second, the debate has ignored the eugenic implications of governmental control over ART. When access to reproductive technologies is restricted, the consequences are dramatic: infertile men and women are rendered unable to procreate, and children who might otherwise have been born with health problems are never born at all. They are eliminated, along with their disabilities, ostensibly for their own good.

Kerry Lynn Macintosh, Brave New Eugenics: Regulating Assisted Reproductive Technologies in the Name of Better Babies, 2010 U. Ill. J.L. Tech. & Pol'y 257, 259 (2010). Do you agree that limiting the use of reproductive technology for the reasons noted by Macintosh can be characterized as a new form of eugenics?

7. *Conditioned nonsupporting father's probation on his not reproducing.*   In State v. Oakley, the Wisconsin Supreme Court affirmed a lower court's decision conditioning David Oakley's probation on his not having additional children during the period of the probation unless he could prove himself capable of supporting his children. 629 N.W.2d 200 (Wis. 2001). Oakley, the father of nine, had been convicted of intentional failure to pay child support, a felony

in Wisconsin. In justifying its decision, the Wisconsin court explained that were Oakley to serve time in prison he would be precluded from reproducing. Therefore, it was just to impose that limitation as a condition of probation. The court further explained that the condition did not unconstitutionally interfere with Oakley's rights:

> [W]e find that the condition is not overly broad because it does not eliminate Oakley's ability to exercise his constitutional right to procreate. He can satisfy the condition of probation by making efforts to support his children as required by law. Judge Hazlewood placed no limit on the number of children Oakley could have. Instead, the requirement is that Oakley acknowledge the requirements of the law and support his present and any future children. If Oakley decides to continue his present course of conduct—intentionally refusing to pay child support—he will face eight years in prison regardless of how many children he has. Furthermore, this condition will expire at the end of his term of probation. He may then decide to have more children, but of course, if he continues to intentionally refuse to support his children, the State could charge him again under §948.22(2). Rather, because Oakley can satisfy this condition by not intentionally refusing to support his current nine children and any future children as required by the law, we find that the condition is narrowly tailored to serve the State's compelling interest of having parents support their children. It is also narrowly tailored to serve the State's compelling interest in rehabilitating Oakley through probation rather than prison. . . .

What differentiates the probation condition placed on David Oakley from that placed on Darlene Johnson (Norplant implantation), supra? The *Oakley* case is discussed in Comment, Devon A. Corneal, Limiting the Right to Procreate, 33 Seton Hall L. Rev. 447 (2003); Tamar Lewin, Father Owing Child Support Loses Right to Procreate, N.Y. Times, July 12, 2001, at A14.

News stories have suggested that limits on procreation have been imposed as probation conditions in about half of the states. (A precise count is impossible because judges' orders in such cases are not generally published.) Sara C. Busch, Conditional Liberty: Restricting Procreation of Convicted Child Abusers and Dead Beat Dads, 56 Case W. Res. L. Rev. 479 (2005).

8. *Conditioning employment on sterilization.*   Some cases of ostensibly consensual sterilization may be compelled and thus, in effect, nonconsensual. This sort of situation was addressed in United Auto Workers v. Johnson Controls, 499 U.S. 187 (1991). Johnson Controls manufactured batteries. Before enactment of the Civil Rights Act of 1964, the company did not employ women in jobs related to the manufacture of batteries. After the company began to employ women in such jobs (warning them of the dangers of exposure to lead should they become pregnant), it learned that eight employees who had become pregnant had levels of lead in their blood beyond the levels recommended by the Occupational Health and Safety Administration as safe for a woman planning to become pregnant. The company then excluded all women "capable of bearing children" from jobs entailing possible exposure to lead. In effect, the policy gave a choice to female employees of child-bearing age working in jobs that could expose them to lead. They could leave their positions or get sterilized. The Supreme Court invalidated the policy as a violation of the Pregnancy Discrimination Act of Title VII. The Court noted the failure of Johnson Controls to limit male employees' exposure to lead. That, the Court concluded, constituted discrimination. The Court disagreed with the company's argument that its

fetal-protection policy fell within the set of exceptions defined as a bona fide occupational qualification (BFOQ):

> We have no difficulty concluding that Johnson Controls cannot establish a BFOQ. Fertile women, as far as appears in the record, participate in the manufacture of batteries as efficiently as anyone else. Johnson Controls' professed moral and ethical concerns about the welfare of the next generation do not suffice to establish a BFOQ of female sterility. Decisions about future children must be left to the parents who conceive, bear, support, and raise them rather than to the employers who hire those parents. Congress has mandated this choice through Title VII, as amended by the PDA. Johnson Controls has attempted to exclude women because of their reproductive capacity. Title VII and the PDA simply do not allow a woman's dismissal because of her failure to submit to sterilization.

Id. at 1207.

9. *Bibliographic note.*   Additional useful references include Sara C. Busch, Conditional Liberty: Restricting Procreation of Convicted Child Abusers and Dead Beat Dads, 56 Case W. Res. L. Rev. 479 (2005) (arguing that conditions on probation that limit or preclude procreation can be justified); Roberta M. Berry, From Involuntary Sterilization to Genetic Enhancement: The Unsettled Legacy of Buck v. Bell, 12 N.D. J.L. Ethics & Pub. Pol'y 401 (1998) (analyzing Buck v. Bell as one of a relatively small set of "horrendously wrong" U.S. judicial decisions and comparing eugenics that supported the decision in *Buck* with contemporary understandings of genetic enhancement); Jana Leslie-Miller, From Bell to Bell: Responsible Reproduction in the Twentieth Century, 8 Md. J. Contemp. Legal Issues 123 (1997) (analyzing Buck v. Bell in its historical context and comparing assumptions beyond the decision to those beyond the biological determinism of Herrnstein and Murray's assertions about race and intelligence in Chapter 8 of their book, The Bell Curve (1994)).

CHALLENGING ISSUES: DISTINGUISHING COERCIVE FROM NONCOERCIVE STERILIZATION OR USE OF CONTRACEPTION

1. Utopia State has passed a new law, called the Sane Family Assistance Plan. The law eliminates an increase in benefits with each additional child to custodial parents on welfare. Previously, the State provided benefit increases to welfare recipients who had another child while on welfare. Moreover, the State has provided that any welfare recipient with more than four children who has an additional child while on welfare will immediately become ineligible for welfare. What do you think of the State's new law? Is it unfair? If so, to whom? See Kimberly A. Smith, Conceivable Sterilization: A Constitutional Analysis of a Norplant/Depo-Provera Welfare Condition, 77 Ind. L.J. 389 (2002).

2. Elisa Jones has been mentally challenged since birth. She is now thirty-three and is pregnant with her tenth child. During the last few years, one or another of her children has been brought to court thirty-six times for "delinquent or unruly behavior." Elisa's mother, with whom Elisa and most of her children live, would like to see Elisa sterilized. When she is asked whether

she wants to be sterilized, Elisa is reported to "giggle and nod." However, it is said that she would likely respond similarly to almost any question asked of her.

Elisa is scheduled to appear in state Juvenile Court this week for a hearing involving one of her children. The judge, who knows Elisa's history and many of her children from previous court appearances, wonders if she might order long-term contraception or sterilization for Elisa. Do you think this is legal? Do you think it is appropriate from an ethical perspective? What other options might be explored?

B.   CONSENSUAL AVOIDANCE OF REPRODUCTION

Increased willingness to rely on contraception contributed to an important demographic change in the nineteenth century—a decrease in family size. Legal historian Michael Grossberg has reported that the fertility rate among white, married women fell from 5.21 in 1860 to 3.56 by the end of the nineteenth century. Michael Grossberg, Governing the Hearth: Law and the Family in Nineteenth-Century America 170 (1985). Methods of contraception available at the time often failed. Some women relied on abortion to limit family size.

Public opposition to contraception intensified at the end of the nineteenth century. Perhaps the most well-known instance of that opposition is the so-called Comstock law, named after Anthony Comstock. Comstock had spearheaded the "morals" campaign that resulted in the law's passage by the federal Congress in 1873. It prohibited use of the U.S. mails to send information about contraception. Such information was categorized as "obscene." Many states enacted similar statutes or others that expressly banned contraception. In the United States, states banned contraception from the middle of the nineteenth century until the middle of the twentieth century (when such laws were declared unconstitutional).

The widespread promulgation of laws in the United States prohibiting contraception and abortion during the last decades of the nineteenth century reflected a moral sentiment of fear for the disintegration of the so-called traditional family. That form of family, itself a product of the Industrial Revolution, shaped domestic life in sharp contrast to life in the marketplace. Among other things, the traditional family valued strong gender differences that identified the marketplace with men, money, and negotiation and identified the home with women, children, love, and duty. Despite lawmakers' efforts to halt the transformation of the family at the end of the nineteenth century, the process of transformation continued. By the 1960s its consequences were undeniable. At the same time, significant segments of society began openly to support dramatic shifts in family life that resulted, by the end of the twentieth century, in the reconstruction of the domestic arena and the laws that govern it.

Beginning in the mid-1960s (in Griswold v. Connecticut, 381 U.S. 479 (1965)), the U.S. Supreme Court decided a set of cases that defined a constitutional right to use contraception. *Griswold* and Eisenstadt v. Baird, which followed seven years later, reflected an evolving reverence in American culture for autonomous individuality within familial settings.

1.   *Contraception*

a.   **Bioethical and Social Perspectives**

> *Janet L. Dolgin, The Family in Transition:*
> *From* Griswold *to* Eisenstadt *and Beyond*
> 82 Geo. L.J. 1519, 1556–1558 (1994)

... [C]omparison of the privacy rights defined in *Griswold* and in *Eisenstadt*[6] is in order. Scholars have argued correctly that privacy, as we understand the term, was largely absent from an earlier American jurisprudence. As Ken Gormley notes, the meaning of privacy—not only for the law, but for the society more generally—is not written in stone. As the social order changes, so does the meaning of notions such as privacy. Before the present century, almost no individual, as such, was ever able to live a life of privacy as the term is used today. Physical constraints made privacy for the individual all but impossible. In addition, people within families were understood as parts of a larger whole, not as separate, potentially unconnected agents. Within the family, people enjoyed neither physical nor moral privacy. Historically in the West, privacy attached at the level of the group, not of the individual.

Physically, homes were cold and unheated, so people slept several in a bed. Toilet and washing activities were also, in this sense, rarely private. Morally, family members were not expected to demand autonomy. The modern notion of privacy, as a right applying to the individual, did not develop fully until the nineteenth century, and then only with regard to people outside the domestic context. For about a century more, people *within* families were defined as "private" vis-à-vis the outside world, but not in relation to each other. "Private life should be lived behind walls," wrote Littre in his mid-nineteenth century Dictionnaire. "No one," he continued, "is allowed to peer into a private home or to reveal what goes on inside." Thus, sometime between the mid-nineteenth and mid-twentieth centuries, the *level* at which society invoked privacy shifted from the group to the individual.

In *Griswold,* the Supreme Court for the first time expressly established the right to privacy as a constitutional matter. The establishment of individual privacy, suggested perhaps in *Griswold*'s subtext, but elaborated expressly in the privacy cases following *Griswold,* depended on the transformation of the family from a universe of enduring connection to a universe more like the market. Privacy has been valued for centuries, but the notion of privacy as attached exclusively or most fittingly to the autonomous individual is a recent innovation in the history of ideas. It is even more recent with regard to people in families. The position that family members are private, or at least have the *right* to be private, one from another, is fundamentally different from the notion that family privacy should be protected from the larger society and the state. But without that underlying transformation in the way families and family relationships are understood, without the extension of the social and legal world of the

---

6. Both *Griswold* and *Eisenstadt* are found in section B(1)(b) of this chapter.

autonomous individual into the world of the family, *Eisenstadt* and the "privacy" cases that followed could not have been written. . . .

Eisenstadt protected a distinct right to privacy, in the sense of a "right to be let alone." However, once the right to privacy attaches to the individual outside the context of a larger, structured group, the right itself changes. The shift is fundamental. The traditional privacy of the family is enjoyed *among* people within a unified group; it is the privacy of relationship that excludes those not part of a particular group. Individual privacy, in contrast, does not involve relationship. It depends on and establishes the separateness of the individual as an agent of action and choice. Thus, the extension of privacy to the individual *qua* individual implies the loss of groups such as the family, which previously mediated between the individual and the larger society and, in particular, between the individual and the state.

Once the individual is afforded privacy within familial units, the family is set free from the ideological underpinnings that allowed it to survive relatively intact since feudal times. As a consequence, the right to privacy *becomes* the right to autonomy; the individual within a family becomes essentially no different from the individual anywhere; and families become collections of people who can choose to join, to leave, or to redesign the contours of the unit itself.

NOTES AND QUESTIONS

1. *Family rights?*   A number of questions are raised by the claim in the preceding article—that the right to family privacy differs from the right to individual privacy in that the first right, but not the second, protects the privacy of *relationship*. Among the questions raised is whether the shift from family privacy to individual privacy situates the right defined in *Eisenstadt,* infra, as a *family* right. If so, it suggests that "families" cannot be defined with reference to fixed roles and relationships except insofar as individuals in families *choose* to adhere to the dictates of fixed roles and relationships.

To what extent do you think that legal rules about contraception (and abortion) should take assumptions about family life into account?

2. *Birth-control movement.*   Near its start, in the early decades of the twentieth century, the birth control movement reflected a combination of positions about families and women that may now seem surprising. In particular, support for the notion that women should have control over their reproduction was joined with the notion that contraception could prove useful as a means of eugenic control. According to Nancy Ehrenreich, early twentieth-century activists such as Margaret Sanger described contraception as a woman's right. But at the same time, Sanger and others within the birth control movement proposed a eugenic agenda that presented birth control, especially for low-income women, as an obligation rather than a right. Nancy Ehrenreich, The Colonization of the Womb, 43 Duke L.J. 492, 522 (1993). This history suggests that the difference between coerced contraception and consensual contraception may sometimes be murky. Camille A. Nelson describes the history of the law's having facilitated the sexual abuse of, and reproductive experimentation on, women who were slaves. Camille A. Nelson, American Husbandry: Legal Norms Impacting the Production of (Re)Productivity, 19 Yale J.L. & Feminism 1 (2007).

b.   Legal Approaches

|| *Griswold v. Connecticut* ||
|| 381 U.S. 479 (1965) ||

Opinion by Mr. Justice DOUGLAS.

Appellant Griswold is Executive Director of the Planned Parenthood League of Connecticut. Appellant Buxton is a licensed physician and a professor at the Yale Medical School who served as Medical Director for the League at its Center in New Haven—a center open and operating from November 1 to November 10, 1961, when appellants were arrested.

They gave information, instruction, and medical advice to *married persons* as to the means of preventing conception. They examined the wife and prescribed the best contraceptive device or material for her use. Fees were usually charged, although some couples were serviced free.

The statutes whose constitutionality is involved in this appeal are §§53–32 and 54–196 of the General Statutes of Connecticut (1958 rev.). The former provides:

> Any person who uses any drug, medicinal article or instrument for the purpose of preventing conception shall be fined not less than fifty dollars or imprisoned not less than sixty days nor more than one year or be both fined and imprisoned.

Section 54–196 provides:

> Any person who assists, abets, counsels, causes, hires or commands another to commit any offense may be prosecuted and punished as if he were the principal offender.

The appellants were found guilty as accessories and fined $100 each, against the claim that the accessory statute as so applied violated the Fourteenth Amendment. . . .

[Many] cases suggest that specific guarantees in the Bill of Rights have penumbras, formed by emanations from those guarantees that help give them life and substance. See Poe v. Ullman, 367 U.S. 497, 516–522 (dissenting opinion). Various guarantees create zones of privacy. The right of association contained in the penumbra of the First Amendment is one, as we have seen. The Third Amendment in its prohibition against the quartering of soldiers "in any house" in time of peace without the consent of the owner is another facet of that privacy. The Fourth Amendment explicitly affirms the "right of the people to be secure in their persons, houses, papers, and effects, against unreasonable searches and seizures." The Fifth Amendment in its Self-Incrimination Clause enables the citizen to create a zone of privacy which government may not force him to surrender to his detriment. The Ninth Amendment provides: "The enumeration in the Constitution, of certain rights, shall not be construed to deny or disparage others retained by the people."

The Fourth and Fifth Amendments were described in Boyd v. United States, 116 U.S. 616, 630, as protection against all governmental invasions "of the sanctity of a man's home and the privacies of life." We recently referred in Mapp v. Ohio, 367 U.S. 643, 656, to the Fourth Amendment as creating a "right to privacy, no less important than any other right carefully and particularly reserved to the people." See Beaney, The Constitutional Right to Privacy, 1962 Sup. Ct. Rev. 212; Griswold, The Right to be Let Alone, 55 Nw. U. L. Rev. 216 (1960). . . .

The present case, then, concerns a relationship lying within the zone of privacy created by several fundamental constitutional guarantees. And it concerns a law which, in forbidding the *use* of contraceptives rather than regulating their manufacture or sale, seeks to achieve its goals by means having a maximum destructive impact upon that relationship. Such a law cannot stand in light of the familiar principle, so often applied by this Court, that a "governmental purpose to control or prevent activities constitutionally subject to state regulation may not be achieved by means which sweep unnecessarily broadly and thereby invade the area of protected freedoms." NAACP v. Alabama, 377 U.S. 288, 307. Would we allow the police to search the sacred precincts of marital bedrooms for telltale signs of the use of contraceptives? The very idea is repulsive to the notions of privacy surrounding the marriage relationship.

We deal with a right of privacy older than the Bill of Rights—older than our political parties, older than our school system. Marriage is a coming together for better or for worse, hopefully enduring, and intimate to the degree of being sacred. It is an association that promotes a way of life, not causes; a harmony in living, not political faiths; a bilateral loyalty, not commercial or social projects. Yet it is an association for as noble a purpose as any involved in our prior decisions.

Reversed.

"Iron city"

Eisenstadt v. Baird
405 U.S. 438 (1972)

Opinion by Mr. Justice BRENNAN.

Appellee William Baird was convicted at a bench trial in the Massachusetts Superior Court under Massachusetts General Laws Ann., c. 272, §21, first, for exhibiting contraceptive articles in the course of delivering a lecture on contraception to a group of students at Boston University and, second, for giving a young woman a package of Emko vaginal foam at the close of his address.

Massachusetts General Laws Ann., c. 272, §21, under which Baird was convicted, provides a maximum five-year term of imprisonment for "whoever . . . gives away . . . any drug, medicine, instrument or article whatever for the prevention of conception," except as authorized in §21A. Under §21A, "[a] registered physician may administer to or prescribe for any married person drugs or articles intended for the prevention of pregnancy or conception. [And a] registered pharmacist actually engaged in the business of pharmacy may furnish such drugs or articles to any married person presenting a prescription from a registered physician." As interpreted by the State Supreme Judicial Court, these provisions make it a felony for anyone, other than a registered physician or pharmacist acting in accordance with the terms of §21A, to dispense any article with the intention that it be used for the prevention of conception. The statutory scheme distinguishes among three distinct classes of distributees— *first*, married persons may obtain contraceptives to prevent pregnancy, but only from doctors or druggists on prescription; *second*, single persons may not obtain contraceptives from anyone to prevent pregnancy; and, *third*, married or single persons may obtain contraceptives from anyone to prevent, not pregnancy, but the spread of disease. This construction of state law is, of course, binding on us. . . .

II

The basic principles governing application of the Equal Protection Clause of the Fourteenth Amendment are familiar. As the Chief Justice only recently explained in Reed v. Reed, 404 U.S. 71, 75–76 (1971):

> In applying that clause, this Court has consistently recognized that the Fourteenth Amendment does not deny to States the power to treat different classes of persons in different ways. . . . The Equal Protection Clause of that amendment does, however, deny to States the power to legislate that different treatment be accorded to persons placed by a statute into different classes on the basis of criteria wholly unrelated to the objective of that statute. A classification "must be reasonable, not arbitrary, and must rest upon some ground of difference having a fair and substantial relation to the object of the legislation, so that all persons similarly circumstanced shall be treated alike."

The question for our determination in this case is whether there is some ground of difference that rationally explains the different treatment accorded married and unmarried persons under Massachusetts General Laws Ann., c. 272, §§21 and 21A. For the reasons that follow, we conclude that no such ground exists. . . .

[W]hatever the rights of the individual to access to contraceptives may be, the rights must be the same for the unmarried and the married alike.

If under *Griswold* the distribution of contraceptives to married persons cannot be prohibited, a ban on distribution to unmarried persons would be equally impermissible. It is true that in *Griswold* the right of privacy in question inhered in the marital relationship. Yet the marital couple is not an independent entity with a mind and heart of its own, but an association of two individuals each with a separate intellectual and emotional makeup. If the right of privacy means anything, it is the right of the *individual*, married or single, to be free from unwarranted governmental intrusion into matters so fundamentally affecting a person as the decision whether to bear or beget a child. See Stanley v. Georgia, 394 U.S. 557 (1969).[10] See also Skinner v. Oklahoma, 316 U.S. 535 (1942); Jacobson v. Massachusetts, 197 U.S. 11, 29 (1905).

---

10. In *Stanley*, 394 U.S., at 564, the Court stated:

Also fundamental is the right to be free, except in very limited circumstances, from unwanted governmental intrusions into one's privacy.

> The makers of our Constitution undertook to secure conditions favorable to the pursuit of happiness. They recognized the significance of man's spiritual nature, of his feelings and of his intellect. They knew that only a part of the pain, pleasure and satisfactions of life are to be found in material things. They sought to protect Americans in their beliefs, their thoughts, their emotions and their sensations. They conferred, as against the Government, the right to be let alone—the most comprehensive of rights and the right most valued by civilized man. Olmstead v. United States, 277 U.S. 438, 478 (1928) (Brandeis, J., dissenting).

See Griswold v. Connecticut, supra; cf. NAACP v. Alabama, 357 U.S. 449, 462 (1958).

On the other hand, if *Griswold* is no bar to a prohibition on the distribution of contraceptives, the State could not, consistently with the Equal Protection Clause, outlaw distribution to unmarried but not to married persons. In each case the evil, as perceived by the State, would be identical, and the underinclusion would be invidious.

Affirmed.

NOTES AND QUESTIONS

1. *First Amendment.*   Justice Douglas concurred in Eisenstadt v. Baird, but would have preferred that the holding be grounded in First Amendment jurisprudence:

> It is irrelevant to the application of these principles that Baird went beyond the giving of information about birth control and advocated the use of contraceptive articles. The First Amendment protects the opportunity to persuade to action whether that action be unwise or immoral, or whether the speech incites to action.

"The teachings of Baird," Justice Douglas asserted, "and those of Galileo might be of a different order; but the suppression of either is equally repugnant." What did Justice Douglas intend here? Was he suggesting that society's readiness to use contraception widely suggested the dawn of a new social age? If so, do you agree with him?

2. *"Emergency" contraception.*   Much controversy has surrounded the approval and use of the so-called morning-after pill. If taken within 24 hours of intercourse, the pregnancy rate is 0.4 percent; if taken within 48 to 72 hours after intercourse, the rate is 2.7 percent. Robert Steinbrook, Waiting for Plan B—The FDA and Nonprescription Use of Emergency Contraception, 350 JAMA 2357 (2004). The emergency contraceptive pill works before implantation of a fertilized egg. However, some critics believe the pill is tantamount to abortion because it can result in the death of a fertilized egg. In 2006, the FDA approved over-the-counter sale of Plan B to women aged 18 and older.

Dr. Steinbrook notes that according to "commonly cited estimates" about half of all pregnancies are not planned. He further reports that in 2000, emergency contraceptive pills were used about 51,000 times. He concludes that that many abortions were thus "averted with the use of emergency contraceptive pills." Id. However, it is not clear that all the women who used this pill would in fact have had abortions had a pregnancy not been precluded through use of the pill.

In 1999, a year after the FDA approved Preven, a morning-after contraceptive made by Gynetics, Inc., Wal-Mart Stores, Inc., based in Bentonville, Arkansas, refused to carry the drug. Wal-Mart explained its refusal as a "business decision." At least one group of pharmacists, Pharmacists for Life International (reported to have about 1,500 members), argues that use of Preven results in abortion. Kristal L. Kuykendall, Wal-Mart: Pill Refused for Business Reasons, Ark. Dem-Gazette, May 15, 1999, at D1. Wal-Mart decided to sell Plan B after the drug's FDA approval in 2006. However, the company permits individual pharmacists to refuse to sell Plan B for reasons of conscience (except in states in which such refusal is illegal).

3. *"Emergency" contraception for young teenagers.*   In 2011, the Secretary of Health and Human Services overrode an FDA decision to allow over-the-counter sales of emergency contraception to girls 16 and younger. (It was apparently the first time that an HHS Secretary openly overruled an FDA decision.) Gardner Harris, Plan to Widen Availability of Morning-After Pill Is Rejected, N.Y. Times, Dec. 7, 2011, www.nytimes.com. FDA scientists had concluded that the drug at issue (Plan B) was safe and effective for use by teenagers. However, the HHS Secretary decided that Teva Pharmaceuticals (the manufacturer of Plan B) had not provided conclusive evidence that the drug should be offered over-the-counter to "all girls of reproductive age." Id.

4. *Health care reform law and contraception.*   Significant dissent emerged in response to a requirement announced by the Obama administration in early 2012 that coverage be provided for contraception and other preventive services, including sterilization and counseling, under the 2010 health care reform law (Patient Protection and Affordable Care Act). Contraception and Insurance Coverage: Religious Exemption Debate, N.Y. Times, May 21, 2012, www.nytimes.com. Religious groups, in particular, balked at the proposition that their health insurance plans would include coverage for contraception. The rule does not compel anyone to use contraception, but it does require insurers to provide it for anyone who wants to use it. Church organizations are exempt from the rule, but affiliated nonprofits, such as hospitals, are obliged to provide contraceptives for women without cost-sharing. Attorneys general from seven states (Florida, Michigan, Nebraska, Ohio, Oklahoma, South Carolina, and Texas) challenged the rule in federal court. A wide set of Catholic organizations and others joined the suits. A U.S. district court judge in Nebraska concluded in Nebraska v. HHS, No. 12-3035 (D. Neb. July 17, 2012), that the plaintiffs lacked standing to sue and, in any event, that the claims were not ripe. Yet, a U.S. district court in Colorado enjoined the federal government from enforcing the contraceptive services mandate against a private company operated by a Catholic family (Newland v. Sebelius, No. 1:12-cv-1123 (D. Colo. July 27, 2012)).

The administration agreed to postpone implementation of the rule for about a year and to impose the obligation on insurers, not employers (thus freeing Catholic hospitals, for instance, from responsibility for obtaining coverage for contraception). Kevin O'Hanlon, Judge Tosses Out Contraception Lawsuit Filed by Nebraska, Six Other States, Lincoln Journal Star, July 17, 2012, www.Journal Star.com. However, imposing the obligation to cover contraceptives on insurers leaves organizations affiliated with religious employers that oppose contraception without protection from the rule's obligation if they self-insure, as many do.

2.   *Abortion*[7]

U.S. law has provided for consensual and nonconsensual sterilization and contraception. Abortion is a different matter. Abortion requires consent. In the twentieth century, the debate about abortion became an ideological battlefield

---

7. The status of fetal and embryonic life is considered in Chapter 3.

in the United States. Through disputes about abortion, society also argued about families, gender, bodies, and the scope of the law's authority to determine people's intimate lives. The abortion issue arose over a century earlier when, for the first time in the United States, states widely criminalized abortion. The common law permitted abortion until quickening (the pregnant woman's first feeling of fetal motion, usually at about four or five months into gestation). In the first half of the nineteenth century, a few states passed statutes prohibiting abortion but when challenged in court these laws were generally invalidated. After 1860, however, states widely promulgated statutes that prohibited or restricted abortion. And in 1873, the federal Congress passed the so-called Comstock Law (named after Anthony Comstock, who lobbied hard for its passage). The law prohibited mailing or importing "any article whatever for the prevention of conception, or for causing unlawful abortion." By this time, public dispute about abortion had begun to implicate much more than abortion per se. The history of abortion in the United States before Roe v. Wade is detailed in N.E.H. Hull & Peter Charles Hoffer, Roe v. Wade: The Abortion Rights Controversy in American History 11–88 (2001); Janet Farrell Brodie, Contraception and Abortion in Nineteenth-Century America (1994); Kristin Luker, Abortion and the Politics of Motherhood 11–91 (1984); Carl H. Degler, At Odds: Women and the Family in America from the Revolution to the Present 227–248 (1980).

Legislative changes regarding abortion appeared in a few states before the Supreme Court's 1973 decision in Roe v. Wade, infra. In the early 1960s, the American Law Institute's Model Penal Code suggested expanding the types of abortions that should be permitted by the states. In 1970, New York's legislature voted to repeal the state's antiabortion statute (permitting abortion only to save the mother's life). In place of that statute, New York promulgated a law that allowed abortions to be performed during the first two trimesters of a pregnancy. Hawaii similarly passed a liberal abortion law before Roe.

Then, in 1973 in Roe, the Court defined a constitutional right to abortion. Since Roe, the Supreme Court has examined and reexamined various dimensions of the right to abortion and has significantly altered the framework within which Roe was constructed.

The politics of abortion intensified dramatically in the aftermath of Roe. The Court's decision became a barometer for measuring public responses to a wide set of issues associated with abortion. These issues related for the most part to questions about the scope and meaning of familial roles and relationships.

a.   Bioethical and Social Perspectives

John Hart Ely, The Wages of Crying Wolf:
A Comment on Roe v. Wade
82 Yale L.J. 920, 923–926 (1973)

Let us not underestimate what is at stake: Having an unwanted child can go a long way toward ruining a woman's life. And at bottom Roe signals the Court's judgment that this result cannot be justified by any good that anti-abortion legislation accomplishes. This surely is an understandable conclusion—indeed it is one with which I agree—but ordinarily the Court claims no mandate to second-guess legislative balances, at least not when the Constitution has designated neither of the values in conflict as entitled to special protection. But even assuming it would be a good idea for the Court to assume this function, *Roe* seems a curious place to have begun. Laws prohibiting the use of "soft" drugs or, even more obviously, homosexual acts between consenting adults can stunt "the preferred life styles" of those against whom enforcement is threatened in very serious ways. It is clear such acts harm no one besides the participants, and indeed the case that the participants are harmed is a rather shaky one. Yet such laws survive, on the theory that there exists a societal consensus that the behavior involved is revolting or at any rate immoral. Of course the consensus is not universal but it is sufficient, and this is what is counted crucial, to get the laws passed and keep them on the books. Whether anti-abortion legislation cramps the life style of an unwilling mother more significantly than anti-homosexuality legislation cramps the life style of a homosexual is a close question. But even granting that it does, the *other* side of the balance looks very different. For there is more than simple societal revulsion to support legislation restricting abortion: Abortion ends (or if it makes a difference, prevents) the life of a human being other than the one making the choice.

The Court's response here is simply not adequate. It agrees, indeed it holds, that after the point of viability (a concept it fails to note will become even less clear than it is now as the technology of birth continues to develop) the interest in protecting the fetus is compelling. Exactly why that is the magic moment is not made clear: Viability, as the Court defines it, is achieved some six to twelve weeks after quickening. (Quickening is the point at which the fetus begins discernibly to move independently of the mother and the point that has historically been deemed crucial—to the extent *any* point between conception and birth has been focused on.) But no, it is *viability* that is constitutionally critical: the Court's defense seems to mistake a definition for a syllogism.

> With respect to the State's important and legitimate interest in potential life, the "compelling" point is at viability. This is so because the fetus then presumably has the capacity of meaningful life outside the mother's womb.

With regard to why the state cannot consider this "important and legitimate interest" prior to viability, the opinion is even less satisfactory. The discussion begins sensibly enough: The interest asserted is not necessarily tied to the question whether the fetus is "alive," for whether or not one calls it a living being, it is an entity with the potential for (and indeed the likelihood of) life. But all of arguable relevance that follows are arguments that fetuses (a) are not recognized as "persons in the whole sense" by legal doctrine generally and (b) are not "persons" protected by the Fourteenth Amendment.

To the extent they are not entirely inconclusive, the bodies of doctrine to which the Court adverts respecting the protection of fetuses under general legal doctrine tend to undercut rather than support its conclusion. And the argument that fetuses (unlike, say, corporations) are not "persons" under the Fourteenth Amendment fares little better. The Court notes that most constitutional clauses using the word "persons"—such as the one outlining the qualifications for the Presidency—appear to have been drafted with postnatal beings in mind. (It might have added that most of them were plainly drafted with *adults* in mind, but I suppose that wouldn't have helped.) In addition, "the appellee conceded on reargument that no case can be cited that holds that a fetus is a person within the meaning of the Fourteenth Amendment." (The other legal contexts in which the question could have arisen are not enumerated.)

The canons of construction employed here are perhaps most intriguing when they are contrasted with those invoked to derive the constitutional right to an abortion. But in any event, the argument that fetuses lack constitutional rights is simply irrelevant. For it has never been held or even asserted that the state interest needed to justify forcing a person to refrain from an activity, *whether or not that activity is constitutionally protected,* must implicate either the life or the constitutional rights of another person. Dogs are not "persons in the whole sense" nor have they constitutional rights, but that does not mean the state cannot prohibit killing them: It does not even mean the state cannot prohibit killing them in the exercise of the First Amendment right of political protest. Come to think of it, draft cards aren't persons either.

> ### Reva Siegel, Reasoning from the Body: A Historical Perspective on Abortion Regulation and Questions of Equal Protection
> #### 44 Stan. L. Rev. 261, 379-380 (1992)

Restrictions on abortion reflect the kind of bias that is at the root of the most invidious forms of stereotyping: a failure to consider, in a society always at risk of forgetting, that women are persons, too. It is a bias that manifests itself in this society's unreflective expectation that women should assume the burdens of bearing and rearing future generations, its tendency to denigrate the work of motherhood, and its readiness to castigate women who seek to avoid maternity as lacking in humanity, proof of which consists in a woman's failure perfectly to subordinate her energies, resources, and prospects to the task of making life—to a degree that men, employers, and the community as a whole most often will not.

This society has "unclean hands" in matters respecting motherhood. While it may possess the power, it sorely lacks the moral grounds to "balance" the rights of women and the unborn as if it were a disinterested bystander to a conflict thrust upon women by nature. We may stand a century away from the attitudes expressed in the nineteenth century campaign, but we are still generations away from any prospect of transcending their ideological or institutional legacy. In a society that viewed women as full and equal citizens—as something more than particularly valuable means to an important social end—the test for determining the constitutionality of abortion-restrictive regulation might be: Has the state asserted its interest in promoting the welfare of the unborn in a fashion consistent with promoting the welfare of women?

In an inchoate fashion, *Roe* embodied this understanding. The Court understood that regulation of women's conduct premised on a theory of fetal personhood would deeply conflict with public recognition of women's personhood. *Roe*'s trimester framework accommodated this conflict practically, but gave only a partial account of its sense. By allowing states to prohibit abortions at the point of fetal viability, the Court hoped to craft a constitutional compromise. . . .

State action on behalf of the fetus in utero must find its constitutional bearings, and constraints, in the community's relation to the citizen in whom unborn life resides. In this sense, the common law criterion of quickening gave surer moral guidance to the regulation of abortion than the "scientific" concept of viability with which *Roe* replaced it. At least the common law criterion of quickening located the unborn internal to a born, sentient being, rather than presenting the unborn as an autonomous life form—an illusion sustained for more than a century now by medical rhetoric. If *Roe* survives in some form, it will be because those charged with expounding federal and state constitutions do not, in their hearts, credit this dehumanizing myth of human genesis. It will be because they recognize that women's lives are required to make potential life recognizable as a person, and recognize that because women are equal citizens too, their labor in bearing life is a gift with which they can endow the community, not a resource the community can expropriate to its use.

> ## Teresa Godwin Phelps, The Sound of Silence Breaking: Catholic Women, Abortion, and the Law
> ### 59 Tenn. L. Rev. 547, 565, 567–568, 569 (1992)

[In this article, Teresa Godwin Phelps explains her decision to talk about abortion with Catholic women, some of whom were feminists. The body of Phelps's article contains interviewees' responses to Phelps's questions about the women's position on abortion and their identity as Catholics. The following excerpt presents the conclusions that Phelps reached in light of the interviews about legal responses to abortion.]

. . . [T]he conversations underscore the paucity of the law's emphasis on rights. The current abortion debate is generally framed using rights language: the fetus or the woman has the superior right to life or to autonomy. A libertarian rights approach to abortion, the one most generally voiced by pro-choice activists, already has been revealed to fall short in cases in which economic factors are present. The rights approach assimilates disparate experience to a false Enlightenment universal. Not surprisingly, it captures most closely the experience of white, educated, middle-class women. . . . [F]or them, the libertarian emphasis on choice was consistent with experience. As a result, the needs of other particular groups of women—especially the poor—were "pruned out" of the pro-choice discourse.

In other words, poor women cannot choose whether to bear a child; their choice is compelled one way or another because of their economic situation.

Similarly, the language of rights fails to encompass the experience and beliefs of many of the women with whom I spoke. For many of them personally, choice had little meaning as long as abortion was a morally unacceptable alternative. And the raw handing to them of "choice" silences them as much as the dictates of the Vatican. It seemingly tells them they have what they need and they should seek no other remedy. This strikes me as demonstrably untrue and unfair. What does the law do for women who have no choice—economically, morally, or otherwise? What does the law do for women who choose or would choose to carry the pregnancy to term? . . .

The legal abortion debate, much like the Church discussion of abortion, focuses on a very limited aspect of a woman's sexuality: her childbearing ability from the moment after conception to the moment after birth. What men and society in general do to a woman's sexuality, how she sees herself, how she comes to respect herself and her body, how she controls her life, how children are supported are, they tell us, beyond the reach of the law. This is not startling news, to be sure. Legal scholars like Robin West have been arguing for years that words on which the law seems fixated like "choice," "autonomy," and "power" are a poor fit for the values necessary for well-being in a woman's life.

If, as we may conclude from these conversations, even some Catholic women, although they would not consider having abortions and although they do not know with certainty when life begins, still do not want abortion made illegal, does this mean we must abandon the law altogether in the abortion question? If it is true, as I believe it is, that rights language utterly fails to conceptualize the reality of pregnancy, in which the pregnant woman and the fetus are interdependent, not autonomous individuals exercising rights against each other, must we abandon all legal language in discussing abortion? And if it is true, and I believe it is, that "law . . . tells stories about the culture that helped shape it and which in turn it helps to shape: stories about who we are, where we came from, and where we are going," what stories does our abortion law tell about our society? . . .

One speaks as a Catholic woman about abortion by first of all speaking, by refusing to succumb to the comforting world of silence. Second, one refuses to accept the current state of the discourse as given. One does not surrender to the dichotomous language of rights but instead raises questions and subjects the rigid positions to insistent scrutiny. One insists that the law on abortion is a law affecting women and children and is thus interrelated to all other laws and practices that concern women and children. . . .

NOTES AND QUESTIONS

1. *Can the debate about abortion be mediated?*   Do you think the debate about abortion in American society can be resolved? If so, how? Thomas H. Murray, former President of the Hastings Center, a center for bioethics scholarship in New York, has suggested that arguments in the debate about abortion follow from deeply held beliefs, and that participants in the debate are generally not open to logical persuasion.

> In my book *The Worth of a Child* I posed a challenge: Imagine some new ethical argument or scientific fact that persuaded nearly everyone on one side of the embryo-as-person debate that they had been mistaken. The other side is right, they would admit. Can you imagine such an argument or act? I cannot. Notice that I did not say which side came up with the persuasive new moral consideration. This is, I believe, not because people are impervious to logic, but because our beliefs about embryos are woven into a complex tapestry of other beliefs—about what it means to be a woman, a man, a child; about families; about the importance of being a nurturing parent. This tapestry of beliefs and commitments affected everything from our attitudes towards sex discrimination in employment to the importance of family leave and educational opportunities for women.

Prepared testimony of Thomas H. Murray before the Senate Judiciary Committee ("Promoting Ethical Regenerative Medicine Research and Prohibiting Immoral Human Reproductive Cloning"), Federal News Service, March 19, 2003.

Teresa Godwin Phelps, in the article printed above, concludes by suggesting that those from all sides of the abortion debate would benefit by undertaking the "essential work" the abortion debate demands "by listening to each other." Phelps, supra, at 569. Phelps, herself a "Catholic feminist," interviewed Catholic women with a variety of views about abortion, but many of the interviewees shared a feminist perspective. Would similar conversations be possible across the much larger divide that separates many pro-choice from many pro-life adherents? See Kristin Luker, Abortion and the Politics of Motherhood (1984) (analyzing interviews with activists from different sides of the debate about abortion).

2. *Changing beliefs about embryos.* Although Murray (quoted in note 1 above) is surely correct that positions about embryos "are woven into a complex tapestry of other beliefs," those "other beliefs" change over time, and thus beliefs about embryos change as well. It was, for instance, only in the nineteenth century that the ontological status of fetal life emerged as a subject of intense theological and biological debate. See James C. Mohr, Abortion in America: The Origins and Evolution of National Policy (1978); John A. Balint, Ethical Issues in Stem Cell Research, 65 Alb. L. Rev. 729 (2002); John T. Noonan, An Almost Absolute Value in History 1, 39 in The Morality of Abortion: Legal and Historical Perspectives (John T. Noonan ed. 1970). Until the appearance of technologies (including, for instance, ultrasonography) that have provided for the observation of embryos, the debate about abortion focused on fetal, rather than embryonic, life.

3. *Questioning abortion jurisprudence.* John Hart Ely's article, supra, argues that, whatever one believes about a woman's right to abortion, the jurisprudence undergirding *Roe* is, at best, shaky. Yet, Ely noted that he himself believed a woman should have a right to terminate a pregnancy. What method would Ely have suggested for effecting that right?

4. *Changing rate of abortion.* In 1972 (the year before the Supreme Court decided Roe v. Wade, infra), about 600,000 abortions were reported in the United States. Seven years after *Roe* about 1.3 million abortions were reported. The number increased until the early 1990s, when it began to fall. Timothy J. Vinciguerra, Notes of a Foot-Soldier, 62 Alb. L. Rev. 1167 (1999). In 2005, there were 8 percent fewer abortions than in 2000. Rachel K. Jones et al., Abortion in the United States: Incidence and Access to Services, 2005, 40 Perspectives on Reproductive Health 6 (2008), http://www.guttmacher.org/pubs/journals/4000608.pdf. In 1999, Dr. Vinciguerra, a fellow of the American College of Obstetrics and Gynecology, suggested several possible explanations for the falling abortion rate in the United States. Abortions were increasingly being performed at points so early in a pregnancy that they were not covered by reporting requirements. The incidence of unintended pregnancies among teenagers was decreasing. And the availability of emergency contraception allowed women to avoid contraceptive devices and to terminate very early pregnancies using drugs rather than surgery.

Between 2000 and 2008, however, the rate of abortion (which decreased overall in the U.S.) increased by 18 percent among poor women. Christian

Nordqvist, Overall Abortion Rate Drops 8% in Eight Years, Rises 18% Among Poor Women in USA, Medical News Today, May 24, 2011, available at http://www.medicalnewstoday.com/articles/226354.php (citing Rachel K. Jones & Megan L. Kavanaugh, Changes in Abortion Rates Betwween 2000 and 2008 and Lifetime Incidence of Abortion, 117 Obstetrics and Gynecology 1263 (2011)). One explanation for the increase in the rate of abortion among low-income women is increasing limitations on access to contraceptive care. Id.

5. *Abortion right cannot be surrendered through contract.*   Not only are coercive abortions not legal, but a woman is not permitted to give up her right to make the abortion decision. In Matter of Baby M., for instance, a surrogate contracted to transfer her right to have an abortion or not to abort a pregnancy to the intending, genetic father. Even the state trial court, which validated the surrogacy contract on all other grounds, invalidated the provision that transferred the abortion right from the pregnant woman to the father. 525 A.2d 1128 (1987), aff'd in part and rev'd in part, 537 A.2d 1227 (1988). (This case is discussed in Chapter 5.)

6. *Considering responses to Roe.* Americans widely assume that the decision of the Supreme Court in Roe v. Wade engendered a wave of opposition to abortion. Linda Greenhouse & Reva B. Siegel, Before (and After) Roe v. Wade: New Questions About Backlash, 120 Yale L.J. 2028, 2034 (2011). Greenhouse and Siegel challenge that narrative by examining the history of responses to abortion in the period before the Court's decision in *Roe.* They locate a wider set of political and social responses that may be as significant as the decision in *Roe* in explaining the intensity of responses to abortion in the period after *Roe.* They conclude that "the powerful preemptive effect of the juricentric narrative [about *Roe*] has blunted curiosity about Roe's roots and its reception." Id. at 2086.

b.   Legal Approaches

|| *Roe v. Wade*[8] ||
|| **410 U.S. 113 (1973)** ||

Opinion by Mr. Justice BLACKMUN.

This Texas federal appeal . . . present[s] constitutional challenges to state criminal abortion legislation. . . .

We forthwith acknowledge our awareness of the sensitive and emotional nature of the abortion controversy, of the vigorous opposing views, even among physicians, and of the deep and seemingly absolute convictions that the subject inspires. One's philosophy, one's experiences, one's exposure to the raw edges of human existence, one's religious training, one's attitudes toward life and family and their values, and the moral standards one establishes and seeks to observe, are all likely to influence and to color one's thinking and conclusions about abortion. . . .

[In Part VI of the opinion, the Court reviewed the history of abortion in some detail, beginning with the positions of the ancient Persians and Greeks.

---

8. Sections of this case concerning the legal and moral status of fetuses are included in Chapter 3.

Part VII reviews the reasons provided for the promulgation of abortion statutes in the United States. Then, beginning in Part VIII, the Court turns to consider abortion laws in light of the Court's privacy jurisprudence.]

VIII

The Constitution does not explicitly mention any right of privacy. In a line of decisions, however, going back perhaps as far as [1891] . . . , the Court has recognized that a right of personal privacy, or a guarantee of certain areas or zones of privacy, does exist under the Constitution. In varying contexts, the Court or individual Justices have, indeed, found at least the roots of that right in the First Amendment; in the Fourth and Fifth Amendments; in the penumbras of the Bill of Rights, Griswold v. Connecticut; in the Ninth Amendment, Id. (Goldberg, J., concurring); or in the concept of liberty guaranteed by the first section of the Fourteenth Amendment, see Meyer v. Nebraska. These decisions make it clear that only personal rights that can be deemed "fundamental" or "implicit in the concept of ordered liberty," Palko v. Connecticut, are included in this guarantee of personal privacy. They also make it clear that the right has some extension to activities relating to marriage, Loving v. Virginia; procreation, Skinner v. Oklahoma; contraception, Eisenstadt v. Baird; family relationships, Prince v. Massachusetts; and child rearing and education, Pierce v. Society of Sisters, Meyer v. Nebraska. This right of privacy, whether it be founded in the Fourteenth Amendment's concept of personal liberty and restrictions upon state action, as we feel it is, or, as the District Court determined, in the Ninth Amendment's reservation of rights to the people, is broad enough to encompass a woman's decision whether or not to terminate her pregnancy. The detriment that the State would impose upon the pregnant woman by denying this choice altogether is apparent. Specific and direct harm medically diagnosable even in early pregnancy may be involved. Maternity, or additional offspring, may force upon the woman a distressful life and future. Psychological harm may be imminent. Mental and physical health may be taxed by child care. There is also the distress, for all concerned, associated with the unwanted child, and there is the problem of bringing a child into a family already unable, psychologically and otherwise, to care for it. In other cases, as in this one, the additional difficulties and continuing stigma of unwed motherhood may be involved. All these are factors the woman and her responsible physician necessarily will consider in consultation.

On the basis of elements such as these, appellant and some *amici* argue that the woman's right is absolute and that she is entitled to terminate her pregnancy at whatever time, in whatever way, and for whatever reason she alone chooses. With this we do not agree. Appellant's arguments that Texas either has no valid interest at all in regulating the abortion decision, or no interest strong enough to support any limitation upon the woman's sole determination, are unpersuasive. The Court's decisions recognizing a right of privacy also acknowledge that some state regulation in areas protected by that right is appropriate. As noted above, a State may properly assert important interests in safeguarding health, in maintaining medical standards, and in protecting potential life. At some point in pregnancy, these respective interests become sufficiently compelling to sustain regulation of the factors that govern the abortion decision. The privacy right involved, therefore, cannot be said to be absolute. In fact, it is not clear to us that the claim asserted by some *amici* that one has an unlimited right to do with one's body as one pleases bears a close relationship to the right of privacy previously articulated in the Court's decisions. The Court has refused to recognize an unlimited right of this kind in the past. Jacobson v. Massachusetts, 197 U.S. 11 (1905) (vaccination); Buck v. Bell, 274 U.S. 200 (1927) (sterilization). [Section IX(A) of the opinion, which discusses the claims about fetal personhood, can be found in Chapter 3.]

X

In view of all this, we do not agree that, by adopting one theory of life, Texas may override the rights of the pregnant woman that are at stake. We repeat, however, that the State does have an important and legitimate interest in preserving and protecting the health of the pregnant woman, whether she be a resident of the State or a nonresident who seeks medical consultation and treatment there, and that it has still *another* important and legitimate interest in protecting the potentiality of human life. These interests are separate and distinct. Each grows in substantiality as the woman approaches term and, at a point during pregnancy, each becomes "compelling."

With respect to the State's important and legitimate interest in the health of the mother, the "compelling" point, in the light of present medical knowledge, is at approximately the end of the first trimester. This is so because of the now-established medical fact . . . that until the end of the first trimester mortality in abortion may be less than mortality in normal childbirth. It follows that, from and after this point, a State may regulate the abortion procedure to the extent that the regulation reasonably relates to the preservation and protection of maternal health. . . .

With respect to the State's important and legitimate interest in potential life, the "compelling" point is at viability. This is so because the fetus then presumably has the capability of meaningful life outside the mother's womb. State regulation protective of fetal life after viability thus has both logical and biological justifications. If the State is interested in protecting fetal life after viability, it may go so far as to proscribe abortion during that period, except when it is necessary to preserve the life or health of the mother.

Measured against these standards [the Texas statute] in restricting legal abortions to those "procured or attempted by medical advice for the purpose of saving the life of the mother," sweeps too broadly. The statute makes no distinction between abortions performed early in pregnancy and those performed later, and it limits to a single reason, "saving" the mother's life, the legal justification for the procedure. The statute, therefore, cannot survive the constitutional attack made upon it here.

XI

To summarize and to repeat:

1. A state criminal abortion statute of the current Texas type, that excepts from criminality only a *lifesaving* procedure on behalf of the mother, without

regard to pregnancy stage and without recognition of the other interests involved, is vocative of the Due Process Clause of the Fourteenth Amendment.

(a) For the stage prior to approximately the end of the first trimester, the abortion decision and its effectuation must be left to the medical judgment of the pregnant woman's attending physician.

(b) For the stage subsequent to approximately the end of the first trimester, the State, in promoting its interest in the health of the mother, may, if it chooses, regulate the abortion procedure in ways that are reasonably related to maternal health.

(c) For the stage subsequent to viability, the State in promoting its interest in the potentiality of human life may, if it chooses, regulate, and even proscribe, abortion except where it is necessary, in appropriate medical judgment, for the preservation of the life or health of the mother.

NOTES AND QUESTIONS

1. *Stages of pregnancy.* With regard to the state's interest in the health of pregnant women, what point did the Court in *Roe* see as "compelling"? Why? What point did the Court see as compelling with regard to the state's interest in protecting potential life? Why? Does this scheme make sense to you? Does it seem commonsensical? Practical? Ethical?

2. *Limits on right to privacy.* In Part VIII of *Roe,* Justice Blackmun justifies the Court's conclusion that the privacy right delineated in the case is not absolute. First, he questions whether the claim that the Constitution protects one's right to "do with one's body as one pleases bears a close relationship to the right of privacy previously articulated in the Court's decisions." Do Skinner v. Oklahoma (about a right to procreate), Griswold v. Connecticut (about a right to contraception), or Eisenstadt v. Baird (about a right to contraception), all cited in Part VIII, suggest such a right? After raising the question, the opinion then asserts that the Court has indeed refused to recognize such a right. To support this assertion, the Court cites Jacobson v. Massachusetts (a 1905 case that validated mandatory inoculation against smallpox—see infra Chapter 12, section B(1)) and Buck v. Bell (see, supra, section A(1)(a)(ii)). Is *Buck* a useful precedent to cite in *Roe* in support of the claim that the state may limit one's right to do what one pleases with one's body? Further, is limiting a woman's right to abortion comparable to limiting a person's right not to be sterilized?

3. *Debate about abortion and views of family.* The word "*family*" or "*familial*" is used seven times in *Roe* (excluding use of the word in citations). In the second paragraph of the opinion (after a summary of the legal issue) the Court explained that "one's attitudes toward life and family and their values" are "likely to influence and to color one's thinking and conclusions about abortion?" Is that correct? How is one's position about abortion likely to reflect one's view of families? Are people who oppose abortion likely to favor different sorts of family relationships than people who favor a right to abortion?

Kristin Luker, who interviewed a group of abortion activists (representing both pro-choice and pro-life positions about abortion), concluded that "[d]ifferent beliefs about the roles of the sexes, about the meaning of parenthood, and about human nature are all called into play when the issue is abortion." Kristin Luker, Abortion and the Politics of Motherhood 158 (1984). Luker explained:

> [T]he values and beliefs of pro-choice diametrically oppose those of pro-life people, as does the logic whereby they arrive at their values. For example, whereas pro-life people believe that men and women are inherently different and therefore have different "natural" roles in life, pro-choice people believe that men and women are substantially equal, by which they mean substantially similar.

Id. at 175–176. Luker explained further that pro-life activists saw the public world of work as a domain more appropriate for men than for women and saw the world of family and motherhood as a domain more suited to women. Id. at 160. Pro-choice people disagreed. Id. at 177.

Luker wrote her book about a decade after *Roe*. Do you think that her description of pro-life and pro-choice activists' views of gender and family life are still accurate?

4. *Views about abortion.*   In *Roe*, the Court explained that people's views of abortion were affected by a number of matters other than their views of family life. The Court correlated views about abortion with people's "philosophy," "experiences," "exposure to the raw edges of human existence," "religious training," and the "moral standards one establishes and seeks to observe." Why do you think that the Court began its opinion with this observation? Does the observation suggest that the Court's view of the case is a product of the Justices' collective experiences, philosophies, and so on? If that is the case, in what sense can the opinion be understood as a reflection of the Constitution? Does it matter if it is not?

The questions raised in this note have in one form or another been discussed in a myriad of articles and books by legal scholars and others. Some useful resources, written just before or after the Court's decision in *Roe*, include John Hart Ely, Democracy and Distrust 1 (1980) (distinguishing interpretive from noninterpretive review of Constitution); Developments in the Law: The Constitution and the Family, 93 Harv. L. Rev. 1156 (1980) (considering importance of Court's adhering to values explicit in the Constitution); Robert Bork, Neutral Principles and Some First Amendment Problems, 47 Ind. L.J. 1 (1971) (arguing that judges should not develop rights not found in the constitutional text).

5. *Ginsburg on* Roe. Professor Ruth Bader Ginsburg (now Justice Ginsburg) suggested in 1985 that Roe v. Wade might have been less controversial had the Court provided a more complete justification for the decision and had the Court not gone as far as it did. Ruth Bader Ginsburg, Some Thought on Autonomy and Equality in Relation to Roe v. Wade, 63 N.C. L. Rev. 375, 376 (1985). Professor Ginsburg noted:

> Roe v. Wade, in contrast to decisions involving explicit male/female classification, has occasioned searing criticism of the Court, over a decade of demonstrations, a stream of vituperative mail addressed to Justice Blackmun, annual

proposals for overruling *Roe* by constitutional amendment, and a variety of measures in Congress and state legislatures to contain or curtail the decision.

Id. at 380. She further suggests that a legislative movement to provide for abortion that began several years before *Roe* might have eventually resembled the no-fault divorce revisions that "swept through the states establishing no-fault divorce as the national pattern." Id. Do you agree with Ginsberg's assessment? Are there any other explanations for the wide differences in social and legal responses to the Court's abortion jurisprudence and its gender-equality jurisprudence?

About ten years after Ruth Bader Ginsburg's article appeared, Justice Blackman was asked about his reaction to criticisms of the *Roe* decision by Ruth Bader Ginsburg and others. Justice Blackmun responded:

> As far as Justice Ginsburg's criticism is concerned, it's a valid point of view to take, but it's an easy one to take after twenty, twenty-five years, in that it could not have been decided back in 1972–73 on the grounds she suggests. William O. Douglas was dead set against approaching the case on that [equal protection] ground, and he would have had enough agreement in the Court that five votes to that effect would never have been achieved. So with all respect to Justice Ginsburg, I just regard her criticism as another proper one as any academic would make of the opinion. She has a right to make it, but she wasn't on the firing line at that time.

The Justice Harry A. Blackmun Oral History Project, Supreme Court Historical Society and the Federal Judicial Center (interview conducted by Prof. Harold Hongju Koh) at 202 (1995), http://lcweb2.10c.gov/diglib/blackmun-public/collection.html.

6. *"Jane Roe" shifts positions.*   "Jane Roe" was 21 years old and pregnant with her third child when she became a plaintiff in Roe v. Wade. She had the child before the decision in the case. That child as well as her first two were adopted by others. In 1980, Norma McCorvey revealed that she was "Jane Roe" in Roe v. Wade. Then in the early 1990s, McCorvey joined the pro-life movement and announced that she regretted her role in *Roe*. In June 2003, she filed a motion with the federal district court in Dallas, Texas, asking "for relief from judgment" and seeking to have *Roe* reopened. She argued that new evidence not considered in *Roe* indicated that abortion had negative consequences for women. The court rejected McCorvey's motion on the ground that it had not been made within a "reasonable time." The Fifth Circuit affirmed the Texas district court's decision, rejecting McCorvey's motion to have *Roe* reopened. McCorvey v. Hill, 385 F.3d 846 (5th Cir. 2004), cert. denied, 543 U.S. 1154 (2005).

7. *Attitudes about abortion.*   A 2010 Gallup Poll found that the majority of Democrats (51 percent) but only a minority of Republicans (26 percent) found abortion "morally acceptable." Independents fell between Democrats and Republicans, with 36 percent of those polled viewing abortion as morally acceptable. Lydia Saad, Four Moral Issues Sharply Divide Americans, Gallup Politics, May 26, 2010, http://www.gallup.com/poll/137357/four-moral-issues-sharply-divide-americans.aspx. A Gallup Poll conducted in 2012 found that 38 percent of Americans found abortion morally acceptable. Interestingly, in the same year, Gallup reported that 89 percent of Americans found birth control morally

acceptable. Frank Newport, Americans, Including Catholics, Say Birth Control Is Morally OK, Gallup Politics, May 22, 2012, http://www.gallup.com/poll/154799/Americans-Including-Catholics-Say-Birth-Control-Morally.aspx

8. *Reading* Casey.   In Planned Parenthood v. Casey, infra, the constitutional jurisprudence of abortion was significantly reconstructed. Yet, the Court in *Casey* did not overrule *Roe* as some had thought it might. As you read *Casey,* consider how this decision does, in fact, redefine a woman's right to terminate a pregnancy.

Planned Parenthood of Southeastern Pennsylvania v. Casey
505 U.S. 833 (1992)

Justice O'CONNOR, Justice KENNEDY, and Justice SOUTER announced the judgment of the Court and delivered the opinion of the Court. . . .

Liberty finds no refuge in a jurisprudence of doubt. Yet 19 years after our holding that the Constitution protects a woman's right to terminate her pregnancy in its early stages, that definition of liberty is still questioned. Joining the respondents as *amicus curiae,* the United States, as it has done in five other cases in the last decade, again asks us to overrule *Roe.*

At issue in these cases are five provisions of the Pennsylvania Abortion Control Act of 1982. . . . The Act requires that a woman seeking an abortion give her informed consent prior to the abortion procedure, and specifies that she be provided with certain information at least 24 hours before the abortion is performed. For a minor to obtain an abortion, the Act requires the informed consent of one of her parents, but provides for a judicial bypass option if the minor does not wish to or cannot obtain a parent's consent. Another provision of the Act requires that, unless certain exceptions apply, a married woman seeking an abortion must sign a statement indicating that she has notified her husband of her intended abortion. The Act exempts compliance with these three requirements in the event of a "medical emergency," which is defined in . . . the Act. In addition to the above provisions regulating the performance of abortions, the Act imposes certain reporting requirements on facilities that provide abortion services. . . .

After considering the fundamental constitutional questions resolved by *Roe,* principles of institutional integrity, and the rule of *stare decisis,* we are led to conclude this: the essential holding of Roe v. Wade should be retained and once again reaffirmed.

It must be stated at the outset and with clarity that *Roe*'s essential holding, the holding we reaffirm, has three parts. First is a recognition of the right of the woman to choose to have an abortion before viability and to obtain it without undue interference from the State. Before viability, the State's interests are not strong enough to support a prohibition of abortion or the imposition of a substantial obstacle to the woman's effective right to elect the procedure. Second is a confirmation of the State's power to restrict abortions after fetal viability, if the law contains exceptions for pregnancies which endanger the woman's life or health. And third is the principle that the State has legitimate interests from the outset of the pregnancy in protecting the health of the woman and the life of the fetus that may become a child. These principles do not contradict one another; and we adhere to each.

II . . .

Men and women of good conscience can disagree, and we suppose some always shall disagree, about the profound moral and spiritual implications of terminating a pregnancy, even in its earliest stage. Some of us as individuals find abortion offensive to our most basic principles of morality, but that cannot control our decision. Our obligation is to define the liberty of all, not to mandate our own moral code. The underlying constitutional issue is whether the State can resolve these philosophic questions in such a definitive way that a woman lacks all choice in the matter, except perhaps in those rare circumstances in which the pregnancy is itself a danger to her own life or health, or is the result of rape or incest.

It is conventional constitutional doctrine that where reasonable people disagree the government can adopt one position or the other. That theorem, however, assumes a state of affairs in which the choice does not intrude upon a protected liberty. . . .

Our law affords constitutional protection to personal decisions relating to marriage, procreation, contraception, family relationships, child rearing, and education. Our cases recognize "the right of the *individual,* married or single, to be free from unwarranted governmental intrusion into matters so fundamentally affecting a person as the decision whether to bear or beget a child." Eisenstadt v. Baird. Our precedents "have respected the private realm of family life which the state cannot enter." These matters, involving the most intimate and personal choices a person may make in a lifetime, choices central to personal dignity and autonomy, are central to the liberty protected by the Fourteenth Amendment. At the heart of liberty is the right to define one's own concept of existence, of meaning, of the universe, and of the mystery of human life. Beliefs about these matters could not define the attributes of personhood were they formed under compulsion of the State.

These considerations begin our analysis of the woman's interest in terminating her pregnancy but cannot end it, for this reason: though the abortion decision may originate within the zone of conscience and belief, it is more than a philosophic exercise. Abortion is a unique act. It is an act fraught with consequences for others: for the woman who must live with the implications of her decision; for the persons who perform and assist in the procedure; for the spouse, family, and society which must confront the knowledge that these procedures exist, procedures some deem nothing short of an act of violence against innocent human life; and, depending on one's beliefs, for the life or potential life that is aborted. Though abortion is conduct, it does not follow that the State is entitled to proscribe it in all instances. That is because the liberty of the woman is at stake in a sense unique to the human condition and so unique to the law. The mother who carries a child to full term is subject to anxieties, to physical constraints, to pain that only she must bear. That these sacrifices have from the beginning of the human race been endured by woman with a pride that ennobles her in the eyes of others and gives to the infant a bond of love cannot alone be grounds for the State to insist she make the sacrifice. Her suffering is too intimate and personal for the State to insist, without more, upon its own vision of the woman's role, however dominant that vision has been in the course of our history and our culture. The destiny of the woman must be shaped to a large extent on her own conception of her spiritual imperatives and her place in society. . . .

III

[In Section III, the Court stresses the importance of heeding stare decisis in reviewing *Roe,* and discusses factors that suggest that a precedent might be overruled.]

IV

From what we have said so far it follows that it is a constitutional liberty of the woman to have some freedom to terminate her pregnancy. We conclude that the basic decision in *Roe* was based on a constitutional analysis which we cannot now repudiate. The woman's liberty is not so unlimited, however, that from the outset the State cannot show its concern for the life of the unborn, and at a later point in fetal development the State's interest in life has sufficient force so that the right of the woman to terminate the pregnancy can be restricted.

That brings us, of course, to the point where much criticism has been directed at *Roe,* a criticism that always inheres when the Court draws a specific rule from what in the Constitution is but a general standard. We conclude, however, that the urgent claims of the woman to retain the ultimate control over her destiny and her body, claims implicit in the meaning of liberty, require us to perform that function. Liberty must not be extinguished for want of a line that is clear. And it falls to us to give some real substance to the woman's liberty to determine whether to carry her pregnancy to full term. We conclude the line should be drawn at viability, so that before that time the woman has a right to choose to terminate her pregnancy. . . .

. . . Consistent with other constitutional norms, legislatures may draw lines which appear arbitrary without the necessity of offering a justification. But courts may not. We must justify the lines we draw. And there is no line other than viability which is more workable. To be sure . . . there may be some medical developments that affect the precise point of viability, but this is an imprecision within tolerable limits given that the medical community and all those who must apply its discoveries will continue to explore the matter. The viability line also has, as a practical matter, an element of fairness. In some broad sense it might be said that a woman who fails to act before viability has consented to the State's intervention on behalf of the developing child.

The woman's right to terminate her pregnancy before viability is the most central principle of Roe v. Wade. It is a rule of law and a component of liberty we cannot renounce. . . .

Yet it must be remembered that Roe v. Wade speaks with clarity in establishing not only the woman's liberty but also the State's "important and legitimate interest in potential life." That portion of the decision in *Roe* has been given too little acknowledgment and implementation by the Court in its subsequent cases. Those cases decided that any regulation touching upon the abortion decision must survive strict scrutiny, to be sustained only if drawn in narrow terms to further a compelling state interest. Not all of the cases decided under that formulation can be reconciled with the holding in *Roe* itself that the State has legitimate interests in the health of the woman and in protecting the potential life within her. In resolving this tension, we choose to rely upon *Roe,* as against the later cases.

Roe established a trimester framework to govern abortion regulations. Under this elaborate but rigid construct, almost no regulation at all is permitted during the first trimester of pregnancy; regulations designed to protect the woman's health, but not to further the State's interest in potential life, are permitted during the second trimester; and during the third trimester, when the fetus is viable, prohibitions are permitted provided the life or health of the mother is not at stake. Most of our cases since *Roe* have involved the application of rules derived from the trimester framework.

The trimester framework no doubt was erected to ensure that the woman's right to choose not become so subordinate to the State's interest in promoting fetal life that her choice exists in theory but not in fact. We do not agree, however, that the trimester approach is necessary to accomplish this objective. A framework of this rigidity was unnecessary and in its later interpretation sometimes contradicted the State's permissible exercise of its powers.

Though the woman has a right to choose to terminate or continue her pregnancy before viability, it does not at all follow that the State is prohibited from taking steps to ensure that this choice is thoughtful and informed. Even in the earliest stages of pregnancy, the State may enact rules and regulations designed to encourage her to know that there are philosophic and social arguments of great weight that can be brought to bear in favor of continuing the pregnancy to full term and that there are procedures and institutions to allow adoption of unwanted children as well as a certain degree of state assistance if the mother chooses to raise the child herself. "The Constitution does not forbid a State or city, pursuant to democratic processes, from expressing a preference for normal childbirth." It follows that States are free to enact laws to provide a reasonable framework for a woman to make a decision that has such profound and lasting meaning. This, too, we find consistent with *Roe*'s central premises, and indeed the inevitable consequence of our holding that the State has an interest in protecting the life of the unborn.

We reject the trimester framework, which we do not consider to be part of the essential holding of *Roe.* Measures aimed at ensuring that a woman's choice contemplates the consequences for the fetus do not necessarily interfere with the right recognized in *Roe,* although those measures have been found to be inconsistent with the rigid trimester framework announced in that case. A logical reading of the central holding in *Roe* itself, and a necessary reconciliation of the liberty of the woman and the interest of the State in promoting prenatal life, require, in our view, that we abandon the trimester framework as a rigid prohibition on all previability regulation aimed at the protection of fetal life. The trimester framework suffers from these basic flaws: in its formulation it misconceives the nature of the pregnant woman's interest; and in practice it undervalues the State's interest in potential life, as recognized in *Roe.* . . .

Roe v. Wade was express in its recognition of the State's "important and legitimate interests in preserving and protecting the health of the pregnant woman [and] in protecting the potentiality of human life." The trimester framework, however, does not fulfill *Roe*'s own promise that the State has an interest in protecting fetal life or potential life. *Roe* began the contradiction by using the trimester framework to forbid any regulation of abortion designed to advance that interest before viability. Before viability, *Roe* and subsequent cases treat all governmental attempts to influence a woman's decision on behalf of the potential life within her as unwarranted. This treatment is, in our judgment, incompatible with the recognition that there is a substantial state interest in potential life throughout pregnancy.

The very notion that the State has a substantial interest in potential life leads to the conclusion that not all regulations must be deemed unwarranted. Not all burdens on the right to decide whether to terminate a pregnancy will be undue. In our view, the undue burden standard is the appropriate means of reconciling the State's interest with the woman's constitutionally protected liberty.

The concept of an undue burden has been utilized by the Court as well as individual Members of the Court, including two of us, in ways that could be considered inconsistent. Because we set forth a standard of general application to which we intend to adhere, it is important to clarify what is meant by an undue burden.

A finding of an undue burden is a shorthand for the conclusion that a state regulation has the purpose or effect of placing a substantial obstacle in the path of a woman seeking an abortion of a nonviable fetus. A statute with this purpose is invalid because the means chosen by the State to further the interest in potential life must be calculated to inform the woman's free choice, not hinder it. And a statute which, while furthering the interest in potential life or some other valid state interest, has the effect of placing a substantial obstacle in the path of a woman's choice cannot be considered a permissible means of serving its legitimate ends. To the extent that the opinions of the Court or of individual Justices use the undue burden standard in a manner that is inconsistent with this analysis, we set out what in our view should be the controlling standard. In our considered judgment, an undue burden is an unconstitutional burden. Understood another way, we answer the question, left open in previous opinions discussing the undue burden formulation, whether a law designed to further the State's interest in fetal life which imposes an undue burden on the woman's decision before fetal viability could be constitutional. The answer is no.

Some guiding principles should emerge. What is at stake is the woman's right to make the ultimate decision, not a right to be insulated from all others in doing so. Regulations which do no more than create a structural mechanism by which the State, or the parent or guardian of a minor, may express profound respect for the life of the unborn are permitted, if they are not a substantial obstacle to the woman's exercise of the right to choose. Unless it has that effect on her right of choice, a state measure designed to persuade her to choose childbirth over abortion will be upheld if reasonably related to that goal. Regulations designed to foster the health of a woman seeking an abortion are valid if they do not constitute an undue burden. . . .

. . . We give this summary [of the undue burden test]:

(a)　To protect the central right recognized by Roe v. Wade while at the same time accommodating the State's profound interest in potential life, we will employ the undue burden analysis as explained in this opinion. An undue burden exists, and therefore a provision of law is invalid, if its purpose or effect is to place a substantial obstacle in the path of a woman seeking an abortion before the fetus attains viability.

(b)   We reject the rigid trimester framework of Roe v. Wade. To promote the State's profound interest in potential life, throughout pregnancy the State may take measures to ensure that the woman's choice is informed, and measures designed to advance this interest will not be invalidated as long as their purpose is to persuade the woman to choose childbirth over abortion. These measures must not be an undue burden on the right.

(c)   As with any medical procedure, the State may enact regulations to further the health or safety of a woman seeking an abortion. Unnecessary health regulations that have the purpose or effect of presenting a substantial obstacle to a woman seeking an abortion impose an undue burden on the right.

(d)   Our adoption of the undue burden analysis does not disturb the central holding of Roe v. Wade, and we reaffirm that holding. Regardless of whether exceptions are made for particular circumstances, a State may not prohibit any woman from making the ultimate decision to terminate her pregnancy before viability.

(e)   We also reaffirm *Roe*'s holding that "subsequent to viability, the State in promoting its interest in the potentiality of human life may, if it chooses, regulate, and even proscribe, abortion except where it is necessary, in appropriate medical judgment, for the preservation of the life or health of the mother." Roe v. Wade.

Justice SCALIA, with whom THE CHIEF JUSTICE, Justice WHITE, and Justice THOMAS join, concurring in the judgment in part and dissenting in part.

. . . The States may, if they wish, permit abortion on demand, but the Constitution does not require them to do so. The permissibility of abortion, and the limitations upon it, are to be resolved like most important questions in our democracy: by citizens trying to persuade one another and then voting. As the Court acknowledges, "where reasonable people disagree the government can adopt one position or the other." The Court is correct in adding the qualification that this "assumes a state of affairs in which the choice does not intrude upon a protected liberty," ibid—but the crucial part of that qualification is the penultimate word. A State's choice between two positions on which reasonable people can disagree is constitutional even when (as is often the case) it intrudes upon a "liberty" in the absolute sense. Laws against bigamy, for example—with which entire societies of reasonable people disagree—intrude upon men and women's liberty to marry and live with one another. But bigamy happens not to be a liberty specially "protected" by the Constitution.

That is, quite simply, the issue in these cases: not whether the power of a woman to abort her unborn child is a "liberty" in the absolute sense; or even whether it is a liberty of great importance to many women. Of course it is both. The issue is whether it is a liberty protected by the Constitution of the United States. I am sure it is not. I reach that conclusion not because of anything so exalted as my views concerning the "concept of existence, of meaning, of the universe, and of the mystery of human life." Rather, I reach it for the same

reason I reach the conclusion that bigamy is not constitutionally protected—
because of two simple facts: (1) the Constitution says absolutely nothing about it,
and (2) the longstanding traditions of American society have permitted it to be
legally proscribed. . . .

Roe's mandate for abortion on demand destroyed the compromises of the
past, rendered compromise impossible for the future, and required the entire
issue to be resolved uniformly, at the national level. . . .

There is a poignant aspect to today's opinion. Its length, and what might be
called its epic tone, suggest that its authors believe they are bringing to an end a
troublesome era in the history of our Nation and of our Court. "It is the
dimension" of authority, they say, to "call the contending sides of national
controversy to end their national division by accepting a common mandate
rooted in the Constitution."

There comes vividly to mind a portrait by Emanuel Leutze that hangs in the
Harvard Law School: Roger Brooke Taney, painted in 1859, the 82d year of his
life, the 24th of his Chief Justiceship, the second after his opinion in *Dred Scott*.
He is all in black, sitting in a shadowed red armchair, left hand resting upon a
pad of paper in his lap, right hand hanging limply, almost lifelessly, beside the
inner arm of the chair. He sits facing the viewer and staring straight out. There
seems to be on his face, and in his deep-set eyes, an expression of profound
sadness and disillusionment. Perhaps he always looked that way, even when
dwelling upon the happiest of thoughts. But those of us who know how the
lustre of his great Chief Justiceship came to be eclipsed by *Dred Scott* cannot
help believing that he had that case—its already apparent consequences for
the Court and its soon-to-be-played-out consequences for the Nation—burning
on his mind. I expect that two years earlier he, too, had thought himself "calling
the contending sides of national controversy to end their national division by
accepting a common mandate rooted in the Constitution."

It is no more realistic for us in this litigation, than it was for him in that, to
think that an issue of the sort they both involved—an issue involving life and
death, freedom and subjugation—can be "speedily and finally settled" by the
Supreme Court, as President James Buchanan in his inaugural address said the
issue of slavery in the territories would be. Quite to the contrary, by foreclosing
all democratic outlet for the deep passions this issue arouses, by banishing the
issue from the political forum that gives all participants, even the losers, the
satisfaction of a fair hearing and an honest fight, by continuing the imposition of
a rigid national rule instead of allowing for regional differences, the Court
merely prolongs and intensifies the anguish.

We should get out of this area, where we have no right to be, and where we
do neither ourselves nor the country any good by remaining.

NOTES AND QUESTIONS

1. *Casey's effect on the holding in* Roe.   In *Casey*, the Court announces that it
is upholding three parts of the "essential holding" in *Roe*. What are those parts?
What part of *Roe* does not survive *Casey*?

2. *"Undue burden" test.*   In Part IV of *Casey*, Justice O'Connor (joined by
Justices Kennedy and Souter) describes a "finding of an undue burden" as "a

shorthand for the conclusion that a state regulation has the purpose or effect of placing a substantial obstacle in the path of a woman seeking an abortion of a nonviable fetus." Does the summary of the undue burden test in Part IV provide practical guidelines for legislators attempting to regulate abortion and for lower courts entertaining disputes about abortion statutes? Is there likely to be agreement about what constitutes "a substantial obstacle in the path of a woman seeking an abortion" before viability? Might the undue burden test be open to abuse by those anxious to effect their view of the state's proper response to abortion?

In Part V of the decision (not printed supra), Justices O'Connor, Kennedy, and Souter[9] analyzed the separate provisions of the Pennsylvania statute at stake in *Casey*. The Justices concluded that the statutory definition of medical emergency placed no undue burdens on the right to abortion. The state statute defined the term as a "condition which, on the basis of the physician's good faith clinical judgment, so complicates the medical condition of a pregnant woman as to necessitate the immediate abortion of her pregnancy to avert her death or for which a delay will create serious risk of substantial and irreversible impairment of a major bodily function." 505 U.S. at 879. The decision then concluded that it was not an undue burden for the state to require a woman seeking an abortion to be informed about "the procedure, the health risks of the abortion and of childbirth, and the 'probable gestational age of the unborn child.'" Id. at 881. Moreover, the Justices opined that it was not an undue burden for the pregnant woman to be provided with information about the fetus, medical help for childbirth, support from the father, and the option of adoption. In addition the Justices concluded that the state may require that a woman wait at least 24 hours after receiving such information before having an abortion; that a one-parent consent requirement for a minor seeking an abortion is constitutional as long as the statute also provides for a judicial bypass option;[10] and that the record keeping and reporting provisions of the statute were constitutional with the exception of that requiring a married woman to give a "'reason for failure to provide notices' to her husband." Id. at 901. The Court refused to uphold the provision of the Pennsylvania statute that required a married woman seeking an abortion to notify her husband. The plurality explained:

> The limited research that has been conducted with respect to notifying one's husband about an abortion, although involving samples too small to be representative, also supports the District Court's findings of fact. The vast majority of women notify their male partners of their decision to obtain an abortion. In many cases in which married women do not notify their husbands, the pregnancy is the result of an extramarital affair. Where the husband is the father, the primary reason women do not notify their husbands is that the

---

9. Justice Stevens joined Justices O'Connor, Kennedy, and Souter in Part V-E (upholding the state's record keeping and reporting requirements except those linked with spousal notification).

10. The judicial bypass option gives a pregnant girl wanting an abortion (but not wanting to inform her parents of the pregnancy and/or not able to obtain a consent from a parent) the opportunity to appear before a judge. If the judge finds the girl adequately mature to make the abortion decision for herself or if an abortion is deemed to be in the best interests of an immature girl, the abortion can proceed without parental notification or consent. See Bellotti v. Baird, 443 U.S. 622 (1979).

husband and wife are experiencing marital difficulties, often accompanied by incidents of violence.

This information and the District Court's findings reinforce what common sense would suggest. In well-functioning marriages, spouses discuss important intimate decisions such as whether to bear a child. But there are millions of women in this country who are the victims of regular physical and psychological abuse at the hands of their husbands. Should these women become pregnant, they may have very good reasons for not wishing to inform their husbands of their decision to obtain an abortion. Many may have justifiable fears of physical abuse, but may be no less fearful of the consequences of reporting prior abuse to the Commonwealth of Pennsylvania. Many may have a reasonable fear that notifying their husbands will provoke further instances of child abuse; these women are not exempt from [the statute's] notification requirement.

505 U.S. at 892.

As some have suggested, the Court's concern about physical abuse seems hard to harmonize with its dismissal of the financial and travel burdens associated with a waiting period especially insofar as the latter burdens may be especially onerous for poor women, rural women, and women of color.

3. *Justice Rehnquist's opinion.*   Then-chief Justice Rehnquist (joined by Justices White, Scalia, and Thomas), concurred in the judgment in part and dissented in part. These Justices wanted to overrule *Roe.*

We believe that *Roe* was wrongly decided, and that it can and should be overruled consistently with our traditional approach to stare decisis in constitutional cases. We would adopt the approach of the plurality in Webster v. Reproductive Health Services, 492 U.S. 490 (1989), and uphold the challenged provisions of the Pennsylvania statute in their entirety.

505 U.S. at 944. Justice Rehnquist and those who joined his opinion would have left the regulation of abortion entirely in the hands of the states.

4. *Abandoning trimester scheme.*   *Casey* rejects the trimester scheme on which the Court relied in *Roe* in favor of a bipartite scheme that focuses on the point of viability. What might justify replacing the scheme delineated in *Roe* with that delineated in *Casey*? The Court asserts that the line dividing a nonviable fetus from a viable fetus is the most "workable" line to focus on in regulating abortion. Does the Court provide other reasons for its choice? What other reasons do you think might have motivated the Court to focus on viability rather than on the trimesters of gestation in constructing a constitutional framework for regulating abortion?

5. *Justice Scalia's opinion.*   Justice Scalia contends that the abortion debate should not be resolved by the judiciary. Who does he believe might better resolve it?

6. *Stenberg v. Carhart.*   Eight years after *Casey,* in Stenberg v. Carhart, 530 U.S. 914 (2000), a majority of the Court relied on the undue burden test in a case involving a so-called "partial birth abortion" statute. Nebraska had passed a law that banned abortions "in which the person performing the abortion partially delivers vaginally a living unborn child before killing the unborn child and completing the delivery." 530 U.S. at 942. The Court held the statute

unconstitutional on two grounds. First, the Nebraska statute provided no exception for safeguarding the health of the mother. Second, relying on the standard defined in *Casey,* the Court concluded that the statute placed an "undue burden" on a woman's right to choose a second trimester abortion. That conclusion followed from the Court's determination that the state's distinction between two types of abortions—"dilation and evacuation" and "dilation and extraction"—and the state's correlative claim that only D&X abortions were included in the category of "partial birth abortions" were not supported by medical evidence.

7. *Amendments to the "Texas Women's Right to Know Act."*   Amendments to the "Texas Women's Right to Know Act," signed into law in 2011, require abortion providers to perform an ultrasound on any woman requesting an abortion. The ultrasound must be done at least 24 hours before the abortion procedure. Further, the provider must show the ultrasound to the pregnant woman and must have her listen to a fetal heartbeat, and the woman must be given an explanation of the ultrasound image. Sherry F. Colb, Some Reflections on the Texas Pre-Abortion Ultrasound Law, a Year After Its Passage, Part One (May 30, 2012) and Part Two (June 6, 2012), Verdict, available at verdict.justia.com. Abortion providers tested the law in federal court. The Fifth Circuit ruled against them. Texas Medical Providers Performing Abortion Services v. Lakey, No. 11-50814 (5th Cir. Jan. 10, 2012) (overturning injunctive relief provided by district court). Colb suggests that the Texas provision mandating that a pregnant woman who wants an abortion be shown an ultrasound of the fetus differs from the informed consent provision upheld in Planned Parenthood v. Casey. She suggests that the ultrasound images that must be shown to pregnant women under the Texas law are far more powerful than written or verbalized information about a fetus and could "traumatize a pregnant woman and prove detrimental to her future mental health." Id., Part Two. Is the Texas ultrasound provision unconstitutional under *Casey's* undue burden test?

8. *Health care reform and abortion.*   Passage of the Patient Protection and Affordable Care Act was almost stymied by abortion opponents, anxious to preclude proposed new state insurance exchanges from offering policies covering abortion. The compromise reached at the time of the law's promulgation resulted in a complicated plan that separates individual premium payments from funds provided by government. In 2011, a bill introduced in the House ("No Taxpayer Funding for Abortion," H.R. 3 (112th Cong. 2d Sess.) would have prohibited federal funds from subsidizing any policies covering abortion, even beyond those offered by state exchanges. A New York Times editorial decried the effort as one that would have resulted in giving government authority over "a medical legal procedure." Editorial, The New Abortion Wars: A Highly Intrusive Federal Bill, N.Y. Times, Jan. 30, 2011, www.nytimes.com.

In 2012, the House considered and rejected a bill that would have prohibited abortions aimed at selecting a baby's gender or race. Prenatal Nondiscrimination Act (PRENDA) of 2012, H.R. 3541 (112th Cong. 2d Sess.). (Passage required two-thirds of those voting.) Open Congress, available at http://www.opencongress.org/bill/112-h3541/show. The bill, referred to as the "Susan B. Anthony and Frederick Douglass Prenatal Nondiscrimination Act of 2011, imposed criminal penalties on any health care professional who "knowingly . . . solicits or accepts funds for the performance of a sex-selection abortion or a race-selection abortion . . . or attempts to do so." Open Congress, available at http://www.opencongress.org/bill/112-h3541/text.

9. *Federal statute prohibiting "partial birth abortions."*   In late 2003, Congress passed a statute prohibiting "partial birth abortions." The statute contains an exception to save the life of the mother but no exception to safeguard the mother's health. The statute was upheld in Gonzales v. Carhart (*Carhart II*), 550 U.S. 124 (2007).

Gonzales v. Carhart (Carhart II)
550 U.S. 124 (2007)

Opinion by Mr. Justice KENNEDY.

These cases require us to consider the validity of the Partial-Birth Abortion Ban Act of 2003 (Act), a federal statute regulating abortion procedures. In recitations preceding its operative provisions the Act refers to the Court's opinion in *Stenberg v. Carhart,* 530 U.S. 914, which also addressed the subject of abortion procedures used in the later stages of pregnancy. Compared to the state statute at issue in *Stenberg,* the Act is more specific concerning the instances to which it applies and in this respect more precise in its coverage. We conclude the Act should be sustained against the objections lodged by the broad, facial attack brought against it.

[The Eighth Circuit (Gonzales v. Carhart) and the Ninth Circuit (Gonzales v. Planned Parenthood) affirmed district court decisions that enjoined enforcement of the Act. . . .]

I . . .

Between 85 and 90 percent of the approximately 1.3 million abortions performed each year in the United States take place in the first three months of pregnancy, which is to say in the first trimester. The most common first-trimester abortion method is vacuum aspiration (otherwise known as suction curettage) in which the physician vacuums out the embryonic tissue. . . .

Of the remaining abortions that take place each year, most occur in the second trimester. The surgical procedure referred to as "dilation and evacuation" or "D&E" is the usual abortion method in this trimester. . . .

[In order to perform a D&E,] a doctor must first dilate the cervix at least to the extent needed to insert surgical instruments into the uterus and to maneuver them to evacuate the fetus. . . .

The abortion procedure that was the impetus for the numerous bans on "partial-birth abortion," including the Act, is a variation of this standard D&E. The medical community has not reached unanimity on the appropriate name for this D&E variation. It has been referred to as "intact D&E," "dilation and extraction" (D&X), and "intact D&X." [Others, in particular those opposing the right to abortion, refer to the procedure as a "partial-birth abortion."] . . . . For discussion purposes this D&E variation will be referred to as intact D&E. The main difference between the two procedures is that in intact D&E a doctor extracts the fetus intact or largely intact with only a few passes [into the woman's uterus with the forceps]. . . .

In an intact D&E procedure the doctor extracts the fetus in a way conducive to pulling out its entire body, instead of ripping it apart. . . .

[In 2000, three years before the Act was passed, the Court invalidated a Nebraska statute that prohibited "partial-birth abortions." Stenberg v. Carhart, 530 U.S. 914 (*Carhart I*). The Court found the Nebraska statute unconstitutional because it provided no exception for safeguarding the health of the mother and because, relying on the standard defined in *Casey*, the statute placed an "undue burden" on a woman's right to choose a second trimester abortion. Another reason for invalidating the Nebraska statute followed from the Court's determination that the state's distinction between two types of abortions—referred to as "dilation and evacuation" and "dilation and extraction"—and the state's correlative claim that only the second sort of abortion was included in the category of "partial birth abortion" were not supported by medical evidence.]

The Act [at issue here] responded to *Stenberg* in two ways. First, Congress made factual findings. Congress determined that this Court in *Stenberg* "was required to accept the very questionable findings issued by the district court judge," but that Congress was "not bound to accept the same factual findings." Congress found, among other things, that "[a] moral, medical, and ethical consensus exists that the practice of performing a partial-birth abortion . . . is a gruesome and inhumane procedure that is never medically necessary and should be prohibited."

Second, and more relevant here, the Act's language differs from that of the Nebraska statute struck down in *Stenberg*.

[Under the Act, physicians who violate it may be fined or imprisoned for not more than two years or both.] . . .

The District Court in *Carhart* concluded the Act was unconstitutional for two reasons. First, it determined the Act was unconstitutional because it lacked an exception allowing the procedure where necessary for the health of the mother. Second, the District Court found the Act deficient because it covered not merely intact D&E but also certain other D&Es.

The Court of Appeals for the Eighth Circuit [affirmed]. . . .

The District Court in *Planned Parenthood* concluded the Act was unconstitutional "because it (1) pose[d] an undue burden on a woman's ability to choose a second trimester abortion; (2) [was] unconstitutionally vague; and (3) require[d] a health exception as set forth by . . . *Stenberg*."

The Court of Appeals for the Ninth Circuit agreed. . . .

II. . . .

The principles set forth in the joint opinion in *Casey* did not find support from all those who join the instant opinion. Whatever one's views concerning the *Casey* joint opinion, it is evident a premise central to its conclusion—that the government has a legitimate and substantial interest in preserving and promoting fetal life—would be repudiated were the Court now to affirm the judgments of the Courts of Appeals. . . .

We assume the following principles for the purposes of this opinion. Before viability, a State "may not prohibit any woman from making the ultimate decision to terminate her pregnancy." It also may not impose upon this right an undue burden, which exists if a regulation's "purpose or effect is to place a substantial obstacle in the path of a woman seeking an abortion before the fetus attains viability." On the other hand, "[r]egulations which do no more than create a structural mechanism by which the State, or the parent or guardian of a minor, may express profound respect for the life of the unborn are permitted, if they are not a substantial obstacle to the woman's exercise of the right to choose." *Casey,* in short, struck a balance. The balance was central to its holding. We now apply its standard to the cases at bar.

III. . . .

We begin with a determination of the Act's operation and effect. A straightforward reading of the Act's text demonstrates its purpose and the scope of its provisions: It regulates and proscribes, with exceptions or qualifications to be discussed, performing the intact D&E procedure. . . .

The Act punishes "knowingly perform[ing]" a "partial-birth abortion." It defines the unlawful abortion in explicit terms.

First, the person performing the abortion must "vaginally delive[r] a living fetus." The Act does not restrict an abortion procedure involving the delivery of an expired fetus. The Act, furthermore, is inapplicable to abortions that do not involve vaginal delivery (for instance, hysterotomy or hysterectomy). The Act does apply both previability and postviability because, by common understanding and scientific terminology, a fetus is a living organism while within the womb, whether or not it is viable outside the womb. We do not understand this point to be contested by the parties.

Second, the Act's definition of partial-birth abortion requires the fetus to be delivered "until, in the case of a head-first presentation, the entire fetal head is outside the body of the mother, or, in the case of breech presentation, any part of the fetal trunk past the navel is outside the body of the mother." The Attorney General concedes, and we agree, that if an abortion procedure does not involve the delivery of a living fetus to one of these "anatomical 'land-marks'"—where, depending on the presentation, either the fetal head or the fetal trunk past the navel is outside the body of the mother—the prohibitions of the Act do not apply.

Third, to fall within the Act, a doctor must perform an "overt act, other than completion of delivery, that kills the partially delivered living fetus." . . .

Respondents contend the [language of the Act is indeterminate], and they thus argue the Act is unconstitutionally vague on its face. . . .

The Act provides doctors "of ordinary intelligence a reasonable opportunity to know what is prohibited." Indeed, it sets forth "relatively clear guidelines as to prohibited conduct" and provides "objective criteria" to evaluate whether a doctor has performed a prohibited procedure. Unlike the statutory language in *Stenberg* that prohibited the delivery of a "'substantial portion'" of the fetus— where a doctor might question how much of the fetus is a substantial portion— the Act defines the line between potentially criminal conduct on the one hand and lawful abortion on the other. Doctors performing D&E will know that if they do not deliver a living fetus to an anatomical landmark they will not face criminal liability. [Thus the Court concludes that the Act is not "unconstitutionally vague on its face."]

We next determine whether the Act imposes an undue burden, as a facial matter, because its restrictions on second-trimester abortions are too broad. A review of the statutory text discloses the limits of its reach. The Act prohibits intact D&E; and, notwithstanding respondents' arguments, it does not prohibit the D&E procedure in which the fetus is removed in parts.

The Act prohibits a doctor from intentionally performing an intact D&E. The dual prohibitions of the Act, both of which are necessary for criminal liability, correspond with the steps generally undertaken during this type of procedure. . . .

. . . The statute [struck down in] *Stenberg* [differs from the Act in that it] prohibited "'deliberately and intentionally delivering into the vagina a living unborn child, or a substantial portion thereof, for the purpose of performing a procedure that the person performing such procedure knows will kill the unborn child and does kill the unborn child.'" The Court concluded that this statute encompassed D&E because "D&E will often involve a physician pulling a 'substantial portion' of a still living fetus, say, an arm or leg, into the vagina prior to the death of the fetus." . . .

Congress, it is apparent, responded to these concerns because the Act departs in material ways from the statute in *Stenberg*. It adopts the phrase "delivers a living fetus, instead of 'delivering . . . a living unborn child, or a substantial portion thereof.'" The Act's language, unlike the statute in *Stenberg*, expresses the usual meaning of "deliver" when used in connection with "fetus," namely, extraction of an entire fetus rather than removal of fetal pieces. The Act thus displaces the interpretation of "delivering" dictated by the Nebraska statute's reference to a "substantial portion" of the fetus. *Stenberg*. . . .

The identification of specific anatomical landmarks to which the fetus must be partially delivered also differentiates the Act from the statute at issue in *Stenberg*. . . . The Act's anatomical landmarks . . . clarify that the removal of a small portion of the fetus is not prohibited. The landmarks also require the fetus to be delivered so that it is partially "outside the body of the mother." To come within the ambit of the Nebraska statute, on the other hand, a substantial portion of the fetus only had to be delivered into the vagina; no part of the fetus had to be outside the body of the mother before a doctor could face criminal sanctions. . . .

[Moreover, the Act's intent requirements] preclude liability from attaching to an accidental intact D&E. If a doctor's intent at the outset is to perform a D&E in which the fetus would not be delivered to either of the Act's anatomical landmarks, but the fetus nonetheless is delivered past one of those points, the requisite and prohibited scienter is not present. . . .

The evidence also supports a legislative determination that an intact delivery is almost always a conscious choice rather than a happenstance, [and the] evidence belies any claim that a standard D&E cannot be performed without intending or foreseeing an intact D&E. . . .

Respondents have not shown that requiring doctors to intend dismemberment before delivery to an anatomical landmark will prohibit the vast majority of D&E abortions. The Act, then, cannot be held invalid on its face on these grounds.

IV. . . .

The question is whether the Act, measured by its text in this facial attack, imposes a substantial obstacle to late-term, but previability, abortions. The Act does not on its face impose a substantial obstacle, and we reject this further facial challenge to its validity.

The Act proscribes a method of abortion in which a fetus is killed just inches before completion of the birth process. . . .

The Act's ban on abortions that involve partial delivery of a living fetus furthers the Government's objectives. No one would dispute that, for many, D&E is a procedure itself laden with the power to devalue human life. Congress could nonetheless conclude that the type of abortion proscribed by the Act requires specific regulation because it implicates additional ethical and moral concerns that justify a special prohibition. Congress determined that the abortion methods it proscribed had a "disturbing similarity to the killing of a newborn infant," and thus it was concerned with "draw[ing] a bright line that clearly distinguishes abortion and infanticide." The Court has in the past confirmed the validity of drawing boundaries to prevent certain practices that extinguish life and are close to actions that are condemned. Glucksberg found reasonable the State's "fear that permitting assisted suicide will start it down the path to voluntary and perhaps even involuntary euthanasia."

Respect for human life finds an ultimate expression in the bond of love the mother has for her child. The Act recognizes this reality as well. Whether to have an abortion requires a difficult and painful moral decision. While we find no reliable data to measure the phenomenon, it seems unexceptionable to conclude some women come to regret their choice to abort the infant life they once created and sustained. Severe depression and loss of esteem can follow. . . .

It is, however, precisely this lack of information concerning the way in which the fetus will be killed that is of legitimate concern to the State. . . . The State has an interest in ensuring so grave a choice is well informed. It is self-evident that a mother who comes to regret her choice to abort must struggle with grief more anguished and sorrow more profound when she learns, only after the event, what she once did not know: that she allowed a doctor to pierce the skull and vacuum the fast-developing brain of her unborn child, a child assuming the human form.

It is a reasonable inference that a necessary effect of the regulation and the knowledge it conveys will be to encourage some women to carry the infant to full term, thus reducing the absolute number of late-term abortions. The medical profession, furthermore, may find different and less shocking methods to abort the fetus in the second trimester, thereby accommodating legislative demand. The State's interest in respect for life is advanced by the dialogue that better informs the political and legal systems, the medical profession, expectant mothers, and society as a whole of the consequences that follow from a decision to elect a late-term abortion. . . .

The Act's furtherance of legitimate government interests bears upon, but does not resolve, the next question: whether the Act has the effect of imposing an unconstitutional burden on the abortion right because it does not allow use of the barred procedure where "necessary, in appropriate medical judgment, for [the] preservation of the . . . health of the mother." The prohibition in the

Act would be unconstitutional, under precedents we here assume to be controlling, if it "subject[ed] [women] to significant health risks" . . .

There is documented medical disagreement whether the Act's prohibition would ever impose significant health risks on women. . . .

The question becomes whether the Act can stand when this medical uncertainty persists. The Court's precedents instruct that the Act can survive this facial attack. The Court has given state and federal legislatures wide discretion to pass legislation in areas where there is medical and scientific uncertainty. . . .

Medical uncertainty does not foreclose the exercise of legislative power in the abortion context any more than it does in other contexts. The medical uncertainty over whether the Act's prohibition creates significant health risks provides a sufficient basis to conclude in this facial attack that the Act does not impose an undue burden.

The conclusion that the Act does not impose an undue burden is supported by other considerations. Alternatives are available to the prohibited procedure. As we have noted, the Act does not proscribe D&E. . . . If the intact D&E procedure is truly necessary in some circumstances, it appears likely an injection that kills the fetus is an alternative under the Act that allows the doctor to perform the procedure. . . .

On the other hand, relying on the Court's opinion in *Stenberg*, respondents contend that an abortion regulation must contain a health exception "if 'substantial medical authority supports the proposition that banning a particular procedure could endanger women's health.'" As illustrated by respondents' arguments and the decisions of the Courts of Appeals, *Stenberg* has been interpreted to leave no margin of error for legislatures to act in the face of medical uncertainty. . . .

. . . The Act is not invalid on its face where there is uncertainty over whether the barred procedure is ever necessary to preserve a woman's health, given the availability of other abortion procedures that are considered to be safe alternatives.

V

The considerations we have discussed support our further determination that these facial attacks should not have been entertained in the first instance. In these circumstances the proper means to consider exceptions is by as-applied challenge. The Government has acknowledged that preenforcement, as-applied challenges to the Act can be maintained. This is the proper manner to protect the health of the woman if it can be shown that in discrete and well-defined instances a particular condition has or is likely to occur in which the procedure prohibited by the Act must be used. In an as-applied challenge the nature of the medical risk can be better quantified and balanced than in a facial attack. . . .

The Act is open to a proper as-applied challenge in a discrete case. Respondents have not demonstrated that the Act, as a facial matter, is void for vagueness, or that it imposes an undue burden on a woman's right to abortion based on its overbreadth or lack of a health exception. For these reasons the judgments of the Courts of Appeals for the Eighth and Ninth Circuits are reversed.

Justice GINSBURG, with whom Justice STEVENS, Justice SOUTER, and Justice BREYER join, dissenting.

... Seven years ago, in Stenberg v. Carhart, the Court invalidated a Nebraska statute criminalizing the performance of a medical procedure that, in the political arena, has been dubbed "partial-birth abortion."[1] With fidelity to the *Roe-Casey* line of precedent, the Court held the Nebraska statute unconstitutional in part because it lacked the requisite protection for the preservation of a woman's health.

Today's decision is alarming. It refuses to take *Casey* and *Stenberg* seriously. It tolerates, indeed applauds, federal intervention to ban nationwide a procedure found necessary and proper in certain cases by the American College of Obstetricians and Gynecologists (ACOG). It blurs the line, firmly drawn in *Casey*, between previability and postviability abortions. And, for the first time since *Roe*, the Court blesses a prohibition with no exception safeguarding a woman's health.

I dissent from the Court's disposition. Retreating from prior rulings that abortion restrictions cannot be imposed absent an exception safeguarding a woman's health, the Court upholds an Act that surely would not survive under the close scrutiny that previously attended state-decreed limitations on a woman's reproductive choices.

I

... In *Stenberg*, we expressly held that a statute banning intact D&E was unconstitutional in part because it lacked a health exception. We noted that there existed a "division of medical opinion" about the relative safety of intact D&E, but we made clear that as long as "substantial medical authority supports the proposition that banning a particular abortion procedure could endanger women's health," a health exception is required. [W]e reasoned, division in medical opinion "at most means uncertainty, a factor that signals the presence of risk, not its absence." [A] statute that altogether forbids [intact D&E] ... consequently must contain a health exception."]

[In section I(B), Justice Ginsburg takes issue with a number of the "congressional findings" on which Congress based the Act.]

II

The Court offers flimsy and transparent justifications for upholding a nationwide ban on intact D&E sans any exception to safeguard a women's health. ...

Ultimately, the Court admits that "moral concerns" are at work, concerns that could yield prohibitions on any abortion. ...

Revealing in this regard, the Court invokes an antiabortion shibboleth for which it concededly has no reliable evidence: Women who have abortions come to regret their choices, and consequently suffer from "[s]evere depression and loss of esteem." Because of women's fragile emotional state and because of the "bond of love the mother has for her child," the Court worries, doctors may

---

1. The term "partial-birth abortion" is neither recognized in the medical literature nor used by physicians who perform second-trimester abortions.

withhold information about the nature of the intact D&E procedure. The solution the Court approves, then, is not to require doctors to inform women, accurately and adequately, of the different procedures and their attendant risks. Instead, the Court deprives women of the right to make an autonomous choice, even at the expense of their safety[9]. . . .

In cases on a "woman's liberty to determine whether to [continue] her pregnancy," this Court has identified viability as a critical consideration. . . .

Today, the Court blurs that line, maintaining that "[t]he Act [legitimately] appl[ies] both previability and postviability because . . . a fetus is a living organism while within the womb, whether or not it is viable outside the womb." Instead of drawing the line at viability, the Court refers to Congress' purpose to differentiate "abortion and infanticide" based not on whether a fetus can survive outside the womb, but on where a fetus is anatomically located when a particular medical procedure is performed.

One wonders how long a line that saves no fetus from destruction will hold in face of the Court's "moral concerns." The Court's hostility to the right *Roe* and *Casey* secured is not concealed. Throughout, the opinion refers to obstetrician-gynecologists and surgeons who perform abortions not by the titles of their medical specialties, but by the pejorative label "abortion doctor." A fetus is described as an "unborn child," and as a "baby;" second-trimester, previability abortions are referred to as "late-term;" and the reasoned medical judgments of highly trained doctors are dismissed as "preferences" motivated by "mere convenience." Instead of the heightened scrutiny we have previously applied, the Court determines that a "rational" ground is enough to uphold the Act. And, most troubling, *Casey*'s principles, confirming the continuing vitality of "the essential holding of *Roe*," are merely "assume[d]" for the moment.

III. . . .

Without attempting to distinguish *Stenberg* and earlier decisions, the majority asserts that the Act survives review because respondents have not shown that the ban on intact D&E would be unconstitutional "in a large fraction of relevant cases." But *Casey* makes clear that, in determining whether any restriction poses an undue burden on a "large fraction" of women, the relevant class is not "all women," nor "all pregnant women," nor even all women "seeking abortions." Rather, a provision restricting access to abortion, "must be judged by reference to those [women] for whom it is an actual rather than an irrelevant restriction." Thus the absence of a health exception burdens all women for whom it is relevant—women who, in the judgment of their doctors, require an intact D&E because other procedures would place their health at risk. . . . It makes no sense to conclude that this facial challenge fails because respondents have not shown that a health exception is necessary for a large fraction of second-trimester abortions, including those for which a health exception is unnecessary: The very purpose of a health exception is to protect women in exceptional cases.

---

9. Eliminating or reducing women's reproductive choices is manifestly not a means of protecting them. When safe abortion procedures cease to be an option, many women seek other means to end unwanted or coerced pregnancies.

If there is anything at all redemptive to be said of today's opinion, it is that the Court is not willing to foreclose entirely a constitutional challenge to the Act. "The Act is open," the Court states, "to a proper as-applied challenge in a discrete case." . . .

The Court envisions that in an as-applied challenge, "the nature of the medical risk can be better quantified and balanced." But it should not escape notice that the record already includes hundreds and hundreds of pages of testimony identifying "discrete and well-defined instances" in which recourse to an intact D&E would better protect the health of women with particular conditions. . . .

The Court's allowance only of an "as-applied challenge in a discrete case" jeopardizes women's health and places doctors in an untenable position. Even if courts were able to carve-out exceptions through piecemeal litigation for "discrete and well-defined instances," women whose circumstances have not been anticipated by prior litigation could well be left unprotected. In treating those women, physicians would risk criminal prosecution, conviction, and imprisonment if they exercise their best judgment as to the safest medical procedure for their patients. The Court is thus gravely mistaken to conclude that narrow as-applied challenges are "the proper manner to protect the health of the woman."

IV. . . .

Though today's opinion does not go so far as to discard *Roe* or *Casey,* the Court, differently composed than it was when we last considered a restrictive abortion regulation, is hardly faithful to our earlier invocations of "the rule of law" and the "principles of stare decisis." Congress imposed a ban despite our clear prior holdings that the State cannot proscribe an abortion procedure when its use is necessary to protect a woman's health. Although Congress' findings could not withstand the crucible of trial, the Court defers to the legislative override of our Constitution-based rulings. A decision so at odds with our jurisprudence should not have staying power.

In sum, the notion that the Partial-Birth Abortion Ban Act furthers any legitimate governmental interest is, quite simply, irrational. The Court's defense of the statute provides no saving explanation. In candor, the Act, and the Court's defense of it, cannot be understood as anything other than an effort to chip away at a right declared again and again by this Court—and with increasing comprehension of its centrality to women's lives. When "a statute burdens constitutional rights and all that can be said on its behalf is that it is the vehicle that legislators have chosen for expressing their hostility to those rights, the burden is undue."

NOTES AND QUESTIONS

1. *Distinguishing* Carhart II.   The Fourth Circuit distinguished *Carhart II* and upheld the district court's invalidation of a Virginia statute that criminalized a form of abortion referred to in the statute as a "partial birth infanticide." Richmond Medical Center for Women v. Herring, 527 F.3d 128 (4th Cir. May 20, 2008). But the circuit court, hearing the case en banc in 2009, reversed the holding of the district court that the statute was not constitutional. 570 F.3d 165 (2009).

The Virginia statute at issue defined the illegal act to occur when a fetus (referred to as a "human infant") "(i) has been born alive but who has not been completely extracted or expelled from its mother, and that (ii) does kill such infant, regardless of whether death occurs before or after extraction or expulsion from its mother has been completed." Va. Code Ann. Sec. 18-2-71.1.B. The statute applied to a fetus expelled or extracted from the mother "past its head" or, in the case of a breech presentation, past its navel. A physician and a women's health clinic sued after *Carhart I* and before *Carhart II*. The challenge was based on the statute's failure to safeguard a woman's health (as required in *Carhart I*). The district court and the Fourth Circuit agreed. Then, however, in *Carhart II*, the Supreme Court upheld the federal "partial-birth" abortion ban even though it did not include an exception to protect a woman's health. The Supreme Court remanded *Herring* to the Fourth Circuit for reconsideration in light of *Carhart II*. On remand, the court again invalidated the statute, but on a different ground. The court concluded that the Virginia statute allowed imposition of liability on a physician who did not intend at the outset of an abortion to perform an intact D&E. In the court's view, this conflicted with a "critical" component of the federal Act, as stated by the Supreme Court in *Carhart II*—the "requirement that a doctor intend at the outset to perform an intact D&E." Then, hearing the case en banc, the Fourth Circuit concluded that the facial challenge to the act failed because the Act could not be categorized as "wholly unconstitutional," and an as-applied challenge failed because the plaintiff did not present "sufficiently concrete circumstances in which the as-applied challenge can be resolved." 570 F.3d at 169.

2. *Might* Carhart II *have a chilling effect on the practice of medicine?*   In *Carhart II,* the Supreme Court arguably provided for a physician's judgment to be displaced by congressional judgment. See George J. Annas, The Supreme Court and Abortion Rights, 356 New Eng. J. Med. 2201 (2007).

3. *Perspective on abortion law.*   Despite the continuing, active debate about abortion in the United States, abortions have now been legal for four decades. A majority of women queried by clinics in Washington state did not realize that abortion had not always been legal. Kate Zernike, 30 Years After Abortion Ruling, New Trends but the Old Debate, N.Y. Times, Jan. 20, 2003, at A1. How, if at all, might this be relevant to the law's regulation of abortion?

4. *Compelled medical treatment.*   One might argue that *Carhart II* can be read to support compelled medical treatment of pregnant women (e.g., compelled cesarean section, compelled blood transfusion). Do you think the Court's decision can be used to support forcing a pregnant woman to have a cesarean section, a blood transfusion, or other unwanted care in the name of a fetus's welfare?

5. *Consequences of a "right to health care."*   Would a constitutional "right to health care" in the United States have changed the outcome in *Carhart II?*

CHALLENGING ISSUES: UNDUE BURDEN TEST

Under the "undue burden" test delineated in *Casey,* as interpreted in *Carhart II,* which, if any, of the following limitations on abortion do you think are unconstitutional?

1. A requirement that any pregnant woman seeking an abortion watch a video showing the gestational development of a fetus;
2. A requirement that any pregnant woman seeking an abortion have an ultrasound;
3. A 48-hour waiting period between the provision of state-mandated information about the gestation of fetuses, the availability of adoption services, and other information designed to promote childbirth over abortion; a 72-hour waiting period;
4. A required information counseling session with a doctor, in which information such as that specified in (3) is conveyed.

Jackson Women's Health Org. v. Currier
2012 U.S. Dist. LEXIS 90393
(USDC SD Miss. July 1, 2012)

[The Jackson Women's Health Organization (the only abortion clinic in Mississippi) asked a U.S. district court to enjoin the enforcement of Mississippi House Bill 1390. The law would result in the clinic's being closed because it did not comply with the law's requirement that all doctors doing abortions be licensed in obstetrics and gynecology and have admitting privileges at a hospital.]

OPINION BY: Daniel P. JORDAN III

This case challenging the constitutionality of Mississippi House Bill 1390 ("the Act") is before the Court on Plaintiffs' Motion for Temporary Restraining Order and/or Preliminary Injunction. Plaintiffs initially feared that the Act, which becomes effective today, would require them to close their doors. After Plaintiffs filed their motion, however, the State renewed the Clinic's license, and Defendants have indicated that no criminal prosecutions will be initiated at this time. Thus, much of the original motion is now moot, and the Clinic will be allowed to open regardless of this Order. Unfortunately, that does not end the issue because the State has informed the Court that it will begin enforcing the Act tomorrow by initiating the administrative process to close the Clinic if it does not comply. Plaintiffs therefore argue, among other things, that requiring them to comply with, or defend against, an allegedly unconstitutional statute will still cause irreparable injury.

The Court has considered the parties' arguments and finds Plaintiffs satisfy the requirements for temporary injunctive relief to maintain the status quo until the newly framed issues can be more thoroughly examined. Thus, Plaintiffs' motion is granted to the extent that any enforcement of the Act is enjoined until July 11, 2012, when a hearing will be held to determine, after further briefing by the parties, whether a preliminary injunction should issue. Plaintiffs' motion for a preliminary injunction will remain pending. Finally, as with many TROs, this Order is not intended to offer a full analysis of the issues.

. . . .

III.   ANALYSIS

Though the debate over abortion continues, there exists legal precedent the Court must follow. Applying that law, the Court finds that a TRO should issue.

A.   Substantial Likelihood of Success on the Merits

While "[t]he Fourteenth Amendment protects a woman's right to choose to terminate her pregnancy prior to viability[, g]overnment regulation of abortions is allowed so long as it does not impose an undue burden on a woman's ability to choose." Victoria W. v. Larpenter, 369 F.3d 475, 483 (5th Cir. 2004) (citing Planned Parenthood of Se. Pa. v. Casey, 505 U.S. 833 (1992)). "A state regulation constitutes an undue burden if it 'has the purpose or effect of placing a substantial obstacle in the path of a woman seeking an abortion of a nonviable fetus.'" Id. (quoting Casey, 505 U.S. at 877).

In this case, Plaintiffs have offered evidence—including quotes from significant legislative and executive officers—that the Act's purpose is to eliminate abortions in Mississippi. They likewise submitted evidence that no safety or health concerns motivated its passage. This evidence has not yet been rebutted. Regarding the effect of the Act, JWHO is the only regular provider of abortions in Mississippi, and as of the Act's effective date, JWHO cannot comply with its requirements. To meet the merits prong, Plaintiffs must show substantial likelihood of success, not certainty. Considering Defendants' response to date, Plaintiffs have met that test.

B.   Substantial Threat of Irreparable Injury

. . . .

Though Defendants have now addressed most of Plaintiffs' original concerns, they have not addressed Plaintiffs' point that the mere threat of closing the clinic—which would be accomplished through the administrative proceedings the State has promised to start—is sufficient irreparable injury. Plaintiffs have likewise suggested that requiring the Clinic to defend itself against an allegedly unconstitutional requirement during the state administrative process is itself an irreparable harm.

At this stage, the Court finds Plaintiffs have satisfied the irreparable-injury prong. . . .

C.   Harm Resulting from a Grant of Injunctive Relief and Public Interest

Defendants offer little more than token opposition to Plaintiffs' position on the final two elements necessary to obtain a TRO, generally arguing that the Clinic would remain open during the state administrative proceedings. But as noted above, question exists as to whether exposure to those proceedings and the threat of closure constitutes sufficient injury. See Ingebretsen v. Jackson Pub. Sch. Dist., 88 F.3d 274, 280 (5th Cir. 1996) ("[T]he public interest [is] not disserved by an injunction preventing . . . implementation [of an unconstitutional statute.]"). Defendants will have an opportunity to address the issues as they now exist, but at this time Plaintiffs have carried their burden on these final elements.

IV.   CONCLUSION

As with any TRO, the relief is temporary and subject to reconsideration before a preliminary injunction is issued. But for the foregoing reasons, the Court finds that Plaintiffs' Motion for Temporary Restraining Order And/Or Preliminary Injunction should be granted to the extent that a Temporary Restraining Order will issue. . . .

NOTES AND QUESTIONS

1. *Jackson Women's Health Org.*   Soon after the TRO-decision in *Jackson Women's Health Org.*, supra, the court concluded that the state had "acted to remove most of the threats originally challenged in the Complaint." The state had "renewed JWHO's license" for a year. Jackson Women's Health Org. v. Currier, 2012 U.S. Dist. LEXIS 97272 (USDC SC Miss. July 13, 2012). Yet the court found that an "irreparable injury" continued to exist because of the possibility that defendants could prosecute plaintiffs in the future "for the days of non-compliance that will begin when the Act takes effect." Id. at 14. Moreover, the district court concluded:

> As for the other factors for injunctive relief, the Court finds that there exists a substantial likelihood of success on the merits and that the threatened injury— the closure of the state's only clinic creating a substantial obstacle to the right to choose—outweighs any harm that will result if the injunction is granted. This is especially true in light of the Defendants' promises that they have no intention to pursue civil or criminal sanctions at this time. Finally, the grant of an injunction will not disserve the public interest, an element that is generally met when an injunction is designed to avoid constitutional deprivations. A preliminary injunction should therefore be entered.

Id. at 16.

2. *State laws limiting right to abortion.*   The statute at issue in *Jackson Women's Health Org.* was one of many state laws passed since 2000 that have limited the right to abortion. A Guttmacher "Policy Review," published in 2012 reports that by 2011 a majority of women of reproductive age in the United States lived in a state that made it difficult to obtain an abortion. The review delineates ten categories of laws that have limited the right to abortion. They include, among other things, laws that require "preabortion counseling that is medically inaccurate or misleading," requiring "a non-medically indicated ultrasound prior to an abortion," "medically inappropriate restrictions on the provision of medication abortion", and "onerous requirements on abortion facilities that are not related to patient safety." Rachel Benson Gold & Elizabeth Nash, Troubling Trend: More States Hostile to Abortion Rights as Middle Ground Shrinks, 15 Guttmacher Policy Review 14, 14–15 (Winter 2012). In 2011, states adopted 92 laws that aimed at limiting abortion. Id. at 16. In the first half of 2012, 15 states enacted 40 laws that limited the right to abortion. Center for Reproductive Rights, 2012 Mid-year Legislative Wrap-up, www.reproductiverights.org.

The so-called "Nelson Amendment" to the Affordable Care Act permitted states to set up state exchanges without providing any coverage for abortion. In the first half of 2012, four states (Alabama, South Carolina, South Dakota, and Wisconsin) had banned insurance coverage of abortion (with restricted exceptions) on their state exchanges. 2012 Mid-year Legislative Wrap-up, supra, at 3. In the same period, state limits on abortion included Georgia's banned abortion at 20 weeks of gestation (HB 954). The law includes very limited exceptions. It explicitly prohibits clinicians from performing abortions even in cases in which there is a risk that the pregnant woman might commit suicide if the pregnancy continues. Id. at 7.

What role, if any, do you think *Carhart II* played in facilitating the trend described here?

=== 6 ===

‖ *Assisting and Monitoring Reproduction* ‖

Throughout U.S. history, the response of lawmakers to reproduction has reflected understandings of family relationships. As the family has changed, legal responses to reproduction have changed accordingly. Sometimes lawmakers have opposed social currents. At other times they have acknowledged and facilitated new social understandings of the family.

In the face of new reproductive technologies, legislators in the United States have been slow to develop comprehensive responses to the social and biological risks these new forms of treatment present for patients and their potential children. As a result, much of the law that does exist has come from judges, resolving specific disputes. As you examine the materials in this chapter, consider why that might be the case.

Consider further how the shifting demographics of family life and changes in understandings of family roles and relationships direct legal responses to assisted reproductive technology (ART) and surrogacy. Think about how responses to assisted reproduction have altered social understandings of family relationships. The material at the beginning of the chapter provides information about relevant changes in demography and in social values.

The following questions relate to issues considered in this chapter. Most do not have clear answers. However, they are useful in focusing attention on the central issues at stake in this area of bioethics.

1. What is a "mother," what is a "father," and what is a "parent"?
2. What is a "family"?
3. Are the forms through which families are created (e.g., surrogacy, the use of donated gametes) likely to shape the relationships that develop between parents and children? For instance, are the relationships within families created through reliance on a contract or through the use of donated gametes or the assistance of a surrogate likely to differ from relationships between parents and children conceived through sexual intercourse between the parents?

4. How do adults' reproductive decisions affect the children born as a result of those decisions? How might those decisions affect other relatives such as siblings or grandparents?

5. Should the right to reproduce be protected as a constitutional right? Should the right to reproduce using technology be protected? If so, should the right to reproduce through cloning be protected?

6. How do the notions of "intention" and "consent" structure social and legal responses to reproduction?

7. Can contemporary reproductive choices and options be categorized as a form of eugenic practice?

8. Do social and legal responses to cases involving assisted reproductive technology and surrogacy reflect society's traditional concern for protecting the best interests of children?

Janet L. Dolgin, The Constitution as Family Arbiter: A Moral in the Mess?
102 Colum. L. Rev. 337, 347–352 (2002)

The modern family arose, in large part, from a confluence of home and work. By the 1960s and 1970s, the values of the marketplace were being applied to, and were redefining, the domestic arena. Family members (especially adults within families) began to understand themselves as autonomous individuals, free to negotiate the terms of their relationships, and as potentially liberated from traditional family roles by the possibility of exercising choice at home, as well as at work. The understandings of personhood and relationship that lay beneath these new understandings of family were not themselves new. They flowed, as did understandings of the traditional family, from the broad ideological arena that empowered and reflected nineteenth century capitalism. By the second half of the twentieth century, however, notions of personhood, previously associated almost exclusively with life outside the home, were appearing within the domestic arena. This process of ideological transformation set the stage for, and was accelerated by, an active revival of feminism, beginning at about the same time. During the last three decades of the twentieth century, the feminist movement, in its liberal and radical guises, presented ideological justification for the reconstruction of American family life.

Increases in divorce, cohabitation, unmarried parentage, and reproductive options (including abortion and contraception) suggest the extent of the shift in understandings of family relationships and the domestic arena that swept the nation in the second half of the twentieth century. Each of those changes was enabled by, or instead itself encouraged, correlative changes in family law, including the promulgation of laws providing for no-fault divorce (beginning in the late 1960s), judicial recognition of prenuptial agreements, allowing a couple to provide before marriage for the terms of a potential divorce (beginning in the early 1970s), decisions of the United States Supreme Court providing for the paternity of unmarried fathers (in the 1970s and 1980s), and a line of Supreme Court cases defining a constitutional right to make reproductive decisions (beginning in the mid-1960s). Increases in divorce, especially, have altered understandings of childhood and transformed many children's lives. In the context of divorce, adults' choices, justified by an ideology that values liberty and freedom within the domestic arena, inevitably affect children. The valuation, or simply the acceptance, of divorce has required society to reconstruct an understanding of family that associated love with lasting commitment and kin relationships with communal solidarity.

These changes have been especially discomforting to a society that sustains a commitment, at least officially, to an understanding of children as innocent and fragile and thus as unprepared to make and effect basic choices about the scope of their domestic relationships. The National Commission on Children, for instance, has found that "parents bear primary responsibility for meeting their children's physical, emotional, and intellectual needs and for providing moral guidance and direction." Yet divorce, for instance, raises complicated questions about the scope of childhood and the appropriate role for children in divorce and post-divorce domestic settings, thus challenging the assumption that children are ill served by the loss of loving kin through parental death, divorce, or separation. In short, the collapse of a world that supported the ideology of traditional families and the reconstruction of domestic life within ongoing families have bred widespread confusion, disagreement, ambiguity and concern.

The elaboration and intermingling of the notions of tradition and modernity have perplexed both society and the law. There is widespread confusion about families in general and especially about children and the implications for children of the "modern" conception of adults within families as autonomous individuals, connected only insofar as, and for as long as, they choose to be connected. Society has been hesitant to redefine children similarly. Yet, the consequences for children of adults' familial choices conflict with traditional understandings of children as treasured, innocent, and vulnerable. For instance, lawmakers struggle, with significant confusion and uncertainty, to harmonize rules that provide for easy divorce with those designed to preserve strong, stable bonds between children and their parents. In attempting to mediate contradictory understandings of adults within families and of children within families, lawmakers are forced to explore and compare various models of family.

A.   ASSISTING REPRODUCTION

The birth—in 1978 in Oldam, England—of a baby conceived in vitro brought public attention to developments in reproductive technology. Approximately 12 percent of couples within the childbearing age group experience infertility. The University of Chicago, Medicine, available at http://www.uchospitals.edu/online-library/content=P01532 (last visited June 15, 2012). By 2010, more than 1 percent of births in the United States involved babies conceived using ART. Centers for Disease Control and Prevention, Assisted Reproductive Technology, available at www.cdc.gov/art/. Infertility treatment did not begin in 1978. In fact, assisted insemination (AI), frequently referred to as artificial insemination, has been used to assist the process of human reproduction for about a century and a half. AI is often not categorized with other forms of assisted reproduction because it is simple to effect, and as a practical matter, can be done without the involvement of a health care professional. A third form of reproductive assistance—so-called traditional surrogacy—depends only on the use of AI. Traditional surrogacy usually involves a "surrogate" who conceives (through AI) and gestates a baby, and who agrees before the baby's conception that she will yield all parental rights to the "intending" parent or parents. Traditional surrogacy is thus not part of the universe of reproductive *technology;* in vitro fertilization (IVF) is. IVF involves retrieval of an egg (often after administration of fertility drugs to cause superovulation). The eggs are fertilized in a petri dish, where embryonic development begins. A few days later, a developing embryo or embryos are inserted into the uterus of the woman who will gestate and give birth to the child. The technique has allowed women whose fallopian tubes are blocked or absent to conceive and gestate a baby. Without the possibility of fertilization outside the body, the woman's eggs (usually fertilized in the fallopian tubes) would not descend into the uterus. In the several decades following the birth of a child conceived in vitro, it has become possible for one woman to gestate and give birth to a child conceived through donors' ova and sperm (generally referred to as gestational surrogacy in cases in which the gestator does not intend to be the social mother), to freeze (cryopreserve) embryos for decades, and perhaps longer, and to thaw them for implantation, gestation, and birth. In 2012, researchers estimated that since the first birth of a child conceived in vitro in 1978, there had been about 5 million such births. James Gallagher, Five Millionth "Test Tube Baby," BBC, July 1, 2012, http://www.bbc.co.uk/news/health-18649582.

Other, more controversial, reproductive techniques include transferring cytoplasm from one woman's egg to those of another (often older) woman whose eggs resist fertilization. This technique results in children with three genetic parents because mitochrondrial DNA is transferred with the ova's cytoplasm. Even more controversial, and apparently never used to create a human child, is somatic cell nuclear transfer (popularly known as cloning).

Today infertility treatment comprises a multibillion-dollar industry. Success rates have increased dramatically; some infertility clinics now report higher pregnancy rates among patients than among couples engaging in unprotected sexual intercourse. However, infertility treatment is not without risks for the mother and child. Some of the risks are biological. Others are social and psychological.

Narrative approaches to fertility medicine capture many of the parameters of infertily care for patients. Aline Kalbian, a religious studies scholar, has offered such an approach. She focuses on what narratives of fertility medicine can explain about patient autonomy and choice for those involved in such care. Aline Kalbian, Narrative ARTifice And Women's Agency, 19 Bioethics 93, 98 (2005). Kalbian considers the claim of some feminists that real autonomy can often not be enjoyed by infertile women in the "context of strongly enforced societal norms about femininity and maternity." Drawing from the work of Arthur Frank and that of Hilde Nelson, Kalbian identifies two distinct narrative approaches to infertility care. One she calls the narrative of hope; the other she calls the narrative of resistance. Neither narrative excludes the other. For some women, encounters with fertility medicine entail both narratives.

Kalbian describes the "hope" narrative as the one most often told by women who turn to infertility medicine. Id. at 102. The narrative leads to only one acceptable ending – pregnancy and the birth of a baby. The hope narrative is supported by fertility clinics which give hope to women and their partners even when the likelihood of success is small. Fertility clinics, Kalbian notes, have a plethora of motives for encouraging this narrative, including a financial interest.

Kalbian suggests that the deep desire of some women to have a baby may encourage them to appropriate a narrative of hope. Their faith in this narrative then virtually compels them to continue with infertility care: "[T]heir intense hope and faith in the potential success of these technologies makes resistance to these technologies difficult or maybe in some cases, impossible." Id. at 104.

Similarly, Sarah Franklin, a British anthropologist, writing at a time when 80 to 85 percent of couples trying IVF did not have a baby, reported that all of the women included in her ethnographic study concluded they had no "choice." They "'had to try.'" Sarah Franklin, Making Miracles: Scientific Progress and the Facts of Life in Reproducing Reproduction: Kinship, Power, and Technological Innovation 102, 106 (Sarah Franklin & Helene Ragone, eds. 1997).

> The assumption that the technique would provide either longed-for offspring or at least peace of mind in having exhausted every avenue of possibility becomes more elusive in the context of having no obvious point of completion of treatment. As failures increase, so do avenues of possibility, as failure often yields diagnostic information of some possible advantage in pinpointing the source of difficulty.

Id. at 109. This is one dynamic underlying the power of the narrative of hope that Kalbian describes. Indeed, Kalbian refers to a "culture of perseverance" within fertility clinics. This observation suggests the second narrative that Kalbian identifies in the context of infertility medicine – the narrative of resistance. Interestingly, she queries what it might mean to resist infertility care without "opposing" it. Kalbian, supra, at 106. She deems the distinction between refusal and opposition significant because it "can help us to reconcile personal interpretations of the role of ARTs with the larger moral significance of these technologies." Id. at 106. Resistance, when it does emerge, can be more than a personal decision. It can be a "political act." To Hilda Nelson, narratives of resistance "'allow oppressed people to refuse the identities imposed on them by their oppressors and to re-identify themselves in more respect-worthy terms.'" Id. at 106-107. By re-shaping their identities through refusal, people can enhance the capacity to exert moral agency. Kalbian adds:

> [F]ree agency in ART-related choices is deeply connected to identity, especially to the extent that identity is shaped by the desire for children. For many feminists, pronatalism, the cultural pressure on women to bear children, can act as a form of oppression. It certainly imposes an identity on women, one that many women, but certainly not all, women embrace.

Id. at 107.

NOTES AND QUESTIONS

1. *Personal narratives.*   Kalbian sees personal narratives as a mode of realigning personal beliefs, values, and preferences in light of dominant beliefs,

values, and preferences. Do you think that a "narrative" approach can be molded into a self-conscious tool for use in reshaping one's own relation to reality? Or must narratives develop unself-consciously as people within broad cultural settings reexamine their own understandings of reality (including the reality of infertility, for instance)?

2. *Feminist responses to ARTs.*   Elsewhere in Narrative ARTifice and Women's Agency, Kalbian suggests that a great deal of feminist opposition to ART assumes or openly argues that women relying on ART are victims of a patriarchy that defines them only as breeders and that discredits their essential personhood if they fail to breed. Kalbian concludes that "[r]esisting medical treatment in any context" demands courage, and that "in the case of fertility medicine, it requires an ability to balance a response to a commercial/techno-logical enterprise with desires that, while profoundly shaped by cultural and societal forces, are experienced as poignantly real."

Others have openly criticized the use of reproductive technology as a mis-guided effort to effect a goal (procreation) that should itself be challenged as a product of cultural hype. In a piece criticizing virtually every aspect of reliance on ARTs to reproduce, Joy Williams writes:

> The human race hardly needs to be more fertile, but fertility clinics are boom-ing. The new millionaires are the hotshot fertility doctors who serve anxious gottahavababy women, techno-shamans who have become the most important aspect of the baby process, giving women what they want: BABIES. . . . [W]omen think of themselves as being *successful, personally fulfilled* when they have a baby, even if it takes a battery of men in white smocks and lots of hor-mones and drugs and needles and dishes and mixing and inserting and implanting to make it so. . . .

Joy Williams, The Case Against Babies 203, 204 in The Best American Essays (Ian Frazier ed. 1997). See also Judith Daar, Regulating Reproductive Technologies: Panacea or Paper Tiger? 34 Hous. L. Rev. 609 (1997) (analyzing ethical and practical implications of assisted reproductive technology).

3. *Legislation requiring accurate reporting.*   In 1992, the U.S. Congress passed the Fertility Clinic Success Rate and Certification Act. 42 U.S.C.A. §§263a-1-7 (2002). The Act requires the Centers for Disease Control and Prevention (CDC) to publish data about the success rates of infertility clinics in the United States. The legislation requires "assisted reproductive technology" programs to report pregnancy success rates to the CDC and requires the CDC to develop a "model program for the certification of embryo laboratories." §263a-2(a)(1).

Among existing federal agencies, only the Food and Drug Administration (FDA) even arguably has authority to regulate ART. The FDA regulates drugs and medical equipment. Whether it has authority to regulate ART is being actively questioned. In 2002, the agency asserted authority over therapeutic and reproductive cloning on the basis of its authority to regulate clinical trial research. President Bush's Council on Bioethics (appointed in November 2001 through Executive Order 13237) has debated the issue but has not reached a clear decision.

4. *How many embryos to implant?*   The story of Nadya Suleman, the so-called Octomom, and her physician, Michael Kamrava, has challenged existing regu-latory schemes with calls for more exacting rules about the number of embryos

that may be implanted in an IVF cycle and for more oversight of infertility treatments. Before giving birth (following infertility care) to eight babies in 2009, Suleman had had six children, all conceived as a result of IVF cycles. Judith Daar, Federalizing Embryo Transfers: Taming the Wild West of Reproductive Medicine? 23 Colum. J. Gender & L. 257, 299 (2012). The Medical Board of California revoked Kamrava's license to practice medicine, after concluding that Kamrava was grossly negligent in his treatment of Suleman and two other patients. The Medical Board of California, News Release, Medical Board of California Revokes License of Former Beverly Hills Physician (June 1, 2011), available at http://www.mbc.ca.gov/board/media/releases_2011_06_01_kamrava.html.

Do you think that the story of Nadya Suleman and her 14 children can be framed as a "narrative of hope," a "narrative of resistance," both, or neither? What additional facts might you want in order to answer the question?

5. *European responses.* ART is available throughout the world (although at least one country—Costa Rica—banned IVF in 2000. That ban has now been lifted. (see next note). In 2006, the European Society of Human Reproduction & Embryology reported that about 1 million ART treatment cycles were being initiated in the world each year. As a result, about 200,000 babies were born annually. http://www.eshre.eu/ESHRE/English/Guidelines-Legal/ART-fact-sheet/page.aspx/1061 (last visited June 15, 2012). Over half of ART cycles worldwide were initiated in Europe, and most of those were carried out in France, Germany, Spain, or the United Kingdom. Id.

In many countries regulation occurred earlier and has been more comprehensive than in the United States. In Britain, for instance, national legislation was enacted soon after the issuance in 1984 of the Warnock Report, named after Mary Warnock, who headed the British Committee of Inquiry into Human Fertilisation and Embryology. The committee was established in 1982. Mary Warnock, A Question of Life: The Warnock Report on Human Fertilisation and Embryology (1984).

A number of disputes not easily resolved through the existing regulatory schemes have suggested the need for amendment and reform. Among these disputes is the case of Dianne Blood. After Blood's husband died of meningitis in 1995, she conceived two boys using her deceased husband's frozen sperm. Under British law at the time, the boy's genetic father could not be their legal father because the children were conceived posthumously. In early 2003, the British Department of Health agreed that that rule was not compatible with the children's rights under Article 8 of the European Convention on Human Rights. That article requires that respect be given to the family life of children such as Blood's sons. Penney Lewis, IVF Proves Fertile Ground for Dispute, Times (London), March 11, 2003, at 7.

Until 2004, Italy was a pioneer in several areas of ART. In February 2004 the Italian Parliament passed a law that bans almost all forms of ART. Italy prohibits gamete donation from any third party, including assisted insemination with donor sperm. European Society of Human Reproduction and Embryology, http://www.eshre.eu/home/page.aspx/2 (last visited June 15, 2012).

6. *Costa Rica bans all IVF treatments.* IVF was legal in Costa Rica between 1995 and 2000 but was banned in 2000 as violative of Article 21 of the nation's constitution which defines "human life" as "inviolable." A challenge to the ban was initiated in 2001 by nine couples in need of infertility treatment. Michael

Cook, Screws Turn on Costa Rica's IVF Ban, BioEdge, Sept. 22, 2012; Michele Catanzaro, Human-rights Court to Rule on Fertility-treatment Ban, Nature, Sept. 14, 2012, www. nature.com. A decade later, the Inter-American Commission on Human Rights concluded that the Costa Rican prohibition on IVF violated several articles in the American Convention on Human Rights. With the hope of having that conclusion enforced, the plaintiffs sought a decision from the Inter-American Court of Human Rights. In December 2012, the Inter-American Court of Human Rights overturned Costa Rica's ban on IVF.

1.   Assisted Insemination

Many decades before the advent of in vitro fertilization or embryo cryopreservation, assisted (or artificial) insemination (AI) involved gamete donation. The technique seems to have been pioneered in 1785 by a Scottish surgeon, John Hunter. Some of the early cases involved insemination with the sperm of the woman's husband. Several reports of insemination using donor sperm in the early twentieth century were greeted with disfavor. By the late 1950s, tens of thousands of children were said to have been conceived using donor sperm. Carmel Shalev, Birth Power: The Case for Surrogacy 58–60 (1989). Until the 1960s, however, the procedure was shrouded in secrecy and was associated with adultery and illegitimacy.

Today AI is used by married couples, unmarried couples, and single people. The process is regulated by law in most states. State laws generally provide that if a woman undergoing AI is married, her husband (if he consents to the procedure) will be the legal father of any child that results. The Uniform Parentage Act, §5 (1973), 9b Uniform Laws Annotated (1987) provides:

> If, under the supervision of a licensed physician and with the consent of her husband, a wife is inseminated artificially with semen donated by a man not her husband, the husband is treated in law as if he were the natural father of a child thereby conceived. The husband's consent must be in writing and signed by him and his wife.

Almost two-fifths of the states have adopted the Uniform Parentage Act. The Uniform Parentage Act, originally set forth in 1973, was revised in 2000 and amended in 2002. The Act now makes it clear that sperm donors are not classed as legal fathers regardless of the marital status of the child's mother. Uniform Parentage Act 702 (2002). (The 2002 version of the Act has been adopted in about nine states.)

The Uniform Status of Children of Assisted Conception Act, §4 (1988), 9b Uniform Laws Annotated 155 (USCACA) provides:

(a) A donor is not a parent of a child conceived through assisted conception.

(b) An individual who dies before implantation of an embryo, or before a child is conceived other than through sexual intercourse, using the individual's egg or sperm, is not a parent of the resulting child.

Section 1 of the USCACA defines a "donor" as an individual "who produces egg or sperm used for assisted conception, whether or not a payment is made for the egg or sperm used, but does not include a woman who gives birth to a resulting child." Only a few of the relevant state statutes consider the legal consequences of a single woman's relying on assisted insemination to conceive a child. See, e.g., Cal. Fam. Code §7613; N.J. Stat. Ann. §9:17-44 (West 1983). Only two states, North Dakota and Virginia, adopted the USCACA.

In recent years, some sperm banks have promised to provide "designer babies," and some of those who approach sperm banks, seeking donated sperm, specify the sort of donor they prefer. One sperm bank in Boston, for instance, requires potential donors to fill out a 24-page questionnaire that asks a wide variety of questions about the potential donor's life and beliefs. Bella English, Birth Control at a Boston Sperm Bank, Boston Globe, May 23, 2002, at D1; www. necryogenic.com. The sperm bank in question, New England Cryogenic, claims to accept one out of every 20 donor applicants, limits donors to men between 18 and 38 years of age, and tests potential donors for a number of communicable or genetically transmissible diseases. New England Cryogenic Center, Inc., http:// www.necryogenic.com/choosing-screening.php (last visited June 15, 2012).

In the United States, commercial markets in sperm and ova have flourished. Moreover, donors usually remain anonymous. This development contrasts with strict rules governing legal adoption in the United States, and it contrasts with prohibitions on anonymous gamete donation in a number of European countries, including Switzerland, Britain, Norway, and Sweden. In those countries, children conceived from donated gametes are granted access to information about donors once the children are 18 years of age. Ross Douthat, The Birds and the Bees (via the Fertility Clinic), N.Y. Times, May 30, 2010, www.nytimes.com.

2. Surrogacy, In Vitro Fertilization, and Gestational Surrogacy

a. Bioethical and Social Perspectives

> **Barbara Bennett Woodhouse, Hatching the Egg:**
> **A Child-Centered Perspective on Parents' Rights**
> 14 Cardozo L. Rev. 1747, 1748-1753, 1767-1768 (1993)

Much has been made recently of the threat to family values posed by children's rights. This Article takes a contrasting view—that it is parents' rights, as currently understood, that undermine those values of responsibility and mutuality necessary to children's welfare. Using narratives drawn from children's stories, literature, popular culture, and case law, I will explore the ways in which legal norms of family and fathering currently fail children. . . .

. . . We adults all understand that something specific is meant by "fathering" a child, just as we know that something different is meant by "mothering." Fathers beget. Mothers bear and nurture. Yet consider Horton the Elephant. Horton is the hero of a beloved story book by the immortal Dr. Seuss. Sit down (preferably with a child) and open the book. On page one, we meet Mayzie Bird, sitting on a red and white spotted egg perched in a scraggly nest in a spindly tree. She is bored with "sitting, just sitting here day after day. It's work! How I hate it! I'd much rather play! I'd take a vacation, fly off for a rest if I could find someone to stay on my nest!" Then Horton the elephant happens by and she pleads with him to give her just a short break, promising to be right back. He resists at first:

> "Why, of all silly things!
> I haven't feathers and I haven't wings.
> ME on your egg? Why, that doesn't make sense. . . .
> Your egg is so small, ma'am, and I'm so immense!"

But turn a few pages and there he sits, perched on the egg, with the tree bowed nearly double under his weight. And sits, and sits, and sits. . . . Although Horton does not know it, the faithless Mayzie has decamped to Palm Beach. Days and months pass and Horton, ever stalwart, stays glued to the nest. He is ridiculed, frozen, rained on, teased, tormented, and even sold—tree, nest, egg, and all—to a circus side-show.

> HORTON STAYED ON THAT NEST!
> He held his head high
> And he threw out his chest. . . .
> "I meant what I said
> And I said what I meant.
> An elephant's faithful
> One hundred per cent!"

After fifty-one weeks, as the egg that Horton has come to think of as "his" is finally hatching, who should appear but Mayzie Bird.

> "But it's MINE!" screamed the bird, when she heard the egg crack.
> (The work was all done. Now she wanted it back.)
> "It's MY egg!" she sputtered. "You stole it from me!
> Get off of my nest and get out of my tree!"

Those parents who are lawyers know that Mayzie is right. She is the egg's genetic mother and Horton is a mere "biological stranger." In most jurisdictions, a mother's pre-birth surrender is not binding. Besides, if the egg is property, then Horton is no more than a gratuitous bailee, and if it is progeny, there is no doctrine of adverse possession in children. As for Mayzie's Palm Beach detour, that is conduct protected by procreational freedoms.

> Poor Horton backed down
> With a sad, heavy heart. . . .
> But at that very instant, the egg burst apart!
> And out of the pieces of red and white shell,
> From the egg that he'd sat on so long and so well,
> Horton the Elephant saw something whizz!
> IT HAD EARS
> AND A TAIL
> AND A TRUNK JUST LIKE HIS!

Now no one in the crowd of bystanders (not even the lawyer parents reading the book) credits Mayzie's claim that the egg belongs to her. To the contrary, these local "lawmakers" name the new animal an "elephant-bird" and shout in unison, "It should be, it should be, it SHOULD be like that! Because Horton was faithful! He sat and he sat!"

The band of spectators recognizes the relationship because Horton has earned it, and also because it is manifest in the baby bird's metamorphosis. On the last pages, the little elephant-bird rides aloft into the future on Horton's trunk, confident as Gunga Din. If anything, it looks more like Horton "belongs" to the tiny, imperious creature than vice versa. But it is clear that their joy in the relationship is mutual. As they return ("happy, one hundred percent!") to the jungle, they are welcomed into the family of families by a smiling crowd of assorted animals with babies tucked in pouches, perched on backs, or slung around necks.

This story captures in visual metaphors how Horton's faithful care of the egg connects him to the baby it contained. Horton has "fathered" the baby bird in an entirely different sense of the word. Dr. Seuss gives us the satisfaction of actually seeing this relationship in tangible form.

Most tantalizing, Dr. Seuss has given us an unexpected dimension of fathering—he has given us father as mother. Horton's gestational experience is very much like pregnancy—the feeling of being expropriated, body and soul, held captive by the needs of the egg, tempted by the option of quitting, but finding the moral consequences unacceptable. Horton does not own the egg; the egg owns him. One thing is sure: after fifty-one weeks of this, Horton has formed a connection to the egg that cannot be ignored. . . .

A number of insights for the authors of children's law are implicit in this fable of fathering and made explicit in this article. First, by making the authority of parenthood contingent on service to children, Horton's story gives legitimacy to adult power over children. Second, by showing that fathers can accept responsibility for mothering, it brings fathers into functional partnership with mothers in the work of nurturing, "liberating" both to care for children. Third, by uncoupling genetics and affiliation, it feeds the larger metaphor of a community of responsibility in which we accept all children as our own.

Law and policy are themselves moral storytellers. Sometimes reinforcing and sometimes in tension with our individual moral calculus, they send messages (through deregulation as much as through regulation) about how we ought to behave. As currently constituted, the legal narratives in family law are in marked dissonance with the competing vision of generational justice so succinctly captured in Horton's story. Where Dr. Seuss placed the egg at the center, law assumes an adult-centric perspective that discounts children's reality. Where Dr. Seuss gave us a parable on sharing the work of gestation, law gives us one extolling individualism and discounting the interdependence and mutuality of family. Finally, in contrast to Horton's tale of functional fathering, law privileges formal definitions of family that fail to acknowledge and sustain functional parenthood, defined as taking care of children. In each of these ways, law cuts against the lessons of attachment through care and responsibility that we tell ourselves and our children in stories like Horton Hatches the Egg. . . .

Changes in cultural consciousness spurred by recent feminism have accelerated a revolution in gender-based views of nurturing. But, paradoxically, feminism has also put the validity of gender neutral views in doubt. On the one hand, a central theme of post-sixties feminism has been the need for men and women to share equally in the unpaid childrearing and homemaking tasks that were formerly assigned to women, and for the community to do its share in supporting the work of family through social supports such as day care and family leave. On the other hand, a new wave of feminist thinkers have questioned their sisters' assumption that men and women are essentially similar and equally adapted to nurturing.

NOTES AND QUESTIONS

1. *Agreements and gestational surrogacy.*   The poignant tale of Horton the elephant presented by Woodhouse provides a frame within which to contemplate the implications of gestational surrogacy (see Johnson v. Calvert, infra), an arrangement through which one woman gestates a fetus conceived from a gamete provided by another woman. In the *Johnson* case, infra, the "gestational mother," the "genetic mother," and the genetic mother's husband (the "genetic father") all intended from the start of the arrangement that the gestator would give the child to the gamete donors who would be the child's social and legal parents. In the Horton story, it is not clear whether Mayzie Bird "intended" to return from Florida after the birth of her genetic birdchild and claim that baby as her own. Would it matter to your sense of justice if Mayzie Bird and Horton had entered into an agreement before Horton served as the equivalent of the egg's gestator, providing, for instance, that Mayzie would compensate Horton and that he would surrender the baby to Mayzie Bird once it hatched? Would it matter to your sense of justice if it became clear that Mayzie Bird didn't surrender her egg from boredom but because she was unable—for some reason relating to bird anatomy—to protect the egg until it hatched?

2. *Permitting/prohibiting paid vs. unpaid surrogacy.*   As part of a long critique of paid and unpaid surrogacy, Margaret Radin suggests that both practices might be questionable on the following grounds:

> Whether surrogacy is paid or unpaid, there may be a transition problem: an ironic self-deception. Acting in ways that current gender ideology characterizes as empowering might actually be disempowering. Surrogates may feel they are fulfilling their womanhood by producing a baby for someone else, although they may actually be reinforcing oppressive gender roles. It is also possible to view would-be fathers as (perhaps unknowing) oppressors of their own partners. Infertile mothers, believing it to be their duty to raise their partners' genetic children, could be caught in the same kind of false consciousness and relative powerlessness as surrogates who feel called upon to produce children for others. Some women might have conflicts with their partners that they cannot acknowledge, either about raising children under these circumstances instead of adopting unrelated children, or about having children at all. These considerations suggest that to avoid reinforcing gender ideology, both paid and unpaid surrogacy must be prohibited.

Margaret Jane Radin, Market-Inalienability, 100 Harv. L. Rev. 1849, 1930–1931 (1987). Do you think that the responses and motivations that Radin delineates are likely to be manifest in real surrogacy arrangements?

Radin further suggests that

> attempting to prohibit surrogacy now seems too utopian, because it ignores a transition problem. At present, people seem to believe that they need genetic offspring in order to fulfill themselves; at present, some surrogates believe their actions to be altruistic. To try to create an ideal world all at once would do violence to things people make central to themselves. This problem suggests that surrogacy should not be altogether prohibited.

Id. at 1932. Do you agree with this suggestion?

Radin additionally postulates that "[c]oncerns about commodification of women and children . . . might counsel permitting only unpaid surrogacy. . . ." Id. at 1932.

3. *Bibliographic note.*   There is a burgeoning literature about surrogacy and its implications. Among many useful books and articles, Martha A. Field's Surrogate Motherhood: The Legal and Human Issues (1988) continues to provide an important treatment of the potential of surrogacy to result in exploitation; Marsha Garrison, Law Making for Baby Making: An Interpretive Approach to the Determination of Legal Parentage, 113 Harv. L. Rev. 835 (2000), proposes an interpretive approach to establishing parentage in cases of technological reproduction generally; Debora L. Spar, The Baby Business: How Money, Science, and Politics Drive the Commerce of Conception (2006), considers the market in babies being created around reproductive technology (including reprogenetics); Jennifer Damelico & Kelly Sorensen, Enhancing Autonomy in Paid Surrogacy, 22 Bioethics 269 (2008), suggest that potential gestational surrogates receive education aimed at "enhancing surrogate autonomy"; Marcelo de Alcantara, Surrogacy in Japan: Legal Implications for Parentage and Citizenship, 48 Fam. Ct. Rev. 417 (2010), reviews legal and policy debates about surrogacy in Japan; Gaia Bernstein, Regulating Reproductive Technologies: Timing, Uncertainty, and Donor Anonymity, 90 B.U.L. Rev. 1189 (2010), argues that a comprehensive scheme regulating ART is needed; and Kristiana Brugger, International Law in the Gestational Surrogacy Debate, 35 Fordham Int'l L.J. 665 (2012), considers how surrogacy can best be regulated in an international context.

b.   Legal Approaches

The following cases raise questions about both the comparative significance of biological parentage in the construction of legal parentage and about the implications of involving third parties in the reproductive process. New Jersey's highest court decided *Baby M* in 1988, just as reproductive technology was becoming available for use in infertility care. The surrogacy arrangement in the *Baby M* case—what is called "traditional" surrogacy—did not involve sophisticated technological assistance. However, the case is important because it has provided a frame for determining parentage in cases including more than two people with claims to parentage. In doing that, the case has served as a model in terms of which courts have assessed claims to parentage in subsequent cases involving ova donation and gestational surrogacy. In fact, in 2009, a New Jersey court applied the ruling in *Baby M* to a case involving a gestational surrogacy arrangement. A.G.R. v. D.R.H., 2009 N.J. Super. Unpub. LEXIS 3250 (Ch. Div. 2009) (see infra this section for discussion of the case).

‖ *In the Matter of Baby M* ‖
‖ **537 A.2d 1227 (N.J. 1988)** ‖

Opinion by WILENTZ, C. J.

[This case was occasioned by a dispute between William and Elizabeth Stern and Mary Beth Whitehead about the parentage of a child conceived with William Stern's sperm and Mary Beth Whitehead's ovum and gestated by Whitehead. The Sterns were married in 1974. They delayed having children until Mrs. Stern completed training to be a physician. At that time, she was diagnosed with multiple sclerosis. In light of medical wisdom at the time, the Sterns concluded that a pregnancy might seriously exacerbate her condition. The Sterns considered adoption but were discouraged when they "learned that because they were of different religions and they were an 'older couple,' adoption of a newborn infant would be extremely difficult." In 1984, they approached the Infertility Center of New York, which connected them with Mary Beth Whitehead. Whitehead had applied to serve as a surrogate for an infertile couple. This would entail her undergoing artificial insemination and, if conception occurred, gestating and giving birth to the baby. Whitehead entered into a contractual agreement (the "surrogate parenting agreement") with William Stern. Among other things, Whitehead agreed to renounce all parental rights in favor of William Stern at the baby's birth. Stern agreed to pay Whitehead $10,000 as well as medical and dental expenses. Whitehead conceived in July 1985. After the birth of the baby, a girl, in March 1986, Whitehead concluded that she was not able to part with the child. During the next several months, the Sterns sought and received an ex parte order that required Whitehead to surrender the child to Stern; Whitehead and her husband left New Jersey for Florida with the child; and the Sterns hired a detective to locate the Whiteheads and the baby. By August 1986, the Whiteheads returned to New Jersey, and litigation to determine the parentage and custody of the child began. In the Matter of Baby M, 525 A.2d 1128 (N.J. Super. 1987).]

Issue: In this matter the Court is asked to determine the validity of a contract that purports to provide a new way of bringing children into a family. For a fee of $10,000, a woman agrees to be artificially inseminated with the semen of another woman's husband; she is to conceive a child, carry it to term, and after its birth surrender it to the natural father and his wife. The intent of the contract is that the child's natural mother will thereafter be forever separated from her child. The wife is to adopt the child, and she and the natural father are to be regarded as its parents for all purposes. The contract providing for this is called a "surrogacy contract," the natural mother inappropriately called the "surrogate mother."

Holding: We invalidate the surrogacy contract because it conflicts with the law and public policy of this State. While we recognize the depth of the yearning of infertile couples to have their own children, we find the payment of money to a "surrogate" mother illegal, perhaps criminal, and potentially degrading to women. Although in this case we grant custody to the natural father, the evidence having clearly proved such custody to be in the best interests of the infant, we void both the termination of the surrogate mother's parental rights and the adoption of the child by the wife/stepparent. We thus restore the "surrogate" as the mother of the child. We remand the issue of the natural mother's visitation rights to the trial court, since that issue was not reached below and the record before us is not sufficient to permit us to decide it de novo.

We find no offense to our present laws where a woman voluntarily and without payment agrees to act as a "surrogate" mother, provided that she is not subject to a binding agreement to surrender her child. Moreover, our holding today does not preclude the Legislature from altering the current statutory scheme, within constitutional limits, so as to permit surrogacy contracts. Under current law, however, the surrogacy agreement before us is illegal and invalid.

II. Invalidity and Unenforceability of Surrogacy Contract

We have concluded that this surrogacy contract is invalid. Our conclusion has two bases: direct conflict with existing statutes and conflict with the public policies of this State, as expressed in its statutory and decisional law.

Rationale

A. Conflict with Statutory Provisions ①

(1) Our law prohibits paying or accepting money in connection with any placement of a child for adoption. Violation is a high misdemeanor. Excepted are fees of an approved agency (which must be a non-profit entity), and certain expenses in connection with childbirth. . . .

[Despite careful structuring of the surrogacy agreement,] Mr. Stern knew he was paying for the adoption of a child; Mrs. Whitehead knew she was accepting money so that a child might be adopted; the Infertility Center knew that it was being paid for assisting in the adoption of a child. The actions of all three worked to frustrate the goals of the statute. It strains credulity to claim that these arrangements, touted by those in the surrogacy business as an attractive alternative to the usual route leading to an adoption, really amount to something other than a private placement adoption for money. . . .

Baby-selling potentially results in the exploitation of all parties involved. Conversely, adoption statutes seek to further humanitarian goals, foremost among them the best interests of the child. The negative consequences of baby-buying are potentially present in the surrogacy context, especially the potential for placing and adopting a child without regard to the interest of the child or the natural mother.

(2) The termination of Mrs. Whitehead's parental rights, called for by the surrogacy contract and actually ordered by the court fails to comply with the stringent requirements of New Jersey law. Our law, recognizing the finality of any termination of parental rights, provides for such termination only where there has been a voluntary surrender of a child to an approved agency or to the Division of Youth and Family Services ("DYFS"), accompanied by a formal document acknowledging termination of parental rights or where there has been a showing of parental abandonment or unfitness. . . .

Rule

In this case a termination of parental rights was obtained not by proving the statutory prerequisites but by claiming the benefit of contractual provisions. From all that has been stated above, it is clear that a contractual agreement to abandon one's parental rights, or not to contest a termination action, will not be enforced in our courts. The Legislature would not have so carefully, so consistently, and so substantially restricted termination of parental rights if it had intended to allow termination to be achieved by one short sentence in a contract.

Since the termination was invalid, it follows, as noted above, that adoption of Melissa by Mrs. Stern could not properly be granted.

(3) The provision in the surrogacy contract stating that Mary Beth Whitehead agrees to "surrender custody . . . and terminate all parental rights" contains no clause giving her a right to rescind. It is intended to be an irrevocable consent to surrender the child for adoption—in other words, an irrevocable

commitment by Mrs. Whitehead to turn Baby M over to the Sterns and thereafter to allow termination of her parental rights. The trial court required a "best interests" showing as a condition to granting specific performance of the surrogacy contract. 217 N.J. Super. at 399–400. Having decided the "best interests" issue in favor of the Sterns, that court's order included, among other things, specific performance of this agreement to surrender custody and terminate all parental rights. . . .

The[] strict [legislative] prerequisites to irrevocability constitute a recognition of the most serious consequences that flow from such consents: termination of parental rights, the permanent separation of parent from child, and the ultimate adoption of the child. Because of those consequences, the Legislature severely limited the circumstances under which such consent would be irrevocable. The legislative goal is furthered by regulations requiring approved agencies, prior to accepting irrevocable consents, to provide advice and counseling to women, making it more likely that they fully understand and appreciate the consequences of their acts.

Contractual surrender of parental rights is not provided for in our statutes as now written. . . . There is no doubt that a contractual provision purporting to constitute an irrevocable agreement to surrender custody of a child for adoption is invalid. . . .

B. Public Policy Considerations

The surrogacy contract's invalidity, resulting from its direct conflict with the above statutory provisions, is further underlined when its goals and means are measured against New Jersey's public policy. The contract's basic premise, that the natural parents can decide in advance of birth which one is to have custody of the child, bears no relationship to the settled law that the child's best interests shall determine custody. . . .

This is the sale of a child, or, at the very least, the sale of a mother's right to her child, the only mitigating factor being that one of the purchasers is the father. Almost every evil that prompted the prohibition on the payment of money in connection with adoptions exists here.

The differences between an adoption and a surrogacy contract should be noted, since it is asserted that the use of money in connection with surrogacy does not pose the risks found where money buys an adoption.

. . . [P]erhaps most important, all parties concede that it is unlikely that surrogacy will survive without money. Despite the alleged selfless motivation of surrogate mothers, if there is no payment, there will be no surrogates, or very few. That conclusion contrasts with adoption; for obvious reasons, there remains a steady supply, albeit insufficient, despite the prohibitions against payment. The adoption itself, relieving the natural mother of the financial burden of supporting an infant, is in some sense the equivalent of payment. . . .

IV. Constitutional Issues

Both parties argue that the Constitutions—state and federal—mandate approval of their basic claims. The source of their constitutional arguments is essentially the same: the right of privacy, the right to procreate, the right to the companionship of one's child, those rights flowing either directly from the fourteenth amendment or by its incorporation of the Bill of Rights, or from the ninth amendment, or through the penumbra surrounding all of the Bill of Rights. They are the rights of personal intimacy, of marriage, of sex, of family, of procreation. Whatever their source, it is clear that they are fundamental rights protected by both the federal and state Constitutions. . . . The right asserted by the Sterns is the right of procreation; that asserted by Mary Beth Whitehead is the right to the companionship of her child. We find that the right of procreation does not extend as far as claimed by the Sterns. As for the right asserted by Mrs. Whitehead, since we uphold it on other grounds (i.e., we have restored her as mother and recognized her right, limited by the child's best interests, to her companionship), we need not decide that constitutional issue. . . .

The right to procreate very simply is the right to have natural children, whether through sexual intercourse or artificial insemination. It is no more than that. Mr. Stern has not been deprived of that right. Through artificial insemination of Mrs. Whitehead, Baby M is his child. The custody, care, companionship, and nurturing that follow birth are not parts of the right to procreation; they are rights that may also be constitutionally protected, but that involve many considerations other than the right of procreation. To assert that Mr. Stern's right of procreation gives him the right to the custody of Baby M would be to assert that Mrs. Whitehead's right of procreation does not give her the right to the custody of Baby M; it would be to assert that the constitutional right of procreation includes within it a constitutionally protected contractual right to destroy someone else's right of procreation.

V. Custody

Having decided that the surrogacy contract is illegal and unenforceable, we now must decide the custody question without regard to the provisions of the surrogacy contract that would give Mr. Stern sole and permanent custody. (That does not mean that the existence of the contract and the circumstances under which it was entered may not be considered to the extent deemed relevant to the child's best interests.) With the surrogacy contract disposed of, the legal framework becomes a dispute between two couples over the custody of a child produced by the artificial insemination of one couple's wife by the other's husband. Under the Parentage Act the claims of the natural father and the natural mother are entitled to equal weight, i.e., one is not preferred over the other solely because he or she is the father or the mother. The applicable rule given these circumstances is clear: the child's best interests determine custody. . . .

There were eleven experts who testified concerning the child's best interests, either directly or in connection with matters related to that issue. Our reading of the record persuades us that the trial court's decision awarding custody to the Sterns (technically to Mr. Stern) should be affirmed since "its findings . . . could reasonably have been reached on sufficient credible evidence present in the record."

VI. VISITATION

The trial court's decision to terminate Mrs. Whitehead's parental rights precluded it from making any determination on visitation. Our reversal of the trial court's order, however, requires delineation of Mrs. Whitehead's rights to visitation. It is apparent to us that this factually sensitive issue, which was never addressed below, should not be determined de novo by this Court. We therefore remand the visitation issue to the trial court for an abbreviated hearing and determination as set forth below. . . .

CONCLUSION

. . . If the Legislature decides to address surrogacy, consideration of this case will highlight many of its potential harms. We do not underestimate the difficulties of legislating on this subject. In addition to the inevitable confrontation with the ethical and moral issues involved, there is the question of the wisdom and effectiveness of regulating a matter so private, yet of such public interest. Legislative consideration of surrogacy may also provide the opportunity to begin to focus on the overall implications of the new reproductive biotechnology—in vitro fertilization, preservation of sperm and eggs, embryo implantation and the like. The problem is how to enjoy the benefits of the technology—especially for infertile couples—while minimizing the risk of abuse. The problem can be addressed only when society decides what its values and objectives are in this troubling, yet promising, area.

The judgment is affirmed in part, reversed in part, and remanded for further proceedings consistent with this opinion.

|| ***Johnson v. Calvert*** ||
|| **851 P.2d 776 (Cal. 1993)** ||

Opinion by PANELLI, J.

In this case we address several of the legal questions raised by recent advances in reproductive technology. When, pursuant to a surrogacy agreement, a zygote[1] formed of the gametes[2] of a husband and wife is implanted in the uterus of another woman, who carries the resulting fetus to term and gives birth to a child not genetically related to her, who is the child's "natural mother" under California law? Does a determination that the wife is the child's natural mother work a deprivation of the gestating woman's constitutional rights? And is such an agreement barred by any public policy of this state?

We conclude that the husband and wife are the child's natural parents, and that this result does not offend the state or federal Constitution or public policy.

Mark and Crispina Calvert are a married couple who desired to have a child. Crispina was forced to undergo a hysterectomy in 1984. Her ovaries

---

1. An organism produced by the union of two gametes. (McGraw-Hill Dictionary of Scientific and Technical Terms (4th ed. 1989), p. 783).

2. A cell that participates in fertilization and development of a new organism, also known as a germ cell or sex cell. (McGraw-Hill Dictionary of Scientific and Technical Terms, supra, p. 2087).

remained capable of producing eggs, however, and the couple eventually considered surrogacy. In 1989 Anna Johnson heard about Crispina's plight from a coworker and offered to serve as a surrogate for the Calverts.

On January 15, 1990, Mark, Crispina, and Anna signed a contract providing that an embryo created by the sperm of Mark and the egg of Crispina would be implanted in Anna and the child born would be taken into Mark and Crispina's home "as their child." Anna agreed she would relinquish "all parental rights" to the child in favor of Mark and Crispina. In return, Mark and Crispina would pay Anna $10,000 in a series of installments, the last to be paid six weeks after the child's birth. Mark and Crispina were also to pay for a $200,000 life insurance policy on Anna's life.

The zygote was implanted on January 19, 1990. Less than a month later, an ultrasound test confirmed Anna was pregnant.

Unfortunately, relations deteriorated between the two sides. Mark learned that Anna had not disclosed she had suffered several stillbirths and miscarriages. Anna felt Mark and Crispina did not do enough to obtain the required insurance policy. She also felt abandoned during an onset of premature labor in June.

In July 1990, Anna sent Mark and Crispina a letter demanding the balance of the payments due her or else she would refuse to give up the child. The following month, Mark and Crispina responded with a lawsuit, seeking a declaration they were the legal parents of the unborn child. Anna filed her own action to be declared the mother of the child, and the two cases were eventually consolidated. The parties agreed to an independent guardian ad litem for the purposes of the suit.

The child was born on September 19, 1990, and blood samples were obtained from both Anna and the child for analysis. The blood test results excluded Anna as the genetic mother. The parties agreed to a court order providing that the child would remain with Mark and Crispina on a temporary basis with visits by Anna. . . .

Because two women each have presented acceptable proof of maternity [under state law—one because she gave birth to the child and the other because she provided the egg from which the child was conceived and is therefore a "genetic" relative to the child], we do not believe this case can be decided without enquiring into the parties' intentions as manifested in the surrogacy agreement. Mark and Crispina are a couple who desired to have a child of their own genes but are physically unable to do so without the help of reproductive technology. They affirmatively intended the birth of the child, and took the steps necessary to effect in vitro fertilization. But for their acted-on intention, the child would not exist. Anna agreed to facilitate the procreation of Mark's and Crispina's child. The parties' aim was to bring Mark's and Crispina's child into the world, not for Mark and Crispina to donate a zygote to Anna. Crispina from the outset intended to be the child's mother. Although the gestative function Anna performed was necessary to bring about the child's birth, it is safe to say that Anna would not have been given the opportunity to gestate or deliver the child had she, prior to implantation of the zygote, manifested her own intent to be the child's mother. No reason appears why Anna's later change of heart should vitiate the determination that Crispina is the child's natural mother.

We conclude that although the Act recognizes both genetic consanguinity and giving birth as means of establishing a mother and child relationship, when the two means do not coincide in one woman, she who intended to procreate the child—that is, she who intended to bring about the birth of a child that she intended to raise as her own—is the natural mother under California law.[10] . . .

. . . Gestational surrogacy differs in crucial respects from adoption and so is not subject to the adoption statutes. The parties voluntarily agreed to participate in in vitro fertilization and related medical procedures before the child was conceived; at the time when Anna entered into the contract, therefore, she was not vulnerable to financial inducements to part with her own expected offspring. As discussed above, Anna was not the genetic mother of the child. The payments to Anna under the contract were meant to compensate her for her services in gestating the fetus and undergoing labor, rather than for giving up "parental" rights to the child. Payments were due both during the pregnancy and after the child's birth. We are, accordingly, unpersuaded that the contract used in this case violates the public policies embodied in Penal Code section 273 and the adoption statutes. For the same reasons, we conclude these contracts do not implicate the policies underlying the statutes governing termination of parental rights. . . .

Finally, Anna and some commentators have expressed concern that surrogacy contracts tend to exploit or dehumanize women, especially women of lower economic status. Anna's objections center around the psychological harm she asserts may result from the gestator's relinquishing the child to whom she has given birth. Some have also cautioned that the practice of surrogacy may encourage society to view children as commodities, subject to trade at their parents' will.

We are all too aware that the proper forum for resolution of this issue is the Legislature, where empirical data, largely lacking from this record, can be studied and rules of general applicability developed. However, in light of our responsibility to decide this case, we have considered as best we can its possible consequences. We are unpersuaded that gestational surrogacy arrangements are so likely to cause the untoward results Anna cites as to demand their invalidation on public policy grounds. Although common sense suggests that women of lesser means serve as surrogate mothers more often than do wealthy women, there has been no proof that surrogacy contracts exploit poor women to

---

10. The dissent would decide parentage based on the best interests of the child. Such an approach raises the repugnant specter of governmental interference in matters implicating our most fundamental notions of privacy, and confuses concepts of parentage and custody. Logically, the determination of parentage must precede, and should not be dictated by, eventual custody decisions. The implicit assumption of the dissent is that a recognition of the genetic intending mother as the natural mother may sometimes harm the child. This assumption overlooks California's dependency laws, which are designed to protect all children irrespective of the manner of birth or conception. Moreover, the best interests standard poorly serves the child in the present situation: it fosters instability during litigation and, if applied to recognize the gestator as the natural mother, results in a split of custody between the natural father and the gestator, an outcome not likely to benefit the child. Further, it may be argued that, by voluntarily contracting away any rights to the child, the gestator has, in effect, conceded the best interests of the child are not with her.

Thus, under our analysis, in a true "egg donation" situation, where a woman gestates and gives birth to a child formed from the egg of another woman with the intent to raise the child as her own, the birth mother is the natural mother under California law.

any greater degree than economic necessity in general exploits them by inducing them to accept lower-paid or otherwise undesirable employment. We are likewise unpersuaded by the claim that surrogacy will foster the attitude that children are mere commodities; no evidence is offered to support it. The limited data available seem to reflect an absence of significant adverse effects of surrogacy on all participants.

The argument that a woman cannot knowingly and intelligently agree to gestate and deliver a baby for intending parents carries overtones of the reasoning that for centuries prevented women from attaining equal economic rights and professional status under the law. To resurrect this view is both to foreclose a personal and economic choice on the part of the surrogate mother, and to deny intending parents what may be their only means of procreating a child of their own genes. Certainly in the present case it cannot seriously be argued that Anna, a licensed vocational nurse who had done well in school and who had previously borne a child, lacked the intellectual wherewithal or life experience necessary to make an informed decision to enter into the surrogacy contract. . . .

KENNARD, J., dissenting.

Dissent:

. . . I agree with the majority that the best interests of the child is an important goal; indeed, as I shall explain, the best interests of the child, rather than the intent of the genetic mother, is the proper standard to apply in the absence of legislation. The problem with the majority's rule of intent is that application of this inflexible rule will not serve the child's best interests in every case.

I express no view on whether the best interests of the child in this case will be served by determining that the genetic mother is or is not the natural mother under California's Uniform Parentage Act. It may be that in this case the child's interests will be best served by recognizing Crispina as the natural mother. But this court is not just making a rule to resolve this case. Because [applicable state law] does not adequately address the situation of gestational surrogacy, this court is of necessity making a rule that, unless new legislation is enacted, will govern all future cases of gestational surrogacy in California. And all future cases will not be alike. The genetic mother and her spouse may be, in most cases, considerably more affluent than the gestational mother. But "[t]he mere fact that a couple is willing to pay a good deal of money to obtain a child does not vouchsafe that they will be suitable parents . . ." It requires little imagination to foresee cases in which the genetic mothers are, for example, unstable or substance abusers, or in which the genetic mothers' life circumstances change dramatically during the gestational mothers' pregnancies, while the gestational mothers, though of a less advantaged socioeconomic class, are stable, mature, capable and willing to provide a loving family environment in which the child will flourish. Under those circumstances, the majority's rigid reliance on the intent of the genetic mother will not serve the best interests of the child. . . .

The allocation of parental rights and responsibilities necessarily impacts the welfare of a minor child. And in issues of child welfare, the standard that courts frequently apply is the best interests of the child. . . . I would apply "the best interests of the child" standard to determine who can best assume the social and legal responsibilities of motherhood for a child born of a gestational surrogacy arrangement.

A.G.R. v. D.R.H.
2009 N.J. Super. Unpub. LEXIS 3250
(Ch. Div. 2009)

[In A.G.R. v. D.R.H., 2009 N.J. Super. Unpub. LEXIS 3250 (Ch. Div. 2009), Judge Schultz looked back 21 years to the state supreme court decision in *Baby M* in order to reach a decision in another surrogacy case with different facts than those of the *Baby M* case. D.R. and S.H, a male, gay couple (legally married in California and registered as domestic partners in New Jersey) entered into an agreement with D.R.'s sister, A.G.R. Under the agreement, A.G.R. agreed to gestate a fetus conceived from S.H.'s sperm and the egg of an anonymous donor. Eight months after embryos were transferred to her body, A.G.R. gave birth to twin girls.

Refusing to distinguish *Baby M* on the grounds that the surrogate there had a genetic and gestational relationship to the child while the surrogate in A.G.R. had only a gestational relationship to the children involved, the court stressed that the *Baby M* court only once mentioned the possible relevance of "the genetic makeup of the infant as it relates to the mother." A.G.R., 2009 N.J. Super. Unpub. LEXIS 3250, at 7. What the *Baby M* court might have done were the facts more like those in A.G.R. is not clear. However, it is important to note that the difference between "traditional" and gestational surrogacy was not a matter of much legal significance in 1988. At that time, gestational surrogacy was only a few years old in the United States, and the first child resulting from gestational surrogacy in Europe was born in England the year after the decision in *Baby M*.]

In moving for summary judgment the defendants claim that because A.G.R. has no genetic link to the children that the instant matter is distinguishable from *Baby M*. This trial judge disagrees. The public policy considerations enumerated above from *Baby M* are far reaching and unrelated to a strict genetic connection. The lack of plaintiff's genetic link to the twins is, under the circumstances, a distinction without a difference significant enough to take the instant matter out of *Baby M*. This court recognizes the many cases cited by defendants from other jurisdictions holding that "gestational carriers" do not have parental rights or at least not when confronted by others claiming to have rights over the children born to the gestational carrier. An example of this would be a California Supreme Court case Johnson v. Calvert, 851 P. 2d 776 (1993). A review of that case is appropriate. In the California case the "intentions as manifested in the surrogacy agreement" were of great importance to the Court, *Johnson,* supra, 851 P. 2d at 782. In *Baby M* the voluntary nature of the parties (thus obviously implying their intent) was of no consequence. The majority in the California case felt that the best interests of the child was "repugnant" as a consideration since it involved unnecessary governmental interference, *Johnson,* supra, 851 P. 2d at 782 n. 10. The best interests of the child were repeatedly mentioned as a concern in *Baby M*. The surrogacy contract in California is not inconsistent with California public policy while it clearly is inconsistent with public policy in New Jersey. The California case took the position that it is disrespectful toward women to not allow them to enter into agreements of this nature, whereas New Jersey law takes a clearly different position that agreements of this nature have a "potential for devastation" to women.

The California court recognized that under their Parentage Act the gestational carrier was a mother since she gave birth, but that the "intended" mother was also a mother under the Act because her eggs were used and thus there was a genetic link. That court had to "break a tie" unlike the instant matter.

If the underlying principles in California were consistent with the principles in New Jersey then the reasoning in the California case upholding the gestational carrier agreement might have been tempting. However, New Jersey's law as expressed in Baby M and the California case had so many conflicting underpinnings that this judge sees no reason to follow the California law or that of other jurisdictions for the same reason.

[Accordingly, the court declared the gestational surrogacy agreement void and identified A.G.R. as the twins' mother. The court identified S.H. as the babies' father.]

K.M. v. E.G.
117 P.3d 673 (SC Cal. 2005)

Opinion by MORENO, J.

We granted review in this case, as well as in Elisa B. v. Superior Court, 117 P.3d 660 and Kristine H. v. Lisa R., 117 P.3d 690, to consider the parental rights and obligations, if any, of a woman with regard to a child born to her partner in a lesbian relationship.

In the present case, we must decide whether a woman who provided ova to her lesbian partner so that the partner could bear children by means of in vitro fertilization is a parent of those children. For the reasons that follow, we conclude that Family Code section 7613, subdivision (b), which provides that a man is not a father if he provides semen to a physician to inseminate a woman who is not his wife, does not apply when a woman provides her ova to impregnate her partner in a lesbian relationship in order to produce children who will be raised in their joint home. Accordingly, when partners in a lesbian relationship decide to produce children in this manner, both the woman who provides her ova and her partner who bears the children are the children's parents.

FACTS

On March 6, 2001, petitioner K.M. filed a petition to establish a parental relationship with twin five-year-old girls born to respondent E.G., her former lesbian partner. K.M. alleged that she "is the biological parent of the minor children" because "[s]he donated her egg to respondent, the gestational mother of the children." E.G. moved to dismiss the petition on the grounds that, although K.M. and E.G. "were lesbian partners who lived together until this action was filed," K.M. "explicitly donated her ovum under a clear written agreement by which she relinquished any claim to offspring born of her donation."

. . . .

In January 1995, Dr. Martin [an infertility specialist with whom E.G. had consulted] suggested using K.M.'s ova. E.G. then asked K.M. to donate her ova, explaining that she would accept the ova only if K.M. "would really be a donor" and E.G. would "be the mother of any child," adding that she would not even consider permitting K.M. to adopt the child "for at least five years until [she] felt the relationship was stable and would endure" . . .

On March 8, 1995, K.M. signed a four-page form on UCSF letterhead entitled "Consent Form for Ovum Donor (Known)." The form states that K.M. agrees "to have eggs taken from my ovaries, in order that they may be donated to another woman." After explaining the medical procedures involved, the form states on the third page: "It is understood that I waive any right and relinquish any claim to the donated eggs or any pregnancy or offspring that might result from them. I agree that the recipient may regard the donated eggs and any offspring resulting therefrom as her own children." The following appears on page 4 of the form, above K.M.'s signature and the signature of a witness: "I specifically disclaim and waive any right in or any child that may be conceived as a result of the use of any ovum or egg of mine, and I agree not to attempt to discover the identity of the recipient thereof." E.G. signed a form entitled "Consent Form for Ovum Recipient" that stated, in part: "I acknowledge that the child or children produced by the IVF procedure is and shall be my own legitimate child or children and the heir or heirs of my body with all rights and privileges accompanying such status."

· · · ·

K.M. admitted reading the form, but thought parts of the form were "odd" and did not pertain to her, such as the part stating that the donor promised not to discover the identity of the recipient. She did not intend to relinquish her rights and only signed the form so that "we could have children." Despite having signed the form, K.M. "thought [she] was going to be a parent."

Ova were withdrawn from K.M. on April 11, 1995, and embryos were implanted in E.G. on April 13, 1995. K.M. and E.G. told K.M.'s father about the resulting pregnancy by announcing that he was going to be a grandfather. The twins were born on December 7, 1995. The twins' birth certificates listed E.G. as their mother and did not reflect a father's name. As they had agreed, neither E.G. nor K.M. told anyone K.M. had donated the ova, including their friends, family and the twins' pediatrician. Soon after the twins were born, E.G. asked K.M. to marry her, and on Christmas Day, the couple exchanged rings.

Within a month of their birth, E.G. added the twins to her health insurance policy, named them as her beneficiary for all employment benefits, and increased her life insurance with the twins as the beneficiary. K.M. did not do the same.

E.G. referred to her mother, as well as K.M.'s parents, as the twins' grandparents and referred to K.M.'s sister and brother as the twins' aunt and uncle, and K.M.'s nieces as their cousins. Two school forms listed both K.M. and respondent as the twins' parents. The children's nanny testified that both K.M. and E.G. "were the babies' mother."

The relationship between K.M. and E.G. ended in March 2001 and K.M. filed the present action. In September 2001, E.G. and the twins moved to Massachusetts to live with E.G.'s mother.

The superior court granted E.G.'s motion to dismiss finding, in a statement of decision, "that [K.M.] . . . knowingly, voluntarily and intelligently executed the ovum donor form, thereby acknowledging her understanding that, by the donation of her ova, she was relinquishing and waiving all rights to claim legal parentage of any children who might result from the in vitro fertilization and implantation of her ova in a recipient (in this case, a known recipient, her domestic partner [E.G.]). . . . [K.M.]'s testimony on the subject of her execution of the ovum donor form was contradictory and not always credible.

. . . .

The Court of Appeal affirmed the judgment, ruling that K.M. did not qualify as a parent "because substantial evidence supports the trial court's factual finding that only E.G. intended to bring about the birth of a child whom she intended to raise as her own."

. . . .

DISCUSSION

K.M. asserts that she is a parent of the twins because she supplied the ova that were fertilized in vitro and implanted in her lesbian partner, resulting in the birth of the twins. As we will explain, we agree that K.M. is a parent of the twins because she supplied the ova that produced the children, and Family Code section 7613, subdivision (b) 2 (hereafter section 7613(b)), which provides that a man is not a father if he provides semen to a Physician to inseminate a woman who is not his wife, does not apply because K.M. supplied her ova to impregnate her lesbian partner in order to produce children who would be raised in their joint home.

The determination of parentage is governed by the Uniform Parentage Act (UPA). (§7600 et seq.) As we observe in the companion case of Elisa B. v. Superior Court, the UPA defines the "'parent and child relationship[, which] extends equally to every child and to every parent, regardless of the marital status of the parents.' (§7602.)"

. . . .

The Court of Appeal in the present case concluded . . . that K.M. was not a parent of the twins, despite her genetic relationship to them, because she had the same status as a sperm donor. Section 7613(b) states: "The donor of semen provided to a licensed physician and surgeon for use in artificial insemination of a woman other than the donor's wife is treated in law as if he were not the natural father of a child thereby conceived." In Johnson [v. Calvert], we considered the predecessor statute to section 7613(b), former Civil Code section 7005. We did not discuss whether this statute applied to a woman who provides ova used to impregnate another woman, but we observed that "in a true 'egg donation' situation, where a woman gestates and gives birth to a child formed from the egg of another woman with the intent to raise the child as her own, the birth mother is the natural mother under California law." We held that the statute did not apply under the circumstances in Johnson, because the husband and wife in Johnson did not intend to "donate" their sperm and ova to the surrogate mother, but rather "intended to procreate a child genetically related to them by the only available means."

The circumstances of the present case are not identical to those in Johnson, but they are similar in a crucial respect; both the couple in Johnson and the couple in the present case intended to produce a child that would be raised in their own home. In Johnson, it was clear that the married couple did not intend to "donate" their semen and ova to the surrogate mother, but rather permitted their semen and ova to be used to impregnate the surrogate mother in order to produce a child to be raised by them. In the present case, K.M. contends that she did not intend to donate her ova, but rather provided her ova so that E.G. could give birth to a child to be raised jointly by K.M. and E.G. E.G. hotly contests this, asserting that K.M. donated her ova to E.G., agreeing that E.G. would be the sole parent. It is undisputed, however, that the couple lived together and that they both intended to bring the child into their joint home. Thus, even accepting as true E.G.'s version of the facts (which the superior court did), the present case, like Johnson, does not present a "true 'egg donation'" situation. K.M. did not intend to simply donate her ova to E.G., but rather provided her ova to her lesbian partner with whom she was living so that E.G. could give birth to a child that would be raised in their joint home. Even if we assume that the provisions of section 7613(b) apply to women who donate ova, the statute does not apply under the circumstances of the present case.

· · · ·

It is true we said in Johnson that "for any child California law recognizes only one natural mother." But as we explain in the companion case of Elisa B. v. Superior Court, this statement in Johnson must be understood in light of the issue presented in that case; "our decision in Johnson does not preclude a child from having two parents both of whom are women. . . ."

DISPOSITION

The judgment of the Court of Appeal is reversed.

NOTES AND QUESTIONS

1. *Surrogacy contracts.* Both the Surrogate Parenting Agreement entered into by William Stern, Mary Beth Whitehead, and Richard Whitehead and the Agreement entered into by William Stern and the Infertility Center of New York are included as appendices to the state supreme court's decision in *Baby M.* Elizabeth Stern did not sign either of these contractual agreements. Why do you think she did not? Richard Whitehead (Mary Beth's husband) did consent to the arrangement in writing. Why do you think he did that?

The Surrogate Parenting Agreement defines the payment to be made by William Stern to Mary Beth Whitehead in the following terms:

> That the consideration for this Agreement, which is compensation for services and expenses, and in no way is to be construed as a fee for termination of parental rights or a payment in exchange for a consent to surrender the child for adoption, in addition to other provisions contained herein, shall be as follows:
>
> (A) $10,000 shall be paid to MARY BETH WHITEHEAD, Surrogate, upon surrender of custody to WILLIAM STERN, the natural and biological father of the child born pursuant to the provisions of this Agreement for surrogate services and expenses in carrying out her obligations under this Agreement;
>
> (B) The consideration to be paid to MARY BETH WHITEHEAD, Surrogate, shall be deposited with the Infertility Center of New York (hereinafter ICNY), the representative of WILLIAM STERN, at the time of the signing of

this Agreement, and held in escrow until completion of the duties and obligations of MARY BETH WHITEHEAD, Surrogate. . . .

(C) WILLIAM STERN, Natural Father, shall pay the expenses incurred by
MARY BETH WHITEHEAD, Surrogate, pursuant to her pregnancy . . .

Do you agree with the New Jersey Supreme Court's conclusion that
"considerable care was taken to structure the surrogacy arrangement so as
not to violate" the state prohibition on paying or accepting money in connection with the adoption of a child? Can you suggest anything else the parties
might have done to structure the arrangement even more carefully in this
regard?

In R.R. v. M.H., 689 N.E.2d 790 (Mass. 1998), a case quite similar to *Baby M,*
the parties entered into an agreement that provided for a transfer of custody
from the surrogate to the biological father and his wife. In that case, the arrangement did not provide for the transfer of parentage. Yet, that difference did not
preclude litigation. As in *Baby M,* the surrogate in *R.R.,* Michelle Hoagland,
decided to retain custody of the baby (conceived through artificial insemination, using the sperm of the intending father, Robert Rascoe). Before the case
reached the state's highest court, the parties agreed that Rascoe and his wife,
Margaret, would retain custody and that Hoagland would enjoy periodic visits
with the child. The Massachusetts court considered only whether the contract
among the parties was enforceable. In this regard, the court refused to validate
compensated surrogacy agreements (even those such as the one at issue in the
case, which presumed to transfer custody but not parentage). The court
"decline[d] on public policy grounds, to apply to a surrogacy agreement of
the type involved . . . the general principle that an agreement between
informed, mature adults should be enforced absent proof of duress, fraud, or
undue influence." 689 N.E.2d at 797.

2. *Constitutional rights and surrogacy.* In *Baby M,* the court referred to
constitutional rights. A number of Supreme Court decisions suggest a right to
procreate, but the Court has never expressly defined such a right. In Skinner v.
Oklahoma, 316 U.S. 535, 541 (1942), the Court referred to reproduction as
"one of the basic civil rights of man," and in Eisenstadt v. Baird, 405 U.S.
438, 453 (1972),[1] the court referred to the right to be "free from unwarranted
governmental intrusion into matters so fundamentally affecting a person as the
decision whether to bear or beget a child." These cases suggest a right to reproduce through sexual intercourse, but do not necessarily suggest a constitutional
right to reproduce using ART or surrogacy.

In Lifchez v. Hartigan, 735 F. Supp. 1361, 1377 (N.D. Ill. 1990), aff'd, 914
F.2d 260 (7th Cir. 1990), a lower federal court recognized a "right to submit to a
medical procedure that may bring about, rather than prevent, pregnancy." In
Lifchez, the court invalidated an Illinois law that prohibited fetal experimentation on the ground that the law could have been interpreted to ban the use
of ART. See Carl H. Coleman, Assisted Reproductive Technologies and the
Constitution, 30 Fordham Urb. L.J. 57 (2002).

3. *Intention of parties.* In contract cases involving disputes occasioned by
reproductive technology, the "intent" of the parties is basic to the interpretive

---

1. These cases are considered in Chapter 5.

process. Is or should the intention of parties who have entered into agreements about reproduction be essential to the resolution of disputes among the parties? What do you think Mary Beth Whitehead "intended" when she applied to be a surrogate? When she entered into the agreement with Stern? When she learned that she was pregnant and when she gave birth? At what point should her intentions be assessed? If intention is assessed at the time that the contract is entered into, has the world of reproduction been moved fully into the world of contract and commerce? Is there any moral difference between assessing intention in cases about conception and birth on the one hand and commercial cases on the other hand?

William Stern and Mary Beth Whitehead discussed the matter of "intention" during a phone conversation that Stern had taped, following his lawyer's advice. The conversation took place after the Whiteheads had fled to Florida with the baby. It was played during the trial. At one point during the conversation Stern invoked the parties' intentions in entering the surrogacy arrangement. "You made an agreement," he told Whitehead. Whitehead responded by asking, "Aren't I allowed to change my mind?" In effect Stern told her "No." "You don't change your mind about things like this, Mary Beth. . . ." (Quoted in Elaine Landau, Surrogate Mothers 98 (1988).)

4. *The language of surrogacy.*   The agreements signed by the parties in *Baby M* refer to William Stern as the "natural father" and to Whitehead as the surrogate. Do you think Whitehead is a "surrogate" and/or a "mother"? That question is more complex in the arrangements that occasioned the disputes at issue in Johnson v. Calvert, K.M. v. E.G., and in A.G.R. v. D.R.H., supra.

5. *Theories of parentage in the* Johnson *case.*   Three California courts rendered decisions in Johnson v. Calvert. No. X633190, slip op. (Cal. Super. Ct., Orange County, Dept. 11, Oct. 22, 1990), aff'd sub nom. Anna J. v. Mark C., 286 Cal. Rptr. 369 (Cal. App. 1991), aff'd sub nom. Johnson v. Calvert, 851 P.2d 776 (Cal. 1993), cert. denied, 510 U.S. 874 (1993). All three held that the Calverts were baby Christopher's legal parents. However, the three courts relied on very different theories in reaching that conclusion. The trial court identified the family through "shared genes" among the baby, Crispina, and Mark. That court referred to Anna Johnson as a "gestational carrier," but a "genetic hereditary stranger" to the child. The appellate court affirmed, relying on a construction of California statutory law. The state supreme court concluded that neither the trial court's biological analysis nor the intermediate appellate court's statutory construction provided firm grounds for resolving the dispute. What theory did the state's highest court rely on to resolve the dispute among the parties?

6. *Favoring genetic or gestational mother?*   Justice Kennard, who dissented from the California Supreme Court's decision in *Johnson,* would have resolved the case by looking to the child's best interests. She asserted that the majority's opinion would always result in a child born as a result of gestational surrogacy being defined under the law as the child of the genetic parents. Is that an accurate reading of the court's decision? (Hint: Read footnote 10 in the court's decision.)

7. *Content of a surrogacy agreement.*   The New Jersey court that decided *A.G.R.,* supra, asserted that, among other things, the court that decided *Baby M.* was concerned that the agreement at issue in the case did not pay attention to

"the fitness of the adoptive parents, the medical history of the birth mother, the feelings of the birth mother, the impact of separation on the child and the best interest of the child." Id., at 6). Do you agree that a surrogacy agreement should provide for all or some of these matters?

8. *New Jersey surrogacy bill.* In the years since *Baby M.* was decided, New Jersey has not passed legislation regulating surrogacy arrangements. In 2012, New Jersey Governor Chris Christie vetoed a bill, the New Jersey Gestational Carrier Agreement Act (S. 1599), that would have denied gestational surrogates a claim to maternity by defining "[t]he intended parent[s]" as the "legal parent[s] of the child" immediately after a child's birth (thus promising to do away with the state's three-day waiting period before legal parentage can be transferred). In vetoing the bill, Christie suggested the need for more far-reaching exploration of the implications of reshaping "the traditional beginnings of the family." Susan K. Livio, Christie Vetoes Bill that Would Have Eased Tough Rules for Gestational Surrogates, www.nj.com, Aug. 8, 2012.

9. *More complicated surrogacy arrangements.* In 1998, the California courts were faced with a surrogacy dispute that involved at least five (and arguably seven) people with claims to the parentage of one child. The case was unusual, however, in that only one of the potential parents sought legal parentage. Buzzanca v. Buzzanca, 72 Cal. Rptr. 2d 280 (Cal. App. 1998), arose as part of divorce proceedings involving Luanne and John Buzzanca. The couple, unable to have a child without assistance, entered into a surrogacy agreement with Pamela Snell. The couple arranged through a California infertility clinic for Snell to become pregnant through anonymously donated gametes. In 1995 Snell gave birth to a baby girl, named Jaycee. The case differed from both *Baby M* and *Johnson* in that neither of the intending parents had a biological connection with the child. The couple's marriage disintegrated before the child's birth. Luanne brought the child home from the hospital. She then sought child support from John, who denied and rejected parentage. The trial court accepted a stipulation that Pamela Snell was not a parent to the child and decided further that neither Luanne nor John was a parent to Jaycee. The court concluded:

> So I think what evidence there is, is stipulated to. And I don't think there would be any more. One, there's no genetic tie between Luanne and the child. Two, she is not the gestational mother. Three, she has not adopted the child. That, folks, to me, respectfully is clear and convincing evidence that she's not the legal mother.

72 Cal. Rptr. 2d at 283. On appeal, the court described the trial court conclusion as "extraordinary" and reversed. The appellate court predicated the Buzzancas' parentage on their parental intentions and defined them, under the law, as the child's natural parents.

How else might Luanne have attained legal parentage of baby Jaycee? Why do you think she pressed to be denominated the baby's "natural" parent?

10. *Naming intentional/genetic parents on birth certificate.* In Culliton v. Beth Israel Deaconess Medical Center, 756 N.E.2d 1133 (Mass. 2001), the highest court in Massachusetts concluded that the genetic, intending parents of a child gestated by a surrogate could be named on the child's birth certificate without the intending parents having to go through an adoption procedure. In *Culliton,*

the genetic, intending parents (Marla and Steven Culliton) and the surrogate (Melissa Carroll) all favored naming the Cullitons as the twins' legal parents. The trial court had concluded (not irrationally in the view of the state's highest court) that it did not have authority to order that the Cullitons be named as the child's legal parents absent a formal adoption proceeding. That judge, the higher court noted,

> acted prudently in seeking to place this case before us as quickly as possible because, as he correctly noted, there is no direct legal "authority for issuing a pre-birth order regarding parentage under the facts of this case." Authority elsewhere is sparse and not altogether consistent.

Id. at 1136. The court concluded:

> Here, where (a) the plaintiffs are the sole genetic sources of the twins; (b) the gestational carrier agrees with the orders sought; (c) no one, including the hospital, has contested the complaint or petition; and (d) by filing the complaint the stipulation for judgment the plaintiffs agree that they have waived any contradictory provisions in contract (assuming those provisions could be enforced in the first place), we conclude that pursuant to the Probate and Family Court's general equity jurisdiction . . . the judge had authority to consider the merits of the relief sought here.

Id. at 1138.

Similarly, in three separate cases, trial courts in Connecticut recognized gestational surrogacy agreements and provided for genetic parents to be named the "biological and legal parents" of babies being gestated by surrogates. See De Bernardo v. Gregory, 2007 Conn. Super. LEXIS 3078 (Nov. 7, 2007), Goad v. Arel, 2007 Conn. Super. LEXIS 3347 (May 24, 2007); Wray v. Samuel, 2007 Conn. Super LEXIS 3349 (April 20, 2007).

11. *California cases and "natural" parentage.* In K.M. v. E.G., supra, and companion cases, Elisa B. v. Superior Court and Kristine H. v. Lisa R., California's highest court made it clear that "natural" parentage is not necessarily identical with "biological" parentage, *Elisa B.,* 117 P.3d at 670, and that a woman who intends to parent a child and who presents herself as that child's parent may be deemed the child's "natural" mother even if she has no biological relation to the child and has not adopted the child. In *Elisa B,* the court recognized Elisa's maternity because she had "actively assisted" Emily, her partner, to become pregnant and had "openly held out" the resulting children "as her natural children." Id. at 85. These cases jettison a series of assumptions about how the law identifies a child's parent(s). What are some of those assumptions?

12. *Dearth of regulation in the United States.* The New Jersey courts entertained the *Baby M* case in the late 1980s. The case raised widespread concern about potential problems raised by surrogacy. Yet, legislatures have been slow to respond, and they vary widely in their response to commercial surrogacy. The practice is permitted and regulated in about 18 states, including Arkansas, Illinois, Washington, and Texas. It is allowed, in some form, in about a dozen states, and it is prohibited, in some form, in about a half-dozen states. Surrogacy contracts are void in some states, and the practice is illegal in others, including Michigan and New York. Tiffany L. Palmer, The Winding Road to the Two-Dad

Family: Issues Arising in Interstate Surrogacy for Gay Couples, 8 Rutgers L.J. & Pub. Pol'y 895, 904–906 (2011); Katherine Drabiak et al., Ethics, Law and Commercial Surrogacy: A Call for Uniformity, 35 J.L. Med. & Ethics 300 (2007). In addition, in recent years, a number of states, including Florida, Illinois, and Texas, have passed laws that provide for gestational surrogacy arrangements.

13. *Ethical obligations of lawyers in cases involving reproductive technology.*   Relationships among the parties to an agreement involving third parties in the reproductive process differ significantly from relationships among family members. One would thus expect that particular ethical obligations fall to attorneys representing clients in such arrangements. What specific ethical obligations would you want to impose on lawyers representing clients in cases occasioned by assisted reproduction and reproductive technology?

14. *Regulation in other countries.*   In Australia, commercial surrogacy is prohibited everywhere. Surrogacy arrangements that do not involve money exchange have recently been accepted in all Australia states except for Tasmania, http://www.legallawyers.com.au/family-law/commercial-surrogacy-laws-in-australia/ (last visited June 15, 2012). In Denmark statutory law precludes the validation of surrogacy agreements. The Child Law (No. 460) of 7 June 2001, Chapter 6. Surrogate Motherhood (Sec. 31). Gestational, but not traditional, surrogacy is permitted in Israel. The law allows paying gestational surrogates. Rhona Schuz, Surrogacy in Israel: An Analysis of the Law in Practice, in Surrogate Motherhood: International Perspectives 35, 36 (Rachel Cook et al. eds. 2003).

Both France and Germany ban commercial surrogacy. http://www.bionews.org.uk/page_92561.asp (last visited June 2, 2011). In Greece commercial surrogacy is not allowed, but "altruistic gestational surrogacy" is permitted. Russia does permit surrogacy by law; Russian law requires a prescription indicating that the person or persons seeking the services of a surrogate are infertile or suffer from a condition that makes childbearing problematic. Find Surrogate Mother.com, www.findsurrogatemother.com. In 2008, the Science Council of Japan, described as an independent group working under the office of the prime minister, continues to press for a legislative response. At least some Japanese couples travel to the United States for reproductive assistance, including assistance with surrogacy arrangements. Surrogate Birth Forum Needed, The Japan Times, May 20, 2008. And in recent years, couples from several countries, including the United States and Canada, have gone to India to find gestational surrogates. There, commercial surrogacy is not subject to significant regulation. Henry Chu, Wombs for Rent, Cheap, L.A. Times, Apr. 19, 2006, at A1.

CHALLENGING ISSUES: PARENTAGE AND SURROGACY

Jane and Bill Malby were unable to have biological children without assistance because Jane had been born without a uterus. They entered into a surrogacy arrangement with Pat Lester, Jane's best friend. Pat agreed to gestate an embryo created from Jane's egg and Bill's sperm, to bear the resulting baby, and at its birth to surrender the baby to Jane and Bill. Pat did not want to be compensated for her part in the arrangement. After the baby's birth, Pat handed the baby over to Jane and expressed delight at having been able to have given the gift of life to the Malbys. The child, a girl, was named Sue Malby. The state, however, refused to list Jane as the legal mother on the child's birth certificate. A state representative explained to Jane, Bill, and Sue that he agreed that the Malbys were the child's parents. (He did not explain why.) However, he said that state law left no option but to have the birth mother listed as the legal mother. The relevant statute (Prohibition of Surrogate Parenthood Agreements) read:

(1)(a) No person, agency, institution, or intermediary may be a party to a contract for profit or gain in which a woman agrees to undergo artificial insemination or other procedures and subsequently terminate her parental rights to a child born as a result.

(2) An agreement which is entered into, without consideration given, in which a woman agrees to undergo artificial insemination or other procedures and subsequently terminate her parental rights to a child born as a result, is unenforceable.

(3) In any case arising under Subsection (1) or (2), the surrogate mother is the mother of the child for all legal purposes, and her husband, if she is married, is the father of the child for all legal purposes.

The state contended that Jane would have to adopt the child in order to become her legal mother. Jane, Bill, and Sue brought suit. What are they likely to argue and how might the courts respond?

Do you think that the state's Prohibition on Surrogate Parenthood Agreements should be amended? If so, how?

3.   Disputes About Embryos

A somewhat different set of questions has developed as a result of the possibility of freezing gametes and embryos for long periods of time and then thawing them for fertilization or gestation. This possibility has led to disputes between gamete donors who together planned to have a child but who changed their minds, and it has led to disputes between gamete donors and infertility clinics.

The first decision by a state's highest court involving the disposition of frozen embryos was Davis v. Davis, decided by the Tennessee Supreme Court in 1992. The court's opinion has provided a model for a number of other courts facing similar disputes. Since *Davis,* a few courts in other states have relied on alternative models that do not stress the significance of contractual agreements in resolving such disputes.

|| ***Davis v. Davis*** ||
|| **842 S.W.2d 588 (Tenn. 1992)** ||

Opinion by Martha Craig DAUGHTREY.

This appeal presents a question of first impression, involving the disposition of the cryogenically-preserved product of in vitro fertilization (IVF), commonly referred to in the popular press and the legal journals as "frozen embryos." The case began as a divorce action, filed by the appellee, Junior Lewis Davis, against his then wife, appellant Mary Sue Davis. The parties were able to agree upon all terms of dissolution, except one: who was to have "custody" of the seven "frozen embryos" stored in a Knoxville fertility clinic that had attempted to assist the Davises in achieving a much-wanted pregnancy during a happier period in their relationship.

I. INTRODUCTION

Mary Sue Davis originally asked for control of the "frozen embryos" with the intent to have them transferred to her own uterus, in a post-divorce effort to become pregnant. Junior Davis objected, saying that he preferred to leave the embryos in their frozen state until he decided whether or not he wanted to become a parent outside the bounds of marriage.

Based on its determination that the embryos were "human beings" from the moment of fertilization, the trial court awarded "custody" to Mary Sue Davis and directed that she "be permitted the opportunity to bring these children to term through implantation." The Court of Appeals reversed, finding that Junior Davis has a "constitutionally protected right not to beget a child where no pregnancy has taken place" and holding that "there is no compelling state interest to justify . . . ordering implantation against the will of either party." The Court of Appeals further held that "the parties share an interest in the seven fertilized ova" and remanded the case to the trial court for entry of an order vesting them with "joint control . . . and equal voice over their disposition."

Mary Sue Davis then sought review in this Court, contesting the validity of the constitutional basis for the Court of Appeals decision. We granted review, not because we disagree with the basic legal analysis utilized by the intermediate court, but because of the obvious importance of the case in terms of the development of law regarding the new reproductive technologies, and because the decision of the Court of Appeals does not give adequate guidance to the trial court in the event the parties cannot agree. . . .

At the outset, it is important to note the absence of two critical factors that might otherwise influence or control the result of this litigation: When the Davises signed up for the IVF program at the Knoxville clinic, they did not execute a written agreement specifying what disposition should be made of any unused embryos that might result from the cryopreservation process. Moreover, there was at that time no Tennessee statute governing such disposition, nor has one been enacted in the meantime. . . .

II. THE FACTS

[The court relates that Mary Sue and Junior Lewis Davis married in 1980. After five tubal pregnancies, Mary Sue was left without either fallopian tube. The Davises were unsuccessful at adopting a child. IVF became their only option in the effort to become parents. The couple went through six rounds of IVF treatment, the last of which occurred in 1988. At that time, seven fertilized ova were frozen for possible future use. In early 1989, however, Junior Davis filed for divorce.]

IV. The "Person" vs. "Property" Dichotomy

[This section of the opinion is printed in Chapter 3. In this section the court concludes that the "preembryos" cannot be categorized as humans, the decision of the trial court to the contrary notwithstanding, and that they cannot be categorized as akin to property as suggested by the decision of the state's intermediate appellate court. Rather, the court concludes that the preembryos "are not, strictly speaking, either 'persons' or 'property,' but occupy an interim category that entitles them to special respect because of their potential for human life."]

V. The Enforceability of Contract

. . . [T]here was initially no agreement between the parties concerning disposition of the preembryos under the circumstances of this case; there has been no agreement since; and there is no formula in the Court of Appeals opinion for determining the outcome if the parties cannot reach an agreement in the future.

In granting joint custody to the parties, the Court of Appeals must have anticipated that, in the absence of agreement, the preembryos would continue to be stored, as they now are, in the Knoxville fertility clinic. One problem with maintaining the status quo is that the viability of the preembryos cannot be guaranteed indefinitely. Experts in cryopreservation who testified in this case estimated the maximum length of preembryonic viability at two years. Thus, the true effect of the intermediate court's opinion is to confer on Junior Davis the inherent power to veto any transfer of the preembryos in this case and thus to insure their eventual discard or self-destruction. . . .

VII. Balancing the Parties' Interests

. . . In this case, the issue centers on the two aspects of procreational autonomy—the right to procreate and the right to avoid procreation. We start by considering the burdens imposed on the parties by solutions that would have the effect of disallowing the exercise of individual procreational autonomy with respect to these particular preembryos.

Beginning with the burden imposed on Junior Davis, we note that the consequences are obvious. Any disposition which results in the gestation of the preembryos would impose unwanted parenthood on him, with all of its possible financial and psychological consequences. . . . In light of his boyhood experiences [including his parents' divorce, his mother's nervous breakdown and his being placed in a home for boys], Junior Davis is vehemently opposed to fathering a child that would not live with both parents. Regardless of whether he or Mary Sue had custody, he feels that the child's bond with the non-custodial parent would not be satisfactory. He testified very clearly that his concern was for the psychological obstacles a child in such a situation would face, as well as the burdens it would impose on him. . . .

Balanced against Junior Davis's interest in avoiding parenthood is Mary Sue Davis's interest in donating the preembryos to another couple for implantation. Refusal to permit donation of the preembryos would impose on her the burden of knowing that the lengthy IVF procedures she underwent were futile, and that the preembryos to which she contributed genetic material would never become children. While this is not an insubstantial emotional burden, we can only conclude that Mary Sue Davis's interest in donation is not as significant as the interest Junior Davis has in avoiding parenthood. . . .

The case would be closer if Mary Sue Davis were seeking to use the preembryos herself, but only if she could not achieve parenthood by any other reasonable means. We recognize the trauma that Mary Sue has already experienced and the additional discomfort to which she would be subjected if she opts to attempt IVF again. Still, she would have a reasonable opportunity, through IVF, to try once again to achieve parenthood in all its aspects—genetic, gestational, bearing, and rearing.

Further, we note that if Mary Sue Davis were unable to undergo another round of IVF, or opted not to try, she could still achieve the child-rearing aspects of parenthood through adoption. . . .

VII. CONCLUSION

In summary, we hold that disputes involving the disposition of preembryos produced by in vitro fertilization should be resolved, first, by looking to the preferences of the progenitors. If their wishes cannot be ascertained, or if there is dispute, then their prior agreement concerning disposition should be carried out. If no prior agreement exists, then the relative interests of the parties in using or not using the preembryos must be weighed. Ordinarily, the party wishing to avoid procreation should prevail, assuming that the other party has a reasonable possibility of achieving parenthood by means other than use of the preembryos in question. If no other reasonable alternatives exist, then the argument in favor of using the preembryos to achieve pregnancy should be considered. However, if the party seeking control of the preembryos intends merely to donate them to another couple, the objecting party obviously has the greater interest and should prevail.

But the rule does not contemplate the creation of an automatic veto, and in affirming the judgment of the Court of Appeals, we would not wish to be interpreted as so holding.

For the reasons set out above, the judgment of the Court of Appeals is affirmed, in the appellee's favor.

NOTES AND QUESTIONS

1. *Balancing parental interests.*   In balancing the interests of Mary Sue Davis and Junior Davis, the court found those of Junior to be stronger. Is that conclusion obvious? Is it objective? Should such a decision be based on objective measures? Can it be?

2. *Contractual provisions involving embryos.*   The court in *Davis* stated clearly that, had the parties entered into a contractual agreement about the embryos, it would have enforced the contract before it would have balanced the parties' interests. Do you agree with the *Davis* court that people should be held to contractual agreements concerning the disposition of their cryopreserved embryos?

In Kass v. Kass, 696 N.E.2d 174 (N.Y. 1998), aff'g 663 N.Y.S.2d 581 (App. Div. 1997), rev'g 1995 WL 110368 (N.Y. Sup. Ct. 1995), New York's highest court committed itself to a contractual analysis in resolving a dispute between a divorcing couple, similar to the dispute between the Davises. Maureen and Steven Kass married in 1988. They entered infertility treatment in 1990 and attempted unsuccessfully to become parents through ten cycles of in vitro fertilization. In 1993, at the time of the last attempt at IVF, five embryos were frozen and stored in the infertility clinic where the couple was being treated. Soon after, Maureen filed for divorce, seeking "sole custody" of the frozen embryos. Steven Kass wanted to donate the embryos to the clinic. He argued that informed consent agreements entered into between himself and Maureen before treatments began precluded Maureen's proposed use of the embryos.

The New York trial court judge held for Maureen on the grounds that the constitutional right to abort or not abort a pregnancy gave Maureen legal control over the frozen embryos in vitro comparable to the control that she would have were the embryos in vivo. Judge Roncallo of the trial court further explained that "[i]f the wife is awarded possession the preembryos will be afforded an opportunity to realize their potential; if the husband is successful such potential will be extinguished as part of a scientific inquiry." 1995 WL 110368, at *2. Yet, the trial court judge also noted that he would have honored an unambiguous contract between the parties if one had existed. In the view of the trial court no such contract did exist. In fact, each of the two higher courts that heard the case acknowledged a potential ambiguity in the informed consent agreements. However, both the intermediate appellate court and the New York Court of Appeals interpreted the agreements so as to resolve the ambiguity. The latter court concluded: "The consents [the Kasses] signed provided for other contingencies [than having a child], most especially that in the present circumstances the pre-zygotes would be donated to the IVF program for approved research purposes." Because the Court of Appeals relied on the consent agreements, it avoided considering questions about the ontological status of the embryos as well as questions about the scope of a constitutional right to make reproductive choices.

3. *Invalidating a consent agreement about embryos.*   Does it make sense to allow couples receiving infertility treatment to determine the disposition of unused embryos through pretreatment contractual agreements? Should these contracts, when they exist, be analyzed as any other contract is analyzed, under usual contract rules?

The third time a state's highest court entertained a dispute about frozen embryos, the Massachusetts Supreme Judicial Court refused to enforce the terms of a consent agreement into which the husband and wife had entered. A.Z. v. B.Z., 725 N.E.2d 1051 (Mass. 2000). This case differed from *Davis* and *Kass* in that the divorcing wife tried to enforce a consent agreement that gave her control of the couple's cryopreserved embryos in the event of divorce. For a variety of reasons, the court concluded that the consent forms that the parties had signed were not valid contractual agreements. More important, the court asserted that even if the parties had entered into an "unambiguous agreement," it would not have enforced a contract that required one party to become a genetic parent against his or her will. After reviewing a variety of state laws and judicial decisions involving reproduction, parentage, and divorce, the court wrote:

> We glean from these statutes and judicial decisions that prior agreements to enter into familial relationships (marriage or parenthood) should not be enforced against individuals who subsequently reconsider their decisions. This enhances the "freedom of personal choice in matters of marriage and family life." Moore v. East Cleveland, 431 U.S. 494, 499 (1977), quoting Cleveland Bd. of Educ. v. LaFleur, 414 U.S. 632, 639–640 (1974).
>
> We derive from existing State laws and judicial precedent a public policy in this Commonwealth that individuals shall not be compelled to enter into intimate family relationships, and that the law shall not be used as a mechanism for forcing such relationships when they are not desired. This policy is grounded in the notion that respect for liberty and privacy requires that individuals be accorded the freedom to decide whether to enter into a family relationship. . . .
>
> In this case, we are asked to decide whether the law of the Commonwealth may compel an individual to become a parent over his or her contemporaneous objection. The husband signed this consent form in 1991. Enforcing the form against him would require him to become a parent over his present objection to such an undertaking. We decline to do so.

Id. at 1059.

4. *Ectogenesis.* Judicial and statutory responses to disputes about frozen embryos only suggest the outlines of possible responses to potential disputes about fetuses or children should artificial wombs become available. Ectogenesis—the process of gestation outside the human body—raises a slew of potentially difficult legal and policy questions. Jessica H. Schultz, Note, Development of Ectogenesis: How Will Artificial Wombs Affect the Legal Status of a Fetus or Embryo, 84 Chi.-Kent L. Rev. 877 (2010). It is presumed that at some point it will become possible to gestate a fetus from conception in an artificial womb, and to move a developing fetus from a woman's uterus so that gestation can continue in an artificial womb. In additional to raising questions about parentage, the second possibility raises troubling questions that could have an impact on the debate about abortion.

5. *British response.* In late 2003, a British court rejected the pleas of two women to preserve frozen embryos produced from their ova and the sperm of their respective former partners. One of the two women, Natallie Evans, had embryos frozen soon after learning that she suffered from ovarian tumors and just before her ovaries were surgically removed. Thus, she viewed the embryos as her last chance to have a genetic child. Her former partner withdrew consent to Ms. Evans's gestating the embryos after the relationship between them fell apart. Similarly, Lorraine Hadley's former partner withdrew his consent to her gestating embryos fertilized with his sperm. The Human Fertilisation and Embryology Act predicates the storage and use of frozen embryos on the consent of both parties. Dr. Michael Wilks, chair of the ethics committee of the British Medical

Association, empathized with the women but opined, in support of the court's decision, that it would not be wise to alter "the rules on consent retrospectively." Michael Horsnell, Frozen Embryos: Judge Ends Women's Hopes of Motherhood, The Times (London), Oct. 2, 2003, at 3. In June 2004, the Appeals Court supported the decision of the court below. Let Her Be Mum, The Sun, June 26, 2004. After losing in the United Kingdom, Evans brought her case to the European Court of Human Rights (Grand Chamber), Evans v. United Kingdom, [2007] 1 FLR 1900, [2007] 2 FCR 5, 22 BHRC 190 (European Ct H. Rts, Grand Chamber). There she argued that relevant British law violated various sections of the European Convention for the Protection of Human Rights ("Convention"). In particular, Evans claimed that British law violated the right of the embryos to life pursuant to Article 2 of the Convention. Holding against Evans, the Grand Chamber found no violation of the Convention in the responses of British law to Evans's case. The court summarized laws about frozen embryos and other aspects of assisted reproduction within the Council of Europe:

> 39. On the basis of the material available to the Court, including the 'Medically Assisted Procreation and the Protection of the Human Embryo Study on the Solution in 39 States' (Council of Europe, 1998) and the replies by the Member States of the Council of Europe to the Steering Committee on Bioethics' 'Questionnaire on Access to Medically Assisted Procreation' (Council of Europe, 2005), it would appear that IVF treatment is regulated by primary or secondary legislation in Austria, Azerbaijan, Bulgaria, Croatia, Denmark, Estonia, France, Georgia, Germany, Greece, Hungary, Iceland, Italy, Latvia, the Netherlands, Norway, the Russian Federation, Slovenia, Spain, Sweden, Switzerland, Turkey, Ukraine and the United Kingdom; while in Belgium, the Czech Republic, Finland, Ireland, Malta, Lithuania, Poland, Serbia and Slovakia such treatment is governed by clinical practice, professional guidelines, royal or administrative decree or general constitutional principles.
>
> 40. The storage of embryos, for varying lengths of time, appears to be permitted in all the above states where IVF is regulated by primary or secondary legislation, except Germany and Switzerland, where in one cycle of treatment no more than three embryos may be created which are, in principle, to be implanted together immediately, and Italy, where the law permits the freezing of embryos only on exceptional, unforeseen medical grounds.
>
> 41. In Denmark, France, Greece, the Netherlands and Switzerland, the right of either party freely to withdraw his or her consent at any stage up to the moment of implantation of the embryo in the woman is expressly provided for in primary legislation. It appears that, as a matter of law or practice, in Belgium, Finland and Iceland there is a similar freedom for either gamete provider to withdraw consent before implantation.
>
> 42. A number of countries have, however, regulated the consent issue differently. In Hungary, for example, in the absence of a specific contrary agreement by the couple, the woman is entitled to proceed with the treatment notwithstanding the death of her partner or the divorce of the couple. In Austria and Estonia the man's consent can be revoked only up to the point of fertilisation, beyond which it is the woman alone who decides if and when to proceed. In Spain, the man's right to revoke his consent is recognised only where he is married to and living with the woman. In Germany and Italy, neither party can normally withdraw consent after the eggs have been fertilised. In Iceland, the embryos must be destroyed if the gamete providers separate or divorce before the expiry of the maximum storage period.

6. *Bibliographic note.* The following articles (within a large and growing literature on disputes about frozen embryos) are useful: Yehezkel Margalit,

To Be or Not to Be (A Parent?—Not Precisely the Question: The Frozen Embryo Dispute, 18 Cardozo J.L. & Gender 355 (2012) (suggesting that disputes about frozen embryos be resolved by a new approach to parentage that provides for options to full legal parentage or nonparentage); Amanda J. Smith, J.B. v. M.B.: New Evidence That Contracts Need to Be Reevaluated as the Method of Choice for Resolving Frozen Embryo Disputes, 81 N.C. L. Rev. 878 (2003) (suggesting that in cases involving disputes about frozen embryos, contracts can safeguard individuals' fundamental rights); Judith Daar, Symposium Remarks: Panel on Disputes Concerning Frozen Embryos, 8 Tex. J. Women & L. 285 (1999) (suggesting that reproduction among those relying on technological assistance be viewed as a process rather than an event). The decision of the European Court of Human Rights in Evans v. United Kingdom is analyzed in Orna Ben-Naftali, International Decision, European Convention for the Protection of Human Rights and Fundamental Freedoms, 102 Am. J. Int'l. L. 128 (2008).

CHALLENGING ISSUES: CRYOPRESERVATION AGREEMENT

In 2005, Becky and David (a married couple) entered into an agreement with the Surrogate Parenting Center (the Center). As a result of surgery, Becky (46 years old at the time) did not produce ova and was unable to gestate a fetus. Through the Center, the couple produced five embryos (using David's sperm and donated ova). Two of the embryos, implanted in the uterus of a surrogate in April 2006, led to the birth of a baby (D) nine months later. The remaining three eggs were cryopreserved. Becky, David, and the Center entered into a "Cryopreservation Agreement" that provided:

> We have been advised and understand that the legal status of the frozen pre-embryos has not been fully determined. In this regard, we acknowledge that we have been advised to seek independent legal counsel concerning our respective rights with regard to each pre-embryo placed in cryopreservation. We agree that because both the husband and wife are participants in the cryopreservation program, any decision regarding the disposition of our pre-embryos will be made by mutual consent. In the event we are unable to reach a mutual decision regarding the disposition of our pre-embryos, we must petition to a Court of competent jurisdiction for instructions concerning the appropriate disposition of our pre-embryos.
>
> We are aware that for a variety of reasons (e.g., our choice, death of both of us, our achieving our desired family size) one or more pre-embryos may remain frozen and will not be wanted or needed by us. By this document, we wish to provide the Center with our mutual direction regarding disposition of our pre-embryos upon the occurrence of any one of the following four (4) events or dates:
>
> A. The death of the surviving spouse or in the event of our simultaneous death.
> B. In the event we mutually withdraw our consent for participation in the cryopreservation program.
> C. Our pre-embryos have been maintained in cryopreservation for five (5) years after the initial date of cryopreservation unless the Center agrees, at our request, to extend our participation for an additional period of time.
> D. The Center ceases its in vitro fertilization and cryopreservation program.

> At the earliest of the above-mentioned events or dates, we authorize and request that . . . our pre-embryos be thawed but not allowed to undergo further development.[2]

Even before D's birth in January 2007, Becky and David separated. David now wants to put the cryopreserved embryos up for adoption. Becky wants to have the embryos gestated by a surrogate and to raise any resulting child or children as the legal mother.

How might a court approach this case?

4. Posthumous Reproduction

The possibility of freezing gametes and embryos has facilitated new forms of posthumous reproduction. Since the beginning of time, some children have been born after the deaths of their fathers. Only in recent decades, however, has it been possible for a child to be born after the death of its mother or to be conceived after the death of its father and mother. In the 1950s it became possible to freeze sperm. That made it possible for a man's frozen sperm to be thawed later—either during the man's life or after his death—and used to fertilize an egg. Embryo cryopreservation became common after the advent of IVF. It is also possible to freeze ova, and a number of pregnancies have resulted from the fertilization of thawed ova. New freezing techniques have significantly increased the success rates of ova cryopreservation.

All these possibilities raise a new set of moral and legal questions. For instance, what is the legal relation between a child and his or her genetic parent who died before the child's conception? Can such a child inherit from the dead parent? Can the child collect Social Security benefits owed to the parent's surviving children? Should posthumous use of gametes be predicated on the gamete donor's having expressly consented to this use? Should posthumous conception be banned whether or not the donor provided consent?

One of the first cases to address some of these issues was decided in France in 1984. In Parpalaix v. CECOS, Trib. Gr. Inst. Creteil, Gazette du Palais (G.P.), Sept. 15, 1984, a French trial court considered the request of Corinne Richard Parpalaix to use the frozen sperm of her recently deceased husband, Alain Parpalaix. Alain, who died of cancer in 1981, had married Corinne several days before his death. Before the marriage but after learning that he suffered from cancer, Alain deposited nine vials of sperm with the Centre d'Etude et de Conservation du Sperme (CECLOS), a government-operated sperm bank near Paris. Alain's parents supported Corinne's efforts to obtain Alain's frozen sperm to conceive a child. The court premised its decision on the notion that Alain's intentions regarding use of his sperm were central to its decision. Although Alain had never expressly asserted that he wanted the sperm used by Corinne to conceive a child after his death, the court found that he had so intended on the basis of its presumptions about Alain's apparent love for and loyalty to his family. The court explained that

---

2. This language is from the "consent and authorization for preembryo cryopreservation contract" at issue in Litowitz v. Litowitz, 48 P.3d 261 (Wash. 2002).

the testimony of Pierre and Danielle Richard, the parents of Corinne Parpalaix, the attitude of Alain Parpalaix, who in the middle of his illness and with the agreement of [Corinne] desired to preserve his opportunity to procreate, an attitude impressively confirmed two days before his death by a religious and civil marriage, the value of the position in this proceeding of Alain Parpalaix's parents, who would have been able to know the deepest intentions of their son, provide a set of testimony and presumptions that establish, without equivocation, the express intent of Corinne Parpalaix's husband to make his wife the mother of a common child, either during his life or after his death.

The court set forth the rule that the sperm donor's intentions would be determinative in deciding whether his sperm could be used posthumously. However, the court did not provide workable guidelines for discerning Alain's intentions. For the *Parpalaix* court, Alain's intentions were not demonstrated through reference to a contract but by the invocation of his love for his wife, parents, and potential child. In late 1984, Corinne was inseminated with Alain's sperm, but she did not become pregnant. *Parpalaix* is described and analyzed in E. Donald Shapiro & Benedene Sonnenblick, The Widow and the Sperm: The Law of Post-Mortem Insemination, 1 J.L. & Health 229 (1986–1987).

Almost a decade later, an intermediate appellate court in California relied heavily on the reasoning in *Parpalaix* to resolve a dispute between a dead man's significant other and his adult children. Hecht v. Superior Court, 20 Cal. Rptr. 2d 275 (Cal. App. 1993), arose after William Kane's suicide on October 30, 1991. Kane had been living with Deborah Hecht for about five years before his death. In the days before he committed suicide, he deposited 15 vials of sperm with a California sperm bank. The documentation that Kane signed authorized the sperm bank to release his sperm to Deborah Hecht or to her physician. In a will, executed in the month before his death, Kane similarly provided that his frozen sperm should be given to Hecht for use after his death. Moreover, in October 1991, Kane wrote to his two children:

> I address this to my children, because, although I have only two, Everett and Katy, it may be that Deborah will decide—as I hope she will—to have a child by me after my death. I've been assiduously generating frozen sperm samples for that eventuality. If she does, then this letter is for my posthumous offspring, as well, with the thought that I have loved you in my dreams, even though I never got to see you born. . . .

Kane's children contested distribution of the sperm to Hecht. Among other things, they argued that any resulting children would be hurt by the impossibility of knowing their father and that such after-born children would disrupt existing family relations. The trial court ordered destruction of the sperm. That order was reversed by the appellate court, which concluded that the sperm was "properly part of decedent's estate." The court relied on *Parpalaix* to answer the claims of Kane's children that public policy concerns should preclude the court's allowing Hecht to use their father's sperm. Thus, in reaching its decision, the court looked both to the contractual documents that Kane left and to its understanding of Kane's (noncontractual) "deepest desire" to have Hecht gestate and give birth to a child conceived from his sperm.

After the appellate court's decision, the probate court ordered distribution of 20 percent of the sperm vials to Hecht (reflecting the will's distribution of property). The appellate court then overturned this decision on the grounds that Kane intended Hecht to receive all his frozen sperm. Hecht v. Kane, 59 Cal. Rptr. 2d 222 (Cal. App. 1996).

$$\| \quad \textit{Astrue v. Capato} \quad \|$$
$$\| \quad \text{132 S. Ct. 2021 (2012)} \quad \|$$

Opinion by GINSBURG, J.

. . . .

I

Karen Capato married Robert Capato in May 1999. Shortly thereafter, Robert was diagnosed with esophageal cancer and was told that the chemotherapy he required might render him sterile. Because the couple wanted children, Robert, before undergoing chemotherapy, deposited his semen in a sperm bank, where it was frozen and stored. Despite Robert's aggressive treatment regime, Karen conceived naturally and gave birth to a son in August 2001. The Capatos, however, wanted their son to have a sibling.

Robert's health deteriorated in late 2001, and he died in Florida, where he and Karen then resided, in March 2002. His will, executed in Florida, named as beneficiaries the son born of his marriage to Karen and two children from a previous marriage. The will made no provision for children conceived after Robert's death, although the Capatos had told their lawyer they wanted future offspring to be placed on a par with existing children. Shortly after Robert's death, Karen began in vitro fertilization using her husband's frozen sperm. She conceived in January 2003 and gave birth to twins in September 2003, 18 months after Robert's death.

Karen Capato claimed survivors insurance benefits on behalf of the twins. The SSA [Social Security Administration] denied her application, and the U.S. District Court for the District of New Jersey affirmed the agency's decision. In accord with the SSA's construction of the statute, the District Court determined that the twins would qualify for benefits only if, as §416(h)(2)(A) specifies, they could inherit from the deceased wage earner under state intestacy law. Robert Capato died domiciled in Florida, the court found. Under that State's law, the court noted, a child born posthumously may inherit through intestate succession only if conceived during the decedent's lifetime.

The Court of Appeals for the Third Circuit reversed. Under §416(e), the appellate court concluded, "the undisputed biological children of a deceased wage earner and his widow" qualify for survivors benefits without regard to state intestacy law. 631 F.3d 626, 631 (2011). Courts of Appeals have divided on the statutory interpretation question this case presents. Compare ibid. and Gillett-Netting v. Barnhart, 371 F.3d 593, 596–597 (CA9 2004) (biological but posthumously conceived child of insured wage earner and his widow qualifies for benefits), with Beeler v. Astrue, 651 F.3d 954, 960–964 (CA8 2011), and Schafer v. Astrue, 641 F.3d 49, 54–63 (CA4 2011) (posthumously conceived child's qualification for benefits depends on intestacy law of State in which wage earner was domiciled). To resolve the conflict, we granted the Commissioner's petition for a writ of certiorari.

II

Congress amended the Social Security Act in 1939 to provide a monthly benefit for designated surviving family members of a deceased insured wage earner. "Child's insurance benefits" are among the Act's family-protective measures. An applicant qualifies for such benefits if she meets the Act's definition of "child," is unmarried, is below specified age limits (18 or 19) or is under a disability which began prior to age 22, and was dependent on the insured at the time of the insured's death.

To resolve this case, we must decide whether the Capato twins rank as "child[ren]" under the Act's definitional provisions. Section 402(d) provides that "[e]very child (as defined in section 416(e) of this title)" of a deceased insured individual "shall be entitled to a child's insurance benefit." Section 416(e), in turn, states: "The term 'child' means (1) the child or legally adopted child of an individual, (2) a stepchild [under certain circumstances], and (3) . . . the grandchild or stepgrandchild of an individual or his spouse [who meets certain conditions]."

The word "child," we note, appears twice in §416(e)'s opening sentence: initially in the prefatory phrase, "[t]he term 'child' means . . . ," and, immediately thereafter, in subsection (e)(1) ("child or legally adopted child"), delineating the first of three beneficiary categories. Unlike §§416(e)(2) and (3), which specify the circumstances under which stepchildren and grandchildren qualify for benefits, §416(e)(1) lacks any elaboration.

A subsequent definitional provision further addresses the term "child." Under the heading "Determination of family status," §416(h)(2)(A) provides: "In determining whether an applicant is the child or parent of [an] insured individual for purposes of this subchapter, the Commissioner of Social Security shall apply [the intestacy law of the insured individual's domiciliary State]."

. . . .

The SSA has interpreted these provisions in regulations adopted through notice-and-comment rulemaking. The regulations state that an applicant may be entitled to benefits "as a natural child, legally adopted child, stepchild, grandchild, stepgrandchild, or equitably adopted child." 20 CFR §404.354. Defining "[w]ho is the insured's natural child," §404.355, the regulations closely track 42 U.S.C. §§416(h)(2) and (h)(3). They state that an applicant may qualify for insurance benefits as a "natural child" by meeting any of four conditions: (1) the applicant "could inherit the insured's personal property as his or her natural child under State inheritance laws"; (2) the applicant is "the insured's natural child and [his or her parents] went through a ceremony which would have resulted in a valid marriage between them except for a legal impediment"; (3) before death, the insured acknowledged in writing his or her parentage of the applicant, was decreed by a court to be the applicant's parent, or was ordered by a court to contribute to the applicant's support; or (4) other evidence shows that the insured is the applicant's "natural father or mother" and was either living with, or contributing to the support of, the applicant. 20 CFR §404.355(a) (internal quotation marks omitted).

As the SSA reads the statute, 42 U.S.C. §416(h) governs the meaning of "child" in §416(e)(1). In other words, §416(h) is a gateway through which all applicants for insurance benefits as a "child" must pass.

III

Karen Capato argues, and the Third Circuit held, that §416(h), far from supplying the governing law, is irrelevant in this case. Instead, the Court of Appeals determined, §416(e) alone is dispositive of the controversy. Under §416(e), "child" means "child of an [insured] individual," and the Capato twins, the Third Circuit observed, clearly fit that definition: They are undeniably the children of Robert Capato, the insured wage earner, and his widow, Karen Capato. Section 416(h) comes into play, the court reasoned, only when "a claimant's status as a deceased wage-earner's child is in doubt." That limitation, the court suggested, is evident from §416(h)'s caption: "Determination of family status." Here, "there is no family status to determine," the court said, so §416(h) has no role to play.

In short, while the SSA regards §416(h) as completing §416(e)'s sparse definition of "child," the Third Circuit considered each subsection to control different situations: §416(h) governs when a child's family status needs to be determined; §416(e), when it does not. When is there no need to determine a child's family status? The answer that the Third Circuit found plain: whenever the claimant is "the biological child of a married couple."

We point out, first, some conspicuous flaws in the Third Circuit's and respondent Karen Capato's reading of the Act's provisions, and then explain why we find the SSA's interpretation persuasive.

A

Nothing in §416(e)'s tautological definition ("'child' means . . . the child . . . of an individual") suggests that Congress understood the word "child" to refer only to the children of married parents. . . .

Nor does §416(e) indicate that Congress intended "biological" parentage to be prerequisite to "child" status under that provision. As the SSA points out, "[i]n 1939, there was no such thing as a scientifically proven biological relationship between a child and a father, which is . . . part of the reason that the word 'biological' appears nowhere in the Act." Notably, a biological parent is not necessarily a child's parent under law. Ordinarily, "a parent–child relationship does not exist between an adoptee and the adoptee's genetic parents." Uniform Probate Code §2-119(a), 8 U. L. A. 55 (Supp. 2011) (amended 2008). Moreover, laws directly addressing use of today's assisted reproduction technology do not make biological parentage a universally determinative criterion. *See, e.g.,* Cal. Fam. Code Ann. §7613(b) (West Supp. 2012) ("The donor of semen . . . for use in artificial insemination or in vitro fertilization of a woman other than the donor's wife is treated in law as if he were not the natural father of a child thereby conceived, unless otherwise agreed to in a writing signed by the donor and the woman prior to the conception of the child."); Mass. Gen. Laws, ch. 46, §4B (West 2010) ("Any child born to a married woman as a result of artificial insemination with the consent of her husband, shall be considered the legitimate child of the mother and such husband.").

We note, in addition, that marriage does not ever and always make the parentage of a child certain, nor does the absence of marriage necessarily mean that a child's parentage is uncertain. An unmarried couple can agree that a child is theirs, while the parentage of a child born during a marriage may be uncertain.

Finally, it is far from obvious that Karen Capato's proposed definition—"biological child of married parents"—would cover the posthumously conceived Capato twins. Under Florida law, a marriage ends upon the death of a spouse. If that law applies, rather than a court-declared preemptive federal law, the Capato twins, conceived after the death of their father, would not qualify as "marital" children.

B

Resisting the importation of words not found in §416(e)—"child" means "the biological child of married parents," Brief for Respondent 9—the SSA finds a key textual cue in §416(h)(2)(A)'s opening instruction: "In determining whether an applicant is the child . . . of [an] insured individual for purposes of this subchapter," the Commissioner shall apply state intestacy law. . . .

Reference to state law to determine an applicant's status as a "child" is anything but anomalous. Quite the opposite. The Act commonly refers to state law on matters of family status. . . .

[A]s originally enacted, a single provision mandated the use of state intestacy law for "determining whether an applicant is the wife, widow, child, or parent of [an] insured individual." All wife, widow, child, and parent applicants thus had to satisfy the same criterion. To be sure, children born during their parents' marriage would have readily qualified under the 1939 formulation because of their eligibility to inherit under state law. But requiring all "child" applicants to qualify under state intestacy law installed a simple test, one that ensured benefits for persons plainly within the legislators' contemplation, while avoiding congressional entanglement in the traditional state-law realm of family relations.

Just as the Act generally refers to state law to determine whether an applicant qualifies as a wife, widow, husband, widower, child or parent, so in several sections the Act sets duration-of-relationship limitations. Time limits also qualify the statutes of several States that accord inheritance rights to posthumously conceived children. No time constraints attend the Third Circuit's ruling in this case, under which the biological child of married parents is eligible for survivor's benefits, no matter the length of time between the father's death and the child's conception and birth.

The paths to receipt of benefits laid out in the Act and regulations, we must not forget, proceed from Congress' perception of the core purpose of the legislation. The aim was not to create a program "generally benefiting needy persons"; it was, more particularly, to "provide . . . dependent members of [a wage earner's] family with protection against the hardship occasioned by [the] loss of [the insured's] earnings." Califano v. Jobst, 434 U.S. 47, 52 (1977). We have recognized that "where state intestacy law provides that a child may take personal property from a father's estate, it may reasonably be thought that the child will more likely be dependent during the parent's life and at his death." Reliance on state intestacy law to determine who is a "child" thus serves the Act's driving objective. True, the intestacy criterion yields benefits to some children outside the Act's central concern. Intestacy laws in a number of States, as just noted, do provide for inheritance by posthumously conceived children, and under federal law, a child conceived shortly before her father's death may be eligible for benefits even though she never actually received her father's support. It was nonetheless Congress' prerogative to legislate for the generality of cases. It did so here by employing eligibility to inherit under state intestacy law as a workable substitute for burdensome case-by-case determinations whether the child was, in fact, dependent on her father's earnings.

. . . .

IV

As we have explained, §416(e)(1)'s statement, "[t]he term 'child' means . . . the child . . . of an individual," is a definition of scant utility without aid from neighboring provisions. That aid is supplied by §416(h)(2)(A), which completes the definition of "child" "for purposes of th[e] subchapter" that includes §416(e)(1). Under the completed definition, which the SSA employs, §416(h)(2)(A) refers to state law to determine the status of a posthumously conceived child. The SSA's interpretation of the relevant provisions, adhered to without deviation for many decades, is at least reasonable; the agency's reading is therefore entitled to this Court's deference under Chevron., 467 U.S. 837.

V

Tragic circumstances—Robert Capato's death before he and his wife could raise a family—gave rise to this case. But the law Congress enacted calls for resolution of Karen Capato's application for child's insurance benefits by reference to state intestacy law. We cannot replace that reference by creating a uniform federal rule the statute's text scarcely supports.

For the reasons stated, the judgment of the Court of Appeals for the Third Circuit is reversed, and the case is remanded for further proceedings consistent with this opinion.

It is so ordered.

NOTES AND QUESTIONS

1. *Decisions about Social Security benefits.*   Before the Supreme Court decided *Astrue v. Capato* (2012), supra, a number of lower courts entertained questions similar to those entertained in *Capato*. In 2002, Massachusetts' highest court, responding to a question certified by the U.S. District Court for the District of Massachusetts, considered the legal paternity of twins conceived after the death of their biological father, Warren Woodward. *Woodward v. Commissioner of Social Security*, 760 N.E.2d 257 (Mass. 2002). Specifically, the federal court asked whether

> a married man and woman arrange for sperm to be withdrawn from the husband for the purpose of artificially impregnating the wife, and the

woman is impregnated with that sperm after the man, her husband, has died, will children resulting from such pregnancy enjoy the inheritance rights of natural children under Massachusetts' law of intestate succession.

The court concluded that the state's intestacy statute provided that a child resulting from posthumous conception may be deemed a "child" for purposes of inheritance if there is a genetic link between the child and the genetic father and if the dead father "affirmatively consented to posthumous conception and to the support of any resulting child." The court noted that a man might have sperm cryopreserved "for a myriad of reasons" that do not include their use after this death. In short, the wife's having proved that her dead husband was the genetic father of the children to which she gave birth was not enough. The court explained the wife's further obligation:

> In the United States District Court, the wife may come forward with other evidence as to her husband's consent to posthumously conceive children. She may come forward with evidence of his consent to support such children. We do not speculate as to the sufficiently of evidence she may submit at trial.

The court explained that its decision recognized three legislative goals: first, protecting the best interests of the children involved; second, providing for the administration of estates, and third, safeguarding the interests of the dead, genetic parent.

Two years after Massachusetts' decision in *Woodward*, the Ninth Circuit rendered a decision in Gillett-Netting v. Barnhart, 371 F. 3d 593 (9th Cir. 2004), rev'g 231 F. Supp. 2d 961 (D. Ariz. 2002). The court reversed a district court holding that had denied Social Security child insurance benefits to Juliet and Piers Netting. The children were conceived by Robert Netting's widow, Rhonda Gillett, about ten months after her husband's death from cancer. After his diagnosis, Robert Netting, fearing that chemotherapy would render him infertile, had had sperm frozen. He made it clear that he hoped his wife would use his sperm to become pregnant even after his death. The Circuit Court, concluding that the twins were Netting's legal children under Arizona law, held that the children were to be deemed dependent on Netting even though they were not conceived until after his death. The court explained:

> Under the [Social Security] Act, a claimant must show dependency on an insured wage earner in order to be entitled to child's insurance benefits. However, the Act statutorily deems broad categories of children to have been dependent on a deceased, insured parent without demonstrating actual dependency. It is well-settled that all legitimate children automatically are considered to have been dependent on the insured individual, absent narrow circumstances not present in this case.

371 F.3d at 598. See also Eng Khabbaz v. Comm'r, Soc. Sec. Admin, 930 A.2d 1180 (N.H. 2007) (child conceived after death of her father was not eligible to inherit from the father under state intestacy law).

2. *Intention and posthumous conception.* The French court in Parpalaix v. CECOS, Trib. Gr. Inst. Creteil, Gazette du Paris (G.P.), Sept. 15, 1984, p. 206 assumed that Alain, in storing sperm, intended that if he were to die, Corinne would use those sperm to conceive a child. Yet, Alain had not made that

intention explicit in any document. In *Hecht,* supra, Kane had left several legal and other documents directing that, after his death, his banked sperm be given to Hecht so that she might conceive a child. Yet, the California intermediate appellate court in *Hecht* relied on its sense of what Kane's intentions must have been in light of the documents as much as it relied directly on the documents (including an agreement entered into with the sperm bank, a will, and a letter to Kane's children). Do you think that the Massachusetts court in *Woodward,* discussed in Note 1, supra, made similar assumptions about Warren Woodward's intentions?

3. *A posthumous sibling.* William Kane's children argued, among other things, that it would be unfair to them and their family were Hecht to produce a posthumous child. Is this concern likely to have been essentially emotional and affective or to have been motivated by concern about the distribution of their father's estate? See Helen S. Shapo, Matters of Life and Death: Inheritance Consequences of Reproductive Technologies, 25 Hofstra L. Rev. 1091 (1997) (reviewing law's treatment of inheritance rights of children, including posthumous children, born as a result of assisted reproduction); Note, Sheri Gilbert, Fatherhood from the Grave: An Analysis of Postmortem Insemination, 22 Hofstra L. Rev. 521 (1993) (concluding that decedent's consent to posthumous use of his sperm should not always be necessary).

4. *The significance of intention.* Judicial responses to cases involving posthumous reproduction often focused on the intentions of the decedent. Why should the decedent's intentions be determinative? Do these cases suggest the readiness of courts to entertain contractual agreements in a wider variety of disputes occasioned by reproductive technology? Or is there something unique about a dead person's frozen gametes that makes reference to the decedent's intentions particularly appropriate? Should there be any limits to a person's right to provide for posthumous reproduction? Might one motive for allowing posthumous reproduction be an interest in allowing people to "live on" through offspring?

5. *British law.* British law provides that a child conceived by a woman using the sperm of her deceased husband would be registered as the man's legal child. The provision applies only if the man had

> consented in writing . . . (i) to the use of his sperm after his death which brought about the creation of the embryo carried by W[ife] or (as the case may be) to the placing in W after his death of the embryo which was brought about using his sperm before his death and (ii) to being treated for the purpose mentioned [registration as the father] . . . as the father of the child.

Human Fertilisation and Embryology Act 2008, Pt 2 (meaning of "father"), Sec. 39, available at http://www.legislation.gov.uk/ukpga/2008/22/section/39#text %3Dsperm

6. *Japanese attitudes.* A survey carried out in Japan in 2007 found a "strong correlation" between support for posthumous reproduction and traditional views of family. Noriyuki Ueda et al., Study of Views on Posthumous Reproduction, Focusing on Its Relation with Views on Family and Religion in Modern Japan, 62 Acta Med. Okayama, 285 (2008), available at http://www.lib.okayama-u.ac.jp/www/acta/pdf/62_5_285.pdf. This finding was linked to concern in

Japan for "family continuity." More specifically, support for posthumous reproduction in Japan correlated with both liberal views about assisted reproduction
generally and conservative views about family tradition. At the time of the survey,
there had only been a handful of cases in Japan involving posthumous reproduction by women using the cryopreserved sperm of deceased husbands. The
researchers found that about two-thirds of survey respondents would provide for
posthumous reproduction by a widow (using her deceased husband's sperm)
only in cases that provided documentation of the decedent's consent. Id. at 292.

CHALLENGING ISSUES: ARRANGING FOR POSTHUMOUS CHILDREN

Three years ago, Susan and Bob Hedweller became patients at the Hap
Infertility Clinic (Hap). The couple had gone through one cycle of IVF treatment when they learned that Bob was suffering from cancer. To ensure that
Susan would be able to continue with the treatment even if Bob became sicker or
died, they decided to have fertilized ova placed in storage. As they were filling
out the facility's informed consent papers, they chatted. All at once, both Susan
and Bob decided that they would like to have the embryos gestated and brought
to life even if they were both to die.

After several serious conversations with Bob's sister, Annette (who agreed
to gestate and give birth to the embryos should Susan not be able to do that),
Susan and Bob provided in writing that they intended to be the legal parents of
any baby or babies that would result from the frozen embryos even if one of them
or both of them had died by the time a baby was actually born.

The next week, ten of Susan's ova were fertilized by Bob's sperm in vitro.
Seven embryos resulted. All of them were frozen. Two days later, Susan and Bob
were driving on Route 28 when the driver of a large oil tanker, heading toward
them, lost control, crossed the center divider on the highway, and crashed into
Susan and Bob's car. Both were killed instantaneously.

About six months later, Annette, though still grieving, asked the doctors at
Hap to implant some of Susan and Bob's embryos in her uterus. This was done,
and Annette became pregnant with twins. During her pregnancy, Annette
learned that one of the babies would be a boy and the other a girl. She was
excited about raising two children, especially because her youngest child had
just left home, and her house seemed too quiet.

While she was pregnant, Annette realized that she might need legal assistance in arranging to have Bob and Susan named as the babies' legal parents.
Annette believed that this is what Bob and Susan would have wanted. Annette
wanted to have Bob and Susan's names on the children's birth certificates and
she hoped that the children would be able to receive survivors' benefits from the
Social Security Administration. She planned to support the children in every way
and assumed that she could gain all the legal rights she needed to raise the
children properly if she were named as a legal guardian for the children.

Annette did a little research on her own. Among other things, she read
Astrue v. Capato as well as some cases that involved disputes between gamete
progenitors and others between intending parents and third parties involve in
the reproductive process.

Armed with a strong will, a deep commitment to fulfill Susan and Bob's wishes, and a bit of legal information, Annette comes to you. She asks whether there will be any insurmountable legal problems with arranging the children's parentage and custody as she wishes. What will you tell Annette? Assume that Annette lives in the state in which you live (as did Bob and Susan).

Do you see any moral problem in allowing Annette to gestate and give birth to the children produced from Susan and Bob's gametes? How would you decide whether this sort of arrangement would be likely to serve the best interests of the prospective children?

5.   Reproductive Cloning[3]

Reproductive cloning presents more complicated social and psychological dilemmas than those associated with most other forms of reproductive technology. In fact, some commentators have even suggested that cloning leads to replication, but not reproduction as we usually think of it.

Cloning differs from other forms of reproduction in that it does not depend on the joining of gametic cells—the sperm and egg. The genome of a clone comes from a somatic cell rather than from two gametic cells. The process is referred to as somatic cell nuclear transfer.

The first mammal cloned was the sheep Dolly, cloned by Ian Wilmut at the Roslin Institute in Scotland in 1997. Since Dolly's birth, many other mammals including cows, mice, and cats have been cloned. No case of human reproductive cloning has been documented, although a religious group, the Raelians, claimed to have cloned a person in late 2002.

People have cloned pets. One California cosmetic surgeon paid $100,000 to a Korean company to have a deceased chihuahua cloned. The project resulted in three dogs, each a clone of the original. The owner told ABC News that the three replacement dogs had "the same habits" as his original dog and surpassed his expectations. Man Clones Beloved Chihuahua: Cloned Pets Cost Grieving Owner a Six Figure Sum, ABCNews (May 19, 2012), available at http://abcnews.go.com/GMA/video/man-clones-beloved-chihuahua-16384939.

Korean researchers claimed in 2005 that they had successfully cloned human embryos. Later, it emerged that the claims were fabricated. In 2011 stem-cell researchers in New York created cloned human embryos by inserting the genetic material of a somatic cell into an egg that *had not been* denucleated. The resulting embryos had three, rather than the normal two chromosome sets and could not be used for reproductive or therapeutic purposes. However, the research has been considered a success insofar as it demonstrated the possibility of creating cloned human embryos. Joe Palca, Researchers Advance Cloning of Human Embryos, NRP, Oct. 5, 2011, available at http://www.npr.org/2011/10/05/141073036/researchers-advance-cloning-of-human-embryos.

A cloning technique, that does not involve the birth of "cloned" children, can be used to allow a woman to have a genetically related child using her own ova but using donated mitochondrial DNA from another woman's ova. This process could be used by a woman attempting to avoid passing on deleterious genes in her own mitochondrial DNA. genes. Antony Blackburn-Starza, Nuffield Council Gives

---

3. Cloning for the production of embryos for research and therapy (nonreproductive cloning) is discussed more fully in Chapter 3.

Green Light to the Prevention of Inherited Mitochondrial Disease, BioNews 661, June 12, 2012, available at http://www.bionews.org.uk/page_150358.asp?dinfo=fLg8CfFCr9VovEQq9KIjA3zi. In 2012, the Nuffield Council on Bioethics in Britain presented a report sanctioning such use of mitochondrial DNA from donated ova to prevent mitochondrial disorders. Were this to happen, the resulting children would have three genetic parents. One of these parents (the ovum donor) would donate only mitochondrial DNA. (British law does not currently allow implementation of the techniques for doing this.) Id.

Cloning adds even more complexity to understandings of family relationships than gestational surrogacy and gamete or embryo donation. From a genetic perspective, the parents of a person who is cloned are also the parents of the resulting clone. And to make things even more complicated, a clone may have a third genetic parent. Cloning depends on the fusing of a somatic cell and an ovum. The cytoplasm in that ovum contains mitochondrial DNA. Thus, unless a clone is created through a somatic cell from the woman whose ovum is used, the clone will have DNA from three individuals: the genetic parents of the person who is being cloned as well as the ovum donor.

Soon after Dolly's birth, President Clinton asked the newly appointed National Bioethics Advisory Commission (NBAC) to study reproductive cloning and suggest appropriate responses. At that time, almost no public attention was paid to the possibility of therapeutic (or nonreproductive) cloning. That possibility became important after the isolation of embryonic stem cells in 1998. In just a few months—genuinely record time—NBAC produced a detailed report with recommendations. NBAC's members did not agree on all the issues surrounding human cloning. However, the group was able to conclude that "any attempt to clone human beings via somatic cell nuclear transfer techniques is uncertain in its prospects, is unacceptably dangerous to the fetus and, therefore, morally unacceptable." Letter from Harold T. Shapiro, Chair, National Bioethics Advisory Commission, to President Clinton (dated June 9, 1997) in Cloning Human Beings, Executive Summary, Report and Recommendations of the National Bioethics Advisory Commission (1997), at I.

In 2002, the President's Council on Bioethics (appointed by President George W. Bush in 2001) issued a report on human cloning. Members of the council did not agree about the ethics of cloning for nonreproductive purposes. They did, however, all agree that cloning to produce children should be prohibited. A selection from the council's summary of its position on reproductive cloning, and a contrasting position, outlined by Lee Silver, follow.

a.   Bioethical and Social Perspectives

> *The President's Council on Bioethics,*
> *Human Cloning and Human Dignity:*
> *An Ethical Inquiry*
> **http://www.bioethics.gov (2002)**

Cloning-to-produce-children might serve several purposes. It might allow infertile couples or others to have genetically-related children; permit couples at risk of conceiving a child with a genetic disease to avoid having an afflicted child; allow the bearing of a child who could become an ideal transplant donor for a particular patient in need; enable a parent to keep a living connection with a dead or dying child or spouse; or enable individuals or society to try to "replicate" individuals of great talent or beauty. These purposes have been defended by appeals to the goods of freedom, existence (as opposed to nonexistence), and well-being—all vitally important ideals.

A major weakness in these arguments supporting cloning-to-produce-children is that they overemphasize the freedom, desires, and control of parents, and pay insufficient attention to the well-being of the cloned child-to-be. The Council holds that, once the child-to-be is carefully considered, these arguments are not sufficient to overcome the powerful case against engaging in cloning-to-produce-children.

First, cloning-to-produce-children would violate the principles of the ethics of human research. Given the high rates of morbidity and mortality in the cloning of other mammals, we believe that cloning-to-produce-children would be extremely unsafe, and that attempts to produce a cloned child would be highly unethical. Indeed, our moral analysis of this matter leads us to conclude that this is not, as is sometimes implied, a merely temporary objection, easily removed by the improvement of technique. . . .

If carefully considered, the concerns about safety also begin to reveal the ethical principles that should guide a broader assessment of cloning-to-produce-children: the principles of freedom, equality, and human dignity. To appreciate the broader human significance of cloning-to-produce-children, one needs first to reflect on the meaning of having children; the meaning of asexual, as opposed to sexual, reproduction; the importance of origins and genetic endowment for identity and sense of self; the meaning of exercising greater human control over the processes and "products" of human reproduction; and the difference between begetting and making. Reflecting on these topics, the Council has identified five categories of concern regarding cloning-to-produce-children. (Different Council Members give varying moral weight to these different concerns.)

① Problems of identity and individuality. Cloned children may experience serious problems of identity both because each will be genetically virtually identical to a human being who has already lived and because the expectations for their lives may be shadowed by constant comparisons to the life of the "original."

② Concerns regarding manufacture. Cloned children would be the first human beings whose entire genetic makeup is selected in advance. They might come to be considered more like products of a designed manufacturing process than "gifts" whom their parents are prepared to accept as they are. Such an attitude toward children could also contribute to increased commercialization and industrialization of human procreation.

③ The prospect of a new eugenics. Cloning, if successful, might serve the ends of privately pursued eugenic enhancement, either by avoiding the genetic defects that may arise when human reproduction is left to chance, or by preserving and perpetuating outstanding genetic traits, including the possibility, someday in the future, of using cloning to perpetuate genetically engineered enhancements.

Troubled family relations. By confounding and transgressing the natural ④ boundaries between generations, cloning could strain the social ties between them. Fathers could become "twin brothers" to their "sons"; mothers could give birth to their genetic twins; and grandparents would also be the "genetic parents" of their grandchildren. Genetic relation to only one parent might produce special difficulties for family life.

Effects on society. Cloning-to-produce-children would affect not only the ⑤ direct participants but also the entire society that allows or supports this activity. Even if practiced on a small scale, it could affect the way society looks at children and set a precedent for future nontherapeutic interventions into the human genetic endowment or novel forms of control by one generation over the next. In the absence of wisdom regarding these matters, prudence dictates caution and restraint.

Conclusion: For some or all of these reasons, the Council is in full agreement that cloning-to-produce-children is not only unsafe but also morally unacceptable, and ought not to be attempted.

> ## *Lee M. Silver, Popular Cloning Versus Scientific Cloning in Ethical Debates*
> ### 4 N.Y.U. J. Legis. & Pub. Pol'y 47, 49–54 (2000–2001)

. . . Scientists have used the technique of somatic cell nuclear transfer (SCNT) to obtain animals that share the same set of genes as ones born previously, and the same protocol could, in theory, be used with humans as well. But simply sharing the same set of genes does not render human beings clones, as the word is popularly used and understood. These popular versions of human cloning are, and always will be, pure fiction.

The word clone, like the word organic, has taken on a public identity very different from its scientific definition. While the popular definition of "organic food," however, is yielding to consensus, the popular conceptualization of what it means to be a clone remains in a state of flux. To be fair, it should be mentioned that even scientists use the term clone in two very different ways: in the first, to describe a single animal conceived through SCNT; and in the second, to describe a whole population of organisms sharing the same genome. . . .

The prospect of human cloning frightens many people. More often than not, however, their fears derive from aspects of the popular conceptualization of cloning that have no basis in reality. Unfortunately, Dr. Ian Wilmut, who brought Dolly into existence, does not help matters when he makes statements such as the following: "I would not support any proposal for copying people. Each child should be wanted as an individual and if you deliberately make a copy I cannot see how that can be the case."

Dr. Wilmut, like all biologists, knows that it is impossible to "copy a person" (as opposed to copying DNA), and yet he invokes this fictitious and inflammatory image to describe the outcome of human reproductive cloning. It is precisely the image that people will be copied, as portrayed in the farcical movie, Multiplicity, that engenders much of the public misunderstanding of the actual scientific process and outcome of biological cloning. If one wishes to educate, rather than obfuscate, it is critical to choose one's words carefully. Scientists who describe cloning inaccurately do society a disservice. I suspect that some do so out of self-interest. Perhaps scientists who hope to use cloning technology for non-reproductive purposes, including animal and human tissue work, feel the need to take what they view as the "moral high ground" in order to protect their own research from public censure.

Cloning has elicited other fears as well. Some people worry that ill-intentioned governments or organizations will clone large numbers of warriors, factory workers, or geniuses beholden to their maker; that cloning will exacerbate the world's population explosion; that cloning will "interfere with evolution"; that clones will be produced for body parts; or that egomaniacs will clone themselves to achieve immortality.

Even some people sufficiently educated to understand the biological process of SCNT hold exaggerated beliefs with respect to the level of similarity between a child conceived through such a process and his or her progenitor. Ethicist Leon Kass expressed commonly held views when he wrote that "cloning creates serious issues of identity and individuality. . . . The cloned individual, moreover, will be saddled with a genotype that has already lived. He will not be fully a surprise to the world."

These fears, however, are groundless because the real biological process of cloning will accomplish so much less than people imagine. Children conceived by SCNT will be indistinguishable—absent DNA testing comparing the child to the progenitor—from children conceived naturally. Like all other children, they will be born as infants emerging from a woman's womb after nine months of gestation. Like all other children, including identical twins, each one will be a unique human being with a unique identity and an unpredictable future. Furthermore, it would be no less an act of murder to remove the heart of such a child for transplantation than it would be to remove any other child's heart, which is precisely the reason why no legitimate medical clinic would consider doing such a thing.

While genes play an important role in guiding the development of our bodies, they do not predetermine the person we will become. It will be no more possible to predict how a cloned child will turn out than to predict how any other child will turn out. It is for this very basic reason, if none other, that real biological cloning will be of no use to governments or egomaniacs. If governments wanted people with certain abilities or skills, it would be quicker and more efficient for them to institute an appropriate system of universal education and identify those citizens who demonstrate the desired characteristics. Egomaniacs, by definition, care only about themselves and no one else; they will quickly lose interest in cloning when they understand that not only will it not allow them to achieve immortality, but also that they could end up with a child who will not follow obediently in their footsteps.

NOTES AND QUESTIONS

1. *Comparing views of the President's Council and Professor Silver.*   Members of the President's Council on Bioethics and Silver express contrasting views about the consequences of cloning for identity and individuality. What's the difference? With which (if either) position do you agree?

2. *Bibliographic note.*   There is an expanding literature on the legal parameters of cloning as a means of reproduction. Useful sources include W. Nicholson Prince II, Am I My Son? Human Clones and the Modern Family, 11 Colum. Sci. & Tech. L. Rev. 119 (2010) (considering complications that cloning creates for understandings of "family"); Comment, Catherine D. Payne, Stem Cell Research and Cloning for Human Reproduction: An Analysis of the Laws, the Direction in Which They May Be Heading in Light of Recent Developments, and Potential Constitutional Issues, 61 Mercer L. Rev. 943 (2010) (considering legal challenges to a legislative prohibition on cloning for reproductive purposes); Jane Maienschein, Cloning and Stem Cell Debates in the Context of Genetic Determinism, 9 Yale J. Health Pol'y L. & Ethics 567 (2009) (stressing importance of understanding the science between commenting on the social implications of matters such as cloning).

b.   Legal Approaches

Several states in the United States have banned reproductive cloning and Congress has entertained a variety of bills that would prohibit all forms of cloning nationally but has passed none of them. Recently, much of the proposed federal legislation has become entangled in a widespread debate about the differences and similarities between reproductive cloning and therapeutic cloning.

A federal ban on cloning might be declared unconstitutional. Legislation that bans all cloning (whether for reproduction, research, or therapy) could be analyzed under the First Amendment (as interfering with scientists' right to do research), the Fifth Amendment (as interfering with due process), and the Fourteenth Amendment (as interfering with due process and equal protection). These issues are considered in detail in Elizabeth Price Foley, The Constitutional Implications of Human Cloning, 42 Ariz. L. Rev. 647 (2000).

The following are among the state codes that ban reproductive cloning.

|| *California*
Health and Safety Code §24185 (2011) ||

Health and Safety Code (2011) §24185. Human reproductive cloning prohibited

(a) No person shall clone a human being or engage in human reproductive cloning.

(b) No person shall purchase or sell an ovum, zygote, embryo, or fetus for the purpose of cloning a human being.

(c) For purposes of this chapter, the following definitions apply:

(1) "Clone" means the practice of creating or attempting to create a human being by transferring the nucleus from a human cell from whatever source into a human or nonhuman egg cell from which the nucleus has been removed for the purpose of, or to implant, the resulting product to initiate a pregnancy that could result in the birth of a human being.

(2) "Department" means the State Department of Health Services.

(3) "Human reproductive cloning" means the creation of a human fetus that is substantially genetically identical to a previously born human

being. The department may adopt, interpret, and update regulations, as necessary, for purposes of more precisely defining the procedures that constitute human reproductive cloning.

Rhode Island
Health and Safety §23-16.4-2 (2011)

Health and Safety §23-16.4-2 (2011)

(a) Prohibition. No person or entity shall utilize somatic cell nuclear transfer for the purpose of initiating or attempting to initiate a human pregnancy nor shall any person create genetically identical human beings by dividing a blastocyst, zygote, or embryo.

(b) Definitions.

(1) "Nucleus" means the cell structure that houses the chromosomes, and thus the genes;

(2) "Oocyte" means the female germ cell, the egg;

(3) "Somatic cell" means any cell of a conceptus, embryo, fetus, child, or adult not biologically determined to become a germ cell; and

(4) "Somatic cell nuclear transfer" means transferring the nucleus of a human somatic cell into an oocyte from which the nucleus has been removed.

(c) Protected research and practices.

(1) Nothing in this section shall be construed to restrict areas of biomedical, microbiological, and agricultural research or practices not expressly prohibited in this section, including research or practices that involve the use of:

(i) Somatic cell nuclear transfer or other cloning technologies to clone molecules, DNA, cells, and tissues;

(ii) Mitochondrial, cytoplasmic, or gene therapy; or

(iii) Somatic cell nuclear transfer techniques to create animals.

(2) Nothing in this section shall be construed to prohibit:

(i) In vitro fertilization, the administration of fertility-enhancing drugs, or other medical procedures used to assist a woman in becoming or remaining pregnant, so long as that pregnancy is not specifically intended to result in the production of a child who is genetically identical to another human being, living or dead;

(ii) Any activity or procedure that results, directly or indirectly in two (2) or more natural identical twins. (R.I. Gen. Laws §23-16.4-4 (2008) contains a "sunset clause" under which the prohibition in §23-16.4-2 expires on July 7, 2010.)

NOTES AND QUESTIONS

1. *Regulating reproductive cloning.* Most but not all commentators have agreed that reproductive cloning of humans should not be permitted, at least at present. Some reach that conclusion because the process does not yet appear safe for the children who might be produced through it. Some suggest that reproductive cloning offers those in the lesbian, gay, bisexual, transgender, and

intersex (LGBTI) community a special opportunity to become parents to genetically related children, and that in consequence, laws preventing reproductive cloning would unconstitutionally deny reproductive rights to members of the LGBTI community. Erez Aloni, From Page to Practice: Broadening the Lens for Reproductive and Sexual Rights: Cloning and the LGBTI Family, 35 N.Y.U. Rev. L. & Soc. Change 1 (2011). Others conclude that reproductive cloning is unethical even if safe because it defies nature, encourages the commodification of people, provides for genetic manipulation and thus for eugenics, and threatens to undermine the identity (and arguably the personhood) of those who are cloned. See, e.g., Sophia Kolehmainen, Human Cloning: Brave New Mistake, 27 Hofstra L. Rev. 557 (1999).

President George W. Bush appointed Leon Kass to chair the President's Council on Bioethics. The Council report on human cloning, supra, argues strongly against reproductive cloning. Council Chair Kass has correlated recent shifts in family life in the United States (of which he is critical) with some of the attractions of cloning:

> Cloning turns out to be the perfect embodiment of the ruling opinions of our new age. Thanks to the sexual revolution, we are able to deny in practice, and increasingly in thought, the inherent procreative teleology of sexuality itself. But, if sex has no intrinsic connection to generating babies, babies need have no necessary connection to sex. . . .
>
> Thanks to our belief that all children should be wanted children (the more high-minded principle we use to justify contraception and abortion), sooner or later only those children who fulfill our wants will be fully acceptable. Through cloning, we can work our wants and wills on the very identity of our children, exercising control as never before. . . .

Leon Kass, The Wisdom of Repugnance, The New Republic (June 2, 1997), at 17.

Other commentators have favored the possibility of human cloning, especially if it is wisely regulated. For instance, Lee Silver, supra, a molecular biologist, and John Robertson, a law professor, have both argued that human cloning should be permitted in certain situations. Robertson suggests that the "strongest case" for reproductive cloning is that of "gametic failure, where a married couple has no other way than cloning to have a genetic kinship relation with the child whom they rear." John A. Robertson, Two Models of Human Cloning, 27 Hofstra L. Rev. 609, 638 (1999).

How would you approach the question as to whether cloning should be permitted?

2. *Best interests of cloned children?* Do you think it would be harmful to a child to be produced through the cloning process? If so, why?

3. *Bibliographic note.* There is a large and expanding literature about the social, psychological, and legal implications of cloning: W. Nicholson Price II, Am I My Son? Human Clones and the Modern Family, 11 Colum. Sci. & Tech. L. Rev. 19 (2010) (discussing the implications of cloned children for understandings of the relationship between parents and children); Robert A. Burt, Constitutional Constraints on the Regulation of Cloning, 9 Yale J. Health Pol'y L. & Ethics 495 (2009) (evaluating possible constitutional challenges to a ban on human embryonic stem cell research and cloning used in the course of such research); John A. Robertson, Embryo Culture and the "Culture of

Life": Constitutional Issues in the Embryonic Stem Cell Debate, U. Chi. Legal F. 1 (2006) (comparing policies in the United States and in Europe, considering therapies that may be derived from research using human embryonic stem cells, and discussing the moral and legal status of embryos); Judith F. Daar, The Prospect of Human Cloning: Improving Nature or Dooming the Species?, 33 Seton Hall L. Rev. 511 (2003) (analyzing moral and legal implications of prohibiting human cloning); Gina Kolata, Clone: The Road to Dolly and the Path Ahead (1998) (offering a journalist's account of the scientific path to the creation of Dolly); Martha C. Nussbaum & Cass R. Sunstein, eds., Clones and Cloning: Facts and Fantasies About Human Cloning (1998) (including an assortment of articles by law professors, political theorists, and others as well as the original paper by Ian Wilmut et al., published in Nature describing the technique used to create the first cloned sheep, Dolly). In addition to scholarly materials, there is a growing collection of fiction about cloning. Among this material is Kazuo Ishiguro, Never Let Me Go (2005) (story of a community of cloned children, created to provide body parts for those from whom they were cloned); Eva Hoffman, The Secret (2001) (telling the emotional and social story of a young woman who had been cloned by and from her willful, successful mother); Martha C. Nussbaum, Little C. in Clones and Clones: Facts and Fantasies About Human Cloning (Martha C. Nussbaum & Cass R. Sunstein eds. 1998) (a short story about a cloned child that frames the importance of the "nurture" side of the nature–nurture dichotomy).

CHALLENGING ISSUES: REGULATION?

The possibility of human cloning has dramatized the importance of regulating (or prohibiting) not only cloning but a variety of other forms of assisted reproduction. Which, if any, of the regulations suggested below should become law, and why? (Potential regulations listed below have been suggested by a group of bioethicists, legal scholars, and others, considering development of an international treaty.) See George J. Annas, Lori B. Andrews & Rosario M. Isasi, The Genetics Revolution: Conflicts, Challenges, and Conundra, 28 Am. J.L. & Med. 151, 154, 155 n.10 (2002).

- It should be criminal to use any cloning technique to begin or try to begin a human pregnancy.
- At least for the next decade, it should be criminal to rely on cloning techniques to develop human embryos for research.
- A license should be required by any health care provider who, or health care institution that
  - provides in vitro fertilization or donor insemination or
  - performs genetic screening on embryos outside the body.
- Provisions should be formulated to ensure that all infertility patients and all gamete donors provide informed consent to any treatment or procedure in which they will be involved.
- No health care provider or facility involved in offering assisted reproduction should be allowed to engage in advertising that could be misleading.

6. Children of ART and Their Best Interests

The interests of children conceived or gestated as a result of surrogacy or reproductive technology have been invoked far more often than they have been seriously considered and protected.

A number of claims have been made about physical harm that may befall children produced through ART. The National Bioethics Advisory Commission recommended to President Clinton in 1997 that the country prohibit human reproductive cloning, at least until the risks of the process are eliminated or significantly decreased. National Bioethics Advisory Commission, Report and Recommendations, Cloning Human Beings, vol. I (1997).

The Commission concluded:

> [A]t this time it is morally unacceptable for anyone in the public or private sector, whether in a research or clinical setting, to attempt to create a child using somatic cell nuclear transfer cloning. The Commission reached a consensus on this point because current scientific information indicates that this technique is not safe to use in humans at this time.

Id. at 106.

Moreover, a number of studies suggest that infertility treatments may carry risks for the children that result. One study published in the New England Journal of Medicine reported more than double (from 4 percent to 9 percent) the incidence of major birth defects in children conceived using IVF and intracytoplasmic sperm injection than among babies not conceived through use of these techniques. M. Hansen et al., The Risk of Major Birth Defects After Intracytoplasmic Sperm Injection and In Vitro Fertilization, 346 New Eng. J. Med. 725 (2002). See also Lars Noah, Assisted Reproductive Technologies and the Pitfalls of Unregulated Biomedical Innovation, 55 Fla. L. Rev. 603 (2003) (suggesting reconsideration of use of fertility drugs); Rebecca L. Skloot, The Other Baby Experiment, N.Y. Times, Feb. 22, 2003, at A17. A 2008 paper published by the Centers for Disease Control and Prevention reported a small increase in the risk of a few birth defects among babies conceived using IVF. Gina Kolata, Picture Emerging on Genetic Risks of IVF, N.Y. Times, Feb. 16, 2009, www.nytimes.com. And a 2012 paper by Urs Scherrer et al. suggested the possibility that children conceived using IVF may have an increased risk of vascular dysfunction. Urs Scherrer, et al., Systemic and Pulmonary Vascular Dysfunction in Children Conceived by Assisted Reproductive Technologies, 125 Circulation, 1890 (2012). Lawmakers in the United States have paid little attention to such reports.

In addition to physical harm, children born as a result of surrogacy or reproductive technology may suffer emotional harm. Lawmakers have not responded consistently to minimize this risk. Courts frequently refer to or consider children's best interests in the context of disputes about parentage and custody occasioned by ART. But almost always in these cases, courts approach the children's best interests without carefully considering the implications of the children's unusual conceptions or births. That is, the cases are treated as if they were run-of-the-mill divorces or disputes over custody between unmarried parents.

The New Jersey courts' approach to the best interests of Baby M is illustrative. In that case, the state's highest court, which reversed the decision of the trial court on almost all grounds, praised the trial court's best-interest determination. The trial court had concluded that the child was best served by giving custody to the father and his wife. In reaching that decision the court reviewed nine criteria established by Dr. Lee Salk, an expert who testified at trial. The trial court's summary follows.

In The Matter of Baby M[4]
525 A.2d 1128 (N.J. Super. Ct. 1987)

. . . [P]erhaps Dr. Salk gives the most quantified definition. He establishes nine criteria in defining "best interests of a child."

1) Was the child wanted and planned for? We now know the Sterns desperately wanted a child. They intended by the contract to have a child. They previously planned for the child by considering Mrs. Stern's own capability, inquiring about adoption and exploring surrogacy. They resolved in favor of surrogacy as the only viable vehicle for them to have a family. Mr. and Mrs. Stern contracted for Mrs. Whitehead's services. They created a nursery and made new wills to provide for the expected child. Mrs. Whitehead wanted to carry a child for a childless couple. It is clear that the Sterns planned for and wanted the child. Mrs. Whitehead did not. Her testimony is quite to that effect.

2) What is the emotional stability of the people in the child's home environment? The Sterns are found to have a strong and mutually supportive relationship. Any familial difficulties are handled through rational decision making. This is good evidence of mutual respect and empathy. Each recognizes and respects the other's needs, desires and goals. There is evidence of successful cooperative parenting of the infant child.

The Whiteheads appear to have a stable marriage now. It was earlier plagued with separations, domestic violence and severe financial difficulties requiring numerous house moves. There was a bankruptcy. Mrs. Whitehead dominates the family. Mr. Whitehead is clearly in a subordinate role. He has little to do with the subject child. Mrs. Whitehead is found to be thoroughly enmeshed with Baby M, unable to separate her own needs from the baby's. This overbearing could inhibit the child's development of independence. The mental health professionals called by the guardian ad litem agree that Mrs. Whitehead may have trouble subordinating her own needs to the child's needs. Mrs. Whitehead has been shown, by clear and convincing proof to this court's satisfaction, to be impulsive, as shown by her unplanned future when dropping out of high school and the removal of her son from a second grade classroom without first making inquiry of the teacher and principal. Another example of impulsiveness is her flight to Florida in violation of a court order. She has been shown, by clear and convincing proof to this court's satisfaction, to be manipulative. Reference need only be made to the tapes of July 15 and 16, 1986. If she was not suicidal, she was certainly manipulative in making the threats to take her life and the baby's life. She has been shown by clear and convincing proof to this court's satisfaction, to be exploitive also. She uses her children for her own ends: witness the bringing of her older daughter to court where the

---

4. Sections of the state supreme court's decision in this case appear in section A(2)(b), supra.

child was terrorized by the crush of media and her fawning use of the media to her own narcissistic ends. It appears she totally failed to consider the impact of the false sex abuse charge on her daughter. The placement of an infant's crib in Tuesday's room is without sensitivity or regard to Tuesday's feelings.

3) What is the stability and peacefulness of the families? Again, the Sterns are found to be living private unremarkable lives. The Whiteheads have known marital discord, domestic violence and many residential moves, although things are tranquil now.

4) What is the ability of the subject adults to recognize and respond to the child's physical and emotional needs? This court finds from clear and convincing proofs presented to it that Mrs. Whitehead has been shown to impose herself on her children. Her emphasis with the infant may impair the parenting of her other two children for whom she has been, with limited exception until now, a good mother. She exhibits an emotional over-investment. It was argued by defendant's counsel that Mrs. Whitehead loved her children too much. This is not necessarily a strength. Too much love can smother a child's independence. Even an infant needs her own space.

The Sterns show sensitivity to the child's needs but at the same time allow her to develop independently. Both families recognize and satisfy the infant's physical needs.

5) What are the family attitudes towards education and their motivation to encourage curiosity and learning? The Sterns have demonstrated the strong role that education has played in their lives. They both hold doctoral degrees in the sciences. Mrs. Stern is a medical doctor. Mrs. Whitehead dropped out of the tenth grade in high school. Mr. Whitehead graduated high school doing enough, as he said, "to get by." Mrs. Whitehead has interposed herself in her son's education, denying the finding of a professional child study team and rejecting their recommendations.

6) What is the ability of the adults to make rational judgments? Mr. Whitehead permits his wife to make most of the important decisions in their family. His active participation in the May 5, 1986 elopement is hardly evidence of cogent thought. Mrs. Whitehead is found to be impulsive especially in crisis circumstances or moments of heightened concern. She doesn't think of the consequences: at age 15½ she dropped out of school; she withdrew her son from second grade for what she perceived to be an affront to him without first inquiring of the teacher or principal; she eloped to Florida in direct violation of a court order, without considering the economic and emotional consequences. She impulsively, not to say maliciously, made an untruthful allegation about Mr. Stern. Mr. & Mrs. Stern have shown a capability to make logical reasoned decisions in all circumstances.

7) What is the capacity of the adults in the child's life to instill positive attitudes about matters concerning health? It is already noted that Mrs. Stern is a pediatrician. The court assumes her skill can but benefit the child. Other than failing to have the child vaccinated when Mrs. Whitehead was in Florida for the first few months of the child's life, which is not to be minimized, there is no evidence that she would convey poor health habits to the child. Mr. Whitehead has been shown to be an episodic alcoholic "binging" for two-week periods approximately every six months. He is doing nothing to eliminate this concern. To infuse a child into such a milieu is problematic.

8) What is the capacity of the adults in the baby's life to explain the circumstances of origin with least confusion and greatest emotional support? Mrs. Whitehead being the parent most invested with the infant's care, in all likelihood would be charged with the task of telling the child of her origin. This court doubts her capability to truthfully report Baby M's origin. She has shown little empathy for the Sterns and their role and even less ability to acknowledge the facts surrounding the original contract. Insofar as emotional support is concerned, the court doubts Mrs. Whitehead could or would subordinate herself for the child's benefit when there is a conflictual circumstance such as relating the child's origin to her. To this day she still appears to reject any role Mr. Stern played in the conception. She chooses to forget that but for him there would be no child. The quality of her reporting capabilities have been tested in these proceedings and are found generally wanting. The Sterns have indicated a willingness to obtain professional advice on how and when to tell his daughter. Important in this equation is the child's trust that will have been constructed between custodial parent and child.

9) Which adults would better help the child cope with her own life? It has been shown that Mrs. Whitehead has trouble coping in crisis. She can manage the routine. The Sterns have shown no aberration in either circumstance.

The court also evaluates the climate in which the child may be exposed with the Whiteheads. In addition to a history of economic and domestic instability with another house move imminent, the reduced level of importance given to education in the Whitehead home and the character trait problems defined by almost all the mental health professionals including Mrs. Whitehead's own chosen experts, Mrs. Whitehead has a genuine problem in recognizing and reporting the truth.

While we here address best interests it is relevant to her entire posture before the court. Doctor Klein, her own expert, said she lies under stress. Dr. Schecter said she is a faulty reporter because of her "I don't know, I can't recall" answers; especially the number of such answers. The court found this to be so to such an extent it became apparent that Mrs. Whitehead testified to what she chose to, exercising a selective memory, intentionally not recalling or outright lying on the witness stand. . . .

. . . She is a good mother for and to her older children. She would not be a good custodian for Baby M.

Johnson v. Calvert[5]
851 P.2d 776 (Cal. 1993)

[Justice Kennard's dissent in this case differs from the majority opinion, see supra, in suggesting the child's best interests, rather than parental intentions, should serve as the determinant of parentage.]

Dissent, KENNARD, J.

When a woman who wants to have a child provides her fertilized ovum to another woman who carries it through pregnancy and gives birth to a child, who is the child's legal mother? Unlike the majority, I do not agree that the

---

5. The majority opinion, printed in section A(2)(b) supra, gives the facts of this case.

determinative consideration should be the intent to have the child that originated with the woman who contributed the ovum. In my view, the woman who provided the fertilized ovum and the woman who gave birth to the child both have substantial claims to legal motherhood. Pregnancy entails a unique commitment, both psychological and emotional, to an unborn child. No less substantial, however, is the contribution of the woman from whose egg the child developed and without whose desire the child would not exist.

For each child, California law accords the legal rights and responsibilities of parenthood to only one "natural mother." When, as here, the female reproductive role is divided between two women, California law requires courts to make a decision as to which woman is the child's natural mother, but provides no standards by which to make that decision. The majority's resort to "intent" to break the "tie" between the genetic and gestational mothers is unsupported by statute, and, in the absence of appropriate protections in the law to guard against abuse of surrogacy arrangements, it is ill-advised. To determine who is the legal mother of a child born of a gestational surrogacy arrangement, I would apply the standard most protective of child welfare—the best interests of the child. . . .

V. MODEL LEGISLATION

The debate over whom the law should recognize as the legal mother of a child born of a gestational surrogacy arrangement prompted the National Conference of Commissioners on Uniform State Laws to propose the Uniform Status of Children of Assisted Conception Act. (9B West's U. Laws Ann. (1992 Supp.) Uniform Status of Children of Assisted Conception Act (1988 Act) pp. 122–137 [hereafter also USCACA].) . . .

The commissioners gave careful consideration to the competing interests of the various participants in assisted conception arrangements, and sought to accommodate those interests in the model legislation. Their overriding concern, however, was the well-being of children born of gestational surrogacy and other types of assisted conception. As the foreword to the model legislation notes, the extraordinary circumstances of these children's births deprive them of parentage in the traditional sense. Thus, the intent of the proposed legislation was to define with precision the legal status of these children as well as to codify the rights of the other participants in a surrogacy arrangement. The commissioners proposed alternative versions of the USCACA: one that would disallow gestational surrogacy and another that would permit it only under court supervision.

In its key components, the proposed legislation provides that "a woman who gives birth to a child is the child's mother" (USCACA, §2) unless a court has approved a surrogacy agreement before conception (USCACA, §5, 6). In the absence of such court approval, any surrogacy agreement would be void. (USCACA, §5, subd. (b).) If, however, the arrangement for gestational surrogacy has court approval, "the intended parents are the parents of the child." (USCACA, §8, subd. (a)(1).) . . .

The USCACA offers predictability in delineating the parentage of children born of gestational surrogacy arrangements. Under the model legislation, if enacted, there would never be a question as to who has the legal responsibility for a child born of a gestational surrogacy arrangement: If the couple who initiated the surrogacy had complied with the provisions of the legislation, they would be the child's legal parents. If they had not, the rights and responsibilities of parenthood would go to the woman who gave birth to the child and her spouse.

Because the California Legislature has not enacted the Uniform Status of Children of Assisted Conception Act, its provisions were not followed in this case.

VI. The Uniform Parentage Act

The only California statute defining parental rights is the Uniform Parentage Act (hereafter also UPA). The Legislature enacted the UPA to abolish the concept of illegitimacy and to replace it with the concept of parentage. The UPA was never intended by the Legislature to govern the issues arising from new reproductive technologies such as gestational surrogacy. Nevertheless, the UPA is on its face broadly applicable, and it is in any event the only statutory guidance this court has in resolving this case. . . .

When a child is born by gestational surrogacy, as happened here, the two women who played biological roles in creating the child will both have statutory claims under the UPA to being the child's natural mother. . . . Here, both Anna, the gestational mother, and Crispina, the genetic mother, have offered proof acceptable under the UPA to qualify as the child's natural mother.

By its use of the phrase "the natural mother," however, the UPA contemplates that a child will have only one natural mother. But the UPA provides no standards for determining who that natural mother should be when, as here, two different women can offer biological proof of being the natural mother of the same child under its provisions. Thus, the UPA by its terms cannot resolve the conflict in this case.

VII. Analysis of the Majority's "Intent" Test

Faced with the failure of current statutory law to adequately address the issue of who is a child's natural mother when two women qualify under the UPA, the majority breaks the "tie" by resort to a criterion not found in the UPA—the "intent" of the genetic mother to be the child's mother.

This case presents a difficult issue. The majority's resolution of that issue deserves serious consideration. Ultimately, however, I cannot agree that "intent" is the appropriate test for resolving this case. . . .

[Among other arguments] the majority[][uses] in support of using the intent of the genetic mother as the exclusive determinant of the outcome in gestational surrogacy cases is that preferring the intending mother serves the child's interests, which are "[u]nlikely to run contrary to those of adults who choose to bring [the child] into being."

I agree with the majority that the best interests of the child is an important goal; indeed, as I shall explain, the best interests of the child, rather than the intent of the genetic mother, is the proper standard to apply in the absence of legislation. The problem with the majority's rule of intent is that application of this inflexible rule will not serve the child's best interests in every case. . . .

VIII. The Best Interests of the Child

The allocation of parental rights and responsibilities necessarily impacts the welfare of a minor child. And in issues of child welfare, the standard that courts frequently apply is the best interests of the child. . . . I would apply "the best interests of the child" standard to determine who can best assume the social and legal responsibilities of motherhood for a child born of a gestational surrogacy arrangement. . . .

Factors that are pertinent to good parenting, and thus that are in a child's best interests, include the ability to nurture the child physically and psychologically and to provide ethical and intellectual guidance. Also crucial to a child's best interests is the "well recognized right" of every child "to stability and continuity."

I would remand the matter to the trial court to undertake [a best interest] evaluation.

NOTES AND QUESTIONS

1. *Comparing children's interests in custody disputes and surrogacy disputes.*   In *Baby M*, the factors that the court considered in determining the child's best interests did not differ from those that might have been considered were the case about a child's custody in the context of a routine divorce. Do you think that other factors are relevant to determining a child's best interests in the context of a dispute occasioned by a surrogacy arrangement? Might the court, for instance, have considered the possible gamut of the child's own developing responses to having been conceived as the result of such an agreement?

In the *Baby M* case, in particular, it was unlikely that the child could have been shielded throughout her childhood from the widespread public attention focused on the parties as the dispute was being litigated and in later years. In fact, for years after the child's birth and long after the court hearings were completed, news media reported on the parties' lives. When Melissa Stern was 16, for instance, Katie Couric interviewed Mary Beth Whitehead on television. Whitehead described for the nation her relationship to her daughter and to the Sterns, noting, among other things, that she did not see the child (by then an adolescent) as much as she would have liked.

At age 22, Melissa Stern was a college student, hoping to become a minister. Apparently, when she was 18, she initiated legal proceedings that allowed Elizabeth Stern to adopt her. Jennifer Weiss, Now It's Melissa's Time, New Jersey Monthly Magazine, March 2007, http://www.reproductivelawyer. com/news/babym.asp (last visited June 23, 2008). In 2007, Melissa told an interviewer that she was "very happy" to have "ended up" with the Sterns. Id.; see also Susannah Cahalan, Tug O' Love Baby M All Grown Up, N.Y. Post, April 13, 2008, http://www.nypost.com/seven/04132008/news/nationalnews/tug_o_love_ baby_m_ all_grown_up_106337.htm (last visited June 23, 2008).

2. *Relying on the best-interest standard.*   In her dissent in Johnson v. Calvert, Justice Kennard concludes that the *parentage* of the child in that case should have been decided through a determination of the child's best interests. The case provides a frame within which to think about some traditional family law rules. Traditionally, family law favored parents over nonparents in disputes about a child's custody and presumed that a child can only have one male parent and one female parent. D. Kelly Weisberg & Susan Frelich Appleton, Modern Family Law 874–880 (2d ed. 2002). These presumptions were challenged by the "family" that presented itself in *Johnson* precisely because gestational surrogacy upsets familiar expectations about biological parentage. Thus, the majority and the dissent both sought to resolve what they perceived as a "tie" between "biological" parents. The majority looked to parental "intention," concluding that in general a child's best interests will, in any event, lie with the person or people who intended from the start to be the child's parent(s). The dissent, in contrast, called for a full best-interest determination to establish parentage. Thus, the dissent completely separated decisions about parentage from decisions about biology, at least in gestational surrogacy cases and presumably in other cases in which more than two people—or perhaps more than one person of one gender—present cognizable claims to biological parentage. See K.M. v. E.G., supra, A(2)(b).

3. *Information about genetic parentage.*   In both *Baby M* and Johnson v. Calvert, the identities of the biological and social parents were apparent. In other cases, especially those involving donated gametes, questions may arise for the children about their genetic parentage. Do you think information about a child's genetic parentage should be available to children conceived through the use of donor gametes?

In the United States, children conceived through use of anonymously donated sperm have generally not been given information about the identities of the donors. In the early 1980s, the Sperm Bank of California was one of the first in the United States to ask sperm donors whether they consented to be contacted by genetic offspring after those offspring reached adulthood. A woman named Claire was the first of those offspring to request a meeting with her genetic father. Claire explained that she had always felt "a bond to him" and was anxious to discover whether his genetic makeup accounted for parts of her being that did not resemble those of her mother or her mother's family. Brian Bergstein, Woman to Meet Sperm Donor Dad, AP, Jan. 30, 2002, http://www.sunsport.net/features/health/ats-ap_health13jan30story?coll+sns%2. Moreover, Internet searches for "donor siblings" (children conceived from the sperm of one man) have become more common and more successful. That is due largely to the efforts of Wendy Kramer, who, anxious to help her son find the man from whose sperm the boy was conceived, created a website that facilitates the search for "donor siblings" and "donor fathers." Janet L. Dolgin, Biological Evaluations: Blood, Genes, and Family, 41 Akron L. Rev. 347 (2008); Kay S. Hymowitz, The Incredible Shrinking Father, 17 City J. (2007), available at http://www.city-journal.org/html/17_2_artificial_insemination.html.

Some children conceived from donor sperm seek the men from whose sperm they were conceived because they want medical information presumably contained in their genetic history. In 2000, a California court compelled an anonymous donor to make his identity known. Johnson v. The Superior

Court, 95 Cal. Rptr. 2d 864 (Cal. Ct. App. 2000), involved a young girl, who was conceived with donor sperm and who suffered from a genetic kidney condition. The court concluded that the sperm donor could be identified and compelled to testify in a suit alleging that the sperm bank had used his sperm despite his having a family history of kidney disease.

Johnson v. Superior Court concerned the right to learn about one's medical history. In addition, some children conceived through donated gametes (eggs as well as sperm) may want sociopsychological information about the gamete donor, and some may want the right to meet the donor. One commentator considered some responses to the likely concerns of children conceived through donor gametes:

> It is important that society as a whole affirm the right to know one's origins. Neil Leighton, a social worker, has argued that children have a right to "the development of a sense of self as a lived narrative blending action and memory [and] to participate in their own histories and their own future." He worries that "children who have no identifiable origin, no identifiable human beginning to their personal narrative may have a sense of alienation in the world in which they find themselves." . . .
>
> . . . It is good . . . when social practices reflect the fact that specific human beings are necessary for any person to come into existence (including, in these instances, both provider and recipients), that individual actions shape the larger social whole, and that cultural development is something individuals participate in rather than something that happens to them. Law and social practice should foster the understanding that what individuals do, even on a small scale, has repercussions beyond themselves and their intimate associates.

Mary Lyndon Shanley, Collaboration and Commodification in Assisted Procreation: Reflections on an Open Market and Anonymous Donation in Human Sperm and Eggs, 36 Law & Soc'y Rev. 257, 269 (2002).

4. *Donor anonymity in France.*   In 2012, the tribunal de Montreuil (Seine-Saint-Denis) denied the request of a 32-year-old woman, conceived through use of anonymously donated sperm, to learn a number of facts about her sperm donor. Among other things, the woman, a lawyer, wanted to know the sperm donor's medical history, the reasons for his donation, and whether her brother was the genetic child of the same donor. The court relied on French legislation that protected the identity of gamete donors from being revealed. Don de Sperme: la Justice Lui Refuse d'Acceder a Ses Origines, Le Nouvel Observateue, June 14, 2012, available at http://tempsreel.nouvelobs.com/societe/20120614.0 BS8711/don-de-sperme-la-justice-lui-refuse-d-acceder-a-ses-origines.html. A year earlier, the French Parliament rejected a proposal by Reselyne Bachelot, a former Health Minister, that the rule protecting donor anonymity be modified on the grounds that such a change would discourage potential donors. Id. After Britain did away with sperm-donor anonymity in 2005, the number of men ready to donate sperm fell dramatically. MacKenna Roberts, Directors of Online Sperm Donor Business Face Criminal Prosecution, BioNews, 511, June 8, 2009, available at http://www.bionews.org.uk/page_45429.asp.

5. *British study of surrogacy.*   A 2002 British study found that the vast majority of surrogates do not find it terribly difficult to hand over the babies they bear to the intending parents. One of the researchers, Fiona MacCallum (of City University in London), explained that she and her coworkers "found only

one instance of the surrogate having slight doubts at this time, with all other mothers reporting no problems." She explained further that the families created through surrogacy arrangements "seem to be characterised by warm relationships and high qualities of parenting." James Meek, Surrogacy "Leads to Better Parenting": First Scientific Study Shows That Families Who Receive the Child Are More Caring and the Handover After Birth Is Not a Problem, Guardian, July 1, 2002, at 5. In 70 percent of the families studied (with children between 9 and 12 months), the surrogate continued to see the child at least once every couple of months.

6. *Donated ova.*   Donated ova are harder to secure than donated sperm and are far more expensive. At present, many ova donors are paid $5,000 for the donation. Ova may cost as much as $50,000. Debora L. Spar, The Baby Business: How Money, Science and Politics Drive the Commerce of Conception xi (2006). The American Society for Reproductive Medicine has opined that payments for ova above $10,000 are inappropriate. The Ethics Committee of the American Society for Reproductive Medicine, Ethics Committee Report: Financial Compensation of Oocyte Donors, 88 Fertility & Sterility 305 (2007). The process of ova donation entails risks for the donor as well as physical discomfort or pain. Often potential donors of ova are given drugs to increase the number of ova that will be produced in a menstrual cycle. Drugs administered to the donor can cause physical discomfort and may entail longer term health risks. At least one study has reported that these drugs may increase the risk of ovarian cancer; later studies, however, have not supported that finding. Moreover, the procedure involved in extracting ova is invasive and thus involves additional risks.

The British Fertilisation and Embryology Authority permits limited payments for egg donors (up to a maximum of £250 per cycle) and also allows licensed clinics to offer discounts for reproductive care to women who donate some of their eggs to other patients. Naomi Pfeffer, Older Mothers and Global/National Responsibilities, BioNews, Feb. 8, 2010, available at http://www.bionews.org.uk/page.asp?obj_id=2567#BMS_RESULT.

A 2003 study of 52 women in an urban center who had donated ova found that more than one-third of the women interviewed would not choose to donate ova again. Among the women included in the study, 44 percent were paid $5,000 for the donation, 16 percent received $3,500, 16 percent received $3,000, and 23 percent received between $2,000 and $2,500. Eleven percent of the women queried said they would donate ova even if not compensated. Alan Mozes, Third of U.S. Egg Donors Unwilling to Donate Again, available at http://story.news.yahoo.com/news?tmpl=story&cid=571&ncid=751&e=2&u=/nm/20030702/hl_nm/women_fertility_dc (visited July 2, 2003).

7. *The cost of IVF—A motive to have multiple embryos implanted.*   By 2012, one IVF cycle in the United States cost about $12,000, and only about 15 states required insurers to cover (or offer coverage for) the procedure. Judith Daar, Federalizing Embryo Transfers: Taming the Wild West of Reproductive Medicine?, 23 Colum. J. Gender & L. 257, 316 (2012). The high cost of IVF has led some patients to pressure fertility clinicians to transfer more embryos in any one IVF cycle than they otherwise would. Id.

8. *Commercial loans for infertility care.*   The high price of infertility care has prompted the development of commercial lending aimed specifically at infertility patients. Indeed, the commercialization of reproduction has taken a new,

explicit turn with the development of "fertility financing" companies. Jessica Silver-Greenberg, In Vitro: a Fertile Niche for Lenders, Wall St. Journal, Feb. 24, 2012, available at http://online.wsj.com/article/SB1000142405297020396080457 7241270123249832.html?mod=googlenews_wsj. Lenders have forged links with infertility physicians. Loans are offered to pay for a variety of expensive infertility treatments, including IVF. The Wall Street Journal reports that some of the "fertility" loans come with interest rates as high as 22 percent. Some infertility doctors have encouraged patients to consider these loans, and some apparently facilitate the process by allowing patients to apply for loans on their websites. Id.

   9. *Donated gametes and health risks.*   Use of third-party gametes can create health risks. Not all laboratories screen donated sperm and eggs for disease. In 1999, the Centers for Disease Control (CDC) found that among "embryo laboratories" responding to a questionnaire, 59 percent (of 232 laboratories) tested sperm for syphilis; about 50 percent tested sperm for hepatitis B, and between 44 percent and 29 percent tested for HIV. Helen M. Alvare, The Case for Regulating Collaborative Reproduction: A Children's Rights Perspective, 40 Harv. J. on Legis. 1, 10–11 (2003). Similarly, egg donors may or may not be tested for a variety of diseases, including HIV, hepatitis, syphilis, gonorrhea, and chlamydia. Id. at 14. Naomi Cahn has summarized the lack of regulation of gamete donation in the United States:

> [T]here is no regulatory agency that oversees individual donors or that monitors gamete banks on a routine basis. Banks and clinics are not required to verify the personal information or much of the medical information that donors provide them, and there is no mechanism for monitoring limits on the number of times that one individual can provide gametic material to another individual. Banks are also not required to monitor what happens to the gametic material once it leaves their offices . . .

Naomi Cahn, Accidental Incest: Drawing the Line – or the Curtain? – for Reproductive Technology, 32 Harv. J.L. & Gender 59, 82-83 (2009).

   In Britain, sperm can be legally donated only through licensed facilities. In support of this rule, the Human Fertilisation and Embryology Authority cites the risks of disease transmission, including HIV, as well as genetic and chromosomal disorders. Licensed facilities in Britain select as donors only about 1 percent of men offering to donate sperm. MacKenna Roberts, Directors of Online Sperm Donor Business Face Criminal Prosecution, BioNews 511, June 8, 2009, available at http://www.bionews.org.uk/page_45429.asp.

   In the United States, state laws aimed at donor screening are inconsistent. Only a few states require sperm and egg screening. See Va. Code Ann. §§32.1-45.3 (Michie 2011); N.H. Rev. Stat. Ann. §§168-B:10, 168-B:14 (2011). Alvare, supra, at 28. Some states require only testing for HIV. No federal laws require that donated embryos or gametes (or the donors themselves) be screened. The Fertility Clinic Success Rate and Certification Act, 42 U.S.C. §263a-1 (2009), mandates fair advertising of clinic success rates. The CDC annually publishes the information reported to it by infertility clinics pursuant to the Act. Alvare, supra, at 28. Moreover, other nations, including Britain and France, limit the number of children who can be created from the sperm of any one donor. There are professional guidelines in the United States, such as those of the American Society for Reproductive Medicine, but the guidelines are not legally enforceable. Jacqueline Mroz, One Sperm Donor, 150 Offspring, N.Y. Times, Sept. 5, 2011, available at www.nytimes.com. In some cases, the families of children conceived through donor sperm have found websites enabling them to locate scores and scores of genetic half-siblings (and in the case of one donor, at least 150 half-siblings). This has created concern about one man's passing a deleterious genetic alteration to large numbers of children as well as concern about "accidental incest" between half-siblings. Id.

Assisted reproduction may present other kinds of health risks to the children. Researchers at Washington University School of Medicine in St. Louis and at Johns Hopkins University discovered that children conceived through IVF (and especially through intracytoplasmic sperm injection) were six times more likely than other children to be affected with Beckwith–Wiederman Syndrome. The syndrome involves an increased risk of developing cancer in early childhood as well as other problems, such as uneven limb development. Amy Dockser Marcus, New Research Suggests Link Between Fertility Treatments and Some Health Problems, Wall St. Journal, Sept. 16, 2003, at D1. A Swedish study reported in The Lancet in 2002 found that IVF puts children at increased risk for neurological problems, including cerebral palsy. The authors suggest that multiple gestation associated with the implantation of more than one embryo is correlated with increased risk of developing such problems. Editor's Choice, Pain & Central Nervous System Week, April 15, 2002, at 7. Even more, the British Royal College of Obstetricians and Gynaecologists reports that the risk of premature birth for twins conceived in vitro is even higher than for twin pregnancies not due to IVF. James Brooks, IVF Slightly Increases Risk of Advserse Outcomes for Mother and Baby, Report Says, BioNews 660, June 11, 2012, available at http://www.bionews.org.uk/page_149744.asp. See also Michele Hansen et al., The Risk of Major Birth Defects After Intracytoplasmic Sperm Infection and In Vitro Fertilization, 346 New Eng. J. Med. 725 (2002) (reporting greater incidence of musculoskeletal and chromosomal defects among children conceived with ART).

There is still uncertainty among experts, however, about the implications of some of the reported correlations between IVF and various health problems in the children born after IVF conception. Moreover, it is unclear whether health risks associated with IVF are caused by the procedure or by some underlying problem or problems connected with parental infertility.

10. *Bibliographic note.*   Additional useful sources include I. Glenn Cohen, Regulating Reproduction: The Problem with Best Interests, 96 Minn. L. Rev. 423 (2011) (suggesting that "best interest" determinations applied to ART issues can erect a smoke screen that masks the issues of deepest importance); Erin Y. Hisana, Gestational Surrogacy Maternity Disputes: Refocusing on the Child, 15 Lewis & Clark L. Rev. 517 (2011) (Pt. VI considers the applicability of the best-interest test to surrogacy disputes); Michelle Dennison, Revealing Your Sources: The Case for Non-Anonymous Gamete Donation, 21 J.L. & Health 1 (2007) (opposing the right to donor anonymity); Ilana Hurwitz, Collaborative Reproduction: Finding the Child in the Maze of Legal Motherhood, 33 Conn. L. Rev. 127 (2000) (suggesting case-by-case review of child's best interests in resolving disputes about children produced using ART).

7.   ART and Discrimination

ART and surrogacy raise three rather different sorts of concerns about discrimination. First, people with various illnesses and disabilities may find it more difficult to gain access to surrogacy and reproductive technology than other people. Second, infertility may itself be categorized as a disability. Third, some commentators (see Roberts, infra) have suggested that at least part of the value attached to reproductive technology stems from an interest among white middle-class people in safeguarding their presumed "genetic heritage."

Decisions about infertility treatment for disabled or ill people also suffering from infertility raise complicated questions. Health care workers are obliged to take patients' disabilities and illnesses into account in making wise treatment decisions. However, a decision to refuse treatment to a disabled or ill patient may be discriminatory. Treatment refusals may, for instance, be motivated by a form of eugenics rather than by an assessment of the patient's (or the patient's potential child's) health and welfare. A number of law review articles have considered whether it might or should be discriminatory to refuse ART to sick or disabled people. See, e.g., Carl H. Coleman, Conceiving Harm: Disability Discrimination in Assisted Reproductive Technologies, 50 UCLA L. Rev. 17 (2002); Taunya Lovell Banks, The Americans with Disabilities Act and the Reproductive Right of HIV-Infected Women, 3 Tex. J. Women & L. 57, 92–95 (1994). The law has almost never addressed the issue directly. In practice, the issue most often arises when HIV-positive patients seek assistance with reproduction. A number of medical societies have changed their official positions about providing ART treatment to HIV-positive patients. In February 2002, the American Society for Reproductive Medicine switched its position and asserted that it is not unethical for a health care provider to assist an HIV-positive patient in reproducing so long as the provider is careful to limit the possibility that the virus will be transmitted to the child or to a partner not infected with the virus. The Society's position was published in its journal. 77 Fertility & Sterility 218, 220 (2002).

Whether infertility is itself a disability is an important, but separate, question. In Bragdon v. Abbott, 524 U.S. 624 (1998), the Supreme Court characterized infertility as a "major life activity." Under the Americans with Disabilities Act of 1990 (ADA), 104 Stat. 327, 42 U.S.C. §§12101 et seq., a person is defined as disabled if the person has "(A) a physical or mental impairment that substantially limits one or more of the major life activities of such individual; (B) a record of such an impairment; or (C) being regarded as having such impairment." Sidney Abbott, the respondent in the case, was HIV-positive since 1986. She sued Dr. Bragdon, a dentist in Bangor, Maine, claiming that his refusal to fill a cavity that he discovered upon routine dental examination was discriminatory and illegal. Abbott had disclosed her HIV status on the dentist's registration form. The Court decided that, due to her HIV-positive status, Abbott was limited in the major life activity of reproduction:

> Conception and childbirth are not impossible for an HIV victim but, without doubt, are dangerous to the public health. This meets the definition of a substantial limitation. The decision to reproduce carries economic and legal consequences as well. There are added costs for antiretroviral therapy, supplemental insurance, and long-term health care for the child who must be examined and, tragic to think, treated for the infection. The laws of some

States, moreover, forbid persons infected with HIV from having sex with others, regardless of consent.

Id. at 641. It is not clear whether the Court's analysis in *Bragdon* applies to someone denied infertility treatment as a result of his or her HIV-positive status. One commentator suggests that "[i]f proof of the specific plaintiff's unwillingness to reproduce is necessary to establish a reproductive disability under *Bragdon,* persons seeking to have children through ARTs could not claim they are disabled because they have medical conditions associated with reproductive risks." Coleman, supra, at 35 (footnote omitted). In Hall v. Nalco, the Seventh Circuit held that employers are precluded by Title VII of the Civil Rights Act of 1964 from firing employees who miss work due to infertility treatments. 534 F.3d 644 (7th Cir. 2008); see also Govori v. Goat Fifty, L.L.C., 2011 U.S. Dist. LEXIS 33708 (S.D.N.Y. 2011) (following *Hall*), Govori v. Goat Fifty, L.L.C., 2012 U.S. Dist. LEXIS 15842 (granting defendants' motion for summary judgment); Kerry van der Burch, Courts' Struggle with Infertility: The Impact of Hall v. Nalco on Infertility-Related Employment Discrimination, 81 U. Colo. L. Rev. 545 (2010) (analyzing *Hall*).

Finally, some commentators have suggested that ART and surrogacy are aimed at and attractive to white middle-class people desirous of having "genetic" children. The following essay by law professor Dorothy Roberts discusses this perspective.

‖ ***Dorothy Roberts, The Genetic Tie*** ‖
62 U. Chi. L. Rev. 209, 244–246 (1995)

One of the most striking features of . . . [the new reproductive] technological efforts to provide parents with genetically related offspring is that they are used almost exclusively by affluent white people. The use of fertility clinics does not correspond to rates of infertility. Indeed, the profile of people most likely to attempt IVF is precisely the opposite of those most likely to be infertile. The people in the United States most likely to be infertile are older, poorer, Black, and poorly educated. Most couples who use IVF services are white, highly educated, and affluent. New reproductive technologies are so popular in American culture not simply because of the value placed on the genetic tie, but because of the value placed on the white genetic tie.

The high cost of fertility treatment largely restricts its availability to only the affluent. The expense of these procedures, however, cannot fully explain the racial discrepancy in their use. There are many Black middle-class infertile couples who could afford them. Besides, inability to afford a medical procedure need not preclude its use. The government could increase the availability of new reproductive technologies to the poor through public funding. As George Annas noted, "although black couples are twice as likely as white couples to be infertile, surrogacy is not promoted for black couples, nor has anyone openly advocated covering the procedure by Medicaid for poor infertile couples." It would also be possible for Black women to enter into informal surrogacy arrangements with Black men without demanding huge fees. Yet there is a stark racial disparity in the use of new reproductive technologies that seems to result from a complex interplay of financial barriers, physician referrals, and cultural preferences.

The public's affection for the white babies that are produced by reproductive technologies legitimates their use. Noel Keane, the lawyer who in 1978 arranged the first public surrogacy adoption, described how this affection influenced the public's attitude toward his clients' arrangement. Although the first television appearance of the contracting parents, George and Debbie, and the surrogate mother, Sue, generated hostility, a second appearance on the Phil Donahue Show with two-month-old Elizabeth Anne changed the tide of public opinion. Keane explained:

> This time there was only one focal point: Elizabeth Anne, blonde-haired, blue-eyed, and as real as a baby's yell. . . .
> The show was one of Donahue's highest-rated ever and the audience came down firmly on the side of what Debbie, Sue, and George had done to bring Elizabeth Anne into the world.

I suspect that a similar display of a curly haired, brown-skinned baby would not have had the same transformative effect on the viewing public. It is hard to imagine a multimillion dollar industry designed to create Black children.

A highly publicized lawsuit against a fertility clinic evidenced revulsion at the technological creation of Black babies. A white woman claimed that the clinic mistakenly inseminated her with a Black man's sperm, rather than her husband's, resulting in the birth of a Black child. The mother, who was genetically related to the child, demanded monetary damages for her injury, which she explained was due to the unbearable racial taunting her daughter suffered. The real harm to the mother, however, was the fertility clinic's failure to deliver the most critical part of its service—a white child. The clinic's racial mix-up rendered the mother's genetic tie worthless. It is highly unlikely that the white mother would have chosen Black features "if allowed the supermarket array of options of blond hair, blue-green eyes, and narrow upturned noses." In the American market, a Black child is indisputably an inferior product.

NOTES AND QUESTIONS

1. *Race and donated gametes.*   Dorothy Roberts, supra, discusses a lawsuit in which a white woman sued an infertility clinic for mistakenly inseminating her with the sperm of a black man rather than with the sperm of her white husband. In another case that arose in 1998 as the result of an infertility clinic's error, two couples, one black and one white, each claimed rights to one child. The two couples were treated on the same day at an infertility clinic in New York. As the result of the clinic error, the white woman (Donna Fasano) was implanted with the embryos of the black couple as well as with at least one embryo formed from her and her husband's gametes. The black woman (Deborah Perry-Rogers) was implanted with embryos formed from her ova and her husband's sperm. Deborah Perry-Rogers did not become pregnant. Donna Fasano became pregnant with twins. The twins, two boys, were born in late 1998. One of the twins appeared to be white and the other appeared to be black. Both couples were informed of the infertility clinic's mistake soon after the error occurred,

during Donna Fasano's pregnancy. However, after the babies' births, the Fasanos claimed that both of the children were theirs and that they desired to raise both boys. Deborah Perry-Rogers and her husband sought genetic testing of the children. That testing revealed that one of the boys was the genetic child of the Rogerses, and the other was the genetic child of the Fasanos. The Fasanos agreed to surrender custody of the Rogerses' child on condition that they were given visitation rights with the boy, whom they saw as their genetic son's brother. The parties entered into a visitation agreement. However, the Rogerses sued in court, seeking sole and exclusive custody of their genetic child.

The New York court held for the Rogerses:

> We agree that under the circumstances presented, the Fasanos lack standing under [N.Y. law] to seek visitation as the child's parents. However, this is not because we necessarily accept the broad premise that in any situation where a parent, possessed of that status by virtue of having borne and given birth to the child, acknowledges another couple's entitlement to the status of parent by virtue of their having provided the genetic materials that created the child, the birth parent automatically gives up all parental rights.
>
> Rather, we recognize that in these rather unique circumstances, where the Rogerses' embryo was implanted in Donna Fasano by mistake, and where the Fasanos knew of the error not long after it occurred, the happenstance of the Fasanos' nominal parenthood over Akeil [the Rogerses' genetic child] should have been treated as a mistake to be corrected as soon as possible, before the development of a parental relationship. It bears more similarity to a mix-up at the time of a hospital's discharge of two newborn infants, which should simply be corrected at once, than to one where a gestational mother has arguably the same rights to claim parentage as the genetic mother. Under such circumstances, the Fasanos will not be heard to claim the status of parents, entitled to seek an award of visitation.

Rogers v. Fasano, 715 N.Y.S.2d 19, 25 (App. Div. 2000). The Fasano–Rogers embryo mix-up as well as other embryo and gamete mix-ups are discussed in Leslie Bender, "To Err Is Human" ART Mix-Ups: A Labor-Based, Relational Proposal, 9 J. Gender Race & Just. 43 (2006).

2. *Gay sperm donors.*   Gay rights groups have expressed concern about discrimination against certain potential gamete donors. In May 2004, the FDA announced that men who had engaged in sex with other men within a five-year period were disqualified as anonymous sperm donors. (The rule does not apply to donations of sperm to recipients who know the donor.) The rule was part of a set of rules relating to tissue donation more broadly. An FDA spokesperson justified the rule by referring to a higher risk of HIV infection among gay men than among other men. Gay rights groups claimed, in response, that HIV infection occurs among all subgroups within the population, and argued as well that the HIV virus can now be detected within 72 hours after testing. Others contend that antibodies to HIV infection may not appear in the human body for up to six months after infection, making negative test results before that time inconclusive. Valerie Richardson, Gays Barred from Sperm Banks, Washington Times, May 21, 2004, at A13.

3. *Infertility care for same-gender couples in Britain.* In Britain, the National Institute for Health and Clinical Excellence (NICE) has updated its guidelines on fertility care so that it expressly includes same-gender couples as eligible for care. In 2008, the Human Fertilisation and Embryology Act revoked a provision

that required a "father" before infertility care would be offered. James Taylor, Changes to NICE Fertility Guideline for Same-sex Couples, BioNews 661 (June 18, 2012), available at http://www.bionews.org.uk/page_151452.asp?dinfo=fLg8CfF Cr9VovEQq9KIjA3zi. NICE concluded that before becoming eligible for government-funded infertility care, lesbians should undergo six cycles of intrauterine insemination for which they pay. This has led to concern that some women will prefer to face the risks of private arrangements than to bear the heavy cost of six inseminations (about £6,000).

B. MONITORING PREGNANCY

1. Medical Intervention During Pregnancy

For the most part, pregnant women, like most patients, have the right to reject medical intervention. Most states allow competent pregnant women to refuse medical care even when the health or life of the fetus is at risk. A small minority of states make an exception to this rule when the fetus is viable and the recommended treatment will benefit both the mother and the fetus. The majority position is represented by the decision in In re Fetus Brown, 689 N.E.2d 397 (Ill. Ct. App. 1997), infra. The minority position is represented by the decision of the Supreme Court of Georgia in Jefferson v. Griffin Spalding County Hospital Authority, 274 S.E.2d 457 (Ga. 1981). In the latter case, Georgia's highest court concluded that a pregnant woman, refusing treatment on religious grounds, was obligated to accept treatment that would benefit her and the near-term fetus. In re Fetus Brown and *Jefferson* are discussed and compared in Note, Bradley J. Glass, A Comparative Analysis of the Right of a Pregnant Woman to Refuse Medical Treatment for Herself and Her Viable Fetus: The United States and United Kingdom, 11 Ind. Int'l & Comp. L. Rev. 507 (2001). See also Comment, Eric M. Levine, The Constitutionality of Court-Ordered Cesarean Surgery: A Threshold Question, 4 Alb. L.J. Sci. & Tech. 229 (1994) (concluding that compelled cesareans should be ruled unconstitutional).

In In re Unborn Child of Samantha Burton, No. 2009 CA 1167 (Fla. Cir. Ct. Mar. 27, 2009), a Florida court followed the model of the Georgia court in *Jefferson* and ordered Samantha Brown, then 25 weeks pregnant, to stay at Tallahassee Memorial Hospital and receive treatment despite her wish to return home to her two young children. The court premised its order on the obligation to safeguard the welfare of the fetus. See Kate Wevers, Burton v. Florida: Maternal-Fetal Conflicts and Medical Decision-Making During Pregnancy, 38 J.L. Med. & Ethics 436 (2010). The court refused Burton's request to transfer to a different hospital. A few days after the court issued its order, a cesarean was performed, and the fetus was delivered dead. Burton v. State, 49 So. 3d 263 (2010). Burton appealed. A state court of appeal entertained the case because the issue was deemed "capable of repetition yet evading review." Id. at 265. The court reversed the trial court decision.

> The test to overcome a woman's right to refuse medical intervention in her pregnancy is whether the state's compelling state interest is sufficient to override the pregnant woman's constitutional right to the control of her person, including her right to refuse medical treatment. Dubreuil, 629 So. 2d 819; Browning, 568 So. 2d 4; Public Health Trust of Dade County v. Wons, 541

So. 2d 96 (Fla. 1989). In addition, where the state does establish a compelling state interest and the court has found the state's interest sufficient to override a pregnant patient's right to determine her course of medical treatment, the state must then show that the method for pursuing that compelling state interest is "narrowly tailored in the least intrusive manner possible to safeguard the rights of the individual." Browning, 568 So. 2d at 14.

Judge Van Nortwick, who concurred, concluded that Burton was also denied a constitutional right to appointed counsel because of the "deprivation of her liberty and violation of her privacy interests." Id. at 7.

In re A.C., 573 A.2d 1235 (D.C. Cir. 1990) (en banc), decided more than two decades ago, remains the most important case involving medical intervention during pregnancy. The case involved a young woman, diagnosed with incurable cancer at 25 weeks' gestation. At first she asked to be kept alive until the fetus would have a better chance to survive. As she rapidly weakened and approached death, she seemed to withdraw her consent to treatment. The hospital sought and received a court order to perform a cesarean section. The surgery was performed. The baby died within hours of its birth; the mother died two days later. The District of Columbia Court of Appeals heard the case en banc after the mother and baby had died.

The court concluded that the cesarean section should not have been performed because it was not clear that the mother had consented and it was not clear that she was no longer competent. The court did not, however, rule out forced treatment in every case involving competent pregnant patients. The court explained:

> Throughout this opinion we have stressed that the patient's wishes, once they are ascertained, must be followed in "virtually all cases," unless there are "truly extraordinary or compelling reasons to override them." Indeed, some may doubt that there could ever be a situation extraordinary or compelling enough to justify a massive intrusion into a person's body, such as a caesarean section, against that person's will. Whether such a situation may someday present itself is a question that we need not strive to answer here.

Id. at 1252.

a.   Bioethical and Social Perspectives

April Cherry, Symposium Remarks:
Maternal-Fetal Conflicts, the Social
Construction of Maternal Deviance,
and Some Thoughts about Love and Justice
8 Tex. J. Women & L. 245, 247–253 (1999)[6]

I first came to this "maternal-fetal conflict" problem very personally during my first semester of law teaching. When the semester started I was six months

---

6. An additional excerpt from Cherry's article is found in section B(2)(a) below (concerning responses to drug and alcohol abuse during pregnancy).

pregnant. It was determined through a sonogram earlier in my pregnancy that I had a condition known as partial placenta previa. Placenta previa is a condition in which the placenta of the pregnant woman covers her cervix either partially or completely. In cases of complete placenta previa, a cesarean section is generally thought to be medically indicated. In these cases, women who go into spontaneous labor may bleed to death. Cases of partial placenta previa often resolve themselves. The placenta can simply change its position during the course of the pregnancy without medical intervention. Consequently, when a pregnant woman is diagnosed with partial placenta previa, a second sonogram is routinely performed in order to determine whether or not the situation has naturally resolved itself. So, during the seventh month of my pregnancy, a second sonogram was performed. Ultrasonography is an amazing technology. It allows doctors and their patients (and the patient's family and friends) to view an image of the fetus in utero. It encourages us to imagine futures with children who are not yet born. In any event, I was presented with a copy of the sonographic image of my fetus (now a fully formed grade-schooler named Olivia). As wonderful as it was to have a copy of this image to take home with me, it was also confusing. So that afternoon, after the sonogram was performed, I walked around the law school confused about this picture, trying to figure out why this picture didn't make sense to me. Finally I came across a colleague, and dear friend of mine, Meg Baldwin, and I said something like, "Meg, what about this is troubling me?" She responded quickly and simply, "You are not in the picture." She had hit the proverbial nail on its head. The free-floating fetus in the picture did not come close to my experience of pregnancy. In no way did it reflect the relationship I had with the fetus growing inside of me—a relationship that was at many times a unitary experience, a relationship that I was having with my own body, and at times a relationship of duality, in which I was as important to it as it was to me. Patricia Williams captured much of my own experience when she wrote, "I do not believe that a fetus is a separate person from the moment of conception. How could it be? It is so interconnected, so flesh-and-blood boned, so completely part of a woman's body. Why try to carve one from the other?"

But the technology shows us a different story, that of the free-floating fetus, unattached to its mother, a singular entity. From the view of the computer screen, the fetus can look like an autonomous being, imbued with both legal and moral rights; a being in need of an advocate to protect it from a potential enemy. From the vantage point of the technology, the fetus, my fetus, could be imagined to be a separate person and a separate patient. All of this talk of "separateness" becomes possible because the technology, by allowing us a peek inside pregnant women's bodies, has allowed both the legal and the medical imagination to perceive separateness where there is, at least in my experience, unity. Hence, I hope that you can see why the issue of "conflicts" between pregnant women and their fetuses has become important to me on many levels. In that law school corridor, not only was I worried about issues of justice for women in some broad sense, I also worried about what was going to happen to me and my fetus when I went to the hospital to deliver my baby. In any event, this is how I come to this topic and the work I do.

II. Two Paradigmatic Cases of Maternal–Fetal Conflict

The issue of "maternal–fetal conflicts" comes up in a course I teach on reproductive rights. We usually see the discussion in two circumstances. The first is the compelled, or forced, medical treatment of pregnant women, usually cesareans or blood transfusions, and the second is the use of illegal drugs by pregnant women.

A.   *The coerced medical treatment of pregnant women*

The first paradigm for the "maternal–fetal conflict" is where the apparent conflict arises between the need of the fetus for particular medical treatment and the pregnant woman's refusal of that treatment as suggested by a physician. Part of the problem with these cases is that often enough, the suggestions for a particular medical treatment are given by a physician who is not the pregnant woman's physician. This detail is important to me. The available data strongly suggest that in the vast majority of maternal–fetal conflict cases, i.e., where doctors and hospitals seek to compel treatment via law, the pregnant women are often poor, unmarried, and women of color. They present for labor and delivery at either public or teaching hospitals. They have received little or no prenatal care, so they do not have a primary obstetrician. The women we are talking about often do not have a trusting relationship with a doctor. In fact, they may have no relationship with doctors, except for when they come to hospitals to deliver their babies.

In the context in which these women are birthing babies, and given poor people's and black people's lack of trust in the medical profession, it does not seem unreasonable for the woman presenting in that situation not to trust the opinion, however learned, of a doctor whom she has just met. The context also helps to explain how these women are labeled as deviant by other actors in the drama and subjected to heightened social control. But more on that later.

In any event, the doctors and hospitals seek to compel treatment. The treatments are usually suggested because the medical staff believes that without treatment, the fetus will die or be born with significant damage, or because the physician does not believe that these women are capable of making an intelligent, informed decision. The treatments range in invasiveness from blood transfusions to cesarean sections. I am inclined to believe that a cesarean section operation is the most invasive. Perhaps in utero fetal therapy is more invasive, but after reading a few descriptions of cesarean sections, I cannot imagine being more invaded, even though we tend to think of cesarean sections as not so dangerous. The cesarean section operation is viewed as a "normal" method of child birthing, because it is done with much frequency. Because cesarean sections have become normalized as a birthing method, we tend to think of them as not very serious. But in fact they are, particularly when compared to a vaginal birth. Cesarean sections are still considered major abdominal surgery, having all the risks associated therewith, including infection and death. Additionally, the maternal mortality rate for cesarean section patients is much higher than for those patients who give birth vaginally. Studies estimate that maternal mortality rates for cesarean delivery are two to four times higher than the maternal mortality rates associated with vaginal delivery. Notwithstanding all of this data, I am not arguing that cesarean sections are not relatively safe surgeries, but they do carry the risks of death and infection. In addition, it may also be important to note that cesarean section deliveries are often performed unnecessarily. For example, in 1991, there were approximately 350,000 unnecessary cesarean section operations performed in the United States. Thus, in the context of the danger of the procedure and its overuse, it makes perfect sense that women, when presented with the option of having a cesarean section, might say, "No, thank you."

Also important in understanding the coerced medical treatment of pregnant women as morally and legally problematic is the demographics, including the race, ethnicity, national origin, and class of the women so coerced. I have already mentioned briefly some of the demographics, but I would like to add a few other facts to the mix. For example, a national survey performed in 1986 by doctors at the University of Illinois College of Medicine found that in a five-year period, at least twenty-one court orders had been sought by hospitals that responded to their surveys. Of those twenty-one court orders sought, courts issued orders compelling treatment of the women in eighteen of the twenty-one cases. Over eighty-five percent of those court orders were obtained within six hours. Eighty-one percent of the women involved were black, Asian, or Latino. Forty-four percent were unmarried. Twenty-five percent did not speak English as their language of choice, or their primary language. Finally, almost all the pregnant women involved were treated in teaching hospitals or were receiving public assistance.

The survey also indicated that in one-third of the cases, the prediction of fetal harm was inaccurate. Despite the inaccuracy of the electronic fetal monitoring technology, physicians and hospitals rely on its data as a safeguard against the often-phantom threat of legal liability for medical malpractice. Physicians and hospitals inform the presiding judge that, without the proposed medical and legal intervention proposed, the fetus will die. Well, in one-third of those cases, the doctors' predictions were wrong. I do not think these predictions of poor outcomes are necessarily the result of doctors' practicing bad medicine. I think the inaccuracy of the predictions is caused by the uncertainty that is intrinsic to medical judgment. As a committee on ethics of the American College of Obstetrics and Gynecology suggested, "The role of obstetrician should be one of an informed educator and counselor weighing the risks and benefits to both patients (the pregnant woman and her fetus) as well as realizing that tests, judgments, and decisions are fallible." Medicine is art as well as science; hence, doctors make mistakes. And given that doctors make mistakes and the law nevertheless enforces their judgments, then I want to ask why don't we allow women to make decisions in these contexts that may have a negative outcome for the fetus? Why doesn't the law support the judgment of women regarding their pregnancies? Why can't a woman make a choice vis-à-vis herself and her fetus that might have a bad outcome? In other words, why can't women make mistakes? What compelled medical treatment means is that doctors get to make choices that affect both a pregnant woman and her fetus all the time, with the force of the law to back them up. Why do we put more faith in the physicians than we do in the women? Why don't we care what women want or need? Where is the justice, love, or compassion for the pregnant woman who is trying to make a difficult decision?

NOTES AND QUESTIONS

1. *Assessing compelled treatment.*   Do you think it is ever justifiable to force treatment on a pregnant woman for her sake? For the sake of her fetus? For the sake of them both? Do you think an obstetrician has an obligation to care for the fetus that is separate from an obligation to care for the pregnant woman? That position is argued in F. A. Chervenak & L. B. McCullough, Perinatal Ethics: A Practical Method of Analysis of Obligations to Mother and Fetus, 66 Obstet. Gynecol. 442 (1985). In contrast, a case discussion, written after the trial court decision in Burton v. State, supra, suggested that judicial discretion in this area (at the trial court level) "may tend to favor compulsory treatment over a woman's right to protect her own bodily integrity." Kate Wevers, Burton v. Florida: Maternal-Fetal Conflicts and Medical Decision-making During Pregnancy, 38 J.L. Med. & Ethics 436, 439 (2010).

2. *Compelled abortion.*   Outrage, expressed widely on the internet, followed the forced abortion of a seven-month fetus in China in 2012. The pregnant woman, Feng Jianmei, and her family did not have the resources to pay the fine exacted for a second child. She was therefore forced to undergo an abortion. A photo of the mother with the aborted fetus beside her was circulated widely on the internet in China and internationally. Protests included calls for the reformation of China's family planning laws and resulted in the government's agreeing to compensate Feng Jianmei with cash. China Pays Family in Forced Abortion Case, Father Says, N.Y. Times, July 11, 2012, www.nytimes.com.

3. *Comparing fetuses and children.*   The federal government has included fetuses in the States Child Health Insurance Program. 42 C.F.R. 457.10 (2012). (Some changes in 42 C.F.R. 457.10, effective on January 1, 2014, do not include changes to the definition of fetus.) Does this suggest that fetuses are children? What about laws that make it a crime to cause the death of a fetus? Should such laws apply to pregnant women? Courts have not used these laws to hold a pregnant woman liable for the death of a fetus she carried. Stallman v. Youngquist, 531 N.E.2d 355 (1988). See Lisa H. Harris & Lynn Paltrow, The Status of Pregnant Women and Fetuses in US Criminal Law, 289 JAMA 1697 (2003). In Tesar v. Anderson, 789 N.W.2d 351 (Wis. App. 2010), a Wisconsin appellate court declined to follow *Stallman.* In *Tesar,* the father of a fetus, born dead as the result of a car accident, sued the mother's insurer on the basis of the mother's negligent driving. The court concluded that public policy did not preclude liability.

4. *Maternal–fetal attachment.*   In recent years, the notion of maternal–fetal attachment has been used to describe the relationship between a pregnant woman and a fetus. Amy Salisbury et al., Maternal-Fetal Attachment, 289 JAMA 1701 (2003). Salisbury et al. note that three scales have been developed that measure maternal–fetal attachment. Id. Although the authors admit that little is known about the development of maternal–fetal attachment and suggest additional studies, they report, among other things, that "maternal mood" correlates with the strength of a pregnant woman's attachment to the fetus, as does the level of psychosocial support given to the pregnant woman. Id. The authors acknowledge that maternal–fetal attachment is likely to be sensitive to diverse factors within different cultural settings. However, they do not suggest that the

very notion of maternal–fetal attachment may reflect cultural biases. Might this notion of maternal–fetal attachment create a presumption over time that a pregnant woman should be happy or that she should strengthen her social and familial support system for the sake of the fetus?

5. *Treating HIV-positive pregnant women.*   Treating HIV-positive pregnant women with antiretroviral drugs can reduce the risk of transmitting the virus to the fetus. Edward M. Connor et al., Reduction of Maternal-Infant Transmission of Human Immunodeficiency Virus Type-I with Zidovudine Treatment, 331 New Eng. J. Med. 1173 (1994). In light of that fact, do you think there should be mandatory HIV testing of pregnant women? See Note, Erin Nicholson, Mandatory HIV Testing of Pregnant Women: Public Health Policy Considerations and Alternatives, 9 Duke J. Gender L. & Pol'y 175 (2002) (noting possibility of voluntary testing combined with program to educate pregnant women about testing and treatment).

Since 1987, the CDC has carried out anonymous population testing to gather data about HIV infection among women of childbearing age. The testing was done on blood collected for other reasons. The testing did not require informed consent because the identity of those whose blood was being tested was unknown. The surveillance program is described in Wendy Chavkin et al., Mandatory Testing of Pregnant Women and Newborns: HIV, Drug Use, and Welfare Policy, 24 Fordham Urb. L.J. 749 (1997). The CDC survey was later suspended, but New York continued testing with state funds.

New York also enacted a statute that provided for nonanonymous testing of newborns for HIV. 10 New York Comp. Codes R. & Regs. §69–1 et seq. (2012). One commentator describes the New York law as "bizarre from a public health standpoint" because testing newborns does not cut down on the transmission of HIV in utero. Andrea Marsh, Testing Pregnant Women and Newborns for HIV: Legal and Ethical Responses to Public Health Efforts to Prevent Pediatric AIDS, 13 Yale J.L. & Feminism 195, 220–221 (2001). Marsh suggests that "[m]andatory newborn testing laws may be the result of a political compromise between forces intent on combating pediatric AIDS and forces attempting to minimize the intrusiveness of testing policies on the privacy of HIV-infected pregnant women." Id. at 221.

b.   Legal Approaches

In Re Fetus Brown
689 N.E.2d 397 (App. Ct. Ill. 1997)

Opinion by THEIS.

The issue before this court is whether a competent, pregnant woman's right to refuse medical treatment, which, in this case involves religiously offensive blood transfusions, may be overridden by the State's substantial interest in the welfare of the viable fetus.

The tensions present in this issue are palpable. Questions of morality and legality converge, requiring consideration of the obligations of a pregnant woman and of the State. As a court, we are asked to determine the proper balance of the mother's common law and constitutional interests in bodily self-determination as against the State's recognized interest in protecting the viable fetus.

[The court then described the facts of the case, noting that Darlene Brown, then 26, required surgery to remove a urethral mass when she was almost 35 weeks pregnant. She lost blood during surgery. After surgery, her hemoglobin level dropped so significantly that her treating physician, Dr. Robert Walsh, opined in a court hearing that if Brown did not receive a transfusion there was only a 5 percent chance that she and the fetus would survive.]

On June 28, 1996, the State filed a petition for adjudication of wardship and a motion for temporary custody of Baby Doe, a fetus. . . .

. . . The court granted the State's petition and appointed the hospital administrator as temporary custodian of Fetus Brown, with the right to consent to any and all blood transfusions for Darlene Brown when advised of such necessity by any attending physician. As alleged in the Browns' later pleadings, Darlene Brown was transfused with six units of packed red blood cells beginning on the night of June 28 and continuing to approximately noon on June 29. Further, Darlene Brown tried to resist the transfusion and the doctors "yelled at and forcibly restrained, overpowered and sedated" her.

On July 8, 1996, the court held a status hearing and found that Darlene Brown had delivered a healthy baby (Baby Doe Brown) on July 1, 1996, and that both baby and mother had been discharged from the hospital. The court then vacated the temporary custody order, dismissed the State's petition, and closed the case.

. . . Darlene Brown contends that, under federal and Illinois law, as a competent adult, she has an absolute right to refuse medical advice and treatment. In contrast, the State urges that its substantial interest in the viable fetus outweighs the minimal invasion presented by the blood transfusion. The public guardian also appeals, seeking guidance regarding its role as protector of fetal rights. . . .

The springboard for this case is the appellate decision in In re Baby Boy Doe, 260 Ill. App. 3d 392, 632 N.E.2d 326, 198 Ill. Dec. 267 (1994). In *Baby Boy Doe*, the appellate court was asked to decide whether the circuit court should balance the rights of the unborn but viable fetus against the right of the competent woman to choose the type of medical care she deemed appropriate, based in part on personal religious considerations.

The *Baby Boy Doe* court first considered the opinion of the Illinois Supreme Court in Stallman v. Youngquist, 125 Ill. 2d 267, 531 N.E.2d 355, 126 Ill. Dec. 60 (1988). In *Stallman,* the court determined that a tort cause of action may not be maintained by a fetus against its mother for the unintentional infliction of prenatal injuries. *Stallman.* In so deciding, the *Stallman* court reasoned that "the law will not treat a fetus as an entity which is entirely separate from its mother." Moreover, the court stated that, in Illinois, a fetus cannot have rights superior to those of its mother. The court thus held that a pregnant woman owes no legally cognizable duty to her developing fetus.

Following the reasoning of *Stallman,* the *Baby Boy Doe* court held that Illinois courts should not engage in a balancing of the maternal and fetal rights such that "a woman's competent choice in refusing medical treatment as invasive as a cesarean section during her pregnancy must be honored, even in circumstances where the choice may be harmful to her fetus." In reaching this decision, the *Baby Boy Doe* court applied the rationale of *Stallman* to determine:

> [A] woman's right to refuse invasive medical treatment, derived from her rights to privacy, bodily integrity, and religious liberty, is not diminished during pregnancy. The woman retains the same right to refuse invasive treatment, even of lifesaving or other beneficial nature, that she can exercise when she is not pregnant. The potential impact upon the fetus is not legally relevant; to the contrary, the *Stallman* court explicitly rejected the view that the woman's rights can be subordinated to fetal rights.

In dicta, however, the *Baby Boy Doe* court left open the question of whether blood transfusions, involving "relatively noninvasive and risk-free" procedures, could permissibly be ordered in such a circumstance. . . .

Most cases [involving refusals of medical treatment] concern competent adults who are not pregnant. Of the cases concerning a pregnant woman, most concern the woman's refusal of medical treatment after the birth of the child, and, thus, the woman's wishes are respected. Although *Baby Boy Doe* was a pregnancy case, the court found the preservation-of-life factor irrelevant as the cesarean section procedure, although necessary for the health of the fetus, was not necessary to preserve the mother's life or health. In fact, the court found that the procedure posed a greater risk to the mother's health. Only in the instant case are we confronted with a situation in which both the pregnant mother and the viable fetus were to benefit from the proposed blood transfusions. We determine that the State's interest in preservation of life continues to concern the life of the decision maker.

Illinois public policy values the sanctity of life. Along with the State's interest in preservation of life, however, must be considered the State's interest in protecting the autonomy of the individual. "The State rarely acts to protect individuals from themselves. . . . This is consistent with the primary function of the State to preserve and promote liberty and the personal autonomy of the individual." Fosmire v. Nicoleau, 75 N.Y.2d 218, 227, 551 N.E.2d 77, 81–82, 551 N.Y.S.2d 876, 880–881 (1990). . . .

. . . [One] State interest is the impact upon third parties. Most cases have considered this interest in the context of the impact upon the minor children of a woman refusing medical treatment. . . .

Some courts have found that the state's interest in the welfare of third parties cannot be determinative of the patient's right to refuse medical treatment. Other courts have declined to go so far, instead holding that where there is no evidence of the minor children's abandonment, such an interest will not override the patient's competent refusal.

Here, the record does not indicate evidence of abandonment of the minor children. Lester Brown, the natural father of the three-year-old, supported Darlene's decision to refuse consent. While there is no evidence in the record regarding the eight-year-old's natural father, Lester Brown as well as his and Darlene's parents all were willing to help support both minor children. Thus, the State's interest in protecting the living minor children is not determinative.

We therefore encounter the ultimate issue, the State's interest in protecting the viable fetus. In Roe v. Wade, the United States Supreme Court explained that the state maintains an "important and legitimate interest in preserving and protecting the health of the pregnant woman . . . [and] the potentiality of human life." In fact, the State maintains "a substantial interest in potential life throughout pregnancy." Planned Parenthood of Southeastern Pa. v. Casey, 505 U.S. 833 (1992). In the abortion context, the state's important and legitimate interest becomes compelling at viability. At that point, the state may restrict abortion, except when necessary to preserve the life or health of the mother. *Roe,* 410 U.S. at 163–64. . . .

To date, a fetus is not considered a minor for purposes of the Illinois Juvenile Court Act. Illinois courts have, however, found viable fetuses to be persons with regard to wrongs caused by third parties, but they have distinguished such injuries from those caused by the mother.

In examining the State's interest in the viable fetus, we note the distinct circumstances of this case. This is not an abortion case in which a pregnant woman seeks to terminate an unwanted pregnancy. Likewise, this case does not involve substance abuse or other abuse by a pregnant woman. And while refusal to consent to a blood transfusion for an infant would constitute neglect, without a determination by the Illinois legislature that a fetus is a minor for purposes of the Juvenile Court Act, we cannot separate the mother's valid treatment refusal from the potential adverse consequences to the viable fetus.

Consequently, following the lead of *Baby Boy Doe* and *Stallman,* and in this case balancing the mother's right to refuse medical treatment against the State's substantial interest in the viable fetus, we hold that the State may not override a pregnant woman's competent treatment decision, including refusal of recommended invasive medical procedures, to potentially save the life of the viable fetus. We disagree with the *Baby Boy Doe* court's suggestion that a blood transfusion constitutes a "relatively noninvasive and risk-free procedure" and find that a blood transfusion is an invasive medical procedure that interrupts a competent adult's bodily integrity. We thus determine that the circuit court erred in ordering Brown to undergo the transfusion on behalf of the viable fetus.

Reversed.

NOTES AND QUESTIONS

1. *State's interest in fetus and in health of pregnant woman.*   In Roe v. Wade, 410 U.S. 113 (1973), and Planned Parenthood of Southeast Pennsylvania v. Casey, 505 U.S. 833 (1992), the Supreme Court found that the state has an interest in protecting fetal life. (Both *Roe* and *Casey* appear in Chapter 5.) In *Roe,* the strength of that interest depended on the relevant trimester of pregnancy. In *Casey,* the Court concluded that the state's interests in the fetus before viability "are not strong enough to support a prohibition of abortion or the imposition of a substantial obstacle to the woman's effective right to elect the procedure." In *Casey,* the Court also declared that from the start of a pregnancy the state has an interest "in protecting the health of the woman and the life of the fetus that may become a child." In the Court's view, "[t]hese principles do not contradict one another." Can you imagine a case in which they might contradict one another? Might the state's interest in the fetus in the abortion context differ from its interest in the fetus in the context of a pregnant woman's refusing medical treatment?

2. *Murder charge.*   In 2004, Melissa Rowland, a pregnant woman in Utah who ignored doctors' warnings that she have a cesarean section to protect twin fetuses, was charged with murder after one of the babies was born dead. According to media reports, the woman had explained to a nurse that she was unwilling to submit to surgery because she did not want to be left with scars. AP, Woman Charged with Murder of Unborn Baby, March 11, 2004, http://news.findlaw.com (visited March 15, 2004). Rowland was charged with murder under a Utah feticide law that defines killing a fetus at any time after conception as a crime. (The statute includes an exception for abortions.)

In 2011, a California woman was charged with murder for causing the death of a four-month old fetus. According to news reports, Nieshia Johnson's pregnant aunt discovered that Neishia, babysitting for the aunt's children, had punished the children by whipping them with a belt. Johnson and her aunt began to fight physically. Johnson then kicked her aunt—then four months pregnant—in the stomach. A few days later, the aunt suffered a miscarriage. A local police detective explained that killing a fetus older than eight weeks gestation can result in a prosecution for murder. Rob McMillan, IE Woman Charged with Killing Unborn Fetus, ABCNews, Apr. 27, 2011, available at http://abclocal.go.com/kabc/story?sectin=news/local/inland_empire&id=8098240. After a jury deadlocked, Johnson pleaded no contest to a charge of assault. In exchange, the district attorney dropped the murder charge. News, Ontario Woman Pleads No Contest in Death of Unborn Baby, Inland Valley Daily Bulletin (Ontario, CA), May 11, 2012, available in Lexis/Nexis News Library.

Many states (38 in 2012) have laws that define killing a fetus as homicide. Fetal Homicide State Laws, Nat'l Conf. State Legislatures, http://www.ncsl.org/issues-research/health/fetal-homicide-state-laws.aspx (last visited Oct. 7, 2012). Almost half of the states (23 states) have laws that define killing a fetus in the earliest stages of gestation as homicide. Id.

2.   Substance Abuse During Pregnancy

In the last decades of the twentieth century, public media reported large numbers of babies born to mothers who were using alcohol or other drugs (especially "crack" cocaine) during pregnancy. There are similarities between discussions about substance abuse during pregnancy and about medical intervention during pregnancy. However, the two matters are distinct. In general, there is a right to be free of unwanted medical intervention. But there is no right to use illegal drugs. Moreover, because many of the drugs at issue in the controversy over drug abuse during pregnancy are illegal, their use can lead to criminal action. In addition, middle-class and wealthier women are generally protected from programs that test and analyze urine or blood for evidence of drug use during pregnancy by the nature of their prenatal care and by assumptions made by the health care system and the state about their lives and behavior. Thus, cases about drug use during pregnancy tend to involve class and racial or ethnic discrimination more openly than cases about medical intervention during pregnancy.

Many state legislatures considered bills dealing with prenatal substance abuse in the decade between 1985 and 1995. During that period, sociolegal commentaries about both prenatal drug use and alcohol use during pregnancy varied widely in the responses they suggested. At one end, commentators argued that women who use drugs or alcohol while pregnant should be stopped from doing so even at the expense of their own liberty. Michael Dorris presents this position in his book, The Broken Cord (1989). Dorris's book describes the consequences for Dorris's own adopted son, Adam, of maternal alcohol use by Adam's biological mother during her pregnancy with Adam. In a forward to Dorris's book, his wife Louise Erdrich (who married Dorris after he adopted Adam) asks: "Once a woman decides to carry a child to term, to produce another human being, has she also the right to inflict on that person Adam's life? Because his mother drank, Adam is one of the earth's damaged." Id. at xvii. Other commentators have stressed a different aspect of state responses to alcohol and drug use during pregnancy. Some commentators have suggested that the effort to criminalize prenatal substance abuse was largely an attack on poor women of color. April Cherry, whose position on coerced medical treatment is printed above, describes responses to prenatal drug abuse as motivated in large part by racism, sexism, and classism. Cherry, infra. Cf. Dorris, supra, at 9.

a.   Bioethical and Social Perspectives

> *April Cherry, Symposium Remarks:*
> *Maternal-Fetal Conflicts, the Social*
> *Construction of Maternal Deviance, and*
> *Some Thoughts about Love and Justice*
> 8 Tex. J. Women & L. 245, 253–255 (1999)[7]

The cases [involving drug-addicted pregnant women] . . . are most often discussed as the case of the pregnant woman addicted to crack as opposed to the one addicted to powder cocaine. We know that in the public mind the difference between the crack user and the powder cocaine user is a racial difference. Because crack is less expensive than powder cocaine, its use is more likely to be associated with poor people, e.g., black folks, than with the wealthier drug users, e.g., white folks. In fact, drug-using and drug-addicted women who have been detained in hospitals or sent to prison out of concern for their fetuses have been largely poor women of color. Judges send these women to jails and prisons with the belief that "preventative detention" will foster fetal welfare. As Sandra Garcia reports, a well-respected state court judge has said that "he would have no compunction regarding ruling outside of sentencing guidelines if a 'doper' came before him during her pregnancy, and that he firmly believed that of the 300 judges who had just attended a conference, the vast majority would rule in ways that would favor fetal health." Unfortunately, "preventative detention" is not necessarily conducive to either maternal or fetal heath. Not only are illicit drugs available in jails and prisons, these institutions generally lack the medical facilities necessary for good prenatal care. Furthermore, shackling a woman during childbirth is not conducive to maternal–infant bonding, thought

---

7. Parts of Cherry's article are printed in section B(1)(a), supra (concerning medical intervention during pregnancy).

to be of prime importance for the infant. It serves merely to punish the woman and show society's contempt for poor, non-English-speaking women of color and their children. If we care about infants as much as we seem to care about fetuses, we might want to reconsider "preventative detention," and consider other ways to encourage maternal and fetal health.

Because the image of "the crack-head" is so racialized, this focus on crack-exposed fetuses and pregnant crack users makes me suspicious. Nevertheless, there is some truth to the charge that women who use crack while pregnant may under many circumstances give birth to babies whose health is, at least initially, compromised. However, the data on the long-term harm [from] maternal crack use is not as conclusive as the public has been led to believe. Although the babies born to women who use crack during their pregnancies may be born with a host of medical problems, it is unclear as to whether these medical problems, other than any drug withdrawal that the infant might suffer, are the result of the maternal crack use, or lack of prenatal care and maternal malnutrition—just plain old poverty. It is also unclear as to whether the initial condition of the newborn born in these circumstances has any long-term effects. At five years old, "crack babies" look a lot like the "non-crack babies" if they are well nourished and live in fairly supportive environments. Therefore, it is highly probable that the crack-baby crisis to which the law has been responding is more myth than reality.

In summary, when we look at the demographics of those pregnant women described as being in conflict with their fetuses, we see that the group is composed of those women who are some of the most disenfranchised in our society and most subject to other forms of reproductive control. We can also see that although physician prediction of fetal harm is often inaccurate, it is nevertheless preferred over the judgment, also often imperfect, of these pregnant women. These factors, especially when taken together, should cause us to question any policy regulating the relationship between pregnant women and their fetuses. History tells us that any such rules will be used against women, particularly women of color, as a tool of social control.

b.   Legal Approaches

|| *Ferguson v. City of Charleston* ||
532 U.S. 67 (2001)

Opinion by STEVENS.

. . . In the fall of 1988, staff members at the public hospital operated in the city of Charleston by the Medical University of South Carolina (MUSC) became concerned about an apparent increase in the use of cocaine by patients who were receiving prenatal treatment.[1] In response to this perceived increase, as of April 1989, MUSC began to order drug screens to be performed on urine

---

1. As several witnesses testified at trial, the problem of "crack babies" was widely perceived in the late 1980s as a national epidemic, prompting considerable concern both in the medical community and among the general populace.

samples from maternity patients who were suspected of using cocaine. If a patient tested positive, she was then referred by MUSC staff to the county substance abuse commission for counseling and treatment. However, despite the referrals, the incidence of cocaine use among the patients at MUSC did not appear to change.

Some four months later, Nurse Shirley Brown, the case manager for the MUSC obstetrics department, heard a news broadcast reporting that the police in Greenville, South Carolina, were arresting pregnant users of cocaine on the theory that such use harmed the fetus and was therefore child abuse.[2] . . . Nurse Brown discussed the story with MUSC's general counsel, Joseph C. Good, Jr., who then contacted Charleston Solicitor Charles Condon in order to offer MUSC's cooperation in prosecuting mothers whose children tested positive for drugs at birth.

[In consultation with local police, the County Substance Abuse Commission, and the Department of Social Services, MUSC adopted Policy 7, concerned with Management of Drug Abuse During Pregnancy.]

. . . The first section, entitled the "Identification of Drug Abusers," provided that a patient should be tested for cocaine through a urine drug screen if she met one or more of nine criteria.[4] It also stated that a chain of custody should be followed when obtaining and testing urine samples, presumably to make sure that the results could be used in subsequent criminal proceedings. The policy also provided for education and referral to a substance abuse clinic for patients who tested positive. Most important, it added the threat of law enforcement intervention. . . .

The threat of law enforcement involvement was set forth in two protocols, the first dealing with the identification of drug use during pregnancy, and the second with identification of drug use after labor. Under the latter protocol, the police were to be notified without delay and the patient promptly arrested. Under the former, after the initial positive drug test, the police were to be notified (and the patient arrested) only if the patient tested positive for cocaine a second time or if she missed an appointment with a substance abuse counselor.[5] In 1990, however, the policy was modified at the behest of the solicitor's office to give the patient who tested positive during labor, like the patient who tested positive during a prenatal care visit, an opportunity to avoid arrest by consenting to substance abuse treatment.

---

2. Under South Carolina law, a viable fetus has historically been regarded as a person; in 1995, the South Carolina Supreme Court held that the ingestion of cocaine during the third trimester of pregnancy constitutes criminal child neglect. Whitner v. South Carolina, 328 S.C. 1, 492 S.E.2d 777 (1995), cert. denied, 523 U.S. 1145, 140 L. Ed. 2d 1104, 118 S. Ct. 1857 (1998).

4. Those criteria were as follows: "1. No prenatal care; 2. Late prenatal care after 24 weeks gestation; 3. Incomplete prenatal care; 4. Abruptio placentae; 5. Intrauterine fetal death; 6. Preterm labor 'of no obvious cause'; 7. IUGR [intrauterine growth retardation] 'of no obvious cause'; 8. Previously known drug or alcohol abuse; 9. Unexplained congenital anomalies."

5. Despite the conditional description of the first category, when the policy was in its initial stages, a positive test was immediately reported to the police, who then promptly arrested the patient.

II

Petitioners are 10 women who received obstetrical care at MUSC and who were arrested after testing positive for cocaine. Four of them were arrested during the initial implementation of the policy; they were not offered the opportunity to receive drug treatment as an alternative to arrest. The others were arrested after the policy was modified in 1990; they either failed to comply with the terms of the drug treatment program or tested positive for a second time. Respondents include the city of Charleston, law enforcement officials who helped develop and enforce the policy, and representatives of MUSC.

Petitioners' complaint challenged the validity of the policy under various theories, including the claim that warrantless and nonconsensual drug tests conducted for criminal investigatory purposes were unconstitutional searches. Respondents advanced two principal defenses to the constitutional claim: (1) that, as a matter of fact, petitioners had consented to the searches; and (2) that, as a matter of law, the searches were reasonable, even absent consent, because they were justified by special non-law-enforcement purposes. The District Court rejected the second defense because the searches in question "were not done by the medical university for independent purposes. [Instead,] the police came in and there was an agreement reached that the positive screens would be shared with the police." Accordingly, the District Court submitted the factual defense to the jury with instructions that required a verdict in favor of petitioners unless the jury found consent. The jury found for respondents.

Petitioners appealed, arguing that the evidence was not sufficient to support the jury's consent finding. The Court of Appeals for the Fourth Circuit affirmed, but without reaching the question of consent. 186 F.3d 469 (1999). Disagreeing with the District Court, the majority of the appellate panel held that the searches were reasonable as a matter of law under our line of cases recognizing that "special needs" may, in certain exceptional circumstances, justify a search policy designed to serve non-law-enforcement ends.[7] On the understanding "that MUSC personnel conducted the urine drug screens for medical purposes wholly independent of an intent to aid law enforcement efforts,"[8] the majority applied the balancing test used in Treasury Employees

---

7. The term "special needs" first appeared in Justice Blackmun's opinion concurring in the judgment in New Jersey v. T. L. O., 469 U.S. 325, 351 (1985). . . . In his concurrence, Justice Blackmun agreed with the Court that there are limited exceptions to the probable-cause requirement, in which reasonableness is determined by "a careful balancing of governmental and private interests," but concluded that such a test should only be applied "in those exceptional circumstances in which special needs, beyond the normal need for law enforcement, make the warrant and probable-cause requirement impracticable. . . ." Ibid. This Court subsequently adopted the "special needs" terminology in O'Connor v. Ortega, 480 U.S. 709, 720, 94 L. Ed. 2d 714, 107 S. Ct. 1492 (1987) (plurality opinion), and Griffin v. Wisconsin, 483 U.S. 868, 873, 97 L. Ed. 2d 709, 107 S. Ct. 3164 (1987), concluding that, in limited circumstances, a search unsupported by either warrant or probable cause can be constitutional when "special needs" other than the normal need for law enforcement provide sufficient justification. See also Vernonia School District 47J v. Acton, 515 U.S. 646, 652-653, 132 L. Ed. 2d 564, 115 S. Ct. 2386 (1995).

8. The majority stated that the District Court had made such a finding. 186 F.3d 469, 477 (CA4 1999). The text of the relevant finding, made in the context of petitioners' now abandoned Title VI claim, reads as follows: "The policy was applied in all maternity departments at MUSC. Its goal was not to arrest patients but to facilitate their treatment

v. Von Raab, 489 U.S. 656 (1989), and Vernonia School Dist. 47J v. Acton, 515 U.S. 646 (1995), and concluded that the interest in curtailing the pregnancy complications and medical costs associated with maternal cocaine use outweighed what the majority termed a minimal intrusion on the privacy of the patients. . . .

We granted certiorari to review the appellate court's holding on the "special needs" issue. Because we do not reach the question of the sufficiency of the evidence with respect to consent, we necessarily assume for purposes of our decision—as did the Court of Appeals—that the searches were conducted without the informed consent of the patients. We conclude that the judgment should be reversed and the case remanded for a decision on the consent issue.

III

Because MUSC is a state hospital, the members of its staff are government actors, subject to the strictures of the Fourth Amendment. New Jersey v. T. L. O., 469 U.S. 325, 335–337, 83 L. Ed. 2d 720, 105 S. Ct. 733 (1985). Moreover, the urine tests conducted by those staff members were indisputably searches within the meaning of the Fourth Amendment. Neither the District Court nor the Court of Appeals concluded that any of the nine criteria used to identify the women to be searched provided either probable cause to believe that they were using cocaine, or even the basis for a reasonable suspicion of such use. Rather, the District Court and the Court of Appeals viewed the case as one involving MUSC's right to conduct searches without warrants or probable cause. Furthermore, given the posture in which the case comes to us, we must assume for purposes of our decision that the tests were performed without the informed consent of the patients.

Because the hospital seeks to justify its authority to conduct drug tests and to turn the results over to law enforcement agents without the knowledge or consent of the patients, this case differs from . . . previous cases in which we have considered whether comparable drug tests "fit within the closely guarded category of constitutionally permissible suspicionless searches." Chandler v. Miller, 520 U.S. 305 (1997).

In [previous] cases, we employed a balancing test that weighed the intrusion on the individual's interest in privacy against the "special needs" that

---

and protect both the mother and unborn child." That finding, however, must be read in light of this comment by the District Court with respect to the Fourth Amendment claim:

> . . . THESE SEARCHES WERE NOT DONE BY THE MEDICAL UNIVERSITY FOR INDEPENDENT PURPOSES. IF THEY HAD BEEN, THEN THEY WOULD NOT IMPLICATE THE FOURTH AMENDMENT. OBVIOUSLY AS I POINT OUT THERE ON PAGE 4, NORMALLY URINE SCREENS AND BLOOD TESTS AND THAT TYPE OF THING CAN BE TAKEN BY HEALTH CARE PROVIDERS WITHOUT HAVING TO WORRY ABOUT THE FOURTH AMENDMENT. THE ONLY REASON THE FOURTH AMENDMENT IS IMPLICATED HERE IS THAT THE POLICE CAME IN AND THERE WAS AN AGREEMENT REACHED THAT THE POSITIVE SCREENS WOULD BE SHARED WITH THE POLICE. AND THEN THE SCREEN IS NOT DONE INDEPENDENT OF POLICE, IT'S DONE IN CONJUNCTION WITH THE POLICE AND THAT IMPLICATES THE FOURTH AMENDMENT.

App. 1247–1249.

supported the program. As an initial matter, we note that the invasion of privacy in this case is far more substantial than in those cases. . . .

. . . In each of those earlier cases, the "special need" that was advanced as a justification for the absence of a warrant or individualized suspicion was one divorced from the State's general interest in law enforcement. . . . In this case, however, the central and indispensable feature of the policy from its inception was the use of law enforcement to coerce the patients into substance abuse treatment. This fact distinguishes this case from circumstances in which physicians or psychologists, in the course of ordinary medical procedures aimed at helping the patient herself, come across information that under rules of law or ethics is subject to reporting requirements, which no one has challenged here. . . .

Respondents argue in essence that their ultimate purpose—namely, protecting the health of both mother and child—is a beneficent one. . . .

While the ultimate goal of the program may well have been to get the women in question into substance abuse treatment and off of drugs, the immediate objective of the searches was to generate evidence for law enforcement purposes in order to reach that goal. The threat of law enforcement may ultimately have been intended as a means to an end, but the direct and primary purpose of MUSC's policy was to ensure the use of those means. In our opinion, this distinction is critical. Because law enforcement involvement always serves some broader social purpose or objective, under respondents' view, virtually any nonconsensual suspicionless search could be immunized under the special needs doctrine by defining the search solely in terms of its ultimate, rather than immediate, purpose. Such an approach is inconsistent with the Fourth Amendment. Given the primary purpose of the Charleston program, which was to use the threat of arrest and prosecution in order to force women into treatment, and given the extensive involvement of law enforcement officials at every stage of the policy, this case simply does not fit within the closely guarded category of "special needs."

The fact that positive test results were turned over to the police does not merely provide a basis for distinguishing our prior cases applying the "special needs" balancing approach to the determination of drug use. It also provides an affirmative reason for enforcing the strictures of the Fourth Amendment. While state hospital employees, like other citizens, may have a duty to provide the police with evidence of criminal conduct that they inadvertently acquire in the course of routine treatment, when they undertake to obtain such evidence from their patients for the specific purpose of incriminating those patients, they have a special obligation to make sure that the patients are fully informed about their constitutional rights, as standards of knowing waiver require.

As respondents have repeatedly insisted, their motive was benign rather than punitive. Such a motive, however, cannot justify a departure from Fourth Amendment protections, given the pervasive involvement of law enforcement with the development and application of the MUSC policy. The stark and unique fact that characterizes this case is that Policy 7 was designed to obtain evidence of criminal conduct by the tested patients that would be turned over to the police and that could be admissible in subsequent criminal prosecutions. While respondents are correct that drug abuse both was and is a serious problem, "the gravity of the threat alone cannot be dispositive of questions concerning what means law enforcement officers may employ to pursue a given purpose." . . .

Accordingly, the judgment of the Court of Appeals is reversed, and the case is remanded for further proceedings consistent with this opinion.

Justice KENNEDY, concurring in the judgment.

I agree that the search procedure in issue cannot be sustained under the Fourth Amendment. . . .

II

In my view, it is necessary and prudent to be explicit in explaining the limitations of today's decision. The beginning point ought to be to acknowledge the legitimacy of the State's interest in fetal life and of the grave risk to the life and health of the fetus, and later the child, caused by cocaine ingestion. Infants whose mothers abuse cocaine during pregnancy are born with a wide variety of physical and neurological abnormalities. . . . There can be no doubt that a mother's ingesting this drug can cause tragic injury to a fetus and a child. There should be no doubt that South Carolina can impose punishment upon an expectant mother who has so little regard for her own unborn that she risks causing him or her lifelong damage and suffering. The State, by taking special measures to give rehabilitation and training to expectant mothers with this tragic addiction or weakness, acts well within its powers and its civic obligations.

The holding of the Court, furthermore, does not call into question the validity of mandatory reporting laws such as child abuse laws which require teachers to report evidence of child abuse to the proper authorities, even if arrest and prosecution is the likely result. That in turn highlights the real difficulty. As this case comes to us, and as reputable sources confirm, . . . we must accept the premise that the medical profession can adopt acceptable criteria for testing expectant mothers for cocaine use in order to provide prompt and effective counseling to the mother and to take proper medical steps to protect the child. If prosecuting authorities then adopt legitimate procedures to discover this information and prosecution follows, that ought not to invalidate the testing. One of the ironies of the case, then, may be that the program now under review, which gives the cocaine user a second and third chance, might be replaced by some more rigorous system. We must, however, take the case as it comes to us; and the use of handcuffs, arrests, prosecutions, and police assistance in designing and implementing the testing and rehabilitation policy cannot be sustained under our previous cases concerning mandatory testing.

Justice SCALIA, dissenting.

There is always an unappealing aspect to the use of doctors and nurses, ministers of mercy, to obtain incriminating evidence against the supposed objects of their ministration—although here, it is correctly pointed out, the doctors and nurses were ministering not just to the mothers but also to the children whom their cooperation with the police was meant to protect. But whatever may be the correct social judgment concerning the desirability of what occurred here, that is not the issue in the present case. The Constitution does not resolve all difficult social questions, but leaves the vast majority of them to resolution by debate and the democratic process—which would produce a decision by the citizens of Charleston, through their elected representatives, to forbid or permit the police action at issue here. The question before us is a narrower one: whether, whatever the desirability of this police conduct, it violates the Fourth Amendment's prohibition of unreasonable searches and seizures. In my view, it plainly does not. . . .

. . . [I]t is not the function of this Court—at least not in Fourth Amendment cases—to weigh petitioners' privacy interest against the State's interest in meeting the crisis of "crack babies" that developed in the late 1980's. I cannot refrain from observing, however, that the outcome of a wise weighing of those interests is by no means clear. The initial goal of the doctors and nurses who conducted cocaine-testing in this case was to refer pregnant drug addicts to treatment centers, and to prepare for necessary treatment of their possibly affected children. When the doctors and nurses agreed to the program providing test results to the police, they did so because (in addition to the fact that child abuse was required by law to be reported) they wanted to use the sanction of arrest as a strong incentive for their addicted patients to undertake drug-addiction treatment. And the police themselves used it for that benign purpose, as is shown by the fact that only 30 of 253 women testing positive for cocaine were ever arrested, and only 2 of those prosecuted. It would not be unreasonable to conclude that today's judgment, authorizing the assessment of damages against the county solicitor and individual doctors and nurses who participated in the program, proves once again that no good deed goes unpunished.

But as far as the Fourth Amendment is concerned: There was no unconsented search in this case. And if there was, it would have been validated by the special-needs doctrine. For these reasons, I respectfully dissent.

NOTES AND QUESTIONS

1. *Considering* Ferguson. Of 30 women arrested under the program challenged in *Ferguson,* 29 were African Americans. See The Drug Testing of Pregnant Women Without Consent Is Unconstitutional, 12 Drug Detection Report, 170 (Oct. 31, 2002). This is not surprising in that the program was put into effect in only one public hospital in Charleston with a largely poor African-American population. Petra Sami, Note, Watered Down Constitutional Rights: A Hospital's Role in Prosecuting Pregnant Women for Drug Use in Ferguson v. City of Charleston, 16 St. John's J.L. Comm. 767 (2002).

Lynn Paltrow, Executive Director of the National Advocates for Pregnant Women, describes practices that were at issue in *Ferguson:* "a draconian program of dragging pregnant and newly delivered mothers out of their hospital beds in chains and shackles had . . . been in effect for five years based on claims of children's rights." Lynn Paltrow, The War on Drugs and the War on Abortion: Some Initial Thoughts on the Connections, Intersections and the Effects, 28 S.U. L. Rev. 201, 232 (2001).

2. *Assumption behind* Ferguson *decision.* For purposes of its analysis in *Ferguson,* the Supreme Court assumed that the patients at MUSC whose urine was tested for evidence of drug use had not consented to the testing. In his

concurring opinion, Justice Kennedy described that assumption as having created "a strange world for deciding the case." 532 U.S. at 91. Arguably, the Court's assuming that the testing was nonconsensual was pivotal in its conclusion that the MUSC policy did not fit into the "special needs" exception to the Fourth Amendment. 532 U.S. at 92–94 (Scalia, J., dissenting); Casenote, Krislen Nalani Chun, Still Wondering After All These Years: Ferguson v. City of Charleston and the Supreme Court's Lack of Guidance over Drug Testing and the Special Needs Doctrine, 24 Hawaii L. Rev. 797, 812–813 (2002).

3. *Nonconsent of* Ferguson *plaintiffs.*   The Supreme Court remanded *Ferguson* on the issue of the plaintiffs' consent. 532 U.S. at 86. In late 2002, the Fourth Circuit decided that the plaintiffs/appellants had not consented to being screened for drugs. Ferguson v. City of Charleston, 308 F.3d 380 (4th Cir. 2002). The court explained:

> For the reasons set forth below, we hold that no rational jury could conclude, from the evidence presented at trial, that Appellants gave their informed consent to the taking and testing of their urine for evidence of criminal activity for law enforcement purposes. Our holding encompasses two determinations: first, that as to most of the Appellants, the record evidence does not support a finding that Appellants knew that their urine was being analyzed for evidence of criminal activity for law enforcement purposes; and second, that the record evidence does not support a finding that Appellants, for Fourth Amendment purposes, voluntarily submitted to the searches.

The court excluded from its holding the case of one plaintiff who had not suffered a Fourth Amendment violation, and it remanded with regard to another plaintiff who might not have been searched pursuant to the program being challenged. 308 F.3d 380, 386–387.

4. *"Special need" doctrine.*   In general, the Fourth Amendment protects people from searches that could result in criminal evidence unless a warrant is first obtained. The Supreme Court relied on the so-called special need exception in a number of decisions that preceded *Ferguson* and that involved questions about the constitutionality of state drug testing programs. These cases include Veronia School District v. Acton, 515 U.S. 646 (1995) (upholding policy of an Oregon school district that tested student athletes for drug use); National Treasury Employees Union v. Von Raab, 489 U.S. 656 (1989) (upholding U.S. Customs Service policy that called for drug testing of certain employees); and Skinner v. Railway Labor Executives' Ass'n, 489 U.S. 602 (1989) (relying on special need exception to uphold Federal Railroad Administration rules that called for drug testing after serious train accidents). However, in 1997, the Court concluded that the special need doctrine did not render constitutional a Georgia program to require drug testing on candidates for public office. Chandler v. Miller, 520 U.S. 305 (1997). The Court concluded that Georgia had not shown enough need for the program "to override the individual's acknowledged privacy interest." Id. at 318.

5. *Risk for fetus of cocaine use by pregnant woman.*   Cocaine use during pregnancy may be less harmful than early reports suggested. Deborah A. Frank et al., Level of Prenatal Cocaine Exposure and Scores on the Bayley Scales of Infant Development: Modifying Effects of Caregiver, Early Intervention, and Birth

Weight, 110 Pediatrics 1143 (2002) (concluding that heavier cocaine use during pregnancy is not an independent risk factor for poorer scores on the Bayley Scales of Infant Development up to two years of age for nonpremature infants). Moreover, many legal acts by pregnant women (such as cigarette smoking or significantly restricting calorie intake) may pose serious risks to a developing fetus. Does this suggest that the focus on criminal aspects of prenatal cocaine use may be motivated, at least in part, by factors other than concern for fetal development? If so, what might those factors be? Cherry provides one answer to this question. Can you think of any others?

6. *Status of fetus.*   The Court in *Ferguson* notes that under South Carolina law, a viable fetus is a "person." 532 U.S. at 71, n.2. In fact, in Whitner v. South Carolina, 492 S.E.2d 777 (1995), the state supreme court categorized prenatal use of cocaine during the last trimester of pregnancy as criminal child neglect. Do you think this holding is constitutional?

The question relates to the applicability of laws mandating that child abuse be reported to the state. Do such laws cover fetuses? Justice Kennedy, who concurred in *Ferguson,* concluded that states can punish a pregnant woman "who has so little regard for her own unborn that she risks causing him or her lifelong damage and suffering." He continued:

> The state, by taking special measures to give rehabilitation and training to expectant mothers with this tragic addiction or weakness, acts well within its powers and civil obligations.
>
> The holding of the Court, furthermore, does not call into question the validity of mandatory reporting laws such as child abuse laws which require teachers to report evidence of child abuse to the proper authorities, even if arrest and prosecution is the likely result. That in turn highlights the real difficulty. As this case comes to us, . . . we must accept the premise that the medical profession can adopt acceptable criteria for testing expectant mothers for cocaine use in order to provide prompt and effective counseling to the mother and to take proper medical steps to protect the child. If prosecuting authorities then adopt legitimate procedures to discover this information and prosecution follows, that ought not to invalidate the testing. One of the ironies of the case, then, may be that the program now under review, which gives the cocaine user a second and third chance, might be replaced by some more rigorous system. We must, however, take the case as it comes to us; and the use of handcuffs, arrests, prosecutions, and police assistance in designing and implementing the testing and rehabilitation policy cannot be sustained under our previous cases concerning mandatory testing.

Justice Scalia, who dissented in *Ferguson,* also suggested that mandatory reporting laws are applicable to fetuses. 532 U.S. at 99.

7. *Expectant fathers.*   Concern about prenatal parental behavior generally has focused on pregnant women and not on expectant fathers. Jeffrey Parness suggests more attention be paid by the law to the harmful prebirth acts of expectant fathers. He refers to expectant fathers who supply cocaine to the mother during pregnancy or expectant fathers who disregard the mother's physician's advice not to have sex during the pregnancy. Jeffrey A. Parness, Pregnant Dads: The Crimes and Other Misconduct of Expectant Fathers, 72 Or. L. Rev. 901 (1993). Parness further suggests that pregnant women might be informed about prebirth paternal support obligations, and that workplace

fetal protection policies should apply to fertile men as well as to women. See United Auto Workers v. Johnson Controls, 499 U.S. 187 (1991) (in this case, the Supreme Court declared a fetal-protection policy facially discriminatory because it banned women of childbearing age but not men from jobs exposing them to lead).

8. *Bibliographic note.*   The following references are useful in considering the issues in this section: Michele Bratcher Goodwin, Precarious Morrings: Typing Fetal Drug Law Policy to Social Profiling, 42 Rutgers L.J. 659 (2011) (suggesting that prosecuting pregnant women for drug addiction with the goal of "winning convictions" in order to "shame and spectacle these women" will not serve the women, their families, or their children); Joanne E. Brosh & Monica K. Miller, Regulating Pregnancy Behaviors: How the Constitutional Rights of Minority Women Are Disproportionately Compromised, 16 Am. J.J. Gender Soc. Pol'y & L. 437 (2008) (arguing that compelling pregnant women to undergo medical treatment is unfair to women in general and to minority women, in particular); Meghan Horn, Note, Mothers Versus Babies: Constitutional and Policy Problems with Prosecutions for Prenatal Maternal Substance Abuse, 14 Wm. & Mary J. of Women & L. 635 (2008) (reviewing social and legal implications of criminal prosecutions of pregnant women who abuse drugs); Kai-Ching Cha, In Utero Exposure to Crack Cocaine: The Swinging Pendulum and the Implications for the Maternal Fetal Conflict, 6 U.C. Davis J. Juv. L. & Pol'y 1 (2001) (suggesting that *Ferguson* "does not go far enough"); Lynn M. Paltrow, Pregnant Drug Users, Fetal Persons, and the Threat to Roe v. Wade, 62 Alb. L. Rev. 999 (1999) (analyzing antichoice motives underlying legal responses to pregnant women who use drugs or alcohol); Dorothy E. Roberts, Punishing Drug Addicts Who Have Babies: Women of Color, Equality, and the Right of Privacy, 104 Harv. L. Rev. 1419 (1991) (describing political and historical settings underlying prosecutions of drug-addicted mothers); Sam S. Balisy, Note, Maternal Substance Abuse: The Need to Provide Legal Protection for the Fetus, 60 S. Cal. L. Rev. 1209, 1220 (1987).

CHALLENGING ISSUES: TESTING PREGNANT WOMEN FOR DRUG USE

The University Medical Center of Great State ("Medical Center") has set up a program to test the urine of pregnant women suspected of drug use. No testing is done without patient consent. Patients are told that the test will reveal use of certain illegal drugs. They are also told that the Medical Center will refer any woman who tests positive to the state Department of Health and Social Services for counseling and any additional treatment deemed necessary by the department. Do you think this program is constitutional? How important is the consent requirement? Do you think a significant number of women who use drugs during pregnancy will give consent? Why might women who use drugs agree to participate? Why might they refuse to participate?

=7=
‖ *Dying* ‖

Sometimes death is a tragedy, at other times it appears to be a welcome relief, and at still other times it is simply a natural, expected, and unquestioned end. Which perspective is prominent depends in the particular case on a number of factors: the age of the person dying, the extent of her pain or suffering, the length of her remaining life (as well as might be predicted), the degree of dependency on others, the extent of any disability she may live with, and the person's own attitude toward continued life. This is not to suggest that these factors *should* play a role, or what *kind or extent* of a role they should play, in determining society's perspective toward the death of a person. On the contrary, to the extent a person's disability affects how society views that person's continued life, we must ask whether unacceptable discrimination may be taking place. If death appears a welcome relief because of a person's suffering, we must ask about the quality of care the person was receiving to see if the suffering might have been avoided. We have to also question whether we can adequately judge how much or how unbearably another person suffers when those assessing the suffering are not experiencing it themselves.

The role the factors just identified may play in determining how society and the law view the death of a particular individual requires rigorous examination. Such examination is especially critical in an age in which death is rendered more and more under our control, or at least our attempted control, by medicine. Such views can affect whether life-sustaining treatment is administered or withheld or withdrawn and whether, in states that allow physicians to aid patients in hastening their deaths (a practice commonly called *physician-assisted suicide*), a prescription for lethal medication is permitted or denied.

We generally are uncomfortable with the possibility that societal views on the death (and by implication the continued life) of a person might affect the provision of medical treatment. As in other areas of medical decision making, the law and medical ethics today generally insist that the autonomy of the patient prevails. Rather than doctors or ethics committees or society at large making decisions about whether an individual must or may receive life-prolonging care, the patient herself is to make such decisions. Constitutional law, common law, and statutory law all recognize that the individual patient has a right to determine the course of her medical treatment, even at the end of life. Although expressing that principle may be simple, applying it is another matter. What if the individual once had decision-making capacity but cannot now express her wishes? How do we respect her autonomy? What if a competent patient expresses a wish to discontinue treatment, but does so in the context of a recent, tragic loss (such as losing the use of her legs through paralysis) that others in her situation have learned to live with and lead full lives? Does respecting the patient's rights in that case mean that doctors must immediately discontinue medical treatment? What if the treatment the patient wishes to receive is extraordinarily expensive and unlikely to prove beneficial? Should she be entitled to it anyway? These are just a sampling of the many questions posed by the materials that follow. In struggling to answer them, we inevitably encounter more than just the individual patient's autonomy; the values of others—family members, physicians, ethics committees, and the larger society—will play some role. What that role is and what it should be are among the central ethical and legal issues surrounding treatment and care at the end of life.

This chapter begins with materials on the withholding or withdrawal of treatment from patients, treatment that might extend their lives. It then addresses the even more controversial situation in which a patient might request assistance from a physician to affirmatively end his life. Some of the general questions that pervade these materials include the following:

1. Should any limitations be placed on a competent person's right to make choices about how and when to die? If so, what should they be and what justifies them?
2. In evaluating decisions by a patient (or a family member on behalf of a patient) to discontinue treatment or to seek physician aid in hastening death, how, if at all, should we take into consideration the quality of life of the patient?
3. The principle of autonomy appears to have become the prevailing ethical and legal standard in end-of-life treatment decisions, but what of the principle of beneficence? How can and should beneficent care of patients figure into these decisions?

The following excerpt provides some general factual background about dying in the United States.

Dewitt C. Baldwin Jr., M.D., The Role of the Physician in End-of-Life Care: What More Can We Do?
2 J. Health Care L. & Pol'y 258 (1999)

In 1900, the average life-expectancy was some 50 years, by 1995, it was estimated to be 75.8 years. In addition, there has been a complete change in the causes of death—from acute, infectious diseases to chronic, long-term illnesses. While people still die suddenly of unexpected causes, such as heart attacks and accidents, the more common trajectories of death consist of patterns of steady decline from a progressive disease such as cancer, with a predictable "terminal phase," or a slow decline with periodic crises and "sudden" death in the case of advanced chronic illness and disabilities, such as congestive heart failure or emphysema.

The nationwide 1996 Gallup Survey indicated that 9 out of 10 adults would prefer to be cared for at home if terminally ill with six months to live. Yet, in 1992, 57% of all deaths occurred in hospitals, with an additional 17% in nursing homes. As some indication of a shift in patterns of care, however, some 17% of deaths in 1995 occurred in hospice care institutions. Indeed, 84% of adults in the Gallup survey expressed interest in a comprehensive program of care, such as hospice. Unfortunately, the median stay in hospice is only 36 days, and shrinking, and some 16% of patients die within 7 days of admission. All of our studies appear to indicate that what people want is to die at home, free of machines, alert yet free of pain and surrounded by family. What they fear most is dying in an institution, alone, hooked up to a machine, in pain, and being a burden to their family.

How realistic is this last fear? From what we know, 90% of adults believe it is the family's responsibility to care for the dying. Yet, "being a burden to family and friends" was cited by 40% of adults as the greatest fear associated with death. Three out of four adults (75%) report that they have experienced the death of a family member or a close friend in the past five years. Unfortunately, 31% of the families in [a recent] study reported losing most of their savings or their major source of income (29%) in the process of caring for the patient, and that a family member often had to quit work or make another major life change.

Until recently, most physicians have focused largely on the treatment and management of pain in terminal patients. And it is true that pain is probably the symptom most patients fear—reported by 45–55% of patients at the end of life. However, nausea, anorexia, constipation, and fatigue, as well as the psychological symptoms of depression and anxiety are frequently reported. What is clear is that few of these symptoms are comprehensively treated outside of a hospice or palliative care service. Pain is usually under treated, (42% of patients in one major study), while the rest tend to be overlooked or ignored.

NOTES AND QUESTIONS

1. *Life expectancy continues to climb.*   In 2009, the average life expectancy in the United States at birth was 78.5; for individuals alive at age 65, the average life expectancy was 19.2 additional years. National Center for Health Statistics. Health, United States, 2011: With Special Feature on Socioeconomic Status and Health (2012).

2. *Where people die—Emerging trends.*   According to the Centers for Disease Control and Prevention (CDC), the percentage of people over 85 who die in hospitals is dropping, from 40 percent in 1989 to 29 percent in 2007. Nineteen percent died at home in 2007, up from 12 percent in 1989. Centers for Disease Control and Prevention, Morbidity and Mortality Weekly Report: QuickStats: Location of Death for Decedents Aged ≥ 85 Years—United States, 1989—2007 (Sept. 23, 2011) at 1285. A similar trend is taking place among the broader population over 65 years of age. Although this matches more clearly the preferences individuals state about where they would like to die, there has also been

a notable increase in the number of individuals over age 85 who die in nursing homes and other long-term facilities, now up to 40 percent. Id. Under what circumstances might dying in a nursing home be considered "dying at home"?

A.   WITHHOLDING OR TERMINATING LIFE-SUSTAINING TREATMENT

In this section we consider constitutional, common law, and statutory rights to refuse life-sustaining treatment by both competent patients and patients who once were competent but have now lost decision-making capacity. Issues surrounding individuals who have never had the capacity to make decisions are covered in Chapter 9. The *Cruzan* case, which is excerpted as the first reading below, is the Supreme Court's only decision on individuals' right to refuse life-sustaining treatment, but many state court cases preceded and then followed *Cruzan*. The state cases and much of the commentary that immediately followed *Cruzan* often described the case as establishing a constitutional "right to die" and assumed that the case resolved many of the fundamental issues concerning the right to refuse treatment. More recent controversies have proved these conclusions premature. The 1997 Supreme Court cases that considered physician-assisted suicide (also included in this chapter) reject the characterization of *Cruzan* as establishing a broad right to die, insisting, instead, on a narrower recognition of a competent individual's right to refuse medical treatment. The 2004 federal appeals court opinion in Blouin v. Spitzer, 356 F.3d 348 (2d Cir. 2004) (discussed briefly) also read *Cruzan* narrowly, casting doubt on whether any federal constitutional protection against burdensome life-sustaining treatment exists for people who have never had decision-making capacity. Finally, controversy in 2003–2004 surrounding the removal of a feeding tube from Terri Schiavo, a Florida woman in a persistent vegetative state (also discussed in this chapter), revealed that the parameters of the right to refuse treatment are still uncertain. At the least, the *Schiavo* case has demonstrated that our society has not reached any settled consensus on many issues related to treatment refusals, even if the medical and legal communities believed otherwise.

1.   Patients Who Have Lost Decision-Making Capacity

Analysis of the rights of incompetent patients to have life-sustaining treatment withdrawn generally begins with an analysis of a competent patient's right to end treatment. Yet the earlier and most prominent court decisions on the "right to die" involved patients who were not competent. Thus, we consider these cases first. Before proceeding, however, we note that although we use in this chapter the words *competent* and *incompetent,* the meanings of these terms are hardly self-evident or uncontroversial. (See Chapter 9 for a discussion of issues of capacity and competency in decision making generally.) They are, nevertheless, commonly used in court opinions and other writings on the subject. By following that common usage, we do not mean to suggest that the world is divided into two categories—those who are capable of making all decisions and those who are capable of making none—although the law in certain instances seems to suggest just that.

a. The Constitutional and Common Law Right to Refuse Treatment

|| *Cruzan v. Director, Missouri Department of Health* ||
497 U.S. 261 (1990)

Chief Justice REHNQUIST delivered the opinion of the Court, in which WHITE, O'CONNOR, SCALIA, and KENNEDY, JJ., joined.

. . . On the night of January 11, 1983, Nancy Cruzan lost control of her car as she traveled down Elm Road in Jasper County, Missouri. The vehicle overturned, and Cruzan was discovered lying face down in a ditch without detectable respiratory or cardiac function. Paramedics were able to restore her breathing and heartbeat at the accident site, and she was transported to a hospital in an unconscious state. An attending neurosurgeon diagnosed her as having sustained probable cerebral contusions compounded by significant anoxia (lack of oxygen). The Missouri trial court in this case found that permanent brain damage generally results after 6 minutes in an anoxic state; it was estimated that Cruzan was deprived of oxygen from 12 to 14 minutes. She remained in a coma for approximately three weeks and then progressed to an unconscious state in which she was able to orally ingest some nutrition. In order to ease feeding and further the recovery, surgeons implanted a gastrostomy feeding and hydration tube in Cruzan with the consent of her then husband. Subsequent rehabilitative efforts proved unavailing. She now lies in a Missouri state hospital in what is commonly referred to as a persistent vegetative state: generally, a condition in which a person exhibits motor reflexes but evinces no indications of significant cognitive function. The State of Missouri is bearing the cost of her care.

After it had become apparent that Nancy Cruzan had virtually no chance of regaining her mental faculties, her parents asked hospital employees to terminate the artificial nutrition and hydration procedures. All agree that such a removal would cause her death. The employees refused to honor the request without court approval. The parents then sought and received authorization from the state trial court for termination. . . . The Supreme Court of Missouri reversed by a divided vote. . . . We granted certiorari to consider the question whether Cruzan has a right under the United States Constitution which would require the hospital to withdraw life-sustaining treatment from her under these circumstances.

At common law, even the touching of one person by another without consent and without legal justification was a battery. Before the turn of the century, this Court observed that "[n]o right is held more sacred, or is more carefully guarded, by the common law, than the right of every individual to the possession and control of his own person, free from all restraint or interference of others, unless by clear and unquestionable authority of law." Union

Pacific R. Co. v. Botsford, 141 U.S. 250, 251 (1891). This notion of bodily integrity has been embodied in the requirement that informed consent is generally required for medical treatment. Justice Cardozo, while on the Court of Appeals of New York, aptly described this doctrine: "Every human being of adult years and sound mind has a right to determine what shall be done with his own body; and a surgeon who performs an operation without his patient's consent commits an assault, for which he is liable in damages." Schloendorff v. Society of New York Hospital, 211 N.Y. 125, 129–130 (1914). The informed consent doctrine has become firmly entrenched in American tort law.

The logical corollary of the doctrine of informed consent is that the patient generally possesses the right not to consent, that is, to refuse treatment. Until about 15 years ago and the seminal decision in In re Quinlan, 70 N.J. 10, *cert. denied sub nom.* Garger v. New Jersey, 429 U.S. 922 (1976), the number of right-to-refuse-treatment decisions was relatively few. Most of the earlier cases involved patients who refused medical treatment forbidden by their religious beliefs, thus implicating First Amendment rights as well as common-law rights of self-determination. More recently, however, with the advance of medical technology capable of sustaining life well past the point where natural forces would have brought certain death in earlier times, cases involving the right to refuse life-sustaining treatment have burgeoned.

In the *Quinlan* case, young Karen Quinlan suffered severe brain damage as the result of anoxia and entered a persistent vegetative state. Karen's father sought judicial approval to disconnect his daughter's respirator. The New Jersey Supreme Court granted the relief, holding that Karen had a right of privacy grounded in the Federal Constitution to terminate treatment. Recognizing that this right was not absolute, however, the court balanced it against asserted state interests. Noting that the State's interest "weakens and the individual's right to privacy grows as the degree of bodily invasion increases and the prognosis dims," the court concluded that the state interests had to give way in that case. The court also concluded that the "only practical way" to prevent the loss of Karen's privacy right due to her incompetence was to allow her guardian and family to decide "whether she would exercise it in these circumstances."

After *Quinlan,* however, most courts have based a right to refuse treatment either solely on the common-law right to informed consent or on both the common-law right and a constitutional privacy right. [The Court here reviewed a number of state court decisions that had developed and applied the right to refuse treatment.] As these cases demonstrate, the common-law doctrine of informed consent is viewed as generally encompassing the right of a competent individual to refuse medical treatment. Beyond that, these cases demonstrate both similarity and diversity in their approaches to decision of what all agree is a perplexing question with unusually strong moral and ethical overtones. State courts have available to them for decision a number of sources—state constitutions, statutes, and common law—which are not available to us. In this Court, the question is simply and starkly whether the United States Constitution prohibits Missouri from choosing the rule of decision which it did. This is the first case in which we have been squarely presented with the issue whether the United States Constitution grants what is in common parlance referred to as a "right to die." . . .

The Fourteenth Amendment provides that no State shall "deprive any person of life, liberty, or property, without due process of law." The principle that a competent person has a constitutionally protected liberty interest in refusing unwanted medical treatment may be inferred from our prior decisions. In Jacobson v. Massachusetts, 197 U.S. 11, 24–30 (1905), for instance, the Court balanced an individual's liberty interest in declining an unwanted smallpox vaccine against the State's interest in preventing disease. Decisions prior to the incorporation of the Fourth Amendment into the Fourteenth Amendment analyzed searches and seizures involving the body under the Due Process Clause and were thought to implicate substantial liberty interests.

Just this Term, in the course of holding that a State's procedures for administering antipsychotic medication to prisoners were sufficient to satisfy due process concerns, we recognized that prisoners possess "a significant liberty interest in avoiding the unwanted administration of antipsychotic drugs under the Due Process Clause of the Fourteenth Amendment." Washington v. Harper, 494 U.S. 210 (1990). Still other cases support the recognition of a general liberty interest in refusing medical treatment. Vitek v. Jones, 445 U.S. 480 (1980) (transfer to mental hospital coupled with mandatory behavior modification treatment implicated liberty interests); Parham v. J.R., 442 U.S. 584 (1979) ("[A] child, in common with adults, has a substantial liberty interest in not being confined unnecessarily for medical treatment").

But determining that a person has a "liberty interest" under the Due Process Clause does not end the inquiry;[7] "whether respondent's constitutional rights have been violated must be determined by balancing his liberty interests against the relevant state interests." Youngberg v. Romeo, 457 U.S. 307, 321 (1982).

Petitioners insist that under the general holdings of our cases, the forced administration of life-sustaining medical treatment, and even of artificially delivered food and water essential to life, would implicate a competent person's liberty interest. Although we think the logic of the cases discussed above would embrace such a liberty interest, the dramatic consequences involved in refusal of such treatment would inform the inquiry as to whether the deprivation of that interest is constitutionally permissible. But for purposes of this case, we assume that the United States Constitution would grant a competent person a constitutionally protected right to refuse lifesaving hydration and nutrition.

Petitioners go on to assert that an incompetent person should possess the same right in this respect as is possessed by a competent person.

The difficulty with petitioners' claim is that in a sense it begs the question: An incompetent person is not able to make an informed and voluntary choice to exercise a hypothetical right to refuse treatment or any other right. Such a "right" must be exercised for her, if at all, by some sort of surrogate. Here, Missouri has in effect recognized that under certain circumstances a surrogate may act for the patient in electing to have hydration and nutrition withdrawn in such a way as to cause death, but it has established a procedural safeguard to assure that the action of the surrogate conforms as best it may to the wishes expressed by the patient while competent. Missouri requires that evidence of the incompetent's wishes as to the withdrawal of treatment be proved by clear and convincing evidence. The question, then, is whether the United States

---

7. Although many state courts have held that a right to refuse treatment is encompassed by a generalized constitutional right of privacy, we have never so held. We believe this issue is more properly analyzed in terms of a Fourteenth Amendment liberty interest.

Constitution forbids the establishment of this procedural requirement by the State. We hold that it does not.

Whether or not Missouri's clear and convincing evidence requirement comports with the United States Constitution depends in part on what interests the State may properly seek to protect in this situation. Missouri relies on its interest in the protection and preservation of human life, and there can be no gainsaying this interest. As a general matter, the States—indeed, all civilized nations—demonstrate their commitment to life by treating homicide as a serious crime. Moreover, the majority of States in this country have laws imposing criminal penalties on one who assists another to commit suicide. We do not think a State is required to remain neutral in the face of an informed and voluntary decision by a physically able adult to starve to death.

But in the context presented here, a State has more particular interests at stake. The choice between life and death is a deeply personal decision of obvious and overwhelming finality. We believe Missouri may legitimately seek to safeguard the personal element of this choice through the imposition of heightened evidentiary requirements. It cannot be disputed that the Due Process Clause protects an interest in life as well as an interest in refusing life-sustaining medical treatment. Not all incompetent patients will have loved ones available to serve as surrogate decisionmakers. And even where family members are present, "[t]here will, of course, be some unfortunate situations in which family members will not act to protect a patient." In re Jobes, 108 N.J. 394, 419 (1987). A State is entitled to guard against potential abuses in such situations. Similarly, a State is entitled to consider that a judicial proceeding to make a determination regarding an incompetent's wishes may very well not be an adversarial one, with the added guarantee of accurate factfinding that the adversary process brings with it. Finally, we think a State may properly decline to make judgments about the "quality" of life that a particular individual may enjoy, and simply assert an unqualified interest in the preservation of human life to be weighed against the constitutionally protected interests of the individual.

In our view, Missouri has permissibly sought to advance these interests through the adoption of a "clear and convincing" standard of proof to govern such proceedings. "The function of a standard of proof, as that concept is embodied in the Due Process Clause and in the realm of factfinding, is to 'instruct the factfinder concerning the degree of confidence our society thinks he should have in the correctness of factual conclusions for a particular type of adjudication.'"

We think it self-evident that the interests at stake in the instant proceedings are more substantial, both on an individual and societal level, than those involved in a run-of-the-mine civil dispute. But not only does the standard of proof reflect the importance of a particular adjudication, it also serves as "a societal judgment about how the risk of error should be distributed between the litigants." The more stringent the burden of proof a party must bear, the more that party bears the risk of an erroneous decision. We believe that Missouri may permissibly place an increased risk of an erroneous decision on those seeking to terminate an incompetent individual's life-sustaining treatment. An erroneous decision not to terminate results in a maintenance of the status quo; the possibility of subsequent developments such as advancements in medical science, the discovery of new evidence regarding the patient's intent, changes in the law, or simply the unexpected death of the patient despite the administration of life-sustaining treatment at least create the potential that a wrong decision will eventually be corrected or its impact mitigated. An erroneous decision to withdraw life-sustaining treatment, however, is not susceptible of correction. . . .

In sum, we conclude that a State may apply a clear and convincing evidence standard in proceedings where a guardian seeks to discontinue nutrition and hydration of a person diagnosed to be in a persistent vegetative state. We note that many courts which have adopted some sort of substituted judgment procedure in situations like this, whether they limit consideration of evidence to the prior expressed wishes of the incompetent individual, or whether they allow more general proof of what the individual's decision would have been, require a clear and convincing standard of proof for such evidence. . . .

The judgment of the Supreme Court of Missouri is
Affirmed.

Justice O'CONNOR, concurring.

I agree that a protected liberty interest in refusing unwanted medical treatment may be inferred from our prior decisions, and that the refusal of artificially delivered food and water is encompassed within that liberty interest. I write separately to clarify why I believe this to be so. As the Court notes, the liberty interest in refusing medical treatment flows from decisions involving the State's invasions into the body. Because our notions of liberty are inextricably entwined with our idea of physical freedom and self-determination, the Court has often deemed state incursions into the body repugnant to the interests protected by the Due Process Clause.

. . . Artificial feeding cannot readily be distinguished from other forms of medical treatment. Whether or not the techniques used to pass food and water into the patient's alimentary tract are termed "medical treatment," it is clear they all involve some degree of intrusion and restraint. Feeding a patient by means of a nasogastric tube requires a physician to pass a long flexible tube through the patient's nose, throat, and esophagus and into the stomach. Because of the discomfort such a tube causes, "[m]any patients need to be restrained forcibly and their hands put into large mittens to prevent them from removing the tube." A gastrostomy tube (as was used to provide food and water to Nancy Cruzan) or jejunostomy tube must be surgically implanted into the stomach or small intestine. Requiring a competent adult to endure such procedures against her will burdens the patient's liberty, dignity, and freedom to determine the course of her own treatment. Accordingly, the liberty guaranteed by the Due Process Clause must protect, if it protects anything, an individual's deeply personal decision to reject medical treatment, including the artificial delivery of food and water.

I also write separately to emphasize that the Court does not today decide the issue whether a State must also give effect to the decisions of a surrogate decisionmaker. In my view, such a duty may well be constitutionally required to protect the patient's liberty interest in refusing medical treatment. Few individuals provide explicit oral or written instructions regarding their intent to refuse medical treatment should they become incompetent. States which decline to consider any evidence other than such instructions may frequently fail to honor a patient's intent. Such failures might be avoided if the State considered an equally probative source of evidence: the patient's appointment of a proxy to make health care decisions on her behalf. . . .

Justice SCALIA, concurring.

... While I agree with the Court's analysis today, and therefore join in its opinion, I would have preferred that we announce, clearly and promptly, that the federal courts have no business in this field; that American law has always accorded the State the power to prevent, by force if necessary, suicide—including suicide by refusing to take appropriate measures necessary to preserve one's life. . . .

[Justice Scalia then argues that the withdrawal of Nancy Cruzan's feeding tube would be equivalent to ordinary suicide, which the state has the authority to prevent–EDS.]

What I have said above is not meant to suggest that I would think it desirable, if we were sure that Nancy Cruzan wanted to die, to keep her alive by the means at issue here. I assert only that the Constitution has nothing to say about the subject. To raise up a constitutional right here we would have to create out of nothing (for it exists neither in text nor tradition) some constitutional principle whereby, although the State may insist that an individual come in out of the cold and eat food, it may not insist that he take medicine; and although it may pump his stomach empty of poison he has ingested, it may not fill his stomach with food he has failed to ingest. Are there, then, no reasonable and humane limits that ought not to be exceeded in requiring an individual to preserve his own life? There obviously are, but they are not set forth in the Due Process Clause. What assures us that those limits will not be exceeded is the same constitutional guarantee that is the source of most of our protection—what protects us, for example, from being assessed a tax of 100% of our income above the subsistence level, from being forbidden to drive cars, or from being required to send our children to school for 10 hours a day, none of which horribles are categorically prohibited by the Constitution. Our salvation is the Equal Protection Clause, which requires the democratic majority to accept for themselves and their loved ones what they impose on you and me. This Court need not, and has no authority to, inject itself into every field of human activity where irrationality and oppression may theoretically occur, and if it tries to do so it will destroy itself.

Justice BRENNAN, with whom Justice MARSHALL and Justice BLACKMUN join, dissenting.

[Justice Brennan's dissent argues that there exists a constitutional due process right to be free of unwanted medical treatment that is fundamental and that belongs to those who are incompetent as well as those who are competent. Because the dissent is lengthy, only a few paragraphs are excerpted here to highlight certain points not made elsewhere–EDS.]

... The only state interest asserted here is a general interest in the preservation of life. But the State has no legitimate general interest in someone's life, completely abstracted from the interest of the person living that life, that could outweigh the person's choice to avoid medical treatment. . . . Thus, the State's general interest in life must accede to Nancy Cruzan's particularized and intense interest in self-determination in her choice of medical treatment. There is simply nothing legitimately within the State's purview to be gained by superseding her decision.

... This is not to say that the State has no legitimate interests to assert here. As the majority recognizes, Missouri has a *parens patriae* interest in providing Nancy Cruzan, now incompetent, with as accurate as possible a determination of how she would exercise her rights under these circumstances. Second, if and when it is determined that Nancy Cruzan would want to continue treatment, the State may legitimately assert an interest in providing that treatment. But until Nancy's wishes have been determined, the only state interest that may be asserted is an interest in safe-guarding the accuracy of that determination.

Accuracy, therefore, must be our touchstone. Missouri may constitutionally impose only those procedural requirements that serve to enhance the accuracy of a determination of Nancy Cruzan's wishes or are at least consistent with an accurate determination. The Missouri "safeguard" that the Court upholds today does not meet that standard. The determination needed in this context is whether the incompetent person would choose to live in a persistent vegetative state on life support or to avoid this medical treatment. Missouri's rule of decision imposes a markedly asymmetrical evidentiary burden. Only evidence of specific statements of treatment choice made by the patient when competent is admissible to support a finding that the patient, now in a persistent vegetative state, would wish to avoid further medical treatment. Moreover, this evidence must be clear and convincing. No proof is required to support a finding that the incompetent person would wish to continue treatment. . . .

[T]he Missouri court imposed a clear and convincing evidence standard as an obstacle to the exercise of a fundamental right. . . . The majority claims that the allocation of the risk of error is justified because it is more important not to terminate life support for someone who would wish it continued than to honor the wishes of someone who would not. An erroneous decision to terminate life support is irrevocable, says the majority, while an erroneous decision not to terminate "results in a maintenance of the status quo." But, from the point of view of the patient, an erroneous decision in either direction is irrevocable. An erroneous decision to terminate artificial nutrition and hydration, to be sure, will lead to failure of that last remnant of physiological life, the brain stem, and result in complete brain death. An erroneous decision not to terminate life support, however, robs a patient of the very qualities protected by the right to avoid unwanted medical treatment. His own degraded existence is perpetuated; his family's suffering is protracted; the memory he leaves behind becomes more and more distorted.

Justice STEVENS filed a separate dissent.

NOTES AND QUESTIONS

1. *The precedential value of* Cruzan.   How might the decision in *Cruzan* be aptly characterized—as upholding a constitutional "right to die" or merely a "right to refuse treatment"? Or does the opinion of former Chief Justice Rehnquist avoid explicit recognition of any constitutional right at all? You may want to come back to this question after reading Washington v. Glucksberg, infra, in which the Court (and again, Chief Justice Rehnquist) explains what the *Cruzan* decision held.

2. *Substantive standards of decision making.*   There are three primary standards by which surrogates (and courts reviewing surrogate decisions) are to

make decisions about withholding or withdrawing treatment: the "substituted judgment" standard, the "subjective" standard, and the "best interests" standard. Descriptions of these standards vary, although they do represent a certain core meaning. Law professor Alan Meisel describes the substituted judgment standard, which was adopted in *Quinlan* and has become the predominant standard, as follows:

> One complicated rendition requires that the surrogate's decision comport with that of the incompetent patient, were he or she competent, taking into account current and future incompetency. The President's Commission [for the Study of Ethical Problems in Medical and Biomedical & Behavioral Research (1983)] supplied a much cleaner version, requiring that the surrogate's decision correspond to what the incompetent patient would have preferred in advance of losing decisionmaking capacity had he or she given thought to the matter. Put most simply, the substituted judgment standard seeks to determine the now-incompetent patient's *probable* wishes concerning treatment.

Alan Meisel, Suppose the Schindlers Had Won the Schiavo Case, 61 U. Miami L. Rev. 733, 744–745 (2007).

The stricter, subjective standard has only been adopted by a few jurisdictions and sometimes only for certain cases. According to Meisel, the subjective standard, "requires knowledge of the patient's *actual* wishes about treatment rather than the substituted judgment standard's determination of *probable* wishes. Under the strictest rendition of the subjective standard, the patient must have actually made a treatment decision while possessing decision making capacity, that is, before the need for the decision actually arose. Furthermore, this decision must have been made in a context of solemnity and not as an offhand comment." Id. at 745.

Some jurisdictions provide that in the event that the patient's preferences about treatment cannot be discerned, the decision for treatment or nontreatment should be made on an analysis of the "best interests" of the patient, which involves a weighing of the benefits and burdens of continued treatment. See, e.g., In re Conroy, 486 A.2d 1209 (N.J. 1985).

How would you categorize Missouri's standard for surrogate decision making, as described by the *Cruzan* court? Which standard do you believe would best replicate the decision the patient would make if competent?

3. *Best interests and dignitary interests.*   As explained in note 2, some jurisdictions allow surrogates to remove life-sustaining treatment on the basis of the patient's best interests when there is an absence of evidence of the patient's probable or actual wishes. Do you think an argument can be made that withdrawal of a feeding tube is in the best interests of a person in a permanent vegetative state? How should the "indignity" of the patient's current state be factored into such an analysis? Should it be?

The situation of the patient in a permanent vegetative state is unique in that it is difficult to conceive of benefits or burdens to the patient from continued treatment, because she can experience nothing. Thus, if such an individual never indicated while competent what she would want in terms of treatment were she to end up in a persistent vegetative state, it is difficult to meet either the autonomy component of surrogate decision making (what she would want) or the beneficence component (what would be best for her). Norman

Cantor suggests that in these circumstances a standard focusing on human dignity is useful and preferred. See Norman L. Cantor, The Permanently Unconscious Patient, Non-Feeding and Euthanasia, 15 Am. J. L. Med. 381 (1989). In this context and other conditions of diminished mental and physical capacity, what do you think respecting "dignity" means? Does it simply require that society respect the individual's own conception of what dignity means? And if it does, does "dignity" collapse into "autonomy"? If instead it has a normative component, what is it? Are certain conditions inherently undignified, such as drooling, incontinence, or severe memory loss? See Lois Shepherd, Dignity and Autonomy after Washington v. Glucksberg, 7 Cornell J.L. & Pub. Pol'y 431 (1998) (excerpted later in the chapter).

4. *Clear and convincing evidence.* What constitutes clear and convincing evidence? This is the evidentiary standard that must be met in Missouri and many other states by a surrogate trying to establish that the patient would choose to have life-prolonging treatment withdrawn (whether the substantive test is substituted judgment, subjective, or best interests). This standard lies somewhere between a "preponderance of the evidence," the standard of proof usually applied in civil cases, and the "beyond a reasonable doubt" standard of criminal cases. The majority opinion in the *Cruzan* case notes that the clear and convincing standard of proof has been defined as evidence that "produces in the mind of the trier of fact a firm belief or conviction as to the truth of the allegations sought to be established, evidence so clear, direct and weighty and convincing as to enable [the factfinder] to come to a clear conviction, without hesitancy, of the truth of the precise facts in issue." 497 U.S. 261 (citing In re Jobes, 108 N.J. 394 (1987)).

The Supreme Court in *Cruzan* points out that the clear and convincing standard places the risk of an erroneous decision on the side of those seeking to terminate life-sustaining treatment. Justice Brennan, in dissent, finds this bias in favor of life unconstitutional. What is his argument? Do you agree or disagree?

___

Since the *Cruzan* decision in 1990, countless decisions have been made outside of courtroom observation and approval to remove feeding tubes and other forms of life support from patients in a persistent vegetative state and patients who are terminally ill. These decisions, made on agreement of the family members of the patient and the patient's health care providers (and sometimes with the aid of an ethics committee at a hospital), are usually guided by state statutes that specify who may act as the patient's surrogate in the absence of a prior designation and under what circumstances medical treatment may be withdrawn. Immunity from liability is generally provided to health care providers who act in good faith in withholding or withdrawing medical treatment under the circumstances designated in the statute. It is the exceptional case that requires court intervention, and then it is usually because the family members or loved ones of the patient are in disagreement.

One such exceptional case received national attention between 2003 and 2005, when the parents of Terri Schiavo, Mary and Robert Schindler, successfully appealed to the Florida legislature and governor to intervene in their daughter's case. Terri Schiavo had been in a persistent vegetative state for ten years when her husband obtained a court order authorizing the removal of her feeding tube. After unsuccessfully appealing this decision and attempting to invoke the jurisdiction of other courts to weigh in on the matter, Terri Schiavo's parents sought the action of the Florida governor to intervene when Terri's feeding tube was removed. The Florida legislature hurriedly passed special legislation, known as Terri's Law, allowing the governor to order the reinsertion of the feeding tube. When a year later the Florida Supreme Court found Terri's Law to be unconstitutional under separation of powers principles, Bush v. Schiavo, 2004 WL 2109983 (Fla. 2004), Terri Schiavo's parents (backed by right-to-life groups and some disability rights groups) achieved passage of extraordinary federal legislation granting federal court jurisdiction over the case. The following excerpt is from the order of the federal district court denying the injunctive relief they sought. At the time the federal legislation had passed, Terri Schiavo's feeding tube had already been removed once again.

Schiavo ex rel. Schindler v. Schiavo
357 F. Supp. 2d 1378 (M.D. Fla., 2005)

ORDER

WHITTEMORE, District Judge.

BEFORE THE COURT is Plaintiffs' Motion for Temporary Restraining Order. In their motion, Plaintiffs seek an order directing Defendants Schiavo and Hospice to transport Theresa Schiavo to Morton Plant Hospital for any necessary medical treatment to sustain her life and to reestablish her nutrition and hydration. This action and Plaintiffs' motion were filed in response to an order of Pinellas County Probate Judge George W. Greer directing Defendant Schiavo, Theresa Schiavo's husband and plenary guardian, to discontinue her nutrition and hydration. . . .

Plaintiffs, the parents of Theresa Marie Schindler Schiavo, brought this action pursuant to a Congressional Act signed into law by the President during the early morning hours of March 21, 2005. The Act, entitled "An Act for the relief of the parents of Theresa Marie Schiavo," provides that the:

> United States District Court for the Middle District of Florida shall have jurisdiction to hear, determine, and render judgment on a suit or claim by or on behalf of Theresa Marie Schiavo for the alleged violation of any right of Theresa Marie Schiavo under the Constitution or laws of the United States relating to the withholding or withdrawal of food, fluids, or medical treatment necessary to sustain life.

JURISDICTION AND STANDING

. . . The plain language of the Act establishes jurisdiction in this court to determine de novo "any claim of a violation of any right of Theresa Schiavo within the scope of this Act." The Act expressly confers standing to Plaintiffs as her parents to bring any such claims.

APPLICABLE STANDARDS

While there may be substantial issues concerning the constitutionality of the Act, for purposes of considering temporary injunctive relief, the Act is presumed to be constitutional.

The purpose of a temporary restraining order, like a preliminary injunction, is to protect against irreparable injury and preserve the status quo until the district court renders a meaningful decision on the merits. A district court may grant a preliminary injunction only if . . . Plaintiffs establish a substantial likelihood of success on the merits, which the court finds they have not done.

. . . This court has carefully considered the Act and is mindful of Congress' intent that Plaintiffs have an opportunity to litigate any deprivation of Theresa Schiavo's federal rights. The Court is likewise mindful of Congress' directive that a *de novo* determination be made "notwithstanding any prior State court determination." In resolving Plaintiffs' Motion for Temporary Restraining Order, however, the court is limited to a consideration of the constitutional and statutory deprivations alleged by Plaintiffs in their Complaint and motion. Because Plaintiffs urge due process violations [that] are premised primarily on the procedures followed and orders entered by Judge Greer in his official capacity as the presiding judge in the dispute between Michael Schiavo and Plaintiffs, their Complaint necessarily requires a consideration of the procedural history of the state court case to determine whether there is a showing of any due process violations. On the face of these pleadings, Plaintiffs have asserted five constitutional and statutory claims. To obtain temporary injunctive relief, they must show a substantial likelihood of success on at least one claim.[3]

A. COUNT I—VIOLATION OF FOURTEENTH AMENDMENT DUE PROCESS RIGHT TO A FAIR AND IMPARTIAL TRIAL

Plaintiffs allege in Count I that Theresa Schiavo's Fourteenth Amendment right to a fair and impartial trial was violated, contending that the presiding judge "became Terri's health care surrogate" and "also purported to act as an impartial trial judge in the same proceeding." They allege that once he "became an advocate for Terri's death, it became impossible for Judge Greer to maintain his role as an impartial judge in order to review his own decision that Terri would want to die." Finally, they allege that "Judge Greer's dual and simultaneous role as judge and health-care surrogate denied Terri a fair and impartial trial." These contentions are without merit.

Florida's statutory scheme, set forth in Chapter 765, contemplates a process for designation of a proxy in the absence of an executed advance directive and provides for judicial resolution of disputes arising concerning decisions made by the proxy. See Fla. Stat. §765.401(1). Where a decision by the proxy is challenged by the patient's other family members, it is appropriate

---

3. Plaintiffs have submitted affidavits of health care professionals regarding Theresa's medical status, treatment techniques and therapies which are available and their opinions regarding how and whether these treatments might improve Theresa's condition. Plaintiffs have not, however, discussed these affidavits in their papers and how they relate to the claimed constitutional deprivations.

for the parties to seek "expedited judicial intervention." Fla. Stat. §765.105. Applying this statutory scheme, the state court appointed Michael Schiavo, Theresa Schiavo's husband, as plenary guardian and proxy for Theresa. Thereafter, a dispute arose between Michael Schiavo and Plaintiffs concerning whether to continue Theresa on artificial life support, and Judge Greer, the presiding judge, was called upon to resolve that dispute.

. . . Plaintiffs offer no authority for their contention that Judge Greer compromised the fairness of the proceeding or the impartiality of the court by following Florida law and fulfilling his statutory responsibilities under Chapter 765 as presiding judge and decision-maker. Plaintiffs' argument is that Judge Greer could not fulfill his judicial duties impartially while at the same time fulfilling his statutory duty to resolve the competing contentions of the parties as surrogate or proxy "to make decisions about life-prolonging procedures."

Plaintiffs' argument effectively ignores the role of the presiding judge as judicial fact-finder and decision-maker under the Florida statutory scheme. By fulfilling his statutory judicial responsibilities, the judge was not transformed into an advocate merely because his rulings are unfavorable to a litigant. Plaintiffs' contention that the statutory scheme followed by Judge Greer deprived Theresa Schiavo of an impartial trial is accordingly without merit. . . .

B. COUNT II—VIOLATION OF FOURTEENTH AMENDMENT PROCEDURAL DUE PROCESS RIGHTS

In Count II, Plaintiffs contend that Theresa Schiavo's Fourteenth Amendment procedural due process rights were violated by Judge Greer's (1) failure to appoint a guardian ad litem, (2) failure to appoint an independent attorney to represent Theresa Schiavo's legal rights, and (3) denial of what Plaintiffs describe as "access to court" by his "fail[ure] to ever meet Terri personally" and failure to "personally assess Terri's level of cognition and her responsiveness."

Initially, the Court finds no authority recognizing as a matter of federal constitutional or statutory right that a state trial judge is required to "personally assess" a ward's "level of cognition and . . . responsiveness." Fla. Stat. §744.3725, on which Plaintiffs rely, is applicable to an action seeking to commit the ward to a facility and other circumstances not relevant to this case. . . .

With respect to Plaintiffs' contention that Judge Greer violated Theresa Schiavo's procedural due process rights by failing to appoint a guardian ad litem, the record belies this contention. . . . [A]ssuming Fourteenth Amendment procedural due process requires the appointment of a guardian ad litem, there would be no constitutional deprivation here because three guardians ad litem were appointed to represent Theresa Schiavo's interests over the course of the litigation.

Plaintiffs' last contention is that Theresa Schiavo's procedural due process rights were violated by Judge Greer's refusal to appoint an independent attorney to represent her interests. The due process clause is implicated when there is a "deprivation of life, liberty or property at the hands of the government." If one or more of these constitutionally protected interests is at stake, as they undoubtedly are in this case, the due process clause requires notice and the opportunity to be heard.

. . . Theresa Schiavo's case has been exhaustively litigated, including an extensive trial, followed by another "extensive hearing at which many highly qualified physicians testified" to reconfirm that no meaningful treatment was available, and six appeals. As the Florida Second District Court of Appeal stated, "few, if any, similar cases have ever been afforded this heightened level of process."

Throughout the proceedings, the parties, represented by able counsel, advanced what they believed to be Theresa Schiavo's intentions concerning artificial life support. In Florida, counsel for Michael Schiavo as Theresa Schiavo's guardian owed a duty of care to Theresa Schiavo in his representation. Finally, with respect to presenting the opposing perspective on Theresa Schiavo's wishes, the Court cannot envision more effective advocates than her parents and their able counsel. Plaintiffs have not shown how an additional lawyer appointed by the court could have reduced the risk of erroneous rulings.

. . . [T]his court concludes that Theresa Schiavo's life and liberty interests were adequately protected by the extensive process provided in the state courts.

C. COUNT THREE—VIOLATION OF FOURTEENTH AMENDMENT RIGHT TO EQUAL PROTECTION OF THE LAW

For the same reasons relief under Count I was not appropriate, the relief sought in Count III via the equal protection clause is without merit. Plaintiff has not established a substantial likelihood of success on the merits of the claims set forth in Count III.

D. COUNTS IV AND V—VIOLATION OF RELIGIOUS LAND USE AND INSTITUTIONALIZED PERSONS ACT (RLUIPA) AND VIOLATION OF FIRST AMENDMENT FREE EXERCISE OF RELIGION CLAUSE

Plaintiffs bring Counts IV and V alleging that Theresa Schiavo's right to exercise her religion has been burdened by the state court's order to remove the feeding tube. . . .

Undoubtedly, Terry Schiavo enjoys, by virtue of 42 U.S.C. §2000-cc(a) [Religious Land Use and Institutionalized Persons Act], a statutorily protected right not to have substantial burdens placed on her religious exercise by the government. The plain language of the statute prohibits government from imposing a substantial burden on the religious exercise of an individual such as Theresa Schiavo. Similarly, the Free Exercise Clause contained in the First Amendment of the Constitution expressly protects the exercise of religion. In their Complaint, Plaintiffs allege that the state court's order imposes a substantial burden on Theresa Schiavo's free exercise of religion. In order to succeed on either claim, however, Plaintiffs must establish that the Defendants were state actors. Plaintiffs' claims fail because neither Defendant Schiavo nor Defendant Hospice are state actors. Moreover, the fact that the claims were adjudicated by a state court judge does not provide the requisite state action for purposes of the statute or the Fourteenth Amendment. See Harvey v. Harvey, 949 F.2d 1127, 1133–34 (11th Cir. 1992) ("Use of

the courts by private parties does not constitute an act under color of
state law.").

This court appreciates the gravity of the consequences of denying injunc-
tive relief. Even under these difficult and time strained circumstances, however,
and notwithstanding Congress' expressed interest in the welfare of Theresa
Schiavo, this court is constrained to apply the law to the issues before it. As
Plaintiffs have not established a substantial likelihood of success on the merits,
Plaintiffs' Motion for Temporary Restraining Order must be DENIED.

NOTES AND QUESTIONS

1. Schiavo *ending*.   In an amended petition, Terri Schiavo's parents
argued that other federal laws prevented the removal of their daughter's feeding
tube, including the Americans with Disabilities Act, the Rehabilitation Act of
1974, and Fourteenth Amendment substantive due process. District Judge
Whittemore denied this petition as well. 358 F. Supp. 2d 1161 (2005). According
to Whittemore, the ADA and Rehabilitation Act did not apply because the
defendants (Terri Schiavo's guardian and husband, Michael Schiavo, and the
hospice where she resided) were either not covered by these statutes or were not
discriminating against Ms. Schiavo on the basis of her disability. The Fourteenth
Amendment substantive due process claim of a "right to life" was rejected by the
Court on the grounds that the "right to life" is only protected by procedural due
process. The Court also rejected a claim that Fourteenth Amendment
procedural due process required that decisions to remove hydration and nutrition from an incompetent person must be supported by "clear and convincing
evidence that the incapacitated person would have made the same decision."
"Contrary to the Plaintiffs' contention," Judge Whittemore wrote, "the
Supreme Court in *Cruzan* did not mandate application of the heightened
clear and convincing evidence standard." 358 F. Supp. 2d 1166–1167. Moreover,
this was already the standard in effect in Florida. The Court wrote: "To the
extent Plaintiffs complain that the quantum of evidence did not rise to the
level of clear and convincing, these claimed evidentiary errors are a matter of
state law, not federal constitutional law." Id. at 1167. The Eleventh Circuit Court
of Appeals affirmed both decisions by the district court, and the U.S. Supreme
Court declined review. Terri Schiavo died on March 31, 2005, 13 days following
the termination of artificial nutrition and hydration.

2. Schiavo *claims*.   Over the course of the seven years during which the
Schindlers fought the removal of Terri Schiavo's feeding tube, they and their
supporters advanced many different claims, of which only some are represented
in the two March 2005 federal district court cases. Although each of these claims
ultimately failed in court, some of them nevertheless found substantial support
among segments of the public as well as from politicians and public officials.
Which of the arguments advanced in federal court do you find the most persuasive? Notice the references to "right to life." Why do you think the *Cruzan*
opinion did not contain a discussion of Nancy Cruzan's right to life? How was
Nancy Cruzan's interest in life protected? What is the significance, if any, of this
distinction?

Consider these other arguments made by those who opposed the removal of Terri Schiavo's feeding tube. Do you find any of these persuasive?

a.   Nutrition and hydration are different from other forms of life-sustaining treatment and should only be discontinued upon very strong proof that it is what the patient would want. Casual statements are not enough—instead, there should be a signed living will or evidence of other very specific statements previously made by the patient that satisfies a "beyond a reasonable doubt" standard.

b.   Even if Terri Schiavo were in a permanent vegetative state (which her parents did not concede), we cannot know for certain what she may or may not experience, and it is inappropriate to judge the quality of the life she lived in that state. In this way, she is just like other people with severe disabilities. If we remove nutrition and hydration from people in a permanent vegetative state, all people with disabilities who cannot be fed orally are at risk. (See signed statement of various disability rights groups posted on the book website, http://www.bioethicsandthelaw.info.)

c.   Guardianship of Terri Schiavo fell to her husband by statute, and then by court order, because of his marriage to Terri. But by 2003, Michael Schiavo was engaged to a woman with whom he had already fathered two children. In these circumstances, guardianship should have been transferred to Terri's parents, and they should have been allowed to take her home and care for her.

   3. *The persistent, or permanent, vegetative state.*   In both the *Cruzan* and *Schiavo* cases—and in *Quinlan,* the first of these treatment refusal cases—the patient was in a persistent vegetative state (although some experts now suggest that we should call patients who have *recently* entered the state as "vegetative" and call those patients for whom the condition is considered *irreversible* as "permanently vegetative"). The Florida statute defines a persistent vegetative state as "a permanent and irreversible condition of unconsciousness in which there is: (a) the absence of voluntary action or cognitive behavior of any kind. (b) an inability to communicate or interact purposefully with the environment." Fla. Stat. §765.101(12) (2002). The term also signifies an official diagnosis of the American Academy of Neurology. Although there are no definite numbers of how many people live in a permanent vegetative state in this country, estimates range between 10,000 and 25,000 adults and 6,000 to 10,000 children. Approximately 4,200 new cases of vegetative state are diagnosed each year in the United States.
   The terms *persistent vegetative state, coma,* and *brain-death* are often the subject of confusion among the general public and even the news media. It seemed to come as a surprise to many watching the *Schiavo* case unfold (and viewing a videotape of Terri Schiavo that was replayed constantly on television) that a person who is in a vegetative state is not asleep. Patients in a vegetative state may have sleep and wake cycles, have open eyes that sometimes even appear to follow an object, and show some reflexes (e.g., in response to light, noise, or pain). They are nevertheless unable to interact in any way with others. Patients in a persistent vegetative state are not terminally ill. Instead, they may live in that condition for 30 or more years, although life expectancy is usually shorter than

this. See generally Bryan Jennett, The Vegetative State: Medical Facts, Ethical and Legal Dilemmas (2002). They are also not brain dead; although they may lack "higher brain" function, their brain stems, which regulate breathing and other autonomic functions, are intact.

For more information on the persistent vegetative state, including statistics, see The Multi-Society Task Force on Persistent Vegetative State, Statement on Medical Aspects of the 'Persistent Vegetative State,' First of Two Parts, 330 New Engl. J. Med. 1499 (1994); The Multi-Society Task Force on the Persistent Vegetative State, Statement on Medical Aspects of the 'Persistent Vegetative State,' Second of Two Parts, 330 New Eng. J. Med. 1572 (1994); American Academy of Neurology, Practice Parameters: Assessment and Management of Patients in the Persistent Vegetative State: Report of the Quality Standards Subcommittee of the American Academy of Neurology, 45 Neurology 1015 (1995); Jean Berube et al., The Mohonk Report: A Report to Congress, Disorders of Consciousness: Assessment, Treatment and Research Needs (2006).

4. *The minimally conscious state.*   Terri Schiavo's parents claimed that she was not in a vegetative state but rather in a recently recognized condition known as the minimally conscious state. Between 112,000 and 280,000 people in the United Sates are estimated to live in a minimally conscious state. The critical difference between a minimally conscious state and a permanent vegetative state is that the former shows some level of cognitive function, whereas a diagnosis of permanent vegetative state means there is no evidence of cognition. The responses of a person in a minimally conscious state may be as simple as any intelligible verbalization or any purposeful behavior—such as reaching for objects—or any appropriate affective response to stimuli or the visual tracking of moving objects. Often such responses are inconsistent and infrequent, making it difficult to distinguish between the purposeful activity of a minimally conscious person and the random movements of the vegetative patient, and requiring serial examinations by a properly trained neurologist.

Expert Dr. Joseph Giacino explains these "disorders of consciousness" as falling along a continuum. He places minimally conscious patients at "an intermediate point along a continuum of consciousness that includes those in VS [vegetative state] on one pole, and those who consistently exhibit meaningful behavioral responses on the other." Until recently, he writes, the category of minimally conscious patients "was indiscriminately lumped together with patients in VS and coma." Joseph T. Giacino, The Minimally Conscious State: Defining the Borders of Consciousness, 150 Progress in Brain Research 381 (2005). This lumping together has contributed to a high rate of inaccurate diagnoses in the past (some estimates put the error rate of diagnoses of minimally conscious patients as in a permanent vegetative state as high as 30 percent to 40 percent). The case of Terry Wallis appears to be one such example.

Following a severe traumatic brain injury, Wallis was diagnosed as permanently vegetative in 1989. He was discharged to a nursing home and, despite reported observations from his family that he could follow simple commands, was never reevaluated by a neurologist. His father's requests for further evaluations were denied as too expensive and unhelpful. Nineteen years later, Wallis experienced a sudden, meaningful recovery that appeared miraculous. After nearly two decades of silence, he began speaking. In fact, a New Yorker article explained that when a medical researcher needed Wallis' Social Security number in 2005 to help him receive assistance, Wallis himself provided it. Jerome Groopman, Silent Minds, The New Yorker (Oct. 15, 2007).

Studying the brain imaging results from special MRI techniques performed on Wallis, researchers have hypothesized that his brain developed "new connections between surviving neurons" that help explain his recovery. Joseph J. Fins, The Minimally Conscious State: Ethics and Diagnostic Nosology, Lahey Clinic Medical Ethics 14 (Fall 2007). In other words, decades after entering what now clearly was not a permanent vegetative state but instead a minimally conscious state, Terry's brain structures experienced new, unexpected growth that may help explain his recovery. Wallis appears to have transitioned from an initial coma, to a vegetative state lasting less than a year into minimal consciousness, and then ultimately, years later, emerging from a minimally conscious state. See also Joseph J. Fins, Nicholas D. Schiff, and Kathleen M. Foley, Late Recovery from the Minimally Conscious State: Ethical and Policy Implications, 68 Neurology 304 (2007).

None of this recent medical research on "disorders of consciousness" has called into question the diagnosis of Terri Schiavo, who underwent extensive and repeated medical examinations by experts, as well as years of unsuccessful, aggressive rehabilitative therapy. But it does open up a number of ethical and legal questions about end-of-life treatment that have received little attention to date. The law in most states is very clear that patients, through advance directives or their surrogates, may withdraw all forms of life support (including artificial nutrition and hydration) in cases of terminal illness and persistent vegetative state. Dan Larriviere and Richard Bonnie, Terminating Artificial Nutrition and Hydration in Persistent Vegetative State Patients, 66 Neurology 1624 (2006). It is often less clear about other conditions, however, either because the statutes do not address those conditions or because there are no reported cases interpreting the common law or constitutional law as applied to those conditions. In the 2001 California case of In re Wendland, 28 P.3d 151, 170 (Cal. 2001), the court noted that "[N]o decision of which we are aware has approved a conservator's or guardian's proposal to withdraw artificial nutrition and hydration from a conscious conservatee or ward." Do you think the law should draw a dividing line between "consciousness" and "no consciousness" in permitting the withholding or withdrawal of life support? If not there, should lines be drawn elsewhere between different conditions? Or should no lines be drawn? Unlike the vast majority of states, Virginia does not differentiate between different health conditions in setting out the guidelines under which health care, of all kinds, can be withheld or withdrawn. See Virginia's Health Care Decisions Act, Va. Code §54.1-2981 et seq. (2009). What are the advantages and disadvantages of this approach?

5. *Advanced dementia.*   In recent years, the medical standard of care for treating individuals with advanced dementia has shifted toward less frequent use of artificial nutrition and hydration, in part because of growing evidence that it may not extend life for these patients. See G.A.K. Pivi et al., Nutrition in Severe Dementia, Current Gerontology and Geriatric Research, Article ID 983056 (2012). Do you think different considerations apply to people who are in a state of minimal consciousness resulting from a traumatic brain injury and those who are experiencing advanced dementia because of Alzheimer's disease? Some states have adopted revisions to their surrogate decision-making laws to specifically recognize advanced dementia or similar end-stage conditions as ones in which life-sustaining treatment can be withheld or withdrawn by an

advance directive or a surrogate decision-maker. See, e.g., Fla. Stat. Chap. 765 (2012).

CHALLENGING ISSUES: SPECIAL REQUIREMENTS FOR WITHDRAWING NUTRITION AND HYDRATION

Consider the following bill submitted for passage by your state legislature. The bill, which goes under the short title the Starvation and Dehydration of Persons with Disabilities Prevention Act, would allow nutrition and hydration to be withdrawn only if certain procedural requirements are met that are in addition to the requirements for removing other forms of life-sustaining treatment.

The proposed statute presumes that each incompetent person has directed her health care providers to supply her with the nutrition and hydration necessary to sustain life. The presumption can only be overcome if:

- The provision of nutrition and hydration would not be beneficial or would be harmful;
- The person has executed an advance directive that "specifically authorizes the withholding or withdrawal of nutrition or hydration"; or
- There is clear and convincing evidence that the incompetent person, when competent, gave "express and informed consent" to withdrawing or withholding nutrition or hydration in the applicable circumstances.

To meet the requirement of "express and informed consent," the patient must have expressed a desire to have treatment withdrawn in the same kind of circumstances in which she later finds herself and must have had general knowledge of the procedure contemplated, the available alternatives to the procedure, and knowledge of the medical condition under which the treatment would be withdrawn. For people who have never been competent (e.g., children), nutrition and hydration can only be withheld or withdrawn if it would not be beneficial or would be harmful.

What do you think of the proposed legislation? What is the rationale for it? Is it justified? Is it constitutional? In this regard, consider the following information (and also ask what other information you would like to know to judge the merits of this proposal):

- It is a felony in your state for a caregiver to fail to feed a disabled or vulnerable adult.
- Surveys taken during the unfolding of the Schiavo controversy in 2005 revealed that a high percentage of Americans (78–82 percent) would not want to be kept alive if they were in a permanent vegetative state. When asked specifically about disconnecting a feeding tube in such condition, the numbers dropped some but were still high—between 61 and 69 percent. Robert J. Blendon, John M. Benson, and Melissa J. Herrmann, The American Public and the Terri Schiavo Case, 165 Arch. Internal Medicine 2580, 2583 (2005).
- With respect to advanced dementia, recent studies show that family members tend to authorize the feeding tube, but they later regret that decision as it becomes burdensome to the patient (e.g., patients with advanced dementia

often pull out their feeding tubes unless they are physically restrained). These same family members say they would not want a feeding tube if they found themselves in similar circumstances. See Guido M. A. Van Rosendaal, M.D. & Marja J. Verhoef, Ph.D., Correspondence, Difficult Decisions for Longterm Tube-Feeding, Canadian Med. Assoc. J. 161 at 798 (Oct. 5, 1999). *See also* Howard Brody, M.D., Ph.D., et al., Withdrawing Intensive Life-Sustaining Treatment—Recommendations for Compassionate Clinical Management, 336 New Eng. J. Med. 652–657 (1997) (describing some of the discomforts and burdens of artificially provided nutrition and hydration).

- In a study of randomly selected, competent nursing home residents, only one-third said they would want a feeding tube if they became unable to eat because of permanent brain damage. This number of positive responses was reduced by a fourth when the participants learned that they might need to be physically restrained to accommodate the feeding tube, and would likely be even smaller if they had been informed about growing evidence of the lack of efficacy of such tubes for patients with dementia. See L. A. O'Brien et al., Nursing Home Residents' Preferences for Life-Sustaining Treatments, 274 JAMA 1775–1779 (1995); L. A. O'Brien et al., Tube Feeding Preferences Among Nursing Home Residents, 12 J. Gen. Intern. Med. 364–371 (1997).

- In one recent study that interviewed hospice nurses concerning their experience with patients who chose to stop eating and drinking because they were ready to die, the nurses reported that 85 percent of such patients died within 15 days, and "[o]n a scale from 0 (a very bad death) to 9 (a very good death), the median score for the quality of these deaths, as rated by the nurses, was 8." Linda Ganzini et al., Nurses' Experiences with Hospice Patients Who Refuse Food and Fluids to Hasten Death, 349 New Eng. J. Med. 4 (2003).

b.   Advance Directives

i.   Bioethical and Social Perspectives

There are basically two types of advance directives: the appointment of a health care surrogate (sometimes called a proxy or health care agent) and a living will (sometimes called an instructional directive), which provides instructions to health care providers or to the surrogate about treatment preferences. Although for years many people working in the field of health care law and bioethics have been urging individuals to execute an advance directive, only 15 to 20 percent of adults in the United States have done so. Muriel R. Gillick, M.D., Advance Care Planning, 350 New Eng. J. Med. 7–8 (Jan. 1, 2004).

> ## *Joanne Lynn, Why I Don't Have a Living Will*
> ### 19 Law, Medicine & Health Care 101, 101–104 (1991)

For a dozen years, my clinical practice has been largely with dying patients, my academic pursuits have focused on medical ethics, and my public service has been mostly at the interface of medicine and law. One would think that I would have "done the right thing" long ago and signed a living will. I have not. This essay is meant to illuminate my reasons. Some of my reasons may apply to others, and I will also mention some concerns that affect others but not me. However, I do not oppose the growth and development of advance directives. Rather, I hope to open the public and professional discussion of how to make decisions for incompetent adults in order to include more varieties of formal and informal advance directives and to force policy-makers to consider how to make decisions for incompetent adults who have no advance directives.

. . . I do not have a living will because I fear that the effects of having one would be worse, in my situation, than not having one. How could this be? A living will of the standard format attends to priorities that are not my own, addresses procedures rather than outcomes, and requires substantial interpretation without guaranteeing a reliable interpreter. Of course, a highly individualized formal advance directive might be able to escape these concerns, as is addressed below. First, however, I will consider the merits of a "standard" living will, such as is available in stationery stores and through the mail.

On its face, a "living will" purports to instruct caregivers to provide no life-sustaining treatment if the person signing it ever were on the verge of dying, with or without treatment, and were unable to make decisions for himself or herself. On the one hand, this is hardly a surprising instruction. Some combination of short life, interminable personal suffering, and adverse effects upon others is enough that virtually all persons would prefer to have had the opportunity to avoid this outcome, even at the cost of an earlier death. I have seen enough suffering that I can readily list all manner of existences that would induce me to accept death rather than have medical treatment to extend life. Not just in my case but in most cases, the text of a living will in standard format rarely tells the physician anything that was not nearly as likely to be true without it. The fact that a person took the time and trouble to sign one and get it to the physician does imply something about that person's character and the seriousness with which he or she approaches these issues, but not much about the individual's preferences and priorities.

As a physician, I use the fact that a person presents a standard-format living will as an opportunity to explore what he or she really means to avoid, what is really feared and hoped for, and who would be trusted to make decisions. This use is exceedingly valuable, but requires no legal standing for the document and does not require that it be treated as the definitive statement of what should be done.

. . . Nevertheless, sometimes living wills do have an impact upon the care plan of all sorts of patients because physicians and other providers inattentively overgeneralize. All too commonly, someone who has a living will is assumed to have requested hospice-type care including a "Do not resuscitate" order, to prefer not to use intensive care, and to have refused curative treatments. This assumption can obviously shape the care plan without there being explicit confirmatory discussion with patient or surrogate. Thus, the living will can also lead to errors of undertreatment.

. . . I, and surely some other patients, prefer family choice *over* the opportunity to make our own choices in advance. The patient himself or herself may well judge the family's efforts less harshly than he or she would judge his or her own decisions made in advance or by the professional caregivers. I have had a number of seriously ill patients say that their next of kin will attend to some choice if it comes up. When challenged with the possibility that the next of kin might decide in a way that was not what the patient would have chosen, the patient would kindly calm my concern with the observation that such an error would not be very important. High [D. M. High, All in the Family: Extended Autonomy and Expectations in Surrogate Health Care Decision-Making, 28 Gerontologist 46–52 (1988 Supplement)] found that patients prefer family decision-making even if they have never discussed preferences with the family. Perhaps this is an important finding, one that should be enabled to find expression in advance directives if that is one mechanism that allows patients to express their views.

This is not the only way that the current focus on advance directives is troubling to a vigorous concept of family life. Families are those who grieve for the patient's suffering and death, who have a history of making decisions that account for the well-being of all concerned, and about whom the patient most likely would have had the most concern. Somehow to imagine that the society *could* or *should* set up systems that remove the family from decision-making is almost outrageous. What if Nancy Cruzan had written a living will that stated that she wanted all treatment stopped if ever she were rendered unconscious for more than three days? Would the society really want caregivers to be obliged to stop treatment then, if her family vigorously objected?

Suppose that Justice Scalia, who wrote forcefully to encourage the requirement that life be sustained in the *Cruzan* case, were afflicted with a terrible, lingering, dying, relying upon all manner of medical torment to sustain life. Suppose also that his family claimed that they knew better what he would have wanted than do those who interpret his public writings and that they want treatment stopped. Should this society really establish systems of care that require that the family's voice be silenced? Surely not. While they might have to discuss their views at some length, surely the voice of a loving family should be prominent.

The idea of family decision-making is further constrained by the common requirement in durable powers of attorney and proxy statutes that there be one solo decision-maker designated. For many families, making a unitary designation is contrary to the family's history of making conjoint decisions and imposes the possibility of generating an unnecessary discord, as someone must be granted disproportionate authority.

. . . For patients and families that would use a next-of-kin surrogate (which is legally authorized without additional formalities in my jurisdiction), who have fairly conventional preferences about the goals and burdens of advanced illness, and who are most comfortable with informal agreements, I do not encourage formal advance directives. . . .

Rebecca Dresser offers a different critique of advance directives than that offered by Joanne Lynn, although their viewpoints do share some similarities. There are situations, according to Dresser, where regardless of what an advance directive might say, family members, physicians, and courts should not follow it. In this regard, she challenges the prevailing ethical and legal viewpoint that respecting the autonomous choices of the competent individual should be the determining principle in resolving later questions about end-of-life treatment when that individual enters a state of incompetency.

Rebecca Dresser, Precommitment: A Misguided Strategy for Securing Death with Dignity
81 Tex. L. Rev. 1823 (2003)

Precommitment is a seductive concept in bioethics. Many see it as a way for people to answer all sorts of biomedical questions about the future, such as whether to participate in dementia research or whether to have children posthumously. Precommitment is most popular as a strategy to resolve questions about the future use of life-sustaining treatment. The living will was an early focus of the death with dignity movement and its successor, the advance treatment directive, is central to medical ethics and law.

Scholars and researchers have analyzed advance directives for more than three decades. Their work exhibits two contradictory themes. First, precommitment remains an alluring strategy for many people worried about end-of-life care. People in this group cling to the notion that advance decisionmaking will deliver them a dignified and merciful death. Many philosophers, clinicians, judges, and legislators belong to this group. At the same time, a second body of work questions the wisdom of the first position. This work describes a host of ethical and practical problems with relying on precommitment to resolve decisions about life-sustaining treatment.

I am part of the second group. In my view, reliance on advance treatment choice is misguided and morally troubling. Although a person's statements about future care can be relevant, they are just one element of a complex situation. In most instances, they offer little guidance to those making decisions at the bedside. And in some cases, such statements should be given less weight than other considerations affecting patient care.

. . . The problem is that much of the philosophical and legal support ignores serious obstacles to putting advance directives into practice. Moreover, advocates of advance directives tend to take a myopic view of the treatment situation. They emphasize the importance of individual choice, while discounting other significant moral and policy considerations. Because of this emphasis, scholars, courts, and legislatures have failed to supply much-needed guidance to physicians, families, and others facing end-of-life questions.

. . . Once writers introduced the advance directive concept, legal authorities moved quickly to incorporate it into policy. This move occurred without study of, or reflection on, the difficulties that might accompany putting advance directive theory into practice. With experience, however, came awareness of these problems. By 2002, empirical research revealed that the reality of advance directives did not conform to their creators' vision.

Studies of advance directives point to several practical problems. First, advance directives are rarely completed. Second, most of the directives that are completed fail to convey meaningful information. Third, people making directives often have a poor understanding of what they are deciding. In particular, they may not envision how they could experience their decisions in a future incapacitated state.

. . . Certain advance directives threaten the welfare of incompetent patients. In these cases, giving priority to the patient's earlier choice would be detrimental to the patient in her current state. Such cases rarely arise in the clinical setting for two reasons. First, the vast majority of advance directives present no real threat to incompetent patients. Most directives express general preferences that fail to constrain decisions at the bedside. Second, those that are more specific rarely request decisions that would harm the incompetent patient.

True conflict situations are rare, but they merit examination. They present most starkly the value choices at stake in applying precommitment to decisions about life-sustaining treatment. The conflict situations fall into two categories. In one, the directive forbids a treatment that would effectively relieve an incompetent patient's pain or discomfort or that would allow the patient to continue a life that appears to have value to her. In the other, the directive prescribes a treatment that would be extremely burdensome to the patient and would not confer a countervailing benefit in the form of a meaningful extension of life. Which should take priority, the advance directive or the incompetent patient's welfare?

Medical ethics and law assign high value to the individual's right to make treatment decisions. Yet ethical and legal principles also support state intervention to shield vulnerable individuals from harm. The parens patriae doctrine recognizes the government's authority to protect the interests of individuals whose age or mental impairment leaves them dependent on others for basic needs. This doctrine underlies the legal requirement that incompetent patients receive treatment that is in their best interests.

Although it is common for courts to declare that the competent individual's preferences should control future treatment, they have not faced direct conflicts between a patient's prior preferences and current best interests. Indeed, in the two cases that came closest to presenting such a conflict, the courts refused to allow the patients' prior wishes to prevail. The cases both involved men who suffered severe brain injuries in car accidents. They had significant physical and mental impairments but were conscious and able to engage in very limited interaction. Neither had a formal advance directive, but before their accidents, both had expressed in no uncertain terms a desire not to be kept alive if they became impaired and dependent on medical interventions. Yet the courts said the men's statements did not constitute the clear and convincing evidence that would allow their treatment to be stopped.

It is possible that the courts would have decided these cases differently if the patients had refused treatment in formal and precise directives. But it is also possible that when courts encounter cases in which directives express treatment choices that would be detrimental to the incompetent patient, they will put the patient's interests first.

In my view, overriding the directive in such circumstances is the more defensible choice.

. . . One justification for overriding the directive is the significant possibility that the advance treatment choice was an uninformed choice. Another is the possibility that the directive conveys an inaccurate account of its maker's true treatment preferences. The empirical data described earlier indicate that these deficiencies are not uncommon. If an advance directive contains uninformed choices or fails to communicate the individual's actual treatment preferences, the directive lacks the moral weight of an autonomous choice.

In theory, an advance directive might be free of these deficiencies. Would a well-informed choice that is accurately stated in a directive—putting aside the question of whether such a directive is possible—supply a sufficient moral warrant for a treatment decision that harms the patient? In my view, giving effect to a harmful directive would be inconsistent with the moral judgments underlying the parens patriae doctrine. Following such a directive could require insensitive and even physically coercive conduct by clinicians, which the law condemns in other contexts. To show respect for vulnerable persons, clinical practice and legal rules should protect patients from prior choices that would harm them in their current state.

A constellation of values supports this approach. They include compassion and empathy for dependent persons, as well as the belief that people with mental disabilities can have lives of meaning and worth. These values account for widely held ethical judgments that incompetent patients should receive humane care and that it would be wrong to withhold beneficial treatments from people simply because they have diminished mental capacity.

In sum, the ethical and legal responsibilities to protect an incompetent patient ought not be suspended because that person once requested an intervention that would now be inhumane or refused an intervention that now offers clear benefit. If a patient can no longer appreciate the values that motivated the precommitment choice, treatment decisions should take into account what now matters to the patient.

NOTES AND QUESTIONS

1. *Family decision making vs. advance directives.*   Lynn prefers more emphasis on family decision making than on advance expressions of patient autonomy in determining what should be done for the incompetent patient who is dying. What reasons does she give for this preference? Do you agree?

2. *Family members' knowledge of patient preferences.*   Do you think Lynn's position is weakened by the fact that studies have shown that family members often don't adequately know or understand a person's desires about end-of-life treatment? Or is Lynn's point more than one of the accuracy of a family member's knowledge of a patient's desires? One scholar who has examined the empirical research reports as follows:

> Surrogate decisionmaking is premised on the belief that surrogates will make medical decisions that reflect patients' preferences. The empirical data indicate, however, that surrogates do a poor job of carrying out patients' wishes. Several studies have examined the accuracy of surrogate decisionmakers by presenting individuals with hypothetical scenarios and asking them to indicate their treatment preferences for each scenario. Potential surrogates are simultaneously asked to predict the preferences of the individuals. These studies consistently demonstrate that the potential surrogates' predictions do not reach a statistically significant degree of agreement with the choices of the individuals. This holds true even when individuals chose people that they would feel most comfortable with as surrogate decisionmakers.

David Orentlicher, The Limitations of Legislation, 53 Md. L. Rev.   1255, 1278 (1994).

3. *Physician preferences.*   Despite the legal recognition of living wills, the opportunity to name a surrogate decision maker, and the statutory designation of a family member to "speak for" (in a sense) the patient when a proxy has not been named, it appears that physician preferences weigh heavily in end-of-life treatment decisions. Orentlicher, supra, concluded in 1994 on the basis of empirical studies that in the event of disagreement between patient preferences and physician preferences, physician preferences prevailed. Id. at 1282–1283. Even when living wills have been executed and are known to physicians, physicians sometimes provide treatment that has been rejected by the terms of the living will; at other times, treatment is withheld when it is desired. Orentlicher concludes: "If physicians continue to believe that they are obligated to make end-of-life medical decisions based on their sense of the patient's best interests rather than on their understanding of the patient's wishes, living wills will have little effect on medical decision making. They will be respected only when they are consistent with the physician's views of the patient's best interests." Id. See also Kellen F. Rodriguez, Suing Health Care Providers for Saving Lives, 20 J. Legal Med. 1 (1999) (discussing a large-scale $28 million SUPPORT study that concluded on the basis of studying 9,100 patients that most physicians did not know about their patients' wishes regarding resuscitation; moreover, even though phase two of the study involved efforts to improve communications between patients and physicians, those efforts were unsuccessful).

4. *Dresser's objections to the living will.*   Dresser points out both practical and theoretical problems with living wills. What are they? On the theoretical side, what are her criticisms of the predominant autonomy-based approach? What does she offer alongside, or in place of, autonomy, to guide decision making in this area?

5. *Why so few people execute living wills.*   As pointed out above, less than 20 percent of the U.S. population has executed living wills. Why is this so? Here are what the authors of an often-cited article about the "failure" of living wills concluded, based on extensive review of existing evidence:

> Thus when we reviewed the five conditions for a successful program of living wills, we encountered evidence that not one condition has been achieved or, we think, can be. First, despite the millions of dollars lavished on propaganda, most people do not have living wills. And they often have considered and considerable reasons for their choice. Second, people who sign living wills have generally not thought through its instructions in a way we should want for life-and-death decisions. Nor can we expect people to make thoughtful and stable decisions about so complex a question so far in the future. Third, drafters of living wills have failed to offer people the means to articulate their preferences accurately. And the fault lies primarily not with the drafters; it lies with the inherent impossibility of living wills' task. Fourth, living wills too often do not reach the people actually making decisions for incompetent patients. This is the most remediable of the five problems, but it is remediable only with unsustainable effort and unjustifiable expense. Fifth, living wills seem not to increase the accuracy with which surrogates identify patients' preferences.

Angela Fagerlin & Carl E. Schneider, Enough: The Failure of the Living Will, 34 Hastings Ctr. Rep. 30 (Mar.-Apr. 2004).

Recent studies reveal that a substantial number of people would give surrogates "leeway" to override their living wills. In one study of 150 mentally

competent dialysis patients, 31 percent indicated they would give their surrogates "complete leeway," and another third would permit some leeway. Ashwini
Sehgal et al., How Strictly Do Dialysis Patients Want Their Advance Directives
Followed? 267 *JAMA* 59 (1992). North Carolina has recently added a section to
its suggested living will form that allows people to indicate whether their
appointed health care agent may "override" their instructions. See N.C. Gen
Stat. §90-321 (2007). Do you think this is a sufficient answer to the evidence
about patient preferences to defer to surrogates? Or are Fagerlin and Schneider
right, that it is time to abandon the living will as the primary legal answer for
making decisions about life-sustaining treatment? Do you have a living will? Why
or why not? Do you want one?

ii. Legal Approaches

In the following case, a Florida district court considers a claim on behalf of
a deceased patient against health care providers who allegedly did not follow her
advance directive refusing treatment.

Scheible v. Joseph L. Morse Geriatric Center, Inc.
988 So. 2d 1130 (Fla. App. 2008)

This case arises out of the death of Madeline Neumann at The Joseph L.
Morse Geriatric Center, a nursing home, in 1995. Mrs. Neumann was admitted
to Morse in December 1992 at the age of 89. At the time, she had an admitting
diagnosis of senile dementia and a seizure disorder. At the time of admission,
Mrs. Neumann's granddaughter, Linda Scheible, presented Morse with a living
will/advance directive previously signed by herself and Mrs. Neumann that
stated there were to be no life-prolonging treatments or resuscitative measures
taken on Mrs. Neumann's behalf if she had a terminal condition or was in the
process of dying. Mrs. Neumann named Linda Scheible as her healthcare
surrogate.

On the evening of October 17, 1995, nursing home staff found Mrs.
Neumann unresponsive in her bed. She was breathing, but staff could not obtain
her vitals. They called 911. EMS arrived, intubated Mrs. Neumann, administered
dopamine, and took her to the hospital. During transport, Mrs. Neumann
attempted to remove the tubing and her hands were placed in physical
restraints. On October 19, 1995, Mrs. Neumann was extubated. She remained
in the hospital until her death on October 23, 1995. The immediate cause of
death was cardiopulmonary arrest.

Appellant filed a complaint against Morse in August 1997 alleging willful
disregard of advance health care directive under chapter 765, Florida Statutes
(1995), willful disregard of the federal patient self-determination act, common
law intentional battery, and violation of the Nursing Home Resident's Rights Act
(section 400.022(1), Florida Statutes (1995)). Appellant later amended the
complaint to add a breach of contract claim[1] and to add Dr. Jaimy Bensimon
and Dr. Jaimy Bensimon, P.A. as defendants, and again later to add a negligence

---

1. The theory of the breach of contract count was that the living will/advance
directive was incorporated into the contract between Mrs. Neumann and Morse for
her care.

claim. Morse succeeded in getting summary judgment granted as to the health care advance directive count and the violation of the federal patient self-determination act count on the grounds that no private cause of action existed under those statutes.

. . . The trial court granted Morse's motion for summary judgment as to violation of nursing home resident's rights, pursuant to [Beverly Enterprises-Fla., Inc. v. Knowles, 766 So. 2d 335 (Fla. 4th D.C.A. 2000)]. The Supreme Court of Florida later upheld this court's decision in *Knowles,* specifically agreeing that section 400.023, Florida Statutes, provides that the personal representative of an estate may bring an action against the nursing home for violation of the patient's bill of rights only when the deprivation or infringement caused the patient's death. Knowles v. Beverly Enters.-Fla., Inc., 898 So. 2d 1, 6 (Fla. 2004).

This case went to jury trial on the battery, negligence, and breach of contract counts. The jury returned a verdict finding Dr. Bensimon not liable for battery or negligence but finding that Morse breached its contract with Mrs. Neumann. The jury awarded $150,000 for breach of contract damages.

. . . Appellant argues that the trial court's ruling was in error because: [(1)-(3) it misinterprets the Nursing Home Resident's Rights Act, rendering its right to refuse care meaningless]; (4) it creates an unconstitutional requirement; and (5) it discriminates unfairly against those who express their constitutional right to health care self-determination by prohibiting life-prolonging treatment.

Appellant's argument presents a question about causation. The theory begins with the premise that Mrs. Neumann was suffering from respiratory arrest when she was found in a non-responsive state by the nursing home staff. Had her wishes been followed and no resuscitative measures been taken, appellant urges she would have expired naturally from that condition. But since she was provided with the care she did not want, appellant argues the immediate cause of her death was cardiopulmonary arrest. The question is therefore whether one who is already in the process of dying has a cause of action based on allegations that resuscitative measures were taken contrary to their expressed will, and the measures result in a manner of death other than that which would have occurred absent those measures. Appellant therefore characterizes the measures taken that prolonged Mrs. Neumann's life as an intervening cause of her death.

Despite appellant's argument, the holding of this court in *Knowles,* and the Supreme Court's opinion affirming it, is that deprivation of the right to refuse health care cannot constitute a legal cause of death for which a plaintiff may sue. In affirming this court's opinion in *Knowles,* the Supreme Court made very clear its agreement that "the plain meaning of the language used in the statute indicates that only personal representatives of the estate of a deceased resident *whose death resulted from the deprivation or infringement of the decedent's rights* may bring an action for damages under the statutory rights scheme." As already noted, appellant attempts to fit her claim into the holding of *Knowles* by characterizing the nursing home's violation of the patient's bill of rights as the supervening cause of a different kind of death than Mrs. Neumann otherwise would have experienced. We hold this characterization to be incorrect.

The breach of Mrs. Neumann's rights that appellant alleged in this count is that measures were taken by nursing home staff to keep her alive that she did not want taken. The immediate wrong suffered was therefore akin to "wrongful prolongation of life." As appellee points out, the Supreme Court of Florida has previously approved of the proposition that finders of fact should not engage in such determinations, such as "to weigh the value of impaired life against the value of nonexistence." Kush v. Lloyd, 616 So. 2d 415, 423 (Fla. 1992) (affirming district court decision rejecting general damages for "wrongful life" claim due to "existential conundrum" raised by the issue).

Affirmed.

NOTES AND QUESTIONS

1. *The gap between living wills and doctors' orders.*   According to newspaper accounts, "When [Neumann] suffered a seizure on Oct. 17, 1995, and nurses were unable to get a pulse, they called Bensimon, then medical director of the roughly 280-bed facility. Even though Neumann's living will said she didn't want life-saving measures to prolong her life, there was no do-not-resuscitate order on her chart." Jane Musgrave, Doctor Not Liable in Case of Living Will, Jury Finds, Palm Beach Post, Mar. 17, 2007. Bensimon, who was 40 minutes away at the time, ordered emergency personnel to be summoned so that a doctor could evaluate Neumann's condition. Laura Parker, In a Crisis, Do-Not-Revive Requests Don't Always Work, USA Today, Dec. 20, 2006. Jurors interviewed following the trial "said Morse should have had better procedures in place to notify staff and others of Neumann's wishes. They said they cleared Bensimon of wrongdoing because they believed he was a compassionate doctor who ordered Neumann to be taken to the hospital to determine whether she could be helped." Musgrave, supra.

The *Scheible* case reveals the problem of translation of a patient's wishes into doctor's orders that staff can follow in an emergency or other circumstances in which the doctor is absent. Often living wills, by their own terms, are effective only when the patient is in a certain condition, such as terminal illness, "when death is imminent," or permanent vegetative state, and require a doctor's certification that that condition exists—a certification often difficult (maybe impossible) to obtain in an emergency situation. See Wright v. Johns Hopkins Health Systems Corp., 353 Md. 568 (Md. App. 1999) (a case similar to this in which no liability was found). Recognition of this problem has led to the adoption in some states of a standard form regarding life-sustaining treatment (and not just resuscitation) that would be placed in a patient's chart and would be signed by the patient's doctor. Emergency personnel and others could follow the orders on this form as they would the more familiar Do Not Resuscitate (DNR) order. See Susan E. Hickman, Charles P. Sabatino, Alvin H. Moss & Jessica Wehrle Nester, The POLST (Physician Orders for Life-sustaining Treatment) Paradigm to Improve End-of-Life Care: Potential State Legal Barriers to Implementation. Also see the website for the Physician Orders for Life-Sustaining Treatment (POLST) Paradigm program, at http://www.ohsu.edu/ethics/polst/.

2. *Legal remedies.*   Neumann's granddaughter was successful only on the contract claim against the nursing home where Neumann resided. What other claims did she bring, and what were the barriers to success? (Some of the reasons why these other claims were unsuccessful are discussed in the case; for others we have to conjecture.)

3. *Wrongful living.*   In the academic literature debating the wisdom of permitting a cause of action for prolongation of life in contradiction of patient

instructions, this potential tort has been named "wrongful living" (similarly, the Florida court in *Scheible* refers to "wrongful prolongation of life"). If a court were to recognize such a tort (which would have to sound in battery or negligence), the injury would presumably be the continuation of life beyond the point at which treatment should have been withheld. Damages, then, might be measured as the difference between no life, or the end of life, and continued life in the condition that the patient had sought to avoid. This possibility should bring to mind the debates considered in Chapter 3 about the wrongful life cause of action for children born with substantial disabilities. Do the same arguments apply for and against recognizing such a cause of action? See generally Philip G. Peters, Jr., The Illusion of Autonomy at the End of Life: Unconsented Life Support and the Wrongful Life Analogy, 45 UCLA L. Rev. 673 (1998) (distinguishing wrongful treatment claims from wrongful life claims); Holly Fernandez Lynch, Michele Mathes & Nadia N. Sawicki, Compliance with Advance Directives, 29 J. Legal Med. 133 (2008) (discussing cases in which plaintiffs claimed, with only limited success, contravention of right to refuse treatment). See also S. Elizabeth Wilborn Malloy, Beyond Misguided Paternalism: Resuscitating the Right to Refuse Medical Treatment, 33 Wake Forest L. Rev. 1035 (1998) (arguing for liability of health care providers for refusing to honor patient choices about treatment refusal). After pointing out that physicians often ignore patient directives about treatment refusal, and courts have been reluctant to impose liability in such situations, Malloy argues that "by failing to impose liability when a patient has decided to refuse treatment, the courts ignore a patient's autonomy interests and impose their own moral judgment on the situation, determining paternalistically that the choice to forgo treatment was incorrect or at least unworthy of respect by the legal system." Id. at 1041.

Do you agree with Malloy that courts should be more willing to impose liability in these situations? If so, how can the concerns of Rebecca Dresser, discussed supra, be accommodated?

4. *Immunity.*   Note that even if a common law cause of action for wrongful living were recognized, states' advance directive statutes generally contain a provision for immunity of health care providers acting in good faith.

5. *Living wills of pregnant women.*   A majority of the states have so-called pregnancy clauses in their advance directive statutes. See, e.g., Ala. Code §22-8A-4(e) (1997). These provisions require that health care providers ignore any provisions in the woman's advance directive that would direct the removal or withholding of life-sustaining treatment. Some of the statutes simply suspend the effect of the pregnant woman's advance directive, whereas others go further and require that treatment be provided. Radhika Rao, Property, Privacy, and the Human Body, 80 B.U. L. Rev. 359, 409-414 (2000). Rao writes that these laws, "literally 'take' the bodies of incompetent pregnant women, treating them as chattel that may be drafted into service as fetal incubators for the state." Id. at 410. What do you think of the propriety of such pregnancy clauses?

6. *The Patient Self-Determination Act.*   The federal Patient Self-Determination Act (referred to in *Scheible*) requires, as a condition to the receipt of federal funds, such as Medicare, that hospitals and other health care facilities and organizations inform patients of their rights regarding end-of-life decision making, including information about the policies of the facility itself so that a patient

might exercise some choice in her provider on the basis of the provider's willingness to honor requests to refuse treatment. 42 U.S.C.A. §1395cc(f)(1), 1396a(a).

CHALLENGING ISSUES: REMOVING ARTIFICIAL NUTRITION AND HYDRATION FROM A MINIMALLY CONSCIOUS OR SEVERELY DISABLED PERSON

Five years ago, Michael sustained debilitating injuries in an automobile accident, with the most serious being a closed head injury that significantly impaired his physical and cognitive abilities, left him unable to walk or talk, and rendered him dependent on a colostomy for defecation and a gastrostomy tube for nutrition. Following his accident, Mary, his wife of 15 years, was appointed his guardian. She has recently petitioned the probate court, over which you preside, for authorization to withdraw Michael's nutritive support. Michael's mother and sister oppose the petition and seek to remove Mary as the guardian.

Conflicting testimony was presented regarding Michael's current level of physical, sensory, emotional, and cognitive function, although all those who have examined Michael agree that he is not in a persistent vegetative state and also that he no longer retains decision-making capacity. At one extreme, Dr. F. testified that Michael has no voluntary control over any of his limbs or any ability to function on a voluntary level and therefore lacks any meaningful interaction with his environment. On the other hand, another physician, Dr. K., testified that Michael could carry out some voluntary motor commands and could recognize faces, respond emotionally, and communicate with others with head nods. You personally visited and questioned Michael at the neurological center where he resides. During that visit, Michael moved both his right arm and right leg on command and responded with appropriate head nods to a series of yes-or-no questions. You have heard testimony from a number of witnesses that there are times when Michael becomes completely withdrawn and does not respond to any stimuli. All experts agree that Michael's level of functioning is unlikely to improve. By all accounts, Michael is not experiencing any type of pain that would outweigh any enjoyment or pleasure he is experiencing.

Mary claimed at trial that Michael had expressed a preaccident preference to decline life-sustaining medical treatment under the present circumstances. In support of this claim, she stated:

> 1. Discussions between Mike and me, regarding what our wishes would be if either of us was ever involved in a serious accident, had a disabling or terminal illness, or was dying of old age, began approximately eight years ago. These discussions occurred on many different occasions. As I indicate below, several were triggered by movies, which we saw together. Mike's position was always the same: he did not want to be kept alive on machines, and he made me promise that I would never permit it.
>
> 2. Some of the conversations that we had about medical care in this context occurred after we watched movies about people who no longer were mentally competent either due to illness, accident, or old age; others involved

people who could no longer do anything for themselves, such as persons who lived in a nursing home and could no longer feed or dress themselves and needed to wear diapers or have other measures taken to continue existing. Mike stated to me on several occasions: "That's bullshit, I would never want to live like that." He also said to me, "Please don't ever let me exist that way because those people don't even have their dignity." I always agreed with Mike because I felt the same way.

3. One movie that always triggered such discussions was "Brian's Song," which, I recall, is a movie about a football player with a terminal illness. Mike said to me after we saw it together: "If I ever get sick don't put me on any machines to keep me going if there is no hope of getting better." He also said that if I ever put him on machines to keep him alive, "I'll always haunt you, Mary." Then he would say, "Do you understand?" I always said "Yes." We watched this movie at least two or three times and had virtually the same discussion each time.

4. Some movies that triggered our discussions were about accidents—car accidents, hunting accidents, or other accidents near home or in water. Mike was an avid hunter and frequently expressed concerned [sic] about a hunting accident. Mike frequently told me that if he ever had an accident from which he would "not recover" and "could not be the same person," he did "not want to live that way." He would say, "Mary, promise me you wouldn't let me live like that if I can't be the person I am right now, because if you do, believe me I'll haunt you every day of your life." I stated my promise to him and made him promise me the same.

5. Mike also made a lot of comments to me about never wanting to live "like a vegetable." He said that if anyone had to live like a vegetable, "their families and doctors should be shot for forcing someone to live like that." He would say, "I'd be pissed if I had to live that way." He also told me that he believed it was unfair to the person who had to be kept alive on machines because that person would always be in pain. He told me that "no one should have to be kept alive if they would never get well again."

6. I am certain that were Mike able to speak today, he would direct that the artificial life support and antibiotic treatments be withdrawn so that he might die in a dignified manner consistent with his explicit wishes expressed to me prior to the accident. It is time that my husband be freed from the ghastly, demeaning existence which he so strongly opposed.

There was also testimony from two of Michael's coworkers, stating that Michael's present condition is not the type referred to in conversations with them before his injury, in which he stated that he would not want to continue living in a vegetative state.

1. How would you decide this case? How would you describe the standards you applied—the subjective standard, substituted judgment? Best interests? (Refer back, if necessary, to the materials following the *Cruzan* case for a discussion of these standards.) Are the patient's preaccident autonomy and his current best interests in conflict or can they be reconciled?

2. Now consider a case involving a law student, Sean, who had read about Michael's case in law school and had signed a living will that stated, "If I'm ever in a condition close to that of Michael [providing full case name and citation], I do not want any life-sustaining treatment, including artificial nutrition and hydration." Sean has suffered an accident that has left him in a very similar condition to Michael's. The rehabilitation center where Sean now resides has petitioned the court for its judgment on how to proceed. The center produces a

copy of Sean's living will, provided to it by Sean's fiancée. Sean's parents object to the withdrawal of artificial nutrition and hydration. They say he recognizes them and responds positively to their visits. How would you decide this case?

CHALLENGING ISSUES: INDIVIDUALIZED LIVING WILLS

What if the living will of a mother of school-aged children, instructed something like this: "In making treatment or non-treatment decisions for me, I direct my health care agent (my spouse) to place primary consideration on what is best for my children in terms of both the financial needs of the family and in terms of their emotional health." If the living will became effective because of a terminal condition and the husband, as health care agent, requested treatment that was burdensome to the patient but may keep her alive for a few additional weeks to allow her children to begin to adjust to the knowledge of their mother's tragic accident, do you think the doctors should comply with the request? What if, instead, he rejected treatment that may be beneficial in extending her life but was very expensive?

CHALLENGING ISSUES: NUTRITION AND HYDRATION: FEEDING BY HAND

Maxine M., a 75-year-old resident of a nursing home, executed a living will five years ago in conformity with the laws of her state. The living will specifies the types of treatment she would like to undergo and those she would like withheld in certain circumstances. The statute in her state expressly permits the withholding of artificially provided nutrition and hydration if the patient has entered an "end stage condition," which has been interpreted by the attorney general of the state to include dementia due to advanced Alzheimer's.

In her sixties, Maxine cared for her father, who had Alzheimer's until his death. When she wrote her living will, she did so with the particular aim of avoiding the fate of her father. In the advanced stages of his disease he became uninterested in eating and did not receive sufficient nutrients until a feeding tube was inserted into his stomach. He did not understand what the feeding tube was for and repeatedly attempted to pull it out. He was eventually placed in restraints, which made him miserable.

Maxine's living will goes further, however, than just refusing a feeding tube. It states that if she enters a state of advanced Alzheimer's and cannot feed herself, she does not want to be fed by hand either. Now at age 75 she is in exactly that state. What do you think the nursing home should do?

2. Competent Patients Who Wish to Refuse Treatment

Although the right of incompetent patients to terminate treatment is premised on the right that competent patients possess, the earliest "right to die" cases involved patients who were not incompetent and were either in a persistent vegetative state, like Quinlan and Cruzan, or were terminally ill. It was not long, however, before courts had to determine the rights of nonterminally ill, competent patients who sought to refuse life-sustaining treatment but met objection from a hospital or physicians. The essential question in such cases is whether any conditions should be placed on a patient's decision to remove life-sustaining treatment, other than competency. Should a court consider the quality of life of the patient seeking withdrawal of treatment? Should a court consider the quality of the care that the patient has been receiving before approving such a request? Compare and contrast the *Bouvia* and *Ms. B* cases, reprinted infra, in these regards. First, however, consider what one scholar has to say about the effects of social prejudice toward people with disabilities in the context of treatment refusals.

a.   Bioethical and Social Perspectives

> ### Paul K. Longmore, Elizabeth Bouvia, Assisted Suicide and Social Prejudice
> **3 Issues L. & Med. 141 (1987)**

The arguments used by American eugenicists were also used in early twentieth century Germany: handicapped persons had "lives without value." They were economically unproductive. They were a burden to society. The German proponents of euthanasia defined as "mentally dead" any person who was, in their terms, unproductive and needed care from another person. From 1934 on under the Nazi regime, German school children were given math problems such as the following:

> A mental patient costs 4 RM each day. A crippled person costs 3.50 RM per day. . . . a) Analyse these figures on the basis of the fact that in Germany there are 300,000 mental patients in institutions. b) On the basis of 4 RM per day what is their total cost each year?

Some eugenicists also obscured the distinction between forced euthanasia at the hands of physicians and a patient's right to die. Nazi euthanasia propagandists even advocated assisted suicide. A 1941 propaganda film, "Ich Klage an" ("I accuse"), presented the story of a woman with multiple sclerosis, who fears not death, but prolonged suffering. A friend yields to her request that he assist her to die. The film's climactic moment at his murder trial becomes an indictment, not of him, but of a law that would condemn someone for an act of mercy. This motion picture was planned as an opening wedge to prepare the German public to accept the program to exterminate disabled people.

The managers of the Nazi euthanasia program pledged that institutionalized disabled persons granted "gnadentod" (deliverance by death) would be carefully chosen through a series of examinations conducted by two doctors. In actual practice, of course, no such medical or procedural care was taken, and persons with disabilities were condemned to death in droves.

. . . Some would argue that the evil of the Nazi euthanasia program was that it paved the way for the genocide of Jews and others. This misses the point. Personnel and techniques were transferred from the institutions where sick and handicapped people were killed to the death camps to carry out the genocide program. There was indeed a connection between German antisemitism and racism and the slaughter of people who were disabled, but another brand of prejudice operated here: virulent contempt of people with disabilities. The scheme aimed at exterminating people with physical, emotional, and developmental disabilities, was first started in Germany and then in the occupied countries. The evil was not that the T4 euthanasia program took a step toward the Holocaust. T4 was a holocaust in and of itself, a handicapped holocaust. That first holocaust grew out of a set of biased social values, subsequently rationalized in a formal ideology, which harbored deep prejudice against persons with disabilities. Those values were paralleled, complemented, and reinforced by German racism.

Many of those values continue to operate today. They appear most notably in discussions of euthanasia and assisted suicide. The point is not that anyone currently advocates a systematic policy of extermination as was implemented in Nazi Germany. Rather, now, as then, and as one finds throughout the modern history of people with disabilities, the same prejudicial social values operate to stigmatize and segregate disabled persons. This bigotry renders them socially dead and then justifies their physical deaths at the hands of representatives of their societies or by so-called voluntary suicide.

... Motion pictures and television overwhelmingly present negative stereotypes of persons with disabilities. But one does not have to look at stories involving major characters with disabilities to find prejudice. In the comedy classic "Annie Hall," Woody Allen has his principal male character say: "I feel that life is divided up into the horrible and the miserable. Those are the two categories. . . . The horrible would be like, I don't know, terminal cases, you know, and blind people, cripples. I don't know how they get through life. It's amazing to me. You know. The miserable is everyone else. So when you go through life, you should be thankful that you're miserable. . . ." Allen's character expresses two common prejudices: he lumps disabled people with those who are terminally ill, and he sees an enormous gulf separating them from "everyone else," much like the chasm between "the great neuropathic family" and the rest of humanity.

The prejudices apparent in fictional film portrayals reappeared in the real life legal case of Elizabeth Bouvia. Her experience epitomizes all of the devaluation and discrimination inflicted on disabled people by society. Because of cerebral palsy, Ms. Bouvia is quadriplegic. When she was five years old, her parents divorced, and her mother was given custody of her. When she was ten, her mother remarried and put her into an institution for handicapped children. For the next eight years, she was shunted from one facility to another. During all that time, her mother rarely visited her. Some parents, to escape the social shame of having a disabled child, adopt society's hostile attitude toward their children and reject them.

At the age of eighteen, Ms. Bouvia decided to make a home for herself in the community. For eight years, in Riverside and then in San Diego, California, she lived independently, assisted by aides she hired to provide housekeeping services and to assist her with her personal needs such as bathing, dressing, and eating. She paid for these aides through a California government program called In-Home Supportive Services (IHSS). Establishment of such programs has been one goal of the independent living movement. Most states still do not have them. In those states, severely disabled adults like Elizabeth Bouvia must spend their lives confined to their families' homes or imprisoned in institutions. Because of her type of disability, Bouvia was legally entitled to the maximum amount available under IHSS. In fact, she received considerably less. State-mandated guidelines supposedly guarantee equal and uniform benefits statewide, but many counties deliberately seek to limit the amount of IHSS granted to disabled residents, sometimes even lying to them about their legal entitlements. Elizabeth Bouvia lived in two of the counties most notorious among disabled Californians for such abuses. The very agencies supposedly designed to enable severely physically handicapped adults like her to achieve independence and productivity in the community become yet another massive hurdle they must surmount, an enemy they must repeatedly battle but can never finally defeat.

Elizabeth Bouvia wanted to get an education. She earned an A.A. at Riverside Community College and a B.A. at San Diego State University. Deciding to pursue a career in social work, she enrolled in the Master's program at San Diego State (SDSU). The course of study included field work experience. The local hospital where she was initially placed for that experience refused to make the "reasonable accommodations" necessary for her to continue there as required by federal law under Section 504 [of the Rehabilitation Act of 1973]. The SDSU School of Social Work refused to back her up. They wanted to place her at a center where she would work only with other disabled people. She refused. Reportedly, one of her professors told her she was unemployable and that, if they had known just how disabled she was, they would never have admitted her to the program. In fact, her disability in no way precluded her from fulfilling the requirements of the program or of her profession. People with more severe disabilities work productively. The professor's statements were not only biased, they were discriminatory, again violating her civil rights under federal law.

Apparently Bouvia was unaware of her legal rights, or perhaps she simply did not have the energy to fight a protracted legal battle against such formidable opponents, especially while she was confronting a series of crises in her personal life. Despairing that she would never achieve the productive professional career she had worked so hard for, she dropped out of school.

Ms. Bouvia never got to the point of confronting the final and most difficult obstacle to work. By getting a job and earning no more than $300 per month, she would have quickly lost her government-financed disability benefits, including the In-Home Supportive Services which made it possible for her to go to work in the first place and would be essential to her continuing to work. This is euphe-mistically called a "work disincentive." It is, in fact, a penalty imposed on dis-abled persons who violate the pervasive social prejudice that they cannot productively contribute to the economy and community and that they should be segregated out of the job market and labor force. Richard Scott, a leading advocate of "aid in dying" and the attorney who has led the fight for Bouvia's supposed legal right to medically assisted suicide, shares that bias. "Quadriple-gics" he said, "cannot work."

. . . Outside school, Elizabeth Bouvia faced other severe stresses. She mar-ried Richard Bouvia but did not report this marriage to the county social service department or the federal Social Security Administration. Had she done so those agencies would have reduced her In-Home Supportive Services and Sup-plemental Security Income benefits. "Able and available" nonhandicapped spouses are expected to provide assistance the government would pay for if the disabled partner were unmarried. This policy prevents or undermines marriages of disabled persons. The euphemism used here is "marriage disincentive," but it too is a punishment for disabled persons who violate the common prejudice that they are unfit to be wives or husbands or lovers or parents or even members of families.

Additional personal stresses struck Ms. Bouvia. Her brother drowned. She became pregnant and then suffered a miscarriage. She saw the film "Whose Life Is It, Anyway?" and became severely depressed. Meanwhile, tensions in her marriage mounted. She and her husband separated. He declared later that he sought a reconciliation, but she, despairing of their relationship, decided to seek a divorce.

At this point, Elizabeth Bouvia checked herself into the psychiatric unit of Riverside County Hospital. She announced her wish to end her life and requested the hospital to assist her. When they refused, she secured the services of a team of Civil Liberties Union lawyers to help her compel the hospital to comply with her wishes. The attorneys brought in three psychiatric professionals to provide an independent evaluation. None of them had any experience or expertise in dealing with persons with disabilities. In fact, Elizabeth Bouvia has never been examined by any psychiatric or medical professional qualified to understand her life experience. She reported to these evaluators the emotionally devastating experiences of the preceding two years. She also said that she wanted to die because of her physical disability. Ignoring all of the emotional blows and the discrimination, her examiners prejudicially concluded that because of her physical condition she would never be able to achieve her life goals, that her disability was the reason she wanted to die, and that her decision for death was reasonable. These same facts were presented to the judge who heard the case in the Riverside Superior Court. He too declared that Ms. Bouvia's physical disability was the sole reason she wished to die.

The trial court judge rejected the petition for assisted suicide, but in 1986, in a second round of litigation, the California court of appeals, despite its tortuous legal and verbal circumlocutions to prove that it was merely upholding the right to refuse medical treatment, in effect, granted her a right to a judicially sanctioned, medically assisted suicide. Typical of discussions regarding disabled people and the right to die, the appellate court ruling is pervaded with ignorance and bias. The court wrote: Ms. Bouvia "suffers from degenerative and severely crippling arthritis." In fact, she has never been formally diagnosed as having arthritis. Her "physical handicaps of palsy and quadriplegia have progressed to the point where she is completely bedridden." In fact, cerebral palsy, which is the cause of her quadriplegia, rather than a separate handicap, is not a progressive condition. "She lies flat in bed and must do so the rest of her life." Her lawyers have assiduously propagated this distortion of the reality of her disability. In fact, she was never bedridden until four years ago, when, in her depressed state, she refused to get out of bed. She has been allowed to languish there ever since. When this case began, her lawyers told the court and the public that she required constant care. In fact, her in-home aides were never on duty more than six hours a day.

The appeals court held that the lower court should have considered the "quality" of the life Elizabeth Bouvia would have to lead. Yet like nearly every other nonhandicapped person connected with this case, they too decided that her physical disability was the lone and exclusive reason that she had found "the quality of her life . . . diminished to the point of hopelessness, uselessness, unenjoyability and frustration."

b. Legal Approaches

|| *Bouvia v. Superior Court* ||
|| 179 Cal. App. 3d 1127 (1986) ||

Opinion by Justice BEACH.

Petitioner, Elizabeth Bouvia, a patient in a public hospital, seeks the removal from her body of a nasogastric tube inserted and maintained against her will and without her consent by physicians who so placed it for the purpose of keeping her alive through involuntary forced feeding.

. . . Petitioner is a 28-year-old woman. Since birth she has been afflicted with and suffered from severe cerebral palsy. She is quadriplegic. She is now a patient at a public hospital maintained by one of the real parties in interest, the County of Los Angeles. Other parties are physicians, nurses and the medical and support staff employed by the County of Los Angeles. Petitioner's physical handicaps of palsy and quadriplegia have progressed to the point where she is completely bedridden. Except for a few fingers of one hand and some slight head and facial movements, she is immobile. She is physically helpless and wholly unable to care for herself. She is totally dependent upon others for all of her needs. These include feeding, washing, cleaning, toileting, turning, and helping her with elimination and other bodily functions. She cannot stand or sit upright in bed or in a wheelchair. She lies flat in bed and must do so the rest of her life. She suffers also from degenerative and severely crippling arthritis. She is in continual pain. Another tube permanently attached to her chest automatically injects her with periodic doses of morphine which relieves some, but not all of her physical pain and discomfort.

She is intelligent, very mentally competent. She earned a college degree. She was married but her husband has left her. She suffered a miscarriage. She lived with her parents until her father told her that they could no longer care for her. She has stayed intermittently with friends and at public facilities. A search for a permanent place to live where she might receive the constant care which she needs has been unsuccessful. She is without financial means to support herself and, therefore, must accept public assistance for medical and other care.

She has on several occasions expressed the desire to die. In 1983 she sought the right to be cared for in a public hospital in Riverside County while she intentionally "starved herself to death." A court in that county denied her judicial assistance to accomplish that goal. She later abandoned an appeal from that ruling. Thereafter, friends took her to several different facilities, both public and private, arriving finally at her present location. Efforts by the staff of real party in interest County of Los Angeles and its social workers to find her an apartment of her own with publicly paid live-in help or regular visiting nurses to care for her, or some other suitable facility, have proved fruitless.

Petitioner must be spoon fed in order to eat. Her present medical and dietary staff have determined that she is not consuming a sufficient amount of nutrients. Petitioner stops eating when she feels she cannot orally swallow more, without nausea and vomiting. As she cannot now retain solids, she is fed soft liquid-like food. Because of her previously announced resolve to starve herself, the medical staff feared her weight loss might reach a life threatening level. Her weight since admission to real parties' facility seems to hover between 65 and 70 pounds. Accordingly, they inserted the subject tube against her will and contrary to her express written instructions.[2]

Petitioner's counsel argue that her weight loss was not such as to be life threatening and therefore the tube is unnecessary. However, the trial court found to the contrary as a matter of fact, a finding which we must accept. Nonetheless, the point is immaterial, for, as we will explain, a patient has the right to refuse any medical treatment or medical service, even when such treatment is labeled "furnishing nourishment and hydration." This right exists even if its exercise creates a "life threatening condition."

Rule:

"[A] person of adult years and in sound mind has the right, in the exercise of control over his own body, to determine whether or not to submit to lawful medical treatment." (Cobbs v. Grant (1972) 8 Cal. 3d 229, 242.) It follows that such a patient has the right to refuse any medical treatment, even that which may save or prolong her life. (Barber v. Superior Court (1983) 147 Cal. App. 3d 1006; Bartling v. Superior Court (1984) 163 Cal. App. 3d 186.) [In *Bartling*, a different division of the appellate court upheld the right of a competent, seriously ill but not terminally ill, adult patient to refuse continued ventilator support even if doing so would hasten death.–Eds.]

. . . At bench the trial court concluded that with sufficient feeding petitioner could live an additional 15 to 20 years; therefore, the preservation of petitioner's life for that period outweighed her right to decide. In so holding the trial court mistakenly attached undue importance to the amount of time possibly available to petitioner, and failed to give equal weight and consideration for the quality of that life; an equal, if not more significant, consideration.

All decisions permitting cessation of medical treatment or life-support procedures to some degree hastened the arrival of death. In part, at least, this was permitted because the quality of life during the time remaining in those cases had been terribly diminished. In Elizabeth Bouvia's view, the quality of her life has been diminished to the point of hopelessness, uselessness, unenjoyability and frustration. She, as the patient, lying helplessly in bed, unable to care for herself, may consider her existence meaningless. She cannot be faulted for so concluding. If her right to choose may not be exercised because there remains to her, in the opinion of a court, a physician or some committee, a certain arbitrary number of years, months, or days, her right will have lost its value and meaning.

Who shall say what the minimum amount of available life must be? Does it matter if it be 15 to 20 years, 15 to 20 months, or 15 to 20 days, if such life has been physically destroyed and its quality, dignity and purpose gone? As in all matters lines must be drawn at some point, somewhere, but that decision must ultimately belong to the one whose life is in issue.

Here Elizabeth Bouvia's decision to forego medical treatment or life support through a mechanical means belongs to her. It is not a medical decision

_____

2. Her instructions were dictated to her lawyers, written by them, and signed by her by means of making a feeble "x" on the paper with a pen in her mouth.

for her physicians to make. Neither is it a legal question whose soundness is to be resolved by lawyers or judges. It is not a conditional right subject to approval by ethics committees or courts of law. It is a moral and philosophical decision that, being a competent adult, is hers alone.

. . . Here, if force fed, petitioner faces 15 to 20 years of a painful existence, endurable only by the constant administrations of morphine. Her condition is irreversible. There is no cure for her palsy or arthritis. Petitioner would have to be fed, cleaned, turned, bedded, toileted by others for 15 to 20 years. Although alert, bright, sensitive, perhaps even brave and feisty, she must lie immobile, unable to exist except through physical acts of others. Her mind and spirit may be free to take great flights but she herself is imprisoned and must lie physically helpless subject to the ignominy, embarrassment, humiliation and dehumanizing aspects created by her helplessness. We do not believe it is the policy of this state that all and every life must be preserved against the will of the sufferer. It is incongruous, if not monstrous, for medical practitioners to assert their right to preserve a life that someone else must live, or, more accurately, endure, for "15 to 20 years." We cannot conceive it to be the policy of this state to inflict such an ordeal upon anyone.

It is, therefore, immaterial that the removal of the nasogastric tube will hasten or cause Bouvia's eventual death. Being competent she has the right to live out the remainder of her natural life in dignity and peace. It is precisely the aim and purpose of the many decisions upholding the withdrawal of life-support systems to accord and provide as large a measure of dignity, respect and comfort as possible to every patient for the remainder of his days, whatever be their number. This goal is not to hasten death, though its earlier arrival may be an expected and understood likelihood. Real parties assert that what petitioner really wants is to "commit suicide" by starvation at their facility [with which the trial court agreed].

Overlooking the fact that a desire to terminate one's life is probably the ultimate exercise of one's right to privacy, we find no substantial evidence to support the court's conclusion. Even if petitioner had the specific intent to commit suicide in 1983, while at Riverside, she did not carry out that plan.

. . . It is not necessary to here define or dwell at length upon what constitutes suicide. Our Supreme Court dealt with the matter in the case of In re Joseph G. (1983) 34 Cal. 3d 429, wherein, declaring that the state has an interest in preserving and recognizing the sanctity of life, it observed that it is a crime to aid in suicide. But it is significant that the instances and the means there discussed all involved affirmative, assertive, proximate, direct conduct such as furnishing a gun, poison, knife, or other instrumentality or usable means by which another could physically and immediately inflict some death-producing injury upon himself. Such situations are far different than the mere presence of a doctor during the exercise of his patient's constitutional rights.

. . . We do not purport to establish what will constitute proper medical practice in all other cases or even other aspects of the care to be provided petitioner. We hold only that her right to refuse medical treatment, even of the life-sustaining variety, entitles her to the immediate removal of the nasogastric tube that has been involuntarily inserted into her body. The hospital and medical staff are still free to perform a substantial if not the greater part of their duty, i.e., that of trying to alleviate Bouvia's pain and suffering.

Petitioner is without means to go to a private hospital and, apparently, real parties' hospital as a public facility was required to accept her. Having done so it may not deny her relief from pain and suffering merely because she has chosen to exercise her fundamental right to protect what little privacy remains to her.

Personal dignity is a part of one's right of privacy. Such a right of bodily privacy led the United States Supreme Court to hold that it shocked its conscience to learn that a state, even temporarily, had put a tube into the stomach of a criminal defendant to recover swallowed narcotics. (Rochin v. California (1952) 342 U.S. 165). Petitioner asks for no greater consideration.

NOTES AND QUESTIONS

1. *Withdrawing treatment vs. assisting in suicide.*   Paul Longmore states that "the California court of appeals, despite its tortuous legal and verbal circumlocutions to prove that it was merely upholding the right to refuse medical treatment, in effect, granted [Bouvia] a right to a judicially sanctioned, medically assisted suicide." Do you agree? The distinction between withdrawing or withholding treatment and assisted suicide has become well settled in the law. See, e.g., *Cruzan,* supra, and *Glucksberg,* infra. Do you think the distinction is sound? Why might an advocate for persons with disabilities have more trouble with the distinction?

2. *Getting the facts right.*   According to Paul Longmore, the appellate court didn't have the facts right in *Bouvia.* If the facts were as Longmore reports them, should the court have decided differently?

3. *The terminally ill and the permanently disabled.*   Should the terminally ill be treated differently from the permanently disabled in questions of the withdrawal of life-sustaining treatment? Longmore suggests that they should; the *Bouvia* court reflects the opposite approach. Which is more convincing?

4. *Update.*   Although the California court permitted Elizabeth Bouvia to have her feeding tube withdrawn, she did not go through with plans to starve herself to death. According to newspaper reports, she "changed her plans almost immediately, when she realized that it would take several painful weeks for her to die." Associated Press, 10 Years After Winning Right to Die, Patient Lives, Orlando Sentinel, Dec. 17, 1993, at A5.

5. *Other cases.*   State v. McAfee, 259 Ga. 579 (1989), is another well-known and controversial case of a competent individual's successful claim for refusing treatment for reasons of quality of life (as opposed to reasons of religion, for example). Larry McAfee, a man with quadriplegia, was determined to have the right to be removed from a ventilator, in addition to medication to address pain that would occur as a result. Following McAfee's successful claim to have his ventilator disconnected, he changed his mind. He explained to an interviewer two years after the court's decision that he had not opted to disconnect the ventilator "because some people came forward and discussed alternative means of living other than in an institution. I told them I would explore those possibilities, which is what I am doing." Are Disabled Joining Death March?, 36 Accent on Living 42, June 22, 1991 (available on Nexis). Psychologist Carol Gill described McAfee as "despairing because he felt he didn't have control over his life even though he kept saying it was because he was paralyzed and had to use a respirator. Activists who know him felt he was really expressing

despair over not having control." 36 Accent on Living, supra. See also McKay v. Bergstedt, 801 P.2d 617 (Nev. 1990) (31-year-old man who had been quadriplegic since age 10 had right to have ventilator removed; desire to die was, according to court, driven by concern about the quality of life following the impending death of his father, who had cared for him). Kenneth Bergstedt died after the district court ruled in his favor but before the state supreme court affirmed that decision. According to the New York Times (Oct. 6, 1990), Bergstedt's father reported that his son had asked him to end his life the previous evening and "that he complied by giving him sedatives and loosening his respirator tube."

Often in law school casebooks one case will follow another because the second either builds on the foundations of the first or gives a clearly different answer to what seems like a very similar question. The following case is reprinted for a different reason. While the British court in the case of *Ms. B* also upholds the patient's right to refuse life-sustaining treatment, the court handles the matter very differently than the *Bouvia* court. As you read the opinion, locate those passages that seek to affirm the value of Ms. B's life and compare those with the passages in *Bouvia* that Longmore (as well as other commentators) have decried as dismissing the value of Bouvia's life. Are these expressions (in either case) appropriate?

Ms B v. An NHS Hospital Trust
[2002] 2 All E.R. 449

Opinion by Dame Elizabeth BUTLER-SLOSS.

1. The Claimant, whom I shall call Ms B, seeks declarations from the High Court in its exercise of the inherent jurisdiction. She claims that the invasive treatment which is currently being given by the respondent by way of artificial ventilation is an unlawful trespass.

2. The respondent is the NHS Hospital Trust (the Trust) responsible for the hospital which is currently caring for Ms B, (the Hospital). . . . Underlying this important issue is the tragic story of an able and talented woman of 43 who has suffered a devastating illness which has caused her to become tetraplegic and whose expressed wish is not to be kept artificially alive by the use of a ventilator.

THE HISTORY

3. Ms B was born on the 6th August 1958 in Jamaica, and has lived in the United Kingdom since the age of 8. She had an unhappy childhood but triumphed over many difficulties to achieve a degree in Social Science and Social Work, and a Masters degree in Public Policy and Administration. She is a qualified Practice Teacher for Social Work, and has a Management Diploma from a London College. She worked as a social worker for a number of local authorities and became a Team Manager. She was appointed in that role to a hospital and

was promoted to Head of Department and Principal Officer for training and
staff development. She is unmarried. She has a close circle of friends and a
godchild to whom she is devoted.

MEDICAL HISTORY

4. On the 26th August 1999, Ms B suffered a haemorrhage of the spinal
column in her neck. She was admitted to the Hospital and a cavernoma was
diagnosed, a condition caused by a malformation of blood vessels in the spinal
cord. She was transferred to another hospital where she stayed for five weeks.
She was informed by doctors that there was a possibility of a further bleed, or
surgical intervention, which would result in severe disability. On the basis of this
advice she executed a Living Will (dated 4th September 1999). The terms of the
Will stated that should the time come when Ms B was unable to give instructions,
she wished for treatment to be withdrawn if she was suffering from a life-threatening condition, permanent mental impairment or permanent unconsciousness. She was, however, also told that the risk of rehaemorrhage was not
particularly great, and so she felt very optimistic about the future. Her condition
gradually improved and after leaving hospital and a period of recuperation, she
returned to work. Thereafter Ms B was in generally good health although she
had some continued weakness in her left arm.

5. At the beginning of 2001, Ms B began to suffer from general weakening
on the left side of her body, and experienced greater numbness in her legs. She
felt unwell on the 12th February 2001, and was admitted to the Hospital in the
early hours of the 13th February 2001. She had suffered an intramedullary
cervical spine cavernoma, as a result of which she became tetraplegic, suffering
complete paralysis from the neck down. On the 16th February 2001 she was
transferred to the Intensive Care Unit (the ICU) of the Hospital. She began
to experience respiratory problems, and was treated with a ventilator, upon
which she has been entirely dependent ever since.

6. Ms B told Dr R (a consultant anaesthetist in the ICU of the Hospital) and
another consultant anaesthetist on about the 24th February 2001 that she had a
Living Will on file, and did not want to be ventilated. The doctors informed her
that the terms of the Living Will were not specific enough to authorise withdrawal of ventilation. On the 23rd March 2001 at another hospital she underwent neurological surgery to remove the cavernous haematoma. After the
operation, her condition improved slightly. She regained the ability to move
her head, and to articulate words. She was however, as she said, bitterly disappointed that the operation had not been more successful. It was at that time that
she first asked for the ventilator to be switched off.

7. On the 26th March 2001 she was assessed by Dr RG, a consultant psychiatrist from another hospital. On the 28th March 2001 Ms B was returned to
the ICU at the Hospital where she remains. She made a request to a consultant
anaesthetist to have the ventilator switched off. On the 5th April 2001, Ms B gave
formal instructions to the Hospital, via her solicitors, that she wished the artificial ventilation to be removed. . . .

8. On the 10th April 2001 she was assessed by Dr L, a consultant psychiatrist
at the Hospital, who concluded she had capacity. On the 11th April 2001 she was
assessed by another consultant psychiatrist at the Hospital, Dr E, who initially

found that Ms B did have capacity. Dr E on the 12th April 2001 then amended her report to state that Ms B did not have capacity, after which Dr L amended his original assessment so as to agree with Dr E. After Dr E's initial opinion, preparations had begun to be made for the ventilator to be turned off. Ms B held discussions with one of the doctors and a lead nurse of the Hospital, and it was agreed that three days should be allowed for Ms B to say goodbye to her family and friends and to finalise her affairs. However, these preparations were called off after Dr E changed her report.

9. Ms B was prescribed antidepressants on the 13th April 2001. She was seen by both Dr E and Dr R on the 30th April 2001. Both doctors stated that on this occasion Ms B said that she was relieved the ventilator had not been switched off. On the 29th May 2001, Ms B participated in assessment for rehabilitation, and agreed to try it. Long-term plans were made for her rehabilitation, with a view to eventually returning home with 24-hour care, or alternatively a residential nursing home. Dr R gave evidence that on the 29th May 2001 Ms B, having been visited by the rehabilitation specialists, was "very cheerful" and "upbeat." She was referred to several spinal units. She received help, which is continuing, from a clinical psychologist. She was re-assessed on the 29th June 2001 by Dr L, and on the 4th July 2001 by Dr E. Their assessments did not provide a firm conclusion as to her mental capacity. On the 12th July 2001 a bronchoscopy was carried out as part of treatment for a left lung collapse. At her request, an independent re-assessment was conducted by Dr RG on the 8th August 2001. He indicated that he did not consider her to be suffering from depression and that he considered her competent to make the decision to discontinue her treatment. Thereafter the Hospital treated Ms B as having capacity to make decisions.

8TH AUGUST TO THE HEARING

10. Ms B made a further Living Will on the 15th August 2001. On the 12th and 25th September two further bronchoscopies were performed with Ms B's consent. She was suffering respiratory distress at the time. The Medical Director considered that there should be involvement from an ethics committee and that assistance should be sought from outside. The Trust did not have an ethics committee and the Health Authority was unable to consider the problem. Between August 2001 and the issue of these proceedings by Ms B on 16 January 2002 the Trust sought advice from various outside sources. The possibility of a one-way weaning programme was suggested by Dr S, a consultant in neuroa-naesthesia and intensive care from another hospital who was consulted. One-way weaning is a programme whereby over a period of time the number of breaths supplied by the ventilator is gradually reduced and the patient's body is allowed to become used to breathing on its own again. Generally if the patient cannot manage on his/her own then the number of breaths is increased. In a one-way weaning programme it would be reduced without going back on the support. Sedation would be given but not so as to cause respiratory depression unless clinically indicated. The clinicians were not prepared to turn off the ventilator. The one-way weaning programme was agreed by the clinicians but with reluctance as an acceptable compromise. It was also agreed that this could be achieved either by sending Ms B to a weaning centre or carrying it out in the ICU.

11. On the 12th November Ms B was offered referral to a weaning centre which she rejected. In the alternative she was offered the programme in the ICU. This she also rejected for two reasons, being the length of the process (about three weeks), and the omission of pain killers as part of the treatment. Ms B made it clear from September 2001 that she did not want to go to a spinal rehabilitation unit. She refused the possibility of a referral to one clinic when her name was near the top of the waiting list in October. She also refused the possibility of a bed in a hospice in December since the hospice would not accept her wish to have her ventilator withdrawn. . . .

[The court then discusses the well-established principle of autonomy in English law, which supports a patient's general right to refuse medical treatment. The court also cites precedent for the proposition that "the principle of the sanctity of human life must yield to the principle of self-determination."]

THE EVIDENCE OF MS B

39. She provided two written statements and gave oral evidence for about an hour and a half. She gave a clear account of her wishes and her feelings. She made it clear in her written and oral evidence that she had never changed her view that she wanted the ventilator withdrawn. It was only during the period that she was assessed as not having capacity to decide that she agreed to consider other possibilities. For the purposes of this case I shall concentrate upon the issues of ambivalence over turning off the ventilator and her rejection of rehabilitation and the one-way weaning programme. [The court then relates Ms. B's testimony on these matters, which is then discussed in the court's analysis below.]

52. At the end of her written statement she set out her feelings as a Christian:

> In many ways the decision to have my treatment withdrawn has been a very difficult one for me as I have been a Christian and a regular church attendee all my life. The dominant view in the church is that that I should wait for God to heal me. Withdrawing ventilation would be seen as throwing in the towel. I have questioned myself about this and it has challenged my integrity. It has been a very difficult process to rationalise what I am doing in the context of my faith but I feel there is no alternative, as I do not have any realistic hope of recovery. I have come to believe that people die and become disabled and God does not always intervene. It has also been difficult for me to contemplate leaving the people I love behind. There has been a lot of talking and crying as no one wants me to die but almost all of them empathise with me and my situation and sincerely wish to respect my wishes, which I have made clear to all.

53. Her wishes were clear and well-expressed. She had clearly done a considerable amount of investigation and was extremely well-informed about her condition. She has retained a sense of humour and, despite her feelings of frustration and irritation which she expressed in her oral evidence, a considerable degree of insight into the problems caused to the Hospital clinicians and nursing staff by her decision not to remain on artificial ventilation. She is, in my judgment, an exceptionally impressive witness. Subject to the crucial evidence of the consultant psychiatrists, she appears to me to demonstrate a very high standard of mental competence, intelligence and ability.

THE MEDICAL EVIDENCE

[The opinion summarizes the evidence given by each doctor; Dr C's is printed here.]

Dr C

57. She made a statement and gave oral evidence. She was the lead clinician and met regularly to discuss Ms B's case with the medical director of the Hospital. She made inquiries of a consultant from another hospital, (Dr D). He told her that it was a matter of consent. She felt that the clinicians always treated Ms B as competent to make decisions. It was however difficult for a patient to make a decision without experiencing a spinal rehabilitation unit. Her dilemma was not to be against the wishes of Ms B but to offer her anything to make her want to live. The four anaesthetists working in intensive care, Dr R, herself and two others discussed how they should approach this situation. It was very difficult and they were and continued to be put under tremendous pressure by the circumstances of this case. She had reluctantly gone along with the proposal of a one-way weaning process. If it was up to her she would not suggest or commence withdrawal of treatment from Ms B. She had studied and spent her professional life trying to do her best to improve and preserve life. She did not feel able to agree with simply switching off Ms B's ventilation. She would not be able to do it. She felt she was being asked to kill Ms B. They had all been looking after Ms B for a long time on a very intimate level. She felt that a lot more needed to be done for these patients.

58. It was clear from their evidence that both the treating clinicians were deeply distressed by the dilemma which had faced them over the year that Ms B had spent in the ICU. They knew her well and respected and liked her. They considered her to be competent to make decisions about her medical treatment. They could not, however, bring themselves to contemplate that they should be part of bringing Ms B's life to an end by the dramatic, (my word), step of turning off the ventilator. As I listened to the evidence of each of them I had the greatest possible sympathy for their position.

CONCLUSION ON MENTAL CAPACITY

89. As I have already said Ms B was a most impressive witness. I therefore considered with especial care the evidence of the two psychiatrists and the submissions of Mr Francis for the Trust. I start with the presumption that Ms B has mental capacity. That presumption was displaced between April and August 2001 in the light of the assessments by Dr E and Dr L, which have not been challenged in this court. Dr RG in August assessed her as mentally competent and the Hospital thereafter treated her as such. Nevertheless, Mr Francis has argued that it is legal capacity which I must consider not the assessment of the mental capacity provided by the doctors. That may be so, but, unless it is an exceptional case, the judicial approach to mental capacity must be largely dependent upon the assessments of the medical profession whose task it is on

a regular basis to assess the competence of the patient to consent or refuse the medical/surgical treatment recommended to the patient. If, as in the present case, two experienced and distinguished consultant psychiatrists give evidence that Ms B has the mental capacity to make decisions, even grave decisions about her future medical treatment, that is cogent evidence upon which I can and should rely. That evidence supports and reinforces the assessment of Ms B's competence in August 2001. No psychiatrist has suggested since August that Ms B is not competent.

90. Mr Francis has pointed to a number of temporary factors which might affect Ms B's competence or erode her capacity: possible evidence of psychological regression; the effect of her grave physical disability; the absence of her experience of rehabilitation which was thought likely to be a positive experience; and the effect of her environment in the ICU. Mr Francis also points to concern about Ms B's history of ambivalence about ventilation and her consent to bronchoscopies.

. . . 92. I reject any suggestion that Ms B's capacity has been impaired by the advent of psychological regression. There is no evidence to support it. I do not consider that Ms B has been ambivalent in her determination to choose her medical treatment and in her wish to cease to have artificial ventilation. She did look at the alternatives and went down the path of rehabilitation when she was deemed incapable of making her own decision. As soon as she was deemed capable she made it clear that she did not want to go to a spinal rehabilitation unit and turned down the opportunity of a place in October last year. Her relief at not having to say goodbye to her family and friends in April is entirely explicable on two grounds. First, it must not be forgotten that she was deemed not competent at that time so it would be unjust of me to place great weight on her emotions. Second, if, contrary to the psychiatric assessment, she was competent, her explanation of relief in not undergoing painful and distressing final good-byes to those she loves, does not seem to me to be incompatible with her long term objective of cessation of artificial ventilation. Equally there is no incompatability in consenting to the bronchoscopies, refusal of which she felt would involve pain and discomfort, which understandably she did not wish to undergo.

93. Mr G's evidence to the effect that one must experience the advantages of rehabilitation is probably excellent advice for the vast majority of paraplegic and tetraplegic patients. His view that not to have experienced rehabilitation means that the patient lacks informed consent cannot be the basis for the legal concept of mental capacity. If Mr G were correct, the absence of experience in the spinal rehabilitation clinic would deny Ms B or any other similar patient the right to choose whether or not to go to one. It is not possible to experience before choosing in many medical situations. That is not the state of the law nor, I assume, would the medical profession accept it for many fundamental and practical reasons.

. . . 95. I am therefore entirely satisfied that Ms B is competent to make all relevant decisions about her medical treatment including the decision whether to seek to withdraw from artificial ventilation. Her mental competence is commensurate with the gravity of the decision she may wish to make. I find that she has had the mental capacity to make such decisions since the 8th August 2001 and that she will remain competent to make such decisions for the foreseeable future. I should however like to underline the wise submission made to me by Mr Jackson that my decision leaves Ms B with a future choice which she can consider freely now that she will be relieved of the burdens of litigation. She is not bound by her past decision and when she goes to the hospital prepared to accept her, she has the right to reflect on what she may wish to do with her life. I would like to add how impressed I am with her as a person, with the great courage, strength of will and determination she has shown in the last year, with her sense of humour, and her understanding of the dilemma she has posed to the Hospital. She is clearly a splendid person and it is tragic that someone of her ability has been struck down so cruelly. I hope she will forgive me for saying, diffidently, that if she did reconsider her decision, she would have a lot to offer the community at large.

REMEDIES

96. In the light of my decision that the Claimant has mental capacity and has had such capacity since August 2001 I shall be prepared to grant the appropriate declarations after discussions with Counsel. I also find that the Claimant has been treated unlawfully by the Trust since August.

97. Throughout the sad developments of this case, all those looking after Ms B have cared for her to the highest standards of medical competence and with devotion. They deserve the highest praise. Ironically this excellent care has to some extent contributed to the difficulties for the Hospital. Ms B has been treated throughout in the ICU in which the medical and nursing team are dedicated to saving and preserving life, sometimes in adverse medical situations. As Dr C said, they are trained to save life. The request from Ms B, which would have been understood in a palliative care situation, appears to have been outside the experience of the ICU in relation to a mentally competent patient. It was seen by some as killing the patient or assisting the patient to die and ethically unacceptable. . . .

98. . . . Ms B was, in my view, placed in an impossible position by the treating clinicians who could not contemplate turning off the ventilator. If they had stopped to consider the likelihood of her being able to breathe unaided they presumably would have endorsed the possibility of success at not greater than 1%. In which case, the one-way weaning process was inevitably going to fail and she would die over three weeks and not in a few hours. I have to say, with some sadness, that the one-way weaning process appears to have been designed to help the treating clinicians and the other carers and not in any way designed to help Ms B. If the one-way weaning process were to be carried out as suggested by the doctors there would be a risk that she would die in discomfort and possibly in pain, even though that is not what they intended. It was obviously, to anyone looking at it from outside the hospital, an unrealistic and unhelpful programme. It was nonetheless supported by the Hospital and by the Trust. No-one stood back, as the solicitors undoubtedly would have done, had they been asked, and considered in an objective way the best way to go forward. The clinicians had clearly become emotionally involved. That situation was entirely understandable. They had with the nursing staff kept Ms B alive and looked after her in every respect including her most intimate requirements. Obviously a relationship built up and it was, in my view, unjust to the team in the ICU that the burden of decision and responsibility for Ms B largely remained in their hands. . . .

99. It is important to draw a careful distinction between the duties of the dedicated team in the ICU of the Hospital caring for Ms B and the Trust

responsible for the working of the Hospital. In my view, the latter should have taken steps to deal with the issue. The failure to do so has led me to the conclusion that I should mark my finding that the Claimant has been treated unlawfully by the NHS Hospital Trust by a small award of damages. I shall not decide the amount until Mr Francis has had an opportunity to make representations if he wishes to do so.

NOTES AND QUESTIONS

1. *Comparing* Bouvia *and Ms. B v. An NHS Hospital Trust.*   How does the court's description of Ms. B compare with the California court's description of Elizabeth Bouvia? How does the tone of the two cases differ? Does this have any significance?

2. *Relevancy of care relationships.*   How does the court describe the relationship between Ms. B and her caregivers? Why was it difficult for her clinician caregivers to support Ms. B's decision to have the ventilator removed? Is this relevant to the outcome of the case? See generally Lois Shepherd, Face to Face: A Call to Replace Compassion with Radical Responsibility, 77 St. John's L. Rev. 445 (2003).

3. *Mental capacity.*   The case of Ms. B focuses on the patient's mental capacity to make decisions about treatment or nontreatment. What are some of the factors the court mentions that might impede an individual's capacity? How does the court handle the question of ambivalence? How does it handle the question whether someone should be required to try rehabilitation before being allowed to make the decision to die?

4. *Weaning program.*   The one-way weaning program offered to Ms. B is described by the court as almost certain death, with the likelihood of discomfort and possibly pain. Why do you think it was even proposed?

5. *The patient's religious views.*   The court talks about Ms. B's religious views in relationship to her treatment refusal. Why do you think it does so? Do you think this is appropriate?

3.   When the Patient or Her Family Wants "Futile" Treatment

‖ ***Causey v. St. Francis Medical Center*** ‖
719 So. 2d 1072 (La. App. 2 Cir. 1998)

Opinion by Judge Brown.

The facts of this end of life drama are not materially disputed. Believing it medically and ethically inappropriate, a physician and hospital withdrew life-sustaining care to a 31-year-old, quadriplegic, end-stage renal failure, comatose patient over the strongly expressed objections of the patient's family. As filed, this action was premised as an intentional battery-based tort. The trial court, however, found that defendants "acted in accordance with professional opinions and professional judgment" and thus this action was covered by the medical malpractice act which required that it first be presented to a medical review panel. Accordingly, the trial court dismissed the action as premature.

Having suffered cardiorespiratory arrest, Sonya Causey was transferred to St. Francis Medical Center (SFMC) from a nursing home. She was comatose, quadriplegic and in end-stage renal failure. Her treating physician, Dr. Herschel R. Harter, believed that continuing dialysis would have no benefit. Although Dr. Harter agreed that with dialysis and a ventilator Mrs. Causey could live for another two years, he believed that she would have only a slight (1% to 5%) chance of regaining consciousness. Because Mrs. Causey's family demanded aggressive life-sustaining care, Dr. Harter sought unsuccessfully to transfer her to another medical facility willing to provide this care.

Dr. Harter enlisted support from SFMC's Morals and Ethics Board. The Board agreed with Dr. Harter's opinion to discontinue dialysis, life-support procedures, and to enter a "no-code" status (do not resuscitate). Mrs. Causey was taken off a feeding tube and other similar devices. The day the ventilator was removed, Mrs. Causey died of respiratory and cardiac failure.

Plaintiffs, the husband, father and mother of Sonya Causey, brought this petition for damages against SFMC and Dr. Harter. Defendants filed an exception of prematurity asserting that this action was covered under Louisiana's Medical Malpractice Act, La. R.S. 40:1299.41 et seq., which requires that malpractice claims be first submitted to a medical review panel before any action can be filed. La. R.S. 40:1299.47. Plaintiffs claim that to discontinue dialysis, remove life-support systems and enter a "no code" order was treatment without consent and an intentional tort not covered by the malpractice act. Finding that defendants made a medical decision, the trial court sustained the exception and dismissed the lawsuit as premature. Plaintiffs have appealed.

Patient participation in medical decision-making is now well-established. Recognizing individual autonomy and the right to self-determination, our state legislature enacted a statute granting a competent, terminally ill person the right to refuse medical treatment. La. R.S. 40:1299.58.1, et seq.

. . . Patients or, if incompetent, their surrogate decision-makers, are [now] demanding life-sustaining treatment regardless of its perceived futility, while physicians are objecting to being compelled to prolong life with procedures they consider futile. The right or autonomy of the patient to refuse treatment is simply a severing of the relationship with the physician. In this case, however, the patient (through her surrogate) is not severing a relationship, but demanding treatment the physician believes is "inappropriate."

The problem is not with care that the physician believes is harmful or literally has no effect. For example, radiation treatment for Mrs. Causey's condition would not have been appropriate. This is arguably based on medical science. Rather, the problem is with care that has an effect on the dying process, but which the physician believes has no benefit. Such life-prolonging care is grounded in beliefs and values about which people disagree. Strictly speaking, if a physician can keep the patient alive, such care is not medically or physiologically "futile"; however, it may be "futile" on philosophical, religious or practical grounds.

Placement of statistical cut-off points for futile treatment involves subjective value judgments. The difference in opinion as to whether a 2% or 9% probability of success is the critical point for determining futility can be explained in terms of personal values, not in terms of medical science. When the medical professional and the patient, through a surrogate, disagree on the worth of pursuing life, this is a conflict over values, i.e., whether extra days obtained through medical intervention are worth the burden and costs.

SFMC had in place a Futile Care Policy which allowed for the discontinuance of medical care over and above that necessary for comfort and support if the probability of improving the patient's condition was slight and would serve only to prolong life in that condition. The inclusion of non-medical persons on the Morals and Ethics Board signals that this is not strictly a physiological or medical futility policy, but a policy asserting values and beliefs on the worth of sustaining life, even in a vegetative condition.

Futility is a subjective and nebulous concept which, except in the strictest physiological sense, incorporates value judgments. Obviously, in this case, subjective personal values of the benefit of prolonging life with only a slight possibility of improvement dictated SFMC's and Dr. Harter's decision. To focus on a definition of "futility" is confusing and generates polemical discussions. We turn instead to an approach emphasizing the standard of medical care.[2]

Physicians are professionals and occupy a special place in our community. They are licensed by society to perform this special role. No one else is permitted to use life-prolonging technology, which is considered by many as "fundamental" health care. The physician has an obligation to present all medically acceptable treatment options for the patient or her surrogate to consider and either choose or reject; however, this does not compel a physician to provide interventions that in his view would be harmful, without effect or "medically inappropriate." In recognizing a terminal patient's right to refuse care, La. R.S. 40:1299.58.1(A)(4) states that the statute is not to be construed "to require the application of *medically inappropriate* treatment or life-sustaining procedures to any patient or to interfere with *medical judgment* with respect to the application of medical treatment or life-sustaining procedures." (Emphasis added). Unfortunately, "medically inappropriate" and "medical judgment" are not defined.

. . . Standards of medical malpractice require a physician to act with the degree of skill and care ordinarily possessed by those in that same medical specialty acting under the same or similar circumstances. Departure from this prevailing standard of care, coupled with harm, may result in professional

---

2. This matter is further complicated by federal legislation, such as the Americans with Disability Act (ADA) and Emergency Medical Treatment and Active Labor Act (EMTALA), that preempts state law and does not recognize a health care provider's right to withdraw life-sustaining care deemed medically inappropriate. Mrs. Causey was both disabled and an emergency patient. In re Baby K., 16 F.3d 590 (4th Cir. 1994), *cert. denied*, 513 U.S. 825 (1994), presents facts similar to this case. The court in *In re Baby K* found that to the extent that state law exempted physicians from providing care they considered medically inappropriate, it conflicted with EMTALA provisions requiring continuous stabilizing treatment for emergency patients and was thus preempted by EMTALA. See, however, distinguishing opinion of Bryan v. Rectors and Visitors of University of Virginia, 95 F.3d 349 (4th Cir. 1996). In *Bryan, supra,* the Fourth Circuit backed off the sweeping statement made in the *Baby K* case that EMTALA imposed upon the hospital an obligation not only to admit a patient for treatment of an emergency condition, which was done, but thereafter to continuously stabilize her condition, no matter how long required. . . . [Instead] EMTALA was found to regulate the hospital's care of the patient only in the immediate aftermath of the act of admitting her for emergency treatment and while it considered whether it would undertake longer-term full treatment. Agreeing with *Bryan*, we find that EMTALA provisions are not applicable to the present case.

malpractice liability. La. R.S. 40:1299.41. A finding that treatment is "medically inappropriate" by a consensus of physicians practicing in that specialty translates into a standard of care. Thus, in this case, whether Dr. Harter and SFMC met the standard of care concerning the withdrawal of dialysis, life-support procedures and the entering of a "no code" status must be determined. If the withdrawal of or the refusal to provide care is considered a "medical procedure," then it may be that the circumstances of this case present an exception to the supreme court's statement in *Lugenbuhl* that "one can hardly argue that it is not below the appropriate standard of care for a doctor or nurse to perform a medical procedure without obtaining any kind of consent." In any event, the Medical Malpractice Act is applicable and the matter should first be submitted to a medical review panel.

For the reasons expressed above, the judgment of the trial court dismissing plaintiffs' action as premature is AFFIRMED. Costs are assessed to plaintiffs-appellants.

Thaddeus Mason Pope, Medical Futility Statutes: No Safe Harbor to Unilaterally Refuse Life-Sustaining Treatment
75 Tenn. L. Rev. 1 (2007)*

. . . 2. PROVIDER REASONS FOR RESISTING TREATMENT

In some circumstances, health care providers resist surrogate requests that "everything be done." Such resistance stems from a significant consensus that some requests for treatment are inappropriate and that health care providers should not comply with them. While no consensus exists on the specific criteria and conditions under which providers may decline to comply with requests for LSMT [life-sustaining medical treatment], the appropriateness of unilateral refusals has long been accepted. In fact, a plethora of professional medical associations have issued policy statements supporting the unilateral withholding and withdrawal of inappropriate LSMT. The policy statements are primarily motivated by four concerns, the most significant of which is professional integrity. Physicians do not want to be indentured servants, "reflexive automatons," "vending machines," "prostitutes," or "grocers" beholden to provide whatever treatment patients or surrogates want. After all, medicine is not a "consumer commodity like breakfast cereal and toothpaste."

The medical profession is a self-governing one with its own standards of professional practice. The "integrity of the medical profession" is an important societal interest that must be balanced against patient autonomy. Indeed, patient autonomy "has never been construed as requiring a health professional to provide a particular type of treatment." Since the medical profession determines the goals and values of medicine, it can judge certain requests as inconsistent with those goals and values.

---

    * The full text of this article was published originally at 75 Tenn. L. Rev. 1 (2007) and this extract is reprinted here by permission of the author and the Tennessee Law Review Association, Inc.

In particular, many health care providers do not consider the practice of medicine to include measures aimed solely at maintaining corporeal existence and biologic functioning. Under these circumstances, providers feel that continued LSMT is just "bad medicine . . . medicine being used for the wrong ends." Moreover, health care providers find it gruesome, distressing, and demoralizing to provide treatment that harms patients.

Second, in addition to professional integrity, providers resist inappropriate treatment requests out of concern for the patient. Continued interventions can be inhumane, invasive, pointless, intrusive, cruel, burdensome, abusive, degrading, obscene, violent, or grotesque. For example, CPR can be painful, causing rib or sternal fractures in a majority of cases. Health care providers want to shorten and ease patient suffering; they do not want to cause or prolong it.

A third reason that providers resist requests for inappropriate treatment is that they do not want to offer false hope. If they acted as though a medically inappropriate option were "available," this would create a psychological burden on surrogates to elect that option regardless of their prior wishes. Naturally, families want to at least take all reasonable measures. Yet, it is unfair and deceptive to offer an option where none actually exists. If health care providers offered ineffective treatment, they would risk losing public confidence.

Lastly, providers resist inappropriate treatment requests in an effort to maximize the utility of scarce resources. Providers want to be good "steward[s]" of both "hard" resources like ICU beds and "soft" resources like health care dollars. While costs have seldom been a consideration in defining when treatment is inappropriate, there is little doubt that costs have been a major impetus for increasing attention on medical futility. Thus, the issue of medically futile treatment is likely to increase in the future as concerns about costs for such treatment grows.

3. LIMITS ON RESISTING TREATMENT

Whatever might be their motivations for stopping LSMT, health care providers generally recognize two important limits on the extent to which they will resist a surrogate's request for LSMT: (1) comfort care and (2) accommodation. First, even when LSMT is stopped, providers will continue to administer comfort care. They will continue to ensure the patient's comfort by providing services that include oral and body hygiene, reasonable efforts to offer food and fluids orally, medication, positioning, warmth, appropriate lighting, and other measures aimed at relieving pain and suffering or respecting the patient's dignity and humanity. In short, stopping treatment does not mean stopping care.

Second, even when they consider continued LSMT to be inappropriate, providers will generally make a short-term accommodation of the surrogate's wishes. Providers will respect patient treatment goals such as providing time to resolve personal matters, grieving, and allowing time to say goodbye. Brain dead patients are oftentimes maintained on life support for several hours or days as a matter of sensitivity to religious, cultural, or moral values.

. . . V. EFFECTS OF THE UNILATERAL DECISION STATUTES

In the early 1990s, health care providers were unwilling to make unilateral decisions to stop LSMT without legal protection. Consequently, over the past eighteen years, state legislatures have promulgated statutes that purport to provide this protection. Now, it is time to assess the effects of these statutes.

While little empirical data exists, there is sufficient evidence to detect four broad trends and identify focused issues for empirical research. The first two trends are reasonably negative, at least from the perspective of statutory effectiveness. First, even in states with comprehensive unilateral decision statutes, many hospitals still do not have futility policies. Second, those few hospitals with futility policies rarely implement them to make a unilateral decision in cases of intractable conflict.

Two additional trends have more positive attributes. First, the unilateral decision statute in one state, Texas, does appear to work. Texas hospitals both have and implement futility policies. Second, unilateral decision statutes appear to facilitate the informal resolution of futility disputes, reducing, although not eliminating, the need to resort to unilateral decision making.

. . . There is an exception to this general failure [of hospitals to implement futility policies by making unilateral decisions]: Texas's statute appears to have had a significant impact since its adoption in 1999. In one study at Baylor University Medical Center in Dallas, researchers found that the statutory authorization gave physicians "more comfort," thereby increasing ethical consultations regarding futility disputes by 67%. Not only did physicians and hospitals across Texas begin the dispute resolution process but also, in approximately two percent of cases that were proven intractable, the providers gave notice that they were going to unilaterally stop LSMT.

A broader study of sixteen Texas hospitals over a five-year period found that, on average, each hospital made the decision to unilaterally stop treatment at least one time each year. Indeed, Texas hospitals unilaterally stopped or decided to stop LSMT, even in the face of significant controversy and mass media coverage urging otherwise. In short, the Texas statute has truly changed provider conduct.

. . . In Texas, when a provider refuses to honor a surrogate's request for continued LSMT, the provider must commence a multi-stage review process. LSMT must be provided during this review process. The first stage entails an ethics committee review of the attending physician's determination. The surrogate must be notified of the ethics committee review process at least forty-eight hours before the committee meets. The surrogate is also entitled to attend the meeting and to receive a written explanation of the committee's decision.

If the ethics committee agrees with the treating physician that LSMT is inappropriate, the provider must attempt to transfer the patient to another provider that is willing to comply with the surrogate's treatment request. The provider is obligated to continue providing LSMT for ten days after the surrogate is given the ethics committee's written decision. If the patient has not been transferred or granted an extension, then the provider may unilaterally stop LSMT on the eleventh day.

. . . Unlike the UHCDA [Uniform Health Care Decisions Act—a model statute adopted in ten states that requires providers generally to comply with patient and health care decisions, but which also has a futility provision] and other unilateral decision statutes which specify vague substantive standards such as "significant benefit," the safe harbor of TADA [Texas Advance Directives Act] is defined solely in terms of process. Texas providers who follow TADA's prescribed notice and meeting procedures are therefore immune from disciplinary action and civil and criminal liability. Because the statute's requirements are concrete and measurable, there is little, if any, uncertainty of compliance.

The TADA is far from perfect. Ten days may not be a reasonable or sufficient time for surrogates to locate an alternative facility willing to accept the patient. There may be procedural due process implications by placing the ultimate decision in the hands of an institutional ethics committee, which is comprised of physicians and administrators who look to the hospital for their economic livelihood. However, these mechanics of the TADA process can and are being considerably refined. The TADA demonstrates that a pure process approach works and that such an approach now serves, and should continue to serve, as a model for other states.

NOTES AND QUESTIONS

1. *"Futility" vs. "medically inappropriate."* The court in *Causey* rejects the term *futile*. Is *medically inappropriate* any more helpful? How is it to be determined what care is medically inappropriate? If it is through standard medical practice, how are the "subjective personal values" that the *Causey* court talks about going to play into any analysis about whether treatment should have been provided?

2. *Ethics boards and committees.* In the *Causey* case, the physicians had consulted the hospital's ethics board. Such committees typically have representation from the lay community, but most members of these committees come from hospital staff. Some see the purpose of ethics committees as simply ensuring that all facets of a problem have been considered and all stakeholders given an appropriate opportunity to weigh in. Other ethics committees work toward a resolution or decision in a matter. This apparently is what the ethics board did in the *Causey* case. What weight, if any, should the court give the decision made by the ethics board?

3. *Focusing on process.* Law professor Thaddeus Pope argues that the Texas statute's emphasis on process makes it superior to statutes that incorporate a substantive standard of "medically inappropriate" treatment. Do you agree? Or does this just shift the decision of what is medically inappropriate to the physician and ethics committee (a decision which is unreviewable by courts)? See Robert D. Truog, Tackling Medical Futility in Texas, 357 New Eng. J. Med. 1 (2007) (discussing the case of Emilio Gonzales, which was the subject of national controversy in 2007).

4. *Preemption and constitutionality of futility statutes.* Pope, supra, points out in another section of his article that uncertainty exists whether these statutes are preempted by federal law (such as the Emergency Medical Treatment and Active Labor Act, the Americans with Disabilities Act, the Rehabilitation Act of 1973, and the Child Abuse Prevention and Treatment Act) and whether they might be unconstitutional (as violating religious freedom, equal protection, the right to life, or the freedom of expression). In a famous case involving Baby K, the federal court of appeals determined that a hospital was required under EMTALA to provide emergency respiratory support to an anencephalic infant although the hospital believed it morally and ethically inappropriate to do so.

In re Baby K, 16 F.3d 590 (1994) (discussed in footnote 2 of *Causey,* reprinted above).

B.   PHYSICIAN AID IN HASTENING DEATH

Through common usage the term *physician-assisted suicide* has come to be understood as involving a physician's prescription, but not administration, of a lethal dosage of medication, which the patient may then choose to self-administer. *Euthanasia* is understood to involve the administration of lethal medication by another; it may be "voluntary" or "involuntary." In this section we consider various bioethical perspectives and the case law of physician-assisted suicide.

Some advocates for physician-assisted suicide prefer to call what they seek by a different term, such as "physician aid in dying," to distinguish the hastening of the patient's death in these circumstances from what we might think of as ordinary suicide, an act that states have long maintained an interest in preventing. According to Compassion & Choices, an organization that describes itself as promoting "choice at the end of life," "Those facing a terminal illness do not want to die but— by definition—*are* dying . . . 'suicide' is a hurtful and derogatory term to both a dying patient and their loved ones." Aid-in-Dying Language Press Kit, Aug. 8, 2008, http://www.compassionandchoices.org/documents/LanguageKIT.pdf.

Although appreciative of this viewpoint, at times this casebook continues to use the term *physician-assisted suicide* because of its commonly understood meaning within the current debate. In other places we use the term *physician aid in hastening death* to avoid misunderstanding about what it is physicians are asked to do in these cases; it is not merely to "aid" the dying.

1.   Bioethical and Social Perspectives

|| *Timothy E. Quill, Death and Dignity: A Case of Individualized Decision Making* ||
|| **324 New Eng. J. Med. 691 (1991)*** ||

Diane was feeling tired and had a rash. A common scenario, though there was something subliminally worrisome that prompted me to check her blood count. Her hematocrit was 22, and the white-cell count was 4.3 with some metamyelocytes and unusual white cells. I wanted it to be viral, trying to deny what was staring me in the face. Perhaps in a repeated count it would disappear. I called Diane and told her it might be more serious than I had initially thought—that the test needed to be repeated and that if she felt worse, we might have to move quickly. When she pressed for the possibilities, I reluctantly opened the door to

---

* Copyright © 1991 Massachusetts Medical Society. All rights reserved.

leukemia. Hearing the word seemed to make it exist. "Oh, shit!" she said. "Don't tell me that." Oh, shit! I thought, I wish I didn't have to.

Diane was no ordinary person (although no one I have ever come to know has been really ordinary). She was raised in an alcoholic family and had felt alone for much of her life. She had vaginal cancer as a young woman. Through much of her adult life, she had struggled with depression and her own alcoholism. I had come to know, respect, and admire her over the previous eight years as she confronted these problems and gradually overcame them. She was an incredibly clear, at times brutally honest, thinker and communicator. As she took control of her life, she developed a strong sense of independence and confidence. In the previous 3 1/2 years, her hard work had paid off. She was completely abstinent from alcohol, she had established much deeper connections with her husband, college-age son, and several friends, and her business and her artistic work were blossoming. She felt she was really living fully for the first time.

Not surprisingly, the repeated blood count was abnormal, and detailed examination of the peripheral-blood smear showed myelocytes. I advised her to come into the hospital, explaining that we needed to do a bone marrow biopsy and make some decisions relatively rapidly. She came to the hospital knowing what we would find. She was terrified, angry, and sad. Although we knew the odds, we both clung to the thread of possibility that it might be something else.

The bone marrow confirmed the worst: acute myelomonocytic leukemia. In the face of this tragedy, we looked for signs of hope. This is an area of medicine in which technological intervention has been successful, with cures 25 percent of the time—long-term cures. As I probed the costs of these cures, I heard about induction chemotherapy (three weeks in the hospital, prolonged neutropenia, probable infectious complications, and hair loss; 75 percent of patients respond, 25 percent do not). For the survivors, this is followed by consolidation chemotherapy (with similar side effects; another 25 percent die, for a net survival of 50 percent). Those still alive, to have a reasonable chance of long-term survival, then need bone marrow transplantation (hospitalization for two months and whole-body irradiation, with complete killing of the bone marrow, infectious complications, and the possibility for graft-versus-host disease—with a survival of approximately 50 percent, or 25 percent of the original group). Though hematologists may argue over the exact percentages, they don't argue about the outcome of no treatment—certain death in days, weeks, or at most a few months.

Believing that delay was dangerous, our oncologist broke the news to Diane and began making plans to insert a Hickman catheter and begin induction chemotherapy that afternoon. When I saw her shortly thereafter, she was enraged at his presumption that she would want treatment, and devastated by the finality of the diagnosis. All she wanted to do was go home and be with her family. She had no further questions about treatment and in fact had decided that she wanted none. Together we lamented her tragedy and the unfairness of life. Before she left, I felt the need to be sure that she and her husband understood that there was some risk in delay, that the problem was not going to go away, and that we needed to keep considering the options over the next several days. We agreed to meet in two days. She returned in two days with her husband and son. They had talked extensively about the problem and the options. She remained very clear about her wish not to undergo chemotherapy and to live whatever time she had left outside the hospital. As we explored her thinking further, it became clear that she was convinced she would die during the period of treatment and would suffer unspeakably in the process (from hospitalization, from lack of control over her body, from the side effects of chemotherapy, and from pain and anguish). Although I could offer support and my best effort to minimize her suffering if she chose treatment, there was no way I could say any of this would not occur. In fact, the last four patients with acute leukemia at our hospital had died very painful deaths in the hospital during various stages of treatment (a fact I did not share with her). Her family wished she would choose treatment but sadly accepted her decision. She articulated very clearly that it was she who would be experiencing all the side effects of treatment and that odds of 25 percent were not good enough for her to undergo so toxic a course of therapy, given her expectations of chemotherapy and hospitalization and the absence of a closely matched bone marrow donor. I had her repeat her understanding of the treatment, the odds, and what to expect if there were no treatment. I clarified a few misunderstandings, but she had a remarkable grasp of the options and implications.

I have been a longtime advocate of active, informed patient choice of treatment or nontreatment, and of a patient's right to die with as much control and dignity as possible. Yet there was something about her giving up a 25 percent chance of long-term survival in favor of almost certain death that disturbed me. I had seen Diane fight and use her considerable inner resources to overcome alcoholism and depression, and I half expected her to change her mind over the next week. Since the window of time in which effective treatment can be initiated is rather narrow, we met several times that week. We obtained a second hematology consultation and talked at length about the meaning and implications of treatment and nontreatment.

She talked to a psychologist she had seen in the past. I gradually understood the decision from her perspective and became convinced that it was the right decision for her. We arranged for home hospice care (although at that time Diane felt reasonably well, was active, and looked healthy), left the door open for her to change her mind, and tried to anticipate how to keep her comfortable in the time she had left.

Just as I was adjusting to her decision, she opened up another area that would stretch me profoundly. It was extraordinarily important to Diane to maintain control of herself and her own dignity during the time remaining to her. When this was no longer possible, she clearly wanted to die. As a former director of a hospice program, I know how to use pain medicines to keep patients comfortable and lessen suffering. I explained the philosophy of comfort care, which I strongly believe in. Although Diane understood and appreciated this, she had known of people lingering in what was called relative comfort, and she wanted no part of it. When the time came, she wanted to take her life in the least painful way possible.

Knowing of her desire for independence and her decision to stay in control, I thought this request made perfect sense. I acknowledged and explored this wish but also thought that it was out of the realm of currently accepted medical practice and that it was more than I could offer or promise. In our discussion, it became clear that preoccupation with her fear of a lingering death would interfere with Diane's getting the most out of the time she had left until she found a safe way to ensure her death. I feared the effects of a violent death on her family, the consequences of an ineffective suicide that would leave her lingering in precisely the state she dreaded so much, and the possibility that a family member would be forced to assist her, with all the legal and personal repercussions that would follow. She discussed this at length with her family. They believed that they should respect her choice. With this in mind, I told Diane that information was available from the Hemlock Society that might be helpful to her.

A week later she phoned me with a request for barbiturates for sleep. Since I knew that this was an essential ingredient in a Hemlock Society suicide, I asked her to come to the office to talk things over. She was more than willing to protect me by participating in a superficial conversation about her insomnia, but it was important to me to know how she planned to use the drugs and to be sure that she was not in despair or overwhelmed in a way that might color her judgment. In our discussion, it was apparent that she was having trouble sleeping, but it was also evident that the security of having enough barbiturates available to commit suicide when and if the time came would leave her secure enough to live fully and concentrate on the present. It was clear that she was not despondent and that in fact she was making deep, personal connections with her family and close friends. I made sure that she knew how to use the barbiturates for sleep, and also that she knew the amount needed to commit suicide. We agreed to meet regularly, and she promised to meet with me before taking her life, to ensure that all other avenues had been exhausted. I wrote the prescription with an uneasy feeling about the boundaries I was exploring—spiritual, legal, professional, and personal. Yet I also felt strongly that I was setting her free to get the most out of the time she had left, and to maintain dignity and control on her own terms until her death.

The next several months were very intense and important for Diane. Her son stayed home from college, and they were able to be with one another and say much that had not been said earlier. Her husband did his work at home so that he and Diane could spend more time together. She spent time with her closest friends. I had her come into the hospital for a conference with our residents, at which she illustrated in a most profound and personal way the importance of informed decision making, the right to refuse treatment, and the extraordinarily personal effects of illness and interaction with the medical system. There were emotional and physical hardships as well.

She had periods of intense sadness and anger. Several times she became very weak, but she received transfusions as an outpatient and responded with marked improvement of symptoms. She had two serious infections that responded surprisingly well to empirical courses of oral antibiotics. After three tumultuous months, there were two weeks of relative calm and well-being, and fantasies of a miracle began to surface.

Unfortunately, we had no miracle. Bone pain, weakness, fatigue, and fevers began to dominate her life. Although the hospice workers, family members, and I tried our best to minimize the suffering and promote comfort, it was clear that the end was approaching. Diane's immediate future held what she feared the most—increasing discomfort, dependence, and hard choices between pain and sedation. She called up her closest friends and asked them to come over to say goodbye, telling them that she would be leaving soon. As we had agreed, she let me know as well. When we met, it was clear that she knew what she was doing, that she was sad and frightened to be leaving, but that she would be even more terrified to stay and suffer. In our tearful goodbye, she promised a reunion in the future at her favorite spot on the edge of Lake Geneva, with dragons swimming in the sunset.

Two days later her husband called to say that Diane had died. She had said her final goodbyes to her husband and son that morning, and asked them to leave her alone for an hour. After an hour, which must have seemed an eternity, they found her on the couch, lying very still and covered by her favorite shawl. There was no sign of struggle. She seemed to be at peace. They called me for advice about how to proceed. When I arrived at their house, Diane indeed seemed peaceful. Her husband and son were quiet. We talked about what a remarkable person she had been. They seemed to have no doubts about the course she had chosen or about their cooperation, although the unfairness of her illness and the finality of her death were overwhelming to us all.

I called the medical examiner to inform him that a hospice patient had died. When asked about the cause of death, I said, "acute leukemia." He said that was fine and that we should call a funeral director. Although acute leukemia was the truth, it was not the whole story. Yet any mention of suicide would have given rise to a police investigation and probably brought the arrival of an ambulance crew for resuscitation. Diane would have become a "coroner's case," and the decision to perform an autopsy would have been made at the discretion of the medical examiner. The family or I could have been subject to criminal prosecution, and I to professional review, for our roles in support of Diane's choices. Although I truly believe that the family and I gave her the best care possible, allowing her to define her limits and directions as much as possible, I am not sure the law, society, or the medical profession would agree. So I said "acute leukemia" to protect all of us, to protect Diane from an invasion into her past and her body, and to continue to shield society from the knowledge of the degree of suffering that people often undergo in the process of dying.

Suffering can be lessened to some extent, but in no way eliminated or made benign, by the careful intervention of a competent, caring physician, given current social constraints.

Diane taught me about the range of help I can provide if I know people well and if I allow them to say what they really want. She taught me about life, death, and honesty and about taking charge and facing tragedy squarely when it strikes. She taught me that I can take small risks for people that I really know and care about. Although I did not assist in her suicide directly, I helped indirectly to make it possible, successful, and relatively painless. Although I know we have measures to help control pain and lessen suffering, to think that people do not suffer in the process of dying is an illusion. Prolonged dying can occasionally be peaceful, but more often the role of the physician and family is limited to lessening but not eliminating severe suffering.

I wonder how many families and physicians secretly help patients over the edge into death in the face of such severe suffering. I wonder how many severely ill or dying patients secretly take their lives, dying alone in despair. I wonder whether the image of Diane's final aloneness will persist in the minds of her family, or if they will remember more the intense, meaningful months they had together before she died. I wonder whether Diane struggled in that last hour, and whether the Hemlock Society's way of death by suicide is the most benign. I wonder why Diane, who gave so much to so many of us, had to be alone for the last hour of her life. I wonder whether I will see Diane again, on the shore of Lake Geneva at sunset, with dragons swimming on the horizon.

|| *Patricia Wesley, Dying Safely* ||
Issues in Law and Medicine 8(3): 467 (1993)

Doctors like to tell stories. Sometimes the story is a brief clinical vignette one physician shares with another over coffee in the nurses' station. Sometimes the story is a literary masterpiece by a renowned physician-artist such as William Carlos Williams, Anton Chekhov, or Walker Percy. And sometimes doctors tell stories designed to revolutionize the heart and soul of medical practice. Such a story, "Death and Dignity: A Case of Individualized Decision Making," appeared in the March 7, 1991, issue of The New England Journal of Medicine. Author Timothy E. Quill, M.D., a Rochester, New York, internist, tells us about his patient Diane, who developed acute leukemia, refused treatment for it, and ultimately asked for and got his aid in killing herself. This story is no simple clinical anecdote, however. While never directly saying so, Dr. Quill offers it as evidence that under certain circumstances, like those in which he and Diane found themselves, physician-assisted suicide can be clinically and ethically "right," and our laws should be changed to permit it.

. . . Dr. Quill's account warrants scrutiny for a number of reasons. It is such an engaging and pretty story! We are made privy to an engrossing medical drama, in which Diane develops acute leukemia, refuses any specific treatment for it, and eventually requests and receives her physician's aid in taking her own life in the final—*presumably* final—days of her illness. Diane is an interesting and feisty woman, and Dr. Quill is a tenderhearted doctor who actually listens to and talks to his patients!

The story also deserves our attention because of where it was published. The New England Journal of Medicine is certainly the most respected medical journal in the United States and arguably in the world. Place of publication alone influenced how this report was received, and granted to assisted suicide a medical elitist cachet it might not otherwise have had. If you want to start the euthanasia train rolling, as at least some of medicine's best and brightest do, there is no better station to leave from than the editorial offices of The New England Journal of Medicine. Given its distinguished birthplace, this account is exactly what the Society for the Right to Die would love to hand out to voters considering the decriminalization of euthanasia. Dr. Kevorkian, with his rusty van and his macabre machinery, is one thing. Dr. Quill and his dragons are quite another and deserve confrontation precisely because of the genteel but deadly power they wield.

. . . All human willing and acting is imbued with complexities and ambiguities that can baffle our best efforts to sort them out. In life's drama, it is often not so easy to decide who does what to whom, when. Who is the actor, and who the acted-upon? Can we ever be sure we have teased apart the many densely intertwined strands of human motivation? Nowhere are these questions more relevant that in the human interaction between physician and patient. How do these questions play out with Diane and her doctors?

The skeptical reader spots the first gap in this seemingly seamless story in this passage:

> Believing that delay was dangerous, our oncologist broke the news to Diane and began to make plans to insert a Hickman catheter and begin induction chemotherapy that afternoon. When I saw her shortly thereafter, she was enraged at his presumption that she would want treatment, and devastated by the finality of the diagnosis. All she wanted to do was go home and be with her family. She had no further questions about treatment and in fact had decided that she wanted none. Together we lamented her tragedy and the unfairness of life.

We are unsure here what news the oncologist broke to Diane—was it confirmation of the diagnosis, information about treatment, or both? Nonetheless, as the sequence of events is described, Diane makes her decision against treatment immediately after talking to the oncologist. By the time Dr. Quill sees her, her mind is already made up. Mutual lamentations about the unfairness of life can wait. What in heaven's name transpired between Diane and the oncologist during their meeting?

. . . Why was she *so* mad, and why no further questions in a personal situation rife with questions of all sorts? Why the rush? Were there other, less obvious reasons for Diane's rage? Justified or not, did her rage at the oncologist influence her decision about treatment? Diane might have profited from a suggestion at this point that it's risky to make a life-and-death decision when one is in a rage. Anger is no friend of clear thinking and careful judgment.

. . . We know very little about Diane, except that she was raised in an alcoholic family, had felt alone for much of her life, and had overcome her own alcoholism and depression. Could her personal background have affected how Diane reacted to her illness and her doctors? Could it have shaped how she reached her decision to forgo treatment and ultimately end her own life?

. . . Throughout Dr. Quill's report, Diane's need to be "in control" is alluded to over and over again. The wish to be responsible for oneself is an admirable trait of a mature individual; it makes "perfect sense," as Dr. Quill notes. However, at times we must surrender some control and tolerate a certain degree of dependence on others. Serious illness is such an occasion. Diane does accept some limited treatment from Dr. Quill, but her fear of losing that valued self-control and becoming dependent on others in a hospital setting is one of her reasons for refusing more aggressive therapy for her leukemia. Such reasoning may be fully compatible with Diane's adult character style, but since it may have carried such a high price tag, we can also wonder about its origins in a more distant, and possibly more traumatic, childhood past as well.

. . . Moving to the more recent past, we note that Diane had vaginal cancer as a young woman, although we are told nothing further about its etiology or treatment. Did this more recent experience echo in the conversations Diane had with herself and her doctors as she confronted a second malignancy? How was she treated then? Was she left with some disfigurement or dysfunction in a part of her body vital to her self-esteem? If her earlier treatment involved modality other than surgery, could she secretly believe that it contributed to the development of her second malignancy, or that they were linked in some other way? How might such a belief affect her treatment decisions at this point?

. . . People with depressive tendencies often feel guilty and self- recrimi-
natory and may seek punishments or limitations of various kinds. Diane was
"convinced" that she would die during treatment for her leukemia. Why?
True enough, the chances for cure are dicey, at best, but why is she "convinced"
she won't make it? Like the word *control,* the word *conviction* also haunts this
narrative. Did Diane become convinced she would die because she saw herself as
deserving of punishment for some crime, real or fantasied? Did she feel that she
did not deserve to survive a second bout with cancer? Skepticism about her
treatment refusal is bolstered by the fact that in my experience, at least, very
few patients forgo initial treatment for a *newly diagnosed,* nonterminal
malignancy.

What role might Dr. Quill have played in Diane's conviction that she was
doomed? Did his knowledge of those four patients who died painful deaths from
similar disorders make it harder for him to keep in mind those who were cured?
Was he thus less likely to probe Diane's conviction that she would perish, and did
he instead mirror it with his own conviction that it was the "right" decision for
her to refuse treatment?

. . . In medicine today, physicians are encouraged to be empathic towards
patients, ascertain and respect their values, and support their choices. There is
much good in such an emphasis, but applied in a stereotyped fashion, without
asking "Why?" "How come?" and "What makes you think that?" nothing can be
more dangerous. The model of the beneficient, paternalistic physician, making
choices in the patient's "best interest," was certainly not value-free. It had its
own costly side effect, namely, the creation of passive and infantilized patients
who end up bitterly disappointed and unable to trust any physician when
magical expectations cannot be met. However, it is frighteningly naive to assume
that when our guide to medical practice is "doing what the patient wants," we
will escape the imposition of the physician's values on the clinical encounter.
Personal values can be sequestered in the question not asked, or the gentle
challenge not posed, when both should have been.

. . . On one level, Diane's request for aid in killing herself does make some
sense. Dr. Quill describes her as someone who wants to call the shots for many
reasons, including the troubling one that she felt alone for much of her life;
perhaps someone like this sees little option but to be in lonely control at the end
as well. Hearing of Diane's suicidal intentions, the skeptic might remember that
advice I told you about earlier: Why is *this* patient saying *this* to *me* at *this* time: Is
she asking a question in the guise of making a statement? Is a trial balloon being
launched, some testing being done? Is Diane asking her doctor: When I become
more ill, more dependent, and when I no longer have that control I prize so
much—and that I suspect *you* prize so much—will you see me as a person of
value? What if I changed my mind and pursued treatment, with the need for
hospital confinement and care by others, would you still see me as worthwhile
even when I might seem worthless to myself?

. . . It is not a neutral act to refer a patient contemplating suicide to the
Hemlock Society. It is putting a loaded gun into the hands of a desperate
person. . . . Remember that Diane was in the midst of a profound crisis. In
such circumstances any suggestion by the physician carries tremendous impact,
often far more than the physician intends. When human beings are in such
straits, they will grasp at anything that offers a way out. This anxious seeking
for quick resolution, while understandable, must be mitigated and resisted by

the physician. At the very least, doctors must be careful about any suggestions they might make, especially when their side effect is death. Would the endgame have been different if Dr. Quill had referred Diane to a self-help support group of cancer patients instead of the Hemlock Society?

. . . Throughout his story, and like many another skilled penman before him, Dr. Quill wants us to believe that he effaced himself as an actor, both in the story he lived and in the story he tells us. Diane is presented as someone who determined her own tragic fate, free of the imprisonment of medical paternalism and what Derek Humphry might call outmoded ideas about the sanctity of life. Closely observed, Dr. Quill's text itself reveals that he was a powerful actor in his story. With his help, Diane dies a politically correct death, accompanied to her grave by all the rhetoric of patient autonomy and medical egalitarianism that litters our intellectual landscape today, and that distracts us from the difficult task of knowing the depths of human willing and acting and of trying to preserve life while we do.

NOTES AND QUESTIONS

1. *Diane's "rational" decision.*   Why did Diane's decision to terminate her life make "perfect sense" to Dr. Quill? How can a doctor evaluate such a decision? Is it appropriate to do so?

2. *Critique of Diane's story.*   What are Dr. Patricia Wesley's primary criticisms of Dr. Quill's story? Can her critique be summarized as saying that autonomy is given too much due and the preservation of life too little, or is it more complicated than that? What concerns does she have that Diane's decision was not completely autonomous, or at least not autonomous in a way that should garner Quill's (and society's) complete deference?

3. *The role of suffering in physician-assisted suicide.*   Dr. Quill is also the author of Care of the Hopelessly Ill: Proposed Clinical Criteria for Physician-Assisted Suicide, 327 New Eng. J. Med. 1380 (1992), in which he directly advocated the legalization of physician prescriptions to hasten death and proposed criteria for its practice. Quill became one of the physician-plaintiffs in the case known as Vacco v. Quill, in which the Supreme Court rejected an equal protection challenge to state bans against physician-assisted suicide. The physician-plaintiffs asserted in that case that "although it would be consistent with the standards of their medical practices to prescribe lethal medication for mentally competent, terminally ill patients who are suffering great pain and desire a doctor's help in taking their own lives, they are deterred from doing so by New York's assisted-suicide ban." Vacco v. Quill, 521 U.S. 793, 797 (1997). Would Diane's situation have fit under this criteria; was she "suffering great pain" when Dr. Quill prescribed the barbiturates? When she used them? Should suffering be a criteria for delineating when physician aid in hastening death might be permitted? If so, should such suffering include mental suffering involving fear of what the future might bring (future physical pain, for example, or loss of "dignity")?

Advocates for a constitutional right to physician-assisted suicide, or merely a legalization of the practice, have largely framed the issue in terms of dignity—insisting that individuals have a right to die with dignity. When you read the Ninth Circuit and Supreme Court opinions of the *Glucksberg* case infra, you'll find that plaintiffs, in arguing for recognition of a constitutional right to physician-assisted suicide, relied heavily on the language in the earlier Supreme Court abortion case of Planned Parenthood v. Casey. *Casey*'s plurality opinion contained language describing the kinds of personal decisions that the Constitution protects as those choices that are "central to personal dignity and autonomy." Autonomy in this context would appear to be fairly clearly about self-determination, but what do advocates of physician-assisted suicide and sympathetic courts mean when they talk about dignity? Here is one view.

> ## Lois Shepherd, Dignity and Autonomy after Washington v. Glucksberg
> ### 7 Cornell J.L. & Pub. Pol'y 431 (1998)

Those who advocate recognition of a constitutional right to physician-assisted suicide can and did appropriate the evocative "dignity and autonomy" language of *Casey*. Assisted suicide advocates, however, use a quite different and more powerful meaning of dignity. . . .

This dignity . . . is not the dignity of philosophers. It is the meaning of dignity that we find in everyday conversation: "the quality of being worthy or honourable; worthiness, worth, nobleness, excellence." When we say that someone acts in a *dignified* manner, we are saying something about her behavior, not merely acknowledging the actor's ability to reflect upon her course of action and to act according to her choice (autonomy). Thus, we might consider an individual who meets an unfortunate fate with her head held high as acting with great dignity; an individual who babbles and cries is undignified. We want our public officials to act with dignity; we call some of them "dignitaries." Our heroes act with dignity. It is not about winning; losers might lose with dignity. It is about deportment. It is about how others perceive us.

The right-to-die movement has appealed to this content-based definition of dignity for a long time. Advocates insist that individuals have the inherent right to die with dignity. The implicit idea is that health care providers too often treat dying patients with aggressive measures that do nothing more than prolong the dying process. By prolonging the dying process, doctors extend the period of time over which the patient suffers from a loss of dignity, suffers from impaired reason or memory, loses control over bodily functions, and becomes increasingly dependent upon others for the most basic needs. Doctors might make the patient's loss of dignity greater by administering heavily sedating medications to ease pain. Pain, it seems, pales in comparison to the burden of indignity. It is not specifically and predominantly pain that we are supposed to want to avoid in our final days, although pain is not discounted, but we are to avoid being helpless, incontinent, incoherent, dependent, drooling, a burden to others, and of poor general deportment. The concept of dignity in the right-to-die movement is laden with strong normative content. It is powerfully attractive. To the extent that dignity embodies a notion of what is worthy, noble, and honorable, almost no one would choose a life, or death, describable by terms meaning the opposite of dignity.

The death with dignity refrain embodies two notions: one, that an individual must have the option to have a dignified *method of death,* and two, that an individual must not *be forced to continue living* without dignity. Both of these concerns influenced the Ninth Circuit's decision to invalidate Washington's ban on physician-assisted suicide. With respect to the first concern, the method of death, the Court discussed evidence offered at trial of people who wished to "die with dignity" having to resort to "gruesome alternatives" because physician assistance was unavailable. One man, "deprived of the chance to die in a dignified manner with his loved ones by his side," shot himself to death, leaving his relatives to clean his "splattered brains off the basement walls." Another patient wished for "the dignity of dying in her own bed, surrounded by the things she loved." Dying in a protracted, drug-induced stupor from medication prescribed to ease intolerable pain, or dying by self-induced suffocation, or jumping off of a bridge are examples of the undignified deaths chosen by desperate patients "deprived of physician assistance."

Regarding the second notion of dignity in the "death with dignity" context, that of dignity in living, the Ninth Circuit focused on the lack of dignity experienced by many individuals who are terminally ill. The Court explicitly recognized that the failing quality of life of the individual takes away his dignity:

> A competent terminally ill adult, having lived nearly the full measure of his life, has a strong liberty interest in choosing a dignified and humane death rather than being reduced at the end of his existence to a childlike state of helplessness, diapered, sedated, incontinent. How a person dies not only determines the nature of the final period of his existence, but in many cases, the enduring memories held by those who love him.

To illustrate the point, the Court related the testimony of one woman who explained how her father, "to whom dignity was very important, lay dying diapered, moaning in pain, begging to die." The Court stated that for such people, "the decision to commit suicide is not senseless, and death does not come too early."

A Michigan state court, in another decision that was ultimately reversed, went even further in its willingness to recognize content-based meaning in the term "dignity" and even in the term "autonomy." The Michigan court in Michigan v. Kevorkian* held that criminalizing physician-assisted suicide was unconstitutional because it violated a person's right to commit "rational" suicide. The opinion noted that "many, if not most" physicians (like the defendant) "accept the fact that under specifically defined conditions the alternative to life serves the best interest of the patient, the surviving family, and society," and that these physicians accept this fact based on "contemporary attitudes about *personal dignity and autonomy,* the quality of life, happiness, and the meaning of life." Let's overlook the *others* referred to in the court's statement—"the surviving family, and society"—because it is certainly far from clear how their best interests should come into play in defining the liberty interests of the individual. That concern aside, the court's statement in *Kevorkian* indicates that physicians accept that the best interests of the patient may be the "alternative to life" (i.e., death),

---

* [No. 93-11482, WL 603212 (Mich. Cir. Ct., Dec. 13, 1993) *rev'd* 527 N.W. 2d 714 (Mich. 1994)—Eds.]

because the patient no longer enjoys dignity and autonomy in life. In this context, the terms dignity and autonomy do not refer to the freedom to make choices (e.g., whether to live or to hasten death). Rather, the terms refer to contemporary attitudes of how one should live an independent life.

Using this line of reasoning, it is possible, indeed appropriate, to judge decisions about whether to choose life or death based upon whether those decisions promote normatively based notions of autonomy as well as dignity. Identifying "choices central to personal dignity and autonomy," then, does not mean that we leave those choices to the individual because we respect her ability and the importance to her self-determination to make them. Instead, we protect choices that, properly made, promote dignity (proper conduct and appearance) and autonomy (independent living). If this is the theoretical underpinning to finding a liberty interest in committing rational suicide, then that liberty interest would be in having *certain* avenues open (i.e., rational, physician-assisted suicide) rather than in having *all* avenues open (i.e., life without dignity). This is about outcomes, not process. The choices made by an individual would be subject to our scrutiny and approval or disapproval as conforming to an expectation about dignified behavior.

Autonomy is not typically so mangled in right-to-die advocacy, although this is standard fare for dignity. The confusion is not limited to lower courts and liberal circuits. Conflicting views of the term dignity are also apparent (and similarly unacknowledged) in Cruzan v. Missouri Department of Health, the other Supreme Court case (besides *Casey*) that the Ninth Circuit relied upon to determine that there was a constitutionally protected right to die. *Cruzan,* the Supreme Court later insisted in *Glucksberg,* was about unwanted medical treatment and the common law of battery, not about a right to die; and the right to withdraw unwanted medical treatment that was assumed (not announced) by the Court in *Cruzan* "was not simply deduced from abstract concepts of personal autonomy" (or dignity, the Court might have added). The Supreme Court Justices, however, were interested in dignity and autonomy in *Cruzan,* even though they did not then, and still have not, shown an awareness of the different ways in which the term dignity is used.

In her concurrence, Justice O'Connor insisted that a competent individual has a right to refuse unwanted artificial feeding and hydration just as she might refuse other forms of forced medical treatment. "Requiring a competent adult to endure such procedures against her will," O'Connor wrote, "burdens the patient's liberty, dignity, and freedom to determine the course of her own treatment." By linking dignity with freedom in decision-making and presupposing that it requires competency, O'Connor uses the understanding of dignity that we find in the abortion cases, dignity as autonomy.

A few pages later, Justice Brennan's dissent used the more restrictive, content-laden definition of dignity. Brennan argued that Nancy Cruzan deserved to "die with dignity." (Of course, what Brennan really meant was that Nancy Cruzan should not have to live without dignity; she was not terminally ill, but in a persistent vegetative state that could have continued for years.) While on the one hand Brennan recognized that decisions about life-prolonging medical procedures are personal, he was clearly not referring to dignity merely in the sense of respecting choices. He noted that "[f]or many, the thought of an ignoble end, steeped in decay, is abhorrent. A quiet, proud death, bodily integrity intact, is a matter of extreme consequence."

It is no wonder, then, with this kind of imprecision, that advocates for a "proud death" have been able to tap into the rich language of abortion decisions referring to choices central to personal dignity and autonomy, even though choice-making in and of itself is not the act that defines dignity for such advocates in the right-to-die context. Rather, it is the actual choice made and the effect that choice will have on the individual that is central to dignity in the death with dignity movement. The assisted suicide advocates do not ignore the ability to choose—because choosing is still central to autonomy, and both dignity and autonomy are appealed to—but dignity and autonomy are not embracing the same value, and may in fact be at odds with one another.

NOTES AND QUESTIONS

1. *The meaning of "dignity."* Lois Shepherd's article expresses concern about the use of the term *dignity* in advocacy for assisted suicide and in the "death with dignity" movement in general. What does dignity mean in this context, and why does she argue that respecting dignity, as defined by the advocates for assisted suicide, is a very different matter than respecting autonomy? Why does this matter?

2. Legal Approaches

In 1997, the Supreme Court of the United States reversed the decisions of two federal courts of appeal that had declared state laws prohibiting assisted suicide unconstitutional as applied to terminally ill patients who wished to hasten their own deaths with medication prescribed by their physicians. The path that the Ninth Circuit case of Compassion in Dying v. Washington took to the Supreme Court (where it became known as Washington v. Glucksberg) illustrates the controversial, close, and deeply divided nature of this debate. In 1994, several physicians practicing in the State of Washington, along with three gravely ill pseudonymous patients, and a nonprofit organization that counsels people considering physician-assisted suicide brought suit in the U.S. District Court seeking to have Washington's assisted suicide statute declared unconstitutional. The District Court did so, but was later reversed by a panel of the Court of Appeals for the Ninth Circuit. The Ninth Circuit reheard the case en banc, reversed the panel's decision (in the opinion reprinted below) and affirmed the District Court. The Supreme Court then reversed the en banc decision. The Supreme Court decision was unanimous, but five Justices wrote separate concurring opinions. Nineteen amicus curiae briefs were filed in the case.

While Washington v. Glucksberg addressed the constitutional challenge to Washington's assisted suicide ban under the Due Process Clause of the Fourteenth Amendment, the related case of Vacco v. Quill, 521 U.S. 793 (1997), coming to the Supreme Court from the Second Circuit Court of Appeals, considered an equal protection challenge to New York's assisted suicide ban. The Court of Appeals held that New York law did not treat equally people in the final stages of terminal illness who wished to hasten their deaths because those who were on life-support systems were allowed to hasten their deaths through removal of those systems, but those who were similarly situated, but not attached to life-sustaining equipment, were not allowed to hasten their deaths by lethal dosages of medication. This unequal treatment, according to the Court of Appeals, was not rationally related to any legitimate state interest. 80 F.3d 716 (1996). The Supreme Court disagreed, concluding that the distinction between assisting suicide and withdrawing life-sustaining treatment is rational. Because of limitations of space, only a brief excerpt from Vacco v. Quill is included following the *Glucksberg* case. Excerpts from the opinions of both the Court of Appeals and the Supreme Court in the *Glucksberg* case are included because they represent such different viewpoints in the highly volatile debate over physician-assisted suicide in the United States. As you read the opinions, assess the merits of the two opinions with respect to the following issues:

1. The characterization of the liberty interest at stake;
2. The proper analysis under the Due Process Clause with respect to assessing the propriety of state intrusion on the claimed right: fundamental rights analysis? Balancing of liberty interests against state interests? Or rational relationship test?;
3. The weight of history;
4. The precedential value of the prior Supreme Court cases of *Casey* (abortion rights) and *Cruzan* (withdrawal of life-sustaining treatment);
5. The strength of the state's interests.

Compassion in Dying v. State of Washington
79 F.3d 790 (9th Cir. 1996)

Opinion by Circuit Judge REINHARDT.

I.

. . . Today, we are required to decide whether a person who is terminally ill has a constitutionally-protected liberty interest in hastening what might otherwise be a protracted, undignified, and extremely painful death. If such an interest exists, we must next decide whether or not the state of Washington may constitutionally restrict its exercise by banning a form of medical assistance that is frequently requested by terminally ill people who wish to die. We first conclude that there is a constitutionally-protected liberty interest in determining the time and manner of one's own death, an interest that must be weighed against the state's legitimate and countervailing interests, especially those that relate to the preservation of human life. After balancing the competing interests, we conclude by answering the narrow question before us: We hold that insofar as the Washington statute prohibits physicians from prescribing life-ending medication for use by terminally ill, competent adults who wish to hasten their own deaths, it violates the Due Process Clause of the Fourteenth Amendment.

II. PRELIMINARY MATTERS AND HISTORY OF THE CASE

The plaintiffs are four physicians who treat terminally ill patients, three terminally ill patients, and a Washington non-profit organization called Compassion In Dying. The four physicians . . . are respected doctors whose expertise is recognized by the state. All declare that they periodically treat terminally ill, competent adults who wish to hasten their deaths with help from their physicians. The doctors state that in their professional judgment they should provide that help but are deterred from doing so by a Washington statute that makes it a felony to knowingly aid another person to commit suicide. . . .

A. Defining the Liberty Interest and Other Relevant Terms

While some people refer to the liberty interest implicated in right-to-die cases as a liberty interest in committing suicide, we do not describe it that way. We use the broader and more accurate terms, "the right to die," "determining the time and manner of one's death," and "hastening one's death" for an important reason. The liberty interest we examine encompasses a whole range of acts that are generally not considered to constitute "suicide." Included within the liberty interest we examine is, for example, the act of refusing or terminating unwanted medical treatment. As we discuss later, . . . a competent adult has a liberty interest in refusing to be connected to a respirator or in being disconnected from one, even if he is terminally ill and cannot live without mechanical assistance. The law does not classify the death of a patient that results from the granting of his wish to decline or discontinue treatment as "suicide." Nor does the law label the acts of those who help the patient carry out that wish, whether by physically disconnecting the respirator or by removing an intravenous tube, as assistance in suicide. Accordingly, we believe that the broader terms—"the right to die," "controlling the time and manner of one's death," and "hastening one's death"—more accurately describe the liberty interest at issue here. Moreover, as we discuss later, we have serious doubts that the terms "suicide" and "assisted suicide" are appropriate legal descriptions of the specific conduct at issue here.

[In section B of the opinion, the Court of Appeals emphasizes that although history is important in assessing whether a particular liberty interest exists, historical analysis is insufficient by itself to decide the matter. In section C, the court surveys historical attitudes toward suicide, beginning with ancient times, and concludes that the history is checkered and includes some acceptance and even praise of certain suicides. It concludes section C by stating that no state currently has a statute prohibiting suicide or attempted suicide although a majority of states do have statutes against assisting suicide–EDS.]

D. Current Societal Attitudes

Clearly the absence of a criminal sanction alone does not show societal approbation of a practice. Nor is there any evidence that Americans approve of suicide in general. In recent years, however, there has been increasingly widespread support for allowing the terminally ill to hasten their deaths and avoid painful, undignified, and inhumane endings to their lives. Most Americans simply do not appear to view such acts as constituting suicide, and there is much support in reason for that conclusion.

Polls have repeatedly shown that a large majority of Americans—sometimes nearing 90%—fully endorse recent legal changes granting terminally ill patients, and sometimes their families, the prerogative to accelerate their death by refusing or terminating treatment. Other polls indicate that a majority of Americans favor doctor-assisted suicide for the terminally ill. In April, 1990, the Roper Report found that 64% of Americans believed that the terminally ill should have the right to request and receive physician aid-in-dying. Another national poll, conducted in October 1991, shows that "nearly two out of three Americans favor doctor-assisted suicide and euthanasia for terminally ill patients who request it." A 1994 Harris poll found 73% of Americans favor legalizing physician-assisted suicide. Three states have held referenda on proposals to allow physicians to help terminally ill, competent adults commit suicide with somewhat mixed results. In Oregon, voters approved the carefully-crafted referendum by a margin of 51 to 49 percent in November of 1994. In Washington and California where the measures contained far fewer practical safeguards, they narrowly failed to pass, each drawing 46 percent of the vote. As such referenda indicate, there is unquestionably growing popular support for permitting doctors to provide assistance to terminally ill patients who wish to hasten their deaths.

. . . Our attitudes toward suicide of the type at issue in this case are better understood in light of our unwritten history and of technological developments. Running beneath the official history of legal condemnation of physician-assisted suicide is a strong undercurrent of a time-honored but hidden practice of physicians helping terminally ill patients to hasten their deaths. According to a survey by the American Society of Internal Medicine, one doctor in five said he had assisted in a patient's suicide. Accounts of doctors who have helped their patients end their lives have appeared both in professional journals and in the daily press.

The debate over whether terminally ill patients should have a right to reject medical treatment or to receive aid from their physicians in hastening their deaths has taken on a new prominence as a result of a number of developments. Two hundred years ago when America was founded and more than one hundred years ago when the Fourteenth Amendment was adopted, Americans died from a slew of illness and infirmities that killed their victims quickly but today are almost never fatal in this nation—scarlet fever, cholera, measles, diarrhea, influenza, pneumonia, gastritis, to name a few. Other diseases that have not been conquered can now often be controlled for years, if not decades—diseases such as diabetes, muscular dystrophy, Parkinson's disease, cardiovascular disease, and certain types of cancer. As a result, Americans are living longer, and when they finally succumb to illness, lingering longer, either in great pain or in a stuporous, semi-comatose condition that results from the infusion of vast amounts of pain killing medications. Despite the marvels of technology, Americans frequently die with less dignity than they did in the days when ravaging diseases typically ended their lives quickly. AIDS, which often subjects its victims to a horrifying and drawn-out demise, has also contributed to the growing number of terminally ill patients who die protracted and painful deaths.

One result has been a growing movement to restore humanity and dignity to the process by which Americans die. The now recognized right to refuse or terminate treatment and the emergent right to receive medical assistance in hastening one's death are inevitable consequences of changes in the causes of death, advances in medical science, and the development of new technologies. Both the need and the capability to assist individuals to end their lives in peace and dignity have increased exponentially.

E.   Prior Court Decisions

Next we examine previous Court decisions that delineate the boundaries of substantive due process. We believe that a careful examination of these decisions demonstrates that there is a strong liberty interest in determining how and when one's life shall end, and that an explicit recognition of that interest follows naturally, indeed inevitably, from their reasoning.

The essence of the substantive component of the Due Process Clause is to limit the ability of the state to intrude into the most important matters of our lives, at least without substantial justification. In a long line of cases, the Court has carved out certain key moments and decisions in individuals' lives and placed them beyond the general prohibitory authority of the state.

. . . A common thread running through these cases is that they involve decisions that are highly personal and intimate, as well as of great importance to the individual. Certainly, few decisions are more personal, intimate or important than the decision to end one's life, especially when the reason for doing so is to avoid excessive and protracted pain.

. . . [W]e believe that two relatively recent decisions of the Court, Planned Parenthood v. Casey, 505 U.S. 833 (1992) and Cruzan v. Director, Missouri Dept. of Health, 497 U.S. 261 (1990), are fully persuasive, and leave little doubt as to the proper result.

F.   Liberty Interest under Casey

In *Casey*, the Court surveyed its prior decisions affording "constitutional protection to personal decisions relating to marriage, procreation, contraception, family relationships, child rearing, and education" and then said:

> These matters, involving the most intimate and personal choices a person may make in a lifetime, choices central to personal dignity and autonomy, are central to the liberty protected by the Fourteenth Amendment. At the heart of liberty is the right to define one's own concept of existence, of meaning, of the universe, and of the mystery of human life. Beliefs about these matters could not define the attributes of personhood were they formed under compulsion of the State.

The district judge in this case found the Court's reasoning in *Casey* "highly instructive" and "almost prescriptive" for determining "what liberty interest may inhere in a terminally ill person's choice to commit suicide." We agree.

Like the decision of whether or not to have an abortion, the decision how and when to die is one of "the most intimate and personal choices a person may make in a lifetime," a choice "central to personal dignity and autonomy." A competent terminally ill adult, having lived nearly the full measure of his life, has a strong liberty interest in choosing a dignified and humane death rather than being reduced at the end of his existence to a childlike state of helplessness, diapered, sedated, incontinent. How a person dies not only determines the nature of the final period of his existence, but in many cases, the enduring memories held by those who love him.

Prohibiting a terminally ill patient from hastening his death may have an even more profound impact on that person's life than forcing a woman to carry a pregnancy to term. The case of an AIDS patient treated by Dr. Peter Shalit, one of the physician-plaintiffs in this case, provides a compelling illustration. In his declaration, Dr. Shalit described his patient's death this way:

> One patient of mine, whom I will call Smith, a fictitious name, lingered in the hospital for weeks, his lower body so swollen from oozing Kaposi's lesions that he could not walk, his genitals so swollen that he required a catheter to drain his bladder, his fingers gangrenous from clotted arteries. Patient Smith's friends stopped visiting him because it gave them nightmares. Patient Smith's agonies could not be relieved by medication or by the excellent nursing care he received. Patient Smith begged for assistance in hastening his death. As his treating doctor, it was my professional opinion that patient Smith was mentally competent to make a choice with respect to shortening his period of suffering before inevitable death. I felt that I should accommodate his request. However, because of the statute, I was unable to assist him and he died after having been tortured for weeks by the end-phase of his disease.

For such patients, wracked by pain and deprived of all pleasure, a state-enforced prohibition on hastening their deaths condemns them to unrelieved misery or torture. Surely, a person's decision whether to endure or avoid such an existence constitutes one of the most, if not the most, "intimate and personal choices a person may make in a life-time," a choice that is "central to personal dignity and autonomy." *Casey,* 505 U.S. at 851. Surely such a decision implicates a most vital liberty interest.

G.   Liberty Interest under Cruzan

In *Cruzan,* the Court considered whether or not there is a constitutionally-protected, due process liberty interest in terminating unwanted medical treatment. The Court said that an affirmative answer followed almost inevitably from its prior decisions holding that patients have a liberty interest in refusing to submit to specific medical procedures. . . . Writing for a majority that included Justices O'Connor and Scalia, Chief Justice Rehnquist said that those cases helped answer the first critical question at issue in *Cruzan,* stating: "The principle that a competent person has a constitutionally protected liberty interest in refusing unwanted medical treatment may be *inferred* from our prior decisions." *Cruzan,* 497 U.S. at 278, 110 S. Ct. at 2851 (emphasis added).

. . . *Cruzan* stands for the proposition that there is a due process liberty interest in rejecting unwanted medical treatment, including the provision of food and water by artificial means. Moreover, the Court majority clearly recognized that granting the request to remove the tubes through which Cruzan received artificial nutrition and hydration would lead inexorably to her death. Accordingly, we conclude that *Cruzan,* by recognizing a liberty interest that includes the refusal of artificial provision of life-sustaining food and water, necessarily recognizes a liberty interest in hastening one's own death.

V.   RELEVANT FACTORS AND INTERESTS

To determine whether a state action that impairs a liberty interest violates an individual's substantive due process rights we must identify the factors relevant to the case at hand, assess the state's interests and the individual's liberty interest in light of those factors, and then weigh and balance the competing interests. The relevant factors generally include: 1) the importance of the various state interests, both in general and in the factual context of the case; 2) the manner in which those interests are furthered by the state law or regulation; 3) the importance of the liberty interest, both in itself and in the context in which it is being exercised; 4) the extent to which that interest is burdened by the challenged state action; and, 5) the consequences of upholding or overturning the statute or regulation.

A.   *The State's Interests*

We analyze the factors in turn, and begin by considering the first: the importance of the state's interests.

[The court discussed each of the following six interests, as summarized herein]:

1. The State's Interest in Preserving Life—The strength of this interest is dependent on the medical condition and wishes of the person whose life is at stake; as the state of Washington and other states have recognized by adopting statutes permitting patients by advance directive or through surrogate decision making to direct the withholding or withdrawal of life-sustaining treatment in instances of a terminal condition or permanent unconsciousness, the state's interest in preserving life are "dramatically diminished" in such circumstances.

2. The State's Interest in Preventing Suicide—This was the primary justification relied upon by the state during the course of litigation but, like the state's interest in preserving life, is diminished in the case of terminally ill, competent adults who wish to die. "In the case of a terminally ill adult who ends his life in the final stages of an incurable and painful degenerative disease, in order to avoid debilitating pain and a humiliating death, the decision to commit suicide is not senseless, and death does not come too early. Unlike 'the depressed twenty-one year old, the romantically devastated twenty-eight year old, the alcoholic forty-year-old,' or many others who may be inclined to commit suicide, a terminally ill competent adult cannot be cured. While some people who contemplate suicide can be restored to a state of physical and mental well-being, terminally ill adults who wish to die can only be maintained in a debilitated and deteriorating state, unable to enjoy the presence of family or friends. Not only is the state's interest in preventing such individuals from hastening their deaths of comparatively little weight, but its insistence on frustrating their wishes seems cruel indeed."

In addition, the court compares physician-assisted suicide to the termination of life-sustaining treatment and other medical practices at the end of life, which the state does not seek to prevent.

Moreover, uncertainty about how long a terminally ill patient actually has to live should not prevent recognition of the right asserted because safeguards could be put in place to prevent error and if an error should occur, "it is likely to benefit the individual by permitting a victim of unmanageable pain and suffering to end his life peacefully and with dignity at the time he deems most desirable."

3. The State's Interest in Avoiding the Involvement of Third Parties and in Precluding the Use of Arbitrary, Unfair, or Undue Influence—While legitimate, these concerns are diminished when the third party providing assistance is a physician, or operating under a physician's direction and supervision and the recipient is a terminally ill patient. Moreover, the concern that the poor and minorities will be exploited

> simply recycles one of the more disingenuous and fallacious arguments raised in opposition to the legalization of abortion. It is equally meretricious here. In fact, as with abortion, there is far more concern that the poor and the minorities, who have historically received the least adequate health care, will not be afforded a fair opportunity to obtain the medical assistance to which they are entitled—the assistance that would allow them to end their lives with a measure of dignity. The argument that disadvantaged persons would receive *more* medical services than the remainder of the population in one and in only one, area—assisted suicide—is ludicrous on its face. So, too, is the argument that the poor and the minorities will rush to volunteer for physician-assisted suicide because of their inability to secure adequate medical treatment.

The court offers a similar analysis with regard to persons with disabilities, adding, "Organizations representing the physically impaired are sufficiently active politically and sufficiently vigilant that they would soon put a halt to any effort to employ assisted suicide in a manner that affected their clients unfairly."

4. The State's Interest in Protecting Family Members and Loved Ones—The state's interest in safeguarding the interests of innocent third parties such as minor children and other dependent family members is almost negligible when the patient is terminally ill and his death is imminent and inevitable.

5. The State's Interest in Protecting the Integrity of the Medical Profession—This interest rests upon a misconception of what doctors have been doing for a considerable time and on the proper function of a physician. Doctors have for decades and probably centuries been discreetly helping terminally ill patients hasten their deaths; now they openly take actions that result in the deaths of their patients through the termination of life-sustaining medical treatment. Many in the profession openly support physician-assisted suicide. While the AMA opposes legalization at this time, it also opposed abortion twenty years ago as in violation of the Hippocratic Oath. [See Chapter 1 for the Hippocratic Oath.–Eds.] As *Roe* shows, a literalist reading of the Hippocratic Oath does not represent the best or final word on medical or legal controversies today. Were we to adhere to the rigid language of the oath, not only would doctors be barred from performing abortions or helping terminally ill patients hasten their deaths, but according to a once-accepted interpretation, they would also be prohibited from performing any type of surgery at all.

6. The State's Interest in Avoiding Adverse Consequences That Might Ensue If the Statutory Provision at Issue Is Declared Unconstitutional— Under this "slippery slope" argument, opponents of assisted suicide argue that a "Pandora's Box" will be opened and before long courts will sanction putting people to death because they are deemed to pose an unjustifiable burden on society. Similar predictions were asserted with respect to recognition of the abortion right—that abortion would substitute for other forms of birth control or become a means of racial genocide—that neither proved true nor stopped the Supreme Court from recognizing the right.

[In the remainder of the opinion, the Court concluded that because the liberty interest in choosing the time and manner of death is at a peak in the case of the terminally ill, while the state interests are generally at a low point in such case, the balancing test means that a total ban on assisted suicide for the terminally ill is unconstitutional, whereas regulation would be permissible.–Eds.]

|| *Washington v. Glucksberg* ||
|| 521 U.S. 702 (1997) ||

Chief Justice REHNQUIST delivered the opinion of the Court.

We begin, as we do in all due process cases, by examining our Nation's history, legal traditions, and practices. In almost every State—indeed, in almost every western democracy—it is a crime to assist a suicide. The States' assisted-suicide bans are not innovations. Rather, they are longstanding expressions of the States' commitment to the protection and preservation of all human life. Indeed, opposition to and condemnation of suicide—and, therefore, of assisting suicide—are consistent and enduring themes of our philosophical, legal, and cultural heritages.

More specifically, for over 700 years, the Anglo-American common-law tradition has punished or otherwise disapproved of both suicide and assisting suicide. [The Court then discusses the English common law prohibition against suicide, which the American colonies adopted, although over time the colonies abolished the harsh penalties of forfeiture of property and ignominious burial.] . . . [T]he movement away from the common law's harsh sanctions did not represent an acceptance of suicide; rather, . . . this change reflected the growing consensus that it was unfair to punish the suicide's family for his wrongdoing. . . .

That suicide remained a grievous, though nonfelonious, wrong is confirmed by the fact that colonial and early state legislatures and courts did not retreat from prohibiting assisting suicide. . . . And the prohibitions against assisting suicide never contained exceptions for those who were near death. Rather, "[t]he life of those to whom life ha[d] become a burden—of those who [were] hopelessly diseased or fatally wounded—nay, even the lives of criminals condemned to death, [were] under the protection of the law, equally as the lives of those who [were] in the full tide of life's enjoyment, and anxious to continue to live." Blackburn v. State, 23 Ohio St. 146, 163 (1872).

The earliest American statute explicitly to outlaw assisting suicide was enacted in New York in 1828, and many of the new States and Territories followed New York's example. . . . By the time the Fourteenth Amendment was ratified, it was a crime in most States to assist a suicide. . . . In this century, the Model Penal Code also prohibited "aiding" suicide, prompting many States to enact or revise their assisted-suicide bans. . . .

Though deeply rooted, the States' assisted-suicide bans have in recent years been reexamined and, generally, reaffirmed. Because of advances in medicine and technology, Americans today are increasingly likely to die in institutions, from chronic illnesses. Public concern and democratic action are therefore sharply focused on how best to protect dignity and independence at the end of life, with the result that there have been many significant changes in state laws and in the attitudes these laws reflect. Many States, for example, now permit "living wills," surrogate health-care decisionmaking, and the withdrawal or refusal of life-sustaining medical treatment. At the same time, however, voters and legislators continue for the most part to reaffirm their States' prohibitions on assisting suicide.

The Washington statute at issue in this case, Wash. Rev. Code §9A.36.060 (1994), was enacted in 1975 as part of a revision of that State's criminal code. Four years later, Washington passed its Natural Death Act, which specifically stated that the "withholding or withdrawal of life-sustaining treatment . . . shall not, for any purpose, constitute a suicide" and that "[n]othing in this chapter shall be construed to condone, authorize, or approve mercy killing. . . ." In 1991, Washington voters rejected a ballot initiative which, had it passed, would have permitted a form of physician-assisted suicide. Washington then added a provision to the Natural Death Act expressly excluding physician-assisted suicide.

California voters rejected an assisted-suicide initiative similar to Washington's in 1993. On the other hand, in 1994, voters in Oregon enacted, also through ballot initiative, that State's "Death With Dignity Act," which legalized physician-assisted suicide for competent, terminally ill adults. Since the Oregon vote, many proposals to legalize assisted-suicide have been and continue to be introduced in the States' legislatures, but none has been enacted. And just last year, Iowa and Rhode Island joined the overwhelming majority of States explicitly prohibiting assisted suicide. Also, on April 30, 1997, President Clinton signed the Federal Assisted Suicide Funding Restriction Act of 1997, which prohibits the use of federal funds in support of physician-assisted suicide.[16]

II

. . . Our established method of substantive-due-process analysis has two primary features: First, we have regularly observed that the Due Process Clause specially protects those fundamental rights and liberties which are, objectively, "deeply rooted in this Nation's history and tradition," id., at 503 (plurality opinion); Snyder v. Massachusetts, 291 U.S. 97, 105 (1934) ("so rooted in the traditions and conscience of our people as to be ranked as fundamental"), and

---

16. [The Court noted that other countries were also debating the issue: Canada, Great Britain, and New Zealand had each recently reaffirmed their prohibition against assisted suicide; the Northern Territory of Australia had legalized assisted suicide and voluntary euthanasia in 1995, but the Australian Senate voted to overturn the Northern Territory's law; and Colombia's Constitutional Court had recently legalized voluntary euthanasia for terminally ill people.–Eds.]

"implicit in the concept of ordered liberty," such that "neither liberty nor justice would exist if they were sacrificed," Palko v. Connecticut, 302 U.S. 319, 325, 326 (1937). Second, we have required in substantive-due-process cases a "careful description" of the asserted fundamental liberty interest. . . .

Turning to the claim at issue here, the Court of Appeals stated that "[p]roperly analyzed, the first issue to be resolved is whether there is a liberty interest in determining the time and manner of one's death," or, in other words, "[i]s there a right to die?" Similarly, respondents assert a "liberty to choose how to die" and a right to "control of one's final days," and describe the asserted liberty as "the right to choose a humane, dignified death," and "the liberty to shape death," As noted above, we have a tradition of carefully formulating the interest at stake in substantive-due-process cases. For example, although *Cruzan* is often described as a "right to die" case, we were, in fact, more precise: We assumed that the Constitution granted competent persons a "constitutionally protected right to refuse lifesaving hydration and nutrition." *Cruzan*, 497 U.S., at 279. The Washington statute at issue in this case prohibits "aid[ing] another person to attempt suicide," and, thus, the question before us is whether the "liberty" specially protected by the Due Process Clause includes a right to commit suicide which itself includes a right to assistance in doing so.

We now inquire whether this asserted right has any place in our Nation's traditions. Here, we are confronted with a consistent and almost universal tradition that has long rejected the asserted right, and continues explicitly to reject it today, even for terminally ill, mentally competent adults. To hold for respondents, we would have to reverse centuries of legal doctrine and practice, and strike down the considered policy choice of almost every State.

. . . Respondents contend that in *Cruzan* we "acknowledged that competent, dying persons have the right to direct the removal of life-sustaining medical treatment and thus hasten death," and that "the constitutional principle behind recognizing the patient's liberty to direct the withdrawal of artificial life support applies at least as strongly to the choice to hasten impending death by consuming lethal medication." Similarly, the Court of Appeals concluded that "*Cruzan*, by recognizing a liberty interest that includes the refusal of artificial provision of life-sustaining food and water, necessarily recognize[d] a liberty interest in hastening one's own death." The right assumed in *Cruzan*, however, was not simply deduced from abstract concepts of personal autonomy. Given the common-law rule that forced medication was a battery, and the long legal tradition protecting the decision to refuse unwanted medical treatment, our assumption was entirely consistent with this Nation's history and constitutional traditions. The decision to commit suicide with the assistance of another may be just as personal and profound as the decision to refuse unwanted medical treatment, but it has never enjoyed similar legal protection. Indeed, the two acts are widely and reasonably regarded as quite distinct. See Vacco v. Quill. In *Cruzan* itself, we recognized that most States outlawed assisted suicide—and even more do today—and we certainly gave no intimation that the right to refuse unwanted medical treatment could be somehow transmuted into a right to assistance in committing suicide.

Respondents also rely on *Casey*. . . . The Court of Appeals, like the District Court, found *Casey* "highly instructive" and "almost prescriptive" for determining "what liberty interest may inhere in a terminally ill person's choice to commit suicide": "Like the decision of whether or not to have an abortion, the decision how and when to die is one of 'the most intimate and personal choices a person may make in a lifetime,' a choice 'central to personal dignity and autonomy.'" Similarly, respondents emphasize the statement in *Casey* that: "At the heart of liberty is the right to define one's own concept of existence, of meaning, of the universe, and of the mystery of human life. Beliefs about these matters could not define the attributes of personhood were they formed under compulsion of the State." *Casey*, 505 U.S., at 851.

By choosing this language, the Court's opinion in *Casey* described, in a general way and in light of our prior cases, those personal activities and decisions that this Court has identified as so deeply rooted in our history and traditions, or so fundamental to our concept of constitutionally ordered liberty, that they are protected by the Fourteenth Amendment. The opinion moved from the recognition that liberty necessarily includes freedom of conscience and belief about ultimate considerations to the observation that "though the abortion decision may originate within the zone of conscience and belief, it is more than a philosophic exercise." *Casey*, 505 U.S., at 852. That many of the rights and liberties protected by the Due Process Clause sound in personal autonomy does not warrant the sweeping conclusion that any and all important, intimate, and personal decisions are so protected, and *Casey* did not suggest otherwise.

The history of the law's treatment of assisted suicide in this country has been and continues to be one of the rejection of nearly all efforts to permit it. That being the case, our decisions lead us to conclude that the asserted "right" to assistance in committing suicide is not a fundamental liberty interest protected by the Due Process Clause. The Constitution also requires, however, that Washington's assisted-suicide ban be rationally related to legitimate government interests. This requirement is unquestionably met here. As the court below recognized, Washington's assisted-suicide ban implicates a number of state interests.

First, Washington has an "unqualified interest in the preservation of human life." *Cruzan*, 497 U.S., at 282. The State's prohibition on assisted suicide, like all homicide laws, both reflects and advances its commitment to this interest. This interest is symbolic and aspirational as well as practical. . . .

Respondents admit that "[t]he State has a real interest in preserving the lives of those who can still contribute to society and have the potential to enjoy life." The Court of Appeals also recognized Washington's interest in protecting life, but held that the "weight" of this interest depends on the "medical condition and the wishes of the person whose life is at stake." Washington, however, has rejected this sliding-scale approach and, through its assisted-suicide ban, insists that all persons' lives, from beginning to end, regardless of physical or mental condition, are under the full protection of the law. As we have previously affirmed, the States "may properly decline to make judgments about the 'quality' of life that a particular individual may enjoy," *Cruzan*, supra, at 282. This remains true, as *Cruzan* makes clear, even for those who are near death.

. . . The State has an interest in preventing suicide, and in studying, identifying, and treating its causes. Those who attempt suicide—terminally ill or not—often suffer from depression or other mental disorders. See New York Task Force 13–22, 126–128 (more than 95% of those who commit suicide had a major psychiatric illness at the time of death; among the terminally ill, uncontrolled pain is a "risk factor" because it contributes to depression). Research indicates, however, that many people who request physician-assisted suicide withdraw that request if their depression and pain are treated. H. Hendin, Seduced by Death: Doctors, Patients and the Dutch Cure 24–25 (1997) (suicidal, terminally ill patients "usually respond well to treatment for depressive illness and pain medication and are then grateful to be alive").... [L]egal physician-assisted suicide could make it more difficult for the State to protect depressed or mentally ill persons, or those who are suffering from untreated pain, from suicidal impulses.

The State also has an interest in protecting the integrity and ethics of the medical profession. In contrast to the Court of Appeals' conclusion that "the integrity of the medical profession would [not] be threatened in any way by [physician-assisted suicide]," the American Medical Association, like many other medical and physicians' groups, has concluded that "[p]hysician-assisted suicide is fundamentally incompatible with the physician's role as healer." And physician-assisted suicide could, it is argued, undermine the trust that is essential to the doctor-patient relationship by blurring the time-honored line between healing and harming.

Next, the State has an interest in protecting vulnerable groups—including the poor, the elderly, and disabled persons—from abuse, neglect, and mistakes. The Court of Appeals dismissed the State's concern that disadvantaged persons might be pressured into physician-assisted suicide as "ludicrous on its face." We have recognized, however, the real risk of subtle coercion and undue influence in end-of-life situations. *Cruzan,* 497 U.S., at 281. . . .

The State's interest here goes beyond protecting the vulnerable from coercion; it extends to protecting disabled and terminally ill people from prejudice, negative and inaccurate stereotypes, and "societal indifference." The State's assisted-suicide ban reflects and reinforces its policy that the lives of terminally ill, disabled, and elderly people must be no less valued than the lives of the young and healthy, and that a seriously disabled person's suicidal impulses should be interpreted and treated the same way as anyone else's.

Finally, the State may fear that permitting assisted suicide will start it down the path to voluntary and perhaps even involuntary euthanasia. The Court of Appeals struck down Washington's assisted-suicide ban only "as applied to competent, terminally ill adults who wish to hasten their deaths by obtaining medication prescribed by their doctors." Washington insists, however, that the impact of the court's decision will not and cannot be so limited. If suicide is protected as a matter of constitutional right, it is argued, "every man and woman in the United States must enjoy it." The Court of Appeals' decision, and its expansive reasoning, provide ample support for the State's concerns. The court noted, for example, that the "decision of a duly appointed surrogate decision maker is for all legal purposes the decision of the patient himself," 79 F.3d, at 832, n.120; that "in some instances, the patient may be unable to self-administer the drugs and . . . administration by the physician . . . may be the only way the patient may be able to receive them," id., at 831; and that not only physicians, but also family members and loved ones, will inevitably participate in assisting suicide, id., at 838, n.140. Thus, it turns out that what is couched as a limited right to "physician-assisted suicide" is likely, in effect, a much broader license, which could prove extremely difficult to police and contain. Washington's ban on assisting suicide prevents such erosion.

This concern is further supported by evidence about the practice of euthanasia in the Netherlands. The Dutch government's own study revealed that in

1990, there were 2,300 cases of voluntary euthanasia (defined as "the deliberate termination of another's life at his request"), 400 cases of assisted suicide, and more than 1,000 cases of euthanasia without an explicit request. In addition to these latter 1,000 cases, the study found an additional 4,941 cases where physicians administered lethal morphine overdoses without the patients' explicit consent. Physician-Assisted Suicide and Euthanasia in the Netherlands: A Report of Chairman Charles T. Canady, *supra*, at 12–13 (citing Dutch study). This study suggests that, despite the existence of various reporting procedures, euthanasia in the Netherlands has not been limited to competent, terminally ill adults who are enduring physical suffering, and that regulation of the practice may not have prevented abuses in cases involving vulnerable persons, including severely disabled neonates and elderly persons suffering from dementia. . . . Washington, like most other States, reasonably ensures against this risk by banning, rather than regulating, assisting suicide.

We need not weigh exactly the relative strengths of these various interests. They are unquestionably important and legitimate, and Washington's ban on assisted suicide is at least reasonably related to their promotion and protection. We therefore hold that Wash. Rev. Code §9A.36.060(1) (1994) does not violate the Fourteenth Amendment, either on its face or "as applied to competent, terminally ill adults who wish to hasten their deaths by obtaining medication prescribed by their doctors."

Throughout the Nation, Americans are engaged in an earnest and profound debate about the morality, legality, and practicality of physician-assisted suicide. Our holding permits this debate to continue, as it should in a democratic society. The decision of the en banc Court of Appeals is reversed, and the case is remanded for further proceedings consistent with this opinion.

It is so ordered.

The following companion case to Washington v. Glucksberg considers whether New York's ban on physician-assisted suicide violated the Equal Protection Clause of the Constitution. The Second Circuit determined that it did, but the Supreme Court reversed.

Vacco v. Quill
521 U.S. 793 (1997)

Opinion by Chief Justice REHNQUIST.

In New York, as in most States, it is a crime to aid another to commit or attempt suicide, but patients may refuse even lifesaving medical treatment. The question presented by this case is whether New York's prohibition on assisting suicide therefore violates the Equal Protection Clause of the Fourteenth Amendment. We hold that it does not.

The Equal Protection Clause commands that no State shall "deny to any person within its jurisdiction the equal protection of the laws." This provision creates no substantive rights. Instead, it embodies a general rule that States must treat like cases alike but may treat unlike cases accordingly. If a legislative classification or distinction "neither burdens a fundamental right nor targets a suspect class, we will uphold [it] so long as it bears a rational relation to some legitimate end."

New York's statutes outlawing assisting suicide affect and address matters of profound significance to all New Yorkers alike. They neither infringe fundamental rights nor involve suspect classifications. Washington v. Glucksberg, at 719–728. These laws are therefore entitled to a "strong presumption of validity."

On their faces, neither New York's ban on assisting suicide nor its statutes permitting patients to refuse medical treatment treat anyone differently from anyone else or draw any distinctions between persons. Everyone, regardless of physical condition, is entitled, if competent, to refuse unwanted lifesaving medical treatment; no one is permitted to assist a suicide.

Generally speaking, laws that apply evenhandedly to all "unquestionably comply" with the Equal Protection Clause.

The Court of Appeals, however, concluded that some terminally ill people—those who are on life-support systems—are treated differently from those who are not, in that the former may "hasten death" by ending treatment, but the latter may not "hasten death" through physician-assisted suicide. This conclusion depends on the submission that ending or refusing lifesaving medical treatment "is nothing more nor less than assisted suicide." Unlike the Court of Appeals, we think the distinction between assisting suicide and withdrawing life-sustaining treatment, a distinction widely recognized and endorsed in the medical profession and in our legal traditions, is both important and logical; it is certainly rational. ("[Professional organizations] consistently distinguish assisted suicide and euthanasia from the withdrawing or withholding of treatment, and from the provision of palliative treatments or other medical care that risk fatal side effects"); Brief for American Medical Association et al. as Amici Curiae 18–25. Of course, as respondents' lawsuit demonstrates, there are differences of opinion within the medical profession on this question.

The distinction comports with fundamental legal principles of causation and intent. First, when a patient refuses life-sustaining medical treatment, he dies from an underlying fatal disease or pathology; but if a patient ingests lethal medication prescribed by a physician, he is killed by that medication. See, e.g., People v. Kevorkian, 447 Mich. 436, 470–472 (1994), cert. denied, 514 U.S. 1083 (1995); Matter of Conroy, 98 N.J. 321, 355, (1985) (when feeding tube is removed, death "result[s] . . . from [the patient's] underlying medical condition").

Furthermore, a physician who withdraws, or honors a patient's refusal to begin, life-sustaining medical treatment purposefully intends, or may so intend, only to respect his patient's wishes and "to cease doing useless and futile or degrading things to the patient when [the patient] no longer stands to benefit from them." Assisted Suicide in the United States, Hearing before the Subcommittee on the Constitution of the House Committee on the Judiciary, 104th Cong., 2d Sess., 368 (1996) (testimony of Dr. Leon R. Kass). The same is true when a doctor provides aggressive palliative care; in some cases, painkilling drugs may hasten a patient's death, but the physician's purpose and intent is, or may be, only to ease his patient's pain. A doctor who assists a suicide, however, "must, necessarily and indubitably, intend primarily that the patient be made dead." Id., at 367.

Similarly, a patient who commits suicide with a doctor's aid necessarily has the specific intent to end his or her own life, while a patient who refuses or discontinues treatment might not. See, e.g., Matter of Conroy, *supra* (patients who refuse life-sustaining treatment "may not harbor a specific intent to die" and may instead "fervently wish to live, but to do so free of unwanted medical technology, surgery, or drugs").

The law has long used actors' intent or purpose to distinguish between two acts that may have the same result. Put differently, the law distinguishes actions taken "because of" a given end from actions taken "in spite of" their unintended but foreseen consequences. Given these general principles, it is not surprising that many courts, including New York courts, have carefully distinguished refusing life-sustaining treatment from suicide. In fact, the first state-court decision explicitly to authorize withdrawing lifesaving treatment noted the "real distinction between the self-infliction of deadly harm and a self-determination against artificial life support." In re Quinlan, 70 N.J. 10, 43, 52, and n.9, *cert. denied sub nom.* Garger v. New Jersey, 429 U.S. 922 (1976). . . .

. . . Logic and contemporary practice support New York's judgment that the two acts are different, and New York may therefore, consistent with the Constitution, treat them differently. By permitting everyone to refuse unwanted medical treatment while prohibiting anyone from assisting a suicide, New York law follows a longstanding and rational distinction.

The judgment of the Court of Appeals is reversed.

It is so ordered.

NOTES AND QUESTIONS

1. *Comparison of two opinions.*   Where, according to the Supreme Court, did the Court of Appeals in Washington v. Glucksberg go wrong in its analysis? Which opinion do you find the most convincing? On what points?

2. *Concern for the depressed or mentally ill.*   Do you agree with the Supreme Court that legalized physician-assisted suicide could make it more difficult for the State to protect from suicidal impulses depressed or mentally ill persons or those who are suffering from untreated pain? Might safeguards be put in place to protect against the use of physician-assisted suicide under these circumstances? Consider Oregon's Death with Dignity Act, reproduced infra. Do Oregon's safeguards appear adequate?

3. *Concern for persons with disabilities.*   A number of advocacy groups for persons with disabilities oppose legalized physician-assisted suicide. Why do you think they do so? Do you agree with the Court of Appeals or the Supreme Court regarding their handling of this issue?

4. *Limiting the right to competent, terminally ill patients.*   The plaintiffs only sought recognition of a constitutional right to assisted suicide for competent, terminally ill patients. Why do you think they limited their claim to this group of individuals? Do you think the claim should be so limited? Could it be? The Supreme Court's opinion gives credence to the State of Washington's "slippery slope" argument—that permitting assisted suicide could start it down the path to voluntary and perhaps even involuntary euthanasia. Do you think this

concern is justified? How did the Court of Appeals handle this argument? [Note: You'll have to look within the Supreme Court's opinion to find some of the Court of Appeals' treatment of this issue, which was contained in footnote 120 of the Court of Appeals' opinion.]

5. *Assisted suicide and abortion.* What are the similarities and the differences between the claimed right to physician-assisted suicide and the right to abortion? Do you think the Supreme Court's jurisprudence on abortion can be reconciled with its decision to decline to recognize a right to physician-assisted suicide?

6. *Terminal sedation.* Law professor David Orentlicher argues that the Court's decision in Washington v. Glucksberg did not, as conventional wisdom would have it, reaffirm the distinction between physician-assisted suicide and withdrawal of life-sustaining treatment. David Orentlicher, The Supreme Court and Terminal Sedation: Rejecting Assisted Suicide, Embracing Euthanasia, 24 Hastings Const. L.Q. 947 (1997). Rather, he submits, the Court endorsed "terminal sedation," which he describes as a form of euthanasia. He writes:

> With terminal sedation, narcotics (e.g., morphine), benzodiazepine sedative drugs (e.g., Valium), barbiturates (e.g., amobarbital) and/or major tranquilizing drugs (e.g., Haldol or Thorazine) are used to sedate the patient. The sedation is maintained until the patient dies, usually within a few days, either from the underlying terminal illness, or from a second step that is often part of terminal sedation—the withholding of nutrition and hydration. Because the sedation leaves the patient with a depressed level of consciousness and stopping the sedation would only result in the patient reexperiencing the suffering, the patient frequently agrees to have food and water withheld rather than having life prolonged for a short time. In cases in which terminal sedation shortens the patient's life, it usually does so by hours or days. For some patients, however, life is shortened by as much as several weeks.
>
> At first glance, terminal sedation seems consistent with well-accepted practices. It is appropriate for physicians to treat the pain and suffering of patients aggressively, even if doing so increases the likelihood that the patient will die. It is also appropriate for patients to refuse life-sustaining treatment, including food and water. Upon closer examination, however, terminal sedation is at times essentially "slow euthanasia."
>
> In many cases, terminal sedation amounts to euthanasia because the sedated patient often dies from the combination of two intentional acts by the physician—the induction of stupor or unconsciousness and the withholding of food and water. Without these two acts, the patient would live longer before eventually succumbing to illness. In other words, if the sedation step and the withholding of nutrition and hydration step are viewed as a total package, we have a situation in which a patient's life is ended by the active intervention of a physician.

Id. at 955-956.

For a different view, see George P. Smith, III, "Today, pain relief—be it physical, mental, social or spiritual—is being recognized more and more as a fundamental human right. . . . If a patient is in a futile condition, efficacious treatment should be given even if the secondary effect of that assistance means hastening life's cruel and inhumane ending. Terminal sedation is just that: recognized treatment. It should not be confused, taxonomically, by denominating it as euthanasia, murder, or assisted suicide. Rather, it is but an act of self-determination."

Abstract, Intractable Pain, Palliative Management and the Principle of Medical Futility, http://papers.ssrn.com/s013/papers.cfm?abstract_id=1166384.

Do you think terminal sedation is euthanasia? No matter how it is denoted, do you think it is acceptable?

7. *Equal protection claim.*   In Vacco v. Quill, the Supreme Court upheld New York's ban on assisted suicide against a challenge that it violated equal protection principles. How does the Court distinguish between assisted suicide and the withdrawal of life support such as a ventilator? Are you convinced by the distinction?

8. *Ethics of care.*   Recall the ethics of care that has emerged as one branch of feminist jurisprudence. (See Chapter 1.) That approach emphasizes relationships, care, and community over rights to autonomy. What do you think an analysis of physician-assisted suicide undertaken within the ethics of care framework would look like? Would an ethics of care ultimately be in favor of or against legalized physician-assisted suicide?

9. *A right to palliative care?*   Justice O'Connor, in a separate concurrence in Washington v. Glucksberg, writes that her agreement that a state may prohibit physician-assisted suicide comes in light of the fact that the state did not impose legal barriers to obtaining medication to alleviate suffering, "even to the point of causing unconsciousness and hastening death." In his separate concurrence, Justice Breyer adds that "were the legal circumstances different—for example, were state law to prevent the provision of palliative care . . . then the law's impact upon serious and otherwise unavoidable physical pain would be more directly at issue" and "the Court might have to revisit its conclusions in these cases." These and other statements in the *Glucksberg* opinions expressing concern for the suffering of dying patients has led some commentators to conclude that the Supreme Court, while unwilling to strike down state laws against assisted suicide, is nevertheless open to exploring a right to palliative care. See Robert A. Burt, The Supreme Court Speaks—Not Assisted Suicide But a Constitutional Right to Palliative Care, 337 New Eng. J. Med. 1234 (1997). But see Lois Shepherd, A Right to Palliative Care? What the U.S. Supreme Court Did and Did Not Say in the Physician-Assisted Suicide Cases, 16 J. Pall. Care 48 (2000).

10. *New York Task Force.*   References in the opinion to the New York Task Force are to the report entitled New York State Task Force on Life and the Law, When Death Is Sought: Assisted Suicide and Euthanasia in the Medical Context 108 (1994), which was prepared by a commission composed of doctors, ethicists, lawyers, religious leaders, and interested laypersons.

As described in the Supreme Court's *Glucksberg* opinion, the State of Oregon in 1994 approved the legalization of physician aid in hastening death through ballot initiative. The following statute permitting and regulating physician prescriptions for hastening death was enacted shortly thereafter. In 2008, the State of Washington adopted a similar measure through a ballot measure called Initiative 1000, now codified at RWC 70.245 (2009).

|| *Oregon Death with Dignity Act* ||

127.800 §1.01. Definitions. [This section defines the following words, among others, for purposes of the act.]

(2) "Attending physician" means the physician who has primary responsibility for the care of the patient and treatment of the patient's terminal disease.

(3) "Capable" means that in the opinion of a court or in the opinion of the patient's attending physician or consulting physician, psychiatrist or psychologist, a patient has the ability to make and communicate health care decisions to health care providers, including communication through persons familiar with the patient's manner of communicating if those persons are available.

(4) "Consulting physician" means a physician who is qualified by specialty or experience to make a professional diagnosis and prognosis regarding the patient's disease.

(12) "Terminal disease" means an incurable and irreversible disease that has been medically confirmed and will, within reasonable medical judgment, produce death within six months.

127.805 §2.01. Who may initiate a written request for medication.

(1) An adult who is capable, is a resident of Oregon, and has been determined by the attending physician and consulting physician to be suffering from a terminal disease, and who has voluntarily expressed his or her wish to die, may make a written request for medication for the purpose of ending his or her life in a humane and dignified manner in accordance with [the act].

(2) No person shall qualify under the provisions of [the act] solely because of age or disability.

127.810 §2.02. Form of the written request.

(1) A valid request for medication under [the act] shall be in substantially the form described in ORS 127.897, signed and dated by the patient and witnessed by at least two individuals who, in the presence of the patient, attest that to the best of their knowledge and belief the patient is capable, acting voluntarily, and is not being coerced to sign the request.

(2) One of the witnesses shall be a person who is not:

   (a) A relative of the patient by blood, marriage or adoption;

   (b) A person who at the time the request is signed would be entitled to any portion of the estate of the qualified patient upon death under any will or by operation of law; or

   (c) An owner, operator or employee of a health care facility where the qualified patient is receiving medical treatment or is a resident.

(3) The patient's attending physician at the time the request is signed shall not be a witness.

(4) If the patient is a patient in a long term care facility at the time the written request is made, one of the witnesses shall be an individual designated by the facility and having the qualifications specified by the Department of Human Services by rule.

127.815 §3.01. Attending physician responsibilities.

(1) The attending physician shall:

(a) Make the initial determination of whether a patient has a terminal disease, is capable, and has made the request voluntarily;

(b) Request that the patient demonstrate Oregon residency pursuant to ORS 127.860;

(c) To ensure that the patient is making an informed decision, inform the patient of:

(A) His or her medical diagnosis;

(B) His or her prognosis;

(C) The potential risks associated with taking the medication to be prescribed;

(D) The probable result of taking the medication to be prescribed; and

(E) The feasible alternatives, including, but not limited to, comfort care, hospice care and pain control;

(d) Refer the patient to a consulting physician for medical confirmation of the diagnosis, and for a determination that the patient is capable and acting voluntarily;

(e) Refer the patient for counseling if appropriate pursuant to ORS 127.825;

(f) Recommend that the patient notify next of kin;

(g) Counsel the patient about the importance of having another person present when the patient takes the medication prescribed pursuant to [the act] and of not taking the medication in a public place;

(h) Inform the patient that he or she has an opportunity to rescind the request at any time and in any manner, and offer the patient an opportunity to rescind at the end of the 15 day waiting period pursuant to ORS 127.840;

(i) Verify, immediately prior to writing the prescription for medication under [the act], that the patient is making an informed decision;

(j) [Fulfill medical record documentation];

(k) Ensure that all appropriate steps are carried out in accordance with [the act] prior to writing a prescription for medication to enable a qualified patient to end his or her life in a humane and dignified manner. . . .

(2) Notwithstanding any other provision of law, the attending physician may sign the patient's death certificate.

127.820 §3.02. Consulting physician confirmation. Before a patient is qualified under [the act], a consulting physician shall examine the patient and his or her relevant medical records and confirm, in writing, the attending physician's diagnosis that the patient is suffering from a terminal disease, and verify that the patient is capable, is acting voluntarily and has made an informed decision.

127.825 §3.03. Counseling referral. If in the opinion of the attending physician or the consulting physician a patient may be suffering from a psychiatric or psychological disorder or depression causing impaired judgment, either physician shall refer the patient for counseling. No medication to end a patient's life in a humane and dignified manner shall be prescribed until the person performing the counseling determines that the patient is not suffering from a psychiatric or psychological disorder or depression causing impaired judgment.

127.840 §3.06. Written and oral requests. In order to receive a prescription for medication to end his or her life in a humane and dignified manner, a qualified patient shall have made an oral request and a written request, and reiterate the oral request to his or her attending physician no less than fifteen (15) days after making the initial oral request. At the time the qualified patient makes his or her second oral request, the attending physician shall offer the patient an opportunity to rescind the request.

127.850 §3.08. Waiting periods. No less than fifteen (15) days shall elapse between the patient's initial oral request and the writing of a prescription under [the act]. No less than 48 hours shall elapse between the patient's written request and the writing of a prescription under [the act]. [Section 3.09 requires certain documentation in the patient's medical record and §3.11 requires the Oregon Department of Human Services to collect certain information and generate reports on the operation of the act.]

127.880 §3.14. Construction of Act. Nothing in [the act] shall be construed to authorize a physician or any other person to end a patient's life by lethal injection, mercy killing or active euthanasia. Actions taken in accordance with [the act] shall not, for any purpose, constitute suicide, assisted suicide, mercy killing or homicide, under the law.

127.885 §4.01. Immunities; basis for prohibiting health care provider from participation; notification; permissible sanctions. Except as provided in ORS 127.890:

(1) No person shall be subject to civil or criminal liability or professional disciplinary action for participating in good faith compliance with [the act]. This includes being present when a qualified patient takes the prescribed medication to end his or her life in a humane and dignified manner.

(2) No professional organization or association, or health care provider, may subject a person to censure, discipline, suspension, loss of license, loss of privileges, loss of membership or other penalty for participating or refusing to participate in good faith compliance with [the act].

(3) No request by a patient for or provision by an attending physician of medication in good faith compliance with the provisions of [the act] shall constitute neglect for any purpose of law or provide the sole basis for the appointment of a guardian or conservator.

(4) No health care provider shall be under any duty, whether by contract, by statute or by any other legal requirement to participate in the provision to a qualified patient of medication to end his or her life in a

humane and dignified manner. If a health care provider is unable or unwilling to carry out a patient's request under [the act], and the patient transfers his or her care to a new health care provider, the prior health care provider shall transfer, upon request, a copy of the patient's relevant medical records to the new health care provider.

[The act also provides that a health care provider, which may include a health care facility, may prohibit another health care provider from participating in the act on its premises and may sanction a health care provider for doing so by loss of staff privileges, termination of lease, or contract.]

Oregon Department of Human Services Summary of Oregon's Death with Dignity Act—2011

Oregon's Death with Dignity Act (DWDA), enacted in late 1997, allows terminally-ill adult Oregonians to obtain and use prescriptions from their physicians for self-administered, lethal doses of medications. The Oregon Public Health Division is required by the Act to collect information on compliance and to issue an annual report. The key findings from 2011 are listed below. The number of people for whom DWDA prescriptions were written (DWDA prescription recipients) and deaths that occurred as a result of ingesting prescribed DWDA medications (DWDA deaths) reported in this summary are based on paperwork and death certificates received by the Oregon Public Health Division as of February 29, 2012. For more detail, please view the figures and tables on our web site at http://public.health.oregon.gov/ProviderPartnerResources/ Evaluation Research/DeathwithDignityAct/Pages/ar-index.aspx.

- As of February 29, 2012, prescriptions for lethal medications were written for 114 people during 2011 under the provisions of the DWDA, compared to 97 during 2010. At the time of this report, there were 71 known DWDA deaths during 2011. This corresponds to 22.5 DWDA deaths per 10,000 total deaths.
- Since the law was passed in 1997, a total of 935 people have had DWDA prescriptions written and 596 patients have died from ingesting medications prescribed under the DWDA.
- Of the 114 patients for whom DWDA prescriptions were written during 2011, 64 (56.1%) ingested the medication; 63 died from ingesting the medication, and one patient ingested the medication but regained consciousness before dying of underlying illness and is therefore not counted as a DWDA death. The patient regained consciousness approximately 14 hours following ingestion and died about 38 hours later. Incomplete ingestion was reported for the patient.
- Nine patients with prescriptions written in previous years ingested the medication during 2011; eight of these patients died from ingesting the medication, and one ingested the medication but regained consciousness before dying of underlying illness and is therefore not counted as a DWDA death. The patient briefly regained consciousness following ingestion and died approximately 30 hours later. Possible medication tolerance was reported

for the patient. Thus, two patients ingesting lethal medication in 2011 awoke and ultimately died of their underlying illness. One patient received their prescription in 2011 and the other received their prescription in 2010.

- Twenty-five (25) of the 114 patients who received DWDA prescriptions during 2011 did not take the medications and died of their underlying illness.
- Ingestion status is unknown for 25 patients for whom DWDA prescriptions were written during 2011. Three of these patients died and follow-up questionnaires were received, but ingestion status could not be determined. For the remaining 22 patients, both death and ingestion status are pending.
- Of the 71 DWDA deaths during 2011, most (69.0%) were aged 65 years or older; the median age was 70 years. As in previous years, most were white (95.6%), well-educated (48.5% had a least a baccalaureate degree), and had cancer (82.4%).
- Most (94.1%) patients died at home; and most (96.7%) were enrolled in hospice care either at the time the DWDA prescription was written or at the time of death. Most (96.7%) had some form of health care insurance, although the number of patients who had private insurance (50.8%) was lower in 2011 than in previous years (68.0%), and the number of patients who had only Medicare or Medicaid insurance was higher than in previous years (45.9% compared to 30.4%).
- As in previous years, the three most frequently mentioned end-of-life concerns were: decreasing ability to participate in activities that made life enjoyable (90.1%), loss of autonomy (88.7%), and loss of dignity (74.6%).
- One of the 71 DWDA patients who died during 2011 was referred for formal psychiatric or psychological evaluation. Prescribing physicians were present at the time of death for six patients (8.5%) during 2011 compared to 18.7% in previous years.
- [D]ata on time from ingestion to death is available for eight of the 71 DWDA deaths during 2011. Among those eight patients, time from ingestion until death ranged from 15 minutes to 1.5 hours.
- Sixty-two (62) physicians wrote the 114 prescriptions provided during 2011 (range 1–14 prescriptions per physician).
- During 2011, no referrals were made to the Oregon Medical Board for failure to comply with DWDA requirements.

NOTES AND QUESTIONS

1. *Regulatory protections; data from operation of the Act.*   Do you think the protections provided in the Oregon Death with Dignity Act are sufficient to allay the bulk of the concerns expressed by the Supreme Court in Washington v. Glucksberg? On the basis of the information provided by the 2011 report, do you think the Act is operating as intended? Do you find any of the information in the report surprising? Do you think it lends support for recognition of a constitutional right to physician-assisted suicide or is it irrelevant to that debate? Is there any further information that you would like to know about the operation of the act? Why do you think that information is important?

2. *Physician involvement.*   The Oregon Act permits the patient's attending physician to be present when the lethal medication is taken, but does not permit the physician to actually administer the medication. What concerns do you think are behind this limitation? Do you think those concerns are justified?

3. *Culture of intolerance toward dependency?*   Loss of independence is the number one reason that patients have chosen, over the years, to use lethal medication under Oregon's Death with Dignity Act, according to their attending physicians. Loss of control over bodily functions is also high. Some critics of the "right to die" or "death with dignity" movement have expressed concern that our culture is overly insistent on people being independent and is intolerant of dependency. Do you agree or does culture have nothing to do with it? If our culture is partly responsible for individuals' desire to hasten death, is there any way to change that?

4. *Constitutional challenges to the Act.*   In 1995, before the Oregon Death with Dignity Act became effective, a federal district court in Oregon held that the Death with Dignity Act violated the Equal Protection Clause of the Fourteenth Amendment because it deprived terminally ill persons of the benefit of laws prohibiting a person from assisting another to end his life. People who were not terminally ill retained those benefits. Lee v. Oregon, 891 F. Supp. 1429 (1995). The district court's decision was later vacated, Lee v. Oregon, 107 F.3d 1382 (9th Cir. 1997) (concluding that plaintiffs lacked Article III standing). Recall the very different equal protection claim in Vacco v. Quill, which won at the appellate level but lost in the Supreme Court. Compare the equal protection arguments for and against the legal availability of physician aid in hastening death. Which do you find most convincing?

5. *Federal challenges to the Act.*   In 2001, then Attorney General John Ashcroft issued a directive that physicians prescribing lethal medication to patients pursuant to Oregon's Death with Dignity Act would be violating the federal Controlled Substances Act (CSA). In Gonzales v. Oregon, 546 U.S. 243 (2006), the U.S. Supreme Court determined that the Attorney General had overstepped his authority in issuing the directive. While, as the majority opinion of Justice Kennedy acknowledged, the dispute was a product of the "political and moral" debate surrounding physician-assisted suicide, the decision to invalidate the directive was based on narrower statutory grounds of interpretation of the CSA. The Attorney General did not, at least without more express direction from Congress, have the power to impose his own view of appropriate medical practice on physicians, whose professional practice is generally regulated by state law. Because it was decided on these narrow grounds, the case did not answer the question whether Congress would have the authority to override the Oregon Death with Dignity Act if it chose to. Possible objections to the constitutionality of such action include Congress' limited authority under the Commerce Clause, the liberty interests of patients under substantive due process, and the First Amendment rights of physicians. Arthur B. LaFrance, Physician Assisted Death: From Rhetoric to Reality in Oregon, 8 Wyoming L. Rev. 333 (2008).

6. *Montana joins the act (sort of).*   In 2009, the Montana Supreme Court ruled that no law or public policy in Montana barred physicians from providing lethal prescriptions to terminally ill, mentally competent adult patients, and that

an existing statutory consent defense to homicide would shield physicians from homicide liability for such acts. Baxter v. Montana, 224 P.3d 1211 (Mont. 2009). The court avoided deciding whether the state's constitution protected a right to physician-assisted suicide, a position advocated by plaintiffs in the case. In 2011, three bills were introduced in the Montana legislature relating to the state supreme court's decision; one was modeled after Oregon's and Washington's laws, two others would have prohibited the same activities. None passed.

CHALLENGING ISSUES: THE PERSON WITH A DISABILITY SEEKING PHYSICIAN-ASSISTED SUICIDE

Hannah B., a 32-year-old Oregon resident with multiple congenital disabilities that render her largely immobile, has recently sought removal of the feeding tube that provides her with nutrition and hydration. Hannah lives at home, where she is cared for by her father and regular home health care providers. Hannah can be fed by mouth, but finds it difficult to swallow, which is why she was being supplementally fed by a nasogastric tube. Her physician of two years has agreed to her request to remove the feeding tube, although he has explained to her that it is unlikely that she will be able to consume enough nutrients on her own to continue living beyond a month or two.

Two weeks after removal of the feeding tube, when Hannah's already low weight has been reduced by ten pounds, she makes an oral request to her doctor for medication for the purpose of ending her life. How should her doctor respond? Is he permitted to prescribe the medication Hannah seeks? If he is permitted, should he? Must he?

CHALLENGING ISSUES: UNIVERSAL ACCESS TO PHYSICIAN-ASSISTED SUICIDE

One of the objections that has been made to permitting physician-assisted suicide is that the practice may involve an evaluation by the physician of the quality of life of the patient, and, by implication, the value of that life over death. If the patient's health permits a good quality of life, but he seeks death, the physician may suspect and treat for depression or counsel delay or some other course of action to avoid the patient's loss of life. On the other hand, if the physician perceives that the patient has a poor quality of life, she will be less likely to deter a patient's desire to hasten death and more likely to assist it. Such judgments about the quality of life of another person, especially when weighed against the possibility of death, are troubling for a number of reasons, among them (1) the history of prejudice against and ignorance about the lives of persons with disabilities, and (2) the fact that the reason advanced most prominently to justify physician-assisted suicide is the patient's autonomy, yet the value judgment of another person seems unavoidable. Could a system be constructed that permitted physician-assisted suicide in a way that avoided these problems?

Consider the following proposal: Every person of majority age is permitted to obtain a lethal dose of medication from a local pharmacy. If we wanted to avoid impetuousness, we could have a waiting period—a person would have to submit a written request for the medication once a week for three weeks or some similar process. We will also assume that there are safeguards in place so that the medication is not easily used to poison someone else. It seems that such a system would satisfy a number of the concerns that opponents of physician-assisted suicide have voiced. The decision to die would appear to be autonomous, without the hint of anyone's agreement that the individual who seeks death has a life that is not worth living. How would you evaluate such a proposal?

=8=
‖ *Death* ‖

Just as the beginning of human life is an unsettled and vigorously debated concept in bioethics and law, so too is the end of human life. Just as crossing the threshold into life has meant the assignment of the full panoply of rights of all living persons, crossing the threshold into death has meant the complete loss of those rights. But the ability to continue the cardiac and respiratory functions of a severely injured or ill person by machine has challenged our society's previously clear lines between life and death. The first part of this chapter considers the definition of death and how one determines when it occurs. The second part is devoted to the treatment of the body of those who are, by all current standards, clearly dead. The overarching questions considered in this chapter include the following:

1. What should be the standard(s) for determining when death has occurred?
2. Is a bright line between life and death possible? Is it desirable?
3. What, if anything, is owed to the individual who once lived? What is owed to his or her family?

A. DEFINITIONS AND DETERMINATIONS OF DEATH

Before the 1970s, death was understood to have arrived upon the total and irreversible cessation of respiratory and cardiac functions. With the advent of medical procedures to artificially continue respiratory and cardiac functions in an individual whose brain function had ceased, combined with the potential to recover and transplant organs from the bodies of those individuals, medical and legal standards of death began to focus on the absence of brain function to determine when death had occurred. All 50 states and the District of Columbia

513

have now adopted, through statute or case law, a definition of death that includes what is commonly known as *brain death,* meaning that death is equated with the cessation of all functions of the brain.

A number of scholars have pointed out that although the term *brain death* has become well-accepted as a colloquial matter, it is misleading because it suggests that there is more than one *type* of death when actually there are two *methods* for determining a singular notion of death. This confusion is exacerbated by common references to removing "life support" from "brain dead" patients who then "die."

1.   *Bioethical and Social Perspectives*

Brain death now appears to be a well-established legal concept, but it remains quite controversial among those considering its ethical grounding. The main impetus in the 1970s and 1980s for adoption of a brain death standard is generally acknowledged to have been organ recovery and transplantation. New technologies allowed the organs of injured patients who had lost brain function to remain oxygenated and therefore viable for transplantation. If not for the desire to continue to provide oxygen to the organs, the mechanisms by which such an individual was receiving artificial respiration and circulation would have been removed, causing within a very short time the cessation of those functions and the satisfaction of the traditional criteria for determination of death, the irreversible loss of cardio-respiratory function.

The "dead donor rule," the rule that vital organs cannot be taken from individuals unless they are dead, prohibited the taking of organs from individuals breathing through artificial means unless an understanding of brain death was adopted. This history contributes to the view of some scholars that "brain death" and, thus our concept of death generally, is a social and legal construct. Others maintain its biological basis. Mixed in with these concerns is recent, growing awareness that the medical standards for determining the cessation of brain function are not as certain and uniform as many people have believed. Consider the following commentaries:

> When we began to consider the legal and moral status of humans with dead brains, we chose to classify them as dead, thus conveying our conviction that it should be legal and ethical, with proper consent, to remove organs that are normally considered necessary to preserve life. In doing so without really understanding what we were doing, we adopted a new and radically different meaning of the word *dead.* While, historically, the word has had a biological definition and no necessary moral and public policy meaning, the new and different meaning had little to do with biology. Obviously, under the new meaning many dead beings have many biological functions (including many living cells and organs). The word *dead* has come to mean—for legal, ethical, and public policy purposes—"having lost full moral standing as a member of the human community." For these purposes—including organ procurement and homicide law—calling someone "dead" merely means that it is morally, legally, and socially acceptable to remove organs (as well as do some other things) and that those who do so are not guilty of murder. Obviously, some of the people called dead for these purposes retain many biologically living functions: their bodies are still living in the biological sense, even if not in the moral and legal

sense. They enter a radically different moral status such that they are no longer full members of the human moral community with all the rights of living members, such as the right not to be killed.

Robert M. Veatch, The Dead Donor Rule: True by Definition, 3 Am. J. Bioethics 10–11 (2003).

After arguing that death is no longer a biological term, but a legal and ethical term, Professor Veatch suggests that the term "dead" be extended to those who have lost higher brain function, in other words, patients whose brain stems are still functioning (and therefore do not meet the current brain death standard) but who permanently lack consciousness because the rest of the brain is not functioning. This would include patients in a persistent vegetative state and infants with anencephaly. The question of who is dead, according to Veatch, would be answered by asking who is a legitimate candidate for potential organ procurement.

Howard Trachtman, M.D. and Professor of Pediatrics, offers an opposing viewpoint:

> I strongly feel that the definition of death focuses on as biological a feature of life as there can be. Along with birth and taxes, death is one of the Big Three, and I do not think there is any validity to the claim that what we regard as death is determined by political considerations. Technological advances in sustaining life might increase the difficulty in making the diagnosis of death. However, this does not impact the undeniable reality of the clinical situation when a person is declared dead. Historically, when cardiac and brain death coincided with one another temporally, there was no discussion. The ability to sustain heart and pulmonary function independently of the brain was perceived as a serious threat to the definition of death. The introduction of the brain-death definition was designed to rectify this difficulty. The definition of brain death—meaning no detectable brain activity in the cortex or brain stem confirmed by electroencephalogram, brain scan, or clinical examination—is still death. Patients who are brain-dead cannot sustain respiratory effort for more than a few minutes, at which point they die; that is, they have cessation of cardiopulmonary activity within minutes of the halting of ventilatory support.
>
> Patients who are in a persistent vegetative state are not dead. This is biology. Diminished quality of life is not synonymous with death. The world's literature is replete with the imagery that suggests the impoverished person, the barren woman, and the parent who loses a child are figuratively dead. There are those who want to add individuals who have irretrievably lost higher cortical function to this list of the "dead." Our hearts go out to these people, but that does not change their biology—they are alive and deserve all the protections of the living. Before abandoning the dead donor rule, let us leave aside the concerns arising from the pressing shortage of organ donors. Instead, let us simply ask this question: in the absence of a request for organ donation, are we ready as a society to put individuals without higher cortical function yet the ability to breathe independently in coffins and bury them? My suspicion is that we are not and that this represents our inherent repugnance for those who would obfuscate about the definition of death.

Howard Trachtman, M.D., Death Be Not Political, 3 Am. J. Bioethics 31 (2003).

Why does Veatch insist that death is a social construct and Trachtman that it is a biological fact? Which do you find more convincing? Might the answer lie in both?

2.   *Legal Approaches*

a.   Adoption of Brain Death Criteria

A majority of states have adopted the Uniform Determination of Death Act, which provides that

> An individual who has sustained either (1) irreversible cessation of circulatory and respiratory functions, or (2) irreversible cessation of all functions of the entire brain, including the brain stem, is dead. A determination of death must be made in accordance with accepted medical standards.

Uniform Determination of Death Act (1980), Uniform Laws Annotated, vol. 12A (West 1996 & Supp. 2003).

Other states have adopted different formulations of the brain death standard, but all have done so. Prior to the adoption of state statutes recognizing brain death, some courts faced the issue of whether brain death should be recognized in cases of homicide. The defendant's argument in such cases was that the victim, while diagnosed as brain dead, was not dead under then-existing legal criteria because he was still breathing, albeit through artificial means, and that what killed the victim was the removal of "life support" systems or the removal of vital organs by physicians. This defense was generally unsuccessful, with the court either judicially adopting a brain death standard for homicide cases (see, e.g., People v. Eulo, 63 N.Y.2d 341 (1984)) or applying traditional causation analysis to conclude that the victim's medical treatment did not constitute an intervening cause to relieve the defendant of criminal liability (see, e.g., State v. Meints, 212 Neb. 410 (1982)).

Note that the Uniform Determination of Death Act does not specify what tests shall be used to determine when death has occurred, but instead defers to "accepted medical standards." A recent survey revealed "wide variability in the practice and determination of brain death among the US News and World Report top 50 institutions for neurology and neurosurgery." D. M. Greer et al., Variability of Brain Death Determination Guidelines in Leading U.S. Neurologic Institutions, 70 Neurology 284–298 (2008). The authors of this report found the results "at once interesting and disturbing. Given the variability of practice in North America, and the world, the accuracy of assessment for brain death across institutions, and even among individual physicians, may be drawn into question."

b.   Accommodation of Religious Beliefs

Although every state has adopted "brain death" as an alternative means of determining the death of an individual, two states, New Jersey and New York, have adopted a sort of "opt-out" of brain death for individuals who object on religious grounds. New Jersey's statute is reprinted below. What do you think of the wisdom of this approach? See also 10 New York Rules and Regulations §400.16(e)(3) (2006) (requiring hospitals to establish "a procedure for the reasonable accommodation of the individual's religious or moral objection to the determination [of brain death] as expressed by the individual, or by the next of kin or other person closest to the individual").

|| *New Jersey Statutes Annotated (1991)* ||

26:6A-2. Recognition of traditional cardio-respiratory criteria
An individual who has sustained irreversible cessation of all circulatory and respiratory functions, as determined in accordance with currently accepted medical standards, shall be declared dead.

26:6A-3. Recognition of modern neurological criteria
Subject to the standards and procedures established in accordance with this act, an individual whose circulatory and respiratory functions can be maintained solely by artificial means, and who has sustained irreversible cessation of all functions of the entire brain, including the brain stem, shall be declared dead.

26:6A-5. Standards and procedures for declaration of death based upon neurological criteria
The death of an individual shall not be declared upon the basis of neurological criteria pursuant to sections 3 and 4 of this act when the licensed physician authorized to declare death, has reason to believe, on the basis of information in the individual's available medical records, or information provided by a member of the individual's family or any other person knowledgeable about the individual's personal religious beliefs that such a declaration would violate the personal religious beliefs of the individual. In these cases, death shall be declared, and the time of death fixed, solely upon the basis of cardio-respiratory criteria pursuant to section 2 of this act.

26:6A-7. Effect on insurance and health benefits
Changes in pre-existing criteria for the declaration of death effectuated by the legal recognition of modern neurological criteria shall not in any manner affect, impair or modify the terms of, or rights or obligations created under, any existing policy of health insurance, life insurance or annuity, or governmental benefits program. No health care practitioner or other health care provider, and no health service plan, insurer, or governmental authority, shall deny coverage or exclude from the benefits of service any individual solely because of that individual's personal religious beliefs regarding the application of neurological criteria for declaring death.

CHALLENGING ISSUES: INDIVIDUALIZED DEFINITIONS OF DEATH TO ACCORD WITH RELIGIOUS BELIEFS

Greta Hamlin, a seven-year-old girl, was brought to the emergency room of a local hospital ten days ago after having sustained serious injuries to her entire body, including her brain. She was placed on a ventilator to sustain her cardio-pulmonary function. An electroencephalogram has revealed the absence of any activity in any part of the brain, including the brain stem. The police have very strong evidence that Greta was the victim of child abuse, and that her parents caused her current physical condition during an episode of domestic violence.

The police want to charge Greta's parents with homicide, but the parents adamantly refuse to allow Greta to be removed from the ventilator, citing their religious belief that death only occurs when a person's heart stops beating. Moreover, the health insurance company covering the cost of Greta's care has informed the hospital that it will refuse to pay for continued hospital care because the medical records the company has received from the hospital staff reveal that she is dead. The company has no obligation, it insists, to pay for the provision of health care services to the dead.

(A) Consider the following questions under the Uniform Determination of Death Act and under New Jersey's law as reprinted above.

1. Is Greta dead? Should she be declared dead by her physician?
2. Can the police charge Greta's parents with homicide?
3. Can Greta's health insurance company refuse payment for any further care?
4. Can Greta's physicians and the hospital remove the mechanical ventilator support systems from Greta on the grounds that she is dead? Can her physicians withdraw ventilator support (and the health insurance company refuse further payment for it) on the grounds that the provision of such care is *futile?* See Chapter 7 for discussion of the concept of futility.

(B) Do New Jersey's statutes relating to determinations of death suggest that death is a social, rather than biological, phenomenon?

c.   Expanding the Class of Those Who Are Considered Dead

i.   The Permanently Unconscious

Professor Veatch and others have for years proposed that people who lack higher brain function and are thus permanently unconscious or insentient be included in the category of those considered dead. Generally, the impetus behind such proposals is the increased number of transplantable organs that would be made available from individuals who are in a persistent vegetative state or infants with anencephaly. In the following case, the Florida Supreme Court considers whether an infant born with anencephaly might be considered dead under Florida law and thus a suitable source for organ donation.

In re T.A.C.P.
609 So. 2d 588 (Fla. 1992)

Opinion by Justice KOGAN.

Is an anencephalic newborn considered "dead" for purposes of organ donation solely by reason of its congenital deformity? . . .

I. FACTS

At or about the eighth month of pregnancy, the parents of the child T.A.C.P. were informed that she would be born with anencephaly. This is a birth defect invariably fatal, in which the child typically is born with only a "brain stem" but otherwise lacks a human brain. In T.A.C.P.'s case, the back of the skull was entirely missing and the brain stem was exposed to the air, except for medical bandaging. The risk of infection to the brain stem was considered very high. Anencephalic infants sometimes can survive several days after birth because the brain stem has a limited capacity to maintain autonomic bodily functions such as breathing and heartbeat. This ability soon ceases, however, in the absence of regulation from the missing brain.

In this case, T.A.C.P. actually survived only a few days after birth. The medical evidence in the record shows that the child T.A.C.P. was incapable of developing any sort of cognitive process, may have been unable to feel pain or experience sensation due to the absence of the upper brain, and at least for part of the time was placed on a mechanical ventilator to assist her breathing. At the time of the hearing below, however, the child was breathing unaided, although she died soon thereafter.

On the advice of physicians, the parents continued the pregnancy to term and agreed that the mother would undergo caesarean section during birth. The parents agreed to the caesarean procedure with the express hope that the infant's organs would be less damaged and could be used for transplant in other sick children. Although T.A.C.P. had no hope of life herself, the parents both testified in court that they wanted to use this opportunity to give life to others. However, when the parents requested that T.A.C.P. be declared legally dead for this purpose, her health care providers refused out of concern that they thereby might incur civil or criminal liability.

The parents then filed a petition in the circuit court asking for a judicial determination. . . .

II. THE MEDICAL NATURE OF ANENCEPHALY

. . . [I]t is clear that anencephaly is distinguishable from some other congenital conditions because its extremity renders it uniformly lethal. Less severe conditions are not "anencephaly." There has been a tendency by some parties and amici to confuse lethal anencephaly with these less serious conditions, even to the point of describing children as "anencephalic" who have abnormal but otherwise intact skulls and who are several years of age. We emphasize that the child T.A.C.P. clearly met the four criteria [identified by the Medical Task Force on Anencephaly]. The present opinion does not apply to children with less serious conditions; they are not anencephalic because they do not have large openings in their skulls accompanied by the complete or near total absence of normal cerebral hemispheres, which defines "anencephaly."

. . . The Task Force reported that the medical consequences of anencephaly can be established with some certainty. All anencephalics by definition are permanently unconscious because they lack the cerebral cortex necessary for conscious thought. Their condition thus is quite similar to that of persons in a persistent vegetative state. Where the brain stem is functioning, as it was here, spontaneous breathing and heartbeat can occur. In addition, such infants may show spontaneous movements of the extremities, "startle" reflexes, and pupils that respond to light. Some may show feeding reflexes, may cough, hiccup, or exhibit eye movements, and may produce facial expressions.

The question of whether such infants actually suffer from pain is somewhat more complex. It involves a distinction between "pain" and "suffering." The Task Force indicated that anencephaly in some ways is analogous to persons with cerebral brain lesions. Such lesions may not actually eliminate the reflexive response to a painful condition, but they can eliminate any capacity to "suffer" as a result of the condition. Likewise, anencephalic infants may reflexively avoid painful stimuli where the brain stem is functioning and thus is able to command an innate, unconscious withdrawal response; but the infants presumably lack the capacity to suffer. It is clear, however, that this incapacity to suffer has not been established beyond all doubt. After the advent of new transplant methods in the past few decades, anencephalic infants have successfully been used as a source of organs for donation. However, the Task Force was able to identify only twelve successful transplants using anencephalic organs by 1990. Transplants were most successful when the anencephalic immediately was placed on life support and its organs used as soon as possible, without regard to the existence of brain-stem activity. However, this only accounted for a total of four reported transplants.

There appears to be general agreement that anencephalics usually have ceased to be suitable organ donors by the time they meet all the criteria for "whole brain death," i.e., the complete absence of brain-stem function. There also is no doubt that a need exists for infant organs for transplantation. Nationally, between thirty and fifty percent of children under two years of age who need transplants die while waiting for organs to become available.

III. Legal Definitions of "Death" & "Life"

. . . The [Florida] statute cited as controlling by the trial court does not actually address itself to the problem of anencephalic infants, nor indeed to any situation other than patients actually being sustained by artificial life support. The statute provides:

> For legal and medical purposes, *where respiratory and circulatory functions are maintained by artificial means of support* so as to preclude a determination that these functions have ceased, the occurrence of death *may* be determined where there is the irreversible cessation of the functioning of the entire brain, including the brain stem, determined in accordance with this section.

§382.009(1), Fla. Stat. (1991) (emphasis added). A later subsection goes on to declare: Except for a diagnosis of brain death, the standard set forth in this section is not the exclusive standard for determining death or for the withdrawal of life-support systems. §382.009(4), Fla. Stat. (1991).

. . . We also note that the 1988 Florida Legislature considered a bill that would have defined "death" to include anencephaly. The bill died in committee. While the failure of legislation in committee does not establish legislative intent, it nevertheless supports the conclusion that as recently as 1988 no consensus existed among Florida's lawmakers regarding the issue we confront today.

The parties have cited to no authorities directly dealing with the question of whether anencephalics are "alive" or "dead." Our own research has disclosed no other federal or Florida law or precedent arguably on point or applicable by analogy.[9]

We thus are led to the conclusion that no legal authority binding upon this Court has decided whether an anencephalic child is alive for purposes of organ donation. In the absence of applicable legal authority, this Court must weigh and consider the public policy considerations at stake here.

IV. COMMON LAW & POLICY

Initially, we must start by recognizing that section 382.009, Florida Statutes (1991), provides a method for determining death in those cases in which a person's respiratory and circulatory functions are maintained artificially. §382.009(4), Fla. Stat. (1991). Likewise, we agree that a cardiopulmonary definition of death must be accepted in Florida as a matter of our common law, applicable whenever section 382.009 does not govern. Thus, if cardiopulmonary function is not being maintained artificially as stated in section 382.009, a person is dead who has sustained irreversible cessation of circulatory and respiratory functions as determined in accordance with accepted medical standards.

The question remaining is whether there is good reason in public policy for this Court to create an additional common law standard applicable to anencephalics. Alterations of the common law, while rarely entertained or allowed, are within this Court's prerogative. However, the rule we follow is that the common law will not be altered or expanded unless demanded by public necessity, or where required to vindicate fundamental rights. We believe, for example, that our adoption of the cardiopulmonary definition of death today is required by public necessity and, in any event, merely formalizes what has been the common practice in this state for well over a century.

Such is not the case with petitioners' request. Our review of the medical, ethical, and legal literature on anencephaly discloses absolutely no consensus that public necessity or fundamental rights will be better served by granting this request.

We are not persuaded that a public necessity exists to justify this action, in light of the other factors in this case—although we acknowledge much ambivalence about this particular question. We have been deeply touched by the

---

9. Some of the parties and amici cite to various other laws establishing civil rights for disabled persons, including section 504 of the federal Rehabilitation Act and the federal Americans with Disabilities Act. We are aware that analogous Florida laws also exist. It is evident, however, that these laws do not apply to the dead. Accordingly, the linchpin question remains whether or not T.A.C.P. was dead at the times in question. We also are not persuaded that Roe v. Wade, 410 U.S. 113 (1973), has any applicability to the facts at hand. By its own terms, *Roe* did not attempt to "resolve the difficult question of when life begins." *Id.* 410 U.S. at 159. We also do not agree that a parental right of privacy is implicated here, because privacy does not give parents the right to donate the organs of a child born alive who is not yet legally dead. Art. I, §23, Fla. Const.

altruism and unquestioned motives of the parents of T.A.C.P. The parents have shown great humanity, compassion, and concern for others. The problem we as a Court must face, however, is that the medical literature shows unresolved controversy over the extent to which anencephalic organs can or should be used in transplants.

There is an unquestioned need for transplantable infant organs. Yet some medical commentators suggest that the organs of anencephalics are seldom usable, for a variety of reasons, and that so few organ transplants will be possible from anencephalics as to render the enterprise questionable in light of the ethical problems at stake—even if legal restrictions were lifted. Others note that prenatal screening now is substantially reducing the number of anencephalics born each year in the United States and that, consequently, anencephalics are unlikely to be a significant source of organs as time passes. And still others have frankly acknowledged that there is no consensus and that redefinition of death in this context should await the emergence of a consensus. . . . Some legal commentators have argued that treating anencephalics as dead equates them with "nonpersons," presenting a "slippery slope" problem with regard to all other persons who lack cognition for whatever reason. Others have quoted physicians involved in infant-organ transplants as stating, "[T]he slippery slope is real," because some physicians have proposed transplants from infants with defects less severe than anencephaly.

We express no opinion today about who is right and who is wrong on these issues—if any "right" or "wrong" can be found here. The salient point is that no consensus exists as to: (a) the utility of organ transplants of the type at issue here; (b) the ethical issues involved; or (c) the legal and constitutional problems implicated.

V. Conclusions

Accordingly, we find no basis to expand the common law to equate anencephaly with death. We acknowledge the possibility that some infants' lives might be saved by using organs from anencephalics who do not meet the traditional definition of "death" we reaffirm today. But weighed against this is the utter lack of consensus, and the questions about the overall utility of such organ donations. The scales clearly tip in favor of not extending the common law in this instance. . . .

Because no Florida statute applies to the present case, the determination of death in this instance must be judged against the common law cardiopulmonary standard. The evidence shows that T.A.C.P.'s heart was beating and she was breathing at the times in question. Accordingly, she was not dead under Florida law, and no donation of her organs would have been legal. . . .

NOTES AND QUESTIONS

1. *Common law definitions of death.*   On what basis does the Florida Supreme Court in In re T.A.C.P. determine that the organs of an anencephalic infant

cannot be donated? Although T.A.C.P.'s condition did not satisfy the requirements of either cardiopulmonary death (because her heart was still beating at the time of the request for donation) or "brain death" under Florida law, the court stated that there was another potential avenue for finding that T.A.C.P. was dead. What was it? Do you think the court was correct in refusing to follow that path? Do you think the court has the power it claims, but refused in this case to exercise, to define life and death? Who should answer the question of when death occurs—the judiciary or the legislature?

2. *Expanding the class of the dead by statute.*   Conversely, if the Florida legislature had passed the bill referred to, would the resulting law have been constitutional? What constitutional infirmities might the bill have had? The bill would have amended the state's brain death statute by adding the following:

> However, when anencephalia exists, it is presumed brain activity does not exist and the criteria for brain death have been fulfilled. "Anencephalia" is defined a developmental anomaly characterized by absence of the cranial vault, and cerebral hemispheres completely missing or reduced to small masses attached to the base of the skull.

Fla. H.B. 1088 (1988). A number of state legislatures have specifically considered including newborns with anencephaly among the dead, although no state has approved any such legislation.

3. *Vulnerable patients?*   One criticism of proposals to permit the harvesting of organs from newborns with anencephaly (either by declaring that they are dead or by permitting an exception to the dead donor rule (as briefly proposed by the Ethics Council of the AMA—see Chapter 3) is that if society is going to adopt a policy of sacrificing some patients' lives for others, then, as Alexander Morgan Capron has written, "it seems very strange—and a very bad precedent—to start with the most vulnerable patients. Unconsenting, incompetent patients who have never had a chance to express their views about whether, if near death but not yet dead, they would want their bodies cut up for purposes of organ donation, are the *least* suitable source." Alexander Morgan Capron, Anencephalic Donors: Separate the Dead from the Dying, 17 The Hastings Ctr. Rep. 5 (Feb. 1987). Capron's view is predicated on a biological understanding of death. Would an understanding of death as a social construct get around his objection?

4. *Utilitarianism.*   What would a utilitarian analysis of this issue look like? It would have to consider the number of infants who could be saved by using organs harvested from infants with anencephaly, as well as the short life of the latter—a life that is not even "experienced" as we normally think of it. But how would a utilitarian analysis factor in "slippery slope" concerns; that is, concerns that less severely disabled newborns or other persons would also be determined to be dead for purposes of organ retrieval? How would utilitarianism confront the criticism that if society declared these individuals "dead," it would, in effect, be saying that it would be appropriate to bury them even though they may still be breathing on their own?

CHALLENGING ISSUES: ADVANCE DIRECTIVES FOR ORGAN DONATION IN THE EVENT THAT AN INDIVIDUAL BECOMES PERMANENTLY UNCONSCIOUS

Support for using infants with anencephaly as organ donors continues among many who have studied the issue, as does opposition to the idea. More recently, however, attention has turned to the idea that individuals might specify, in an advance directive or by similar means, that they wish to be used as an organ donor in the event that they enter into a persistent vegetative state or other form of permanent unconsciousness. Just as with proposals for using newborns with anencephaly, the legal method for accomplishing this in a way that a physician recovering vital organs would not be committing homicide would be either (1) to create an exception to the dead donor rule for those who have expressly provided that they wish their organs to be taken although they are still alive or (2) to allow such individuals to be declared dead, in effect with their consent about when such a declaration might be properly made. These proposals appear at least to avoid the problem of vulnerability associated with patients who have never been conscious or competent. Moreover, they seem quite consonant with the movement in recent decades toward honoring advance directives and otherwise respecting patients' wishes regarding the kind of treatment (or lack thereof) they would like to receive should they find themselves in certain physical states generally associated with an absence of any quality of life. The latter of the two approaches would appear to allow individuals to define for themselves when they should be considered "dead." What do you think about this proposal, which would seem to endorse the idea that death is neither a biological nor a social concept, but an *individual* one?

ii.   Donation After Cardiac Death

When the Uniform Determination of Death Act and similar legal standards for death were adopted in the 1970s and 1980s, the "traditional" criteria for determining death, irreversible cessation of cardiac and respiratory function, were restated with little discussion because of the consensus surrounding them. That comfortable state of affairs has dissolved as new possibilities for using the bodies of the newly deceased for organ donation now seem to demand that we ask exactly when that "moment" of death occurs. Although most transplantable organs from deceased donors have come from patients who have satisfied the criteria for "brain death," in the last 20 years it has become accepted medical practice to recover organs from donors after the irreversible cessation of circulatory and respiratory functions, called variously (and confusingly) "circulatory," "cardiopulmonary," "cardiocirculatory," or "cardiac" death. James L. Bernat, The Boundaries of Organ Donation after Circulatory Death, 359 New Eng. J. Med. 669–671 (2008). In 2006, organs were recovered from 645 donors following cardiac death, accounting for 8 percent of all deceased donors. Robert Steinbrook, Organ Donation after Cardiac Death, 357 New Eng. J. Med. 209–213 (2007).

The reason such patients had not been considered a viable source of organs prior to this time is because of the swift loss of blood flow to the organs once death has occurred. But if the patient's death is, in effect, "scheduled," an organ procurement team can be ready to take the organs as soon as death is pronounced. The ideal candidate is one who is highly dependent on a ventilator who has—or in the event of incapacity, whose family has—decided on its removal. A 2005 national conference of experts on the subject, as well as a report issued by the Institute of Medicine and guidelines adopted by the Joint Commission (the hospital accrediting body) and the United Network for Organ Sharing, reveal consensus on the following issues:

> (1) Irreversibility of cessation of circulatory and respiratory functions means that these functions will not resume *spontaneously,* rather than that they cannot with intervention (mechanical ventilation) be resumed. The limited data available suggests that spontaneous resuscitation can be ruled out after 2 minutes. Routinely waiting until it would be impossible to resuscitate the patient with artificial means would seriously compromise the organs intended for recovery. The waiting times currently adopted in various institutional protocols fall between 2 and 5 minutes.
>
> (2) The decision to withdraw or withhold life support should be made separately from and prior to the decision to donate, so that the decision to end life support is not influenced by the possibility of donation; the physician who declares death must not be a member of the organ recovery or transplant team, and the latter should not be present during the withdrawal of life-sustaining measures.
>
> (3) In order to best preserve the health and therefore transplantability of organs, certain interventions (such as the administration of pharmacological agents) may be performed on the patient prior to death, as long as the patient (or, as appropriate, surrogate decisionmaker) gives informed consent, even though such interventions do not benefit the patient but are solely for the purpose of organ procurement.

J. L. Bernat et al., Report of a National Conference on Donation after Cardiac Death, 6 Am. J. Transplant. 281–291 (2006); Robert Steinbrook, Organ Donation after Cardiac Death, 357 New Eng. J. Med. 209–213 (2007).

This developing practice of organ donation after cardiac death is not without its critics. Some express concern about the conflict of interest that physicians and other care providers may face in the knowledge that hastening one person's death is expected to benefit another patient (even when care is taken that the procurement team and those providing patient care are kept separate). There is also concern about medical interventions that do not benefit the patient and may not actually be agreed to by the patient because of the patient's incapacity, but are consented to by the patient's surrogate or family. Most of the current criticism, however, appears to revolve around the definition of "irreversibility" and whether, as one critical editorial put it, "the medical profession has been gerrymandering the definition of death to carefully conform with conditions that are most favorable for transplantation." Robert D. Truog & Franklin G. Miller, The Dead Donor Rule and Organ Transplantation, 359 New Eng. J. Med. 674–675 (2008). A 2008 Denver Children's Hospital report of three successful transplants in infants of hearts obtained from donors who died from cardiocirculatory causes prompted the following commentary:

> Virtually all observers have assumed that donation after cardiac death could, in principle, provide any vital organs except hearts. If someone is pronounced dead on the basis of irreversible loss of heart function, after all, it would not be possible for heart function to be restored in another body. Some have

suggested defining death as the impossibility of autoresuscitation, which means that the heart cannot restart spontaneously even if it could be started by means of external stimulation. Calling such a heart "irreversibly stopped" may be defensible if no attempt will be made to restart the heart. However, one cannot say a heart is irreversibly stopped if, in fact, it will be restarted.

. . . It is impossible to transplant a heart successfully after irreversible stoppage: if a heart is restarted, the person from whom it was taken cannot have been dead according to cardiac criteria.

. . . This means that under current law, it is not possible to procure a transplantable heart after cardiac death.

Robert M. Veatch, Donating Hearts after Cardiac Death—Reversing the Irreversible, 359 New Eng. J. Med. 672–673 (2008).

Veatch suggests two options for changing the law to make the transplantation of hearts after cardiac death legally possible: creating exceptions to the dead donor rule, or changing the definition of death to include a brain-based pronouncement of death that would encompass permanent unconsciousness (this second option would limit the patients from whom donation could take place). Veatch prefers the second option, as noted in section c(i) above; for a contrasting view, consider what the following authors have to say:

> Many will object that transplantation surgeons cannot legally or ethically remove vital organs from patients before death, since doing so will cause their death. However, if the critiques of the current methods of diagnosing death are correct, then such actions are already taking place on a routine basis. Moreover, in modern intensive care units, ethically justified decisions and actions of physicians are already the proximate cause of death for many patients—for instance, when mechanical ventilation is withdrawn. Whether death occurs as the result of ventilator withdrawal or organ procurement, the ethically relevant precondition is valid consent by the patient or surrogate. With such consent, there is no harm or wrong done in retrieving vital organs before death, provided that anesthesia is administered. With proper safeguards, no patient will die from vital organ donation who would not otherwise die as a result of the withdrawal of life support. Finally, surveys suggest that issues related to respect for valid consent and the degree of neurologic injury may be more important to the public than concerns about whether the patient is already dead at the time the organs are removed.

Robert D. Truog & Franklin G. Miller, The Dead Donor Rule and Organ Transplantation, 359 New Eng. J. Med. 674–675 (2008).

NOTES AND QUESTIONS

1. *Irreversibility.* What do you think of the developing medical consensus that "irreversible" loss of cardiocirculatory function in the definition of death means that spontaneous resuscitation is not possible and no attempt at resuscitation will be made? Doesn't this mean we could have two patients with the exact same physical condition, and one might be alive and the other dead? What do you think of Veatch's argument that hearts cannot be legally transplanted after cardiac death?

2. *How long to wait?* Under the Denver Children's Hospital research protocol, in which pediatric heart transplants took place using hearts following

donors' cardiac death, the observation period between the end of circulatory function and the removal of organs was shortened to less than the prevailing norm of two to five minutes. In the first of the three transplants, physicians waited 3 minutes before death was declared and organ recovery begun, but in the other two, the process was reduced to 1.25 minutes. This was justified as reducing injury to the organs and "based on the longest reported period before autoresuscitation of a child or adult, 60 seconds." Mark M. Boucek et al., Pediatric Heart Transplantation after Declaration of Cardiocirculatory Death, 359 New Eng. J. Med. 709–714 (2008). Who should determine what the appropriate amount of time is before declaration of death and on what basis?

   3. *Options.*   What do you think is the best course of action to ensure the legality of organ donation practices following cardiac death: (a) continue with our current definition of death, interpreting it to encompass existing protocols (as appears to be the practice currently); (b) modify the definition of death; or (c) create exceptions to the dead donor rule?

B.   TREATMENT OF THE DECEASED BODY

1.   Anatomical Gifts

All 50 states and the District of Columbia have adopted some form of the Uniform Anatomical Gift Act (UAGA), which allows an individual while alive to make a gift of an organ for transplantation or research. The gift becomes effective upon the individual's death. The original UAGA was adopted in 1968, revised in 1987, and then most recently revised in 2006 (although further revisions occurred in 2007, the current Act is still referred to as the "2006 UAGA"). As of Fall 2012, 47 states, including the District of Columbia, have adopted the 2006 revision.

a.   Summary of Uniform Anatomical Gift Act (2006)

The 2006 UAGA specifies, among other things:

   (a) *who can make a gift of their own body, or parts thereof*—Generally, an adult prior to death, an emancipated minor, or a minor authorized under state law to apply for a driver's license.
   (b) *who can make a gift of another's body, or parts thereof*—Generally, a hierarchy is established beginning with an agent of the donor ("donor" meaning the individual whose body or parts are donated), then the donor's spouse, adult children, parents, adult siblings, adult grandchildren, grandparents, guardians, or "any other person having the authority to dispose of the decedent's body." When there is more than one individual in a class (e.g., three adult siblings) to which the decision has fallen, then one member of the class can make the decision if there is no known objection from the others; if there is a known objection, then the decision must be made by a majority of the class.

(c) *how the gift may be made*—A signed writing, an indication on a driver's license, by a will, orally if the donor is terminally ill.

(d) *rules for amending or revoking anatomical gifts*—A revocation does not bar another person from making a gift of that person's body if authorized to do so.

(e) *rules for refusing to make an anatomical gift*—A donor may refuse to make an anatomical gift in much the same manner (documentation, etc.) that a gift may be made. In contrast to a revocation, an effective refusal does bar another person from making a gift of a decedent's body.

(f) *to whom a gift may be made*—In the absence of a specific designation by the donor, body parts will be distributed in conformity with federal regulations regarding the allocation of organs to tissue banks and organ procurement organizations.

(g) *separate roles for physicians*—"Neither the physician who attends the decedent at death nor the physician who determines the time of the decedent's death may participate in the procedures for removing or transplanting a part from the decendent."

(f) *required efforts to secure gifts*—Organ procurement organizations must make a reasonable search for a record of an anatomical gift or for the availability of any person who may be authorized to make a gift. (Federal law requires, as a condition of receiving Medicare and Medicaid funding, that all hospitals refer deaths or near deaths to organ procurement organizations, and that they "[e]nsure, in collaboration with the designated OPO, that the family of each potential donor is informed of its options to donate organs, tissues, or eyes or to decline to donate." 42 C.F.R. §482.45.)

b.   Important Recent Revisions to the UAGA

One of the more important changes in the 2006 revision to the Uniform Anatomical Gift Act is Section 8, reprinted below as adopted by the State of Georgia:

Georgia Revised Uniform Anatomical Gift Act
Ga. Stat. §§44-5-140 et seq. (2008)

§44-5-146. Preclusive effect of anatomical gift, amendment, or revocation

(a) Except as otherwise provided in subsection (g) of this Code section and subject to subsection (f) of this Code section, in the absence of an express, contrary indication by the donor, a person other than the donor is barred from making, amending, or revoking an anatomical gift of a donor's body or part if the donor made an anatomical gift of the donor's body or part under Code Section 44-5-143 or an amendment to an anatomical gift of the donor's body or part under Code Section 44-5-144.

(b) A donor's revocation of an anatomical gift of the donor's body or part under Code Section 44-5-144 is not a refusal and does not bar another person specified in Code Sections 44-5-142 and 44-5-147 from making an anatomical gift of the donor's body or part under Code Section 44-5-143 or 44-5-148.

(c) If a person other than the donor makes an unrevoked anatomical gift of the donor's body or part under Code Section 44-5-143 or an amendment to an anatomical gift of the donor's body or part under Code Section 44-5-144, another person may not make, amend, or revoke the gift of the donor's body or part under Code Section 44-5-148.

(d) A revocation of an anatomical gift of a donor's body or part under Code Section 44-5-144 by a person other than the donor does not bar another person from making an anatomical gift of the body or part under Code Section 44-5-143 or 44-5-148.

(e) In the absence of an express, contrary indication by the donor or other person authorized to make an anatomical gift under Code Section 44-5-142, an anatomical gift of a part is neither a refusal to give another part nor a limitation on the making of an anatomical gift of another part at a later time by the donor or another person.

(f) In the absence of an express, contrary indication by the donor or other person authorized to make an anatomical gift under Code Section 44-5-142, an anatomical gift of a part for one or more of the purposes set forth in Code Section 44-5-142 is not a limitation on the making of an anatomical gift of the part for any of the other purposes by the donor or any other person under Code Section 44-5-143 or 44-5-148.

(g) If a donor who is an unemancipated minor dies, a parent of the donor who is reasonably available may revoke or amend an anatomical gift of the donor's body or part.

(h) If an unemancipated minor who signed a refusal dies, a parent of the minor who is reasonably available may revoke the minor's refusal.

The 2006 UAGA has met considerable criticism over two provisions, Sections 14 and 21, which give organ procurement organizations some measure of influence over medical treatment decisions for individuals who are potential donors.

Section 14 concerns examinations to determine if a potential donor meets medical criteria for donation. Section 14 states:

> When a hospital refers an individual at or near death to a procurement organization, the organization may conduct any reasonable examination necessary to ensure the medical suitability of a part that is or could be the subject of an anatomical gift for transplantation, therapy, research, or education from a donor or prospective donor. During the examination period, measures necessary to ensure the medical suitability of the part may not be withdrawn unless the hospital or procurement organization knows that the individual has expressed a contrary intent.

Section 21 of the 2006 UAGA concerns conflicts between anatomical gifts and advance directives. It has already been revised. It originally stated:

> If a prospective donor has a declaration or advance health care directive, measures necessary to ensure the medical suitability of an organ for transplantation

or therapy may not be withheld or withdrawn from the prospective donor, unless the declaration expressly provides to the contrary.

Upon criticism that the section improperly overrode patient's autonomy as expressed through advance care planning documents, it was revised to state:

> If a prospective donor has a declaration or advance health care directive and the terms of the declaration or directive and the express or implied terms of a potential anatomical gift are in conflict with regard to the administration of measures necessary to ensure the medical suitability of a part for transplantation or therapy, the prospective donor's attending physician and prospective donor shall confer to resolve the conflict. If the prospective donor is incapable of resolving the conflict, an agent acting under the prospective donor's declaration or directive, or, if none or the agent is not reasonably available, another person authorized by law other than this [act] to make health care decisions on behalf of the prospective donor, shall act for the donor to resolve the conflict. The conflict must be resolved as expeditiously as possible. Information relevant to the resolution of the conflict may be obtained from the appropriate procurement organization and any other person authorized to make an anatomical gift for the prospective donor under Section 9. Before resolution of the conflict, measures necessary to ensure the medical suitability of the part may not be withheld or withdrawn from the prospective donor if withholding or withdrawing the measures is not contraindicated by appropriate end-of-life care.

According to some commentators, these provisions—even as revised—inappropriately transfer to organ procurement agencies decision-making authority for some aspects of medical care for still living patients. See Ana S. Iltis, Michael A. Rie, & Anji Wall, Organ Donation, Patients' Rights, and Medical Responsibilities at the End of Life 37 Crit. Care Med. 310-315 (2009). Iltis et al., explain:

> Some observers have applauded the revised version of section 21, claiming that it resolves previous concerns with EOL [end of life] care. We argue that both section 14, which was not revised, and the revised version of section 21 remain problematic. No procedure is specified and no particular right to support or representation throughout the process of conferring to resolve a conflict is accorded to patients or their surrogates, who may not understand or have the resources to clearly articulate and enforce their wishes, and who may feel manipulated. Some observers have voiced concerns regarding fairness, manipulation, and transparency in the informed consent process for organ donation. Patients who do not have surrogates or family members with whom physicians may confer are offered no additional protection to ensure that their EOL wishes are respected. This circumstance would also apply to wards of the state whose health care was under the direct supervision of courts of law. There is no recognition of patients as being the final source of authority over themselves. It is reasonable to ask whether families should be required to endure a process of conferring on a matter they see as clear and that does not aim to benefit the patient. It also is debatable whether patients who do not have surrogates, which may be a significant percentage of patients in some intensive care units, should have EOL wishes expressed in an advance directive ignored if there is no surrogate to defend those wishes vigorously.
>   . . . Some people not only are willing to donate organs after death but give high priority to making an anatomical gift and would want interventions initiated or prolonged while they are living, if necessary for donation. Others

are willing to donate after death but do not give high priority to donation and would not want additional interventions before death to make organ donation possible or would defer these decisions to their designated surrogates. Donor cards do not permit these preferences to be expressed. In the present process of securing consent to organ donation via donor cards and registries, insufficient information is provided about OPO life support policies and the possible premortem implications of becoming a donor (as affirmed by UAGA 2006). The consent remains ethically and legally questionable because individuals are unable to make and express a decision about whether and to what extent they want their donor status to influence their EOL care. It is unreasonable to hold that a willingness to make a postmortem anatomical gift implies consent for premortem care or transfers decision making authority to an OPO.

Id.

NOTES AND QUESTIONS

1. *Family overrides.*   According to the Official Commentary of the National Conference of Commissioners on Uniform State Laws,

Section 8 [the reprinted portion of the Georgia statute, above] substantially strengthens the respect due a decision to make an anatomical gift. While the 1987 Act provided that a donor's anatomical gift was irrevocable (except by the donor), until quite recently it had been a common practice for procurement organizations to seek affirmation of the gift from the donor's family. This could result in unnecessary delays in the recovery of organs as well as a reversal of a donor's donation decision. Section 8 intentionally disempowers families from making or revoking anatomical gifts in contravention of a donor's wishes. Thus, under the strengthened language of this [act], if a donor had made an anatomical gift, there is no reason to seek consent from the donor's family as they have no right to give it legally. See Section 8(a). Of course, that would not bar, nor should it bar, a procurement organization from advising the donor's family of the donor's express wishes, but that conversation should focus more on what procedures will be followed to carry out the donor's wishes and on answering a family's questions about the process rather than on seeking approval of the donation. A limited exception applies if the donor is a minor at the time of death. In this case, either parent may amend or revoke the donor's anatomical gift. See Section 8(g).

Why do you think health care providers have been reluctant to rely on a legally valid document specifying the donor's anatomical gift and have instead sought consent to organ donation from the donor's family? Do you think new Section 8 of the 2006 UAGA will be effective in reversing this common practice? Do you think that is a worthy goal?

2. *Respecting donors' autonomy or increasing the number of gifts?*   Notice the effect of several of the provisions of Section 8: (a) family members can donate a deceased donor's organs after the donor has revoked a prior gift document, (b) an anatomical gift of a specified part does not prevent family members from donating other parts of the donor's body (absent the donor's express contrary indication), and (c) donation by parents can take place after a minor's death, even if the minor signed a refusal to make a gift. Is there any tension in these

provisions between honoring the donor's autonomy and increasing the number of gifts? Do you think they strike the right balance between these goals?

3. *Donor cards vs. Advance Directives.*   What do organ donors consent to when they sign a donor card? According to Iltis et al. the first version of 2006 UAGA presumed that donors have consented to an override of their advance directive in cases of conflict—life-sustaining treatment would not be withheld or withdrawn unless the advance directive expressly stated that its provisions prevailed over a donor gift. Iltis et al. see little improvement in the 2007 revision. Why?

4. *Default position in favor of continuing "life support systems."*   During the examination period to determine the medical suitability of organs (Section 14) and while any conflict between an advance directive and potential anatomical gift are resolved (Section 21), "measures necessary to ensure the medical suitability" of an organ cannot be withheld or withdrawn. Does this "default" position in favor of continued use of "life support systems" amount to a presumption of consent to organ donation until there has been an explicit refusal? If not a presumption of consent, what about a "presumption of intent to donate organs"? See Joseph L. Verheijde, Mohamed Y Rady, & Joan L. McGregor, The United States Revised Uniform Anatomical Gift Act (2006): New Challenges to Balancing Patient Rights and Physician Responsibilities, 2 Phil., Ethics, & Humanities in Med., 19 (2007) (arguing that "[t]he premises underlying the subtle progression of the Revised UAGA (2006) towards the presumption about how to dispose of one's organs at or near death can pave the way for an affirmative 'duty to donate' to the detriment of human liberty in a free society).

c.   Limited Presumed Consent Laws

The severe and constant shortage of human organs for transplantation (see Chapter 14) has prompted a number of proposals over the years to increase donations. One such proposal is understood under the name *presumed consent.* Although the terms of a presumed consent program can vary, the general idea is that every individual is presumed to have consented to the donation of some or all of his organs upon his death and would have to "opt out" of that donation by executing some kind of document equivalent to what the current program expects for donations.

In the United States, a few states have promulgated presumed consent laws with regard to specific organs such as corneas and pituitary glands. Those laws may not, however, be deemed constitutional. Consider the following two cases, which present very different views on the permissibility of a provision from earlier versions of the Uniform Anatomical Gift Act providing that in certain instances, a medical examiner may remove the corneas of a decedent in the absence of objection by the next of kin. This is in essence a limited form of presumed consent.

The 2006 UAGA eliminated the presumed consent provision relating to corneas in the possession of coroners. A number of states adopting the 2006 UAGA have, however, retained the cornea provision. See, e.g., N.C. Gen Stat. §130A-412.3; see generally David Orentlicher, Presumed Consent to Organ

Donation: Its Rise and Fall in the United States, 2008, http://papers.ssrn.com/s013/papers.cfm?abstract_id=1207862.

State v. Powell
497 So. 2d 1188 (Fla. 1986)

Opinion by Justice OVERTON.

This is a petition to review a circuit court order finding unconstitutional section 732.9185, Florida Statutes (1983), which authorizes medical examiners to remove corneal tissue from decedents during statutorily required autopsies when such tissue is needed for transplantation. The statute prohibits the removal of the corneal tissue if the next of kin objects, but does not require that the decedent's next of kin be notified of the procedure. [F]or the reasons expressed below, [we] find that the statute is constitutional.

The challenged statute provides:

Corneal removal by medical examiners.—

(1) In any case in which a patient is in need of corneal tissue for a transplant, a district medical examiner or an appropriately qualified designee with training in ophthalmologic techniques may, upon request of any eye bank authorized under §732.918, provide the cornea of a decedent whenever all of the following conditions are met:

(a) A decedent who may provide a suitable cornea for the transplant is under the jurisdiction of the medical examiner and an autopsy is required in accordance with §406.11.

(b) No objection by the next of kin of the decedent is known by the medical examiner.

(c) The removal of the cornea will not interfere with the subsequent course of an investigation or autopsy.

(2) Neither the district medical examiner nor his appropriately qualified designee nor any eye bank authorized under §732.918 may be held liable in any civil or criminal action for failure to obtain consent of the next of kin.

The trial court decided this case by summary judgment. The facts are not in dispute. On June 15, 1983, James White drowned while swimming at the city beach in Dunellon, Florida. Associate Medical Examiner Dr. Thomas Techman, who is an appellant in this cause, performed an autopsy on James' body at Leesburg Community Hospital. On July 11, 1983, Anthony Powell died in a motor vehicle accident in Marion County. Medical Examiner Dr. William H. Shutze, who is also an appellant in this cause, performed an autopsy on Anthony's body. In each instance, under the authority of section 732.9185, the medical examiner removed corneal tissue from the decedent without giving notice to or obtaining consent from the parents of the decedent.

James' and Anthony's parents, who are the appellees in this case, each brought an action claiming damages for the alleged wrongful removal of their sons' corneas and seeking a judgment declaring section 732.9185 unconstitutional.

In its judgment, the trial court noted that section 732.9185 "has as its purpose the commendable and laudable objective of providing high quality cornea tissue to those in need of same," but declared the statute unconstitutional on the grounds that it (1) deprives survivors of their fundamental personal and property right to dispose of their deceased next of kin in the same condition as lawful autopsies left them, without procedural or substantive due process of law; (2) creates an invidious classification which deprives survivors of their right to equal protection; and (3) permits a taking of private property by state action for a non-public purpose, in violation of article X, section 6(a), of the Florida Constitution. The court concluded that the state has no compelling interest in non-consensual removal of appellees' decedents' corneal tissue that outweighs the survivors' right to dispose of their sons' bodies in the condition death left them. For the reasons expressed below, we reject these findings.

In addressing the issue of the statute's constitutionality, we begin with the premise that a person's constitutional rights terminate at death. See Roe v. Wade, 410 U.S. 113 (1973). If any rights exist, they belong to the decedent's next of kin.

Next, we recognize that a legislative act carries with it the presumption of validity and the party challenging a statute's constitutionality must carry the burden of establishing that the statute bears no reasonable relation to a permissible legislative objective. In determining whether a permissible legislative objective exists, we must review the evidence arising from the record in this case.

The unrebutted evidence in this record establishes that the State of Florida spends approximately $138 million each year to provide its blind with the basic necessities of life. At present, approximately ten percent of Florida's blind citizens are candidates for cornea transplantation, which has become a highly effective procedure for restoring sight to the functionally blind. As advances are made in the field, the number of surgical candidates will increase, thereby raising the demand for suitable corneal tissue. The increasing number of elderly persons in our population has also created a great demand for corneas because corneal blindness often is age-related. Further, an affidavit in the record states:

> Corneal transplants are particularly important in newborns. The brain does not learn to see if the cornea is not clear. There is a critical period in the first few months of life when the brain "learns to see." If the cornea is not clear, the brain not only does not "learn to see," but the brain loses its ability to "learn to see." Hence, corneal transplant in children must be made as soon as practicable after the problem is discovered. Without the medical examiner legislation, there would be virtually no corneal tissue available for infants and these children would remain forever blind.

The record reflects that the key to successful corneal transplantation is the availability of high-quality corneal tissue and that corneal tissue removed more than ten hours after death is generally unsuitable for transplantation. The implementation of section 732.9185 in 1977 has, indisputably, increased both the supply and quality of tissue available for transplantation. Statistics show that, in 1976, only 500 corneas were obtained in Florida for transplantation while, in 1985, more than 3,000 persons in Florida had their sight restored through corneal transplantation surgery.

The record also demonstrates that a qualitative difference exists between corneal tissue obtained through outright donation and tissue obtained pursuant to section 732.9185. In contrast to the tissue donated by individuals, which is largely unusable because of the advanced age of the donor at death, approximately eighty to eighty-five percent of tissue obtained through medical examiners is suitable for transplantation. The evidence establishes that this increase in the quantity and quality of available corneal tissue was brought about by passage of the statute and is, in large part, attributable to the fact that section 732.9185 does not place a duty upon medical examiners to seek out the next of kin to obtain consent for cornea removal. An affidavit in the record reveals that, before legislation authorized medical examiners in California to remove corneas without the consent of the next of kin, the majority of the families asked by the Los Angeles medical examiner's office responded positively; however, approximately eighty percent of the families could not be located in sufficient time for medical examiners to remove usable corneal tissue from the decedents. An autopsy is a surgical dissection of the body; it necessarily results in a massive intrusion into the decedent. This record reflects that cornea removal, by comparison, requires an infinitesimally small intrusion which does not affect the decedent's appearance. With or without cornea removal, the decedent's eyes must be capped to maintain a normal appearance.

Our review of section 732.9185 reveals certain safeguards which are apparently designed to limit cornea removal to instances in which the public's interest is greatest and the impact on the next of kin the least: corneas may be removed only if the decedent is under the jurisdiction of the medical examiner; an autopsy is mandated by Florida law; and the removal will not interfere with the autopsy or an investigation of the death. Further, medical examiners may not automatically remove tissue from all decedents subject to autopsy; rather, a request must be made by an eye bank based on a present need for the tissue.

We conclude that this record clearly establishes that this statute reasonably achieves the permissible legislative objective of providing sight to many of Florida's blind citizens.

We next address the trial court's finding that section 732.9185 deprives appellees of a fundamental property right. All authorities generally agree that the next of kin have no property right in the remains of a decedent. Although, in Dunahoo v. Bess, 146 Fla. 182, 200 So. 541 (1941), this Court held that a surviving husband had a "property right" in his wife's body which would sustain a claim for negligent embalming, we subsequently clarified our position to be consistent with the majority view that the right is limited to "possession of the body . . . for the purpose of burial, sepulture or other lawful disposition," and that interference with this right gives rise to a tort action. Kirksey v. Jernigan, 45 So. 2d 188, 189 (Fla. 1950). More recently, we affirmed the district court's determination that the next of kin's right in a decedent's remains is based upon "the personal right of the decedent's next of kin to bury the body rather than any property right in the body itself." The view that the next of kin has no property right but merely a limited right to possess the body for burial purposes is universally accepted by courts and commentators. . . .

Under the facts and circumstances of these cases, we find no taking of private property by state action for a non-public purpose in violation of article X, section 6, of the Florida Constitution. We note that the right to bring an action in tort does not necessarily invoke constitutional protections. Decisions of the United States Supreme Court have clearly established that the loss of a common law right by legislative act does not automatically operate as a deprivation of substantive due process. Tort actions may be restricted when necessary to obtain a permissible legislative objective.

Appellees also assert that their right to control the disposition of their decedents' remains is a fundamental right of personal liberty protected against unreasonable governmental intrusion by the due process clause. Appellees argue that, because the statute permits the removal of a decedent's corneas without reference to his family's preferences, it infringes upon a right, characterized as one of religion, family, or privacy, which is fundamental and must be subjected to strict scrutiny. Appellees rely upon a line of decisions from the United States Supreme Court which recognize the freedom of personal choice in matters of family life as one of the liberties protected by the due process clause. Appellees also point out that the United States Supreme Court has found rights to personal privacy in connection with activities relating to marriage, Boddie v. Connecticut, 401 U.S. 371 (1971); procreation, Skinner v. Oklahoma, 316 U.S. 535 (1942); contraception, Griswold v. Connecticut, 381 U.S. 479 (1965); abortion, Roe v. Wade; and child-rearing and education, Pierce v. Society of Sisters, 268 U.S. 510 (1925). According to appellees, the theme which runs through these cases, and which compels the invalidation of section 732.9185, is the protection from governmental interference of the right of free choice in decisions of fundamental importance to the family.

We reject appellees' argument. The cases cited recognize only freedom of choice concerning personal matters involved in existing, ongoing relationships among living persons as fundamental or essential to the pursuit of happiness by free persons.

We find that the right of the next of kin to a tort claim for interference with burial, established by this Court in *Dunahoo,* does not rise to the constitutional dimension of a fundamental right traditionally protected under either the United States or Florida Constitution. Neither federal nor state privacy provisions protect an individual from every governmental intrusion into one's private life, especially when a statute addresses public health interests.

The record contains no evidence that the appellees' objections to the removal of corneal tissues for human transplants are based on any "fundamental tenets of their religious beliefs." Wisconsin v. Yoder, 406 U.S. at 218, 92 S. Ct. at 1534. "[T]he very concept of ordered liberty precludes allowing every person to make his own standards on matters of conduct in which society as a whole has important interests." *Id.* at 215–16.

We also reject the trial court's finding that section 732.9185 creates an invidious classification regarding the next of kin of deceased persons. "Legislatures have wide discretion in passing laws that have the inevitable effect of treating some people differently from others." Parham v. Hughes, 441 U.S. 347 (1979). We find that the statute's effect on the next of kin is incidental and does not offend equal protection.

In conclusion, we hold that section 732.9185 is constitutional because it rationally promotes the permissible state objective of restoring sight to the blind.

Newman v. Sathyavaglswaran
287 F.3d 786 (9th Cir. 2002)

Opinion by FISHER.

Parents, whose deceased children's corneas were removed by the Los Angeles County Coroner's office without notice or consent, brought this 42 U.S.C. §1983 action alleging a taking of their property without due process of law. The complaint was dismissed by the district court for a failure to state a claim upon which relief could be granted. We must decide whether the long-standing recognition in the law of California, paralleled by our national common law, that next of kin have the exclusive right to possess the bodies of their deceased family members creates a property interest, the deprivation of which must be accorded due process of law under the Fourteenth Amendment of the United States Constitution. We hold that it does. The parents were not required to exhaust postdeprivation procedures prior to bringing this suit. Thus, we hold that they properly stated a claim under §1983.

I.   FACTUAL AND PROCEDURAL BACKGROUND

. . . Following their deaths, the Office of the Coroner for the County of Los Angeles (the coroner) obtained possession of the bodies of the children and, under procedures adopted pursuant to California Government Code §27491.47 as it then existed,[3] removed the corneas from those bodies without the knowledge of the parents and without an attempt to notify them and request consent. The parents became aware of the coroner's actions in September 1999 and subsequently filed this §1983 action alleging a deprivation of their property without due process of law in violation of the Fourteenth Amendment.

II.   PROPERTY INTERESTS IN DEAD BODIES

The Fourteenth Amendment prohibits states from "depriving any person of life, liberty, or property, without due process of law." U.S. Const. amend. XIV, §1. At the threshold, a claim under §1983 for an unconstitutional deprivation of property must show (1) a deprivation (2) of property (3) under color of state law. . . . If these elements are met, the question becomes whether the state afforded constitutionally adequate process for the deprivation. Here, it is uncontested that the coroner's action was a deprivation under color of state law. The coroner argues, however, that the dismissal of the parents' complaint was proper because they could not have a property interest in their children's corneas. . . .

C.   *The Right to Transfer Body Parts*

The first successful transplantation of a kidney in 1954 led to an expansion of the rights of next of kin to the bodies of the dead. In 1968, the National Conference of Commissioners on Uniform State Laws approved the Uniform Anatomical Gift Act (UAGA), adopted by California the same year, which grants next of kin the right to transfer the parts of bodies in their possession to others for medical or research purposes. The right to transfer is limited. The California

---

3. California Government Code §27491.47(a) stated:

Notwithstanding any other provision of law, the coroner may, in the course of an autopsy, remove and release or authorize the removal and release of corneal eye tissue from a body within the coroner's custody, if . . . the coroner has no knowledge of objection to the removal. . . .

UAGA prohibits any person from "knowingly, for valuable consideration, purchasing or selling a part for transplantation, therapy, or reconditioning, if removal of the part is intended to occur after the death of the decedent. . . ."

In the 1970s and 1980s, medical science improvements and the related demand for transplant organs prompted governments to search for new ways to increase the supply of organs for donation. . . . Many perceived as a hindrance to the supply of needed organs the rule implicit in the UAGA that donations could be effected only if consent was received from the decedent or next of kin. . . . [S]ome states passed "presumed consent" laws that allow the taking and transfer of body parts by a coroner without the consent of next of kin as long as no objection to the removal is known. California Government Code §27491.47, enacted in 1983, was such a law.[10]

III. DUE PROCESS ANALYSIS

"To provide California non-profit eye banks with an adequate supply of corneal tissue," §27491.47(a) authorized the coroner to "remove and release or authorize the removal and release of corneal eye tissue from a body within the coroner's custody" without any effort to notify and obtain the consent of next of kin "if . . . the coroner has no knowledge of objection to the removal." . . .

In analyzing whether the implementation of that law by the coroner deprived the parents of property, we define property as "the group of rights inhering in the citizen's relation to the physical thing, as the right to possess, use and dispose of it. . . . In other words, it deals with what lawyers term the individual's 'interest' in the thing in question."

In two decisions the Sixth Circuit, the only federal circuit to address the issue until now, held that the interests of next of kin in dead bodies recognized in Michigan and Ohio allowed next of kin to bring §1983 actions challenging implementation of cornea removal statutes similar to California's. Whaley v. County of Tuscola, 58 F.3d 1111 (6th Cir. 1995) (Michigan); Brotherton v. Cleveland, 923 F.2d 477 (6th Cir. 1991) (Ohio). The Sixth Circuit noted that courts in each state had recognized a right of next of kin to possess the body for burial and a claim by next of kin against others who disturb the body. Those common law rights, combined with the statutory right to control the disposition of the body recognized in each state's adoption of the UAGA, was held to be sufficient to create in next of kin a property interest in the corneas of their deceased relatives that could not be taken without due process of law. . . .

We agree with the reasoning of the Sixth Circuit and believe that reasoning is applicable here. Under traditional common law principles, serving a duty to protect the dignity of the human body in its final disposition that is deeply rooted in our legal history and social traditions, the parents had exclusive and legitimate claims of entitlement to possess, control, dispose and prevent the violation of the corneas and other parts of the bodies of their deceased children. . . .

Because the property interests of next of kin to dead bodies are firmly entrenched in the "background principles of property law," based on values

---

10. In 1998, §27491.47(a)(2) was amended to require that the coroner obtain written or telephonic consent of the next of kin prior to removing corneas. . . .

and understandings contained in our legal history dating from the Roman Empire, California may not be free to alter them with exceptions that lack "a firm basis in traditional property principles." . . .

When the coroner removed the corneas from the bodies of the parents' deceased children and transferred them to others, the parents could no longer possess, control, dispose or prevent the violation of those parts of their children's bodies. To borrow a metaphor used when the government physically occupies property, the coroner did not merely "take a single 'strand' from the 'bundle' of property rights: it chopped through the bundle, taking a slice of every strand." This was a deprivation of the most certain variety. . . .

IV. POSTDEPRIVATION PROCESS

. . . [W]e reverse the district court's dismissal of the parents' complaint and remand for proceedings in which the government's justification for its deprivation of parents' interests may be fully aired and appropriately scrutinized.

NOTES AND QUESTIONS

1. *The constitutional claims.* Why does the Florida Supreme Court reject the plaintiffs' constitutional claim? How would you rate a family's interest in controlling disposition of a loved one's remains as compared to other interests the U.S. Supreme Court has determined support recognition of a fundamental right (e.g., marriage, childrearing)? In Newman v. Sathyavaglaswaran, in contrast to the decision in *Powell*, the Ninth Circuit determined that the parents did have a property interest in their children's corneas that could not be invaded absent due process of law. Which opinion do you find more convincing?

2. *Federal/state split.* Courts in at least two other states have upheld the constitutionality of cornea removal statutes similar to Florida's. See Georgia Lions Eye Bank, Inc. v. Lavant, 255 Ga. 60 (1985); Tillman v. Detroit Receiving Hospital, 138 Mich. App. 683 (1984). But two federal appellate circuits that have addressed the issue have disagreed. In addition to *Newman,* see Brotherton v. Cleveland, 923 F.2d 477 (6th Cir. 1991) and Whaley v. County of Tuscola, 58 F.3d 111 (6th Cir. 1995). The federal–state court split is made even more apparent by the California appellate court's refusal in a 2007 case to follow *Newman.* In Perryman v. County of Los Angeles, 63 Cal. Rptr. 3d 732 (Cal. App. 2007), the state appellate court criticized the Ninth Circuit's *Newman* decision for declaring that California's property rights extended to possession of bodies. This determination, according to the state court, was in contravention of existing California precedent. The court wrote, "To find a section 1983 violation, the federal court is supposed to *apply* state law, not *rewrite* it. The *Newman* court shrugged off over 100 years of California case authority to write an entirely new rule regarding property rights in dead bodies. It is, at this point, a federal rule, not a state rule, and we decline to follow it." Id. at 740.

3. *Additional facts in Powell v. State.* Justice Shaw, in dissent, stated that the *Powell* case should not have been decided on summary judgment because many

factual issues were in dispute. How the record might have been developed may, in his view, have had some bearing on the legal issues decided by the Supreme Court. For example, Shaw points out that one of the boy's parents (Appellee White) had testified as follows in his deposition:

> He was called to the hospital where his son's body had been taken and met with appellant Gauger. . . . Appellant Gauger told him that the son's death was a simple accidental drowning with no suggestion of foul play. However, he was told state law required an autopsy be performed and that the body was to be shipped to another county for that autopsy. Appellee White objected strenu-ously to the autopsy but believed he had no recourse under the law and asked that the intrusion be kept to a minimum. Appellant Gauger told him it would only be necessary to make a small incision into the chest to probe the lungs. Nothing was said of cornea removal and he only learned of it when he viewed his son's body at the funeral home following the return of the body after the autopsy. The body's eyes, particularly the right eye, were noticeably sunken into the skull. The funeral director explained this sunken condition of the eyes as caused by the cornea removal.

Do the facts as alleged in this deposition testimony surprise you? Would they make a difference in how you assessed the legal basis for the claims made by the appellees?

4. *Nonvoluntary tissue harvest under the 2006 UAGA.*   As noted above, the latest version of the UAGA eliminates the presumed consent provision relating to corneas in the possession of coroners. However, there is a still a possibility of harvesting tissue for transplant without consent when the medical examiner has authority to dispose of a decedent's body. Norman Cantor writes:

> The drafters' comments on the 2006 UAGA concede that even under the new Section 22(b) some unconsented tissue harvests may continue. Those com-ments point out that the newest hierarchy of people authorized to consent to tissue removal includes, at the end of the list in new Section 9(10), "any other person having authority to dispose of the decedent's body." . . . Where a med-ical examiner is authorized to dispose of a corpse—as when a forensic autopsy is performed and no one claims the body—medical examiners might still permit the harvesting of tissue or organs.

Norman L. Cantor, After We Die: The Life and Times of the Human Cadaver (2010).

5. *Bioethical perspectives.*   The opinion in *Powell* contains portions of anal-ysis with a decidedly utilitarian bent. Is this inevitable when the scrutiny placed on legislation is merely the rational relationship test? What would an opinion that was informed more by the bioethical perspective of Principlism have emphasized? Might it have caused the case to have come out differently? What if the primary concern were distributive justice?

In regard to the latter concern, a recent Los Angeles Times investigation into close to 600 cases of unconsented cornea removal in a 12-month period revealed that over 80 percent of the donors were persons of color, and most were homicide victims. In addition, the eye bank that harvested the organs under the authoriza-tion of the coroner charged transplant centers a processing fee 1200 percent higher than the amount it paid to the coroner's office. Michele Goodwin, Rethinking Legislative Consent Law? 5 DePaul J. Health Care L. 257, 259–260

(2002) (arguing that evidence on corneal donations via presumed consent legislation does not comport with notions of distributive justice).

6. *"Presumed consent" laws in other countries.*   In a few other countries, the law provides for "presumed consent" to the use of organs after death. In Austria, for instance, organs can be removed from a dead person's body for transplantation even if there is no express consent in the deceased's medical records. Belgium similarly passed a law providing for presumed consent. In Belgium a person can "opt out" of the consequences of presumed consent by making his or her wishes known at a local town hall. Brazil passed a presumed consent law in 1997 but repealed it within two years. Carol J. Roberts, Presumed Consent for Organ Procurement—Does It Have a Future in the U.S.?, 35 J. Neuroscience Nursing 107 (2003). In countries relying on "presumed consent," the rate of cadaveric organ donation is about 25 percent higher than in "express consent" countries. Ori Scott & Eyal Jacobson, Implementing Presumed Consent for Organ Donation in Israel, 9 IMAJ 777 (2007), Scott and Jacobson report:

> The existence of a presumed consent law shifts the question that the donors and their families face. Instead of asking families if they have a reason to believe that the deceased would have agreed to donate, they are asked whether they think the deceased would have objected to the donation. Moreover, with regard to public opinion, presumed consent laws and changing the default from "No" to "Yes" actually reflect a social norm concerning the expected course of action, although the right to refuse the donation still exists. This last assumption regarding the social norm has been proven correct; in contrast to the U.S and Great Britain where about 40–50% of the families refuse the donation of their beloved ones' organs, in France the rate of family refusal is about 30% and in Spain as low as 20%.

Id. at 778.

Yet, a correlation between the presence of presumed consent laws and rates of donation is not conclusive evidence that the system in fact increases the rate of donation. That may be a consequence of many other factors. See Amber Rithalia et al., Impact of Presumed Consent for Organ Donation on Donation Rates: A Systematic Review, 338 BMJ a3162 (2009) (concluding that while "[t]he available evidence suggests that presumed consent is associated with increased organ donation rates, even when other factors are accounted for, . . . it cannot be inferred from this that the introduction of presumed consent legislation per se will lead to an increase in organ donation rates" as other factors, such as the availability of potential donors, transplantation services, wealth, and public attitudes, may also play a role).

7. *Relevance of family law.*   The organ donation process is affected by family law. Under both the 1987 UAGA and the 2006 UAGA, a potential donor's spouse can consent or refuse to consent to posthumous organ donation on behalf of the deceased as long as he or she is not precluded by the donor's own anatomical gift or refusal or is otherwise superseded in the statutory hierarchy (e.g., by an appointed health care agent). What qualifies as a "spouse?" Hawaii amended its anatomical gift act to treat reciprocal beneficiaries as spouses with regard to organ donations from the body of a deceased partner. Haw. Rev. Stat. Ann. §327-3 (Michie 2000). Similarly, in Vermont, Maine, and elsewhere, a partner in a "civil union" would be treated as a spouse for purposes of organ donation

decisions. California has not provided specifically for anatomical gift decisions by surviving cohabitants, but the state does allow domestic partners to make medical decisions for one another. This right could easily be extended to include the right to make decisions about organ donations. In other states, the right of an unmarried party to make a posthumous decision about a deceased partner's donating organs is less clear. Roderick T. Chen & Alexandra K. Glazier, Can Same-Sex Partners Consent to Organ Donation?, 29 Am. J.L. & Med. 31 (2003); Me. Rev. Stat. tit. 22, Secs 2843-A(D)(1-A), 2846, 2949(1)(C) (2011).

2. Autopsies and Other Uses of Human Corpses

|| **Janicki v. Hospital of St. Raphael**
744 A.2d 963 (Conn. Super. 1999) ||

Opinion by Judge BLUE.

INTRODUCTION

In 1993, during the Battle of Mogadishu in Somalia, American servicemen repeatedly risked their lives to rescue the bodies of their slain comrades. M. Bowden, Black Hawk Down: A Story of Modern War (Atlantic Monthly Press 1999). This is an ancient military tradition, going back to the battle fought over the body of Patroklos on the plains of Troy. It is also a powerful illustration of the symbolic importance that the bodies of the dead have for the hearts and minds of the living. This is a case involving such emotions.

In 1996, the plaintiff, Marcia Janicki, gave birth at the Hospital of St. Raphael (the hospital) to a stillborn nonviable fetus that she had carried for approximately nineteen weeks. She alleges that she expressly instructed the hospital not to dissect the fetus and that the hospital performed a dissection anyway. The hospital argues that it was legally entitled to perform a dissection, regardless of the mother's instructions. Each side, unencumbered by binding precedent, claims the high moral ground. The difficult judicial task in this case of first impression is to ascertain the correct legal standards and proceed accordingly.

. . . The parties' characterization of the subject of the dissection here seems to have been framed, at least in part, by tactical legal considerations. Thus, at argument, the hospital characterized the subject as "tissue." The hospital analogized it, rather infelicitously, to a tumor taken from a patient. In the hospital's opinion, "tissue" can be freely subjected to pathological testing regardless of the patient's instructions to the contrary. Janicki is somewhat more wide ranging in her characterization. Her complaint repeatedly refers to the subject of the dissection as a "child." The emotional appeal that such a characterization might have for a jury aside, this terminology seemingly attempts to capture the legal ground staked out by statutory and case law (discussed below) that the body of a (once living) human being who has died cannot ordinarily be subjected to an autopsy without the consent of the next of kin. . . .

Neither of these characterizations is appropriate. The fetus here was not a "child" because it never became viable and never had a separate living existence. On the other hand, it was not "tissue," at least in the sense in which that term is usually understood. It was tissue only in the broad sense that it was "an aggregate of cells." Webster's Third New International Dictionary 2399 (1971). That definition, however, is so broad as to include every living thing, including the entire person of a living human being. Webster explains that the term is usually applied to aggregates of cells "that form one of the structural materials out of which the body of a plant or an animal is built up." Id. The term, so defined, would not be applicable here, since we are dealing with an entire fetus (and one which the mother wished to remain entire) and not just one of the structural materials of a fetus, such as a biopsy sample or a bodily organ. Moreover, the symbolic importance of the fetus is obviously vastly different from that of ordinary tissue. It is unlikely in the extreme that a woman who has carried a fetus for nineteen weeks will view that fetus, stillborn or not, in the same way that she would, for example, view a tumor removed from her body.

For all these reasons, the fetus here cannot be characterized as either "tissue" or a "child." It was a separate physical entity, although not, in this case, a living one. It will help to keep this characterization in mind as the plaintiff's causes of action are reviewed.

[The court next approved dismissal of the medical malpractice and detrimental reliance claims of the plaintiff. The medical malpractice claims were dismissed because there were no allegations of improper medical treatment of the plaintiff. The detrimental reliance count was dismissed for insufficient pleading.]

THE COUNTS OF NEGLIGENT INFLICTION OF EMOTIONAL DISTRESS

Janicki's third and eleventh counts, directed at the hospital and Reguero [her attending physician] respectively, allege negligent infliction of emotional distress. This is the true battleground of the case. Connecticut, of course, has long recognized a cause of action for negligent infliction of emotional distress. . . . Because the hospital and Reguero are represented by the same counsel and submit identical arguments, they will jointly be referred to as "the hospital."

A.   THE STANDARD OF CONDUCT
1.   *The Common Law*

No reported judicial decision dealing with the unauthorized autopsy of a stillborn child has been discovered by counsel or the court. A number of arguably analogous cases can, however, be found. These cases involve: (1) tort claims involving autopsies of corpses of human beings who have been born alive; (2) property claims involving tissue specimens (in the ordinary sense of the word tissue); and (3) domestic relations claims involving human preembryos. These analogies will be considered in turn.

a.   Human Corpses

Historically, the law of human corpses has been an oddity. English law for a very long time recognized the anomalous rule that there can be no property in a corpse. Thus, Blackstone stated that, "though the heir has a property in the monuments and escutcheons of his ancestors, yet he has none in their bodies or ashes; nor can he bring any civil action against such as indecently at least, if not impiously, violate and disturb their remains, when dead and buried." 2 W. Blackstone, Commentaries on the Laws of England (1807) p. 429. Under this rule, stealing a corpse, which by definition has no owner, was not a felony. The "no property" rule remains the law in England today. See Dobson v. North Tyneside Health Authority, [1997] 1 W.L.R. 596, (C.A. 1996). *Dobson,* however, recognizes that . . . "persons charged by the law with the duty of interring the body have a right to the custody and possession of it until it is properly buried." (Internal quotation marks omitted.) . . .

American courts, especially in the last century, have not been receptive to the "no property" rule. Most courts in this country now recognize that the next of kin have at least a "quasi-property" right in a decedent's body for purposes of burial or other lawful disposition. See Brotherton v. Cleveland, 923 F.2d 477, 481 (6th Cir. 1991), and authorities cited therein. The reach of this "quasi-property" right is uncertain. What is important, for present purposes, is that American courts have recognized a rule that, "where a nonofficial autopsy is performed without the consent of those who have the quasi-right of property in the corpse . . . the one responsible for such act is liable in damages." 22A Am. Jur. 2d 44, Dead Bodies §66 (1988).

Is the body of a stillborn fetus entitled to less consideration in this regard than the body of a once living human being? A stillborn fetus does not have survivors in the same legal sense that a once living human being has survivors (never having lived, it cannot have an estate) but, as we have just seen, the mother nevertheless retains at least a quasi-property right in the body. The real question that must be addressed is not one of property but one of symbolism. The body of a once living human being is entitled to respect because of its symbolic import, if for no other reason. It is hardly a stretch to conclude that the body of a stillborn fetus should be entitled to similar respect for the same reason. To address the facts at hand, a mother who has carried a fetus for nineteen weeks can understandably view its body as symbolic not only of the physical presence that she once felt in her own body but also of the hopes and dreams she once had for the future. Symbols are an important, perhaps vital, part of human existence, and all of us, to some extent, live by them. Think of the flag or, for that matter, of the law itself. It is not improper for the law to recognize the existence and legitimacy of such emotions.

b.   Tissue Specimens

The evolving law concerning tissue samples is one of enormous complexity but relatively little applicability to this case. The California Supreme Court has held, in a controversial decision, that patients do not retain a sufficient property interest in excised cells to support a cause of action for conversion. Moore v. Regents of the University of California, 51 Cal. 3d 120, 134–47 (1990), *cert. denied,* 499 U.S. 936 (1991) . . . Whether or not one thinks that a physician may appropriately use a patient's cells for medical research without the patient's permission—the issue in *Moore*—most people would agree that the use of a stillborn fetus for medical research without parental permission raises much graver issues. The fetus, at a minimum, has a much greater symbolic import than a small group of cells, and is entitled to a greater respect because of that import.

c.   Preembryos

The law governing the disposition of preembryos (often referred to as "frozen embryos"), articulated in a well-known domestic relations case, is unusually helpful because of its reasoning.

. . . Davis v. Davis, 842 S.W.2d 588 (Tenn. 1992), *cert. denied,* 507 U.S. 911, 113 S. Ct. 1259, 122 L. Ed. 2d 657 (1993) remains the only case attempting "to lay out an analytical framework for disputes between a divorcing couple regarding the disposition of frozen embryos." The analytical framework that it lays out is useful in the context of the instant case. A preembryo, like the fetus in question here (and unlike a fetus in utero) is not contained in the physical body of the mother. Again, like the fetus in question here, it is not a "person" within the meaning of the law. And, most importantly, it is a creation of human reproduction, and occupies a position on the emotional (and perhaps moral) spectrum far removed from that of ordinary tissue.

There are at least two important differences between preembryos and the fetus in question here, but those differences cut in different directions. First, of course, the fetus here was nonviable and stillborn and thus did not have the potential for human life enjoyed by a preembryo. It will be recalled, however, that the potential for human life is only one of two reasons for the "special respect" identified by the Ethics Committee of the American Fertility Society. The other reason for that "special respect" is the fact that preembryos have a "symbolic meaning for many people." (Internal quotation marks omitted.) That symbolic meaning plainly exists here.

A second difference between preembryos and the fetus in question here adds to the symbolic import at issue in this case. The fetus in question here had a gestational age of nineteen weeks. A mother who has carried a fetus for nineteen weeks, even one that (as it appears) did not have the potential for life, is likely to develop an emotional attachment that she would not necessarily develop for a preembryo never implanted in her body. The symbolic value of the fetus here is likely, in this sense, to be even more considerable.

For these reasons, the common law should recognize that the fetus in question here, while not a person, was not "property" or "tissue" either. Instead, it occupied an intermediate category in the law entitled to a special respect that would not be given ordinary tissue. The hospital concedes that it had an obligation to turn the fetus over to Janicki for burial. The well-established line of authority dealing with unauthorized autopsies on human corpses teaches us that this conceded duty is accompanied by another duty, namely that of preserving the body. The fact that the fetus here was entitled to a "special respect" not accorded ordinary tissue means, at a minimum, that the hospital and its physicians were not entitled to dissect it in the teeth of the mother's express instructions to the contrary.

Because of [the diversity of parental views on the symbolic importance of the stillborn fetus] it would be inappropriate, at least in the context of the present case, to mandate that a physician obtain affirmative parental consent in order to perform a fetal dissection. It is, however, appropriate to mandate that, in cases not involving the chief medical examiner, a fetal dissection cannot be performed in defiance of express maternal *prohibition*. By expressly prohibiting a dissection, the mother has effectively indicated that she considers the fetus to have significant symbolic importance. Her wishes are entitled to the law's respect. Janicki has appropriately alleged a breach of the applicable standard of conduct.

[Section B of the opinion discussed the issue of proximity in Janicki's emotional distress claim, concluding that the fact that Janicki did not witness the negligent conduct complained of did not preclude her recovery as a matter of law.]

NOTES AND QUESTIONS

1. *Characterization of the fetus.*   How does the court characterize the stillborn fetus for purposes of this case? Do you agree with that characterization?

2. *Reconciling* Powell *and* Janicki. Are State v. Powell and Janicki v. St. Raphael reconcilable? Is the answer to this simply that one deals with a constitutional claim and the other is about a common law tort? Or that one is against the state and the other a private actor? Or might the discussion contained in *Janicki* inform or challenge the analysis contained in *Powell* regarding the existence of a constitutional right to direct the disposition of family member's remains?

3. *Consent for autopsies.*   The *Janicki* court draws back from requiring affirmative parental consent for an unofficial autopsy, limiting its holding to a requirement that the hospital not ignore an express maternal prohibition. Do you think the court should have gone further to require affirmative parental consent to such autopsies? For whose benefit are they performed anyway?

4. *Contrasting case.*   In Walker v. Firelands Community Hospital, 170 Ohio App. 3d 785 (2007), patients brought a class action against a hospital and former morgue employee for improper storage and disposal of fetal remains following a miscarriage or stillborn birth. Apparently unbeknownst to the hospital, the morgue employee had, over a period of ten years, stored up to approximately 88 intact fetal specimens commingled in three containers filled with formalin. The court held that patient-plaintiffs had no cause of action under Ohio law, declining to extend an existing cause of action for interference with the burial of a dead body to cover a fetus at, or less than, 20 weeks' gestation. Patients were also unable to satisfy Ohio's requirements for negligent infliction of emotional distress absent proof that they were bystanders or experienced fear associated with physical consequences to themselves.

5. *Exhibitions of human bodies.*   First appearing in the 1990s, plastinated human body exhibits have toured museums around the world, drawing in millions of viewers but generating controversy at the same time. Dr. Gunther von Hagens of Germany created the first exhibit, "Body Worlds," using a technique he developed called "plastination," which allows the bodies to be preserved and exhibited without their skin to reveal bones, muscles, organs, and nerves. The bodies are often positioned in athletic poses (playing badminton, for example) or otherwise interesting or provocative poses (one male body, for example, holds his removed skin). Although immensely popular, the exhibits have been subject to criticism that they show disrespect for the dead. In addition, controversy has surrounded the origination of some of the bodies; in particular, whether the bodies were expressly donated for this purpose.

CHALLENGING ISSUES: PRACTICING INTUBATION ON THE NEWLY DECEASED

One practice of some hospital emergency departments has recently come under increased scrutiny and debate. That is the practice of using newly deceased patients to practice resuscitation techniques, including intubation. There is, in such instances, absolutely no benefit to the already deceased patient. The consent of the family might be sought, but it is understandably a distressing time for the family. Consent may be denied and the intrusion resented. While there is no benefit to the deceased patient, there is also no mutilation or alteration of the body. Do you think such a practice could subject a hospital or its medical staff to tort liability? On what theory? If a state legislature endorsed the practice through permissive legislation, do you think a family member could successfully claim that such a law was unconstitutional? Why or why not?

For information and commentary on hospital policies and professional guidelines, see Marta Karczewska, Ethical Issues in the Emergency Department: Consent for Procedure Training on Newly Deceased Patients, 12 McGill J. Med. 116–119 (2009).

> ## Katheryn D. Katz, Parenthood from the Grave: Protocols for Retrieving and Utilizing Games from the Dead or Dying
> ### 2006 U. Chi. Legal F. 289 (2006)

When physicians face a request to remove sperm from a dead or dying male or ovarian tissue from a woman who has suffered sudden death or is declared brain-dead, the physician is presented with ethical and legal issues of profound dimensions but scant direction as to the proper course of action. The pleas of a bereaved spouse or parents arise from the tragic circumstances, which evoke compassion and an understandable desire to lessen the survivor's suffering. Nevertheless, acceding to a request for gamete retrieval raises questions of who, if anyone, may give consent, what informed consent means in these circumstances, and whether the dead or dying have procreative rights that must be respected.

. . . Physicians in the United States who receive requests for PMGR [post-mortem gamete retrieval] have little to guide them in determining whether to accede to the requests. The mere technical feasibility of PMGR does not warrant the procedure's use. There are ethical, moral, and legal questions that must be answered before a physician may take sperm from a male corpse or gametes from a deceased female so that these deceased may reproduce. There is an abundance of medical and legal literature discussing PMGR, but there is scant legal authority directly on point in the United States. If we look for governing law on the legality of PMGR and subsequent use of the gametes for conception, the most cited authority is the case of Diane Blood, decided by the courts of Great Britain.

The Human Fertilisation and Embryology Authority ("HFEA") in Great Britain prevented Diane Blood from storing or utilizing sperm taken from her dying husband because Mr. Blood had not given his written permission after having had a proper opportunity to receive counseling. Mrs. Blood then sought permission to export the sperm to Belgium, where the law would permit her to use the sperm. The HFEA ruled that Mrs. Blood was barred from taking the sperm abroad for use on the ground that she should not be able to avoid the specific requirements of the Human Fertilisation and Embryology Act by exporting the sperm to a country to which she had no connection.

Mrs. Blood sought judicial review of the Authority's decision. In the litigation that followed, the Court of Appeal upheld the HFEA on the issue of consent but found that Mrs. Blood had the right to export the sperm under the European Community Treaty, which guarantees freedom of movement for goods and medical services among member states. As a result of the High Court's finding that HFEA was incompatible with the European Convention on Human Rights, Mrs. Blood eventually was able to have two sons using the frozen sperm. Yet, after their birth Mrs. Blood could not place her deceased husband's name on her sons' birth certificates because HFEA declared that any baby conceived after his father's death had no biological father for the purposes of succession and inheritance. Eventually, Mrs. Blood succeeded in getting the Act amended to provide that children conceived postmortem would be recognized as the legal heirs of their deceased father.

The international publicity generated by Mrs. Blood's effort to have children with her late husband demonstrates how compelling the facts may be when a loved one dies suddenly before he or she has had a chance to become a parent. The legal resolution of the case, however, is of little help in the United States, where the very idea of a central licensing authority for reproductive technology is anathema to our belief in state, as opposed to federal, control of medical practice and parentage issues. Of course, in the case of reproductive technology there is virtually no oversight of any kind. In any event, it is difficult to imagine Americans submitting their reproductive decisions to government authority.

The American Society for Reproductive Medicine ("ASRM") has determined that medical personnel do not have to honor a surviving spouse's request for PMGR if the patient has not given prior consent or else made his wishes known. The ASRM avoids the issue of whether PMGR is permissible by stating that "such requests pose judgmental questions that should be answered within the context of the individual circumstances and applicable state laws." Inasmuch as there are few applicable state laws, the ASRM's statement provides little guidance but may be read to permit PMGR. There is some legislative and judicial direction on issues such as inheritance after posthumous conception, the status of cryopreserved pre-embryos, and parentage when donated gametes are used to achieve pregnancy, but nothing specifically addresses PMGR.

. . . Protocols or standards for PMGR have been developed against a background debate on the ethics of retrieval and reflect various positions advanced in that debate. . . . The difference between the most restrictive and the more permissive positions is whether explicit prior consent of the deceased or incompetent is required or, as in the permissive protocols, reasonably inferred consent fulfills the need for consent. The most permissive position would create a presumption in favor of PMGR in the absence of evidence that the decedent made his or her opposition clear while alive. Even those who adopt the most expansive stance toward PMGR do so in the belief that they espouse what the decedent would have wanted, had he or she thought about the matter. Whichever protocol is adopted, the other guidelines are sufficiently exclusionary that they have "dramatically" reduced the number of postmortem gamete retrievals performed. . . . Current hospital protocols regarding PMGR ask the question: who has the right to request retrieval? By this question it is meant, who has the right to consent to PMGR? Among most of those who have considered the issue there is a shared conclusion that laws governing organ donation or autopsies do not apply to PMGR, that organ donation and gamete retrieval are not ethically equivalent. Arguably the Uniform Anatomical Gift Act ("UAGA"), adopted in some form by all fifty states, authorizes the postmortem retrieval of gametes for use in assisted reproduction in the absence of a clear objection by the subject before he or she died. Since the Act defines "part" as "an organ, tissue, eye, bone, artery, blood, fluid or other portion of the human body," it has been argued that a wife should have the right to obtain her husband's sperm postmortem. Further, it is the case that autopsies and organ harvesting have immediate consequences to the dead body and may be more "invasive, destructive and disfiguring" than sperm retrieval. Nevertheless, gamete retrieval followed by artificial insemination or IVF has ongoing important effects that affect the deceased's family and his or her own legacy. In the words of Anne Reichman Schiff, posthumous conception "recasts the content and contours of the deceased's life." She adds that when it occurs without the person's consent, it deprives an individual of "the right to be the conclusive author of a highly significant chapter of his or her life."

Further, the purpose of organ donation is to preserve life and is for the medical benefit of the recipient of the organ. The purposes of donation under the UAGA are "transplantation, therapy, medical or dental research, education, research, or advancement of medical or dental science." Utilization of a decedent's gametes creates life and is for the benefit of a healthy individual. With PMGR, the recipient, who is usually the next of kin and would be the one to give consent to procurement of the sperm, stands to benefit personally. Moreover, it has also been suggested that "there is no strong social argument in favor of bringing additional children into the world."

Because of the legal uncertainty surrounding disposition of gametes, the safest course of action is to require (1) that the one making the request is the decedent, that is, a decedent who has made a specific request when competent and of age and (2) that the intended recipient is a spouse. While such a practice may ignore the desires of others, such as parents or lovers, to have the decedent's lineage continue, it has the virtue of a bright-line rule and avoids speculation about the deceased's intentions. No right of parents to control the reproductive decisions of their adult progeny is recognized in the law. The parents' desire to have a grandchild with the genes of the deceased—that is, to "prolong" the deceased's life though postmortem conception, or to simply continue their lineage—is not among the recognized legal interests.

On the other hand, the law recognizes that families are often formed outside of marriage; therefore, someone who had explicit permission for PMGR and utilization of the gametes might have a valid claim against the institution that denied a request. There is legal precedent for cases in which sperm was given premortem to a paramour.

Since the purpose of the request for PMGR is to achieve a pregnancy, consent to PMGR requires not just consent to the gamete retrieval but evidence of the deceased's desire to achieve procreation. Some protocols demand explicit prior authorization; they specify that the consent must be that of the deceased and must have been given premortem. At least one medical institution specifies that it must be documented in writing.

Recognizing that prospective authorization for PMGR is unlikely, other guidelines allow for "reasonably inferred" consent.

. . . Some of the current guidelines are both benevolent and intrusive. A common feature of these protocols is a one-year waiting period and quarantine on the use of gametes. The one-year period is believed to be "the initial period of psychological adjustment and bereavement after the loss of a loved one." We are told that "this one-year quarantine . . . lets women go through the grieving process." Further, the wife is to undergo medical and psychological consultations which "should include a basic assessment of the psychological status of the wife, family, social and financial support systems as well as a discussion of the implications of raising the child as a single parent without its genetic father." Moreover, there should be discussion of disclosing to the child the method of conception. What is not mentioned is the fact that the child will have no legal father and will not be recognized as an heir.

It is expected that the waiting period and the counseling that the wife is to receive will enable her to make a more "rational" decision when the period of grief has passed. This rationale assumes that everyone grieves in the same way and that there is a point at which grief ends. Both of these assumptions are questionable and reveal a linear approach to a process which is more chaotic than straightforward. Further, no matter how benign the intentions behind the one-year quarantine, it presents a serious barrier to the procreative hopes of a recipient who suffers from premature ovarian failure, is at the outer limit of her reproductive years, or has some other condition that demands immediate rather than later use of the sperm.

. . . If we look at PMGR through the lens of reproductive rights, we must first determine whose procreative rights are at issue. The dead are not usually thought of as having rights that survive death, but, as noted above, procreative rights are exceptional. Moreover, we do honor the wishes of the dead as to the disposition of property even though we could just as easily say that death ends all property rights. We do not speak of our deceased loved ones as corpses even though metaphysically the decedent has left the body. If an individual has expressed clear intention to procreate with a particular individual or not to procreate, then those wishes should be honored in the same way that testamentary provisions receive deference. Of course, if a testamentary provision violates public policy it will not honored. If utilization of the gametes would result in consanguinity, for example, the provision would be invalid. The difficulty is that in most instances where there is a request for PMGR, the deceased has left no instructions.

. . . The drafters of the former Uniform Status of Children of Assisted Conception Act ("USCACA") denied legal parentage to any child conceived after the death of the donor. In other words, the donor of the gametes is not considered a parent of the resulting child. That means that the child would be considered a non-marital child even if the parents were married. It also means that the child would not be entitled to Social Security benefits, military service benefits, or other benefits from the deceased parent and would not be able to bring a wrongful death action for the death of that parent. In order to avoid disinheriting his child, the donor would have to have specific provisions in his or her will recognizing and providing for posthumously conceived children.

The Uniform Parentage Act ("UPA") provides that if assisted reproduction occurred after a provider of ova, sperm, or genetic material for an embryo died, that provider will not be considered a parent unless he has given written consent to be treated as a parent. Four states have adopted the UPA and a number of states are considering adopting the Act. A number of other states have already adopted legislative changes that limit the inheritance rights of posthumously conceived children.

NOTES AND QUESTIONS

1. *Application of Uniform Anatomical Gift Act.*   What do you think of the argument that the UAGA, through its general provisions regarding organ and tissue donation, covers PMGR? Are the basic principles and understandings on which the UAGA is based the same or different than for PMGR? Consider various scenarios that might challenge the conclusion that the UAGA, as currently written, covers PMGR. For example, if the UAGA covers postmortem sperm retrieval, would it allow the parent of a minor to consent to donation for purposes of insemination in a gestational surrogate? See Bethany Spielman, Pushing the Dead into the Next Reproductive Frontier: Post Mortem Gamete Retrieval under the Uniform Anatomical Gift Act, 37 J. Law Med. Ethics 331–343 (2009) (discussing In re Matter of Daniel Thomas Christy, Johnson County Case No. EQV068545 (Sept. 14, 2007), a ruling from an Iowa district court that the UAGA applied to the request by parents of a deceased man to retrieve his sperm for use by his fiancée).

CHALLENGING ISSUES: POSTMORTEM GAMETE RETRIEVAL

Dr. A is on call in the emergency room one evening when paramedics bring in a man who has been severely injured in an automobile accident. Although Dr. A and her team do everything they can to treat the man's injuries, they are unable to save his life. When Dr. A tells the man's wife that he has died, the wife has an unusual request. She and her husband had been trying to start a family. She would still like to conceive and bear her husband's child. She asks

Dr. A to retrieve some of her husband's sperm for purposes of procreation through assisted reproductive technologies.

Because her husband's death has occurred within the last 24 hours, it is medically possible to retrieve and cryogenically preserve his sperm for these purposes. The American Society for Reproductive Medicine has described the techniques that may be used, including "stimulated ejaculation, microsurgical epididymal sperm aspiration (MESA) or testicular sperm extraction (TSE)." http://www.asrm.org/Media/Ethics/posthum.html (last visited Sept. 10, 2004).

1. Imagine you are hospital counsel. The hospital has no policy on PMGR. What would you advise Dr. A if she came to you for advice?

2. Now you have been asked to help the ethics committee of the hospital to devise a policy on PMGR. What advice would you give them on the following issues (and any others you might determine to be important): a) requirement and form of donor consent, b) who may request PMGR, c) whether there should be a waiting period prior to the permitted utilization of the gamete.

3. Now imagine you are a state legislator. Do you think legislation in this area would be helpful? What would it say, in broad terms?

= 9 =

‖ *Medical Decision Making for Others* ‖

From its start, bioethics as a contemporary discipline identified autonomy as a foundational principle. In the United States, this focus harmonized with a deeply ingrained concern for protecting individual liberty. In addition, privileging autonomy seemed a reasonable response to the revelation of a series of abuses of peoples' bodies and minds in the name of medical science. Many, although not all, of these abuses involved "experimentation" (sometimes the experimentation was combined with clinical "care," sometimes not).

The Nuremberg Code, developed by the judges who presided over the trial of Nazi doctors after World War II, declared the "voluntary consent of the human subject" to be absolutely essential to any human subject research project. The Nuremberg Code, II Trials of War Criminals Before the Nuremberg Military Tribunals Under Control Council Law (see Chapter 11). The so-called Common Rule, adopted by the U.S. government in the mid-1970s to protect the subjects of research involving humans, requires researchers to obtain the consent of subjects or of their "legally authorized representative[s]" (see Chapter 11, section (C)(2)).

In 1979, the Belmont Report: Ethical Principles and Guidelines for the Protection of Human Subjects of Research, produced by the National Commission for the Protection of Human Subjects of Biomedical and Behavioral Research, identified three "basic ethical principles." These include "respect for persons, beneficence and justice." "Respect for persons" depends on treating individuals as "autonomous agents." Yet, the Belmont commissioners recognized the impossibility of privileging autonomy as a core bioethical principle without providing in some way for people who lack capacity to entertain autonomous choices. Thus, the Report further provides that "persons with diminished autonomy are entitled to protection." (The text of the Report is available at http://videocast.nih.gov/pdf/ohrp_belmont_report.pdf and can be found in Chapter 11, section (C)(2)).

By the early 1970s, states in the United States began to apply the informed consent principle to clinical health care settings. (The history of this development is presented in Chapter 2.) One option sometimes followed in research settings—refusing to include subjects without capacity in the study—does not work in clinical settings. Some patients clearly lack decision-making capacity. This group includes people with advanced dementia, infants, and people with serious disorders of consciousness, including those in a coma or in a persistent vegetative state. For such patients, the law accepts the decisions of authorized surrogates. However, capacity rests on a continuum, and capacity assessments can be challenging.

Moreover, in some cases, a patient may seem capable as a general matter but not with regard to a specific medical decision that he or she actually faces. And sometimes capacity is challenged because a patient refuses recommended care or insists on care that is not recommended. In such cases, the effort to respect patient autonomy may seem to be in conflict with concern for the patient's welfare.

Special issues shape considerations of medical decision making for children. Very young children raise one set of challenges. Older children, who enjoy some, or even significant, decision-making capacity occasion different, but equally complicated, questions. Section G considers medical decision making for children.

As you think about the materials in this chapter, consider the following conundrums:

1. As a general matter, should patient autonomy be privileged over beneficence?
2. Should beneficence (a patient's welfare) be privileged over autonomy?
3. Or should autonomy and beneficence be balanced? If so, are there broad principles that should guide the process of affecting that balance? Or must any effort to balance patient autonomy against patient welfare (where the two seem to be in conflict) be carried out without the help of broad principles—in light of each individual patient's situation?
4. Do you think there is an age after which children should be presumed capable of making their own medical decisions? Does your answer depend on the sort of health care at issue? Does it depend on the maturity of a particular child? How would you assess a child's maturity?
5. Should the state be more, or differently, responsible for protecting the health of children than that of adults? If so, why?

A.   CHALLENGING AUTONOMY?

For the most part, bioethicists, clinicians, and lawyers have continued to see autonomy as key to protecting patients and subjects of human research. However, in the last few decades, a subtle challenge to autonomy's ubiquity has appeared. (The notion of autonomy was always modified to address the needs of patients clearly lacking capacity.)

Challenges to patient autonomy have focused on cases in which displacing autonomy with beneficence would seem to serve a patient's welfare. U.S. law respects the right of capable patients to reach their own medical decisions. Capable patients have the right to make their own health care decisions, even if clinicians, family members, or others deem those decisions to be unwise or downright harmful. Explicit legal exceptions to that general rule are rare, although in a few cases, courts have ordered care against the wishes of pregnant women. (See Jefferson v. Griffin Spalding County Hospital Authority, 274 S.E.2d 457 (Ga. 1981); In re A.C., 573 A.2d 1235 (D.C. Cir. 1990) (en banc); and see also Chapter 6, Part B(1)).

However, limitations on patients' decision-making autonomy are much more common than the law would suggest. So, for instance, clinicians may call for capacity determinations because a patient seems peculiar (but not clearly to lack capacity). Sometimes, intrusions on patient autonomy are unselfconscious efforts on the part of clinicians, family members, or others (such as clergy) to safeguard a patient's welfare. Yet, informal pressure may be hard to distinguish from manipulation. Patient "refusals" lead to capacity assessments far more often than patient "consents." Most of the "refusal" cases involve patients whose capacity was challenged because their medical decisions ran counter to those of their caregivers. (The case of Mary Northern, below, is of this sort).

NOTES AND QUESTIONS

1. *Capacity assessments.*   Sometimes assessing capacity is simple. Patients without consciousness, patients under three years of age, and patients with advanced Alzheimer disease are not capable of medical decision making. But in many cases, assessing capacity can be a subtle art. Paul S. Appelbaum, a psychiatrist, has outlined four standards to be used in capacity determinations; each of the four is generally reflected in legal determinations of decision-making capacity. Paul S. Appelbaum, Assessment of Patients' Competence to Consent to Treatment, 357 New Eng. J. Med. 18 (2007). The standards delineated by Appelbaum assess a patient's ability to 1. "communicate a choice"; 2. "understand relevant information"; 3. "appreciate the situation and its consequences"; and 4. "reason about treatment options." Id. at 1836. Appelbaum cautions clinicians that one should presume capacity in the absence of a reason to challenge a patient's capacity to make his or her own medical decisions. In Appelbaum's view most assessments of a patient's capacity can be carried out by the patient's treating physician but psychiatric consultation may be sought if the patient is mentally ill or if the case is "complex" for other reasons. What, if anything, would you add to Appelbaum's standards? Would you eliminate or alter any of them?

2. *Re-constructing standards for assessing capacity.*   Law professor Elyn Saks has shaped a standard for assessing competency in light of her conclusion that existing standards (circa the early 1990s) resulted in competent people losing the right to choose among medical options on incompetency grounds, Elyn R. Saks, Competency to Refuse Treatment, 69 N.C.L. Rev. 945 (1991). Saks wrote:

> [A standard that assumes that] competency is incompatible only with patently false beliefs . . . supports [some] controversial conclusions. For example, a

> psychiatric patient's belief that medication will not work does not render the
> patient incompetent to refuse the medication. And a patient may be competent
> even though he refuses medication because he does not believe he is ill or
> because he believes he is bad and deserves to suffer.

Id. at 947–948. Saks notes an important difference between the decisions of two
judges in a case (infra, pp. 572–579) asking a Tennessee court to decide whether
a patient whose doctors recommended amputation of her feet was competent to
refuse that recommendation. Saks wrote:

> In *Northern* . . . the majority and the concurring judge divided over whether
> Mrs. Northern needed to accept her doctors' view that she would die without
> the amputation of her gangrenous feet. The majority required her to accept the
> truth of her doctors' beliefs; the concurrence, only the fact of the doctors'
> beliefs. Because only the fact of the doctors' beliefs was indisputable, only
> the concurring judge's opinion accorded to those beliefs their proper signifi-
> cance. Both opinions, nevertheless, could correctly base their findings of
> incompetence on Mrs. Northern's failure to recognize that her feet were
> black, dead, and odorous.

Id. at 981.

3. *Influencing capable patients: "nudging" and "hovering."* A serious
informed consent conversation may inevitably "influence" a patient's choices.
However, there is a continuum that ranges from respect for patient autonomy to
manipulating patients' choices to disregarding the choices of capable patients.
Recently, a number of articles in professional journals have suggested the benefits of "nudging" patients or "hovering" over them, both in informed consent
contexts and in other health care settings. It is important to consider where
"nudging" and "hovering" fall on the continuum and why they might seem
attractive options in clinical care.

David Asch and his colleagues suggest that various modes of "hovering
over people in their daily lives" can help ensure that they take prescribed medications, practice healthy habits (such as good eating and not smoking), and
receive needed care when various "biometric assessments" indicate potential
problems. David A. Asch, Ralph W. Muller & Kevin G. Wolpp, Automated
Hovering in Health Care—Watching Over the 5000 Hours, New Eng. J. Med.,
June 21, 2012, available at www.nejm.org. "Hovering" may interfere with autonomy but the term suggests a concerned parent rather than an untoward intrusion. Do you think the sort of "hovering" that Asch and colleagues recommend
is appropriate? If so, as a general matter or only in certain types of cases?

In a "Symposium on Nudge," authors discussed "Nudging Healthy Lifestyles," and "Nudging Smokers," among other things. Symposium on Nudge,
3 Eur. J. Risk Reg. (Jan. 2012), available at http://ssrn.com/abstract=2005672.
One article in the issue attributed the use of the notion of "nudge" to
"libertarian paternalism." Adam Burgess, 'Nudging' Healthy Lifestyles: The
UK Experiments with the Behavioural Alternative to Regulation and the Market,
3 Eur. J. Risk Reg. (Jan. 2012), available at http://papers.ssrn.com/s013/
papers.cfm?abstract_id=2005672. The notion of nudging, previously relied
on by behavioral economists, entered popular discourse through Richard H.
Thaler and Cass R. Sunstein's book Nudge: Improving Decisions About Health,
Wealth, and Happiness (2009). "Nudging" people with regard to health has

been recommended as a tool for shaping people's decisions so as to serve their interests without undermining their autonomy. Introduction, 3 Eur. J. Risk Reg., Symposium, supra. The term *nudge,* much like the term *hover,* suggests a kindly, if somewhat overbearing, parent whose interests are firmly focused around the presumptive needs of his or her child. Does use of terms such as *nudge* and *hover* serve to limit autonomy without presuming openly to do so? If so, should such efforts be encouraged or discouraged?

Evan Slinger and Iyle Powys Whyte have focused on some discomforting parameters of nudging by government. Slinger and Whyte suggested that such efforts can be more nefarious than beneficent, but because they typically occur below people's radar, the process of having been "nudged" may go unnoted. Does nudging assume the inability of those who presumptively need nudging to make their own choices wisely? And does it thus infantilize those it aims to influence? Id. These concerns similarly underlie most efforts to limit patient autonomy in the name of patient welfare. Interestingly, "hovering" and "nudging" assume patient capacity and are generally not taken to represent untoward interference with patient autonomy.

The next section considers situations in which patient autonomy is successfully challenged (or clearly absent), and surrogates make medical decisions in a patient's stead.

B.   WHO ARE SUBSTITUTE DECISION MAKERS AND WHEN SHOULD THEY ACT?

1.   *Bioethical and Social Perspectives*

> *Thaddeus Mason Pope, Health Law and Bioethics: Pressing Issues and Changing Times: Surrogate Selection: An Increasingly Viable, but Limited, Solution to Intractable Futility Disputes*
> 35 St. Louis U.J. Health L. & Pol'y 183, 206–208 (2010)

There are three basic types of surrogates, corresponding to the three basic ways through which surrogates get their decision-making authority. First, the patient herself can designate her surrogate in an advance directive. This type of agent is normally referred to as an "agent" or "attorney-in-fact." Second, the court can appoint a surrogate. This type of surrogate is normally referred to as a "guardian" or "conservator." Third, if neither of these is available, the health-care provider can designate a surrogate pursuant to rules for default decision makers. This type of surrogate is normally referred to as a "surrogate" or "proxy."

1.   PATIENT-DESIGNATED SURROGATES: AGENTS AND ATTORNEYS-IN-FACT

Every state legislature has established a decision-making process that allows competent patients to appoint an agent to decide about healthcare in the event that they become unable to decide for themselves. This appointment can be made through a simple form typically referred to as an advance directive or durable power of attorney for healthcare. Furthermore, even if a patient has not undertaken the execution formalities to appoint an agent, they can often designate a surrogate, even orally. Such a designation is made directly by the patient to healthcare providers, letting them know whom the patient wants to speak on her behalf.

Upon a determination that the patient has lost capacity, the agent typically has the right to make all healthcare decisions that the patient could have made for herself, unless the patient has explicitly limited the agent's authority. And providers must comply with the healthcare decisions made in good faith by an agent to the same extent that they must comply with decisions made by the patient herself.

2.   PHYSICIAN-DESIGNATED SURROGATES: DEFAULT SURROGATES AND PROXIES

If the patient has neither appointed an agent nor designated a surrogate, or if none is reasonably available at the time a decision must be made, then the healthcare provider can designate a surrogate. The provider makes the designation on the patient's behalf pursuant to default surrogate statutes in almost every state. These statutes specify a priority list of individuals whom the physician should or must designate. Typically, at the top of this hierarchy are the patient's spouse, adult child, parent, and adult sibling. These relatives are likely not only to know the convictions and beliefs of the patient but also to be concerned for the patient. Since most patients do not engage in adequate advance care planning, default surrogates are the most numerous type of surrogate.

3.   COURT-DESIGNATED SURROGATES: GUARDIANS AND CONSERVATORS

The final way in which a person can become a substitute decision maker for a patient is to get appointed by a court. For patients without capacity, it is sometimes necessary to petition a court to appoint a guardian or conservator. The petition is usually filed by a relative or by the administrator of a long-term care facility where the patient resides. After the appointment, the court supervises the guardian's choices on behalf of the patient, to ensure that the patient is getting appropriate medical care. Because this process can be cumbersome and expensive, comparatively few surrogates are guardians.

NOTE

1. *Pressures on surrogates.* The law focuses on who should serve as a surrogate decision maker and on the parameters of a surrogate's decision-making authority. For those who do serve in this role, the pressures can be enormous.

Elizabeth Vig and co-authors examined the consequences of serving as a surrogate decision maker for a patient without capacity. They referred to one study reporting that a significant number (about one-third) of surrogates who made decisions for seriously ill loved ones developed posttraumatic stress disorder symptoms. Elizabeth K. Vig et al., Surviving Surrogate Decision-Making: What Helps and Hampers the Experience of Making Medical Decisions for Others, 22 J. Gen. Internal Med. 1274 (2007). Researchers also found that surrogates' distress at having to make difficult decisions was often, although not always, lessened by the presence of an advance directive that gave the surrogate a sense of what the patient would want. Decision making for surrogates was also eased by clinicians' including them in conversations about the patient's medical situation and by clinicians' responding to surrogate's questions. Id.

2. Legal Approaches

For many years, New York was among a small minority of U.S. states that did not provide for family members to make health care decisions for patients without capacity. Then, in 1991, the Health Care Proxy Law, Art. 29-C, NY Pub. Health L., provided for people, while competent, to prepare advance directives. The health proxy law allowed people to appoint "proxy" decision makers who would become responsible for medical decision making should the principal become incapable of participating in his or her own medical decisions. The proxy law was of significant help, but it did not provide for the majority of cases in which patients without capacity had not, in fact, executed an advance directive while still competent. Finally, in 2010, New York enacted the Family Health Care Decisions Act (FHCDA). This statute provided for the appointment of surrogate decision makers for patients without advance directives. The state's model proxy form and sections of the FHCDA follow.

> ## State of New York, Department of Health, Health Care Proxy
> http://www.health.ny.gov/forms/doh-1430.pdf

(1) I, _____ hereby appoint _____ (name, home address and telephone number) as my health care agent to make any and all health care decisions for me, except to the extent that I state otherwise. This proxy shall take effect only when and if I become unable to make my own health care decisions.

(2) Optional: Alternate Agent

If the person I appoint is unable, unwilling or unavailable to act as my health care agent, I hereby appoint_____(name, home address and telephone number) as my health care agent to make any and all health care decisions for me, except to the extent that I state otherwise.

(3) Unless I revoke it or state an expiration date or circumstances under which it will expire, this proxy shall remain in effect indefinitely. (Optional: If you want this proxy to expire, state the date or conditions here.) This proxy shall expire (specify date or conditions): _____

(4) Optional: I direct my health care agent to make health care decisions according to my wishes and limitations, as he or she knows or as stated below. (If you want to limit your agent's authority to make health care decisions for you or to give specific instructions, you may state your wishes or limitations here.) I direct my health care agent to make health care decisions in accordance with the following limitations and/or instructions (attach additional pages as necessary): _____

In order for your agent to make health care decisions for you about artificial nutrition and hydration (nourishment and water provided by feeding tube and intravenous line), your agent must reasonably know your wishes. You can either tell your agent what your wishes are or include them in this section. See instructions for sample language that you could use if you choose to include your wishes on this form, including your wishes about artificial nutrition and hydration.

(5) Your Identification (please print)

Your Name _____
Your Signature _____
Date _____
Your Address_____

(6) Optional: Organ and/or Tissue Donation

I hereby make an anatomical gift, to be effective upon my death, of: (check any that apply)
■ Any needed organs and/or tissues
■ The following organs and/or tissues_____
■ Limitations_____

If you do not state your wishes or instructions about organ and/or tissue donation on this form, it will not be taken to mean that you do not wish to make a donation or prevent a person, who is otherwise authorized by law, to consent to a donation on your behalf.

Your Signature _____
Date_____

(7) Statement by Witnesses (Witnesses must be 18 years of age or older and cannot be the health care agent or alternate.) I declare that the person who signed this document is personally known to me and appears to be of sound mind and acting of his or her own free will. He or she signed (or asked another to sign for him or her) this document in my presence.

[followed by spaces within which to document the date, names, addresses, and signatures of each of two witnesses]

The Family Health Care Decisions Act
Chapter 8, Laws of New York, 2010, N.Y. Public Health Law Article 29-CC

[In 2010, after many years of legislative disagreement and consequent inaction, New York passed the Family Health Care Decisions Act. The Act provides for surrogate decision making for patients without capacity who did not prepare an advance directive while still capable.]

§2994-d. Health care decisions for adult patients by surrogates.

1. Identifying the surrogate. One person from the following list from the class highest in priority when persons in prior classes are not reasonably available, willing, and competent to act, shall be the surrogate for an adult patient who lacks decision-making capacity. However, such person may designate any other person on the list to be surrogate, provided no one in a class higher in priority than the person designated objects:

(a) A guardian authorized to decide about health care pursuant to article eighty-one of the mental hygiene law;

(b) The spouse, if not legally separated from the patient, or the domestic partner;

(c) A son or daughter eighteen years of age or older;

(d) A parent;

(e) A brother or sister eighteen years of age or older;

(f) A close friend.

2. Restrictions on who may be a surrogate. An operator, administrator, or employee of a hospital or a mental hygiene facility from which the patient was transferred, or a physician who has privileges at the hospital or a health care provider under contract with the hospital may not serve as the surrogate for any adult who is a patient of such hospital, unless such individual is related to the patient by blood, marriage, domestic partnership, or adoption, or is a close friend of the patient whose friendship with the patient preceded the patient's admission to the facility. If a physician serves as surrogate, the physician shall not act as the patient's attending physician after his or her authority as surrogate begins.

3. Authority and duties of surrogate.

(a) Scope of surrogate's authority.

(i) Subject to the standards and limitations of this article, the surrogate shall have the authority to make any and all health care decisions on the adult patient's behalf that the patient could make.

(ii) Nothing in this article shall obligate health care providers to seek the consent of a surrogate if an adult patient has already made a decision about the proposed health care, expressed orally or in writing or, with respect to a decision to withdraw or withhold life-sustaining treatment expressed either orally during hospitalization in the presence of two witnesses eighteen years of age or older, at least one of whom is a health or social services practitioner affiliated with the hospital, or in writing. If an attending physician relies on the patient's prior decision, the physician shall record the prior decision in the patient's medical record. If a surrogate has already been designated for the patient, the attending physician shall make reasonable efforts to notify the surrogate prior to implementing the decision; provided that in the case of a decision to withdraw or withhold life-sustaining treatment, the attending physician shall make diligent efforts to notify the surrogate and, if unable to notify the surrogate, shall document the efforts that were made to do so.

(b) Commencement of surrogate's authority. The surrogate's authority shall commence upon a determination, made pursuant to section twenty-nine hundred ninety-four-c of this article, that the adult patient lacks decision-making capacity and upon identification of a surrogate pursuant to subdivision one of this section. In the event an attending physician determines that the patient has regained decision-making capacity, the authority of the surrogate shall cease.

(c) Right and duty to be informed. Notwithstanding any law to the contrary, the surrogate shall have the right to receive medical information and medical records necessary to make informed decisions about the patient's health care. Health care providers shall provide and the surrogate shall seek information necessary to make an informed decision, including information about the patient's diagnosis, prognosis, the nature and consequences of proposed health care, and the benefits and risks of an alternative to proposed health care.

4. Decision-making standards.

(a) The surrogate shall make health care decisions:

(i) in accordance with the patient's wishes, including the patient's religious and moral beliefs; or

(ii) if the patient's wishes are not reasonably known and cannot with reasonable diligence be ascertained, in accordance with the patient's best interests. An assessment of the patient's best interests shall include: consideration of the dignity and uniqueness of every person; the possibility and extent of preserving the patient's life; the preservation, improvement or restoration of the patient's health or functioning; the relief of the patient's suffering; and any medical condition and such other concerns and values as a reasonable person in the patient's circumstances would wish to consider.

(b) In all cases, the surrogate's assessment of the patient's wishes and best interests shall be patient-centered; health care decisions shall be made on an individualized basis for each patient, and shall be consistent with the values of the patient, including the patient's religious and moral beliefs, to the extent reasonably possible.

5. Decisions to withhold or withdraw life-sustaining treatment. In addition to the standards set forth in subdivision four of this section, decisions by surrogates to withhold or withdraw life-sustaining treatment shall be authorized only if the following conditions are satisfied, as applicable:

(a)

(i) Treatment would be an extraordinary burden to the patient and an attending physician determines, with the independent concurrence of another physician, that, to a reasonable degree of medical certainty and in accord with accepted medical standards, (A) the patient has an illness or injury which can be expected to cause death within six months, whether or not treatment is provided; or (B) the patient is permanently unconscious; or

(ii) The provision of treatment would involve such pain, suffering or other burden that it would reasonably be deemed inhumane or extraordinarily burdensome under the circumstances and the patient has an irreversible or incurable condition, as determined by an attending physician with the independent concurrence of another physician to a reasonable degree of medical certainty and in accord with accepted medical standards.

(b) In a residential health care facility, a surrogate shall have the authority to refuse life-sustaining treatment under subparagraph (ii) of paragraph (a) of this subdivision only if the ethics review committee, including at least one physician who is not directly responsible for the patient's care, or a court of competent jurisdiction, reviews the decision and determines that it meets the standards set forth in this article. This requirement shall not apply to a decision to withhold cardiopulmonary resuscitation.

(c) In a general hospital, if the attending physician objects to a surrogate's decision, under subparagraph (ii) of paragraph (a) of this subdivision, to withdraw or withhold nutrition and hydration provided by means of medical treatment, the decision shall not be implemented until the ethics review committee, including at least one physician who is not directly responsible for the patient's care, or a court of competent jurisdiction, reviews the decision and determines that it meets the standards set forth in this subdivision and subdivision four of this section.

(d) Providing nutrition and hydration orally, without reliance on medical treatment, is not health care under this article and is not subject to this article.

(e) Expression of decisions. The surrogate shall express a decision to withdraw or withhold life-sustaining treatment either orally to an attending physician or in writing.

NOTES AND QUESTIONS

1. *List of surrogates.* The Family Health Care Decisions Act, supra, lists those with authority to make medical decisions for a patient without capacity, in order of priority. Would you have formulated the list differently either with regard to those on it or with regard to their prioritization?

2. *Model acts.* In 1993, the National Conference of Commissioners on Uniform State Laws passed the Uniform Health Care Decisions Act (UHCD Act). A year later, the model act gained approval from the American Bar Association House of Delegates. The Act has been adopted in a few states and has been used as a broad model in one or two others. The Act provides for decisions by surrogates in cases in which a patient is not capable and has not designated a surrogate decision maker. Priority is given to the patient's spouse, if not legally separated, followed by an adult child, a parent, or an adult sibling. Section 5. UHCD Act. If none of these people is available, then the Act looks to an adult who was close to the patient—who "exhibited special care and concern for the

patient"—and who knows about the "patient's personal values." In making decisions for a patient, a surrogate is directed to look first to any "instructions" that the patient left. If the patient's wishes while competent are not known, the surrogate may consider the patient's best interests. In doing this, the surrogate is directed to "consider the patient's personal values." Id.

C. MAKING DECISIONS FOR NEVER-CAPABLE PATIENTS

Most adult patients without capacity once had capacity, but not all did.[1] This section considers surrogate decision making for patients who do not and never did have capacity.

Although it may be possible to discern with at least some degree of accuracy (or, alternatively, we may be able to convince ourselves that we can discern) what the wishes of a patient might be with respect to life-sustaining treatment when she was at one time competent, how do we go about determining what a person who has never been competent would decide? Should we use the substituted judgment approach, and try to decide as that person would decide, or should we abandon that approach as unworkable and rely instead on an objective "best interest" test? How would you evaluate what the court did in the following case?

> ## *Superintendent of Belchertown State School v. Saikewicz*
> ### Supreme Judicial Court of Massachusetts, 373 Mass. 728, 370 N.E.2d 417 (1977)

On April 26, 1976, William E. Jones, superintendent of the Belchertown State School (a facility of the Massachusetts Department of Mental Health), and Paul R. Rogers, a staff attorney at the school, petitioned the Probate Court for Hampshire County for the appointment of a guardian of Joseph Saikewicz, a resident of the State school. Simultaneously they filed a motion for the immediate appointment of a guardian ad litem, with authority to make the necessary decisions concerning the care and treatment of Saikewicz, who was suffering with acute myeloblastic monocytic leukemia. The petition alleged that Saikewicz was a mentally retarded person in urgent need of medical treatment and that he was a person with disability incapable of giving informed consent for such treatment.

. . . The judge below found that Joseph Saikewicz, at the time the matter arose, was sixty-seven years old, with an I.Q. of ten and a mental age of approximately two years and eight months. He was profoundly mentally retarded. The record discloses that, apart from his leukemic condition, Saikewicz enjoyed generally good health. He was physically strong and well built, nutritionally nourished, and ambulatory. He was not, however, able to communicate verbally,

---

1. Special problems occasioned by medical decision making for children are considered in Part G of this chapter.

resorting to gestures and grunts to make his wishes known to others and responding only to gestures or physical contacts. In the course of treatment for various medical conditions arising during Saikewicz's residency at the school, he had been unable to respond intelligibly to inquiries such as whether he was experiencing pain. It was the opinion of a consulting psychologist, not contested by the other experts relied on by the judge below, that Saikewicz was not aware of dangers and was disoriented outside his immediate environment. As a result of his condition, Saikewicz had lived in State institutions since 1923 and had resided at the Belchertown State School since 1928. Two of his sisters, the only members of his family who could be located, were notified of his condition and of the hearing, but they preferred not to attend or otherwise become involved.

On April 19, 1976, Saikewicz was diagnosed as suffering from acute myeloblastic monocytic leukemia. . . . The disease is invariably fatal. Chemotherapy, as was testified to at the hearing in the Probate Court, involves the administration of drugs over several weeks, the purpose of which is to kill the leukemia cells. This treatment unfortunately affects normal cells as well. One expert testified that the end result, in effect, is to destroy the living vitality of the bone marrow. Because of this effect, the patient becomes very anemic and may bleed or suffer infections, a condition which requires a number of blood transfusions. In this sense, the patient immediately becomes much "sicker" with the commencement of chemotherapy, and there is a possibility that infections during the initial period of severe anemia will prove fatal. Moreover, while most patients survive chemotherapy, remission of the leukemia is achieved in only thirty to fifty per cent of the cases. Remission is meant here as a temporary return to normal as measured by clinical and laboratory means. If remission does occur, it typically lasts for between two and thirteen months although longer periods of remission are possible. Estimates of the effectiveness of chemotherapy are complicated in cases, such as the one presented here, in which the patient's age becomes a factor. According to the medical testimony before the court below, persons over age sixty have more difficulty tolerating chemotherapy and the treatment is likely to be less successful than in younger patients. This prognosis may be compared with the doctors' estimates that, left untreated, a patient in Saikewicz's condition would live for a matter of weeks or, perhaps, several months. According to the testimony, a decision to allow the disease to run its natural course would not result in pain for the patient, and death would probably come without discomfort.

[Detailed findings of the probate judge as to the costs and benefits of allowing Saikewicz to undergo chemotherapy are set out in the full opinion of the case.]

Concluding that, in this case, the negative factors of treatment exceeded the benefits, the probate judge ordered on May 13, 1976, that no treatment be administered to Saikewicz for his condition of acute myeloblastic monocytic leukemia except by further order of the court. The judge further ordered that all reasonable and necessary supportive measures be taken, medical or otherwise, to safeguard the well-being of Saikewicz in all other respects and to reduce as far as possible any suffering or discomfort which he might experience.

Saikewicz died on September 4, 1976, at the Belchertown State School hospital. Death was due to bronchial pneumonia, a complication of the leukemia. Saikewicz died without pain or discomfort.

The question what legal standards govern the decision whether to administer potentially life-prolonging treatment to an incompetent person encompasses two distinct and important subissues. First, does a choice exist? That is, is it the unvarying responsibility of the State to order medical treatment in all circumstances involving the care of an incompetent person? Second, if a choice does exist under certain conditions, what considerations enter into the decision-making process?

We think that principles of equality and respect for all individuals require the conclusion that a choice exists. For reasons discussed at some length [above], we recognize a general right in all persons to refuse medical treatment in appropriate circumstances. The recognition of that right must extend to the case of an incompetent, as well as a competent, patient because the value of human dignity extends to both.

This is not to deny that the State has a traditional power and responsibility, under the doctrine of parens patriae, to care for and protect the "best interests" of the incompetent person.

. . . The "best interests" of an incompetent person are not necessarily served by imposing on such persons results not mandated as to competent persons similarly situated. It does not advance the interest of the State or the ward to treat the ward as a person of lesser status or dignity than others. To protect the incompetent person within its power, the State must recognize the dignity and worth of such a person and afford to that person the same panoply of rights and choices it recognizes in competent persons. If a competent person faced with death may choose to decline treatment which not only will not cure the person but which substantially may increase suffering in exchange for a possible yet brief prolongation of life, then it cannot be said that it is always in the "best interests" of the ward to require submission to such treatment. Nor do statistical factors indicating that a majority of competent persons similarly situated choose treatment resolve the issue. The significant decisions of life are more complex than statistical determinations. Individual choice is determined not by the vote of the majority but by the complexities of the singular situation viewed from the unique perspective of the person called on to make the decision. To presume that the incompetent person must always be subjected to what many rational and intelligent persons may decline is to downgrade the status of the incompetent person by placing a lesser value on his intrinsic human worth and vitality.

. . . We believe that both the guardian ad litem in his recommendation and the judge in his decision should have attempted (as they did) to ascertain the incompetent person's actual interests and preferences. In short, the decision in cases such as this should be that which would be made by the incompetent person, if that person were competent, but taking into account the present and future incompetency of the individual as one of the factors which would necessarily enter into the decision-making process of the competent person.

. . . The two factors considered by the probate judge to weigh in favor of administering chemotherapy were: (1) the fact that most people elect chemotherapy and (2) the chance of a longer life. Both are appropriate indicators of what Saikewicz himself would have wanted, provided that due allowance is taken for this individual's present and future incompetency. . . . With regard to the second factor, the chance of a longer life carries the same weight for Saikewicz as for any other person, the value of life under the law having no relation to intelligence or social position. Intertwined with this consideration is the hope that a cure, temporary or permanent, will be discovered during the period of extra weeks or months potentially made available by chemotherapy. The guardian ad litem investigated this possibility and found no reason to hope for a dramatic breakthrough in the time frame relevant to the decision.

The probate judge identified six factors weighing against administration of chemotherapy. Four of these, Saikewicz's age, 67, the probable side effects of treatment, the low chance of producing remission, and the certainty that treatment will cause immediate suffering were clearly established by the medical testimony to be considerations that any individual would weigh carefully. A fifth factor, Saikewicz's inability to cooperate with the treatment, introduces those considerations that are unique to this individual and which therefore are essential to the proper exercise of substituted judgment. The judge heard testimony that Saikewicz would have no comprehension of the reasons for the severe disruption of his formerly secure and stable environment occasioned by the chemotherapy. He therefore would experience fear without the understanding from which other patients draw strength. The inability to anticipate and prepare for the severe side effects of the drugs leaves room only for confusion and disorientation. The possibility that such a naturally uncooperative patient would have to be physically restrained to allow the slow intravenous administration of drugs could only compound his pain and fear, as well as possibly jeopardize the ability of his body to withstand the toxic effects of the drugs.

The sixth factor identified by the judge as weighing against chemotherapy was "the quality of life possible for him even if the treatment does bring about remission." To the extent that this formulation equates the value of life with any measure of the quality of life, we firmly reject it. A reading of the entire record clearly reveals, however, the judge's concern that special care be taken to respect the dignity and worth of Saikewicz's life precisely because of his vulnerable position. The judge, as well as all the parties, were keenly aware that the supposed ability of Saikewicz, by virtue of his mental retardation, to appreciate or experience life had no place in the decision before them. Rather than reading the judge's formulation in a manner that demeans the value of the life of one who is mentally retarded, the vague, and perhaps ill-chosen, term "quality of life" should be understood as a reference to the continuing state of pain and disorientation precipitated by the chemotherapy treatment. Viewing the term in this manner, together with the other factors properly considered by the judge, we are satisfied that the decision to withhold treatment from Saikewicz was based on a regard for his actual interests and preferences and that the facts supported this decision.

NOTES AND QUESTIONS

1. *Standard of decision making.* What standard did the court use in the *Saikewicz* case to determine that withholding chemotherapy treatment from Saikewicz was proper? Does the court follow a substituted judgment approach or a best interests approach or perhaps some hybrid of the two?

2. *Assessing mental age.*   Justice Liacos noted in *Saikewicz* that the trial court judge had determined that Joseph Saikewicz had an I.Q. of 10 and the mental age of a two-year-eight-month-old child. How does one make sense of that information in deciding what would be best for Mr. Saikewicz? Do you think that a two-and-a-half-year-old child resembles Mr. Saikewicz? How might Joseph Saikewicz differ mentally or emotionally from such a child and what, if any, relevance might those differences have in approaching decision making for a patient such as Mr. Saikewicz?

CHALLENGING ISSUES: WITHHOLDING ANTIBIOTICS FOR TREATMENT OF PNEUMONIA IN A NEVER-COMPETENT PATIENT

Jared K., a 24-year-old man who has been severely mentally disabled since a young age due to a childhood infection, has lived in a group home for much of his life. He is minimally interactive with his surroundings and is fed by a gastric tube. His father is his guardian. Two days ago Jared became ill with what his doctors suspect is pneumonia, but his father refuses to have any diagnostic testing done on Jared to determine the cause of his illness and refuses the administration of antibiotics, which the doctors believe could easily treat the pneumonia, if that is what Jared has, with no adverse side effects. The ethics advisory committee of the hospital met this morning and agreed, nearly unanimously, that the attending physician should honor the patient's refusal, through the proxy of his father, of antibiotic therapy. The ethics committee explains its agreement with the decision to withhold treatment as honoring the decision of the patient's proxy, which should be followed unless clearly not in the patient's best interests. Many of the members of the ethics committee stated that they would choose not to be treated in circumstances similar to the patient's. One member of the ethics committee, however, disagrees with the decision and has sought the opinion of the group home's lawyer (which is you). There is little time to act. What would you do?

D.   DECISIONS FOR PATIENTS WHO HAVE LOST CAPACITY

Decision making for patients who have lost capacity is often very challenging. The issue is covered in detail in Chapter 7. That chapter reviews many cases that call for end-of-life decisions for patients who once had capacity, no longer do, and who did not prepare an advance directive while capable. A set of well-known cases involving young women, each of whom suffered a period of anoxia (due to a different cause in each case), then entered a persistent vegetative state, and remained in that state for years, helped shape the law's responses to end-of-life decision making for patients who have lost capacity. These cases include In re Quinlan, 70 N.J. 10, cert. denied sub nom.; Garger v. New Jersey, 429 U.S. 922 (1976); Cruzan v. Director, Missouri Department of Health, 497 U.S. 261 (1999);

and Schiavo ex rel. Schindler v. Schiavo, 357 F. Supp. 2d 1378 (M.D. Fla. 2005). In each case, relatives of the patient (in two cases—*Quinlan* and *Cruzan*—the patient's parents, and in one—*Schiavo*—the patient's husband) asked that life-sustaining care be ended. Each story differs from the other two, and each court entertained somewhat different questions than the other two. But in each case, the wishes of an incompetent patient's relatives were assessed in light of the presumptive wishes of the once capable patient, as well as other matters. None of the patients in these cases left a formal advance directive. Thus, in none of the three cases was it possible clearly to discern the relevant wishes of the patient before she lost capacity.

Often, cases involving patients without capacity but who, when competent, prepared advance directives, are less discomforting for surrogate decision makers (see Note 1, Section B(1), supra). However, that is not always the case. Advance directives may not cover all contingencies—including the one that happens to be at issue for the no-longer-competent patient. But even when an advance directive does describe the situation at hand and does delineate the formerly competent person's preferences for responding to that situation, conundrums can arise. Sometimes a surrogate may not be able to carry out the wishes expressed in a patient's advance directive. Elizabeth Vig and colleagues, supra, tell of the distress experienced by one surrogate when she was not able to facilitate her husband's preference that he die at home.

In addition, it may not be easy to determine *whose* wishes are expressed in an advance directive. That is, one may ask whether the person who prepared the advance directive is the *same* person for whom medical decisions must be made. Stephen Latham described the case of his own father, who developed Alzheimer disease. Latham suggested that his father was enjoying life, indeed, that he was "perfectly happy" with his everyday life. This notwithstanding, Latham reports that his father, before he developed Alzheimer disease, would not have wished to have lived the way he was in fact living. Latham identified a philosophical debate about whether "the previous desires of someone who is essentially not here anymore should rule in our present context." Stephen R. Latham, Living Wills and Alzheimer's Disease, 23 Quinn. Prob. L.J. 425, 430–431 (2010). (Parts of Latham's article are reprinted in Chapter 2.)

E.   PATIENTS WITH SOME (OR FULL) CAPACITY: REFUSING RECOMMENDED CARE

This section considers the stories of several patients whose right to make autonomous health care decisions was challenged even though the patients in question enjoyed significant (or arguably full) capacity. In at least some cases of this sort, substitute decision makers seem to act with the patient's best interests in mind. But that is not necessarily what happens. It may be especially difficult to determine "best interests" if one tries to fit a patient's stated (but elided) wishes into the best-interest equation.[2]

---

2. Cases involving substitute decisions for patients who seemed clearly to lack decision-making capacity are considered in Chapter 2 and Chapter 7.

Each of the patients considered in this section refused care that clinicians recommended. In each case, the patient seems to have enjoyed significant capacity. Yet, in each case, the patient's capacity was challenged. It seems likely—although we know of no formal survey providing statistical evidence—that cases involving challenges to the competence of patients who enjoy at least some capacity have been occasioned in cases involving patients' refusing care recommended by clinicians far more often than in cases involving patients' consenting to such care.

‖ *Dax Cowart's Story* ‖

The story of Dax Cowart's medical care was occasioned by events that occurred in the early 1970s, before the appearance of contemporary laws and policies about the significance of safeguarding patient autonomy.[3] The story (never brought to court) is important, however, for a number of reasons. First, it illustrates powerfully the implications of eliding a patient's wishes about his or her care. Second, Dax's story became an important factor in stimulating policymakers and legislatures to create rules that protect patient autonomy. Dax, who recovered from the severe burns that rendered him a long-term patient, later went to law school and, among other things, became an advocate for the right of patients to refuse case.

Dax was a young, active man, recently discharged from military service as a pilot, when he returned home to Texas and began to work in his father's real estate business. In July 1973, Dax was severely burned over more than two-thirds of his body as the result of a gas explosion that killed his father almost at once. Dax was brought by ambulance to a hospital where he was treated for many months. His repeated requests to have extremely painful treatments stopped were ignored by his clinicians. Dax's mother (who would be Dax's legal surrogate decision maker in most states today were Dax deemed incompetent) was deeply committed to Dax's surviving, despite Dax's own protests and his obvious pain. (In 1973, when Dax was burned, physicians were far less likely to provide patients with adequate pain control than is the case today.) Hospital psychiatrists affirmed Dax's competence. Yet, his stated wishes that medical treatments be stopped were not implemented.

Dr. Robert B. White, one of the psychiatrists who examined Dax, concluded that Dax's wish to discontinue care was "in great measure logical and

---

3. Robert Burt's 1979 book, Taking Care of Strangers, presented Dax Cowart's story. In the book, Burt refers to Dax as David G. Since that time, Dax has told his story. Much of the discussion here is drawn from Case Studies in Bioethics, 5 Hastings Cent. Rpt. 9 (1975) (hereinafter *Case Studies*); and from Confronting Death: Who Chooses, Who Controls (a dialogue between Dax Cowart and Robert Burt), 28 Hastings Cent. Rpt. 14 (1998) (referred to in the text as "Dialogue"). In addition, there are two videos available about Dax's case. One ("Please Let Me Die") was made in 1974 and the second ("Dax's Case") was made in 1984.

rational." Robert B. White, A Demand to Die, 5 Hastings Cent. Rpt 9 (1975). White further explained:

> I found myself in sympathy with his wish to put an end to his pathetic plight. On the other hand, the burden on this mother would be unthinkable if he left the hospital, and none of us who were responsible for his care could bring ourselves to say, "You're discharged; go home and die."

Id. at 9.

A video about Dax's care and about some of what happened to him while he was a patient shows Dax in astonishing pain. As his body was dipped into disinfectant solution, he screamed in agony. The only lawyer who seems to have been involved represented the family in a negligence case against the company responsible for the explosion that burned Dax and killed his father. That lawyer, a friend of the Cowart family, was interviewed; that interview forms part of one of the videos about Dax's story. The lawyer asserted that he needed a living plaintiff to achieve a significant financial award. (Many students and others who watch the video are startled by the lawyer's straightforward financial strategizing about Dax's life.) In any event, Dax's requests to terminate treatment against the wishes of his mother and the medical judgment of his physicians went unmet.

In a 1998 dialogue with law professor Robert Burt, Dax Cowart explained that the agonizing pain he endured was the primary reason that he wanted to terminate care even though he knew that he would almost certainly die without that care. He noted as well that he was concerned about continuing to live given the quality of life he expected to have. At the time, Dax was unable to walk, had had the distal part of his fingers on each hand amputated, and had lost his sight. Later, he regained the ability to walk. In 1998, Dax acknowledged that he was simply wrong about the consequences of his lasting disabilities for the course of his life: "With that quality of life," he explained, "it did not seem that I would ever want to live. I have freely admitted for many years now that I was wrong about that." Dialogue, at 17. Dax further acknowledged that he was a happy man. He had gone to law school and practiced law. He participated in physical activities such as karate. Yet, he concluded that despite all of this, his physicians should have allowed him to terminate treatment and die.

NOTES AND QUESTIONS

1. *A surrogate's choices?* What options faced those who directed Dax Cowart's fate while he was being treated for the burns he suffered? Which of these options would you find most acceptable?

2. *When is the end of the day?* In the 1998 dialogue with Robert Burt (see footnote 3, supra), Burt asked Cowart how he would speak with someone in a situation that resembled his situation in 1973 and 1974. He replied: "[W]ere I called to that patient's bedside, I would want to ask why he or she wanted to refuse treatment. I would expect that one of the answers might be the pain. I would then say, 'If that were addressed, would that change things for you?'" Confronting Death: Who Chooses, Who Controls (a dialogue between Dax Cowart and Robert Burt), 28 Hastings Cent. Rpt. 14, 18 (1998). Later in the conversation, when

pressed by Burt about how to respond to a patient who continued to refuse care, Cowart replied:

> When is the end of the day? Is the end of the day at the end of one day, at the end of one week, or at the end of one year? To answer truthfully, I don't think I can say when it is without knowing more about the circumstances. For me, one hour was an eternity, with the pain I was going through. Certainly no longer than one day under those circumstances. There may be times when we would want to extend that. . . . But the problem I see in doing that is that I don't believe our health care providers would be honest about letting go of a patient earlier than whatever we set up as the maximum time. . . . [U]ntil we break out of the paternalistic mode, I can't see our physicians allowing patients to exercise their free choice unless they're legally bound to.

Id. at 19.

3. *Other responses?* Dax Cowart's clinicians and his closest relative, his mother, agreed that care should be continued. If they had disagreed, do you think that would have given added weight to Dax's position, largely ignored in fact? Had Dax managed to bring his case to court, what do you think should have been relevant to the court's decision?

State v. Northern
563 S.W.2d 197 (Ct App., Middle Sec. Tenn. 1978)

Opinion by Todd

[Mary Northern was a 72-year-old poor woman. She lived alone in rural Tennessee and had "no available help from relatives." She suffered thermal burning of her feet after she self-treated frostbite. This led to gangrene and to hospitalization. Her clinicians concluded that saving Mary Northern's life depended on amputation of both feet. Mary refused to consent. A proceeding was initiated pursuant to the state's Protective Services for Elderly Persons law. The law defined "protective services" as "services which are necessary to maintain mental and physical health and which an elderly person is unable to perform or obtain for himself." The provision further stated that "[i]f an elderly person does not consent to the receipt of protective services, or if he withdraws his consent, the services shall be terminated, unless the department determines that the elderly person lacks capacity to consent."]

On January 24, 1978, the Tennessee Department of Human Services filed this suit alleging that Mary C. Northern was 72 years old, with no available help from relatives; that Miss Northern resided alone under unsatisfactory conditions as a result of which she had been admitted to and was a patient in Nashville General Hospital; that the patient suffered from gangrene of both feet which required the removal of her feet to save her life; that the patient lacked the capacity to appreciate her condition or to consent to necessary surgery.

Attached to the complaint are identical letters from Drs. Amos D. Tackett and R. Benton Adkins which read as follows:

> Mrs. Mary Northern is a patient under our care at Nashville General Hospital. She has gangrene of both feet probably secondary to frost bite and then thermal burning of the feet. She has developed infection along with the gangrene of her

feet. This is placing her life in danger. Mrs. Northern does not understand the severity or consequences of her disease process and does not appear to understand that failure to amputate the feet at this time would probably result in her death. It is our recommendation as the physicians in charge of her case, that she undergo amputation of both feet as soon as possible.

On January 24, 1978, the Chancellor appointed a guardian ad litem to defend the cause and to receive service of process pursuant to Rule 4.04(2) T.R.C.P.

On January 25, 1978, the guardian ad litem answered as follows:

The Respondent, by and through her guardian ad litem, states as follows:
1. She is 72 years of age and a resident of Davidson County, Tennessee.
2. She is presently in the intensive care unit of General Hospital, Nashville, Tennessee, because of gangrenous condition in her two feet.
3. She feels very strongly that her present physical condition is improving, and that she will recover without the necessity of surgery.
4. She is in possession of a good memory and recall, responds accurately to questions asked her, is coherent and intelligent in her conversation and is of sound mind.
5. She is aware that the Tennessee Department of Human Services has filed this complaint, knows the nature of the complaint, and does not wish for her feet to be amputated.
6. There is no psychiatric report of her mental capacity, and there is nothing in the hospital or court record to support the statement that she lacks the capacity to realize the need for protective services.
7. The Court should not grant the relief sought by the Department of Human Services until a psychiatric report of the Respondent's present mental state has been made a part of this record, and the Court finds that the Respondent lacks the mental capacity to consent to medical treatment.
8. The Court is without jurisdiction to grant the relief to award physical custody of the respondent to the Department of Human Services absent a finding that the Respondent is guilty of a crime, or absent a finding that the Respondent lacks sufficient mental capacity in accordance with T.C.A. 33-501 et seq. (Mentally Retarded Person), and/or T.C.A. 33-601 et seq., (Mentally Ill Person).

. . . .

On January 26, 1978, there was filed in this cause a letter from Dr. John J. Griffin, reporting that he found the patient to be generally lucid and sane, but concluding:

Nonetheless, I believe that she is functioning on a psychotic level with respect to ideas concerning her gangrenous feet. She tends to believe that her feet are black because of soot or dirt. She does not believe her physicians about the serious infection. There is an adamant belief that her feet will heal without surgery, and she refused to even consider the possibility that amputation is necessary to save her life. There is no desire to die, yet her judgment concerning recovery is markedly impaired. If she appreciated the seriousness of her condition, heard her physicians' opinions, and concluded against an operation, then I would believe she understood and could decide for herself. But my impression is that she does not appreciate the dangers to her life. I conclude that she is incompetent to decide this issue. A corollary to this denial is seen in her unwillingness to consider any future plans. Here again I believe she was utilizing a psychotic mechanism of denial.

> This is a schizoid woman who has been urged by everyone to have surgery. Having been self-sufficient previously (albeit a marginal adjustment), she is continuing to decide alone. The risks with surgery are great and her life-style has been permanently disrupted. If she has surgery there is a tremendous danger for physical and psychological complications. The chances for a post-operative psychosis are immense, yet the surgeons believe an operation is necessary to save her life. I would advise delaying surgery (if feasible) for a few days in order to attempt some work for strengthening her psychologically. Even if she does not consent to the operation after that time, however, I believe she is incompetent to make the decision.

. . . .

On January 28, 1978, a certified transcript was filed, and two members of this Court heard argument on behalf of the parties and on behalf of a proposed amicus curiae, after which it was announced that this Court would act under §27-327 T.C.A. to investigate the facts.

On the same date two members of this Court heard testimony of the three doctors previously mentioned and visited the patient in the intensive care unit of the hospital. . . .

On the same date, January 28, 1978, this Court entered an order reciting the following:

> From all of the above the Court Finds:
>   1. That the respondent is not now in "imminent danger of death" in the extreme sense of the words, but that her present condition is such that "imminent danger of death" may reasonably be expected during her continued hospitalization.
>   2. That both feet of respondent are severely necrotic and affected by wet gangrene, an infection which probably will result in death unless properly treated by amputation of the feet.
>   3. That the probability of respondent's survival without amputation is from 5% to 10%; and the probability of survival after amputation is about 50%, with possible severe psychotic results.
>   4. That, with or without amputation, the prognosis of respondent's condition is poor.
>   5. That respondent is an intelligent, lucid, communicative and articulate individual who does not accept the fact of the serious condition of her feet and is unwilling to discuss the seriousness of such condition or its fatal potentiality.
>   6. That, because of her inability or unwillingness to recognize the actual condition of her feet which is clearly observable by her, she is incompetent to make a rational decision as to the amputation of her feet.
>   7. That respondent has no wish to die, but is unable or unwilling to recognize an obvious condition which will probably result in her death if untreated.

This Court is therefore of the opinion that a responsible individual should be named with authority to consent to amputation of respondent's feet when urgently recommended in writing by respondent's physicians because of the development of (symptoms) indicating an emergency and severe imminence of death.

. . . .

The first assignment of error asserts that [the operative statute] is unconstitutional.

. . . .

Title 14, Chapter 23, T.C.A. is a valid exercise of legislative authority of the sovereign State of Tennessee in providing protection for its incompetent citizens.

Also . . . the brief of appellant states:

> Such actions by the Court were injurious to the appellant because they deprived her of her right to make her own decisions—regardless as to whether death might be a probable consequence—as to whether she was willing to surrender control of her own person and life.

This controversy arises from the fact that Miss Northern's attending physicians have determined that all of the soft tissue of her feet has been killed by frostbite, that said dead tissue has become infected with gangrene and that the feet must be removed to prevent loss of life from spreading of gangrene and its effects to the entire body. Miss Northern has refused to consent to the surgery.

The physicians have determined, and the Chancellor and this Court have found, that Miss Northern's life is critically endangered; that she is mentally incapable of comprehending the facts which constitute that danger; and that she is, to that extent, incompetent, thereby justifying State action to preserve her life.

As will be observed from the bill of exceptions, a member of this Court asked Miss Northern if she would prefer to die rather than lose her feet, and her answer was "possibly." This is the most definitive expression of her desires in this record.

The patient has not expressed a desire to die. She evidences a strong desire to live and an equally strong desire to keep her dead feet. She refuses to make a choice.

If the patient would assume and exercise her rightful control over her own destiny by stating that she prefers death to the loss of her feet, her wish would be respected. The doctors so testified; this Court so informed her; and this Court here and now reiterates its commitment to this principle.

For the reasons just stated, this is not a "right to die" case.

. . . .

The sixth assignment of error raises the question of the sufficiency of evidence on the issue of capacity to consent.

Any alleged insufficiency of evidence has been adequately supplied by the hearing before this Court on January 28, 1978. Any alleged insufficiency in interrogation of the patient by the psychiatrist was supplied by the testimony of the psychiatrist before this Court on January 28, 1978 and the interview of the patient conducted by judges of this Court and preserved as part of the record of proceedings on January 28, 1978.

This Court is satisfied from the testimony and from its own examination of the patient, both orally and visually, that the evidence is adequate in the challenged respects.

The sixth assignment of error is respectfully overruled.

. . . .

The appellant has filed . . . supplemental assignments of error, of which the first is:

> 1. The statute, T.C.A. §§14-2301, et seq., is impermissibly vague; and, therefore, void and unconstitutional. The two phrases used in the statute, "imminent

danger of death" and "capacity to consent" have not been defined in the statute nor is the Court given any assistance to determine when either standard has been met in the legal context, rather than a medical context.

In the judgment of this Court, the words "imminent danger of death" are no more vague than is consistent with the nature of the subject matter.

. . . .

"Imminent danger of death" should be reasonably interpreted to carry out the purposes of the statute. For an authorization to mildly encroach upon the freedom of the individual, a relatively mild imminence or danger of death may suffice. On the other hand, the authorization of a drastic encroachment upon personal freedom and bodily integrity would require a correspondingly severe imminence of death.

In the present case, the Chancellor was not called upon to act until the imminence of death was moderately severe. By the time of the hearing before this Court, the imminence of death had lessened somewhat but remained real and appreciable. Accordingly this Court, recognizing a present real and appreciable imminence of death, made provision for drastic emergency measures to be taken only in event of severe and urgent imminence of death.

Appellant also [complains] of [the] vagueness of the meaning of "capacity to consent." Capacity means mental ability to make a rational decision, which includes the ability to perceive, appreciate all relevant facts and to reach a rational judgment upon such facts.

Capacity is not necessarily synonymous with sanity. A blind person may be perfectly capable of observing the shape of shall articles by handling them, but not capable of observing the shape of a cloud in the sky.

A person may have "capacity" as to some matters and may lack "capacity" as to others.

In 44 C.J.S. Insane Persons §2, pp. 17, 18, partial insanity is defined as follows:

> Partial insanity. Although it is hard to define the invisible line that divides perfect and partial insanity, the law recognizes a state of mind called "partial insanity," that is, insanity on a particular subject only, sometimes denominating it "insane delusion" or "monomania." The use of the term, however, has been criticized. Partial insanity has been said to be the derangement of one or more of the facilities of the mind which prevents freedom of action. Ordinarily it is confined to a particular subject, the person being sane on every other. The degree of insanity, as partial or total, is to be measured by the extent and number of the delusions existing in the mind of the person in question. . . .

In the present case, this Court has found the patient to be lucid and apparently of sound mind generally. However, on the subjects of death and amputation of her feet, her comprehension is blocked, blinded or dimmed to the extent that she is incapable of recognizing facts which would be obvious to a person of normal perception.

For example, in the presence of this Court, the patient looked at her feet and refused to recognize the obvious fact that the flesh was dead, black, shriveled, rotting and stinking.

The record also discloses that the patient refuses to consider the eventuality of death which is or ought to be obvious in the face of such dire bodily deterioration.

As described by the doctors and observed by this Court, the patient wants to live and keep her dead feet, too, and refuses to consider the impossibility of such a desire. In order to avoid the unpleasant experience of facing death and/or loss of feet, her mind or emotions have resorted to the device of denying the unpleasant reality so that, to the patient, the unpleasant reality does not exist. This is the "delusion" which renders the patient incapable of making a rational decision as to whether to undergo surgery to save her life or to forego surgery and forfeit her life.

The physicians speak of probabilities of death without amputation as 90 to 95% and the probability of death with surgery as 50–50 (1 in 2). Such probabilities are not facts, but the existence and expression of such opinions are facts which the patient is unwilling or unable to recognize or discuss.

If, as repeatedly stated, this patient could and would give evidence of a comprehension of the facts of her condition and could and would express her unequivocal desire in the face of such comprehended facts, then her decision, however unreasonable to others, would be accepted and honored by the Courts and by her doctors. The difficulty is that she cannot or will not comprehend the facts.

The first supplemental assignment of error is respectfully overruled.

The second supplemental assignment of error is as follows:

> 2. The Chancellor erred by denying the Appellant her rights to substantive and procedural due process. The entire legal proceedings involve in this case and on appeal are unprecedented; the order of the Chancellor granting the appeal but refusing the automatic stay of thirty days allowed by the Rules is one example of the procedural wrongs which was not in accordance with the established legal practice, and contrary to the expected procedure to be followed. The proposed amputation will not only permanently deprive the Appellant of her two limbs, but most likely will significantly and irreparably alter her personality for the worse, and make her mentally and physically dependent upon the State.

Whatever the propriety or impropriety of the action of the Chancellor in attempting to effectuate his action in spite of the appeal, the error, if any, has been rendered harmless by the action of this Court, after appeal, in reviewing and modifying his actions.

This Court does not recognize that it has been guilty of any improper deviation from correct procedure. The gravity of the condition of the patient and the resultant emergency in time required the unusual action of the Court . . . and the unusual acceleration of hearings and actions taken.

This Court is painfully and acutely aware of the possible tragic results of amputation. According to the doctors, the patient has only a 50% chance of surviving the surgery; and, if she survives, she will never be able to walk and may suffer severe mental and emotional problems.

On the other hand, the doctors testified, and this Court finds, that the patient's chances of survival without amputation are from 5% to 10%—a rather remote and fragile chance. Moreover, as testified by the doctors and found by this Court, even if the patient should survive without amputation, she will never walk because the dead flesh will fall off the bones of her feet leaving only bare bones.

The second supplemental assignment of error is respectfully overruled.

. . . .

It is, therefore, ordered, adjudged and decreed that

1. Mary C. Northern is in imminent danger of death if she does not receive surgical amputation of her lower extremities and she lacks the capacity to consent or refuse consent for such surgery.

2. That Honorable Horace Bass, Commissioner of Human Services of the State of Tennessee or his successor office is hereby designated and authorized to act for and on behalf of said Mary C. Northern in consenting to surgical amputation of her lower extremities and of exercising such custodial supervision as is necessarily incident thereto at any time that Drs. Amos D. Tackett and R. Benton Adkins join in signing a written certificate that Mary C. Northern's condition has developed to such a critical stage as to demand immediate amputation to save her life. The previous order of this Court is likewise so modified.

As modified, the order of the Chancellor is affirmed. The cause is remanded for further appropriate proceedings including fixing of such additional guardian ad litem fee as may be appropriate.

Modified, Affirmed and Remanded.[4]

DROWOTA, Judge, concurring.

While I am in complete agreement with the opinion of the Court, I believe it worth-while to try to elucidate and emphasize the central issue around which this entire litigation revolves: Is Miss Mary Northern at this time mentally and emotionally competent to decide whether or not to permit amputation of her gangrenous feet? There appears to be some confusion, reflected in some of the arguments advanced to us, as to what this issue means and how this Court has treated it in the instant case. The arguments of both the guardian ad litem and the amicus curiae at times suggest that the crux of the matter is the legal question of whether an individual possesses the right to accept or reject medical treatment in a life-threatening situation, sometimes popularly referred to as a "right to die." In this opinion, I would like to make it clear that this Court has little or no quarrel with such a legal principle, and that the crux of this case is the issue of Miss Northern's competence, gauged to the best of the Court's ability from the facts presented to us, to exercise her legal right to choose.

. . . .

In the instant case, the Court found that Miss Northern does not have the capacity to decide whether her feet should or should not be amputated. This finding is not based on any belief by this Court that a competent adult should not be permitted to reject lifesaving treatment. It is not, as has been argued to us, based on any idea of this Court that any person who refuses treatment we subjectively think a "normal" or "rational" person would choose is "incompetent" merely because of that refusal. It is based on the Court's finding that Miss Northern is unable or unwilling to comprehend even dimly certain very basic facts, without which no one, whether elderly lady, doctor, or judge, would be

---

4. On May 1, 1978, Mary Northern died in a Nashville hospital as the result of a clot from the gangrenous tissue migrating through the bloodstream to a vital organ. Because of complications rendering surgery more dangerous, the proposed surgery was never performed.

competent to make such a decision. These facts include the appearance of her feet, which are disfigured, coal black, crusty, cracking, oozing, and rancid. Yet, Miss Northern looks at them and insists that nothing is wrong. Also included is the fact that her doctors are of the opinion that her life is in danger, yet she has expressed no understanding of either the gravity or the consequences of her medical condition. Again, this Court respects Miss Northern's right to disagree with medical opinions and advice. Again, if this Court in good faith could find that she perceived as facts that her feet do look and smell as they do, and that her doctors are telling her that she needs surgery to save her life, we would not interfere with whatever decision she made regardless of how much it conflicted with the substance of her medical advice or with what we ourselves might have chosen. But from our honest evaluation of the facts and evidence of this case, we have been forced to conclude that Miss Northern does not comprehend such basic facts and hence is currently incompetent to decide this particular question. While this finding was made more difficult by Miss Northern's apparent ability to grasp facts not related to the condition of her feet, it is nonetheless correct.

NOTES AND QUESTIONS

1. *"Limited incompetence."*   The *Northern* court explains that Dr. John Griffin found Mary Northern to have been "generally lucid and sane" but that she was "functioning on a psychotic level with respect to ideas concerning her gangrenous feet." Does that make sense to you? What other explanations might there be for Mary's responses?

The *Northern* court referred to two members of the court's visiting Ms. Northern in the hospital. A fascinating transcript of that meeting raises essential questions about decision making for a patient who seems competent in every regard except that relating to health care decisions facing him or her. Judge Todd notes in his opinion, supra, that,

> The patient has not expressed a desire to die. She evidences a strong desire to live and an equally strong desire to keep her dead feet. She refuses to make a choice.
>   If the patient would assume and exercise her rightful control over her own destiny by stating that she prefers death to the loss of her feet, her wish would be respected.

The interview "proceeding" included Mary Northern, Judge Todd and Judge Drowota (joined as well by the Rev. Sorrow, described as a frequent visitor of Ms. Northern in the hospital):

> Judge Drowota: —Should we let you die, or would you rather live your life without your feet?
> Mary Northern (MN):   I am giving my feet a chance to get well.
>
> . . . .
>
> MN: You are pretty handsome; it's rather nice to have all you handsome men come at you, this morning.

Mr. Sorrow: Can they look at your feet?

MN: NO, no. Can you see me?

Judge Todd: I think maybe you better see your feet.

MN: You know where they are? . . . They are there.

[Mary describes the judges' interest in looking at her feet as "sadism." A nurse reveals Mary Northern's feet. Mary asserts that her feet are "getting well."]

Judge Todd: Would you—would you just bear with us just for one more thing?

MN: You want to establish your point. . . . You got your points all in writing and established it. . . .

Judge Todd: Yes, ma'am. If the time comes that you have to choose between losing your feet and dying would you rather just go ahead and die than lose your feet? . . .

MN: It's possible—It's possible only if I—Just forget it. I—You are making me sick talking.

   . . . .

Judge Todd: She wants to live and have her feet.

Rev. Sorrow: That's exactly what she wants.

MN: This is ridiculous. I am tired. . . .

Because Mary Northern did not (and apparently self-consciously would not) say that she preferred death to life without her feet, the court concluded that she was not competent to refuse the amputation. Do you agree? How else might you interpret Mary Northern's refusing to voice the formula required by the court— that she preferred death to the amputation?

2. *After amputation?*   In fact, Mary Northern died with her feet intact. However, had her feet been amputated—a response that would probably have extended Mary Northern's life—how would this poor, elderly woman have cared for herself? The case suggests a vital need for clinicians to work closely with social workers and lawyers in providing for the most general welfare of patients such as Mary Northern.

3. *Deciding for Ms. Northern?*   Had Mary Northern had family members who supported her decision to refuse the amputation, do you think that the case would have been brought to court? What, if any, difference would it have made if Mary had had a spouse or child who supported her refusal? If you had been appointed the guardian ad litem for Mary Northern, how would you have responded to her situation?

Bouvia v. Superior Court
225 Cal. Rptr. 297 (Cal. Ct. App. 1986)

This case is found in Chapter 7, pp. 457–460, supra, and discussed in Chapter 2, pp. 87–88, supra. As you reread *Bouvia*, consider the parameters along which her story resembles that of Dax Cowart or Mary Northern and the parameters along which it differs from their stories.

NOTE AND QUESTIONS

1. *Distinguishing* Bouvia *from* Northern.   *Bouvia* was among the first legal cases in which a court sided with a competent patient who wished to die—Bouvia's wish, reportedly, was grounded on her disabilities. Elizabeth Bouvia was asking that the public hospital in which she resided pull a nasogastric tube through which she was receiving nutrition and permit her to die of starvation. The court relied on the right of a capable adult to make autonomous decisions about health care (including food and water). Does it make sense to conclude that Bouvia was capable but that Mary Northern was not? What else might distinguish the court's responses in the two cases?

CHALLENGING ISSUE: DECISION MAKING BY AND FOR A WOMAN WITH ANOREXIA NERVOSA[5]

Anne is an intelligent 32-year-old former medical student. She has had an eating disorder for over 20 years and has been diagnosed with a very serious form of anorexia nervosa. She has also abused alcohol for about a decade.

Anne seems to have a lovely family. Her childhood appears to have been happy, with a devastating exception. From about the age of 4 until about 11, Anne was sexually abused. Her parents were not aware of the abuse until much later.

Anne was first hospitalized for eating problems when she was 15. After nine months, she was discharged and, although her weight was low, seemed able to live a satisfying life. She began a difficult course of medical study. However, after two years she entered into a bad relationship with a man named John and started to drink. She dropped out of school. When she was 26, Anne was again hospitalized with eating problems. She has remained seriously ill since that time and has been in and out of hospitals. In the last six years, Anne has spent several periods of time in eating disorder units and one period of two months in an alcohol treatment unit. Four years ago, John left Anne. Then, last year, one of Anne's best friends died in an automobile accident. Just before Anne's latest hospitalization, she was drinking as much as a bottle of hard liquor every day. During this period, the alcohol constituted her only source of calories. Anne now says that her refusal to eat is not specifically intended as a form of suicide. However, she has acknowledged that she will die if she does not receive nutrition.

Last year, Anne attempted on two occasions to complete an advance directive that provided that she not be forcibly fed should she reach the sort of condition that she has now reached. During the last year, several of her physicians have concluded that Anne had the capacity to authorize an advance directive, but several others have concluded that she lacked the requisite capacity. In any event, Anne signed an advance directive about six months ago. The next day she was admitted to an eating disorder unit for assessment. Dr. Perkins, chief of the unit, opined that Anne was severely ill with anorexia nervosa but that treatment could help her. She remained in Dr. Perkins's unit

---

5. Anne's story is based on an actual case, decided in Britain in 2012. A Local Authority v. E, [2012] EWHC 1639 (COP) (Royal Courts of Justice, June 15, 2012), available at http://www.documentcloud.org/documents/369203-anorexiaruling.html#document/p14.

for two weeks. After her release, she became increasingly sick. She was detained about two months ago and forcibly fed for a week. Feeding was discontinued because of Anne's objection.

Now, Anne's parents have concluded that professional care is unlikely to help their daughter. They want Anne to live, but they do not believe that she is likely to be cured. They have concluded that Anne should be allowed to refuse food and thus call an end to many years of great suffering. Anne's physicians are also skeptical about the ultimate value of forced feeding, but they are ready to support a decision to feed Anne forcibly. However, one expert has opined that there are treatments available that might help Anne.

At present, Anne is hospitalized and has been receiving palliative care for about three weeks. She is receiving high doses of opiates and is not being forcibly fed. Her body mass index (BMI) is 11. A person with a BMI below 12 is at risk for sudden cardiac death.

Do you think that a court could (legally) or should (morally) order that Anne be forcibly fed?

Do you think that Anne's "true identity" is masked by her illness? If so, how might a court (or any other decision maker for Anne) interested in discerning Anne's best interests do that? Are the elements of her "true identity" to be found in Anne at age 10, before her eating disorder developed? Or at age 20, when she was underweight but not seriously so and was successfully attending medical school? Or in her present situation? Are all of those periods as well as others in Anne's life relevant to a portrait of Anne's identity for purposes of deciding whether or not to force feed Anne now?

F.   CLINICAL ETHICS COMMITTEES

The New Jersey court that decided the case of Karen Ann Quinlan in 1976 suggested that hospitals develop ethics committees to entertain disputes among patients, clinicians, and/or patients' kin. In re Matter of Quinlan, 355 A.2d 647, *cert. denied sub nom.* Garger v. New Jersey, 429 U.S. 922 (1976).[6] In *Quinlan,* New Jersey's highest court sided with Karen Ann's father and permitted the discontinuation of assisted respiration for Karen, who had entered a persistent vegetative state years earlier as a result of an extended period of anoxia. Justice Hughes, who decided the case for New Jersey's highest court, explicitly suggested near the end of his opinion in *Quinlan* that hospitals should focus on providing "a regular forum for more input and dialogue in individual situations and to allow the responsibility of these judgments to be shared." 355 A.2d at 668. In the view of Justice Hughes, ethics committees provided a good model. He noted that such committees were likely to be interdisciplinary, could assist in "review[ing] the individual circumstances of ethical dilemma[s], and would offer "assistance and safeguards for patients and their medical caretakers." *Id.*

As Justice Hughes noted, ethics committees existed in some hospitals when he entertained the *Quinlan* case. However, the decision foreshadowed widespread construction of ethics committees in hospitals and nursing homes. In

---

6. *Quinlan* is considered as well in Chapter 7, Section A(1)(a).

1982, five years after *Quinlan* was decided, ethics committees with authority to participate in clinical decision making existed in about one percent of U.S. hospitals. Diane E. Hoffmann, Regulating Ethics Committees in Health Care Institutions—Is it Time?, 50 Md. L. Rev. 746, 747, n.3 (1991). In 1986 Maryland began the first state to pass legislation that required hospital ethics committees. *Id.* at 748, n.10. By the early 1990s, a majority of U.S. hospitals had ethics committees. Susan M. Wolf, Ethics Committees and Due Process: Nesting Rights in a Community of Caring, 50 Md. L. Rev. 798, 799–800 (1991). And in 1992 the hospital accreditation board (the Joint Commission on Accreditation of Healthcare Organizations) required all hospitals to have institutional mechanisms for resolving ethical disputes.

Ethics committees have served to limit resort to litigation in resolving disputes about patient care. Originally, they served in an advisory role. Increasingly, they have become an integral part of decision making in cases involving challenging ethical questions or disputes about patient care. They serve a number of functions, depending on the state and the particular hospital. Among other things these committees may help resolve disputes between patients or patients' surrogates and clinicians or disputes between members of a hospital's staff. They often provide education in medical ethics to clinicians and others involved in patient care, including patients' family members, and some of them help develop or review hospital policies. Further, a hospital ethics committee may evaluate clinicians' decisions about how best to provide for a patient's needs. They can be of significant assistance in facilitating decision making for patients lacking capacity. Clinicians, patients, or others may seek an ethics committee consultation. In general, the committees are not tightly regulated by state law, and the consequences of their deliberations have not been systematically subjected to formal assessment. In most states, hospital ethics committees can include physicians, nurses, clergy, social workers, various therapists, and a member, or more, representing the lay public. Committee members are usually appointed by the hospital in which the committee operates.[7]

Widespread development of palliative care units in U.S. hospitals in the last couple of decades has furthered the need for ethics committees. Palliative care services focus on limiting pain and ensuring patient comfort. Palliative care includes curative care more often than does hospice care, although palliative care focuses on mitigating pain. However, the American Academy of Hospice and Palliative Medicine (AAHPM) describes both hospice and palliative care doctors as focusing on patients' "quality of life while treating their symptoms." See AAHPM home, available at http://www.aahpm.org/learn/default/patienteducation.html. Palliative care services now exist in more than half of hospitals in the United States. Matt Sedensky, AP, Hospitals Add Palliative Teams at Feverish Pace, Time: Healthland, available at http://healthland.time.com/2012/06/04/u-s-hospitals-adding-palliative-care-teams-at-a-feverish-pace/. A significant percentage of cases considered by hospital ethics committees involve patients receiving palliative care. Mark P. Aulisio & Robert M. Arnold, Role of the Ethics Committee: Helping to Address Value Conflicts or Uncertainties, 134 Chest 417 (2008), available at http://chestjournal.chestpubs.org/content/134/2/417.full.

---

7. We are grateful to Tracy Dunbrook, Visiting Assistant Professor of Law at the Maurice A. Deane School of law at Hofstra University, for sharing her insights about hospital ethics committees with us.

A number of states have imbued ethics committees with special powers, pursuant to statutory law. Often these powers relate directly to seriously ill patients facing end-of-life issues. For instance, Texas has given significant power to ethics committees under the Texas Advance Directives Act (TADA). The law, enacted in 1999, defined an extrajudicial role for hospital ethics committees that allows them to engage in the decision-making process for patients who are terminally ill or who are suffering from an irreversible condition. Tex. Health and Safety Code, Sec. 166.002 et. seq, Sec. 166.031 (2011). Dr. Robert Fine, who played a role in the construction of TADA, notes that "in practice it is a disagreement with patient surrogates that leads to utilization of the full dispute resolution process." Robert L. Fine, Point: The Texas Advance Directives Act Effectively and Ethically Resolves Disputes About Medical Futility, 136 Chest 963, 965 (2009). TADA has significantly limited the number of disputes about medical decisions that end up in court.

The Texas law, which gives ethics committees the authority to withdraw life-sustaining care from terminal patients, may relieve some family members of the burden of making that decision. (The procedural requirements included in the Texas law are delineated in Chapter 7, Section A(3).) Robert Fine reported that family members sometimes seem to find comfort in being freed from the heavy burden of life-and-death decision making for a loved one. Accordingly, in Fine's view, many surrogates in this situation seemed to say: "If you are asking us to agree with the recommendation to remove life support from our loved one, we cannot. However, we do not wish to fight the recommendation in court, and if the law says it is okay to stop life support, then that is what should happen." Robert L. Fine, Resolution of Futility by Due Process: Early Experience with the Texas Advance Directives Act, 138 Ann. Internal Med. 743 (2003).

On the other hand TADA has critics. Dr. Robert Truog has argued that TADA gives "life-and-death decision making" to committees largely composed of hospital clinicians. Truog suggests that insofar as committee members are generally closely acquainted with the clinicians whose decisions they are reviewing, a conflict-of-interest inheres in the composition of the committees. And committee members "typically work for the same hospital or university [as do those whose decisions they review] and are economically dependent on the financial well-being of those institutions." Robert D. Truog, Counterpoint: The Texas Advance Directives Act Is Ethically Flawed: Medical Futility Disputes Must Be Resolved by a Fair Process, 136 Chest 968, 969 (2009). Truog cites one survey that found that in the vast majority (more than 90 percent) of 47 cases brought to an ethics committee in Texas, the committee agreed with the clinicians. Accordingly, Truog would prefer that the membership of ethics committees more adequately reflect the diversity of local communities. Further, he faults TADA for significantly usurping the role of courts in protecting those treated unfairly. In Texas, judicial review of ethics committee decisions can be sought only for the purpose of extending the time provided for locating an alternative placement for the patient. Id. at 968.

In testimony before President's Bush's Council on Bioethics, law professor Thaddeus Pope suggested that TADA may be unconstitutional because, among other things, it violates procedural due process protections. For instance, ethics committees are generally not neutral. Thaddeus Mason Pope, Transcript, President's Council on Bioethics, Medical Futility: Institutional and Legislative

Initiatives,   Sept.   12,   2008,   http://thaddeuspope.com/images/PCBE__
Transcripts_September_12,_2008___Session_5__Medical_Futility__Institu.pdf.
(TADA's constitutionality has been challenged but without success. See Rebuttal
from Dr. Fine, 136 Chest 971 (2009).)

In general, Pope described surrogate decision makers in the United States
as "increasingly likely to make demands that [patients'] providers determine are
inappropriate" and "at the same time . . . providers are increasingly likely to
resist these demands." Further, Pope explained: "[M]ore surrogate insistence
combined with more provider resistance leads to more intractability. So, that's
the general situation in the United States." Id.

Yet, Nancy Dubler suggests that ethics committees can successfully resolve
conflicts between clinicians and family members of a patient without capacity.
Dubler has described such cases as the most challenging that ethics committees
face and has noted the usefulness of alternative dispute resolution methods in
responding to such conflicts.

> ### Nancy Neveloff Dubler, See You Out of Court? The Role of ADR in Health Care: A "Principled Resolution": The Fulcrum of Bioethics Mediation
> #### 74 L. & Contemp. Probs. 177, 185–187 (2011)

Bioethics mediation is one of the tools of CEC [Clinical-Ethics Consulta-
tion], a subspecialty of bioethics, and an example of applied ethics in which a
trained professional, generally a physician, nurse, social worker, lawyer, or philosopher, acts as a consultant to the medical team to address discomforts about
care planning and the implementation of previously forged care agreements.

In bioethics mediation, a principled resolution reflects a clinical plan of
action agreed upon by relevant stakeholders and chosen from among multiple
morally permissible options that fall within the spectrum of acceptable clinical,
ethical, and legal outcomes. Bioethics conflict is almost always about the
"proper" or "appropriate" plan for future care. The parties generally include
the attending physician, other members of the healthcare team, and some advocate for the patient. This advocate can be a family member or friend. Sometimes
the patient is alone without family, such as an "unbefriended elderly" or "unre-
presented patient." The mediation is largely with non-patient advocates because
capacitated adult patients have the legal right to accept or reject medical alternatives even if their decisions are thought to be wrong by others. Thus, bioethics
mediation often addresses situations in which the adult patient is allegedly
incapacitated, is clearly incapacitated, or is a minor or an otherwise legally
compromised person.

The bioethics mediator is always neutral to the particular case, but is likely
to be known to the medical staff. Indeed, case-mediation requests often come
from satisfied repeat users of the service. One of the differences between bioethics mediation and other sorts of mediation is that the mediator is generally a
member of the CEC team, giving her access to the healthcare institution, the
right to intervene in the case, and the power to write a note in the medical chart,
which is the legal record of the patient's care. In the chart note, the bioethics
mediator notes the principled resolution as the consensus reached and,

therefore, the CE recommendation. In general, the physician, who has the legal authority and responsibility for the patient's care, will be a part of the mediation; thus committed to the consensus, she will write any orders as needed to effectuate the resolution.

The bioethics mediator recognizes that there are always multiple options for the plan of care. This may be in distinct contrast to the medical providers who more often tend to see only the best plan. This is not surprising because physicians are trained to evaluate medical data and act to reach the optimum goal. It goes counter to training, instinct, and paternalistic habits to see nonmedical factors as relevant and valid. Even as physicians and practitioners began increasingly to recognize that medical choices reflect personal values and history, they still jockeyed to maintain control of the decision-making process. They did so out of the lofty motive to do what is in the "best interest" of the patient and the not-so-elevated characteristic of having no real experience in sharing power. The mediator helps the parties to maximize options either by defining actually distinct end points or by introducing new timetables that better permit the accumulation of data. Thus the bioethics mediator plays the crucial role of opening space and time for considering other factors.

Consider the following vignette of a large, loving, and chaotic family (let us say) from Bosnia in which the healthcare proxy, the oldest son, is decompensating at the imminent death of his mom and is drinking heavily. He has had a number of clashes with the nursing staff in the ICU; some of the staff are merely wary and some are actively scared of him. The mediator and the attending physician have tried to move the family, all seventeen of them who are present, to accept the fact that mom is dying. The oldest son (the healthcare proxy) finally explodes and demands that the physician give mom a special tonic she used to take when she lived at home. Left to her own devices, the physician is likely to reject this out of hand. Nothing has prepared her for the experience of providing an unknown substance to a dying patient. However, the mediator has been at this for some time and says the following:

> How lucky is your mom to have family who love her so much, are willing to spend so much time and effort to make her better. Now, I hear the doctor saying that this tonic is unlikely to help your mom, that she is dying and beyond the help of any medicine. However, it might be possible for the pharmacy to analyze this tonic and if they agree that it could not harm her, we might be able to give it to the patient.

By stroking, repeating, and reinforcing, the bioethics mediator has bought some time, supported the family (or at least the oldest son), deflected the annoyance and punitive reaction of the physician, and, with a bit of luck and a call on the "favor bank" at the pharmacy, would make this action possible. Her logic, from the bioethics perspective, is simple:

> The patient was given the tonic at home as her family believed that it would help cure her ailment. She is now dying and cannot be discharged home where the family could continue with old remedies. But, as the patient is dying, the potential that this tonic will actively harm her is limited. Receiving the tonic supports the patient's and the family's beliefs and their explanatory model of illness, and it offers the son and family a sense of peace that they supported her well-being.

Now, this person is an obtunded, ventilator-dependent, dying patient: what harm could this tonic possibly cause? The bioethics mediator's action on behalf of the family changes the power structure, unpacks the enmity between staff and family, and calms the oldest son. In bioethics mediation the process is part of the product.

Bioethics mediation stands in the tradition of mediation in that it searches for consensus in chaos. The type of mediation described in the paragraph above is somewhat similar to the idea of the "permanent umpire"—a selected and fixed arbitrator who would give instant mediation and assist in ongoing dispute resolution. Bioethics mediation is a sort of hybrid between traditional mediation and the presence of a "permanent umpire."

NOTES AND QUESTIONS

1. *Limits on ethics committees powers?*   Some of the cases brought to hospital ethics committees are difficult and heart wrenching. Ethics committees have significant power to entertain and assist in resolving conflicts among surrogate decision makers (or patients) and clinicians as well as among members of a hospital staff. However, their determinations are not final insofar as they do not preempt court review. What sorts of powers would you want to give to ethics committees? Would you—and if so, how would you—want to limit those powers?

2. *Bioethics mediation.*   Nancy Dubler's article, supra, illustrates how bio-ethics mediation works. The excerpt provides one example, involving a dying woman from Bosnia whose family requests help that differs from that typically provided by U.S. clinicians. In general, how do you think that bioethics medi-ation might usefully differ from other forms of mediation commonly employed in nonhospital settings?

3. *Words of caution.*   Some physicians take strong exception to practices encouraged by laws such as TADA. Dr. Yashar Hirshaut, an oncologist in New York City, asserts that referring to very ill people as "terminal," rather than as people with advanced disease, shifts clinicians' focus from treating the disease toward a process aimed at easing death. In Hirshaut's view, the label ("terminal") reflects a dehumanization of patients that then justifies practices that facilitate death. An interview with Dr. Hirshaut by Yitzchok Frankfurter can be found at Life and the Bridge in Between Illness, Ami Magazine 69 (Apr. 4, 2011).

If Dr. Hirshaut is correct, what factors (in addition to the alleviation of pain) do you think might encourage legislatures and hospitals to develop palliative care and hospice services?

4. *Bibliographic note.*   Additional discussion of hospital ethics committees can be found in Joanna K. Weinberg, Institutional Ethics Committees: Should We Kill All the Lawyers? The Role of Lawyers on Hospital Ethics Committees, 21 Ann. Health L. 181 (2012); Meir Katz, When Is Medical Care "Futile"? The Institutional Competence of the Medical Profession Regarding the Provision of Life-Sustaining Medical Care, 90 Neb. L. Rev. 1, 22–25 (2011); David Braggish, The Ethics Consultation, 23 Quinn. Prob. L.J. 432 (2010).

G.   SPECIAL ISSUES WHEN CHILDREN ARE PATIENTS

Medical decision making for children raises special issues. Even defining the developmental stages of childhood and adolescence is complicated, and assessing capacity may be difficult, especially for children in the middle years of childhood. Individuals develop in different ways, at different rates. And social understandings of childhood and adolescence have shifted dramatically during the last several centuries. In addition, views about medical decision making for children generally reflect assumptions about the place and role of children within families. As the so-called traditional family that developed in the century and a half after the start of the Industrial Revolution has been widely transformed into the contemporary family of "choice," the scope and meaning of childhood have changed.

1.   Introduction: The Parameters of Childhood and Parents as Decision Makers

a.   Bioethical and Social Perspectives

Children under 3 years of age differ significantly in their needs, capacities, and interests from children of 7, and both groups differ dramatically from children of 13 or 14. By age 16 or 17, adolescents may resemble adults more than they resemble younger children.

Childhood can be divided into at least four developmental stages. The boundaries between these stages are not absolute, and different theorists divide and describe the stages of childhood differently. The stages of childhood are preceded by a gestational stage that includes the period from conception through birth. A period of infancy extends from birth until about 2. Ages 3 through 5 can be defined as "early childhood"; 6 through 11 as middle childhood; and 12 through 19 as adolescence. See John S. Dacey & John F. Travers, Human Development: Across the Lifespan 7 (4th ed. 1999).

Development during childhood is not a product of biology alone. Rather, it is the consequence of complicated interactions among biological, sociological, cultural, psychological, environmental, and economic factors. Virtually all psychologists agree that development during childhood shapes the resulting adult's character and choices. However, a variety of psychological "schools" provide different theories through which to make sense of the connection between a child's many experiences and the adult that that child becomes.

Sigmund Freud, for instance, theorized that differences in personality originate in childhood sexual experience, read broadly.

> There seems no doubt that germs of sexual impulses are already present in the new-born child and that these continue to develop for a time, but are then overtaken by a progressive process of suppression; this in turn is itself interrupted by periodical advances in sexual development or may be held up by individual peculiarities. Nothing is known for certain concerning the regularity and periodicity of this oscillating course of development.

Unlike Freud, who focused on the psychosexual development of personality, the Swiss cognitive psychologist Jean Piaget focused on the development of intellect. Piaget identified four stages of increasingly advanced cognitive development. The first stage, occurring between birth and about age 2, Piaget called the sensory motor stage. During this stage children learn to manipulate objects that they can see. The second Piagetian stage involves what Piaget called pre-operational thought. Children between 2 and 7 become capable of simple logical thinking. During the third stage (the concrete operational stage), children between ages 7 and 11 develop an expanded capacity to use symbols, including those involved in speech, and develop a more sophisticated understanding of causation. During the last stage of child development (the formal operational stage), according to Piaget, children between ages 11 and 15 become capable of pure thought, including the ability to draw hypotheses and to theorize. See Wallace J. Mlyniec, A Judge's Ethical Dilemma: Assessing a Child's Capacity to Choose, 64 Fordham L. Rev. 1873 (1996).

Other psychologists have constructed other approaches to the study of child development and of development through the life span. Some useful references include Abraham Maslow, Motivation and Personality (1987) (focusing on the development of needs); B.F. Skinner, Beyond Freedom and Dignity (1971) (stressing the importance of environment in learning in his stimulus–response theory of human behavior); Erik Erikson, Childhood and Society (2d ed. 1963); Erik Erikson, Identity Youth and Crisis (1968) (constructing a psychosocial theory of human development). See Dacey & Travers, supra, at 25–43 (summarizing theories of development).

Such efforts to describe and explain child development reflect a variety of assumptions about children within families, and thus about families. The so-called traditional family that developed during the early years of the Industrial Revolution treasured children, and understood them as vulnerable and innocent. Historian Carl Degler described the differentiation of childhood and adulthood as the most important development in the construction of the nineteenth-century family. Degler explained:

> [C]hildhood itself was perceived as it is today, as a period of life not only worth recognizing and cherishing but extending. Moreover, simply because children were being seen for the first time as special, the family's reason for being, its justification as it were, was increasingly related to the proper rearing of children.

Carl N. Degler, At Odds: Women and the Family in America from the Revolution to the Present 66 (1980). In large part, the vision of childhood shaped by the nineteenth century has survived the vast social changes of the last two centuries.

NOTE

1. *Bibliographic note.*   Philippe Aries has documented the development of childhood from the fifteenth or sixteenth century. Philippe Aries, Centuries of Childhood: A Social History of Family Life (Robert Baldick trans. 1962). The history of childhood in the United States is considered in Mary Ann Mason, From Father's Property to Children's Rights: The History of Child Custody of the United States (1994); Viviana A. Zelizer, Pricing the Priceless Child: The

Changing Social Value of Children (1985); Carl A. Degler, At Odds, Women and the Family in America: From the Revolution to the Present (1980); a useful compendium of essays on children's health is Ruth E.K. Stein, ed., Health Care for Children: What's Right, What's Wrong, What's Next (1997).

The following sources provide additional insight into the shifting scope of childhood in contemporary Western society: Neil Postman, The Disappearance of Childhood (1982, 1994); Felton Earls, Children: From Rights to Citizenship, 633 Annals of the Am. Acad. of Polit'l & Soc. Sci. 6 (2011); Janet L. Dolgin, The Fate of Childhood: Legal Models of Children and the Parent–Child Relationship, 61 Alb. L. Rev. 345 (1997).

b. Legal Approaches

Two cases—decided by the same court in the same year—have suggested the scope of social assumptions about children and about the parent–child relationship in the United States. The first case, Bellotti v. Baird, 443 U.S. 622 (1979), is about the right of minor girls to terminate a pregnancy. The second case, Parham v. J.R., 442 US 584 (1979), is about a parent's right to institutionalize a child in a state mental facility without judicial review. Even that brief description suggests a disparity in perspective between the two cases: in *Bellotti,* the Court focused on a child's right to health care; in *J.R.,* it focused on a parent's right to direct a child's health care.

Bellotti involved a constitutional challenge to a Massachusetts law that limited a minor girl's right to consent to an abortion. The law, enacted in 1974 provided, in part:

> If the mother is less than eighteen years of age and has not married, the consent of both the mother and her parents [to an abortion to be performed on the mother] is required. If one or both of the mother's parents refuse such consent, consent may be obtained by order of a judge of the superior court for good cause shown, after such hearing as he deems necessary. Such a hearing will not require the appointment of a guardian for the mother. If one of the parents has died or has deserted his or her family, consent by the remaining parent is sufficient. If both parents have died or have deserted their family, consent of the mother's guardian or other person having duties similar to a guardian, or any person who had assumed the care and custody of the mother is sufficient. . . .

The Court explained:

> Among the questions certified to the Supreme Judicial Court was whether §12S permits any minors—mature or immature—to obtain judicial consent to an abortion without any parental consultation whatsoever. The state court answered that, in general, it does not. . . .
>
> We think that, construed in this manner, §12S would impose an undue burden upon the exercise by minors of the right to seek an abortion. As the District Court recognized, "there are parents who would obstruct, and perhaps altogether prevent, the minor's right to go to court." There is no reason to believe that this would be so in the majority of cases where consent is withheld. But many parents hold strong views on the subject of abortion, and young pregnant minors, especially those living at home, are particularly vulnerable to their parents' efforts to obstruct both an abortion and their access to court. It would be unrealistic, therefore, to assume that the mere existence of a legal

right to seek relief in superior court provides an effective avenue of relief for some of those who need it the most.

We conclude, therefore, that under state regulation such as that undertaken by Massachusetts, every minor must have the opportunity—if she so desires—to go directly to a court without first consulting or notifying her parents. If she satisfies the court that she is mature and well enough informed to make intelligently the abortion decision on her own, the court must authorize her to act without parental consultation or consent. If she fails to satisfy the court that she is competent to make this decision independently, she must be permitted to show that an abortion nevertheless would be in her best interests. If the court is persuaded that it is, the court must authorize the abortion. If, however, the court is not persuaded by the minor that she is mature or that the abortion would be in her best interests, it may decline to sanction the operation.

The second case, also decided by the U.S. Supreme Court in 1979, challenged a Georgia statute that provided for the *"voluntary"* admission of a child to a Georgia state mental hospital in cases in which the child's parent(s) or guardian sought such admission and the relevant facility's superintendent approved the admission. The Court declined appellees' due process challenge, specifically denying the child plaintiffs in *J.R.* the right to a "formal, adversary, pre-admission hearing" before admission to a state mental hospital. The Court explained:

> In defining the respective rights and prerogatives of the child and parent in the voluntary commitment setting, we conclude that our precedents permit the parents to retain a substantial, if not the dominant, role in the decision, absent a finding of neglect or abuse, and that the traditional presumption that the parents act in the best interests of their child should apply. . . .
>
> It is not necessary that the deciding physician conduct a formal or quasi-formal hearing. A state is free to require such a hearing, but due process is not violated by use of informal, traditional medical investigative techniques.

NOTES AND QUESTIONS

1. *Difficulty defining childhood.   Bellotti* and *J.R.,* read together, suggest a society struggling with inconsistent understandings of childhood and of the parent–child relationship. The two cases can be distinguished with reference to differences between decisions about abortion and decisions about institutionalizing children. However, focusing on that distinction rather than on understandings of children and parents that underlie each case may serve to disguise a fundamental uncertainty in society about what children are and about how children do or should relate to parents.

In *Bellotti,* the Court noted the conclusion of the district court that some parents might "obstruct, and perhaps altogether prevent, the minor's right to go to court." The Court explained that nothing suggested that such parents constituted a "majority of the cases where consent is withheld." Despite this, the Court concluded that "[i]t would be unrealistic . . . to assume that the mere existence of a legal right to seek relief in superior court provides an effective avenue of relief for some of those who need it the most." In light of that conclusion, the Court interpreted the Constitution to require a state to provide a pregnant minor seeking an abortion with the opportunity "to go directly to a court without first consulting or notifying her parents."

In *J.R.,* the Court similarly considered a minority of parents who might seek to institutionalize a child for reasons unrelated to the child's best interests. The Court reasoned, however, that the possibility of parental abuse or neglect did not give cause to "discard wholesale those pages of human experience that teach that parents generally do act in the child's best interests."

How do you explain the different weight the Court gives to the need to protect against the possibility, however small, of parental abuse in *Bellotti* and in *J.R.?* Does this difference simply reflect perceived differences between a decision about abortion and a decision about institutionalizing children? If that is the case, how does one distinguish the two sorts of decisions? Aren't the possible consequences of unwarranted institutionalization very damaging to a child? If so, can the case of institutionalizing a child still be distinguished from that of a pregnant minor seeking an abortion through reference to the seriousness of consequences for the minor involved?

2. *Judicial assumptions about the parent–child relationship.* *Bellotti* grants children more room to effect their own choices than *J.R.,* but that difference may not be grounded on a different vision of children as much as on a different vision of the parent–child relationship. In *Bellotti,* the Court extended what several commentators have described as a sort of burdened autonomy to minors seeking abortions. A girl relying on the so-called judicial bypass option outlined in *Bellotti* is likely to receive judicial consent to abort an unwanted pregnancy. However, the girl is not free to effect her own choice without adult involvement. Instead, she is allowed to substitute judicial permission for parental permission to abort.

The Court appears to presume that the parent–child relationship may be so dysfunctional that the minor must be given some alternative option to parental consent or notification. Thus, in theory, the decision does not necessarily assume that children are competent to deal with the sort of choices about abortion that the law extends to adult women, but that it is too likely that minors facing an unwanted pregnancy will often not be able or willing to rely on parental support and guidance. Curiously, however, in light of assumptions about childhood that undergird *Bellotti,* one result of the judicial bypass option is that a girl relying on it is asked to exhibit a degree of initiative and competence rarely asked of adults seeking abortions or any other form of medical care. Ironically, one consequence of allowing children to bypass parental authority in favor of other sorts of adult authority is that the children who manage to locate and invoke alternative sources of authority are forced, in the process, to grow up. Excellent accounts of the process required of a minor seeking permission in court for an abortion are found in Rachel Rebouche, Parental Involvement Laws and New Governance, 34 Harv. J.L. & Gender 175 (2011); J. Shoshanna Ehrlich, Grounded in a Reality of Their Lives: Listening to Teens Who Make the Abortion Decision Without Involving Their Parents, 18 Berkeley Women's L.J. 61 (2003); J. Shoshanna Ehrlich, Journey Through the Courts: Minors, Abortion and the Question for Reproductive Fairness, 10 Yale J.L. & Feminism 1 (1998).

3. *Right to postadmission hearing.* Justice Brennan, who dissented in Parham v. J.R., agreed with the majority "that the District Court erred in interpreting the Due Process Clause to require preconfinement commitment hearings in all cases in which parents wish to hospitalize their children." But he disagreed "with the Court's decision to pretermit questions concerning the postadmission procedures due Georgia's institutionalized juveniles." He

concluded that a child such as J.R. had a right to "at least one postadmission hearing." 442 U.S. at 626. He explained further that under the Constitution, Georgia "may postpone formal commitment hearings, when parents seek to commit their children." However, he concluded, "the State cannot dispense with such hearings altogether. Our cases make clear that, when protected interests are at stake, the fundamental requirement of due process must provide reasonably prompt postdeprivation hearings." 442 U.S. at 634.

4. *Assumptions about parents.*   In a footnote, the *J.R.* Court explained that it would first "deal with the issues arising when the natural parents of the child seek commitment to a state hospital," and would then "deal with the situation presented when the child is a ward of the state." 442 U.S. at 600, n.11. Justifying the conclusion that parents are likely to serve their children's interests, the Court asserted that the law has "historically . . . recognized that natural bonds of affection lead parents to act in the best interest of their children." It would thus seem that the Court's decision is predicated on the strength and consistency of parents' "natural bonds of affection" for their children. How then can one make sense of the Court's later assertion that "we cannot assume that when the State of Georgia has custody of a child it acts so differently from a natural parent in seeking medical assistance for the child"?

In his dissent, Justice Brennan questioned the Court's presumption that no significant difference distinguishes a commitment by a parent or parents from a commitment by the state:

> To my mind, there is no justification for denying children committed by their social workers the prior hearings that the Constitution typically requires. In the first place, such children cannot be said to have waived their rights to a prior hearing simply because their social workers wished them to be confined. The rule that parents speak for their children, even if it were applicable in the commitment context, cannot be transmuted into a rule that state social workers speak for their minor clients. The rule in favor of deference to parental authority is designed to shield parental control of child rearing from state interference. The rule cannot be invoked in defense of unfettered state control of child rearing or to immunize from review the decisions of state social workers. The social worker–child relationship is not deserving of the special protection and deference accorded to the parent–child relationship, and state officials acting in loco parentis cannot be equated with parents.
>
> Second, the special considerations that justify postponement of formal commitment proceedings whenever parents seek to hospitalize their children are absent when the children are wards of the State and are being committed upon the recommendations of their social workers. The prospect of preadmission hearings is not likely to deter state social workers from discharging their duties and securing psychiatric attention for their disturbed clients. Moreover, since the children will already be in some form of state custody as wards of the State, prehospitalization hearings will not prevent needy children from receiving state care during the pendency of the commitment proceedings. Finally, hearings in which the decisions of state social workers are reviewed by other state officials are not likely to traumatize the children or to hinder their eventual recovery.
>
> For these reasons, I believe that, in the absence of exigent circumstances, juveniles committed upon the recommendation of their social workers are entitled to preadmission commitment hearings. As a consequence, I would hold Georgia's present practice of denying these juveniles prior hearings unconstitutional.

442 U.S. at 637–638.

5. *What are children?*   If you recently arrived in the United States from another galaxy and knew nothing about the notion of "children" in U.S. society, would you have a sense of how the society in which you have landed understands children after having considered *Bellotti* and *J.R.*? Would you be able to describe accurately the society's view of the "parent–child relationship"? Would you feel troubled that parents have authority to make medical decisions for children in most circumstances, at least until the children are well into the adolescent period? Would you conclude that children (at least above a certain age) should make their own medical decisions? Or that parents should always make those decisions? Or, on the model of *Bellotti,* would you conclude that some other adult(s) should be authorized to make medical decisions for children, at least in certain situations?

2.   Medical Decision Making for Children

Both Bellotti v. Baird and Parham v. J.R., supra, provide a constitutional frame that gives lower courts and legislatures considerable scope to resolve questions about medical decision making for children and adolescents variously.

Such questions reflect many of the concerns raised by medical decision making in general. However, the governing assumption that allows adults to make their own medical decisions—respect for their autonomous individuality—does not pertain in the case of children—especially young children. The younger the child, the less likely it is that the child will be viewed as autonomous and thus capable of making his or her own medical decisions. As a result, medical decision making for children almost invariably involves children in their relation to adults. Often those adults are the children's parents. They may also be other relatives, legal guardians, health care professionals, lawyers, or judges. In the main, however, understandings of familial relationships, especially those between parents and children, are central to legal decisions about medical decisions for children considered too young to make medical decisions independently.

a.   Bioethical and Social Perspectives

i.   Children and Surrogates: Refusing and Consenting to Care

Generally, decisions for young children are made by their parents or guardians. Medical decision making for adolescents occasions complex questions.

Even for a very young child, serious ethical questions sometimes emerge about a parent's medical decisions for his or her child. The consequences of parental (or other adult) consent (or refusal to consent) to care for young children may be particularly complicated if one attempts to discern the choices the child involved will have wanted to have been made once he or she is mature. That effort would seem especially important in certain sorts of cases—for instance, those in which a parent consents to genital surgery on a baby born with ambiguous genitalia. Some commentators suggest that because surgery is risky and not medically necessary in such cases, the law should not provide for substituted judgments in these cases. Note, Kishka-Kamari Ford, "First, Do No Harm"—The Fiction of Legal Parental Consent to Genital Normalizing Surgery on Intersexed Infants, 19 Yale L. & Pol'y Rev. 469, 477–479 (2001).

> ## Rhonda Gay Hartman, Coming of Age: Devising Legislation for Adolescent Medical Decision Making
> ### 28 Am. J.L. & Med. 409, 422–426 (2002)

Collectively, legislation that affords legal decision-making to minors for medical care raises a number of important points for examination in shaping policy and devising—or revising—legislation. First, there is no indication that the policies underpinning current statutes have considered the actual decision-making ability of adolescents to decide treatment for STDs [sexually transmitted diseases], mental health, or because they have graduated from high school or have married. . . .

While scientific findings suggest that adolescents possess levels of cognitive capacities—as measured by Piagetian stage and task-specific schema—which are ignored by the empirical and normative values that influence legal policy regarding minors, those findings do not evidence the same capacities for minors less than fourteen years of age. Scientific studies suggest that minors demonstrate decision-making comparable to young adults by age fourteen in healthcare decision-making [and] pregnancy decision-making. . . .

It is also unclear whether policy-makers intuitively realize a difference in decision-making between adolescents and children. Perhaps they intended to empower older minors with language such as "minors shall have the right to decide medical care," leaving no discretion to medical practitioners. This fails to explain, however, legislation that focuses not on the minor, but on the healthcare provider who may "examine, prescribe for or treat a minor" in the absence of parental consent or notification without risk of liability. In other words, questions remain as to whether legislative policy is aimed at protecting providers, who decide that it is professionally and ethically appropriate to treat an adolescent patient in the absence of parental consent, from liability or to facilitate decision-making by adolescents. These policy points compel clarification for developing a legislative framework to effectively govern adolescent medical decision-making.

Second, adolescents require guidance for fostering responsible decision-making. Studies with adolescents and physicians have suggested that adult involvement in adolescent decision-making is valued and beneficial. However, a crucial point for policy consideration is the scope of adult guidance and whether the adolescent or the state should decide who provides the guidance. Statutes requiring parent notification or consent for an adolescent's abortion, which the U.S. Supreme Court has upheld under the federal Constitution, are a paradigmatic example. While adult involvement could provide an adolescent with emotional sustenance and support in making this difficult decision, a policy point that should be considered is whether the state should dictate through notification and consent requirements that a parent provide the guidance, or whether the adolescent is capable to choose for herself the adult with whom she would be most comfortable in seeking guidance. Studies have shown that the person to whom most adolescents prefer to turn for guidance in pregnancy decision-making, as well as in medical decisionmaking in general, is a parent.

Studies also suggest that adolescents facing unplanned pregnancies demonstrate decision-making ability comparable to young adults in the same situation.

State legislation that requires parental involvement in abortion and medical decision-making attempts to foster a policy of strengthening parent and child relationships. Whether (and how) the state should attempt to achieve this goal, however, is questionable. The nature and strength of any parent–child relationship arguably rests with the parents who have the primary responsibility for minors' care and nurturance. Worthy of examination, then, is whether legislating the dynamic of this relationship accomplishes the policy goal or whether, in effect, it merely makes medical practitioners' provision of care for adolescent patients more difficult. Indeed, legislation indicates a trend toward yielding to physicians' judgments regarding whether a parent should be notified. Recent legislation delegates to physicians a responsibility to expend "reasonable efforts" to assist minors in accepting parental involvement. . . .

Conflicts are inherent in legislative provisions that strive for balance between promotion of family ties and adolescent autonomy, and they heighten with respect to confidentiality. . . . While family unity and parental ties are legitimate state interests, they should not be furthered at the expense of all personal rights or conflicting interests. Reported findings from a study of physicians who care for adolescent patients ranked family support and harmony "considerably less persuasive in justifying disclosure of confidential patient information." Results from a study of adolescent patients indicate that adolescents regard confidentiality as "the most important characteristic" in their decision to access medical care. In response, Massachusetts mandates the confidentiality of the minor's medical information unless the minor consents, and only allows provider notification to parents when the condition is "so serious that the minor's life or limb is endangered," thereby promoting the mental and physical well-being of minors as the primary policy goal.

Third, refusal of unwanted medical treatment is noticeably absent from the statutory provisions that afford legal autonomy to adolescents for medical decision-making. Empowerment in decision-making to choose treatment—including self-image and self-esteem—wanes in meaning without the corollary ability to refuse it. The ability to refuse unwanted treatment becomes especially meaningful for critically-ill and chronically-ill adolescents who understand their diagnosis and prognosis, and desire to decline vigorous measures. The absence from current legislation suggests that this point has not garnered adequate, if any, attention from policy-makers, despite federal and state laws that expressly protect refusals of treatment as central to the liberty right exercised by adults for medical decision-making.

Alicia Ouellette, Shaping Parental Authority over Children's Bodies
85 Ind. L.J. 955, 960–964 (2010)

A.   WESTERNIZING ASIAN EYES

I heard about the first case [discussed here] while attending a presentation at a local hospital. There, a white plastic surgeon spoke glowingly about surgery he elected for his adopted Asian daughter. She came to his family with eyes that he deemed problematic because, like the eyes of many people of Asian descent, his daughter's eyes lacked a fold in the upper eyelid. As a result, he thought she looked sleepy and he was concerned that her eyes closed completely when she smiled. He proudly reported that he had solved the problem by having his daughter's eyes surgically shaped through a procedure called blepharoplasty. He was thrilled with the results. His beautiful daughter now has big round eyes that stay open and shine, even when she smiles, and make her look more like her new western family. The adoptive father seemed certain that his decision to use surgery to shape his daughter's eyes would improve her life.

Although blepharoplasty is among the most common procedures performed by plastic surgeons in the United States, it carries risks. Originally designed "specifically to westernize the eyelid at the patient's request," the procedure is done on an outpatient basis. After the patient is sedated and anesthetized, the surgeon makes an incision above the eyelid and removes excessive skin, tissue under the skin, and fat pads. The surgeon then sutures the incision and packs the eye with a light dressing. Once the wound heals, the incision disappears in the newly formed crease. In addition to the usual risks of surgery, eye-shaping surgery poses the risk of hematoma, asymmetry, and drooping. Recovery may be uncomfortable. A woman who had the procedure as an adult said that after the operation "she had to sleep in a semi-standing position and 'when you lay down, it feels like the swelling is burying you.'"

B.   HORMONES FOR STATURE

In the summer of 2004, the Food and Drug Administration (FDA) approved HGH treatments for children who are very short but otherwise healthy. Although the FDA approved the use of HGH in healthy children only when the child's predicted adult height is at or below five feet for females, and five feet, four inches for males, or 2.25 standard deviations below the mean for the child's age and sex, the FDA decision does not regulate off-label prescription of HGH to children who do not fall within the FDA guidelines.

As a result, pediatricians today "hear parents ask for [H]GH because their son (and it's usually sons) is as 'short as I was in grade school,' or 'is the shortest one on the team.'" Other parents "are seeking the drug-and no doubt obtaining it-for use in children who are of normal height and even for use in some who are tall, in the hopes that the drug will enable them to grow tall enough to become successful basketball players." Although some doctors refuse parental requests for HGH for healthy children, others defer to parental choice. Thus a parent with financial means who can find a willing provider can administer HGH to his son to give him a better shot at making the varsity basketball team.

A course of treatment with HGH requires subcutaneous injections three to six times a week over the course of four or five years. On average, the hundreds of injections will increase a child's adult height by about one and one-half inches. The treatment will not make a short person tall; a child who would have been five feet tall as an adult without the injections would likely be five feet, one and one-half inches or five feet, two inches after treatment. And the treatment's long-term risks are not well understood. It is clear that the treatment may cause musculoskeletal pain and aggravation of kidney problems. It poses long-term risks of diabetes, hypertension, and cancer.

In addition to physical risks, the artificially administered HGH may cause children psychological or psychosocial harm. Although parents and physicians often believe that giving a child an inch or two extra of adult height will increase a child's self-esteem and social status, the evidence is to the contrary. Studies show that in the long run, the psychosocial adaptation and self-esteem of treated children is comparable to a placebo group, and repeated injections increase the child's negative self-image and associated stigmatization of height as a defining feature of the child's existence.

C.   LIPOSUCTION ON A TWELVE-YEAR-OLD

Brooke Bates was twelve years old when her parents persuaded a plastic surgeon to use liposuction to remove thirty-five pounds of fat and fluid from her body. Brooke and her parents were initially thrilled with the results, but the surgery did not keep Brooke from putting weight back on. When the weight returned in less than a year, the parents returned Brooke to the operating room for a tummy tuck. A year later, her parents took her to Mexico for gastric lap band surgery after their family doctor advised against the procedure.

Brooke may be the youngest known person to have been shaped by liposuction, but she is not the only child on whom the procedure has been used. The American Society of Plastic Surgeons reports 3979 cases of liposuction on patients between the ages of thirteen and nineteen in 2008. Liposuction is not an effective treatment for obesity in any patient, adult or child. Clinical studies have demonstrated that lipoplasty does not reduce the risk of heart disease or diabetes and that it does not increase metabolism. It is an intervention designed to sculpt contours into a person's body by removing pockets of fat. The surgery itself poses the risk of infection, embolism, puncture wounds in the organs, seroma, nerve compression, changes in sensation, swelling, skin necrosis, burns, fluid imbalance, toxicity from anesthesia, and even death.

NOTES AND QUESTIONS

1. *Mature minors.*   Although a few states have incorporated the so-called mature minor doctrine into statutory law, see, infra, subsection (b) of this Section, most states that recognize the doctrine do so under common law principles. In theory, mature minors, identified variously by their age, maturity, intelligence, and responsibility, may make their own health care decisions regardless of their status. Some courts also take into account the character of the procedure or treatment being considered. It is presumed that greater capacity is required for decision making about more serious conditions. Doctors rendering treatment to mature minors are free from liability for failing to secure parental consent.

Lawrence Schlam and Joseph Wood have noted that in spite of the mature minor doctrine, courts traditionally presumed the state's power to protect minors in cases involving disputes about a minor's right to consent to health care: "Courts seldom allow minors under the age of sixteen to make decisions regarding their own medical treatment." Lawrence Schlam & Joseph P. Wood, Informed Consent to the Medical Treatment of Minors: Law and Practice, 10 Health Matrix 141, 158 (2000). However, courts generally protect doctors who rely on mature minor rules. Id. at 163.

2. *Regulation of pediatric "shaping" care?* Do you think that the medical treatments described in the article by Alicia Oulette—cases that Oulette calls "shaping cases"—should be precluded by law? Should they be regulated by law? If so, what sort of regulation makes sense?

3. *Children's "assent."* The Committee on Bioethics of the American Academy of Pediatrics recognized the particular difficulties that the informed consent doctrine presents to those caring for children's health. The Committee concluded that the doctrine has "only limited direct application in pediatrics," and thus recommended that in general those caring for children's health needs rely on "parents or other surrogates" to provide "informed permission" and on children to provide "assent" "whenever appropriate." American Academy of Pediatrics, Committee on Bioethics, Informed Consent, Parental Permission, and Assent in Pediatric Practice, 95 Pediatrics 314 (1995).

Assent refers to the compliance of a minor, not old enough (or mature enough) to provide legal "consent." In the committee's view, physicians' seeking children's assent (when the children are too young and immature to provide "consent" for themselves) would "empower children to the extent of their capacity." Seeking assent involves "developmentally appropriate" explanations of the child's condition. A child's refusal to assent may be ethically binding in a few situations, including that of research or intervention not directly beneficial to the patient. Finally, the committee concluded that children of at least age 14 may be as capable as adults of making decisions about health care. Id.

Do you think the practice of seeking assent from children too young to provide consent serves a useful purpose? How is a child who assents to a treatment likely to feel if his or her parent or guardian refuses to consent or if the child refuses to assent but the parent or guardian consents? Should health care workers only seek children's assent after they have a fairly good idea as to how the child's parent or guardian is likely to respond? Might it be possible to involve children in the decision-making process without asking them to assent to or refuse to assent to treatment? Or, as a practical matter, is the effort to obtain a child's assent valuable because it is likely to result in the child and his or her clinicians entering into a dialogue about the child's condition?

4. *Placebos marketed for children.* Caring for a hypochondriacal child apparently convinced a Maryland woman of a need for children's placebos. She responded by marketing child-friendly sugar tablets under the brand name Obecalp (placebo, spelled backward). Christie Aschwanden, Experts Question Placebo Pill for Children, N.Y. Times, May 27, 2008, at F5. Jennifer Buettner, who created Obecalp, declares on the company's website that she turned to placebos after she "learn[ed] of the massive over prescribing and lack of efficacy in children's drugs," http://www.inventedbyamother.com/ (last visited Aug. 5, 2012).

Placebos occasion many ethical issues. Will treating children's complaints with pills, for instance, condition children to want and expect drugs for every minor complaint? Moreover, parents who knowingly give their children placebos are engaging in deception. Might such deception generalize to other, more problematic contexts? One family physician, interviewed by Aschwanden, suggested that sick children are more likely to benefit from a hug than from a sugar pill. Might parents who distribute placebos to sick children do that at the expense of old-fashioned forms of parental love?

5. *"Ashley's treatment."* In January 2007, the parents of a child named Ashley revealed the child's story to the media. Born with static encephalopathy, Ashley has, and according to physicians will always have, the mental capacity of a three-month-old. Ashley is cared for by her parents, at home. They call her their "pillow angel." When Ashley was about six, her parents sought medical help from two physicians at Seattle Children's Hospital. The result (referred to by Ashley's parents as "Ashley's Treatment") limited the child's future growth and reproductive development. The treatment included administration of hormones, a hysterectomy, and treatment to preclude future breast development. Ashley's parents have described the treatment:

> Unlike what most people thought, the decision to pursue the Ashley Treatment was not a difficult one. Once we understood the options, problems, and benefits, the right course was clear to us. Ashley will be a lot more physically comfortable free of menstrual cramps, free of the discomfort associated with large and fully-developed breasts, and with a smaller, lighter body that is better suited to constant lying down and is easier to be moved around.
>
> Ashley's smaller and lighter size makes it more possible to include her in the typical family life and activities that provide her with needed comfort, closeness, security and love: meal time, car trips, touch, snuggles, etc.

The Ashley Treatment: Towards a Better Quality of Life for "Pillow Angels," http://ashleytreatment.space.live.com/ (updated Mar. 25, 2007; last visited June 25, 2008).

In May 2007, after an investigation by the Washington Protection and Advocacy System, Seattle Children's Hospital acknowledged that sterilizing Ashley without a court order violated state law and stated that it would not again sterilize a disabled child or provide growth attenuation therapy without obtaining permission from a court. Amy Burkholder, "Pillow Angel": Surgery Broke Law, CNN.com (May 8, 2007).

In 2012, when Ashley was 14, her father told a journalist that Ashley was 54 inches tall and weighed 65 pounds and that she was expected to stay at that weight. He concluded that the treatment had resulted in "every intended benefit to Ashley," including "smaller size, no menstrual discomfort, and no breast issues." According to Ashley's father (who refers to himself publically as AD—Ashley's Dad), he was in contact with six other families who had obtained the same treatment for a child with problems similar to Ashley's. Ed Pilkington, The Ashley Treatment: "Her Life Is as Good as We Can Possibly Make It," The Guardian, Mar. 15, 2012, http://www.guardian.co.uk/society/2012/mar/15/ashley-treatment-email-exchange.

Can you justify the parents' decision to seek the therapy? Can you justify the doctors' having provided the treatment that the parents sought? Or the hospital's having authorized the care in question? Could Ashley's parents have found alternative means of caring for her? Might it sometimes be advantageous to alter a presumptively "normal" body in some way, for example, by precluding growth, as in Ashley's case; by limiting a sense, such as sight or hearing; or by amputating a limb? If so, who should be allowed to make that decision in the case of a child?

Ashley's story has been widely reported. See, e.g., S. Matthew Liao et al., The Ashley Treatment, 37 Hastings Center Rep. 16 (Mar. 1, 2007); Peter Singer, A Convenient Truth, N.Y. Times (op-ed), Jan. 26, 2007 (justifying treatment of the child); "Pillow Angel" Doctor Speaks on Controversial Care, Grand Rapids Press, Jan. 14, 2008 (pediatrician defends treatment). Ashley's parents have described her story and her life at http://ashleytreatment.space.live.com/. A group of disability activists have responded critically to Ashley's story. A Disability Community's Response to Ashley's Treatment, http://www.katrinadisability.info/ashley.html. Alicia Oullette also tells Ashley's story in the article excerpted, supra.

b.   Legal Approaches

i.   Statutory Responses

> **Rhode Island Gen. Laws §23-4.6-1 (2012)**
> **Idaho Code §39-3801 (2012)**
> **Cal. Fam. Code, Div. 11. Minors. Part 4 (2012)**

RHODE ISLAND GEN. LAWS §23-4.6-1 (2012)

Any person of the age of sixteen (16) or over or married may consent to routine emergency medical or surgical care. A minor parent may consent to treatment of his or her child.

IDAHO CODE §39-3801 (2012)

§39-3801. Infectious, contagious, or communicable disease—Medical treatment of minor 14 years of age or older—Consent of parents or guardian unnecessary

Notwithstanding any other provision of law, a minor fourteen (14) years of age or older who may have come into contact with any infectious, contagious, or communicable disease may give consent to the furnishing of hospital, medical and surgical care related to the diagnosis or treatment of such disease, if the disease or condition is one which is required by law, or regulation adopted pursuant to law, to be reported to the local health officer. Such consent shall not be subject to disaffirmance because of minority. The consent of the parent, parents, or legal guardian of such minor shall not be necessary to authorize hospital, medical and surgical care related to such disease and such parent, parents, or legal guardian shall not be liable for payment for any care rendered pursuant to this section.

CAL. FAM. CODE, DIV. 11. MINORS. PART 4 (2012)

§6920. Minor's capacity to consent to medical or dental care without consent of parent or guardian

Subject to the limitations provided in this chapter, notwithstanding any other provision of law, a minor may consent to the matters provided in this chapter, and the consent of the minor's parent or guardian is not necessary. . . .

§6922. Consent by minor 15 or older living separately

(a) A minor may consent to the minor's medical care or dental care if all of the following conditions are satisfied:

(1) The minor is 15 years of age or older.

(2) The minor is living separate and apart from the minor's parents or guardian, whether with or without the consent of a parent or guardian and regardless of the duration of the separate residence.

(3) The minor is managing the minor's own financial affairs, regardless of the source of the minor's income.

(b) The parents or guardian are not liable for medical care or dental care provided pursuant to this section.

(c) A physician and surgeon or dentist may, with or without the consent of the minor patient, advise the minor's parent or guardian of the treatment given or needed if the physician and surgeon or dentist has reason to know, on the basis of the information given by the minor, the whereabouts of the parent or guardian.

§§6924–6929. [These sections delineate additional groups of children who can consent to medical care in light of particular circumstances and conditions. These groups include, for instance, children 12 or older, consenting to "mental health treatment or counseling or residential shelter services"; girls 12 or older, consenting to treatment needed as the result of an alleged rape; and minors consenting to treatment "related to the prevention or treatment of pregnancy."]

NOTES AND QUESTIONS

1. *Statutory "mature minor" provisions.*   As the statutes in this section suggest, states have not responded consistently to the task of determining the age at which minors are deemed capable of consenting to their own medical care. Every state now grants certain minors the right to consent to medical care or to certain sorts of medical care. Some of the exceptions depend on the character of the condition from which the minor suffers or is thought to suffer. Others depend on the status of the minor. Minors whose status renders them capable of consenting to care under state law may include those who are married, legally emancipated, or serving in the armed forces, and those who are themselves parents. Abigail English et al., Center for Adolescent Health and the Law, State Minor Consent Statutes: A Summary (2d ed. 2003). In addition, as the statutes, supra, indicate, states often allow minors to consent to certain forms of health care but not others. Minors may, for instance, be allowed to consent to care (sometimes including diagnosis and treatment) for drug or alcohol abuse, for sexually transmitted diseases, for contraceptive assistance, and for certain reportable contagious diseases but not for many other common conditions and illnesses. B. Jessie Hill, Medical Decision Making by and on Behalf of Adolescents: Reconsidering First Principles, 15 J. Health Care L. & Pol'y 37 (2012); Abigail English & Madlyn Morreale, Children's Health Symposium: A Legal and Policy Framework for Adolescent Health Care: Past, Present, and Future, 1 Hous. J. Health L. & Pol'y 63, 81 (2001).

Some state laws that allow minors to consent to specific types of care do not give minors authority to refuse the same care. In Maryland, for instance, minors are authorized to consent to treatment for drug or alcohol abuse, but they are not authorized to refuse the same care. Hill, supra, at 44. The aim, it would seem, is to make it more, rather than less, likely that minors in need of care for substance abuse will get that care.

2. *Reach of mature minor provisions.*   The Idaho statute, supra, provides that a child of 14 or older may consent to care relating to "any infectious, contagious, or communicable disease." Assume a 15-year-old child is hospitalized with a contagious disease. While in the hospital, it is discovered that the child is also suffering from a condition that needs attention and that is not "infectious, contagious, or communicable." Must parental consent be obtained and if so is it not virtually certain that the parent will learn of the condition for which the child originally sought care? Should this matter?

Some analysts have suggested that in cases involving conflict between an older minor patient and a parent, doctors should refer minor patients who appear to be "mature" to courts for assessment. See, e.g., Melinda T. Derish & Kathleen Vanden Heuvel, Mature Minors Should Have the Right to Refuse Life-Sustaining Medical Treatment, 28 J.L. Med. & Ethics 109, 118–119 (2002). Alternatively, the conflict could be considered by a clinical ethics committee. Others have suggested that the decision as to a minor patient's maturity should rest with the doctor who should be protected from liability for a good faith conclusion regarding the patient's maturity. In Belcher v. Charleston Area Medical Center, 422 S.E.2d 827, 838 (1992) the court explained:

> Whether [a] child has the capacity to consent depends upon the age, ability, experience, education, training, and degree of maturity or judgment obtained by the child, as well as upon the conduct and demeanor of the child at the time of the procedure or treatment. The factual determination would also involve whether the minor has the capacity to appreciate the nature, risks, and consequences of the medical procedure to be performed, or the treatment to be administered or withheld. Whether there is a conflict between the intentions of one or both parents and the minor, the physician's good faith assessment of the minor's maturity level would immunize him or her from liability for the failure to obtain parental consent.

In cases involving adolescent patients who disagree with their parents about treatment options, what do you see as the comparative advantages and disadvantages of referring such minors to courts or of permitting doctors to decide whether such patients are mature?

3. *Confidentiality.*   Even when children are allowed to consent to health care, they may not enjoy the privilege of confidentiality. Difficult questions arise when health care is provided pursuant to a minor's consent and then the minor's parent or parents request information about the nature of the minor's condition and the form of treatment provided. Doctors who rely on a minor's consent to treatment generally are obliged to protect the patient's confidentiality. However, there are a number of exceptions that may require physicians to breach confidentiality. The most important exception arises in cases of suspected child abuse or neglect. In every state, the duty to report child abuse and neglect supersedes rules of confidentiality involving children's health care. J. Shoshanna Ehrlich, Grounded in the Reality of Their Lives: Listening to Teens Who Make the Abortion Decision without Involving Their Parents, 18 Berkeley Women's L.J. 61, 70 n.34 (2003). California's statutory provision, §6922

supra, provides that minors "15 or older living separately" may consent to their own health care. Yet, the section allows a doctor or dentist caring for a patient in this category to "advise the minor's parent or guardian of the treatment given or needed" even if the minor has not consented to revelation of confidential information to a parent or guardian. Do you think these provisions make sense? What are the advantages and disadvantages of allowing a minor to consent to health care but revealing information about the minor's condition and treatment to his or her parents or guardian?

4. *School board policy on notifying parents.*   Sometimes school officials may be encouraged or required to reveal health-related information about students to their parents. In 2008, the Board of Education in Howard County in Maryland promulgated a regulation that seems at odds with state law (which allows adolescents to undergo pregnancy testing, to receive contraception, and to be treated for sexually transmitted diseases without informing parents). Susan DeFord, Pregnancy Notification Policy Alarms Some Health Experts, The Wash. Post, Feb. 3, 2008, at C12. Under the regulation, any school employee made aware of a student's pregnancy must inform the school's counselor or nurse who must, in turn, make sure that the girl's parents are told of the pregnancy. Id. Critics of the new regulation have worried that it might result in pregnant girls avoiding prenatal care.

5. *Consent and minors' treatment for alcohol or drug abuse.*   Complicated issues arise for children in need of treatment for alcohol or drug abuse. A majority of states allow minors to consent to such treatment. Richard Boldt, Adolescent Decision Making: Legal Issues with Respect to Treatment for Substance Misuse and Mental Illness, 15 J. Health Care L. & Pol'y 75 (2012). Even among states allowing minors to consent to care for alcoholism and substance abuse, rules vary widely. Some states expressly remove "the disability of minority" from minors in need of such treatment. Fla. Stat. Sec. 3997.601 (2012). New York recognizes "the important role of the parents or guardians" in "treating a minor for chemical dependence on an inpatient, residential, or outpatient basis." NY CLS Men. Hyg. Sec. 22.11 (2012). However, if seeking consent from a parent or guardian would, in the judgment of a doctor, "have a detrimental effect on the course of treatment of a minor who is voluntarily seeking treatment for chemical dependence," then treatment can be offered without the consent of the parents or guardian. Id.

6. *Medical emergency exception to parental consent requirement.*   If the mature minor exception is not applicable, doctors are generally not permitted to treat children without consent from the child's parent or guardian. However, there is a broad statutory exception for medical emergencies. Generally, statutes provide that medical care may be provided to a child regardless of age without the consent of the child's parent or guardian if, in the judgment of the health care provider, the minor's health or life will be risked if care is not rendered quickly. See, e.g., Minn. Stat. Ann. §144.344 ("Emergency Treatment") (LexisNexis 2007).

7. *Decision making for newborns.*   Medical decision making for newborns invariably precludes relying on the patient's wishes. The American Medical Association, Council on Ethical and Judicial Affairs, Opinion 2:215, opines that the primary concern in making decisions about life support for seriously

ill newborns should be "what is best for the newborn" (issued June 1994 based on the report "Treatment Decisions for Seriously Ill Newborns," adopted June 1992). The association's opinion delineates five factors that should be considered: first, the likelihood that treatment will succeed; second, the risks of treatment and nontreatment; third, the likely extension of life if treatment is successful; fourth, the pain that is likely to attend treatment; and fifth, the "anticipated quality of life" for the baby if treatment is administered and if it is withheld. The opinion further provides that "[p]hysicians must provide full information to parents of seriously ill newborns regarding the nature of treatments, therapeutic options and expected prognosis with and without therapy, so that parents can make informed decisions for their children about life-sustaining treatment." See Pierucci et al., End-of-Life Care for Neonates and Infants: The Experience and Effects of a Palliative Care Consultation Service, 108 Pediatrics 653 (2001) (considering value of palliative care for terminally ill children in first year of life).

8. *British law.*   The age of majority in Britain, generally, is 18. However, the English Family Law Reform Act of 1969 (§8) grants children who are 16 and 17 the right to consent to medical treatment. Such children have full authority to consent to "any surgical, medical or dental treatment which, in the absence of consent, would constitute a trespass to his person." Although the right to consent to treatment is generally assumed to encompass the right to refuse treatment, English courts have not always taken that view in the case of 16-and 17-year-olds. Alastair Bissett-Johnson & Pamela Ferguson, International Commentaries: Consent to Medical Treatment by Older Children in English and Scottish Law, 12 J. Contemp. Health L. & Pol'y 449, 456–457 (1996). See also Robert L. Stenger, Exclusive or Concurrent Competence to Make Medical Decisions for Adolescents in the United States and United Kingdom, 14 J.L. & Health 205 (1999–2000). Why do you think the right to consent to treatment might be differentiated from the right to refuse treatment in the case of a 16- or 17-year-old? See Note 1, supra.

In 2004, the Department of Health in the United Kingdom promulgated guidelines that permit physicians to provide contraceptive services to minor girls without parental consent. Kaiser Daily Reproductive Health Report, British Health Department Issues Guidelines Allowing Abortions for Girls Under 16 Without Parental Consent, Aug. 2, 2004, available at www.kaisernetwork.org. The guidelines provide:

> A doctor or health professional is able to provide contraception, sexual and reproductive health advice and treatment, without parental knowledge or consent, to a young person aged under 16, provided that:

> > She/he understands the advice provided and its implications. Her/his physical or mental health would otherwise be likely to suffer and so provision of advice or treatment is in their best interest.

> However, even if a decision is taken not to provide treatment, the duty of confidentiality applies, unless there are exceptional circumstances. . . .

U.K. Dept. of Health, Best Practice Guidance for Doctors and Other Health Professionals on the Provision of Advice and Treatment to Young People

Under 16 on Contraception, Sexual and Reproductive Health, July 29, 2004, available at http://www.dh.gov.uk/en/Publicationsandstatistics/Publications/ PublicationsPolicyAndGuidance/Browsable/DH_4867521 (last visited June 26, 2012).

The guidelines provide that confidentiality for minors is not "absolute." Otherwise confidential information about a minor may be revealed (in line with local child protection protocols) if "a health professional believes that there is a risk to the health, safety or welfare of a young person or others which is so serious as to outweigh the young person's right to privacy. . . ." Id. The issue is further considered in Children, Parental Responsibility, Medical Treatment of Children, Butterworths Family L. Service (Feb. 3, 2012), available in Lexis/Nexis, UK Law Journals.

In 2011, the Department of Health of the UK included among the goals of the nation's Primary Care Trusts and Local Authorities the provision of contraception to "under sixteens," as well as "rapid access to testing and treatment for sexually transmitted infections including blood borne viruses," and providing "rapid access" to emergency contraception through community pharmacy schemes, and walk-in centers. Department of Health, United Kingdom, Standard 4: Growing Up Into Adulthood (2011), available at http://www.dh.gov. uk/en/Publicationsandstatistics/Publications/PublicationsPolicyAndGuidance/ Browsable/DH_4867521 (last visited July 23, 2012).

A group of U.K. researchers studied parental attitudes toward making a vaccine that prevents some forms of human papillomavirus available to girls under 16 without parental consent. About the same percentage of respondents asserted that they would not require parental consent as asserted that they would require it. (The respondent group was small and thus may not be representative of the U.K. population as a whole.) Loretta Brabin et al., Semi-Qualitative Study of Attitudes to Vaccinating Adolescents Against Human Papillomavirus Without Parental Consent, 7 BMC Pub. Health 20 (2007), available at http://www. pubmedcentral.nih.gov/picrender.fcgi?artid=1804267&blobtype=pdf.

9. *Sterilization.*   In the United States, federal law precludes federal programs from sterilizing anyone under 21 years of age. The same regulations preclude federal programs from sterilizing anyone defined as mentally incompetent. 42 C.F.R. 50.203 (2012). (See Chapter 5, section A(1)(b), for discussion of "informed consent requirement" for those eligible to give consent to sterilization.)

ii.   Judicial Responses

‖   ***Curran v. Bosze***   ‖
566 N.E.2d 1319 (Ill. 1990)

Opinion by CALVO.

Allison and James Curran are 3½-year-old twins. Their mother is Nancy Curran. The twins have lived with Ms. Curran and their maternal grandmother since their birth on January 27, 1987.

The twins' father is Tamas Bosze. Ms. Curran and Mr. Bosze have never been married. As a result of an action brought by Ms. Curran against Mr. Bosze concerning the paternity of the twins, both Mr. Bosze and the twins underwent a blood test in November of 1987. The blood test confirmed that Mr. Bosze is the father of the twins. On February 16, 1989, Mr. Bosze and Ms. Curran entered into an agreed order (parentage order) establishing a parent–child relationship. The parentage order states that Ms. Curran "shall have the sole care, custody, control and educational responsibility of the minor children." . . .

Mr. Bosze is the father of three other children: a son, age 23; Jean Pierre Bosze, age 12; and a one-year-old daughter. Ms. Curran is not the mother of any of these children. Each of these children has a different mother. Jean Pierre and the twins are half-siblings. The twins have met Jean Pierre on two occasions. Each meeting lasted approximately two hours.

Jean Pierre is suffering from acute undifferentiated leukemia (AUL), also known as mixed lineage leukemia. Mixed lineage leukemia is a rare form of leukemia which is difficult to treat. . . . Jean Pierre was treated with chemotherapy and went into remission. Jean Pierre experienced a testicular relapse in January 1990, and a bone marrow relapse in mid-June 1990. [His doctor] has recommended a bone marrow transplant for Jean Pierre.

Mr. Bosze asked Ms. Curran to consent to a blood test for the twins in order to determine whether the twins were compatible to serve as bone marrow donors for a transplant to Jean Pierre. Mr. Bosze asked Ms. Curran to consent to the twins' undergoing a bone marrow harvesting procedure if the twins were found to be compatible. After consulting with the twins' pediatrician, family members, parents of bone marrow donors and bone marrow donors, Ms. Curran refused to give consent to the twins' undergoing either the blood test or the bone marrow harvesting procedure.

On June 28, 1990, Mr. Bosze filed an emergency petition in the circuit court of Cook County. The petition informed the court that Jean Pierre "suffers from leukemia and urgently requires a [bone] marrow transplant from a compatible donor. Without the transplant he will die in a short period of time, thereby creating an emergency involving life and death." The petition stated that persons usually compatible for serving as donors are parents or siblings of the recipient, and Jean Pierre's father, mother, and older brother had been tested and rejected as compatible donors.

According to the petition, "[t]he only siblings who have potential to be donors and who have not been tested are the children, James and Allison." The petition stated Ms. Curran refused to discuss with Mr. Bosze the matter of submitting the twins to a blood test to determine their compatibility as potential bone marrow donors for Jean Pierre. The petition stated the blood test "is minimally invasive and harmless, and no more difficult than the paternity blood testing which the children have already undergone." According to the petition, there would be no expense involved to Ms. Curran. . . .

Neither justice nor reality is served by ordering a 3½-year-old child to submit to a bone marrow harvesting procedure for the benefit of another by a purported application of the doctrine of substituted judgment. Since it is not possible to discover that which does not exist, specifically, whether the 3½-year-old twins would consent or refuse to consent to the proposed bone marrow harvesting procedure if they were competent, the doctrine of substituted judgment is not relevant and may not be applied in this case.

Several courts from sister jurisdictions have addressed the issue whether the consent of a court, parent or guardian, for the removal of a kidney from an incompetent person for transplantation to a sibling, may be legally effective. . . .

In Strunk v. Strunk (Ky. 1969), 445 S.W.2d 145, the Kentucky Court of Appeals, in a 4 to 3 decision, determined that a court of equity had the power to permit a kidney to be removed from a mentally incompetent ward of the State, upon the petition of his committee, his mother, for transplantation into his 28-year-old brother who was dying from a kidney disease. The ward of the State was a 27-year-old man who had the mental capacity of a six-year-old.

The mother petitioned the county court for authority to proceed with the kidney transplant. The county court "found that the operation was necessary, that under the peculiar circumstances of this case it would not only be beneficial to [the ward's brother] but also beneficial to [the ward] because [the ward] was greatly dependent upon [his brother], emotionally and psychologically, and that [the ward's] well-being would be jeopardized more severely by the loss of his brother than by the removal of a kidney." . . .

[T]he *Strunk* court was of "the opinion that a chancery court does have sufficient inherent power to authorize the operation. The circuit court having found that the operative procedures in this instance are to the best interest of [the ward] and this finding having been based upon substantial evidence, we are of the opinion the judgment should be affirmed."

In Hart v. Brown (Super. 1972), 29 Conn. Supp. 368, 289 A.2d 386, the parents of identical twins, age 7 years and 10 months, sought permission to have a kidney from the healthy twin transplanted into the body of the seriously ill twin who was suffering from a kidney disease. The parents brought a declaratory judgment action, as parents and natural guardians of the twins, seeking a declaration that they had the right to consent to the proposed operation. Guardians ad litem for each of the twins were appointed. Defendants in the declaratory judgment action were the physicians and the hospital at which the proposed kidney transplantation operation was to take place; the defendants had refused to use their facilities unless the court "declare[d] that the parents and/or guardians ad litem of the minors have the right to give their consent to the operation upon the minor twins."

The court in *Hart* concluded it had the power to determine that the parents have the right to consent to the operation. . . .

Although purporting to apply the doctrine of substituted judgment, the *Hart* court did not inquire as to what the 7½-year-old minors would do if the minors were competent. The *Hart* court instead determined that "the natural parents would be able to substitute their consent for that of their minor children after a close, independent and objective investigation of their motivation and reasoning." . . .

In each of the foregoing cases where consent to the kidney transplant was authorized, regardless whether the authority to consent was to be exercised by the court, a parent or a guardian, the key inquiry was the presence or absence of a benefit to the potential donor. Notwithstanding the language used by the courts in reaching their determination that a transplant may or may not occur, the standard by which the determination was made was whether the transplant would be in the best interest of the child or incompetent person.

The primary benefit to the donor in these cases arises from the relationship existing between the donor and recipient. In *Strunk,* the donor lived in a State institution. The recipient was a brother who served as the donor's only connection with the outside world. In . . . *Hart* . . . , there was evidence that the sibling relationship between the donor and recipient was close. In [*Hart*], both parents had given their consent.

We hold that a parent or guardian may give consent on behalf of a minor daughter or son for the child to donate bone marrow to a sibling, only when to do so would be in the minor's best interest. . . .

Ms. Curran has refused consent on behalf of the twins to the bone marrow transplant because she does not think it is in their best interests to subject them to the risks and pains involved in undergoing general anesthesia and the harvesting procedure. While Ms. Curran is aware that the risks involved in donating bone marrow and undergoing general anesthesia are small, she also is aware that when such risk occurs, it may be life-threatening. . . .

It is a fact that the twins and Jean Pierre share the same biological father. There was no evidence produced, however, to indicate that the twins and Jean Pierre are known to each other as family. . . .

This court shares the opinion of the circuit court that Jean Pierre's situation "evokes sympathy from all who've heard [it]." No matter how small the hope that a bone marrow transplant will cure Jean Pierre, the fact remains that without the transplant, Jean Pierre will almost certainly die. The sympathy felt by this court, the circuit court, and all those who have learned of Jean Pierre's tragic situation cannot, however, obscure the fact that, under the circumstances presented in the case at bar, it would be neither proper under existing law nor in the best interests of the 3½-year-old twins for the twins to participate in the bone marrow harvesting procedure. . . .

Circuit court affirmed.

NOTES AND QUESTIONS

1. *Parental disagreement.* Curran v. Bosze raises difficult issues. Some of them are not specific to children; others are. In general, the law does not require one person to undergo medical procedures to save another. Because the potential donors in the case were only 3½ years old, they were incapable of consenting (or even assenting) to become donors. Thus, the decision falls to their parent or parents. The parentage order denominating Mr. Bosze as the children's father provided that Ms. Curran would remain the custodial parent, but that she would consult and confer with Mr. Bosze "in all matters of importance relating to the health . . ." of the children. The mother's decision to refuse the father's requested testing of the children as potential bone marrow donors suggests the sort of difficulties that can develop between two parents should they disagree about health decisions for their children.

2. *Comparing substituted judgment and best interest standards.* Because the 3½-year-old children in Curran v. Bosze were clearly too young to provide informed consent to a medical procedure, the court turned to alternative sources of consent. The court examined the substituted judgment standard and determined it could not be differentiated from a best-interest standard in cases (such as *Curran* itself) in which the party involved was never capable of the sort of understanding needed to give informed consent to health care,

either because of very young age or because of life-long mental incapacity of some sort. Yet, a major part of the court's best interest analysis follows from the fact that the children's mother was opposed to the children's being tested for compatibility and to their serving as bone marrow donors. The court turned to the expert testimony of Dr. Bennett Levanthal, a professor of psychiatry and pediatrics, who opined that "the single most salient issue" in the case was that the mother objected to the twins' being tested and to their serving as donors. He explained: "The mother's inability for whatever reason to concur and to support this process probably puts the—not probably, almost certainly[—]puts the children at very serious risk for having adverse psychological consequences or results of this procedure." Presumably, similar reasoning could not be as easily applied to a different case in which the children were themselves in need of medical care. In this sort of case, the mother's "inability . . . to concur" might be balanced by the benefits of providing treatment. One task in cases such as *Curran* is to disentangle the position that a child's custodial parent should make the sort of decision at issue in the case and an assessment that that parent's opposition to the proposed procedures would significantly undermine the children's best interests. The two are interconnected, but they are not identical.

3. *Minors' consent to cessation of life-sustaining treatment.*   Special questions have arisen with regard to the scope for "mature minors" to decide to reject life-sustaining treatment. In 1994, a Florida judge allowed a 15-year-old who had had two liver transplants to stop taking antirejection medication. The case was initiated as a neglect petition against the boy's mother who, over time, was convinced that her son had the right to reject life-sustaining treatment. The case was never reported but was discussed widely in news media and has been considered in law reviews. See, e.g., Paul Arshagouni, Introduction, 9 J. Health Care L. & Pol'y 315 (2007); Note, The Mature Minor Doctrine: Do Adolescents Have the Right to Die?, 11 Health Matrix 687, 687–689 (2001); Note, Joan-Margaret Kun, Rejecting the Adage "Children Should Be Seen and Not Heard"—The Mature Minor Doctrine, 16 Pace L. Rev. 423, 423–425 (1996). In considering this case and others that resemble it, Paul Arshagouni, supra, focuses expressly on the conflict between wanting to grant older (and "mature") adolescents the right to make their own health care decisions and wanting to protect them from bad decisions—decisions seeming to undercut the child's welfare. Id. at 338. Even more, for Arshagouni, the "problem" with an approach that allows "mature minors" to make their own medical decisions is that, in fact, courts often elide the minor's maturity and look to see whether the minor's decision seems wise: "If the decision is 'appropriate,' the court deems the minor 'mature.' It follows that where the court determines the decision 'inappropriate,' it will deem the minor immature." Id. at 339.

4. *Parent and child disagree about child's care.*   In Matter of Thomas B., 152 Misc. 2d 96, 99 (Family Court, Cattaraugus County, N.Y. 1991), a New York family court ruled that parents can force a child to undergo medical diagnosis and treatment even if the child objects. Thomas B., whose father had recently died of cancer, was diagnosed with a tumor at the age of 15. His doctors recommended that a biopsy of the tumor be performed, but Thomas objected to a biopsy because he was afraid of needles. Thomas B.'s mother wanted the biopsy done. She sought a court order. The child's law guardian communicated the boy's position to the court but concluded that the recommended procedure was

in the child's best interests. The New York Family Court agreed with the law guardian and with Thomas B.'s mother and ordered that the boy submit to the recommended diagnostic procedure despite his own refusal to consent. The court wrote:

> Under Public Health Law §2504 (1) "[a]ny person who is eighteen years of age or older . . . may give effective consent for medical, dental, health and hospital services for himself or herself." An implicit corollary of that provision is that a person under 18 years of age may not give effective consent for such services. If a person under 18 years of age may not give effective consent, it follows logically that such a person may not effectively withhold consent, either. Generally, an infant "is universally considered to be lacking in judgment, since his normal condition is that of incompetency."

Does *Thomas B.* conflict with *Bellotti,* discussed supra, pp. 590–594 Is an adolescent more capable of making a decision about abortion than a decision about whether to submit to a diagnostic procedure recommended by a doctor? See Note, Jennifer E. Chen, Family Conflicts, The Role of Religion in Refusing Medical Treatment for Minors, 58 Hastings L.J. 643 (2007) (suggesting that in cases of conflict about medical decisions involving adolescents, courts should rely on a "triadic balancing" that considers the interests of the minor, the parents, and the state).

5. *Religious grounds for refusing care.*   Patients with religious reasons for refusing care constitute a subset of "refusal" cases. The health care system almost always facilitates the treatment choices of adults who refuse care for religious reasons (as for virtually every other reason). In the case of children, the decision to refuse care for religious reasons is more complicated because of the child's apparent and/or legal lack of capacity to consent to health care decisions. Such cases often involve a complicated triangle involving parent, child, and state.

Sometimes in religious refusal cases, the parent and the minor patient agree that treatment should not be administered, but the hospital seeks court acquiescence. In re Application of Long Island Jewish Medical Center, 557 N.Y.S.2d 239 (Sup. Ct. 1990) was a case of this sort. Philip Malcolm, a boy of almost 18, was admitted to Long Island Jewish Medical Center with serious symptoms, including anemia. He was diagnosed with rhabdomyosarcoma, a pediatric cancer of the tissue that is to become muscle.

Phillip appeared to need an immediate blood transfusion to deal with severe anemia. In addition, chemotherapy and radiation treatment were recommended but could not be undertaken unless the hospital received consent for blood transfusions. It was estimated that Phillip had a 20 to 25 percent chance of survival if he received treatment, and would die, in pain, probably within a month, if he did not. Phillip, his mother, and his stepfather were all members of Jehovah's Witnesses. They refused to consent to blood transfusions because the procedure was proscribed by their religion. Long Island Jewish Medical Center petitioned for authorization to provide treatment. A court hearing was held the day after Phillip's admission.

Both Theodore Venable and Joan Venable, Phillip's stepfather and mother, testified at the hearing that their religion precluded their consenting to blood transfusions for Phillip. Phillip testified that in his view if he consented to a transfusion, he would lose the chance for everlasting life. He did, however, add that if the court ordered the transfusion, he would not be responsible for the decision. The court described Phillip as follows:

> Phillip is in his last year at the High School of Art and Design, where he is studying industrial design. He has never been away from home and has never dated a girl. He consults his parents before making decisions and when asked whether he considered himself an adult or a child, he responded "child." There was no evidence that Phillip had been urged by his parents to make his own decision regarding blood transfusions.

Phillip's lawyer argued that Phillip was almost 18, that he was an intelligent boy, and that he had a due process right to make medical decisions "consistent with his values and convictions before he loses the right to control what is done to his body." The court noted that the highest courts in Illinois and in Tennessee had endorsed the position that a "mature minor" be allowed to refuse life-saving medical treatment:

> The Supreme Court of Illinois said, "If the evidence is clear and convincing that the minor is mature enough to appreciate the consequences of her actions, and that the minor is mature enough to exercise the judgment of an adult, then the mature minor doctrine affords her the common law right to consent to or refuse medical treatment." Tennessee has also accepted the "mature minor" doctrine. The Supreme Court of Tennessee noted that the mature minor doctrine is not a recent development in Tennessee law. It stated, "recognition that minors achieve varying degrees of maturity and responsibility (capacity) has been part of the common law for well over a century."

In addition, the court acknowledged that New York statutory law provided for invocation of the mature minor doctrine in various settings, including that of mental health care, and treatment for substance abuse and for sexually transmitted diseases. Yet the court refused Phillip's request to refuse treatment:

> While this court believes there is much merit to the "mature minor" doctrine, I find that Phillip Malcolm is not a mature minor. Therefore, his refusal to consent to blood transfusions is not based upon a mature understanding of his own religious beliefs or of the fatal consequences to himself. It is recommended that the Legislature or the appellate courts take a hard look at the "mature minor" doctrine and make it either statutory or decisional law in New York State.

The court authorized the hospital to administer blood to Phillip during the course of chemotherapy, whenever it was medically necessary to do so.

Might it have been preferable for the court to have stressed Phillip's own statement that if he were subjected to *court-ordered* transfusions, he would not lose the right to everlasting life because he would not bear responsibility for the decision? Would the latter approach have acknowledged Phillip's maturity in a way that the court's actual approach did not?

6. *Australian case involving parental refusal of blood transfusion for four year old.* In 2012, the Supreme Court in South Australia rejected the decision of the parents of a four-year-old girl with leukemia and ordered that a blood transfusion be administered. The parents, both Jehovah's Witnesses, refused blood

for their child on religious grounds. Linda Starr, Minors and Refusal of Treatment: Who Decided in the Best Interests of the Child?, 20 Australian Nursing Journal 31 (2012). Although parents have authority to make medical decisions for their children, the case conditioned authority on a requirement that parents act in the best interests of their children.

7. *Bibliographic note.*   Useful articles on the age of consent for health care decision making include Michele Goodwin & Naomi Duke, Capacity and Autonomy: A Thought Experiment on Minors' Access to Assisted Reproductive Technology, 34 Harv. J.L. & Gender 503 (2011); Rhonda Gay Hartman, Gault's Legacy: Dignity, Due Process, and Adolescents' Liberty Interests in Living Donation, 22 N.D. J.L. Ethics & Pub. Pol'y 67 (2008); Jennifer Rosato, Using Bioethics Discourse to Determine When Parents Should Make Health Care Decisions for Their Children: Is Deference Justified?, 73 Temple L. Rev. 1 (2000); Lawrence Schlam & Joseph P. Wood, Informed Consent to the Medical Treatment of Minors: Law and Practice, 10 Health Matrix 141 (2000).

CHALLENGING ISSUES: INVOLUNTARY ADMINISTRATION OF PSYCHOTROPIC MEDICATION TO A MINOR

Selona is 14. Last month, she was visiting at the home of her friend, Gayle, when Gayle's mother made offensive comments about Selona's mother. Selona tried to call her mother but did not get an answer. She ran into the bathroom and ingested 15 tablets of amoxicillin and 5 Motrin. Selona then told Gayle what she had done and asked Gayle to call 911. Selona was taken to Parklane Hospital. She told the emergency room personnel that she was "stressed" and that she had had a physical altercation with her mother about three months earlier. Selona did not have a psychiatric history.

After Selona was released from Parklane Hospital, her parents had her admitted as a voluntary patient to Clearview Hospital, a psychiatric facility. Physicians at Clearview wanted to treat Selona with psychiatric medications. Her parents refused to consent. As a result, the hospital converted Selona's admission status to "involuntary" based on the certifications of two physicians that she posed a risk of harm to herself and others. The hospital then sought an order that permitted it to administer several psychotropic medications, including risperidone, lithium, and Depakote, to Selona. Selona and her parents opposed the administration of these medications. The drugs' side effects include weight gain, sedation, akathisia (motor restlessness), a decrease in blood pressure that could cause dizziness, hypothyroidism, cognitive impairment, hair loss, and liver function abnormalities.

A hearing was then held. At the hearing, Dr. George, Selona's treating psychiatrist at Clearview, alleged that Selona had a "mood disorder, not otherwise specified." Dr. George further testified that Selona might develop a more serious psychiatric disorder if not treated. He explained that although Selona had not shown any suicidal tendencies while at Clearview, she should be medicated to prevent future problems. Selona's parents were not made parties to the proceeding. They attended the hearing but did not testify. The trial court granted the hospital's petition. The court explained that "parents may not deprive their child of life-saving treatment."

Mental Hygiene Legal Services has appealed on behalf of Selona. State law provides that:

> [s]ubject to regulations of the commissioner of mental health governing the patient's right to object to treatment . . . the consent of a parent or guardian or the authorization of a court shall be required for the non-emergency administration of psychotropic medications to a minor residing in a hospital.

The appellate court found no evidence suggesting that Selona had a life-threatening condition. The court, reversing the trial court's decision, rejected the hospital's petition to medicate Selona.

Do you agree with the appellate court? What other options might the hospital have had?

CHALLENGING ISSUES: MATURE MINORS

Bob had muscular dystrophy for most of his childhood years. He used a wheelchair. At age 17, he became ill with a cold. Due to his underlying illness, potential consequences of the cold were serious. One afternoon, he began to choke and could not breathe. His father brought him to General Hospital where he was admitted, intubated, and sent to the pediatric intensive care unit. The next day the tube was removed, and Bob began to breathe on his own, although with great difficulty. After hearing the treating physicians' assessment of Bob's prognosis, his parents stated in writing that Bob should not be reintubated or resuscitated should he again suffer from respiratory failure while in the hospital. A "Do Not Resuscitate" order was attached to Bob's chart. Later that day Bob stopped breathing. The hospital staff did not resuscitate him, and he soon died.

After Bob's death his parents sued the hospital. Among other things, they argued that their son was a mature minor and his consent should have been obtained before a "Do Not Resuscitate" order was issued.

Do you think the treating physicians should have obtained Bob's consent? What do you think a court should consider in deciding the case?

=10=
‖ *Discrimination in Health Care* ‖

Discrimination in health care can take many forms, from differential treatment in health care access, insurance access, medical treatment decisions, and provider–patient relationships. This chapter introduces readers to the topic of discrimination in health care by focusing on various groups of people who have been subjected to one or more forms of documented discrimination in health care—discrimination on the basis of class, race or ethnicity, gender, immigrant status, sexual orientation or gender identity, disability, older age, and genetics. Legal protection against discrimination on these and other bases has varied and, where it exists, it has been somewhat haphazard.

The following questions might be kept in mind while reading the materials in this chapter.

1. Which groups of people do you think are most likely to have less than full access to health care, or more likely to suffer discriminatory treatment?
2. What do you think are the relative weights of the following contributing causes to discrimination in access and treatment: poverty, geography, characteristics of the patient, patient preferences; health care provider preferences; politicians' preferences; religious beliefs; cultural assumptions of patients or of health care providers; patients' health status; all or most of the above; or other factors?
3. How can one discern whether (or when) *more* health care is *better* health care?
4. To what extent (or when) does "good" health care depend on "good" relationships between patients and health care providers?

A. CLASS

Access to health care is limited—often with dire consequences—for 45 to 50 million people in the United States who have no health insurance. Those without public or private health coverage are not cut off from health care completely, but as Prof. Timothy Jost has stated, "persons who are uninsured get less health care, get it later, and suffer greater mortality and morbidity because of their failure to receive health care in a timely fashion." Timothy Stoltzfus Jost, Private or Public Approaches to Insuring the Uninsured: Lessons from International Experience with Private Insurance, 76 N.Y.U. L. Rev. 419, 419 (2001). The Affordable Care Act of 2010 (discussed more fully in Chapter 14) is designed to increase access to health care for people who have been uninsured by expanding access and affordability of insurance—through an expansion of Medicaid eligibility on the public insurance side, and, in the private insurance market, through federal subsidies, insurance exchanges, and a prohibition on insurance coverage denial or pricing due to preexisting health conditions. Because of the fuller treatment of this issue in Chapter 14, the materials here on discrimination in health care because of class are brief.

> ## Mary Anne Bobinski, Health Disparities and the Law: Wrongs in Search of a Right
> ### 29 Am. J.L. & Med. 363, 373–374 (2003)

The perhaps unexpected influence of socioeconomic factors [on health] can be seen when comparing the data on life expectancy in the United States with that found in other countries. It is well established, for example, that the United States lags behind other countries in the length and quality of life. The life expectancy for women in the United States is lower than it is in eighteen other countries; in life expectancy for men, the United States ranks twenty-fifth.

The explanation, according to HHS, is that "inequalities in income and education underlie many health disparities." Socioeconomic status, as measured either by income or level of education, is strongly correlated with health status. As noted in Healthy People 2010:

> [i]n general, population groups that suffer the worst health status also are those that have the highest poverty rates and the least education. Disparities in income and education levels are associated with differences in the occurrence of illness and death, including heart disease, diabetes, obesity, elevated blood level, and low birth weight. Higher incomes permit increased access to medical care, enable people to afford better housing and live in safer neighborhoods, and increase the opportunity to engage in health-promoting behaviors.[1]

As if socioeconomic disparities in health were not serious enough on their own, they are also closely associated with racial and ethnic disparities in health. A greater proportion of non-whites than whites are likely to live below the poverty level. Less than ten percent of whites live below the poverty level, a little more than ten percent of Asian/Pacific Islanders live below this level and nearly thirty percent of African-Americans and Hispanics are impoverished. African-Americans and Hispanics are less likely than whites to have completed more than twelve years of education. Health disparities associated with socioeconomic

---

1. Prof. Bobinski here provides an *id.* citation to Donna E. Shalala, *Message from the Secretary*, 1 U.S. Dep't of Health & Human Serv. (HHS), Healthy People 2010 (2000), at 12.–EDS.

factors thus have a disproportionate impact on the health of African-Americans and Hispanics.

Finally, a number of researchers contend that societies with greater inequalities in wealth are less healthy than societies with greater income equality. A new movement has adopted the view that this correlation implies causation—that there is something about social income disparities that affects the health of a population. Harvard School of Public Health Professors Ichiro Kawachi and Bruce P. Kennedy argue in a recent book that unbridled capitalism in the United States has led to income disparities which negatively affect the health of our society. This argument has drawn a vigorous critique, but it appears to have influenced the Healthy People 2010's analysis of the determinants of health. It remains to be seen whether law in general and public health law in particular can be an effective tool in addressing behavioral and socioeconomic determinants of health.

B. RACE AND ETHNICITY

No analysis of racial and ethnic discrimination in the United States, whether in the health care context or in other contexts, can be complete without consideration of class factors. Thus, this subsection and the one that precedes it should be understood as part and parcel of a larger whole.

1. *Bioethical and Social Perspectives*

|| *Sidney D. Watson, Health Law Symposium: Foreword* ||
48 St. Louis U. L.J. 1, 4–5, 7 (2003)

[A] 1999 study by Kevin A. Schulman and colleagues published in the New England Journal of Medicine entitled The Effect of Race and Sex on Physicians' Recommendations for Cardiac Catheterization [attracted much media attention]. The researchers studied 720 primary care physicians who each viewed a videotaped patient interview to determine whether the patient should be referred for cardiac catheterization. The eight patient-actors who appeared in the videos used the same script, had the same clinical symptoms, history, source of insurance and income, wore the same clothes, and even bore a dramatic physical resemblance to each other. The research model controlled tightly for every variable except race and sex. Among the eight actors were four whites, four African-Americans, four women and four men. The Schulman study found a statistically significant difference in referral rates based upon the race and gender of the patients—the patient's race and gender affected the likelihood of primary care physicians referring the patient for cardiac catheterization. The Schulman study, which also published the photos of its actor-patients in the New England Journal of Medicine, put a face and a touch of humanity on the statistical studies. It provided vivid, graphic evidence that racial and ethnic disparities in care are about race and ethnicity and not primarily attributable to socioeconomic status and the patient's source of insurance. . . .

Dr. [David] Williams[2] . . . looks at the growing body of recent literature on racial and ethnic disparities in health care access and quality. While multiple factors contribute to the racial and ethnic disparities in care—geographic maldistribution of health resources in mostly white neighborhoods, institutional policies of private hospitals and health systems, and patients' trust, knowledge and prior experiences with the health care system—discrimination by health care professionals plays an important, albeit unconscious and unintentional, role. As Dr. Williams' statistics graphically show, white Americans, as a group, hold negative perceptions about Africans, Hispanics and Asians. Not only do white health care professionals bring these misconceptions to their work, medical care is rendered under the kind of constraints—time pressure, brief encounters, and the need to manage complex, cognitive tasks—that are likely to enhance reliance on negative stereotyping because there is simply not enough time available to get to know each patient.

> ## *Joel Teitelbaum & Sara Rosenbaum,*
> ## *Medical Care As a Public Accommodation:*
> ## *Moving the Discussion to Race*
> ## 29 Am. J.L. & Med. 381, 382–383 (2003)

The Civil Rights Act of 1964 represents a watershed moment in U.S. civil rights policy. Addressing discrimination in such areas as employment, housing, federally assisted programs and public accommodation, the Act was intended to remedy discrimination in a broad array of settings. The term "place of public accommodation" under the Act essentially reaches enterprises that sell their services to the general public and whose activities affect commerce. Specifically, the Act reaches inns, hotels and motels, restaurants and food establishments and places of exhibition or entertainment, such as theaters and arenas. The definition found in the Act parallels common law concepts of public accommodation as understood at the time.

The definition of a place of public accommodation under the Act did not, and does not today, include medical care providers and facilities. Where medical care services are concerned, the Act applies only if there is evidence of the receipt of "federal financial assistance" within the meaning of the Act. Furthermore, the concept of federal financial assistance has tended to focus on direct payments to institutional healthcare providers such as hospitals and nursing homes. Indeed, the history of Title VI indicates the lengths to which policy makers went to narrowly construe the reach of the law concerning private physicians. In his excellent history of Title VI, David Barton Smith describes the extent to which the potential reach of Title VI into directly federally assisted medical practices nearly caused the defeat of Medicare by Southern senators. Smith's book also chronicles the promises that the Johnson Administration made not to classify Medicare physician payments as a form of assistance. Despite the fact that physicians plied their trade to the paying public, courts viewed physicians in private practice as outside the realm of a place of public

---

2. Referring to David R. Williams, Race, Health and Health Care, 48 St. Louis U. L.J. 13 (2003).–Eds.

accommodation; the "kid gloves" treatment that was the hallmark of legal rulings carried over into the broader reaches of U.S. civil rights policy as well.

. . . Although the importance of the federal financial provisions of Title VI can hardly be overstated, every effort was made immediately following enactment of the law to clarify the limitations of its reach where office-based medical practice was concerned. Despite the fact that both the common law and state statutes regulating the conduct of institutional healthcare providers were evolving to include an explicit duty of care, at least in certain narrowly defined circumstances, private medical practices remained untouched.

Sidney D. Watson, Section 1557 of the Affordable Care Act: Civil Rights, Health Reform, Race, and Equity
55 How. L.J. 855 (2012)

. . . Attending to issues of race and equity in this time of health insurance expansion and reform is critical because, in America, health insurance and health care remain racially and ethnically segregated with one health care system serving disproportionately white patients with private insurance and a different "safety net" system serving minority patients with Medicaid and the uninsured. Private health insurers and health care providers rely on a variety of business practices that operate to segregate and exclude minority patients from mainstream medical care. These policies may not have the intent of discriminating on the basis of race and ethnicity—in fact, most are motivated by economic and profit maximization concerns—but they operate to disproportionately exclude and segregate people of color. For example, health insurers avoid selling private plans in minority neighborhoods because residents tend to be sicker, less educated, poorer, and thus, they are more risky to insure. Health care providers avoid locating in minority neighborhoods due to the higher percentages of uninsured residents. Health insurers offer one set of plans and networks to privately insured patients and a different set for those with Medicaid. Most private physicians either refuse outright to treat Medicaid patients or restrict the number of Medicaid patients they accept.

Because the ACA [Affordable Care Act] continues the tradition of Medicaid for the poor and a variety of private insurance offerings for wealthier Americans, it has the potential to perpetuate America's dual track medical care with one system serving mostly white patients with private insurance and a different system for poorer, mostly minority patients with Medicaid. In fact, the ACA may exacerbate this two-tier system by creating a third tier of moderate-income Americans, half of whom are people of color, who obtain their health insurance through the new Exchanges using federal tax credit subsidies. By maintaining multiple sources of health insurance, the ACA may serve to reinforce and further segregate patients along racial lines. Similarly, the ACA's commitment to expanding the number and capacity of community health centers and other alternative providers may reinforce the racial segregation that has emerged over the last thirty years in which special "safety net" providers serve minority neighborhoods while mainstream providers operate in more affluent white communities.

The Act contains an important new provision specifically aimed at documenting racial disparities, including racial segregation in health insurance and health care delivery. The ACA requires that federally funded health insurers and health care providers collect and report data about the race, ethnicity, and language of the patients they serve. While data collection is necessary—and long overdue—to document the extent of racial segregation in health insurance and delivery, reporting alone is unlikely to eliminate racial and ethnic segregation in health care, even when combined with the ACA's new health insurance coverage provisions and workforce initiatives.

. . . The ACA includes a broad new health care specific civil rights mandate: Section 1557 prohibits health insurers and health care providers from discriminating on the basis of race and ethnicity along with gender, disability, and age. This new antidiscrimination protection prohibits not only intentional discrimination but also facially neutral policies and practices that have an unjustified disproportionate racial impact, including those that segregate along racial lines. While Title VI of the 1964 Civil Rights Act has long prohibited federally funded health care providers and Medicaid from using facially neutral policies that have a disproportionate adverse racial impact, Section 1557's antidiscrimination mandate reaches many more health insurance, health care, and public health activities. It offers an important new anti-discrimination tool for identifying and dismantling health care segregation.

. . . The Johnson Administration used [a similar opportunity to combine expanded federal funding with civil rights remedies] to de-segregate the nation's hospitals. That effort succeeded because the civil rights expectations were clear and easily verified. The hospitals knew what was expected of them and knew they had to both dismantle segregation and also put into place new policies before the new federal Medicare dollars would begin to flow. An inter-governmental taskforce, supplemented by local community members, served as the eyes and ears of the federal level effort.

Much can be gleaned from the language of Section 1557 because it uses familiar civil rights language that has established legal meaning. However, implementing regulations are needed. . . .

> ## Ruqaiijah Yearby, Breaking the Cycle of "Unequal Treatment" with Health Care Reform: Acknowledging and Addressing the Continuation of Racial Bias
> ### 44 Conn. L. Rev. 1281 (2012)

. . . In 2002, the groundbreaking Institute of Medicine Study, Unequal Treatment: Confronting Racial and Ethnic Disparities in Healthcare ("IOM study"), noted that some health care providers, such as physicians, were influenced by a patient's race, which, in turn, created a barrier to African-Americans' access to health care. Not only did this racial bias prevent African-Americans from accessing health care services, it caused African-Americans to have poor health outcomes. The IOM study also found evidence of poorer quality of care for minority patients in studies of cancer treatment, treatment of cardiovascular disease, and rates of referral for clinical tests, diabetes management, pain management, and other areas of care. Ten years after the publication of this sweeping study, racial bias continues to drive racial disparities in health care, and as a result, access to health care remains unequal. Racial bias in health care operates on three different levels: interpersonal, institutional, and structural.

Interpersonal bias is the conscious (explicit) and/or unconscious (implicit) use of prejudice in interactions between individuals. Interpersonal bias is best illustrated by physicians' treatment decisions based on racial prejudice, which results in the unequal treatment of African-Americans. According to Rene Bowser's seminal article, Racial Profiling in Health Care: An Institutional Analysis of Medical Treatment Disparities, these racial disparities in treatment often lead to racial disparities in mortality rates between African-Americans and Caucasians. Institutional bias operates through organizational structures within institutions, which "establish separate and independent barriers" to health care services. According to Brietta Clark, institutional bias is best demonstrated by hospital closures in African-American communities.[3] Finally, operating at a societal level, structural bias exists in the organizational structure of society, which "privile[ges] some groups . . . [while] denying others access to the resources of society," including health care. An example of structural bias is the provision of health care based primarily on ability to pay, rather than on the needs of the patient.

Unfortunately, the government often ignores the significance of racial bias in causing racial disparities in health care, and by extension, overall health, even though such biases are among the causes identified in numerous government reports, initiatives, and empirical research studies conducted over the past decade. The Patient Protection and Affordable Care Act ("ACA") exemplifies the government's failure to acknowledge the interconnectedness of racial bias and racial disparities. Although the Patient Protection Act explicitly mentions disparities in health care and provides several mandates to address these disparities, it fails to acknowledge or target the root causes of racial disparities-racial bias. Therefore . . . the ACA will not fully equalize access to health care for minorities. In fact, the Act may exacerbate the existing problem of racial disparities because it proposes individual and community based solutions that will not put an end to interpersonal, institutional, and structural racial bias, which cause racial disparities in health care. . . .

NOTES AND QUESTIONS

1. *Limitations of traditional responses.* Louise Trubek and Maya Das suggest that traditional responses to eliminate racial disparities in health care have stalled in recent years. Louise G. Trubek & Maya Das, Achieving Equality: Healthcare Governance in Transition, 29 Am. J.L. & Med. 395 (2003). The first traditional response—a "civil rights litigation approach" under Title VI of the Civil Rights Act of 1964—has suffered from lack of success in court and a paucity of lawyers ready to carry the burden of this work. The second traditional response focused on increasing the number of minority physicians. This effort has slowed in recent years as affirmative action programs have faced limits under the law.

---

3. Referring to Brietta R. Clark, Hospital Flight From Minority Communities: How Our Existing Civil Rights Framework Fosters Racial Inequality in Healthcare, 9 DePaul J. Health Care L. 1023, 1029 (2005)–Eds.

The third traditional response—local efforts to improve access to primary and preventive health care—has had limited success and has not expanded into a regional or national effort. The authors find promise in a new approach (the "disease management" approach). This approach focuses on improving the quality of care for all patients, especially with reference to specific diseases, including diabetes, asthma, and heart disease. The authors explain the advantages of the approach: "Disease management programs are able to improve the quality of care by focusing on educating patients and providing scientifically based, uniform clinical care for specific conditions." Id. at 401.

Both Professors Watson and Yearby (in separate articles, supra) see some promise in the Affordable Care Act's attempts to decrease discrimination in health care on the basis of race and ethnicity. What are the different mechanisms contained in the ACA that might achieve this goal? What, according to these authors, are the shortfalls to the ACA's approach?

2. *Connections between racial and class disparities in health care.*   Some of the conclusions of the study comparing responses to white and African-American cardiac patients described by Sidney Watson, supra, were retracted (in light of criticisms of the statistical methodology upon which the researchers had relied). Still, however, the study succeeded in making the American public aware of racial disparities in health care.

M. Gregg Bloche wonders about the study's wide political impact (despite the partial retraction of its conclusions):

> Why has racial bias in the clinical judgments physicians made on behalf of equivalently insured and socio-economically situated Americans generated a greater political response than has the racially unequal impact of allowing more than forty million Americans to go without medical coverage? And, why have racial disparities in health status—a thing distinct from health care provision and not much influenced by it—received less political attention than has racial bias in physician judgment?

M. Gregg Bloche, Race and Discretion in American Medicine, 1 Yale J. Health Pol'y, L. & Ethics 95, 98 (2001). Bloche suggests the answer to his questions lies in the public's comparative readiness to tolerate disparities resulting from class differences than those that seem to be the direct result of racism. He explains: "As a matter of law—and of politics—we tend to treat racial disparities in Americans' enjoyment of myriad goods, services, and benefits as less troublesome when they are mediated through socio-economic differences than when they arise from the overt bigotry of identifiable actors." Id. at 98.

3. *Disparities in health care for Native Americans.*   Disparities in health care for Native Americans exist but are often forgotten or ignored in public discourse and in efforts to respond generally to disparities in health care. One commentator suggests this may be the result of an erroneous belief that the Indian Health Service provides adequate care for most members of the Native American population. Ruth J. Katz, Addressing the Health Care Needs of American Indians and Alaska Natives, 94 Am. J. Pub. Health 13 (Jan. 1, 2004), 2004 WL 11254746. Over half of the Native American (including the Alaskan native) population has income below 200 percent of the federal poverty line; of these, almost half are uninsured. And only about half of the low-income Native American population without health coverage has access to the Indian Health Service. Katz notes there

are many Native Americans that the Indian Health Service does not reach. Some of these are not members of tribes recognized by the federal government; others live too far from Indian Health Service sites to rely on them.

A report prepared by the Office of the General Counsel, U.S. Commission on Civil Rights, documents some of the factors responsible for the poor health status of the Native American population. Broken Promises: Evaluating the Native American Health Care System, U.S. Comm'n on Civil Rights (Draft Report, July 2, 2004), available at http://www.usccr.gov (last visited July 21, 2004). The report concludes that the health status of Native Americans "lags behind" the health status of other groups in the United States. The report attributes this to a combination of social, cultural, financial, and structural limits to health care access that Native Americans face. In short, discrimination against the group is compounded by inadequate clinical facilities and insufficient federal funding.

4. *Discrimination and genetic information.* Correlations between deleterious genetic alterations and race or ethnicity carry the potential for discrimination in health care. Commentators are vociferously debating the consequences of research results suggesting that genetic differences correlate with race and ethnicity. See, e.g., Richard S. Cooper et al., Race and Genomics, 348 New Eng. J. Med. 1166, 1169 (2003) (questioning the "value of continental race as a classification scheme" in explaining differences in the incidence of health and disease); Esteban Gonzalez Burchard et al., The Importance of Race and Ethnic Background in Biomedical Research and Clinical Practice, 348 New Eng. J. Med. 1170, 1171 (2003) (suggesting the costs of linking "race or ethnic background with genetics" is lower than the costs of not doing so). Broad genetic claims— such as the suggestion that some "races" are weaker than others—must be evaluated carefully and critically. Among other things, claims of that sort have the potential to exacerbate racism by justifying it. It is known, for instance, that African Americans suffering from specific conditions are referred for care less often than whites suffering from the same condition. For instance, African Americans with end-stage renal disease are referred for transplantation less often than whites in the United States. Similarly, they are referred less often for cardiac catheterization. Burchard et al., supra, at 1171. In these cases, differences in care result from bias and discriminatory practice rather than from genetic differences between the populations. But the suggestion that genetic differences explain health differences broadly could be used as implicit or explicit justification for providing less care to members of groups identified as prone genetically to illness generally or to particular illnesses.

2. Legal Approaches

Hall v. Bio-Medical Application, Inc.
671 F.2d 300 (8th Cir. 1982)

Opinion by HENLEY.

Plaintiff Robert Hall is a black male resident of Little Rock, Arkansas, who suffers from kidney disease and requires hemodialysis treatment several times a week. From March, 1978 to May, 1979 Hall received his treatment, as prescribed by his physician, Dr. Brewer, at Bio-Medical Application (BMA), an outpatient hemodialysis facility. Plaintiff asserts that during this time he and other black patients were subjected to racial discrimination by the staff of BMA, and that on May 18, 1979 an incident occurred in which the nurse supervisor, Melanie Flannigan, called him a "black son of a bitch" and removed him from the dialysis machine, leaving the dialysis needles in his arm. Plaintiff left the facility and later removed the needles himself, causing a substantial blood loss. After the May 18 incident, plaintiff continued in the care of Dr. Brewer, but received his hemodialysis treatment at the Baptist Medical Center.

. . . [The plaintiff] charg[ed] defendants with violating 42 U.S.C. §1981 [which prohibits discrimination in the making and enforcement of contracts by reason of race, color, or national origin–EDS.], medical malpractice, and intentional infliction of emotional distress. The district court . . . found that plaintiff had failed to sustain his burden of proof with respect to the §1981 claim and the claim of intentional infliction of emotional distress. However, judgment was entered for plaintiff on his pendent claim of medical malpractice in the amount of $4,500.00. Plaintiff now appeals the denial of his §1981 claim. . . . Defendants cross-appeal the court's finding of medical malpractice. We affirm the judgment of the district court.

I. §1981

Plaintiff first contends that the trial court erred in denying his §1981 claim. The district court stated in its findings of fact and conclusions of law that plaintiff had failed to meet the applicable burden of proof requirements as set forth in Texas Department of Community Affairs v. Burdine, 450 U.S. 248 (1981). In support of his contention, plaintiff relies on affidavits and testimony of former employees of BMA who stated that white patients were given priority in scheduling, that black patients were treated with less sensitivity and disciplined more severely than white patients, that black patients' dialysis had on occasion been rushed, and that nurse Flannigan made disparaging racial remarks. Plaintiff also argues that the May 18 incident described above further supports a finding of unlawful discrimination resulting in the deprivation of his protected right "to make and enforce contracts."

After reviewing the record, we conclude that if plaintiff established a prima facie case of unlawful discrimination, defendants effectively rebutted it by articulating a legitimate, nondiscriminatory reason for plaintiff's termination as a client of BMA; and further, that plaintiff failed to show this reason to be a mere pretext for discrimination. Defendants offered evidence, and the district court found, that plaintiff had on several occasions become disruptive and had used obscene and abusive language. For example, on September 8, 1978 Hall became upset and shouted obscenities when he demanded to speak to Flannigan, who had left for the day. His hemodialysis was terminated early because he threatened to remove the dialysis needles himself. On September 13, he again became angry when a BMA employee refused to discuss the September 8 incident, and left without receiving his treatment. The district court also found that on May 14, 1979 plaintiff called the BMA social worker and threatened to cause some trouble, a threat he repeated on May 16 when he reported for his treatment. Finally, on May 18, Hall became angry and used obscene language after he was asked to hang up an extension phone while Flannigan was engaged in a long distance call. It was at this point that Flannigan called plaintiff a "black son of a bitch" and removed him from the machine.

Although Flannigan's behavior was clearly unprofessional, we conclude that plaintiff's repeated disruptive and abusive conduct constituted a legitimate nondiscriminatory justification, which was not shown to be pretextual, for terminating his contractual relationship with BMA. . . .

III. DEFENDANTS' CROSS-APPEAL

Defendants contend that the trial court erred in finding defendants liable to plaintiff for medical malpractice based on the May 18 incident. It is submitted that the procedure used to disconnect plaintiff from the hemodialysis machine was routine and that the needles were left in place in case plaintiff returned to the machine to finish his treatment. Instead, Hall refused all offers of assistance, left the facility, and removed the needles himself.

The district court was not unaware of defendant's provoking behavior, and allocated forty per cent of the fault to plaintiff pursuant to Arkansas' comparative fault statute. However, defendants' justification of the medical procedure used to disconnect plaintiff from the hemodialysis machine overlooks the court's emphasis on Flannigan's overall treatment of Hall. "Her behavior did not conform to the high standards we necessarily expect of those in the nursing profession. . . . Under extreme provocation, she engaged in language and conduct . . . unacceptable in a highly trained professional." We find sufficient evidence to support the district court's findings with respect to plaintiff's claim of medical malpractice.

The judgment of the district court is affirmed.

|| ***42 U.S.C. 18116*** ||
**Codification of Section 1557 of the Patient Protection
and Affordable Care Act**[4]

§18116. NONDISCRIMINATION

(a) *In General*

Except as otherwise provided for in this title (or an amendment made by this title), an individual shall not, on the ground prohibited under title VI of the Civil Rights Act of 1964 (42 U.S.C. 2000d et seq.), title IX of the Education Amendments of 1972 (20 U.S.C. 1681 et seq.), the Age Discrimination Act of 1975 (42 U.S.C. 6101 et seq.), or section 794 of title 29, be excluded from participation in, be denied the benefits of, or be subjected to discrimination under, any health program or activity, any part of which is receiving Federal financial assistance, including credits, subsidies, or contracts of insurance, or under any program or activity that is administered by an Executive Agency or any

---

4. Pub. L. 111-148, title I, §1557, Mar. 23, 2010, 124 Stat. 260.

entity established under this title (or amendments). The enforcement mechanisms provided for and available under such title VI, title IX, section 794, or such Age Discrimination Act shall apply for purposes of violations of this subsection.

(b)   Continued Application of Laws

Nothing in this title (or an amendment made by this title) shall be construed to invalidate or limit the rights, remedies, procedures, or legal standards available to individuals aggrieved under title VI of the Civil Rights Act of 1964 (42 U.S.C. 2000d et seq.), title VII of the Civil Rights Act of 1964 (42 U.S.C. 2000e et seq.), title IX of the Education Amendments of 1972 (20 U.S.C. 1681 et seq.), section 794 of title 29, or the Age Discrimination Act of 1975 [42 U.S.C. 6101 et seq.], or to supersede State laws that provide additional protections against discrimination on any basis described in subsection (a).

(c)   Regulations

The Secretary may promulgate regulations to implement this section.

NOTES AND QUESTIONS

1. *An alternative explanation?*   In Hall v. Bio-Medical Application, Inc., the Eighth Circuit concluded that Hall's angry, disruptive behavior at Bio-Medical Application (BMA) provided a "legitimate nondiscriminatory justification" for BMA's ending its contractual relationship with Hall. Is this alternative explanation of BMA's response to Hall adequate in light of the nurse supervisor's having referred to Hall as a "black son of a bitch"? Do you think the court should have considered whether Hall's behavior was a reasonable response to blatant racism?

2. *Section 1557 of ACA.*   Note that the nondiscrimination section of the ACA (Section 1557, supra) delineates the prohibited grounds of discrimination by reference to already existing civil rights statutes. Sidney Watson explains,

> Section 1557's textual density is the byproduct of its tendency to cross reference to Title VI and three other existing civil rights laws: Title IX, which prohibits sex discrimination in federally funded school activities; the Age Discrimination Act of 1975, which prohibits age discrimination in federally funded programs; and Section 504 of the Rehabilitation Act, which prohibits disability discrimination in federally funded programs. These other three civil rights statutes are modeled on Title VI, and courts have interpreted the terms they have in common, in pari materia, as having the same legal meaning.

Sidney D. Watson, Section 1557 of the Affordable Care Act: Civil Rights, Health Reform, Race, and Equity, 55 How. L. J. 855, 871 (2012). Although inelegant, Section 1557's reliance on these other federal civil rights statutes, which have already established legal meanings, "is evidence of the Congressional intent that this new civil rights statute is to prohibit both intentional and disparate impact discrimination." Id. at 870.

This "new civil rights statute" will also reach many more health care providers and other participants in the health care market than Title VI. Watson explains that Section 1557 contains

> a more expansive statutory definition of "[f]ederal financial assistance" than does Title VI and its companion civil rights statutes, defining federal financial assistance to include, rather than exclude, "credits, subsidies or contracts of insurance." This inclusion of "contracts of insurance" makes clear that Section 1557 reaches physicians and other health care providers who accept Medicare Part B insurance, making irrelevant HHS's specious conclusion that Medicare is an excluded "contract of insurance" for purposes of Title VI. Moreover, Section 1557's specificity that federal financial assistance includes "credits" and "subsidies" unequivocally establishes that Section 1557's antidiscrimination mandate covers private insurance companies, physicians, and other providers who will be receiving new federal tax credits and subsidies authorized by the ACA.

Id. at 873.

3. *Suits for retaliatory discharge of "whistleblowers."* A postgraduate ophthalmology resident, terminated from his position at New York Hospital, brought suit against the hospital in federal court. The terminated resident alleged that he was fired for protesting the hospital's failure to care adequately for two African-American patients. Hall v. New York Hospital, 2003 U.S. Dist. LEXIS 22039 (S.D.N.Y. 2003), aff'd 117 Fed. Appx. 790 (2d Cir. 2004). The resident, Dr. Michael Hall, described two incidents during the summer of 1997 involving African-American children needing eye surgery. Dr. Hall alleged that in each case the child received inadequate care because of the child's race. He alleged further that after he complained to two doctors, they "sought to engender plaintiff's resignation or to terminate his employ in naked retaliation for [his] whistle blowing activities." The court dismissed plaintiff's claim, brought under 42 U.S.C. §1981, because Dr. Hall "failed to allege racial animus or discriminatory intent." However, the court allowed that had plaintiff presented such allegations, his case would have been heard.

> In the present case, although plaintiff is not a member of a racial minority, the Second Circuit has held that whites have standing to sue under §1981.... Furthermore, a number of courts, including this one, have recognized that an employee who has been the subject of retaliatory discharge because of his or her efforts to vindicate the §1981 rights of racial minorities may bring an action under §1981.
>
> Plaintiff alleges that he was unlawfully terminated from the hospital's Ophthalmology Residency Program in retaliation for his actions wherein he "sought to vindicate the rights" of two black patients. Plaintiff's §1981 claims are based solely on two allegations: (1) In July 1997, a black patient he was treating lost an eye because "several senior physicians, all of whom were white, intentionally refused to authorize the transfer of the patient to another medical facility"; and (2) On August 11, 1997, "various senior physicians ... all of whom were white ... intentionally refused to assist plaintiff in his attempt to treat the child." Plaintiff claims that as a result of his spoken and written protests "decrying the obvious departure from the duty of care owed to the black patient," he was terminated from his position.

It was not clear that the physicians in question were aware that either patient was African American:

Nowhere in his complaint does plaintiff claim that he informed any hospital physicians that his two patients were black, or that he specifically complained of disparate treatment provided to blacks as compared to whites, or that the issue of race was ever discussed in connection with his patients' care or his complaints about their treatment.

In another case, however, a "whistleblower" health care provider could, under the court's analysis in Hall v. New York Hospital, proceed with a §1981 claim. That could happen, if, for instance, a hospital were to "retaliate" against the whistleblower for informing hospital supervisors about discriminatory treatment of members of a racial minority by hospital health care providers.

4. *Disparities in health care correlating with race and gender.*   Analysis of disparities in health care among various ethnic and racial groups becomes more complicated when gender is brought into the account. In general, women's health has been assessed through models developed in light of men's health problems. For instance, far more women perceive themselves to be at risk for breast cancer than for coronary disease (long framed as a "man's" disease); yet, in fact, ten times more women die of heart disease or stroke than of breast cancer. Ron Winslow, New Guidelines Tackle Women's Heart Risks, Wall St. Journal, Feb. 5, 2004, at D1. Moreover, about half of the people who suffer from cardiovascular disease are women. Yet, women are not diagnosed or treated as often as men are. World Heart Federation, http://www.world-heart-federation.org/what-we-do/go-red-for-women/why-go-red.

In 2004, the Kaiser Family Foundation reported a number of facts about the comparative health status of white, Latina, and African-American women in the United States, Issue Brief: An Update on Women's Health Policy: Racial and Ethnic Disparities in Women's Health Coverage and Access to Care: Findings from the 2001 Kaiser Women's Health Survey, The Kaiser Family Foundation, March 2004, available at http://www.kff.org/womenshealth/whp031004pkg.cfm (visited Mar. 28, 2004). Self-assessments of health status differed markedly among the three groups, with 13 percent of white women, 29 percent of Latinas, and 20 percent of African-American women describing their health status as "fair or poor." Moreover, about 16 percent of African-American women between 18 and 64, as compared with 12 percent of white women, and 10 percent of Latinas, are reported to be physically limited in routine activities such as school, work, and housework. Id. Sidney D. Watson, Section 1557 of the Affordable Care Act: Civil Rights, Health Reform, Race, and Equity, 55 How. L. J. 855, 871 (2012).

The Issue Brief found many differences in health or health care among women on the basis of their ethnic or racial identity. These included differences in insurance coverage, access to care, dealing with the costs of health care, and perceptions as to the quality of care. The Issue Brief concludes:

> There is increasing evidence that the underlying racial and ethnic inequities in health care extend beyond the logistic and economic factors. In a large-scale analysis of racial and ethnic disparities, the Institute of Medicine concluded that ". . . evidence suggests that bias, prejudice, and stereotyping on the part of healthcare providers may contribute to the differences in care." While this does not account for the multiple disparities that women of color experience, it is an area that providers and other health care professionals can address to close some of the access and coverage gaps.

Gender discrimination in health care is further considered in the next subsection.

CHALLENGING ISSUES: DISPARITIES IN HEALTH CARE: RACE AND GENDER

You are an assistant to Senator Pat Ralson from Utopian State. Senator Ralson is committed to increasing access to health care for all people in the country. At this time, Senator Ralson is anxious to have more information about factors that correlate with limited access to health care. She believes it is much easier to "fix" a problem if one knows what causes the problem. Several weeks ago, Senator Ralson asked you to do some preliminary research.

In beginning this work, you have come across a study involving more than 1,000 pregnant women that examined which women were more or less likely to receive epidurals for pain management during labor and delivery.[5] The study reported that race (defined as "white versus nonwhite") was "not a significant risk factor for nonreceipt of epidural procedures during childbirth." However, the study found that ethnicity was correlated with nonuse of epidurals during normal deliveries. In particular, the study reported that the chance of a Hispanic woman not receiving an epidural was two times that of a white woman. The study also found that women with private health insurance were more likely to receive epidurals than other women; this latter finding did not surprise you as much as the finding about the comparatively low rate of epidurals received by Hispanic women having babies. You are concerned about the report and would like to understand it. Senator Ralson has told you that she has some funds for research on issues related to health care access. You would like to propose a study aimed at explaining the results of the report about nonreceipt of epidurals on the basis of ethnicity. What factors would you want to investigate that might explain the correlation between nonreceipt of epidurals and Hispanic ethnicity?

C. GENDER

	Karen H. Rothenberg, Gender Matters: Implications	
	for Clinical Research and Women's Health Care	
	32 Hous. L. Rev. 1201, 1206, 1208–1209, 1211, 1213 (1996)	

For the most part, the lack of knowledge about women's health has resulted from our failure to research women's health issues. . . .

Science has a long history of viewing men as the standard by which all things are measured. "Like the pronoun 'he,' it was taken for granted that

---

5. See Martin J. Atherton, Veronica DeCarolis Feeg & Azza Fouad El-Adham, Race, Ethnicity, and Insurance as Determinants of Epidural Use: Analysis of a National Sample Survey, 22 Nursing Economics 6 (Jan. 1, 2004), 2004 WL 71790227.

the white male subject stood for all of us." Because the research community views men as the norm, they see differences in women as unknown variables that tend to confound results. For example, women present factors such as menstrual cycles, pregnancy, teratogenic liability, and menopause. Some researchers argue that these factors complicate research and add excess costs to experimentation. Paradoxically, "scientists seem to be confirming that women's bodies are different and more difficult to study. But then by simply extending their male-drawn conclusions to women, they are implying that—with a few obvious exceptions—women's bodies are the same as men's." These assumptions have discouraged studies on females and have fostered ignorance concerning the special needs of women. . . .

Perhaps the most shocking example of the exclusion of women from the clinical study of a health condition that almost exclusively affects women was a project that examined the impact of obesity on breast and uterine cancer. The study participants were all men. For twenty years, women were also excluded from the Baltimore Longitudinal Study of Aging, one of the largest studies of the natural process of aging. Six years after women were permitted to participate, a report of the study findings entitled "Normal Human Aging" was published. It is considered the definitive study of aging in the United States. It contains no data on women. . . .

The effects of exclusion from clinical research are far reaching. All women suffer the consequences of studies that include only men, or that include women, but do not adequately analyze any gender-related differences. . . .

Several well-known studies of cardiovascular disease considered only male subjects. Although they have had a significant impact on the treatment and prevention of heart disease in men, these studies have not produced definitive information about prevention and treatment of women's heart disease. In fact, the lack of research on women's health and gender-blind health conditions in women may have a dangerous effect. Based on the findings of studies of heart disease and cholesterol that included men only, the American Heart Association recommended a diet that could actually elevate the risk of heart disease for women. . . .

Bias has also been reported in studies that evaluate the relationship between the gender of a physician and the offering of gender-sensitive diagnostic practices, such as breast exams, pap smears, and mammograms. Women who reported having a male physician as their usual provider were less likely to receive pap tests and mammograms than women who reported having a female physician as their usual care provider. . . .

The most difficult physician–patient relationships tend to be between male physicians and female patients. Some research has shown that male physicians may discourage information exchange with female patients. For example, compared to male physicians, female physicians engage in significantly more positive talk, partnership-building, question-asking, and information-giving. Similarly, when with female physicians, patients talk more during the medical visit and appear to participate more actively in the medical dialogue. The longest visits are between female physicians and female patients and the shortest between male physicians and female patients.

NOTES AND QUESTIONS

1. *Female and male voices.*   Psychologist Carol Gilligan has suggested that men and women differ in the way they approach moral issues. Gilligan has described males as stressing autonomy and abstract rules while women more often rely on context, and focus on connections among people. Carol Gilligan, In a Different Voice: Psychological Theory and Women's Development (1982). Professor Rothenberg has summarized some possible consequence of this difference, noting that some feminists have concluded "that many traditional legal doctrines and practices are based on male values of autonomy and abstraction and fail to value the positive 'feminine' concerns of responsibility, relationship, and essential connectedness. . . ." Karen H. Rothenberg, New Perspectives for Teaching and Scholarship: The Role of Gender in Law and Health Care, 54 Md. L. Rev. 473, 481 (1995).

In light of that assessment, what effect is the gender of a patient in comparison with that of the physician likely to have on a patient's ability to reach an informed consent to recommended health care? Are female patients more likely to feel comfortable asking questions of female than of male physicians? (What about male patients?) If this is true, what, if anything, would it mean for health policy?

2. *Gender and domination.*   Some feminist theorists have concluded that the essential reality of gender must be understood in light of the widespread social subordination of women and the dominance of men. See, e.g., Catherine MacKinnon, Feminism Unmodified: Discussions on Life and Law (1987). MacKinnon's work is now 25 years old. Do you think her assessment, if once valid, is still so? If there are gender differences of this nature in the context of health care, how might the law best respond?

3. *Discrimination in health insurance pricing and coverage.*   In 2012, the National Women's Law Center, an advocacy organization for women, published a report showing that women are commonly charged more for health insurance than men in the individual market, even when maternity coverage is excluded. National Women's Law Center, Turning to Fairness: Insurance Discrimination Against Women Today and the Affordable Care Act, Mar. 16, 2012, http://www.nwlc.org/sites/default/files/pdfs/nwlc_2012_turningtofairness_report.pdf. In the group health insurance market, employers may be charged higher premiums by insurance companies if they employ a large percentage of women. Some of the report's conclusions:

> • Gender rating, the practice of charging women different premiums than men, results in significantly higher rates charged to women throughout the country. In states that have not banned the practice, the vast majority, 92%, of best-selling plans gender rate, for example, charging 40-year-old women more than 40-year-old men for coverage. Only 3% of these plans cover maternity services.
> • Based on an average of currently advertised premiums and the most recent data on the number of women in the individual health insurance market, the practice of gender rating costs women approximately $1 billion a year.
> • There is such wide variation in differences women are charged both within and across states—even with maternity care excluded—that it is difficult to see how actuarial justifications could explain the difference. For example, one plan examined in Arkansas charges 25-year-old women 81% more than men for coverage while a similar plan in the same state only charges women 10% more for coverage than men.

The Report notes that some states have banned gender rating in insurance markets and/or have required insurers to cover maternity care. The Affordable Care Act will do both, on a national scale, beginning in 2014 (except that existing plans sold outside of the ACA's health exchanges will be "grandfathered" with respect to coverage matters).

Why do you think the Report took care to make the last point in the bulleted list, above? What argument can be made in support of gender rating? Do you find it persuasive?

4. *More on gender discrimination.* Additional material about gender discrimination against women is found in Chapter 5 (Assisting and Manipulating Reproduction) and Chapter 6 (Avoiding Reproduction).

D.   IMMIGRANT STATUS

> *Janet L. Dolgin & Katherine R. Dieterich,*
> *When Others Get Too Close: Immigrants, Class,*
> *and the Health Care Debate*
> 19 Cornell J. Law & Public Pol'y 283 (2010)

. . . The great majority of hospitals in the United States are required to screen, and if needed, to treat patients arriving at emergency rooms for care. Congress passed the law mandating such care, the Emergency Medical Treatment and Labor Act (EMTALA), in order to prevent hospitals from dumping people without the ability to pay, and thereby to ensure that everyone would have access to emergency medical care. EMTALA applies to any hospital with an emergency room that accepts Medicare payments.

EMTALA applies to "any individual" arriving at a hospital's emergency room for emergency medical care or who is in labor. The statute requires hospitals to "provide for an appropriate medical screening examination" to determine whether an "emergency medical condition" or labor exists. If a hospital identifies an emergency condition or labor, it is precluded from discharging or transferring patients who have not been stabilized.

Within these parameters, hospitals are obliged to provide the same level of care to undocumented immigrants that they provide to anyone else. At present, however, there is virtually no reimbursement guarantee. Between 2005 and 2008, limited funds, referred to as "Section 1011 funds," were available to compensate providers for emergency care to undocumented immigrants. Even this limited funding was not available to reimburse providers for needed continuing care of a patient who was stabilized. After 2008, unused funds remained available to reimburse hospitals for uncompensated emergency care. A bill to reauthorize Section 1011 funding through 2012 is currently in committee.

Hospitals have faced significant expenses caring for patients in this situation. Federal law and various accreditation standards make hospitals responsible for identifying and affecting an "appropriate discharge" for each patient. However, it is virtually impossible to locate a long-term care facility willing to provide care for a patient with serious needs and no health care coverage or resources. Undocumented immigrants are not eligible for federally-funded health care. It can therefore be especially challenging for hospitals to provide an appropriate discharge for an undocumented immigrant-patient in need of continuing care after he or she has been stabilized. Hospitals may be forced to bear huge economic burdens in such cases, at least in the majority of states in which Medicaid excludes undocumented immigrants from coverage. It also creates dangerous health risks for undocumented immigrants in need of continuing care.

. . . Recognition of American anxieties about undocumented immigrants reached center-stage in the national health care reform debate in the spring of 2009 when Senator Max Baucus of Montana, Chair of the Senate Finance Committee at the time, announced that if Congress were to pass a law creating a national health care program, it would not include coverage for "undocumented aliens, undocumented workers." Baucus described any proposal to provide such coverage as "too politically explosive." He added that if coverage were provided at all for undocumented immigrants ("undocumented aliens, undocumented workers"), it would not be through a federally-funded program. Rather, it might come in the form of "charity care."

Baucus's assertions about undocumented immigrants were especially significant for two unrelated reasons. First, millions of people among those without health coverage in the United States are undocumented immigrants. Second, during the spring of 2009, it was widely assumed that the Obama administration's hope for health care reform rested largely in Baucus's hands.

Senator Baucus's unapologetic declaration about the exclusion of undocumented immigrants from a new, federally-funded health care program seemed clearly to suggest that public opposition to extending health care coverage to undocumented immigrants was widespread and strong enough that including undocumented immigrants would have risked undermining the entire health care reform enterprise.

Clearly, Baucus assumed broad social anxiety about undocumented immigrants competing for social benefits. Such anxiety is evident in responses from readers of a Dallas Morning News story reporting Baucus's declaration that undocumented immigrants would not be beneficiaries of public health care coverage. These responses ranged from anger at the issue (e.g., suggesting that illegal immigrants be shot at the border), to gratitude to Baucus (e.g., noting unfairness of Americans not getting free health care while illegal immigrants do), to skepticism that Baucus's promise, even if fulfilled, would actually benefit the nation (e.g., expressing worry about the [citizen] children of "illegal aliens" "show[ing] up on the numbers . . . [as] uninsured").

Among responses to the story that described undocumented immigrants as unwelcome competition, many focused on the possibility that "citizens" might lose social benefits (health care, in particular) because of the expense incurred in treating undocumented immigrants. Some responses expressed concern about "citizens" losing jobs as a result of immigrants ready to work at low wages.

Moreover, beneath the worry about losing social benefits, was a still deeper concern. This underlying concern reflected a pervasive anxiety within the middle class, and especially among those sitting at the lower edges of the middle class, about losing their standing in the nation's complicated, opaque socioeconomic hierarchy. Access to health care and other social benefits plays a major part in defining and in establishing a person's socioeconomic status. Thus, people anxious about the risk of losing their socioeconomic status are likely to be especially concerned about losing or competing for health care and other social benefits.

NOTES AND QUESTIONS

1. *Exclusion of undocumented immigrants from Affordable Care Act/new immigrants from Medicaid.* Senator Baucus's declaration (discussed in Dolgin & Dieterich, supra) was correct. The Affordable Care Act of 2010 explicitly excludes undocumented immigrants from purchasing insurance through the health insurance exchanges (see Section 1312 (f)(3), limiting access to the health insurance exchanges to "lawful residents") and from any federal subsidies for the purchase of insurance (see Section 1412(d)). At the same time, the federal government intends to severely cut payments it has made in the past to hospitals which treat a disproportionate share of the poor and uninsured (these monies are known as "disproportionate share hospital" funds). The premise for this reduction is that more people will be insured under operation of the ACA, and thus hospitals should have less in unreimbursed costs. This assumption, however, does not account for the approximately 11 million people now living in the United States illegally, who are generally poor and uninsured. Nina Bernstein, Hospitals Fear Cuts in Aid for Care to Illegal Immigrants, N.Y. Times, July 26, 2012. See also Note, Michelle Nicole Diamond, Legal Triage for Healthcare Reform: The Conflict Between the ACA and EMTALA, 43 Colum. Hum. Rts. L. Rev. 255 (2011). An executive at a neighborhood hospital in New York City that serves poor and uninsured populations, many of them immigrants, reported that she was told by Congressional staffers in Washington that "they understand that this is a problem, but immigration is just too hot touch."

Note that even immigrants who are legally in the United States are not eligible for Medicaid (except in emergencies) for their first five years in the country. This provision was included in the Personal Responsibility and Work Opportunity Reconciliation Act of 1996 (known as "welfare reform"). Some states do cover such individuals with their own funds. See Rachel Benson Gold, 6(2) The Guttmacher Report on Public Policy, Immigrants and Medicaid After Welfare Reform (May 2003), http://www.guttmacher.org/pubs/tgr/06/2/gr060206.html.

How do we make sense of the different approaches taken by the ACA and EMTALA on the issue of care for undocumented immigrants? What are the social and political influences on health care policy affecting both undocumented immigrants and new "legal" immigrants? Why is this issue "just too hot to touch?" Bernstein, supra.

CHALLENGING ISSUE: HOSPITAL DEPORTATIONS

Felipe Valdez, a 31-year-old undocumented immigrant from Guatemala, worked as a landscape gardener in Florida when he was hit by an uninsured drunk driver. He suffered traumatic brain injury among other serious medical problems. He was taken to the emergency department of Memorial Medical Center (Memorial), a non-profit Florida hospital, where he received excellent care for several months before being transferred to a nursing home. He returned to the hospital emergency department after his condition deteriorated in the nursing home. He has been there ever since, now more than three years since the accident. Although his prognosis was initially very poor, he did eventually recover significant cognitive facilities, able to understand and communicate at the level of a nine-year-old. The cost of Valdez's hospital care has exceeded $1.5 million.

At this point, Valdez no longer needs hospitalization, but still requires rehabilitative care for traumatic brain injury and nursing care. Because federal law precludes the hospital from discharging Valdez without an appropriate plan for transfer, the hospital has been seeking, but cannot find, a rehabilitation facility or nursing home willing to take him, because he is indigent, but ineligible for Medicaid as an undocumented immigrant.

Memorial is now planning to arrange to send Valdez back to Guatemala. It has secured a letter from a Guatemalan health official that states in very general terms that a hospital system there will accept and evaluate Mr. Valdez and transfer him to an appropriate facility in Guatemala following evaluation. The hospital is seeking a court order permitting it to transport Valdez to Guatemala at the hospital's expense.

If you were the judge hearing this case, would you grant the order? What would you want to know before you would grant the order and what kind of evidence would be sufficient to supply that information?

Suppose now that you are hospital counsel. The court, on the basis of the letter from the Guatemalan health official, has authorized the hospital to transport Valdez to Guatemala, with a suitable escort and necessary medical support for the trip. Valdez's guardian (a cousin by marriage) has filed a notice of appeal and a motion to stay the trial court's transport order. The order is not yet stayed, however, and even if the stay is granted, it won't be for a few hours. Hospital administration urges that Valdez be put in a private plane immediately, accompanied by a nurse, before the order can be stayed. How would you respond?

(This Challenging Issue is drawn from Dolgin & Dieterich, supra, with some additional facts added from the actual case, Montejo v. Martin Mem'l Med. Ctr., Inc., 874 S0.2d 654 (Fla. Dist. Ct. App. 4th Dist. 2004).)

E.   SEXUAL ORIENTATION OR GENDER IDENTITY

Discrimination in health care against people because of their sexual orientation or gender identity can take many overt and subtle forms, as the following excerpt on nursing home treatment reveals. Compared to race, national origin, gender, or disability, protection against discrimination on this basis has received less attention and even less legal action. That appears to be changing.

Evelyn M. Tenenbaum, Sexual Expression and Intimacy between Nursing Home Residents with Dementia: Balancing the Current Interests and Prior Values of Heterosexual and LGBT Residents
21 Temp. Pol. & Civ. Rts. L. Rev. 459 (2012)

. . . It is estimated that there are approximately three million lesbian, gay, bisexual, and transgender (LGBT) elders in this country and that this number will grow to four million by 2030. This group of elders has its own unique concerns due to a long history of discrimination.

Despite the size of this population, there is little hard data on the treatment of LGBT elders and their access to health care facilities, including nursing homes. This lack of data can be attributed to the "widespread failure of governmental and academic researchers to include questions about sexual orientation and gender identity in their studies of the aged." Informal surveys and anecdotal evidence suggest that LGBT elders suffer discrimination in hospitals, assisted living facilities, and nursing homes. Some of this discrimination may be unintentional because "[m]ost health care professionals are completely unaware of the specific needs of this population."

Many gay and lesbian elders learned to hide their identities when they were young to avoid overt discrimination. Some have remained hidden as a vestigial coping mechanism. The discrimination in health and social services systems may prompt elders in nursing homes to resume or continue hiding their identities to avoid isolation and stigmatization. This can have dire consequences. Research has shown that "managing stigma over long periods of time results in higher risks of depression and suicide, addictions, and substance abuse."

Nursing homes can also make it difficult for same-sex partners to visit, increasing isolation and loneliness for gay and lesbian residents. The Nursing Home Reform Act (NHRA) does not require the nursing home to provide the same access to LGBT partners and spouses that it provides to heterosexual spouses.[6] Legal protections against other forms of discrimination are also inadequate, and the protections that do exist are costly and difficult to pursue. For example, a federal regulation promulgated under the NHRA gives nursing home residents the "right to be free of . . . discrimination, and reprisal from the facility in exercising his or her rights." But courts are divided on whether nursing home residents can enforce the provisions of the NHRA. And only a few

---

6. Tenenbaum's note here provides,

The NHRA provides that a nursing home must "permit immediate access" to a resident's "immediate family and other relatives," subject to the resident's right to deny them admission. 42 U.S.C. §§1395i-3(c)(3)(B), 1396r(c)(3)(B) (2006). Federal law does not recognize same-sex spouses as family members. Defense of Marriage Act (DOMA), 1 U.S.C. §7 (2006); 28 U.S.C. §1738C (2006). If a visitor is not a family member, the nursing home can impose reasonable restrictions. 42 C.F.R. §483.10(j)(viii) (2011); cf. 10 N.Y. Comp. Codes R. & Regs. tit. 10, §415.3(e)(2)(f)(3) (2012) (requiring that a nursing home assure privacy during visits from a "spouse, relative or partner" who "resides in a location out of the facility"). Advocating for equal access in nursing homes may now be easier because new federal regulations enacted in January 2011 require that federally funded hospitals provide equal visitation access to LGBT persons. 42 C.F.R. §482.13(h) (2011).–Eds.

states have laws protecting against discrimination in nursing homes based on sexual orientation.

Gay and lesbian nursing home residents may have additional concerns due to religious issues. For example, a Catholic nursing home may refuse to allow same-sex relationships because they are contrary to the doctrines of the Catholic Church. Evangelical Christian staff members at secular nursing homes may also raise objections to assisting residents in pursuing their same-sex relationships.

Demented nursing home patients face additional concerns. Dementia reduces sexual inhibitions and, therefore, demented nursing home residents may not be able to hide their sexual orientation. The Hebrew Home for the Aged at Riverdale—a nursing home at the forefront in encouraging sexual expression among its residents—trains staff to accept the patient's sexual preferences. However, many nursing homes are not prepared to deal with same-sex relationships, and gay and lesbian residents may be subject to isolation, harassment, and discrimination by the other residents, administration, and staff.

There may also be a conflict between a demented resident's former lifestyle and his current desire for a same-sex relationship in the nursing home. Some gay men and lesbian women "desperately want[] a conventional life with a wife [or husband] and children." They prioritize their religion over their sexuality and live a lifetime without disclosing their sexual orientation. In this type of case, should the patient's prior critical interest—suppressing his sexual orientation due to his religion—control or his new interest in having a same-sex relationship in the nursing home? Given the patient's lifetime emphasis on his religion, this may be the type of situation where the patient's critical interest should be given more weight, especially if the spouse, family, and friends continue to visit the patient in the nursing home.

Nursing homes should develop policies to address LGBT issues. They should be encouraged to educate health care staff to accept the sexual orientation of their residents and to raise awareness of the needs of the elderly gay and lesbian population. Staff should also be encouraged to discuss their religious, moral, and cultural values. If the staff member cannot provide a supportive environment to those having same-sex relationships, the staff member should be moved to an area of the nursing home where sexual relationships are not a concern. Nursing homes founded upon religious principles that reject homosexuality should be required to reveal their policies so that patients are aware of them before they enter.

NOTES AND QUESTIONS

1. *What does the ACA have to say?* The antidiscrimination provision of the ACA, section 1557, supra, has been recently interpreted by the Office of Civil Rights (OCR) within the Dep't of Health and Human Services as protecting individuals against discrimination on the basis of sexual orientation or gender identity. In the summer of 2012, the OCR issued a response to a letter from the National Center for Lesbian Rights seeking clarification on the scope of section 1557 (42 U.S.C. 18116). That section provides that no individual shall be excluded from participation in, denied the benefits of, or be subjected to discrimination on the grounds prohibited by various existing civil rights statutes (which cover race, color, national origin, sex, age, and disability) in any health

programs and activities receiving federal financial assistance or that is administered by the federal executive or established by the ACA. The letter, from Leon
Rodriguez to Maya Rupert, dated July 12, 2012, states,

> We agree that Section 1557's sex discrimination prohibition extends to claims
> of discrimination based on gender identity or failure to conform to stereotypical
> notions of masculinity or femininity and will accept such complaints for inves-
> tigation. Section 1557 also prohibits sexual harassment and discrimination
> regardless of the actual or perceived sexual orientation or gender identity of
> the individuals involved.

The letter is available at http://www.nachc.com/client//OCRLetterJuly2012
.pdf. What do you think such an interpretation will mean for how nursing
homes must treat residents in the future?

2. *Bibliographic note.*   For more on the challenges faced by lesbian, gay,
bisexual, or transgender people, see Jaime E. Hovey, Note, Nursing Wounds:
Why LGBT Elders Need Protection from Discrimination and Abuse Based on
Sexual Orientation and Gender Identity, 17 Elder L. J. 95 (2009) (discussing the
types of discrimination elder LGBT people face in nursing homes and examining federal and state law responses).

F.   PEOPLE WITH DISABILITIES

1.   Bioethical and Social Perspectives

Mary Crossley, Becoming Visible: The ADA's Impact on Health Care for Persons with Disabilities
52 Ala. L. Rev. 51, 57-60 (2000)

When Congress enacted the Americans with Disabilities Act ("ADA") in
1990, it included the underlying legislative "findings and purposes" in the
statute itself and stated as one of its findings that "discrimination against individuals with disabilities persists in such critical areas as . . . health services." Congress went on to announce that it was the ADA's purpose "to provide a clear and
comprehensive national mandate for the elimination of discrimination against
individuals with disabilities." Based on these statements, one would surmise that
in 1990 Congress believed that all was not well when it came to the ability of
Americans with disabilities to access and receive needed health services. Indeed,
the voluminous legislative history that underpins the ADA includes ample testimony regarding the barriers that people with disabilities faced in obtaining
health care. . . .

As anticipated by commentators writing at the time of the ADA's passage,
the statute generally has been a powerful tool for addressing denials of access to
medical treatment for persons with disabilities, denials that often reflect health
care providers' prejudices and fears. A provider's refusal to treat a person based
on that person's disability is probably the most direct and overt form of disability

discrimination in the health care context, and it is a form of discrimination that can predictably lead to both adverse physical consequences for the individual who may not be able to obtain needed medical treatment and psychic harm flowing from the overt rejection by the health care provider.

The Supreme Court's first case interpreting the ADA, Bragdon v. Abbott, exemplifies the statute's application to this type of situation. In that case, dentist Randon Bragdon refused to fill a cavity of Sidney Abbott, a woman with HIV infection, in his office. Abbott sued under Title III of the ADA, which prohibits disability discrimination by the operator of a place of public accommodation, a term that expressly includes the "professional office of a health care provider." While the dentist argued that providing the requested services in his office would pose a "direct threat" of HIV transmission to him, the district court rejected this reasoning and granted summary judgment to the plaintiff. The court's analysis indicates that—absent a "direct threat" or some other defense—a refusal to provide dental treatment to an individual based on the individual's disability constitutes an ADA violation.

The question of when the direct threat defense may be invoked ultimately went to the Supreme Court, which addressed whether deference should be paid to the individual judgment of a health care provider regarding the existence of a significant risk of transmission. The Court concluded that the existence of significant risk and direct threat, while it should be determined from the standpoint of the person who refuses to provide treatment, must be assessed based on objective medical or scientific information. To put it simply, a health care provider cannot avoid ADA liability for refusal to treat merely by pointing to his good faith belief that treatment would pose a direct threat to him, unless that belief is also supported by objective evidence. The Supreme Court's judgment thereby reinforces the principle that subjective prejudices and irrational fears are not a legitimate basis for depriving individuals with disabilities of access to treatment. . . .

While refusal to treat cases arising under the ADA have most commonly been brought by plaintiffs with HIV infection, the statute's protection of the right of an individual not to be denied access to medical treatment based on disability has also come into play in cases involving individuals with other disabilities, including hearing impairments and Alzheimer disease. And for the person who might be turned away from a doctor's office, dentist's office, or hospital because of a disability, this is a crucial protection that enables him to access health care treatment necessary to preserve his life or health or to increase his functioning.

2.   Legal Approaches

|| ***Sumes v. Andres*** ||
|| **938 F. Supp. 9 (D.D.C. 1996)** ||

Opinion by GREENE.

This case involves claims under the section 504 of the Rehabilitation Act of 1973, 29 U.S.C. §794, and the D.C. Human Rights Act ("DCHRA"), D.C. Code

§1-2519.[1] Because the parties sharply contest the factual background of this case, the Court will briefly outline each side's version of the facts. Plaintiff is a deaf woman who was pregnant at the time relevant to the instant action. Plaintiff visited the office of defendant, an obstetrician, seeking prenatal care. During the visit, plaintiff was accompanied by her mother, who was interpreting for her. Plaintiff asserts that as soon as defendant walked into the examining room and was told by plaintiff's mother that plaintiff was deaf, he stepped back and said "all deaf people are high risk," refused to treat plaintiff, and said that she should go to a high risk center. According to plaintiff, plaintiff's mother then told defendant that plaintiff was not feeling well and might have a fever, and inquired if he could examine her briefly and stabilize her if necessary before they went to another center. Defendant refused and left the room. Plaintiff maintains that defendant never asked about her health or medical history, and did not perform an examination at any time.

According to defendant, his practice is limited to low risk patients. He will not treat individuals who have symptoms such as fever and nausea unless such an individual is a prior patient of his. Plaintiff was not a prior patient of his, and according to defendant, she had never previously seen an obstetrician or gynecologist. Defendant maintains that he referred plaintiff to a high risk center after plaintiff's mother had told him that plaintiff was not feeling well and had been feverish. He testified that he was also concerned that her deafness might be the result of some underlying congenital condition that he did not feel qualified to evaluate. He thus maintains that the reason he did not treat plaintiff is because she appeared to be suffering from a medical condition that was outside of the area of his specialty. He points to the fact that plaintiff was in fact suffering from another condition—when she went to a hospital after defendant declined to treat her, she was diagnosed with a kidney infection. He also notes that her deafness is a result of a congenital condition, Waardenburg Syndrome. However, he concedes that he was not aware of the fact that plaintiff suffered from this condition until the present lawsuit was initiated.

The parties have stipulated to the following facts: (1) that plaintiff is a "disabled person" as defined by the Rehabilitation Act and has a "disability" as defined by the D.C. Human Rights Act; (2) defendant receives "federal financial assistance" through the Medicaid program and thus is subject to the Rehabilitation Act; and (3) at the time of plaintiff's visit to defendant's office, she was one to two months pregnant. . . .

To prevail on the Rehabilitation Act claim, plaintiff must show: (a) she is a disabled person, (b) she was "otherwise qualified" to receive treatment from defendant, (c) defendant refused to treat her "solely by reason of" her disability, and (d) defendant receives federal financial assistance. In light of the parties' stipulations, the issues for the Court to resolve are whether plaintiff was "otherwise qualified" to receive treatment from defendant and whether defendant refused to treat plaintiff "solely by reason of" her disability.

Under the Rehabilitation Act, an individual is "qualified" to receive services if she "meets the essential eligibility requirements for the receipt of such

---

1. Plaintiff's request for injunctive relief—which included a claim under the Americans with Disabilities Act, 42 U.S.C. §§12181–12189—was resolved on summary judgment. Both parties waived their right to a jury trial and therefore, the trial was presented to the bench.

services." In the provision of medical services, the issue becomes whether "there is no factor apart from the mere existence of disability that renders that participant unqualified for the [services]."

A health care provider may consider any genuine medical risks associated with plaintiff's disability, but he "must also consider whether it is possible to make reasonable accommodations to enable the patient to [be treated] despite those risks." Accordingly, a provider "may not withhold medical benefits, without reasonable accommodation, solely based on a participant's disability, but may only act pursuant to a bona fide medical reason."

Plaintiff must first make a prima facie showing that she was otherwise qualified to be treated; the burden then shifts to defendant to show that plaintiff was not in fact qualified. Generally, when undertaking an "otherwise qualified" inquiry, "courts should normally defer to the reasonable medical judgments of public health officials." However, "[a] strict rule of deference would enable doctors to offer merely pretextual medical opinions to cover up discriminatory decisions." Thus, a plaintiff may prevail if she can show that the reason given by defendant is a pretext or that it "encompasses unjustified consideration of the handicap itself."

The Court finds that plaintiff visited the office of defendant while she was pregnant, and thus was qualified to receive prenatal care. The Court finds nothing about her disability that would disqualify her from receiving such care from defendant. Nor was she suffering from any other condition that would preclude defendant from treating her. Therefore, the Court finds that plaintiff was "otherwise qualified" within the meaning of the Rehabilitation Act.

The Court also finds that defendant refused to treat plaintiff solely by reason of her disability. The Court credits the evidence presented by plaintiff that immediately upon learning she was deaf, defendant refused to treat her. The Court finds that defendant made such a refusal before he learned that plaintiff was suffering from a fever and before he questioned plaintiff about her medical or family history. To the extent that plaintiff may have been sweating or shivering, the Court finds that defendant's failure to take her temperature or to ask her any questions about her illness undermines any claim that the reason he refused to treat her was because he believed she was suffering from a condition that he was not qualified to treat. Furthermore, the fact that she was later diagnosed with a kidney infection is irrelevant, because defendant had no knowledge of that condition when he refused to treat her. Nor could he have had such knowledge because of his failure to ask her any questions about her symptoms or medical history. The Court finds that he had no "bona fide medical reason" for refusing to treat plaintiff and thus concludes that the sole reason defendant refused to treat her was because she was deaf. Accordingly, the Court finds in favor of plaintiff on the Rehabilitation Act claim.

[For the most part, the court's analysis of the plaintiff's D.C. Human Rights Act claim parallels its analysis of her claim under §504 of the Rehabilitation Act of 1973.] . . .

The remaining issue for the Court to resolve is the amount of damages that should be awarded to plaintiff. After plaintiff left the defendant's office, she proceeded directly to the emergency room where she received the necessary attention for what was later diagnosed as a kidney infection. Thus, plaintiff suffered no physical or medical injury from defendant's refusal to treat her.

However, plaintiff may recover compensatory damages for humiliation, embarrassment, and emotional pain and suffering under both statutes. A finding of humiliation and embarrassment flows naturally from a finding of discrimination.

Plaintiff testified that defendant's actions towards her made her feel angry, irritated, dismissed, and like less of a person. The Court credits this testimony. Furthermore, at the time of defendant's discriminatory acts, plaintiff was pregnant, was at defendant's office for her first visit to an obstetrician-gynecologist, and was waiting in the examining room disrobed, except for a hospital gown, from the waist down. Upon consideration of these facts, the Court believes that an award of compensatory damages in the amount of $10,000 is appropriate. . . .

For the above-stated reasons, the Court concludes that defendant violated the Rehabilitation Act and the D.C. Human Rights Act when he refused to treat plaintiff on July 18, 1994. Accordingly, the Court shall enter judgment in favor of plaintiff in the amount of $10,000.

NOTES AND QUESTIONS

1. *Discrimination against HIV-positive patients.* As Mary Crossley, supra, reports, most plaintiffs in refusal-to-treat cases brought under the Americans with Disabilities Act have been HIV-positive. One such case commenced in 2002 involved an Arizona surgeon and the clinic with which he worked. In 2004, the surgeon entered into an agreement with the Department of Justice, in settlement of a claim made under the ADA by an HIV-positive patient. The suit claimed that the surgeon had refused to operate on the patient's shoulder because the surgeon feared the risk of HIV infection. As part of a consent decree, the surgeon agreed to pay $120,000 to the patient and $20,000 to the government. In addition, the defendant/surgeon's clinic (specializing in sports medicine, among other things) agreed to have each of its medical employees trained in the treatment of HIV-positive patients. The clinic further agreed to effect a policy providing for the termination of any employee refusing to treat a patient because of that patient's HIV-positive status. Surgeon Who Refused to Treat HIV-Positive Man Settles Suit, 19 AIDS Policy and Law 8 (2004); Robert Anglen, Doctor Settles with HIV-Positive Patient, The Arizona Republic, Feb. 10, 2004, at 10B.

2. *Insurance company limit on coverage for treatment of AIDS.*   In Doe v. Mutual of Omaha, 179 F.3d 557 (7th Cir. 1999), cert. denied, 528 U.S. 1106 (2000), plaintiffs relied on the ADA to challenge the insurance company's policy of putting a cap on benefits related to treatment for AIDS or AIDS-related conditions. Judge Posner, for the Seventh Circuit, reversed the district court in dismissing the suit. Crossley, supra, comments:

> [T]he court pointed out, Mutual of Omaha sold policies to the plaintiffs, apparently on the same terms and with the same coverage limitations provided to other insureds—the policies were simply less valuable to the plaintiffs because of the cap on AIDS coverage.
>
> Without discussing the point explicitly, the court thus implicitly recognizes that the plaintiffs are complaining of the AIDS cap's disparate impact on people with the disabling condition AIDS. Other courts, in suits challenging as

discriminatory a provision uniformly included in insurance policies have reasoned explicitly that, because all insureds are subject to the same provision, no discrimination has occurred. Such courts fail to recognize the application of disparate impact theory to insurance practices; just because everyone is treated the same does not mean that a practice is nondiscriminatory.

Crossley, supra, at 80–81. How might one justify the decision not to apply disparate impact theory to an insurance provision such as that at issue in *Mutual of Omaha?* How might you argue that such a provision should not be justified?

3. *Decisions against treatment on "futility" grounds and other "end of life" issues.* See Chapter 7 for further exploration of concerns about disability discrimination relating to issues of withdrawing or withholding life-sustaining treatment.

CHALLENGING ISSUES: ACCOMMODATING PATIENTS WHO ARE DISABLED

Kayla Royce is being treated by Dr. Gary Taylor for a rather complicated dermatological condition that seems to become worse at times of stress in Kayla's life. Kayla is especially concerned about the condition because it has begun to leave scars on her arms. She is worried that the condition may spread, and about the possibility that it might be caused by allergies or that it might be contagious. Kayla is also concerned about any risk the skin condition might pose to her two-year-old son.

Kayla is deaf and relies primarily on a combination of sign language and lip reading to communicate with others. During Kayla's four visits to Gary Taylor's office, the doctor has communicated with Kayla through writing and lip reading; he has also relied on the National Relay Service when using the telephone. In addition, Kayla's hearing-impaired sister, Beth, has accompanied Kayla to the doctor's office and has served as an interpreter. However, Beth is not trained to interpret between hearing and deaf people and was unfamiliar with some medical language that Dr. Taylor used in conversations with Kayla.

Under the Americans with Disabilities Act (ADA), a doctor's office is defined as a place of public accommodation. Under the statute, a place of public accommodation is required to provide equal services to disabled people as are provided to other people. The regulations implementing the ADA provide that for hearing-impaired people this may involve providing

> [q]ualified interpreters, notetakers, computer-aided transcription services, written materials, telephone handset amplifiers, assistive listening devices, assistive listening systems . . . or other effective methods of making aurally delivered materials available to individuals with hearing impairments.

28 C.F.R. §36.303(b)(1).

Kayla believes that Dr. Taylor should provide her with a trained interpreter (at no extra cost to her). Do you think Kayla should be provided for in this way? If so, do you think that Kayla should have to request such assistance if she wants it or do you think that Dr. Taylor should offer to provide such assistance to her before she asks for it?

G.   CHILDREN WHO ARE SICK OR DISABLED

1.   Bioethical and Social Perspectives

Martha A. Field, Killing "The Handicapped"—Before and after Birth
16 Harv. Women's L.J. 79, 81–83, 96–97 (1993)

The story of the Bloomington Baby Doe provides a context in which to think about the [nontreatment of handicapped newborns]. It was an important case historically, partly because it first turned substantial public attention to the nontreatment problem. Moreover, the case illustrates well many of the difficult and recurring issues.

In 1982 a baby was born in Bloomington, Indiana, who had a blocked esophagus—a medical condition that prevented him from swallowing. The usual course would have been to correct the condition by operating so that the child could ingest food and drink, and in the interim to feed him intravenously. The operation was neither new nor experimental; it had at least a ninety-percent success rate. This baby—who came to be known as Baby Doe—also happened to have Down syndrome, so it was reasonably projected that he would have some mental retardation. (The extent of retardation is usually not apparent at such an early age and was not apparent in this case.)

Because of his retardation, the parents decided that the operation should not be performed and that the baby should not be fed intravenously. The doctors' Hippocratic Oath prohibited the giving of a lethal injection, so the baby was slowly starved in the far corner of the newborn ward. (Phenobarbital and morphine were administered to aid with the baby's pain.) A pediatrician and nurse, along with others, sought a court order to feed the infant, but the judge ruled that the parents, acting together with doctors, were entitled to let the child die.

When the case was publicized, families came forward who wanted to adopt the baby. Surprising as it seems to some people, there is in fact a well-developed adoption market for Down syndrome children. Would-be adopters include parents of other Down syndrome children and others who have had some contact with mental retardation and believe that parenting children with retardation can be rewarding. But the parents of Baby Doe resisted the adoption offer, saying that they had decided to let their baby die not to fulfill their own selfish interests, but because they believed that course would be in the best interests of the child. On this basis, they claimed, they also had the right to resist the offer of adoption. . . .

I believe that recognizing parental discretion over the life of newborns who have handicaps is not only immoral and unwise, but also illegal under constitutional and statutory law. But because the Supreme Court has not passed on the issue, and other courts' opinions on the subject are rare, the law today has not fully developed. . . .

What would be the consequences of holding that giving parents special discretion applicable only to children with handicaps is prohibited discrimination? First, if a government were to allow killing of newborns up to three days old because the parents were distressed, the discretion should extend to parents of nonhandicapped children as well as children with disabilities. But, in fact, today no right of infanticide is recognized for parents of nonhandicapped newborns; they are prosecuted if they kill their newborn child. If they were to decide against necessary medical treatment, doctors or the hospital would go to court and get an order to treat over their objection.

On the other hand, if parents' freedom to choose extended only to the freedom to protect themselves with contraception, then abortion for handicap could be prevented as well—indeed, it would have to be.

For purposes of this argument I take no position on what is the moment at which parental discretion should begin or end, saying simply that whatever the line is for the nonhandicapped, that same line must apply to "the handicapped" as well. . . .

If the nondiscrimination principle is used to resolve the Baby Doe debate, as I think it should be, it is worth noting that it resolves the two major problems in administering a Baby Doe rule—which newborns will be covered, and how long the right will last. It is no longer necessary to identify a special vulnerable category, because all newborns will be given life on the same basis. And requiring that handicapped newborns be treated like a group more like the legislators and like the majority—the nonhandicapped—provides some safeguard against the right being extended for too long a period of time. Predictably it would be the rare jurisdiction that would move to enact parental discretion after birth, when that discretion applied to newborns without disabilities as well as to those with them. The equal protection/antidiscrimination approach often serves this function of assuring fairer treatment of vulnerable or unpopular groups.

Mary Crossley, *Of Diagnoses and Discrimination: Discriminatory Nontreatment of Infants with HIV Infection* 93 Colum. L. Rev. 1581, 1618, 1624–1627 (1993)

A fundamental ethical question posed by both the Baby Doe controversy and [other, similar cases involving newborns with life-threatening but treatable conditions and with other, nontreatable or less treatable underlying conditions such as HIV-infection] . . . is what standards should guide medical decision-makers making treatment choices for an infant incapable of making its own autonomous choices. The general model of medical decisionmaking . . . requires physician deference to patient autonomy and thus does not suit treatment decision-making for a disabled infant. . . .

[T]he danger of quality of life standards that either consider the social worth of a disabled infant or measure the infant's life against an "acceptable" life lies in their subjectivity and variability. These characteristics describe a moral landscape in which "slippery slope" objections carry considerable force, particularly when surrounding circumstances (such as movements towards health care rationing and the social stigma attached to HIV infection . . .) increase the danger that morally unacceptable decisions may be made. In other words, once we accept that the burdens an individual imposes on society are a valid consideration in deciding whether to provide medical treatment to that individual, how are we to assess how severe the burden must be before we

ethically can consider it? Should the burdens a prisoner or a chronically mentally ill person imposes factor into decisions whether those persons should
receive life-saving medical treatment? If not, where and how should the line
be drawn?

Another approach accepts the validity of considering an infant's quality of
life, but attempts to conduct the assessment solely from the infant's own
perspective. This quality of life approach directs that treatment decisions accord
with the "best interests of the child," so that the only relevant benefits and
burdens to be weighed are those experienced by the child. . . . [T]his best interests of the child standard recognizes that in some cases medical treatment and
continued life may impose a burden on an infant that is not outweighed by any
benefits to be gained by continued life. Moreover, this standard accepts that an
infant's mental and physical condition, including the effects of any disability,
should weigh in the benefits–burdens calculus.

Not only does the best interests standard limit consideration of benefits
and burdens to those experienced by the infant; it also seeks to weigh alternatives from the disabled infant's point of view. In other words, the proper comparison is not between the quality of life experienced by a "normal" infant and
the quality of life expected for this disabled infant, but between this infant's
prospective quality of life and no life at all. Thus, a severe disability may justify
withholding medical treatment from an infant, but only when the burdens
resulting from the disability are so extreme that, from the infant's perspective,
continued life offers no overriding benefit.

While even advocates of a best interests standard have acknowledged its
"staggering problems of interpretation and application," including the
potential influence of the decision-maker's subjective biases, many commentators have embraced it as the morally preferable approach to making treatment
decisions because it seeks to focus exclusively and realistically on the infant's
welfare.

By focusing on the child's interests, this standard avoids morally dubious
utilitarian justifications based on the well-being of other interested parties, such
as parents, siblings, or even of society at large; and by giving full weight to the
child's interests, this approach can justify nontreatment in certain cases without
having to make the (usually pernicious) assumption that the child is a nonper-
son with no standing in the human community.

This approach also best satisfies the principle of justice by holding medical
decisions for disabled newborns to the same standard—a best interests
standard—as medical decisions for other noncompetent patients who have
not previously expressed their autonomous desires regarding treatment choices.

Anita Silvers & Leslie Pickering Francis, *Playing God with Baby Doe: Quality of Life and Unpredictable Life Standards at the Start of Life*
25 Ga. St. U. L. Rev. 1061 (2009)

CAPTA [Child Abuse Prevention and Treatment Act] protection for
infants with disabilities has been criticized for interfering with parents' rights
to decide what is in the best interests of their child. This objection begs the

question, however, by failing to acknowledge that the impetus for developing protection for infants with disabilities arose from cases in which the parents' motivation appeared compromised, prompted by the prospect of disability to misjudge what was in the child's best interest, or to discount the child's interest for that reason. While parents have the right to shape their children, children are not their parents' property but are entrusted to them. Both the regulations formulated under Section 504 [of the Rehabilitation Act of 1973], and the CAPTA directives, aim at circumstances in which parents, either from ignorance or ill will, do not merit that trust.

Consideration of the fate of the original Baby Doe, as well as of the future open to him had he lived (a future his parents apparently were ignorant about, or else ignored), illuminates how disability bias operates and the importance of confronting it. This was a case in which the parents were influenced by the obstetrician who delivered the baby and also delivered a deeply gloomy prognosis about the quality of the child's future life. While their obstetrician advised the parents to withhold treatment, other physicians, including the family's doctor, as well as the hospital administration, disagreed.

As to which of these competing views would have survived the test of time, Kopelman[7] writes in 2005 that "Baby Doe died in 1982; as more has been learned about trisomy 21, there has been greater agreement about the duty to provide life-saving treatments for infants with this condition." Yet this way of putting the facts may be misread as suggesting that from 1982 to 2008, accurate judgment about the quality of life attainable by individuals with Down syndrome improved due to greater scientific understanding of the chromosomal anomaly, trisomy 21, which is correlated with Down syndrome. But this is not so.

No knowledge about the biology of trisomy 21 has caused the elevation of social status and expansion of opportunity that over the past quarter century has enriched the quality of life of people with Down syndrome now can enjoy in the United States. In earlier times, the inability of such individuals to read, to live independently, and to contribute as citizens, were claimed as incontrovertible fact. Today many citizens with Down syndrome engage in all these activities.

Instead, federal protection against disability discrimination during the past quarter century now offers more equitable opportunity to people with Down syndrome. We know that individuals with Down can learn to read only because those born after the middle of the 1970s were given full access to schooling where they were taught to read. Their generation was the earliest to be afforded an education equivalent to that offered to nondisabled children. Learning that people with trisomy 21 can read was not a matter of learning about trisomy 21 (no one has correlated any part of the triplicated chromosome with reading ability or its absence), but rather a matter of learning about (and eliminating) the effects of disability discrimination on educational opportunity. Ironically, had parents of children with trisomy 21 born in the early 1980s all made the same mistaken assessment of their children's potential as Baby Doe's parents did, greater knowledge about the capabilities of individuals with trisomy 21 likely would not have been achieved, nor would the greater agreement on the duty to save these children's lives that, according to Kopelman, now prevails.

---

7. Referring to Loretta M. Kopelman, Are the 21-Year-Old Baby Doe Rules Misunderstood or Mistaken?, 115 Pediatrics 797 (2005).–Eds.

. . . Hindsight into the baselessness of past prognostications of the social burdensomeness of disability does not seem to have led to nonbiased procedures for deliberating about medical treatment of anomalous infants today. Commentators agree that cases of extreme prematurity have replaced cases of congenital anomalies such as trisomy 21 or spina bifida in the center of debates about which infants should be treated aggressively. Diagnosed with trisomy 21, there was no doubt that the original Baby Doe was disabled. In contrast, there is much more variation in outcomes for extreme prematurity: an extremely premature or very low birthweight or extremely low birthweight infant may later be diagnosed with a disability, but the nature and degree of impairment, if any, may not be evident in the first hours, days or weeks of life. The conditions of these infants therefore should be less likely to lend themselves to incautiously pessimistic prognostications. Yet the opposite response to them seems to prevail, making them as subject to dire predictions about the value of their prospective lives as infants with traditional disabling conditions have been.

About 1.4% of U.S. babies are born with birth weights of less than 1,500 grams. Various reports show the incidence of cerebral palsy (CP) among this group as 7–10% of very low birth weight infants (1,250 to 1,500 grams) and 7–17% of extremely low birthweight infants (under 1,250 grams), with the effects of CP ranging from relatively mild below the knee lameness to quadriplegia. Different studies set the risk of major neurosensory or neurological disability at from 12% to 50% for extreme prematurity. About 40% of extremely low birth weight children have IQs of less than seventy, an outcome correlated as well with severe intraventricular hemorrhage. Various antenatal events may stimulate fetal inflammatory responses that can injure immature cerebral white matter. Further, there is evidence that certain therapeutic interventions are associated with adverse neurodevelopmental outcomes. Studies also suggest that extremely premature infants with parenting, social and environmental risk factors are at increased risk for neurodevelopmental disabilities.

Although extremely low birthweight babies sometimes suffer from conditions that may lead to disability (for example, patent ductis arteriosis, retinopathy of prematurity, respiratory distress syndrome) or worse, these conditions are not themselves diagnoses of disability, or disabling anomalies, as trisomy 21 and spina bifida (except sometimes for a low or incomplete lesion) are. These conditions may or may not lead to disability, as may other medical problems associated with prematurity. Thus neither extreme prematurity nor extremely low birthweight, nor diagnoses associated with prematurity such as those mentioned above, actually qualify infants as "disabled" and thereby as categorically entitled to the life-saving services designated by CAPTA's famous fourteen words. Although it was evident that the original Baby Doe would prove to be cognitively impaired, it was (and still is) impossible to tell at birth whether the disability of a baby with trisomy 21 will be mild, moderate or severe. Predictions about the future abilities and disabilities of premature neonates are even more tenuous, especially as the occasioning of disabling impairments in them is not very well understood.

. . . A telling illustration of the tenuousness of such predictions is the current commentary concerning the cost of supporting the Los Angeles octuplets. For example, a well-known physician told television audiences that "[t]here is a relatively small chance that all eight of th[e]se kids will grow up to be normal adults. There's going to be a chance of cerebral palsy, developmental delays[—]emotionally, mentally [—]vision problems, hearing problems." In the context of questions about their mother's relying on public aid, such a comment conjures up visions of extraordinary demands on the welfare system, imposed by the presence of (possibly eight more) disabled individuals brought into the world.

Yet the precise probability of the manifestation of any of this list of conditions is unclear, nor is there a perspicacious basis for the claim that they have just a relatively small chance of growing up nondisabled. Notice that this is a very different claim than that they have a higher than typical risk of not doing so. For one thing, as octuplets their risk of disability presumably should be calculated with some reference to the outcomes of other octuplet live births. The last octuplet birth in the United States was ten years ago, and the seven surviving ten-year-olds are not disabled. Further, almost all birth weights of the recently born octuplets are greater than the birth weight of the largest octuplet of ten years ago, and unlike their predecessors all were weaned off ventilators soon after birth. As extremely low birth weight and ventilator dependence in neonates are correlated with ensuing disability, statistically speaking the new octuplets are much less likely than their nondisabled ten-year-old predecessors to have disabilities. Not to mention the improvements in medical care for preterm neonates that have been achieved in the past ten years. Yet even physicians who should understand these probabilities seem to issue hyperbolic warnings about the prospective burden of disability such infants may impose on society, nor are there professional guidelines or a standard of community practice to restrain them from doing so.

. . . [A] clear historical record exists to show how vagueness about risk encourages exaggerating the burdensomeness of living with disability and sometimes curtails disabled people's access to social opportunity and even to life itself. Yet the ethics of incertitude in medical prognosis, applying statistics drawn from research on cohorts to make prognoses about individual cases, is not very well researched.

Compared to the volume of bioethics literature criticizing supposedly unfortunate influences of the Baby Doe rules on physicians' freedom to judge, not a lot has been written about how, in doing so, physicians should deal with uncertainty about prospects of disability in Baby Doe cases without opening the door to the deleterious effects of disability discrimination. Model guidelines for avoiding disability discrimination in deliberating about courses of medical intervention for extremely low birth weight or extremely premature infants thus would be helpful in facilitating ethical decision making. But the feasibility and success of such a program depends on how far physicians and hospitals have progressed since the initial Baby Doe cases in distancing themselves from disability discrimination. In this regard, too, the prognosis for future Baby Does is obscure.

NOTES AND QUESTIONS

1. *Legal response to withholding treatment from newborns.*   The *Baby Doe* case, described in Martha Field's article, supra, generated widespread debate about the treatment of disabled newborns. One result of that debate was the Child Abuse Amendments of 1984, Pub. L. No. 98-457, 98 Stat. 749 (codified as

amended 42 U.S.C. §§5101–5106 (2004)). The law, an amendment to the Child Abuse Prevention and Treatment Act, required states to set up procedures for responding to cases in which treatment was being withheld from disabled newborns for the state to be eligible for the receipt of funds geared toward the prevention of child abuse and neglect. The legislation gave the Department of Health and Human Services authority to devise regulations for implementing the law. The current regulations, 45 C.F.R. §1340.15, printed infra, are referred to as the Baby Doe rules. The excerpt from Anita Silvers and Leslie Pickering Francis calls out some in the medical establishment for suggesting that the rules are no longer needed—as if the attitudes that were present before the Baby Doe regulations were not widespread or have been eradicated. What do Silvers and Francis suggest changed those attitudes? What category of newborns do they identify as now at risk of discrimination?

2. *HIV-infected children.* Crossley's article, supra, focuses on medical and legal responses to HIV-infected newborns in the early years of the HIV/AIDS crisis. During that time, older children who were HIV positive and or who had AIDS also faced discrimination in medical, educational, and other environments. In the 1980s, soon after AIDS was recognized, a number of school districts decided either to bar HIV-positive children and children with AIDS or to treat them differently from other children. Since that time, a number of changes have occurred—in both medicine and law—to alter the societal treatment of children with HIV. Maternal-fetal transmission of HIV has been dramatically reduced through medical treatment, and the Americans with Disabilities Act of 1990 has been interpreted to cover HIV-positive status. See Bragdon v. Abbott, 524 U.S. 62 (1998). Discrimination is not completely eradicated, however, as revealed in a case from 2011 involving the denial of admission of an HIV-positive teenager to a boarding school for which he appeared to be otherwise qualified. The school, Milton Hershey, entered a settlement agreement with the child, his mother, and the U.S. Justice Department, which, upon investigating the complaint, found that the school had violated the ADA. The settlement agreement can be found at http://www.ada.gov/milton-hershey_sa_aids.htm.

3. *Conflict over treatment decisions.* Differences of opinion between parents and physicians involving HIV-infected children have sometimes resulted in legal action. In re Nikolas, 720 A.2d 562 (Me. 1998), involved a dispute between the state of Maine and a mother who rejected a doctor's treatment recommendations for her HIV-infected son. The Supreme Court of Maine supported the trial court's holding in favor of the mother's right to make her son's treatment decision and thus denied the state's petition for a child protection order. Judge Wathen for the Maine court concluded:

> We emphasize that the decision required the trial court to weigh the interests of the State, the child, and the parents, and to balance the benefits and risks of treatment against the benefits and risks of declining treatment. If the child's health should change, if the treatment efficacy should be demonstrated to be better than it is now known to be, or if better treatment options should become available, that balance could shift in favor of treatment. Neither the parents nor the State should assume that the trial court's decision, affirmed by our opinion today, is necessarily the final word on treatment for Nikolas.

Id. at 568. One commentator has concluded that Maine law would have permitted the judge to have held for the state. That it did not, she explains, was probably a product of the court's "sympathy for [the mother's] plight more than a sense that the law was on her side." Kimberly Mutcherson, No Way to Treat a Woman: Creating an Appropriate Standard for Resolving Medical Treatment Disputes Involving HIV-Positive Children, 25 Harv. Women's L.J. 221, 270 (2002). Mutcherson argues that the mother in In re Nikolas would not have become the object of a state petition for a protective order against her had she not been poor and comparatively uneducated. Mutcherson asserts that this mother "presented an easy target for a system that perhaps found it difficult to imagine that a woman in [her] situation could make an informed decision about her child's healthcare." *Id.* at 276. If you agree with Mutcherson's assessment, how might a state handle such cases?

4. *Practical usefulness of Child Abuse Amendments of 1984.* Many queries have been raised about the practical usefulness of the Child Abuse Amendments of 1984. Martha Field, in other, unprinted parts of her article, defines reliance on state enforcement as a problem because some states do not carry out that task with care. More particularly, she asserts that child protective services may defer to hospitals, thus undermining the deterrence value of rules aimed at monitoring hospital responses to disabled babies. In addition, the rules seem nebulous enough to allow hospital decision makers wide scope for responding to disabled newborns. Mary Crossley, considering how the Child Abuse Amendments and regulations apply to an HIV-positive infant also suffering from some other life-threatening condition, concludes that the mandate of the rules remains "elusive." Crossley, *supra,* at 1630. As a starting position, the rules require hospitals to treat the infant's life-threatening condition. However, notes Crossley, the exception relating to treatment that will "merely prolong dying" might apply. At the time when there were no effective treatments for AIDS, the infant might be viewed as in the process of "dying" from that underlying condition. The Department of Health and Human Services has interpreted the exception to exclude cases in which a condition may become life-threatening at some point in the future. It is not clear, however, as Crossley explains, whether the infant's HIV status should be taken as evidence that the infant is in the process of dying or that the infant has a condition that may one day become life-threatening.

For additional analyses of the Child Abuse Amendments of 1984, see Thomas William Mayo, Health Care Law, 55 SMU L. Rev. 1113 (2002); Comment, James W. Curry, The Federal Policy on the Selective Non-Treatment of Severely Handicapped Neonates: A Compassionate Response to the Death of Baby Doe?, 25 Cumb. L. Rev. 631 (1994).

5. *Limits of parent's right not to have a child.* Martha Field added an appendix to her article, "Killing the Handicapped . . . ," supra, that stimulates debate about the limitations of a parent's right to choose not to have children. Field lists what she describes as "different moments in the developmental process that might be adopted as the cut-off for parental discretion." Field, supra, at 104. She begins with the moment of sexual intercourse. Were the right to choose precluded at this point, then contraception would be impermissible. Next she asks about the moment of conception, of implantation, and so on. She then asks whether the parent's right to choose should extend to the moment of birth, or even later. The last option on Field's list is "sixty years after birth," followed by "etc." With regard to a forty-year-old child, Field asks:

> Should parents or guardians have the right to terminate the life of a conscious adult child because of mental retardation or other handicaps? Usually more is

required before their decision to do so could be controlling. Persons who have disabilities, like others, should not be allowed to die through another person's decision unless they satisfy the criteria regarding "right to die" that the state applies to all persons.

Field, supra, at 137.

2. *Legal Approaches*

---

45 C.F.R. 1350.15 (Services and Treatment for Disabled Infants)

(a) Purpose. The regulations in this section implement certain provisions of the Act, including section 107(b)(10) governing the protection and care of disabled infants with life-threatening conditions.

(b) Definitions.

(1) ... The term "medical neglect" includes, but is not limited to, the withholding of medically indicated treatment from a disabled infant with a life-threatening condition.

(2) The term "withholding of medically indicated treatment" means the failure to respond to the infant's life-threatening conditions by providing treatment (including appropriate nutrition, hydration, and medication) which, in the treating physician's (or physicians') reasonable medical judgment, will be most likely to be effective in ameliorating or correcting all such conditions, except that the term does not include the failure to provide treatment (other than appropriate nutrition, hydration, or medication) to an infant when, in the treating physician's (or physicians') reasonable medical judgment any of the following circumstances apply:

(i) The infant is chronically and irreversibly comatose:

(ii) The provision of such treatment would merely prolong dying, not be effective in ameliorating or correcting all of the infant's life-threatening conditions, or otherwise be futile in terms of the survival of the infant; or

(iii) The provision of such treatment would be virtually futile in terms of the survival of the infant and the treatment itself under such circumstances would be inhumane.

(3) Following are definitions of terms used in paragraph (b)(2) of this section:

(i) The term "infant" means an infant less than one year of age. The reference to less than one year of age shall not be construed to imply that treatment should be changed or discontinued when an infant reaches one year of age, or to affect or limit any existing protections available under State laws regarding medical neglect of children over one year of age. In addition to their applicability to infants less than one year of age, the standards set forth in paragraph (b)(2) of this section should be consulted thoroughly in the evaluation of any issue of medical neglect involving an infant older than one year of age who has been continuously hospitalized since birth, who was born extremely prematurely, or who has a long-term disability.

(ii) The term "reasonable medical judgment" means a medical judgment that would be made by a reasonably prudent physician, knowledgeable about the case and the treatment possibilities with respect to the medical conditions involved. . . .

(c) Eligibility requirements.

(1) . . . [T]o qualify for a basic State grant under . . . the Act, a State must have programs, procedures, or both, in place within the State's child protective service system for the purpose of responding to the reporting of medical neglect, including instances of withholding of medically indicated treatment from disabled infants with life-threatening conditions. . . .

NOTES AND QUESTIONS

1. *Discrimination against disabled children.*   Disabled children not only face discrimination in access to care at the start of life but also throughout life. In large part, the problems faced by disabled children seeking access to health care resemble those faced by disabled adults in similar situations. Several challenges to various government rules and regulations have depended on the Americans with Disabilities Act (ADA), 42 U.S.C. §§12101 et seq. (2000), which prohibits discrimination against disabled people by state government and in places of public accommodation. See, e.g., Helen L. v. DiDario, 46 F.3d 325 (3d Cir. 1995) (relying on ADA to require state Department of Public Welfare to provide health care services to disabled adult in her own home, not just in an expensive nursing home). A few cases involving children have challenged Medicaid's rules as discriminatory against those who are disabled. Skubel v. Fuoroli, 113 F.3d 330 (2d Cir. 1997), involved two children, both with serious mental and physical disabilities and both in need of constant nursing care. Both children had to be accompanied by a nurse to join in educational and community activities. Medicaid paid all or a substantial part of each child's nursing care costs. However, a Medicaid regulation limited coverage of nursing care to that provided within the child's residence. The regulation thus prevented such children from attending school or participating in social activities outside the home. The Second Circuit invalidated the regulation, concluding that it constituted an unreasonable interpretation of Congress's intention in creating Medicaid. "There does not appear to be any rational connection," the Second Circuit concluded, "between the regulation and the purpose to be served by the statute governing home nursing services. The restriction ignores the consensus among health care professionals that community access is not only possible but desirable for disabled individuals." Id. at 336. See also Detsel v. Sullivan, 895 F.2d 58 (2d Cir. 1990) (similarly invalidating Medicaid regulation that precluded Medicaid funds for child's nursing home care outside child's home). A useful summary of the law's responses to discrimination against disabled children, including a discussion of *Skubel,* can be found in Linda C. Fentiman, Health Access for Children with Disabilities, 19 Pace L. Rev. 245 (1999).

2. *Drugs and unintentional discrimination against children.*   An unintentional form of discrimination affects children who are given drugs that have been tested on adults but not comparably tested (or not tested at all) on children. Both the Food and Drug Administration in the United States and regulators in Britain have expressed concern about medications given to children to treat depression. In the last decade of the twentieth century, prescriptions of anti-depressants for children and adolescents rose threefold. Following reports of an increased suicide risk among children taking antidepressants, the FDA has warned that patients given antidepressants (regardless of age) should be monitored for a risk of suicide. In Britain, regulators have specified that only one drug (Prozac) is currently deemed appropriate for the treatment of depression in children. Robert McGough, Diagnoses of Youth Depression, Drug Prescriptions Rise Sharply, Wall St. J., May 5, 2004, at D2, col. 5.

3. *Children diagnosed with Attention Deficit Hyperactivity Disorder.*   A great deal of legal, medical, and social controversy has surrounded the diagnosis of children with Attention Deficit Hyperactivity Disorder (ADHD) and the treatments that often follow that diagnosis. As many as 17 percent of American children of school age are being diagnosed with the condition. Yet, some experts estimate that no more than 2 percent of the children in school are seriously overactive or inattentive. George Archibald, Schools Push Too Many Mood Drugs, House Told, Nation, May 7, 2003, at A3 (quoting testimony of Dr. William B. Carey, director of behavioral pediatrics at Children's Hospital of Philadelphia to a House subcommittee on educational reform). Ritalin and other psychotropic drugs are being prescribed routinely for children diagnosed with ADHD. There is significant disagreement among experts about the efficacy and consequences of long-term Ritalin use. The American Academy of Pediatrics and the National Institute of Mental Health support medicating children diagnosed with ADHD. However, some experts have concluded that drugs are not always as useful as other forms of therapy, including behavioral therapy, for children diagnosed with ADHD. Susan L. Pollet, Legal Implications of Attention Deficit/Hyperactivity Disorder, N.Y.L.J., May 9, 2003, at 4.

Diagnosing ADHD is as much an art as a science. Many commentators have suggested that the diagnosis and subsequent marginalization of children so diagnosed reflects a failure of schools and parents to deal with children at the active end of normal behavior as much as it reflects the identification of children with a treatable illness. See Victor W. Henderson, Stimulant Drug Treatment of the Attention Deficit Disorder, 65 S. Cal. L. Rev. 397, 408 (1991) (concluding that the diagnostic validity of attention deficit disorder is "unsettled").

A number of parents with school-aged children, diagnosed with ADHD, have refused to treat their children with drugs, and as a result have faced the possibility that their children would be expelled or suspended from school, or even that they would be deprived of custody of their children. Three case stories involving parental refusal to treat children diagnosed with ADHD are collected in Amy L. Komoroski, Stimulant Drug Therapy for Hyperactive Children: Adjudicating Disputes Between Parents and Educators, 11 B.U. Pub. Int. L.J. 97 (2001).

Perhaps the readiness of schools and health care workers to diagnose children with ADHD reflects broad social problems more than it reflects the actual prevalence of the condition. To the extent that society is uncertain about the range of childhood behaviors, it becomes tempting to medicalize children who are particularly problematic because they are more energetic, more demanding, more aggressive, or less focused than the majority of children.

A few class action suits have been filed against the American Psychiatric Association (APA) and Novartis Pharmaceuticals Corp., the supplier of Ritalin in the United States. See, e.g., Vess v. Ciba-Geigy Corp., 317 F.3d 1097 (S.D. Cal. 2003); Hernandez v. Ciba-Geigy Corp., 200 F.R.D. 285 (S.D. Tex. 2001). These suits are described in Iris Lan, Pharmaceuticals: Conspiracy to Increase Ritalin Profits Alleged, 29 J.L. Med. & Ethics 100 (2001). The suits allege that the APA and Novartis conspired, among other things, to define ADD and ADHD so broadly that physicians would write more and more prescriptions for Ritalin. Lan concludes by noting that some experts see the "real problem" as misdiagnosis rather than a conspiracy between the APA and Novartis. Lan explains:

> The Clinical Practice Guidelines for the diagnosis of ADHD, given by the American Academy of Pediatrics, affirms the attitude of most physicians that ADHD is a complicated condition that should be diagnosed only after a very thorough evaluation of the child's home, school, and social life. In the era of managed care, however, physicians and nurses must make quick diagnoses and prescriptions, often to the detriment of a thorough evaluation.

Id. at 101–102.

H. ELDERLY PEOPLE[8]

Access to health care for elderly people is in large part limited by the same factors that limit access to health care for younger people. These factors include social and economic status, insurance options, and the proximity of clinical care. Those factors are often products of class, race, and geography. For instance, one study of access to health care among elderly people in rural areas within the United States notes that outcome differences in the health care received by elderly people in rural areas and in urban areas "generally relate to an imbalance of volume, staff support, equipment, and choice." Thomas C. Rosenthal & Chester Fox, Access to Health Care for the Rural Elderly, 284 JAMA 2034, 2034 (2000). Those in rural areas are less likely than their urban counterparts to have easy access to hospitals, to have a choice of Medicare managed care programs, or to have specialists to whom they can turn for assistance. Id.

In addition, elderly people may be precluded from full access to health care because of discriminatory assumptions about their physical and mental abilities—what Betty Friedan refers to as the "mystique of age." "Even the most prescient of those who have studied aging until now," Friedan suggests, "can only view it as it is actually experienced in our society today."

> They can only surmise the damage imposed by the lack of purposeful roles for older people in our society, the restricted, isolating environment even for those

---

8. This section can be read in conjunction with Chapter 14 (concerned with social justice issues in health care generally).

still living in the communities of the young, the forces that *impose* the victim state upon us. . . .

How then do we move beyond the youth model of decline that binds so many gerontologists and society itself?

Betty Friedan, The Fountain of Age 127, 128 (1993).

1.   Unequal Paternalism

a.   Bioethical and Social Approaches

|| *Linda S. Whitton, Ageism: Paternalism and Prejudice* ||
46 DePaul L. Rev. 453, 453–455 (1997)

Betty Anderson is a seventy-year-old widow whose husband died two years ago leaving her financially well set with a three-hundred-thousand-dollar house and over one million dollars in investments. Several months ago Mrs. Anderson's children admitted her to Sunnyvale Retirement Center, and now she wants to return home. You have been contacted by Mrs. Anderson for legal advice.

You discover upon meeting Betty Anderson that she is a well-dressed, articulate woman. After initial pleasantries, she describes to you in narrative fashion her life of the past two years. Mrs. Anderson states that following her husband's death she was quite depressed, became prescription drug dependent, and often had a few too many cocktails in the afternoon. Her children, claiming they were having her house repainted, took her to Sunnyvale to live "temporarily." Now, she observes, they rarely visit, and when questioned about the status of her house, they respond with ever-changing excuses for why she cannot return home.

At the conclusion of your interview with Mrs. Anderson, you speak with Mr. Cory, the Social Services Director of Sunnyvale. Mr. Cory explains that Mrs. Anderson was admitted to Sunnyvale four months ago under authority granted to her son in a durable power of attorney. Attached to the power of attorney was a physician's letter certifying that, in the physician's opinion, Mrs. Anderson was incapacitated and unable to act in her own best interests. Mr. Cory also informs you that Mrs. Anderson's son has filed a petition for guardianship over Mrs. Anderson. When asked whether he believes Mrs. Anderson would be capable of living independently in her own home, Mr. Cory replies that she has made remarkable progress at Sunnyvale. He attributes her state of well-being to proper diet and the cessation of her former substance abuse. He expresses concern that if Mrs. Anderson returns home she may get lonely and depressed again and fall back into her old pattern of living. Mr. Cory admits, though, that currently there is no apparent reason why Mrs. Anderson could not live on her own. Upon further investigation, you discover that Mrs. Anderson's son has already sold her home and all of her furnishings, and that the guardianship hearing is only two weeks away.

The foregoing scenario was presented to law students in an Elder Law class as the basis for a comprehensive semester project. The fact pattern, based on a real life situation, is surprisingly not unique. The students were instructed to identify the legal issues raised by Mrs. Anderson's circumstances and to research and develop a strategy for her legal representation. They were also asked to consider the consequences, both legal and nonlegal, of planning for Mrs. Anderson's future in an environment of eroding family trust. Included in their responsibilities as Mrs. Anderson's lawyer would be the particularly difficult task of informing her of the sale of her house and identifying options for her future living arrangements.

The students were required to make an oral presentation of their conclusions and recommendations at the end of the semester. As the professor anticipated, the class discussed issues related to the validity and scope of the durable power of attorney and defense strategies for the guardianship proceeding. Unanticipated, however, were the students' recommendations concerning how an attorney should advise Mrs. Anderson about her options for the future.

A majority of the students did not even consider the purchase of another house to be a viable option for Mrs. Anderson. The most common suggestions focused on finding a "nice apartment" in a retirement community where Mrs. Anderson would be less likely to become "lonely and depressed" again. Some even suggested that it might be best not to object to the guardianship proceeding, but to negotiate instead for limited guardianship so that a supervisory mechanism would be in place should Mrs. Anderson "fall off the wagon."

Surprised by these responses after a semester of consciousness raising about ageism and stereotyping, the Elder Law professor then asked the students to reconsider the initial fact situation with one alteration in the facts: If Mrs. Anderson were thirty-five years old instead of seventy, would your advice change? Changing this one fact, the age of the client, was a catalyst for exploring previously unexamined attitudes. The class noted that if Mrs. Anderson had been thirty-five, rather than seventy, years old, concerned family members probably would have encouraged her to enroll in a rehabilitation program or to seek psychological counseling, rather than admitting her to a nursing home. In this changed context, a recommendation that Mrs. Anderson permanently give up her home because of grief-related depression would seem unreasonable if made by family members and outrageous if encouraged by her lawyer. Nonetheless, those same actions and recommendations were previously viewed as at least palatable for a woman of seventy.

NOTES AND QUESTIONS

1. *Assumptions about aged people.* Do you agree with the Elder Law students referred to in Linda Whitton's article, who concluded that the 35-year-old Mrs. Anderson should be treated differently and counseled differently than the 70-year-old Mrs. Anderson? Why or why not?

2. *Gerontophobia and professional ageism.* Whitton describes "gerontophobia" as a consequence of a combination of fear and blame. She recalls the conclusions about gerontophobia of Harold Sheppard, Presidential Counselor on Aging during Jimmy Carter's presidency. Sheppard saw antagonism to the elderly as a combination of envy (of rich elders) and resentment (of needy elders). By 1990, Sheppard concluded that the public viewed the elderly as

"greedy." Whitton remarks: "Stated another way, the public mood had shifted from mere envy and resentment to blame." Whitton, supra, at 469.

Whitton notes that geriatrics is not a field of choice among medical students. Medical school fellowships in geriatrics are so unpopular that it is not always possible to find recipients for them. Id. at n.108. She attributes the comparative scarcity of health care providers concerned with elderly populations to "professional ageism." Whitton, supra, at 472.

"Professional ageism" can develop in the guise of compassionate concern or in the form of outright contempt. Whitton explains:

> . . . Derogatory labels for elderly patients include: "gomers" (an acronym for "Get Out of My Emergency Room"), "crocks," and "dirt balls." Patronizing language which infantilizes older patients is also common. As one nursing home resident observed:
>
>> Why do you think the staff insists on talking baby talk when speaking to me? I understand English. I have a degree in music and am a certified teacher. Now I hear a lot of words that end in "y." Is this how my kids felt? My hearing aid works fine. There is little need for anyone to position their face directly in front of mine and raise their voice with those "y" words.
>
>> Other forms of compassionate ageism are manifested in treatment protocols which encourage dependency and decrease autonomy. Classic examples are daily routines in long-term care facilities that provide few choices for residents regarding their schedules and activities, or worse, the overuse of restraints.
>
>> Sometimes, there may be a fine line between compassionate ageism, which strips a patient of self-respect and autonomy, and "therapeutic nihilism," which results in undertreatment or nontreatment of the elderly. . . .

Id. at 473.

Is "compassionate ageism" necessarily paternalistic? If so, can it ever be justified? Might "compassionate ageism" be justified because elderly people suffer from physical and mental decline more often than younger people do? More specifically, does the need of some elderly people for help justify differential treatment of those (such as the woman quoted above who resents being spoken to as if she were two years old) who may be physically disabled but who are mentally competent? Would your answers be different depending on the percentage of elderly people actually in need of help with life activities? In fact, the percentage of people over 65 in nursing homes is very small—about 5 percent.

3. *An "age mystique."* In The Fountain of Age (1993), Betty Friedan comments that as she commenced research for a book about growing older she felt a deep "dread of age and personal denial." That dread and denial dissipated as Friedan located study after study that suggested a "new truth about age"—that, despite popular stereotypes, aging may involve growth and development much as do other stages of the lifespan. Id. at 10. Yet, she found even many gerontologists refused to acknowledge the reality of "productive aging." Discussants at one conference in Austria in 1983 "wanted only to talk about Alzheimer's,

senility, and nursing homes. They vehemently objected to discussing age in terms of any kind of 'productivity.'" Id. at 25–26.

Friedan notes that even those providing service to elderly people too often assume negative images of senior citizens. One nurse/social worker explained to Friedan that programs providing "compassionate services and patronizing diversions" for seniors are often "really ageist and work toward increased dependence of the elderly and increased segregation as opposed to working toward integration and independence." Id. at 58 (quoting unnamed nurse/social worker). Friedan's interviewee explained further that the large services industry aimed at offering compassionate care to seniors has "added to the problem" by working "toward securing enough resources to keep themselves and their programs funded." Id.

Friedan delineates an "age mystique," comparable to the "feminine mystique," described in her well-known book about women. The age mystique, which "distorts our view of aging," is illustrated in several psychological studies that examined images of age among people 25 to 40, 40 to 60, and over 70. Id. at 60. The two younger groups saw seniors as likely to be alone, inactive, unpleasant, and incompetent. People over 70 were more likely to see seniors as active and engaged. However, all three groups were more likely to describe 75-year-olds as "senile" and 35-year-olds as "forgetful" for similar omissions (e.g., forgetting to buy an item on a supermarket shopping list). One researcher commented that older people, anxious to separate themselves from disabilities associated with old age, tend to exaggerate symptoms of senility in others to stress differences between themselves and others perceived as senile.

In general, some symptoms are routinely ascribed to age if exhibited by elderly people and to other causes if exhibited by younger people. Muriel Oberleder, a gerontologist, noted that many of the symptoms of senility (e.g., depression, disorientation) are symptoms of anxiety throughout the lifespan. Id. at 60–61.

4. *Sexuality in later years.* John DeLamater and Morgan Still report on a study of sexuality in later life. The study, conducted under the auspices of the American Association of Retired Persons, received data from 1,384 men and women 45 years of age or older. John D. DeLamater & Morgan Still, Sexual Desire in Later Life, 42 J. Sex. Research 138 (2005). The authors note that cultural images suggesting that sexuality is "unnatural" in old age become self-fulfilling. They report that sexual desire does diminish with age, but it diminishes much later in life than is popularly thought.

A study of 69 elderly people in Ireland concluded that the population studied viewed sexuality as an important dimension of life. The study attributed nonsexuality among some study participants to factors such as illness or the lack of a sexual partner. Neil Cotter, Sexual Dynamos: Survey Reveals Pensioners Love Staying Naughty into Their 90s, Mirror (U.K.), Aug. 31, 2005.

5. *Responses of health care providers to elderly people.* A variety of studies suggests that health care workers respond differently to elderly people than to younger people. Many of the differences are subtle and may be hard for elderly patients to identify expressly. Whitton, supra, at 474–475, describes a number of these studies. In one, for instance, social workers treated cancer patients under 65 differently than cancer patients over 65. Among other things, younger patients were given more individual treatment and more service generally

than were patients over 65. Whitton, supra (citing Elizabeth A. Rohan et al., The Geriatric Oncology Patient, 23 J. Gerontological Soc. Work 201 (1994)). Similar patterns characterize psychiatric care of competent, elderly people. Those responses may be grounded in the assumption that elderly people are stagnant and cannot engage actively in the processes of life.

6. *Stereotypes.*   One author, writing about the place of the elderly in the criminal justice system, notes various examples of stereotypic thinking about older people in the legal literature. William E. Adams, Jr., The Intersection of Elder Law and Criminal Law: More Traffic Than One Might Assume, 30 Stetson L. Rev. 1331 (2001). The sorts of stereotypes of elderly people that Adams describes within the context of the criminal justice system suggest similar stereotypes that shape responses to elderly people within the health care system.

Adams refers, for instance, to a law review note called Blue Hairs in the Bighouse: The Rise in the Elderly Inmate Population, Its Effects on the Overcrowding Dilemma and Solutions to Correct It, 26 New Eng. J. Crim & Civ. Confinement 225 (2000). Adams elaborates: "The first line of this note continues the troubling characterization of older persons, exemplified by the title and starting in a stereotypical fashion by stating, 'When one thinks of the elderly, one envisions images of a fragile old man or woman needing help to carry groceries. . . . '" At least arguably the stereotypic image is especially surprising and troubling in that the author of the Note openly aimed to counter stereotypes. Id. at 1333–1334. The Note's title and first sentence suggest the extent to which such images are internalized within society.

Adams further suggests that among those discussing crimes committed by older people, disproportionate attention has been paid to shoplifting even though older people are actually less likely to shoplift than younger people. Id. at 1345. The stereotype, explains Adams, is based on the mistaken belief that elderly shoplifters—because they are elderly—are poor and/or suffer from dementia.

CHALLENGING ISSUES: AUTONOMY AND AGE

In her book The Fountain of Age (1993), Betty Friedan quotes one gerontologist presenting at a conference in 1988. The gerontologist explained: "Some older people don't want to make their own choices. . . . Some people are not capable of being empowered. Should we force them to be autonomous, whether they want to be or not? Let's talk about the right of the elderly to give up empowerment and autonomy, and the responsibility of professionals and institutions to make the decisions for them." Id. at 127.

Do you agree with this assertion? Why or why not?

b.   Legal Approaches

A variety of laws ostensibly promulgated to protect elderly people may be grounded in discriminatory understandings of age and may actually harm elderly people. One form of "reporting law" suggests the character of the problem.

By the early 1990s, all the states had passed laws mandating reporting of elder abuse. In theory, these laws are comparable to laws mandating that child abuse be reported. Elder abuse laws aim generally to safeguard vulnerable elderly people from abuse by a variety of caretakers and others, including family members, professional caretakers in home settings, and caretakers in institutional settings. Reporting laws are aimed at revealing abuse so that action can be taken to stop it.

The complicated motivations behind and consequences of laws mandating that elder abuse be reported are evident in a peculiar variety of reporting law: A majority of the states now require mandated reporters to report *self-neglect*. This sort of provision suggests a significant limitation in the right of elderly people to effect their own choices about matters such as food, clothing, medication, and health care generally. The Nevada and Ohio statutes, although different, both provide for mandatory reporting of self-neglect.

Nev. Rev. Stat. Ann., Crimes Against the Person: Abuse, Neglect, Exploitation, and Isolation of Older Persons (2008)

§200.5091. Policy of state

It is the policy of this state to provide for the cooperation of law enforcement officials, courts of competent jurisdiction and all appropriate state agencies providing human services in identifying the abuse, neglect, exploitation and isolation of older persons and vulnerable persons through the complete reporting of abuse, neglect, exploitation and isolation of older persons and vulnerable persons.

§200.5092. Definitions

As used in NRS 200.5091 to 200.50995, inclusive, and section 1 of this act, unless the context otherwise requires: . . .

    4. "Neglect" means the failure of:

        (a) A person who has assumed legal responsibility or a contractual obligation for caring for an older person or a vulnerable person or who has voluntarily assumed responsibility for his care to provide food, shelter, clothing or services which are necessary to maintain the physical or mental health of the older person or vulnerable person; or

        (b) An older person or a vulnerable person to provide for his own needs because of inability to do so.

    5. "Older person" means a person who is 60 years of age or older.

    7. "Vulnerable person" means a person 18 years of age or older who:

        (a) Suffers from a condition of physical or mental incapacitation because of a developmental disability, organic brain damage or mental illness; or

        (b) Has one or more physical or mental limitations that restrict the ability of the person to perform the normal activities of daily living.

§200.5093. Reports: Voluntary and mandatory; investigation; penalty

    1. Any person who is described in subsection 4 and who, in his professional or occupational capacity, knows or has reasonable cause to

believe that an older person has been abused, neglected, exploited or isolated shall:

(a) Except as otherwise provided in subsection 2, report the abuse, neglect, exploitation or isolation of the older person to:

(1) The local office of the Aging Services Division of the Department of Health and Human Services;

(2) A police department or sheriff's office;

(3) The county's office for protective services, if one exists in the county where the suspected action occurred; or

(4) A toll-free telephone service designated by the Aging Services Division of the Department of Health and Human Services; and

(b) Make such a report as soon as reasonably practicable but not later than 24 hours after the person knows or has reasonable cause to believe that the older person has been abused, neglected, exploited, or isolated.

[Subsection 4 of the provision lists mandatory reporters. The list includes, among others, doctors, dentists, dental hygienists, psychiatrists, psychologists, marriage and family therapists, coroners, social workers, and funeral home or mortuary owners and employees. Others may, but are not required to, report elder abuse and neglect.]

Ohio Rev. Code Ann. Adult Protective Services (2008)

§5101.60 Definitions.

As used in sections 5101.60 to 5101.71 of the Revised Code: . . .

(B) "Adult" means any person sixty years of age or older within this state who is handicapped by the infirmities of aging or who has a physical or mental impairment which prevents the person from providing for the person's own care or protection, and who resides in an independent living arrangement. An "independent living arrangement" is a domicile of a person's own choosing, including, but not limited to, a private home, apartment, trailer, or rooming house. . . .

(H) "In need of protective services" means an adult known or suspected to be suffering from abuse, neglect, or exploitation to an extent that either life is endangered or physical harm, mental anguish, or mental illness results or is likely to result. . . .

(K) "Neglect" means the failure of an adult to provide for self the goods or services necessary to avoid physical harm, mental anguish, or mental illness or the failure of a caretaker to provide such goods or services. . . .

§5101.61 Duty to report abuse, neglect or exploitation of adult. . . .

Any attorney, physician, osteopath, podiatrist, chiropractor, dentist, psychologist, any employee of a hospital . . . , any nurse licensed under Chapter 4723 of the Revised Code, any employee of an ambulatory health facility, any employee of a home health agency, any employee of an adult care facility . . . , any employee of a community alternative home . . . , any employee of a nursing home, residential care facility, or home for the aging, . . . any senior service provider, any peace officer, coroner, clergyman, any employee of a community mental health facility, and any person engaged in social work or counseling having reasonable cause to believe that an adult is being abused, neglected, or exploited, or is in a condition which is the result of abuse, neglect, or exploitation shall immediately report such belief to the county department of job and family services. . . .

   (B) Any person having reasonable cause to believe that an adult has suffered abuse, neglect, or exploitation may report, or cause reports to be made of such belief to the department.

NOTES AND QUESTIONS

   1. *Reporting self-neglect.*   The Nevada and Ohio reporting statutes, supra, require designated reporters to inform certain state authorities about self-neglect by an older person. There is, however, a potentially important difference between the two statutes in their assertions about whose self-neglect must be reported. What is that?

   Statutes such as Nevada's and Ohio's, which require designated reporters to inform the state about elderly people engaging in activities deemed neglect-ful even though the very same activities would likely not be interpreted to warrant intervention if carried out by younger people, have been promulgated by a majority of the states. Sana Loue questions the purpose of such statutory provisions. She describes an elderly woman whose doctor observes that she is not consuming adequate calories to maintain good nutrition. The woman is not poor, and there is no evidence that some other person is responsible for her poor nutrition. Loue comments: "Under Ohio law, for instance, the physician must now determine whether this woman's failure to provide a greater level of nutrition for herself constitutes a 'failure . . . to provide . . . the goods or services necessary to avoid physical harm, mental anguish, or mental illness' so as to render her nonintake of food reportable neglect." Sana Loue, Elder Abuse and Neglect in Medicine and Law: The Need for Reform, 22 J. Legal Med. 159, 179 (2001).

   2. *Assumptions behind self-neglect reporting.*   Mandatory reporting laws about elder abuse follow the model of reporting laws relating to child abuse. The need to report child abuse is predicated on the state's responsibility and authority to protect a presumptively fragile, innocent population. In the context of elder abuse, as the self-neglect laws printed above suggest, the central assumption— that those being "protected" cannot care for themselves—may often be inappropriate. Certainly elder people are sometimes subjected to abusive or neglectful treatment by family members and other caretakers. Moreover, negative, social images of elderly people do sometimes encourage elder abuse. However, self-neglect reporting laws—especially laws such as Nevada's that "protect" all people over a certain age, "presume incompetence." Id. at 181. As Loue explains:

> The right of a competent adult to refuse medical treatment is a long-recognized legal principle. . . . [B]ehavior that might be viewed as different or eccentric if performed by a younger person potentially could be construed as self-neglect when engaged in by an elderly individual. . . . State protective statutes that

encompass all individuals at or above a specified minimum age, without more, would seem to be violative of this premise and reflective of "ageism."

Id. at 181–182.

3. *Bibligraphic note.*   Joseph W. Barber, Note: The Kids Aren't All Right: The Failure of Child Abuse Statutes as a Model for Elder Abuse Statutes, 16 Elder L.J. 107 (2008). This note details differences between the character of elder abuse and child abuse, and, for that reason, criticizes states for having modeled elder abuse statutes on child abuse statues. Jennifer L. Wright, Protecting Who from What, and Why, and How?: A Proposal for an Integrative Approach to Adult Protective Proceedings, 12 Elder L.J. 53 (2004) (suggesting that adult guardianships and parens patriae civil commitment proceedings be integrated).

2.   *Talk of Rationing*

The increasing costs of health care have motivated some theorists to suggest that health care be rationed. One group of commentators has suggested that people above a certain age be denied health care that depends on public financing. At a 1989 conference run by the National Legal Center for the Medically Dependent and the Disabled, Daniel Callahan explained: "While individual elderly people may want more, and could even benefit from more, we will have done our duty to them in our public entitlement programs if we could get through a full life span, by which I mean the late 70's or early 80's" (quoted in Nat Hentoff, Prologue: The Indivisibility of Life xiv in Set No Limits (Robert L. Barry & Gerard V. Bradley eds. 1991)). A variety of responses to Callahan, all critical, can be found in Robert L. Barry & Gerard V. Bradley, Set No Limits: A Rebuttal to Daniel Callahan's Proposal to Limit Health Care for the Elderly (1991).

Robert Binstock and Stephen Post have suggested that in the early 1980s popular understandings of elderly people began to change in American culture. Binstock and Post contend that before that time, aged people were viewed as "poor, frail, socially dependent, objects of discrimination, and above all deserving." Robert H. Binstock & Stephen G. Post, Old Age and the Rationing of Health Care in Too Old for Health Care?: Controversies in Medicine, Law, Economics, and Ethics 1 (Robert H. Binstock & Stephen G. Post eds. 1991). The authors describe this as the foundation of a "compassionate" view of elderly people. Toward the end of the twentieth century, according to Binstock and Post, a contrasting perspective developed. From this perspective, the elderly are viewed as a "powerful group" presenting a "burdensome responsibility" to the larger society. Id. at 2.

The elderly population suffers from poor health and chronic conditions (including arthritis, hypertension, hearing impairments, heart disease, cataracts and diabetes) more than others. The U.S. Department of Health and Human Services reports that in 2000, 9 percent of the total population assessed their health as fair or poor and 27 percent of the elderly did so. Moreover, 54 percent of the elderly reported having some form of physical and nonphysical disability in 1997, and almost three-quarters of those over age 80 reported having at least one disability. Administration on Aging, U.S. Dep't of Health and Human Services, A Profile of Older Americans: 2002, at 12. There is little difference between elderly men and women with regard to their own assessments of their health, but there are differences among ethnic and racial groups. Just over 40 percent of elderly African Americans and just over 35 percent of elderly Hispanics assessed their health as fair or poor as compared with 26 percent of elderly whites. Id. 130. Olmsted v. L.C. ex rel. Zimring, 527 U.S. 581 (1999).

Those favoring age-based rationing make a set of assumptions about the elderly and the sort of medical care they require and receive that may not be accurate. For instance, one assumption—that elderly patients do not benefit as much or as often from medical intervention as do younger people—has been challenged. Second, although elderly people are more often disabled or ill than younger people, rates of disability among a diverse group of elderly Americans have declined at an accelerating pace since the late 1980s. NIH News Release, Dramatic Decline in Disability Continues for Older Americans, May 7, 2001, http://www.nia.nih.gov/NewsAndEvents/PressReleases/PR200110507Dramatic. htm. Moreover, a 2008 study supported by the National Institute of Aging found that between 1993 and 2002, rates of cognitive impairment among people over 70 decreased (from 12.2 percent in 1993 to 8.7 percent in 2002). The researchers found a correlation between lower cognitive impairment and higher levels of education and financial status. National Institute on Aging Press Release, Study Finds Improved Cognitive Health Among Older Americans, Feb. 25, 2008, http:// www.nia.nih.gov/NewsAndEvents/PressReleases/PR20080225coghealth.htm.

Society does spend more on the health needs of elderly people than of other people. Yet, the elderly are not a homogenous group, and old age is not an accurate predictor of the outcome of clinical interventions, even though some factors that do correlate with the success of medical interventions are related to age.

> *Life expectancy* is one measure that is a superior predictor of the efficacy of medical care. Obviously, advancing age indicates a shorter life expectancy; but the underlying disease and its prognosis are far more important criteria to keep in mind when making decisions on the basis of life expectancy.

Dennis W. Jahnigen & Robert H. Binstock, Economic and Clinical Realities: Health Care for Elderly People 28, in Binstock & Post, supra.

Andrew H. Smith & John Rother, Older Americans and the Rationing of Health Care
140 U. Pa. L. Rev. 1847, 1852–1855 (1992)

Arguments in favor of age-based rationing are founded on more than economics. Medical benefit, productivity, equality, natural life-span, and intergenerational justice are just a few of the bases cited in support of age-based rationing.

The medical benefit argument asserts that older people cannot, because of their physical condition, benefit from certain treatments. While it is true that advanced age is statistically associated with reduced likelihood of a favorable medical outcome, it is, as a single factor, a highly undependable clinical outcome predictor. In fact, physiologic age does not correlate at all well with chronological age. Older people are extremely heterogeneous, both physiologically and psychologically—more so than younger adults. For this reason, an arbitrary age-based cutoff for certain medical services is inappropriate if the goal is to target treatments to those who can benefit from them.

Some would justify the withholding of expensive medical services to older persons on the basis of the decreased productivity of the elderly. Such commentators implicitly question what return society will realize from its investment in care, particularly life-sustaining care, for the older persons. Some may argue that excluding older persons from treatment could result in greater returns for society, were those dollars invested in more "worthy," productive workers. This view presents a demeaning, monetary vision of the value of human life that is not acceptable in an egalitarian society. If we believe that all human life is sacred, and equally deserving of protection, then access to care should not be determined by what society may gain from permitting an individual to regain her health.

Restrictions on health care services to older Americans have been suggested to follow from application of the "principle of equality" to health care spending. This suggestion is based upon the idea that individuals should have the opportunity to live to the same age as others—that there is a prima facie right to a minimum number of life-years. This perspective, as some formulate it, would support limitation of health care for the elderly to provide services that would allow all, to the extent possible, to reach at least a certain age. Here persons are treated as sums of life-years, not as individual human entities; individuals' lives are not recognized as equally, but uniquely, precious.

Perhaps the most widely discussed justification for rationing life sustaining health care for the elderly is the "natural life-span" view articulated by Daniel Callahan. He argues that the cost of health care for the elderly will inevitably deprive younger generations not only of adequate health care, but of many other things they need to realize their full life experience.

Callahan calls for a policy—age based rationing—that will allow young people the opportunity to become old, proceeding along the following lines. The elderly know that much of their own welfare depended upon the work and contributions of earlier generations. They should not place the young in the difficult position of forcing them to make sacrifices. The elderly should lead the way, and allow the needs of the young to take precedence over their own needs. Callahan describes this state of affairs as "both gracious and fair." Callahan advances the notion of a "natural lifespan," a lifespan that is normative rather than just a statistical average. He defines the natural lifespan as "one in which life's possibilities have on the whole been achieved and after which death may be understood as a sad, but nonetheless relatively acceptable event." Once one has lived this natural lifespan, roughly figured to be about the late seventies or early eighties, one should not receive expensive, life sustaining medical treatment. Callahan proposes that those who continue to live on past the natural lifespan should receive only supportive and palliative care.

The concept of a "natural life-span" is hard to defend in an age when so many people continue to lead active and healthy lives at age eighty and older. To attempt to establish an age at which everyone will have accomplished everything of significance is, inevitably, a hopeless enterprise. As noted above, the older population is far too heterogeneous to permit such a calculation, unless one is prepared to completely ignore individual human potential. One need only note the activities and accomplishments of such octogenarians and nonagenarians as

Bertrand Russell, Pablo Picasso, Isaac Bashevis Singer, Konrad Adenauer, and many others to doubt the wisdom of restricting medical treatment for those who have lived past their "natural life-span."

Callahan's approach views life as a matter of what one does—the tasks one completes. But this view is quite limited. It has been observed that life may be as much about being as doing, that life may "consist as much of relating to others as of completing tasks."

Finally, the argument for age-based rationing as a matter of intergenerational justice, as drawn by Callahan, Lamm, and others, is unduly one-sided. As Thomasma observes, "intergenerational justice cuts both ways." It is the elderly, who through their investment of "human capital," who through their sacrifices, created the vast range of resources and services younger people now enjoy. Greene aptly notes that any economic analysis that takes into account the elderly's investment in human capital would find that they have received less than a competitive return on their investment. We might well ask what kind of justice it is that would deprive elderly citizens of the results of medical research when their taxes financed those discoveries, and their personal sacrifices (such as those made in America's wars) preserved our opportunity to gain the rewards of a free and prosperous society.

George P. Smith II, Distributive Justice and Health Care
18 J. Contemp. Health L. & Pol'y 421, 427–428 (2002)

The moral and social costs of age-based rationing are indisputably very high, as the elderly would receive less than their economic due as a return on their prior investment to society. Indeed, the harshest criticism against rationing is seen in the misperception that health care will be withheld or withdrawn based solely on economic decisions.

Rationing health care to the elderly is based traditionally upon a cost–benefit analysis that views the elderly as poor investments per health care dollar, or as a use of scarce resources with limited returns. The basic argument advanced here is that other segments of the population have more of a potential return on the investment of health care dollars than the elderly. Rationing does not mean necessarily the withholding of all medical care. Instead, expensive treatments should be abandoned when the chances of positive, rehabilitative results are minimal. Thus, the primary negative implication for age-based rationing is the demeaning notion of placing a monetary value on an elderly person's life.

Chronological age alone, as the determinative factor, fails as a practical approach in making health care decisions because of the great divergence between theory and practice. Instead, other variables, such as quality of life and health factors, are as equally important in determining treatment for the elderly. The utilitarian view of health care advocates balancing many different factors such as public and private benefits, predicted cost savings, risks involved and necessary trade-offs. In contrast, others argue a functional approach to rationing where the functional status of the person takes precedence over any utilitarian balancing. No doubt, the best gatekeeping ethic is to be found in the inherent physician-patient relationship—a relationship based on mutual trust and access to health care information which then allows treatment to be consistent with a patient's preferences or recovery potential. The major factor in addressing health care rationing should not be age. Rather, the course of a patient's treatment should be dependent solely upon his individual medical condition and shaped always by the goal of humane, loving care which reduces human suffering, enhances the common good, as well as safeguards the dignity of the human spirit especially in end-game situations.

NOTES AND QUESTIONS

1. *Rationing health care.*   What arguments favor rationing health care for the aged? What arguments disfavor rationing health care for the aged?

2. *A natural life span.*   Do you think that the notion of a "natural lifespan," proposed by Dan Callahan and discussed in the article, supra, by Andrew Smith and John Rother, is compelling?

In Older Americans and the Rationing of Health Care, Andrew Smith and John Rother note the accomplishments of several well-known individuals during their eighth, ninth, and tenth decades of life. They note, for instance, that the British philosopher Bertrand Russell (1872–1970) published an important work (Political Ideals) at the age of 91 and worked actively in the political area until he died at 97; Pablo Picasso (1881–1973) created great art in the second half of his ninth decade of life; Isaac Bashevis Singer (1904–1991) published an important novel (The Death of Methuselah) when he was 84; and Konrad Adenauer (1876–1967) published a four-volume autobiography *after* he retired at age 87 from his post as Chancellor of the Federal Republic of Germany. These bibliographic facts are offered by Smith and Rother to dispute Callahan's understanding of a natural life span, after which death is deemed acceptable, albeit sad. Do you think that full health care for the elderly should depend on proof that old people (or the oldest of old people) lead socially productive lives? Does this sort of evidence challenge Callahan's notion of a natural life span?

3. *Government programs for the elderly: Medicare and Medicaid—A brief summary.* The Medicare program was created by Congress in 1965 as an amendment to the Social Security Act (Title 18), to provide for the health care needs of elderly people. At the time, slightly more than half of the over-65 population in the United States had no insurance coverage for health care. When the program commenced (July 1, 1966), 19 million people enrolled. It is expected that in 2030, 77 million people will be enrolled. http://cms.hhs.gov/about/history/mcaremil.asp. Medicare is available to people aged 65 and over and eligible for Social Security; to disabled people eligible for Social Security or Railroad Retirement benefits; to people with Amyotrophic Lateral Sclerosis; and to people suffering from end-stage kidney disease. Within these groups Medicare eligibility does not depend on economic status. The Medicare program has significantly increased access to health care for elderly people, although it has not eliminated inequalities in health care among those eligible for the program.

The original Medicare program contained two parts (which still exist, though other parts have been added). Part A provides for hospitalization. More specifically, Part A covers inpatient hospital care, some skilled nursing home care, and some home health care and hospice care. Part B provides coverage for doctors' services (although not routine care), as well as a variety of other outpatient medical and surgical services. Part A is financed by a federal payroll tax; Part B by general federal funds in combination with copayments and premiums paid by enrollees. In 2008, most enrollees paid $96.40 per month (and a deductible of $135/year) for Part B coverage. There is now, however, a sliding scale. In 2008, Part B enrollees earning more than $82,000 (or couples earning more than $164,000 annually) paid more. Parts A and B (the so-called Original Medicare Plan) do not cover many services and supplies. Among other things, they do not cover dental care, hearing aids, drugs, and many screening tests and vaccinations. Other options have been added to Medicare over the years. The Balanced Budget Act of 1997 brought several crucial changes to the operation of Medicare. Among them was the creation of Medicare Part C, which offers a variety of managed care options to Medicare enrollees. At the end of the twentieth century, more than 16 percent of Medicare enrollees had opted for Part C (now referred to as Medicare Advantage). Elderly people who can afford it may purchase Medigap insurance to cover services and supplies not covered under Medicare.

Another limitation of the original Medicare program—its failure to cover prescription drugs—was criticized and debated for years. During the early years of the twenty-first century, the AARP (formerly the American Association of Retired Persons) worked actively for passage of a Medicare prescription drug benefit. John Rother, Commentary: Advocating for a Medicare Prescription Drug Benefit, 3 Yale J. Health Pol'y L. & Ethics 279 (2003). In 2003, Congress passed legislation that added an optional prescription drug benefit to Medicare. Medicare Prescription Drug, Improvement, and Modernization Act of 2003, 117 Stat. 2066 (2003).

Elderly people enrolled in Medicare, but unable to meet the cost-sharing requirements of the Medicare system or to purchase supplemental coverage, may be eligible for coverage from Medicaid. Medicaid, also enacted in 1965 as an amendment to the Social Security Act (Title 19), provides federal matching funds for state programs that provide health coverage for poor people. However, the reach of the program is limited, and not all poor people are eligible for Medicaid coverage. Income eligibility for Medicaid coverage varies among the states.

Medicare pays for limited stays in skilled nursing facilities. It covers 100 days of care (20 days in full and 80 in part), following at least a three-day hospitalization. Medicaid does cover long-term care services. It pays for almost half of all nursing home expenses incurred in the United States, and the program pays for about 40 percent of the cost of long-term care for people of all ages. At one time some elderly people engaged in what is known as "Medicaid estate planning." That became much more difficult after passage of the Deficit Reduction Act of 2005, Pub. L. No. 109-171, 120 Stat. 4 (codified in scattered sections of 42 U.S.C. and 20 U.S.C.). DRA limited the possibility of "spending down" so as to become eligible for Medicaid's long-term care benefit. Among other things, it placed a cap ($500,000 or $750,000 at the discretion of the state) on home equity that can be sheltered; it extended the "look-back" period (during which transfers of assets are not recognized for eligibility purposes) to five years; and it altered the penalty period so as to discourage attempts at asset transfer.

I. GENETIC DISCRIMINATION

**Sonia M. Suter, *The Allure and Peril of Genetics
Exceptionalism: Do We Need Special Genetics
Legislation?*
79 Wash. U. L. Q. 669 (2001)**

. . . Legal and bioethics scholars have written extensively about the dangers of genetic discrimination by insurers, employers, and society. The media also describe and scientists increasingly point out the perils of genetics. The public has absorbed these messages. My students, friends, family, and cocktail-party acquaintances are well-versed on the possible sources of genetic discrimination. Policy makers, attuned to public sentiment, are no less aware of these fears. Responding to the public's increased concerns about genetic discrimination and privacy, legislators have been extremely active in promoting genetics legislation. Although a few states have had narrow versions of genetics legislation in place since the 1970s, forty-six states currently have some form of legislation that protects genetic information, most of it enacted within the past decade. In addition, numerous genetics bills have been introduced in Congress since 1995, though none of them has become law. Both former President Clinton and President Bush have weighed in on the need for protections against genetic discrimination. To put it simply, public fears of genetics research have intensified with the speed of genetic sequencing. As we confront the newly-sequenced human genome, it is time to reassess the publicly shared discourse about the ethical, legal, and social implications of genetics. Nearly all discussions of the threats of genetics explicitly or implicitly suggest that the problems are as new and fresh as the technology underlying it. In other words, we face a brave new world not only of technology, but of social controversy. In the rush to identify and focus on the social implications, most discussions skip over the initial and essential questions: Is there really anything new here? Are we really in a brave new world of social and ethical issues, or does the new technology simply ask us to reexamine long-standing, persistent, and thorny social issues that we have never resolved?

. . . Various persuasive arguments can be made for protecting genetic information. But this fact alone does not offer a principled account for protecting only genetic information (or indeed for protecting all genetic information). The real issue is whether these arguments apply only to genetic information. After examining the different rationales that motivate genetics legislation, I argue that they do not apply to all genetic information, but more importantly, they apply equally to other types of medical information. In short, there is a grossly imperfect fit between the justifications for carving out special protections for genetic information and the category of genetic information because genetic information is both over- and under-inclusive with respect to its legislative purposes. This imprecise fit, particularly the under-inclusiveness, suggests the line between genetic and nongenetic information is not morally compelling. Although under- and over-inclusiveness is inherent in rule or law making, it is not necessarily a fatal flaw. . . . To assess the propriety of legislation that only protects genetic information, we must consider the degree of over- and under-inclusiveness and the interests they implicate. [T]he costs of some degree of over-inclusiveness with genetic information are small, and in any case, legislative definitional fine-tuning can minimize the problem to some extent. The real concern, however, is the under-inclusiveness of genetic information, which applies to virtually every justification.

. . . The most frequent justification for [genetic] legislation is to prevent genetic discrimination. At heart, this is a fairness argument. We cannot control the genes we inherit. Like race, our genetic information is an immutable trait, for which we should not be penalized. Many believe that allowing insurers, employers, or other groups to discriminate on the basis of genetic information compounds personal misfortunes outside our control. They contrast genetic risk factors with those we can control, such as smoking, speeding, or drinking, the burdens of which many believe we should bear.

Genetic discrimination is also a concern because certain characteristics of genetic information make it particularly vulnerable to insurance or employment discrimination. It is like a "future diary" that predicts one's "likely medical future." Indeed, it can be highly predictive. If you have the gene for HD [Huntington's Disease], for example, you will almost certainly develop the disease if you live long enough. Others worry that genetic information is prone to discrimination because it can be misunderstood. Our problematic history with genetics only intensifies these fears. A related concern is that genetic discrimination can lead to forms of racial, ethnic, or gender bias when discrimination is based on a gene that predominantly affects discrete groups. For example, the breast cancer genes are most common in women of Askenazi Jewish descent.

. . . The much more problematic aspect of the imprecise fit of genetics legislation to its underlying concerns is its under-inclusiveness. This problem infects virtually every justification in favor of protecting genetic information, raising serious questions about the validity of limiting these protections to just genetic information. . . . For example, consider the argument that genes are not in our control. Genetics, it turns out, proves to be an inadequate proxy for what is not in our control. Although we cannot control the genes we inherit, we cannot control a great many other risk factors, such as in utero exposures, environmental conditions, or drunk drivers, which may have profound effects on our future health. Moreover, many risk factors, which seem very much in one's control, may be less so than we imagine. Addictive behavior is influenced by genetic elements, as well as many social elements outside of our control, such as family, socioeconomic status, and culture. Controlling one's weight, for example, is not solely a matter of willpower. Even addiction to smoking has genetic elements. Thus, genetics does not function satisfactorily as an exclusive category for risks outside our control.

Genetic information is also an under-inclusive category with respect to other concerns that inspire genetic nondiscrimination laws. For example, genetic information is not alone in its predictive capacity. Before the advent of protease inhibitors, HIV infection virtually ensured the future development of AIDS. Similarly, significant asbestos exposure leads to a high risk of lung cancer. Worries that insurers or employers will discriminate based on genetic information apply equally to other medical information. Indeed, we know with certainty that insurers use medical information to discriminate (i.e., to make risk-based distinctions). And to the extent that people view genetic discrimination as a proxy for race or gender discrimination, protecting genetic information is under-inclusive. Racial discrimination has occurred through the use of other proxies for race. For example, before it was illegal, some insurers tried to engage in geographic red-lining—failing to sell insurance in certain locations. In addition, employers use medical information in the workplace to test fitness for duty and susceptibility to workplace hazards. And although we may worry about misinterpretations of genetic information, sadly, evidence shows that insurers and employers are careless and imprecise in their use of other actuarial data and risk information. While that may only inspire greater fear with regard to genetic information, it emphasizes problems with the underwriting system and employer use of medical information generally, not specifically with respect to genetics. Finally, concerns that fears of discrimination will prevent individuals from participating in medical research or treatment for conditions such as mental illness or cancer also justify the protection of other medical information.

. . . More troubling, and less immediately obvious, is that the unintended inequities of genetics legislation exacerbate social inequities. Although genetic risks transcend socioeconomic class, nongenetic risks frequently do not. Many nongenetic risks have sociological components related to poverty and environmental hazards, some of which are not in one's control. For example, numerous studies demonstrate that people of color and low income communities face disproportionate environmental impacts in the United States. Some sources of such environmental risks include "hazardous waste sites, incinerators, chemical factories, and sewage treatment plants," which are placed disproportionately in these lower-income communities. Minorities and the poor also face high levels of lead exposure. Continuous exposure to such environmental hazards poses increased risks of "cancer, asthma, chronic bronchitis, emphysema and other respiratory diseases, reproductive and birth defects, immunological problems, and neurological defects." In addition, low socioeconomic status is disproportionately associated with "virtually all of the chronic diseases that are the leading causes of mortality"; infectious diseases, such as HIV or tuberculosis; traumatic injuries and death; and developmental delay and other disabilities.

As a result, the poor, which includes many minorities, are more likely to face nongenetic risks than the middle or upper classes. Many of these risks can be measured through high cholesterol, high blood pressure, high blood levels of lead or other toxins, etc. If insurers, for example, can make actuarial decisions on the basis of evidence of nongenetic risks, but not genetic risks, we allow discrimination that will disproportionately disadvantage these vulnerable populations. Or to put it differently, we ask the least advantaged to bear their own nongenetic risks alone, even as we ask everyone, including them, to subsidize genetic risks. Given that many environmental hazards, as well as other health risks, are linked to poverty and low socioeconomic status, there is reason to be concerned about the social impact of a policy that only protects genetic risks, but does not protect the risks that most profoundly affect the poor and minorities.

Finally, although genetic risk factors transcend socioeconomic status, the individuals currently most concerned about genetic discrimination may not represent the full socioeconomic spectrum. Genetic discrimination is primarily on the minds of those interested in genetic testing for research or clinical purposes, whose basic health care needs have usually been met. As a result, genetic discrimination is principally a concern of the middle to upper classes, who have financial resources for testing and jobs and insurance they fear losing. This group of well-educated, well-off individuals has lobbied heavily for genetics legislation. In contrast, the groups most vulnerable to health risks associated with poverty and environmental hazards do not have the same political voice or cohesiveness. There is a danger that the strong political voice of the first group outshadows the interests of more vulnerable, but less politically powerful groups. In short, genetics-specific legislation becomes another middle-class entitlement.

NOTES AND QUESTIONS

1. *Genetic exceptionalism.*   Sonia Suter argues that state and (at that time proposed, now enacted) federal legislation aimed at reducing genetic discrimination is under- and overinclusive. What does she mean by underinclusive? According to Suter, what are the social justice implications of such underinclusiveness?

2. *The Genetic Information Non-Discrimination Act (GINA).*   This federal act, promulgated in 2008 (Pub. L. No. 110-233), prohibits employers, group health plans, and health insurance companies from various forms of discrimination on the basis of genetic information. Insofar as information about deleterious genetic alterations has been attributed to familial, ethnic, and racial groups, GINA may be protective of both individuals and groups with which they are identified.

Under GINA, protected information is defined to include information about an "individual's genetic tests," "the genetic tests of family members of such individual," and "the manifestation of a disease or disorder in family members of such individual." Employers are prohibited from discriminating on the basis of genetic information with regard to hiring and compensation. Group health plans and health insurers are prohibited from using genetic information in enrollment decisions or premium adjustments. Moreover, group health plans and health insurers are precluded from requiring or asking individuals to submit to genetic testing.

GINA specifically categorizes genetic information as "health information." That requires plans to conform with Health Insurance Portability and Accountability Act (HIPAA) privacy provisions with regard to genetic information.

See generally Mark A. Rothstein, Is GINA Worth the Wait? 36 J.L. Med. & Ethics 174 (2008).

3. *The Affordable Care Act of 2010.*   A very popular provision of the Affordable Care Act (ACA), embraced by legislators of various political affiliations, prohibits insurance companies from denying coverage or charging higher premiums to individuals with preexisting health conditions. Preexisting conditions are health conditions that exist before an insurance plan is purchased or an individual enrolled in an employer plan. Health insurers have long denied coverage of preexisting conditions, or sometimes simply denied insurance at all because of a preexisting condition. Beginning in September 2010, the ACA prohibits insurers from excluding children under age 19 from coverage because

of a preexisting condition. Beginning in 2014, insurers cannot deny coverage or charge higher premiums to anyone because of preexisting conditions. Between 2010 and 2014, a new, temporary federal program was established to offer insurance to uninsured adults with preexisting conditions through state-based high-risk insurance pools. States have discretion to determine how premiums will be set and other operational aspects of the plans, within federally prescribed limits. Health Policy Brief: Updated: Pre-Existing Condition Insurance Plan, Health Affairs, Nov. 30, 2010, available at http://www.healthaffairs.org/healthpolicybriefs/brief.php?brief_id=34.

Prior to the passage of the ACA, the Health Insurance Portability and Accountability Act of 1996 enacted some important, although limited, restrictions on a health insurer's ability to limit coverage of preexisting medical conditions for adults. The focus of the HIPAA restrictions is portability of insurance for individuals when changing jobs. State laws may provide additional or more generous protections in some cases. For a succinct and accessible summary of the HIPAA rules about portability of health coverage, see U.S. Dep't of Labor, FAQs about Portability of Health Coverage and HIPAA, at http://www.dol.gov/ebsa/faqs/faq_consumer_hipaa.html#.UH15966gbjU.

Do the new restrictions on insurance discrimination for preexisting conditions satisfy the concerns expressed by Suter, supra, about the underinclusiveness of genetic discrimination legislation?

4. More on genetics and genomics.   The issues of genetic exceptionalism and genetic discrimination are also discussed in Chapter 4.

= PART III =

BIOETHICS AND THE COMMUNITY

=11=

Human Subject Research and Experimental Health Care

This chapter bridges Part II of this book, which focuses on the individual, and Part III, which raises issues about community. Its topic covers issues that mediate clearly between the two, as individual research subjects or patients receiving experimental health care provide benefits to the community in the advancement of medical knowledge.

Much of the field of bioethics today focuses on issues at the beginning and at the end of life—issues about reproduction and dying. The origins of the field itself, though, are traced by some scholars to issues of human experimentation. In 1966, Henry Beecher published an exposé of contemporary research abuses in the United States that, according to some observers, marked the introduction of outside scrutiny into the world of doctor and patient—the introduction of governments, ethicists, lawyers, and patient advocates. See David Rothman, Strangers at the Bedside 1–4 (1991). What is perhaps most telling about the times in which Beecher published his indictment of medical research is that the 22 questionable research studies that he exposed had not been kept secret at all, but were contained in the pages of prestigious medical journals, so confident and insular was the world of medical research. The insularity of that world was shaken. There would be far fewer assumptions that doctors always have the interests of their patients at heart and that medical knowledge is so esoteric that laypeople cannot make judgments about the priorities and practices of the profession. Public attention brought to bear on these and other research abuses led to a federal regulatory oversight scheme that covers much but not all medical research in the United States. As you will see in this chapter, it is far from ideal. Questionable research practices continue. Moreover, the research landscape has become far more competitive and commercial in recent years, creating strong financial incentives to disregard or at least discount patient safety.

Financial incentives, aside, however, there are still "purer" motivations in research that place research subjects at risk of harm or coercion. The primary issue in human subject research is how to permit medical progress, which nearly everyone agrees requires some experimentation on humans, and yet still protect the individual human subject. The material at the beginning of this chapter reveals a history of physician-researchers placing their emphasis between the two squarely on medical progress, to the undeniable detriment of their patients and others who might be the subjects of their research. Although the abuses of the Nazi doctors, described below, may lie at one extreme, each decade of experimentation since then seems to contain its own abuses, even as ethical codes and regulatory protections are refined and strengthened. On the one hand, the goal of protection of individual subjects appears now to be a high priority, but in practice attaining that goal appears elusive for reasons explored in this chapter. Some of these challenges are age-old and intrinsic to the nature of human subject research, as evidenced by the following questions you will encounter throughout the chapter:

1. What *can* be properly asked of a volunteer? What is the appropriate balance between the benefits of research and the risks to the individual (concerns about beneficence and nonmaleficence)?
2. Can a patient truly understand the risks and benefits to participation in research? Can she understand the distinction between therapy intended to benefit her and research intended to lead only to knowledge (concerns about autonomy)?
3. How should the burdens of research be fairly distributed? Do certain populations need extra protection from potential exploitation? Do certain populations need or deserve less (concerns about justice)?

Other challenges are more specific to the changing context in which research now takes place:

4. How can the many present-day conflicts of interest between researcher and subject be appropriately managed?
5. How do ethical standards for research in the United States apply when U.S.-led research is conducted in developing countries?
6. How are research subjects to be protected when it is their DNA, rather than their body, that is the subject of study and manipulation?

Following the initial materials on the historical, theoretical, and contemporary context in which medical research takes place, the chapter examines ethics codes and legal regulations in some detail. Legal cases are rather sparse in this field, although there are some recent reported cases that may mark the beginning of more judicial oversight in this area. One of these, Grimes v. Kennedy Krieger Institute, Inc., 782 A.2d 807 (Md. 2001), involves children, a population of special concern and special regulations. Following the materials on research involving children, four other populations are considered and questions asked about whether different rules should apply to them—but rules that provide *less* rather than *more* protection for individual research subjects. These are individuals who have given biological samples on which research might be conducted, military personnel, populations in developing countries, and the terminally ill.

A. BIOETHICAL AND SOCIAL PERSPECTIVES

> *Jay Katz, Human Sacrifice and Human Experimentation: Reflections at Nuremberg*
> **22 Yale J. Int'l L. 401 (1997)**

The Doctors' Trial was the first of twelve trials that followed the Nuremberg trial of the major war criminals by the International Allied Military Tribunal. Conducted by American judges, the Doctors' Trial focused on experimentation on human beings during the Nazi regime. Evidence of the experiments was presented over many months in excruciating detail. I have reviewed the record many times and still find it devastatingly painful to read.

Most notorious among the experiments was Dr. Sigmund Rascher's work on the effects of high altitude on human survival. On May 15, 1941, Rascher wrote to Heinrich Himmler:

> During [a medical selection course in which] research on high altitude flying played a prominent part [we learned that English fighter planes were able to reach higher ceilings than we could]. [R]egret was expressed that no experiments on human beings have so far been possible for us because such experiments on human beings are very dangerous and nobody is volunteering. I therefore put the serious question: is there any possibility that two or three professional criminals can be made available for these experiments? . . . The experiments, in which the experimental subject of course may die, . . . are absolutely essential . . . and cannot . . . be carried out on monkeys, because monkeys offer entirely different test conditions.

Dr. Rudolf Brandt, on behalf of Himmler, responded promptly: "I can inform you that prisoners will, of course, be gladly made available for the high-flight researches. . . . I want to use the opportunity to extend my cordial wishes to you on the birth of your son."

In Rascher's report on one of these experiments, he described in graphic detail the fate of

> A 37-year-old Jew in good general condition who [at ever increasing altitudes] began to perspire and to wiggle his head [and to suffer from severe] cramps. . . . [B]reathing increased in speed and [he] became unconscious. . . .
> Severest cyanosis developed . . . and foam appeared at the mouth. . . . After breathing had stopped the electrocardiogram was continuously written until the action of the heart had come to a complete standstill. About 1/2 hour [later,] dissection was started.

The freezing experiments, many fatal, were even more brutal, if that is possible. The subjects were immersed in ice water for hours on end. They pleaded to be shot to escape their unbearable agony. As I read these accounts, I could almost hear their agonizing pleas. These and the many other experiments, conducted at Auschwitz and elsewhere, bear testimony to the brutality inflicted on "lives not worth living" and therefore expendable.

Rascher, in his report, was delighted that the heart actions he had recorded "will [prove to be of] particular scientific interest, since they were written down with an electrocardiogram to the very end." For him the experiment represented another triumph in the 100-year history of human sacrifice for the sake of the advancement of knowledge.

Experimentation with human beings antedates the Nazis. Its roots go back to antiquity, but in the 1850s, human research increased in magnitude unprecedented during the millennia of medical history. Academic physicians observed with envy the discoveries in physics and chemistry that had resulted from systematic, objective investigations, and they adopted the methodologies of the physical sciences so that medicine would also become a respected scientific discipline. At the same time, doctors lost sight of the fact that it is one thing to experiment with atoms and molecules and quite another to do so with human beings. Once, while reflecting on the inhumanity of Auschwitz, my thoughts took me back to these beginnings of medical research. I was struck by how quickly physicians accepted these new ways of conducting research with human beings, never asking whether fellow human beings, particularly patients, should be subjected to these novel practices and, if so, with what safeguards.

The initial advances in knowledge that resulted from such scientific investigations, which promised to alleviate human suffering to an extent previously unknown, seemed to justify the means employed. The uncharted moral path led only once to Auschwitz; yet, on many other occasions down the road, human beings would pay a considerable price for the sake of medical progress.

The early fruits of medical research were spectacular. The bacterial etiology of many diseases was proven, resulting in cures never before the lot of mankind. Investigations of the use of X-rays to see the previously invisible revolutionized diagnostic techniques. Experiments with various anesthetic agents led to remarkable advances in surgery.

These experiments were largely conducted in public hospitals with the poor, with children, women, prostitutes, the elderly—that is, with the disadvantaged, the downtrodden. Albert Moll, in his remarkable book Ärztlich Ethik, published in 1902, described many experiments conducted with patient-subjects throughout Europe and the United States during the late nineteenth century. He was particularly troubled by experimentation with the terminally ill, who frequently served, as they still do, as subjects of research. Since they would soon die anyway, learning from them seemed self-evidently the right thing to do. In reading these accounts my mind turned again to the Auschwitz subjects, who were also terminal cases—"lives not worth living"—soon to be reduced to ashes.

Human research and its contributions to the advancement of knowledge captured the imagination of doctors. The promise that omnipotence would replace the earlier struggle against impotence, and the promise of fame, academic advancement, and perhaps even economic fortune, loomed large in physicians' minds.

But the intrusion of research into the clinical practice of medicine required keeping the two enterprises separate. Patients went to doctors to be helped and not to serve as research subjects. Crucial distinctions needed to be made between clinical care and human research for the advancement of science. Instead, the boundaries between therapy and research became blurred. The "therapeutic illusion"—that research would in some undefined ways benefit subjects—contributed to this obfuscation.

... When medical science and medical practice became intertwined, a new ethical question should have been raised: Are physicians' obligations to their patient-subjects different from their obligations to their patients? But only a few remarkable physicians considered that question, and their concerns were not heeded.

... For many reasons, physicians have preferred to view human experimentation merely as an extension of medical practice. In 1916 the Harvard physician Walter Cannon recommended to the House of Delegates of the American Medical Association that it endorse the importance of obtaining patient consent and cooperation in human experimentation. His proposal, however, was not brought up for consideration. One influential physician observed that "it would open the way for a discussion of the importance of obtaining the consent of the patient before any investigations are carried on which are not primarily for the welfare of the patient."

And this is only half the story. Disclosure in these contexts would require discussions with patient-subjects of the uncertainties inherent in therapeutic medicine as well; and, if that were to happen, the question would arise: Why should not patients be similarly informed? Physicians feared that their authority to make decisions on behalf of patients would be undermined and patients' best interests would be detrimentally affected. Doctors viewed such prospects, as they still do, as a threat to the traditional practice of medicine. They valued silence, their own and their patients', for silence maintains authority.

The Doctors' Trial, as never before, confronted the world with agonizing accounts of what physician-scientists can do and justify when respect for human dignity is totally abrogated. Their conduct was so aberrational, almost unbelievable, that the prosecution and judges found it difficult to sort out the implications of what had transpired in the concentration camps in terms of medicine's past and future.

... [T]he Tribunal articulated a vision of the limits of scientific medical research that was clear and unambiguous. To be sure, its pronouncement would eventually require elaboration and modification, but it was the uncompromising clarity of its vision about the primacy of consent that proved so disturbing to the medical community.

... They did not know that for decades their code would make little impact on research practices; that many violations would continue to occur in the United States and elsewhere. For example, the Tuskegee Syphilis Study, begun in 1932, in which the lives and health of many African-Americans were ruined, was not stopped until 1972. That study had been conducted by the U.S. Public Health Service with 400 uninformed African-American men in order to gather data on the natural history of untreated syphilis from its inception to death. The study should never have begun, and it surely should have been stopped in the early 1940s when effective treatment for some of the late manifestations of syphilis became available.

Or consider the experimental injection of live cancer cells into uninformed elderly patients at the Brooklyn Jewish Chronic Disease Hospital. Or consider the experimental injection of plutonium into uninformed pregnant women to learn whether plutonium crosses the placental barrier, conducted at a time when little was known about plutonium and its dangers. Or consider the total body radiation experiments with terminally ill patients at the Cincinnati University Hospital. The plutonium and radiation experiments were conducted during the Cold War and were justified on grounds of national defense, an argument that had also been advanced by the Nazi physicians for what they had done. Finally, consider more recent drug studies to determine the toxicity of new cancer treatments, which were presented to patient-subjects not as research but as "new and promising frontier treatments."

These experiments were not comparable to the Nazi research, for care was generally taken to keep physical harm to a minimum. In putting it this way, I want to make distinctions between the deliberate torture that accompanied the concentration camp research and the care taken to minimize physical harm to the extent possible in contemporary research. With respect to consent, however, we still have a long way to go in learning the lessons that the Nazi experience should teach us. As one American research scientist put it, "I am aware of no investigator (myself included) who was actively involved in research involving human subjects in the years before 1964 who recalls any attempts to secure voluntary or informed consent according to Nuremberg's standards."

In giving preeminence to "voluntary consent" in the conduct of research, the judges sought to admonish investigators to become more respectful of subjects' dignitary interests in making their own decisions in interactions with investigators. Implementation of that objective remains the unfinished legacy of the Nuremberg judges. For the regulations that now require consent will not adequately protect the rights of subjects to self-determination unless the mindsets of physician-investigators embrace these rights as a new Hippocratic commitment.

Vulnerable subjects are compelled by their necessitous circumstances to place their trust in physicians whom they consider care givers, not investigators. The problem of "trust" surfaced in one of the studies conducted by the President's Advisory Committee on Human Radiation Experiments during the Cold War, in which we assessed attitudes toward research among many hundreds of patient-subjects who as recently as 1994 were enrolled in research projects. We discovered that patient-subjects believed that "an [experimental] intervention would not even be offered if it did not carry some promise of benefit [for them]," and that the consent process was "a formality" to which they need not give much thought.

The lesson to be learned from our findings is clear: Consent will never be truly informed or voluntary unless patient-subjects are disabused of that belief. Their rights can be protected only if physician-investigators acknowledge that their patient-subjects view them as physicians and not investigators, and that they, the doctors themselves, have the responsibility to challenge that trust in research settings. Patient-subjects must be told that their own and their physician-investigators' agendas are not the same. Research is not therapy.

This is a formidable undertaking and a consequential one, about which I have written extensively. It takes time, may impede research because of too many refusals, and may thereby make some experiments impossible to conduct. Choices have to be made between the relentless pursuit of medical progress and the protection of individual inviolability. The latter, however, will be given the weight it deserves only if doctors learn to respect patient-subjects as persons with minds of their own and with the capacity to decide for themselves how to live their medical lives. Their choices may or may not include a willingness for altruistic self-sacrifice, but such choices must take precedence [over] the advancement of science.

Guido Calabresi, Reflections on Medical Experimentation in Humans
98 Daedalus 387–393 (1969)

The problem of experimentation on humans necessarily looks rather different to one who has concentrated on accident law than it does to the doctor or even to the jurisprude. The torts professor sees the possibility of a choice between the life, well-being, or comfort of a given patient and the lives or well-being of unknown future patients. He is immediately struck that the issue in medical experimentation is the risking of lives to save other lives while in accident law, almost always, the issue is the taking of lives simply because saving them costs too much.

In torts law, we have become accustomed to the fact that many activities are permitted, even though *statistically* we know they will cost lives, since it costs too much to engage in these activities more safely or to abstain from them altogether. We have grade crossings, even though we know that with grade crossings a certain number of people will be killed each year and even though grade crossings could be eliminated relatively easily. We use automobiles— knowing that they cost us fifty thousand lives each year—because to use safer, slower means of transport would be far too costly in terms of pleasures and profits forgone. Worse even than that, we use automobiles with relatively cheap (but relatively dangerous) tires, airports with relatively cheap (but relatively dangerous) control systems, and so on *ad infinitum*. And we do this because we deem the lives taken to be cheaper than the costs of avoiding the accidents in which they are taken.

From the perverse standpoint of accident law, then, the whole fury about medical experimentation would seem to be a tempest in a teapot. Surely it is more justifiable to take some lives in order to save more lives than it is to take lives simply to save money, as we do in the accident field. But this view, I fear, is far too superficial. Even in the accident field, there are many occasions when we do treat life as a pearl beyond price. When a known individual is trapped in a coal mine, we try to rescue him at enormous money cost and even at the risk of many other lives. Yet if we always gave human life the value we give to the life of the man in the coal mine, we would surely abolish grade crossings, make cars and airports much safer, and perhaps even forbid "non-essential" driving completely. What is the meaning of this apparent paradox? And what does it tell us about medical experimentation?

The first possible explanation has to do with statistics. Somehow a man is less a man to us when he is simply a number. We know the man trapped in the coal mine, just as we often know the patient subjected to experimentation. The statistical accident victim we do not know, and so we can ignore him. But that is not in itself an adequate explanation. The statistical victim is just as real as the man in the coal mine. If we want to be fully rational, we must admit to ourselves that he has as much of a family as a known victim, that he and they suffer as much when he is killed, and that only a willful ignoring of reality enables us to treat him as less real than the man trapped in the coal mine.

But perhaps this willful ignoring of statistical victims is less foolish, though no more "rational," than it might seem at first glance. We are committed to "humanism," to the dignity of the individual, and to human life. Much of the fabric of our society depends on our belief in this commitment, as do most of our traditional and "cherished" liberties. Accident law indicates that our commitment to human life is not, in fact, so great as we say it is; that our commitment to life-destroying material progress and comfort is greater. But this fact merely accentuates our need to make a bow in the direction of our commitment to the sanctity of human life (whenever we can do so at a reasonable total cost). It also accentuates our need to reject any societal decisions that too blatantly contradict this commitment. Like "free will," it may be less important that this commitment be total than that we believe it to be there.

Perhaps it is for these reasons that we save the man trapped in the coal mine. After all, the event is dramatic, the cost, though great, is unusual; and the effect in reaffirming our belief in the sanctity of human lives is enormous. The effect of such an act in maintaining the many societal values that depend on the dignity of the individual is worth the cost. Abolishing grade crossings might save more lives and at a substantially smaller cost per life saved, but the total cost to society would be far greater and the dramatic effect far less. . . .

It should be clear that the foregoing does not mean that individual human life is not valued highly. Nor, certainly, does it suggest that we are indifferent to when and how society should choose to sacrifice lives. Quite the contrary; it indicates that there is a deep conflict between our fundamental need constantly to reaffirm our belief in the sanctity of life and our practical placing of some values (including future lives) above an individual life. That conflict suggests, at the very least, the need for a quite complex structuring to enable us *sometimes* to sacrifice lives, but hardly ever to do it blatantly and as a society, and above all to allow this sacrifice only under quite rigorous controls. . . . I suggest that the problem with human experimentation lies in the fact that, unlike accidents, it has seemed to be quite unamenable to most of the complex "indirect" controls over takings of lives we have so far developed in our society.

In the field of accidents, much of the control over the taking of human lives is accomplished by what economists call the market. Limbs and lives are given a money value; the activities that take lives or limbs in accidents pay the victims; and people quite coldly decide whether it is cheaper to install a safety device or to pay for the accidents that occur because the safety device is missing. Despite the enormous oversimplification of the foregoing example (the effect of "fault" in determining accident payments, for instance, is ignored), it indicates how "accidents" are controlled in an indirect fashion which, nonetheless, takes into account both the value of lives taken and the cost of saving them.

The beauty of the market device is that no one seems to be making the decisions to take lives and, therefore, no blatant infringement of the commitment to human life as sacred occurs. Moreover, when society *does* enter into the accident field directly, it is usually to impose more stringent prohibitions, regulations, or safety standards than the market would bring about. We do not allow drunken driving—any more than we allow murder—even though the drunk may be perfectly willing to compensate his victim. The consequence is that collective societal action seems always to be directed toward preserving the individual life rather than taking it, and our commitment is further strengthened. . . .

Other elements of accident law serve to reduce still further the blatantness of the taking. In many situations, the victim can be said to have, to some extent at least, consented to the risk. Consent is often actually very dubious. Are we, in fact, free to avoid driving cars? Is a tunnel-digger free to engage in a safer occupation? And is there any consent at all when a pedestrian is run down by a car? But these questions are neither here nor there. They would be crucial were free consent the keystone of the system (as it may have to be in medical experiments). Where, however, consent serves merely to lessen further the directness of a taking that is already controlled by a seemingly impersonal system, even semi-free consent suffices to support the belief that our society prizes individual lives above all.

. . . Finally, the temporal juxtaposition of decisions to avoid accidents and lives taken serves to make "accidental" takings of lives seem less blatant. At the time a decision to adopt a safety device is to be made, the cost of the device is both present and real; the accident costs to be saved may also be statistically known; but the lives themselves are in the future and seem conjectural. Once again, if the decision is made against the device, even the individual making the decision—let alone society—does not seem to be choosing "certainly" to destroy lives.

In medical experiments, much of this process seems reversed. It is the lives to be saved by the experiment that seem future and conjectural, while the life to be risked or taken is both present and real.

. . . No one has purposefully chosen the market method of controlling accidents, and no one, in our society, has the clear responsibility for making radical changes in the method. These facts happily leave us with the feeling that no one is directly responsible for any specific life taken and that neither as individuals nor as a society do we choose against lives in order to save money. Yet it remains true that we are unlikely to want to scrap the system of control that luckily has come into being. And to say this is precisely to say that a method which gives *satisfactory* control of the choice between lives and cost is operating without anyone bearing the onus of having purposefully chosen the method, let alone the onus of seeming to destroy individual lives for the sake of money. Since no adequate control system over medical experiments has arisen by itself, we cannot avoid the onus of working purposefully toward establishing a control system. This indicates that we will not end with so psychologically satisfactory a result as we have in the field of accidents. But, if anything, this fact heightens the need for establishing a system in which the actual choice over the taking of lives is as diffuse as possible.

Thus, the question remains as to whether or not we can find a control system in the medical experiment field that affords an adequate balancing of present against future lives and is still sufficiently indirect and self-enforcing as to avoid clear and purposive choices to kill individuals for the collective good.

NOTES AND QUESTIONS

1. *Individual inviolability vs. the common good.* Many debates now taking place about how medical research should be conducted assume that the individual research subject must have consented to her inclusion in the research. Voluntary consent is the cornerstone of current research ethics. Thus, as you will see in later materials in this chapter, there are issues about what kind of information must be given to research subjects to ensure that their consent is "informed," but there is no question that consent must be obtained.

The excerpt presented above by Jay Katz explains that such was not the case historically. Clearly in earlier times medical researchers did not accept the view that "individual inviolability" takes precedence over medical progress. Today's practices, he fears, still provide little real protection to patient-subjects, who trust their doctors to have only the interests of their patients in mind. Guido Calabresi's article contrasts sharply with the writings of Katz. He challenges the idea that "individual inviolability," to use Katz's term, is presumptively the prevailing good. What is his argument and how does he support it? What kind of control system does he suggest we might need for pursuing medical research? As you read the remainder of the material in the chapter, consider how the current regulatory system for medical research fulfills or does not fulfill the needs he identifies.

2. *Lessons from the past?*   Katz's article describes some of the Nazi experiments as well as contemporaneous and more recent experiments conducted in the United States that have received universal condemnation, for example, the Tuskegee Syphilis Study, the Brooklyn Jewish Chronic Disease Hospital cancer experiments, and the Cincinnati radiation experiments (one of among many radiation experiments of the post–World War II research era). In other passages of the article, Katz expresses some hesitation about making comparisons between the Nazi experiments and other human research, but concludes that it is acceptable to do so. What value, if any, do you think knowledge and discussion of the Nazi experiments have on evaluations of past practices in the United States? What about comparisons made between such experiments and current practices?

3. *The Guatemala Study.*   Information about past research abuses continues to surface. In November 2010, President Barack Obama asked the Presidential Commission for the Study of Bioethical Issues to investigate a recently discovered study on sexually transmitted diseases funded by the U.S. National Institutes of Health that took place in Guatemala from 1946 to 1948. The U.S. government formally apologized to the government of Guatemala, the study's survivors, and descendants of those affected by the research. According to the Commission's Report, "Subjects were exposed to syphilis, gonorrhea, and chancroid, and included prisoners, soldiers from several parts of the army, patients in a state-run psychiatric hospital, and commercial sex workers." Presidential Commission for the Study of Bioethical Issues, Ethically Impossible: STD Research in Guatemala from 1946 to 1948, 2011, available at http:// www.bioethics.gov/ cms/sites/default/filesEthicallyImpossible_PCSBI.pdf. The report detailed "gross violations of ethics" including blatant lack of informed consent, deliberate infection with sexually transmitted diseases, and enrollment of what are now referred to as "vulnerable populations," including prisoners, soldiers, and even children. Press Release, President's Bioethics Commission Releases Result of Its Historical Investigation of the 1940s U.S. Public Health Service STD Studies in Guatemala, Sept. 13, 2011, available at http:// www.bioethics.gov/cms/ node/308. These actions were clearly wrong according to ethical standards at the time, as the Report noted:

> The history of U.S.-supported experimentation undertaken to advance medical knowledge and protect national security is complex with evolving ethical standards and norms. Nonetheless, the experiments in Guatemala starkly reveal

that, despite awareness on the part of government officials and independent medical experts of then existing basic ethical standards to protect against using individuals as a mere means to serve scientific and government ends, those standards were violated.

Id., at 7. The Report also concluded that many government officials and leading academic scientists in both the United States and Guatemala supported or were involved in the study. Id.

4. *Research results from past unethical experiments.* As horrific as some past experiments have been, they may on occasion have actually produced some information of interest to current scientists. Do you think it is ethically acceptable for present researchers to use data derived from past unethical experimentation?

B. CURRENT PRACTICES

The "control system," as Guido Calabresi might call it, that has developed to balance medical progress (and the improvement of present and future lives) and individual inviolability is a complex and largely private one. As we will see in further detail in this chapter, regulation at the federal level largely consists of delegating the review of research protocols to institutions at which the research is being conducted. This is done through Institutional Review Boards (IRBs), some of whose recent lapses are the subject of the following excerpt. The two excerpts following Beh's provide further insight into the current climate of medical research, which is riddled with conflicts of interest, both potential and actual.

> *Hazel Glenn Beh, The Role of Institutional Review Boards in Protecting Human Subjects: Are We Really Ready to Fix a Broken System?*
> **26 Law & Psychol. Rev. 1 (2002)**

A number of . . . well-publicized incidents occurring in the past two or three years have demonstrated the flaws in the current system. These studies have shaken public confidence in human subject research and, in each, criticism was lodged against local IRBs as well as researchers. These events include the death of Jesse Gelsinger, an eighteen-year-old volunteer with an inherited liver disorder, who died during a gene therapy experiment at the University of Pennsylvania; allegations that as many as twenty participants in a study conducted at the Fred Hutchinson Cancer Center may have died unnecessarily during the course of a twelve-year-long cancer treatment study because scientists ignored clear evidence that the treatment did not work and actually harmed subjects; and the death of twenty-four-year-old Ellen Roche, a healthy research volunteer who died within days of inhaling an unapproved drug used to induce asthma-like symptoms. Though these incidents have recently drawn national attention to the issue of human subject research, they are by no means isolated events. Indeed, some suggest that these incidents occur more frequently than believed and that they result from fundamental failures in the system designed to protect human subjects. Lawsuits in these cases may invite more courts to examine the national system of human subject protections and prompt changes.

In 2001, the Seattle Times published a five-part investigative report describing "Protocol 126," a blood cancer experiment conducted over a twelve-year period in the 1980s and 1990s at the premier Fred Hutchinson Cancer Research Center. The Seattle Times reported that perhaps as many as twenty subjects likely died prematurely as a result of the failed experiment that continued despite evidence that the protocol did not work and was leading to premature deaths. According to the Seattle Times, various entities were to blame. It condemned the principal investigators who ignored the mortality rates that exceeded conventional treatment. It explained that perhaps the investigators and Fred Hutchinson were motivated by their own financial interests in Genetic Systems, a company that held a financial stake in the antibodies developed to diagnose or treat infectious disease and cancer. This information was not revealed to the patients or the IRB. Though the IRB inquired into the possible financial conflicts of interests among the researchers with a financial stake in the success of the protocol, the researchers denied the conflict and the IRB failed to pursue a fuller investigation. More revealing of systemic failure, the Seattle Times blamed the center's IRB as well as the external agencies tasked with oversight of the study. These entities allegedly failed in their singular responsibility to protect the human subjects from ill-conceived or unreasonably dangerous experimentation. Moreover, Fred Hutchinson's IRB allegedly failed to exercise independent leadership and oversight, and thereby failed to perform the duties mandated by federal law. For example, the Seattle Times pointed to instances where the IRB's concerns were ignored, it approved protocol changes with only a perfunctory review, and most alarmingly, where the criticism voiced by IRB members within the institution was chilled through intimidation. The lead researcher chastised the IRB when he stated that in addition to the IRB members' responsibility to review the ethical considerations of the study, they were also required to assist the researchers and not hinder the research.

. . . Recently, the University of Pennsylvania also became embroiled in a public controversy arising out of human subject experimentation. In September 1999, eighteen-year-old Jesse Gelsinger died while participating in a University of Pennsylvania Phase I clinical trial testing a new gene therapy treatment for ornithine transcarbamylase ("OTC") deficiency, a rare, genetic liver disorder. Although many individuals with OTC die in infancy, Gelsinger, suffering from a milder form, was able to manage it with a low protein diet supplemented by medication. Gelsinger's physicians recommended the gene therapy trial conducted at the University of Pennsylvania, and eight days after the infusion of a genetically altered virus by the researchers, Gelsinger died. His father reported that he and his son believed that the experimental procedures offered therapeutic potential. In the words of one commentator, however, "there was virtually no chance" that the experiment—which researchers insisted on calling a therapy trial—would provide him with any therapeutic benefit. The study intended to evaluate the safety of the procedure, rather than the treatment's effectiveness. The possibility of improvement from this study was overstated, whereas the risks were understated in the consent form. Moreover, the Gelsingers were not informed that "at the time the study commenced, in more than 390 clinical trials of gene therapy in the last decade, no one had ever been cured," and in addition, the consent form failed to "disclose that in earlier versions of the same experiments on monkeys, the monkeys had died."

Reportedly, evidence suggested that there were earlier problems and that the studies were not yielding favorable results. Of the seventeen patients treated prior to Gelsinger, only three showed any sign of improvement or benefit. More-over, the virus given to Gelsinger "spread far beyond his liver, where it was supposed to correct the defect in his cells. Within the liver it had bound to immune cells far more than to the hepatocytes it was meant to target." In addi-tion, Gelsinger's attorneys alleged that the researchers may have had substantial conflicts of interest due to their financial interests in the company that owned the product being tested. These interests were undisclosed to the participants in the study.

. . . Gelsinger's estate filed suit against the researchers, the university and its officials, including the bioethicist who advised the project. The suit alleged that the researchers failed to obtain informed consent, concealed prior adverse events, and failed to disclose that the institution and the director of the gene therapy institute would profit from the school's discovery because both had a financial interest in the company that sponsored the gene research. The Gel-singer family settled the suit with the University of Pennsylvania.

On June 3, 2001, Ellen Roche, a healthy volunteer, died following her par-ticipation in an asthma study conducted by Johns Hopkins University. As a participant in the study, Roche inhaled hexamethonium, a substance that has not been "approved by the FDA for use in humans, and has never been approved by the FDA for administration via inhalation." The ensuing federal investigation required Johns Hopkins to immediately suspend all federally funded research, with limited exceptions, until specific corrective actions were taken.

As with the Protocol 126 and Gelsinger incidents, critics claimed the IRB was partly responsible. The determination letter issued by the Office of Human Research Protections [which monitors human subject research funded by federal agencies] noted the IRB's failure to adequately review the experiment, and particularly to evaluate the use of hexamethonium. The IRB neglected to acquire literature, "available [through] routine MEDLINE and internet data-base searches," on the known lung toxicity of hexamethonium. . . . OHRP also criticized the IRB's approval of an informed consent document that, among other shortcomings, "failed to adequately describe the research procedures" and the "reasonably foreseeable risk and discomforts." Remarkably, OHRP also determined that the IRB neglected to review research at a convened meeting.

> ## Trudo Lemmens & Paul B. Miller, The Human Subjects Trade: Ethical and Legal Issues Surrounding Recruitment Incentives
> ### 31 J.L. Med. & Ethics 398 (2003)

A PriceWaterhouseCoopers report has suggested that in order to maintain levels of profitability, pharmaceutical companies will have to launch, on average, between twenty-four and thirty-four new drugs per year. This in part explains why as of 1999 more than 450 medicines were under development for heart disease, cancer, and stroke, and why a further 191 were being developed for Alzheimer's, arthritis, and depression. This also explains in part the surge in numbers of physicians involved in clinical trials: 30,000 more physicians were involved in clinical trials in the United States in 1998 than a decade earlier, an increase of 600 percent. Over the same period, there has been a 60 percent increase in numbers of community-based clinical trials conducted. As the latter data indicate, community-based physicians, most often remunerated through monetary incentives, are increasingly competing with researchers in academic institutions for access to research subjects. The conduct of clinical trials is shifting from the teaching hospitals of academic institutions to the offices of private physicians and CROs [Contract Research Organizations].

How the above-noted trends translate in terms of numbers of subjects enrolled per annum in research can unfortunately only be guessed at. No official numbers are available in the United States or Canada. This in itself is an indication of the troubling lacunae in the oversight of research. In order to understand the importance of regulation and oversight, as well as the human significance of existing pressures on the system, it is surely essential that we know how many people participate in research. Adil E. Shamoo has estimated—based on U.S. National Institutes of Health (NIH) data on expenditures per subject and available statistics on gross private investment in research—that approximately 18,000,000 people participate in research each year in the United States, which amounts to approximately 6 percent of the population.

> # *Jesse A. Goldner, Dealing with Conflicts of Interest in Biomedical Research: IRB Oversight As the Next Best Solution to the Abolitionist Approach*
> ## 28 J.L. Med. & Ethics 379 (2000)

Conflicts of interest, of course, are by no means merely financial—at least in the narrowest sense of that word. The true issue may not necessarily be one of a physician's honesty or integrity but, rather, one of his or her unconscious biases and influences, which may be subtle and difficult to detect. Some such conflicts, however, can be equally insidious. Motivation to conduct research is an enormously complex matter that no doubt differs among individuals. At one end of the spectrum may be the altruistic, unselfish incentive to improve the lives of others. At the other is the arguably crass, but surely comprehensible, human desire to improve one's financial situation and level of creature comforts by amassing and spending capital. Between these lies a range of potential sources of motivation: the simple joy that comes from successful efforts and progress, the satisfaction felt when work is finally developed and completed, the desire to produce insights, and the quest for recognition through publications and professional advancements. Finally, institutional work environments themselves can generate immense pressures.

THE PRICES WE PAY AND THE NEED FOR CHANGE

Concerns about the implications of unchecked conflicts of interest extend beyond the issue of the need to protect individual research subjects from inappropriate perils engendered by such conflicts. These conflicts, far too frequently, can lead to deficiencies in the validity of the data obtained and, thus, in the robustness of the analyses that result: that is, bad research. When this occurs, of course, the harm that transpires is not solely to the research subjects themselves—whose health and safety are put at risk—but also to individuals in the population at large who later may pass up more efficacious therapy in favor of intervention modalities that are seemingly effective, but only because the bad research supports them. The problem, however, extends even beyond members of this broader group that may be harmed. The result of conflicts of interest and bad research is that public confidence and trust in the entire research enterprise vanishes. This has implications for the willingness of individuals to participate as subjects in research, for the public to financially support research efforts, and ultimately for our very ability to continue to alleviate suffering, conquer disease, and treat painful medical conditions.

Finally, given what we know about human nature, we need to recognize that despite the existence of sound arguments that favor maximum efforts to prohibit conflicts of interest in biomedical research, the political reality is such that we simply may be unable to effectuate such a strategy. The abolitionist position, preferable though it is, may be impracticable in the current environment, where both institutions and individual investigators have so much at stake in maintaining some semblance of the status quo. Conflicts of interest may well be unavoidable. Consequently, the very most we can do is eliminate some, minimize those that remain, and provide adequate education to increase the likelihood that conflicts will be recognized and managed appropriately.

INDIVIDUAL CONFLICTS OF INTEREST

. . . The issue of individual conflicts of interest ordinarily arises when an investigator conducts a clinical study in which he or she has a financial interest. The investigator's financial interest in the research may manifest itself in a variety of ways. . . .

A. Per Capita Payments and Finder's Fees

The first situation in which an investigator's conflict of interest may arise involves clinical trials sponsored by pharmaceutical manufacturers. It is a common practice in the pharmaceutical industry to pay investigators for their recruiting of subjects on a per capita basis. To obtain a sufficient number of patient-subjects in an acceptable period of time, manufacturers offer investigators financial incentives to enter patients into studies. One commentator estimates that remuneration levels are as high as $3,000 per subject. Another indicates that such levels typically range from $2,000 to $5,000 per subject. These payments purportedly are intended to offset medical expenses incurred by the subject's participation, as well as the data management costs incurred by the investigator, but the amounts involved typically exceed these costs. In an academic setting, the researcher commonly uses money in excess of that required for conducting the study to purchase supplies and equipment or to support travel to scientific meetings. In addition, this money is often used to fund research efforts that may not have been judged sufficiently important or scientifically rigorous to warrant funding by government agencies via the standard peer review process. But particularly outside of academic environments, the money left over after study-related expenses have been met will remain in the researcher-physician's pocket.

In addition to the per capita payments, pharmaceutical sponsors frequently offer investigators, or their staff, incentives to boost subject enrollment. These incentives may be financial, often in the form of bonus payments per subject enrolled; or they may be non-financial, such as granting the investigator authorship on a corresponding study paper, providing the research site with office or medical equipment, or offering gifts such as books. There are several reasons, inherent in how the pharmaceutical industry operates, why sponsors offer these types of incentives. First, sponsors are pushing tight enrollment deadlines. These shorter deadlines reflect the pharmaceutical companies' desire to be as profitable as possible. The time for a drug patent starts running when the patent application is filed, which is prior to the clinical testing of the drug. Sponsors seek to shorten the testing phase so that they may recoup research and development costs before similar drugs appear on the market. Second, there is an intensified search for subjects. Sponsors need increasing numbers of subjects who meet particular eligibility criteria to fill more and larger clinical trials. As a result of these pressures, pharmaceutical sponsors must offer researchers incentives to meet the sponsors' needs. . . .

B.   Gifts From Industry Sponsors

Another conflict of interest stemming from links with the pharmaceutical industry is the research-related gift. Gifts from companies to academic and other investigators can be in the form of biomaterials, discretionary funds, and support for students, research equipment or trips to professional meetings. A study in the Journal of the American Medical Association found that 43 percent of researchers who responded to a survey had received a research-related gift in the last three years. Of those researchers who had received a gift, 66 percent reported that the gift was important to their research. The survey results also suggest that corporate gifts may have been associated with a variety of donor restrictions and expectations. For example, some donors expected pre-publication review of any articles or reports stemming from the use of the gift, while others expected ownership of all patentable results from research in which the gift was used. In addition to difficulties stemming from the donor's expectations, research-related gifts are problematic in that they may cause an investigator to choose to develop or pursue one protocol over another out of a desire for future gifts. Alternatively, if an investigator is dependent on the gifts—similar to 13 percent of surveyed investigators who indicated that the gift was "essential" to their research—he or she may be inclined to publish or emphasize favorable results or minimize unfavorable aspects of a study, irrespective of the data, in order to help assure future gifts and support from a particular company.

Research indicates that, despite physician claims to the contrary, gifts have an effect on physicians. For example, a study published in the medical journal Chest examined the impact of an all-expense-paid trip to a resort hosting a seminar sponsored by a pharmaceutical company on physician prescribing patterns. The majority of the physicians interviewed insisted that this elaborate gift would not influence their prescribing decisions. The study demonstrated, however, that this promotional technique, used by some pharmaceutical companies, was associated with a significant increase in the prescribing of the promoted drugs at the institution studied. Thus, such enticements clearly influenced the behavior of the physicians in clinical practice. If minor gifts influence the prescribing conduct of physicians, then more major gift incentives are likely to have a pernicious effect on the projects physician-researchers pursue and the way in which researchers report outcomes. This is why it is important for universities and other research institutions to control the existence of this type of conflict of interest by maintaining an appropriate policy regarding gifts from industry.

C.   *Stock Ownership and Similar Financial Interests*

A financial conflict of interest in the research setting may also occur when an investigator holds stock in, or serves as a paid consultant to, the manufacturer whose drugs or devices are under investigation. As noted earlier, a concern with these types of arrangements stems from the fear that the potential for profit may subtly affect an investigator's interpretation of his or her research or that the promise of large profits could affect the way the investigator presents his or her findings publicly. The potential for monetary gain could also influence the investigator's view of ethical issues. For example, if an investigator perceives the possible risk involved in the study to be great, he or she may attempt to offer the subjects higher levels of compensation as an inducement to enter the study. If the investigator is still unsuccessful in enrolling subjects, he or she may target institutions with populations such as the mentally ill or mentally retarded as a source of subjects. Even in situations where the potential for profit does not affect the investigator's work product, the perception of bias may linger in the minds of other investigators and lay observers. In 1998, a comprehensive study of bias resulting from financial conflicts of interest was reported in an article published in the New England Journal of Medicine. This study surveyed eighty-nine investigators who had published research on calcium channel antagonists and found that 96 percent of the supportive authors had financial ties to the manufacturers. Only 60 percent of the authors of neutral papers and 37 percent of the authors of critical papers were found to have such ties. In addition, only two of the seventy papers analyzed in the study included disclosures of the investigator's financial relationship with the manufacturer. In part, as a result of this demonstration of the potential for bias, a relatively recent study indicated that some 15 percent of journals now require disclosure of stock ownership of companies the author is evaluating. . . .

D.   *Conflicts of Interest Related to the Academic Research Environment*

All financial conflicts of interest facing individual investigators are not as overt as stock ownership, per capita payments, and gifts from pharmaceutical companies. There are, for example, conflicts of interest embedded in the highly competitive nature of academic research. Investigators often pursue clinical research in order to build their reputations and academic standing. In addition, investigators at different institutions may pursue the same clinical research simultaneously. Since recognition, future research grants, and job prospects generally go to those who publish first, and since criteria used to appoint, evaluate, and promote faculty emphasize publication output, investigators experience tremendous pressure to conduct and conclude research quickly. This pressure to produce continues unremittingly throughout an investigator's career. Therefore, an investigator's research may eventually fall prey to his or her desire for recognition. Although the investigator's motivations may not necessarily be directly or even largely financial in these situations, conflicts may stem as much from the desire for recognition or advancement as from corresponding increases in compensation.

University researchers also face financial conflicts of interest as a result of the passage of the Bayh-Dole Act in 1980, which "encourages academic institutions supported by federal grants to patent and license new products developed by their faculty members and to share royalties with the researchers." The National Institutes of Health (NIH) has a standard process for determining who can take title to an invention and file a patent application. After notifying the NIH of an invention, the awardee institution has two years to determine if it will do so, and the researcher himself will share in any profits. If the institution does not elect to take title, then the NIH can choose to do so, in which case the individual inventor also is guaranteed a portion of any royalties received. However, if the NIH does not take title, then the researcher-inventor himself may file for a patent.

After the researcher files for a patent, he or she may form a biotechnology company or enter into a joint venture with these types of companies. The stock options and directors' fees from these corporations may far exceed the salaries that the researchers receive from their universities. The potential for commercialization may create incentives for academic researchers to pursue areas of research that are likely to result in patentable inventions. At the least, it is encouraging researchers to think from a business perspective instead of a purely scientific one. Although this is an acceptable purpose, inadequate attention may have been given to conflicts of interest issues, which will always be a concern in an entrepreneurial environment. . . .

II. INSTITUTIONAL CONFLICTS OF INTEREST

Many academic medical centers are finding themselves squeezed for clinical revenue due to a combination of lower levels of government payments through Medicare and Medicaid and an increase in competition for managed care dollars from nonacademic medical centers. As a result, the temptation to emphasize research dollars as a source of funding may well increase. Historically, federal and state governments provided funding for scientific research while the contributions from private industry were minuscule. More recently, funds received from private industry have helped sustain many of these research budgets, which had previously declined. Although there is a strong incentive for universities to seek funding from private research companies, there is also a potential conflict of interest from the affiliation because medical entrepreneurialism is not only a goal of individual researchers, but also of the universities themselves. Conflict-of-interest issues arise as a result of the tension between a desire to make contributions to improve medical treatment and the universities' financial interest in research.

The passage of the Bayh-Dole Act has also compounded institutional conflicts of interest. Under the Act, sponsoring universities are given intellectual property rights in the inventions created with federal funding. These rights are then freely transferable to private companies. The purpose of the Bayh-Dole Act was to establish uniform vesting of patent rights in inventions resulting from federally funded research as well as to encourage the commercialization of such inventions. The result, however, has been to give academic institutions and researchers intellectual-property rights. Thus, the institution may potentially obtain valuable patent rights as a direct result of research conducted at the university. Furthermore, the passage of the Bayh-Dole Act has also strengthened the ties between academic institutions and for-profit industries because academic institutions need an avenue to facilitate the movement of new products, such as drugs or devices, from the institution to the marketplace. Such ongoing relationships, however, may prove to be problematic in the long run as universities may become increasingly tempted to lose their objectivity.

NOTES AND QUESTIONS

1. *Conflicts of interest.*   Identify the various conflicts of interest that arise in the context of medical research. How many potential conflicts can you name? What are the potential harms of such conflicts? As you read the following materials, consider how conflicts of interest are handled in the ethical codes, federal regulations, and cases applying principles of tort law.

2. *Reducing the impact of conflicts of interest.*   Although the various conflicts of interest that may inhere in medical research have recently received much attention, most of the solutions or "reforms" that have been adopted have focused on the disclosure of such potential conflicts to IRBs considering whether to approve a research protocol, relying on the researcher's institution to "manage, reduce, or eliminate" conflicting interests. See, e.g., Responsibility of Applicants for Promoting Objectivity in Research for Which PHS Funding is Sought, 42 U.S.C. 216, 289b-1, 299c-3 (1995). A 2008 investigation spearheaded by Senator Charles Grassley of Iowa revealed egregious examples of underreporting industry payments by researchers. Dr. Joseph Biederman, a world-renowned child psychiatrist at Harvard University, reportedly earned over $1.6 million in consulting fees from pharmaceutical companies between 2000 and 2007, but reported little of this to his IRB. The revelation was particularly startling not only because of the large amount of money involved and its hidden nature, but also because

Biederman, along with some of his colleagues, profited so greatly from promoting the controversial prescription of antipsychotic medications to children with bipolar disorder, a condition once thought to be present only in the adult population. Gardiner Harris & Benedict Carey, Researchers Fail to Reveal Full Drug Pay, N.Y. Times, June 8, 2008, at A1.

Originally introduced by Senator Grassley in 2007, the Physicians Payment Sunshine Act, passed with the Affordable Care Act of 2010, will be implemented when the Centers for Medicare and Medicaid adopt final regulations. The law requires pharmaceutical, medical device, and biological and medical supply manufacturers to report for public disclosure any payments or gifts to physicians and teaching hospitals in excess of $10, as well as certain ownership or investment interests held by physicians or members of their immediate families.

Do you think disclosure should be made to the human subjects of research themselves? What do you think subjects would make of them? Do you think the focus of future attempts to reduce the impact of conflicts of interest should be on disclosure of the conflicts or their reduction or elimination?

3. *American Medical Association and finders' fees.*   According to law professor and physician Bill Sage,

> It has taken medicine relatively long to recognize and respond to the conflict of interest inherent in research payments to ordinary physicians. The American Medical Association's first opinion on conflicts of interest in research emphasized that "remuneration received by the researcher . . . be commensurate with the efforts of the researcher on behalf of the company." This rule had the unintended consequence of favoring payments to physicians who work really hard to get their patients to participate in studies—with a much higher attendant risk that the patient's original course of care will be altered as a result—over payments made to physicians who maintain a passive but perhaps less harmful attitude. Sensing this danger, the AMA clarified its position in a subsequent opinion, stating bluntly that "offering or accepting payment for referring patients to research studies (finder's fees) is unethical."

William M. Sage, Some Principles Require Principals: Why Banning "Conflicts of Interest" Won't Solve Incentive Problems in Biomedical Research, 85 Tex. L. Rev. 1413, 1458–1459 (2007).

4. *The dual role of physician and researcher and therapeutic misconception.*   The term *therapeutic misconception* is widely used to describe the confusion that research subjects may have regarding the purpose and therefore operation of research trials in which they're involved. They tend to assume, even if told otherwise, that "decisions about their care are being made solely with their benefit in mind"—an inappropriate assumption, write the authors who originally coined the term, "because of the inherent conflicts between the role of investigator and the role of physician-caretaker." Paul S. Appelbaum et al., The Therapeutic Misconception: Informed Consent in Psychiatric Research, 5 Int. J. Law Psychiatry 319–329 (1982).

Consider what Jay Katz has written about the dual role of doctor and researcher:

> Physician-investigators must see themselves as scientists only and not as doctors. In conflating clinical trials and therapy, as well as patients and subjects, as if both were one and the same, physician-investigators unwittingly become double

agents with conflicting loyalties. . . . Moreover, since loyalty to the research protocol will take precedence over faithfulness to the therapeutic mission, and since physician-investigators will tend to view the person before them as a patient and not as a subject, the tragic fact that human beings are used for the ends of others can readily become obliterated. It is then not surprising that physician-investigators, without fully knowing it, become confused about the nature of their task, as well as about their perceptions of themselves and their patient-subjects.

The investigators who appear before patient-subjects as physicians in white coats create confusion. Patients come to hospitals with the trusting expectation that their doctors will care for them. They will view an invitation to participate in research as a professional recommendation that is intended to serve their individual treatment interests. It is that belief, that trust, which physician-investigators must vigorously challenge so that patient-subjects appreciate that in research, unlike therapy, the research question comes first.

Jay Katz, Human Experimentation and Human Rights, 38 St. Louis U. L.J. 7 (1993).

For readings on the therapeutic misconception of cancer patients, see C. Daugherty et al., Perceptions of Cancer Patients and Their Physicians Involved in Phase I Trials, 13 J. Clin. Oncol. 1062–1072 (1995) (reporting survey results of cancer patients and concluding that their enrollment in Phase I trials is motivated by the hope of therapeutic benefit rather than for altruistic reasons); M. Miller, Phase I Cancer Trials: A Collusion of Misunderstanding, 30 Hastings Ctr. Rep. 34–43 (Jul.-Aug. 2000). Miller writes,

It seems to me that we [physician-researchers] do not view Phase I trials as an extension of medical practice, nor adopt the oxymoronic language of 'therapeutic research,' deliberately or with the aim of deceiving subjects into thinking that they are patients. Rather, we do so unwittingly and in order that we may continue to see ourselves as compassionate physicians even as we perform duties in service of dispassionate science.

CHALLENGING ISSUES: LESSONS FROM LEGAL ETHICS?

How do other professions handle conflicts of interest, and is there any wisdom in following their example? Like physician-researchers, members of the legal profession are subject to serious conflicts of interest in their professional work— for example, when the interests of their clients conflict, or the interests of a current client and former client conflict, or when the lawyers themselves have interests in conflict with their representation of a client. Certain of these types of conflicts may, under the principles of legal ethics, be considered "nonconsentable." The thought is that in some situations, no amount of disclosure can result in adequate protection of the client's interests. The attorney is prohibited in such situations from even asking the client to consent to the representation.

Should the dual role of doctor and researcher be considered either so detrimental to the patient-subject or too difficult for the patient-subject to adequately understand that it should be "nonconsentable"?

If "physician-investigators must see themselves as scientists only and not as doctors," as Katz suggests, wouldn't that mean that the patient-subject had no doctor and thus had to obtain one? What might be gained or lost from a requirement that a subject of research have his or her own independent physician in regards to the proposed research protocol?

For more on this subject, see Lois Shepherd & Margaret Foster Riley, In Plain Sight: A Solution to a Fundamental Challenge in Human Research, 40 J.L. Med. & Ethics 970 (2012).

C.   LEGAL APPROACHES

1.   Ethics Codes

The Nuremberg Code, created and adopted by the tribunal that judged the Nazi doctors, established for the first time clear limits on medical research. As such, it has been highly influential in the establishment of regulations governing human subject research and in evaluating the ethical and legal propriety of particular practices. The Code does not, however, have the force of binding law.

> **The Nuremberg Code**
> **II Trials of War Criminals Before the Nuremberg Military Tribunals Under Control Council Law No. 10, 181–182 (1946–1949)**

1. The voluntary consent of the human subject is absolutely essential. This means that the person involved should have legal capacity to give consent; should be so situated as to be able to exercise free power of choice, without the intervention of any element of force, fraud, deceit, duress, overreaching, or other ulterior form of constraint or coercion; and should have sufficient knowledge and comprehension of the elements of the subject matter involved as to enable him to make an understanding and enlightened decision. This latter element requires that before the acceptance of an affirmative decision by the experimental subject there should be made known to him the nature, duration, and purpose of the experiment; the method and means by which it is to be conducted; all inconveniences and hazards reasonably to be expected; and the effects upon his health or person which may possibly come from his participation in the experiment. The duty and responsibility for ascertaining the quality of the consent rests upon each individual who initiates, directs, or engages in the experiment. It is a personal duty and responsibility which may not be delegated to another with impunity.

2. The experiment should be such as to yield fruitful results for the good of society, unprocurable by other methods or means of study, and not random and unnecessary in nature.

3. The experiment should be so designed and based on the results of animal experimentation and a knowledge of the natural history of the disease or other problem under study that the anticipated results will justify the performance of the experiment.

4. The experiment should be so conducted as to avoid all unnecessary physical and mental suffering and injury.

5. No experiment should be conducted where there is a prior reason to believe that death or disabling injury will occur; except, perhaps, in those experiments where the experimental physicians also serve as subjects.

6. The degree of risk to be taken should never exceed that determined by the humanitarian importance of the problem to be solved by the experiment.

7. Proper preparations should be made and adequate facilities provided to protect the experimental subject against even remote possibilities of injury, disability, or death.

8. The experiment should be conducted only by scientifically qualified persons. The highest degree of skill and care should be required through all stages of the experiment of those who conduct or engage in the experiment.

9. During the course of the experiment the human subject should be at liberty to bring the experiment to an end if he has reached the physical or mental state where continuation of the experiment seems to him to be impossible.

10. During the course of the experiment the scientist in charge must be prepared to terminate the experiment at any stage, if he has probable cause to believe, in the exercise of the good faith, superior skill and careful judgement required of him that a continuation of the experiment is likely to result in injury, disability, or death to the experimental subject.

The Belmont Report is the foundational document of U.S. research ethics principles. It was issued in 1979 by the National Commission for the Protection of Human Subjects of Biomedical and Behavioral Research (usually called simply the "National Commission") in response to the charge issued under the National Research Act of 1974 (Pub. L. 93-348) "to identify the basic ethical principles that should underlie the conduct of biomedical and behavioral research involving human subjects and to develop guidelines which should be followed to assure that such research is conducted in accordance with those principles."

|| ***The Belmont Report*** ||
National Commission for the Protection of Human Subjects of Biomedical and Behavioral Research (1974)

ETHICAL PRINCIPLES & GUIDELINES FOR RESEARCH INVOLVING HUMAN SUBJECTS

Scientific research has produced substantial social benefits. It has also posed some troubling ethical questions. Public attention was drawn to these questions by reported abuses of human subjects in biomedical experiments, especially during the Second World War. During the Nuremberg War Crime Trials, the Nuremberg code was drafted as a set of standards for judging physicians and scientists who had conducted biomedical experiments on concentration camp prisoners. This code became the prototype of many later codes intended to assure that research involving human subjects would be carried out in an ethical manner.

The codes consist of rules, some general, others specific, that guide the investigators or the reviewers of research in their work. Such rules often are inadequate to cover complex situations; at times they come into conflict, and they are frequently difficult to interpret or apply. Broader ethical principles will provide a basis on which specific rules may be formulated, criticized and interpreted.

Three principles, or general prescriptive judgments, that are relevant to research involving human subjects are identified in this statement. Other principles may also be relevant. These three are comprehensive, however, and are stated at a level of generalization that should assist scientists, subjects, reviewers and interested citizens to understand the ethical issues inherent in research involving human subjects. These principles cannot always be applied so as to resolve beyond dispute particular ethical problems. The objective is to provide an analytical framework that will guide the resolution of ethical problems arising from research involving human subjects.

This statement consists of a distinction between research and practice, a discussion of the three basic ethical principles, and remarks about the application of these principles.

A.   *Boundaries Between Practice and Research*

It is important to distinguish between biomedical and behavioral research, on the one hand, and the practice of accepted therapy on the other, in order to know what activities ought to undergo review for the protection of human subjects of research. The distinction between research and practice is blurred partly because both often occur together (as in research designed to evaluate a therapy) and partly because notable departures from standard practice are often called "experimental" when the terms "experimental" and "research" are not carefully defined.

For the most part, the term "practice" refers to interventions that are designed solely to enhance the well-being of an individual patient or client and that have a reasonable expectation of success. The purpose of medical or behavioral practice is to provide diagnosis, preventive treatment or therapy to particular individuals. By contrast, the term "research" designates an activity designed to test an hypothesis, permit conclusions to be drawn, and thereby to develop or contribute to generalizable knowledge (expressed, for example, in theories, principles, and statements of relationships). Research is usually described in a formal protocol that sets forth an objective and a set of procedures designed to reach that objective.

When a clinician departs in a significant way from standard or accepted practice, the innovation does not, in and of itself, constitute research. The fact that a procedure is "experimental," in the sense of new, untested or different, does not automatically place it in the category of research. Radically new procedures of this description should, however, be made the object of formal research at an early stage in order to determine whether they are safe and effective. Thus, it is the responsibility of medical practice committees, for example, to insist that a major innovation be incorporated into a formal research project.

Research and practice may be carried on together when research is designed to evaluate the safety and efficacy of a therapy. This need not cause any confusion regarding whether or not the activity requires review; the general rule is that if there is any element of research in an activity, that activity should undergo review for the protection of human subjects.

B. Basic Ethical Principles

The expression "basic ethical principles" refers to those general judgments that serve as a basic justification for the many particular ethical prescriptions and evaluations of human actions. Three basic principles, among those generally accepted in our cultural tradition, are particularly relevant to the ethics of research involving human subjects: the principles of respect of persons, beneficence and justice.

1. Respect for Persons

Respect for persons incorporates at least two ethical convictions: first, that individuals should be treated as autonomous agents, and second, that persons with diminished autonomy are entitled to protection. The principle of respect for persons thus divides into two separate moral requirements: the requirement to acknowledge autonomy and the requirement to protect those with diminished autonomy.

An autonomous person is an individual capable of deliberation about personal goals and of acting under the direction of such deliberation. To respect autonomy is to give weight to autonomous persons' considered opinions and choices while refraining from obstructing their actions unless they are clearly detrimental to others. To show lack of respect for an autonomous agent is to repudiate that person's considered judgments, to deny an individual the freedom to act on those considered judgments, or to withhold information necessary to make a considered judgment, when there are no compelling reasons to do so.

However, not every human being is capable of self-determination. The capacity for self-determination matures during an individual's life, and some individuals lose this capacity wholly or in part because of illness, mental disability, or circumstances that severely restrict liberty. Respect for the immature and the incapacitated may require protecting them as they mature or while they are incapacitated.

Some persons are in need of extensive protection, even to the point of excluding them from activities which may harm them; other persons require little protection beyond making sure they undertake activities freely and with awareness of possible adverse consequence. The extent of protection afforded should depend upon the risk of harm and the likelihood of benefit. The judgment that any individual lacks autonomy should be periodically reevaluated and will vary in different situations.

In most cases of research involving human subjects, respect for persons demands that subjects enter into the research voluntarily and with adequate information. In some situations, however, application of the principle is not obvious. The involvement of prisoners as subjects of research provides an instructive example. On the one hand, it would seem that the principle of respect for persons requires that prisoners not be deprived of the opportunity to volunteer for research. On the other hand, under prison conditions they may be subtly coerced or unduly influenced to engage in research activities for which they would not otherwise volunteer. Respect for persons would then dictate that prisoners be protected. Whether to allow prisoners to "volunteer" or to "protect" them presents a dilemma. Respecting persons, in most hard cases, is often a matter of balancing competing claims urged by the principle of respect itself.

2.   Beneficence

Persons are treated in an ethical manner not only by respecting their decisions and protecting them from harm, but also by making efforts to secure their well-being. Such treatment falls under the principle of beneficence. The term "beneficence" is often understood to cover acts of kindness or charity that go beyond strict obligation. In this document, beneficence is understood in a stronger sense, as an obligation. Two general rules have been formulated as complementary expressions of beneficent actions in this sense: **(1)** do not harm and **(2)** maximize possible benefits and minimize possible harms.

The Hippocratic maxim "do no harm" has long been a fundamental principle of medical ethics. Claude Bernard extended it to the realm of research, saying that one should not injure one person regardless of the benefits that might come to others. However, even avoiding harm requires learning what is harmful; and, in the process of obtaining this information, persons may be exposed to risk of harm. Further, the Hippocratic Oath requires physicians to benefit their patients "according to their best judgment." Learning what will in fact benefit may require exposing persons to risk. The problem posed by these imperatives is to decide when it is justifiable to seek certain benefits despite the risks involved, and when the benefits should be foregone because of the risks.

The obligations of beneficence affect both individual investigators and society at large, because they extend both to particular research projects and to the entire enterprise of research. In the case of particular projects, investigators and members of their institutions are obliged to give forethought to the maximization of benefits and the reduction of risk that might occur from the research investigation. In the case of scientific research in general, members of the larger society are obliged to recognize the longer term benefits and risks that may result from the improvement of knowledge and from the development of novel medical, psychotherapeutic, and social procedures.

The principle of beneficence often occupies a well-defined justifying role in many areas of research involving human subjects. An example is found in research involving children. Effective ways of treating childhood diseases and fostering healthy development are benefits that serve to justify research involving children—even when individual research subjects are not direct beneficiaries. Research also makes it possible to avoid the harm that may result from the application of previously accepted routine practices that on closer investigation turn out to be dangerous. But the role of the principle of beneficence is not always so unambiguous. A difficult ethical problem remains, for example, about research that presents more than minimal risk without immediate prospect of direct benefit to the children involved. Some have argued that such research is inadmissible, while others have pointed out that this limit would rule out much research promising great benefit to children in the future. Here again, as with all hard cases, the different claims covered by the principle of beneficence may come into conflict and force difficult choices.

3. Justice

Who ought to receive the benefits of research and bear its burdens? This is a question of justice, in the sense of "fairness in distribution" or "what is deserved." An injustice occurs when some benefit to which a person is entitled is denied without good reason or when some burden is imposed unduly. Another way of conceiving the principle of justice is that equals ought to be treated equally. However, this statement requires explication. Who is equal and who is unequal? What considerations justify departure from equal distribution? Almost all commentators allow that distinctions based on experience, age, deprivation, competence, merit and position do sometimes constitute criteria justifying differential treatment for certain purposes. It is necessary, then, to explain in what respects people should be treated equally. There are several widely accepted formulations of just ways to distribute burdens and benefits. Each formulation mentions some relevant property on the basis of which burdens and benefits should be distributed. These formulations are (1) to each person an equal share, (2) to each person according to individual need, (3) to each person according to individual effort, (4) to each person according to societal contribution, and (5) to each person according to merit.

Questions of justice have long been associated with social practices such as punishment, taxation and political representation. Until recently these questions have not generally been associated with scientific research. However, they are foreshadowed even in the earliest reflections on the ethics of research involving human subjects. For example, during the 19th and early 20th centuries the burdens of serving as research subjects fell largely upon poor ward patients, while the benefits of improved medical care flowed primarily to private patients. Subsequently, the exploitation of unwilling prisoners as research subjects in Nazi concentration camps was condemned as a particularly flagrant injustice. In this country, in the 1940's, the Tuskegee syphilis study used disadvantaged, rural black men to study the untreated course of a disease that is by no means confined to that population. These subjects were deprived of demonstrably effective treatment in order not to interrupt the project, long after such treatment became generally available.

Against this historical background, it can be seen how conceptions of justice are relevant to research involving human subjects. For example, the selection of research subjects needs to be scrutinized in order to determine whether some classes (e.g., welfare patients, particular racial and ethnic minorities, or persons confined to institutions) are being systematically selected simply because of their easy availability, their compromised position, or their manipulability, rather than for reasons directly related to the problem being studied. Finally, whenever research supported by public funds leads to the development of therapeutic devices and procedures, justice demands both that these not provide advantages only to those who can afford them and that such research should not unduly involve persons from groups unlikely to be among the beneficiaries of subsequent applications of the research.

C. Applications

Applications of the general principles to the conduct of research leads to consideration of the following requirements: informed consent, risk/benefit assessment, and the selection of subjects of research. [Due to space limitations, only selected portions are included here.–EDS.]

1. Informed Consent

Respect for persons requires that subjects, to the degree that they are capable, be given the opportunity to choose what shall or shall not happen to them. This opportunity is provided when adequate standards for informed consent are satisfied.

While the importance of informed consent is unquestioned, controversy prevails over the nature and possibility of an informed consent. Nonetheless, there is widespread agreement that the consent process can be analyzed as containing three elements: information, comprehension and voluntariness.

Information. Most codes of research establish specific items for disclosure intended to assure that subjects are given sufficient information. These items generally include: the research procedure, their purposes, risks and anticipated benefits, alternative procedures (where therapy is involved), and a statement offering the subject the opportunity to ask questions and to withdraw at any time from the research. Additional items have been proposed, including how subjects are selected, the person responsible for the research, etc.

However, a simple listing of items does not answer the question of what the standard should be for judging how much and what sort of information should be provided. One standard frequently invoked in medical practice, namely the information commonly provided by practitioners in the field or in the locale, is inadequate since research takes place precisely when a common understanding does not exist. Another standard, currently popular in malpractice law, requires the practitioner to reveal the information that reasonable persons would wish to know in order to make a decision regarding their care. This, too, seems insufficient since the research subject, being in essence a volunteer, may wish to know considerably more about risks gratuitously undertaken than do patients who deliver themselves into the hand of a clinician for needed care. It may be that a standard of "the reasonable volunteer" should be proposed: the extent and nature of information should be such that persons, knowing that the procedure is neither necessary for their care nor perhaps fully understood, can decide whether they wish to participate in the furthering of knowledge. Even when some direct benefit to them is anticipated, the subjects should understand clearly the range of risk and the voluntary nature of participation.

A special problem of consent arises where informing subjects of some pertinent aspect of the research is likely to impair the validity of the research.

In many cases, it is sufficient to indicate to subjects that they are being invited to participate in research of which some features will not be revealed until the research is concluded. In all cases of research involving incomplete disclosure, such research is justified only if it is clear that (1) incomplete disclosure is truly necessary to accomplish the goals of the research, (2) there are no undisclosed risks to subjects that are more than minimal, and (3) there is an adequate plan for debriefing subjects, when appropriate, and for dissemination of research results to them. Information about risks should never be withheld for the purpose of eliciting the cooperation of subjects, and truthful answers should always be given to direct questions about the research. Care should be taken to distinguish cases in which disclosure would destroy or invalidate the research from cases in which disclosure would simply inconvenience the investigator.

Comprehension. The manner and context in which information is conveyed is as important as the information itself. For example, presenting information in a disorganized and rapid fashion, allowing too little time for consideration or curtailing opportunities for questioning, all may adversely affect a subject's ability to make an informed choice. . . .

Voluntariness. An agreement to participate in research constitutes a valid consent only if voluntarily given. This element of informed consent requires conditions free of coercion and undue influence. Coercion occurs when an overt threat of harm is intentionally presented by one person to another in order to obtain compliance. Undue influence, by contrast, occurs through an offer of an excessive, unwarranted, inappropriate or improper reward or other overture in order to obtain compliance. Also, inducements that would ordinarily be acceptable may become undue influences if the subject is especially vulnerable. . . .

2. Assessment of Risks and Benefits

. . . *The Nature and Scope of Risks and Benefits.* The requirement that research be justified on the basis of a favorable risk/benefit assessment bears a close relation to the principle of beneficence, just as the moral requirement that informed consent be obtained is derived primarily from the principle of respect for persons. The term "risk" refers to a possibility that harm may occur. However, when expressions such as "small risk" or "high risk" are used, they usually refer (often ambiguously) both to the chance (probability) of experiencing a harm and the severity (magnitude) of the envisioned harm.

The term "benefit" is used in the research context to refer to something of positive value related to health or welfare. Unlike, "risk," "benefit" is not a term that expresses probabilities. Risk is properly contrasted to probability of benefits, and benefits are properly contrasted with harms rather than risks of harm. Accordingly, so-called risk/benefit assessments are concerned with the probabilities and magnitudes of possible harm and anticipated benefits. Many kinds of possible harms and benefits need to be taken into account. There are, for example, risks of psychological harm, physical harm, legal harm, social harm and economic harm and the corresponding benefits. While the most likely types of harms to research subjects are those of psychological or physical pain or injury, other possible kinds should not be overlooked.

The Systematic Assessment of Risks and Benefits. It is commonly said that benefits and risks must be "balanced" and shown to be "in a favorable ratio." The metaphorical character of these terms draws attention to the difficulty of making precise judgments. Only on rare occasions will quantitative techniques be available for the scrutiny of research protocols. However, the idea of systematic, nonarbitrary analysis of risks and benefits should be emulated insofar as possible. . . .

Finally, assessment of the justifiability of research should reflect at least the following considerations: **(i)** Brutal or inhumane treatment of human subjects is never morally justified. **(ii)** Risks should be reduced to those necessary to achieve the research objective. It should be determined whether it is in fact necessary to use human subjects at all. Risk can perhaps never be entirely eliminated, but it can often be reduced by careful attention to alternative procedures. **(iii)** When research involves significant risk of serious impairment, review committees should be extraordinarily insistent on the justification of the risk (looking usually to the likelihood of benefit to the subject—or, in some rare cases, to the manifest voluntariness of the participation). **(iv)** When vulnerable populations are involved in research, the appropriateness of involving them should itself be demonstrated. A number of variables go into such judgments, including the nature and degree of risk, the condition of the particular population involved, and the nature and level of the anticipated benefits. **(v)** Relevant risks and benefits must be thoroughly arrayed in documents and procedures used in the informed consent process.

3.   Selection of Subjects

. . . Justice is relevant to the selection of subjects of research at two levels: the social and the individual. Individual justice in the selection of subjects would require that researchers exhibit fairness: thus, they should not offer potentially beneficial research only to some patients who are in their favor or select only "undesirable" persons for risky research. Social justice requires that distinction be drawn between classes of subjects that ought, and ought not, to participate in any particular kind of research, based on the ability of members of that class to bear burdens and on the appropriateness of placing further burdens on already burdened persons. Thus, it can be considered a matter of social justice that there is an order of preference in the selection of classes of subjects (e.g., adults before children) and that some classes of potential subjects (e.g., the institutionalized mentally infirm or prisoners) may be involved as research subjects, if at all, only on certain conditions.

Injustice may appear in the selection of subjects, even if individual subjects are selected fairly by investigators and treated fairly in the course of research. Thus injustice arises from social, racial, sexual and cultural biases institutionalized in society. Thus, even if individual researchers are treating their research subjects fairly, and even if IRBs are taking care to assure that subjects are selected fairly within a particular institution, unjust social patterns may nevertheless appear in the overall distribution of the burdens and benefits of research. . . .

Some populations, especially institutionalized ones, are already burdened in many ways by their infirmities and environments. When research is proposed that involves risks and does not include a therapeutic component, other less burdened classes of persons should be called upon first to accept these risks of research, except where the research is directly related to the specific conditions of the class involved. Also, even though public funds for research may often flow in the same directions as public funds for health care, it seems unfair that populations dependent on public health care constitute a pool of preferred research subjects if more advantaged populations are likely to be the recipients of the benefits.

NOTES AND QUESTIONS

1. *Common requirements for ethical research.* The Nuremberg Code and the Belmont Report have some age on them and, by the nature of their creation are not subject to revision. Nevertheless, the general principles enunciated in them have had considerable staying power. Compare the two documents. What would you list as the common requirements for ethical research between them? See E. J. Emanuel, D. Wendler & C. Grady, What Makes Clinical Research Ethical? 283 JAMA 2701 (2000).

2. *Declaration of Helsinki.* In 1964, the World Medical Association adopted what is known as the Declaration of Helsinki to provide a set of guidelines for medical research involving human subjects. The World Medical Association, founded in 1947, is a voluntary international confederation of national medical associations. The Declaration of Helsinki has undergone five revisions since its original adoption, becoming more specific with each revision and also more protective of the human subjects of research. It even expresses concern about animal welfare and the environment. Prior to Spring 2008, the FDA required compliance with the Declaration of Helsinki in clinical trials conducted in foreign countries if those trials were to be used as support for an investigational new drug application or marketing approval for a drug or biologic product. The 2000 amendments to the Declaration, however, were controversial for two main reasons. They limited placebo-controlled trials to those where no existing proven therapy exists, with exceptions for compelling reasons or for research of minor conditions in studies involving no additional serious risk of harm to patients" (paragraph 29 of the Declaration, as clarified by a later-added footnote). And they required access by research subjects to the best proven treatments following completion of the study (paragraph 30). In response, in April 2008, the FDA changed its rules to no longer require compliance with the Declaration and instead to allow foreign clinical trials if conducted according "Good Clinical Practice" (GCP). The revised rule provides:

> GCP is defined as a standard for the design, conduct, performance, monitoring, auditing, recording, analysis, and reporting of clinical trials in a way that provides assurance that the data and reported results are credible and accurate and that the rights, safety, and well-being of trial subjects are protected. GCP includes review and approval (or provision of a favorable opinion) by an independent ethics committee (IEC) before initiating a study, continuing review of an ongoing study by an IEC, and obtaining and documenting the freely given informed consent of the subject (or a subject's legally authorized representative, if the subject is unable to provide informed consent) before initiating a study.

Dept. of Health & Human Services, Food and Drug Administration, 21 C.F.R. 312.120 (2008). What do you think will be the effect of this rule change? Who would you expect to benefit from the new rule? The issue of different standards for trials conducted by U.S. companies in foreign countries is explored further in section 4.

3. *Legal effect?*   Neither the Nuremberg Code nor the Declaration of Helsinki has been formally adopted by governmental entities in the United States, and the Belmont Report is not "law." The *Grimes* case, reprinted below in section 3, as well as a number of other legal cases, has taken such declarations into account in determining what duties might be owed by researchers toward research subjects. What influence do you think such codes or declarations should have on a court's assessment of the duties owed under tort law to research subjects?

2.   Federal Regulations

> ### Carla M. Stalcup, Reviewing the Review Boards: Why Institutional Review Board Liability Does Not Make Good Business Sense
> #### 82 Wash. U. L.Q. 1593, 1596–1600 (2004)

The United States followed [the] international example[s of the Nuremberg Code and Declaration of Helsinki], beginning with the NIH establishing internal policies regarding research with human subjects, which were the first of their kind in the nation. These policies were later codified as federal regulations issued by the Department of Health, Education, and Welfare (now the Department of Health and Human Services (DHHS)) in July of 1974. In that same year, Congress enacted the National Research Act of 1974. The Act created the National Commission for the Protection of Human Subjects of Biomedical and Behavioral Research (National Commission). . . . To oversee human-subject protection, the National Commission also established the Office for the Protection of Research Risks (OPRR) (now the Office for Human Research Protections (OHRP)) within the NIH. In 1978, the National Commission published the Belmont Report. . . .

Seeing the need for explicit federal guidance, in 1981 the DHHS revised the regulations for protecting human subjects and codified them at Title 45, Part 46 of the Code of Federal Regulations. In 1991, wanting even more concrete federal safeguards, the DHHS adopted the Federal Policy for the Protection of Human Subjects as part of the revisions. These collective regulations became known as the "Common Rule" and have been promulgated by the seventeen federal agencies that conduct, support, or regulate human-subject research.[1]

The Common Rule is a set of federal regulations that incorporates the ethical principles and guidelines of the Belmont Report and standardizes human-subject protections among the different federal agencies and departments. Additional protections for vulnerable populations—pregnant women,

---

1. [The FDA does not follow the Common Rule in its regulation of research of investigative drugs or medical devices, but applies its own set of regulations for the protection of human subjects similar but not identical to the Common Rule.–EDS.]

handicapped or mentally disabled persons, prisoners, and children—have also been adopted by the DHHS. The responsibility of enforcing institutional compliance with the Common Rule has been delegated to the OHRP.

There are three essential requirements of the Common Rule: (1) assurances, (2) institutional review boards, and (3) informed consent. First, any institution that conducts federally funded human research must submit a written assurance to the sponsoring agency that its researchers will comply with all of the requirements of the Common Rule.

Second, the Common Rule mandates that all research institutions that receive federal funds for human research establish one or more IRBs. IRBs are composed of at least five members with varying backgrounds. An IRB reviews the proposed research protocols and informed consent forms in light of institutional commitments and regulations, applicable law, and standards of professional conduct and practice. As such, an IRB needs members with expertise in these different areas; an IRB cannot consist entirely of members of one profession, and at least one member must not be affiliated with the institution in any way.

In reviewing research, an IRB is allowed to approve, require modifications of, or disapprove research protocols, and must notify the investigators and the institution in writing of its decision regarding the proposed research activity. If the IRB disapproves a research protocol, it must give a statement of the reasons for its decision and allow the investigator an opportunity to respond in person or in writing. An IRB must also conduct continuing review of ongoing research at intervals appropriate to the degree of risk, but not less than once per year.

Before approving research, the IRB must ensure that the following criteria are satisfied: (1) the risks to subjects are minimized; (2) the risks to subjects are reasonable relative to the anticipated benefits; (3) subject selection is equitable; (4) informed consent is sought from each prospective subject or a legal guardian thereof; (5) informed consent will be appropriately documented; (6) provisions exist for monitoring data to ensure subject safety; and (7) provisions exist to protect the privacy and confidentiality of subjects. In addition, an IRB or the affiliated institution should maintain documentation of the IRB's activities, including all research proposals reviewed, minutes of IRB meetings, records of continuing review, and correspondences between the IRB and investigators.

Last, the Common Rule requires informed consent, whereby an investigator must obtain legally effective informed consent before involving a human being as a research subject. For consent to be considered valid, the prospective subject or her legal representative must have sufficient opportunity to consider whether to anticipate, and the consent information must be stated in language understandable to the subject or the representative. Informed consent forms cannot include language that waives or appears to waive any of the subject's legal rights, or releases or appears to release the investigator, the sponsor, the institution, or its agents from liability for negligence. Each subject must also be provided with a description of the research; an explanation of risks, benefits, and alternatives; a discussion of confidentiality; a list of contact people; and a statement that participation is voluntary and may be discontinued at any time.

A hypothetical research protocol follows the partial regulations appearing below to allow you to work through the regulations at a detailed level. It can be tedious work to read regulations in the absence of a context or a question that you are trying to answer. For this reason, you might want to skim the regulations first, then look at them in more detail in the context of the hypothetical, as you try to answer the questions raised by the proposed protocol.

> ## Code of Federal Regulations Title 45 —Public Welfare Subtitle A—Department of Health and Human Services Subchapter A—General Administration Part 46 —Protection of Human Subjects
> ### Revised January 15, 2009; Effective July 14, 2009

SUBPART A—BASIC HHS POLICY FOR PROTECTION OF HUMAN RESEARCH SUBJECTS

Sec. 46.101 To what does this policy apply?

(a) Except as provided in paragraph (b) of this section, this policy applies to all research involving human subjects conducted, supported or otherwise subject to regulation by any federal department or agency which takes appropriate administrative action to make the policy applicable to such research. This includes research conducted by federal civilian employees or military personnel, except that each department or agency head may adopt such procedural modifications as may be appropriate from an administrative standpoint. It also includes research conducted, supported, or otherwise subject to regulation by the federal government outside the United States. . . .

(b) Unless otherwise required by department or agency heads, research activities in which the only involvement of human subjects will be in one or more of the following categories are exempt from this policy: . . .

(4) Research, involving the collection or study of existing data, documents, records, pathological specimens, or diagnostic specimens, if these sources are publicly available or if the information is recorded by the investigator in such a manner that subjects cannot be identified, directly or through identifiers linked to the subjects. . . .

(f) This policy does not affect any state or local laws or regulations which may otherwise be applicable and which provide additional protections for human subjects. . . .

Sec. 46.102 Definitions. [This section provides definitions, including the following:]

(d) *Research* means a systematic investigation, including research development, testing, and evaluation, designed to develop or contribute to generalizable knowledge. Activities which meet this definition constitute research for purposes of this policy, whether or not they are conducted or supported under a program which is considered research for other purposes. . . .

(f) *Human subject* means a living individual about whom an investigator (whether professional or student) conducting research obtains

(1) Data through intervention or interaction with the individual, or

(2) Identifiable private information.

Intervention includes both physical procedures by which data are gathered (for example, venipuncture) and manipulations of the subject or the subject's environment that are performed for research purposes. Interaction includes communication or interpersonal contact between investigator and subject. Private information includes information about behavior that occurs in a context in which an individual can reasonably expect that no observation or recording is taking place, and information which has been provided for specific purposes by an individual and which the individual can reasonably expect will not be made public (for example, a medical record).

Private information must be individually identifiable (i.e., the identity of the subject is or may readily be ascertained by the investigator or associated with the information) in order for obtaining the information to constitute research involving human subjects.

Sec. 46.107 IRB membership.

(a) Each IRB shall have at least five members, with varying backgrounds to promote complete and adequate review of research activities commonly conducted by the institution. The IRB shall be sufficiently qualified through the experience and expertise of its members, and the diversity of the members, including consideration of race, gender, and cultural backgrounds and sensitivity to such issues as community attitudes, to promote respect for its advice and counsel in safeguarding the rights and welfare of human subjects. In addition to possessing the professional competence necessary to review specific research activities, the IRB shall be able to ascertain the acceptability of proposed research in terms of institutional commitments and regulations, applicable law, and standards of professional conduct and practice. The IRB shall therefore include persons knowledgeable in these areas. If an IRB regularly reviews research that involves a vulnerable category of subjects, such as children, prisoners, pregnant women, or handicapped or mentally disabled persons, consideration shall be given to the inclusion of one or more individuals who are knowledgeable about and experienced in working with these subjects.

(b) Every nondiscriminatory effort will be made to ensure that no IRB consists entirely of men or entirely of women, including the institution's consideration of qualified persons of both sexes, so long as no selection is made to the IRB on the basis of gender. No IRB may consist entirely of members of one profession.

(c) Each IRB shall include at least one member whose primary concerns are in scientific areas and at least one member whose primary concerns are in nonscientific areas.

(d) Each IRB shall include at least one member who is not otherwise affiliated with the institution and who is not part of the immediate family of a person who is affiliated with the institution.

(e) No IRB may have a member participate in the IRB's initial or continuing review of any project in which the member has a conflicting interest, except to provide information requested by the IRB.

(f) An IRB may, in its discretion, invite individuals with competence in special areas to assist in the review of issues which require expertise beyond or in addition to that available on the IRB. These individuals may not vote with the IRB. . . .

Sec. 46.111 Criteria for IRB approval of research.

(a) In order to approve research covered by this policy the IRB shall determine that all of the following requirements are satisfied:

(1) Risks to subjects are minimized: (i) by using procedures which are consistent with sound research design and which do not unnecessarily expose subjects to risk, and (ii) whenever appropriate, by using procedures already being performed on the subjects for diagnostic or treatment purposes.

(2) Risks to subjects are reasonable in relation to anticipated benefits, if any, to subjects, and the importance of the knowledge that may reasonably be expected to result. In evaluating risks and benefits, the IRB should consider only those risks and benefits that may result from the research (as distinguished from risks and benefits of therapies subjects would receive even if not participating in the research). The IRB should not consider possible long-range effects of applying knowledge gained in the research (for example, the possible effects of the research on public policy) as among those research risks that fall within the purview of its responsibility.

(3) Selection of subjects is equitable. In making this assessment the IRB should take into account the purposes of the research and the setting in which the research will be conducted and should be particularly cognizant of the special problems of research involving vulnerable populations, such as children, prisoners, pregnant women, mentally disabled persons, or economically or educationally disadvantaged persons.

(4) Informed consent will be sought from each prospective subject or the subject's legally authorized representative, in accordance with, and to the extent required by Sec. 46.116.

(5) Informed consent will be appropriately documented, in accordance with, and to the extent required by Sec. 46.117.

(6) When appropriate, the research plan makes adequate provision for monitoring the data collected to ensure the safety of subjects.

(7) When appropriate, there are adequate provisions to protect the privacy of subjects and to maintain the confidentiality of data.

Sec. 46.116 General requirements for informed consent.

Except as provided elsewhere in this policy, no investigator may involve a human being as a subject in research covered by this policy unless the investigator has obtained the legally effective informed consent of the subject or the subject's legally authorized representative. An investigator shall seek such consent only under circumstances that provide the prospective subject or the representative sufficient opportunity to consider whether or not to participate and that minimize the possibility of coercion or undue influence. The information that is given to the subject or the representative shall be in language understandable to the subject or the representative. No informed consent, whether oral or written, may include any exculpatory language through which the subject or the representative is made to waive or appear to waive any of the subject's legal rights, or releases or appears to release the investigator, the sponsor, the institution or its agents from liability for negligence. . . .

[The regulations also specify a list of disclosures that must be made to the potential research subject and the required written form of the subject's consent.—Eds.]

NOTES AND QUESTIONS

1. *Federal oversight.* Until recently, research that was not funded by one of the federal agencies that had adopted the Common Rule and did not involve a drug or device under FDA regulation was not covered. Now, the Office for Human Research Protections (OHRP), a subsidiary of HHS, requires all entities receiving federal funding implement a "federal wide assurance" by which the institution agrees to apply federal rules to all research it carries out regardless of funding as well as to employ an IRB registered with OHRP. 112. See 45 C.F.R. §§46.101–46.103 (2010).

In the event of noncompliance with the regulations, the research institution may be required by the sponsoring federal agency to take corrective action or, in more egregious cases, to cease their federally sponsored projects. But federal oversight is usually absent in any meaningful way, with the current system largely dependent on the work of the IRBs. See Sharona Hoffman, Continued Concern: Human Subject Protection, the Institutional Review Board, and Continuing Review, 68 Tenn. L. Rev. 725 (2001). Although IRBs have come under much criticism of late for providing too little protection for human research subjects, no alternative system has been proposed that has received serious consideration. Even providing more federal oversight of the work of the existing 3,000 to 5,000 IRBs in the United States is difficult to contemplate. See id. at 734–735. Sharona Hoffman writes, "Because there are thousands of IRBs in the United States, and tens of thousands of clinical trials are being conducted at any given time, even doubling or tripling the number of federal agency inspections will not meaningfully improve the continuing protection of clinical trial enrollees." Id. at 735. Can you think of other potential avenues for improving the protection of research subjects that don't require more federal resources?

2. *Research that is not covered.* Not all research conducted in the United States falls within the federal oversight regulations. Research that is not funded by or does not take place in an institution funded by one of the federal agencies that have adopted the Common Rule or does not involve a drug or device under FDA regulation is not covered. Do you think all research should be subject to federal regulatory oversight?

3. *State regulation of research?* Human subject protection need not be the exclusive province of federal regulation. As you will see in the *Grimes* case below, state tort law may also impose duties on researchers for the protection of research subjects. In a unique move by the state legislature following the *Grimes* case, Maryland adopted a statute that requires researchers within the state to

comply with the federal regulations whether or not they are recipients of federal funding. Md. Code Ann., Health Gen. §13-2001-04 (Supp. 2003).

4. *Revisions and proposed revisions.*   In 2009, a Subpart E was added to the federal regulations to require registration of IRBs with the Department of Health and Human Services. More significantly, in July 2011, DHHS issued an Advance Notice of Proposed Rulemaking (ANPRM) titled "Human Subjects Research Protections: Enhancing Protections for Research Subjects and Reducing Burden, Delay, and Ambiguity for Investigators," seeking comment on certain proposed changes to the Common Rule. The proposed changes are, according to DHHS, "the most extensive since the Department of Health, Education, and Welfare published proposed rules for the protection of human subjects involved in research on August 14, 1979." http://www.hhs.gov/ohrp/humansubjects/index.html. They would, among other things, involve:

1. Revising the existing risk-based framework to more accurately calibrate the level of review to the level of risk.
2. Using a single Institutional Review Board review for all domestic sites of multi-site studies.
3. Updating the forms and processes used for informed consent.
4. Establishing mandatory data security and information protection standards for all studies involving identifiable or potentially identifiable data.
5. Implementing a systematic approach to the collection and analysis of data on unanticipated problems and adverse events across all trials to harmonize the complicated array of definitions and reporting requirements, and to make the collection of data more efficient.
6. Extending federal regulatory protections to apply to all research conducted at U.S. institutions receiving funding from the Common Rule agencies.
7. Providing uniform guidance on federal regulations.

DHHS News Release, available at http://www.hhs.gov/news/press/2011pres/07/20110722a.html.

5. *Compensation for injuries.*   Inevitably, some people are injured or die from research participation. Coverage of medical care and compensation for research-related injuries are essentially voluntary in the United States, unless an injured subject successfully sues for relief. Although some research institutions have taken it upon themselves to establish a compensation plan system, a survey of compensation-for-injury policies implemented by American medical schools found that 72 percent said that they do not provide monetary compensation and another 11 percent do so only on a discretionary basis. See David B. Resnik, J.D., Ph. D., Compensation for Research Related Injuries, 27 J. Legal Med. 263 (2006) (omitting citations). In August 2011 the Presidential Commission for the Study of Bioethical Issues recommended studying methods for compensating people who are injured during research. The Commission's Report noted,

> This Commission is not the first to study the question of compensation for injuries incurred in the course of research participation. The Presidential Commission for the Study of Ethical Problems in Medicine and Biomedical and Behavioral Research in 1982 and NBAC [National Bioethics Advisory

Commission] in 2001 explored this issue and called on the government to study the feasibility and need for requiring treatment or compensation for medical costs in the United States. The Institute of Medicine in 2002, also recommended that "organizations conducting research should compensate any research participant who is injured as a direct result of participating in research, without regard to fault." Over the last several decades, almost all other developed nations, and many transnational standard-setting bodies, have instituted policies to require researchers or sponsors to provide treatment or compensation for treatment for research subjects' injuries.

Presidential Commission for the Study of Bioethical Issues, Moral Science: Protecting Participants in Human Subjects Research, Dec. 15, 2011.

CHALLENGING ISSUES: RESEARCH PROTOCOL TO WITHDRAW MEDICATION FROM PATIENTS WITH SCIHZOPHRENIA

Imagine that you are on an IRB of a prestigious university and the following research study has been proposed for your review. The study is to be conducted by an institute at the university that combines treatment, research, and training in the care of individuals with acute psychotic symptoms.[2]

Schizophrenic patients who have recovered from their psychotic disorders will be withdrawn from medication with the expectation that many patient-subjects will experience a relapse. The study's objective is to predict better such relapses, especially in those patient-subjects who exhibit severe symptoms such as bizarre behavior, self-neglect, hostility, depressive mood, and tendency to suicide. Thus, the research would lead to a better understanding about what types of patients need continuous antipsychotic medication and which patients can function without medication. The antipsychotic medication in current use causes certain side effects, one of which is tardive dyskinesia, "a syndrome consisting of involuntary and potentially irreversible movements for which no known treatment exists." Many schizophrenic patients request withdrawal of medication because of these side effects.

In the protocol's section on "Potential Benefits," the investigators note:

> Since no study shows 100 percent relapse in schizophrenics withdrawn from antipsychotics, unquestioned maintenance treatment may for any particular patient involve much risk and little benefit. At present, there is little consistent data regarding predictive factors for patients at low risk of relapse without pharmacotherapy.
>
> One important improvement over previous studies is that relapse is defined as the elevation of psychiatric symptoms to the severe or extremely severe level. Thus, minor symptom fluctuations that might often be inconsequential are not considered relapses. In contrast to the studies that defined the period of observation by the necessity to increase medication to avoid a possible relapse, we can be certain that any symptoms that we isolated actually did precede a clear relapse.
>
> Clinical relapse or psychotic exacerbation can be expected to occur in at least some of our patient-subjects. However, since most of our patients have been requesting drug withdrawal for months, and since our knowledge as to

2. This problem is drawn generally from a research study that took place at the University of California, Los Angeles, described in Jay Katz, Human Experimentation and Human Rights, 38 St. Louis U. L.J. 7, 41–51 (1993).

which acute schizophrenic patients will relapse following drug withdrawal is very meager, we feel this risk is justified, especially in view of the risk of tardive dyskinesia with longer-term antipsychotic use. Withdrawal from antipsychotic medication one year after the psychotic episode is not unusual in standard psychiatric practice for patients with acute nonchronic schizophrenia, since little clear evidence exists regarding longer-term prophylactic effects for this nonchronic population.

It should be noted that although continuous use of the antipsychotic medication may cause tardive dyskinesia, with permanent side effects, many psychiatrists also believe that a relapse can have serious permanent effects on patients.

The study would take place in two phases. In the first phase, patient-subjects would be randomly assigned to one of two groups; the first receiving a standardized dose of antipsychotic medication, the second receiving a placebo. This would go on for 12 weeks, then the groups' treatment would be reversed for the following 12 weeks, with those who had been receiving the placebo now receiving the medication and those who had been receiving the medication now receiving the placebo. When patients received the antipsychotic medication, they would receive a standardized, rather than an individualized dose of medication, which could either cause relapse or unnecessary side effects depending on the patient.

During the second phase of the study all of the patient-subjects would receive no medication and would be followed for at least one year. If a patient-subject experienced severe recurrences in symptomatology, then the patient would be withdrawn from the study. The patient-subjects could also withdraw from the study on their own accord, a requirement of all research subjected to the federal regulations.

The consent form submitted to the IRB for approval states:

> The purpose of this study is to take people like me off medication in a way that will give the most information about the medication, its effects on me, on others and on the way the brain works. An inactive substance (a placebo) or an active medication will be randomly administered during the first 24 weeks of the study and after that, all medication will be stopped, although I will continue to receive regular care at the University After Care Clinic.
>
> Blood will be drawn from me at regular intervals during the study. I understand that during blood drawing, I may experience pain from the needle prick, a small amount of bleeding, infection or black and blue marks at the site of the needle mark which will disappear in about 10 days.
>
> I understand that because of the withdrawal of active medication, I may become worse during this study and that either a relapse of my initial symptoms or new symptoms may occur. I understand that I will not be charged for the active medication or the placebo that I am provided during this study. If I do show a significant return of symptoms, I understand the clinic staff will use active medication again to improve my condition. If I would require hospitalization during this study, although this is not likely, I understand that the clinic staff would help to arrange an appropriate hospitalization but the research project would not pay for the hospitalization.
>
> I understand that I may benefit from this study by being taken off medication in a careful way while under close medical supervision. The potential benefits to science in this study are that it will increase my doctor's knowledge of the relationship between the medication, its effect on people such as myself, and on the way the brain functions in certain forms of mental illness.
>
> I understand that my condition may improve, worsen, or remain unchanged from participation in the study.

1. As a member of the IRB, what questions would you have for investigators regarding the research project? Would you approve it?

2. Does the consent form adequately disclose the risks to the patient-subject? The risk–benefit ratio for the patient-subject?

3. Do you think it would be clear to patient-subjects that if they enroll in the study, they will not be receiving the same individualized care they would receive if they were simply being treated by a doctor who was not involved in research? How might such treatment differ?

4. The regulations require IRBs to conduct continuing review at intervals appropriate to the degree of risk, but not less than once per year. 45 C.F.R. §46.109(e). Suppose you are reviewing the study in its fifth year. At this point, 88 percent of the patient-subjects who have been enrolled in the study have suffered a relapse. Would the consent form need to be altered on the basis of this information? In what way? Would you allow the project to go forward?

5. You are not a scientist or an employee of the university on whose IRB you sit. The other members of the IRB, however, are all scientists and employees of the university. Is this permitted? What might be the effect of this composition of the IRB membership?

6. Suppose that instead of withdrawing patient-subjects from medication, the research protocol called for testing the effectiveness of an alternative antipsychotic medication. Further, suppose that a number of the physician-investigators and the university had a financial interest in the new drug they were developing. Would that financial interest have to be disclosed to the research subjects under the IRB regulations? What do you think is the *least* disclosure that the physician-investigators could get by with and still be in compliance with the IRB regulations?

3. Common Law

When research is conducted by a physician-researcher in the context of providing medical care to a patient-subject, the latter will have available the traditional medical malpractice/tort law framework to redress grievances stemming from the physician's negligence, although the standard of care may differ because of the research component to the relationship. (The standard of care owed by physician-researchers is still undetermined. See generally Carl H. Coleman, Duties to Subjects in Clinical Research, 58 Vand. L. Rev. 387 (2005).) In the following two cases, however, a doctor–patient relationship is never established. These cases explore the issue of what duties a researcher might owe to a research subject outside the context of ongoing medical treatment.

‖ *Grimes v. Kennedy Krieger Institute, Inc.* ‖
366 Md. 29, 782 A.2d 807 (2001)

CATHELL, J.

We initially note that these are cases of first impression for this Court. For that matter, precious few courts in the United States have addressed the issues presented in the cases at bar. . . .

In these present cases, a prestigious research institute, associated with Johns Hopkins University, based on this record, created a nontherapeutic research program[2] whereby it required certain classes of homes to have only partial lead paint abatement modifications performed, and in at least some instances, including at least one of the cases at bar, arranged for the landlords to receive public funding by way of grants or loans to aid in the modifications. The research institute then encouraged, and in at least one of the cases at bar, required, the landlords to rent the premises to families with young children. In the event young children already resided in one of the study houses, it was contemplated that a child would remain in the premises, and the child was encouraged to remain, in order for his or her blood to be periodically analyzed. In other words, the continuing presence of the children that were the subjects of the study was required in order for the study to be complete. Apparently, the children and their parents involved in the cases sub judice were from a lower economic strata and were, at least in one case, minorities.

The purpose of the research was to determine how effective varying degrees of lead paint abatement procedures were. Success was to be determined by periodically, over a two-year period of time, measuring the extent to which lead dust remained in, or returned to, the premises after the varying levels of abatement modifications, and, as most important to our decision, by measuring the extent to which the theretofore healthy children's blood became contaminated with lead, and comparing that contamination with levels of lead dust in the houses over the same periods of time. In respect to one of the protocols presented to the Environmental Protection Agency and/or the Johns Hopkins Joint Committee on Clinical Investigation, the Johns Hopkins Institutional Review Board (IRB), the researchers stated: "To help insure that study dwellings are occupied by families with young children, City Homes will give priority to families with young children when renting the vacant units following R & M [Repair and Maintenance] interventions."

The same researchers had completed a prior study on abatement and partial abatement methods that indicated that lead dust remained and/or returned to abated houses over a period of time. In an article reporting on that study, the very same researchers said: "Exposure to lead-bearing dust is particularly hazardous for children because hand-to-mouth activity is recognized as a major route of entry of lead into the body and because absorption of lead is inversely related to particle size" . . .

Apparently, it was anticipated that the children, who were the human subjects in the program, would, or at least might, accumulate lead in their blood from the dust, thus helping the researchers to determine the extent to which the various partial abatement methods worked. There was no complete and clear explanation in the consent agreements signed by the parents of the children that the research to be conducted was designed, at least in significant part, to measure the success of the abatement procedures by measuring the extent to which the children's blood was being contaminated. It can be argued that the researchers intended that the children be the canaries in the mines but

---

2. . . . Nontherapeutic research generally utilizes subjects who are not known to have the condition the objectives of the research are designed to address, and/or is not designed to directly benefit the subjects utilized in the research, but, rather, is designed to achieve beneficial results for the public at large (or, under some circumstances, for profit).

never clearly told the parents. (It was a practice in earlier years, and perhaps even now, for subsurface miners to rely on canaries to determine whether dangerous levels of toxic gasses were accumulating in the mines. Canaries were particularly susceptible to such gasses. When the canaries began to die, the miners knew that dangerous levels of gasses were accumulating.)

The researchers and their Institutional Review Board apparently saw nothing wrong with the research protocols that anticipated the possible accumulation of lead in the blood of otherwise healthy children as a result of the experiment, or they believed that the consents of the parents of the children made the research appropriate. . . .

The provisions or conditions imposed by the federal funding entities, pursuant to federal regulations, are conditions attached to funding. As far as we are aware, or have been informed, there are no federal or state (Maryland) statutes that mandate that all research be subject to certain conditions. Certain international "codes" or "declarations" exist (one of which is supposedly binding but has never been so held) that, at least in theory, establish standards. We shall describe them, infra. Accordingly, we write on a clean slate in this case. We are guided, as we determine what is appropriate, by those international "codes" or "declarations," as well as by studies conducted by various governmental entities, by the treatises and other writings on the ethics of using children as research subjects, and by the duties, if any, arising out of the use of children as subjects of research.

Otherwise healthy children, in our view, should not be enticed into living in, or remaining in, potentially lead-tainted housing and intentionally subjected to a research program, which contemplates the probability, or even the possibility, of lead poisoning or even the accumulation of lower levels of lead in blood, in order for the extent of the contamination of the children's blood to be used by scientific researchers to assess the success of lead paint or lead dust abatement measures. Moreover, in our view, parents, whether improperly enticed by trinkets, food stamps, money or other items, have no more right to intentionally and unnecessarily place children in potentially hazardous nontherapeutic research surroundings, than do researchers. In such cases, parental consent, no matter how informed, is insufficient. . . .

The research relationship proffered to the parents of the children the researchers wanted to use as measuring tools, should never have been presented in a nontherapeutic context in the first instance. Nothing about the research was designed for treatment of the subject children. They were presumed to be healthy at the commencement of the project. As to them, the research was clearly nontherapeutic in nature. The experiment was simply a "for the greater good" project. The specific children's health was put at risk, in order to develop low-cost abatement measures that would help all children, the landlords, and the general public as well.

The tenants involved, presumably, would be from a lower-rent urban class. At least one of the consenting parents in one of these cases was on public assistance, and was described by her counsel as being a minority. The children of middle class or rich parents apparently were not involved. . . .

The research project at issue here, and its apparent protocols, differs in large degree from, but presents similar problems as those in the Tuskegee Syphilis Study conducted from 1932 until 1972, the intentional exposure of soldiers to radiation in the 1940s and 50s, the tests involving the exposure of

Navajo miners to radiation, and the secret administration of LSD to soldiers by the CIA and the Army in the 1950s and 60s. The research experiments that follow were also prior instances of research subjects being intentionally exposed to infectious or poisonous substances in the name of scientific research. They include the Tuskegee Syphilis Study, aforesaid, where patients infected with syphilis were not subsequently informed of the availability of penicillin for treatment of the illness, in order for the scientists and researchers to be able to continue research on the effects of the illness, the Jewish Hospital study,[8] and several other post-war research projects. Then there are the notorious use of "plague bombs" by the Japanese military in World War II where entire villages were infected in order for the results to be "studied"; and perhaps most notorious, the deliberate use of infection in a nontherapeutic project in order to study the degree of infection and the rapidity of the course of the disease in the Rose and Mrugowsky typhus experiments at Buchenwald concentration camp during World War II. These programs were somewhat alike in the vulnerability of the subjects; uneducated African-American men, debilitated patients in a charity hospital, prisoners of war, inmates of concentration camps and others falling within the custody and control of the agencies conducting or approving the experiments. In the present case, children, especially young children, living in lower economic circumstances, albeit not as vulnerable as the other examples, are nonetheless, vulnerable as well. It is clear to this Court that the scientific and medical communities cannot be permitted to assume sole authority to determine ultimately what is right and appropriate in respect to research projects involving young children free of the limitations and consequences of the application of Maryland law. The Institutional Review Boards, IRBs, are, primarily, in-house organs. In our view, they are not designed, generally, to be sufficiently objective in the sense that they are as sufficiently concerned with the ethicality of the experiments they review as they are with the success of the experiments. . . . Here, the IRB, whose primary function was to insure safety and compliance with applicable regulations, encouraged the researchers to misrepresent the purpose of the research in order to bring the study under the label of "therapeutic" and thus under a lower safety standard of regulation. The IRB's purpose was ethically wrong, and its understanding of the experiment's benefit incorrect.

The conflicts are inherent. This would be especially so when science and private industry collaborate in search of material gains. Moreover, the special relationship between research entities and human subjects used in the research will almost always impose duties.

I. The Cases

Two separate negligence actions involving children who allegedly developed elevated levels of lead dust in their blood while participating in a research study with respondent, Kennedy Krieger Institute, Inc., (KKI) are before this Court. Both cases allege that the children were poisoned, or at least exposed to the risk of being poisoned, by lead dust due to negligence on the part of KKI.

---

8. Generally known as the Jewish Chronic Disease Hospital study where chronically ill and debilitated patients were injected with cancer cells without their consent.

Specifically, they allege that KKI discovered lead hazards in their respective homes and, having a duty to notify them, failed to warn in a timely manner or otherwise act to prevent the children's exposure to the known presence of lead. Additionally, plaintiffs alleged that they were not fully informed of the risks of the research. . . .

The Consent Form [used by the research institute] states in relevant part:

PURPOSE OF STUDY:

As you may know, lead poisoning in children is a problem in Baltimore City and other communities across the country. Lead in paint, house dust and outside soil are major sources of lead exposure for children. Children can also be exposed to lead in drinking water and other sources. We understand that your house is going to have special repairs done in order to reduce exposure to lead in paint and dust. On a random basis, homes will receive one of two levels of repair. We are interested in finding out how well the two levels of repair work. The repairs are not intended, or expected, to completely remove exposure to lead.

We are now doing a study to learn about how well different practices work for reducing exposure to lead in paint and dust. We are asking you and over one hundred other families to allow us to test for lead in and around your homes up to 8 to 9 times over the next two years provided that your house qualifies for the full two years of study. Final eligibility will be determined after the initial testing of your home. We are also doing free blood lead testing of children aged 6 months to 7 years, up to 8 to 9 times over the next two years. We would also like you to respond to a short questionnaire every 6 months. This study is intended to monitor the effects of the repairs and is not intended to replace the regular medical care your family obtains. . . .

BENEFITS

To compensate you for your time answering questions and allowing us to sketch your home we will mail you a check in the amount of $5.00. In the future we would mail you a check in the amount of $15 each time the full questionnaire is completed. The dust, soil, water, and blood samples would be tested for lead at the Kennedy Krieger Institute at no charge to you. *We would provide you with specific blood-lead results. We would contact you to discuss a summary of house test results and steps that you could take to reduce any risks of exposure.*

[Emphasis added.]

. . . [Appellants] contend, contrary to the trial courts' findings, that KKI owed a duty to warn appellants of the presence of lead-based paint and dust because: (1) a "special relationship" existed between the parties; (2) of the contractual duty created by the consent agreement; (3) the danger was foreseeable; and (4) a Federal regulation exists, which created such a duty.

. . . Initially, we note that we know of no law, nor have we been directed to any applicable in Maryland courts, that provides that the parties to a scientific study, because it is a scientific, health-related study, cannot be held to have entered into special relationships with the subjects of the study that can create duties, including duties, the breach of which may give rise to negligence claims. We also are not aware of any general legal precept that immunizes nongovernmental "institutional volunteers" or scientific researchers from the responsibility for the breaches of duties arising in "special relationships." Moreover, we, at the very least, hold that, under the particular circumstances testified to by the parties, there are genuine disputes of material fact concerning whether a special relationship existed between KKI and Ericka Grimes, as well as between KKI and Ms. Higgins and Myron Higgins. Concerning this issue, the granting of the summary judgment motions was clearly inappropriate. When a "special relationship" can exist as a matter of law, the issue of whether, given certain facts, a special relationship does exist, when there is a dispute of material fact in that respect, is a decision for the finder of fact, not the trial judge. We shall hold initially that the very nature of nontherapeutic scientific research on human subjects can, and normally will, create special relationships out of which duties arise. Since World War II the specialness or nature of such relationships has been frequently of concern in and outside of the research community.

As a result of the atrocities performed in the name of science during the Holocaust, and other happenings in the World War II era, what is now known as the Nuremberg Code evolved. Of special interest to this Court, the Nuremberg Code, at least in significant part, was the result of legal thought and legal principles, as opposed to medical or scientific principles, and thus should be the preferred standard for assessing the legality of scientific research on human subjects. Under it, duties to research subjects arise.

IV. The Special Relationship

B.   The Sufficiency of the Consent Form

[In its analysis of the claims of the appellants, the court held that there were existing questions of fact regarding whether a duty to the appellants would arise under either tort or contract principles, and thus summary judgment was inappropriate. Some portions of the opinion relating specifically to the sufficiency of the consent form and whether a "special relationship" existed between the researchers and subjects that created duties of care are reprinted below.]

The consent form did not directly inform the parents of the fact that it was contemplated that some of the children might ingest lead dust particles, and that one of the reasons the blood of the children was to be tested was to evaluate how effective the various abatement measures were.

A reasonable parent would expect to be clearly informed that it was at least contemplated that her child would ingest lead dust particles, and that the degree to which lead dust contaminated the child's blood would be used as one of the ways in which the success of the experiment would be measured. The fact that if such information was furnished, it might be difficult to obtain human subjects for the research, does not affect the need to supply the information, or alter the ethics of failing to provide such information. A human subject is entitled to *all* material information. The respective parent should also have been clearly informed that in order for the measurements to be most helpful, the child needed to stay in the house until the conclusion of the study. Whether assessed by a subjective or an objective standard, the children, or their surrogates, should have been additionally informed that the researchers anticipated that, as a result of the experiment, it was possible that there might be some accumulation of lead in the blood of the children. The "informed" consent was not valid because full material information was not furnished to the subjects or their parents.

C. Special Relationship

... In Case Number 129, Ms. Higgins ... signed a Consent Form in which KKI agreed to provide her with "specific blood-lead results" in respect to her child and to discuss with her "a summary of house test results and steps that [she] could take to reduce any risks of exposure." She contends that this agreement between the parties gave rise to a duty owed by KKI to provide her with complete and accurate information. Pursuant to the plans of the research study, KKI collected dust samples in the Federal Street property on May 17, 1994, July 25, 1994, and November 3, 1994. KKI informed Ms. Higgins of the dust sample results by letters dated June 24, 1994, September 14, 1994, and February 7, 1995, respectively. Although KKI had recorded high levels of lead concentration in the dust samples collected by the Cyclone vacuum during the May 17, 1994 visit, KKI failed to disclose this information to Ms. Higgins in the letter dated June 24, 1994. Instead, KKI relied on the results obtained from the dust wipe samples collected and informed her that there was no area in her house where the lead level was higher than what might have been found in a completely renovated house.

Ms. Higgins contends that KKI knew of the presence of high levels of lead-based paint and dust in the Federal Street property as early as December of 1993, that even after Level II intervention such high levels still existed as of June of 1994, and that it was not until she received a letter dated September 14, 1994 that KKI specifically informed Ms. Higgins of the fact that her house had elevated lead levels. This was after her child, Myron, was diagnosed with elevated levels of lead in his blood.

Specifically, Ms. Higgins contends that KKI was negligent in its failure to inform her of its knowledge of the high levels of lead dust recorded by both XRF testing in December 1993 and from the samples collected via the Cyclone vacuum in May 1994 and that this withholding of information combined with KKI's letter dated June 24, 1993, informing her solely of the lower results of the samples collected by dust wipe methodology, was misleading to her as a participant in the study. KKI does not argue the facts as appellant presents them. Instead, it argues that no duty to inform existed because although the Cyclone readings were high, they were not an indication of a potential hazard because the clearance levels were based on dust wipe methodology and the dust wipe results were not above the clearance levels. Looking at the relevant facts of Case Number 129, they are susceptible to inferences supporting the position of appellant, Ms. Higgins. Accordingly, for this reason alone, the grant of summary judgment was improper.

As we indicated earlier, the trial courts appear to have held that special relationships out of which duties arise cannot be created by the relationship between researchers and the subjects of the research. While in some rare cases that may be correct, it is not correct when researchers recruit people, especially children whose consent is furnished indirectly, to participate in nontherapeutic procedures that are potentially hazardous, dangerous, or deleterious to their health. As opposed to compilation of already extant statistics for purposes of studying human health matters, the creation of study conditions or protocols or participation in the recruitment of otherwise healthy subjects to interact with already existing, or potentially existing, hazardous conditions, or both, for the purpose of creating statistics from which scientific hypotheses can be supported, would normally warrant or create such special relationships as a matter of law.

It is of little moment that an entity is an institutional volunteer in a community. If otherwise, the legitimacy of the claim to noble purpose would always depend upon the particular institution and the particular community it is serving in a given case. As we have indicated, history is replete with claims of noble purpose for institutions and institutional volunteers in a wide variety of communities.

Institutional volunteers may intend to do good or, as history has proven, even to do evil and may do evil or good depending on the institution and the community they serve. Whether an institutional volunteer in a particular community should be granted exceptions from the application of law is a matter that should be scrutinized closely by an appropriate public policy maker. Generally, but not always, the legislative branch is appropriately the best first forum to consider exceptions to the tort laws of this State—even then it should consider all ramifications of the policy—especially considering the general vulnerability of subjects of such studies—in this case, small children. In the absence of the exercise of legislative policymaking, we hold that special relationships, out of which duties arise, the breach of which can constitute negligence, can result from the relationships between researcher and research subjects.

VI. PARENTAL CONSENT FOR CHILDREN TO BE SUBJECTS OF POTENTIALLY HAZARDOUS NONTHERAPEUTIC RESEARCH

. . . The issue of the parents' right to consent on behalf of the children has not been fully presented in either of these cases, but should be of concern not only to lawyers and judges, but to moralists, ethicists, and others. The consenting parents in the contested cases at bar were not the subjects of the experiment; the children were. Additionally, this practice presents the potential problems of children initiating actions in their own names upon reaching majority, if indeed, they have been damaged as a result of being used as guinea pigs in nontherapeutic scientific research. Children, it should be noted, are not in our society the equivalent of rats, hamsters, monkeys, and the like. Because of the overriding importance of this matter and this Court's interest in the welfare of children—we shall address the issue.

Most of the relatively few cases in the area of the ethics of protocols of various research projects involving children have merely assumed that a parent can give informed consent for the participation of their children in nontherapeutic research. The single case in which the issue has been addressed, and resolved, a case with which we agree, will be discussed further, infra.

It is not in the best interest of a specific child, in a nontherapeutic research project, to be placed in a research environment, which might possibly be, or which proves to be, hazardous to the health of the child. We have long stressed that the "best interests of the child" is the overriding concern of this Court in matters relating to children. Whatever the interests of a parent, and whatever the interests of the general public in fostering research that might, according to a researcher's hypothesis, be for the good of all children, this Court's concern for the particular child and particular case, over-arches all other interests. It is, simply, and we hope, succinctly put, not in the best interest of any healthy child to be intentionally put in a nontherapeutic situation where his or her health may be impaired, in order to test methods that may ultimately benefit all children. . . .

When it comes to children involved in nontherapeutic research, with the potential for health risks to the subject children in Maryland, we will not defer to science to be the sole determinant of the ethicality or legality of such experiments. The reason, in our view, is apparent from the research protocols at issue in the case at bar. Moreover, in nontherapeutic research using children, we hold that the consent of a parent alone cannot make appropriate that which is innately inappropriate. . . .

Based on the record before us, no degree of parental consent, and no degree of furnished information to the parents could make the experiment at issue here, ethically or legally permissible. It was wrong in the first instance.

VII. CONCLUSION

. . . We hold that in Maryland a parent, appropriate relative, or other applicable surrogate, cannot consent to the participation of a child or other person under legal disability in nontherapeutic research or studies in which there is any risk of injury or damage to the health of the subject.

We hold that informed consent agreements in nontherapeutic research projects, under certain circumstances can constitute contracts; and that, under certain circumstances, such research agreements can, as a matter of law, constitute "special relationships" giving rise to duties, out of the breach of which negligence actions may arise. We also hold that, normally, such special relationships are created between researchers and the human subjects used by the researchers. Additionally, we hold that governmental regulations can create duties on the part of researchers towards human subjects out of which "special relationships" can arise. Likewise, such duties and relationships are consistent with the provisions of the Nuremberg Code.

The determination as to whether a "special relationship" actually exists is to be done on a case by case basis. The determination as to whether a special relationship exists, if properly pled, lies with the trier of fact. We hold that there was ample evidence in the cases at bar to support a fact finder's determination of the existence of duties arising out of contract, or out of a special relationship, or out of regulations and codes, or out of all of them, in each of the cases.

We hold that on the present record, the Circuit Courts erred in their assessment of the law and of the facts as pled in granting KKI's motions for summary judgment in both cases before this Court. Accordingly, we vacate the rulings of the Circuit Court for Baltimore City and remand these cases to that court for further proceedings consistent with this opinion.

ON MOTION FOR RECONSIDERATION PER CURIAM

The Court has considered the motion for reconsideration and the submissions by the various amici curiae. The motion is denied, with this explanation.

. . . Much of the argument in support of and in opposition to the motion for reconsideration centered on the question of what limitations should govern a parent's authority to provide informed consent for the participation of his or her minor child in a medical study. In the Opinion, we said at one point that a parent "cannot consent to the participation of a child . . . in nontherapeutic research or studies in which there is any risk of injury or damage to the health of the subject." As we think is clear from Section VI of the Opinion, by "any risk," we meant any articulable risk beyond the minimal kind of risk that is inherent in any endeavor. The context of the statement was a non-therapeutic study that promises no medical benefit to the child whatever, so that any balance between risk and benefit is necessarily negative. . . .

NOTES AND QUESTIONS

1. *Theories of recovery in* Grimes.   What legal theories did the plaintiffs in *Grimes* advance to support a duty on the part of the researchers to warn plaintiffs about increased levels of lead dust in their homes? What did the Court hold in respect of these theories?

2. *Significance of* Grimes *case.*   The *Grimes* case is highly significant in at least three respects: (1) its holding that a "special relationship" might exist between the researchers and subjects under the facts of the case (an issue for the trier of fact), and that, ordinarily, such a special relationship *will* exist between researchers and subjects; (2) its view of the inadequacy of the federal IRB oversight system now in place, and in particular its protection of children subjects; (3) its implicit comparisons of the lead paint abatement study to past, highly egregious research abuses (only a portion of which is excerpted above). In a later court filing, KKI complained, that "What Kennedy Krieger and its dedicated scientists sought to do here bears no resemblance whatsoever to the atrocious examples of study participants being affirmatively poisoned and/or intentionally deceived about the availability and appropriateness of medical attention." Grimes v. Kennedy Krieger Inst., Inc., Appellee's Motion for Partial Reconsideration and Modification of Opinion (Sept. 17, 2001), quoted in Hazel Glenn Beh, The Role of Institutional Review Boards in Protecting Human Subjects: Are We Really Ready to Fix a Broken System? 26 Law & Psychol. Rev. 1 (2002). Do you agree that the comparisons were unfair?

3. *Continuing duties to research subjects.*   Could KKI's continuing duties to the research subjects (which would include warning the parents of the presence of dangerous lead levels in their homes) have been eliminated by a properly drafted informed consent obtained at the inception of the study? Presumably not for children, as the court held that parents cannot consent to their children's participation in nontherapeutic research that holds more than a minimal risk. But what if the research subjects were not children but another group of individuals who might be harmed by elevated lead in the blood? Is a waiver of continuing duties on the part of researchers permissible? What do the federal regulations provide with respect to this issue?

4. *Conflicts of interest.*   Not all conflicts of interests are as clear to identify as the economic interests of the researcher versus the health interests of the subject. How would you characterize the potential conflict of interest inherent in the study conducted by KKI in the *Grimes* case? According to the court, would that conflict of interest need to be disclosed to the research subjects or their surrogates? In this regard, consider the following exchange between the court and KKI's counsel at oral argument, set out in a footnote to the *Grimes* opinion:

> *The Court:* Kennedy had a reason not to tell these parents that their kids were exposed to something dangerous, because if they did the parents might leave and the kids wouldn't stay in the study to be studied down the road. That's sort of what bothers me an awful lot. If you inform the participants in the

study that a danger has arisen, the participants leave the house and they're no longer in the study and the study gets skewered. And it very specifically says in the consent agreement that they're going to test for lead dust . . . seven or eight times after the repairs are made and it very specifically says that the results of testing of the house will be shared with the parents. They assert that you didn't do it. . . .

The Respondent: . . . They were all told within the time frame of the study itself. . . . Kennedy did nothing to hold back information to keep people in the study. They clearly told everybody if there was some lead in their dust during the study. . . .

The Court: When you talk about during the study you're talking about the last day, that includes the last day of the study, which is twenty-four months down the line. . . . Under your theory, if the study went on for ten years, it would be O.K. to tell them on the last day after the ten years. . . .

The Respondent: If the participant had no reason to expect that the results would be forthcoming sooner. . . .

What do you think of the Respondent's suggestion about when the test results regarding elevated levels of lead dust would have to be disclosed to the research subjects? Would you have been comfortable making that argument on behalf of KKI?

5. *Duties to provide information.*   In Ande v. Rock, 647 N.W. 2d 265 (Wis. App. 2002), the parents of two minor children with cystic fibrosis sued state employees, including researchers, for failing to inform them of their first child's positive test results for cystic fibrosis in time for them to pursue alternative methods of treatment to lessen the severity of the progression of the child's illness and to avoid the conception of the second child. The first child, C.E.A., was part of a research protocol that required the parents of half of the newborns in the study to be told if their child tested positive for cystic fibrosis, so that an investigational nutritional plan of treatment could be initiated for those children, while the parents of the other half of the children who were tested would not be told, as those children would constitute the "blinded control" group. C.E.A. was in the second group and her parents were therefore not told of her positive test result. The parents and children sued state actors for medical malpractice and under §1983 for a violation of their property and/or liberty interests under the United States Constitution. (Other claims, such as a duty to warn, were dismissed on procedural grounds for lack of timely notice.) The Wisconsin Court of Appeals affirmed the trial court's dismissal of the Andes's medical malpractice claim because of the absence of a physician–patient relationship, and the dismissal of the Andes's federal claims because the claimed constitutionally protected interests, if they existed, were not established well enough to preclude qualified immunity for government officials. Government officials enjoy qualified immunity "for the performance of discretionary functions if the official's conduct does not violate a clearly established federal statutory or constitutional right." 647 N.W.2d at 273. "Accordingly," wrote the court, "if a reasonable person in the position of the defendants could have believed that the manner in which he or she conducted the cystic fibrosis study did not violate the plaintiffs' rights at the time the test on C.E.A. was conducted and that not informing the Andes of the test results until 1995 did not violate the Andes's liberty or property interests, qualified immunity protects the defendants from liability arising from the Andes's claims brought under federal law." Id. The court found that a reasonable person could so believe.

What do you think of the research study that was the subject of the Andes's suit? Are such control group studies necessary for the proper conduct of scientific research? If so, do you think the following document that the plaintiffs alleged was given to them in explanation of the cystic fibrosis study would be adequate to inform the parents of their child's participation?

> One-half of the blood samples are tested for CF before the babies are one month old. The remaining blood samples are partially tested at this time. Testing on these blood samples is completed when the children are 4 years old. Positive test results are reported to your child's doctor.
>
> If the CF research test is done, you may contact your doctor, certified nurse-midwife, or the CF specialist at (608) 263-8555 for the result.

Does this consent form clearly explain to parents that their child may be tested for CF, that that test may be positive and yet neither they nor the child's doctor would be informed of the results?

In any event, the Ande v. Rock court gave little consideration to the informed consent claim because, it said, the injuries alleged by the plaintiffs did not stem from the failure to obtain consent but the failure to disclose test results.

6. *Other tort and contract claims in research.*   In Abney v. Amgen, 443 F.3d 540 (6th Cir. 2006), plaintiffs who participated in a clinical trial sued the drug manufacturer for continued access to the drug after the trial was terminated. The plaintiffs brought contract and promissory estoppel claims based on a statement in the informed consent document that participants "may elect to continue treatment for up to an additional 24 months." They also claimed a breach of fiduciary duty. The trial court denied their request for a preliminary injunction and the appellate court affirmed. The fiduciary duty claim was denied because the manufacturer (Amgen) could not have been said to have undertaken a duty to act primarily for the benefit of the plaintiffs. The contract and promissory estoppel claims held more potential under the court's assessment, but not when made against Amgen, who had not signed the informed consent document. The university conducting the research and its IRB might have presented better legal targets for the contract/promissory estoppel claims, but the plaintiffs had not named them as defendants.

D.   SPECIAL POPULATIONS

1.   Children

> ### Lainie Friedman Ross, Children as Research Subjects: A Proposal to Revise the Current Federal Regulations Using a Moral Framework
> 8 Stan. L. & Pol'y Rev. 159, 159–160, 165–166, 167 (1997)

[Paul] Ramsey's position was that children should never participate as research subjects in "non-therapeutic research" (that is, research which has no direct benefit for the children-subjects). Ramsey argued that for research to be moral, the subject must give his informed consent. Since the child cannot give informed consent, his parents must act as his surrogate. However, parental responsibility to their child is fiduciary, and to authorize their child's participation is a breach of this duty.

Richard McCormick rejected Ramsey's argument using a natural law approach and concluded that parental consent "is morally valid precisely insofar as it is a reasonable presumption of the child's wishes." McCormick held that there are "certain identifiable valuables that we ought to support, attempt to realize, and never directly suppress because they are definitive of our flourishing and well-being." The child, then, would want to participate as a research subject because he ought to do so. That is, the child would choose to participate because:

To pursue the good that is human life means not only to choose and support this value in one's own case, but also in the case of others when the opportunity arises. In other words, the individual ought also to take into account, realize, make efforts in behalf of the lives of others also, for we are social beings and the goods that define our growth and invite to it are goods that reside also in others.

Ramsey rebutted McCormick's argument on the grounds that it was too broad and would justify compulsory altruism. At the extreme, if McCormick's arguments are valid, "then anyone and not only children may legitimately be entered into human experimentation without his will [consent.]"

Ramsey's second argument against using children as research subjects is based on the Kantian principle that persons should never be treated solely as a means, but always simultaneously as an end. Ramsey argued that the use of a child as a subject in research which offers no direct therapeutic benefit treats the child solely as a means. While it may serve useful societal goals, it fails to serve the child-subject's own interests, and thus, cannot morally be performed.

McCormick objected to this argument because it presumes an atomistic view of humans. Since humans are social beings, their good transcends their individual good. Accordingly, participation as a research subject is consistent with treating the child as an end. The problem with this argument, as McCormick himself realized, is that it can require the participation of adults in research projects to which they do not give their consent, and while McCormick tolerates this enforced Good Samaritanism, most ethicists and legal scholars do not.

The debate initiated by McCormick and Ramsey continues unabated. The primary motivation for refuting Ramsey's position is that excluding children from research will have long-term negative consequences for the wellbeing of children in general. Ramsey himself realized that prohibiting children from participating in all nontherapeutic research threatens to leave children as "therapeutic orphans." His solution was to exhort researchers to "sin bravely": the trustworthy researcher was the one who did "not deny the moral force of the imperative he violates." . . .

To justify a child's participation as a research subject, I refute Ramsey's arguments and show that the child's participation is consistent with the modified principle of respect. Consider again nontherapeutic low risk research. This research presents no more risk than that which a child typically experiences (or, using Ackerman's standard, such research presents no more risk than that which is encountered in many activities to which parents typically expose their children for educational purposes). Many activities in a typical child's life, in fact, will present greater risks and harms, including such routine activities as participation in contact sports and traveling as a passenger in the family car. Not only is it impossible to live in a risk-free world, but it also would be contrary to the pursuit of a meaningful life plan. The development of autonomy requires that children be allowed to take some risks. Parents are morally and legally authorized to decide which risks their child can take and in what settings. Parental authorization or prohibition of a child's participation in this type of research, then, is not abusive or neglectful.

Parents must also respect their children's developing personhood. They do this by helping their children become autonomous individuals capable of devising and implementing their own life plans. Given the minimal amount of risk which the proposed research entails, the child's participation will not interfere with the child's developing personhood even if she is forced to participate against her will. Their decision to override their child's dissent is not abusive; parents legitimately override their child's decisions in many daily activities. This is one way in which parents steer their child's development into the person she will become.

In other words, a child's participation in minimal risk research which offers no direct therapeutic benefit, even if she dissents, is consistent with the modified principle of respect. Although parents should always consider their child's opinion in their decisionmaking, parents ought to have final decisionmaking authority about whether their child participates in such research. . . .

When research entails more than a minor increase over minimal risk and does not offer the prospect of proportionate benefit, then the participation of children-subjects is immoral and the physician-researchers must be prohibited from using children-subjects. The child's parents, or the state as parens patriae, must prohibit the child's participation. Even if the research is reviewed by a national committee, the decision to balance the well-being of a particular child against the possibility of significant societal benefit is a utilitarian calculus which fails to respect the developing personhood of the individual child. All children should be prohibited from participating in such research, regardless of their competency and despite the utility of the research.

NOTES AND QUESTIONS

1. *Comparing approaches of Ramsey and McCormick.*   Lainie Friedman Ross contrasts the positions of Paul Ramsey and Richard McCormick with regard to nontherapeutic research involving children. What's the difference between Ramsey's approach and McCormick's approach?

Does the *Grimes* opinion more closely reflect the view of Paul Ramsey or of Richard McCormick? Note the Court's additional statement on its denial of reconsideration. It appears to acknowledge that its "no-risk" standard for nontherapeutic research in children is at odds with the federal regulations on research (and widespread practice) that allow children to be enrolled in research without prospect of benefit to them if the research presents "minimal risk" or even, in some limited instances, more than minimal risk. See 45 C.F.R. 46 (Subpart D) (2009). But the Court's apparent attempt to clarify its position vis a vis the regulations fails. While in one sentence the Court appears to accept some minimal risk, it then suggests that in nontherapeutic research of the sort conducted in *Grimes,* any risk would cause the balance between risk and benefit to be negative (and therefore unacceptable). See Leonard H. Glantz, Nontherapeutic Research with Children: Grimes v. Kennedy Krieger Institute, 92 Am. J. Pub. Health 1070 (2002).

2. *When is research nontherapeutic?* The research at issue in *Grimes* is considered by the court to be nontherapeutic, and thus subject to more stringent safety regulations, because it is not expected to nor intended to benefit the research subjects. KKI disputed this issue, saying that the children were able to live in a house that had had the partial lead abatement repairs performed, although KKI did not specifically contend that the children had moved into such housing from less desirable housing. In any event, the Court found the argument of benefit to the individual children lacking.

Lainie Friedman Ross suggests that the authority of parents to consent to their children's participating in human subject research should sometimes be permitted even if there is no direct therapeutic benefit to the child. Do you agree with her conclusion? If you do, how do you justify allowing children to be used in research that will not directly benefit them?

More specifically, Friedman Ross would allow parents to consent to their children's participating in *low-risk* nontherapeutic research. Do you think that the research at issue in *Grimes* was "low risk"?

3. *Benefits to others.* Rehabilitating otherwise uninhabitable housing at less cost arguably benefited not just society at large but the group of Baltimore residents of whom these children were members. The IRB regulations and other sources of ethical and legal standards for research do not credit any such benefits. Should they? If so, would group representation in the planning and implementation of such a study lend it more legitimacy? See Larry I. Palmer, What Is Urban Health Policy and What's Law Got To Do with It? 15 Geo. J. Pov. L. & Pol'y 635 (2008).

On a related issue, although the federal regulations relating to the protection of human research subjects (the IRB regulations) indicate that special precautions are in order for "vulnerable" populations, and includes within this category, "economically or educationally disadvantaged persons," see 45 C.F.R. §46.111(b), there are not, in fact, special rules or guidelines for this population as there are for children, prisoners, and pregnant women. See T. Howard Stone, The Invisible Vulnerable: The Economically and Educationally Disadvantaged Subjects of Clinical Research, 31 J.L. Med. & Ethics 149 (2003). Should there be?

4. *Balancing the benefits and harms of doing research on children.* The most pressing need for research on children involves diseases specific to children (e.g., infantile leukemia, certain congenital conditions) and diseases that manifest differently in children and in adults (e.g., AIDS). Moreover, it is difficult and risky to extrapolate from research about the effects of drugs on adult patients to the effects of the same drugs on children. Yet, drugs tested on adults and approved by the FDA may be used "off label" to treat children. The FDA has recognized the widespread use of "off label" drugs to treat pediatric patients as a problem:

> The absence of pediatric safety information in product labeling poses significant risks for children. Inadequate dosing information exposes pediatric

patients to the risk of adverse reactions that could be avoided with an appropriate pediatric dose. The lack of pediatric safety information in product labeling exposes pediatric patients to the risk of age-specific adverse reactions unexpected from adult experience.

Department of Health and Human Services, FDA, Regulations Requiring Manufacturers to Assess the Safety and Effectiveness of New Drugs and Biological Products in Pediatric Patients, 63 FR 66632, Dec. 2, 1998, at 66632.

The unintended consequence of heightened protection for children (subpart D of the federal regulations) and pregnant women (subpart B) has been the dearth, until relatively recently, of clinical trials testing the efficacy and safety of pharmaceuticals on these populations (and also on women in general). Pressure by advocacy groups has caused a change in FDA policies that now encourage clinical trials on these populations. *See* I. Glenn Cohen, Therapeutic Orphans, Pediatric Victims? The Best Pharmaceuticals for Children Act and Existing Pediatric Human Subject Protection, 58 Food & Drug L.J. 661 (2003); Karen H. Rothenberg, Gender Matters: Implications for Clinical Research and Women's Health Care, 32 Hous. L. Rev. 1201 (1996). The Food and Drug Administration Modernization Act of 1997 (FDAMA), 111 Stat. 2296, offered incentives (in the form of extra patent protections) to drug manufacturers for carrying out pediatric trials. The provisions expired in 2002 but were largely reenacted—again with the creation of a voluntary system for testing—as part of the Best Pharmaceuticals for Children Act (BPCA), 115 Stat. 1408 (codified as amended in scattered sections of 21 U.S.C.). The Pediatric Research Equity Act (PREA), passed in 2003, required drug manufacturers submitting new drug applications to provide data about the safety and efficacy of drugs for pediatric populations. The act provides for a number of exemptions. See Holly Fernandez Lynch, Give Them What They Want?, 16 Ann. Health L. 79 (2007) (providing a full account of congressional and agency provisions aimed at encouraging pediatric testing). Fernandez Lynch notes that, "[b]etween the passage of the FDAMA in 1997 and the passage of PREA in 2003, the number of child subjects nearly tripled as pharmaceutical companies began to 'think pediatric.' However, the question now is whether child subjects will be adequately protected in this new environment. . . ." Id. at 97.

5. *Bibliographic note.*   Other useful references include Larry I. Palmer, Genetic Health and Eugenics Precedents: A Voice of Caution, 30 Fla. St. U. L. Rev. 237, 241–257 (2003); David M. Smolin, Nontherapeutic Research with Children: The Virtues and Vices of Legal Uncertainty, 33 Cumb. L. Rev. 621 (2002); Bernard M. Dickens, The Legal Challenge of Health Research Involving Children, 6 Health L.J. 131 (1998); Briar McNutt, The Under-Enrollment of HIV-Infected Foster Children in Clinical Trials and Protocols and the Need for Corrective State Action, 20 Am. J.L. & Med. 231 (1994); Francoise Baylis & Jocelyn Downie, An Ethical and Criminal Law Framework for Research Involving Children in Canada, 1 Health L.J. 39 (1993).

CHALLENGING ISSUES: EXPERIMENTAL CARE

An infant girl was born last week at Newfield Hospital. The baby, named Sally, is the child of Sue and Peter Tomkins. She suffers from a fatal heart condition and is almost certain to die very shortly. Only a heart transplant could possibly save the baby, but it is very unlikely that a suitable heart can be found in time.

A week before Sally's birth, Newfield's relevant bioethics committee gave its approval to the hospital's performing animal-to-human transplants. Dr. Lee Barlon, a surgeon at Newfield, requested hospital permission to replace Sally's diseased heart with a baboon heart, the first such procedure for a newborn. The few earlier adult recipients of simian hearts had died within a few days of transplant. It is unknown whether the drugs usually administered to transplant patients to limit rejection would preclude rejection of a nonhuman heart. Dr. Leslie Sother, another surgeon at Newfield, has opined that the baboon heart would be rejected by Sally's body within two weeks of the proposed transplantation.

Do you think the hospital should contemplate proceeding with the transplantation? If the baby's parents consent to the surgery, should that be deemed adequate justification for going ahead with this controversial transplant procedure? A baboon will have to be killed in order to supply the heart for transplantation; does that factor into your decision?

For further discussion of a case resembling this one, see Howard S. Schwartz, Bioethical and Legal Considerations in Increasing the Supply of Transplantable Organs from UAGA to "Baby Fae," 10 Am. J.L. & Med. 397 (1985).

CHALLENGING ISSUES: HUMAN NEUROSTEM CELL THERAPY

James was born six weeks premature with neonatal hypoxic-ischemic injury. The condition involves brain injury in neonates. Possible consequences include learning disabilities, mental retardation, and cerebral palsy. Researchers would like to insert human neurostem cells (HNSC) into James's brain. There is some evidence that this would limit the disabilities caused by his condition. In particular, experiments using neonatal mice suggest that the stem cell therapy might limit or reverse the neurological deficits that can be caused by hypoxic-ischemic injury. Inserting HNSC into James's brain would require the use of general anesthesia. This alone would render the therapy more than minimally risky. It is not known whether the actual insertion of the stem cells would have negative effects for the boy.

Do you think a clinical trial should be carried out? If so, how should a subject population be selected?

Whereas certain populations, such as children, pregnant women, prisoners, adults lacking mental capacity, and the economically disadvantaged, have long been seen as needing special protection in research participation, other populations have either received less protection or been the subject of advocacy for less or different protection, as the following materials show.

2.   *Donors of Biological Samples*

|| *Greenberg v. Miami Children's Hospital*
Research Institute
264 F. Supp. 2d 1064 (S.D. Fla. 2003) ||

[See Chapter 2, section A(2) and Chapter 13, section E(2), for reprinted excerpts of the case. *Greenberg* developed out of a joint effort between patients' families and researchers to find the genetic alterations associated with Canavan disease, a fatal genetic condition afflicting young children. The plaintiffs sued the researcher and institutions with which he was associated when they learned that blood, urine, and tissue samples supplied to the researcher were the basis for a patent he and the relevant institutions obtained. The patent gave them ownership rights to "any activity related to the Canavan disease gene, including without limitation: carrier and prenatal testing, gene therapy and other treatments for Canavan disease and research involving the gene and its mutations." As noted in Chapter 2, the parties in *Greenberg* entered into a confidential settlement agreement in 2003, shortly before the case was scheduled to go to trial.–Eds.]

NOTES AND QUESTIONS

1. Greenberg's *approach to research on biological samples.*   In *Greenberg*, the Court noted that "[A]lthough Federal regulations do mandate that consent must be obtained from the subjects of medical research, the informed consent does not cover more than the research itself"—in other words, the duty of informed consent in this context does not cover disclosure of economic interests. The Court distinguishes the case from Moore v. Regents, 703 P.2d 479 (Cal. 1990) (discussed in Chapter 13), because that case "involved a physician breaching his duty when he asked his patient to return for follow-up tests after the removal of the patient's spleen because he had research and economic interests. . . . Defendants here are solely medical researchers and there was no therapeutic relationship as in *Moore*." The Court also distinguished the case from *Grimes* because "there was no actual human experimentation as part of an ongoing relationship." It further noted the practical implications of a duty to disclose economic interests as a requirement of informed consent in this case:

> First, imposing a duty of the character that Plaintiffs seek would be unworkable and would chill medical research as it would mandate that researchers constantly evaluate whether a discloseable event has occurred. Second, this extra duty would give rise to a type of dead-hand control that research subjects could hold because they would be able to dictate how medical research progresses. Finally, these plaintiffs are more accurately portrayed as donors rather than objects of human experimentation, and thus the voluntary nature of their submissions warrants different treatment.

Do you agree that research on specimens is fundamentally different from research on the living human body? In what ways is it similar? How should that affect the nature of informed consent that should be required?

2. *Federal regulations.*   When the Common Rule was initially devised, ethical issues surrounding research using human tissues samples were not given much serious attention. Nevertheless, the existing definitions and regulations of the Common Rule do supply some guidance with respect to research on stored samples. Consent from participants is currently not required for research on clinically derived specimens (such as blood taken for diagnostic purposes) as long as they are not individually identifiable or for "downstream" research, such as when specimens are shared by researchers for studies not originally contemplated—again, as long as they are not individually identifiable by the current investigator. Office for Human Research Protection, Dep't of Health & Human Servs., Guidance on Research Involving Coded Private Information or Biological Specimens 3 (2008), available at http:// www.hhs.gov/ohrp/humansubjects/ guidance/cdebiol.pdf.

But the notion that human tissue samples are truly "deidentifiable" has been called into question with new DNA research. As one author states, "DNA is as individually identifying as a fingerprint, and so nearly any individual cell could theoretically be traced back to its source." Natalie Ram, Assigning Rights and Protecting Interests: Constructing Ethical and Efficient Legal Rights in Human Tissue Research, 23 Harv. J.L. & Tech. 119, 131–132 (2009). Furthermore, data derived from genetic material not only reveals information about the person it came from but their relatives as well.

Recently the NIH, as a condition of research funding, began to require researchers to share large datasets containing coded human genotype and phenotype data. (*Genotype* refers to the genetic make-up of an organism, whereas *phenotype* refers to actual observed properties of the organism.) Because it was coded, the data shared through the NIH GWAS ("Genome-Wide Association Studies") data repository did not retain identifying information of the human subject from whom the genomic data had retrieved; nevertheless, the investigator who originally collected the specimens could determine identities through a code. Based on the belief that the identities of the human subjects could not be determined without knowledge of the code of the original investigator (who was required to give assurances of privacy protection), the GWAS datasets were made available to the public through the internet. In August 2008, the potential for breach of confidentiality became apparent. A new bioinformatic method revealed that it was possible, if enough genomic data on an individual was available from another source, to determine whether that individual participated in a particular study (such as for a particular disease or condition, like alcoholism). The NIH quickly shut down public access to the datasets, which are now available only to researchers. NIH Background Fact Sheet on GWAS Policy Update, Feb. 28, 2008, available at http://grants.nih.gov/ grants/gwas/index.htm.

Given the recent recognition that biological samples cannot be guaranteed anonymity, along with the great expansion of genomic research, new approaches to research on biospecimens and related data have been proposed from various quarters. In 2011, DHHS released an Advance Notice of Proposed Rule-making, in which it sought comment on a set of proposed changes to the Common Rule, some of which would affect research on biospecimens. For all biospecimens collected in the future (whether "leftover" pathological specimens or otherwise), research could only be conducted if consent were obtained from the individual for research. A general written consent at the time of initial collection, however, even one that is obtained as a part of consent for care upon admission to a hospital, would be sufficient, and it could cover all future research uses. According to the Advance Notice, "this standardized general consent form would permit the subject to say no to all future research. In addition, there are likely to be a handful of special categories of research with biospecimens that, given the unique concerns they might raise for a significant segment of the public, would be dealt with by check-off boxes allowing subjects to separately say yes or no to that particular type of research (e.g., perhaps creating a cell line, or reproductive research)." Deidentification would no longer be the central issue it is today in determining whether research can be conducted or not; concerns about informational risks would be handled through standard data security mechanisms. Research conducted under these rules would not require IRB approval. 76 Fed. Reg. 44512 (July 26, 2011).

What do you think are the pros and cons of this proposed approach?

3. *Havasupai case.*   In 2010, members of the Havasupai tribe and Arizona State University reached a $700,000 settlement after years of litigation regarding the tribe's claims that ASU researchers misused tribe members' blood samples supplied for research on diabetes. Although the consent form signed by individual participants described general studies involving "the causes of behavioral/medical disorders," tribal leaders complained that the group had been approached only for research on diabetes and would not have agreed to the samples' use in later research on schizophrenia, inbreeding, and theories of human migration, the latter of unique concern to the tribe because the findings contradicted its traditional story of origin. Due to the case's settlement, the strength of the legal claims—fraud, breach of fiduciary duty, negligence, and trespass, among others—is unknown, although both *Greenberg* and Moore v. Regents, 703 P.2d 479 (Cal. 1990), suggest the plaintiffs faced substantial hurdles. See Michelle M. Mello & Leslie E. Wolf, The Havasupai Indian Tribe Case—Lessons for Research Involving Stored Biologic Samples, 363 New Eng. J. Med. 204 (2010); Katherine Drabiak-Syed, Lessons from Havasupai Tribe v. Arizona State University Board of Regents: Recognizing Group, Cultural, and Dignitary Harms As Legitimate Risks Warranting Integration into Research Practice, 6 J. Health & Biomedical L. 175, 175–176 (2010).

The Department of Health and Human Services has recently catalogued the kinds of risk that inhere in research as physical, psychological, and informational:

> Physical risks are the most straightforward to understand—they are characterized by short term or long term damage to the body such as pain, bruising, infection, worsening current disease states, long-term symptoms, or even death. Psychological risks can include unintentional anxiety and stress including feelings of sadness or even depression, feelings of betrayal, and exacerbation of underlying psychiatric conditions such as post traumatic stress disorder. . . . Informational risks derive from inappropriate use or disclosure of information, which could be harmful to the study subjects or groups. For instance, disclosure of illegal behavior, substance abuse, or chronic illness might jeopardize current or future employment, or cause emotional or social harm. In general, informational risks are correlated with the nature of the information and the degree of identifiability of the information.

76 Fed. Reg. 44512 (July 26, 2011). Do these classifications capture what appeared to be at stake for the Havasupai tribe? Whether information was

"identifiable" by researchers to particular individuals was not the concern. Can you imagine any objections that you might have to certain kinds of research on your "deidentified" biological samples? Should you be allowed to prevent the use of your samples in such research? Even if individuals are able to refuse consent to use of their biological samples (not a given, as the discussion in Note 2 points out), how can group interests be protected? Should they be?

4. *Newborn blood spot cases.*   In addition to common law theories of liability and federal regulations governing research, genetic privacy statutes may also determine the research that can be conducted on biospecimens. In Bearder v. Minnesota, 806 N.W.2d 766 (Minn. 2011), the state supreme court held that Minnesota's genetic privacy law restricted the use of research on blood samples collected under newborn screening statutes. The parents of 25 children sued the state for allowing their children's newborn blood samples to be used in research without their consent as long as they were deidentified. The state's contract with the medical laboratories that conducted the screening permitted such research. The court noted that "As of December 31, 2008, there were more than 800,000 newborn screening samples in storage, dating back to samples taken as early as 1997. More than 50,000 blood samples have been used in studies for purposes beyond the initial screening of the newborn children." The Court held that the blood samples were "genetic information," as that term was used in the state's genetic privacy act, and thus, unless otherwise expressly provided by law, the state was required to obtain informed consent before it could use, store, or disseminate the blood samples that remained after the newborn health screening was complete.

A similar case was brought in Texas. In both cases, the states agreed to destroy the blood samples. Amy Harmon, Havasupai Case Highlights Risks in DNA Research, N.Y. Times, Apr. 21, 2010. Harmon quotes parent Andrea Beleno, of Austin, Texas: "The nurses asked me if they could give my son a pacifier. They asked me if they could give him formula. No one asked me if his DNA could be stored in a state database."

What if the state *had* asked Beleno? Should parents be allowed to consent to submitting their children's biological specimens to biobanks for research? What might be some arguments for treating children's specimens differently than adults?

3.   *Experiments on Military Personnel*

|| ***Minns v. United States*** ||
|| **155 F.3d 445 (4th Cir. 1998)** ||

Niemeyer, Circuit Judge.

In preparation for Operation Desert Storm and the Persian Gulf War, the United States military inoculated its servicemen and exposed them to toxins and pesticides in anticipation of possible biological and chemical attacks by Iraq. The wives and children of three servicemen claim in this case that the military negligently administered and used "investigational" and defective drugs on the three servicemen, causing their children, who were born after the War, serious birth defects.

. . . All three children suffer from Goldenhar's Syndrome, a rare birth defect producing deformity, including asymmetry of the face and body, a partially developed or lopsided ear, internal fistulas, and, in some cases including these children, esophageal malformations and the absence of an anal opening. The families of these children recognize that scientific studies about the effects of the administered drugs and pesticides are in process and will not be concluded until later in 1998 or in 1999. Based on preliminary results from some studies, however, they believe that the toxins to which the servicemen were exposed were possibly stored in the servicemen's semen and passed on to their wives, where the toxins were stored in fatty tissue and ultimately were released during pregnancy to the fetus. The deformed children were born from one to two-and-one-half years after the servicemen were exposed to the toxins and pesticides.

The wives and children presented claims for damages to the Office of the Judge Advocate General under the Military Claims Act, 10 U.S.C. §2731 et seq. After the Judge Advocate General disallowed their claims, they filed these actions to review the Judge Advocate General's decisions and to assert claims under the Federal Tort Claims Act, 28 U.S.C. §§1346(b), 2671 et seq.

. . . Through enactment in 1948 of the Federal Tort Claims Act ("FTCA"), Congress waived the sovereign immunity of the United States for certain torts that otherwise could be proved against it. The FTCA did not create new causes of action but merely accepted liability against the United States for circumstances that otherwise "would bring private liability into existence." Indeed, the FTCA expressly states that the United States is liable for tort claims "in the same manner and to the same extent as a private individual under like circumstances."

Relying on this operation of the FTCA, the Supreme Court concluded in Feres [v. United States, 340 U.S. 135 (1950)], that even after enactment of that Act, servicemen could not sue the government because "[w]e know of no American law which ever has permitted a soldier to recover for negligence, against either his superior officers or the Government he is serving."

. . . The wives and children of the three servicemen involved in this case do not attempt to take issue with the conclusion that under the *Feres* doctrine the three servicemen do not have claims against the government for damages under the FTCA. But they argue that, as wives and children of servicemen, they are not barred from prosecuting a claim under the FTCA based on the United States' negligent acts directed *at them*. They observe that if they are not allowed to prosecute their tort claims under the FTCA, they have no remedy at all for their damages. . . .

While justifications for the *Feres* doctrine include the fact that compensation is provided to servicemen through a no fault comprehensive benefit scheme and the fact that a serviceman's relationship to the government is a "distinctively federal" one, its principal justification focuses on the unique relationship between the government and its military personnel:

> Although the Court in *Feres* based its decision on several grounds, in the last analysis, *Feres* seems best explained by the peculiar and special relationship of the soldier to his superiors, the effects of the maintenance of such suits on

discipline, and the extreme results that might obtain if suits under the Tort Claims Act were allowed for negligent orders given or negligent acts committed in the course of military duty.

United States v. Shearer, 473 U.S. 52, 57 (1985). The military has a unique need to operate under special regulations and rules of order to ensure "unhesitating and decisive action by military officers and equally disciplined responses by enlisted personnel." This discipline "would be undermined by a judicially created remedy exposing officers to personal liability at the hands of those they are charged to command." Accordingly, consistent with the structure created by the Constitution, which leaves control of the military to the Legislative and Executive Branches, "Congress has created, and [the Supreme] Court has long recognized two systems of justice, to some extent parallel: one for civilians and one for military personnel." . . . [E]ven where a judicial action does not "contest the wisdom of broad military policy," the *Feres* doctrine requires courts to reject actions which are "the *type* of claims that, if generally permitted, would involve the judiciary in sensitive military affairs at the expense of military discipline and effectiveness." If a suit requires deep inquiry into military decisions or would strongly impact military discipline, the *Feres* doctrine will bar it.

[M]ost courts have adopted a "genesis" test for evaluating whether the *Feres* doctrine applies to derivative genetic injury claims of servicemen's children based on governmental negligence in exposing the servicemen to dangerous substances. Under this test, if a non-serviceman's injury finds its "genesis" in the injury suffered by a serviceman incident to service, then the *Feres* doctrine bars the non-serviceman's suit. Stated otherwise, if the non-serviceman's suit is based on essentially the same facts as the potential serviceman's suit or the non-serviceman's suit could not have happened "but for" the serviceman's cause of action, then under the genesis principle the *Feres* doctrine precludes the suit.

Because the genesis test well accords with the primary purpose of the *Feres* doctrine and is applicable to factual circumstances similar to those presented in this case, we now join the other circuits which have adopted it as their test for evaluating tort claims of non-military personnel that derive from servicemen's relationships with the government.

Turning to the circumstances before us, the military decided to inoculate its servicemen, including the three servicemen involved in this case, and to expose them to drugs and pesticides in anticipation of possible biological and chemical attacks by Iraq. Even if the military had been negligent in carrying out this program, the families of the servicemen agree that the *Feres* doctrine prevents the servicemen themselves from suing the United States under the FTCA. They maintain, however, that because they are wives and children of servicemen, not servicemen themselves, their claims are not barred by *Feres*. But they overlook the fact that, in advancing their own negligence suits, they rely upon the same negligent acts that allegedly impacted the servicemen.

Under the chain of causation that these wives and children assert, the military's negligence in implementing and administering the inoculation program to the servicemen resulted in making them carriers of the toxins to their wives and ultimately to their newborn children. This negligence in implementing and administrating the program to the servicemen thus was the "genesis" and the "but for" cause of the injuries to the wives and children. To establish the liability of the United States, the wives and children would have to challenge the decisions and acts of military personnel in preparing for war, and their suits would thus entail second-guessing decisions and acts that were indisputably "incident to military service." If allowed to proceed, their suits would place the courts in exactly the position that the *Feres* doctrine was designed to avoid.

. . . The plaintiffs make a separate argument that the government's failure to warn was an independent act of negligence which was not derivative of servicemen's claims but which directly affected the plaintiffs. Similarly, however, this allegation arises out of the general failure to warn about the risks associated with a military decision made to protect soldiers during an impending war. Questioning the military's decision not to warn either the soldiers or their families about the possible risks of inoculation or exposure to pesticides would again create the court-intrusion problem that the *Feres* doctrine aims to avoid. Courts would be questioning strategies, defense preparations, and the military's control of information, contrary to their authority.

. . . [T]he decision whether to warn soldiers and their families of the potential effects of inoculations and pesticides . . . amounted to a judgment call. The decision whether to warn about the effects of inoculations and pesticides implicates other military decisions such as whether to risk alerting the enemy about war preparations and whether to give a warning that might be harmful to cohesion, particularly when the decision had already been made to use the drugs. The decision falls equally at the core of the discretionary function exception.

. . . Our rulings in these cases leave the wives and children of the three returning servicemen without a judicial remedy, even if their claims have merit. As the plaintiffs readily acknowledge, scientific studies have not yet demonstrated the necessary causal link between the servicemen's inoculations and pesticide exposure and their children's birth defects. If scientists are able to demonstrate that this link exists, the matter might become an appropriate one for the serious consideration of Congress. Congress has a long history of providing warranted relief for the impact of military service on veterans and their families, and to remedy the service-related injuries of our veterans and their families is a proper and noble function of the Legislative Branch.

NOTES AND QUESTIONS

1. *United States v. Stanley.*   The military actions at issue in the *Minns* case—inoculation of servicemen and exposure of servicemen to pesticides—were presumably to protect the health of the servicemen before they encountered combat. The injuries allegedly suffered by the children of the servicemen would therefore have been an unintended consequence of the experimental "treatment." The facts in the Supreme Court case of United States v. Stanley, 483 U.S. 669 (1987), are quite different. In that case, the plaintiff, an Army master sergeant stationed at Fort Knox, Kentucky, volunteered in 1958 to participate in what he understood to be a program designed to test the effectiveness of certain protective clothing and equipment against chemical warfare. Instead, without his knowledge or consent, he was allegedly administered doses of LSD as part of an Army study to test the effects of LSD on humans. Stanley did not learn of his exposure to LSD until 1978, when he received a letter from the Army identifying him as one of the

"volunteers" who participated in the 1958 tests. The Army was at this date soliciting his participation in a study of the long-term effects of the LSD exposure. Stanley claimed that since his 1958 exposure to LSD he had suffered hallucinations, periods of incoherence and memory loss, and personality changes that led, among other things, to the dissolution of his marriage. Stanley's claim against the U.S. government under the Federal Tort Claims Act was dismissed by the district court as barred under the *Feres* doctrine. The Supreme Court considered whether Stanley nevertheless had a *Bivens* action—an action for damages that can arise directly under the Constitution against individual governmental officers. *See* Bivens v. Six Unknown Fed. Narcotics Agents, 403 U.S. 388 (1971). The Court held that the same factors that bar a serviceman's action for damages under the FTCA under *Feres* apply to a *Bivens* action, so that there is no remedy available against individual officers for injuries that arise out of the course of activity incident to military service. Justice O'Connor and Justice Brennan wrote separate stirring dissents to the decision to disallow the *Bivens* action. O'Connor wrote:

> In my view, conduct of the type alleged in this case is so far beyond the bounds of human decency that as a matter of law it simply cannot be considered a part of the military mission. The . . . judicial exception to an implied remedy for the violation of constitutional rights . . . surely cannot insulate defendants from liability for deliberate and calculated exposure to otherwise healthy military personnel to medical experimentation without their consent, outside of any combat, combat training, or military exigency, and for no other reason than to gather information on the effect of lysergic acid diethylamide on human beings.
>
> No judicially crafted rule should insulate from liability the involuntary and unknowing human experimentation alleged to have occurred in this case. . . . If [the principle of voluntary consent of the human subject] is violated the very least that society can do is to see that the victims are compensated, as best they can be, by the perpetrators. I am prepared to say that our Constitution's promise of due process of law guarantees this much.

In your view, do *Minns* and *Stanley* implicate the same considerations or should the suit in one be allowed to go forward and not the other? Where do you think the perimeter of immunity for military actions lies? Should distinctions be made between actions affecting servicemen and those affecting civilians? Between the good faith or bad faith intentions of the officers implementing the research or experimental programs? Between negligence and intentionality?

2. *Regulatory protections.* Despite the limitations they face in tort recovery for research injuries, military personnel do receive some protection from research abuses in the form of regulation. The Department of Defense (DoD) adopted the Common Rule in 1991. The DoD and individual military service branches have also adopted additional procedural protections to reduce the coercive pressures that may be exerted on or perceived by lower-ranked military personnel. There remain circumstances, however, under which waivers of informed consent can be obtained by the Secretary of Defense. The applicable regulations are somewhat of a labyrinth. For recent summaries and critiques, see Efthimios Parasidis, Human Enhancement and Experimental Research in the Military, 44 Conn. L. Rev. 1117 (2012); Jennifer Siegal, Advancing Ethical Research Practices in the Military 24(4) Health Lawyer 1 (2012); Catherine L. Annas & George J. Annas, Enhancing the Fighting Force: Medical Research on American Soldiers, 25 J. Contemp. Health L. & Pol'y 283 (2009).

4.   Research Among Populations of Developing Countries

In 2000, the Declaration of Helsinki was amended to require that new treatments be tested against the "best current" treatment, rather than placebos, unless no proven treatment exists (paragraph 29 of the Declaration). In this regard, the World Medical Association took the lead in condemning research conducted in developing nations that does not offer subjects proven treatments, but only offers them investigational treatments or a placebo. (In 2008, the FDA explicitly rejected the applicability of paragraph 29 to foreign trials by U.S. drug companies conducted to support an investigational new drug application or marketing proposal. Dept. of Health & Human Services, Food and Drug Administration, 21 C.F.R. 312 (2008). See section C(1), supra.)

In response to protests that there was not sufficient justification for abandoning the traditional placebo arm of the clinical trial when no harm comes from use of the placebo, the WMA adopted a clarification in 2002 (see footnote to paragraph 29). The clarification stated that placebos could still be used when necessary to establish the safety or efficacy of an experimental therapy or when the experimental therapy is being investigated for a "minor condition" and receiving the placebo will not pose "any additional risk of serious or irreversible harm" to the research subject.

The clarification affirmed, however, that in all other cases the new method should be tested against the best current method, which is the ethical, although not legal, standard for research conducted in the United States and other developed countries (often referred to as "equipoise," although definitions of the term vary). Paragraph 29 essentially condemns the conduct of research on subjects in developing countries by researchers from developed countries that would be considered unethical if conducted within the researchers' own country. The revision suggests that research ethics should be universal. If not, isn't the research exploitative?

The impetus for the revision of the Declaration was the conduct of controversial clinical trials in the late 1990s on pregnant women in several developing African countries to test an experimental drug therapy regimen that was less expensive than the proven AZT therapy in preventing HIV transmission from mother to infant. The investigational therapy was tested against a placebo, rather than the proven AZT therapy. Thus, even though proven therapies existed, they were not offered in either arm of the trial. Those pregnant women assigned to the control group had no opportunity for any beneficial treatment. Supporters of the research pointed out that they would not anyway, because the poverty of the women and their countries meant that proven AZT therapy was out of the question. So, they asked, how were these women and children harmed? In fact, weren't all the research subjects benefited in being given a 50 percent chance to receive the investigational treatment that had the potential to substantially reduce the risk of HIV transmission?

Critics of the research study charged that an unacceptable double standard was at work. In the United States, the new therapy would have been tested against the proven therapy, since one existed, and there would have been no placebo arm. According to these critics, pregnant women in developing countries were being exploited for the gain of U.S. researchers and their corporate partners and, to the extent the drugs might later be used in the United States but still be financially outside the reach of developing countries, the women were being exploited for the benefit of U.S. patients.

What do you think of the ethical acceptability of conducting such research? If you think the Declaration states an appropriate ethical standard, how should one determine what the "best current" treatment is? Can local conditions be taken into account? In particular, may this requirement be satisfied by providing the "best current" treatment available locally, with economic considerations taken into account? Or does the "best current" treatment mean the best treatment in the world?

The permissibility of "double standards" for research conducted in developing countries is further limited by paragraph 30 of the Declaration, which also, in 2004, was reaffirmed. That paragraph requires that research subjects be given the best proven treatment at the conclusion of the study.

Comparisons have been made by some commentators between the African AIDS clinical trials and the Tuskegee Syphilis Study. Are the comparisons apt?

For more discussion of these issues, see Brian Vastag, Helsinki Discord? A Controversial Declaration, 284 JAMA 2983 (2000); David Orentlicher, Universality and Its Limits: When Research Ethics Can Reflect Local Circumstances, 30 J.L. Med. & Ethics 403 (2002); Ruth Faden & Nancy Kass, Editorial, HIV Research, Ethics, and the Developing World, 88 Am J. Pub. Health 548 (1998); Mervyn Susser, Editor's Note, The Prevention of Perinatal HIV Transmission in the Less-Developed World, 88 Am. J. Pub. Health 547 (1998).

5. The Terminally Ill

Children are seen as particularly vulnerable to exploitation because they have little control and even little input regarding what will be done to them. Perhaps we also afford them more protection because they are young, near the beginning of life, and thus harm done to them through research may have permanent and long-lasting effects. We also tend to think of children as among the most innocent of populations and therefore, perhaps, more deserving of protection from harm.

But now contrast the situation of the terminally ill adult who appears to be close to the end of life. Desperate for a research breakthrough, for a miracle even, some will try anything, or at least accept greater risks in treatment. Should we afford them less protection to allow them to grab at any hope, or should we maintain the same protections for them, the same benefit-to-risk ratios, the same certainties of safety provided by required clinical trials, for example? Should we focus on their vulnerability to exploitation or their decreased life span? Is this a "nothing to lose" proposition?

In the mid-1980s, AIDS activists successfully pushed the FDA to make certain investigational drugs available for treatment and sale to AIDS patients outside of participation in clinical trials; in other words, before the drugs were proven safe and effective. George Annas offered the following commentary back in 1989.

> *George J. Annas, Faith (Healing), Hope,*
> *and Charity at the FDA: The Politics*
> *of AIDS Drug Trials*
> 34 Vill. L. Rev. 771 (1989)

Today the most likely subject of medical experimentation is not the prisoner or even the soldier, but the patient with a disease.

All patients, particularly terminally ill patients, deserve protection from those who want to prey on their desperation for profit. People with AIDS have a lot to lose, including their health, their lives, their dignity, and their money. They can be and have been viciously exploited. Because many victims of AIDS are members of disenfranchised groups that have traditionally been rightfully suspicious of government's view of them, they may be at special risk for exploitation by those who proclaim that the government and orthodox medicine is in a conspiracy to deny them treatment. . . .

The second reason why encouraging the use of unproven drugs is bad public policy is that denying death ultimately serves no purpose (other than providing temporary false hope). . . . It is not compassionate to hold out false hope to a terminally ill patient and thereby induce that patient to spend his last dollar on unproven "remedies." If anything, such strategy seems aimed primarily at treating the guilt of a society that has done little to meet the real needs of AIDS victims by giving us the comforting illusion that we are doing something to help.

The third reason why making unproven drugs available is counterproductive public policy is that, if unproven remedies are made easily available it will be impossible to do scientifically valid trials of new drugs. Those suffering from AIDS will be unwilling to participate in randomized clinical trials, and those who are randomized to an arm of the study they do not like will take the drugs they "believe in" on the sly, making any valid finding from the study impossible.

. . . It is not "compassionate" to make quack remedies easily available to those who can pay for them. Real compassion demands that we allocate the money and staff necessary to do real scientific research, and that when valid clinical trials demonstrate that a therapy is "safe and effective," we make it available to all who need it, regardless of their ability to pay. Compassion does not counsel us to supply dying patients with fabulous promises and foolish drugs.

NOTES AND QUESTIONS

1. *Autonomy vs. beneficence/nonmaleficence.*   Annas's commentary sounds themes that go beyond the AIDS epidemic. Fatal diseases of all kinds bring requests for "treatment," even when the drugs or devices or procedures are "experimental" and unproven. To what extent do you think we should defer to patients' "autonomous choices" to submit to unproven therapies?

2. *Constitutional rights?*   Terminally ill patients have clamored for less protection (or rather, less restriction) from the FDA for years, not merely in connection with the AIDS epidemic. For example, in the 1970s a group of terminally

ill cancer patients sought to enjoin the FDA from preventing them from obtaining laetrile from across the borders of Mexico and Canada. They were ultimately unsuccessful; the Supreme Court upheld the FDA's regulation as reasonable, stating that neither effectiveness nor safety is irrelevant to the terminally ill. See United States v. Rutherford, 442 U.S. 544 (1979).

More recently, an advocacy group for terminally ill patients seeking access to drugs that have passed initial Phase I testing challenged FDA restrictions as infringing on their constitutional rights. While the district court dismissed the group's claims, a divided panel for the Third Circuit Court of Appeals reversed, concluding that "where there are no alternative government-approved treatment options, a terminally ill, mentally competent adult patient's informed access to potentially life-saving investigational new drugs determined by the FDA after Phase I trials to be sufficiently safe for expanded human trials warrants protection under the Due Process Clause." 445 F.3d 470, 486 (D.C. Cir. 2006). This decision was then reversed en banc, in the following case, and the Supreme Court denied cert.

Abigail Alliance for Better Access to Developmental Drugs v. Eschenbach
495 F.3d 695 (2007)

GRIFFITH, Circuit Judge.

The Abigail Alliance for Better Access to Developmental Drugs (the "Alliance") is an organization of terminally ill patients and their supporters that seeks expanded access to experimental drugs for the terminally ill. The Food, Drug, and Cosmetic Act ("FDCA" or "Act"), however, generally prohibits access to new drugs unless and until they have been approved by the Food and Drug Administration ("FDA"). See 21 U.S.C. §355(a). Gaining FDA approval can be a long process. First, an experimental drug's sponsor (e.g., a drug company) must submit an application for approval. Because no drug may be approved without a finding of "substantial evidence that the drug will have the effect it purports or is represented to have," an application must contain "full reports of investigations which have been made to show whether or not such drug is safe for use and whether such drug is effective in use." Such reports rely in large measure on clinical trials with human subjects.

. . . Clinical testing for safety and effectiveness requires three or sometimes four phases. See 21 C.F.R. §312.21. Phase I involves the initial introduction of a new drug into human subjects. A Phase I study usually consists of twenty to eighty subjects and is "designed to determine the metabolism and pharmacologic actions of the [new] drug in humans, the side effects associated with increasing doses, and, if possible, to gain early evidence on effectiveness." Although gathering data on effectiveness may be part of Phase I, its primary focus is to determine whether the drug is safe enough for continued human testing. Phase II studies are "well controlled" and "closely monitored" clinical trials of no more than several hundred subjects, used to evaluate both the "effectiveness of the drug for a particular indication" and its "common short-term side effects and risks."

Phase III studies are expanded clinical trials of several hundred to several thousand subjects designed to "gather . . . additional information about effectiveness and safety that is needed to evaluate the overall benefit–risk relationship of the drug and to provide an adequate basis for physician labeling."

. . . Terminally ill patients need not, however, always await the results of the clinical testing process. The FDA and Congress have created several programs designed to provide early access to promising experimental drugs when warranted. For example, under the "treatment IND [investigational new drug]" program, the FDA may approve use of an investigational drug by patients not part of the clinical trials for the treatment of "serious or immediately life-threatening disease [s]" if there exists "no comparable or satisfactory alternative drug or other therapy;" if "[t]he drug is under investigation in a controlled clinical trial;" and if the drug's sponsor "is actively pursuing marketing approval of the investigational drug with due diligence." The FDA reserves the right, however, to deny any treatment IND request if (1) the agency believes there is no "reasonable basis" to conclude that the drug is effective; or (2) granting the request "[w]ould . . . expose the patient[] . . . to an unreasonable and significant additional risk of illness or injury." Sponsors may not profit from any approved treatment IND program and may only "recover costs of manufacture, research, development, and handling of the investigational drug."[4]

. . . [When a "citizen petition" submitted by the Alliance to the FDA yielded no results], the Alliance turned to the courts, arguing that the United States Constitution provides a right of access to experimental drugs for its members. In a complaint that mirrored much of its earlier submissions to the FDA, the Alliance argued that the FDA's lengthy clinical trials, combined with the "FDA's restrictions on pre-approval availability[,] amount to a death sentence for these [terminally ill] patients." Nor, the Alliance argues, are the FDA's exceptions to the clinical testing process sufficient to provide the terminally ill the access they need because they "are small, when they exist at all," and the ban on profits prevents many drug sponsors from participating. . . . As framed by the Alliance, we now consider:

> Whether the liberty protected by the Due Process Clause embraces the right of a terminally ill patient with no remaining approved treatment options to decide, in consultation with his or her own doctor, whether to seek access to investigational medications that the [FDA] concedes are safe and promising enough for substantial human testing.

---

4. The FDA has several other regulatory programs designed to hasten research of the safety and effectiveness of drugs for terminally or severely ill patients and allow early access where scientifically and medically warranted. For example, under its "Fast Track" program, the agency has "established procedures designed to expedite the development, evaluation, and marketing of new therapies intended to treat persons with life-threatening and severely-debilitating illnesses, especially where no satisfactory alternative therapy exists." 21 C.F.R. §312.80. Fast Track allows the FDA to waive its IND application requirement if it is "unnecessary or cannot be achieved," id. §312.10, and even allows a waiver request to be made "[i]n an emergency . . . by telephone or other rapid communication," id. The "Accelerated Approval" program provides a truncated approval process for "certain new drug products that have been studied for their safety and effectiveness in treating serious or life-threatening illnesses and that provide meaningful therapeutic benefit to patients over existing treatments." Id. §314.500. The FDA categorizes some new drugs, including nearly all cancer drugs, as "priority drugs" and seeks to accelerate their availability.

Appellants' Br. at 1. That is, we must determine whether terminally ill patients have a fundamental right to experimental drugs that have passed Phase I clinical testing. If such a right exists, the Alliance argues that both 21 C.F.R. §312.34(b)(3) (preventing access to experimental drugs for terminally ill patients where there is insufficient evidence of effectiveness or where there is an unreasonable risk of injury) and 21 C.F.R. §312.7 (prohibiting drug manufacturers from profiting on the sale of experimental drugs) must be subjected to strict scrutiny because they interfere with a fundamental constitutional right. We do not address the broader question of whether access to medicine might ever implicate fundamental rights.

    . . . In [*Washington v. Glucksberg*, 521 U.S. 702 (1997)], the Supreme Court described its "established method of substantive-due-process analysis" as having "two primary features."

> First, we have regularly observed that the Due Process Clause specially protects those fundamental rights and liberties which are, objectively, deeply rooted in this Nation's history and tradition and implicit in the concept of ordered liberty, such that neither liberty nor justice would exist if they were sacrificed. Second, we have required in substantive-due-process cases a careful description of the asserted fundamental liberty interest.

We will assume arguendo that the Alliance's description of its asserted right would satisfy *Glucksberg*'s "careful description" requirement. Looking to whether the Alliance has demonstrated that its right is deeply rooted in this Nation's history, tradition, and practices, the Alliance's claim for constitutional protection rests on two arguments: (1) that "common law and historical American practices have traditionally trusted individual doctors and their patients with almost complete autonomy to evaluate the efficacy of medical treatments"; and (2) that FDA policy is "inconsistent with the way that our legal tradition treats persons in all other life-threatening situations." Appellants' Br. at 31. More specifically, the Alliance argues that the concepts of self-defense, necessity, and interference with rescue are broad enough to demonstrate the existence of the fundamental right they seek—a right for "persons in mortal peril" to "try to save their own lives, even if the chosen means would otherwise be illegal or involve enormous risks."

    . . . Although the Alliance contends that it only wants drugs that "are safe and promising enough for substantial human testing," i.e., drugs that have passed Phase I testing, current law bans access to an experimental drug on safety grounds until it has successfully completed all phases of testing. . . . Thus, to succeed on its claim of a fundamental right of access for the terminally ill to experimental drugs, the Alliance must show not only that there is a tradition of access to drugs that have not yet been proven effective, but also a tradition of access to drugs that have not yet been proven safe.

    Examining, as we are required to do under *Glucksberg*, our Nation's history, legal traditions, and practice with respect to the regulation of drugs for efficacy and safety, we conclude that our Nation has long expressed interest in drug regulation, calibrating its response in terms of the capabilities to determine the risks associated with both drug safety and efficacy.

    Drug regulation in the United States began with the Colonies and States when the Colony of Virginia's legislature passed an act in 1736 that addressed the dispensing of more drugs than was "necessary or useful" because that practice had become "dangerous and intolerable." Edward Kremers, Kremers and Urdang's *History of Pharmacy* 158 (4th ed. 1976). The Territory of Orleans (Louisiana) passed an act in 1808 requiring a diploma and an examination before permitting pharmacists to dispense drugs; Louisiana also prohibited the sale of deteriorated drugs and restricted the sale of poisons. *Id.* at 182–84, 214. South Carolina enacted legislation in 1817 requiring pharmacists to obtain licenses, Kremers, *supra,* at 184, 214, followed by Georgia in 1825 and Alabama in 1852, *id.* at 214. By 1870, at least twenty-five states or territories had statutes regulating adulteration (impure drugs), and a few others had laws addressing poisons. *Id.* at 216. In the early history of our Nation, we observe not a tradition of protecting a right of access to drugs, but rather governments responding to the risks of new compounds as they become aware of and able to address those risks.

The current regime of federal drug regulation began to take shape with the Food, Drug, and Cosmetic Act of 1938. The Act required that drug manufacturers provide proof that their products were safe before they could be marketed. See *id.* The new Act also prohibited false therapeutic claims. Notably, the drug industry "strenuously objected" to the 1938 Act "ostensibly on the ground that it would deprive the American people of the right to self-medication," Harry A. Toulmin, Jr., *Law of Foods, Drugs and Cosmetics* 8–9 (2d ed. 1963)—an argument not unlike the Alliance's position of today.

We end our historical analysis where the Alliance would prefer it begin—with the 1962 Amendments to the FDCA. Undoubtedly, as the Alliance argues at length, Congress amended the FDCA in 1962 to explicitly require that the FDA only approve drugs deemed effective for public use. Thus, the Alliance argues that, prior to 1962, patients were free to make their own decisions whether a drug might be effective. But even assuming arguendo that efficacy regulation began in 1962, the Alliance's argument ignores our Nation's history of drug safety regulation described above. Nor can the Alliance override current FDA regulations simply by insisting that drugs which have completed Phase I testing are safe enough for terminally ill patients. Current law bars public access to drugs undergoing clinical testing on safety grounds. The fact that a drug has emerged from Phase I with a determination that it is safe for limited clinical testing in a controlled and closely-monitored environment after detailed scrutiny of each trial participant does not mean that a drug is safe for use beyond supervised trials. FDA regulation of post-Phase I drugs is entirely consistent with our historical tradition of prohibiting the sale of unsafe drugs.

. . . A prior lack of regulation suggests that we must exercise care in evaluating the untested assertion of a constitutional right to be free from new regulation. But the lack of prior governmental regulation of an activity tells us little about whether the activity merits constitutional protection. . . . Indeed, creating constitutional rights to be free from regulation based solely upon a prior lack of regulation would undermine much of the modern administrative state, which, like drug regulation, has increased in scope as changing conditions have warranted.

. . . The Alliance next turns to several common law doctrines, arguing that barring access to experimental drugs for terminally ill patients is "inconsistent with the way that our legal tradition treats persons in all other life-threatening situations." Specifically, the Alliance argues that three doctrines—(1) the doctrine of necessity; (2) the tort of intentional interference with rescue; and (3) the right to self-defense—each support the recognition of a right to self-preservation. Such a right to self-preservation, the Alliance believes, would permit "persons in mortal peril . . . to try to save their own lives, even if the chosen means would otherwise be illegal or involve enormous risks." Specifically, in this case, the Alliance believes that a right to self-preservation would give the terminally ill a constitutionally protected right of access to experimental drugs.

Looking first to the Alliance's necessity argument, the Alliance invokes the common law doctrine, which "traditionally covered the situation where physical forces beyond the actor's control rendered illegal conduct the lesser of two evils." *United States v. Oakland Cannabis Buyers' Cooperative,* 532 U.S. 483, 490 (2001). The Alliance offers, however, little detail about how necessity would apply to its case. (E.g., would terminally ill patients have a right to force drug companies to provide them with experimental drugs?) Nonetheless, the Supreme Court's analysis of the common law doctrine of necessity in *Oakland* leaves little room for the Alliance's argument that common law necessity could justify overriding the Food, Drug, and Cosmetic Act.

In *Oakland,* a group of patients seeking access to marijuana for medicinal purposes argued that "because necessity was a defense at common law, medical necessity should be read into the Controlled Substances Act." The Supreme Court rejected that argument because "[u]nder any conception of legal necessity, one principle is clear: The defense cannot succeed when the legislature itself has made a determination of values." Although the Court limited its analysis to the statutory issue and did not address the defendant's constitutional arguments, the learning of *Oakland* is clear. Congress may limit or even eliminate a necessity defense that might otherwise be available. That is precisely what the FDCA has done.

. . . The Alliance next invokes the tort of intentional interference with lifesaving efforts, which the Restatement of Torts defines as "intentionally prevent[ing] a third person from giving to another aid necessary to his bodily security." But that is not this case. The Alliance seeks access to drugs that are experimental and have not been shown to be safe, let alone effective at (or "necessary" for) prolonging life. Indeed, the Alliance concedes that taking experimental drugs can "involve enormous risks." In essence, the Alliance insists on a constitutional right to assume any level of risk. It is difficult to see how a tort addressing interference with providing "necessary" aid would guarantee a constitutional right to override the collective judgment of the scientific and medical communities expressed through the FDA's clinical testing process. Thus, we cannot agree that the tort of intentional interference with rescue evidences a right of access to experimental drugs.

Finally, the Alliance looks to traditional self-defense principles to support its proposed constitutional right. The common law doctrine of self-defense provides that "[o]ne who is not the aggressor . . . is justified in using a reasonable amount of force against his adversary when he reasonably believes (a) that he is in immediate danger of unlawful bodily harm from his adversary and (b) that the use of such force is necessary to avoid this danger." 2 Wayne R. LaFave, *Substantive Criminal Law* §10.4 (2d ed. 2003). Self-defense typically arises when a victim is being attacked by an aggressor and uses reasonable force to overcome immediate danger. The Alliance argues that self-defense permits victims to assume two types of risk: (1) the risk that the victim will kill the attacker; and (2) the risk that "[f]ighting back may dramatically increase the . . . harm" to the victim. So, the argument goes, if victims of crimes are allowed to assume these risks in defending their lives, terminally ill patients should also be allowed to assume the risk that an experimental drug may hasten their deaths.

That self-defense principles should be applied in the medical context is evidenced, the Alliance argues, by the Supreme Court's abortion jurisprudence. The Alliance does not look to the "right of personal privacy" addressed in *Roe v. Wade*, 410 U.S. 113, 152, (1973). Instead, the Alliance argues that *Roe* "recognized another, entirely separate right to abortion: a woman's right to abort a fetus at any stage of a pregnancy if doing so is necessary to preserve her life or health." "That right," the Alliance argues, "is grounded in traditional self-defense principles rather than privacy. . . ." Applying that concept here, the Alliance argues that because its terminally ill members are in immediate danger of harm from cancer, they can use whatever medical means are necessary to defend themselves. Thus, they argue, even if a medical treatment might otherwise be prohibited by law, the doctrine of self-defense justifies access to that treatment, just as self-defense justifies an assault victim using physical force otherwise prohibited by law.

This analogy also fails because this case is not about using reasonable force to defend oneself (as in most cases involving self-defense), nor is it about access to life-saving medical treatment. This case is about whether there is a constitutional right to assume, in the Alliance's own words, "enormous risks" in pursuit of potentially life-saving drugs. Unlike the cases in which the doctrine of self-defense might properly be invoked, this case involves risk from drugs with no proven therapeutic effect, which at a minimum separates this example from the abortion "life of the mother" exception. Because terminally ill patients cannot fairly be characterized as using reasonable force to defend themselves when they take unproven and possibly unsafe drugs, the Alliance's desire that the terminally ill be free to assume the risk of experimental drugs cannot draw support from the doctrine of self-defense.

. . . [W]e conclude that the Alliance has not provided evidence of a right to procure and use experimental drugs that is deeply rooted in our Nation's history and traditions.

[The court next concludes that the FDA regulations meet rational basis scrutiny.—Eds.]

. . . Although in the Alliance's view the FDA has unjustly erred on the side of safety in balancing the risks and benefits of experimental drugs, this is not to say that the FDA's balance can never be changed. The Alliance's arguments about morality, quality of life, and acceptable levels of medical risk are certainly ones that can be aired in the democratic branches, without injecting the courts into unknown questions of science and medicine. Our Nation's history and traditions have consistently demonstrated that the democratic branches are better suited to decide the proper balance between the uncertain risks and benefits of medical technology, and are entitled to deference in doing so. . . . [O]ur holding today ensures that this debate among the Alliance, the FDA, the scientific and medical communities, and the public may continue through the democratic process.

For the foregoing reasons, the judgment of the district court is affirmed.

ROGERS, Circuit Judge, with whom Chief Judge GINSBURG joins, dissenting:
. . . In the end, it is startling that the oft-limited rights to marry, to fornicate, to have children, to control the education and upbringing of children, to perform varied sexual acts in private, and to control one's own body even if it

results in one's own death or the death of a fetus have all been deemed fundamental rights covered, although not always protected, by the Due Process Clause, but the right to try to save one's life is left out in the cold despite its textual anchor in the right to life. This alone is reason the court should pause about refusing to put the FDA to its proof when it denies terminal patients with no alternative therapy the only option they have left, regardless of whether that option may be a long-shot with high risks. The court is on even weaker footing when it relies upon the risks entailed in medical procedures to wrest life-and-death decisions that once were vested in patients and their physicians. The court commits a logical error of dramatic consequence by concluding that the investigational drugs are somehow not "necessary." While the potential cures may not prove sufficient to save the life of a terminally ill patient, they are surely necessary if there is to be any possibility of preserving her life. . . .

NOTES AND QUESTIONS

1. *A negative right to health care?*   In an essay discussing the potential implications had Alliance won, law professor John Robertson characterizes its claim as a negative right to health care which, he writes, "while a far cry from a positive right to universal coverage," is "not to be sneered at." John Robertson, Controversial Medical Treatment and the Right to Health Care, 36 Hastings Ctr. Rep. 15–20 (Nov.-Dec. 2006). He describes a negative right to health care as "the right of a patient and doctor to pursue a course of treatment of their choosing without interference by the government." Id. If recognized in the context of the Abigail Alliance case, it would have meant that the FDA would have had to provide compelling reasons why an informed patient should "be denied investigational drugs outside of Phase II studies if the drug maker and the patient's physician are willing to provide them." Id.

If there is a negative right to health care, in what other contexts might it be implicated? If a right of access to experimental drugs were recognized for the terminally ill, would it also have to be recognized for patients who are seriously but not terminally ill? Robertson suggests that a negative right to health care could support a right of access to medical marijuana (a claim rejected in Raich v. Gonzales, 500 F.3d 850 (2007)) or to treatments using embryonic stem cells (the use of which might be prohibited under a state law), or to the ability to pay for organs.

Whether the right Abigail Alliance claimed was a right to health care or right to life, or however it may be denominated, do you think the FDA should have been put to the test of persuading the court that its restrictions on access to drugs were narrowly tailored to further a compelling interest? Or was the court correct to reject the Alliance's claim on the basis that no right existed?

2. *Drug safety.*   How many drugs that have passed Phase I testing eventually make it to market? According to a 2007 commentary in JAMA,

> Only 5% of all cancer drugs that enter clinical testing are approved for patient use; among cancer drugs assessed in phase 2 trials, only 30% proceed to phase 3 assessment. During clinical trials for all drugs from 1981–1992, attrition (ie, abandonment) occurred for 3 reasons: safety concerns (including toxicity) averaged 20.5%; lack of efficacy averaged 35.3%; and economics averaged 31.8%.

Peter D. Jacobson & Wendy E. Parmet, A New Era of Unapproved Drugs: The Case of Abigail Alliance v. Von Eschenbach, 297 JAMA 205 (2007). Does this data affect your assessment of the claims of Abigail Alliance?

3. *Enrollment in clinical trials and public health.*   In addition to safety concerns, another objection to greater access to unproven drugs is that patients would be less willing to enroll in randomized clinical trials if they could access the drugs outside of trials, and randomized clinical trials are necessary to determine the safety and efficacy of new drugs in the interest of public health. (In a clinical trial, patients have no guarantee they will be assigned to the arm providing the new drug rather than a placebo or existing treatment.) Would there be ways to respond to this concern and still expand access to new drugs outside of Phase II and Phase III testing?

4. *Postapproval studies.*   In 2012, the Institute of Medicine completed a report, requested by the FDA, that considers how the agency should approach the issue of post-approval efficacy and safety of drugs—in other words, how drugs are actually working once in use and over the drug's "life-cycle." Institute of Medicine, Report: Ethical and Scientific Issues in Studying the Safety of Approved Drugs, May 1, 2012, http://books.nap.edu/openbook.php?record_id=13219&page=R1. The Report urged the FDA to consider itself a "public health agency," in balancing two central obligations, the public health obligation "to protect people from unsafe medicines" and the obligation "to safeguard the rights and interests of research participants." (see Report Brief, http://www.iom.edu/Reports/2012/Ethical-and-Scientific-Issues-in-Studying-the-Safety-of-Approved-Drugs/Report-Brief.aspx). It concluded that observational studies can do much of the work postapproval, as long as effective and transparent strategies for collecting data are in place. The committee concluded that the FDA may also at times

> be justified in requiring studies that could expose patients to heightened risk—but only if a public health question of pressing importance is at stake, if no other study design could supply the needed evidence, and if the FDA relies on the research findings in a timely fashion in formulating its regulatory response. In addition, appropriate safeguards to protect patients' rights and interests must be in place to ensure that the additional risk is acceptable, and the study should employ a well-designed informed consent process tailored for the unique aspects of the postmarketing setting.

5. *Other claims to access.*   In the 2008 case Gulvanson v. PTC Therapeutics, Inc., 303 Fed. Appx. 128, 129 (3d Cir. 2008), the Third Circuit overturned the district court's decision to grant a preliminary injunction for a teenager with Duchenne Muscular Distrophy (DMD) who was refused access to a Phase 2a clinical trial for the drug PTC124. According to the Third Circuit opinion, the District Court abused its discretion in granting Gunvalson's motion under a theory of promissory estoppel because ultimately the claim was not likely to succeed on the merits. The pleadings failed to allege reliance on clear and definite promises of access to the experimental drug. See Seema Shah, Patricia Zettler (FNd1), From a Constitutional Right to a Policy of Exceptions: Abigail Alliance and the Future of Access to Experimental Therapy, 10 Yale J. Health Pol'y, L. & Ethics 135, 159–160 (2010).

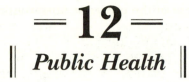

= 12 =
‖ *Public Health* ‖

While much of this casebook focuses on an individual patient's experience with medical care and those who provide it, this chapter has a different bent. Public health is a subject that is concerned less with any particular individual's health and more with the health of a population. This does not mean, of course, that the individual is irrelevant. An individual suspected of carrying a highly contagious and dangerous disease is of particular interest to public health authorities, who may wish to test, quarantine, or treat him to protect others. But public health authorities, generally local and state agencies operating under the state's inherent police powers, seek to serve the public broadly through measures to prevent the spread of disease and illness.

"Contemporary Americans," writes law professor Wendy Parmet, "who are used to thinking of illness as a personal and private matter, are apt to forget that almost all societies have public policies for the control and alleviation of disease." Wendy E. Parmet, Health Care and the Constitution: Public Health and the Role of the State in the Framing Era, 20 Hastings Const. L.Q. 267 (1992). Public health measures can be traced from the Hellenic and Roman eras through the Middle Ages and Renaissance and, in the United States, from the colonial period. Id. As Parmet writes of U.S. history, "As far back as 1629, the General Court of Massachusetts Bay Colony acted to protect the public health by limiting the number of passengers on each ship carrying migrants to the new colony." Id. at 287–288.

Threats to the public's health have changed over the years—for example, smallpox and typhoid have been replaced with HIV/AIDS and SARS; tuberculosis, once thought near eradication, has returned. Health threats from personal habits such as smoking and unhealthy eating habits, in addition to contagious disease, have come to occupy much of the attention of public health officials in recent years. Activities of public health programs have shifted over the years as well. Large-scale sanitation programs, once the work of public health programs, have become the province of engineers; likewise, environmental and occupational harms have become the responsibility of other governmental agencies. But eliminating or reducing disease, illness, and poor health in the population, whatever form it takes, remains the central purpose of public health laws and programs.

How does bioethics relate to public health concerns? In many ways. Most obviously, a particular individual may pose a threat or perceived threat to the health of a population if that individual carries an infectious disease. Efforts to immunize against certain diseases, test for them, and isolate an individual to protect others' health raise questions about the extent to which the government may intrude into the privacy of an individual's health affairs, invade his bodily integrity, and restrict his liberty. Where should the line be drawn between the state's ability to protect the public health and an individual's ability to freely go about his life undisturbed?

In addition to concerns about the privacy and liberty interests of the individual, public health efforts directed toward individuals also raise important issues of equal treatment. Thus, even if an individual's liberty may properly be circumscribed because of the threat she poses to others, how should we respond to uneven treatment among individuals who pose similar threats? How should we handle a health threat when it appears to come from an already marginalized group? Does such a situation call for exceptional measures to protect against social stigma?

The allocation of resources is also an important area in which questions of ethics in public health arise. When choices must be made about which public health problems to focus on and how to direct our resources to address them, we might examine these decisions not only in pragmatic terms (e.g., asking whether our resources are being efficiently used), but also with an eye toward what is the more ethical choice (e.g., asking whether we have a responsibility to direct our resources toward alleviating one problem rather than another).

Both in practice and in theory, each of these primary concerns is related. As seen in a number of the readings that follow, the field of public health law continually raises questions about the intersection of individual rights and public responsibilities. Although much of general bioethics discourse focuses on the rights of individuals as against state intrusions of individual liberty (and therefore that aspect of this chapter's readings will seem familiar), increasing attention is being focused on whether the public (acting through the state) has any *responsibilities* to protect its members from contagious disease and other threats to their health. This question is particularly sharpened when the state's efforts at disease prevention restrict individual liberties, without also addressing the health care and other needs of those affected or the conditions that make particular groups vulnerable to disease, such as poverty and homelessness.

A full examination of the ethics of public health would require coverage of many more topics than can be addressed in this chapter. As with each chapter in this book, choices had to be made. We have tended in this chapter to focus on challenges posed by contagious disease (naturally occurring or possibly occurring through bioterrorism), and to consider primarily the authority of states and their public health authorities to order individuals to undertake certain actions, such as vaccination, testing, treatment, quarantine, or isolation. But we have also included readings that look not just at individual rights, but that examine the ethics of public health decisions from the viewpoint of responsibility—responsibilities of governments, of institutions, and of individuals.

The following questions recur in one form or another in the materials in this chapter:

1. How should the state's interest in protecting the public's health be balanced against an individual's rights to autonomy, bodily integrity, and privacy?
2. Even when intrusions of an individual's liberty seem justified, in what manner and by what process should those intrusions be made?
3. What responsibilities do state public health authorities—and governments generally—owe to the healthy, the sick, and those at risk of disease?

A.   THE INTERSECTION OF BIOETHICS AND PUBLIC HEALTH

1.   Bioethical and Social Perspectives

As the following article suggests, the law of public health and the activities of public health authorities have received to date comparatively little attention by those interested in bioethics, whose writings more frequently focus on the individual patient–provider relationship. That appears to be changing, however, and this article provides some possible directions that new bioethical inquiries might take in the public health arena. Following the article is a problem that asks you to apply what you have learned about bioethical analysis to the public health issue of syringe availability.

> *Charles B. Smith, Margaret P. Battin,*
> *Jay A. Jacobson, Leslie P. Francis,*
> *Jeffrey R. Botkin, Emily P. Asplund,*
> *Gretchen J. Domek, & Beverly Hawkins,*
> *Are There Characteristics of Infectious*
> *Diseases That Raise Special Ethical Issues?*
> **4 Developing World Bioethics 1, 2–3, 12–16**
> **(May 2004)**

INTRODUCTION

Historically, infectious diseases such as plague, smallpox, typhoid, cholera, tuberculosis and leprosy have been the cause of enormous fear and social distress. Because most of these diseases were thought to be contagious and often occurred in dramatic epidemics, societies addressed these diseases as public health problems, and the needs and rights of populations and communities for protection by improved sanitation, quarantine, immunization, disease screening and directed therapy have typically been the primary ethical concerns of public health practitioners and legislators. In contrast, the field of bioethics that emerged in the late 1960's has increasingly emphasized the rights of individual patients to autonomous decision making, the avoidance of harm, and the obligation of the practitioner to act in the best interests of the individual patient. Generally, bioethicists have focused on cases that involved chronic, debilitating and life-ending diseases such as cancer, organ failure, congenital abnormalities and addictions, while little attention has been given to the discussion of ethical issues related to the control and management of infectious diseases.

With the appearance of AIDS in the early 1980's the separation between the population-wide concerns of public health and the individual practitioner/patient orientation of bioethics began to close. Zuger identified AIDS as the "first disease on record to spawn a huge, vocal, visible, angry grassroots patients' rights movement that changed the course of history." AIDS activists have been very effective in forcing public health officials and legislators to consider the rights of patients to privacy, autonomous decision making regarding their care, and the rights of infected patients to justice in the distribution of healthcare resources. Conversely, the relation of AIDS communicability to specific human behaviors has forced individual practitioners to be more open about questioning patients' private behaviors, to be more concerned with educating patients and the public about high risk behaviors, and to consider classical public health methods for reducing communicability. In many ways, AIDS and many other infectious diseases require us to consider the patient as both a *victim* with individual needs and rights, and as a potential *vector* of disease that is of concern to the community.

Unfortunately, AIDS, and possibly the often-associated infectious disease tuberculosis, are among the very few examples of infectious diseases where public health policy makers and modern bioethicists have begun to have useful dialogue to explore new ethical paradigms.

. . . We . . . propose that the ethical issues raised by infectious diseases are often related to these diseases' powerful ability to engender fear in individuals and panic in populations. This fear and panic often leads to rapid, emotionally driven decision making about the care of individual patients and about public health policies, even when these decisions challenge generally accepted medical-ethics principles such as patient autonomy, non-maleficience, beneficience and justice. . . .

VI.   Host Susceptibility

The general health of the host determines susceptibility to many infectious diseases. While some infectious diseases, such as the Ebola virus and small pox, are so virulent that they will attack all humans regardless of their general health status, susceptibility to most infectious diseases is highly linked to the general health of the host. Susceptibility to infection and the resulting morbidity and mortality to such common infectious diseases as tuberculosis, enteric pathogens, and acute respiratory tract diseases is highly correlated with nutrition and general health status. The relatively high mortality rates for the common infant diarrhoeas and childhood respiratory tract infections seen in malnourished children in poor African nations and in wartime refugee camps dramatically illustrate this association. This realisation leads to frequent debate about the just and ethical distribution of community resources. It has been argued that available but limited resources should first of all go to providing adequate nutrition before resources are spent on more expensive and possibly less effective medical services. . . .

VII.   COMMUNITY SUSCEPTIBILITY

The general health of the community environment determines susceptibility to many infectious diseases. The social and environmental health status of communities includes the provision of sanitation, hygiene, availability of clean air, water, and food, adequate nutrition and control of mosquitoes and other vectors of infectious diseases. This social infrastructure has significant effects on the susceptibility of community members to infectious diseases. The strong association of poverty and poor environmental health with infectious diseases raises the ethical issues of justice and human rights. In a sense, the patient is both the individual and the community.

The World Health Organization estimates that at least two thirds of the world's population lacks safe sanitation and one quarter lacks access to safe water. It is not surprising then, that in these undeveloped communities infantile diarrhoea is a major contributor to those infectious diseases that continue to be the major cause of death worldwide. The poverty-associated crowding and lack of hygiene in central Africa has for more than 100 years been associated with a very high rate of meningococcal meningitis. In the 1996 outbreak, more than 15,000 Africans died of this acute and often fatal infection.

Poverty-related lack of hygiene and associated increased susceptibility to infectious diseases continues to be a problem even in highly developed countries such as France and the US. Outbreaks of tuberculosis, diphtheria and louse-borne trench fever have recently been observed in the homeless populations of several US cities.

In most wars, morbidity and mortality from infectious diseases has exceeded that of military actions, and war-associated refugee camps continue to suffer from high attack rates and mortalities from measles, cholera, infantile diarrhoeas, acute respiratory tract diseases and malaria. This phenomenon illustrates the effect of war-related disruptions of community socio-economic conditions on infectious diseases. The public realization that this link exists can generate considerable fear and influence decisions to abandon communities during times of war and create refugee crises. Although not a direct form of bio-warfare, the military strategy of disrupting social, economic and public health systems and encouraging refugee migrations has the same effect of precipitating outbreaks of infectious diseases and killing large numbers of civilians.

VIII. HIGH SOCIO-ECONOMIC IMPACT

Infectious diseases may lead to deterioration in community socioeconomic status. In this regard, there is a tremendous amount at stake. The link between low community economic status and susceptibility to infectious diseases goes both ways. For centuries we have been aware of the devastating effect that worldwide epidemics, such as the plague and influenza, can have on local and even world economies. The outbreak of bubonic plague in Europe in the mid-14th century killed one third of Europe's population, and the effects on local and regional commerce were devastating. The 1918 worldwide influenza epidemic killed 21 million people, an effect on mortality and economic development that rivaled that of the First World War. This raises issues of the economic responsibility of societies to maintain conditions that discourage infections and to treat outbreaks.

Most recently, we have come to realize and to fear the destructive effects the AIDS epidemic is having on the economies of countries where as many as 25% of the working age population can be taken out of the work force by this infection. This fear of continued spread of the HIV infection and resulting AIDS mortality has been compounded by the realization and fear that the resulting decline in socio-economic and public health services is associated with epidemics of tuberculosis and other infectious diseases. These fears have led some community leaders to publicly deny the existence of some infectious disease epidemics, such as AIDS and SARS, a violation of the truth-telling ethic that has seriously delayed and obstructed needed community public health control measures.

The recent Macroeconomics and Health Report to the World Health Organization recognized the synergy between economic development and infectious diseases by emphasizing the principal point that economic growth is not possible without a healthy population. This realization may hopefully generate a more just distribution of resources between the rich and poor nations. In the 2002 meeting of the World Health Assembly, the Commission on Macroeconomics and Health reported that the world now has the capability of ending poverty and poverty-associated diseases for the first time in history. The cost to the rich developed countries would only be one cent out of every $10 of gross national product.

CONCLUSION

Although many of the characteristics of infectious diseases mentioned in this paper might be present in non-infectious diseases, taken together they comprise a group of traits that raise distinctive ethical concerns. Our historical attitudes toward infectious diseases have been shaped by countless years of public health officials contending with them; but they have not been central in recent bioethics. Only now, as diseases like HIV/AIDS, multi-drug resistant tuberculosis, SARS, West Nile virus, and other emerging and reemerging diseases come to the fore, are we pressed to re-examine the ethical principles to which we have been appealing. We believe that a new paradigm for ethics of infectious diseases will evolve as public health policy makers and ethicists give increased consideration to the rights of individuals, and bioethicists give increased consideration to the competing needs to prevent spread of communicable diseases.

NOTES AND QUESTIONS

1. *Ethical analysis of public health activities.*   How do these authors explain the relative lack of attention that bioethics study has paid to public health issues? Why do they think this should change? What would such attention add to consideration of public health issues?

2. *Questioning the responsibilities of developed countries.*   What do these authors identify as the major causes of continued devastation of human life by infectious diseases? The authors appear to suggest that at least part of the responsibility for eliminating those causes lies with "rich developed countries." Do you agree or disagree? Is this a matter merely of politics or a matter of ethics?

3. *Biowarfare.*   What is biowarfare? How is it related to war? How is it related to bioterrorism?

2.   Legal Approaches

Consider the information provided in the following article about access to sterile syringes by injection drug users. The questions that follow the article ask you to apply an analysis of the ethics of various legal impediments to syringe access.

> ## Scott Burris, Steffanie A. Strathdee, & John S. Vernick, Lethal Injections: The Law, Science, and Politics of Syringe Access for Injection Drug Users
> ### 37 U.S.F. L. Rev. 813 (2003)

Access to sterile syringes through syringe exchange programs (SEPs) has been associated with decreased rates of needle sharing, decreased prevalence and incidence of blood borne infections such as HIV and hepatitis B and C, and increased rates of entry into drug treatment among injection drug users (IDUs). There is no evidence that such programs increase crime, drug use or the number of discarded needles on the street. Pharmacies, syringe vending machines, and deregulating syringe access can further expand sterile syringe coverage to IDUs, thereby increasing the potential to achieve these positive public health outcomes.

Despite its public health value, however, syringe access has been politically controversial in the United States. In our political culture, driven by symbols and perceptions, improved syringe access has been painted as "soft on drugs," a retreat from zero tolerance that will be seen as an endorsement of drug use. Polls continue to show that only a little more than half of respondents support enhanced syringe access—a majority, but evidently one that is too narrow or uncommitted to counterbalance the intense symbolic force of the syringe access issue in policy-making. Syringe access, then, is quite a familiar public health policy dilemma: science and professional judgment point to an intervention that is unsettling, if not absolutely unacceptable, to a significant part of the United States public and its political leaders.

Syringe access is regulated by state law. The legal regulation of syringe access varies from state to state but takes one or more of three forms: syringe prescription laws and regulations; other pharmacy regulations or miscellaneous statutes imposing a variety of restrictions on the sale of syringes by pharmacists or others; and drug paraphernalia laws prohibiting the sale or possession of items intended to be used to consume illegal drugs.

. . . Since the beginning of the HIV epidemic, twelve states . . . have deregulated the sale or possession of at least some number of syringes. In others, . . . efforts at deregulation ha[ve] been unsuccessful. To date, no state that has liberalized syringe access in response to HIV has rescinded the change, but change continues to be a controversial matter in states that maintain restrictive access policies.

NOTES AND QUESTIONS

1. *Bioethics inquiry of laws affecting syringe access.*   The article by Charles B. Smith, et al., excerpted above, suggests that "generally accepted medical ethics principles such as patient autonomy, non-maleficience, beneficience, and justice" should be critically applied to public health policies. How would you do so in evaluating the ethical propriety of a syringe exchange program (where injection drug users can exchange used syringes for sterile ones)? How would you evaluate a syringe exchange program under a utilitarian analysis?

2. *Ethics of the professional.*   If a state law restricted syringe access to those who had a physician prescription, do you think a physician would be acting ethically to write a prescription for syringes if requested by an injection drug user?

3. *State law variations.*   State law on syringe access varies widely. Research the law in your state. Do you think it is ethically sound? If not, do you think it would be politically feasible to change it? Why or why not?

4. *Drug-injecting risk compared between cities.*   A recently published study examined data from 2004 to 2006 to compare the risk of infection behaviors of injection drug users (IDUs) in New York City, which had large-scale syringe exchange programs and pharmacy availability without a prescription, and Newark, New Jersey, where syringe exchange and nonprescription purchase were illegal at the time. The Newark IDUs were (even after controlling for various differences between city populations) much more likely to report syringe sharing, to be HIV seropositive (three times more likely), and positive for hepatitis B (four times more likely) and hepatitis C (three times more likely). Alan Neaigus et al., Greater Drug Injecting Risk for HIV, HBV, and HCV Infection in a City Where Syringe Exchange and Pharmacy Syringe Distribution Are Illegal, 85 J. Urban Health 301 (2008).

B.   CONTROL AND PREVENTION OF INFECTIOUS DISEASE

1.   Vaccination

|| *Jacobson v. Commonwealth of Massachusetts* ||
197 U.S. 11 (1905)

Opinion of the court by Mr. Justice HARLAN.

[T]he plaintiff in error, Jacobson, was proceeded against by a criminal complaint in one of the inferior courts of Massachusetts. The complaint charged that on the 17th day of July, 1902, the board of health of Cambridge, being of the opinion that it was necessary for the public health and safety, required the vaccination and revaccination of all the inhabitants thereof who had not been successfully vaccinated since the 1st day of March, 1897, and provided them with the means of free vaccination; and that the defendant, being over twenty-one years of age and not under guardianship, refused and neglected to comply with such requirement. [The jury found the defendant guilty and he was sentenced to pay a fine of $5.]

The authority of the state to enact this statute is to be referred to what is commonly called the police power,—a power which the state did not surrender when becoming a member of the Union under the Constitution. Although this court has refrained from any attempt to define the limits of that power, yet it has distinctly recognized the authority of a state to enact quarantine laws and "health laws of every description"; indeed, all laws that relate to matters completely within its territory and which do not by their necessary operation affect the people of other states. According to settled principles, the police power of a state must be held to embrace, at least, such reasonable regulations established directly by legislative enactment as will protect the public health and the public safety.

. . . The defendant insists that his liberty is invaded when the state subjects him to fine or imprisonment for neglecting or refusing to submit to vaccination; that a compulsory vaccination law is unreasonable, arbitrary, and oppressive, and, therefore, hostile to the inherent right of every freeman to care for his own body and health in such way as to him seems best; and that the execution of such a law against one who objects to vaccination, no matter for what reason, is nothing short of an assault upon his person. But the liberty secured by the Constitution of the United States to every person within its jurisdiction does not import an absolute right in each person to be, at all times and in all circumstances, wholly freed from restraint. There are manifold restraints to which every person is necessarily subject for the common good. On any other basis organized society could not exist with safety to its members. Society based on the rule that each one is a law unto himself would soon be confronted with disorder and anarchy. . . .

Applying these principles to the present case, it is to be observed that the legislature of Massachusetts required the inhabitants of a city or town to be vaccinated only when, in the opinion of the board of health, that was necessary for the public health or the public safety. The authority to determine for all what ought to be done in such an emergency must have been lodged somewhere or in somebody; and surely it was appropriate for the legislature to refer that question, in the first instance, to a board of health composed of persons residing in the locality affected, and appointed, presumably, because of their fitness to determine such questions. To invest such a body with authority over such matters was not an unusual, nor an unreasonable or arbitrary, requirement. Upon the principle of self-defense, of paramount necessity, a community has the right to protect itself against an epidemic of disease which threatens the safety of its members. It is to be observed that when the regulation in question was adopted smallpox, according to the recitals in the regulation adopted by the board of health, was prevalent to some extent in the city of Cambridge, and the disease was increasing. . . . The liberty secured by the 14th Amendment, this court has said, consists, in part, in the right of a person "to live and work where he will" (Allgeyer v. Louisiana, 165 U.S. 578); and yet he may be compelled, by force if need be, against his will and without regard to his personal wishes or his pecuniary interests, or even his religious or political convictions, to take his place in the ranks of the army of his country, and risk the chance of being shot down in its defense. It is not, therefore, true that the power of the public to guard itself against imminent danger depends in every case involving the control of one's body upon his willingness to submit to reasonable regulations established by the constituted authorities, under the sanction of the state, for the purpose of protecting the public collectively against such danger.

. . . If there is any such power in the judiciary to review legislative action in respect of a matter affecting the general welfare, it can only be when that which the legislature has done comes within the rule that, if a statute purporting to have been enacted to protect the public health, the public morals, or the public safety, has no real or substantial relation to those objects, or is, beyond all question, a plain, palpable invasion of rights secured by the fundamental law, it is the duty of the courts to so adjudge, and thereby give effect to the Constitution.

[No one can] confidently assert that the means prescribed by the state to that end has no real or substantial relation to the protection of the public health and the public safety. Such an assertion would not be consistent with the experience of this and other countries whose authorities have dealt with the disease of smallpox.[1] And the principle of vaccination as a means to prevent the spread of smallpox has been enforced in many states by statutes making the vaccination of children a condition of their right to enter or remain in public schools.

. . . Since, then, vaccination, as a means of protecting a community against smallpox, finds strong support in the experience of this and other countries, no court, much less a jury, is justified in disregarding the action of the legislature simply because in its or their opinion that particular method was—perhaps, or possibly—not the best either for children or adults.

. . . The defendant offered to prove that vaccination "quite often" caused serious and permanent injury to the health of the person vaccinated; that the

---

1. The Court's footnote here describes the vaccination programs of England and other European countries and provides statistical data about the utility of the vaccine in reducing incidences of the disease and mortality rates.–EDS.

operation "occasionally" resulted in death; that it was "impossible" to tell "in any particular case" what the results of vaccination would be, or whether it would injure the health or result in death; that "quite often" one's blood is in a certain condition of impurity when it is not prudent or safe to vaccinate him; that there is no practical test by which to determine "with any degree of certainty" whether one's blood is in such condition of impurity as to render vaccination necessarily unsafe or dangerous; that vaccine matter is "quite often" impure and dangerous to be used, but whether impure or not cannot be ascertained by any known practical test; that the defendant refused to submit to vaccination for the reason that he had, "when a child," been caused great and extreme suffering for a long period by a disease produced by vaccination; and that he had witnessed a similar result of vaccination, not only in the case of his son, but in the cases of others.

These offers, in effect, invited the court and jury to go over the whole ground gone over by the legislature when it enacted the statute in question. The legislature assumed that some children, by reason of their condition at the time, might not be fit subjects of vaccination; and it is suggested—and we will not say without reason—that such is the case with some adults. But the defendant did not offer to prove that, by reason of his then condition, he was in fact not a fit subject of vaccination at the time he was informed of the requirement of the regulation adopted by the board of health. It is entirely consistent with his offer of proof that, after reaching full age, he had become, so far as medical skill could discover, and when informed of the regulation of the board of health was, a fit subject of vaccination, and that the vaccine matter to be used in his case was such as any medical practitioner of good standing would regard as proper to be used. The matured opinions of medical men everywhere, and the experience of mankind, as all must know, negative the suggestion that it is not possible in any case to determine whether vaccination is safe. Was defendant exempted from the operation of the statute simply because of his dread of the same evil results experienced by him when a child, and which he had observed in the cases of his son and other children? Could he reasonably claim such an exemption because "quite often," or "occasionally," injury had resulted from vaccination, or because it was impossible, in the opinion of some, by any practical test, to determine with absolute certainty whether a particular person could be safely vaccinated?

. . . We are not prepared to hold that a minority, residing or remaining in any city or town where smallpox is prevalent, and enjoying the general protection afforded by an organized local government, may thus defy the will of its constituted authorities, acting in good faith for all, under the legislative sanction of the state. If such be the privilege of a minority, then a like privilege would belong to each individual of the community, and the spectacle would be presented of the welfare and safety of an entire population being subordinated to the notions of a single individual who chooses to remain a part of that population. We are unwilling to hold it to be an element in the liberty secured by the Constitution of the United States that one person, or a minority of persons, residing in any community and enjoying the benefits of its local government, should have the power thus to dominate the majority when supported in their action by the authority of the state.

. . . Until otherwise informed by the highest court of Massachusetts, we are not inclined to hold that the statute establishes the absolute rule that an adult must be vaccinated if it be apparent or can be shown with reasonable certainty that he is not at the time a fit subject of vaccination, or that vaccination, by reason of his then condition, would seriously impair his health, or probably cause his death. No such case is here presented. It is the cause of an adult who, for aught that appears, was himself in perfect health and a fit subject of vaccination, and yet, while remaining in the community, refused to obey the statute and the regulation adopted in execution of its provisions for the protection of the public health and the public safety, confessedly endangered by the presence of a dangerous disease.

The judgment of the court below must be affirmed. . . .

NOTES AND QUESTIONS

1. *Fines vs. forcible vaccination.*   Note that Jacobson was not compulsorily vaccinated but was instead subject to a fine. Does the Court's reasoning require this outcome? If the Massachusetts statute in question had permitted forcible vaccination rather than provide a fine, would the Court's reasoning in this case have upheld its constitutionality? Do you think such a statute should be considered constitutional? How does compulsory vaccination compare to forced sterilization as permitted by Buck v. Bell (see Chapter 5)? Note that both *Jacobson* and Buck v. Bell refer to the power of the government to draft individuals into the armed forces as support for the public health measure at issue in the case. Is the comparison to the draft apt?

2. *Scientific evidence.*   How does the Court handle the question of the scientific evidence in support of compulsory vaccination? Note that it affirms the lower court's decision to disallow Jacobson's offer to prove the existence of contrary opinions about the vaccine's safety and efficacy. How should we evaluate the deference apparently given to the legislature in light of the possibility that information about science can be shaped by political forces?

3. *Current constitutional analysis.*   *Jacobson* was obviously decided before Roe v. Wade and other privacy rights cases, which required a more stringent review of state action impinging on the bodily integrity of the individual (e.g., Roe v. Wade, 410 U.S. 113 (1973) (strict scrutiny/compelling state interest); Planned Parenthood v. Casey, 505 U.S. 833 (1992) (undue burden); and In re Cruzan, 497 U.S. 261 (1990) (suggesting a balancing test)). What do you think a current analysis of the *Jacobson* facts would look like? Would the result be different?

4. *Current state of law on vaccinations.*   All states now require proof of certain vaccinations prior to a child's enrollment in school. Exemptions from immunization are generally provided for children for whom a particular immunization is medically contraindicated or if the parents object on religious (and in some states simply "personal" or "moral") beliefs. The Supreme Court has upheld mandatory vaccination as a condition for public school attendance. Zuch v. King, 260 U.S. 174 (1922). The exemption for immunizations that are medically contraindicated are probably constitutionally required (see *Jacobson*), but the exemption for religious reasons unlikely so. See Prince v. Massachusetts, 321 U.S. 158 (1944) ("The right to practice religion freely does not include liberty to expose the community or the child to communicable disease or the latter to ill health or death.") See also Wright v. De Witt Sch. Dist., 385 S.W.2d 644 (Ark.

1965) (individuals' freedom to act according to their religious beliefs is subject to the state's health regulation requiring smallpox vaccination as prerequisite to attending school). See generally Lawrence O. Gostin, Public Health Law: Power, Duty, Restraint 210 (2000).

5. *HPV vaccine.*   In June 2006, the FDA approved a vaccine for females, aged 9 to 26, against human papillomavirus (HPV), a sexually transmitted virus that can, in rare cases without proper screening, cause cervical cancer. Although deaths from cervical cancer worldwide are estimated at over 200,000, fewer than 4,000 occur in the United States, where proper screening and treatment are very effective. Shortly after the vaccine was approved, legislative proposals to make the vaccine mandatory for girls prior to school enrollment were introduced in a substantial number of states. Met with strong opposition, the proposals were adopted in only two jurisdictions (Washington, DC and Virginia) and included generous "opt out" provisions. Renee Gerber, Mandatory Cervical Cancer Vaccinations, 35 J. L. Med. & Ethics 495 (2007); Gail Javitt, Deena Berkowitz & Lawrence O. Gostin, Assessing Mandatory HPV Vaccination: Who Should Call the Shots?, 36 J.L. Med. & Ethics 384 (2008).

Opposition to mandatory HPV vaccination has generally focused on one or more of the following concerns: (1) there is uncertainty about the long-term safety and effectiveness of the vaccine; (2) in contrast to other vaccines mandated by the states (with the exception of tetanus), HPV is neither highly contagious nor "associated with significant morbidity and mortality occurring shortly after exposure." Javitt et al., at 389; (3) because the virus is sexually transmitted, some critics of mandatory vaccination argue that it is for parents to decide whether their daughters should be vaccinated; (4) mandatory vaccination of females only is suspect when males also can become infected with and spread HPV. Finally, Merck, the maker of the vaccine (sold under the name Gardasil) has been soundly criticized for its aggressive marketing and lobbying efforts, which many claim have caused vaccination deployment to occur too quickly. The HPV vaccine is very expensive compared to others: in 2008, it cost at least $360 for a three-dose series. Elizabeth Rosenthal, Drug Makers' Push Leads to Vaccines' Fast Rise, N.Y. Times, Aug. 2, 2008, at A1.

In October 2011, the Centers for Disease Control and Prevention's Advisory Committee on Immunization Practices announced its recommendation that males aged 11 to 21 also be vaccinated against HPV. The American Academy of Pediatrics echoed this recommendation in February 2012. American Academy of Pediatrics, HPV Vaccine Recommendations, 129 Pediatrics 602 (2012).

6. *H1N1 and mandatory vaccinations of health care workers.*   In 2009, the spread of the H1N1 strain of influenza (otherwise known as swine flu) prompted hospitals around the United States, and even some states, to impose mandatory vaccination on their health care workers. Such efforts did not go unopposed. In New York, four nurses working for public hospitals filed suit to enjoin an emergency regulation adopted by the New York State Hospital Review and Planning Council requiring H1N1 and seasonal flu vaccinations for all state health care workers or risk losing employment. In October 2009, nurses were granted a temporary restraining order. This halted the vaccinations, and soon thereafter New York suspended the directive due to a vaccine shortage. See Daniel Goodman & Christopher Webster, The Mandatory Vaccination of Health Care Workers, Law Practice Today (Apr. 21), available at http://www.americanbar.org/

newsletter/publications/law_practice_today_home/law_practice_today_archive/
april11/the_mandatory_vaccination_of_health_care_workers.html.   Institutions
that allow opt-outs but then require clear identification of who has not received
a vaccination (such as through special badges or the requirement to wear a mask)
must take precautions that such measures do not stigmatize health care workers or
reveal private health information about them. Id.; Service Employees International
Union, Local 121 RN v. Los Robles Regional Medical Center (2009 U.S. Dist. LEXIS
111489). For a discussion of the legal arguments on the topic of mandatory vaccination, see Christine Nero Coughlin et al., When Doctors Become "Patients":
Advocating a Patient-Centered Approach for Health Care Workers in the Context
of Mandatory Influenza Vaccinations and Informed Consent, 45 Wake Forest L.
Rev. 1551 (2010).

7. *Vaccination and autism.*   In response to burgeoning autism diagnoses
among children (1 in every 150 children today as compared to 1 in every 10,000
children 20 years ago), a recent grassroots movement has emerged advocating for
the discontinuance or alteration of childhood vaccinations—specifically, the
vaccine for measles, mumps, and rubella (MMR)—because of a putative link
between those vaccines and autism. The beginnings of the movement can perhaps
be traced to a 1998 article in the medical journal The Lancet suggesting that the
MMR vaccine caused autism. See http://www.thelancet.com/journals/lancet/
article/PIIS0140673697110960/fulltext. However, a 2011 editorial in the British
Medical Journal found that the evidence produced in the 1998 article was "fraudulent" and that there was "[c]lear evidence of falsification of data." See http://
abcnews.go.com/Health/Autism/link-vaccine-autism-link-fraud-british-medical-
journal/story?id=12547823#.UCkn76OfgVp. Moreover, the Federal Circuit in
Cedillo v. Dept of Health & Human Services, 617 F.3d 1328 (2010), affirmed
the decision of the lower court of federal claims known as the "Vaccine Court"
that no viable theory that vaccines cause autism had been presented. The decision
affected approximately 5,000 such claims under the National Vaccine Injury Compensation Program. See Lauren L. Haertlein, Immunizing Against Bad Science: The
Vaccine Court and the Autism Test Cases, 75 Law & Contemp. Probs. 211 (2012).

2.   Quarantine and Isolation

Quarantine and Isolation: Lessons Learned from SARS
Institute for Bioethics, Health Policy and Law, University of Louisville School of Medicine (2003)

Concern over and the practice of avoiding persons with contagious diseases has been documented in the most ancient of texts and writings, including
the Old Testament (avoiding lepers) and the works of Thucydides (c. 460–400
B.C.E.), Hippocrates (c. 460–370 B.C.E.), and Galen (c. 130–200 C.E.). One of
the earliest uses of quarantine-and-isolation-type measures to control the movement of sick persons is said to have taken place in 532 C.E., when the Emperor

Justinian of the Eastern Roman Empire commanded that persons arriving into the capital city of Constantinople (current day Istanbul, Turkey) from "contaminated localities" be housed in special facilities to be "cleansed."

. . . Quarantine and isolation measures in the U.S. were at first similar to those used in Europe and were not uniform or coordinated. The control of communicable diseases that were largely attributed to immigration or trade from abroad was dealt with primarily by local authority, and only secondarily by state or federal authority. In Boston, for example, a city ordinance required that all ships attempting to disembark in the harbor first stop at the harbor entrance to be checked for sick persons; somewhat later, a "house" on Rainsford's Island in the harbor was designated for the detention of persons with "contagious diseases."

In New York City, a more elaborate system of medical inspection and detention was developed, centered off Staten Island, that included the inspection of all incoming ships, cargo, and passengers for contagion. Persons considered to have a disease at the time considered "quarantinable" (e.g., cholera, yellow fever, plague, leprosy, smallpox) by a quarantine officer were admitted for mostly palliative care to an isolation hospital located at the quarantine station, staffed by physicians, nurses, and orderlies. Persons with less serious contagious diseases (e.g., measles, scarlet fever) were sent to a Marine Hospital on Ellis Island. The detention or isolation period was usually determined by the disease at issue, including what was known about the disease's incubation period and degree of infectiousness. A similar disease control system was established by the New York City Health Departments, with the department's staff of inspectors, physicians, and special police force having the authority to inspect all persons within the city who were reported to be sick and to remove to the city's quarantine island certain persons with contagious disease.

. . . In the twentieth century there were many cases in which quarantine and isolation—including both mandatory and voluntary measures—were used by public health officials in the U.S. and other countries in an attempt to control communicable diseases. Sometimes these measures were quite controversial. A sample of some of the more prominent cases illustrates the varying ways that public health officials have used quarantine and isolation.

In 1907, an apparently healthy woman, Mary Mallon, was involuntarily admitted to the New York City Health Department's Detention Hospital, and held there, with the subsequent affirmation of a New York court, for a total of three years based upon concerns about her infectious state for typhoid fever. The conditions for her release specified that she not engage in any occupation that would bring her into contact with food, but she accepted a job as a cook at a hospital, which later had dozens of cases of typhoid. Mary Mallon was again involuntarily admitted to a number of New York area hospitals and institutions "without any prospect of again being released." In Ms. Mallon's case, public health officials concluded that only isolation for the remainder of her life would effectively control the risk of typhoid transmission.

In the fall and winter of 1918, divergent approaches to quarantine and isolation were used in response to an influenza pandemic (often referred to as the "Spanish Flu") that killed between 20 and 40 million persons worldwide, including hundreds of thousands in the U.S. Inconsistent control measures were implemented in most U.S. jurisdictions, including mass graves for the dead; suspension or closure of public gathering places (e.g., churches, schools, shops); prohibitions on public gatherings (e.g., funerals, meetings); ordinances against spitting, coughing, or sneezing in public; and the quarantine of suspected influenza cases or the isolation of sick persons. . . . [I]rrationality about some of the control measures, such as orders to close some public gathering places (e.g., churches) but not others (e.g., saloons), appeared to undermine the public's confidence in health officials and their policies.

NOTES AND QUESTIONS

1. *Unequal treatment.*   Mary Mallon (otherwise known as "Typhoid Mary") lived on North Brother Island in isolation, as ordered by the state of New York, for 26 years, until her death in 1938. Judith Walzer Leavitt's book on Mallon's experience searches for answers to her unique treatment—for there were a number of healthy typhoid carriers in the state who were never ordered into isolation. She writes,

> The policies governing healthy carriers answer some of the questions about the particular detention of Mary Mallon. The somewhat ambiguous guidelines—written after her second incarceration—stated that carriers "need not be retained in hospitals or institutions if not desired. They will be sent home if home conditions are satisfactory." The vagueness of how "satisfactory" was to be determined left room for significant maneuvering and permitted health officials to make decisions about healthy carriers that incorporated a range of considerations. They could, for example, differentiate between Mary Mallon, whom health officials did not trust to behave in the public's interest, possibly because of her blatantly resistant behavior, and other healthy carriers, like Alphonse Cotils, whose resistance was quieter and whose home conditions and personal attributes seemed to predict closer compliance with the health codes.
>
> Although two healthy carriers might have borne equally dangerous pathogenic bacteria as identified in the laboratory, they were not necessarily treated equally in practice. According to the equivocal health department protocols, the carriers' social condition and even their psychological responses could be applied alongside the laboratory reports to evaluate the dangers they presented and to determine ways to protect the public from the dangers they posed. Health officers judged the home conditions, sanitary facilities, and the individual's tractability as they determined the proper regulation of healthy typhoid bacilli carriers.

Judith Walzer Leavitt, Typhoid Mary: Captive to the Public's Health 57–60 (1996). What are the advantages and disadvantages of such indeterminate rules?

2. *Lifetime isolation.*   Do you think there are any conditions under which lifetime isolation would be legally and ethically permissible?

In the spring of 2003, a number of countries (especially Canada, China, Hong Kong, Singapore, Taiwan, and Vietnam) were hit with a new epidemic of unknown cause and no known cure called SARS (Severe Acute Respiratory Syndrome). Quarantine and isolation were used to an unprecedented international extent to limit the transmission of the disease. The link between the efficacy of those quarantine and isolation efforts and employment security and wage replacement is discussed in the following excerpt from a report produced in cooperation with the U.S. Centers for Disease Control.

> *Quarantine and Isolation: Lessons
> Learned from SARS*
> **Institute for Bioethics, Health Policy and Law,
> University of Louisville School of Medicine
> (2003)**

Quarantine resulted in the confinement of thousands of individuals who were well enough to work and who needed to work to support themselves and their families. Because the success of quarantine depended on compliance by the affected individuals, all of the countries we studied took some steps to provide for income replacement and employment security of individuals in quarantine. SARS-based discrimination in employment was a problem in all of the countries we studied; health care workers were among those suffering the most discrimination. Bad economic conditions associated with SARS also resulted in unemployment. Governmental responses varied. For example, in Hong Kong, sick leave was granted to individuals in home confinement. Canada passed a law prohibiting the discharge of employees under quarantine absent proof that a business downturn necessitated the elimination of positions and providing compensation for individuals absent from work for at least five days and physicians affected by hospital closures due to quarantine.

ISSUES TO CONSIDER

C.3.1. In general, under current U.S. law, employees without a contrary contractual provision may be discharged for being in quarantine. Laws need to be enacted to prohibit discrimination and to provide for the job security of individuals in quarantine.

C.3.2. With the exception of those contractually entitled to paid sick leave, employees in the U.S. are not eligible for income replacement due to quarantine under any federal or state law. Providing income replacement for employees and self-employed persons is essential to ensure a high rate of compliance with quarantine.

C.3.3. To promote adherence to quarantine, individuals in quarantine need to be held harmless for various consequences of lost income, and therefore measures need to be explored that would, for example, provide for insurance and rent payments and protect against repossession for missed car payments.

NOTES AND QUESTIONS

1. *Economic security and wage replacement.* Do you agree that the government should provide economic benefits to individuals who must forgo income because of a requirement to be quarantined or isolated? Why or why not? If you do agree, is it for practical reasons or do you think these measures may be ethically required?

2. *Avian flu and suggested use of the military.* Over the past decade or so, avian influenza has been considered by the Centers for Disease Control and

Prevention and other domestic and international public health organizations to pose a potential major threat to human health. Although highly contagious among birds, the virus does not usually infect humans. During a 2008 outbreak in animals (an "epizootic"), however, a number of cases found in humans raised serious concerns. Most of these cases were traced to direct contact with infected birds, usually poultry. Human-to-human infection is rare. According to the CDC, there have been "reported human cases of avian influenza A (H5N1) in Asia, Africa, the Pacific, Europe and the Near East. Indonesia and Vietnam have reported the highest number of H5N1 cases to date. Overall mortality in reported H5N1 cases is approximately 60%." Centers for Disease Control and Prevention, Avian Influenza: Current H5N1 Situation (Sept. 24, 2008), available at http://www.cdc.gov/flu/avian/outbreaks/current.htm. Studies have shown that this recent strain of bird flu (H5N1) is similar to the H1N1 virus that caused the flu pandemic in 1918. If H5N1 mutates in the same way as the H1N1 virus, it could infect tens of millions of people and spread rapidly around the world. In 2005, when the threat of a possible pandemic reaching the United States seemed more likely than today, President Bush stated that if the flu reached the United States, areas of outbreak would be quarantined, possibly with military force. To use the military for these purposes could require a change in U.S. law. Moreover, many have criticized relying on federal responses over local government authority due to the slow response of the federal government to Hurricane Katrina relief in 2005; the suggestion that the military might be involved added fuel to those criticisms. Bioethics scholar and commentator George Annas criticized Bush's plan on a number of grounds, including the following:

> [Q]uarantine and isolation are often falsely equated, but the former involves people who are well, the latter people who are sick. Sick people should be treated, but we don't need the military to force treatment. Even in extremes like the anthrax attacks, people seek out and demand treatment. Sending soldiers to quarantine large numbers of people will most likely create panic, and cause people to flee (and spread disease), as it did in China where a rumor during the SARS epidemic that Beijing would be quarantined led to 250,000 people fleeing the city that night.
>
> Not only can't we evacuate Houston, we cannot realistically quarantine its citizens. The real public health challenge will be shortages of health care personnel, hospital beds, and medicine. Plans to militarize quarantine miss the point in a pandemic. The enemy is not sick or exposed Americans—it is the virus itself.

George Annas, Bush's Risky Flu Pandemic Plan, The Boston Globe, Oct. 8, 2005. What other arguments might be made against use of the military in this situation? Arguments in favor of it?

3.   Tuberculosis: A Modern Case Study

Tuberculosis was the leading cause of death in the United States 100 years ago. But around the 1950s, the development of antibiotics to treat tuberculosis, along with improvements in living conditions such as sanitation and nutrition, caused a sharp decline in cases of tuberculosis, and an expectation of its eventual eradication. Unexpectedly, however, the 1980s saw increasing numbers of cases, especially among the poor, the homeless, prison populations, and individuals living with HIV infection. Public health authorities had an additional challenge in curbing the spread of tuberculosis in this new epidemic—the fact that a number of individuals were now infected with a form of tuberculosis that was resistant to the traditional antibiotics. See generally Karen H. Rothenberg & Elizabeth C. Lovey, Something Old, Something New: The Challenge of Tuberculosis Control in the Age of AIDS, 42 Buff. L. Rev. 715 (1994). The following case is about the efforts of public health authorities in the city of Newark, New Jersey, to isolate and treat one such individual.

a.   Legal Approaches

City of Newark v. J.S.
279 N.J. Super. 178, 652 A.2d 265 (1993)

Opinion by GOLDMAN, J.S.C.

This case presents novel issues surrounding a resurging public health catastrophe, tuberculosis (TB). . . .

On October 22, 1993, Newark filed a verified complaint with the emergent duty judge and obtained a temporary commitment order and an order to show cause. Newark sought a final order "committing [J.S.] to [a local hospital] until the State Commissioner of Health shall be satisfied that the person has recovered to the extent that he will not be a menace to the community or to members of his household or that the person will so conduct himself that he will not constitute such a menace." This opinion amplifies oral findings rendered at the conclusion of the commitment hearing.

The defendant, J.S., is a 40-year-old African-American male suffering from TB and HIV disease. Hospital authorities requested that Newark intervene when J.S. sought to leave the hospital against medical advice. J.S. was found dressed in street clothes, sitting in the hospital lobby. Once he wandered to the pediatrics ward. He had a prior history of disappearances and of releases against medical advice, only to return via the emergency room when his health deteriorated. Allegedly, J.S. failed to follow proper infection control guidelines or take proper medication when in the hospital and failed to complete treatment regimens following his release. In March of 1993 J.S. had been discharged and deposited in a taxicab, which was given the address of a shelter to which he was to be driven. J.S. was given an appointment at a TB clinic a bus trip away from the shelter. J.S.'s Supplemental Security Income check was being delivered to another hospital, so he had no money. He did not keep his TB clinic appointment and was labeled as "non-compliant."

A sputum sample confirmed that J.S. had active TB. TB is a communicable disease caused by a bacteria or bacilli complex, mycobacterium (M.) tuberculosis. One of the oldest diseases known to affect humans, it was once known as consumption or the great "white plague" because it killed so many people. Human infection with M. tuberculosis was a leading cause of death until antituberculous drugs were introduced in the 1940s. While it can affect other parts of the body, such as lymph nodes, bones, joints, genital organs, kidneys, and skin, it most often attacks the lungs. It is transmitted by a person with what is called active TB by airborne droplets projected by coughing or sneezing. When the organism is inhaled into the lungs of another, TB infection can result. Usually this happens only after close and prolonged contact with a person with active TB. Most of those who become infected do not manifest any symptoms because the body mounts an appropriate immune response to bring the infection under control; however, those infected display a positive tuberculin skin test. The infection (sometimes called latent TB) can continue for a lifetime, and infected persons remain at risk for developing active TB if their immune systems become impaired.

Typical symptoms of active TB include fatigue, loss of weight and appetite, weakness, chest pain, night sweats, fever, and persistent cough. Sputum is often streaked with blood; sometimes massive hemorrhages occur if TB destroys enough lung tissue. Fluid may collect in the pleural cavity. Gradual deterioration occurs. If active TB is not treated, death is common.

Only persons with active TB are contagious. That active state is usually easily treated through drugs. Typically a short medication protocol will induce a remission and allow a return to daily activities with safety. A failure to continue with medication may lead to a relapse and the development of MDR-TB (multiple drug resistant TB), a condition in which the TB bacilli do not respond to at least two (isoniazid and rifampin) of the primary treatments, so that the active state is not easily cured and contagiousness continues for longer periods. . . .

Active TB of the lungs is considered contagious and requires immediate medical treatment, involving taking several drugs. Usually, after only a few days of treatment, infectiousness is reduced markedly. After two to four weeks of treatment, most people are no longer contagious and cannot transmit TB to others even if they cough or sneeze while living in close quarters. Usually exposure over a prolonged time is required, and less than thirty per cent (30%) of family members living closely with an infected person and unprotected by prophylactic drugs will become infected by the patient with active TB. On the other hand, transmission has been known to occur with as little as a single two-hour exposure to coughing, sneezing, etc., of a person with active TB. To cure TB, however, continued therapy for six to twelve months may be required. Failure to complete the entire course of therapy risks a relapse and the development of MDR-TB. . . .

TB is more serious in persons with impaired immune systems, which can result from poor health, chronic abuse of alcohol or drugs, old age, chemotherapy for cancer, or HIV infection. New Jersey's statutory scheme for dealing with TB dates from 1912 when the predecessor to N.J.S.A. 30:9-57 was first adopted. Only minor amendments have been made since 1917.

This law allows me to enter an order committing a person to a hospital if he or she is "suffering from" TB and "is an actual menace to the community." Notice of the hearing is required and was provided. Neither the statute nor the implementing regulation, N.J.A.C. 8:57-1.10, provides any guidance on the procedures to follow when such applications are made, nor what standards are to be used in issuing such orders. There is no case law in New Jersey providing guidance on these and many other related issues.

The regulatory schemes in other jurisdictions vary widely. There are older schemes like that in New Jersey which provide little or no guidance. There are those that provide detailed procedural details to guarantee due process while still allowing detention, isolation, quarantine, or confinement in the most extreme cases.

[The court then noted the procedural protections available to individuals under New York's more recently amended public health statutes; New York's approach to the problem was considered relevant "because the magnitude of Newark's TB problem is exceeded only by New York City."–EDS.]

Newark's attempt to protect the health of its citizenry is an archetypical expression of police power. Ogden v. Gibbons, 22 U.S. (9 Wheat) 1, 6 L. Ed. 23 (1824) (dicta that a state has the power "to provide for the health of its citizens" by quarantine). Cf., Jacobson v. Massachusetts, 197 U.S. 11, 25 S. Ct. 358, 49 L. Ed. 643 (1905) (compulsory vaccinations upheld against substantive due process challenge because societal interest in health can overcome individual rights). The claim of "disease" in a domestic setting has the same kind of power as the claim of "national security" in matters relating to foreign policy. Both claims are very powerful arguments for executive action. Both claims are among those least likely to be questioned by any other branch of government and therefore subject to abuse. The potential abuse is of special concern when the other interest involved is the confinement of a human being who has committed no crime except to be sick.

Due process limits police power. The Fourteenth Amendment requires "that deprivation of life, liberty or property by adjudication be preceded by notice and opportunity for hearing appropriate to the nature of the case." Mullane v. Central Hanover Trust Co., 339 U.S. 306, 317 (1950). The parameters of due process require an analysis of both the individual and governmental interests involved and the consequences and avoidability of the risks of error and abuse. Here the clash of competing interests is at its peak. Hardly any state interest is higher than protecting its citizenry from disease. Hardly any individual interest is higher than the liberty interest of being free from confinement. The consequences of error and abuse are grave for both the state and the individual.

The United States Supreme Court has recognized that "civil commitment for any purpose constitutes a significant deprivation of liberty that requires due process protection." Addington v. Texas, 441 U.S. 418, 425 (1979). Our Supreme Court in In re S.L., 94 N.J. 128 (1983) had occasion to collect authority on what this meant. A person has the right to notice, counsel, and must be afforded the opportunity to present opposing evidence and argument, and to cross examine witnesses. Illness alone cannot be the basis for confinement. To justify confinement it must be shown that the person is likely to pose a danger to self or to others. State v. Krol, 68 N.J. 236, 257, 344 A.2d 289 (1975). The proofs must show that there is a "substantial risk of dangerous conduct within the foreseeable future." Id., at 260. These proofs must be shown by clear and convincing evidence. Addington v. Texas, supra, 441 U.S. at 434. The terms of confinement must minimize the infringements on liberty and enhance autonomy. State v. Krol, supra, 68 N.J. at 257–58. Periodic reviews are required. State v. Fields, 77 N.J. 282 (1978). Lesser forms of restraint must be used when they would suffice to fulfill the government interests.

. . . The ADA also limits discrimination by government. Title II, 42 U.S.C.A. §12131, applies the ADA to all governmental agencies. "[N]o qualified individual with a disability shall, by reason of such disability, be . . . subjected to discrimination by any such entity." At first blush one might not consider involuntary confinements as subject to the ADA. Usually we think of discrimination in employment, housing, schools, transportation, public accommodations and the like. Yet for government to try to confine someone based upon his or her illness alone is as wrongful an act of discrimination as denying him or her a service from government. If public entities are barred from subjecting disabled persons to discrimination, can it be seriously doubted but that they are barred from involuntarily confining them?

Whether someone with TB is disabled was answered by School Board of Nassau County, Florida v. Arline, 480 U.S. 273 (1987). In *Arline* the primary issue was whether a person with TB could be considered a "handicapped individual" within the meaning of the Rehabilitation Act of 1973, as amended, 29 U.S.C.A. §701. In the ADA "disability" was used by Congress instead of "handicap" to reflect currently accepted terminology. The ADA's definition of "disability" was intended to be the same as the definition of "handicapped" under the Rehabilitation Act and the Fair Housing Act. Thus, the *Arline* analysis applies to the ADA.

In *Arline*, a school teacher had latent TB for twenty years but then had three relapses into active TB within two years. Following her last relapse and allegedly fearful of another, the school board fired Ms. Arline. The board claimed that it was concerned about the potential risk to children if she should have another relapse. The United States joined with the school board and argued that the "mere belief that an individual is contagious—whether reasonable or not" justified the exclusion of the handicapped. The argument was that the reason for the discrimination was the fear of contagion rather than the disability. The Supreme Court responded to this argument forcefully:

> We do not agree with petitioners that, in defining a handicapped individual under §504, the contagious effects of a disease can be meaningfully distinguished from the disease's physical effects on a claimant such as this. Arline's contagiousness and her physical impairment each resulted from the same underlying condition, tuberculosis. It would be unfair to allow an employer to seize upon the distinction between the effects of a disease on others and the effects of a disease on a patient and use that distinction to justify discriminatory treatment.
>
> Nothing in the legislative history of §504 suggests that Congress intended such a result. That history demonstrates that Congress was as concerned about the effect of an impairment on others as it was about its effect on the individual.

480 U.S. at 282.

Allowing fears to justify adverse treatment would render §504 meaningless and would honor the most appalling prejudice in our society. The Supreme Court explained: "[s]ociety's accumulated myths and fears about disability and disease are as handicapping as are the physical limitations that flow from actual impairment."

... Congress intended the ADA to apply to communicable diseases when it provided that to be protected by the ADA a person must be "qualified" and defined "qualified" as one who does "not pose a direct threat to the health or safety of others. . . ." 42 U.S.C.A. §12113(b). This standard of "direct threat" means that discrimination is permissible only if necessary to avoid a significant risk to other persons, a risk that cannot be eliminated by a reasonable accommodation. 42 U.S.C.A. §12111(3).

Accordingly, the ADA and its regulations require that a health officer seeking to infringe upon a diseased person's liberty by imposing detention, confinement, isolation or quarantine, must first establish, by clear and convincing evidence, that the person poses a significant risk of transmitting disease to others with serious consequences. This is not materially different from the words of N.J.S.A. 30:9-57, which requires proof that J.S. "is an actual menace to the community. . . ."

While opinions of public health authorities must be respected, their decisions must be based upon the latest knowledge of epidemiology, virology, bacteriology, and public health. No court can substitute its medical judgment for those authorities brought to its attention or by the evidence before it. Public health decisions must be accorded due deference, *Arline*, supra, 480 U.S. at 288 ("[C]ourts normally should defer to the reasonable medical judgments of public health officers.") Nonetheless, such deference is not appropriate if those powers are exercised in an "arbitrary, unreasonable" manner. *Jacobson*, supra, 197 U.S. at 28. Courts must guard against the risk that governmental action may be grounded in popular myths, irrational fears, or noxious fallacies rather than well-founded science.

The isolation of the chronically ill and of those perceived to be contagious appears across cultures and centuries, as does the development of complex and often pernicious mythologies about the nature, cause and transmission of illness. Tuberculosis is no exception.

The best way to guard against such risks is to demand an individualized, fact-specific determination as to the person under consideration. This is the key to all decision-making under the ADA. . . . Thus proof that this specific person (and not similar persons) poses a significant risk to others, a risk that may not be merely speculative, theoretical, remote or even "elevated," is required. In addition, the least restrictive means should be used to achieve the clearly defined public health goal. This is precisely what, in this context, "reasonable accommodation" means within the ADA. "A person who poses a significant risk of communicating an infectious disease to others in the workplace will not be otherwise qualified for his or her job if reasonable accommodation will not eliminate that risk." *Arline*, supra, 480 U.S. at 287, n.16.

[The court then looked to the New Jersey statute providing the standards and procedures for civil commitment due to mental illness. In particular, the court noted that persons whose confinement is sought must by statute be provided counsel, an expeditious hearing, adequate notice of the hearing, discovery before the hearing, and an independent medical examination paid for by the committing authority. The person has the right to be present at the hearing, to cross-examine witnesses, and to present testimony. The hearing must be on the record and evidence provided under oath. Periodic court reviews are mandated. All proofs must be shown by clear and convincing evidence.–Eds.]

. . . [T]o the extent that current laws regarding the commitment of those with TB are so ancient that they fail to meet modern standards of due process or the mandates of the ADA, it is the responsibility of our courts to ensure that there are procedures to ensure the rights of individuals whose proposed confinement invokes the judicial process. There is no need to declare the New Jersey TB control statute (N.J.S.A. 30:9-57) unconstitutional so long as it is interpreted to be consistent with the Constitution. There is no reason to find it in violation of the ADA so long as it is interpreted to be consistent with the ADA. It must be remembered that this statute was first enacted in 1912, yet it had provisions requiring notice and a judicial hearing. The statute required proof that the person be "an actual menace to the community or to members of his household." The Legislature intended to permit the confinement of someone with TB but only under circumstances consistent with due process. Many of the rights we now recognize were unheard of in 1912. The ADA did not exist. Declaring the statute unconstitutional and leaving citizens of New Jersey with no shield against the rare person with TB who poses a true significant risk to others would be the true frustration of legislative intent. Therefore I construe N.J.S.A. 30:9-57 so as to include those rights necessitated by contemporary standards of due process and by the ADA. Such a construction effectuates the legislative intent.

The first step of the individualized analysis required here is to define precisely what Newark seeks. During the active phase of TB, isolation of J.S., as opposed to confinement or imprisonment, is what is required. If J.S. lived in a college dormitory with other roommates, different quarters would have to be found for him. If J.S. lived in a private home and could be given a private bedroom or others in the household could be given prophylactic antibiotic therapy, confinement to his own home might be appropriate. J.S. is homeless, and a shelter where he would risk infecting others, including those with impaired immune systems, would probably be the worst place for him to stay.

Because active TB can be serious and can be potentially contagious by repeated contact, there are few options for the homeless with active TB.[10] There is no question but that J.S. has active TB. There is no question but that he poses a risk to others who may be in contact with him, particularly in close quarters. Because he is homeless, there is no suggestion of any other place he could stay that would be less restrictive than a hospital.

The hearing I conducted was designed to comport to all the requirements of due process and with all the requirements of a commitment hearing under [the New Jersey statutes regarding civil commitment for mental illness]. I believe my conclusions also satisfy the ADA and *Arline*, that judicial decisions in this area be based upon, "(a) the nature of the risk (how the disease is transmitted), (b) the duration of the risk (how long is the carrier infectious), (c) the severity of the risk (what is the potential harm to third parties), and (d) the probabilities the disease will be transmitted and will cause varying degrees of harm." 480 U.S. at 288.

I find that J.S. presents a significant risk to others unless isolated. Hospital confinement is the least restrictive mode of isolation proposed to me. The only request at this time is that J.S. be confined until he has shown three negative sputum tests demonstrating that his TB is no longer active. This is narrow, limited, and very reasonable, but because the time period for treatment is indefinite, I will initially set an initial court review to be held in three weeks . . . unless J.S. has earlier been determined to have gone into remission from active TB. In that event J.S. will be released immediately unless Newark seeks confinement for another reason.

---

10. The defendant has not argued here that some state action has caused his homelessness and put him in the very position that results in the need for confinement. If J.S. would suggest some other alternative to hospitalization that would impose less restrictions but would achieve the same public health objective, then Newark would have the burden of showing why this less restrictive alternative was not selected.

At the [next] hearing, Newark will have the burden of proving the need for further confinement. . . . In the interim I will utilize the well-established procedures New Jersey has in place for civil commitments of the mentally ill. Although some procedures may not apply to the confinement of those with contagious diseases like TB, until and unless a more specific law is enacted, the only available and constitutional mechanism is to use these tested mental health statutes, court rules, and the case law thereunder. This is certainly preferable to declaring N.J.S.A. 30:9-57 unconstitutional and leaving no authority whatsoever to fulfill an essential public police power. . . .

Newark also wanted J.S. ordered to provide sputum samples and take his medication as prescribed. The testimony was that a forced sputum sample requires a bronchoscopy, a procedure involving sedation and requiring separate informed consent because of its risks. No facts were shown to justify such a diagnostic procedure where it might cause harm to J.S. As to continued treatment, testimony showed that the medications were quite toxic, dangerous, and some required painful intramuscular administration. J.S. is being asked to take many pills causing numerous side effects, including nausea and pain. The efficacy of the drugs will be unknown until receipt of sensitivity reports.

These facts cannot justify a remedy as broad as Newark seeks. J.S. has the right to refuse treatment even if this is medically unwise. Matter of Farrell, 108 N.J. 335, 347 (1987) (people have the right of self-determination regarding their own bodies). He must remain isolated until he is no longer contagious. Contagiousness cannot be assessed unless he gives sputum samples. While he can refuse to provide sputum samples and refuse bronchoscopy, his release from isolation may be delayed, as he will be unable to satisfy the conditions of release. The same is true with his refusal to take medication. If he refuses, he may not get better. If J.S. continues to suffer from active TB, he will be unable to satisfy the conditions of release.

On the other hand if J.S. cooperates with his caregivers, provides sputum samples, and takes his medication willingly, then upon his improvement, Newark will have a difficult time proving that he needs confinement because he is not cooperative.[12] His in-hospital conduct will go a long way towards demonstrating his ability to follow medical therapy once released and will be considered if after his active TB is cured, J.S.'s confinement is sought because his alleged failure to follow continued therapy will make him a future risk. I would then have to consider an order analogous to those permitted under N.J.S.A. 30:4-27.15c, which would simply require J.S. to take his medication.[14]

---

12. In order to fulfill the requirement of using the least restrictive alternative, public health officials will usually have to show that they attempted step-by-step interventions, beginning with voluntary DOT [directly observed therapy; i.e., the medication is taken when the patient is directly observed by a health care worker], supplemented by incentives (e.g., food or money as a reward for taking medication) and enablers (e.g., travel assistance). Commitment is an absolute last resort.

14. This is precisely what subsequently happened here. At the November 30, 1993, review hearing, Newark presented additional expert testimony and J.S.'s updated medical records showing the situation unchanged. But thereafter, J.S. began to take his medication faithfully and his active TB was arrested. On January 10, 1994, J.S. was released from confinement pursuant to a consent order in which he agreed to DOT and agreed to being committed again if he failed to take his medicine. This consent order was approved in open court in J.S.'s presence as there was no longer any need for isolation once he no longer suffered from active TB.

NOTES AND QUESTIONS

1. *Deference regarding health risk evaluations.*   Does the standard of deference toward the decisions of public health authorities appear to have changed since Jacobson v. Massachusetts? How?

2. *Procedural due process.*   New Jersey's statute regarding the isolation of individuals infected with tuberculosis had not changed much since 1912 and offered little in the way of procedural protections for the person whose confinement was sought by public health authorities. Do you think the New Jersey Superior Court was correct to adopt for these types of cases (that of contagious disease) the procedures provided by statute for commitment on the basis of mental illness? Should it have instead simply declared the existing tuberculosis statute unconstitutional? Why or why not? To what extent is the court declaring that the procedural protections it is willing to read into the statute are *constitutionally required?*

3. *Americans with Disabilities Act.*   The court in Newark v. J.S., following the Supreme Court's *Arline* decision (whose subject was the related Rehabilitation Act of 1973), determined that J.S. was disabled and therefore came under the provisions of the act. However, he would not be "qualified" for the protections of the act if he "pose[d] a direct threat to the health or safety of others." Does the ADA, according to this court, offer J.S. any protection? Of what sort?

4. *Testing and treatment compared to confinement.*   In the end, the court in Newark v. J.S. determines that it will order confinement for J.S. at the hospital, but it will not order that J.S. provide sputum samples or take medication. Why does the court draw the line between these two requested orders? Is the distinction justified?

5. *Voluntary compliance/consent or coercion?*   This case, unlike most, gives us a follow-up to events since the original decision made at the initial hearing (see footnote 14). We know that J.S. eventually began complying with the testing and medical treatment sought by the public health authorities. At the time he was released he no longer had active TB, although continued compliance with his medication regimen would be necessary to cure him of the disease and prevent his becoming contagious again. The court tells us that it entered a consent order under which J.S. agreed to DOT (directly observed therapy) and recommitment if he failed to take his medicine. This postscript to the case raises a number of questions, among them:

(A)   The court indicated in its opinion regarding the original order that it could not order that J.S. submit to testing and medication. But the court also notes that continued confinement will provide J.S. with a strong incentive to comply with the same. When the court in footnote 14 then tells us that J.S. began to voluntarily comply with testing and medication, what are we to understand by the term "voluntary"?

(B)   Along the same lines, how should we understand J.S.'s "consent" (recognized in the consent order) that he continue to take medication under DOT and that he agreed to recommitment if he didn't comply? Should J.S. have been given "incentives" and "enablers" as described in the court's footnote 12? If he wasn't, and consented to DOT only because he wanted to avoid recommitment, has the state used the "least restrictive alternative"?

6. *Demographics.*   A law review article that appeared around the time of the Newark v. J.S. case revealed certain demographic dimensions of reemerging TB infection:

> Approximately seventy percent of all TB cases occur among ethnic or racial minorities. For the years 1985 to 1992, TB cases increased about 26.8% in non-Hispanic blacks, increased by 74.5% in Hispanics, but decreased by 9.9% in non-Hispanic whites. For cases reported in the year 1992 alone, 28.6% occurred in non-Hispanic whites while 71.3% occurred in minorities. The reasons for the excess rates of TB in minorities stem from the higher prevalence of latent TB infection in these populations due to crowded substandard housing, homelessness, substance abuse, and limited access to health care.

Karen H. Rothenberg & Elizabeth C. Lovey, Something Old, Something New: The Challenge of Tuberculosis Control in the Age of AIDS, 42 Buff. L. Rev. 715 (1994). More recent statistics show a similar story: in 2007, 83 percent of all reported TB cases in the United States occurred in racial and ethnic minorities. See http://www.cdc.gov/tb/publications/factsheets/specpop/resources_TB_Minorities.htm. In 2010, among American-born individuals, 67 percent of TB cases were observed in minorities, while among foreign-born individuals, 95 percent of TB cases were observed in minorities. See http://www.cdc.gov/tb/publications/factsheets/specpop/resources_TB_Blacks.htm. How, if at all, should these statistics be factored into an ethical analysis of the activities of public health authorities to confine individuals or mandate therapy to eliminate their contagiousness? More specifically, should the ability of the state to restrict individuals' liberties to protect the public's health be dependent in some part on its efforts to reduce the susceptibility of those individuals to disease? With respect to J.S., the City of Newark presumably provided both for hospitalization and for treatment. Do you think it could have provided for confinement in a less hospitable environment, without treatment? (In this regard, consider the case of civil commitment of sexual predators for the public's protection, discussed below in section C(1).)

7. *HIV and tuberculosis.*   Public health departments are not the only place from which calls come for isolating contagious individuals. Rothenberg and Lovey point out that the same groups that argued successfully *against* isolation of individuals infected with HIV (i.e., advocacy groups on behalf of HIV-infected individuals) are making the case *in favor* of isolating those people with infectious TB. HIV-infected individuals are particularly susceptible to tuberculosis because of their weakened immune system, which also causes the disease to wreak havoc quickly, and often fatally. Therefore some groups seek the isolation of those with TB to protect people with HIV. Rothenberg & Lovey, supra, at 716. In this regard, prison inmates have been successful in several suits to require mandatory testing of all inmates for TB and isolation of those who are contagious. See, e.g., Vega v. Sielaff, 1992 WL 88146 (S.D.N.Y. 1992). Do you think different policies on isolation are justified for HIV infection and tuberculosis?

b.   Bioethical and Social Perspectives

In Newark v. J.S., the court tells us that J.S. is African American. Why do you think the court includes this information? Is it relevant? How much do we in fact know about J.S.? How much *should* we know? Discussions about the appropriateness of isolation or quarantine often center around certain principles, be they constitutional principles of self-determination or bodily integrity (as protected by the Fourteenth Amendment of the Constitution), or bioethics principles such as autonomy, confidentiality, justice, and so on (such as the "principles" that make up the approach of "Principlism" discussed in Chapter 1). In the following excerpt, John Arras makes the argument for more attention to the details of the stories of the people involved and how individuals experience a particular situation.

> ## John D. Arras, Principles and Particularity: The Role of Cases in Bioethics
> ## 69 Ind. L.J. 983 (1994)

During [the] early period in the development of bioethics as a field, the case study emerged as an object of serious consideration. At first, case studies were often employed in the traditional manner as illustrations of how a particular ethical theory might bear on moral problems. For example, a case involving the use of placebos in medical research would be used as a prism through which to view the salient features of Kantian or rule utilitarian reasoning. Many, however, increasingly used case studies not just as illustrations, but as objects of interest in their own right. Case studies posed intellectual and moral problems that called for a solution. It was important to get the right (or at least an acceptable) answer, not simply in order to exhibit the properties of one's favorite theory, but to help determine the fates of living, breathing individuals, many of whom posed moral dilemmas of excruciating difficulty. The moral philosopher was fast becoming an "applied ethicist," and the ethicist was no longer an isolated theorist, but was now enmeshed in the problems, dilemmas, and crises of professional life. Indeed, the theorist was well on his or her way to becoming a consultant, moving from being a detached observer to a player in the professionals' drama.

The case studies that developed in the literature of this period shared two salient features. First, professionals tended to define them. Second, the case studies were brief and "thin." Except for legal cases, the cases presented for consideration in the bioethics literature rarely exceeded a few paragraphs. Crucial medical facts (for example, the patient's diagnosis, options, and prognosis as affected by various treatment choices) would be presented, the shape of the ethical quandary would be sketched, and the care provider's position clarified. Such cases seldom painted a more fleshed out portrait of the various actors and the implications of the choices before them. The audience of such case studies often had extremely limited information about, for example, the patients' perception of their disease and the meaning of treatment options as mediated by their social and family history, race, economic class, prior medical encounters, and psychological characteristics.

A typical example of this "bare bones" approach to case studies, drawn from the experience of my colleague Nancy Dubler, might have gone something like this:

> The medical housestaff at a public hospital in the Bronx confronts a difficult case involving a "problem patient." Mr. Jones is an IV drug user who also happens to be infected with HIV and tuberculosis. The TB has been diagnosed as being of the multi-drug resistant variety, and thus poses a serious threat of potentially lethal infection to anyone coming into casual contact with Mr. Jones. The problem is that the patient insists upon leaving his room so he can be free to wander the corridors and lobby of the hospital. The staff are extremely upset and worried that these expeditions outside of his room will lead to the infection of other patients, caregivers, or hospital visitors.

As presented, this case poses a conflict among the patient's individual rights, the public's legitimate interest in protection from harm, and the hospital's fiduciary obligations to its patients and employees. Where should the line be drawn between civil liberties and public health? Would it be ethically justifiable to lock the patient in his room against his will? . . .

[Later in this article, Arras provides the following "thicker" version of the case presented above to reveal the importance of "enhanced particularity for ethical analysis."–Eds.]

> The patient AB is a 42 year old Hispanic male. He has known that he is HIV-positive since 1989. He has been and continues to be an intravenous drug user. He was found by the Emergency Medical Service team in early April 1992, wandering and disoriented with a tourniquet still attached to his arm. He was brought to the hospital to rule out TB and endocarditis because of an active cough and a temperature of 105 degrees.
>
> Upon admission to the hospital, the patient's previous admissions were not immediately discovered because his two prior chart histories in the record room were linked to two different names and sets of personal data. Because of his admitting condition, however, and an X-ray that showed severe upper lobe infiltrates, he was placed in a single room and initially begun on INH, RIF, PZA, and EMB.
>
> Once the patient's medical history was reconstructed from the previous admissions, he was shown to have had two admissions in the previous three months and to be HIV-positive. He had received three or four weeks of therapy during that time, although none of it was consecutive. TB had been first diagnosed in January, it was sensitive to all drugs. A drug-resistant strain was confirmed upon sputum culture in March during his second admission; the organism was identified as resistant to INH and PZA. Upon the third admission, as on the prior two admissions, AB was placed in a negative pressure isolation room and ordered not to leave this space. When his prior drug sensitivities became available, he was placed on a six-drug regimen that included parenteral amikacin.
>
> The patient refused to stay in his room. He had been promised that a television and a telephone would be connected. When neither happened, he went in search of both. He also complained that the room was very cold and uncomfortable. After he had been found in the elevators and in the lobby of the hospital, the nurses took away his clothes. He was again found wandering in the hall. At that point the resident on duty called the guard and had the patient handcuffed to the bed by his hands and feet. He was also "posied," confined by a bed jacket with straps that were tied to the bed.
>
> The room was in fact quite cold, as is often the case with negative pressure, highly ventilated rooms. In addition, blankets were in very short supply in the

hospital. As some patients were being given a stack of sheets in lieu of blankets, the nurses did not feel that they could give this particular patient more blankets. Even if the supply had been adequate, staff might not have been forthcoming. Once he had been gowned, cuffed, and posied, AB was quite cold and miserable.

The next morning after the patient had been released from restraints for breakfast and was again found in the lobby, the resident called for a guard and asked the Department of Health for a detention order; it was issued.

During this time the staff caring for the patient had no special protections. No "microspore" masks were available. The rumor in the hospital was that some would be available soon. The most effective masks, however, would be available only for special technicians such as those doing induced sputum cultures. Masks at the next level of effectiveness would be available to the general staff. At this point, none were available except for those "liberated" from a nearby hospital. The resident in charge of the patient was pregnant and very afraid of contracting TB; she had, therefore, not actually seen or spoken to him.

Once the detention order was issued, the hospital placed the patient under "one-to-one" surveillance with a guard beside the door at all times. The cost of such supervision is approximately $100,000 per year.

Once the guard had been posted, the patient began refusing medications selectively. Some of the refusals seemed random. Some, however, were comprehensible. For example, he refused to take amikacin. The administration of this medication can be either intramuscular or intravenous. Assuming that there were no available veins to administer the drug intravenously, the staff had begun the intramuscular administration that he regularly refused because of the pain and discomfort. They then discovered that it was, indeed, possible to administer the medication intravenously. He did not refuse the medication in this form.

Approximately one week after admission, AB was shifted to a different single room that was less cold. He was also provided with a television and a working telephone. After four weeks of treatment, his fever abated, and he felt much better. He began to talk about leaving the hospital. He also began pulling out the intravenous drips used to administer the amikacin. His last three smears were negative, but his X-ray continued to show a large upper lobe infiltrate.

In the first encounter with Mr. AB, the issue was simple: Should the patient be permitted to roam the corridors and lobby of the hospital where he might infect others with a potentially lethal strain of TB, or should he be forcibly detained in his room or, if necessary, on his bed? While the above "thicker" description of the case poses the same question, it reveals particularities about the patient's life in the hospital and his relations with others that might fundamentally alter one's attitude towards the case and the patient.

NOTES AND QUESTIONS

1. *Thin vs. thick stories.*   What does Arras's second version of the story of Mr. AB add to explain his noncompliance with the measures imposed to protect others from exposure to TB? What version of this story would you likely receive from the nurses and physicians at the hospital? From the public health authorities?

2. *Do details make a difference?*   How might such details factor into a *solution* to the problem presented by Mr. AB? To the problem presented by J.S.?

c.   Public Policy

Considerations of public policy, of course, are present in both cases (legal and ethical) considered above, because how individuals will be treated, and how attempts to isolate or quarantine them will be viewed, depends in part on the policies that have been adopted by governmental agencies and private institutions in response to the problem of which these individuals are but one example. In the next reading, we look at public policy from a different perspective by looking at the effects of policies on an entire population rather than just one individual—in this case, the prison population of Siberia. The global dimensions of infectious disease control, the influence of organizations from richer, more developed countries on the health problems of poorer, less developed countries, and the issue of what "cost effective" means are all present in this story told of the 1990s tuberculosis epidemic inside some of Russia's prisons.

> ## *Paul Farmer & Nicole Gastineau Campos,*
> ## *Rethinking Medical Ethics: A View from Below*
> ### 4 Developing World Bioethics 17, 29–32 (May 2004)

[A] doubling of incarceration rates occurred after the collapse of the Soviet Union. The infamous gulag came to be more than three times as full in "democratic" Russia, with Siberian incarceration rates exceeding, at one point, 1000 per 100,000 population (only the United States rivals this ratio). Overcrowding, poor ventilation, interruption of medical supplies and salaries for overworked prisons staff, and malnutrition led to explosive epidemics of tuberculosis within Russia's prisons. . . . In some senses, the Russian epidemics were more reminiscent of the prison-seated outbreaks documented in New York beginning in the late 1980s: although HIV was not a factor in the Russian epidemics, they were, as in New York, prison-based and involved strains of highly drug-resistant *Mycobacterium tuberculosis*, the organism that causes the disease.

Into this dramatic and novel situation came, for the first time, non-Russian aid agencies and non-governmental organisations. To date, there have been few thorough studies of this stunning development, but such analyses are important to our understanding of what is occurring within prison walls today. By the mid 1990s, such organisations were prominent players in post-Soviet states, all of which had seen catastrophic deterioration in their social safety nets and medical systems. The non-governmental organisations were mostly European and North American, and in the postperestroika disarray they had something their Russian . . . partners did not then have: money and clout. The ability of these aid organisations to shape responses to epidemic tuberculosis in Siberia was significant, and they insisted on what they termed the most "cost-effective" approach, the one endorsed by international tuberculosis experts, including the World Health Organization: directly observed therapy with "first-line" anti-tuberculous drugs. But some of the Russian prison physicians objected, as did members of Russia's large and crumbling tuberculosis-treatment infrastructure: the prisoner-patients had drug-resistant tuberculosis and would not be cured by standard first-line regiments; some Russian specialists made other objections. These voices were drowned in an undercurrent of censorious opinion from the international experts and the non-governmental agencies, which, flush with resources and backed by international expert opinion, insisted on giving all prisoners the same doses of the same first-line drugs.

In Siberia and other pilot sites, the treatment outcomes were nothing short of catastrophic: less than half of all patients were deemed cured (expected cure rates for supervised therapy of drug-susceptible tuberculosis exceed 95%). Worse, prisoner-patients who were not cured by therapy with first-line drugs emerged from this treatment, if they survived, with "amplified" resistance. That is, their prognosis had worsened dramatically even if they were to be afforded care with the right drugs. But the non-Russian groups, whether international tuberculosis experts or aid groups, did not concede that they had made an error. Instead, they pressed on, delivering precisely the same medications even to prisoner-patients with documented multi-drug-resistant tuberculosis.

More delegations visited Siberia in 1998. Members of at least one delegation pointed out that drug resistance was not the *likely* cause of treatment failure, it was the cause *already documented.* Somewhat discreetly, it would seem, the lead non-governmental organisation had sent sputum samples for drug-susceptibility testing to at least two reference laboratories in Western Europe. Both laboratories confirmed that patients within Siberian prisons were sick from highly resistant strains of *M. tuberculosis*—strains resistant to precisely those drugs being administered, under direct supervision, by the non-governmental organisations who had been chastising Russian experts for their lack of knowledge of modern tuberculosis control.

Well before 2000, tuberculosis had become the leading cause of death in Russian prisons. In Siberian facilities, surviving prisoners had become less and less treatable, and those with multi-drug-resistant tuberculosis were cohorted behind barbed wire and declared altogether "untreatable." But this was not the case: multi-drug-resistant tuberculosis is treatable with other, more expensive drugs; data from a slum in Peru and rural Haiti have made it clear that such efforts can succeed in settings far poorer than Siberia. The real debate was not about the efficacy of therapy but about its costs.

By 2001, the lead non-governmental organisation appeared to yield to growing pressure from prisoners, their guards, and expert opinion: it would work with its Russian partners to treat patients with multi-drug-resistant tuberculosis with the drugs to which their strains had been shown to be susceptible. It took the organisation well over a year to procure the drugs, but early in 2002 it announced the programme was to commence treatment right away. The need was great: in a single oblast in Western Siberia, an estimated 2000 prisoner-patients were warehoused with active multi-drug-resistant tuberculosis. But although the drugs began to arrive in Siberia, no treatment occurred in the ensuing year. In September 2003, the lead organisation issued a press release: they were pulling out of Siberia. As of today, not a single prisoner has been treated, by non-governmental organisations based in Siberia for a decade, for multi-drug-resistant tuberculosis, although thousands, perhaps more, have died of this disease. The press release blames Russian officials, particularly those in the Ministry of Health, for their intransigence, but it is likely that careful study of what occurred will come to a somewhat different conclusion.

The story is a sad one, but it will become sadder: circulating strains of multi-drug-resistant *M. tuberculosis* will mean that prisoner detainees are exposed to epidemic strains of highly drug-resistant tuberculosis and then do not receive care when they need it. But that will not change the fact that the initial approach of the non-governmental organisations was incorrect: multi-drug-resistant tuberculosis cannot be cured with regimens based on the very drugs to which infecting strains are resistant, but these patients' prognosis can be worsened by such practices, even if proper therapy later becomes available. Since international authorities had endorsed these practices they should have been the first to acknowledge the error and to make pledges to help correct it. But no mea culpa has been issued from any interested party.

All interested parties, including those willing to underline the ethical lapses involved, must be part of a broader movement not merely to point to such lapses, masked or acknowledged, but also to address them. In the case of multi-drug-resistant tuberculosis in Russian prisons, that means staying and seeing these patients through treatment that is effective, not "cost-effective." The fact that prisoners with drug-resistant tuberculosis were given drugs that were wholly ineffective is a reminder that concepts such as "cost effectiveness" are in fact ideological constructs. The example is one of many and serves, too, as a reminder of the most pressing questions for modern medical ethics.

NOTES AND QUESTIONS

1. *What happened.*   According to these authors, what went wrong in the treatment of prisoners with tuberculosis in Siberia? Who were the institutional actors and how did they interact, and with what effect on individual patients?

2. *Relevance to bioethical inquiry.*   Compared to the voluminous writings within the field of bioethics on topics such as physician-assisted suicide and embryonic stem cell research, there is very little written on subjects such as the treatment in the 1990s of the tuberculosis epidemic of Siberian prisons. Why do you think that is? How is what happened in Siberia relevant to the study of bioethics in the United States? What lessons for U.S. bioethics do the authors suggest?

3. *Tuberculosis in U.S. prisons.*   Tuberculosis is also a problem in American prisons, where conditions are often overcrowded. As Rothenberg and Lovey point out, prisoners are three times more likely to be exposed to tuberculosis than the general population. Karen H. Rothenberg & Elizabeth C. Lovey, Something Old, Something New: The Challenge of Tuberculosis Control in the Age of AIDS, 42 Buff. L. Rev. 715 (1994). Lest we think of the problem of prison tuberculosis as being of concern only to prisoners and guards, we have to realize that hundreds of thousands of prisoners are released each year into the general public. Id.

4. AIDS: The Exception?

As far as modern epidemics go, the AIDS virus has been and continues to be more devastating than the recurrence of tuberculosis. In many ways, however, it has been treated differently by public health authorities than other infectious diseases. Coercive measures have been largely forgone in favor of more cooperative modes of reducing transmission, such as education and voluntary, anonymous testing. States generally have some program of "partner notification," in which an HIV-infected individual's sexual partners or needle-sharing contacts are notified that they may have been exposed to HIV, although these programs take many forms, and sometimes depend on the infected individual himself carrying through with the notification.

Some commentators have charged that such treatment represents unjustified "exceptional" treatment, perhaps because of pressures brought to bear by highly vocal, activist groups who unduly influenced the policies that were put in place. Wendy Parmet suggests other explanations:

> . . . Perhaps the most serious and difficult debate about the coercive powers and HIV concerned the use of wide-scale mandatory testing. For many reasons, this was never implemented. No doubt, the timing of the HIV epidemic played some role in the initial rejection of mandatory testing. Arriving after the Civil Rights movements, Watergate, the birth of the gay rights movement and even the revelations about the Tuskegee experiments, HIV made its appearance at a time when the public was especially sensitive to claims of individual rights and particularly skeptical of government authority. But even more important than the zeitgeist, perhaps, was the reality that given the fact that HIV was transmitted by private behaviors, and that an individual remained infectious throughout his or her life, it was difficult to see how mandatory testing could aid efforts to thwart the disease's spread. Rather, by the late 1980s most public health officials had come to believe that the trust of those infected and the cooperation of communities at risk was key to protecting the public against HIV, and both of these could and would be undermined by the imposition of coercive measures. As Professor Samuel Bagenstos has written,

>> [W]hen public health officials forewent coercive measures in their responses to AIDS, their position reflected less a capture by an important interest group than a hardhearted calculation that an epidemic spread by the intimate conduct of particular segments of the community simply could not be brought under control by measures that failed to pay attention to the interests of those segments of the community.

Wendy E. Parmet, Quarantine Redux: Bioterrorism, AIDS, and the Curtailment of Individual Liberty in the Name of Public Health, 13 Health Matrix 85 (2003).

It remains to be seen what the future holds for the use of coercive measures to control the spread of infectious disease. Was HIV/AIDS an exception? Or did the experience with HIV/AIDS change in fundamental ways the approach that public health authorities will take with respect to preventing the spread of other infectious diseases, even those whose transmission is not limited to the exchange of bodily fluids? That is, will future efforts at disease control exhibit similar sensitivity to issues of confidentiality and concerns about discrimination, and weigh more heavily in favor of encouraging voluntary efforts rather than mandatory actions to curb the spread of disease?

The era of special treatment for HIV/AIDS may be waning. In September 2006, the CDC revised its recommendations for HIV testing. Replacing earlier recommendations that testing be done on "high risk individuals," patients in acute-care settings, and pregnant women, these more recent recommendations call for testing to become a routine part of medical care for people aged 13 to 64, regardless of risk, "similar to screening for other treatable conditions." CDC, Revised Recommendations for HIV Testing of Adults, Adolescents, and Pregnant Women in Health-Care Settings, Morbidity and Mortality Weekly Report, Sept. 22, 2006. In addition, the CDC recommended that requirements for pretest counseling and separate written consent (mandatory in some states) be dropped. A number of states have revised their laws to follow these recommendations. See John G. Bartlett et al., Opt-Out Testing for Human Immunodeficiency Virus in the United States, 300 JAMA 945–951 (2008). The recommendations were adopted to increase early detection of HIV both for delivery of care and to facilitate prevention by individuals' changing their own behaviors upon knowledge of positive status. Id. According to the CDC, approximately 25 percent of HIV-positive individuals in the United States are unaware of their infected status. Kaiser Daily HIV/AIDS Report, May 8, 2006, available at http://www.kaisernetwork.org/daily_reports/rep_index.cfm?DR_ID=37075. The emerging practice may be routine testing for HIV, but that testing is still entirely voluntary, rather than mandatory.

The reemergence of tuberculosis in substantial numbers in the early 1990s in New York revealed that state's willingness to use certain coercive measures in the name of public health, such as directly observed therapy and at times, isolation (as we saw in New Jersey, in Newark v. J.S.), suggesting that traditional public health measures of testing, isolation, and quarantine have not been abandoned in those situations where they are believed to be warranted. The country's response to perceived threats of bioterrorism, as considered in the next section, suggest much the same.

5. Bioterrorism

In the wake of the terrorist attacks on the World Trade Centers in New York City on September 11, 2001, and the dissemination of anthrax a month later, federal and state governmental authorities began a critical examination of their ability to respond to similar attacks that might occur in the future, including attacks that might directly be targeted toward the public's health. Part of this examination would include questions about resources, communication systems, and mobility, but a substantial issue was what powers the government, especially state governments, had under existing law to direct or restrain individuals' activities to contain the harm that might be done to the population's health. The following excerpt from Lawrence Gostin explains the development of a model statute crafted for state adoption to replace what a number of policymakers and scholars believe are outdated and insufficient state statutes. A portion of the model act then follows that pertains to testing, isolation, and quarantine. The reporting obligations imposed on physicians and pharmacists in Article III of the Model Act are then discussed and critiqued, along with other provisions, in an excerpted article written by one of the Model Act's critics.

> **Lawrence O. Gostin, The Model State Emergency Health Powers Act: Public Health and Civil Liberties in a Time of Terrorism**
> **13 Health Matrix 3 (Winter, 2003)**

Safeguarding the public's health, safety, and security took on new meaning and urgency after the attacks on the World Trade Towers in New York and the Pentagon in Washington, D.C. on September 11, 2001. On October 4, 2001, a Florida man named Robert Stevens was diagnosed with inhalational anthrax. The intentional dispersal of anthrax through the U.S. postal system in New York, Washington, Pennsylvania and other locations resulted in five confirmed deaths, hundreds treated, and thousands tested. The potential for new, larger, and more sophisticated attacks have created a sense of vulnerability. National attention has urgently turned to the need to rapidly detect and react to bioterrorism, as well as to naturally occurring infectious diseases.

In the aftermath of September 11th, the President and the Congress began a process to strengthen the public health infrastructure. The Center for Law and the Public's Health (CLPH) at Georgetown and Johns Hopkins Universities drafted the Model State Emergency Health Powers Act ("MSEHPA" or the "Model Act") at the request of Centers for Disease Control and Prevention (CDC) and in collaboration with members of national organizations representing governors, legislators, attorneys general, and health commissioners. Because the power to act to preserve the public's health is constitutionally reserved primarily to the states as an exercise of their police powers, the Model Act is designed for state—not federal—legislative consideration. It provides responsible state actors with the powers they need to detect and contain a potentially catastrophic disease outbreak and, at the same time, protects individual rights and freedoms. Thirty-six states and the District of Columbia have introduced legislative bills based on the MSEHPA; thirty-nine states and the District of Columbia have enacted or are expected to shortly enact a version of the Model Act.

‖ *Model State Emergency Health Powers Act* ‖ (as of December 21, 2001)

ARTICLE 1 TITLE, FINDINGS, PURPOSES, AND DEFINITIONS

Section 104 Definitions

(a) "Bioterrorism" is the intentional use of any microorganism, virus, infectious substance, or biological product that may be engineered as a result of biotechnology, or any naturally occurring or bioengineered component of any such microorganism, virus, infectious substance, or biological product, to cause death, disease, or other biological malfunction in a human, an animal, or another living organism in order to influence the conduct of government or to intimidate or coerce a civilian population. . . .

(c) "Contagious disease" is an infectious disease that can be transmitted from person to person.

(d) "Infectious disease" is a disease caused by a living organism or other pathogen, including a fungus, bacteria, parasite, protozoan, or virus. An infectious disease may, or may not, be transmissible from person to person, animal to person, or insect to person. . . .

(m) A "public health emergency" is an occurrence or imminent threat of an illness or health condition that:

(1) is believed to be caused by any of the following:

(i) bioterrorism;

(ii) the appearance of a novel or previously controlled or eradicated infectious agent or biological toxin;

(iii) [*a natural disaster;*]

(iv) [*a chemical attack or accidental release; or*]

(v) [*a nuclear attack or accident*]; and

(2) poses a high probability of any of the following harms:

(i) a large number of deaths in the affected population;

(ii) a large number of serious or long-term disabilities in the affected population; or

(iii) widespread exposure to an infectious or toxic agent that poses a significant risk of substantial future harm to a large number of people in the affected population.

ARTICLE IV DECLARING A STATE OF PUBLIC HEALTH EMERGENCY

[Section 401] Declaration

A state of public health emergency may be declared by the Governor upon the occurrence of a "public health emergency" as defined in Section 1-103(m) [1-104(m)?]. Prior to such a declaration, the Governor shall consult with the public health authority and may consult with any additional public health or other experts as needed. The Governor may act to declare a public health emergency without consulting with the public health authority or other experts when the situation calls for prompt and timely action.

[Section 405] Termination of Declaration

[This section requires the Governor to terminate the declaration of a state of public health emergency when the conditions under which it was declared no longer exist; provides for automatic termination of the declaration after 30 days unless renewed by the Governor; and permits the state legislature by a majority vote in both chambers to terminate the declaration.]

ARTICLE VI SPECIAL POWERS DURING A STATE OF PUBLIC HEALTH EMERGENCY: PROTECTION OF PERSONS

[Section 601] Protection of Persons

During a state of public health emergency, the public health authority shall use every available means to prevent the transmission of infectious disease and to ensure that all cases of contagious disease are subject to proper control and treatment.

[Section 602] Medical Examination and Testing

During a state of public health emergency the public health authority may perform physical examinations and/or tests that are necessary for the diagnosis or treatment of individuals. . . .

(b) Medical examinations or tests must not be such as are reasonably likely to lead to serious harm to the affected individual.

(c) The public health authority may isolate or quarantine, pursuant to Section 604, any person whose refusal of medical examination or testing results in uncertainty regarding whether he or she has been exposed to or is infected with a contagious or possibly contagious disease or otherwise poses a danger to public health.

[Section 603] Vaccination and Treatment

[This section contains provisions parallel to Section 602, allowing public health authorities to vaccinate and treat persons, with the exception of those for whom vaccination or treatment is reasonably likely to lead to serious harm to the individual. In addition, those individuals who "are unable or unwilling for reasons of health, religion, or conscience to undergo" vaccination or treatment may be isolated or quarantined pursuant to Section 604.]

[Section 604] Isolation and Quarantine

(b) Authorization. During the public health emergency, the public health authority may isolate . . . or quarantine . . . an individual or groups of individuals. This includes individuals or groups who have not been vaccinated, treated, tested, or examined pursuant to Sections 602 and 603. The public health authority may also establish and maintain places of isolation and quarantine, and set rules and make orders. Failure to obey these rules, orders, or provisions shall constitute a misdemeanor.

(c) Conditions and principles. The public health authority shall adhere to the following conditions and principles when isolating or quarantining individuals or groups of individuals:

(1) Isolation and quarantine must be by the least restrictive means necessary to prevent the spread of a contagious or possibly contagious disease to others and may include, but are not limited to, confinement to private homes or other private and public premises.

(2) Isolated individuals must be confined separately from quarantined individuals.

(3) The health status of isolated and quarantined individuals must be monitored regularly to determine if they require isolation or quarantine.

(4) If a quarantined individual subsequently becomes infected or is reasonably believed to have become infected with a contagious or possibly contagious disease he or she must promptly be removed to isolation.

(5) Isolated and quarantined individuals must be immediately released when they pose no substantial risk of transmitting a contagious or possibly contagious disease to others.

(6) The needs of persons isolated and quarantined shall be addressed in a systematic and competent fashion, including, but not limited to, providing adequate food, clothing, shelter, means of communication with those in isolation or quarantine and outside these settings, medications, and competent medical care.

(7) Premises used for isolation and quarantine shall be maintained in a safe and hygienic manner and be designed to minimize the likelihood of further transmission of infection or other harms to persons isolated and quarantined.

(8) To the extent possible, cultural and religious beliefs should be considered in addressing the needs of individuals, and establishing and maintaining isolation and quarantine premises.

(d) Cooperation. Persons subject to isolation and or quarantine shall obey the public health authority's rules and orders; and shall not go beyond the isolation or quarantine premises. Failure to obey these provisions shall constitute a misdemeanor.

[Section 605] Procedures for Isolation and Quarantine

During a public health emergency, the isolation and quarantine of an individual or groups of individuals shall be undertaken in accordance with the following procedures.

(a) Temporary isolation and quarantine without notice.

(1) Authorization. The public health authority may temporarily isolate or quarantine an individual or groups of individuals through a written directive if delay in imposing the isolation or quarantine would significantly jeopardize the public health authority's ability to prevent or limit the transmission of a contagious or possibly contagious disease to others.

(2) Content of directive. The written directive shall specify the following: (i) the identity of the individual(s) or groups of individuals subject to isolation or quarantine; (ii) the premises subject to isolation or quarantine; (iii) the date and time at which isolation or quarantine commences; (iv) the suspected contagious disease if known; and (v) a copy of Article 6 and relevant definitions of this Act.

(3) Copies. A copy of the written directive shall be given to the individual to be isolated or quarantined or, if the order applies to a group of individuals and it is impractical to provide individual copies, it may be posted in a conspicuous place in the isolation or quarantine premises.

(4) Petition for continued isolation or quarantine. Within ten (10) days after issuing the written directive, the public health authority shall file a petition pursuant to Section 605(b) for a court order authorizing the continued isolation or quarantine of the isolated or quarantined individual or group of individuals.

(b) Isolation or quarantine with notice.

(1) Authorization. The public health authority may make a written petition to the trial court for an order authorizing the isolation or quarantine of an individual or groups of individuals.

(2) Content of petition. [This section requires the information required for a "directive" under §605(a)(2), along with a sworn affidavit of the public health authority concerning compliance with the act.]

(3) Notice. Notice to the individuals or groups of individuals identified in the petition shall be accomplished within twenty-four (24) hours in accordance with the rules of civil procedure.

(4) Hearing. [requiring a hearing within five days of filing the petition, or ten under extraordinary circumstances]

(5) Order. The court shall grant the petition if, by a preponderance of the evidence, isolation or quarantine is shown to be reasonably necessary to prevent or limit the transmission of a contagious or possibly contagious disease to others.

(i) An order authorizing isolation or quarantine may do so for a period not to exceed thirty (30) days.

(ii) [specifying required content of order]

(6) Continuances. Prior to the expiration of an order issued pursuant to Section 605(b)(5), the public health authority may move to continue isolation or quarantine for additional periods not to exceed thirty (30) days each. The court shall consider the motion in accordance with standards set forth in Section 605(b)(5).

(c) Relief from isolation and quarantine.

(1) Release. An individual or group of individuals isolated or quarantined pursuant to this Act may apply to the trial court for an order to show cause why the individual or group of individuals should not be released. The court shall rule on the application to show cause within forty-eight (48) hours of its filing. If the court grants the application, the court shall schedule a hearing on the order to show cause within twenty-four (24) hours from issuance of the order to show cause. The issuance of an order to show cause shall not stay or enjoin an isolation or quarantine order.

(2) Remedies for breach of conditions. An individual or groups of individuals isolated or quarantined pursuant to this Act may request a hearing in the trial court for remedies regarding breaches to the conditions of isolation or quarantine. A request for a hearing shall not stay or enjoin an isolation or quarantine order.

(i) Upon receipt of a request under this subsection alleging extraordinary circumstances justifying the immediate granting of relief, the court shall fix a date for hearing on the matters alleged not more than twenty-four (24) hours from receipt of the request.

(ii) Otherwise, upon receipt of a request under this subsection the court shall fix a date for hearing on the matters alleged within five (5) days from receipt of the request.

(5) [allowing public health authorities for good cause to move the court to extend the time for a hearing]

(d) [requiring record of proceedings and the conduct of proceedings in a way to allow all parties to participate]

(e) Court to appoint counsel and consolidate claims.

(1) Appointment. [requiring appointment of counsel at state expense]

(2) Consolidation. [allowing consolidation of proceedings where individual proceedings are impractical]

ARTICLE VIII MISCELLANEOUS

[Section 804] Liability

[This section eliminates the liability of the state and public health authority and their agents, as well as private persons and corporations acting under their direction, for death or injury unless caused by gross negligence or willful misconduct]

> ## Ken Wing, Policy Choices and Model Acts: Preparing for the Next Public Health Emergency
> ### 13 Health Matrix 71, 74–75, 81 (2003)

I have no doubt that all states need to collect and analyze data on infectious diseases and other public health risks quickly and effectively. I also have no doubt that the states should structure and empower some agency to respond to identified public health risks. Indeed, all states do so in one way or another. My questions concerning the reporting requirements, the public health authority, and the broad investigational powers that would be created under the "model act," however, are . . . : why should a state create such an extensive system of reporting and in this particular manner? Anyone familiar with the experience of tracking AIDs and HIV exposure knows that mandatory disclosure of individual-identifying data can be counterproductive (not to mention politically volatile). If I'm reading the language of Article III correctly, the "model act" would take that information collection to unprecedented extreme. Every doctor and every pharmacist would become an enforcement arm for a public health authority. This would be no little or infrequent matter, as these providers would be required to report all potential causes of public health emergencies— within 24 hours. The extent of the power of the public authority to investigate these reports is not clear from the "model act" but, as written, it is virtually without limit. As such, it is notable—and somewhat ironic—that there are no provisions for the protection of confidentiality or privacy written into the statute, although, in a later article of the "model act" the authors have had the foresight to immunize public officials from liability for exceeding their powers.

More to the point, is there any evidence—from the events of September 11, 2001, or otherwise—that suggests such laws should be in place? Are state or local agencies even equipped to handle this volume of information? What would be the impact on the behavior of people seeking medical attention? Again, interesting ideas are interesting ideas, but a proposed solution to a problem—let alone a "model act"—has to be tied to some assessment of the problem and its underlying causes. Why enact this type of legislation at this time? Many states have enacted comparable regulatory requirements but in much more limited circumstances—reporting of gun shot wounds for instance—and under much more carefully prescribed limits on the government's investigational response. Even those programs are controversial. State and local public health agencies have long struggled to maintain a user-friendly public image and a posture that emphasizes their public health—not their public safety character. The public health authority created by the "model act" would permanently obliterate that distinction. Do the authors of the "model act" really think we need this sort of regulatory apparatus? Why? Again I find myself reading a "model act" and looking for something that should be there but is not.

. . . I can think of circumstances under which some individuals may have to be isolated or quarantined involuntarily. There might even be extraordinary circumstances under which isolation or quarantine should be mandated on the basis of a "group"—although again I find myself wondering exactly what the authors meant by such terminology in Articles V and VI. I also can imagine events that would necessitate some massive marshalling of medical resources, both public and private. But why create the regulatory apparatus for doing so in advance? Why do so in such plenary and heavy-handed terms? Is there any reality-based evidence that American providers need to be regulated in such a fashion during an emergency? Why not improve education and communication and funding such that providers can and will do what the "model act" would simply require under penalty of criminal sanctions? Again I reflect on what we learned in the Fall of 2001 about the behavior in a public health emergency of government officials, medical care providers, businesses and property owners, and thousands of ordinary Americans. Neither then, nor now, do I find myself wishing that the Model State Emergency Health Powers Act had been in effect. There are some things I do wish had been in existence during the Fall of 2001 which will be implemented for the next comparable scenario: more funding for state and local health departments, new procedures for communicating across jurisdictions and from public health to public safety agencies, better training for emergency medical personnel, and so on. I find little to suggest that what we need is the ability to quickly suspend civil rights and to grant public health officials unlimited power to command and control all public and private resources. If my state is ever faced with a public health emergency, I would prefer that we respond to it on a case-by-case basis and in the ad hoc way anticipated under our constitutional system.

NOTES AND QUESTIONS

1. *The individual's threat to public health.*   Under the Model State Emergency Health Powers Act, what must the public health authority show regarding the threat an individual poses to the public health to obtain a court order for the isolation or quarantine of an individual, and by what standard of proof must the authority prove it? Isn't the standard enunciated in Newark v. J.S. considerably higher? Is the difference in standards and burdens of proof justified by the existence of a "public health emergency?" Do you think the Model Act passes constitutional muster? (Recall that the New Jersey court in Newark v. J.S. suggested certain requirements for the conditions of isolation for the state's action to fall within the permissible bounds of the U.S. Constitution's protection of individual liberties.)

2. *Scientific basis for belief of contagion.*   How much scientific evidence about the public health threat (e.g., the existence of disease, its effects, its method of transmission, the reliability of testing to prove contagiousness) must the public health authority have, and how much must it present to the court to obtain orders for vaccination, testing, treatment, or isolation?

In this connection, consider the U.S.'s experience with the swine flu epidemic of 1976. On the advice of the CDC that early outbreaks of the influenza could lead to an epidemic of huge proportions, President Gerald Ford implemented a plan of voluntary immunization of the American public at great cost ($134 million) and, at the insistence of vaccine manufacturers, Congress agreed to underwrite the vaccine manufacturers' liability exposure. Larry Gostin, Public Health Law: Power, Duty, Restraint 185–187 (2000). Gostin writes:

> On October 1, 1976, the first vaccinations were given and, ten days later, three elderly people in Pittsburgh died shortly after receiving the vaccine. Despite health officials' claims that the deaths were not causally related to the vaccine, the media started a "body count" mentality. On October 14, the president and his family received immunizations on primetime television to reassure the public.
>
> In November, a physician in Minnesota reported a case of ascending paralysis, called Guillain-Barré syndrome (GBS). After surveillance revealed an increased incidence of GBS, the swine flu immunization program was brought to an end on December 16, with the president's reluctant agreement; 45 million people had been vaccinated.
>
> . . . The swine flu immunization program provides an intriguing account of policymaking in circumstances of uncertainty. Many commentators held government scientists primarily responsible. For example, in a controversial report commissioned by Secretary [of Health, Education, and Welfare, Joseph] Califano, Richard Neustadt and Harvey Fineberg found that health officials manipulated their constitutional superiors to comply with "expert" recommendations by their assumed air of arrogance: overconfidence among scientific experts spun from meager evidence, conviction fueled by personal agendas, and zeal by scientists to make their lay superiors do right.
>
> In retrospect, health officials did err in recommending a massive immunization campaign with substantial economic costs and potential harmful effects in circumstances of scientific uncertainty. The available data were inadequate to predict whether swine flu would be contained within narrow outbreaks or would become a more serious epidemic.
>
> . . . The swine flu epidemic is instructive in many ways, but it still fails to answer the critical question of whether, in the face of scientific uncertainty, it is better to err on the side of excess caution or aggressive intervention. Consider the appropriate response to suspected bioterrorism with a microbial agent such as anthrax or smallpox. In an emergency, to whom should vaccines be made available and under what circumstances would the government be justified in mandating vaccination? The costs both of action and of inaction are evident: the costs of inaction, if the risk materializes, are lost lives, but the costs of overreaction, if the risk is exaggerated, are wasted public funds and unnecessary burdens of vaccine-induced injury and diminished autonomy.

Id.

3. *Defining a public health emergency.*   How many deaths or disabilities must be anticipated before the governor of a state acting under the Model Act may declare a public health emergency? Does that number vary according to the size of the "affected population" (an undefined term in the act)? In other words, would it be possible to declare a public health emergency if there were concern of an outbreak of TB or hepatitis in a small island population—where the number of anticipated deaths or disabilities would be small as compared to the state population, but large when considered as a percentage of the island population? If a public health emergency could be declared in such a situation, could it likewise be declared in connection with an outbreak of contagious

disease in a prison population? Why might a state wish to declare the public health emergency in the former situation but not the latter?

4. *Social services.*   What reasons might a person have for avoiding a properly obtained order for isolation? Does the Model Act adequately provide for the needs (medical care, food, lost wages) of isolated individuals? What about their dependents, if any?

5. *Testing.*   As in Newark v. J.S., under the Model Act individuals are not subjected to mandatory testing—in other words, they can refuse to be tested, but then they may be subject to isolation or quarantine. The Model Act states that the public health authority may isolate or quarantine any person whose refusal of medical examination or testing "results in uncertainty regarding whether he or she has been exposed to or is infected with a contagious or possibly contagious disease or otherwise poses a danger to public health." Couldn't that cover everybody?

6. *Criticisms of the MSEHP Act.*   Ken Wing offers a number of criticisms of the Model Act; what are they? What are the lessons that might be learned from handling of the AIDS epidemic, or from the handling of the September 11, 2001, terrorist attacks on the World Trade Center and the anthrax contaminations that followed? See also George J. Annas, Bioterrorism, Public Health, and Civil Liberties, 346 New Eng. J. Med. 1337–1342 (2002) for another outspoken critic's view of the Model Act. Lawrence Gostin, one of the principal authors of the Model Act, defends the act against criticisms in Lawrence O. Gostin, The Model State Emergency Health Powers Act: Public Health and Civil Liberties in a Time of Terrorism, 13 Health Matrix 3 (2003).

7. *Federal vs. state response to bioterrorism.*   The recent attention to state public health statutes to respond to a public health emergency such as might be brought on by a bioterrorist act is, in some critics' minds, misdirected attention. Rather, they see the threat posed by bioterrorism together with the high rate of travel among U.S. residents as calling for a *federal* response. See Wing, supra; Annas, supra. Federal law currently permits the government to control the movement of persons into the country and between states to prevent the spread of communicable disease and allows in some instances for apprehension, examination, and detention of infected individuals. See 42 U.S.C. §§264 and 266 and corresponding regulations.

C.   OTHER PUBLIC HEALTH CHALLENGES

Public health officials have long been concerned with challenges to population health that do not come from the threat of infectious disease, but that arise instead from other sources, such as inherited characteristics or unhealthy habits such as smoking. In this section we look at three very different subjects— civil commitment of "sexually violent predators," drug testing of beneficiaries of government assistance, and obesity. These topics raise some of the same issues as traditional public health subjects—such as questions of individual liberties and personal and public responsibilities. But they also raise different questions, such as whether they are even properly understood as public health concerns and how far the reach of public health authority extends.

1.   *Civil Commitment of "Sexually Violent Predators"*

In the last decade or so a number of state legislatures have passed statutes permitting the civil commitment of convicted sex offenders after they have completed their criminal sentence. Such statutes do not tie civil commitment to the original criminal sentence, such as a condition of probation or parole, but provide for an entirely separate determination made in civil courts that the individual has a mental condition that makes him or her dangerous to the public. Upon such determination, these individuals can be committed to a mental facility for an indeterminate period of time, until they no longer pose a danger to others. In 1997, the U.S. Supreme Court upheld Kansas's Sexually Violent Predator Act. As you read the following case, consider in what ways the civil commitment of sex offenders is like and unlike the quarantine or isolation of individuals because of the danger they pose to others. Is this issue properly one of criminal law or civil law? Are states using the apparatus and legal tradition of public health law to good or ill effect?

|| *Kansas v. Hendricks* ||
|| **521 U.S. 346 (1997)** ||

Opinion of the Court by Justice THOMAS.

The Kansas Legislature enacted the Sexually Violent Predator Act (Act) in 1994 to grapple with the problem of managing repeat sexual offenders.

. . . The Act defined a "sexually violent predator" as:

> any person who has been convicted of or charged with a sexually violent offense and who suffers from a mental abnormality or personality disorder which makes the person likely to engage in the predatory acts of sexual violence.

A "mental abnormality" was defined, in turn, as a

> congenital or acquired condition affecting the emotional or volitional capacity which predisposes the person to commit sexually violent offenses in a degree constituting such person a menace to the health and safety of others.

. . . Hendricks admitted that he had repeatedly abused children whenever he was not confined. He explained that when he "get[s] stressed out," he "can't control the urge" to molest children. Although Hendricks recognized that his behavior harms children, and he hoped he would not sexually molest children again, he stated that the only sure way he could keep from sexually abusing children in the future was "to die." Hendricks readily agreed with the state physician's diagnosis that he suffers from pedophilia and that he is not cured of the condition; indeed, he told the physician that "treatment is bull—."

Kansas argues that the Act's definition of "mental abnormality" satisfies "substantive" due process requirements. We agree. Although freedom from physical restraint "has always been at the core of the liberty protected by the Due Process Clause from arbitrary governmental action," that liberty interest is not absolute. The Court has recognized that an individual's constitutionally protected interest in avoiding physical restraint may be overridden even in the civil context:

> [T]he liberty secured by the Constitution of the United States to every person within its jurisdiction does not import an absolute right in each person to be, at all times and in all circumstances, wholly free from restraint. There are manifold restraints to which every person is necessarily subject for the common good. On any other basis organized society could not exist with safety to its members.

Jacobson v. Massachusetts, 197 U.S. 11, 26 (1905). Accordingly, States have in certain narrow circumstances provided for the forcible civil detainment of people who are unable to control their behavior and who thereby pose a danger to the public health and safety. We have consistently upheld such involuntary commitment statutes provided the confinement takes place pursuant to proper procedures and evidentiary standards. It thus cannot be said that the involuntary civil confinement of a limited subclass of dangerous persons is contrary to our understanding of ordered liberty.

The challenged Act unambiguously requires a finding of dangerousness either to one's self or to others as a prerequisite to involuntary confinement. Commitment proceedings can be initiated only when a person "has been convicted of or charged with a sexually violent offense," and "suffers from a mental abnormality or personality disorder which makes the person likely to engage in the predatory acts of sexual violence." Kan. Stat. Ann. §59- 29a02(a) (1994).

. . . A finding of dangerousness, standing alone, is ordinarily not a sufficient ground upon which to justify indefinite involuntary commitment. We have sustained civil commitment statutes when they have coupled proof of dangerousness with the proof of some additional factor, such as a "mental illness" or "mental abnormality." . . . Statutory requirements [such as these] serve to limit involuntary civil confinement to those who suffer from a volitional impairment rendering them dangerous beyond their control. The Kansas Act is plainly of a kind with these other civil commitment statutes: It requires a finding of future dangerousness, and then links that finding to the existence of a "mental abnormality" or "personality disorder" that makes it difficult, if not impossible, for the person to control his dangerous behavior. Kan. Stat. Ann. §59-29a02(b) (1994).

Hendricks nonetheless argues that our earlier cases dictate a finding of "mental illness" as a prerequisite for civil commitment. He then asserts that a "mental abnormality" is *not* equivalent to a "mental illness" because it is a term coined by the Kansas Legislature, rather than by the psychiatric community. Contrary to Hendricks' assertion, the term "mental illness" is devoid of any talismanic significance. Not only do "psychiatrists disagree widely and frequently on what constitutes mental illness," but the Court itself has used a variety of expressions to describe the mental condition of those properly subject to civil confinement. . . . We have traditionally left to legislators the task of defining terms of a medical nature that have legal significance. . . . Hendricks' diagnosis as a pedophile, which qualifies as a "mental abnormality" under the Act, . . . plainly suffices for due process purposes.

We granted Hendricks' cross-petition to determine whether the Act violates the Constitution's double jeopardy prohibition or its ban on *ex post facto* lawmaking. The thrust of Hendricks' argument is that the Act establishes criminal proceedings; hence confinement under it necessarily constitutes punishment. He contends that where, as here, newly enacted "punishment" is predicated upon past conduct for which he has already been convicted and forced to serve a prison sentence, the Constitution's Double Jeopardy and *Ex Post Facto* Clauses are violated. We are unpersuaded by Hendricks' argument that Kansas has established criminal proceedings.

. . . As a threshold matter, commitment under the Act does not implicate either of the two primary objectives of criminal punishment: retribution or deterrence. The Act's purpose is not retributive because it does not affix culpability for prior criminal conduct. Instead, such conduct is used solely for evidentiary purposes, either to demonstrate that a "mental abnormality" exists or to support a finding of future dangerousness.

. . . Nor can it be said that the legislature intended the Act to function as a deterrent. Those persons committed under the Act are, by definition, suffering from a "mental abnormality" or a "personality disorder" that prevents them from exercising adequate control over their behavior. Such persons are therefore unlikely to be deterred by the threat of confinement.

. . . Furthermore, commitment under the Act is only *potentially* indefinite. The maximum amount of time an individual can be incapacitated pursuant to a single judicial proceeding is one year. §59-29a08. If Kansas seeks to continue the detention beyond that year, a court must once again determine beyond a reasonable doubt that the detainee satisfies the same standards as required for the initial confinement. This requirement again demonstrates that Kansas does not intend an individual committed pursuant to the Act to remain confined any longer than he suffers from a mental abnormality rendering him unable to control his dangerousness.

. . . Where the State has "disavowed any punitive intent"; limited confinement to a small segment of particularly dangerous individuals; provided strict procedural safeguards; directed that confined persons be segregated from the general prison population and afforded the same status as others who have been civilly committed; recommended treatment if such is possible; and permitted immediate release upon a showing that the individual is no longer dangerous or mentally impaired, we cannot say that it acted with punitive intent. We therefore hold that the Act does not establish criminal proceedings and that involuntary confinement pursuant to the Act is not punitive. Our conclusion that the Act is nonpunitive thus removes an essential prerequisite for both Hendricks' double jeopardy and *ex post facto* claims.

[Later portions of the opinion find other affirmities in Hendricks's double jeopardy and *ex post facto* claims.]

NOTES AND QUESTIONS

1. *A divided Court.*   The decision in Hendricks was five to four, with Justice Breyer writing the dissenting opinion. All members of the Court essentially agreed that states have the power "to confine persons who, by reason of a mental disease or mental abnormality, constitute a real, continuing, and serious danger

to society." Kennedy, J., concurring, 521 U.S. at 372. But the dissenters found the Kansas statute violated the Due Process and Ex Post Facto Clauses because it was not tailored to fit the "nonpunitive civil aim of treatment," which the state conceded was possible in Hendricks's case (i.e., he was not considered "untreatable" and yet he was given little or no treatment). The statute further did not consider less restrictive alternatives, it delayed treatment until after the individual's criminal sentence was served, and it applied to crimes committed prior to the passage of the act.

2. *Treatability and treatment.*   According to the majority opinion, if Hendricks's mental abnormality were considered "untreatable," civil commitment would still be permissible, even lifetime commitment. The majority acknowledged that incapacitation by itself (without treatment, where treatment is not possible) may be a legitimate end of civil law, and cites for this purpose Compagnie Francaise de Navigation a Vapeur v. Louisiana Bd. of Health, 186 U.S. 380 (1902), in which the court permitted involuntary quarantine of persons suffering from communicable diseases. How do you think the issues of treatability and treatment should factor into a constitutional analysis of sexually violent predator statutes? An ethical analysis?

3. *Public health precedents.*   In addition to citing the public health case of *Compagnie Francaise,* the majority also cites Jacobson v. Massachusetts, the early vaccination case. Are the analogies sound? How is the issue of civil confinement of sexual predators similar to or different from other public health activities?

4. *What and who defines mental abnormalities?*   The Court states that dangerousness alone is "ordinarily" not enough to commit an individual to indefinite civil confinement. But what must there be in addition to dangerousness? In *Hendricks,* pedophilia was a sufficient "mental abnormality." In Foucha v. Louisiana, 504 U.S. 71 (1992), however, the Court held that antisocial personality disorder (along with dangerousness) was not sufficient to civilly commit a person who had been acquitted on the basis of insanity. Bruce Winnick reconciles these cases by emphasizing the Court's characterization of Hendricks's pedophilia as a condition that rendered him unable to control his behavior, whereas in *Foucha,* antisocial personality disorder was not characterized in the same way. Those who are able to control their behavior are more appropriately dealt with by the criminal law, whereas those who cannot control their behavior are more appropriately dealt with by the civil law. Bruce Winnick, Sex Offender Law in the 1990s: A Therapeutic Jurisprudence Analysis, 4 Psychol. Pub. Pol'y & L. 505 (1998). But doesn't a statute such as Kansas's permit the latter to be confined first by criminal law and then by civil law?

In any event, Winnick suggests this reading of the case is preferable to understanding it as requiring more complete deference to state legislatures to define whatever category of "mental abnormality" coupled with dangerousness they wish to confine individuals postincarceration. He asks in this regard whether a state might constitutionally establish a category of "violent hotheads," or, in light of recent terrorist activities that include what many would consider "crazy," such as suicide bombing attempts, "violent terrorists." What do you think?

5. *Federal civil commitment statute.*   In United States v. Comstock, 130 S. Ct. 1949 (2010), the Supreme Court held that the federal government had the

authority, under the Necessary and Proper Clause, to enact a federal civil commitment program for already-in-custody mentally ill, sexually dangerous persons beyond the conclusion of their sentences. The law in question in *Comstock* was the Adam Walsh Child Protection and Safety Act, 18 U.S.C. §4248. The Court did not address any claims that the statute denied equal protection, procedural or substantive due process, or other constitutional rights. Justice Breyer, who had dissented in *Hendricks,* wrote the majority opinion, explaining that the Court "assume[s] for argument's sake that the federal Constitution would permit a State to enact this statute, and we ask solely whether the Federal Government, exercising its enumerated powers, may enact such a statute as well." Id. at 1956.

2. *Drug Testing for Government Benefits*

|| *Lebron v. Wilkins* ||
820 F. Supp. 1273 (M.D. Fla. 2011)

Mary S. SCRIVEN, District Judge

The question presented is whether Section 414.0652, Florida Statutes, which requires all applicants for a class of federal welfare benefits to submit to suspicionless drug testing, is constitutional under the Fourth and Fourteenth Amendments.

Issue:

BACKGROUND

Plaintiff in this case, Luis Lebron, applied to the Florida Department of Children and Families ("DCF") for benefits under the federal Temporary Assistance for Needy Families ("TANF") program in July 2011 to support himself and his minor child. Plaintiff has sole custody of his four-year-old son and is an undergraduate student at the University of Central Florida with prior military service. Though Plaintiff attests that he has never used illegal drugs, Section 414.0652 requires him to submit to drug testing as a condition of eligibility for TANF benefits.

. . . After holding hearings on welfare reform, the Florida Legislature enacted legislation in 1998 that required DCF to develop and implement a "Demonstration Project" to study and evaluate the "impact of the drug-screening and drug-testing program on employability, job placement, job retention, and salary levels of program participants" and to make "recommendations, based in part on a cost benefit analysis, as to the feasibility of expanding the program," including specific recommendations for implementing such an expansion.

. . . The results of the Demonstration Project confounded the expectations of the researchers, who observed that "evidence of drug abuse in Florida is substantially lower than the percentages reported in other research on this topic." . . . [D]rug use among the tested TANF population was found to be significantly lower than drug use among welfare recipients in other national studies. The results also showed significantly lower rates of drug use among this population than the rate of drug use among the population of Florida at large, which was recently estimated at 8.13 percent.

. . . The preliminary results of the Demonstration Project were reported to the Legislature in an Evaluation Report that recommended that the project not be expanded because of the high costs of drug testing "compared with the benefits derived" and because of the "minimal differences in employment and earnings between those who showed evidence of current substance abuse and those who did not." The Legislature apparently did not undertake further testing or expanded testing, and the Demonstration Project expired on June 30, 2001, pursuant to a statutory sunset provision.

In 2011, the Florida Legislature resurrected the concept of drug testing TANF applicants. No new studies were conducted, and no new data specific to the Florida welfare population was offered. Instead, legislative staff officials turned again to the Demonstration Project, evaluated its data and considered other issues implicated by the proposed suspicionless drug testing program. Staff analyses provided to the Florida House of Representatives and the Florida Senate considered the legal ramifications of drug testing, citing a number of cases raised by the parties in the filings before this Court. The House analysis cited the line of United States Supreme Court cases dealing with suspicionless drug testing of individuals and noted that the issue had been successfully challenged as unconstitutional in Michigan in the precise context of welfare recipients. [Marchwinski v. Howard, 113 F. Supp. 2d 1134 (E.D. Mich. 2000), *aff'd* 60 Fed. Appx. 601 (6th Cir. 2003)–EDS.]

Despite the failure of the Demonstration Project to uncover evidence of rampant drug abuse among TANF applicants; despite the conclusion of researchers that drug use did not adversely impact any of the goals of the TANF program, including employability, earning capacity or independence from social assistance; despite the fact that the study revealed no financial efficacy; despite the legal ramifications; and, despite the express recommendation that the project not be continued or expanded, Florida enacted Section 414.0652 on May 31, 2011.

. . . The preliminary results from the drug testing conducted pursuant to Section 414.065 reveal even lower drug use among TANF applicants than demonstrated by the results of the Demonstration Project. Evidence adduced on this record suggests that preliminary tests show that only about 2 percent of TANF applicants tested positive in the first month of drug testing.

DISCUSSION

. . . The Supreme Court has "routinely treated urine screens taken by state agents as searches within the meaning of the Fourth Amendment," Ferguson v. City of Charleston, 532 U.S. 67, 77 n.9 (2001), regardless of whether the person subjected to the test has the opportunity to refuse it. *See* Chandler v. Miller, 520 U.S. 305, 313 (1997) (drug testing of prospective political candidates considered to be a search); Vernonia Sch. Dist. 47J v. Acton, 515 U.S. 646 (1995); (policy requiring high school students to sign a form consenting to testing in order to play sports considered a search); Bd. of Educ. of Indep. Sch. Dist. No. 92 of Pottawatomie Cnt. v. Earls, 536 U.S. 822 (2002) (policy requiring middle school and high school students to consent to drug testing as a condition for participation in extracurricular activities held a search).

In short, this case ... concerns the collection of an individual's urine, an act that necessarily entails intrusion into a highly personal and private bodily function, and the subsequent urinalysis, which can reveal a host of private medical facts about that individual. The intrusion here also extends well beyond the initial passing of urine. Positive drug tests are not kept confidential in the same manner as medical records; they are shared with third-parties, including DCF, medical reviewers and counselors for the Florida Abuse Hotline. More troubling, positive test results are memorialized, perhaps indefinitely, in a database that the State admits can be accessed by law enforcement. This potential interception of positive drug tests by law enforcement implicates a "far more substantial" invasion of privacy than in ordinary civil drug testing cases. In light of the inherently investigative character of the drug test and binding legal authority, the Court rejects the argument that a drug test taken pursuant to Section 414.0652 is not a search within the meaning of the Fourth Amendment.

... Because Florida's drug testing program authorizes suspicionless searches, Florida must establish that the interests it advances to demand such searches without probable cause or reasonable suspicion meet the "Special Needs" exception to the Fourth Amendment.

Special Needs:

... The State maintains that the following interests qualify as special needs: (1) ensuring that TANF funds are used for their dedicated purpose, and not diverted to drug use; (2) protecting children by "ensuring that its funds are not used to visit an 'evil' upon the children's homes and families"; (3) ensuring that funds are not used in a manner that detracts from the goal of getting beneficiaries back to employment; (4) ensuring that the government does not fund the "public health risk" posed by the crime associated with the "drug epidemic."

These goals are undeniably laudable objectives. However, these stated goals can be found nowhere in the legislation, and with good reason: the State's commissioned study undercuts each of these rationales as a likely feature of the proposed legislation. As noted, researchers found a lower rate of drug usage among TANF applicants than among current estimates of the population of Florida as a whole. This would suggest that TANF funds are no more likely to be diverted to drug use or used in a manner that would expose children to drugs or fund the "drug epidemic" than funds provided to any other recipient of government benefits. The researchers also found no evidence that TANF recipients who screened and tested positive for the use of illicit substances were any less likely to find work than those who screened and tested negative.

... Though the State speaks in generalities about the "public health risk, as well as the crime risk, associated with drugs" being "beyond dispute," it provides no concrete evidence that those risks are any more present in TANF applicants than in the greater population. Rather, the evidence suggests that those risks are less prevalent among TANF applicants. The Court, therefore, rejects the suggestion that the inchoate public health or crime risks assertions incanted by the State justify the Fourth Amendment intrusions mandated by Section 414.0652.

Nor is the drug testing analogous to the preventative drug testing program approved of in *Earls*. In *Earls*, as in prior and subsequent public school drug testing cases, the subjects of the drug tests were vulnerable students, and the school district's custodial or tutelary responsibility towards those students justified early, preventative intervention through drug testing. The Supreme Court also considered evidence of a "nationwide drug epidemic" that had "grown worse" since its decision in *Vernonia* in 1995 upholding the constitutionality of drug testing of student athletes. Specifically, the Court pointed out that "the number of 12th graders using any illicit drug increased from 48.4 percent in 1995 to 53.9 percent in 2001. The number of 12th graders reporting they had used marijuana jumped from 41.7 percent to 49.0 percent during that same period."

. . . When the asserted concerns regarding public safety, the wellbeing of children and the employment of TANF applicants are stripped away, the State is left with only one alleged special need: the interest in preserving public funds by ensuring that money that is intended for one purpose is not used instead to purchase illegal drugs. Again, this is a commendable governmental purpose, and one that courts have found relevant to the special needs analysis.

. . . The State has not shown by competent evidence that any TANF funds would be saved by instituting a drug testing program. The State, of course, concedes the substantial cost of administering the program; everyone who tests negative must be reimbursed for the cost of the drug test. Fla. Stat. §414.0652(2)(a). Thus, millions of TANF dollars will be spent funding drug tests.

. . . [T]he State invokes the government's general interest in fighting the "war on drugs" and the associated ills of drug abuse generally to contend that TANF funds should not be used to fund the drug trade. The Court agrees. But, if invoking an interest in preventing public funds from potentially being used to fund drug use were the only requirement to establish a special need, the State could impose drug testing as an eligibility requirement for every beneficiary of every government program. Such blanket intrusions cannot be countenanced under the Fourth Amendment.

. . . As the State has failed to demonstrate a special need for its suspicionless drug testing statute, the Court finds no need to engage in the balancing analysis—evaluating the State's interest in conducting the drug tests and the privacy interests of TANF applicants.

ACCORDINGLY, the Court finds that Plaintiff has shown a substantial likelihood of success on the merits of this action.

[The Court also finds that Plaintiff has demonstrated that he will suffer irreparable harm in the absence of preliminary injunctive relief and that a grant of preliminary injunction serves the public interest and outweighs whatever minimal harm a preliminary injunction might visit upon the State. The Plaintiff's Motion for Preliminary Injunction is GRANTED.]

NOTES AND QUESTIONS

1. *Recent legislative activity.* Until very recently, drug testing as a precondition for receipt of government benefits was an almost unheard-of phenomenon. As of April 2008, only one state—Michigan—had attempted to impose drug testing on welfare recipients, and this attempt was struck down as an unconstitutional search under the Fourth Amendment by the U.S.

Court of Appeals for the Sixth Circuit, *Marchwinski v. Howard*, 113 F. Supp. 2d 1134 (E.D. Mich. 2000), aff'd 60 Fed. Appx. 601 (2003). But in recent years, more and more states have sought to impose such programs or at the very least, have contemplated them. As of May 2012, seven states had passed mandatory drug testing or screening programs for applicants for or recipients of public assistance, including TANF, Supplemental Nutrition Assistance, and Medicaid. In 2011 and 2012, over half of the states were considering such proposals in their legislatures. See the website for the National Conference of State Legislatures at http://www.ncsl.org/issues-research/human-services/drug-testing-and-public-assistance.aspx.

2. *The public health connections.* What public health justifications might be offered in support of such drug testing? Do you find them convincing? If you do, what kind of evidence would you want before concluding that the intrusion into individuals' privacy is justified by these public health aims? According to the *Lebron* case, the State of Florida had some problems with its evidence of drug use by TANF recipients; what were they? Would your support or rejection of such programs depend on whether they offered treatment for those testing positive? On whether they required suspicion of drug use vs. applying to all applicants/recipients? Are there any public health arguments that can be made against such programs?

3. The Obesity "Epidemic"

> ### Colin Hector, Nudging Towards Nutrition? Soft Paternalism and Obesity-Related Reform
> ### 67 Food & Drug L.J. 103 (2012)

1. The Prevalence of Obesity in America

A number of researchers have contended that obesity rates grew rapidly since the 1980s, and projected that these rates would continue to climb without preventative measures. For instance, in their short "Facts About Obesity in the United States," the CDC bluntly states that "[o]besity rates are soaring in the U.S." and that "[b]etween 1980 and 2000, obesity rates doubled among adults." This claim is consistent with research that has shown obesity rates sharply increasing, from 15.0% of the United States population in 1980, to an incredible 30.9% of the population in 2000. In line with these findings, Dr. James O. Hill predicted that "[i]f obesity is left unchecked . . . almost all Americans will be overweight by 2050." Although the CDC's more recent data shows that obesity rates have increased only marginally over the last 10 years, the organization warns that obesity remains "a national epidemic," with more than 72 million American adults obese.

In response, other scholars have argued that the notion of an obesity "epidemic" that began in the 1980s is based on questionable science. Some academics have claimed that obesity rates are inherently misleading due to the primary manner in which obesity is measured. Generally, obesity is determined by an individual's body mass index (BMI), which is derived from an individual's weight and height. If an adult individual's BMI is between 25 and 29, they are classified as "overweight," and a person with a BMI of over 30 is classified as "obese." A common criticism of using body mass to determine obesity is that individuals who are heavier due to above-average muscle mass are characterized in the "overweight" and "obese" categories. Skeptics have also contended that estimates of obesity prevalence may be considerably skewed because BMI fails to account for natural variations in body size and composition, particularly with respect to age and ethnicity. Thus, these arguments suggest that obesity rates based on BMI may include many individuals who do not carry an amount of excess body fat that warrants the "obese" classification.

However, the observation that BMI is an imperfect measurement of body fat when it comes to particular individuals does not necessarily lead to the conclusion that BMI is a poor indicator of body fat across a general population. . . .

2.   Consequences of Obesity

Even if BMI is a relatively accurate indicator of body fat, there is still the more important question of whether the BMI thresholds of 25 for "overweight" and 30 for "obese" reflect legitimate health concerns. Some critics have contended that the health consequences at these BMI levels are negligible at best, and in many cases may actually be correlated with lower health risks. Professor J. Eric Oliver, in *Fat Politics: The Real Story Behind America's Obesity Epidemic*, contends that the notion of an overweight and obesity "epidemic" is at least partly the result of the National Institute of Health (NIH) changing the threshold point for "overweight" from a BMI of 27.8 for men and 27.3 for women, to a BMI of 25 for both sexes. Oliver and others claim that these changes, which were implemented in 1998, ran contrary to studies demonstrating that increased mortality was not evident until well beyond a BMI of 30. Hence, these arguments suggest a disconnect between the current BMI standards for "overweight" and "obese," and the CDC's definition of these terms as "ranges of weight that are greater than what is considered healthy for a given height."

Skepticism over the health consequences of "overweight" and "obese" BMI levels has become the central battleground of the obesity research controversy. In large part, this has been the result of a vociferous response to the oft-cited statistics that 300,000 or 400,000 Americans die annually from obesity-related deaths. The 300,000 figure comes from studies published in 1993 and 1999, and the 400,000 statistic comes from a later study by CDC researchers that was published in 2004. All of these studies have come under considerable scrutiny, and have been criticized based on their methodology and findings.

. . . Adding to the furor over the obesity death statistics, in 2005 a study led by CDC researcher Kathleen Flegal estimated annual obesity-related deaths in the United States at the much lower number of 111,909, with the vast majority of deaths occurring in individuals with a BMI of 35 or greater. In addition, these researchers found that being overweight (but not obese) was associated with a slight *reduction* in mortality. . . .

Unsurprisingly, the disagreements over the health-related consequences of obesity have led to a similar controversy regarding the cost of obesity to the American economy. A 2001 report by the Surgeon General estimated the costs of overweight and obesity at $117 billion, including both direst costs such as healthcare ($61 billion) and indirect costs such as loss of productivity ($56 billion). Later research has suggested that overweight and obesity related healthcare costs have steadily risen. For instance, a 2003 study estimated the annual cost of medical spending attributable to overweight and obesity related health problems at $78.5 billion, with roughly half paid by government-sponsored programs. And more recent studies have estimated that current obesity-related health care costs may have risen to more than $147 billion dollars.

B.   *Policy Implications*

. . . The politicization of obesity research is particularly salient with respect to the discussion over the root causes of obesity. Despite the complexities inherent in studying this topic, the large body of research concerning the causes of obesity has been increasingly framed in terms of two narratives. The first is the narrative of personal responsibility, which posits that obesity is largely the result of personal choices that are the responsibility of each individual. This narrative has been embraced by anti-regulatory politicians, as well as the food and beverage industry. For instance, one of the more notable recent obesity-related bills, which sought to forbid consumers from bringing lawsuits against food companies, was presented squarely within the narrative of personal responsibility. The bill was tellingly entitled The Personal Responsibility in Food Consumption Act, and described by one Representative as saying "[d]on't run off and file a lawsuit if you are fat . . . [l]ook in the mirror because you're the one to blame."

The second narrative frames obesity as the result of an unhealthy or "toxic" food environment that induces unhealthy eating behaviors. This narrative looks at obesity as the result of behaviors that are induced by characteristics of modern society. Accordingly, this narrative emphasizes many of the environmental causes of obesity. Although once confined to a small number of academics and researchers, this view has gained considerable traction among the wider public and with pro-regulatory politicians.

II.   SOFT PATERNALISM AS A FRAMEWORK FOR APPROACHING OBESITY-RELATED REFORM

. . . Soft paternalism is a regulatory framework that draws on the insights of behavioral economics in order to develop policies that encourage people to make better decisions. Although soft paternalism involves an element of government intervention, it adheres to the fundamental principle that consumers should be relatively free to make "bad" choices. Richard H. Thaler and Cass R. Sunstein, in their book Nudge: Improving Decisions About Health Wealth, and Happiness (Nudge), illustrate the soft paternalism framework with the idea of the "nudge." A nudge, the authors write, is any contextual change "that alters people's behavior in a predictable way without forbidding any options or significantly changing their economic incentives." Thus, while a nudge may encourage people to make a specific choice, it is not a mandate.

A.   *Behavioral Economics and Bounded Rationality*

Behavioral economics rests on the basic insight that people act in predictably irrational ways. . . . Critical to this endeavor is the idea that people have systematic biases that influence their decision making, often to their detriment. By integrating these biases into economic models, behavioral economics replaces the idea of "full rationality" with the more realistic concept of "bounded rationality." Thus, a central challenge for behavioral economics is identifying the forces that cause people to behave in a predictably irrational manner, and analyzing what can be done to mitigate or overcome these biases. . . .

1.   Hyperbolic Discounting and Visceral Factors

. . . First, people have a systematic, often considerable preference for smaller rewards now over larger gains later. . . . This behavior—known as hyperbolic discounting—raises serious questions about consumer rationality. . . .

Second, the tendency to make these sorts of irrational decisions is reinforced by the impact of visceral factors, such as hunger, thirst, and current mood.

Considered together, hyperbolic discounting and the influence of visceral factors provide a helpful framework for understanding consumption decisions that lead to obesity. The heavy emphasis people place on immediate rewards, and the drive to satisfy motivational states, militates in favor of behavior that results in short-term pleasure at the expense of long-run adverse health consequences. . . .

2.   The Status Quo Bias and the Power of Defaults

A second area of concern for behavioral economists regards the way in which the presentation of choices to consumers can influence decision making. In contrast to the model of rational deliberation, research has shown that how choices are presented, or framed, can have a powerful effect on the choices people make, One of the most important findings in this area is that people demonstrate a consistent preference for existing conditions—whether it be incumbent politicians, healthcare plans, or current policies—than rational models would predict, even when the costs of switching are low.

The existence of this "status quo bias" raises the importance of default options. As expected, people have a systematic tendency to pick the option that is presented as the "default." Accordingly, the effect of a change in defaults can lead to striking results. For example, in countries where people must affirmatively choose to be an organ donor, the percentage of donors averages 15 percent. By contrast, when people must opt-out of being a donor, the percentage of donors is 98 percent. . . .

The importance of default options has also been demonstrated in the context of obesity-related consumption behaviors. Some important defaults concern the physical layout of food options at the point of purchase. *Nudge*, for example, begins with an anecdote of how the placement of food and beverage options in a school cafeteria can influence what students consume. Other defaults relate to the manner in which food is packaged. For instance, researcher Brian Wansink has conducted several studies demonstrating that consumption behavior can be greatly influenced by the portion size that food is provided in.

B. Specific Policy Recommendations

Since the Nutrition Labeling and Education Act of 1990, the United States has required certain nutritional disclosures on food and beverage products. Nutrition labeling is currently being reevaluated, making now an opportune time to consider changes to food labels that reflect some of the insights of behavioral economics. . . . To the extent that people's ability to make rational decisions is displaced by hyperbolic discounting and visceral factors, information should be presented in a way that highlights potential long-term consequences. . . .

. . . Another area in which soft paternalism may support an optimization of defaults involves portion size norms. Although optimizing default portion sizes could be directly established through a mandate, or limited to state-controlled locations such as school cafeterias, they may also be accomplished by regulations that fall under the ambit of soft paternalism. David R. Just and Collin R. Payne, in an article exploring the relationship between obesity and behavioral economics, suggest two ways in which portion sizes may be altered without resort to mandates. First, they argue that legal reforms concerning food and beverage advertisements could result in better product packaging. By reforming the law to allow manufacturers to advertise that their product packaging can discourage overeating, the authors contend that marketplace competition would likely lead to more sensible packaging and portion sizes. Second, the authors suggest that packaging and portion sizes could be better optimized by the use of a certification system. As with organic foods, these certificates could encourage food manufactures to reformulate packaging so that it better encourages healthy levels of consumption.

Pelman v. McDonald's Corp.
237 F. Supp. 2d 512 (S.D.N.Y. 2003)

Opinion by District Judge SWEET.
. . . The plaintiffs have alleged that the practices of McDonalds in making and selling their products are deceptive and that this deception has caused the minors who have consumed McDonalds' products to injure their health by becoming obese. Questions of personal responsibility, common knowledge and public health are presented, and the role of society and the courts in addressing such issues.

The issue of determining the breadth of personal responsibility underlies much of the law: where should the line be drawn between an individual's own responsibility to take care of herself, and society's responsibility to ensure that others shield her? Laws are created in those situations where individuals are somehow unable to protect themselves and where society needs to provide a buffer between the individual and some other entity—whether herself, another individual or a behemoth corporation that spans the globe. Thus Congress provided that essentially all packaged foods sold at retail shall be appropriately labeled and their contents described. Also as a matter of federal regulation, all alcoholic beverages must warn pregnant women against their use. Congress has gone further and made the possession and consumption of certain products criminal because of their presumed effect on the health of consumers.[2]

This opinion is guided by the principle that legal consequences should not attach to the consumption of hamburgers and other fast food fare unless consumers are unaware of the dangers of eating such food. As discussed, *infra*, this guiding principle comports with the law of products liability under New York law. . . . If consumers know (or reasonably should know) the potential ill health effects of eating at McDonalds, they cannot blame McDonalds if they, nonetheless, choose to satiate their appetite with a surfeit of supersized McDonalds products. On the other hand, consumers cannot be expected to protect against a danger that was solely within McDonalds' knowledge. Thus, one necessary element of any potentially viable claim must be that McDonalds' products involve a danger that is not within the common knowledge of consumers. . . . [P]laintiffs have failed to allege with any specificity that such a danger exists.

CLAIMS

The plaintiffs allege five causes of action as members of a putative class action of minors residing in New York State who have purchased and consumed McDonalds' products. Counts I and II are based on deceptive acts and practices in violation of the Consumer Protection Act, New York Gen. Bus. Law §§349 and 350, and the New York City Administrative Codes, Chapter 5, 20-700 et seq. Count I alleges that McDonalds failed to adequately disclose the ingredients and/or health effects of ingesting certain of their food products with high levels of cholesterol, fat, salt, and sugar; described their food as nutritious; and engaged in marketing to entice consumers to purchase "value meals" without disclosing the detrimental health effects thereof. Count II focuses on marketing techniques geared toward inducing children to purchase and ingest McDonalds' food products. Count III sounds in negligence, alleging that McDonalds acted at least negligently in selling food products that are high in cholesterol, fat, salt, and sugar when studies show that such foods cause obesity and detrimental health effects. Count IV alleges that McDonalds failed to warn the consumers of McDonalds' products of the ingredients, quantity, qualities and levels of cholesterol, fat, salt, and sugar content and other ingredients in those products, and that a diet high in fat, salt, sugar, and cholesterol could lead to obesity and health problems. Finally, Count V also sounds in negligence,

---

2. In the interest of consistency and integrity, it should be noted that the author of this opinion publicly opposed the criminalization of drugs. This belief is based upon the notion that, as long as consumers have adequate knowledge about even harmful substances, they should be entitled to purchase them, and that the issue should be one of health, rather than of the criminal law. The same logic must apply in the situation of fast food, which is arguably less harmful and certainly less demonized than drugs that have been made illegal—unless, of course, this is the opening salvo in the "War on Big Macs."

alleging that McDonalds acted negligently in marketing food products that were physically and psychologically addictive.

[The district court dismissed all of the plaintiffs' claims, for lack of specificity or because defendants owed no duty to warn consumers of well-known attributes of its products. However, the complaint was dismissed with leave to amend and, in the following passages, the court suggested which argument of plaintiffs, if properly pled, had the greatest chance of success.–EDS.]

I.   Plaintiffs' Claim that McDonalds' Products Are More Dangerous than the Average Hamburger, Fries, and Shake

For the first time in their opposition papers, the plaintiffs attempt to show that overconsumption of McDonalds is different in kind from, for instance, overconsumption of alcoholic beverages or butter because the processing of McDonalds' food has created an entirely different—and more dangerous—food than one would expect from a hamburger, chicken finger or french fry cooked at home or at any restaurant other than McDonalds. They thus argue that McDonalds' food is "dangerous to an extent beyond that which would be contemplated by the ordinary consumer who purchases it, with the ordinary knowledge common to the community as to its characteristics." Restatement (Second) Torts §402A, cmt. I. If true, consumers who eat at McDonalds have not been given a free choice, and thus liability may attach.

. . . [P]laintiffs argue that McDonalds' products have been so altered that their unhealthy attributes are now outside the ken of the average reasonable consumer. They point to McDonalds' ingredient lists to show that McDonalds' customers worldwide are getting much more than what is commonly considered to be a chicken finger, a hamburger, or a french fry.

For instance, Chicken McNuggets, rather than being merely chicken fried in a pan, are a McFrankenstein creation of various elements not utilized by the home cook. A Chicken McNugget is comprised of, in addition to chicken:

> water, salt, modified corn starch, sodium phosphates, chicken broth powder (chicken broth, salt and natural flavoring (chicken source)), seasoning (vegetable oil, extracts of rosemary, mono, di- and triglycerides, lecithin). Battered and breaded with water, enriched bleached wheat flour (niacin, iron, thiamine, mononitrate, riboflavin, folic acid), yellow corn flour, bleached wheat flour, modified corn starch, salt, leavening (baking soda, sodium acid pyrophosphate, sodium aluminum phosphate, monocalcium phosphate, calcium lactate), spices, wheat starch, dried whey, corn starch. Batter set in vegetable shortening. Cooked in partially hydrogenated vegetable oils, (may contain partially hydrogenated soybean oil and/or partially hydrogenated corn oil and/or partially hydrogenated canola oil and/or cottonseed oil and/or corn oil). TBHG and citric acid added to help preserve freshness. Dimethylpolysiloxane added as an anti-foaming agent.

In addition, Chicken McNuggets, while seemingly a healthier option than McDonalds hamburgers because they have "chicken" in their names, actually contain twice the fat per ounce as a hamburger. It is at least a question of fact as to whether a reasonable consumer would know—without recourse to the

McDonalds' website—that a Chicken McNuggets contained so many ingredients other than chicken and provided twice the fat of a hamburger.

This argument comes closest to overcoming the hurdle presented to plaintiffs. If plaintiffs were able to flesh out this argument in an amended complaint, it may establish that the dangers of McDonalds' products were not commonly well known and thus McDonalds had a duty toward its customers.

NOTES AND QUESTIONS

1. *Personal and public responsibilities.* Compare and contrast the approaches represented by the *Pelman* case and the "soft paternalism" advocated by Colin Hector. Where do these approaches place responsibility for health? How do these approaches value personal freedom?

2. *Personal responsibility for one's costs.* The government, through a number of programs, pays for many of the costs associated with health problems brought about by unhealthy eating habits and sedentary behaviors. Private insurance companies also bear some of the burden although they presumably pass the cost on to those who pay insurance premiums. Might an argument be made that those people who are obese must bear the costs associated with their own obesity (e.g., higher premiums or a larger copay in their insurance)? How convincing is that argument? How would it apply to children?

Notice that the same argument has been made for other behaviors of "choice." For example, some have argued that parents who choose to bear a child with a costly genetic disability should have to bear any costs associated with that disability if the parents could have avoided the genetic condition. See Eric Rakowski, Who Should Pay for Bad Genes?, 90 Cal. L. Rev. 1345 (2002). Should this suggestion be viewed similarly?

3. *More on fast-food lawsuits and other legal efforts relating to obesity.* The *Pelman* plaintiffs amended their complaint to include several causes of action, each of which was based on New York's Consumer Protection Act. Although this amended complaint was then dismissed by the federal district court on the grounds that plaintiffs had failed to adequately allege causation, the appellate court, in Pelman v. McDonald's Corp., 396 F.3d 508 (2005), reversed, allowing the following claims to proceed: (1) defendant misled plaintiffs to believe its foods were part of a healthy lifestyle, (2) defendant failed to disclose that its foods were substantially less healthy than represented by advertising, and (3) defendant engaged in unfair and deceptive practices by promising nutritional brochures to customers and then not supplying them. Proving causation remains the biggest hurdle for plaintiffs. In 2010, the plaintiff consumers in *Pelman* lost a motion for class certification. 272 F.R.D. 82 (S.D.N.Y. 2010).

In response to *Pelman* and similar lawsuits filed against fast-food restaurants, the U.S. Congress considered but did not pass the Personal Responsibility in Food Consumption Act, H.R. 339, 108th Congress (2003) (introduced in 2004 and 2005 as well), which would have eliminated any liability of food companies on the basis of claims of injury relating to weight gain or obesity. Some states, however, passed similar limited liability legislation.

Other state and local government action has been focused on improving school lunch menus and physical education requirements, and limiting access to sugary drinks sold in vending machines in schools. In 2006, New York City became the first city in the United States to ban the use of trans fats in restaurant cooking; California joined at the state level with a bill passed in 2008. Jennifer Steinhauer, California Bans Restaurant Use of Trans Fats, N.Y. Times, July 26, 2008. Most recently, New York City banned restaurants from selling sugar-sweetened drinks in cups larger than 16 ounces. Michael M. Grynbaum, Health Panel Approves Restriction on Sale of Large Sugary Drinks, N.Y. Times, Sept. 13, 2012.

3. *Patient Protection and Affordable Care Act.*   The health reform law passed in 2010 includes a number of provisions aimed at addressing obesity:

> Several of the more obvious provisions in the bill that tackle obesity are the following: improved nutrition labeling in fast food restaurants, which will list calories and provide information on other nutrients; the Childhood Obesity Demonstration Project, which gives grants to community-based obesity intervention programs; and Community Transformation Grants, which funds community-based efforts to prevent chronic diseases. Other parts of the new law take a rather broader approach and have the potential to reduce obesity because they are focused on prevention. For example, health plans and health insurance issuers are required to provide coverage for evidence-based items or preventive services (including obesity screening and nutritional counseling) that have a rating of "A" or "B" in the current recommendations of the United States Preventive Services Task Force. PPACA prohibits the use of cost-sharing for such services. That is, there are no co-payments or deductibles when clinicians screen patients for obesity and offer or refer them to comprehensive, intensive behavioral interventions to promote improvement in weight status. In addition, employers are allowed to reward employees, in the form of a discount or rebate of a premium or contribution, a waiver of all or part of a costsharing mechanism, or the absence of a subcharge (an extra fee), for participating in a wellness program that is reasonably designed to promote health or prevent disease. In other words, PPACA permits employers to lower insurance premiums by up to 30 percent for employee participation in certain health promotion and disease prevention programs, or for meeting certain health standards.

Y. Tony Yang & Len M. Nichols, Obesity and Health System Reform: Private vs. Public Responsibility, 39 J. Law, Med. & Ethics 380 (2011) (concluding that "the new freedoms PPACA grants to employers and health plans to use financial incentives for participation in wellness programs that emphasize good weight control may be among the more promising elements of the law as it now stands").

4. *Children and cholesterol-lowering drugs.*   Recent prescription data reveals that children are increasingly being prescribed adult medications to treat problems related to obesity, such as Type 2 diabetes, high blood pressure, high cholesterol, and acid reflux. And the American Academy of Pediatrics has come out with a recommendation that more children, age eight and up, be given cholesterol-reducing drugs. Stephanie Saul, Weight Drives the Young to Adult Pills, Data Says, N.Y. Times, July 26, 2008. According to the Times, "While the drugs do help treat the conditions, some doctors fear they are simply a shortcut fix for a problem better addressed by exercise and diet. Even so, some pharmaceutical companies are developing new versions, including flavored ones, of adult medications for children." Id.

CHALLENGING ISSUES: BANNING SCHOOL VENDING MACHINES

Suppose that you are a member of the board of education of a school district contemplating a ban on vending machines in your schools. While you recognize that growing childhood overweight and obesity rates are a public health problem nationwide, you also understand the position of some, that parents and children—rather than the "nanny state"—should be ultimately responsible for the food those children ingest. Additionally, you are sensitive to the economics of the measure—particularly in these cash-strapped days—and realize that keeping vending machines in school may augment (or at least maintain) economic dividends for the school district, in the form of vending sales, corporate sponsorships, and corporate advertising revenues. How would you vote? What if the measure did not ban vending machines outright, but merely prohibited the sale of certain items?

CHALLENGING ISSUES: AVOIDING OBESITY BY AVOIDING SOME BIRTHS?

Suppose in the future that it is possible to identify a genetic variation that predisposes a person to obesity. Should physicians and genetic counselors make that test available to parents as a part of routine prenatal testing? Should insurance cover it? Is there more information that you would want to make that decision? If so, what would it be?

=13=
‖ *The Business of Health Care* ‖

This chapter focuses on the business of health care from an ethical perspective. The first part introduces questions about the ethical considerations that should guide health care providers and businesses, as well as the ethical considerations that should guide legal regulation of those providers and businesses. When health care delivery is understood as a business—rather than a relationship of trust between individual provider and patient—where do bioethical concerns fit? What work can they accomplish? Are bioethics to be counterbalanced by business ethics or free market ideals?

The second part focuses on the influence of financial incentives and business interests on medical treatment decisions for individual patients. Because most of health care is purchased through public or private insurance, rather than through payment directly from the patient, reimbursement arrangements can easily lead to either over- or underutilization of services. Both knowing what is the "right" amount of these services and then structuring private and public actions to achieve that amount are a continuing challenge.

Whereas the materials in the second part focus on health care delivery and financing for insured patients, we turn in the third part to the uninsured and underinsured with readings on billing and collection practices.

Then in the last two parts we address actions taken by health care providers and businesses to protect and advance their interests through mechanisms to control health care markets and to secure and protect property rights in the development, production, and sale of products related to health care, such as drugs and genetic tests.

A.   ETHICS AND THE BUSINESS OF HEALTH CARE

	Mark A. Hall, A Corporate Ethics of "Care"	
	in Health Care	
	3 Seattle J. for Soc. Justice 417 (2004)	

Health care is a uniquely personal and value-laden service that people often receive in a condition of great anxiety and vulnerability. Therefore, we hope that the corporations that deliver this service care for us personally, rather than see us only as a means to make money. Many people will initially react that a "caring corporation" is an oxymoron, so let me begin by defining what I think that this might mean. I take the term "care" to mean a feeling or attitude rather than an action. Thus, care does not simply mean the mechanistic aspects of delivering medical services as in the phrase, "health care delivery system." Instead, it means delivering health care with a caring attitude—as in the contrast between "caring and curing." In short, the question is whether health care corporations can be expected to have a genuine concern for the well-being of their customers and communities, rather than treating health care purely as a business transaction.

Care matters because in every corporate environment, various mechanisms of legal oversight exist to protect against opportunistic behavior and to promote social objectives. Legal controls, however, invite corporations to follow only the letter and not the spirit of the law and to follow the letter of the law only so far as it is likely to be enforced. Rather than trying to police all possible forms and instances of circumvention, it would be more efficient to foster a corporate culture or climate that motivates behavior consistent with public policy. This analytical point is one of the major insights of the social norms branch of legal scholarship. People refrain from littering and help out their neighbors in need not because the law requires it, but in response to social norms. The same can be true for corporations. A culture of caring about the right set of goals and outcomes can be a more powerful and systemic influence on corporate behavior and attitudes than any overtly regulatory regime.

In medicine there are strong reasons to value an ethic of caring. The vulnerability of patients and the suffering caused by illness create imperative moral conditions that compel an ethic of compassion. Traditionally, this morality has been fostered through the professional ethics that apply to individual physicians and nurses. Now that health care delivery has become "corporatized," we must also look to institutions for ethical attributes of caring. We might have good reasons to be deeply skeptical of whether this is feasible for reasons captured in the historical prohibition of the "corporate practice of medicine." In prior eras, it was thought that the ethical and compassionate practice of medicine was inherently incompatible with the profit orientation and bureaucratic rationality of corporations, which, in the words of one court, "tend to debase" the ethics of the profession. Despite these concerns, however, we have come to accept the necessity, or at least the inevitability, of the corporate dominance of health care delivery. Therefore, we desperately hope that the basic rationale for the corporate practice prohibition is wrong and hope that health care corporations can foster an ethic of caring.

[After explaining the limited importance of "for-profit" vs. "nonprofit" status and ethics codes for promoting a caring culture, Hall suggests measuring and reporting care, as laid out in the following sections.–EDS.]

[T]aking a clue from the field of health care quality measurement, I propose that the best way to foster a caring culture is by objectively measuring and reporting the ultimate outcome in which we are interested. If caring could be measured in some fashion, then corporations could be rated and compared based upon their cultures of caring. Measuring care would provide managers with a metric upon which they could focus. This would make it more feasible for managers to care about caring and to ultimately do something about it. My proposal goes beyond others, however, by using measures of caring as more than a tool for strictly internal management. Thus, I propose making caring a visible basis for comparison among competing organizations.

Because health care institutions are so acutely conscious of their reputations, comparing corporations based on their cultures for caring has the potential to work wonders. This acute sensitivity to corporate reputations creates a unique opportunity to use market mechanisms to promote socially desired goals. Although this strategy works reasonably well for reputations regarding the quality of care, the market forces bearing on reputations for caring are imperfect. Hospitals, for instance, compete primarily for physicians, not directly for patients. Moreover, there are reasons to suppose that physicians are imperfect agents for a patient's desire to have compassionate nurses. Generally speaking, physicians care more about efficiency and technical competency than about the emotive aspects of a patient's experience. Therefore, hospitals that promote themselves based on the caring quality of their nursing staff will receive only limited rewards for their efforts. Instead, competitive pressures bearing on hospitals may tend to promote less, rather than more, caring by the nursing staff.

This lack of market incentive to foster a reputation for caring is similar to other kinds of market defects that health economists have noted restrict information about the quality of products or services. The solution for health care is the same as the solution for consumer products—to encourage or to require better production and dissemination of information about the characteristic of interest. In the health care sector, there are numerous points of leverage for amplifying or steering market forces in more socially desired directions. For example, mechanisms of accreditation, standards for tax exemption, conditions for participation in Medicare, and direct regulation of hospitals and health insurers would all amplify and steer the market in a more socially conscious direction.

One example of how these mechanisms have been used to address the general corporate ethos relates to the amorphous concept of "community benefit" under charitable tax exemption laws. In the 1980s, the tax exempt status of nonprofit hospitals came under attack because of the low level of true charity care that they were delivering beyond merely absorbing the bad debts and contractual discounts that all hospitals incur. To fortify the argument that hospitals deserve an exemption for community benefits other than charity care, several leaders in the voluntary hospital sector formulated an inventory of community benefits that served as a template for what nonprofit hospitals should be doing in areas such as public education, community representation on the board of trustees, and maintaining a full range of services. This helped to focus the attention of nonprofit managers on advancing these dimensions of community orientation.

Doing something similar for the amorphous concept of caring might create a strong incentive for managers to foster a culture of caring. After all, no health care institution wants to be known as uncaring or as less caring than its competitors. We see this strategy already working with the widespread use of satisfaction measures; it is now commonplace to receive satisfaction surveys from all sorts of providers both within and outside of health care. Purchasers, managers, and regulators have all found that measuring and reporting satisfaction is a strong motivator to improve service quality.

The same can be true for constructs as subjective and interpersonal as caring. Questions about caring are already often part of satisfaction surveys. They are also a part of a validated research tool to measure the ethical climate of corporations. A research team at Wake Forest University has developed several scales that rate trust in physicians and health insurers. Trust is an ethical and interpersonal construct that is closely akin to caring, and several of the items in these trust scales refer specifically to caring. These measures have been tested, validated, and have been shown to have a strong psychometric reliability; they are now being widely used by institutions and physician groups to evaluate and to improve relationships with patients.

The next step would be to further develop and standardize the components of the measures that refer to caring. Among other tasks, this would require agreeing on what the principal objects of caring should be for different types of health care organizations. For instance, these organizations might be expected to care not only about their customers but also about their communities. For each of these points of reference, it is necessary to make a decision about what these organizations should be expected to care about. These will be difficult issues to resolve, but if a general consensus can be reached, then the technical task of reducing these goals to a practical survey measure can be readily accomplished. Moreover, health care organizations could be encouraged or required by various means to report their caring scores. . . .

> ## Joshua E. Perry, Physician-Owned Specialty Hospitals and the Patient Protection and Affordable Care Act: Health Care Reform at the Intersection of Law and Ethics
> ### 49 Am. Bus. L.J. 369 (2012)

I.   ETHICS AND THE BUSINESS OF MEDICINE

The delivery of health care is, "at its roots, a helping enterprise"—a business permeated with the concept of care—that has historically been characterized by individual and corporate commitments to serving the best interests of others, not a reductionist pursuit of profit maximization driven by advertising campaigns, efforts to increase sales, and strategies for capturing market share. It was this more expansive view of the health care business as a helping profession with its clinical boundaries governed by a robust ethical tradition that led

Troyen Brennan to argue nearly twenty years ago that the goal of health policy should be "moral consistency between the realm of clinical interventions and access to the institutions that provide them."

II. PHYSICIAN-OWNED SPECIALTY HOSPITALS

Physician-owned specialty hospitals are health care delivery businesses that are either partially or fully owned by physician-investors who limit the services provided to three primary specialties: cardiac, orthopedic, or other surgical procedures. Limiting their practice to these high-profit-margin services has resulted in health care delivery centers that constitute many successful businesses providing tens of thousands of jobs, millions of dollars in state and federal tax revenues—which nonprofit general hospitals do not pay—and hundreds of millions of dollars in cumulative payroll. However, these specialty hospitals treat a lower percentage of severely ill patients than do their general hospital competitors, suggesting that these physician-owned specialty hospitals either intentionally skim the cream off the top of the patient population or intentionally limit their technological and personnel capacity so they are equipped to treat only the healthiest and least costly sector of cardiac, orthopedic, or surgical patients. Moreover, due to differences in staffing levels, employee compensation, and the use of single-occupancy rooms, physician-owned facilities have higher costs than do general hospitals and result in higher utilization rates and greater requests for Medicare reimbursement. Nonetheless, for their physician-owners, who have seen personal incomes decline over the last decade, these investments offer a practice environment where MDs—not MBAs—control administrative decisions that impact patient care and produce increased earning opportunities.

Ron Winslow's investigation of the Heart Hospital of New Mexico, which opened in 1999, offers an illustration of conflicts created by physician-owned specialty hospitals. At its inception, local cardiologists owned forty-one percent of Heart Hospital, a stand-alone cardiac center, in partnership with MedCath Inc., a publicly traded nationwide operator of cardiovascular clinics. . . .

Two primary reasons reportedly prompted the cardiac physician-investors to invest in the upstart hospital. First, during the preceding decade they had seen their income erode dramatically. From 1989 to 1999, the Medicare reimbursement fee for a common cardiac diagnostic procedure had been reduced by sixty-two percent, while the fee for triple-bypass surgery had been cut by thirty-nine percent. Meanwhile, hospitals during the same decade had begun retaining a greater percentage of what Medicare paid. For example, in 1989, hospitals kept approximately sixty percent of the Medicare reimbursement for bypass surgery, with the remainder passing through to the heart surgeon. In 1999, however, general hospitals were keeping as much as eighty-five percent, with the remainder being paid to the surgeon. The second motivating factor for those physicians who would invest in and practice at Heart Hospital was purported to be control. The emergence of managed care in the 1970s had, by the mid-1990s, left physicians and surgeons weary of having their judgment challenged by "cost-obsessed hospital and managed-care bureaucrats." It is reasonable to infer that when MedCath invited cardiologists to invest in and practice at Heart Hospital, the entrepreneurial opportunity presented a solution both to the problem of declining incomes and to the cardiologists' administrative frustration over bureaucratic second-guessing and other real or perceived practice inefficiencies.

... Neither the climate that fueled the frustration nor the response of physician-investors was consistent with the hallmarks of ethical health policy Brennan seems to have in mind when he describes "providers [who are] actively cognizant of the nature of their activities (as part of a group process) and the collective impact of their individual actions." Deeper analysis of the physician-owned specialty hospital industry reveals costs to both the system of health care delivery and the individual patient.

A.   Systematic Costs

... A 2005 MedPAC [Medicare Payment Advisory Commission] report concluded that physician-owned specialty hospitals obtain most of their patients by taking market share away from community hospitals. Moreover, the report revealed that physician-owned specialty hospitals treat a higher percentage of patients who are less sick, and therefore less costly and more profitable, than patients receiving similar treatments at general hospitals. Coupled with the finding that most specialty hospitals treat few, if any, Medicaid patients, the MedPAC report speculated that if the specialty hospital industry were to continue to grow without additional regulation, community hospitals attempting to compete with specialty hospitals could find their profits adversely impacted, which could have a negative ripple effect on their ability to provide charity care and other less financially rewarding medical services. MedPAC's data analysis also disputed the specialty hospitals' claim that, through specialization, they were able to have lower overall costs than full-service community hospitals. Likewise, a 2005 report issued by Michael Leavitt, Secretary of the Department of Health and Human Services (HHS), also found that specialty hospitals generally treat a less-sick patient population with "lower severity levels."

B.   Patient Costs

... In January 2008, HHS's Office of Inspector General (OIG) issued a report on physician-owned specialty hospitals and their ability to manage medical emergencies. Out of the 109 specialty hospitals the OIG reviewed, only fifty-five percent had an emergency department. Of those, more than half were equipped with only one emergency bed. Additionally, while ninety-three percent of the physician-owned specialty hospitals were found to have nurses on duty and physicians on call twenty-four hours a day, seven hospitals failed to meet the Conditions of Participation (CoP) promulgated by the CMS [Centers for Medicare & Medicaid Services]. Given that so many of the physician-owned specialty hospitals lack the capacity to offer complete, on-site emergency services or the availability of trained personnel, it is not surprising that the OIG report found that sixty-six percent of these facilities instruct their staff to dial 9-1-1 as an official component of their medical emergency response protocol.

The use of 9-1-1 "to obtain medical assistance to stabilize a patient" seemingly constitutes a violation of the CMS's CoP, which state that a hospital receiving Medicare funds may not rely on 9-1-1 emergency services as a substitute for its own emergency services. Moreover, the OIG's investigation revealed that twenty-two percent of all physician-owned specialty hospitals do not even have a policy or protocol in place that addresses patient emergencies, including appropriate use of response equipment, initial life-saving treatment, or transfer of patients to full-service hospitals. This too constitutes a violation of the CMS's CoP. . . .

III.   A CASE STUDY FOR ETHICAL HEALTH CARE POLICY

Legislative efforts addressing the constellation of issues raised by physician-owned specialty hospitals can be traced to the Medicare antifraud and abuse legislation of the 1970s and early 1980s that attempted to eliminate perverse incentives that were contributing to overutilization of health care services and concomitant rising costs.

. . . Congress soon passed the "Ethics in Patient Referrals Act," which had been sponsored by U.S. Representative Fortney H. (Pete) Stark and primarily targeted self-referrals to facilities furnishing clinical laboratory services. The reforms were expanded in 1993 to cover self-referrals to facilities offering additional health services, including inpatient and outpatient hospital services.

Together, these efforts to prohibit physician self-referral would become more widely known as the Stark Laws. Originally intended to prevent physicians from making patient referrals to any institution in which the physician enjoyed any financial connection, legislative compromises resulted in the insertion of an exception that would permit physicians to own an interest in a general facility if the "financial interest was in the entire hospital and not merely in a distinct part or department of the hospital." Such compromise was possible because it was assumed by Congress that physicians with an ownership interest in a "whole hospital"—offering a diversity of services—would be less likely to have clouded judgment due to the dilution of potential economic gains in the context of a full-service, general hospital. This exception notwithstanding, the Stark Laws were clear in their prohibition against physicians with an ownership interest in a distinct hospital subdivision referring their Medicare patients to that subdivision.

By capitalizing on the "whole hospital exception" in the Stark Laws—laws that otherwise were clear in their prohibition of similar physician self-referral schemes—the number of physician-owned specialty hospitals, often similar in size and scope to hospital departments, tripled to 100 between 1990 and 2003. . . .

On March 23, 2010, President Barack Obama signed into law the PPACA, which includes section 6001, "Limitation on Medicare Exception to the Prohibition on Certain Physician Referrals for Hospitals." "[F]erociously complex," the 2000-page systematic health care overhaul was heralded as "the most significant piece of domestic legislation to emerge from Washington in decades." Although the details are described below, section 6001 essentially amends the Social Security Act to prohibit new or expanded physician-owned specialty hospitals from filing Medicare claims if a financial relationship exists between the referring physician and the hospital receiving the government reimbursement. For advocates of physician-owned specialty hospitals, however, the "illogical and unfortunate" legislation was predicted to "virtually destroy over 60 hospitals" that were currently under development and stifle any future growth of those facilities already in existence. Predictably, interested parties opposed to physician-owned specialty hospitals viewed section 6001 as "a good [law] that will stem the tide of an entrepreneurial approach to medicine that is potentially fatal."

A.   What Does Section 6001 Do?

Section 6001 of the PPACA amends section 1877 of the Social Security Act—that is, the Stark Laws—in ways that impact both physician-owned specialty hospitals already in existence, as well as those under development. For those physician-owned specialty hospitals currently operating with Medicare certification, the new law prohibits increases to the number of operating rooms, procedure rooms, and beds for which the hospital is licensed, unless narrow exceptions can be met.[1] Moreover, the legislation addresses conflict-of-interest concerns by requiring disclosures to make the operation of these facilities more transparent.

In this same spirit of transparency, the new law also requires physician-owned specialty hospitals to make available to HHS a detailed annual report on the identity of investors and the nature and extent of all investment terms. Additionally, these facilities will have to disclose all ownership and investment interests to specific patients, as well as post general disclosure notices on websites and public advertising alerting the public to the hospital's status as physician-owned.

Finally, the reforms address concerns related to the legitimacy of a physician's investment and patient safety. In a subsection entitled "Ensuring bona fide investment," the legislation curbs the ability of these facilities to expand the pool of physician-investors, while also explicitly forbidding an array of fraudulent investment terms and conditions. The law addresses safety by requiring all physician-owned specialty hospitals without twenty-four-hour onsite physicians to secure signed consent from patients. Moreover, physician-owned specialty hospitals relying on dialing 9-1-1 emergency services supplied by other, full-service area hospitals will have to provide baseline stabilization treatments and have the capacity to transfer patients to full-service hospitals without reliance upon 9-1-1 emergency transfer services.

C.   In What Ways Does the Reform Legislation Reflect Ethical Health Care Policy?

1.   Nonmaleficence

Considered narrowly, the medical ethics mandate to "do no harm" applies to the treatment an individual physician provides for an individual patient at the bedside. Yet, more broadly applied, the principle can be used to interrogate the

---

1. Perry later details that, "Going forward, any physician-owned specialty hospital seeking to expand its capacity will have to match or outpace the percentages of Medicaid patients being treated at non-physician-owned facilities." 49 Am Bus. L. J. at 410.–Eds.

systems and institutions that constitute the health care delivery mechanisms throughout society and to determine whether a systematic harm is being perpetrated. Phrased more positively, a concern for beneficence would argue for a more concerted effort by policy makers to promote Brennan's conception of the traditional altruistic commitment between a physician and her patient both in light of individual patients and the broader good of all potential patients. In the context of physician-owned specialty hospitals—or any component of the health care system—two questions are operative. First, are individual patients being harmed? Second, are broader, perhaps less immediately recognizable, harms being done to the health care system and the professionals who inhabit it? . . .

2.   Conflicts of Interest

In addition to the ethical concerns over unnecessary harms that threaten individual patients, an entire class of non-Medicare-eligible patients, and full-service hospitals, another fundamental ethical concern addressed by the new legislation is the issue that Brennan frames as systematic resource limitations in the allocation of services, which manifests in this context as a physician's conflicting pecuniary interests. This conflict of interest, which is to a certain extent unavoidable, has been at the heart of medical ethics and professionalism norms throughout the history of health care, especially in the United States, where the entrepreneurial, money-making potential of health care delivery has been well-documented. At some level, a conflict will always exist between a physician's need for personal income and the patient's need for medical treatment. Thus, the question may simply boil down to whether physician-owned specialty hospitals exacerbate or reduce this inherent challenge to the "altruism of healing." On May 17, 2006, in a Senate Finance Committee hearing considering the issue of physician-owned specialty hospitals, Senator Charles Grassley pondered the fundamental questions of "whether [physician-owned specialty hospitals] serve the best interest of the patients being treated at them, or if they are serving the best interests of the physicians who own and operate them."

Appropriating an ethical health care policy framework might reformulate the question to ask specifically, do institutions promote a patient-centered commitment that reinforces the physician's ethical duty? Or do these facilities only further confuse the physician's judgment when the physician is making determinations about treatments and tests that may or may not be necessary?

[S]ome measure of conflicting financial interest is unavoidable. Physicians must eat. Staff must be paid. Medical school loans are a reality. Yet, physician-owned specialty hospitals unnecessarily create an additional layer of pecuniary conflict that policy makers, guided by the ethical concerns raised in this article, could reasonably decide to ban retroactively and completely, consistent with the Stark legislation's original intent, which was to prevent physicians from referring Medicare patients to any institutions in which they had a financial connection.

3.   Bona Fide, Transparent Ownership

Proponents of physician-owned specialty hospitals are tireless in claiming that their entrepreneurial efforts are consistent with the best ideals of a competitive, free-market environment that rewards efficiency and innovation. Additionally, their insistence that a motivation beyond profit taking can be found in a good-faith desire for both greater physician autonomy and freedom from large hospital and conglomerate bureaucracies is compelling. Indeed, it is completely reasonable for physicians to desire professional freedom from the frustrations of administrative hassles and clinical empowerment to exercise control and develop specific competencies over those practice dynamics that will result in the highest levels of patient care. The desire to "own" their own practice, in the sense of controlling it, seems both reasonable and consistent with enduring ethical concerns over individual autonomy and self-determination on the part of professional health care providers. And yet, such individual interests are in tension with Brennan's vision of a "healing community" that recognizes the interconnected and collective impact of medical practice.

Indeed, American medicine's history of kickback deals and fiscally reckless self-referral practices renders it difficult to see only this silver lining of hospital ownership that proponents proffer. Copious amounts of data confirm that financial interests influence medical decision making. Hence, those provisions of section 6001 designed to monitor whether physician-ownership deals will indeed be "bona fide investments" appear to be justified by the concerns of a health care policy guided by ethical considerations.

CONCLUSION

"Ethics in its broadest sense," Professor Larry Churchill observes, "concerns how we live and the choices we make." Brought to bear in the context of practical policy deliberations, such normative reflections facilitate review of the array of values in play and the commitments of the various participants. Contemplation of ethical concerns, ultimately, makes it possible to understand more fully the operative principles underlying stakeholders' positions, as well as their implications and likely consequences if adopted.

NOTES AND QUESTIONS

1. *Getting corporations to care.* Do you agree with Mark Hall that it is desirable to have health care corporations that care about their customers and communities? If it is desirable, then why won't market forces produce such corporate cultures? What roles might the law play in fostering such values?

2. *Litigation over PPACA's section 6001.* In 2010, the Physician Hospitals of America, a trade association, together with a physician-owned hospital, sued DHHS seeking to enjoin implementation and enforcement of section 6001 on the grounds that the new law violated their due process and equal protection rights under the Fifth Amendment of the Constitution. Physician Hospitals of America v. Sebelius, 781 F.Supp.2d 431 (2011). The court granted the government's summary judgment motion, determining that the law survived rational basis review, did not result in an unconstitutional, retroactive taking, and was not void for vagueness. The district court's decision was subsequently vacated on the grounds that it lacked subject-matter jurisdiction because plaintiffs

were required first to proceed with available administrative procedures. 691 F.3d 649 (5th Cir. 2012). In the district court, the Secretary of DHHS offered four justifications for Section 6001: "(1) physician ownership leads to over-utilization of services, (2) physician ownership results in greater healthcare expenditures, (3) referral patterns undermine public and community hospi-tals, which provide uncompensated care and other services not typically offered by POHs [physician-owned hospitals], and (4) POHs provide inade-quate emergency care."

Drawing on the work of Joshua Perry, supra, if you were to explain these justifications in ethical terms, what would that explanation look like (e.g., does the charge of overutilization of services suggest problems of fairness, harms to individuals, or something else)? How might you advance an ethical argument for the *plaintiffs'* position?

3. *Business ethics and health care organizations.* Patricia H. Werhane, an expert in business and professional ethics, argues that Milton Friedman's edict on the social responsibility of business is wrong, but can be useful none-theless in thinking about the ethics of health care organization. Patricia H. Werhane, Business Ethics, Organization Ethics, and Systems Ethics for Health Care, in N. Bowie, ed., Blackwell Guide to Business Ethics (2002). Here is Friedman's edict:

> There is one and only one social responsibility of business—to use its resources and engage in activities designed to increase its profits so long as it stays within the rules of the game, which is to say, engages in open and free competition without deception or fraud.

Id.

Under this edict, "managers' first duties and fiduciary duties are to owners or shareholders." Id. According to Werhane, "Friedman's depiction of the rela-tionship between ethics and business has been influential in changing the model of contemporary healthcare delivery. . . . Yet there are a number of dif-ficulties with this argument even as it applies to the practice of commerce or business, and even greater difficulties when applied without qualification to healthcare management and delivery." Id.

One of these difficulties is the fact that many of the most successful for-profit business appear to operate under a different principle. Werhane discusses the conclusions of scholars studying "visionary companies"—companies that are considered "the premier organization in their industries, as being widely admired by their peers, and as having a long track record of making a significant impact on the world around them." Id. (citing J. Collins & J. Porras, Built to Last (1994)). According to Collins and Porras:

> Contrary to business school doctrine, "maximizing shareholder wealth" or "profit maximization" has not been the dominant driving force or primary objective through the history of the visionary companies. Visionary companies pursue a cluster of objectives, of which making money is only one—and not necessarily the primary one. Yes, they seek profits, but they are equally guided by a core ideology—core values and a sense of purpose beyond just making money. Yet, paradoxically, the visionary companies make more money than the more purely profit-driven comparison companies.

Id. (citing J. Collins & J. Porras, Built to Last (1994)). Drawing on these conclusions, Werhane suggests that Friedman's edict be rewritten for health care organizations to read:

> There is one and only one social responsibility of any healthcare organization: to use its professional and economic resources and engage in activities designed to treat and improve the health of its patient populations so long as it stays within the rules of game.

Id. What do you think?

CHALLENGING ISSUES: CAN PHARMA CARE?

Consider the following real-life situation from several decades ago.

In 1978, Dr. P. Roy Vagelos, then head of the Merck research labs, received a provocative memorandum from a senior researcher in parasitology, Dr. William C. Campbell. Dr. Campbell had made an intriguing observation while working with ivermectin, a new antiparasitic compound under investigation for use in animals.

According to scholars writing about the decision faced by the Merck executive,

> Campbell thought that ivermectin might be the answer to a disease called river blindness that plagued millions in the Third World. But to find out if Campbell's hypothesis had merit, Merck would have to spend millions of dollars to develop the right formulation for human use and to conduct the field trials in the most remote parts of the world. Even if these efforts produced an effective and safe drug, virtually all of those afflicted with river blindness could not afford to buy it. Vagelos, originally a university researcher but by then a Merck executive, had to decide whether to invest in research for a drug that, even if successful, might never pay for itself.

Thomas Donaldson & Patricia H. Werhane, Ethical Issues in Business: A Philosophical Approach (8th ed. 2008) (citing The Business Enterprise Trust (1991)).

Consider these additional facts, also provided by Donaldson and Werhane:

> *The disease:* River blindness is caused by a parasitic worm carried on a fly that breeds along fast-flowing rivers in parts of Africa, the Middle East, and Latin America. Those affected by the parasite suffer from extreme itching and skin infections and, when the worms eventually invade the eyes, blindness. In 1978, approximately 340,000 people were blind because of the disease, and about 18 million people were infected, although with varying degrees of symptom severity. Two different drugs were currently known to kill the parasite, but with serious accompanying side effects.
>
> *The company:* Merck & Co., Inc. was founded in Germany in the late 1600s. In 1978, it was an American company and one of the largest pharmaceutical companies in the world, employing over 28,000 people. The company "spent a great deal of money on research because it knew that its success ten and twenty years in the future critically depended upon present investments. The company deliberately fashioned a corporate culture to nurture the most creative, fruitful research. Merck scientists were among the best-paid in the industry, and were

given great latitude to pursue intriguing leads." Id. The words of George W. Merck, son of the company's founder, "formed the basis of Merck's overall corporate philosophy." Id. He said, "We try never to forget that medicine is for the people. It is not for the profits. The profits follow, and if we have remembered that, they have never failed to appear. The better we have remembered it, the larger they have been." Id.

The discovery: Ivermectin had recently been proved to be a powerful compound to treat parasites in animals, and Merck was successfully pursuing approvals for its use as a veterinary drug. Whether it would be possible to formulate the drug for safe human use, however, was uncertain. Moreover, development of the drug would be costly, had little potential to make money for the company, and carried some risks. Among the risks were that the discovery of adverse health effects in human trials could hurt reception of the drug for animal use, and that a black market in the human drug, if ultimately developed and distributed in developing countries, would undercut sales of the veterinary drug.

Suppose the decision whether Merck should proceed in developing ivermectin to combat river blindness in humans is left up to Dr. Vagelos. What do you think he should decide? Why?

Do you think law should influence decisions of this type and, if so, how?

B. INCENTIVIZING AND CONTROLLING MEDICAL TREATMENT DECISIONS

During the last half-century, the essential goals of providing health care have not changed, but the practical aspects of providing health care have changed due to technological developments and to shifts in the socioeconomic organization of health care delivery.

Physicians rely more on tests and less on clinical examinations than they did a half-century ago. They are more likely to work in specialties and subspecialties and thus less likely to have long-term relationships with their patients or to know their patients' families. And they are much more likely to look to third parties for compensation than was the case five decades ago. Whereas doctors were once compared with other comforters of body and soul (including faith healers, psychologists, and clergy), they are now compared as well with engineers and plumbers. Comparison of a doctor's accuracy and efficiency is not only to other doctors, but to machines. Atul Gawande reports, for instance, that a first-rate Swedish cardiologist was far less proficient (and more expensive) than a computer at reading electrocardiograms. Atul Gawande, Complications: A Surgeon's Notes on an Imperfect Science (2002).

Writing in 1995, Marc Rodwin points to three changes in medical practice that challenge the idea that physicians are and can be fiduciaries for patients: "(1) a shift in influence over doctors from patients to other groups; (2) a shift in authority from doctors to managed care organizations; and (3) a growing concern with groups rather than individuals." Marc A. Rodwin, Strains in the Fiduciary Metaphor: Divided Physician Loyalties and Obligations in a Changing

Health Care System, 21 Am. J.L. and Med. 241, 253–254 (1995). These changes are still present and evolving. Rodwin continues:

> Groups other than patients now have growing influence over physicians. Integrated health care systems and managed care organizations often control the flow of patients to doctors. Third-party payers and managed care organizations control the flow of payments to physicians and set policies on what services are covered, rates of reimbursement, and the standard of care. Quality reviewers and other parties are establishing protocols that set parameters that define the work of doctors. For-profit hospitals need to promote a return for their shareholders and not-for-profit hospitals, which have to compete with for-profit hospitals, are often forced to adopt similar financial policies. Both are beginning to use economic criteria to assess the performance of physicians and decide whether to maintain or expand their hospital privileges. These trends make it easier for parties other than patients to hold doctors accountable to their interests and in the process weaken accountability to patients.

Id.

1.   Managed Care

Physicians have always faced conflicts of interest in their work. However, the character and breadth of the conflicts have altered in the last several decades as a fee-for-service system has been largely replaced by one involving various forms of managed care. Under the fee-for-service system, physicians' remuneration increased as they did *more* procedures and provided *more* treatment to patients. Within the world of managed care, physician compensation is more likely to increase as fewer procedures are ordered and fewer treatments are rendered to patients. As a consequence, doctors often feel themselves caught between the demands of payers and the demands of healing.

The following readings describe some of the more prominent features of managed care during its heyday of the 1980s and 1990s. They also describe the managed care "backlash" from physicians, patients, media, and ultimately state legislatures. Much of this backlash originated from a perception that many of the practices of managed care organizations were unethical.

a.   Bioethical and Social Approaches

Dionne Koller Fine, Physician Liability and Managed Care: A Philosophical Perspective
19 Ga. St. U. L. Rev. 641, 647–649,
662–663, 665–666 (2003)

Managed care attempts to control health care costs by controlling physician behavior and limiting patients' utilization of services through a variety of techniques. Therefore the term managed care "can be used to include virtually any financing arrangement where there is third-party management or supervision that attempts in some structured way to oversee quality and, particularly, the costs of services delivered to the plan's beneficiaries." Courts have noted that MCOs [managed care organizations] often wear two hats, providing administrative support for an insurance plan, including making determinations of eligibility or coverage, and acting "as an arranger and provider of medical treatment." Therefore, MCOs integrate financing and delivery of health care. Managed care encompasses many different types of health care delivery structures, including Health Maintenance Organizations (HMOs), Preferred Provider Organizations (PPOs), and Independent Practice Associations (IPAs). The principles underlying the different managed care structures, however, are the same.

MCOs use many techniques to force physicians and patients to consider the costs of care. For instance, MCOs often require preauthorization for certain services, restrict access to specialists, deny payment for services provided outside of their provider "network," and restrict coverage for prescription drugs. Many MCOs pay physicians on a capitated basis, whereby physicians agree to receive a fixed monthly fee per enrolled patient from the MCO, regardless of what services patients ultimately need and receive. MCOs also frequently offer participating physicians bonus incentives tied to certain utilization levels.

One of an MCO's primary cost containment tools is utilization review, which "is designed to evaluate the medical necessity and appropriateness of health services from the payer's perspective, in light of norms of acceptable practice." Utilization review is "based on two assumptions: that there are wide variations in the use of many medical services; and that careful review of medical care can eliminate wasteful, unnecessary care or harmful care." It mainly consists of prior review, before services are delivered, and concurrent review and case management. Prior review includes "pre-admission review" before hospitalization for elective procedures, "admission review" for emergency admissions, review during hospital admission to determine the length of stay, and "pre-procedure review" to determine the appropriateness of certain recommended procedures. In addition to these techniques for standard plan participants, MCOs have case managers who closely monitor treatment for high-cost plan members suffering from costly or chronic conditions. . . .

The primary ethical objection to managed care is that the cost-containment strategies that MCOs commonly employ alter the traditional physician–patient relationship. Critics assert that physicians can no longer exclusively act as the patient's advocate and consider the patient's needs without regard to considerations of cost. Because of the structure of many MCO–physician contracts, physicians' incomes are put in conflict with the well-being of their patients. Critics also assert that MCOs induce physicians to deny necessary treatment, unlike the fee-for-service model. Accordingly, MCOs force physicians to ration care at the bedside, a role critics point out is unethical. An additional ethical problem stems from the fact that MCOs are for-profit enterprises. "These institutions have conflicting roles in their attempt to function both as traditional businesses, which have financial obligations to shareholders, and as medical entities, which have duties to uphold the best interests of patients." The emphasis on the bottom line provides a strong incentive for such companies to enroll only healthy participants, who are likely to have lower health care costs, and avoid enrolling chronically ill or disabled individuals. Commentators refer to this incentive as "cream skimming," and it raises significant issues regarding health care coverage options for the most vulnerable members of society. Additionally, MCOs lack organizational ethics that would draw from work that has been done in corporate ethics. As MCOs continue to grow, there must be some investigation and development of organizational ethics in light of the tension between the MCO's for-profit status and the patient-centered ethic of medicine. . . .

. . . Managed care fundamentally changes a physician's obligations and incentives with respect to providing health care and also puts in direct conflict the physician's traditional ethical and legal obligations toward her patient and the physician's obligation to control health care costs. . . .

Traditional notions of fidelity to patients, reflected in medical ethics as well as the law, require physicians to promote their patients' interests above all others. Yet the economics of health care make this requirement unrealistic. This long-standing indifference to the cost of health care is now untenable because it requires the physician to deliver care with resources that he does not control.

> [A] particular medical morality has developed. The physician is duty bound to treat the patient with greatest respect. The physician must maintain a loyalty to the patient and engender the patient's trust. The patient must "come first" even if this requires some self-effacement and sacrifice on the part of the physician. . . . Other concerns should not intrude on this relationship. The moral code of beneficence works best if it is isolated from the usual concerns of the liberal state, especially the competitive market.[155]

The law reinforces this isolation of the medical profession and its ethics from the consequences of the costs of the care it delivers. The result is that the law exposes the physician to potential liability for "failing to do the impossible."

In summary, the general policy problem stems from the fact that the law with respect to physician liability does not fully account for changes that have arisen as a result of the change from fee-for-service medicine to managed health care. This conflict takes on greater importance because the physician is not simply put in an ethical dilemma by managed health care. She faces potential legal liability and severe economic harm.

> ## Elizabeth A. Pendo, Images of Health Insurance in Popular Film: The Dissolving Critique
> ### 37 J. Health L. 267 (2004)

There's nothing more thrilling than nailing an insurance company!
—Deck Shifflet, *The Rainmaker*

Hollywood has a new villain—the private health-insurance system. Viewers of the 1997 film *As Good As it Gets* probably remember the profane outburst of Helen Hunt's character describing her private insurance coverage—a health maintenance organization (HMO)—and its failure to provide appropriate medical treatment for her sick child. One probably also remembers that the audience cheered. The scene, viewed by millions, attracted an extraordinary amount of attention. Even President Clinton referred to the scene in a speech presenting

---

155. Troyen Brennan, *Just Doctoring: Medical Ethics in the Liberal State*, 48 (1991).

the Patient's Bill of Rights in 1998, joking that the film is "going to be disqualified for an Academy Award because it's too close to real life."

Three additional films show that the tremendous audience response to this scene was not a fluke. They signal a new and unexplored focus on private health insurance, now dominated by managed care and its relationship to healthcare, in contemporary mainstream films. Sidney Lumet's *Critical Care,* Francis Ford Coppola's *The Rainmaker,* and Nick Cassavetes's *John Q* each center on negative and disturbing images of modern insurance companies from the perspective of a doctor, a lawyer, and a parent. Each portrays the inner workings of these companies and the victimization of patients and their families as a result of insurer policies and practices. The narratives also reflect common public perceptions about private health insurance, such as: the link between lack of coverage and lack of access to care, including life-saving care; the perverse and distorting effect of certain managed care reimbursement arrangements on treatment decisions; and the loss of adequate health coverage for workers and their families.

. . . Prior to these films, no mainstream film villanized the health-insurance industry as a central element of the plot. Why did private health insurers emerge as villains in popular films in the late 1990s? Each of these films offers a sharp critique of the current state of health insurance and its relationship to healthcare; but is the system really failing in the ways these films suggest? If so, what can we learn from the solutions these films offer?

. . . Despite inaccuracies and omissions, which tend to capitalize on public mistrust and misperceptions, the premises raised by the films have significant factual support. There is a link between lack of coverage and lack of access to care; reimbursement arrangements may distort treatment decisions, and certainly are believed to do so; and workers and their families are losing adequate health coverage. Moreover, they tell an important symbolic or emotional truth about the gross disparities between the treatment of the uninsured and the insured, even though the specifics of each of the stories may not be complete or factually true.

These films capture the intensity of the managed care backlash at its height, and dramatize certain truths—symbolic or emotional, if not always literal—about the consumer experience of managed care. A close reading reveals that despite their passionately critical tone, these films actually put forward solutions that are highly individualist and conservative, rather than inclusive and systemic. Although each film appears to be a daring and defiant attack on the healthcare system and its institutions, in reality the films do not threaten the status quo in any meaningful way. Instead, the resolution of each of the narratives comes about through the actions of one individual—one good doctor, one good attorney taking one good case, and, most disturbingly, one good father with a gun—and resolves the situation of one patient.

[This critique] of these films is significant because it resonates with similar shifts in current healthcare policy, evidenced by the turn toward consumer-driven health plans. Since the first of these films was released in 1997, healthcare costs have again risen dramatically, and "we are back to health care inflation with a vengeance."

The term "consumer-driven health plan" describes a variety of different approaches to providing employee health benefits that share two common themes: the employer makes a fixed, rather than variable, dollar contribution toward the employee's health benefits; and the consumer assumes a greater degree of choice and risk in choosing and paying for healthcare. For example, under a "defined contribution" approach, instead of offering a specific health insurance plan or a choice of plans for a set annual premium, an employer provides a specific contribution that the employee can use to purchase the plan of his choice, either from a menu of options provided by the employer, or, in its most pure form, from the Yellow Pages. Any shortfall between the amount of the employer's defined contribution and the cost of the chosen health plan is borne by the employee.

Another emerging approach is the combination of a high-deductible catastrophic health insurance policy—typically $1,500 or more for an individual—with some form of tax-exempt employee spending account that the consumer can use to satisfy all or part of the deductible. It is unknown whether consumer-driven plans can control costs for employers and empower consumers to make better and more efficient choices as claimed, and initial consumer response to such plans is mixed. Notwithstanding some skepticism, many employers report that they will use more consumer-oriented strategies in healthcare benefits in the coming years.

Consumer-driven health plans tout individual choice and freedom as the solution to a variety of problems with the current system of health coverage and care. In this context, "choice" also includes individual responsibility to make the right choices in terms of price and quality and the individual obligation to bear the consequences of such choices. It remains to be seen whether consumer-driven plans will enable individual consumers to make better or more appropriate choices and whether "choice" as conceived will lead to better financial or health outcomes for consumers. Moreover, concern that consumer-driven plans will not address systemic issues such as the increasingly high cost of healthcare and the growing crisis of uninsurance and underinsurance, or whether the plans will disproportionately disadvantage the chronically ill, remain to be addressed.

Much like how the films raise the critical issues but allow the dramatic tension to dissipate into private and individualistic resolutions, the current healthcare crisis raises fundamental and systemic issues that are simply not addressed by private, nonsystemic options, such as emerging consumer-driven health plans. How do you protect yourself as a consumer in the current healthcare system? The films suggest you should have a doctor like Werner Ernst, a lawyer like Rudy Baylor, or a parent like John Archibald. Similarly, the shift toward consumer-directed health plans suggests you should simply make better choices.

NOTES AND QUESTIONS

1. *Ethical objections to managed care.*   According to Dionne Koller Fine, supra, what are the main ethical objections to managed care? How are these objections manifested in the films discussed by Elizabeth Pendo, supra? What is Pendo's criticism of the "solutions" offered by these films? How does she compare these Hollywood solutions to consumer-driven reforms?

2. *Patient Bill of Rights.*   The bill referred to in Pendo, supra, would have amended the Public Health Service Act and ERISA to provide protections to

consumers in managed care plans, such as access to specialists and emergency care and certain procedural safeguards, such as an appeals process, to address claims. Although different versions of the bill (called the Bipartisan Patient Protection Act, Senate Bill 1052 in the 2001–2002 Congress) made some progress in Congress, it ultimately failed to pass.

b. Legal Approaches

|| *Neade v. Portes* ||
739 N.E.2d 496 (Ill. 2000)

Opinion by McMorrow . . .

According to the allegations in plaintiff Therese Neade's complaint, plaintiff's husband, Anthony Neade, had a family history of heart disease, suffered from hypertension and a high cholesterol count, smoked heavily and was overweight. In 1990, at age 37, Mr. Neade began to exhibit symptoms of coronary artery blockage. Specifically, Mr. Neade experienced chest pain extending into his arm and shortness of breath. Mr. Neade's primary care physician, Steven Portes, M.D., hospitalized Mr. Neade from August 10 through August 13, 1990. During this hospitalization, Mr. Neade received several tests, including a thallium stress test and an electrocardiogram (EKG). Dr. Thomas Engel (not a party to this appeal) found the results of the tests to be normal and diagnosed Mr. Neade with hiatal hernia and/or esophagitis. Mr. Neade was thereafter discharged.

After his hospitalization, Mr. Neade visited Dr. Portes on August 17, August 28 and September 24, 1990, at the Primary Care Family Center (Primary Care), complaining of continued chest pain radiating to his neck and arm. Relying on the results of the thallium stress test and EKG taken during Mr. Neade's hospitalization, Dr. Portes informed Mr. Neade that his chest pain was not cardiac related. In October 1990, Mr. Neade returned to Dr. Portes, this time complaining of stabbing chest pain. At the request of Dr. Portes, his associate, Dr. Huang, examined Mr. Neade. Dr. Huang recommended that Mr. Neade undergo an angiogram—a test that is more specific for diagnosing coronary artery disease than a thallium stress test. Dr. Huang was employed on a part-time basis at Primary Care and had no hospital privileges. Dr. Portes, as Mr. Neade's primary care physician, was responsible for ordering any necessary hospitalization or additional tests. Despite Dr. Huang's recommendation, Dr. Portes did not authorize an angiogram for Mr. Neade.

Mr. Neade again returned to Primary Care in June 1991, complaining of chest pain. Dr. Portes asked Dr. Schlager, another part-time physician at Primary Care, to examine Mr. Neade. After this examination, Dr. Schlager also recommended that Mr. Neade undergo an angiogram, but Dr. Portes, relying on the thallium stress test, did not authorize the angiogram and advised Dr. Schlager that Mr. Neade's chest pain was not cardiac related. Subsequently, on September 16, 1991, Mr. Neade suffered a massive myocardial infarction caused by coronary artery blockage. Nine days later, Mr. Neade died.

Plaintiff's complaint alleges that Dr. Portes was the president of Primary Care and, as such, negotiated contracts with various organizations on behalf of himself and the clinic. Chicago HMO, of which Mr. Neade was a member, was one of the organizations with which Dr. Portes had contracted for the provision of services. According to plaintiff's complaint, Dr. Portes personally negotiated with Chicago HMO in 1990 and 1991 and agreed that Dr. Portes and his group would receive from Chicago HMO, inter alia, $75,000 annually. The $75,000 was to be used by Dr. Portes and his group to cover costs for patient referrals and outside medical tests prescribed for Chicago HMO members. This fund was termed the "Medical Incentive Fund."

Pursuant to the contract between Dr. Portes, Primary Care and Chicago HMO, any portion of the Medical Incentive Fund that was not used for referrals or outside tests would be divided at the end of each year between Primary Care's full time physicians and Chicago HMO, with the physicians receiving 60% of the remaining money and Chicago HMO receiving 40%. If the Medical Incentive Fund was exhausted prior to the end of the year, Dr. Portes and his group would be required to fund any additional consultant fees and outside tests. Plaintiff and Mr. Neade were not informed of this arrangement between Dr. Portes, Primary Care and Chicago HMO.

Count I of plaintiff's amended complaint alleges that Dr. Portes' reliance on the thallium stress test and EKG and his failure to authorize an angiogram constituted medical negligence which proximately resulted in Mr. Neade's death. In count I, plaintiff alleged facts regarding the Medical Incentive Fund. Count II of plaintiff's amended complaint alleges that Dr. Portes had a fiduciary duty to act in good faith and in the best interest of Mr. Neade, and that he breached that duty by refusing to authorize further testing, by refusing to refer Mr. Neade to a specialist and by refusing to disclose to the Neades Dr. Portes' financial relationship (including the Medical Incentive Fund) with Chicago HMO. Count II further alleges that Dr. Portes breached his fiduciary duty by entering into a contract with Chicago HMO that put his financial well-being in direct conflict with Mr. Neade's physical wellbeing. . . .

The primary issue in this appeal is whether plaintiff can state a cause of action for breach of fiduciary duty against Dr. Portes for Dr. Portes' failure to disclose his interest in the Medical Incentive Fund. A fiduciary relationship imposes a general duty on the fiduciary to refrain from "seeking a selfish benefit during the relationship." Illinois courts have recognized a fiduciary relationship between a physician and his patient, but Illinois courts have never recognized a cause of action for breach of fiduciary duty against a physician. . . .

Courts in other jurisdictions have dismissed claims for breach of fiduciary duty when those claims are duplicative of medical negligence claims. Such claims for breach of fiduciary duty have also been dismissed where they constitute an impermissible recasting of a medical negligence claim, even though plaintiff's complaint did not include a medical negligence claim. The appellate court in the case at bar discussed decisions from Minnesota, Colorado, Arizona and New Mexico. Each of these jurisdictions held that a breach of fiduciary duty claim is duplicative of a negligence claim. . . .

In a case involving facts similar to the case at bar, the United States Supreme Court recently refused to recognize a breach of fiduciary duty under ERISA. Pegram v. Herdrich, 530 U.S. 211, 147 L. Ed. 2d 164, 120 S. Ct. 2143 (2000). In *Herdrich,* the plaintiff, a member of the Carle Clinic Association,

P.C., Health Alliance Medical Plans, Inc., and Carle Health Insurance Management Co., Inc. (collectively Carle), an HMO, visited her primary care physician complaining of groin pain. The following week, the physician found an inflamed mass in the plaintiff's abdomen. The physician required the plaintiff to wait eight days to receive an ultrasound at a Carle facility over 50 miles away. In the interim, the plaintiff's appendix ruptured, causing peritonitis. The plaintiff filed a suit for both medical malpractice against her physician and breach of fiduciary duty against Carle. The breach of fiduciary duty claim alleged that Carle's act of providing incentives for its physicians to limit medical care and procedures constituted a breach of fiduciary duty under ERISA. The Supreme Court reversed the Seventh Circuit's determination that the plaintiff stated a cause of action for breach of fiduciary duty under ERISA. The Supreme Court noted the nature of a breach of fiduciary claim against an HMO physician. The Court stated:

> The defense of any HMO would be that its physician did not act out of financial interest but for good medical reasons, the plausibility of which would require reference to standards of reasonable and customary medical practice in like circumstances. That, of course, is the traditional standard of the common law. . . . Thus, for all practical purposes, every claim of fiduciary breach by an HMO physician making a mixed decision [about a patient's eligibility for treatment under an HMO and the appropriate treatment for the patient] would boil down to a malpractice claim, and the fiduciary standard would be nothing but the malpractice standard traditionally applied in actions against physicians.

We find the reasoning in the foregoing cases persuasive in analysis of the case at bar and decline to uphold plaintiff's breach of fiduciary duty claim. The appellate court held that because plaintiff pled different facts in support of her breach of fiduciary duty claim from those facts pled in her medical negligence claim, she stated two separate causes of action. Though many of the facts pled in counts I and II are identical, in her breach of fiduciary duty claim, plaintiff did plead the additional fact that Dr. Portes failed to disclose the Medical Incentive Fund. However, as our appellate court . . . stated, it is operative facts together with the injury that we look to in order to determine whether a cause of action is duplicative. In the case at bar, the operative fact in both counts is Dr. Portes' failure to order an angiogram for Mr. Neade. Plaintiff alleges in both counts that Mr. Neade's failure to receive an angiogram is the ultimate reason for his subsequent death. Plaintiff also alleges the same injury in both her medical negligence claim and her breach of fiduciary duty claim, namely, Mr. Neade's death and its effect on plaintiff and her family. We determine that plaintiff's breach of fiduciary duty claim is a re-presentment of her medical negligence claim.

In order to sustain a breach of fiduciary duty claim against Dr. Portes, plaintiff would have to allege, inter alia, that: (1) had she known of the Medical Incentive Fund she would have sought an opinion from another physician; (2) that the other physician would have ordered an angiogram for Mr. Neade; (3) that the angiogram would have detected Mr. Neade's heart condition; and (4) that treatment could have prevented his eventual myocardial infarction and subsequent death. In order to prove the second element, plaintiff would have been required to present expert testimony that the expert, after examining Mr. Neade and considering his history, would have ordered an angiogram.

This requirement relates to the standard of care consideration—the first prong in a traditional medical negligence claim—under which a physician is held to "the reasonable skill which a physician in good standing in the community would use." That is precisely what plaintiff must prove to support her breach of fiduciary duty claim. As the Supreme Court stated in *Herdrich,* the breach of fiduciary duty claim "would boil down to a malpractice claim, and the fiduciary standard would be nothing but the malpractice standard traditionally applied in actions against physicians." Thus, we need not recognize a new cause of action for breach of fiduciary duty when a traditional medical negligence claim sufficiently addresses the same alleged misconduct. The breach of fiduciary duty claim in the case at bar would be duplicative of the medical negligence claim. . . .

Our decision to refrain from permitting the creation of this new cause of action finds additional support in statutory law. The Illinois legislature has placed the burden of disclosing HMO incentive schemes on HMOs themselves. The Illinois General Assembly recently enacted the Managed Care Reform and Patient Rights Act (hereinafter, the Managed Care Act), which states: "Upon written request, a health care plan shall provide to enrollees a description of the financial relationships between the health care plan and any health care provider." The Managed Care Act, effective on January 1, 2000, requires that managed care organizations disclose physician incentive plans to patients. Thus, the legislature has chosen to put the burden of disclosing any financial incentive plans on the HMO, rather than on the physician. The legislature has put the burden of disclosure on the entities that create financial incentive plans and require physicians to adhere to them. If the legislature had wished to place the burden of disclosing financial incentives on physicians, it could have done so.

Moreover, the outcome that would result if we were to allow the creation of a new cause of action for breach of fiduciary duty against a physician in these circumstances may be impractical. For example, physicians often provide services for numerous patients, many of whom may be covered by different HMOs. In order to effectively disclose HMO incentives, physicians would have to remain cognizant at all times of every patient's particular HMO and that HMO's policies and procedures. . . . If we were to recognize a breach of fiduciary duty claim in the context of the case at bar, we fear the effects of such a holding may be unworkable.

Plaintiff and the appellate court rely on Current Opinions of the Council on Ethical and Judicial Affairs of the American Medical Association (AMA) in support of the argument that plaintiff can state a cause of action for breach of fiduciary duty against Dr. Portes for his failure to disclose the Medical Incentive Fund. Specifically, they rely on Opinion 8.132 entitled "Referral of Patients: Disclosure of Limitations," which states:

> Physicians must assure disclosure of any financial inducements that may tend to limit the diagnostic and therapeutic alternatives that are offered to patients or that may tend to limit patients' overall access to care. Physicians may satisfy this obligation by assuring that the managed care plan makes adequate disclosure to patients enrolled in the plan.

AMA Council on Ethical and Judicial Affairs, Current Op. 8.132 (1995–2000).

As previously noted in this opinion, the Illinois legislature determined that disclosure to patients is to be made by managed care plans. . . .

We decline to recognize a new cause of action for breach of fiduciary duty against a physician for the physician's failure to disclose HMO incentives in a suit brought against the physician for medical negligence. We hold that, under the facts in the case at bar, a breach of fiduciary duty claim is duplicative of a medical negligence claim. The injuries suffered by plaintiff as a result of Dr. Portes' medical care are sufficiently addressed by application of traditional concepts of negligence. . . .

The appellate court held that evidence of the Medical Incentive Fund may be relevant in the event that Dr. Portes testifies in the medical negligence trial. The appellate court noted that, in general, a witness may be cross-examined on issues relating to interest and bias, and found that "issues concerning Dr. Portes' financial gain go to his credibility." We agree. Therefore, we hold that evidence of the Medical Incentive Fund may be relevant if Dr. Portes testifies at trial. The relevance and admission of such evidence is for the discretion of the trial court. . . .

For the foregoing reasons, we hold that plaintiff may not state a cause of action for breach of fiduciary duty against Dr. Portes.

Dissent by HARRISON . . .

The right to assert claims for breach of fiduciary duty and negligence in the same professional malpractice action is not unfettered. When the same operative facts support a negligence count and a count for breach of fiduciary duty based on the same injury to the client, the counts are identical and the fiduciary duty count should be dismissed as duplicative. In this case, however, the negligence and breach of fiduciary duty counts asserted by plaintiff are not identical. As the appellate court correctly recognized,

> It is conceivable that a trier of fact could find both that Dr. Portes was within the standard of care and therefore not negligent in relying on the thallium stress test and the EKG in deciding that an angiogram was not necessary and also that Dr. Portes did breach his fiduciary duty in not disclosing his financial incentive arrangement and, as a proximate result thereof, Neade did not obtain a second opinion, suffered a massive coronary infarction, and died.

When my colleagues write that "the injuries suffered by plaintiff as a result of Dr. Portes' medical care are sufficiently addressed by application of traditional concepts of negligence" it is clear to me that this distinction has been lost on them. Dr. Portes' failure to disclose that he had a financial incentive to deny the test recommended by his two associates and required by plaintiff's husband triggers separate policy considerations and constitutes an independent wrong.

Physicians have professional, ethical, moral and legal obligations to provide appropriate medical care to their patients and should not allow the exercise of their medical judgment to be corrupted or controlled. At a time when HMO's are playing an ever-increasing role in how patient care is administered, these obligations are being tested as never before. In response, AMA guidelines now require physicians to assure disclosure to patients of any financial inducements that may tend to limit the diagnostic and therapeutic alternatives that are offered to patients or that may tend to limit patients' overall access to care. In addition, according to documentation and deposition testimony in this case, current standards of care require a physician to divulge his financial interests in withholding care to a patient so that the patient can make an informed decision about the quality of care he is receiving and the physician's motivation in taking care of him.

> ## Karl Kronebusch, Mark Schlesinger, & Tracy Thomas, Managed Care Regulation in the States: The Impact on Physicians' Practices and Clinical Autonomy
> ### 34 J. Health Pol. Pol'y & L. 219 (2009)

[The] "backlash" against managed care was accompanied by a wave of negative media coverage and an outpouring of state regulation. Between 1990 and 1999, the states adopted more than a thousand distinct regulatory provisions concerning managed care. Many states adopted "clusters" of regulations covering a wide range of managed care practices, and some states passed legislation in virtually every year their legislature was in session, including states with deep-rooted conservative ideologies and those with a limited managed care presence.

Most health policy analysts, however, have concluded that this state regulation was much ado about nothing. Anecdotal reports and interviews with plan administrators and state officials reveal few instances in which these regulations are said to have changed managed care practices. Although laws regulating "early" postdelivery discharges have increased maternal hospital stays, empirical studies of the impact of specific regulations concerning direct access to ob-gyn specialists revealed no change in the delivery of screening services, and any-willing-provider requirements have had only modest impacts on the performance of health plans. The most comprehensive of these initial empirical assessments, based on consumers' reports about their health care experiences, concluded that "overall, patient protection laws had little or no effect on either trust, satisfaction with care or utilization." To be sure, there is considerable evidence that various managed care restrictions have been loosened since the late 1990s. But most analysts attributed this change to market pressures on plans rather than seeing it as any consequence of government intervention.

Legislative initiatives may have proven ineffective because states did not appropriate sufficient resources to enforce the laws. Indeed, Frank Sloan and Mark Hall (2002) report that in 60 percent of the states that adopted new regulations, the state agency responsible for their enforcement was not authorized to hire any new staff to pursue this mission. Moreover, there was significant uncertainty about the applicability of state regulations to managed care organizations under the provisions of the Employee Retirement Income Security Act (ERISA) of 1974, which allows states to regulate insurance and, by implication, managed care but also exempts "self-insured" employer plans from state regulation. Given these many limitations on effective regulation, it is possible that state legislators' rush to enact managed care legislation was little more than symbolic politics, designed to quiet political demands from angry constituents, but never intended to have much real impact on health insurers or medical practice. Certainly its impact remained unnoticed by most consumers, who remain disenchanted with managed care and whose experiences appear to be unaffected by regulation.

But there is one other possibility. Perhaps managed care regulation only *appears* to be ineffective because past research has not appropriately assessed its consequences. Interviews with plan administrators are likely to yield self-serving responses, downplaying the influence of regulations to forestall more interventions. Assessing the impact of individual regulatory initiatives is difficult when states adopt clusters of regulations. And consumer reports about medical care may miss many of the crucial dimensions of access and quality, about which patients remain at best poorly informed.

. . . By relying on physician reports about their day-to-day experiences in their own practices, rather than their assessment of either managed care or state regulation, we can construct estimates of the consequences of regulation, while minimizing any biases that would otherwise be introduced by strategic responses.

. . . Our findings offer some new insights into the dynamics of managed care and its consequences. It has been noted by many recent observers that managed care became less restrictive over the past five years. This "loosening up" has generally been attributed to changing conditions in the medical marketplace and, especially, the role of employer and employee demand for less restrictive insurance products. Our results indicate that state regulation also contributed to these evolving differences in managed care. The impediments to regulatory impacts that we identified above, including the general difficulties of enforcement and the limitations on the states associated with ERISA, do not appear to have prevented state regulation from having an impact. Indeed, other studies suggest that in practice, state regulation of managed care may induce changes in plan behavior and provider decisions that affect a broad range of patients, including those patients who are in self-insured employer plans that are nominally exempt from state regulation.

Understanding past lessons from managed care regulation is more than a matter of historical interest; it is likely to have future policy import as well. Regulation of managed care practices is now firmly established and is unlikely to be eliminated. Moreover, when Medicare, Medicaid, or SCHIP programs contract with private plans, their contractual requirements can be devised in part based on the lessons from states' regulatory experiences. These two mechanisms allow government at both the state and federal level to respond to revived concerns about managed care, should these return to the policy agenda in the future.

Our suggestion that managed care practices may evoke policy makers' renewed attention may surprise many readers, since managed care was widely characterized as "fallen on hard times," left with an "empty toolbox," or essentially "dead" just a few years ago. But reports of managed care's demise were considerably exaggerated. In the first place, though the increase in state regulation during the mid- to late 1990s did coincide with a reduction in some constraints on clinical practice, the oft-repeated claim that physicians had recaptured their lost autonomy was never accurate to begin with. For example, although specialists reported increasing levels of clinical autonomy between 1997 and 2001, they also reported comparable increases in physician profiling, or the monitoring of clinicians' treatment patterns, during that same period. And primary care physicians reported no change at all in their clinical autonomy during these years.

Equally important, managed care plans adapted to the expanded regulatory constraints by shifting the nature of their external review to focus on clinical choices involving high-cost cases. Although this considerably narrowed the number of cases affected by external review, the reduced impact of managed care was offset by a contemporaneous increase in the management of pharmaceutical benefits. Over the past few years, these new incarnations of managed care practices appear to be increasingly affecting access to medical care: between 2003 and 2007, access problems attributed by the American public to health plan practices increased by more than 9 percent, leading analysts to conclude that "the return of health plan prior authorization requirements for certain services may be a contributing factor."

The political response to this "second coming" of managed care is likely to take a different form than that precipitated by the managed care backlash of the mid-1990s. Because plans are avoiding the sorts of interventions that are most evident to the public (restrictions on maternity stays or emergency room use), the debate around a new generation of managed care regulation is more likely to be among policy specialists and focused on substantive detail, rather than the more symbolically political response of the first wave of managed care regulations (Gerber and Teske 2000). Because a second generation of managed care regulations can build on the first, it is also likely to differ from the initial efforts; policy makers will now be able to draw on more than a decade of experience with regulatory implementation and enforcement. The political and programmatic contexts will matter as well, especially given the level of public and professional concern about various managed care practices, and the other issues and policy proposals that may provide "windows of opportunity" for fresh attention to these concerns.

Our finding that managed care regulation does appear to affect medical practice should be heartening to those who have campaigned for such regulation. The complexity of managed care practices, and of medical care itself, makes this domain hardly the most promising setting for regulatory success. The states have dedicated only limited resources to enforcing these regulations, and the applicability of certain forms of state regulation to employment-related health plans is potentially limited by ERISA. The pattern of positive outcomes reported here is thus all the more striking, and it challenges those critics who had dismissed managed care reform as impractical given those limitations.

NOTES AND QUESTIONS

1. *"Medical necessity."*   Haavi Morreim argues that managed care organizations "practice medicine much more than they should, primarily because health care contracts are largely founded on the concept of medical necessity." Haavi Morreim, Playing Doctor: Corporate Medical Practice and Medical Malpractice, 32 U. Mich. J.L. Reform 939, 944–950 (1999). That is, as long as coverage decisions depend on judgments about whether medical care (including proposed treatments, diagnoses, etc.) is "necessary," and as long as many patients are precluded from receiving proposed care if their health coverage plans refuse

to pay the cost of the care, "plans will continue to practice medicine routinely rather than sparingly." Id. at 1010. As Morreim further comments, "medical necessity," is vague, and can be interpreted broadly or narrowly. Can you think of any different criteria that might replace the notion of "medical necessity" in plans' decisions about coverage?

2. *Lawsuits against MCOs and the complication of ERISA.*   *Neade* did not involve an employer-funded managed care organization, which would have subjected the plaintiff's claims to additional limitations under the Employee Retirement Income Security Act of 1974. In Pegram v. Herdrich, 530 U.S. 211 (2000), rev'g 154 F.3d 362 (7th Cir. 1998), referred to in *Neade,* the Supreme Court upheld the dismissal of a breach of fiduciary claim against an ERISA managed care organization on the grounds that mixed treatment and eligibility decisions made by MCO physicians are not subject to fiduciary duties. Later, in Aetna Health Inc. v. Davila, 542 U.S. 200 (2004), the Supreme Court further limited the legal claims that can be brought against ERISA insurance plans by holding that ERISA totally preempted state tort claims for such plans. This means that plaintiffs (alleging that recommended treatment was not provided) cannot sue their employer-sponsored MCO in state court; moreover, because they must now sue pursuant to ERISA, they are limited to awards that cover the dollar value of denied services. Justice Ginsburg, who (with Justice Breyer) concurred, noted that she joined "the rising judicial chorus urging that Congress and [this] Court revisit what is an unjust and increasingly tangled ERISA regime. DiFelice v. Aetna U.S. Health Care, 346 F.3d 442, 453 (CA3 2003) (Becker, J., concurring)." For a succinct explanation of the case and discussion of its public health implications, see Sara Rosenbaum & Joel Teitelbaum, Aetna Health, Inc. v. Davila: Implications for Public Health Policy, 199 Public Health Rep. 510 (2004).

See also Wickline v. State, 192 Cal. App. 3d 1630 (1986), an early, non-ERISA case brought against Medi-Cal, a California medical assistance program, in which the plaintiff sued for recovery for medical complications from early hospital discharge. The court concluded that Medi-Cal was not liable for the discharge decision and that the "decision to discharge" is "the responsibility of the patient's own treating doctor." Id. at 1645, and that if, "in his medical judgment, it was in his patient's best interest that she remain in the acute care hospital setting for an additional four days beyond the extended time period originally authorized by Medi-Cal, [he] should have made some effort to keep Wickline there." Id. at 1645–1646.

3. *Class action suits.*   In recent years, a number of class action suits have been filed against managed care companies. Kathy Cerminara assesses these suits in light of their providing people without personal resources and skill adequate to sue large managed care companies with the capacity to do so:

> Class actions provide a way for covered individuals to assert their voices, since many of these individuals can neither play a role in negotiating their coverage contracts nor exit their current coverage arrangements. Class actions permit a concerted assertion of concerns. They facilitate the expression of dissatisfaction that does not garner respect or response in the marketplace.

Kathy L. Cerminara, Taking a Closer Look at the Managed Care Class Actions: Impact Litigation as an Assist to the Market, 11 Ann. Health L. 1, 9 (2002).

Compare and contrast the approach of class actions to redressing grievances about managed care practices to the solutions represented in the films Elizabeth Pendo, supra, discusses.

Among the cases to which Cerminara refers are Grijalva v. Shalala, 946 F. Supp. 747 (D. Ariz. 1996), 152 F.3d 1115 (9th Cir. 1998), cert. granted and remanded for reconsideration, 526 U.S. 1096 (1999) (suit against Secretary of the Department of Health and Human Services by group of Medicare recipients, alleging Secretary failed adequately to monitor HMOs providing Medicare benefits) and Romero v. Prudential Insurance Co., C.A. No. 00-00-2592 (E.D. Pa., filed May 22, 2000) (alleging, among other things, that those hired by the company to make decisions about medical necessity were not sufficiently trained).

4. *"Gag" clauses.*   Among the most severely criticized forms of control that managed care companies have offered to or imposed on physicians were so-called gag clauses. These contractual clauses banned physicians from talking to patients about certain treatment options not covered by the HMO either because of the expense involved or for some other reason. Such clauses are now prohibited in virtually every state. Why do you think that, among all the various financial incentives and other forms of control that managed care companies have exercised, gag clauses were nearly universally rejected? Gag clauses are considered in Kristin L. Jensen, Releasing Managed Care's Chokehold on Healthcare Providers, 16 Ann. Health L. 141 (2007); Joan H. Krause, The Brief Life of the Gag Clause: Why Anti-Gag Legislation Isn't Enough, 67 Tenn. L. Rev. 1 (1999).

2.   Gainsharing and Other Health Care Financing and Delivery Initiatives

Most lawmakers and commentators have long assumed that underutilization (encouraged by the promise of individual or institutional financial gain) will diminish the quality of care. Law professor Richard Saver, however, criticizes the "more-must-be-better view of health care" and suggests that "gainsharing" may be as successful in hospital settings as it sometimes has been in industrial settings. Saver defines gainsharing as "a formal reward and participation system in which workers share financially in productivity improvements achieved by their organization as a result of the workers' contributions." Richard Saver, Squandering the Gain: Gainsharing and the Continuing Dilemma of Physician Financial Incentives, 98 Nw. U. L. Rev. 145 (2003). Saver delineates three general consequences of gainsharing:

> (1) workers collaborate with management and each other through committees, group projects, and similar activities designed to generate ideas for improving productivity in their specific work areas; (2) workers participate in actual decision-making for productivity reforms . . . ; and (3) workers as a group receive a direct financial bonus for any cost-savings and/or productivity gains the organization may experience.

Id. at 147.

In his article, Saver describes a successful "gainsharing" plan at General Tire. Workers convinced the company to spend more to develop equipment that ultimately saved the company money. The workers were motivated by the company's Saving Time and Resources (STAR) program under which employee teams were rewarded for innovations that saved the company money. Saver notes that a similar program at a hospital would probably be illegal. The Medicare-Medicaid statute bans hospitals from providing bonuses to physicians for reducing hospital services to Medicare or Medicaid patients. Saver argues, however, that well-designed physician incentives constitute a "critical step" toward the reform of health care delivery in the United States.

Since Saver's analysis of gainsharing, the Affordable Care Act of 2010 has created a Medicare gainsharing program under which providers (various combinations of hospitals, physicians, nursing homes, and others) can form Accountable Care Organizations (ACOs) to share in cost savings. An ACO takes responsibility for the overall care of their Medicare patients, of which they must serve a minimum of 5,000. To the extent the ACO produces savings by coordinating care, eliminating unnecessary costs, reducing hospitalizations, and so on, while still meeting expectations for quality clinical performance, Medicare shares those savings with the ACO. The following excerpt comes from the Federal Register publication of the final rule establishing ACOs.

> ## Department of Health and Human Services
> ## Centers for Medicare & Medicaid Services,
> ### 76 Federal Register 67802, 42 CFR Part 425

ACTION: Final rule.

SUMMARY: This final rule implements section 3022 of the Affordable Care Act which contains provisions relating to Medicare payments to providers of services and suppliers participating in Accountable Care Organizations (ACOs) under the Medicare Shared Savings Program. Under these provisions, providers of services and suppliers can continue to receive traditional Medicare fee-for-service (FFS) payments under Parts A and B, and be eligible for additional payments if they meet specified quality and savings requirements.

DATES: These regulations are effective on January 3, 2012.

I. D. Public Comments Received on the Proposed Rule

[Response to comments "that the Shared Savings Program has similar characteristics to some forms of managed care where it is possible to achieve savings through inappropriate reductions in patient care."]

Response: It is important to note that the Shared Savings Program is not a managed care program. Medicare FFS beneficiaries retain all rights and benefits under traditional Medicare. Medicare FFS beneficiaries retain the right to see any physician of their choosing, and they do not enroll in the Shared Savings Program. Unlike managed care settings, the Shared Savings Program "assignment" methodology in no way implies a lock in or enrollment process. To the contrary, it is a process based exclusively on an assessment of where and from whom FFS beneficiaries have chosen to receive care during the course of each performance period. The program is also not a capitated model; providers and suppliers continue to bill and receive FFS payments rather than receiving lump sum payments based upon the number of assigned beneficiaries. The design of the Shared Savings Program places the patient at the center. It encourages physicians, through the eligibility requirements, to include their patients in decision making about their health care. . . . Lastly, in order for an ACO to share in savings the ACO must meet quality standards and program requirements that we will be monitoring. We will monitor the ACO's compliance with these requirements, as described in section II.H. of this final rule, with a special focus on ACOs that attempt to avoid at-risk patients. The purpose of the Shared Savings Program is to achieve savings through improvements in the coordination and quality of care, and not through avoiding certain beneficiaries or placing limits on beneficiary access to needed care.

NOTES AND QUESTIONS

1. *Compromises with health industry.*   The final ACO rule differed in important respects from that originally proposed. As reported in Kaiser Health News, "ACOs are a key provision in the health law to slow rising health costs while delivering high-quality care to Medicare beneficiaries." Phil Galewitz & Jenny Gold, HHS Releases Final Regulations for ACOs, Kaiser Health News, Oct. 20, 2011, http://www.kaiserhealthnews.org/stories/2011/october/20/accountable-care-organization-rules-regulations.aspx. But early interest by physicians and other providers faded when the original proposed rule was published. Some of the concessions to the health industry included in the final rule were a track for participating in an ACO without the risk of losing money; a reduction in quality measures of performance from 65 to 33; and identification of beneficiaries likely to be assigned to the ACO, as opposed to only retrospective assignment based on use of primary care services.

2. *Early figures.*   In July 2012, the DHHS published a news release announcing that 89 new ACOs had entered into agreements with the Centers for Medicare and Medicaid (CMS), bringing the number of organizations participating in the Shared Savings program to 154, and the number of Medicare beneficiaries receiving care from these organizations to more than 2.4 million. DHHS, News Release, HHS announces 89 new Accountable Care Organizations, July 9, 2012, available at http://www.hhs.gov/news/press/2012pres/07/20120709a.html.

3. *"Managed Care" vs. "Accountable Care."*   How does "accountable care" differ from "managed care?" What structural differences appear to have been implemented to avoid the perceived abuses of 1990s-styled MCOs?

In a 2012 JAMA article, health policy expert Ezekiel Emanuel, M.D., Ph.D., notes that although managed care did succeed in controlling costs, its "strategy was to pay less, not work with physicians to provide truly high-quality managed care." He argues that ACOs may succeed where MCOs failed because "Today is different from the 1990s—physicians and others in the health system know more, have better data, guidelines, and metrics; and despite antagonisms, can collaborate better." Ezekiel J. Emanuel, Why Accountable Care Organizations Are Not 1990s Managed Care Redux, 307 JAMA 2263–2264 (2012). One important knowledge point Emanuel emphasizes is that "nearly two-thirds of health care costs are concentrated in 10% of patients, so to control costs, the focus needs to be on these patients, not the 50% of the population that is relatively healthy and uses just 3% of the health care dollars." Id.

3. Doctors' Entrepreneurial Activities

In the first part of this chapter, you read about the growth of physician-owned hospitals as physicians have sought entrepreneurial activities to replace some of the income lost to managed care practices. Susan Shapiro (at the time, a senior research fellow with the American Bar Foundation) has delineated the following entrepreneurial activities in which doctors now engage:

- dispensing of drugs or medical products;
- fee splitting or kickbacks for referrals or ping-pong referrals with specialists and other practitioners;
- self-referral to medical facilities—home health care agencies, medical laboratories, pharmacies, nursing homes, x-ray and diagnostic imaging facilities, medical equipment suppliers, dialysis centers, physical therapy and rehabilitation facilities, ambulatory surgery centers, radiation therapy facilities, and the like—in which they have a financial interest;
- kickbacks, rebates, gifts, prizes, free meals, and paid trips from medical suppliers, laboratories, and pharmaceutical companies; and
- payments by hospitals for admitting patients or even outright purchases by hospitals of a physician's practice.

Susan P. Shapiro, Bushwhacking the Ethical High Road: Conflict of Interest in the Practice of Law and Real Life, 28 Law & Soc. Inquiry 87, 163–167 (2003). Id. at 166. How might these activities harm a doctor's patients? Might any of these entrepreneurial activities be advantageous to patients? More generally, why should doctors—or should they not—be precluded from entering the marketplace as freely as those involved in other sorts of businesses?

In the following excerpt, Steven Wales reports the results of studies appearing to show that physicians' treatment choices are substantially influenced by their financial self-interest. Such studies led to the Stark Laws, which have been expanded by the Affordable Care Act to cover physician-owned hospitals, as described in Perry, supra.

> *Steven D. Wales, The Stark Law: Boon or Boondoggle? An Analysis of the Prohibition on Physician Self-Referrals*
> **27 Law & Psychol. Rev. 1, 5–7 (2003)**

... The Office of the Inspector General (OIG) for the Department of Health and Human Services (HHS) issued the results of a study in 1989.

The study found that patients of referring physicians who own or invest in independent clinical laboratories received 45% more clinical laboratory services than ... Medicare patients in general. ... OIG also concluded that patients of physicians known to be owners or investors in independent physiological laboratories used 13% more physiological testing services than all Medicare patients in general.

These numbers are remarkable. Forty-five percent more services were performed when the doctor stood to gain by referral. The implication is that physicians, even those acting entirely in good faith, are likely to err on the side of referrals when they have a financial incentive to generate business.

Later studies provide further evidence that physicians' treatment choices may be influenced by the money to be made: self-referring physicians used imaging examinations "at least four times more often" than other physicians; physicians earning bonuses based on business generated increased the number of lab tests per patient 23%, the number of X-rays 16%, and total charges 20%; physicians who owned imaging technology used it "significantly more often" than those who did not, generating as much as 6.2 times higher average imaging charges than those who referred imaging exams to radiologists; patients of self-referring physicians used physical therapy and rehabilitation facilities 39 to 45% more than other patients and net revenue was 30 to 40% higher in physician-owned facilities; finally, the differences in referral rates between physician-owners of diagnostic imaging facilities and nonowners was greatest for costly, high technology services—self-referring doctors referred patients for simple X-rays no more than other doctors, but "ordered 54% more MRI scans, 27% more CT scans, 37% more nuclear medicine scans, 27% more echocardiograms, 22% more ultrasound services, and 22% more complex X-rays."

It should be noted that these studies were not as convincing as they may appear. Many commentators rejected these studies as inconclusive. Some said, for example, that the numbers "do not necessarily lead to the conclusion that physicians with ownership interests in facilities overutilize those facilities." Instead, critics argued:

> these studies fail to address issues, such as whether a physician who refers patients to a facility he owns has a greater knowledge of the services that facility provides, or whether the greater number of tests provided at physician-owned facilities reduces the overall costs per patient. Thus these commentators contend that the studies, in the aggregate, do not conclusively prove that physician joint ventures lead to an unnatural market or a lower quality of care. Rather they argue that the studies at most show an interdependence between a physician's ownership interest in a facility and the possibility he or she will refer patients to that facility more often than nonowner physicians. . . .

Nevertheless, these studies had an impact on the public and on Congress. In 1989, Congress passed Stark I [Ethics in Patient Referral Act] to specifically address the self-referral problem. Stark I prohibited "physician referrals under Medicare for clinical lab services when the referring physician has a financial relationship with the lab unless the terms of certain statutory or regulatory exceptions are met." Stark I also required entities to self report various ownership and referral arrangements. In 1993 that law was expanded by a portion of the Omnibus Budget and Reconciliation Act of 1993, or "Stark II." Stark II prohibited physician self-referrals under Medicare and Medicaid not only to clinical lab services, but also to ten other categories of Designated Health Services (DHS).

Fla. Stat. §456.052 (Disclosure of Financial Interest by Production)
(2012)

(1) A health care provider shall not refer a patient to an entity in which such provider is an investor unless, prior to the referral, the provider furnishes the patient with a written disclosure form, informing the patient of:

(a) The existence of the investment interest.

(b) The name and address of each applicable entity in which the referring health care provider is an investor.

(c) The patient's right to obtain the items or services for which the patient has been referred at the location or from the provider or supplier of the patient's choice, including the entity in which the referring provider is an investor.

(d) The names and addresses of at least two alternative sources of such items or services available to the patient.

(2) The physician or health care provider shall post a copy of the disclosure forms in a conspicuous public place in his or her office.

(3) A violation of this section shall constitute a misdemeanor of the first degree, punishable as provided [under relevant Florida statutory law]. In addition to any other penalties or remedies provided, a violation of this section shall be grounds for disciplinary action by the respective board.

NOTES AND QUESTIONS

1. *Stark Laws.*   In the excerpt above, Steven Wales reports data showing that doctors are much more likely to refer patients for testing when the doctors have financial incentives. Is that necessarily bad? Might not doctors (as the quote at the end of Wales's article suggests) know more about the services provided by laboratories or testing services in which they have an interest and thus be more likely to consider the potential advantages of such services for patients?

As Wales points out, Stark I and Stark II (known together as the Stark Law or Stark Laws) only apply to self-referrals involving Medicare and Medicaid patients. Thus, as Wales notes, a physician can avoid the reach of the Stark Law by refusing to accept Medicare and Medicaid patients. 27 Law & Psychol. Rev. 1, n.54. Wales wonders whether enough physicians with ancillary investments might eventually choose private entrepreneurial activities over federal payments so as to avoid the Stark Law, with the consequence that Medicare and Medicaid patients would find it increasingly difficult to find physicians to treat them. What does the Perry article, supra, have to say on this question with respect to physician-owned specialty hospitals?

2. *Disclosure.*   The Florida rule on "disclosure of financial interest by production" requires health care workers, when referring patients to entities in which they have an interest, to disclose that fact to patients. Do you think that effectively precludes abuses due to doctors' conscious or unconscious self-interest? At what sorts of abuses is the statute aimed?

The Physicians Payment Sunshine Act, passed with the Affordable Care Act of 2010, requires pharmaceutical, medical device, and biological and medical supply manufacturers to report for public disclosure any payments or gifts to physicians and teaching hospitals in excess of $10, as well as certain ownership or investment interests held by physicians or members of their immediate families.

3. *Additional statutes.*   A number of additional federal and state statutes aim to limit fraud and abuse within the world of health care. Federal and state anti-kickback statutes differ from Stark in a number of ways. These statutes are not restricted to physician referrals. The federal anti-kickback statute, which prohibits payment to induce or reward referrals of items or services payable by a federal health care program, is a criminal statute, whereas Stark is civil. See 42 U.S.C. §1320a-7b(b). Under the federal anti-kickback statute scienter must be proven. The Stark Law provides for strict liability. The Health Insurance Portability and Accountability Act extended the anti-kickback statute to cover all federal programs providing health care. Sec. 241(a), 110 Stat. 2016. The Civil False Claims Act is a third federal statute aimed at controlling fraud and abuse in the provision of health care. 31 U.S.C. §3729. The statute provides a cause of action against anyone who presents a false claim to the government.

4. *Fraud statutes vs. offering financial incentives to physicians.*   Arti Rai suggests that legislators have depended on fraud statutes when their real aim was to control the quality and cost of health care, because fraud statutes are accepted and acceptable whereas the "government lacks effective mechanisms for addressing these problems [of cost and quality] directly." Arti K. Rai, Health Care Fraud and Abuse: A Tale of Behavior Induced by Payment Structure, 30 J. Legal Studies 579 (2001). Rai states that "the shibboleth of fraud and abuse was introduced in the political arena largely because more direct efforts at cost control, such as enrolling all seniors in some form of managed care, were seen as politically untenable." Id. at 582. Rai then suggests that cost and quality concerns can be addressed better through offering financial incentives to physicians than through laws aimed at fraud. Rai analogizes the situation to that of changes in patent law after 1980 that provided an incentive for university researchers to compete by encouraging the patenting of research funded with public money. As a result, private companies have invested heavily in biomedical research done by university scientists. Thus, Rai recommends the development of financial incentives that would encourage doctors to take cost considerations into account in providing care. This is one of the aims of the new ACOs, the development of which has required waivers of certain fraud and abuse provisions.

Other useful analyses of fraud and abuse laws can be found in David A. Hyman, Health Care Fraud and Abuse Market Change, Social Norms, and the Trust "Reposed in the Workmen," 30 J. Legal Stud. 531 (2001); the article considers how changes in the medical marketplace make enforcement of fraud and abuse laws very complicated.

5. *Physicians selling supplements.*   Some physicians have become drug and vitamin salespersons, providing their patients with advice about over-the-counter drugs and supplements and then selling such drugs and supplements to patients. Supplements present special problems because, unlike over-the-counter drugs, they are not categorized as medicine under the normal

regulatory authority of the FDA. Ford Fessenden & Christopher Drew, Bottom Line in Mind, Doctors Sell Ephedra, N.Y. Times, Mar. 31, 2003, at A3. To remove a supplement from the market, the FDA must show that it poses an unreasonable risk to health or safety. Fessenden and Drew report on one Texas doctor, concerned about the rising costs of practice and diminishing payments to his practice, who joined with his spouse, a pediatrician, to open a weight loss program in Etowah, Tennessee. The couple sold dietary supplements, some of which included ephedra, a powerful stimulant that has been linked with scores of deaths. Despite widespread publicity that followed dozens of deaths attributed to the use of ephedra, the Tennessee doctor's practice flourished. The doctor, who says he "should be rewarded" for helping his patients lose weight, got the supplements from Wellness International Network Ltd. Wellness urged doctors to market its products with the claim that they could thus make up for diminished income as a result of managed care payments. In early 2003, a group of doctors working with Wellness wrote to Tommy Thompson, Secretary of Health and Human Services, urging him to allow ephedra to remain on the market. The doctors' letter did not mention the profits they make by selling ephedra to weight-loss patients. Id.

This newspaper story suggests that at least some physicians, concerned about the effect of managed care on their annual income, and perhaps also concerned about preserving their freedom to practice medicine without bureaucratic involvements, paperwork, and external pressure to treat more patients more quickly, are tempted to "make up for" some of the consequences of managed care by engaging in entrepreneurial activities that lie outside the traditional domain of doctoring. To what extent do you think physicians are influenced by *expectations* they had (before they entered the field or in their early years of practice) that never materialized (or that were deflected) due to the advent of managed care? To what extent does the complex reality of medicine-as-business justify doctors' selling unregulated supplements for a profit?

In what regard, if at all, are your responses to these questions affected by knowing that in early 2004, the FDA prohibited the sale of supplements containing ephedra?

In 2006, the 10th Circuit reversed a district court decision that had enjoined the FDA from enforcing its prohibition against Nutraceutical Corporation (which made and sold ephedra) selling products containing even low doses of ephedra. Nutraceutical Corp. v. von Eschenbach, 459 F.3d 1033 (2006) rev'g Nutraceutical Corp. v. Crawford, 364 F. Supp. 2d 1310 (D. Utah 2005). The 10th Circuit concluded that the FDA was correct in performing a "risk–benefit analysis" in determining whether ephedra presented "an 'unreasonable risk of illness or injury'" and that it satisfied the burden of proving that ephedra did pose an "unreasonable risk of illness or injury" even when taken in low doses. The court concluded:

> The FDA's extensive research identified the dose level at which ephedrine alkaloids present unreasonable risk of illness or injury to be so minuscule that no amount of EDS [ephedrine-alkaloid dietary supplements] is reasonably safe. The FDA reasonably concluded that there is no recommended dose of EDS that does not present an unreasonable risk. . . .

> We find that the FDA correctly followed the congressional directive to analyze the risks and benefits of EDS in determining that there is no dosage level of EDS acceptable for the market. Summary judgment for plaintiffs was therefore improper, and summary judgment for defendants should have been entered. Accordingly, the district court's decision is reversed, and we remand for entry of judgment in favor of defendants. . . .

Id. at 1043–1044.

6. *Physicians as retailers?*   A former Australian Medical Association president, who operated a health food store next to her medical practice, responded to criticism by asking why physicians should be held to a different standard than other professionals. She noted, in particular, the absence of objection to veterinarians selling pet food or to physiotherapists selling exercise equipment. Matthew Franklin, Phelps Defends Doctors' Right to Sell Vitamins, The Australian, Sept. 22, 2006, at 3.

7. *Industry gifts to physicians.*   Physicians who accept gifts from industry recognize the potential for bias, but may believe that the actualization of that bias is a matter of self-conscious choice and can thus be easily avoided. Yet, a 2003 article in the Journal of the American Medical Association asserts that bias can occur even if physicians are conscious of the risk of being influenced by industry gifts and believe they are unaffected by the gifts, and even if the gifts are very small, in effect "trinkets." Jason Dana & George Loewenstein, A Social Science Perspective on Gifts to Physicians from Industry, 290 JAMA 252 (2003). The authors suggest that physician bias (effected as a consequence of gifts from industry) accounts for expensive treatment choices. The implications are especially disconcerting because many "new," more expensive drugs (76 percent between 1989 and 2000 according to FDA estimates) are not significantly more effective than older drugs that cost less. Id.

A 2006 article in the Journal of the American Medical Association argues that voluntary constraints have not adequately contained conflicts of interest stemming from the relationship between physicians and industry (including especially pharmaceutical companies and manufacturers of medical devices). Troyen A. Brennan et al., Health Industry Practices That Create Conflicts of Interest, 295 JAMA 429 (2006). The authors recommend that academic medical centers prohibit all gifts from industry to physicians and prohibit pharmaceutical companies from providing drug samples directly to physicians; that committees selecting formulary drugs and medical devices for hospitals and medical groups exclude physicians who maintain any financial relationship with the relevant industry; that industry not be allowed to pay (directly or through a subsidiary) for any programs providing continuing medical education (CME) credit; that faculty at academic medical centers be precluded from serving on industry speakers bureaus or as ghostwriters for industry; and that contracts setting up consulting or research relationships between industry and medical academics should be permitted but carefully regulated. Id.

8. *Comparison to bioethicists' conflicts.*   In considering conflicts of interest imposed on physicians by managed care, comparison can be made to bioethicists who accept remuneration from pharmaceutical companies. Carl Elliott described a campaign assembled by Eli Lilly to promote an expensive drug (Xigris) against much cheaper competitor drugs. Lilly hired bioethicists and medical school

doctors to study the ethics of drug rationing. Carl Elliott, Not-So-Public Relations, Slate Magazine, Dec. 15, 2003. "It is," explained Elliott, "a brilliant strategy. There is no better way to enlist bioethicists in the cause of consumer capitalism than to convince them they are working for social justice." Elliott asks, suggestively, whether there is "anything wrong" with bioethicists' taking money from pharmaceutical companies if there is no express effort made by the companies to influence the bioethicists' work. What do you think? Do you think the implications of Elliott's interpretation are accurate, overly harsh, or not strong enough?

CHALLENGING ISSUES: HEALERS AND BUSINESS MANAGERS: REGULATING PHYSICIANS

For the most part, the work of physicians (and other health care providers) in the United States has been defined and regulated differently from the work of most actors in the marketplace. Read the three statements that follow and then consider whether you think that the work of physicians and other health care providers should or should not be regulated differently than the work of business people is regulated.

> As Professor Baruch A. Brody has noted, physicians function in two roles vis-à-vis their patients: (1) the "professional" role, and (2) the "honest businessman" role. As a "professional," the physician serves primarily in a fiduciary role. . . .
>
> On the other hand, under the "honest businessman" model, the physician/patient relationship is essentially a business relationship in which the physician acts in his or her own economic self interest. . . . [I]n the "honest businessman role," the physician is expected "to pursue his or her economic interests by providing necessary quality services in an honest fashion." Moreover, in this latter role, it is appropriate for physicians to provide their patient with cost-effective care in accordance with the cost containment goals of the patient's health plan. In the "professional" role, the physicians are responsible for serving the interests of their patient by providing care that meets the needs of their patient. In the "honest businessman" role, however, the physician is primarily concerned with the economics of medicine. While there may be some tension between these two roles, it is also possible to reconcile them. And it is not per se immoral or unethical for a physician to balance the patient's needs and desires against the costs of proposed treatments.

Leonard J. Nelson, Helling v. Carey Revisited: Physician Liability in the Age of Managed Care, 25 Seattle U. L. Rev. 775, 781–782 (2002).

> Although medical-care consumers stand to gain financially from [incentive payments] . . . , there is widespread and legitimate fear that incentive payments may lead physicians to offer inferior care. Any consideration of physician incentive plans must take that fear seriously and analyze it closely. Such analysis may begin with the assumption that physicians generally desire to give their patients excellent medical care. Very small incentives should not overcome that cast of mind, and should not pose a threat to patients, even though they may guide physicians toward cost-saving innovations over time. On the other hand, consumers should certainly be afraid of the potential for certain incentive plans to impact adversely on individual clinical decisions. . . . We may refer to the degree to which a given incentive plan impacts upon particular clinical decisions as its intensity. Very intense incentive programs are those which have the greatest potential to impact upon individual clinical decisions made by physicians.

Stephen R. Latham, Regulation of Managed Care Incentive Payments to Physicians, 22 Am. J.L. & Med. 399, 409 (1996).

> Estimates vary, but even the most conservative say that up to 25 percent of the health care procedures provided in this country are unnecessary. . . .
>   . . . The overall rate of surgery done in the United States is twice as high as surgery levels for the United Kingdom and 50 percent higher than the rate of surgery in Canada. Hysterectomies, in general, are done in this country at a rate that is six times higher than Japan's and four times higher than Sweden's. Coronary bypass operations—a procedure whose net impact has been repeatedly challenged—are done in this country at a rate ten times higher than in Great Britain.

George C. Halvorson, Strong Medicine 184–185 (1993).

C.　CHARGING AND COLLECTING PAYMENT

1.　Bioethical and Social Approaches

> ### Beverly Cohen, The Controversy over Hospital Charges to the Uninsured—No Villains, No Heroes
> #### 51 Vill. L. Rev. 95 (2006)

Beginning in March 2003, the Wall Street Journal ran a series of articles focusing on hospitals that charge uninsured patients inflated hospital rates and aggressively hound them to make collections. The articles emphasized the draconian collections methods used by some hospitals, including residential foreclosures and even "body attachments," where the patient debtors were jailed until they could pay bail.

At the same time, a number of investigational reports were being published showing the devastating effects of overwhelming medical debt on families, coupled with census figures showing an ever-rising number of uninsured in this country. One such report by The Commonwealth Fund announced findings in June 2003 that hospitals' reluctance to lower charges to the uninsured resulted in long term debt for the affected families. The report also announced that the problem was apparently caused by unclear federal laws and regulations that had the unintended effect of discouraging hospitals from offering services at free or reduced rates to the uninsured.

During the summer of 2004, the increased attention to the issue of excessive hospital charges to the uninsured resulted in a wave of class action lawsuits across the nation. Uninsured patients alleged that hospitals charged them substantially higher rates than the hospitals accepted from private insurance plans, Medicare and Medicaid for comparable services. The lawsuits also alleged that the hospitals failed to advise the uninsured patients of available options for charity care, and then aggressively pursued the patients to make collection on the exorbitant bills.

Also in the summer of 2004, the Committee on Energy and Commerce of the House of Representatives held a hearing to review hospital billing and collections practices for the uninsured. The hearing followed a year-long investigation of the issue, wherein the Committee collected detailed information from twenty hospital systems on their billing and collections practices. Thus began an intensive examination of a healthcare anomaly that was not appreciated by the general population of healthcare consumers, but which was generally known and accepted by the healthcare industry for decades: the only segment of society that pays full and undiscounted charges for hospital care is the uninsured—the very segment of the population that is least able and likely to pay full charges for medical care. Governmental agencies in charge of regulating healthcare have known this, the hospital industry has known this and private insurers and HMOs have known this; nonetheless, these entities have done little or nothing to complain about the inequity or press for reform.

. . . America first became aware of the issue of exorbitant hospital charges for the uninsured through a series of Wall Street Journal ("Journal") articles beginning in March 2003. The articles began by telling the story of Quinton White, a seventy-seven year-old retired dry-cleaning worker suffering from kidney and heart ailments who was paying off a hospital debt that his now-deceased wife had incurred twenty years previously when she was treated for cancer at Yale-New Haven Hospital. The article, Twenty Years and Still Paying, described how the original $18,740 hospital bill had blossomed to nearly $55,000 after the addition of interest and fees. The hospital, through its attorney, put a lien on Mr. White's modest home and seized most of his bank account. Over time, Mr. White paid the hospital close to the amount of the original bill, but $39,000 still remained, with interest alone reaching $33,000.

. . . A later Journal article gave concrete comparisons between hospital charges and the rates paid by governmental programs and private insurers. This article told the story of Paul Shipman, an uninsured individual who ended up spending twenty-one hours at the Inova Fairfax Hospital in Fairfax, Virginia, when he experienced chest pains. Mr. Shipman ended up having a stent installed to prop open one of the arteries to his heart. The Journal reported that as a result of this procedure, Mr. Shipman received a $29,500 hospital bill, plus a $1000 bill for the ambulance trip, a $7000 bill from the cardiologist who performed the stent procedure and several thousand dollars in additional bills for the emergency room visit. The twenty-one hours of medical care cost Mr. Shipman nearly $40,000, an exorbitant bill by any standard.

The Journal then compared the Shipman bills to what the hospital would receive for the same services from private insurers, Medicare and Medicaid. While insurance plans might pay a "case based" rate (a flat dollar amount corresponding to a given diagnosis that covers all of the care the patient receives at the hospital), the uninsured receive a bill with line by line charges for every item, down to band-aids and aspirins. The two systems of pricing result in huge differentials to the bills.

. . . At about the same time that the Journal was giving the public a dramatic picture of the devastating consequences of medical debt for the uninsured, a number of investigational reports were being published that conclusively established the failure of hospitals to provide charity care to this population. Although the researchers were examining hospitals located in different geographical areas, their findings were shockingly similar: hospitals did not tell the uninsured about charity care, did not offer charity care, did not discount bills to the uninsured and aggressively pursued payment.

. . . For the past twenty years, health insurers, managed care plans and governmental programs have all sought to drive down their rates for hospital care, which often comprises the largest segment of expense for healthcare insurers. [T]he only patient group that did not benefit from the drive down of hospital rates was the uninsured. The employed population largely came to receive health insurance benefits through their employers' health benefit plans. The age sixty-five and older population became covered by Medicare. The extremely indigent often met the state's criteria to qualify for Medicaid. All these groups paid discounted hospital rates or case based rates. A portion of the middle class, however, either newly unemployed or not covered by an employer sponsored health benefit plan, did not qualify for Medicaid and was not old enough to be covered by Medicare. It was only this group of uninsured patients that was left to pay full charges when they received hospital services.

. . . Beginning in the summer of 2004, uninsured patients across the United States commenced a number of class action lawsuits against hospitals alleging excessive charges and overly aggressive collections practices. The litigations were coordinated by Richard F. Scruggs, the Oxford, Mississippi, attorney who had successfully represented plaintiffs in the tobacco class actions. By January 2005, more than seventy such lawsuits had been commenced in federal courts in more than forty states, with more than 600 hospitals named as defendants. Dozens of similar class actions were also commenced in state forums.

For the most part, the various state and federal complaints made the same allegations. The chief claim was that by receiving federal charitable tax exemption under §501(c)(3) of the Internal Revenue Code, the hospitals had entered into an express or implied contract with the federal government obliging them to provide charity care. Plaintiffs alleged that when they were billed excessive charges for hospital services and were aggressively pursued by the hospitals for collection, the hospitals were in breach of their charitable obligations. Plaintiffs also asserted various state and federal claims against the hospitals for breach of express or implied charitable duties, breach of the duty of good faith and fair dealing, breach of charitable trust and unjust enrichment, but these claims were premised, at least in part, upon the same legal theory that the hospitals' charitable tax exemption under §501(c)(3) created an express or implied contract with the government to furnish charity care.

. . . The early decisions rendered by the district courts in the class actions challenging hospitals' billing and collections practices have been almost unanimously in favor of the hospitals. . . .

. . . Fatal to plaintiffs' federal tax claims was the district courts' uniform rulings that the grant of a §501(c)(3) charitable tax exemption does not create a contract between the recipient and the federal government. . . . Based on this finding, the courts ruled that the grant of a federal charitable tax exemption could not give rise to a claim for breach of contract or breach of an implied contractual duty of good faith and fair dealing. The district courts further held that even assuming, arguendo, a contract existed, §501(c)(3) does not give rise to a private right of action and that plaintiffs lacked standing to assert such a claim. In addition, the courts ruled that §501(c)(3) does not contain language demonstrating intent to create a trust, so that there was no basis to claim breach of a charitable trust. To the extent that unjust enrichment or constructive trust claims were premised upon the existence of a contract under §501(c)(3), the district courts dismissed those counts as well.

. . . As a result of the numerous class action dismissals in the federal forums, the focus of the class actions has been shifting to state courts. In contrast to the ruling on the federal claims, some early results on the state claims have been favorable for the plaintiffs. The Connecticut Superior Court in Ahmad v. Yale-New Haven Hospital, Inc. sustained plaintiffs' state law claims against Yale-New Haven Hospital based upon Connecticut's bed fund law and the state's unfair trade law. An Illinois state court ruled in Servedio v. Our Lady of the Resurrection Medical Center that state law claims alleging consumer fraud, unfair practices and breach of contract were adequately pleaded.

. . . It is possible that the inconsistent results in the state and federal forums on the state law claims signal merely that the state forums will be more receptive to plaintiffs' state causes of action. It is equally likely, however, that the state actions will yield mixed results. These state claims necessarily depend upon unique state interpretations of common law or upon particular language of state statutes, so that one state's outcome does not necessarily predict what will happen in others.

. . . The exposé on hospital billing and collections practices for the uninsured has not been a proud chapter in healthcare history. Had it not been for a single reporter at the Journal, it is possible that the issue of hospital charges for the uninsured might still remain largely hidden from public view. While it is understandable that hospitals legitimately may have believed that tampering with their charge schedules to give rate relief to the uninsured would have exposed them to anti-kickback risk and threatened them with lower Medicare reimbursements, this does not excuse hospitals for their silence. Nor could regulatory concerns ever justify practices like those by the Carle Foundation, which first treated an uninsured patient for attempted suicide and then later had him arrested for not paying his bill.

The government and the private insurance industry also are not free from blame. They too were certainly aware that a substantial segment of middle America was being victimized by exorbitant hospital charges, but failed to take action to publicize the issue or lobby for change. While the class action lawyers may assert that they acted swiftly to attempt to right this wrong, in fact they flooded into the federal courts with legal theories that were plainly unsupportable under current law. [One] court aptly described the federal claims as "bootless" and "without basis in law," and referred to the plaintiffs as "hav[ing] lost their way." So far, all that the class actions have accomplished is to drain thousands of dollars out of hospitals for defense costs that could have been allocated to charity care.

2. *Legal Approaches*

To address some of the perceived abuses in collection and billing practices of hospitals, the Patient Protection and Affordable Care Act of 2010 added new, additional requirements that hospitals must meet to be as recognized as tax-exempt under §501(c)(3). Hospitals failing to meet these requirements may incur tax penalties (a new remedy available to the Internal Revenue Service) in addition to loss of tax-exempt status. If a hospital organization operates more than one facility, each facility must meet the requirements. These new requirements are found in §501(r), reprinted in part below, along with §501(c)(3).

|| *26 U.S.C. §§501(c)(3) and 501(r) (2010)[2]* ||

SECTION 501

(c) List of exempt organizations

(3) Corporations, and any community chest, fund, or foundation, organized and operated exclusively for religious, charitable, scientific, testing for public safety, literary, or educational purposes, or to foster national or international amateur sports competition (but only if no part of its activities involve the provision of athletic facilities or equipment), or for the prevention of cruelty to children or animals, no part of the net earnings of which inures to the benefit of any private shareholder or individual, no substantial part of the activities of which is carrying on propaganda, or otherwise attempting, to influence legislation (except as otherwise provided in subsection (h)), and which does not participate in, or intervene in (including the publishing or distributing of statements), any political campaign on behalf of (or in opposition to) any candidate for public office.

(r) Additional requirements for certain hospitals
(1) In general

A hospital organization to which this subsection applies shall not be treated as described in subsection (c)(3) unless the organization—

(A) meets the community health needs assessment requirements described in paragraph (3),

(B) meets the financial assistance policy requirements described in paragraph (4),

(C) meets the requirements on charges described in paragraph (5), and

(D) meets the billing and collection requirement described in paragraph (6).

(3) Community health needs assessments
(A) In general

An organization meets the requirements of this paragraph with respect to any taxable year only if the organization—

(i) has conducted a community health needs assessment which meets the requirements of subparagraph (B) in such taxable year or in either of the 2 taxable years immediately preceding such taxable year, and

(ii) has adopted an implementation strategy to meet the community health needs identified through such assessment.

(B) Community health needs assessment

A community health needs assessment meets the requirements of this paragraph if such community health needs assessment—

---

2. Subsection (r) was added to 26 U.S.C. §501 by the Patient Protection and Affordable Care Act, Pub. L. 111-148, 124 Stat. 119, 855–858 (2010), as amended by the Health Care and Education Reconciliation Act of 2010, Pub. L. 111-152 (2010) §9007(a).

(i) takes into account input from persons who represent the broad interests of the community served by the hospital facility, including those with special knowledge of or expertise in public health, and

(ii) is made widely available to the public.

(4) Financial assistance policy

An organization meets the requirements of this paragraph if the organization establishes the following policies:

(A) **Financial assistance policy**

A written financial assistance policy which includes—

(i) eligibility criteria for financial assistance, and whether such assistance includes free or discounted care,

(ii) the basis for calculating amounts charged to patients,

(iii) the method for applying for financial assistance,

(iv) in the case of an organization which does not have a separate billing and collections policy, the actions the organization may take in the event of non-payment, including collections action and reporting to credit agencies, and

(v) measures to widely publicize the policy within the community to be served by the organization.

(B) **Policy relating to emergency medical care**

A written policy requiring the organization to provide, without discrimination, care for emergency medical conditions (within the meaning of section 1867 of the Social Security Act (42 U.S.C. 1395dd)) to individuals regardless of their eligibility under the financial assistance policy described in subparagraph (A).

(5) Limitation on charges

An organization meets the requirements of this paragraph if the organization—

(A) limits amounts charged for emergency or other medically necessary care provided to individuals eligible for assistance under the financial assistance policy described in paragraph (4)(A) to not more than the amounts generally billed to individuals who have insurance covering such care, and

(B) prohibits the use of gross charges.

(6) Billing and collection requirements

An organization meets the requirement of this paragraph only if the organization does not engage in extraordinary collection actions before the organization has made reasonable efforts to determine whether the individual is eligible for assistance under the financial assistance policy described in paragraph (4)(A).

Press Release: Treasury Releases Proposed Guidance to Ensure Patient Access to Financial Assistance from Charitable Hospitals

June 22, 2012 (Available at http://www.treasury. gov/press-center/press-releases/Pages/tg1621.aspx)

[In this press release, the Department of Treasury summarized the key elements of the proposed regulations under Section 501(r) as follows.]

Establishment and Disclosure of Financial Assistance Policy. Each tax-exempt hospital must establish a financial assistance policy that clearly describes the eligibility criteria for receiving financial assistance and how to apply for it. Consistent with the statute, the proposed regulations do not provide substantive requirements for a financial assistance policy regarding eligibility or amount of assistance, giving hospitals flexibility to determine the most effective way to serve their particular communities. Additionally, the proposed regulations describe how a hospital must widely publicize its financial assistance policy to ensure that community members are aware that aid is available.

Limitation on Collection Actions. A tax-exempt hospital is prohibited from engaging in certain collection methods (for example, reporting a debt to a credit agency or garnishing wages) until it makes reasonable efforts to determine whether an individual is eligible for the financial assistance it offers. Under these proposed rules, charitable hospitals must:

- Provide patients with a plain language summary of the financial assistance policy before discharge and with the first three bills;
- Give patients at least 120 days following the first bill to submit an application for financial assistance before commencing certain collection actions;
- Give the patient an additional 120 days (for 240 days total) to submit a complete application;
- If a patient is determined eligible for financial assistance during these 240 days, refund any excess payments made before applying for aid and seek to reverse any collections actions already commenced.

Limitation on Charges. A hospital may not charge individuals eligible for its financial assistance more for medically necessary care than the amounts generally billed to insured individuals. To help hospitals comply with this requirement when they do not know whether a patient is eligible for assistance, the proposed regulations provide a safe harbor. If a person has not applied for financial assistance, the hospital may bill the person at its usual charges, provided the hospital is reaching out to determine whether the person is eligible for financial assistance. If the person is eligible for aid, the hospital must refund any excess payments already made.

Non-Discriminatory Emergency Medical Care Policy. Each hospital must have a written policy requiring the hospital to provide emergency medical care without discriminating against patients who may need financial assistance. To simplify hospitals' compliance with this requirement, the proposed regulations provide that a policy that is consistent with the requirements of the Emergency Medical Treatment and Active Labor Act (EMTALA) is generally sufficient. The proposed rules require the policy to prohibit debt collection activities in the emergency department or in other hospital venues where collection activities could interfere with treatment.

NOTES AND QUESTIONS

1. *Ethical analysis.*   Beverly Cohen's article, supra, is quite critical of the hospital industry, government, private insurance industry, and class action

attorneys with respect to their actions, or inaction, relating to billing and collection practices of hospitals. Do you agree with her assessment? Does Section 501(r), as implemented by the proposed regulations, meet the criticisms of hospital billing and collection processes? Would you favor more or less, or merely different, ways of addressing the problems described by Cohen?

Note that Section 501(r) only affects nonprofit hospitals, which in 2011 made up 59 percent of the hospitals in the United States and 68 percent of Medicare beds. Issue Brief, The Network for Public Health Law, New Requirements for Nonprofit Hospitals Provide Opportunities for Health Department Collaboration, last updated Oct. 2011, available at http://www.networkforphl.org/ _asset/fqmqxr/CHNAFINAL.pdf. Do you think similar rules should apply to for-profit hospitals?

2. *Hospital defense.* In Congressional hearings beginning in the summer of 2003, hospitals defended their billing and collection practices in large part by arguing that Medicare regulations and federal anti-kickback laws restricted their ability to charge less than their uniform charge structure to uninsured patients and required them to vigorously pursue collection efforts. Cohen, supra, at 115–116. Beverly Cohen, in one part of her article, credits this defense as having some merit:

> While there is no question that many hospitals have not acted charitably with regard to uninsured patients, it also appears that, contrary to the denials by HHS [Dept. of Health and Human Services], hospitals had legitimate reasons for believing that lowering charges for the uninsured and underinsured or failing to take aggressive collections activities would expose themselves to regulatory risk. CMS's [Centers for Medicare and Medicaid Services] and the OIG's [Office of Inspector General] Advisory Opinions, Bulletins, Fraud Alerts, audit findings and even their express statements at the congressional hearing support the hospitals' position that waiving cost sharing or forgiving debt created regulatory risk. Although the hospitals' defenses with regard to the uninsured are substantially weaker than their defenses regarding Medicare beneficiaries, there are some legitimate bases supporting the hospitals' reluctance to discount charges or forgive debt.

Id. at 118.

In response to this claim, in February 2004, the Secretary of DHHS issued a letter assuring hospitals that they "can provide discounts to uninsured and underinsured patients who cannot afford their hospital bills and to Medicare beneficiaries who cannot afford their Medicare cost-sharing obligations." See News Release, Text of Letter from Tommy G. Thompson, Secretary of Health and Human Services, to Richard J. Davidson, President, American Hospital Association, February 19, 2004, available at http://archive.hhs.gov/news/press/ 2004pres/20040219.html. Around the same time, the OIG released a guidance explaining federal regulations connecting to this issue and stating that "No OIG authority prohibits or restricts hospitals from offering discounts to uninsured patients who are unable to pay their hospital bills." https://oig.hhs.gov/fraud/ docs/alertsandbulletins/2004/FA021904hospitaldiscounts.pdf.

3. *Charges for care in the for-profit hospital market and for out-of-network care.* New Section 501(r) of the tax code, supra, added by the ACA, provides a regulatory solution to the problem of billing the uninsured more than publicly or privately insured patients. This solution only applies to nonprofit hospitals and

also does not address the problem of insured patients seeking care outside of their insurance plan's network of preferred providers. Another (or additional) approach would be to apply principles of contract law to the payment of medical services. Barak D. Richman, Mark A. Hall & Kevin A. Schulman, Overbilling and Informed Financial Consent—A Contractual Solution, 367 New Eng. J. Med. 396 (2012). Richman et al. propose that prices in the health care setting can be assigned by understanding medical services as being provided under an implied contract. "An implied-contracts approach would obligate a patient to pay whatever amount a prudent patient and provider would have agreed to, given appropriate time and information." Id.

4, *Collections in the emergency departments.*   The Department of Treasury's proposed rules require hospitals to have a policy in place "to prohibit debt collection activities in the emergency department or in other hospital venues where collection activities could interfere with treatment." Press Release, supra. This regulation appears aimed at recent upfront bill collection efforts by hospitals. A report from Kaiser Health News, in collaboration with the Washington Post, stated that, "[l]ast year, about 80,000 emergency-room patients at hospitals owned by HCA, the nation's largest for-profit hospital chain, left without treatment after being told they would have to first pay $150 because they did not have a true emergency." Phil Galewitz, Hospitals Demand Payment Upfront From ER Patients With Routine Problems, Kaiser Health News, Feb. 20, 2012, available at http://www.kaiserhealthnews.org/stories/2012/february/19/hospitals-demand-payment-upfront-from-er-patients.aspx. According to HCA's spokesperson, the practice "has been a successful part of helping to reduce crowding in emergency rooms and to encourage appropriate use of scarce resources."

The State Attorney General for Minnesota recently sued Accretive Health, a company that helps hospitals process and collect payments, for practices that were allegedly far more aggressive than HCA's. The suit included claims for violation of federal and state health records privacy laws, Minnesota debt collection statutes, and Minnesota consumer protection laws. In a complaint filed in the U.S. District Court of Minnesota (Civil File No. 12-145 RHK/JJK), the State of Minnesota alleged a number of unsavory practices on the part of Accretive. Below are a few paragraphs from the 80-plus-page Second Amended Complaint, filed in early July 2012:

89. A hospital emergency room is and should be a solemn place. It is a place of medical trauma and emotional suffering, both for patients and their families. It is a place where patients and their families are especially vulnerable. It is a place where husbands lose wives, wives lose husband, parents lose children, and children lose parents. Many Americans face life-changing events in the emergency room.

90. Accretive prepared a document called the "Accretive Secret Sauce." The cover states: "You've never seen ASS like ours!" and "Check out our ASS!" The Secret Sauce states that typical hospitals do not collect money in the emergency room but that one of Accretive's Secret Sauce ingredients is to make bedside collections visits in the emergency room to extract money from patients. In the document, Accretive claims that its "Secret Sauce" results in a 15 percent collection rate from patients in the emergency room. . . .

92. Accretive orchestrated and implemented at hospitals in Minnesota a scheme of aggressive collections of past due balances and current bills in the emergency room. Minnesota patients received bedside collection visits—both from Accretive employees and from hospital employees under Accretive's control, supervision, management, training, direction, and oversight—while suffering from

serious medical injuries and ailments, including but not limited to chest pain, strokes, blood clots, labored breathing, diabetic attacks, escalated heart rates, elevated blood pressure, kidney stone attacks, disorientation and while hemorrhaging blood. Some patients were asked to pay money while in so much pain they thought they might die and/or while in medical distress and under duress. . . .

Accretive and the State of Minnesota reached a settlement within a month of the filing of the Second Amended Complaint. Under the settlement agreement, Accretive agreed to pay a $2.5 million fine and refrain from doing business in the State for six years. Elizabeth Stawicki, Hospital Debt Collector Settles Minnesota Case for $2.5 Million, Kaiser Health News, July 31, 2012, available at http://www.kaiserhealthnews.org/stories/2012/july/31/accretive-minnesota-lawsuit.aspx.

5. *Bibliographic note.*   A succinct explanation of how hospitals set their prices and how they are paid can be found in Uwe E. Reinhardt, The Pricing of U.S. Hospital Services: Chaos Behind a Veil of Secrecy, 25 Health Affairs 57 (2006).

D. CONTROLLING THE PRACTICE OF MEDICINE AND PROTECTING HEALTH CARE MARKETS

1.   Corporate Practice of Medicine

Physicians and other health care providers have for many years promoted the view that the practice of medicine was not like other businesses and should not fall under corporate control by laypeople who knew nothing of its science or art. This view is most clearly embodied in the "corporate practice of medicine doctrine," described in the first reading below. But while this understanding may suggest that the practice of medicine is "above" the world of business—and, certainly, plenty of health care providers genuinely lament the intrusion of cost and payment considerations into their medical treatment decision—it is clear that physicians and other providers have also engaged, individually and collectively, in business practices to protect their market share and exploit their market power—such as noncompetition agreements and other restraints of trade. The materials that follow raise questions about how one should view these activities from an ethical perspective.

a.   Bioethical and Social Approaches

> ## E. Haavi Morreim, Playing Doctor: Corporate Medical Practice and Medical Malpractice
> **32 U. Mich. J.L. Reform 939, 944–950 (1999)**

Although the doctrine banning corporate practice of medicine is largely a common law phenomenon arising during the 1930s, its roots go back earlier. Around the turn of the century, when allopathic physicians were competing with myriad other healers, newly enacted licensing laws required physicians to complete prescribed learning, pass examinations, and demonstrate the good character expected of a professional. Thereafter, quality of care rose and competition diminished. During the early part of the century, however, two new kinds of practice arrangements, contract practice and corporate practice, won the condemnation of the American Medical Association because they seemed to bode a diminution of physicians' growing stature and a retreat to the previous chaos.

In contract practice, corporations such as lumber and mining companies hired physicians to care for their employees, particularly in places like the Pacific Northwest, where physicians were not abundant. Although it ensured better access to care, it also limited patients' choice of physicians and meant that the corporation, rather than the physician, might decide how many patients would be seen.

In corporate practice, corporations marketed professional services (ranging from medicine and law to optometry and dentistry) to the public under their own brand name. Corporate practice was deemed particularly offensive, with images (and sometimes the reality) of crass commercialism. Courts ruling on these arrangements during the 1930s identified several potential hazards as they pointed to licensure laws and held that only licensed individuals, not corporations, can practice medicine, optometry, dentistry, law, or other professions. For present purposes, two of those hazards seem most pertinent. First, where physicians are employees, courts feared that laymen with no particular knowledge of medicine could dictate how many patients the physician would see, which treatments he could use, and other matters that courts believed should be left to a physician's professional discretion. After all, the defining criterion of an employment relationship, as distinct from an independent contractor relationship, is the level of control that the employer can exert over the employee. . . .

Second, the employment relationship was seen to divide the physician's loyalties. Instead of owing fealty exclusively to his patients' best interests, the employee–physician would also have duties to promote the best interests of his corporate master.

Since the 1930s, explicit exceptions to the ban on corporate practice have been numerous. In many states, whatever is left of the doctrine is simply ignored, although a few states still enforce their corporate practice bans. In the current market, however, two things seem obvious. First, early courts' concerns about lay interference in clinical practice, and about division of physicians' loyalties, are as vital today as ever. Medical ethics literature is filled with commentators' worries about both. Second, earlier courts' specific focus on employment as the keystone of concern is now an anachronism. MCOs do not need to employ a physician in order to control him. They can exercise enormous influence—some would say control—over medical judgments simply by deciding what they will and will not provide or pay for, particularly when they inform providers and patients in advance about their plans to deny coverage. Care has grown so costly that without assurance of funding, many providers will refuse to offer treatments and many patients will decline to seek them.

Accordingly, the questions concerning corporate practice of medicine have evolved. Instead of asking whether corporations should be permitted to employ physicians, we must now examine the "nouveau-corporate practice," and inquire whether health plans' broader panoply of economic controls, shy of actual employment, constitutes the practice of medicine; to what extent any such practice of medicine is (un)desirable; and whether MCOs should be, literally, directly liable for classic medical malpractice when they practice medicine.

b. Legal Approaches

Berlin v. Sarah Bush Lincoln Health Center
688 N.E.2d 106 (Ill. 1997)

Opinion by NICKELS.

Plaintiff, Richard Berlin, Jr., M.D., filed a complaint for declaratory judgment and a motion for summary judgment seeking to have a restrictive covenant contained in an employment agreement with defendant, Sarah Bush Lincoln Health Center (the Health Center), declared unenforceable. The circuit court of Coles County, finding the entire employment agreement unenforceable, granted summary judgment in favor of Dr. Berlin. The circuit court reasoned that the Health Center, as a nonprofit corporation employing a physician, was practicing medicine in violation of the prohibition on the corporate practice of medicine. A divided appellate court affirmed. . . .

The central issue involved in this appeal is whether the "corporate practice doctrine" prohibits corporations which are licensed hospitals from employing physicians to provide medical services. We find the doctrine inapplicable to licensed hospitals and accordingly reverse. . . .

CORPORATE PRACTICE OF MEDICINE DOCTRINE

The corporate practice of medicine doctrine prohibits corporations from providing professional medical services. Although a few states have codified the doctrine, the prohibition is primarily inferred from state medical licensure acts, which regulate the profession of medicine and forbid its practice by unlicensed individuals. The rationale behind the doctrine is that a corporation cannot be licensed to practice medicine because only a human being can sustain the education, training, and character-screening which are prerequisites to receiving a professional license. Since a corporation cannot receive a medical license, it follows that a corporation cannot legally practice the profession.

The rationale of the doctrine concludes that the employment of physicians by corporations is illegal because the acts of the physicians are attributable to the corporate employer, which cannot obtain a medical license. The prohibition on the corporate employment of physicians is invariably supported by several public policy arguments which espouse the dangers of lay control over professional judgment, the division of the physician's loyalty between his patient and his profitmaking employer, and the commercialization of the profession. . . .

APPLICABILITY OF DOCTRINE TO HOSPITALS IN OTHER JURISDICTIONS

Although the corporate practice of medicine doctrine has long been recognized by a number of jurisdictions, the important role hospitals serve in the health care field has also been increasingly recognized. Accordingly, numerous jurisdictions have recognized either judicial or statutory exceptions to the corporate practice of medicine doctrine which allow hospitals to employ physicians and other health care professionals . . . .

. . . We decline to apply the corporate practice of medicine doctrine to licensed hospitals. The instant cause is distinguishable from [earlier decisions]. None of those cases specifically involved the employment of physicians by a hospital. More important, none of those cases involved a corporation licensed to provide health care services to the general public. . . .

. . . The Medical Practice Act contains no express prohibition on the corporate employment of physicians. Rather, the corporate practice of medicine doctrine was inferred from the general policies behind the Medical Practice Act. Such a prohibition is entirely appropriate to a general corporation possessing no licensed authority to offer medical services to the public. . . . However, when a corporation has been sanctioned by the laws of this state to operate a hospital, such a prohibition is inapplicable.

The legislative enactments pertaining to hospitals provide ample support for this conclusion. For example, the Hospital Licensing Act defines "hospital" as:

> any institution, place, building, or agency, public or private, whether organized for profit or not, devoted primarily to the maintenance and operation of facilities for the diagnosis and treatment or care of . . . persons admitted for overnight stay or longer in order to obtain medical, including obstetric, psychiatric and nursing, care of illness, disease, injury, infirmity, or deformity. . . .

[A number of state] statutes clearly authorize, and at times mandate, licensed hospital corporations to provide medical services. We believe that the authority to employ duly-licensed physicians for that purpose is reasonably implied from these legislative enactments.

In addition, we find the public policy concerns which support the corporate practice doctrine inapplicable to a licensed hospital in the modern health care industry. The concern for lay control over professional judgment is alleviated in a licensed hospital, where generally a separate professional medical staff is responsible for the quality of medical services rendered in the facility.

Furthermore, we believe that extensive changes in the health care industry [in the last six decades], including the emergence of corporate health maintenance organizations, have greatly altered the concern over the commercialization of health care. In addition, such concerns are relieved when a licensed hospital is the physician's employer. Hospitals have an independent duty to provide for the patient's health and welfare.

We find particularly appropriate the statement of the Kansas Supreme Court that "it would be incongruous to conclude that the legislature intended a hospital to accomplish what it is licensed to do without utilizing physicians as independent contractors or employees. . . . To conclude that a hospital must do so without employing physicians is not only illogical but ignores reality." Accordingly, we conclude that a duly-licensed hospital possesses legislative authority to practice medicine by means of its staff of licensed physicians and is excepted from the operation of the corporate practice of medicine doctrine.

NOTES AND QUESTIONS

1. *Assessing reasons for corporate practice doctrine.* How does the court in *Berlin* distinguish cases decided in earlier years? Do you think that the distinction makes sense?

To which public policy concerns supporting the corporate practice of medicine prohibition did the *Berlin* court refer in rejecting the applicability of the prohibition in *Berlin*? Why are those concerns not considered relevant to hospitals?

2. *Future relevance of doctrine.* By the 1970s and 1980s, the corporate practice of medicine doctrine, although not obsolete, was becoming less consequential. The health care industry, encouraged by private payers and government alike to coordinate care and reduce costs, has undergone substantial integration. Many more physicians are employed by institutions—hospitals or health systems—than in the past, and that trend is likely to continue. Nevertheless, it is worth asking whether the doctrine has any ethical underpinnings that are worth recognizing and preserving in the new world of health care delivery and financing. What do you think? In considering this question, think about whether the practice of medicine is different from the practice of other professions–or whether it should be.

3. *Restraint of trade.* Justifications for the corporate practice of medicine doctrine can be understood as rooted in ethics. Yet it is also protective of the medical profession and its practitioners. In the case of In re American Medical Association, 94 F.T.C. 701 (1979), the FTC determined that a provision of the AMA's Principles of Medical Ethics that restricted the right of its members to enter into certain contractual agreements presented an unreasonable restraint on trade, and accordingly ordered the AMA to eliminate the provision in question. The AMA's official interpretations of the challenged provision forbade physicians from working for any group (including any hospital) that might sell "the services of that physician . . . for a fee"; condemned physicians' taking positions with "lay" entities that resulted in the lay entity's profiting from the physicians' services; and declared it unethical for physicians to take salaried jobs in hospital emergency rooms. The case was eventually appealed to the U.S. Supreme Court. By an equally divided vote, the Court affirmed a Second Circuit decision that upheld the FTC's order with small modifications. American Medical Ass'n v. Federal Trade Comm'n, 638 F.2d 443 (2d Cir. 1980), aff'd per curiam (by a divided vote), 455 U.S. 676 (1982). The case is described in detail in Jeffrey F. Chase-Lubitz, The Corporate Practice of Medicine Doctrine, 40 Vand. L. Rev. 445, 475–478 (1987).

Other useful articles include Mark A. Hall & Carl E. Schneider, Patients as Consumers: Courts, Contracts and the New Medical Marketplace, 106 Mich. L. Rev. 643 (2008); James F. Blumstein, Of Doctors and Hospitals: Setting the Analytical Framework for Managing and Regulating the Relationship, 4 Ind. Health L. Rev. 209 (2007).

4. *Narcotic treatment programs and corporate practice doctrine.*   The corporate practice of medicine doctrine has created particular problems for narcotics treatment programs (NTPs). These programs, which provide methadone maintenance therapy to counteract addiction to heroin, are usually owned by people not themselves doctors. In California, the legislature enacted a law that specifically exempts NTPs from the state's corporate practice of medicine doctrine. Cal. Bus. & Prof. Code 2401(c) (amended by Chapter 231) (described in Carla G. McClurg, Health and Welfare: Chapter 321, 33 McGeorge L. Rev. 305 (2002)). The amendment was stimulated by passage of Proposition 36 (effective in 2001), which diverts nonviolent drug offenders from prison into treatment programs. Proposition 36: Drugs, Probation and Treatment Program, http:// www.ss.ca.gov/elections/sov/2000_general/measures.pdf (visited Jan. 22, 2004). Chapter 321 allows NTPs in California to employ physicians; however, the NTP is precluded by the law from interfering with the professional judgment of doctors it hires. In other states, NTPs are prohibited even though they must comply with HHS and FDA regulations regarding dosage and delivery, and by the Department of Drug and Alcohol Programs. McClurg, at 308.

See also California Ass'n of Dispensing Opticians v. Pearle Vision Center, 143 Cal. App. 3d 412 (1983) (affirming preliminary injunction for licensed opticians against a franchise of vision centers; defendant-vision centers, although not licensed to practice optometry, operated as though they were). The case is discussed in Arnold J. Rosoff, The Corporate Practice of Medicine Doctrine: Has Its Time Passed? 12 Health L. Dig. 1, 4 (1984).

2.   Noncompetition Agreements and Other Restraints of Trade

|| *Central Indiana Podiatry v. Krueger* ||
882 N.E.2d 723 (Ind. 2008)

BOEHM, Justice.

We hold that noncompetition agreements between a physician and a medical practice group are not per se void as against public policy and are enforceable to the extent they are reasonable. To be geographically reasonable, the agreement may restrict only that area in which the physician developed patient relationships using the practice group's resources.

From 1996 until 2005, podiatrist Kenneth Krueger was employed by Central Indiana Podiatry, P.C. (CIP) under a series of written employment agreements that were renewed every one or two years. Each agreement contained provisions restricting Krueger's activities after any termination. For two years after leaving CIP's employ, Krueger would be prohibited from divulging the names of patients, contacting patients to provide podiatric services, and soliciting CIP employees. Krueger also would be prohibited from practicing podiatry for two years within a geographic area defined as fourteen listed central Indiana counties and "any other county where [CIP] maintained an office during the term of this Contract or in any county adjacent to any of the foregoing counties." CIP maintained an office in two unlisted counties, and another twenty-seven counties are contiguous to one or more of these sixteen. The restricted area thus consisted of forty-three counties, essentially the middle half of the state.

At some point, Krueger worked at CIP's offices in Clinton, Marion, Howard, Tippecanoe, and Hamilton counties. By 2005, he was working three days each week at the Nora office in Indianapolis (Marion County), and one day each at the Lafayette (Tippecanoe) and Kokomo (Howard) offices. In 2005, a Kokomo office employee reported to CIP that Krueger had attempted to kiss her at the office. While CIP was investigating the incident, Krueger, concerned that he might be terminated, obtained an electronic copy of the names and addresses of patients treated at the Nora office. CIP terminated Krueger on July 25, 2005.

In September 2005, Krueger entered into an employment agreement to practice podiatry with Meridian Health Group, P.C. in Hamilton County. Hamilton is immediately north of Marion County and is one of the counties listed in Krueger's noncompetition agreement. Krueger provided a copy of the CIP patient list to Meridian, and along with other Meridian employees, created a letter announcing his employment with Meridian "approximately 10 minutes from [Krueger's] previous office" in northern Marion County. This letter was mailed to patients on September 30, 2005.

When it learned of the letter CIP sought injunctive relief against Krueger and damages from Krueger and Meridian, claiming that Krueger's employment violated the geographic limitations. . . .

Krueger argues that the noncompetition agreement is void as against public policy because noncompetition agreements involving physicians interfere with the physician–patient relationship. There is some force to this contention. Noncompetition agreements are justified because they protect the investment and good will of the employer. In many businesses, the enforceability of a noncompetition agreement affects only the interests of the employee and employer. A noncompetition agreement by a physician involves other considerations as well. Unlike customers of many businesses, patients typically come to the physician's office and have direct contact with the physician. If an agreement forces a physician to relocate outside the geographic area of the physician's practice, the patients' legitimate interest in selecting the physician of their choice is impaired. Moreover, the confidence of a patient in the physician is typically an important factor in the relationship that relocation would displace. In both respects physicians are unlike employees in many businesses. The legal framework applicable to these relationships needs to take these differences into account.

Whether physicians should be prohibited from entering into noncompetition agreements is essentially a policy question. Three states have statutes prohibiting physician noncompetition agreements. In the absence of any Indiana legislation on this point, Krueger points to an American Medical Association ethics opinion discouraging but not prohibiting noncompetition agreements. Krueger also cites a recent Tennessee Supreme Court case, Murfreesboro Medical Clinic, P.A. v. Udom, which relied largely on the AMA opinion in holding that essentially all physician noncompetition agreements violate public policy. 166 S.W.3d 674, 684 (Tenn.2005). For the reasons expressed below, we disagree, and note that the Tennessee legislature has since acted to permit physician noncompetition agreements.

The AMA's views of noncompetition agreements between physicians were in place when we upheld such agreements in Raymundo v. Hammond Clinic Ass'n, 449 N.E.2d 276 (Ind.1983). At that time, we rejected the claim that "public policy precludes medical doctors from entering into or enforcing non-competition covenants," and we adopted a reasonableness standard for physician noncompetition agreements. *Raymundo* is consistent with the substantial majority of United States jurisdictions in permitting reasonable restrictions.

This Court has long held that noncompetition covenants in employment contracts are in restraint of trade and disfavored by the law. We construe these covenants strictly against the employer and will not enforce an unreasonable restriction. For the reasons noted above, agreements by physicians should be given particularly careful scrutiny. . . .

[W]e agree with the Court of Appeals that CIP demonstrated that the agreement served the legitimate interest of preserving patient relationships developed with CIP resources and to that extent served a legitimate interest of CIP.

Although CIP has asserted a legitimate interest served by the noncompetition agreement, to be enforceable, the noncompetition agreement must also be reasonable in terms of the time, activities, and geographic area restricted. The parties accept two years as a reasonable period of time and dispute only the reasonableness of the geographic restriction. The trial court found the noncompetition agreement "invalid, unenforceable and geographically unreasonable." The Court of Appeals agreed that the geographic restriction "covers a significant portion of Indiana," but upheld the geographic restriction, finding that it was reasonable in light of CIP's several locations and evidence that CIP offices drew patients from surrounding counties. . . .

Whether a geographic scope is reasonable depends on the interest of the employer that the restriction serves. . . . An employer has invested in creating its physician's patient relationships only where the physician has practiced. We agree with the courts that have held that noncompetition agreements justified by the employer's development of patient relationships must be limited to the area in which the physician has had patient contact.

The record does not support any inference that Krueger used CIP's resources to establish relationships throughout the approximately forty counties the agreement identifies by name or description. Because that is the area sought to be restricted by the agreement, the agreement is clearly overbroad. If a noncompetition agreement is overbroad and it is feasible to strike the unreasonable portions and leave only reasonable portions, the court may apply the blue pencil doctrine to permit enforcement of the reasonable portions. The blue pencil doctrine permits excising language but not rewriting the agreement. CIP chose to define its geographic scope in terms of counties rather than the radius from the workplace used in *Raymundo* or some smaller area. . . . Because Marion, Tippecanoe, and Howard are named counties in which the record established that Krueger worked in the two years preceding his termination, the geographic scope is sustainable as to them.

However, the geographic scope is unreasonable to the extent it reaches contiguous counties. The Nora office in northern Marion County is nearly forty miles from parts of contiguous Johnson County. As one would expect, and as the dissent observes, the record established that some patients cross county lines for podiatry services. But there is nothing to suggest the improbable flow of a substantial number of podiatry patients from Johnson County across a heavily trafficked metropolitan area to Nora. . . .

Krueger argues, and the trial court held, that the Indiana Administrative Code "obligat[ed]" Krueger "to provide written notice to his former patients that he had changed practice groups" and that "CIP implicitly authorized Krueger to utilize its patient list to accomplish this task." The Indiana Board of Podiatric Medicine's Standards of Professional Conduct provide that a podiatrist shall "[g]ive reasonable written notice to a patient or to those responsible for the patient's care when the podiatrist withdraws from a case so that another practitioner may be employed by the patient or by those responsible for the patient's care."

. . . These provisions do not either justify or call into question the validity of a restriction on the area in which a podiatrist may practice. They merely require notice to patients that the move will take place.

. . . The parties' arguments regarding whether a preliminary injunction would disserve the public interest are largely the same as those regarding whether physician noncompetition agreements should be void as against public policy. CIP also argues that an injunction would not harm the public because CIP provided qualified physicians to meet the needs of all patients who would have seen Krueger. Because physician noncompetition covenants are not per se unenforceable and because CIP looked after the needs of its patients, a preliminary injunction would not have disserved the public interest.

The trial court's order denying CIP a preliminary injunction is affirmed except as to Marion, Tippecanoe, and Howard counties, and this case is remanded to the trial court for disposition of CIP's remaining claims.

NOTES AND QUESTIONS

1. *Physician noncompetititon agreements.* The Indiana Supreme Court in *Central Indiana Podiatry* held that physician noncompetition agreements are not per se unenforceable, but are instead to be judged by a reasonableness standard (as are other noncompetition agreements), although physician agreements "should be given particularly careful scrutiny." What do you think of this approach? What do you think "particularly careful scrutiny" means?

2. *Blue-penciling.* Courts will sometimes engage in blue-penciling to salvage a noncompetition agreement that is overly broad, as the court in *Central Indiana Podiatry* did. This means that the court will strike through unreasonable provisions but will not rewrite provisions. Knowing this, attorneys for companies seeking noncompetition agreements from employees and others (such as the seller of a business) will commonly write noncompetition agreements with a list of expanding geographical areas, for example, defining the location in which the physician will not practice as (a) city, (b) county, (c) intrastate region, (d) state, (e) region of country, (f) the United States, (g) North America, (h) the world. This allows a court to strike through those locations on the list that are not necessary to protect the legitimate interests of the company and thus are void, while preserving the noncompetition agreement in its essential elements. What do you think of this practice? Do you think agreements written in this way will cause those bound by such agreements to restrict their practice more severely than legally warranted?

Is writing an agreement in this manner ethical as a general matter and as applied specifically to physicians? How does it compare to asking patients to sign an unenforceable waiver of their right to sue for malpractice?

3. *Redefining the "learned professions" in relationship to restraints of trade.*   Related to the decline of the corporate practice of medicine doctrine has been the recategorization of the so-called learned professions (including law and medicine) for various legal purposes. In 1975, the U.S. Supreme Court concluded that a county bar association (as part of the "learned professions") was not thereby exempt from the reach of antitrust law. The case involved the legality of a minimal fee schedule for lawyers developed by a bar association in Virginia. Goldfarb v. Virginia State Bar, 421 U.S. 773 (1975). Several years later, in Arizona v. Maricopa County Medical Society, the Court concluded that fee agreements among doctors violated the Sherman Act. 457 U.S. 332 (1982). The Court explained that "the fact that doctors—rather than nonprofessionals—are the parties to the price-fixing agreements [does not] support the [doctors'] position."

One commentator described the "re-envisioning of the business of medical care" in *Maricopa County* to define the profession in terms not unlike those that would describe "the business of selling wholesale rubber and steel to the automobile industry." Sara Rosenbaum, The Impact of United States Law on Medicine as a Profession, 289 JAMA 1546, 1553 (2003). According to Rosenbaum, the fact that the U.S. Department of Justice has extended to doctors some room to negotiate price through provider networks should not be seen as a revivification of the exemption once enjoyed by doctors as members of a learned profession. In her view, *Maricopa County* and surrounding events "fundamentally transformed the business of medicine." Id. at 1553.

See also Wilk v. Am. Med. Ass'n, 895 F.2d 352 (7th Cir. 1990) (holding AMA ethical standard prohibiting "professional association" between members and chiropractors was an unreasonable restraint of trade in violation of the Sherman Act because its purpose was to bar entry by competitors).

E.   HEALTH CARE "PRODUCTS" AND DISCOVERIES

1.   *Manufacturing and Marketing*

a.   Bioethical and Social Perspectives

> *Heidi Li Feldman, Pushing Drugs:*
> *Genomics and Genetics, the Pharmaceutical*
> *Industry and the Law of Negligence*
> 42 Washburn L.J. 575, 575–576, 581–582,
> 587–589 (2003)

MDM [market-driven manufacturing] is a well-documented, much practiced activity, although American courts do not recognize MDM as a discrete category of conduct. The basic idea of MDM is that marketing considerations should continuously control every aspect and stage of a product's lifecycle. When a company engages in MDM, it completely inverts the conception of product design, development, and dissemination that seems natural to those unfamiliar with modern producer practices. Somebody thinking rather loosely about products manufacturing might well think the process goes as follows. A person or group of people notice a need or desire other people seem to have and envision a product that would fulfill the need or gratify the desire. These people then invent that product and manufacture it. The inventors/manufacturers then turn to other people to get their product into a distribution chain—wholesaler to jobber to sales representatives to retailers, for example. The retailers sell the product to the ordinary consumer.

MDM essentially turns this simple picture upside down. A modern corporation often starts by fanning or instilling desires or needs in the general population, thereby stimulating or creating demand for a product the company has not yet fully envisioned. Only after development of demand does the company invest in design, tailoring its product to the now-felt needs and desires that the company itself has promoted. . . .

II.   A CASE STUDY OF PHARMACEUTICAL MDM . . .

From the mid-twentieth century to the century's end, the pharmaceutical industry enjoyed two major rounds of success. The first included the development of antibiotics and vaccines; the second, the development of drugs to control, if not cure, chronic serious health problems such as depression, high cholesterol, and high blood pressure. By the beginning of the twenty-first century, however, drug companies were no longer reaping such large profits from these two waves of drug development. Both legal and market forces have led to the decline. On the legal side, patent protection for many twentieth century "wonder drugs" has expired. On the market side, both private and public insurers have pressured physicians, pharmacies, and patients to use generics or less expensive versions of branded drugs, part of a larger effort to control health care costs overall. Hospitals too are trying to escape traditional purchasing systems that are financed by pharmaceutical manufacturers. They seek independent bargaining power to negotiate lower drug costs.

So, the pharmaceutical industry has lost some luster, both in terms of the sector's stock performance and in terms of maintaining a reputation for producing "wonder drugs." Manufacturers have addressed the decline in profitability through a combination of tactics, which create a climate infused with risk of harm, one that will only be exacerbated when the first pharmacogenomic drugs hit the market. For example, drug companies routinely pay insurance plans to increase the use of their products: the drug company pays the insurance plan to add its drug to lists of recommended drugs that are distributed to physicians and pharmacies. Drug companies also give physicians and pharmacies direct financial reward for switching a patient from a rival's product to their own. While many companies use these and other components of MDM for their pharmaceuticals, one drug maker, Pfizer, has used MDM to become, according to the Financial Times, the "world's largest pharmaceutical group." "Pfizer has become the first company to capture more than 10% of the worldwide prescription pharmaceutical market." This success is not unrelated to Pfizer's much remarked upon MDM. . . .

Originally, Neurontin was FDA-approved only for epilepsy. In 2002, Pfizer gained approval for Neurontin as a treatment for managing pain associated with shingles, the only additional FDA-approved use for the drug. Currently, the Boston United States Attorney's Office, "states[,] and the District of Columbia are investigating" potentially illegal promotion of off-label usage of Neurontin during the period Warner-Lambert merchandised the drug. Discovery has uncovered memoranda from 1995 and 1996 documenting the decision by Warner-Lambert's "new product committee" not to conduct large clinical trials required for FDA approval of Neurontin for treatment of migraines and social phobia. The committee decided instead to perform small studies and place the results in medical journals. A 1995 company memorandum stated "that 25 percent of Neurontin prescriptions were" for off-label usage. In 2001, the majority of all Neurontin prescriptions written in the United States—roughly three-quarters of them—were for off-label uses. Sales figures for Neurontin in 2001 were $1.75 billion. In 2002, it appears that approximately eighty percent of Neurontin prescriptions were written for conditions other than epilepsy, the FDA-approved indication; and early estimates show that Neurontin has reached two billion dollars in sales in 2002.

The memoranda documenting the activities of Warner-Lambert executives were released by the attorney for a private plaintiff, Dr. David Franklin, M.D.—a former Parke-Davis "medical liaison"—now suing Pfizer.[2] According to press reports, Franklin, "alleges he was forced to participate in a national marketing campaign in which he and others made exaggerated or false claims about the safety and efficacy of the drug." Franklin also claims that "illegal promotion of the drug defrauded the federal government out of hundreds of millions of dollars in Medicaid payments."

Other documents uncovered in Franklin's suit and reported in the press further detail Warner-Lambert's MDM strategy: allegedly, the company provided ghost-written journal articles for physicians to publish under their own names and rewarded the largest potential prescribers with all-expense-paid weekend trips to a Florida beach resort (in addition to expenses, each physician allegedly received a $250 honorarium).

NOTES AND QUESTIONS

1. *Proposed new cause of action against pharmaceuticals.*   Heidi Li Feldman concludes Pushing Drugs, supra, by proposing that courts recognize a cause of action for negligent pharmaceutical market-driven manufacturing (MDM). A drug company, in her view, should be protected from liability if it "engage[s] in MDM as [would] a person of ordinary caution and prudence, with due regard for the safety of others. . . . If cogent legal arguments can be brought to bear on this issue, then a cause of action for negligent pharmaceutical MDM poses no special difficulties for courts to administer." Feldman, supra, at 598. Finally, Feldman suggests that such a new cause of action is especially called for in light of the likelihood of a new generation of gene-specific drugs that may

---

2. See United States ex rel. Franklin v. Parke-Davis, infra, subsection E(1)(b)—Eds.

prove to be largely safe and effective or that may "set [the stage] for a new round of pharmaceutically induced injuries." Id. at 599. Assuming the risk Feldman identifies, what other mechanisms might be considered to limit that risk?

2. *Pharmaceuticals' profits and costs.*   The pharmaceutical industry attributes the high cost of drugs in the United States to a combination of factors, including primarily the arduous trial-and-error work needed to develop a new drug and the long period it takes to receive marketing approval for a new drug from the FDA. Most potential new drugs do not reach the market. Commentators outside the industry attribute the high cost of drugs in the United States to other factors, including large profits for the pharmaceuticals and the enormous sums given to promotional budgets. Andrew Harris, Recent Congressional Responses to Demands for Affordable Pharmaceuticals, 16 Loy. Consumer L. Rep. 219 (2004); Henry Grabowski, Pharmaceuticals: Politics, Policy and Availability: Patents and New Product Development in the Pharmaceutical and Biotechnology Industries, 8 Geo. Pub. Pol'y Rev. 7 (2003).

Jatin and Nitin Roper report that in 2004 the marketing budget of the U.S. pharmaceutical industry was $57.5 billion. Of that, something over a third was devoted to "detailing" (visits paid by pharmaceutical industry "reps" to physicians); a little more than a quarter was spent on drug samples, given to doctors for distribution to patients; and about 7 percent was spent on direct-to-consumer advertising. Jatin Roper & Nitin Roper, Pharmaceutical Industry Marketing to Physicians, Healthcare Policy, Clinical Correlations, NYU Internal Medicine Blog, June 8, 2008, available at http://www.clinicalcorrelations.org/?p=737 (last visited July 7, 2008) (citing M.A. Gagnon & J. Lexchin, The Cost of Pushing Pills, PLoS Med (2008)).

3. *Industry gifts and payments to physicians.*   Jatin and Nitin Roper also note that marketing to physicians "works":

> Gifts of any value to physicians create a tacit expectation that they return the favor; these incentives may result in bias in clinical decision-making that affects patient health and increases health care costs. Many doctors agree that gifts influence other practitioners, but insist that they do not affect their own practices. The public, meanwhile, is as appalled with drug companies wooing doctors as they are with lobbyists "donating" money to politicians' campaigns. In 2002 the pharmaceutical industry, fearing national legislation, voluntarily limited their marketing gifts to those of less than $100 in value, while explicitly allowing unfettered drug sample distribution, "ghostwriting," and unlimited payments for physician speakers. The magnitude of these payments is staggering and continues to increase. In Minnesota, where most monetary gifts to physicians are publicly reported, at least 700 providers received more than $10,000 between 1997 and 2005, while the average internal medicine doctor received $1000, and the average cardiologist $2300.

Id. (citing G. Harris & J. Roberts, Doctors' Ties to Drug Makers Are Put on Close View, N.Y. Times, Mar. 21, 2007). Academic medical centers have begun to set policies that prohibit or limit gifts from industry to physicians. Id. In 2006, JAMA published a policy proposal recommending that even small gifts from industry to physicians be banned. The authors suggest, more particularly, changes in, or elimination of, "common practices related to . . . pharmaceutical samples, continuing medical education, funds for physician travel, speakers bureaus, ghostwriting, and consulting and research contracts." Troyen A. Brennan et al., A Policy Proposal for Academic Medical Centers, 295 JAMA 429 (2006). In 2010, as part of the Patient Protection and Affordable Care Act, Congress enacted the Physician Payment Sunshine Act, which requires pharmaceutical and device companies to report physician compensation, ownership, and investment interests. Those regulations will go into effect in 2013.

4. *Food companies' solicitation of physicians.*   Food companies have begun to mimic the marketing schemes of pharmaceutical companies. Some send representatives directly to physicians' offices to suggest that patients be advised of the health benefits of specific foods. Katy McLaughlin & Jane Spencer, Take Two Grass-Fed Steaks and Call Me in the Morning, Wall St. Journal, May 25, 2004, at D1, 2004 WL-WSJ 56930072. Physicians are being provided with samples of healthy snacks much as they have long been provided with drug samples. Moreover, food companies employ physicians who speak about the health benefits of the companies' products at medical conferences. Some food companies are working with pharmaceuticals so that sample drugs are distributed together with food coupons or packaged foods. Do you see anything problematic about this practice? Are doctors trained to evaluate the claims food companies are making? How might it matter if they are not?

b.   Legal Approaches

> ## United States ex rel. David Franklin v. Parke-Davis
> ### 147 F. Supp. 2d 39 (D. Mass. 2001)

Opinion by SARIS.

In this qui tam action under the False Claims Act ("FCA"), 31 U.S.C. §3729–33, Relator Dr. David Franklin alleges, among other things, that his former employer engaged in a fraudulent scheme to promote the sale of the drug Neurontin for "off-label" uses (i.e., uses other than those approved by the Food and Drug Administration) and that this illegal marketing campaign caused the submission of false claims to . . . the federal government for Medicaid reimbursement. The Defendant has moved for dismissal based on Relator's failure to plead a claim of fraud with particularity pursuant to Fed. R. Civ. P. 9(b) and his failure to state a claim upon which relief may be granted pursuant to Fed. R. Civ. P. 12(b)(6). . . .

Relator David Franklin ("Franklin" or "Relator") is a former employee of Defendant Parke-Davis, a division of Warner-Lambert Company. . . .

At the time of the events in question, Warner-Lambert Company was a corporation engaged in the manufacture and sale of pharmaceutical and consumer products. Defendant Parke-Davis was the company's pharmaceutical products division, which manufactured, marketed, and conducted research relating to prescription drugs. . . .

Under the Food, Drug, and Cosmetics Act ("FDCA"), 21 U.S.C. §§301–97, new pharmaceutical drugs cannot be distributed in interstate commerce unless the sponsor of the drug demonstrates to the satisfaction of the Food and Drug Administration ("FDA") that the drug is safe and effective for each of its intended uses. Once a drug is approved for a particular use, however, the

FDA does not prevent doctors from prescribing the drug for uses that are different than those approved by the FDA. Allowing physicians to prescribe drugs for such "off-label" usage "is an accepted and necessary corollary of the FDA's mission to regulate [pharmaceuticals] without directly interfering with the practice of medicine." Though physicians may prescribe drugs for off-label usage, the FDA prohibits drug manufacturers from marketing or promoting a drug for a use that the FDA has not approved. A manufacturer illegally "misbrands" a drug if the drug's labeling includes information about its unapproved uses. If the manufacturer intends to promote the drug for new uses in addition to . . . those already approved, the materials on off-label uses must meet certain stringent requirements and the manufacturer must resubmit the drug to the FDA testing and approval process.

Whether a drug is FDA-approved for a particular use will largely determine whether a prescription for that use of the drug will be reimbursed under the federal Medicaid program. Reimbursement under Medicaid is, in most circumstances, available only for "covered outpatient drugs." Covered outpatient drugs do not include drugs that are "used for a medical indication which is not a medically accepted indication." A medically accepted indication, in turn, includes a use "which is approved under the Federal Food Drug and Cosmetic Act" or which is included in specified drug compendia. Thus, unless a particular off-label use for a drug is included in one of the identified drug compendia, a prescription for the off-label use of that drug is not eligible for reimbursement under Medicaid.

Neurontin, which is the brand name for the drug gabapentin, was approved by the FDA in 1994 for use as an adjunctive treatment for epilepsy in doses from 900 to 1800 mg per day. Neurontin is also used for a number of off-label purposes. For example, Neurontin is prescribed for pain control, as monotherapy for epilepsy, for control of bipolar disease, and as treatment for attention deficit disorder. According to Relator, 50% of Neurontin's sales in 1996 are attributable to off-label uses. Of those sales, Relator estimates that 50% (or 25% of Neurontin's total sales) were reimbursed by the government either indirectly through Medicaid or directly through purchases by the Veterans Administration.

Accupril, which is the brand name for the drug quinipril, is an angiotensin converting enzyme (ACE) inhibitor that has been approved for the control of hypertension and as a treatment for heart failure.

During the events in question, neither Neurontin nor Accupril were eligible for reimbursement from Medicaid when prescribed for an off-label use because neither drug's off-label uses were included in one of the compendia specified by [federal law]. . . . The crux of Relator's allegations is that the Defendant engaged in an extensive and far-reaching campaign to use false statements to promote increased prescriptions of Neurontin and Accupril for off-label uses which caused the filing of false claims for reimbursement by the federal government.

Relator alleges that he was hired by Parke-Davis onto a team of "medical liaisons." While medical liaisons are ordinarily connected to the research divisions of the manufacturer, Parke-Davis's medical liaisons were exclusively employed as sales and promotion personnel.

Parke-Davis's medical liaisons, including Relator, were instructed to make exaggerated or false claims concerning the safety and efficacy of Parke-Davis drugs for off-label uses. They were also trained to convey that Neurontin could be prescribed for its various off-label uses in amounts of up to 4800 mg per day— far above the maximum dosage of 1800 mg per day approved by the FDA. To bolster their representations to physicians, medical liaisons were encouraged to misrepresent their scientific credentials and to pose as research personnel, rather than as sales representatives.

Relator also alleges the doctors were rewarded with kickbacks for prescribing large quantities of Parke-Davis drugs. These alleged kick-backs took various forms. For instance, some doctors were allegedly paid sums of money which were ostensibly compensation for drug studies. However, Relator alleges these studies were shams and had no scientific value. Other doctors were allegedly paid sums of money under the guise of being compensated for their services as "consultants" or "preceptors" or for participating in a "speakers bureau." Doctors were also allegedly given cash payments for small record-keeping tasks, such as allowing Parke-Davis access to information about the doctors' patients who were receiving Neurontin. There are also allegations that doctors prescribing large amounts of Parke-Davis drugs were given gifts such as travel and tickets to the Olympics.

According to Relator, when questions arose concerning the availability of reimbursement for prescriptions for off-label uses of Parke-Davis drugs, medical liaisons were instructed to coach doctors on how to conceal the off-label nature of the prescription. Relator also alleges that Parke-Davis took numerous actions to conceal its activities from the FDA, including shredding documents, falsifying documents, and encouraging medical liaisons to conduct their marketing activities without leaving a "paper trail" that might be discovered by the FDA. . . .

Qui tam actions under the FCA must comply with Fed. R. Civ. P. 9(b), which requires that "the circumstances constituting fraud . . . shall be stated with particularity." Relator must, at a minimum, set forth the "'who, what, when, where, and how' of the alleged fraud." To pass Rule 9(b) muster, the complaint must plead with particularity the time, place and contents of the false representations as well as the identity of the person making the false representations and what he obtained with them. The particularity requirement of Rule 9(b) serves the purposes of enabling defendants to prepare meaningful defenses to charges of fraud, preventing conclusory allegations of fraud from serving as a basis for strike suits and fishing expeditions, and protecting defendants from groundless charges that may damage their reputations.

The requirements of Rule 9(b), however, must be read in conjunction with Fed. R. Civ. P. 8(a), which requests "a short and plain statement of the claim" for relief. Thus, while Relator must allege the circumstances of the fraud, he is not required to plead all of the evidence or facts supporting it. . . .

Viewed in light of the disclosure, Relator's complaint contains allegations of fraud sufficient to satisfy Rule 9(b): Counts II and IV describe a scheme of fraud designed to increase the submission of off-label prescriptions for Neurontin for payment by Medicaid; and Count VI describes false statements made to physicians to induce off-label prescriptions for Neurontin. As far as the "who" in these counts is concerned, the disclosure identifies by name the individuals at Parke-Davis who instructed the medical liaisons on how to fraudulently promote off-label use of Neurontin. It also lists the medical liaisons by name. In addition, the disclosures and exhibits identify the physicians who were contacted and allegedly given false information and kickbacks in return for increasing their off-label use of Neurontin. Relator adequately identifies the "what" by alleging that Defendant's conduct resulted in the submission of numerous Neurontin prescriptions that were ineligible for reimbursement under Medicaid because they were prescribed for an off-label use. The "when" of Relator's complaint is confined to the time-frame during which Relator was employed as a Parke-Davis medical liaison in its Northeast Customer Business Unit. Finally, the "how" of the alleged fraud is detailed in the portions of the complaint and disclosure that describe a fraudulent marketing campaign conducted by Parke-Davis in which kickbacks and unlawful and misleading marketing were allegedly used to encourage doctors to increase their use of Neurontin for unapproved purposes.

Dr. Franklin cites at least eleven specific examples of fraudulent statements which medical liaisons (including himself) were trained to give to physicians, and did give to physicians, to induce the purchase of Neurontin for off-label uses, including the following:

- Upon order of the company and as a result of training of medical liaisons, Dr. Franklin "deliberately contrived reports to mislead physicians into believing that a body of data existed that demonstrated the effectiveness of Neurontin in the treatment of bipolar disease." In fact, no data existed at all to support the use of Neurontin in bipolar disease.

- Dr. Franklin was trained and instructed to actively deceive physicians with contrived data, falsified "leaks" from clinical trials, scientifically flawed reports, or "success stories" that stated that Neurontin was highly effective in the treatment of a variety of pain syndromes. No such body of evidence existed.

- He was instructed to advise physicians that Parke-Davis had developed a large body of data to support the use of Neurontin as mono-therapy. This was an "outright lie" and left patients unknowingly without good seizure control.

- Medical liaisons were instructed to tell physicians that a great deal of data existed that supported the safe use of Neurontin at levels that exceed 4800 mg per day. However, clinically significant safety data existed at dosing levels at only 1800 mg per day.

- Parke-Davis provided medical liaisons with slides that stated that Neurontin was effective for the treatment of Attention Deficit Disorders but no data existed to support that claim. . . .

When considered alongside the disclosure, the complaint amply details both a general framework of the purported Medicaid fraud and provides more specific information on the individuals, locations, the precise statements alleged to be false and time-frames involved. The complaint therefore satisfies the requirements of Rule 9(b) with respect to the off-label sale of Neurontin for Medicaid reimbursement (Counts II, IV, and VI). . . .

Count IX alleges the illegal promotion of Accupril. According to Franklin, the medical liaisons were told to tell physicians, including those at the Veterans Administration, that if a patient is on any other ACE inhibitor but Accupril, the studies showed that these patients would have more heart attacks, require more procedures, and die sooner. Relator alleges there was no credible scientific data to support these claims. (Disclosure at 28.) However, unlike the claims involving

Neurontin, the Disclosure does not identify the liaisons involved in the fraud, the doctors who were given false information, or any false claims made. It is dismissed.

NOTES AND QUESTIONS

1. *Allegations in* Franklin.   What were the specific illegalities in which the plaintiff in *Franklin* alleged that the pharmaceutical company defendant had engaged?

2. *Subsequent events.*   In 2003, the district court in Massachusetts denied Parke-Davis's motion for summary judgment with regard to Franklin's allegations under the False Claims Act. Franklin had alleged that Parke-Davis "'caused to be presented' claims for reimbursement for off-label prescriptions that were ineligible for coverage under Medicaid." United States ex rel. Franklin v. Parke Davis, 2003 U.S. Dist. Lexis 15754 (2003). In May 2003, the Wall Street Journal reported that the filing alleged that Parke-Davis was paying substantial sums of money to doctors (in at least one case, over $300,000). In exchange, the doctors agreed to promote off-label uses of Neurontin to other doctors. David Armstrong, Technology & Health: Maker of Epilepsy Drug Sued, Wall St. Journal, May 30, 2003, at B4.

In 2004, Warner-Lambert (by then owned by Pfizer) agreed to a settlement that involved paying over $400 million. Among other things the company agreed to pay $280 million as a criminal fine for violations of the Food, Drug and Cosmetic Act. Franklin was to receive over $26 million as a result of the settlement. David Armstrong & Assa Wilde Mathews, Pfizer Case Signals Tougher Action on "Off-Label" Drug Use, Wall St. Journal, May 14, 2004, at B1.

However, in 2008, in a case against Pfizer filed by consumers and health insurers, plaintiffs claimed that for several years after Pfizer's purchase of Warner-Lambert in 2000, Pfizer either changed or refused to release reports showing that Neurontin was not effective as a response to several off-label conditions. Keith J. Winstein, Suit Alleges Pfizer Spun Unfavorable Drug Studies, Wall St. Journal, Oct. 10, 2008, http://www.wsj.com. The claim conflicts with Pfizer's public commitment to publish "medically or scientifically significant results" of every study conducted by the company, regardless of a study's results. Id. And in 2010, Pfizer was ordered to pay $142 million for violations of federal racketeering laws and to pay $65 million for violations of California's unfair competition laws due to illegal promotion of Neurontin. Despite these successes in the courtroom, there is considerable evidence that the government investigation and large settlements have had very little effect on drugmaker behavior and physician activity. See Aaron S. Kesselheim et al., False Claims Act Prosecution Did Not Deter Off-Label Drug Use in the Case of Neurontin, 30 Health Affairs 2318 (2011). These authors note: "[One] limitation of the False Claims Act is that although some settlements—particularly those against pharmaceutical manufacturers—have led to billions of dollars in recoveries, the deterrent effect may be muted because the size of these settlements are dwarfed by the potential financial gains from thwarting the law." Id.

3. *Pharmaceuticals' advertising directed at consumers.*   Direct-to-consumer pharmaceutical advertising of nonprescription and prescription drugs raises

additional ethical and practical questions. The first product advertised directly to consumers by the pharmaceutical industry (Upjohn's Rogaine) was aimed at controlling hair loss. Elizabeth C. Melby, The Psychological Manipulation of the Consumer-Patient Population Through Direct-to-Consumer Prescription Drug Advertising, 5 Scholar 325 (2003). Advertisements for prescriptions drugs, in particular, have become much more widespread in the last decade.

Meredith B. Rosenthal et al., Promotion of Prescription Drugs to Consumers, 346 New Eng. J. Med. 498, 499–510 (2002), report that pharmaceutical companies advertise only a small percentage of their drugs directly to consumers. The authors did not, however, definitively explain why pharmaceutical companies advertise some products but not others directly to consumers. They do note that such advertising tends to involve drugs that treat chronic conditions and drugs with few and mild side effects. Id. The drugs advertised to consumers include "antidepressants, antihistamines, antihyperlipidemics, and antiinflammatory agents." Id. In general, companies do not advertise to consumers drugs with patents about to expire. Exceptions have emerged in the case of old drugs approved for new uses. Id.

The practice of direct-to-consumer advertising concerns physicians because, among other things, it requires them to respond to patient questions about products advertised directly to consumers. This can upset traditional expectations about the doctor–patient relationship. Rosenthal et al. report that about one-quarter of patients surveyed by independent consultants reported that they had initiated discussions with their physicians about drugs they saw advertised on television. However, less than one-quarter of those actually received prescriptions for the drug in question.

What advantages, if any, do you see to such advertising for those to whom the advertisements are directed? What disadvantages, if any?

4. *Bibliographic note.*   Margaret Z. Johns, Informed Consent: Requiring Doctors to Disclose Off-Label Prescriptions and Conflicts of Interest, 58 Hastings L.J. 967 (2007). Johns suggests that physicians should disclose off-label prescribing and conflicts of interest occasioned by industry marketing practices. Volume 35(2) of the Hofstra Law Review (2006) contains several papers that were presented at the 2006 Hofstra conference, "Biomedical Research and the Law: The Pharmaceutical Industry and Its Relationship with Government, Academia, Physicians and Consumers."

2.   Patents and Property Rights[4]

As you read this subsection, consider whether a health care provider's commitment to relieve suffering is antithetical to the sort of commercialism implied by obtaining a patent. Does it depend on what is being patented? Does it depend on what uses can (or presumably will) be made of the thing being patented? Does it matter that a physician (or other health care provider) is involved in research as well as caring for patients or that he or she is committed only to research and engages in no patient care?

In 1955, soon after the media learned that trials for Jonas Salk's polio vaccine had been successful, Salk explained in an interview with Edward R.

---

4. Further consideration of patenting life forms is found in Chapter 3. Chapter 4 includes extensive discussion of ethical issues relating to human genetics and genomics.

Murrow that he did not own the new vaccine. Rather, Salk explained, "the people" own it. To patent the vaccine, in Salk's view, was unthinkable. It was tantamount to patenting the sun.[5] Yet, in 1987, Salk applied for a patent on an AIDS vaccine. He assigned commercial rights to the vaccine to Immune Response Corp. Equitable May Back AIDS Vaccine Development, Chemical Week, July 8, 1987 (available on LEXIS, news library). Many things changed for researchers between 1955 and 1987. At least for Salk, commercialization of such vaccines, unimaginable in 1955, had become a reality 30 years later. By the end of the twentieth century, many patents were being issued to protect researchers' interests in living forms.

a.   Bioethical and Social Perspectives

> ### Margo A. Bagley, Patent First, Ask Questions Later: Morality and Biotechnology in Patent Law
> 45 Wm. & Mary L. Rev. 469, 490–491, 518–519 (2003)

Eventually, . . . courts began refusing to impose the requirement [that "useful" within the meaning of the patent statute includes an element of moral utility]. The courts acknowledged that it was an area in which Congress could legislate, but that such determinations were not the proper purview of the judiciary or the USPTO [the U.S. Patent and Trademark Office]. In 1998, however, the moral utility doctrine seemed on the verge of revival when the USPTO threatened to invoke the requirement in response to receiving a controversial patent application. The application, filed by activist Jeremy Rifkin and biologist Stuart Newman, claimed the invention of human–animal chimera, creatures made, in theory, by blending human cells with those of various animals such as mice, chimpanzees, pigs, or baboons. The applicants actually have not made such creatures, nor do they want anyone else to make them. Rather, their purpose in filing the application was to provoke a debate and force Congress, the courts, or the USPTO to draw the line on patent-eligible subject matter.

Shortly after receiving the chimera application, the USPTO issued a media advisory entitled Facts on Patenting Life Forms Having a Relationship to Humans. In the advisory, the Office cited Justice Story's quote in Lowell v. Lewis and posited that "inventions directed to human/non-human chimera could, under certain circumstances, not be patentable because, among other things, they would fail to meet the public policy and morality aspects of the utility requirement." Nevertheless, by its own admission in a more recent statement, the USPTO has acknowledged that it is without authority to deny a patent based on morality or public policy concerns and has actually issued several patents that encompass humans.

---

5. This story is told in many places with slight differences. See, e.g., Symposium: The Human Genome Project, DNA Science and the Law, 51 Am. U. L. Rev. 371, 377 (2002) (remarks of Q. Todd Dickinson); IAVI's Intellectual Property Agreements for AIDS vaccine, IAVI (The Newsletter of International Aids), http://www.iavi.org/science.

... In contrast to the U.S. "patent first" approach, the EPC (covering all European Union states plus others) contains an express morality-based patent eligibility bar. EPC Article 53 states: "European patents shall not be granted in respect of: (a) Inventions the publication or exploitation of which would be contrary to 'ordre public' or morality. . . ." Article 53(a) provides not only a basis for EPO examiners to reject a patent application, but also provides that any member of the public can lodge an opposition to the grant of a patent on this or any other patentability basis, at any time within nine months of the publication of the EPO decision to issue the patent.

b.   Legal Approaches

|| *Diamond v. Chakrabarty* ||
447 U.S. 303 (1980)

Opinion by BURGER.

In 1972, respondent Chakrabarty, a microbiologist, filed a patent application, assigned to the General Electric Co. The application asserted 36 claims related to Chakrabarty's invention of "a bacterium from the genus Pseudomonas containing therein at least two stable energy-generating plasmids, each of said plasmids providing a separate hydrocarbon degradative pathway." This human-made, genetically engineered bacterium is capable of breaking down multiple components of crude oil. Because of this property, which is possessed by no naturally occurring bacteria, Chakrabarty's invention is believed to have significant value for the treatment of oil spills. Chakrabarty's patent claims were of three types: first, process claims for the method of producing the bacteria; second, claims for an inoculum comprised of a carrier material floating on water, such as straw, and the new bacteria; and third, claims to the bacteria themselves. The patent examiner allowed the claims falling into the first two categories, but rejected claims for the bacteria. His decision rested on two grounds: (1) that micro-organisms are "products of nature," and (2) that as living things they are not patentable subject matter under 35 U.S.C. §101.

Chakrabarty appealed the rejection of these claims to the Patent Office Board of Appeals, and the Board affirmed the examiner on the second ground. Relying on the legislative history of the 1930 Plant Patent Act, in which Congress extended patent protection to certain asexually reproduced plants, the Board concluded that §101 was not intended to cover living things such as these laboratory created micro-organisms.

The Court of Customs and Patent Appeals, by a divided vote, reversed on the authority of its prior decision in In re Bergy which held that "the fact that microorganisms . . . are alive . . . [is] without legal significance" for purposes of the patent law. . . . Since then, *Bergy* has been dismissed as moot, leaving only *Chakrabarty* for decision.

II

The Constitution grants Congress broad power to legislate to "promote the Progress of Science and useful Arts, by securing for limited Times to Authors

and Inventors the exclusive Right to their respective Writings and Discoveries."
Art. I, §8, cl. 8. The patent laws promote this progress by offering inventors
exclusive rights for a limited period as an incentive for their inventiveness
and research efforts. The authority of Congress is exercised in the hope that
"[the] productive effort thereby fostered will have a positive effect on society
through the introduction of new products and processes of manufacture into
the economy, and the emanations by way of increased employment and better
lives for our citizens."

The question before us in this case is a narrow one of statutory interpretation requiring us to construe 235 U.S.C. §101, which provides:

> Whoever invents or discovers any new and useful process, machine,
> manufacture, or composition of matter, or any new and useful improvement
> thereof, may obtain a patent therefor, subject to the conditions and require-
> ments of this title.

Specifically, we must determine whether respondent's micro-organism
constitutes a "manufacture" or "composition of matter" within the meaning
of the statute. . . .

[T]his Court has read the term "manufacture" in §101 in accordance with
its dictionary definition to mean "the production of articles for use from raw or
prepared materials by giving to these materials new forms, qualities, properties,
or combinations, whether by hand-labor or by machinery." Similarly, "composition of matter" has been construed consistent with its common usage to
include "all compositions of two or more substances and . . . all composite articles, whether they be the results of chemical union, or of mechanical mixture, or
whether they be gases, fluids, powders or solids." In choosing such expansive
terms as "manufacture" and "composition of matter," modified by the comprehensive "any," Congress plainly contemplated that the patent laws would be
given wide scope.

The relevant legislative history also supports a broad construction. The
Patent Act of 1793, authored by Thomas Jefferson, defined statutory subject
matter as "any new and useful art, machine, manufacture, or composition of
matter, or any new or useful improvement [thereof]." The Act embodied
Jefferson's philosophy that "ingenuity should receive a liberal encouragement."
Subsequent patent statutes in 1836, 1870, and 1874 employed this same broad
language. In 1952, when the patent laws were recodified, Congress replaced the
word "art" with "process," but otherwise left Jefferson's language intact. The
Committee Reports accompanying the 1952 Act inform us that Congress
intended statutory subject matter to "include anything under the sun that is
made by man."

This is not to suggest that §101 has no limits or that it embraces every
discovery. The laws of nature, physical phenomena, and abstract ideas have
been held not patentable. Thus, a new mineral discovered in the earth or a
new plant found in the wild is not patentable subject matter. Likewise, Einstein
could not patent his celebrated law that $E=mc^2$; nor could Newton have patented
the law of gravity. Such discoveries are "manifestations of . . . nature, free to all
men and reserved exclusively to none."

Judged in this light, respondent's micro-organism plainly qualifies as patentable subject matter. His claim is not to a hitherto unknown natural

phenomenon, but to a nonnaturally occurring manufacture or composition of matter—a product of human ingenuity "having a distinctive name, character [and] use." . . .

Here . . . the patentee has produced a new bacterium with markedly different characteristics from any found in nature and one having the potential for significant utility. His discovery is not nature's handiwork, but his own; accordingly it is patentable subject matter under §101.

IV

Two contrary arguments are advanced, neither of which we find persuasive. [The Court rejected the argument that "the terms 'manufacture' or 'composition of matter' do not include living things." Petition had so argued on the ground that if this were not the case, there would have been no need for Congress to have promulgated the 1930 Plant Patent Act or the 1970 Plant Variety Protection Act. The Court concluded that Congress did not pass either act for the reason asserted by petitioner.] . . .

The petitioner's second argument is that micro-organisms cannot qualify as patentable subject matter until Congress expressly authorizes such protection. His position rests on the fact that genetic technology was unforeseen when Congress enacted §101. From this it is argued that resolution of the patentability of inventions such as respondent's should be left to Congress. The legislative process, the petitioner argues, is best equipped to weigh the competing economic, social, and scientific considerations involved, and to determine whether living organisms produced by genetic engineering should receive patent protection. . . .

. . . Congress has performed its constitutional role in defining patentable subject matter in §101; we perform ours in construing the language Congress has employed. In so doing, our obligation is to take statutes as we find them, guided, if ambiguity appears, by the legislative history and statutory purpose. Here, we perceive no ambiguity. The subject-matter provisions of the patent law have been cast in broad terms to fulfill the constitutional and statutory goal of promoting "the Progress of Science and the useful Arts" with all that means for the social and economic benefits envisioned by Jefferson. Broad general language is not necessarily ambiguous when congressional objectives require broad terms. . . .

A rule that unanticipated inventions are without protection would conflict with the core concept of the patent law that anticipation undermines patentability. Mr. Justice Douglas reminded that the inventions most benefiting mankind are those that "push back the frontiers of chemistry, physics, and the like." Congress employed broad general language in drafting §101 precisely because such inventions are often unforeseeable.

To buttress his argument, the petitioner, with the support of amicus, points to grave risks that may be generated by research endeavors such as respondent's. The briefs present a gruesome parade of horribles. Scientists, among them Nobel laureates, are quoted suggesting that genetic research may pose a serious threat to the human race, or, at the very least, that the dangers are far too substantial to permit such research to proceed apace at this time. We are told that genetic research and related technological developments may spread pollution and disease, that it may result in a loss of genetic diversity, and that its practice may tend to depreciate the value of human life. These arguments are forcefully, even passionately, presented; they remind us that, at times, human ingenuity seems unable to control fully the forces it creates—that, with Hamlet, it is sometimes better "to bear those ills we have than fly to others that we know not of."

It is argued that this Court should weigh these potential hazards in considering whether respondent's invention is patentable subject matter under §101. We disagree. The grant or denial of patents on micro-organisms is not likely to put an end to genetic research or to its attendant risks. The large amount of research that has already occurred when no researcher had sure knowledge that patent protection would be available suggests that legislative or judicial fiat as to patentability will not deter the scientific mind from probing into the unknown any more than Canute could command the tides. Whether respondent's claims are patentable may determine whether research efforts are accelerated by the hope of reward or slowed by want of incentives, but that is all.

What is more important is that we are without competence to entertain these arguments—either to brush them aside as fantasies generated by fear of the unknown, or to act on them. The choice we are urged to make is a matter of high policy for resolution within the legislative process after the kind of investigation, examination, and study that legislative bodies can provide and courts cannot. That process involves the balancing of competing values and interests, which in our democratic system is the business of elected representatives. Whatever their validity, the contentions now pressed on us should be addressed to the political branches of the Government, the Congress and the Executive, and not to the courts.

. . . Our task . . . is the narrow one of determining what Congress meant by the words it used in the statute; once that is done our powers are exhausted. Congress is free to amend §101 so as to exclude from patent protection organisms produced by genetic engineering. Cf. 42 U.S.C. §2181(a), exempting from patent protection inventions "useful solely in the utilization of special nuclear material or atomic energy in an atomic weapon." Or it may choose to craft a statute specifically designed for such living things. But, until Congress takes such action, this Court must construe the language of §101 as it is. The language of that section fairly embraces respondent's invention.

Accordingly, the judgment of the Court of Customs and Patent Appeals is Affirmed.

NOTES AND QUESTIONS

1. *From morality to utility.*   As the Court makes clear in *Chakrabarty*, §101 of the U.S. Patent Act provides for patents to be issued for "useful" inventions. Although U.S. courts once took morality into account in determining an invention's utility, that is no longer the case. Margo Bagley, supra, explains the shift from a focus on morality to one on utility alone to have corresponded with shifts in social morality and the multiplication of "difficulties in defining morally acceptable inventions." 45 Wm. & Mary L. Rev. at 489. Do you think that the diversity of views that attends many moral issues in the United States would make it impractical (or unfair) for Congress to predicate the granting of patent

applications on the moral implications or "moral utility" of the innovation described in the application?

2. *How far does the reasoning of* Chakrabarty *extend?*   Do you think *Chakrabarty* provides for granting patents on any living organism that has been genetically engineered? Can *Chakrabarty* be read to suggest that a human being might be patentable?

3. *The Harvard oncomouse.*   In 1988, the USPTO granted a patent on what has become known as the Harvard oncomouse. (The patent application was sponsored by Harvard University.) The oncomouse had been modified so as to become especially likely to develop cancer. The patent was the first on a mammal. U.S. Patent No. 4,736,866 (issued Apr. 12, 1988). The story of the Harvard oncomouse is told by Linda J. Demaiine & Aaron Xavier Fellmeth, Reinventing the Double Helix: A Novel and Nonobvious Reconceptualization of the Biotechnology Patent, 55 Stan. L. Rev. 303 (2002). In Europe, where the European Patent Office (EPO) has a morality clause, the application for a patent on the oncomouse was hotly contested. Among other arguments, those opposing the EPO's granting a patent argued that the genetically predisposed mouse would suffer. The patent was granted by the EPO because on balance the patent was seen to result in more good than harm, largely because the oncomouse promised to help in the search for a cure for cancer.

4. *Patenting mice.*   By the 1990s, researchers began to respond to concern about the effects of patenting mice—especially high prices and limits on the use of mice by patent holders. GenPharm, for instance, was charging $80 to $150 per mouse for certain genetically modified mice. Harold Varmus, a Nobel Prize winner and, later, director of the NIH, helped organize geneticists to respond. In 1993, the NIH set up a laboratory of genetically altered mice that would in theory give researchers equal access. However, in the late 1990s, DuPont (which had been granted a patent on mice altered through a certain gene-insertion method) refused to allow researchers to share the technique without the company's agreement. Varmus (by then Director of NIH) refused to agree to DuPont's terms. Negotiations followed. Eventually DuPont agreed to allow use of the modified mice by NIH researchers and NIH grantees at nonprofit institutions. Eliot Marshall tells the story in more detail in A Deluge of Patents Creates Legal Hassles for Research, 287 Science 255 (2000).

5. *Patenting "cybrids" (animal-humans).*   The USPTO has issued patents on chimeras, including a transgenic swine that includes a gene encoding for a human protein. See Gregory R. Hagen & Sebastien A. Gittens, Patenting Part-Human Chimeras, Transgenics and Stem Cells for Transplantation in the United States, Canada, and Europe, 14 Rich. J.L. & Tech. 11, at P54 (2008), available at http://law.richmond.edu/jolt/v14i4/article11.pdf. Hagen and Gittens note:

> At the same time it has granted patents on . . . part-human materials, the USPTO denies that it has any principled way of deciding which animal–human combinations are patentable. . . . President George W. Bush and many members of Congress sought to definitively prevent the creation and patenting of certain chimeras through legislation, with the Human Chimera Prohibition Act of 2005. The Act expressly stated its ethical concerns that some chimeras blur the lines between human and animal, male and female, parent

and child, and one individual and another individual, threatening the respect for human dignity and the integrity of the human species. The Act would have prohibited the creation of various types of chimeras (including a human embryo into which a non-human cell, or any component part of a non-human cell, was inserted); but it was not passed by Congress.

Id. at P55.

Although human cells and organs are often essential to research and sometimes lead to significant profits for researchers and for the biotechnology industry and pharmaceutical companies, individuals whose cells and organs are used in research rarely share in those profits. Moore v. Regents of the University of California, 793 P.2d 479 (Cal. 1990), represents one of the first cases involving a dispute about the commercial use of a patient's cells. The California Supreme Court rejected John Moore's property claims to his spleen cells but concluded that Moore had not been adequately informed about the use to which his doctors intended to put his cells. The case has been widely debated. It raises a number of issues about patients' and research subjects' rights as well as about doctor–patient trust.

Moore v. Regents of the University of California
793 P.2d 479 (Cal. 1990)

[John Moore was treated for leukemia by Dr. David Golde at the UCLA Medical Center. In subsequent years, he was asked to travel from his home in Seattle to Los Angeles for what he thought were follow-up health care examinations. In fact, doctors and researchers were collecting samples of Moore's white blood cells for research uses. Later the research institution patented a cell line that had significant commercial potential. The patent application named Dr. Golde and another researcher as the inventors of the valuable cell line. Moore's doctor and others made millions of dollars from the lymphokines produced from Moore's cells. Moore, who had never been told of the aspect of his "treatment" that related to the doctors' research, sued his doctor and the research institution for tort conversion and for use of his body tissue without his informed consent.–EDS.]

PANELLI, Justice.

We granted review in this case to determine whether plaintiff has stated a cause of action against his physician and other defendants for using his cells in potentially lucrative medical research without his permission. Plaintiff alleges that his physician failed to disclose preexisting research and economic interests in the cells before obtaining consent to the medical procedures by which they were extracted. . . . We hold that the complaint states a cause of action for breach of the physician's disclosure obligations, but not for conversion . . . .

A.   Breach of Fiduciary Duty and Lack of Informed Consent

Moore repeatedly alleges that Golde failed to disclose the extent of his research and economic interests in Moore's cells before obtaining consent to the medical procedures by which the cells were extracted. These allegations, in our view, state a cause of action against Golde for invading a legally protected interest of his patient. This cause of action can properly be characterized either as the breach of a fiduciary duty to disclose facts material to the patient's consent or, alternatively, as the performance of medical procedures without first having obtained the patient's informed consent.

Our analysis begins with three well-established principles. First, "a person of adult years and in sound mind has the right, in the exercise of control over his own body, to determine whether or not to submit to lawful medical treatment." Second, "the patient's consent to treatment, to be effective, must be an informed consent." Third, in soliciting the patient's consent, a physician has a fiduciary duty to disclose all information material to the patient's decision.

These principles lead to the following conclusions: (1) a physician must disclose personal interests unrelated to the patient's health, whether research or economic, that may affect the physician's professional judgment; and (2) a physician's failure to disclose such interests may give rise to a cause of action for performing medical procedures without informed consent or breach of fiduciary duty.

To be sure, questions about the validity of a patient's consent to a procedure typically arise when the patient alleges that the physician failed to disclose medical risks, as in malpractice cases, and not when the patient alleges that the physician had a personal interest, as in this case. The concept of informed consent, however, is broad enough to encompass the latter. "The scope of the physician's communication to the patient . . . must be measured by the patient's need, and that need is whatever information is material to the decision." . . .

B.   Conversion

Moore also attempts to characterize the invasion of his rights as a conversion—a tort that protects against interference with possessory and ownership interests in personal property. He theorizes that he continued to own his cells following their removal from his body, at least for the purpose of directing their use, and that he never consented to their use in potentially lucrative medical research. Thus, to complete Moore's argument, defendants' unauthorized use of his cells constitutes a conversion. As a result of the alleged conversion, Moore claims a proprietary interest in each of the products that any of the defendants might ever create from his cells or the patented cell line.

No court, however, has ever in a reported decision imposed conversion liability for the use of human cells in medical research. While that fact does not end our inquiry, it raises a flag of caution. In effect, what Moore is asking us to do is to impose a tort duty on scientists to investigate the consensual pedigree of each human cell sample used in research. To impose such a duty, which would affect medical research of importance to all of society, implicates policy concerns far removed from the traditional, two-party ownership disputes in which the law of conversion arose. Invoking a tort theory originally used to determine whether the loser or the finder of a horse had the better title, Moore claims ownership of the results of socially important medical research, including the genetic code for chemicals that regulate the functions of every human being's immune system. . . .

"To establish a conversion, plaintiff must establish an actual interference with his *ownership* or *right of possession* . . . . Where plaintiff neither has title to the property alleged to have been converted, nor possession thereof, he cannot maintain an action for conversion." . . .

Since Moore clearly did not expect to retain possession of his cells following their removal, to sue for their conversion he must have retained an ownership interest in them. But there are several reasons to doubt that he did retain any such interest. First, no reported judicial decision supports Moore's claim, either directly or by close analogy. Second, California statutory law drastically limits any continuing interest of a patient in excised cells. Third, the subject matters of the Regents' patent—the patented cell line and the products derived from it—cannot be Moore's property.

Neither the Court of Appeal's opinion, the parties' briefs, nor our research discloses a case holding that a person retains a sufficient interest in excised cells to support a cause of action for conversion. We do not find this surprising, since the laws governing such things as human tissues, transplantable organs, blood, fetuses, pituitary glands, corneal tissue, and dead bodies deal with human biological materials as objects sui generis, regulating their disposition to achieve policy goals rather than abandoning them to the general law of personal property. It is these specialized statutes, not the law of conversion, to which courts ordinarily should and do look for guidance on the disposition of human biological materials.

Lacking direct authority for importing the law of conversion into this context, Moore relies, as did the Court of Appeal, primarily on decisions addressing privacy rights. One line of cases involves unwanted publicity. These opinions hold that every person has a proprietary interest in his own likeness and that unauthorized, business use of a likeness is redressible as a tort. But in neither opinion did the authoring court expressly base its holding on property law . . . .

Not only are the wrongful-publicity cases irrelevant to the issue of conversion, but the analogy to them seriously misconceives the nature of the genetic materials and research involved in this case. Moore, adopting the analogy originally advanced by the Court of Appeal, argues that "[i]f the courts have found a sufficient proprietary interest in one's persona, how could one not have a right in one's own genetic material, something far more profoundly the essence of one's human uniqueness than a name or a face?" However, as the defendants' patent makes clear—and the complaint, too, if read with an understanding of the scientific terms which it has borrowed from the patent—the goal and result of defendants' efforts has been to manufacture lymphokines. Lymphokines, unlike a name or a face, have the same molecular structure in every human being and the same, important functions in every human being's immune system. Moreover, the particular genetic material which is responsible for the natural production of lymphokines, and which defendants use to manufacture lymphokines in the laboratory, is also the same in every person; it is no more unique to Moore than the number of vertebrae in the spine or the chemical formula of hemoglobin.

. . . The next consideration that makes Moore's claim of ownership problematic is California statutory law, which drastically limits a patient's control over excised cells. Pursuant to Health and Safety Code section 7054.4, "[n]otwithstanding any other provision of law, recognizable anatomical parts, human tissues, anatomical human remains, or infectious waste following conclusion of scientific use shall be disposed of by interment, incineration, or any other method determined by the state department [of health services] to protect the public health and safety." Clearly the Legislature did not specifically intend this statute to resolve the question of whether a patient is entitled to compensation for the nonconsensual use of excised cells. A primary object of the statute is to ensure the safe handling of potentially hazardous biological waste materials. Yet one cannot escape the conclusion that the statute's practical effect is to limit, drastically, a patient's control over excised cells. By restricting how excised cells may be used and requiring their eventual destruction, the statute eliminates so many of the rights ordinarily attached to property that one cannot simply assume that what is left amounts to "property" or "ownership" for purposes of conversion law.

It may be that some limited right to control the use of excised cells does survive the operation of this statute. There is, for example, no need to read the statute to permit "scientific use" contrary to the patient's expressed wish. A fully informed patient may always withhold consent to treatment by a physician whose research plans the patient does not approve. That right, however, as already discussed, is protected by the fiduciary-duty and informed-consent theories.

Finally, the subject matter of the Regents' patent—the patented cell line and the products derived from it—cannot be Moore's property. This is because the patented cell line is both factually and legally distinct from the cells taken from Moore's body. Federal law permits the patenting of organisms that represent the product of "human ingenuity," but not naturally occurring organisms. (Diamond v. Chakrabarty (1980) 447 U.S. 303, 309–310.) Human cell lines are patentable because "[l]ong-term adaptation and growth of human tissues and cells in culture is difficult—often considered an art . . . ," and the probability of success is low. It is this *inventive effort* that patent law rewards, not the discovery of naturally occurring raw materials. Thus, Moore's allegations that he owns the cell line and the products derived from it are inconsistent with the patent, which constitutes an authoritative determination that the cell line is the product of invention. Since such allegations are nothing more than arguments or conclusions of law, they of course do not bind us.

. . . Finally, there is no pressing need to impose a judicially created rule of strict liability, since enforcement of physicians' disclosure obligations will protect patients against the very type of harm with which Moore was threatened. So long as a physician discloses research and economic interests that may affect his judgment, the patient is protected from conflicts of interest. Aware of any conflicts, the patient can make an informed decision to consent to treatment, or to withhold consent and look elsewhere for medical assistance. As already discussed, enforcement of physicians' disclosure obligations protects patients directly, without hindering the socially useful activities of innocent researchers.

For these reasons, we hold that the allegations of Moore's third amended complaint state a cause of action for breach of fiduciary duty or lack of informed consent, but not conversion.

BROUSSARD, Justice, concurring and dissenting.

. . . When it turns to the conversion cause of action . . . the majority opinion fails to maintain its focus on the specific allegations before us. Concerned that the imposition of liability for conversion will impede medical research by innocent scientists who use the resources of existing cell repositories—a factual setting not presented here—the majority opinion rests its holding, that a conversion action cannot be maintained, largely on the proposition that a patient generally possesses no right in a body part that has already been removed from his body. Here, however, plaintiff has alleged that defendants interfered with his legal rights before his body part was removed. Although a patient may not retain any legal interest in a body part after its removal when he has properly consented to its removal and use for scientific purposes, it is clear under California law that before a body part is removed it is the patient, rather than his doctor or hospital, who possesses the right to determine the use to which the body part will be put after removal. If, as alleged in this case, plaintiff's doctor improperly interfered with plaintiff's right to control the use of a body part by wrongfully withholding material information from him before its removal, under traditional common law principles plaintiff may maintain a conversion action to recover the economic value of the right to control the use of his body part. Accordingly, I dissent from the majority opinion insofar as it rejects plaintiff's conversion cause of action . . . .

Greenberg v. Miami Children's Hospital Research Institute
264 F. Supp. 2d 1064 (S.D. Fla. 2003)

[See Chapter 2, section A(2) for the facts of this case. The case developed out of a joint effort between patients' families and researchers to find the genetic alterations associated with Canavan disease, a fatal genetic condition. The plaintiffs sued the researcher and institutions with which he was associated when they learned that blood samples supplied to the researcher were the basis for a patent he and the relevant institutions obtained. The patent gave them ownership rights to "any activity related to the Canavan disease gene, including without limitation: carrier and prenatal testing, gene therapy and other treatments for Canavan disease and research involving the gene and its mutations." As noted in Chapter 2, the parties in *Greenberg* entered into a confidential settlement agreement in 2003, shortly before the case was scheduled to go to trial.–EDS.]

C.   UNJUST ENRICHMENT

. . . Plaintiffs allege that MCH [Miami Children's Hospital Research Institute] is being unjustly enriched by collecting license fees under the Patent. Under Florida law, the elements of a claim for unjust enrichment are (1) the plaintiff conferred a benefit on the defendant, who had knowledge of the benefit; (2) the defendant voluntarily accepted and retained the benefit; and (3) under the circumstances it would be inequitable for the defendant to retain the benefit without paying for it. The Court finds that Plaintiffs have sufficiently alleged the elements of a claim for unjust enrichment to survive Defendants' motion to dismiss.

While the parties do not contest that Plaintiffs have conferred a benefit to Defendants, including, among other things, blood and tissue samples and soliciting financial contributions, Defendants contend that Plaintiffs have not suffered any detriment, and note that no Plaintiff has been denied access to Canavan testing. Furthermore, the Plaintiffs received what they sought—the successful isolation of the Canavan gene and the development of a screening test. Plaintiffs argue, however, that when Defendants applied the benefits for unauthorized purposes, they suffered a detriment. Had Plaintiffs known that Defendants intended to commercialize their genetic material through patenting and restrictive licensing, Plaintiffs would not have provided these benefits to Defendants under those terms.

Naturally, Plaintiffs allege that the retention of benefits violates the fundamental principles of justice, equity, and good conscience. While Defendants claim that they have invested significant amounts of time and money in research, with no guarantee of success and are thus entitled to seek reimbursement, the same can be said of Plaintiffs. Moreover, Defendants' attempt to seek refuge in the endorsement of the U.S. Patent system, which gives an inventor rights to prosecute patents and negotiate licenses for their intellectual property[,] fails[] as obtaining a patent does not preclude the Defendants from being unjustly enriched. . . . The Complaint has alleged more than just a donor–donee relationship for the purposes of an unjust enrichment claim. Rather, the facts paint a picture of a continuing research collaboration that involved Plaintiffs also investing time and significant resources in the race to isolate the Canavan gene. Therefore, given the facts as alleged, the Court finds that Plaintiffs have sufficiently pled the requisite elements of an unjust enrichment claim and the motion to dismiss for failure to state a claim is DENIED as to this count. . . .

E.   CONVERSION

The Plaintiffs allege . . . that they had a property interest in their body tissue and genetic information, and that they owned the Canavan registry in Illinois which contained contact information, pedigree information and family information for Canavan families worldwide. They claim that MCH [Miami Children's Hospital] and [researcher] Matalon converted the names on the register and the genetic information by utilizing them for the hospitals' "exclusive economic benefit." The Court disagrees and declines to find a property interest for the body tissue and genetic information voluntarily given to Defendants. These were donations to research without any contemporaneous expectations of return of the body tissue and genetic samples, and thus conversion does not lie as a cause of action.

In Florida, the tort of "conversion is an unauthorized act which deprives another of his property permanently or for an indefinite time." . . . Using property given for one purpose for another purpose constitutes conversion.

First, Plaintiffs have no cognizable property interest in body tissue and genetic matter donated for research under a theory of conversion. This case is similar to Moore v. Regents of the University of California, where the Court declined to extend liability under a theory of conversion to misuse of a person's excised biological materials. 793 P.2d 479, 488 (Cal. 1990). The plaintiff in Moore alleged that he had retained a property right in excised bodily material used in research, and therefore retained some control over the results of that research.

The California Supreme Court, however, disagreed and held that the use of the results of medical research inconsistent with the wishes of the donor was not conversion, because the donor had no property interest at stake after the donation was made. ("No court has ever in a reported decision imposed conversion liability for the use of human cells in medical research."). The Court also recognized that the patented result of research is "both factually and legally distinct" from excised material used in the research.

Second, limits to the property rights that attach to body tissue have been recognized in Florida state courts. For example, in State v. Powell the Florida Supreme Court refused to recognize a property right in the body of another after death. Similarly, the property right in blood and tissue samples also evaporates once the sample is voluntarily given to a third party.

Plaintiffs rely on Pioneer Hi-Bred v. Holden Foundation (S.D. Iowa, Oct. 29, 1987), *aff'd,* 35 F.3d 1226 (8th Cir. 1994), for their assertion that genetic information itself can constitute property for the purposes of the tort of conversion. In that case, the Court held that a corn seed's property interest in the genetic message contained in a corn seed variety is property protected by the laws of conversion. Plaintiffs argue that giving permission for one purpose (gene discovery) does not mean they agreed to other uses (gene patenting and commercialization). Yet, the Pioneer court recognized that, "where information is gathered and arranged at some cost and sold as a commodity on the market, it is properly protected as property." This seemingly provides more support for property rights inherent in Defendants' research rather than the donations of Plaintiffs' DNA. Finally, Plaintiffs cite a litany of cases in other jurisdictions that have recognized that body tissue can be property in some circumstances. See, e.g., Brotherton v. Cleveland, 923 F.2d 477, 482 (6th Cir. 1991) (aggregate of rights existing in body tissue is similar to property rights); York v. Jones, 717 F. Supp. 421, 425 (E.D. Va. 1989) (couple granted property rights in their frozen embryos). These cases, however, do not involve voluntary donations to medical research.

Additionally, the Florida statute on genetic testing is cited by Plaintiffs in support of their contention that persons who contribute body tissue for researchers to use in genetic analysis do not relinquish ownership of the results of the analysis. This statute, however, is inapplicable under a common law theory of conversion, because by its plain meaning, it only provides penalties for disclosure or lack of informed consent if a person is being genetically analyzed. Plaintiffs have not cited any case that interprets the statute as applying to an analogous factual situation, and this Court's investigation did not find any relevant case either. Moreover, even assuming, arguendo, that the statute does create a property right in genetic material donated for medical research purposes, it is unclear whether this confers a property right for conversion, a common law cause of action.

Finally, although the Complaint sets out that Plaintiff Greenberg owned the Canavan Registry, the facts alleged do not sufficiently allege the elements of a prima facie case of conversion, as the Plaintiffs have not alleged how the Defendants' use of the Registry in their research was an expressly unauthorized act. The Complaint only alleges that the Defendants "utilized the information and contacts for their exclusive economic benefit." Compl. There [are] no further allegations of the circumstances or conditions that were attached to the Defendants' use of the Canavan Registry. Nor are there any allegations about any of the Plaintiffs' entitlement to possess the Registry.

The Court finds that Florida statutory and common law do not provide a remedy for Plaintiffs' donations of body tissue and blood samples under a theory of conversion liability. Indeed, the Complaint does not allege that the Defendants used the genetic material for any purpose but medical research. Plaintiffs claim that the fruits of the research, namely the patented material, was commercialized. This is an important distinction and another step in the chain of attenuation that renders conversion liability inapplicable to the facts as alleged. If adopted, the expansive theory championed by Plaintiffs would cripple medical research as it would bestow a continuing right for donors to possess the results of any research conducted by the hospital. At the core, these were donations to research without any contemporaneous expectations of return.

Consequently, the Plaintiffs have failed to state a claim upon which relief may be granted on this issue. Accordingly, this claim is DISMISSED.

F.   MISAPPROPRIATION OF TRADE SECRETS

The Plaintiffs' final claim is that MCH misappropriated a trade secret—the registry of people who had Canavan disease. Florida's Trade Secrets Act defines a trade secret as: information, including a formula, pattern, compilation, program, device, method, technique, or process, that: (a) Derive(s) independent economic value, actual, or potential, from not being generally known to, and not being readily ascertainable by proper means by, other persons who can obtain economic value from its disclosure or use; and (b) Is the subject of efforts that are reasonable under the circumstances to maintain its secrecy.

Whether a particular type of information constitutes a trade secret is a question of fact and cannot be resolved on a motion to dismiss. Del Monte Fresh Produce Co. v. Dole Food Co., 136 F. Supp. 2d 1271, 1294 (S.D. Fla. 2001). Florida courts have repeatedly held that lists comprising information, such as names of patients, blood donors, and customers can qualify as trade secrets. . . . However, to qualify as a trade secret, information that the Plaintiff seeks to protect must derive economic value from not being readily ascertainable by others and must be the subject of reasonable efforts to protect its secrecy.

At the outset, Defendants dismiss Plaintiffs' characterization of the Canavan registry as a trade secret. First, Defendants assert that Plaintiffs have not alleged that the registry belonged to any Plaintiff. Second, Defendants argue that the registry itself was not alleged to have any independent "economic value" for the purposes of Florida law since the Complaint does not allege the registry had any economic value derived from the confidentiality. Finally, a trade secret must be the subject of efforts "reasonable under the circumstances to maintain its secrecy." Defendants claim that there is nothing in the Complaint which indicates that any efforts were made to keep secret the Registry.

Plaintiffs counter Defendants' assertion that the Canavan registry is not a trade secret because it had value, in that it streamlined Matalon's research and was treated as confidential because it contained confidential information such as contact details, pedigree, and familial information for families worldwide.

While it is clear that the Complaint does allege that the Plaintiffs Greenberg and NTSAD [National Tay-Sachs and Allied Diseases Association, Inc.] created the list, "expending time, money, and other efforts," other key indicia of a trade secret are missing. Plaintiffs do not allege that the list derived economic value from not being generally known to others. The Complaint merely states that it had "substantial economic value" in streamlining Matalon's research. Second, there is no allegation that the Plaintiffs undertook measures to keep the list confidential. Plaintiffs only allege that there was an "expectation that it would remain confidential."

Even assuming, arguendo, that the Court finds that the Canavan Registry is a trade secret, Plaintiffs have not sufficiently alleged how the trade secret was misappropriated. . . .

The Canavan Registry was not misappropriated by MCH because there is no allegation that MCH knew or should have known that the Canavan Registry was a confidential trade secret guarded by Plaintiffs, and furthermore, that Matalon had acquired through improper means. Plaintiffs' theory that Defendants misappropriated the Registry once Matalon and MCH chose to use the Registry beyond the use for which it was authorized does not pass muster, since there was no explicit authorization that the Registry be used for a certain purpose in the first place. Plaintiffs cannot donate information that they prepared for fighting a disease and then retroactively claim that it was a protected secret.

Accordingly, the Court finds that Plaintiffs have failed to state a claim regarding misappropriation of trade secret as they have not sufficiently alleged the requisite elements to convert the Registry into an actionable trade secret. This claim is therefore DISMISSED.

NOTES AND QUESTIONS

1. *Patenting genetic information.* Within a decade after the U.S. Supreme Court decided *Chakrabarty,* infra, Craig Venter, then a scientist at the National Institutes of Health, filed patent applications for hundreds of DNA fragments identified with the use of gene-decoding tools. James Watson, also working for NIH at the time, actively opposed the effort to patent genetic information. Since that time, thousands of patent applications for genes have been submitted, mostly by biotechnology companies. Many have been approved. See Arthur Allen, Who Owns My Disease, 26 Mother Jones 52 (2001).

Not all researchers involved in identifying genetic alterations have attempted to patent the results of their work. Francis Collins, who later became head of the Human Genome Project, and a colleague identified the gene alteration associated with cystic fibrosis. The work was done at the University of Michigan. The University received a patent, but made the decision to preclude exclusive licensing agreements and to charge only a small sum for each test performed. Collins asserts that genomic information should not belong to anyone and should not be patented. See Peter Gorner, Parents Suing Over Patenting of Genetic Test, Chicago Tribune, Nov. 19, 2000, at C1.

In contrast to this approach, the University of Utah and Myriad Genetics, which received a patent for two genetic alterations associated with breast cancer, charge thousands of dollars for the tests. Id. The University and Myriad's patents were recently challenged in a lawsuit brought against them (and the U.S. Patent and Trademark Office) by various medical organizations, researchers, genetics counselors, and patients in an effort coordinated by the American Civil Liberties Union. In August 2012, the U.S. Court of Appeals, Federal Circuit, upheld the patents on the two isolated genes against arguments that they were unpatentable as "products of nature." Assoc. for Molecular Pathology v. U.S. Patent and Trademark Office, 689 F.3d 1303 (2012). The opinion is lengthy, including an explanation of the science behind the patents. In the case, the government did not defend the UPSTO's long-standing position that isolated genes were patentable, suggesting that to be patent-eligible subject matter the genes generally must be altered. The court rejected that argument, stating that "isolated DNAs . . . have a markedly different chemical structure compared to native DNAs," and that an isolated DNA molecule is "worlds apart" from one visualized through a microscope. Id. at 1331. With respect to the potential adverse effects from allowing patents on isolated genes, the court wrote: "The dissent mentions possible "adverse effects" that may occur if isolated DNAs are held to be patent eligible. But, respectfully, it is the adverse effects on innovation that a holding of ineligibility might cause. Patents encourage innovation and even encourage inventing around; we must be careful not to rope off far-reaching areas of patent eligibility." Id. at 1333.

In November 2012, the Supreme Court granted certiorari limited to the question, "Are human genes patentable?" Association for Molecular Pathology v. Myriad Genetics, Inc., 2012 WL 4508118 (U.S. Nov 30, 2012). For a discussion of the case, see Douglas L. Rogers., After Prometheus, Are Human Genes Patentable? (December 5, 2012), available at SSRN: http://ssrn.com/abstract=2185984 or http://dx.doi.org/10.2139/ssrn.2185984.

2. *Providing for the common good?*   In addition to the allegations about informed consent (see Chapter 2, section A(2)), unjust enrichment, conversion, and the misappropriation of trade secrets, the *Greenberg* plaintiffs also alleged that defendants breached their fiduciary duty to the plaintiffs. The court makes reference to the holding of the Maryland Supreme Court in Grimes v. Kennedy Krieger Inst., 782 A.2d 807, 834–835 (Md. 2001), (see Chapter 11, section C(3)), that researchers and the institutions with which they are affiliated become fiduciaries of research subjects. However, the *Greenberg* court concluded that the plaintiffs did "not sufficiently allege[] the second element [in a fiduciary relationship] of acceptance of trust by Defendants and therefore have failed to state a claim." Thus, of the five claims raised by plaintiff, the court dismissed four, holding that plaintiffs could only proceed to trial with regard to their unjust enrichment claim. Why do you think courts (and litigants) might tend to shape cases such as *Greenberg* with reference to laws about property?

Daniel and Debbie Greenberg, the named plaintiffs in the case, had apparently hoped that testing for Canavan disease would be offered at little or no cost, much as testing for Tay-Sachs disease is offered. The Canavan Foundation had to stop offering free genetic screening after it learned that it would have to pay royalties to the patent holders. See Peter Gorner, Court Allows Suit on Use of Dead Kids' DNA for Patent, Chicago Tribune, June 8, 2003, at 13; Peter Gorner, Parents Suing Over Patenting of Genetic Test, Chicago Tribune, Nov. 19, 2000, at C1. Jon Merz, a bioethicist at the University of Pennsylvania, asserts that "[a]mong scientists and researchers, Canavan is an outlandish case. The families deserve to be treated better. I hope the courts are going to do well by them." Gorner, supra, June 8, 2003.

Would you approve of a requirement that research institutions and individual researchers, benefitting financially from the use of patients' and/or research subjects' body tissues, donate some part of the value of the product for the common good?

3. *Patients' obtaining gene patents.*   Another couple, faced with the diagnosis of a serious genetic condition (pseudozanthoma elasticum—PXE) in two of their children, collected DNA samples from families affected by the condition and when the gene was identified, themselves became patent holders. The couple, Sharon and Patrick Terry, wanted to ensure that discovery of the PXE gene would be used to help families affected by the condition. Sharon Terry explained to an interviewer for Mother Jones magazine: "We didn't want to do the science without the ethics, and the only way to make it all work was to have control of it ourselves." Arthur Allen, Who Owns My Disease, 26 Mother Jones 52 (2001). Allen reports concern among scientists about patients' patenting genetic information. One researcher explained: "The scientist might not care about the money from the patent, but his institution probably will." Id.

4. *Making tests for rare genetic conditions available.*   At present, there is no genetic test available for a large number of identified genetic alterations associated with disease or disability. Much of the genetic information in question has been patented, but tests have not been developed because the related conditions are considered too rare to make testing commercially profitable. Two doctors at the University of Iowa College of Medicine in Iowa City, concerned that their ophthalmology patients are unable to obtain tests for genetic alterations that have been identified, have started a program at the university that provides tests for eye conditions. No one makes money from the tests. The doctors have asked 72 patent holders for permission to provide the tests at cost. By August 2003, a dozen had responded. None of these owners (including pharmaceutical companies and medical centers) opposed the idea, although some wanted more information. The doctors running the testing program hope for federal legislation that will help ensure the availability of testing for rare genetic alterations. Ron Winslow, Researchers Have Plan for Genetic Eye Tests, Ignored by Industry, Wall St. Journal, Aug. 29, 2003, at B1.

5. *Consequences for research?*   In responding to plaintiffs' conversion claim, the *Greenberg* court wrote: "If adopted, the expansive theory championed by Plaintiffs would cripple medical research as it would bestow a continuing right for donors to possess the results of any research conducted by the hospital."

The California Supreme Court noted a similar concern in Moore v. Regents, supra. Among the policy concerns that prompted the court to deny Moore's conversion claim was the "important policy consideration . . . that we not threaten with disabling civil liability innocent parties who are engaged in socially useful activities, such as researchers who have no reason to believe that their use of a particular cell sample is, or may be, against a donor's wishes." The court quoted a report of the Office of Technology Assessment to Congress: "Uncertainty about how courts will resolve disputes between specimen sources and specimen users could be detrimental to both academic researchers and the infant biotechnology industry. . . ."

Do you think that the potentially beneficial use for society of a patient's cells in cases such as *Moore* should be determinative? Would the court's conclusions about Moore's interests in his body samples be different if the researchers' goals were not apparently laudable and socially useful? Should legal conclusions about a person's ownership rights in his or her body parts (including cells and genetic information obtained from those cells) be dependent on the *sort of use* a researcher wants to make of those body parts? Would it matter if Dr. Golde and his co-researchers had no aims beyond financial gain? Might the court have assumed too much about the usefulness of the research?

6. *Calling for new legal approaches to biotechnology.* Jonathan Kahn explains that the law's entry into the world of biotechnology is occurring without adequate conceptual resources. He suggests that "where control of commercially valuable information increasingly implicates personal identity, existing principles of property law and informed consent are simply inadequate to the task of dealing with the resulting legal issues in a complete and satisfying manner." Jonathan Kahn, Biotechnology and the Legal Constitution of the Self: Managing Identity in Science, the Market, and Society, 51 Hastings L.J. 909, 910–911 (2000). Kahn, following the position of the appellate court in *Moore,* suggests that the law focus on the usefulness of the tort of appropriation of identity instead of on informed consent and conversion claims:

> Specifically, the court made the intriguing and potentially radical move of extending principles of appropriation to Moore's DNA as constitutive of his identity. A fuller analysis of Moore's case suggests that, just as DNA may be recognized under principles of appropriation as constitutive of one's identity, so too might the law accord a measure of recognition to other significant affiliations—such as race, class, gender, religion, or ethnicity—as fundamentally constitutive of one's individual identity. By focusing on identity-constitutive affiliations, the concept of appropriation may shift the legal debate from one over "group rights" to one of "rights through groups"—that is, to consider how legal treatment of groups through which individuals derive, construct, and/or maintain significant aspects of their identity implicates individual rights.

Id. at 912.

7. *Genetic information.* Potential uses of genetic information and information from human tissues are enormous. Researchers are anxious to gain access to such information. In 1998, the Icelandic Parliament voted to permit the government to extend a license to deCODE Genetics, a private company, to set up an electronic database containing genealogical and genetic information about people with records in Iceland's national health care system. David Winickoff writes:

> By seizing control of the medical records of all Icelandic citizens, the government exploited its citizens' health information. In the Notes to the Act [the Health Sector Database (HSD Act)], the Icelandic Parliament asserts that "[d]ue to the nature of the data and their origin [Icelandic health records] cannot be subject to ownership in the usual sense. Institutions, companies or individuals cannot therefore own the data [because] they exist primarily due to the treatment of patients." This language is mere formalism: access, use, and control are nothing but the traditional incidents of property. Thus, the

government markets this personal medical information at the same time as it denies that the information can be owned.

Next, the government, still denying the proprietary aspects of the information, declared the "[r]ecorded data on the health of the Icelandic people [to be] a natural resource which should be preserved and used to yield benefits as far as possible." Once considered a private record between patient and doctor, medical records have become a collective resource to be mined. The Parliament explained that: "[i]t is . . . fair and a duty to utilise the data in the interests of the health sciences and to promote public health. This can best be done by the government authorising the creation and operation of a single centralised database, in which these data would be collected and where they would be processed."

. . . .Besides the impropriety of transferring value from the individual to a company while trying to convince the donors that what they are donating is worthless, the Act gives little assurance that this donation will "promote public health" or benefit the people of Iceland.

David E. Winickoff, Governing Population Genomics: Law, Bioethics, and Biopolitics in Three Case Studies, 43 Jurimetrics J. 187, 206-207 (2003).

Two years after the Icelandic government granted the license for the population database, Beth Israel Deaconess Medical Center in Boston entered into a collaboration with Ardais Corporation under which the hospital would transfer tissue samples from patients along with coded information about these patients to the company. Ardais agreed to pay the hospital for organizing and transferring the information. Winickoff, supra, questions the appropriateness of asking patients to participate in the program:

The BI [Beth Israel] consent form states that "there will be no direct benefit" to participants in the program, but that "society may benefit from research using your tissue by learning more about what causes diseases, how to prevent them, how to treat them, and how to cure them." To support this refusal to include patients as recipients of the financial returns, one might argue that because benefits of the research will accrue to society in the forms of scientific progress, therapies, and drugs, additional compensation of patients is unnecessary. The contribution of tissue costs the patient nothing, whereas the contribution of researchers—like labor, capital, and inventiveness—is more deserving of reward.

This reasoning is certainly familiar, but it likely overstates the contributions of researchers in relation to those of tissue sources. Further, who is really benefitting from this "altruism," and by how much? Hospitals are able to generate rents from these materials, and the commercial value of companies like Ardais consists almost exclusively in their control over this tissue and medical information. There is no denying that the private sector brings important therapies to patients, but considering the increasingly important role that this material plays in the world of commercial genomics, is this "trickle-down" approach sufficient and equitable consideration for the provision of such an indispensable input? Should the hospital do nothing to ensure that the commercial value generated by the research protocol at least inures to the community of patients directly?

Id. at 216-217.

The path for deCODE has sometimes been bumpy as it has made the computer database operational. In 2002, for instance, the company postponed operations due to disagreements with state regulators about the sort of data that could be reported and disagreements with hospitals about funding transfer of relevant information. Alison Abbott, Icelandic Database Shelved as Court Judges Privacy in Peril, 429 Nature 118, May 13, 2004, available at http://www.nature.com/nature. In 2003, the supreme court of Iceland ruled that health information concerning a dead man could not be placed in the Icelandic computer database against the wishes of his surviving child. *Id.* For a description of deCODE's work and research projects in Iceland, see Emily Singer, Genomics into Drugs, Technology Review, Apr. 12, 2006 (interviewing Kari Stefansson, founder and CEO of deCODE Genetics), http://www.technologyreview.com/Biotech/16689/; Corie Lok, Translating Iceland's Genes into Medicine, http://www.technologyreview.com, Sept. 12–14, 2004 (last visited Aug. 23, 2004).

If you were designing a database such as that approved by the Icelandic parliament or that established by the Beth Israel-Ardais collaboration, how would go about insuring fairness, transparency, privacy, and respect for autonomy?

=14=

Social Justice: Access to Care, Distribution of Care, and the Social Determinants of Health

This chapter focuses on questions about social justice and health care. The World Health Organization characterizes social justice as "a matter of life and death. It affects the way people live, their consequent chance of illness, and their risk of premature death." World Health Organization, Closing the Gap in a Generation: Health Equity Through Action on the Social Determinants of Health (Preface), p. 3, available at http://whqlibdoc.who.int/publications/2008/9789241563703_eng.pdf.

Our use of the notion of social justice as it relates to health is expansive. It includes a concern with fair access to health care, with fair systems for distributing health care, and with just distributions of social resources such as education, nutritious food, and a safe environment that hold enormous consequences for the health status of individuals and of populations. Considering issues of social justice as they affect health status facilitates discourse that combines the insights of medical ethics in a clinical context and of an ethics of public health. A perspective grounded in a notion of social justice is concerned with both the health of individuals and with the health status of communities.

Access to health care—both preventative care and care for illness—is essential to health. A recent study of the relation between health status and Medicaid coverage is illustrative. Researchers found that states that expanded Medicaid coverage after 2000 reported a reduction in deaths among low-income adults (below the age of Medicare eligibility) of more than 6 percent. Benjamin D. Sommers, Katherine Baicker & Arnold M. Epstein, Mortality and Access to Care Among Adults After State Medicaid Expansions, New Eng. J. Med., July 25, 2012, www.nejm.org. Individuals' stories are telling. Susan Sered and Rushika Fernandapulle note in their book, Uninsured in America, that "Edna" (whom they had interviewed a couple of years earlier) opened a conversation with them by reporting: "'I'm great, feeling much better. I have full-blown diabetes now

and they amputated a toe.'" Edna was better, despite her serious health problems because she had finally gained access to health care. After her health
problems became life-threatening, resulting in emergency surgery and medical
care, Edna was able to enter the health care system. Susan Starr Sered & Rushika
Fernandapulle, Uninsured in America 198 (2005).

Yet, achieving and sustaining good health requires more than access to
health care. Access to care is necessary, but it is not sufficient. Good health also
depends on a wide set of social and economic factors, broadly referred to as the
social determinants of health. These include environmental, social, and economic factors that relate indirectly, but powerfully, to health status. A British
team, charged with studying inequalities in health at the end of the twentieth
century, offered 39 recommendations for improving health. Only three were
linked directly to access to health care.[1] The other recommendations were
aimed at reducing disparities in income and education, increasing employment
opportunities, and improving housing conditions, nutrition, and environmental safety.

In short, access to health care and comparatively good living conditions are
both essential to health, but it has proved easier to broaden access to health
care—to provide preventive services and medical care to those who are sick—
than to respond effectively to inequalities that result from the social determinants of health. Social justice calls for both responses.

As you study the issues addressed in this chapter, consider the following
broad questions:

1. What factors are most likely to determine access to health care in the
    United States today?
2. What factors are most likely to determine access to *good* health care?
    Are the factors that facilitate access to care different from the factors
    that result in *good* care?
3. What are the most important social determinants of health that affect
    the health of individuals and of populations?
4. What are the essential elements of a just process for the distribution of
    health care resources?

A.   SCOPE OF THE OBLIGATION TO TREAT

The United States has recognized a general right to health care only fleet-
ingly and has not broadly implemented such a right.[2] Even the Patient Protection and Affordable Care Act, largely validated by the Supreme Court in 2012
(see Part D, infra), has significant gaps, and will not provide health care coverage
for millions of people.

---

1. The 39 recommendations are included as an Appendix in Michael Marmot,
The Status Syndrome 259 (2004).
2. Section C of this chapter reviews responses to a right to health care in the
United States.

Professor Eleanor Kinney has documented differences in positions about health care as a right within the United States and as described in a variety of international documents. Eleanor D. Kinney, Recognition of the International Human Right to Health and Health Care in the United States, 60 Rutgers L. Rev. 335 (2008). The U.S. Constitution gives Congress authority to provide for the general welfare. Art. 1, §8, cl. 1. However, that constitutional provision has not been interpreted by the U.S. Supreme Court as the source of a general right to health care. Maher v. Roe, 432 U.S. 464 (1977), suggests clearly that the Supreme Court does not interpret the Constitution as requiring that everyone has access to health care. In that case, the Court declared that "the Constitution imposes no obligation on the states to pay . . . any of the medical expenses of indigents." 432 U.S. at 469. The case concerned a specific issue—financing of abortions through the Medicaid program—but the basic principle delineated in the case extends beyond abortions.

Moreover, in the United States, physicians are not required to begin to treat or to continue treating patients. They cannot, however, refuse to take on or to continue to treat patients if their reasons are illegal, for example, discriminatory as defined by law. Beyond that, the only limitation on a physician's right to refuse to continue seeing a patient is that the patient must be given notice and time to find alternative care.

Payton v. Weaver
182 Cal. Rptr. 225 (Ct. App. Cal. 1982)

Opinion by GRODIN.

Occasionally a case will challenge the ability of the law, and society, to cope effectively and sensitively with fundamental problems of human existence. This is such a case. Appellant, Brenda Payton, is a 35-year-old black woman who suffers from a permanent and irreversible loss of kidney function, a condition known as chronic end stage renal disease. To stay alive, she must subject herself two or three times a week to hemodialysis (dialysis). . . .

Brenda has other difficulties. Unable to care for her children, she lives alone in a low-income housing project in West Oakland, subsisting on a $356 per month Social Security check. She has no family support; one brother is in prison and another is a mental patient. She confesses that she is a drug addict, having been addicted to heroin and barbiturates for over 15 years. She has alcohol problems, weight problems and, not surprisingly, emotional problems as well.

Despite these difficulties Brenda appears from the record to be a marvelously sympathetic and articulate individual who in her lucid moments possesses a great sense of dignity and is intent upon preserving her independence and her integrity as a human being. At times, however, her behavior is such as to make extremely difficult the provision of medical care which she so desperately requires.

The other principal figure in this case is respondent John C. Weaver, Jr., a physician specializing in kidney problems. He conducts his practice through respondent Biomedical Application of Oakland, Inc. (BMA), which operates an outpatient dialysis treatment unit on the premises of respondent Providence Hospital.

Dr. Weaver began treating Brenda in 1975 when, after the birth of Brenda's twin daughters, her system rejected a transplanted kidney. He has been treating her ever since. To her, "Dr. Weaver is and was and still is the man between me and death . . . other than God, I don't think of nobody higher than I do Dr. Weaver."

On December 12, 1978, Dr. Weaver sent Brenda a letter stating he would no longer permit her to be treated at BMA because of her "persistent unco-operative and antisocial behavior over . . . more than . . . three years . . . her per-sistent refusal to adhere to reasonable constraints of hemodialysis, the dietary schedules and medical prescriptions . . . the use of barbiturates and other illicit drugs and because all this resulted in disruption of our program at BMA."

In the latter part of 1978, Brenda applied for admission to the regular dialysis treatment programs operated by respondents Alta Bates and Herrick Hospitals, and was refused.

For several months Dr. Weaver continued to provide Brenda with necessary dialysis on an emergency basis, through Providence. On April 23, 1979, he again notified her by letter that he would no longer treat her on an outpatient basis. This letter led to Brenda's filing of a petition for mandate to compel Dr. Weaver, BMA, and Providence to continue to provide her with outpatient dialysis ser-vices. That litigation was settled by a stipulated order which called for continued treatment provided Brenda met certain conditions: that she keep all appoint-ments at their scheduled time; that she refrain from use of alcohol and drugs; that she maintain prescribed dietary habits; and that she "in all respects coop-erate with those providing her care and abide by her physician's prescribed medical regimen." Later, a sixth stipulation was added: that Brenda would "enter into and participate in good faith in a program of regular psychotherapy and/or counseling."

Dr. Weaver and BMA continued treatment of Brenda as an outpatient pursuant to the stipulation, but on March 3, 1980, Dr. Weaver, contending that Brenda had failed to fulfill any part of the bargain, again notified her that treatment would be terminated. He provided her with a list of dialysis providers in San Francisco and the East Bay, and volunteered to work with her counsel to find alternative care.

Brenda then instituted a second proceeding, again in the form of a petition for writ of mandate, naming Herrick and Alta Bates Hospitals as respondents, along with Dr. Weaver, BMA and Providence. . . .

The trial court, after a lengthy evidentiary hearing, found that Brenda had violated each and every condition which she had accepted as part of the stipu-lated order providing for continued treatment, and that finding is basically undisputed. There was evidence that Brenda continued, after the stipulated order, to buy barbiturates from pushers on the street at least twice a week; that she failed to restrict her diet, gaining as much as 15 kilograms between dialysis treatments; that she continued to be late and/or miss appointments; that due primarily to missed appointments she had 30 emergencies requiring hospitalization in the 11 months preceding trial; that she would appear for treatment in an intoxicated condition; that she discontinued her program of counseling after a brief period; and, as the trial court found, she displayed in general "gross non-cooperation with her treating physician, BMA of Oakland and Providence Hospital." The trial court found that her behavior in these respects was "knowing and intentional."

Brenda's behavior was found to affect not only Dr. Weaver but the other patients and the treating staff as well. Dialysis treatment is typically provided to several patients at a time, all of them connected to a single dialysis machine. There was evidence that Brenda would frequently appear for treatment late or at unscheduled times in a drugged or alcoholic condition, that she used profane and vulgar language, and that she had on occasion engaged in disruptive behavior, such as bothering other patients, cursing staff members with obscenities, screaming and demanding that the dialysis be turned off and that she be disconnected before her treatment was finished, pulling the dialysis needle from the connecting shunt in her leg causing blood to spew, and exposing her genitals in a lewd manner. The trial court found that during the times she has sought treatment "her conduct has been disruptive, abusive, and unreasonable such as to trespass upon the rights of other patients and to endanger their rights to full and adequate treatment," and that her conduct "has been an imposition on the nursing staff." The court determined that, on balance, the rights and privileges of other patients endangered by Brenda's conduct were superior to the rights or equities which Brenda claimed. . . .

We begin our analysis by considering the trial court's conclusion that Dr. Weaver and the clinic with which he is associated have no present legal obligation to continue providing Brenda with dialysis treatment. . . .

. . . Brenda relies upon the general proposition that a physician who abandons a patient may do so "only . . . after due notice, and an ample opportunity afforded to secure the presence of other medical attendance."

The trial court found, however, that Dr. Weaver gave sufficient notice to Brenda, and discharged all his obligations in that regard, and that finding, also, is amply supported. Dr. Weaver supplied Brenda with a list of the names and telephone numbers of all dialysis providers in San Francisco and the East Bay, and it is apparent from the record that nothing would have pleased him more than to find an alternative facility for her, but there is no evidence that there is anything further he could have done to achieve that goal under the circumstances.

During the proceedings, the trial court observed that Dr. Weaver "is one of the most sensitive and honest physicians that I have been exposed to either in a courtroom or out of a courtroom," that he was "in fact sensitive to [Brenda's] needs, that he has attempted to assist her to the best of his medical abilities, that he continues to have concern for her as a person and has continued to serve her medical needs," and that "[the] man has the patience of Job." It appears that Dr. Weaver has behaved according to the highest standards of the medical profession, and that there exists no basis in law or in equity to saddle him with a continuing sole obligation for Brenda's welfare. The same is true of the clinic, the BMA.

We turn now to Brenda's contention that Herrick and Alta Bates Hospitals violated their obligations under Health and Safety Code section 1317 [to provide "emergency services and care . . . to any person requesting such services or care."] . . .

. . . While end stage renal disease is an extremely serious and dangerous disease, which can create imminent danger of loss of life if not properly treated, the need for continuous treatment as such cannot reasonably be said to fall within the scope of section 1317. There are any number of diseases or conditions which could be fatal to the patient if not treated on a continuing basis. If a patient suffering from such a disease or condition were to appear in the emergency room of a hospital in need of immediate life-saving treatment, section 1317 would presumably require that such treatment be provided. But it is unlikely that the Legislature intended to impose upon whatever health care facility such a patient chooses the unqualified obligation to provide continuing preventive care for the patient's lifetime.

It does not necessarily follow that a hospital, or other health care facility, is without obligation to patients in need of continuing medical services for their survival. . . . [W]here such a hospital contains a unique, or scarce, medical resource needed to preserve life, it is arguably in the nature of a "public service enterprise," and should not be permitted to withhold its services arbitrarily, or without reasonable cause. . . . And, while disruptive conduct on the part of a patient may constitute good cause for an individual hospital to refuse continued treatment, since it would be unfair to impose serious inconvenience upon a hospital simply because such a patient selected it, it may be that there exists a collective responsibility on the part of the providers of scarce health resources in a community, enforceable through equity, to share the burden of difficult patients over time, through an appropriately devised contingency plan.

Whatever the merits of such an approach might be in a different factual context, however—and we recognize that it poses difficult problems of administration and of relationship between hospitals and physicians—it cannot serve as a basis for imposition of responsibility upon these respondents under the circumstances present here. Apart from the fact that the record does not demonstrate to what extent respondent hospitals are the sole providers of dialysis treatment in the area accessible to Brenda, her present behavior, as found by the trial court, is of such a nature as to justify their refusal of dialysis treatment on either an individual or collective basis. Whatever collective responsibility may exist, it is clearly not absolute, or independent of the patient's own responsibility.

NOTES AND QUESTIONS

1. *Options for Brenda Payton?*   In a part of Payton v. Weaver not printed, supra, the California court "confront[ed] . . . [a] fundamental question posed by Brenda's challenge . . . : what alternatives exist for assuring that Brenda does not die from lack of treatment as a result of her uncooperative and disruptive behavior[?]" The court then delineated three options: an involuntary conservatorship ("appropriate in the case of persons 'gravely disabled as a result of mental disorder or impairment by chronic alcoholism'"); a different type of involuntary conservatorship under the state's Probate Code (providing that "[a] conservator . . . may be appointed for a person who is unable properly to provide for his or her personal needs for physical health, food, clothing, or shelter"); and a voluntary conservatorship, also under the state's Probate Code. Which option seems best?

2. *Portrait of the doctor in Payton.*   The court in Payton v. Weaver describes Dr. Weaver as a dedicated, compassionate doctor. Do you think the court would have (or should have) decided the case differently had Dr. Weaver been less impressive? Might the decision in *Weaver* encourage less compassionate

physicians to refuse to treat or to provide inadequate care to patients whom they do not like? See Stella L. Smetanka, Who Will Protect the "Disruptive" Dialysis Patient, 32 Am. J.L. Med. 53 (2006) (providing perspective of dialysis patient viewed as disruptive).

3. *What might it mean to call a patient noncompliant?*   Sometimes in cases in which a patient's failure to recover is attributed to "noncompliance" the patient is not "bad" or foolish," but may instead be burdened by limited resources. Paul Farmer has described some of the complicated implications of concluding that a patient's noncompliance is to blame for his or her continuing illness:

> Certainly, patients may be noncompliant, but how relevant is the notion of compliance in rural Haiti [where Farmer has worked]? Doctors may instruct their patients to eat well. But the patients will "refuse" if they have no food. They may be told to sleep in an open room and away from others, and here again they will be "noncompliant" if they do not expand and remodel their miserable huts. They may be instructed to go to a hospital. But if hospital care must be paid for in cash, as is the case throughout Haiti, and the patients have no cash, they will be deemed grossly negligent.

Paul Farmer, Pathologies of Power: Health, Human Rights, and the New War on the Poor 151 (2005).

4. *Physician response to patients who litigate.*   Although doctors are permitted to terminate their relationships with patients (unless their motivation is illegal as defined by a law), some doctors in recent years have sought more proactive responses to litigious patients.

In late 2003, a group of physicians in Texas launched a website called DoctorsKnowUs.com. That site provided physicians with access to the names of prospective patients who were or had been plaintiffs in malpractice lawsuits in the state or elsewhere. Plaintiffs who had brought meritorious lawsuits were included on the list along with others who had commenced frivolous suits. A New York Times article described one man who was put on the list because he sued a hospital and doctor. The man's 39-year-old wife had died of a brain tumor that was not diagnosed. The man suggested that his failure (after his name appeared on the list) to find a doctor willing to treat his 18-year-old son for a minor problem could have been "retaliatory." General counsel to the Texas Medical Association disclaimed any knowledge about the group that set up the website but explained that the site's existence served as evidence of physicians' "frustration" in the face of "lawsuit abuse." Ralph Blumenthal, In Texas, Hire a Lawyer, Forget About a Doctor?, N.Y. Times, Mar. 5, 2004, at A12, col. 5.

Less than a week after several national newspapers described the website, it was closed. The site posted a message announcing its cessation (in March 2004) and expressing hope that the "controversy" it had engendered would result in changes that would prove fair to both doctors and patients. Id.

A similar set of issues was raised by an abandonment suit brought by Patricia and George Thompson against the Scripps Clinic (a group medical practice) after Scripps transferred the Thompsons to an alternative provider. Scripps Clinic v. Superior Court, 108 Cal. App. 4th 917 (2003). Scripps had acted in response to a malpractice action that the Thompsons had brought against two of Scripps' doctors. The court held for the Thompsons—not because it was illegal for Scripps to end its relationship with the Thompsons following initiation of their malpractice suit but because there was a two-week period during which the Thompsons were left without coverage. The court wrote:

> It has long been the law in California that a physician can lawfully abandon a patient "'only . . . after due notice, and an ample opportunity afforded to secure the presence of other medical attendance.'" (Payton v. Weaver (1982) 131 Cal. App. 3d 38, 45). . . .
>
> Scripps contends that because it gave adequate notice to the Thompsons and because Health Net transferred them to [another] Medical Group, the Thompsons did not raise a triable issue of fact as to breach. We disagree. As we discussed above, there was a two-week hiatus between the time Scripps denied the Thompsons access to its physicians for nonemergency services and the time the Thompsons were assigned to [the second clinic]. The Thompsons raised a triable issue of fact as to whether they were given ample time to retain other physicians.

Id. at 932.

The California appellate court held, however, that Scripps had the right, as a general matter, to end its relationship with the Thompsons, and moreover, to end it on the ground that the Thompsons had brought suit against the clinic. Id. at 932.

5. *Rules regarding Medicare's coverage of dialysis.*   In 2008, the Centers for Medicare and Medicaid Services (CMS) amended the rules regarding Medicare's coverage of dialysis care. The rules now give patients the right to be informed by a dialysis facility about policies regarding routine and involuntary transfer. 42 C.F.R. 494.70(b)(1) (2012). Moreover, patients can be discharged or transferred only if (among other things):

(4) The facility has reassessed the patient and determined that the patient's behavior is disruptive and abusive to the extent that the delivery of care to the patient or the ability of the facility to operate effectively is seriously impaired, in which case the medical director ensures that the patient's interdisciplinary team—

(i) Documents the reassessments, ongoing problem(s), and efforts made to resolve the problem(s), and enters this documentation into the patient's medical record;

(ii) Provides the patient and the local ESRD Network with a 30-day notice of the planned discharge;

(iii) Obtains a written physician's order that must be signed by both the medical director and the patient's attending physician concurring with the patient's discharge or transfer from the facility;

(iv) Contacts another facility, attempts to place the patient there, and documents that effort; and

(v) Notifies the State survey agency of the involuntary transfer or discharge.

42 C.F.R. 494.180(f)(i-v) (2012). The Federal Register noted one commenter who argued, citing Payton v. Weaver, that "existing case law" reveals "the inability of the law to assist the abandoned patients who manifest extreme non-compliance." The response noted that a patient who exhibited "psychosocial needs" that might be manifest through "disruptive behavior" would be assessed monthly by an "interdisciplinary team." The commenter noted as well that

facilities are required to have "discharge policies" that guide them in cases of involuntary discharge. 73 Fed. Reg. 20393 (Apr. 15, 2008).

B. ALLOCATING HEALTH CARE

1. Allocating Scarce Resources

This section and the next focus on implications of explicit systems and implicit assumptions that undergird the distribution of limited resources in the world of health care. It considers, in particular, laws related to the allocation of organs for transplantation. Those laws provide one of the few legal models in the United States aimed explicitly at allocating a scarce resource.

Einer Elhauge, Allocating Health Care Morally
82 Cal. L. Rev. 1449, 1451-1453 (1994)

[G]iven society's limited resources, the absolutist position that no beneficial health care should ever be denied is untenable. Nonetheless, no health care system can survive unless it avoids ongoing tradeoffs between health needs and monetary costs by imposing a budgetary constraint derived outside the moral paradigm. The author also concludes that the principle that everyone should receive a minimum of adequate care lacks a concrete affirmative meaning sufficient to guide health care allocations. However, the absence in the health care context of important negative reasons for refraining from an equal distribution of societal resources supports defining adequate care roughly as the level of health care enjoyed by the middle class. . . .

Health law policy suffers from an identifiable pathology. The pathology is not that it employs four different paradigms for how decisions to allocate resources should be made: the market paradigm, the professional paradigm, the moral paradigm, and the political paradigm. The pathology is that, rather than coordinate these decisionmaking paradigms, health law policy employs them inconsistently, such that the combination operates at cross-purposes. . . .

This inconsistency results in part because, intellectually, health care law borrows haphazardly from other fields of law, each of which has its own internally coherent conceptual logic, but which in combination results in an incoherent legal framework and perverse incentive structures. In other words, health care law has not—at least not yet—established itself to be a field of law with its own coherent conceptual logic, as opposed to a collection of issues and cases from other legal fields connected only by the happenstance that they all involve patients and health care providers.

In other part, the pathology results because the various scholarly disciplines focus excessively on their favorite paradigms. Scholars operating in the disciplines of economics, medicine, political science, and philosophy each tend to assume that their discipline offers a privileged perspective. This leads them either to press their favored paradigm too far or to conceptualize policy issues solely in terms of what their paradigm can and cannot solve.

Instead, health law policy issues should be conceived in terms of comparative paradigm analysis. Such analysis focuses on the strengths and weaknesses of the various decisionmaking paradigms, determining which is relatively better suited to resolving various decisions, and then assigning each paradigm to the roles for which it is best suited. It is from this comparative perspective that this Article analyzes the promise and limits of the moral paradigm for allocating health care resources. . . .

The moral paradigm denies that the questions of what resources should be devoted to and within health care are matters that should be resolved by the market, professional judgment, or political forces. Instead, decisions about when health care should be provided call for moral inquiry because they affect profound matters of life, death, and health. As we will see, the principles guiding this moral inquiry are varied, including the immorality of allowing death and suffering, the obligation to treat everyone as equals, and the importance of respecting individual autonomy. Often these principles conflict. Moreover, different moral philosophers emphasize different principles and reach different conclusions about their interpretation. One thus cannot speak of a moral paradigm in the sense of one monolithic set of universally agreed moral principles for guiding medical resource allocation. What unites the various positions I will group under the moral paradigm is not their uniformity but their insistence that allocation decisions should be derived from moral analysis, rather than dictated by market forces, professional judgment, or political accountability.

NOTES AND QUESTIONS

1. *A "moral paradigm."* Einer Elhauge proceeds to delineate a "concrete proposal" for constructing a health care plan that reflects a "moral paradigm." If you were constructing such a proposal, what concrete elements would you want to have incorporated in the broad plan?

2. *Scarce resources and survival at sea.* In 1842, an American court decided a case, United States v. Holmes, 26 F. Cas. 360, 1 Wall Jr. 1 (1842), about a shipping disaster. The case is often taught in introductory courses in criminal law. Among other things, it raises questions about "necessity" as a defense.

United States v. Holmes did not involve health care, but it did involve decisions about how to allocate scarce resources crucial to life. The story of Holmes began when an American ship, the William Brown, en route from Liverpool to Philadelphia in 1841, hit an iceberg near Newfoundland. A number of passengers and crew escaped onto a longboat. However, there were so many people on the longboat that all were at risk of dying. The defendant participated, along with other members of the crew, in throwing 16 passengers overboard. The only "principle of selection" was apparently the mate's direction to the crew "not to part man and wife, and not to throw over any women."

The court (which sentenced the defendant to six months in jail and a $20 fine) wrote:

> [There should be] some mode of selection fixed, by which those in equal relations may have equal chance for their life. By what mode, then, should selection be made? The question is not without difficulty; nor do we know of any rule

prescribed, either by statute or by common law, or even by speculative writers on the law of nature. In fact, no rule of general application can be prescribed for contingencies which are wholly unforeseen. There is, however, one condition of extremity for which all writers have prescribed the same rule. When the ship is in no danger of sinking, but all sustenance is exhausted, and a sacrifice of one person is necessary to appease the hunger of others, the selection is by lot. This mode is resorted to as the fairest mode, and, in some sort, as an appeal to God, for selection of the victim.

When the selection has been made by lots, the victim yields of course to his fate, or, if he resist, force may be employed to coerce submission. Whether or not "a case of necessity" has arisen, or whether the law under which death has been inflicted have been so exercised as to hold the executioner harmless, cannot depend on his own opinion; for no man may pass upon his own conduct when it concerns the rights, and especially, when it affects the lives, of others. . . .

What do you think the people on the longboat described in United States v. Holmes should have done? In Judge Baldwin's view, how should "sacrificial" victims be selected in a situation of disaster?

An even more remarkable story than that of Holmes is memorialized in a British case, Regina v. Dudley & Stephens, 14 Q.B.D. 273 (1884). The case also involved a disaster at sea, and it involved survival cannibalism. *Dudley & Stephens* resembled *Holmes* in that it was occasioned by a sinking ship. Four crew members were forced to abandon their yacht. Together they entered a dinghy with limited supplies and little hope of being found. In fact, they were picked up by a passing ship several days after they were forced to abandon the yacht. However, before they knew that they would shortly be rescued—with scanty supplies and hope of rescue dwindling—the yacht's captain and mate killed and ate 17-year-old Richard Parker, who had served as cabin boy on the yacht. After being picked up and returned to England, Dudley and Stephens were charged with murder. A full analysis of the case is found in A.W. Brian Simpson, Cannibalism and the Common Law (1984).

Does survival cannibalism provide any insights (positive or negative) into the fair distribution of scarce resources?

3. *Japanese clinicians in internment camps.* Don Nakayama and Gwenn Jensen have described the impressive response of clinicians of Japanese ancestry to the health hazards faced by those incarcerated in internment camps by the U.S. government in the period following Japan's attack on Pearl Harbor. Don K. Nakayama & Gwenn M. Jensen, Professionalism Behind Barbed Wire: Health Care in World War II Japanese-American Concentration Camps, 103 J. Nat'l Med. Assoc. 358 (Apr. 2011). Over 100,000 people of Japanese ancestry were forcibly placed in internment camps, where "they were exposed . . . to environmental and endemic health conditions." Id. at 360.

Doctors and nurses [of Japanese ancestry] were conscripted by the US government that imprisoned them. They worked behind barbed wire and under guard towers to maintain the health and well-being of their communities displaced from their homes on the West Coast. Their altruism and self-sacrifice under demanding conditions are excellent examples of commitment to serve and medical professionalism.

Id. at 358. Many of the physicians who provided care in the camps were trained in U.S. medical programs. Nakayama and Jensen report that these clinicians were especially impressive as providers of care insofar as they complemented Western training with "traditional Japanese values of loyalty, respect for elders, and self-sacrifice for the family." Id. at 358. The authors contrast the service of these clinicians with that of contemporary physicians who "refuse to see Medicare or Medicaid patients, much less those without health insurance, or—more troubling—highly fatal contagious diseases such as AIDS." Id. at 363. Nakayama and Jensen suggest that in seeking to train students to become humanistic physicians, training programs might look to cultural traditions that stress the "concept of belonging to the human community." Id. at 363.

4. *Patients' habits and limits on care.*   In 2004, an arm of Britain's National Health Service recommended that infertility clinics offer three free cycles of IVF to couples in which the woman is between 23 and 39 years old. Yet, less than half of Britain's health trusts have followed the recommendation. Women's Health: Health Information & More, http://www.womens-health.co.uk/ivf-nhs.html (last visited July 13, 2012). Private IVF is quite costly. In consequence, some British women are going to other countries, including India, Spain, and the Czech Republic for infertility care. And at least five of the health trusts do not offer IVF at all. Jeremy Laurance, The Independent, June 7, 2011, available in Lexis/Nexis, News Library.

Some of the health trusts exclude free care for women who smoke or who are obese. Id.; Mark Henderson, Infertile Couples Denied Full IVF as NHS Offers Them Just One Chance, The Times (London), June 24, 2008; News, Smokers Lose Out at IVF Clinics, Birmingham Post, June 23, 2008. One Labor member of Parliament expressed concern about banning obese women from free IVF treatments but less concern about banning women who smoke. She explained that smoking, more than weight, is within an individual's control. News, supra. Is that correct? The bans raise questions about the proper distinction between medical advice for patients with particular traits or habits and excluding such patients from care or, as in Britain, from free care.

5. *Retail health clinics.*   In the last several years, retail clinics, offering limited services, have opened in retail stores, pharmacies, and groceries throughout the country. These clinics, largely staffed by physicians' assistants and nurse practitioners, treat common conditions such as strep throat and sinus infections. Some offer immunizations and preventive care. Sarah Barr, Market Trends: Limited Service Clinic Expansion Likely, 16 BNA Health Care Policy Report Banner 617, May 5, 2008. By 2012 CVS Caremark pharmacies housed more than 600 retail health care clinics.

Such clinics offer convenient, comparatively inexpensive care, but they raise concerns about quality of care. Critics have suggested that walk-in clinics in pharmacies and retail stores may ill-serve certain patient groups. Children and adolescents, they suggest, may not benefit from the inconsistent care likely to follow reliance on limited service retail clinics. Moreover, critics worry that problems presented, and care received, at retail clinics may not be entered on patients' medical records. Those favoring such clinics note that at least some of them transmit electronic records to a provider named by the patient. Id. A few states, including Rhode Island and Illinois, have begun to consider regulating retail health clinics. Insurance companies now reimburse over 40 percent of retail clinic patients for some part of the cost of care. Id.

In 2012, Notre Dame University joined with Take Care Health Systems (Walgreens' clinic division) to provide a "wellness center" for the University's employees. The Notre Dame clinic offers primary care, physical therapy, and some additional services. Capsules, the KHN Blog, Notre Dame On-Campus Retail Clinic Opens, But Without Birth Control, Kaiser Health News, July 18, 2012, http://capsules.kaiserhealthnews.org/. Interest in such clinics may soar within the next few years, as the Affordable Care Act increases the number of people with health care coverage. CVS Caremark Outpaces Wal-Mart and Walgreen in Retail Health Clinics, Trefis, July 2, 2012, available in Lexis/Nexis, News Library. The Notre Dame center is to include a pharmacy. However, it will not make contraception available. Id.

In general, do retail clinics provide a preferred model for increasing access to good health care? In responding, it might be important to know whether such clinics substitute for doctor visits or provide health care services for people who might not otherwise see any health care provider.

6. *Rationing health care.* Proposals to ration health care resources raise thorny issues. Howard Brody suggests that instead of focusing only on rationing, we might be well served by focusing as well on the containment of waste. Howard Brody, From an Ethics of Rationing to an Ethics of Waste Avoidance, 366 New Eng. J. Med. 1949 (2012). Brody defines waste broadly to include much more than acts of intentional fraud. Waste may also result from presenting expensive treatments as useful long before their usefulness has, in fact, been demonstrated. Brody illustrates this phenomenon with a very expensive form of treatment that was used for metastatic breast cancer (chemotherapy and then autologous bone marrow transplantation). The treatment was terribly hard on patients. Yet it cured virtually no one. Id. at 1950. Useless, but expensive, treatments may be a consequence, opines Brody, of physicians' "habit[s] or financial self-interest or . . . flawed evidence." Id.

7. *Limiting services to the elderly.* Especially troubling questions have been occasioned in response to the high cost of health care for elderly people and even more for dying people of any age. This is not a new theme. Several decades ago, at a conference run by the National Legal Center for the Medically Dependent and the Disabled, Daniel Callahan declared: "While individual elderly people may want more, and could even benefit from more, we will have done our duty to them in our public entitlement programs if we could get through a full life span, by which I mean the late 70's or early 80's" (quoted in Nat Hentoff, Prologue: The Indivisibility of Life xiv in Set No Limits (Robert L. Barry & Gerard V. Bradley eds. 1991)). A variety of responses to Callahan, all critical, can be found in Robert L. Barry & Gerard V. Bradley, Set No Limits: A Rebuttal to Daniel Callahan's Proposal to Limit Health Care for the Elderly (1991).

Robert Binstock and Stephen Post have suggested that in the early 1980s popular understandings of elderly people began to change in American culture. Binstock and Post contend that before that time, aged people were viewed as "poor, frail, socially dependent, objects of discrimination, and above all deserving." Robert H. Binstock & Stephen G. Post, Old Age and the Rationing of Health Care in Too Old for Health Care?: Controversies in Medicine, Law, Economics, and Ethics 1 (Robert H. Binstock & Stephen G. Post eds. 1991). The authors describe this as the foundation of a "compassionate" view of elderly people. Toward the end of the twentieth century, according to Binstock and

Post, a contrasting perspective developed. From this perspective, the elderly are viewed as a "powerful group" presenting a "burdensome responsibility" to the larger society. Id. at 2.

Those in the elderly population suffer from poor health and chronic conditions (including arthritis, hypertension, hearing impairments, heart disease, cataracts, and diabetes) more frequently than other people. However, those favoring age-based rationing make a set of assumptions about the elderly and the sort of medical care they require and receive that may not be accurate. For instance, one assumption—that elderly patients do not benefit as much or as often from medical intervention as do younger people—has been challenged. Second, although elderly people are more often disabled or ill than younger people, rates of disability among a diverse group of elderly Americans have declined at an accelerating pace since the late 1980s. NIH News Release, Dramatic Decline in Disability Continues for Older Americans, May 7, 2001, http://www.nia.nih.gov/NewsAndEvents/PressReleases/PR200110507Dramatic.htm. Moreover, a 2008 study supported by the National Institute of Aging found that between 1993 and 2002, rates of cognitive impairment among people over 70 decreased (from 12.2 percent in 1993 to 8.7 percent in 2002). The researchers found a correlation between lower cognitive impairment and higher levels of education and financial status. National Institute on Aging Press Release, Study Finds Improved Cognitive Health Among Older Americans, Feb. 25, 2008, http://www.nia.nih.gov/NewsAndEvents/PressReleases/PR20080225coghealth.htm.

Society does spend more on the health needs of elderly people than of other people. Yet, the elderly are not a homogenous group, and old age is not an accurate predictor of the outcome of clinical interventions, even though some factors that do correlate with the success of medical interventions are related to age.

> Life expectancy is one measure that is a superior predictor of the efficacy of medical care. Obviously, advancing age indicates a shorter life expectancy; but the underlying disease and its prognosis are far more important criteria to keep in mind when making decisions on the basis of life expectancy.

Dennis W. Jahnigen & Robert H. Binstock, Economic and Clinical Realities: Health Care for Elderly People 28, in Binstock & Post, supra.

What arguments favor rationing health care for the aged? What arguments disfavor rationing health care for the aged?

8. *A natural life span.*   Daniel Callahan has suggested that there is a natural life span. Andrew Smith and John Rother, highly critical of the notion that rationing should begin once that life span has been reached, note the accomplishments of several well-known individuals during their eighth, ninth, and tenth decades of life. They note, for instance, that the British philosopher Bertrand Russell (1872–1970) published an important work (Political Ideals) at the age of 91 and worked actively in the political arena until he died at 97; Pablo Picasso (1881–1973) created great art in the second half of his ninth decade of life; Isaac Bashevis Singer (1904–1991) published an important novel (The Death of Methuselah) when he was 84; and Konrad Adenauer (1876–1967) published a four-volume autobiography after he retired at age 87 from his post as Chancellor of the Federal Republic of Germany. These bibliographic facts are offered by

Smith and Rother to dispute Callahan's understanding of a natural life span, after which death is deemed acceptable, albeit sad. Do you think that full health care for the elderly should depend on proof that old people (or the oldest of old people) lead socially productive lives? Does this sort of evidence challenge Callahan's notion of a natural life span?

CHALLENGING ISSUES: NOT ENOUGH VENTILATORS

A long-feared pandemic has become a reality. The United States as well as the global community must respond to millions of patients, ill with a serious form of influenza. Many have died. Many more may die. The condition involves severe respiratory distress. Many patients require ventilator support. Unfortunately, there simply are not enough ventilators to provide for the population of influenza patients in need of ventilator assistance. There are not even enough health care providers to keep the existing ventilators functioning adequately.

You have become a member of a government committee charged with fairly allocating existing ventilators. The committee has met once. Half of the session was devoted to laments from committee members about the fact that a plan of action was not put in place years before the crisis developed. You agree. But those laments do not substitute for the pressing need to develop a plan of action in response to an existing crisis.

How would you allocate ventilators among those who need them? What factors seem most important in such an allocation plan? Would you categorize anyone as not eligible for ventilator support?

2. Medical Tourism

At one time, medical tourism involved patients from non-Western countries seeking health care, mostly in the United States and Europe. See, e.g., Steven Findlay, U.S. Hospitals Attracting Patients from Abroad, USA Today, July 22, 1997, at 1A. Now medical tourism and the outsourcing of medical services and medical goods are being presented as alternatives to domestic care for U.S. residents. Each mode of medical tourism raises questions about the fair allocation of scare medical resources globally.

The extent of the migration for health care outside the United States is unknown. However, books and public media provide information about the availability of health care outside the United States, its cost as compared with the cost of the same sort of care in the United States, and information about accommodations and plane fares. Specific medical facilities and practitioners outside the United States are known for providing care for one condition or another. One law review article reports that South African hospitals offer "medical safaris" that combine plastic surgery with vacation time; Mexico offers low-cost dental care; and in 2005, one hospital in Bangkok, Thailand, provided care for tens of thousands of U.S. patients most of whom received noncosmetic services. Nicolas P. Terry, Medical Tourism and Outsourcing, 29 W. New Eng. L. Rev. 421, 424–425 (2007).

U.S. residents who go abroad for health care generally choose to do so because it seems that they can receive care comparable to that available in the

United States for less money. Josef Woodman reported in Patients Beyond Borders (2007) that heart bypass surgery, which at the time cost $130,000 in the United States, cost $10,000 in India and $9,000 in Malaysia; hip replacement, which cost $43,000 in the United States, cost $9,000 in India and $12,000 in Thailand and Singapore. Id. at 7. He reported comparable savings for various dental procedures performed in Mexico and Costa Rica. Insurers have begun to pay for care outside the United States. Jonathan Edelheit, president of the Medical Tourism Association, described as an industry group, explained that the "largest U.S. insurers" and companies that self-insure have become interested in adding offshore options for those whose health care they cover. Mark S. Kopson, Medical Tourism, 3 J. Health & Life Science L. 147 (2010); Bruce Einhorn, Outsourcing the Patients, Business Week, Mar. 13, 2008.

There are conflicting claims about the comparative quality of care provided within the United States and abroad. Terry reports that "[f]or every story about the risks of medical tourism there are countervailing endorsements from satisfied patients." Terry, supra, at 464.

Additional concern has focused on legal remedies if malpractice occurs during treatment abroad. Large malpractice awards are rare in many foreign countries, and a patient harmed by malpractice abroad may be precluded from bringing suit in a U.S. court against a health care provider abroad. Medical malpractice recoveries may be much lower in countries to which Americans go for health care than they are in the United States. For instance, the average recovery in the United States is more than 12 times that in Thailand and more than 6 times that in Mexico. *See* Nathan Cortez, Recalibrating the Legal Risks of Cross-Border Health Care, 10 Yale J. Health Pol'y L. & Ethics 1 (2010); Philip Mirrer-Singer, Medical Malpractice Overseas: The Legal Uncertainty Surrounding Medical Tourism, 70 Law & Contemp. Prob. 211 (2007).

At present, Medicare and Medicaid do not pay for overseas care. However, a number of large companies are beginning to cover employees who choose to have elective surgery overseas, and a few Blue Cross plans pay for overseas care. Michele Masucci & Scott Simpson, Outsourcing Care, 238 N.Y. L.J. 11, Dec. 17, 2007. Glen Cohen has identified a number of insurers (private and governmental) in the United States that are offering (or contemplating offering) an option to receive care outside the country. I. Glen Cohen, Protecting Patients with Passports: Medical Tourism and the Patient-Protective Argument, 95 Iowa L. Rev. 1467 (2010).

> In 2006, Newsweek reported that at least forty U.S. corporations signed on to a medical-tourism plan offered by United Group Programs, a health insurer in Boca Raton, Florida. West Virginia recently debated legislation that would have given its public employees incentives to use medical tourism, and there have even been proposals to get Medicare and Medicaid beneficiaries to use the health care services of foreign countries. In sharp contrast, Texas has used its regulatory powers over health insurers to prevent those operating in the state from offering a plan that requires patients to travel to a foreign country to receive a particular healthcare service.

Id. at 1473-74.

In contrast with medical tourism, the outsourcing of medical services and goods may occur without patients even knowing about it. By 2005, 6 percent of U.S. hospitals had outsourced functions related to information technology.

Terry, supra, at 439–440. An even larger percentage of U.S. hospitals outsource imaging. Advantages include lower costs as well as nighttime coverage through outsourcing to radiologists in far-off time zones. Moreover, pharmaceutical companies are conducting an increasingly large number of clinical trials outside the United States. Medical transcription is being outsourced to the Philippines, India, and Pakistan, among other places. This has occasioned concern about privacy and about quality of the product (particularly if the person working on a transcription is not fluent with U.S. colloquialisms, names, and places.) Medical Transcription Companies, Outsourcing of Medical Transcription, http://www.topmedicaltranscription.com/Content21/Outsourcing-of-medical-transcription.htm (last visited Dec. 10, 2012). In theory, U.S. and international law protect human subjects outside the United States. However, supervision and inspection may be less carefully carried out. Id. at 453–455.

Medical tourism and outsourcing are discussed in Nathan Cortez, Embracing the New Geography of Health Care: A Novel Way to Cover Those Left Out of Health Reform, 84 S. Cal. L. Rev. 859 (2011); Nicolas P. Terry, Medical Tourism and Outsourcing, 29 W. New Eng. L. Rev. 421 (2007); Note, Kerrie S. Howze, Medical Tourism: Symptom or Cure?, 41 Ga. L. Rev. 1013 (2007); Note, Philip Mirrer-Singer, Medical Malpractice Overseas: The Legal Uncertainty Surrounding Medical Tourism, 70 Law & Contemp. Prob. 211 (2007). Josef Woodman's Patients Beyond Borders: Everybody's Guide to Affordable, World-Class Medical Tourism (2007) is a "how-to" book for the prospective medical tourist; Michele Masucci & Scott Simpson, Outsourcing Care, 238 N.Y. L.J. 11, Dec. 17, 2007.

NOTES AND QUESTIONS

1. *Socioeconomic implications of medical tourism.*   In assessing medical tourism, how relevant would it be to know that the residents of the countries to which medical tourists typically go for less costly health care than that available in their home countries may not themselves have access to the forms of care provided to paying tourists? Does proposing medical tourism as a good option to costly health care in the United States serve to undermine efforts to make the American health care system more affordable by presenting apparent reasonable options?

2. *Benefits of medical tourism.*   Two U.S. radiologists, writing in the Journal of Law and Health, concluded that offshore teleradiology, as an adjunct to onsite radiology services, offers significant benefits and is likely to become increasingly important. Eric M. Nyberg & Charles F. Lanzieri, American Diagnostic Radiology Moves Offshore: Where is the "Internet Wave" Taking This Field?, 20 J.L. & Health 253 (2006/2007). Offshore radiology raises important questions about physicians' training, licensure, quality assurance, and reciprocal certification. Nyberg and Lanzieri suggest that,

> The process of international cooperation to create a commonly recognized medical profession certification may already be in its early stage. In 2000, the International Association of Medical Regulatory Authorities (IAMRA) was formed, of which the United States National Board of Medical Examiners is a

member. In 2002, IAMRA initiated a taskforce to look at creating an internationally recognized "medical passport" to be given to highly qualified medical
practitioners which was modified to a "Fast Track Credentials System."
However, this international credentialing is still in the planning process.

Id. at 263.

3. *Medical tourism and experimental care.* Some people travel abroad to
receive treatments not available in their home countries (for any price). An
entrepreneurial health care facility in Hangzhou, China (Beike Biotechnology)
has attracted patients from the United States and elsewhere. The facility offers
stem-cell therapy to treat a wide variety of conditions that elude most forms of
care. One couple from Georgia traveled to Hangzhou in search of a cure for
their baby daughter, born with optic nerve hypoplasia. The condition, caused by
a failure of the optic nerve to develop during gestation, results in blindness or
significantly reduced sight. The couple paid $23,000 to have the child treated
with infusions of stem cells extracted from cord blood. Louisa Lim, Stem-Cell
Therapy in China Draws Foreign Patients, NPR, Mar. 19, 2008. Dr. Sean Hu, who
created Beike Biotechnology, reports that the treatment has helped many
patients with a variety of conditions, but he cannot explain why. The results
that Dr. Hu reports do not seem to have been produced elsewhere. Do you
see this doctor as a brilliant maverick or as a profiteer, charging far more for
treatments than the cost of the treatments to him?

3.   Allocating Organs for Transplantation

Widespread debate, sometimes acrimonious, has focused on how best to procure and allocate organs for transplantation. Federal and state responses are
suggestive of the challenges raised by efforts to allocate scare resources fairly.

As a practical matter, the history of legal responses to organ donation
began in 1954, when the first successful human kidney transplantation was
performed. By the late 1960s human livers and hearts were also being successfully transplanted.

In 1968, the National Conference of Commissioners on Uniform State Law
presented the Uniform Anatomical Gift Act. The Act provided that people at
least 18 years of age be permitted to arrange that their organs be donated at their
death. An individual's wish to become a cadaver donor can be indicated through
a will or through other means, including a statement on the person's driver's
license. The 1968 version was widely promulgated by the states. At present, it is in
effect in some form in every state.

The commissioners revised the Act in 1987 and again in 2006. The 1987
version prohibits the sale of organs. It also precludes family members from
reversing the wishes of dead relatives regarding posthumous organ donation.
This version was intended to "simplify the manner of making an anatomical
gift." (Uniform Anatomical Gift Act, Prefatory Note (amended 1987).) Among
other things, witnesses need not sign the "document of gift," and consent from
the donor and from a donor's next-of-kin is not needed if medical personnel
make a "reasonable effort" to discern the views of the next-of-kin. Id. §4. The
1987 version, adopted in some form in about half of the states, has not been as

widely promulgated as the earlier version. The 2006 revision strengthens language precluding family members and others from reversing an individual's decision to become an anatomical donor after death. However, in the case of minor donors, either parent, upon the minor's death, can revoke the minor's decision to donate. The 2006 revision also provides for "refusals." Should an individual sign such a refusal, others are precluded from later donating the individual's organs or tissues. Uniform Anatomical Gift Act (2006), available at http://www.anatomicalgiftact.org.

In 1984, Congress passed the National Organ Transplant Act, Pub. L. No. 98-507, 98 Stat. 2339 (1984) (codified at 42 U.S.C. §§273-274 (2004) (NOTA)). The Act makes it illegal to pay for an organ "if the transfer affects interstate commerce." 42 U.S.C. §274e (2000). The Act also set up an organ procurement system, administered by the Organ Procurement and Transplantation Network. The United Network for Organ Sharing (UNOS), a private, nonprofit existing registry, was selected to run the network. Amendments to NOTA in 1990 focused on the need for a national system for organ sharing. NOTA was next amended in 2004, Organ Donation and Recovery Improvement Act of 2004, Pub. L. No. 108-216. The 2004 amendments focus on increasing the number of live donors. Among other things, the 2004 provisions provide for grants to states, organ procurement organizations (OPOs) and other "entities" to reimburse nonmedical expenses of live donors; for the establishment of a "public education program" to encourage live donations; and for grants to OPOs and hospitals to improve coordination of organ donations.

Regional OPOs follow guidelines set by UNOS in allocating organs. To some extent, allocation guidelines are organ specific. General criteria include organ and recipient compatibility, recipient health, the likelihood that the transplantation will succeed, and the length of time the potential recipient has been on the waiting list. In addition, a recipient closer to the donor geographically is generally preferred over one less proximate to the donor.

Today thousands of ill people in need of organ transplants remain on waiting lists for years. Under the UNOS policy, a patient's "waiting time" begins when the patient is put on the list. That decision, if transplantation is desired by the patient, is made by the patient's physician, exercising his or her own judgment. Thus, in some part, a patient's wait time depends on his or her doctor's readiness to suggest organ donation and, if the patient approves of this route, actively to take steps to have the patient's name placed on the waiting list.

Almost 115,700 people were on the UNOS waiting list in December 2012. In the first three-quarters of the year, only about 21,000 transplants were performed. (http://optn.transplant.hrsa.gov/data/default.asp). About 79 percent of the transplants performed were done with organs from deceased donors. The remaining 21 percent of the transplants involved organs from living donors. Id. Most people remaining on the UNOS waiting list need kidneys (almost 94,700 people); others need pancreases, livers, intestines, hearts, and lungs. OPTN data. Id. (last visited December 10, 2012).

Strict rules govern the allocation of organs to potential donees listed with UNOS. However, it is legal for donors to designate a specific recipient, thus bypassing the UNOS waiting list.

a.   Bioethical and Social Perspectives

	Michele Goodwin, Empire: Empires of the Flesh:	
	Tissue and Organ Taboos	
	60 Ala. L. Rev. 1219, 1242–1245 (2009)	

[R]ecent studies by Dr. Arthur Matas and others provide compelling data that the best organ transfers for recipient health come from living donors. The focus of public policy must be how best to frame incentive models for living donations while preserving autonomy; weeding out fraud, corruption, and coercion; and promoting good health.

. . . .

Let us place organ dynamics and demand in perspective. The National Kidney Foundation reports that there are 485,000 people in the United States with end-stage renal disease (ESRD). Nearly 350,000 of these people are on dialysis and over 85,000 will die from ESRD. Clearly, the demand for organs exceeds the number of those persons who currently wait on the transplant lists. Rationing helps to explain why only 100,000 are on the United States transplant waitlist rather than one-half million. Most sobering are the economic figures: nearly twenty-five percent of Medicare's budget is spent on ESRD and dialysis.

Who pays? Federal dollars and insurance currently take up the costs for organ transplants as well as dialysis. For this reason, benefits would accrue if the federal government moved individuals off of dialysis and transplanted them. By most studies, in two years, even with paying for the organ, the government would recoup costs and in year three begin to save millions of dollars. . . .

[A]ltruism and markets coexist in the reproductive realms of ova donation and selling, as well as adoption through both state-facilitated foster care to adoption processes and private adoptions that involve lawyers, brokers, and agencies. In these scenarios as well as my proposal, altruism competes minimally with markets. Indeed, my proposal only expands the realm of permissible coexisting spheres of markets and altruism, which already consist of other essential, though non-biological "goods" and services, including food, clothing, health care, and medical insurance.

Beyond increasing the supply of organs, incentives for organ sharing will likely benefit society in several meaningful ways. First, there is an incentive to avoid buying organs on the black market. Black market organ shopping has the advantage of a reduced wait time but exposes the purchasers and sellers to numerous health and social risks. In black markets, the risks are high. Too many variables remain irresolvable; the sellers' health histories cannot be confirmed, unfavorable past social conduct (that can impact the quality of an organ) is unlikely to be disclosed, and there is no medical follow-up. Nor can the purchaser be sure that the seller is a voluntary participant in the transplant transaction. For black market sellers, the future is equally bleak. Because of their complicity in an illegal act—selling an organ—there is a disincentive to report any abuses experienced in the process. After the transaction, follow-up care is unlikely to be available.

Second, a more reliable system emerges with the use of incentives. Currently, the altruistic procurement system is mired by delays, deaths, unpredictability, and unreliability. By introducing a market-based system to coexist with altruistic donation, greater reliability is introduced to the larger complex of organ procurement and distribution. Greater reliability is likely to inspire greater confidence, trust, and respect for the organ procurement system.

Third, incentives will likely promote better health outcomes for potential sharers and recipients. Those interested in receiving a payment for sharing T&O [tissue and organs] will have an incentive to stay healthy during their lives so that their organs will be "picked" for transplantation. Likewise, because their organs have a real value, there is an incentive in maintaining their health. The benefits of healthier living are well-documented in scientific and medical literature. Beyond reducing medical costs, healthier eating and living increases life span, vitality, and productivity. Healthier people are less likely to become obese and suffer the secondary stresses of diabetes, hypertension, high blood pressure, chronic fatigue, alcoholism, and drug abuse. The benefits here inure not simply to the individual, but extend also to families' and sharers' communities.

Fourth, economically disadvantaged individuals might receive better screening for illnesses. Currently, participants in reproductive markets incorporate medical care, psychological evaluations, and sometimes therapy into their negotiation processes. Medical screening and support has evolved into a standard benefit associated with the adoption and surrogacy processes. Similarly, in the context of organ selling, medical screenings to determine the health and vitality of the sellers will likely be a health benefit to participants and not simply a moment of objectification.

NOTES AND QUESTIONS

1. *Alternative options to current organ donation system.*   Adam Kolber, A Matter of Priority, 55 Rutgers L. Rev. 671, 725–726 (2003), has suggested encouraging donor registration by developing a system that would provide those registering as prospective donors with allocation priority. Does this alternative seem preferable to that suggested by Michele Goodwin or to the existing system which relies on altruistic donation? Which of the alternative systems seems more compelling morally? Which seems more likely to provide the largest supply of organs for transplantation?

2. *Addition of a compensation system.*   In a 2004 article, Goodwin suggested that were a compensation system for the allocation of organs added to the present system based on altruism, access to organs donated through altruistic donors could be allocated, in whole or in part, to people unable to afford to participate in the compensation system, thereby increasing the availability of organs for poorer patients (Altruism's Limits: Law, Capacity, and Organ Commodification, 56 Rutgers L. Rev. 305 (2004)). Do you agree? What was Goodwin assuming?

3. *Objections to an incentive system.*   In the 2009 article (printed in part, supra), Michele Goodwin describes some of the objections that scholars have raised to an incentive system for procuring organs for donation. Some have warned that potential altruistic donors might refrain from donating were the donation system to offer incentives. Id. at 1245–1246. More specifically, organ

donation can be a deeply meaningful act. For instance, one donor of bone marrow for an unrelated leukemia patient commented that donating an organ gave her a fundamentally important connection to some "other." Shelby Allen, Gift of Life: 2 Strangers, Yet 2 Twins, N.Y. Times, Sept. 24, 2002, at F5. If one is paid for donating an organ, the donation is transformed from an altruistic and relational connection into a commercial deal.

Goodwin notes that other scholars have expressed concern about the loss of human dignity for donors and donees that might result from incentives, but she suggests that that might be balanced against the benefit of a larger organ supply. More particularly, an incentive system inevitably occasions questions about ownership of organs and tissue. Id. at 1245–1246. Arthur Caplan, head of the Division of Bioethics at New York University, has cautioned that providing payment for organ donations might result in donors caving in to pressure from relatives anxious to participate in the financial gain. Carol M. Ostrom, How Far Is Too Far in the Search for Organ Donors?, Seattle Times, Mar. 22, 2004, available at http://seattletimes.nwsource.com (visited Mar. 23, 2004). A somewhat different view has been expressed by S. Gregory Boyd, who referred to the "tyranny of the gift"—the guilt of organ recipients. Boyd suggested that a market in organs would allow recipients to mitigate or extinguish their guilt through payments. Comment, S. Gregory Boyd, Considering a Market in Human Organs, 4 N.C. J.L. & Tech. 416, 471 (2003).

4. *Keeping patients on UNOS waiting lists.*   The Washington Post reported in 2008 that about a third of patients on the UNOS waiting list were classified as "inactive" and that some of them had been in that category for several years. An individual categorized as inactive is not eligible to receive an organ. The reasons for the classification, which include a patient's being too ill to receive an organ or not ill enough, vary, Rick Stein, A Third of Patients on Transplant List Are Not Eligible; How Accurate Is the Waiting List?, Washington Post, Mar. 22, 2008, available in Lexis/Nexis News Library. Critics have suggested that the practice of keeping patients not eligible to receive an organ on the waiting list for long periods may be aimed at encouraging people to become living donors, at helping fundraising efforts, or at providing support for desired shifts in organ-procurement policies. Id.

5. *A commercial market in organs?*   In 1984, the American Medical Association's Council on Ethical and Judicial Affairs concluded that "it is not ethical to participate in a procedure to enable a living donor to receive payment, other than for the reimbursement of expenses necessarily incurred in connection with removal." Code of Medical Ethics, E-2.15. At that time, the AMA sanctioned limited payments to the family members of dead organ donors who had agreed during life to have payment transferred to family members. By the early years of the twenty-first century, however, the AMA began to consider a more extensive payment system. At about the same time, the Department of Health and Human Services considered providing for payment to both living and deceased organ donors. Barbara Carton, Doctors, U.S. Government Move Closer to Backing Payment When Organs Are Donated, Wall St. Journal, Feb. 14, 2002, at B1. A few transplant centers in the United States reward living donors who provide an organ for a stranger by allowing a loved one of the donor to move ahead on an organ waiting list. Amy Dockser Marcus, Doctors Try Radical Approaches to

Combat Organ Shortage, Wall St. Journal, May 6, 2003, at D1. An interdisciplinary group of ethicists, transplant professionals, and others who attended the International Congress on Ethics in Organ Transplantation in December 2002 in Munich, Germany, accepted a resolution urging countries to study establishing a commercial market in organs. The group was motivated, in part, by the existence of an illegal market in organ sales. Janet Radcliffe Richards, a bioethicist at University College in London, noted that in the existing "altruistic" system, doctors and hospitals make money from the donation process, but donors, alone, are unpaid. Jim Warren, Commerce in Organs Acceptable in Some Cultures, Guidelines Needed, Ethics Congress Recommends, 13 Transplant News, Jan. 15, 2003. Yet, in 2009, the Council of Europe issued a report strongly opposing the sale of organs for transplantation and calling for a U.N. treaty. The report concentrated on "transplant tourism" by people from wealthier countries in poorer countries. Report Calls for Global U.N. Pact to Ban Organ Sales, Trend Daily News (Oct. 14, 2009), available in Lexis/Nexis, News Library.

Before the federal and state governments in the United States banned the purchase and sale of organs, a Virginia man, H. Barry Jacobs, announced that he would serve as a mediator between those needing organs and those willing to donate organs. Jacobs set up International Kidney Exchange Ltd. The organization would buy healthy kidneys for $10,000 and then sell them to those in need for the cost of the organ, related expenses, and a fee ranging from $2,000 to $5,000 to the company. Months after the plan was announced, Virginia banned organ sales. The federal government followed suit soon thereafter. Curtis E. Harris & Stephen P. Alcorn, To Solve a Deadly Shortage: Economic Incentives for Human Organ Donation, 16 Issues L. & Med. 213, 231 (2001). Harris and Alcorn reject the revivification of an unregulated commercial market for organs but suggest that "a controlled market, akin to the radio and television industry" would avoid the most serious consequences of an open market while increasing the availability of needed organs. Id. at 232. They suggest that the project begin with the creation of a regulated market in posthumous organs. They propose rules that would "allow a contractual agreement for monies to be paid to the donor's estate upon death and the retrieval of fit organs." Id. at 232. They even suggest the possibility that contractual agreements be market driven so that, for instance, the price of an organ in a contract with an athlete (presumably a healthy donor) would be more than the price owed someone judged less fit. Id. at 233. The authors do not explain whether, or if so, how, the contract term would be altered if the athletic donor developed a sedentary lifestyle before dying—or how that sort of thing might be, or whether it should be, monitored.

Others, in the United States and abroad, favor the development of a regulated commercial market in organs. Gavin Carney, an Australian kidney specialist and professor at the Australian National University, urges the legalization of organ sales. The nation's Health Minister, while acknowledging that Australia has one of the lowest organ donation rates in the world, rejected Carney's suggestion. A representative of Transplant Australia, a charity supporting organ donation, acknowledged that the average waiting time for a kidney in Australia is four years; yet, concerned, among other things, about potential exploitation of poor people, the group rejected Carney's proposal. Doctor Pushes Australia Organ Sales, http://www.nowpublic.com/world/doctor-pushes-australian-organ-sales.

See also David Schwark, Organ Conscription: How the Dead Can Save the Living, 24 J.L. & Health 323 (2011); Sally Satel, Death's Waiting List, N.Y. Times, May 15, 2006 (proposing development of a regulated organ market in the United States).

Do you think that establishing a market system for organ donations is ethical? To what extent does your response depend on a presumption that such a system would be effective or not?

6. *Illegal markets in organs.*   Poor Europeans from Serbia, Spain, Italy, Greece, and elsewhere are using online resources to advertise their readiness to sell organs, including kidneys and lungs. The trade is illegal, but desperate for money, people are offering to sell organs for money. One Serbian father who had lost his job offered to sell a kidney for $40,000. Prosecution is very rare, in part because surgery generally occurs in countries other than the home country of the seller or the buyer. Dan Bilefsky, Black Market for Body Parts Spreads Among the Poor in Europe, N.Y. Times, June 29, 2012, available at www.nytimes.com.

7. *Nonconsensual sale of organs, some from prisoners in China.*   In 2006 the sale of human organs was prohibited by the Chinese Health Ministry. Sunny Woan, Buy Me a Pound of Flesh, 47 Santa Clara L. Rev. 413, 413 (2007). In 1993, China had admitted that at least some organs from executed prisoners were being sold. Many of these organs were used for transplants to high Chinese officials, other Chinese citizens, and foreigners with cash. Some claim that the numbers involved may be much higher than officials admit. In 1998, Harry Wu, a human rights activist, was able to videotape the offer by two Chinese nationals, negotiated in New York City, to sell Chinese prisoners' organs, including kidneys, lungs, livers, and corneas. Wu claimed at the time that the prisoners involved had not consented to the use of their organs after death and that the Chinese government may have enlarged the categories of crimes that can be punished with execution so as to increase the supply of organs available.

Before 2006, public media reported a variety of unsettling stories about the sale of organs from Chinese prisoners. The Guardian (London) reported that a 40-year-old Malaysian paid for the kidney of a 19-year-old Chinese prisoner apparently executed for drug trafficking. Time Magazine reported in 1998 that a pair of corneas from an executed Chinese prisoner cost about $5,000; kidneys cost about $20,000 each; and a liver cost about $40,000. The price for the kidney, the article noted, included the costs of the surgery. In 2012, Chinese health officials declared that the practice of taking organs from executed prisoners will be stopped within a few years. China to End Transplanting Inmate Organs, UPI, Mar. 23, 2012, available in Lexis/Nexis, News Library.

Doctors in the United States, faced with patients appearing for aftercare following transplant surgery in China, had questions about their moral obligations. Some treated such patients even though they considered the donations for money as morally wrong. One doctor explained that his job was to provide the care these patients needed, not to "punish them." Do you agree with this assessment? See Craig S. Smith, Quandary in U.S. Over Use of Organs of Chinese Inmates, N.Y. Times, Nov. 11, 2001, at A1; Thomas Fuller, Transplant Lifeline to Death Row: Organs of Executed Convicts in China Sold to Malaysians, The Guardian, June 16, 2000; Christine Gorman (reported by Elaine Rivera and Mia Turner), Body Parts for Sale: An FBI Sting Operation Uncovers What

Chinese Activists Say Is a Grisly Trade: Human Organs for Cash, Time, Mar. 9, 1998, at 76; Cesar Chelala, Prospect of Discussions on Prisoners' Organs for Sale in China, 350 The Lancet 1307, Nov. 1, 1997.

    8. *New sources of organs.*   Several potential sources of organs for transplantation that do not require human donors seem to be on the horizon. It may become possible to grow human organs for transplantation outside the body. A number of research avenues have been opened. Regenerative medicine has recently focused on research involving embryonic stem cells. Scientists in Scotland and in Japan isolated in mice what is called an "immortality gene" because it provided for the indefinite growth of laboratory stem cells. Turning Back the Bio Clock, Wired News, Mar. 13, 2004, available at http://www.wired.com/medtech/health/news/2004/03/62660 (last visited July 26, 2012). The discovery encouraged researchers to intensify the search for a similar human gene. Moreover, in 2007, two teams of researchers, one led by James Thomson in the United States and the second by Shinya Yamanaka in Japan, announced almost simultaneously that they had reprogrammed human skin cells to act like embryonic stem cells. The resulting cells were deemed capable of becoming any sort of adult tissue. Karen Kaplan, Stem Cell Milestone Achieved; Scientists Coax Mature Human Cells to Behave Like Embryonic Ones, a Step That May Bridge the Ethical Divide, Los Angeles Times, Nov. 21, 2007, available in Lexis/Nexis News Library. Much work is needed before the procedure will be medically useful, but in theory, these rejuvenated cells (referred to as induced pluripotent stem cells) can be used to achieve the goals of regenerative medicine. It is, for instance, hoped that these cells can be developed into organs for transplantation. Were that possible, a ready supply of histocompatible organs would become available for patients in need of organ replacement. Pro-life adherents praised the research for offering the possibility of developing therapeutically useful stem cells that can be obtained without destroying blastocysts. Scientists have already repaired some organs (grown on artificial "scaffolds," using the patient's own stem cells). The technique has been employed to repair tracheas and skeletal muscles, among other organs. Jeremy Laurance, We Will "Grow" All Organs to Order in Future, Says Pioneering Surgeon, The Independent, Mar. 9, 2012, available in Lexis/Nexis, News Library.

    Xenotransplantation—the transplantation of animals' cells and organs—may provide another source of treatment for humans. Doctors now treat a few human conditions with pig parts, including, for instance, heart valves. The use of animal organs raises several medical problems as well as concern from animal rights groups about the usurpation of animals.

    Some headway is being made against the two primary medical problems presented by the use of animal organs to treat humans: acute rejection and the possibility of introducing animal viruses into human populations. Researchers hope that pig organs will one day be used to repair spinal cord injuries, to treat diabetes, and to replace livers, kidneys, and hearts, either permanently or temporarily while the recipients await human organs. Nell Boyce, Down on the Organ Farm, 134 U.S. News & World Report, June 16, 2003, at 47. One Boston laboratory bred a pig lacking a sugar molecule (present in pigs but absent in humans). Without that sugar molecule, primates do not recognize a transplanted organ as foreign. It is hoped that this will prove to be the case for humans. After insertion of one such pig heart into a baboon, the animal lived for 83 days. Dr. David Sachs, whose lab conducted the research, explained that a human trial would be possible only after a baboon with a transplanted heart lived for a year. Jessica Fargen, Hog-Wild Pig Organs, The Boston Herald, Oct. 29, 2006; David K.C. Cooper, Novel Genetic Modifications Could Mitigate Rejection Problems Created by the Use of Pig Organs in Humans. A Brief History of Cross-species Organ Transplantation, 25 Baylor U. Med. Cent. Proceedings 49 (2012).

In addition to these options, work continues on the development of artificial organs. In early 2004, an FDA panel approved an artificial heart for short-term use, generally for patients awaiting human hearts. The device is a descendant of the Jarvik heart, implanted in Dr. Barney Clark, a Seattle dentist, in 1982. Dr. Clark survived on the device for over 3 months. In 2006, the FDA approved Abiomed Inc.'s artificial heart for implantation in people with advanced heart failure and ineligible for a heart transplantation. The device weighs about two pounds and is operated by an external power transfer coil that recharges an internal battery. FDA News: FDA Approves First Totally Implanted Permanent Artificial Heart for Humanitarian Uses, Sept. 5, 2006, http://www.fda.gov/NewsEvents/Newsroom/PressAnnouncements/2006/ucm108724.htm (last visited July 27, 2012). In 2012, doctors in Boston implanted a total artificial heart into a 66-year-old man who suffered from late-stage cardiac amyloidosis. Physicians hoped that the man would survive until a matching donor heart becomes available. 1st SynCardia Total Artificial Heart Implant Performed in New England, PR Newswire, July 11, 2012, available in Lexis/Nexis, News Library.

9. *Assessing consent of family members of comatose patients.* Ethicists have expressed concern about family members agreeing to the donation of organs from comatose kin who never consented to be organ donors. Two medical ethicists (David Wendler and Ezekiel Emanuel) have suggested that family members only be permitted to agree to the donation of organs in such a case if the donation will be to a nonrelative. Transplant Medicine: Ethicists Say Troubling Living Donor Cases Need Guidelines, Medical Letter on the CDC & FDA via http://www.NewsRx.com, Mar. 7, 2004, available in Lexis/Nexis News Library. Wendler and Emanuel addressed the issue with reference to a report from UCLA about a 20-year-old firefighter who was not expected to recover from a brain injury. The young man was not brain dead, and he had not consented to organ donation. Yet, his parents were allowed to give consent for the man to serve as a kidney donor for a sick cousin. Several days after the surgery, doctors removed the donor from a ventilator. He soon died. After this case was reported in public media, several groups of medical ethicists recognized a need to develop ethical guidelines for handling such cases.

The British Medical Association has opined that, in a presumed consent system, organ donation should proceed (if the patient did not opt out of donation) unless doing that would create "severe distress" to the patient's family. Glyn Davies & John Fabre, Presumed Consent to Organ Donation Is Not the Right Path for Wales to Take, The Western Mail, Dec. 19, 2011, available in Lexis/Nexis, News Library. Do you agree with the Association's position?

Do you think the right of family members to consent to organ donation should be judged differently than their right to consent to the termination of life support for a relative who had not previously expressed his or her wishes about either matter?

10. *Expense of transplantation.* Organ transplantation raises two sorts of rationing questions. This section has focused on allocating scarce organs. A second set of questions arises in light of the expense of most organ transplantations. These questions become especially pressing in those cases in which the chances of success are rated poorly. See Lars Noah, Triage in the Nation's Medicine Cabinet: The Puzzling Scarcity of Vaccines and Other Drugs, 54 S.C. L. Rev. 371, 385–386 (2002). Noah notes that some commentators have asked whether organ transplantation—especially the most risky and most expensive transplantations—"represents a sensible expenditure of scarce health care resources." One commentator summarized the issue in the context of heart transplantations in South Africa in the 1990s:

In July 1995, I saw an emotional debate on heart transplantation on South African television. The debate featured Dr. Barnard, who was arguing for the continuation of heart transplantation at Groote Schuur Hospital and in other South African hospitals. It struck me as odd that heart transplants were considered a priority when twenty miles from Groote Schuur was a squatter settlement where nearly 500,000 lived in abject poverty. I was then assisting on a project at the settlement that aimed to prevent kwashiorkor in infants and provide contraceptive methods to women living in shacks that had neither running water nor electricity. The relevance of high technology medicine in the "New" South Africa is in question. The progressive, humanistic, and compassionate goals of transplant medicine jar with South Africa's stated goal of striving to reflect, in every sector, the nation's unity and commitment to an equitable distribution of resources.

Alexandria K. Niewijk, Tough Priorities, 29 Hastings Ctr. Rpt. 42 (Nov.-Dec. 1999). Similar questions can be raised in the United States today.

CHALLENGING ISSUES: REGULATION OF A COMMERCIAL MARKET IN ORGANS?

Pete is a good friend of yours. He has been ill with kidney disease for many years. Now he has been told that his only chance for long-term survival lies with a kidney transplant. You have been tested (as have Pete's siblings and parents), and none of you would be a suitable donor. Pete believes that he should be allowed to purchase a kidney at a fair price from a willing seller. He is anxious to begin lobbying in favor of a system that would provide for the sale and purchase of kidneys and certain other organs (e.g., parts of livers). Pete has asked you to draft a model statute that he might present to legislators. You are ambivalent about the issue but agree to draft the statute. You explain to Pete that you expect to reach a firmer sense of your own moral assessment of a commercial market in organs as you begin working on the draft and that Pete should know that after further contemplation of the issue you may decide that you cannot help him with this project. You decide to begin by listing the advantages and disadvantages of a market in organs and then to construct statutory provisions that might eliminate or lessen the disadvantages of a commercial market in organs. Your first question is whether a commercial market in organs should include both living and cadaver donors.

b.   Legal Approaches

i.   Statutory Responses

|| *Organ Procurement and Transplantation Network* ||
42 U.S.C.S. §274 (2012)

(a) Contract authority of Secretary. . . . The Secretary shall by contract provide for the establishment and operation of an Organ Procurement and Transplantation Network which meets the requirements of subsection (b). The amount provided under such contract in any fiscal year may not exceed $7,000,000. Funds for such contracts shall be made available from funds available to the Public Health Service from appropriations for fiscal years beginning after fiscal year 1984.

(b) Functions. . . .

(2) The Organ Procurement and Transplantation Network shall—

(A) establish in one location or through regional centers—

(i) a national list of individuals who need organs, and

(ii) a national system, through the use of computers and in accordance with established medical criteria, to match organs and individuals included in the list, especially individuals whose immune system makes it difficult for them to receive organs,

(B) establish membership criteria and medical criteria for allocating organs and provide to members of the public an opportunity to comment with respect to such criteria,

(C) maintain a twenty-four-hour telephone service to facilitate matching organs with individuals included in the list,

(D) assist organ procurement organizations in the nationwide distribution of organs equitably among transplant patients,

(E) adopt and use standards of quality for the acquisition and transportation of donated organs, including standards for preventing the acquisition of organs that are infected with the etiologic agent for acquired immune deficiency syndrome,

(F) prepare and distribute, on a regionalized basis (and, to the extent practicable, among regions or on a national basis), samples of blood sera from individuals who are included on the list and whose immune system makes it difficult for them to receive organs, in order to facilitate matching the compatibility of such individuals with organ donors,

(G) coordinate, as appropriate, the transportation of organs from organ procurement organizations to transplant centers,

(H) provide information to physicians and other health professionals regarding organ donation,

(I) collect, analyze, and publish data concerning organ donation and transplants,

(J) carry out studies and demonstration projects for the purpose of improving procedures for organ procurement and allocation,

(K) work actively to increase the supply of donated organs,

(L) submit to the Secretary an annual report containing information on the comparative costs and patient outcomes at each transplant center affiliated with the organ procurement and transplantation network,

(M) recognize the differences in health and in organ transplantation issues between children and adults throughout the system and adopt criteria, polices, and procedures that address the unique health care needs of children,

(N) carry out studies and demonstration projects for the purpose of improving procedures for organ donation procurement and allocation, including but not limited to projects to examine and attempt to increase transplantation among populations with special needs, including children and individuals who are members of racial or ethnic minority groups, and among populations with limited access to transportation, and

(O) provide that for purposes of this paragraph, the term "children" refers to individuals who are under the age of 18.

> ### *United Network for Organ Sharing*
> **http://optn.transplant.hrsa.gov/**
> **policiesAndBylaws/policies.asp**

Organ Distribution Policy, Provisions 3.1 et seq. can be found at http://optn. transplant.hrsa.gov/policiesAndBylaws/policies.asp (last visited July 13, 2012); provisions 3.5 et seq. can be found at http://optn.transplant.hrsa.gov/Policiesand Bylaws2/policies/pdfs/policy_7.pdf (last visited July 13, 2012).

3.1.1 OPO. An Organ Procurement Organization (OPO) is an organization, accepted as a member, and authorized by the Centers for Medicare and Medicaid Services (CMS) to procure organs for transplantation. For each OPO, CMS defines a geographic procurement territory within which the OPO concentrates its procurement efforts. No OPO is limited to or granted exclusive procurement rights to procure organs in its territory.

. . . .

3.1.4 Waiting List. The Waiting List is the computerized list of candidates who are waiting to be matched with specific donor organs in hopes of receiving transplants. Waiting List candidates are registered on the Waiting List by member transplant centers. The candidate's transplant program shall be responsible for ensuring the accuracy of candidate ABO data on the waiting list. Each transplant program shall implement and operate procedure for providing online verification of a candidate's ABO data on the waiting list against the source documents by an individual other than the person initially entering the candidate's ABO data in UNetSM. The transplant program shall maintain records documenting that such separate verification of the source documents against the entered ABO has taken place and make such documentation available for audit. Upon entry of the candidate's waitlist data, the candidate will be added to the waitlist but will not be listed as an active candidate until separate verification of the candidate's ABO data has taken place.

3.1.4.1 All transplant candidate interactions will be required to be completed through UNetSM by transplant programs. The Organ Center will facilitate candidate listings and modifications in the event of computer and/or Internet failure. When the Organ Center facilitates a candidate's listing or modification due to computer and/or Internet failure, the transplant center will be required to submit a statement explaining the event.

3.1.4.2 Each transplant candidate must be ABO typed on two separate occasions prior to listing. Two separate occasions is defined as two samples, taken at different times, sent to the same or different labs.

3.1.4.3 Transplant candidates shall only be listed on UNetSM with the candidate's actual blood type.

3.1.5 UNOS Match System. The UNOS Match System is the computerized algorithm used to prioritize patients waiting for organs. It eliminates potential recipients whose size or ABO [blood] type is incompatible with that of a donor and then ranks those remaining potential recipients according to the ranking system approved by the UNOS Board.

. . . .

3.5 Allocation of Deceased Kidneys. Deceased kidneys must be allocated according to the following policies. The final decision to accept a particular organ will remain the prerogative of the transplant surgeon and/or physician responsible for the care of the candidate. This allows physicians and surgeons to exercise their medical judgment regarding the suitability of the organ being offered for a specific candidate; to be faithful to their personal and programmatic philosophies about such controversial matters as the importance of cold ischemia time and anatomic anomalies; and to give their best assessment of the prospective recipient's medical condition at the moment. If an organ is declined for a candidate, a notation of the reason for that decision must be made on the appropriate form and submitted promptly.

[Many of the provisions in section 3.5 concern the consequences of antigen matches and mismatches for donation.]

3.5.6.1 Local Allocation. With [certain defined] exceptions . . . all kidneys will be allocated first to local patients . . . ["the locale where the kidneys are procured"].

. . . .

3.5.11 The Point System for Kidney Allocation. [Points are given to a candidate for "time of waiting," "quality of antigen mismatch," age (points are given to pediatric candidates), among other things.]

. . . .

3.5.11.6 A candidate will be assigned 4 points if he or she has donated for transplantation within the United States his or her vital organ or a segment of a vital organ (i.e., kidney, liver segment, lung segment, partial pancreas, small bowel segment). To be assigned 4 points for donation status under Policy 3.5.11.6, the candidate's physician must provide the name of the recipient of the donated organ or organ segment, the recipient's transplant facility and the date of transplant of the donated organ or organ segment, in addition to all other candidate information required to be submitted under policy. . . . When multiple transplant candidates assigned 4 points for donation status are eligible for organ offers under this policy, organs shall be allocated for these patients according to length of time waiting.

NOTES AND QUESTIONS

1. *Organ procurement organizations.*   The United Network for Organ Sharing (UNOS) first entered into a contract with the Health Resources and Services Administration of HHS to administer the Organ Procurement and Transplantation Network in 1986. It has been under contract with HHS ever since. All

binding UNOS policies must be approved by HHS. http://www.unos.org (last visited July 26, 2012).

At the center of the organ donation system are OPOs, authorized to operate through contracts with the federal government and at work throughout the country. Most operate independently. About 13 percent of OPOs, however, are based in hospitals. Each OPO is responsible for a specified "donation service area" (DSA). Akinlolu Ojo (of the Scientific Registry of Transplant Recipients) and coauthors describe the work of OPOs to include

> spend[ing] a considerable amount of time, energy, and money establishing a positive donation environment in the donor hospitals within their DSAs. Specifically, OPO staff members educate hospital medical, nursing, and administrative personnel regarding potential donor identification, the donor and family consent process, and donor maintenance care prior to actual organ recovery. They work to develop strong, trusting, and collaborative relationships with the hospital's trauma, critical care, neurosurgical, and neurological specialists, because these individuals play a critical role in the success of the overall donation process. Additionally, OPOs also strive to establish collegial, supportive relationships with the medical examiner or coroner within whose jurisdiction they are located. These relationships are critical in the effort to maximize donation while meeting the needs and requirements of these important officials.

Akinlolu O. Ojo et al., Organ Donation and Utilization in the USA, 4 Am. J. Transplant 27 (2004).

If you were given the opportunity to interview an OPO official to learn concretely what OPO personnel do, what sorts of questions would you ask? What would you want to know about OPO goals and strategies, for instance?

2. *Allocation criteria.*   The UNOS policy provides that allocation criteria include factors such as length of time on the organ waiting list, tissue type, immune status, geographic distance between donor and recipient, and tissue match and blood type. For certain organs, UNOS also takes into account the urgency of the potential recipient's medical situation (for patients waiting for lungs, hearts, livers, and intestines). UNOS's centralized computer gives transplant professionals continuous information about organ availability. Transplant Living, Matching Organs, http://www.transplantliving.org/before-the-transplant/about-organ-allocation/matching-organs/ (last visited July 13, 2012). Organs entered into the system are offered to the first candidate on the list (determined in light of the allocation criteria noted, supra). If that candidate does not get the organ for any one of a number of reasons, the organ is offered to the next candidate. Id.

3. *Amendment to discriminatory allocation criteria.*   Although the pre-2003 UNOS criteria were not explicitly discriminatory, they resulted (for reasons related to tissue compatibility) in comparatively fewer African Americans and Hispanics receiving needed organs than others on the list. In 2003, the UNOS changed the criteria for matching organ donors and recipients so as to provide access to minorities in need of organs comparable to their percentage of the total population needing organs. The change involved discounting one of four genetic markers (the human leukocyte antigen-B (HLA-B) marker) previously considered in the matching process. In consequence, organ donations to

minorities have increased by about 6 to 7 percent. The increase in transplant failure due to rejection increased, but only minimally, as a result of the change in allocation criteria. Organ Donation: Organ-Matching Criteria Change Increases Number of Available Transplant Kidneys, Health & Med. Week, Feb. 23, 2004.

About half of the people on the organ waiting list are minorities. Jennifer Wider, Organ Donation: A Crisis Among Minorities, Society for Women's Health Research, Apr. 10, 2008, http://www.womenshealthresearch.org/site/News2?page=NewsArticle&id=7471. Minority women, more likely than others to suffer from lung, pancreas, kidney, and liver failure, are among those most in need of organs for transplantation. Id. In late 2007 of those awaiting organs for transplantation, 28 percent were Blacks. Blacks received 19.3 percent of organs transplanted in the same year. In part, the disparity seems to result from Blacks' suspicions about the trustfulness of the organ allocation system. Michele Goodwin & Nevin Gewertz, Rethinking Colorblind State Action: A Thought Experiment on Racial Preferences, 72 L. & Contemp. Probs. 251 (2009).

A number of commentators have pointed to a variety of additional causes for the disproportionately small number of African Americans and Hispanics in need of organs who actually receive organs. Among the explanations are institutional racism resulting in African Americans and Hispanics not being put on organ waiting lists as quickly as others would be or not having their names placed on the lists at all. Goodwin asserts that "many African Americans on dialysis are unaware that an organ transplant was a viable option for them, and while better physician–patient communication helps to alleviate the problem, the allocation protocols further exacerbate racial disparities." Michele Goodwin, Altruism's Limits: Law, Capacity, and Organ Commodification, 56 Rutgers L. Rev. 305 (2004).

4. *"Service fees."*   Although the National Organ Transplantation Act and the Uniform Anatomical Gift Act prohibit individuals from buying or selling organs, "service fees" may be exchanged between hospitals and OPOs for organs and cadavers to be used for research purposes. Some commentators view these fees, as exchanged in fact, as tantamount to illegal payments. See, e.g., Michele Goodwin, Commentary: Commerce in Cadavers Is an Open Secret, Los Angeles Times, Mar. 11, 2004. Goodwin asserts that the body parts exchanged pursuant to such service fees are often used to promote commercial ends.

5. *Relevance in organ allocation as cause of organ failure.*   The UNOS Ethics Committee (General Considerations in Assessment for Transplant Candidacy) has addressed the case of the potential organ recipient whose organ failure resulted from behavior (alcohol or drug abuse, smoking, eating disorders, etc.). The committee suggests that people within this group should not thereby be definitively excluded from consideration as organ recipients. The committee added, however, that more "discussion of this issue in a societal context may be warranted." OPTN, Resources, OPTN/UNOS Ethics Committee General Consideration in Assessment for Transplant Candidacy, http://optn.transplant.hrsa.gov/resources/bioethics.asp?index=5 (last visited July 13, 2012).

Other patients have apparently been denied a place on organ waiting lists because of drug use unrelated to organ failure. Timothy Garon, a California musician, took marijuana with medical approval (legal in California). Marijuana does not harm the liver. However, three times Garon was denied a place on a transplant list. The medical facilities in question did not explain those denials.

One facility had agreed to reconsider its decision if Garon (then desperately ill) agreed to participate in a 60-day drug treatment program. Garon was too ill to comply. In addition, one of the facilities that refused to put Garon on the transplant list took a history of drug use into account in making decisions about a patient's eligibility to receive an organ. Gene Johnson & Cherie Black, Pot Eased Suffering, May Have Cost His Life: Legal Medical Marijuana Use Bars Transplant, Seattle Post-Intelligencer, May 2, 2008, http://seattlepi .nwsource.com/local/361630_marijuana03.html?source=mypi.

ii.   Judicial Responses

|| *Flynn v. Holder* ||
|| 665 F.3d 1048 (9th Cir. 2011, amended 2012) ||

[This case is found in Chapter 2, pp. 115–119, supra.]

NOTES AND QUESTIONS

1. *Living donors.*   Organs, including kidneys as well as parts of lungs and livers, can now be donated by living people. The risks of this sort of surgery can be very serious (even including death), although the likelihood of death occurring is small. The most usual negative consequence for a donor is pain. Organ donation can result also in infection, and there may be some risk that the donor will him- or herself need the organ donated at some future time. In 2002, a healthy 56-year-old man died after donating part of his liver to his brother. The case raises troubling questions for health care workers, in particular, who have been taught "First do no harm," but who are being asked to perform procedures on healthy individuals that pose potentially grave dangers to these people. Denise Grady, New Yorker Dies After Surgery to Give Liver Part to Brother, N.Y. Times, Jan. 15, 2002, at A17.

2. *Living Organ Donor Network.*   The Living Organ Donor Network, organized by a group of transplant professionals, has developed a plan to encourage and support living donors that does not involve payment. The network has set up a registry of living kidney donors so that their health can be monitored for life. In addition, the plan involves providing disability and medical insurance to cover any donors who become disabled or ill as a result of the donation. Deborah L. Shelton, Group Will Track, Insure Live Organ Donors, 43 Am. Medical News, Oct. 9, 2000, at 36. The website of the National Kidney Registry: Facilitating Living Donor Transplants, reported in late 2012 that between 2008 and 2012, it had facilitated 544 transplants. www.kidneyregistry.org (last visited Oct. 6, 2012).

3. *Website matching donors and recipients.* In early 2004, Paul Dooley, a Massachusetts businessman, created MatchingDonors.com (last visited Oct. 6, 2012). The site matches people willing to donate organs while alive with people in need of organs. Potential donees pay several hundred dollars each month for

subscription rights. MatchingDonors.com has been severely criticized for creating hopes that will not be met and for charging sums not available to most people needing organs. Carol M. Ostrom, How Far Is Too Far in the Search for Organ Donors?, Seattle Times, Mar. 21, 2004, available at http://seattletimes .nwsource.com (visited Mar. 24, 2004).

LifeSharers is another organization involved in connecting potential donors with people in need of organs. Members of the prospective donor group agree to donate organs after death in exchange for the right to receive an organ through LifeSharers should they need one. Only if no LifeSharers member needs an available organ is the organ made available generally to those registered with UNOS.

Some critics have balked at the notion of an organ "club." Although membership in LifeSharers is free, and the group does not restrict membership, other organ "clubs" might be more restrictive in their membership. Under UNOS rules, donors are allowed to designate a named recipient, but they are not allowed to designate a group of potential recipients, defined by race, religion, or any other factor.

4. *Incentives for bone marrow donations.*   Flynn v. Holder was occasioned by an interest in finding bone marrow donors for rare bone marrow cells. More-MarrowDonors.org, a nonprofit organization, developed plans for a pilot program to motivate potential bone marrow donors with incentives such as scholarships and housing allowances worth $3,000. Litigation Backgrounder, Institute for Justice, http://www.ij.org/bone-marrow-backgrounder-3 (last visited July 11, 2012).

Less than a third of people needing a bone marrow transplantation have a family member who is a matching donor. About three-quarters of Caucasians in need of an unrelated bone marrow donor find one. Other ethnic groups do not fare as well. One quarter of African Americans needing an unrelated donor locate one. MoreMarrowDonors.org, http://moremarrowdonors.org/ ?page_id=87 (last visited July 11, 2012).

The named plaintiff, Doreen Flynn, had five children. Three had Fanconi anemia. Those with the condition often need a bone marrow transplant. Id. Other plaintiffs included Dr. John Wagner, who specialized in doing bone marrow transplantation at the University of Minnesota. MoreMarrowDonors.org joined the case as a plaintiff as did Akiim DeShay, an African American who had survived leukemia and who served on the board of MoreMarrowDonors.org. (Several additional people joined the suit as plaintiffs.)

5. *From bone marrow to solid organs?*   Before *Flynn*, about 2 percent of the population had joined the national bone marrow registry. MoreMarrowDonors .Org, http://moremarrowdonors.org/?page_id=87 (last visited July 11, 2012). If the *Flynn* opinion, in fact, results in a significant increase in people who join the registry (at least within the area of the country covered by the Ninth Circuit) will that provide grounds for considering plans to compensate donors of solid organs such as kidneys? Should it?

6. *Bibliographic note.*   Information about UNOS is available at http://www. unos.org (visited Dec. 10, 2012). Other useful references include Hayley Cotter, Increasing Consent for Organ Donation: Mandated Choice, Individual

Autonomy, and Informed Consent, 21 Health Matrix 599 (2011); Theodore C. Bergstrom et al., One Chance in a Million: Altruism and the Bone Marrow Registry, 99 Am. Econ. Rev. 1390 (2009); Michele Goodwin, The Body Market: Race, Politics & Private Ordering, 49 Ariz. L. Rev. 599 (2007); AMA, Financial Incentives Could Improve Organ Donation and Reduce Donor-Receipt Gap, June 16, 2008, http://www.ama-assn.org/ama/pub/category/18674.html; Adam J. Kolber, A Matter of Priority: Transplanting Organs Preferentially to Registered Donors, 55 Rutgers L. Rev. 671 (2003); Comment, Samantha A. Wilcox, Presumed Consent Organ Donation in Pennsylvania: One Small Step for Pennsylvania, One Giant Leap for Organ Donation, 107 Dick. L. Rev. 935 (2003); Shelby E. Robinson, Comment, Organs for Sale? An Analysis of Proposed Systems for Compensating Organ Providers, 70 U. Colo. L. Rev. 1019 (1999); Carol M. Ostrom, How Far Is Too Far in the Search for Organ Donors? Seattle Times, Mar. 21, 2004, available at http://seattletimes.nwsource.com/cgi-bin (visited Mar. 23, 2004).

CHALLENGING ISSUE:[3] ALLOCATING ORGANS FOR TRANSPLANTATION

Assume that you have been given responsibility for deciding how to allocate organs for transplantation. You decide that decisions about how to allocate organs can only be reasonably made after you discern who—if anyone—owns body parts.

How would you go about deciding who owns or should have a right to donate body parts?

How would you consider the question about ownership of or a right to donate body parts from a Kantian perspective?[4] How would you consider the question if you were behind a Rawlsian "veil of ignorance"? Situated behind Rawls' veil of ignorance you would have no relevant information about potential donors and recipients. You would not know whether you or any specific others had "good" body parts, and you would not know whether you or any specific others would one day need body parts.

Colavito v. New York Organ Donor Network, Inc.
486 F.3d 78 (2007)

Opinion by SACK.

The plaintiff's decedent, Robert Colavito ("Colavito"), suffering from grave kidney disease, was the intended recipient of two kidneys from the body of his late close friend, Peter Lucia. The New York Organ Donor Network ("NYODN") sent one of Lucia's kidneys to Florida, where Colavito resided. But contrary to the wishes of the Lucia family, the NYODN designated the other kidney for another recipient before it was known whether the first one could be

---

3. This Challenging Issue is based on questions asked by Guido Calabresi in An Introduction to Legal Thought: Four Approaches to the Allocation of Body Parts, 55 Stan. L. Rev. 2113, 2143–2144 (2003).

4. The Kantian perspective is summarized in Chapter 1, supra, pp. 15–17.

successfully transplanted to Colavito. When Colavito's doctor discovered that the kidney sent to Florida was damaged and therefore incapable of being transplanted successfully, he tried to obtain the second Lucia kidney from NYODN. That one, however, was by then in the process of being implanted in the other patient. Colavito, thinking that he had an enforceable right to the second kidney, brought suit against the defendants for fraud, conversion, and violation of New York Public Health Law. . . .

The district court . . . granted summary judgment to the defendants on the merits of Colavito's fraud claim. ("Colavito I"). It also concluded that a public policy against recognizing property rights in human corpses barred Colavito's attempt to state a cause of action for common law conversion or under the New York Public Health Law. . . .

Colavito appealed to this Court. We affirmed with respect to the fraud claim, but certified to the New York Court of Appeals questions as to whether, under New York law, Colavito could maintain the causes of action for conversion or pursuant to the New York Public Health Law. ("Colavito II"). Specifically, we asked

> (1) Do the applicable provisions of the New York Public Health Law vest the intended recipient of a directed organ donation with rights that can be vindicated in a private party's lawsuit sounding in the common law tort of conversion or through a private right of action inferred from the New York Public Health Law? (2) Does New York Public Health Law immunize either negligent or grossly negligent misconduct? (3) If a donee can bring a private action to enforce the rights referred to in question 1, may the plaintiff recover nominal or punitive damages without demonstrating pecuniary loss or other actual injury?

The New York Court of Appeals accepted the certified questions. In its subsequent response to the questions ("Colavito III") the Court concluded that although the intended recipient of a donated organ might have a common law right to it under New York law, no such right exists for the "specified donee of an incompatible kidney." The court also decided that whether or not a private cause of action exists under the New York Public Health Law for the disappointed intended recipients of organ donations, it is available only to those who fall within the statutory term "donee," which the court read the statute to "define[] as someone who needs the donated organ." The court concluded that inasmuch as Colavito could gain no medical benefit from the organs in question, he did not "need" them and therefore was not covered by the Act.

The Court, "under the circumstances of this case," decided certified question no. 1—"Do the applicable provisions of the New York Public Health Law vest the intended recipient of a directed organ donation with rights that can be vindicated in a private party's lawsuit sounding in the common law tort of conversion or through a private right of action inferred from the New York Public Health Law?"—in the negative. The Court concluded that in light of its answer to question no. 1, it was not required to answer questions no. 2—"Does New York Public Health Law immunize either negligent or grossly negligent misconduct?"—or no. 3—"If a donee can bring a private action to enforce the rights referred to in question 1, may the plaintiff recover nominal or punitive damages without demonstrating pecuniary loss or other actual injury?" . . .

This leaves us a single further question for resolution. The Court of Appeals, as a basis both for answering our first question and deciding that the other two questions need not be addressed, assumed—understandably, in light of the facts and the language of our prior opinion—that Lucia's kidneys were incompatible with Colavito's immune system, thus preventing the organs from being successfully transplanted to Colavito. That assumption underlies the Court of Appeals' conclusion that Colavito had no common law property right in the incompatible kidney (common law conversion) and did not "need" it. But neither the district court in Colavito I, nor we in Colavito II, ever actually decided whether there was a "genuine issue" of "material fact," Fed. R. Civ. P. 56(c), that would require a trial as to whether Lucia's kidneys and Colavito's immune system were compatible. Colavito himself refused to concede that a successful transplant was impossible. . . . We cannot decide the propriety of the district court's grant of the defendants' motion for summary judgment without determining whether compatibility remains a genuine issue of material fact in this case.

Ordinarily, we "will not review an issue the district court did not decide." However, "whether we do so or not is a matter within our discretion."

We think this is an appropriate case in which to exercise our discretion to decide this issue in the first instance. Colavito's contention throughout has been that compatibility is immaterial. . . . We have nonetheless noted that "the evidence strongly suggests that . . . the Lucia kidneys were . . . useless to" Colavito. Indeed, there is ample evidence to that effect. At the same time, Colavito himself presented no evidence to the district court that would have raised a genuine issue with respect to compatibility. The notion that Lucia's second kidney might have been successfully transplanted to Colavito is, on the evidence in the district court record, speculative at best. A party may not defeat a Rule 56 motion based on conjecture alone.

Because we conclude as a matter of law that Colavito could not have derived a medical benefit from the organ and did not "need" it, we also conclude that in light of the New York Court of Appeals' answer to our first certified question, he had no cause of action under either the New York common law of conversion or the New York Public Health Law. The defendants were therefore entitled to summary judgment.

Accordingly, we affirm the district court's grant of summary judgment to the defendants on all of Colavito's claims.

QUESTION

1. *Alternative facts.* Do you think that the Second Circuit would have decided *Colavito* differently had there been no question about problems of tissue incompatibility were one of Lucia's kidneys given to Colavito?

C.   HEALTH CARE AS A RIGHT?

1.   *Bioethical and Social Perspectives*

|| *Mariah McGill, The Human Right to Health Care in the State of Vermont*
 37 Ver. B.J. & L. Dig. 28, 28–29 (2011) ||

WHAT IS THE HUMAN RIGHT TO HEALTH CARE?

The United States played a pivotal role in the creation of the United Nations and the drafting of the Universal Declaration of Human Rights. But it has often lagged behind other nations in recognizing human rights, including the right to health care, in its own domestic context. In 1943, President Franklin Delano Roosevelt included the "right to adequate medical care and the opportunity to achieve and enjoy good health" in his proposal for a "Second Bill of Rights." The United Nations Commission on Human Rights, chaired by Eleanor Roosevelt, later enshrined the right to health in the Universal Declaration of Human Rights, which was adopted by the United Nations General Assembly in 1948 and applies to all member nations including the United States.

Article 25 of the Universal Declaration of Human Rights declares that "everyone has the right to a standard of living adequate for the health and well-being of himself and of his family, including food, clothing, housing and medical care and necessary social services." The right to health is also recognized in a number of other international instruments, including the Constitution of the World Health Organization (WHO) of which the United States is a member, and the Convention on the Elimination of All Forms of Racial Discrimination, which the United States Senate ratified in 1994. The WHO Constitution states that the "enjoyment of the highest attainable standard of health is one of the fundamental rights of every human being without distinction of race, religion, political belief, economic or social condition" and goes on to declare that "governments have a responsibility for the health of their peoples which can be fulfilled only by the provision of adequate health and social measures."

Article 12 of the International Covenant on Economic, Social and Cultural Rights (ICESCR), which the United States signed in 1977 but has not yet ratified, also recognizes a right to the "enjoyment of the highest attainable standard of physical and mental health." The right to health is not limited to the right to receive medical treatment. It can be understood as the right to a health system encompassing health care and the underlying determinants of health including adequate food, safe housing and sanitation, healthy work and environmental conditions and access to health-related information and education. However, this article focuses specifically on the human right to health care.

The Covenant requires governments to progressively realize the right to health, as well as other economic and social rights. This means that the Covenant recognizes that governments may be constrained due to limited resources from immediately implementing all aspects of the right to health. Nonetheless, governments must take a series of affirmative steps that will over time lead to the full enjoyment of the right to health as quickly as possible.

The United States has not yet ratified the ICESCR, however, as a signatory it "is obliged to refrain from acts which would defeat the object and purpose" of the treaty. Additionally, as a member of the United Nations, the United States is required to report on its progress on human rights, including economic, social, and cultural rights, to the United Nations Human Rights Council every four years. Further, the United States is subject to the worldwide mandate of the Special Rapporteur on the Right to Health appointed by the United Nations Human Rights Council. The Special Rapporteur investigates and presents annual reports to the United Nations on implementation of the right to health and has incorporated the work of the United Nations Committee on Economic, Social and Cultural Rights to define the content of that right.

The Committee on Economic, Social and Cultural Rights is responsible for monitoring implementation of the ICESCR and, through country reports and a General Comment has defined the right to health. Under international law, governments have the responsibility to respect, protect, and fulfill the right to health. First, governments must respect the right to health by refraining from direct violations of the right to health, such as preventing dissemination of health information or putting up roadblocks preventing access to hospitals. Second, they must protect the right to health by protecting individuals from third-party violations by, for example, regulating hospitals, health professionals, and pharmaceuticals. Finally, governments must fulfill the right to health by taking affirmative steps to move towards realizing the right to health, such as providing health services.

The Committee has identified four elements necessary to achieving the right to health: availability, accessibility, acceptability, and quality. According to the Committee, governments must make health facilities, goods, and services available to all in their territory. They must also make health care accessible by eliminating physical and economic barriers and preventing discrimination in the provision of health care services. Acceptability is the principle that health care should follow ethical guidelines and be culturally appropriate. Quality is the principle that governments have a duty to ensure that health care services are safe, effective, and efficient.

In addition to the four substantive elements, the Committee has also identified four procedural protections: non-discrimination, participation, access to remedies, and information. According to the Committee, governments must ensure that there is no discrimination in the provision of health care and ensure that people have an opportunity to participate in decisions regarding their own health care as well as on health care policy. Governments must also provide adequate information on medical services and public health to make participation meaningful and provide avenues for people to hold decision makers accountable.

Norman Daniels, The Ethics of Health Reform:
Why We Should Care About Who Is Missing Coverage
44 Conn. L. Rev. 1057, 1062–1064 (2012)

Cuba . . . has a life expectancy roughly equal to the United States, despite being much, much poorer than the United States, to say nothing of being the focus of economic attacks by the United States for decades. The state of Kerala, in India, is much poorer even than Cuba, but its health measures are the best of any state in India, and rival those of richer developed countries. How is that possible? What this says to me is that policy differences across countries matter a lot. What you see in the graph are countries with a lot of variation in health outcomes, even among wealthy countries. It is a well-known fact that the United States ranks only about fiftieth in life expectancy in the world. Even among other industrial countries the United States does not compare well. This can be attributed to several factors. In particular, significant economic inequality in the United States produces health inequalities, and that means that economically disadvantaged people in the United States have a lower heath status and that equals out to a lower life expectancy.

Nonetheless, life expectancy is really somewhat independent of universal coverage as an issue. The Whitehall Studies in the United Kingdom are illustrative. Whitehall is the headquarters for the British Civil Service. Starting about twenty years after the introduction of universal coverage in Britain, people began to ask the questions: What difference does universal coverage make? Is it reducing health inequalities in society? Whitehall then began large studies of typical parts of the population, including all the workers in the British Civil Service.

What is striking about these data is that these are all individuals with universal coverage in the British health care system. They are all people who are not so poor that they are deprived, regardless of their occupations. They are people with basic levels of education, and yet, researchers found what is called a socioeconomic gradient of health. People with almost twice the relative mortality rate, but who are in the blue-collar group fared much worse in longevity and health status than people who are in the best-off groups—administrative occupations consisting of professionals, executives, and clerical workers. This forms a socioeconomic gradient of health.

Put into words, that gradient says something like, "the richer you are, or the higher your occupational status, the longer and healthier your life." That kind of gradient is present in every age group in the study in the United Kingdom. It is also found in every country in the world where it has been measured. This is a very robust finding, and one that no one challenges, so then the questions become: What is causing it? Why are we getting this result? This socioeconomic gradient of health is, after all, just a correlation; it doesn't show causation. Some part of the gradient may be explained by sicker people being selected for lower status and worse paying jobs, but that is not the majority of the story, especially if the gradient includes education and occupational status rather than just income.

If we go back to my earlier thesis and look at those three principles of justice that Rawls said came out of his theory, we actually get a model for what health would look like for one part of the world, given the distribution of some of the social determinants. But what I did not mention was some of the data about what those determinants are. They include things like income and wealth inequality in society, educational inequality, inequality in participation in political activities, lack of access to health or health care, and inequalities in that access depending on wealth. What one finds in every country are variations in the distribution of these kinds of goods, and they produce health inequalities in those societies.

What I am suggesting is that if you had a just social arrangement, it would shrink the inequalities, flatten the socioeconomic gradient, and it might in fact help improve the overall health level of the population by improving the bottom line. That would be a very good outcome if it were true. The way I think of this is through the slogan "social justice is good for our health."

> ## Scott Burris, From Health Care Law to the Social Determinants of Health: A Public Health Law Research Perspective
> ### 159 U. Pa. L. Rev. 1649, 1649, 1651, 1653–1654 (2011)

Research over the past three decades has demonstrated that population health is shaped powerfully by "the contexts in which people live, learn, work, and play"—also called "social determinants of health" or "fundamental social causes of disease." . . .

. . . [E]ven as health lawyers and health care policy experts celebrate the enactment of the Patient Protection and Affordable Care Act. . . . We have at least two good reasons to keep social determinants in mind: first, the relatively dismal state of population health in the United States is not caused primarily by a lack of health care, and second, even universal health care access will not make us substantially healthier as a society. Health care is a huge part of the American economy and undeniably a public good, but the stakes are too high for the public—and health law scholars—to continue neglecting the robust social structures that are shaping America's well-being. Compared to other countries with our resources, and even some countries without them, we are doing poorly, and it is well past time we all got sick of it.

In the United States, discussion of inequitable health outcomes has largely focused on racial disparities. These widespread differences in health outcomes by race are an instance of health inequality, but only that. Because we so rarely collect statistics or conduct analysis by class in this country, we have largely treated the health inequality problem as solely one of race for policy purposes. It is not. Race and class both are at work here.

The gradient also appears in population-level analyses of the relationship between social inequality and a wide range of health and social outcomes (crime rates, educational performance, etc.). It turns out that both U.S. states and the countries of the world line up along the gradient when their levels of social inequality are plotted against their respective health and social problems; as inequality within a state or country increases, so too does the severity of a country's or state's health and social problems. A rising tide may lift all boats, but the choppy waters of inequality make the sailing tougher for everyone: even the best-off in an unequal society tend to be worse off than the average person in a more equal one. Thus, the richest Americans do not live as long as the richest Swedes and Japanese. This can help explain the fundamental health care policy anomaly in the U.S. system: why we are number one in health care spending and number thirty in health outcomes. Inequality evidently pulls everyone down.

The social production of health is sufficiently complex to preclude simple causal attributions. No one is arguing that inequality directly causes ill health or other pathological social outcomes. Yet consistent correlations across populations between health and various forms of social and economic inequality leave little room for doubt that social arrangements account for an important fraction of population health. Efforts to find the mechanisms of these effects are ongoing. A recent book by sociologists Richard Wilkinson and Kate Pickett[5] provides many examples of more or less well-founded causal hypotheses. For example, they suggest that the relationship between inequality and homicide (which appears both between countries and among U.S. states) can be explained at least in part by the imperative among young men to gain social status in environments that offer few other means of doing so. Social epidemiologists have studied the effect of social position over the life course, pointing to the powerful effects of early childhood deprivation on lifetime health. Bruce Link and Jo Phelan have conceived of the process in terms of access to the basic resources people need to thrive, while others, more biologically inclined, have documented the powerful role of stress across the life course in connecting social position to health outcomes. The WHO Commission on the Social Determinants of Health sums up social determinants and their workings in holistic terms:

> The poor health of the poor, the social gradient in health within countries, and the marked health inequities between countries are caused by the unequal distribution of power, income, goods, and services, globally and nationally, the consequent unfairness in the immediate, visible circumstances of peoples [sic] lives—their access to health care, schools, and education, their conditions of work and leisure, their homes, communities, towns, or cities—and their chances of leading a flourishing life. This unequal distribution of health-damaging experiences is not in any sense a "natural" phenomenon but is the result of a toxic combination of poor social policies and programmes, unfair economic arrangements, and bad politics. Together, the structural determinants and conditions of daily life constitute the social determinants of health and are responsible for a major part of health inequities between and within countries.

Responding to the findings of this social epidemiology is perhaps the true "grand challenge" of our time in public health.

NOTES AND QUESTIONS

1. *Universal access to health care in Vermont.* Mariah McGill describes Vermont's remarkable success in passing Act 128 ("An Act Relating to Health Care Financing and Universal Access to Health Care in Vermont"). (Act 128 is available at http://www.leg.state.vt.us/DOCS/2010/ACTS/ACT128.PDF). The Act proclaims:

---

5. The reference is to Richard Wilkinson & Kate Pickett, *The Spirit Level: Why Greater Equality Makes Societies Stronger* (Bloomsbury Press 2009)–Eds.

It is the policy of the state of Vermont to ensure universal access to and coverage for essential health services for all Vermonters. All Vermonters must have access to comprehensive, quality health care. Systemic barriers must not prevent people from accessing necessary health care. All Vermonters must receive affordable and appropriate health care at the appropriate time in the appropriate setting, and health care costs must be contained over time.

Act 128, Sec. 2 ("Principles for Health Care Reform"). Act 128 created a "commission on health care reform." Dr. William Hsiao, a consultant hired by the commission, designed health care plans for the state and suggested that Vermont construct a "public/private single payer health care system with a standard benefits package and a uniform system of payment." McGill, supra, at 29. In 2011, the state legislature promulgated H.202. This law includes many of Hsiao's suggestions. *See* McGill, supra at and Vermont's Act No. 48 available at http://www.leg.state.vt.us/DOCS/2012/ACTS/ACT048.PDF. Implementation of the Act is to occur in tandem with implementation of the Patient Protection and Affordable Care Act in Vermont. Then, in 2017, the state hopes to replace a state health benefits exchange with a universal health care system ("Green Mountain Care").

2. *Law and the social determinants of health.*   In sections of Scott Burris's article not printed above, he describes two ways in which law is relevant to the social determinants of health. First "law helps structure and perpetuate the social conditions that we describe as 'social determinants.'" In addition, "law acts as a mechanism or mediator through which social structures are transformed into levels and distributions of health." Id. at 1655–1656. In an earlier co-authored article, Burris et al. suggest:

Laws and legal practices contribute to the development, and influence the stability, of social conditions that have been associated with population health outcomes (i.e., law contributes to the creation and perpetuation of fundamental social determinants of health); and law operates as a pathway along which broader social determinants of health have an effect (i.e., law is one of the social systems through which more fundamental social characteristics work to create health effects). Consideration of existing data in epidemiology and the social science of law supports the plausibility and usefulness of this framework.

Scott Burris, Ichiro Kawachi & Austin Sarat, Health, Law, and Human Rights: Background and Key Concepts: Integrating Law and Social Epidemiology, 30 J.L. Med. & Ethics 510 (2002).

3. *Access to coverage under the Patient Protection and Affordable Care Act.*   Norman Daniels notes that the Patient Protection and Affordable Care Act (ACA) significantly expands coverage, but it does not provide universal coverage. However, he concludes that it may be "the only politically available way to provide access to coverage in this, the largest privately-based insurance country." Daniels, supra, at 1066. Yet, in another sort of politico-economic system, publically funded coverage could have been constructed. That would have avoided the need for the so-called individual mandate, the central concern in most of the litigation that challenged the constitutionality of the ACA. More specifically, construction of a one-payer system, not dependent on the preservation of a private insurance industry, would have avoided the need for a mandate.

4. *Individual and structural determinants of health.*   Erika Blacksher, a philosopher, has assessed arguments that blame poor health on the patient and arguments that blame poor health on societal structural factors. Blacksher has concluded that both individual agency and structural determinants of health play important parts in creating or preserving health. The effort to bring health to populations must include the work of individuals, and that of various "agents of population health," that is "bodies of collective action" that develop the social conditions necessary for good health. See footnote 6, infra.

CHALLENGING ISSUE: INDIVIDUAL AND COMMUNAL RESPONSIBILITY[6]

In 2006, West Virginia took advantage of an option offered by the Deficit Reduction Act of 2005, Pub. L. 109-171, Sec. 6044, to limit benefits available to many state Medicaid recipients. Adults who entered into an agreement with West Virginia (for themselves and their children) became entitled to an "enhanced" set of Medicaid benefits. The agreement required beneficiaries, among other things, to agree to health screening tests, engage in programs designed to improve health, and keep appointments with clinicians. Those who did not sign onto the agreement would receive a "basic" benefit package that limited the number of prescription drugs a child could get in any month and placed new restrictions on care for vision, hearing, and teeth. The basic package also did away with coverage for orthotics, nutrition education, smoking cessation and mental health care, among other things.

You have been asked to assess the plan from the perspective of social justice. How do you think those who favor the plan do that? How do you think those who dislike the plan do that?

D.   ACCESS TO CARE: THE PATIENT PROTECTION AND AFFORDABLE CARE ACT

1.   Social and Bioethical Perspectives

In Spring 2010, Congress passed and the President signed the Patient Protection and Affordable Care Act. Patient Protection and Affordable Care Act, Pub. L. No. 111-148, 24 Stat. 119 (2010), as amended by Health Care and Education Reconciliation Act, Pub. L. No. 111-152, 124 Stat. 1029 (2010). The Act, referred to here as the ACA, represented a significant expansion of access to health care by offering Medicaid eligibility to adults as well as children earning up to 133 percent (or 138 percent with permissible adjustments) of the federal poverty

---

6. This Challenging Issue is based on a discussion in Erika Blacksher's article, Health Reform and Health Equity: Sharing Responsibility for Health in the United States, 39 Hofstra L. Rev. 41, 53–54 (2010). West Virginia's program is described in Judith Solomon (Center on Budget and Policy Priorities), West Virginia's Medicaid Changes Unlikely to Reduce State Costs or Improve Beneficiaries' Health, May 31, 2006, available at http://www.cbpp.org/files/5-31-06health.pdf.

level and federal subsidies to join insurance plans on state exchanges for those earning up to 400 percent of the federal poverty level. (In Nat'l Fed. Indep. Bus. v. Sebelius, infra, the Court declared it unconstitutional to require states to expand their Medicaid programs (or risk losing all Medicaid funding) as required by the ACA.)

The ACA did not promise universal coverage for everyone living in the United States. The largest group excluded was undocumented immigrants. Moreover, the Act did not promise a major overhaul of the nation's health care coverage system. It did not include a public option, and it preserved the central role of private insurance companies as health insurers.

Nevertheless, many considered passage of the ACA a remarkable achievement in a nation that for over a century had failed, despite many efforts, to provide more universal coverage for the population. Seven U.S. presidents, including Coolidge, Franklin Roosevelt, Harry Truman, Lyndon Johnson, Jimmy Carter, and Bill Clinton had attempted to reform the nation's health care system. None succeeded. When Barack Obama was elected President in late 2008, about 50 million people in the United States were without health care coverage. Obama's commitment to health care coverage reform was facilitated at first by a Democratic-controlled Congress. Then, a special election to replace deceased Senator Ted Kennedy in Massachusetts led to the election of a Republican and the loss of the sixtieth vote for the health reform law. Democrats devised a complicated plan to save the law. It involved the House's voting on a bill that the Senate had already passed and then responding to outstanding concerns with a second bill, passed through reliance on the reconciliation process (which does not require a super-majority vote). President Obama signed the two bills in March 2010. Almost immediately, intense opposition followed from within Congress and from among many in the public. A group of state attorneys general commenced suit, arguing that significant parts of the ACA were not constitutional. And the 112th Congress, elected in November 2010, brought a large Republican majority to the House. The House began its session with a bill—offered symbolically, since its defeat in the Senate and a veto by the President were certain—to repeal the ACA. H.R. 2, 112th Cong. (2011).

Opposition to the ACA coalesced variously around concern that the law would give too much control to the federal government, would deprive the citizenry of liberty (i.e., health care choices), and would unfairly burden the middle-class with higher taxes.

Two specific legal arguments sat at the center of most of the litigation about the ACA. One involved the claim that the ACA's so-called "individual mandate" exceeded Congress's authority under the Commerce Clause. The other involved the imposition on states of the ACA's expansion of Medicaid. The mandate was deemed necessary because the Act's implementation depended on the participation of for-profit insurance companies. More specifically, the individual mandate required most people to have health care coverage or to pay a fine (described variously as a "penalty" and as a "tax"). The fine was not large; however, opponents contended that penalizing people who failed to act (that is people who failed to obtain health coverage) exceeded Congress's Commerce Clause power. In June 2012, five members of the U.S. Supreme Court agreed with that conclusion. However, in an opinion authored by Chief Justice Roberts, a majority of the Court validated the individual mandate as a tax. Nat'l Fed. Indept Bus. et al., v. Sebelius, infra. (Justice Roberts, alone, concluded that the mandate exceeded Congress's Commerce Clause powers but could be upheld as a tax.) The second important issue at stake in the case involved the expansion of Medicaid to cover everyone with an income below 133 percent of the federal poverty level (or 138 percent with adjustments allowed for by federal law). Seven members of the Court invalidated the provision that required states to join an expanded Medicaid program or risk losing all federal Medicaid funds.

> ## Sara Rosenbaum, Realigning the Social Order: The Patient Protection and Affordable Care Act and the U.S. Health Insurance System
> ### 7 J. Health & Biomed. L. 1, 11-16 (2011)

. . . The [Affordable Care] Act rests on four structural pillars. The first pillar, the heart of the law, is an individual mandate that requires "applicable" individuals to maintain "minimum essential health coverage" or face certain financial penalties. This requirement to secure affordable coverage or face a financial penalty creates the type of robust risk pool on which fundamental health insurance reform can be built. Further, the mandate operates as the quid pro quo for both the insurance market reforms and a system of premium and cost sharing subsidies for taxpayers, who purchase a "qualified health plan" through a state health insurance exchange. Subsidies are made available for taxpayers with incomes between 100 and 400 percent of the federal poverty level and who are ineligible for other forms of "minimum essential coverage," such as employer-sponsored health benefits or Medicaid. Premium subsidies and cost-sharing assistance, targeted at individuals with incomes below 250 percent of the federal poverty level, are financed through advanced tax credits; these tax credits are calculated at the time of enrollment into a qualified health plan through an exchange. Tax credits are based on the prior year's income and can be recouped for any premium month in which the advance tax credit pay exceeds the amount of credit for which the individual qualifies based on current monthly income.

The second pillar is comprised of the sweeping and preemptive federal reforms aimed at transforming the insurance and employee health benefit plan market through major restructuring of the Public Health Service Act, ERISA, and the Internal Revenue Code. These reforms, which build upon the more limited non-discrimination standards contained in the 1996 HIPAA legislation, are aimed at regulating multiple practices by insurers and health plans (with a series of exceptions for "grandfathered health plans"). Of primary importance are reforms that halt discrimination against the sick in both the individual and group health markets by explicitly prohibiting the use of pre-existing condition exclusions and discriminatory enrollment practices based on health status, as well as excessive waiting periods before coverage begins in the case of persons with pre-existing conditions. The market reforms also guarantee the availability and renewability of insurance, bar rescissions except in the case of misrepresentation and bad faith, extend dependent coverage to age twenty-six, and require coverage of certain federally designated preventive services without patient cost sharing. To make coverage more transparent, the reforms require disclosure of information and the use of plain language and uniform terms in plan documents, mandate quality reporting, and alter the pricing of health insurance coverage by establishing federal medical loss ratios for both individual and group health insurance. To make coverage fairer for people who have significant health needs that prompt coverage denials, the Act establishes an external appeals process as a right and revises the internal appeals procedures currently used by ERISA-governed employee health benefit plans and state regulated insurers. The Act standardizes and improves coverage through the establishment of a federal requirement that all health plans in the individual and small group markets, one hundred full-time employees or fewer, cover certain "essential health benefits," and the Act establishes certain patient protections governing access to health care. Finally, the Act establishes coverage for the routine health care costs patients participating in clinical trials incur. Most reforms apply to both the state-regulated individual and group health insurance markets, as well as to the self-insured employer-sponsored health benefit plans, thereby importing the reforms into ERISA.

The third pillar is the establishment of state health insurance exchanges whose purpose is to organize a shopping market for individual and small group health plan products. States can elect to establish their own exchanges or defer to a default federal exchange. States may also consolidate their individual and group health insurance exchanges, operate subsidiary and multi-state regional exchanges, and open their exchanges to larger employers. Exchanges may be public or private non-profit entities, and they are obligated to carry out certain functions. Exchanges are expected to certify and recertify health plans sold as qualified health plans in the individual or small group markets. They are required to maintain a toll-free assistance hotline as well as an internet website for enrollees, facilitate health plan enrollment, assign quality ratings to health plans, present health plan options in a standardized format, oversee the services of health insurance Navigators, and make available electronic calculators to enable individuals to determine the cost of their plans after applying advance tax credits. Exchanges also bear the responsibility for enrolling eligible individuals in Medicaid and the Children's Health Insurance Program, certifying individuals who are exempt from the individual mandate, and supporting consumer assistance needs, including linking consumers to grievance and appeals systems. In addition, exchanges are accountable for assisting employers in their use of the small group market.

The final pillar is a restructuring of Medicaid to extend coverage to all non-elderly low income persons who are legal residents or citizens. The predominant group to benefit from this change is non-elderly adults historically excluded from Medicaid as a result of their personal characteristics. For instance, these adults have traditionally not qualified for Medicaid due to the absence of minor children in the home as a result of being an older or childless adult. An alternative explanation for exclusion from a state's Medicaid program is that the adult's household income, which while below the federal poverty level, nonetheless exceeds the state's eligibility standard for low income non-pregnant adults.

NOTE AND QUESTION

1. *Medicaid and the Supreme Court decision in NFIB v. Sebelius.* Sara Rosenbaum, supra, asserted that the restructuring of Medicaid "essentially closes Medicaid's last remaining coverage gap for the poor." Id. at 16–17. What do

you think becomes of that assertion in light of the Supreme Court's decision in NFIB v. Sebelius, infra, in which the Court allowed states to opt out of the ACA's expanded Medicaid program without forfeiting participation in Medicaid as that program existed before the Act's implementation?

2.   Legal Approaches

a.   The Patient Protection and Affordable Care Act (ACA)

The health care reform package, passed in 2010, includes three acts. The main act is the Patient Protection and Affordable Care Act. The Health Care and Education Reconciliation Act, passed about three weeks after the Affordable Care Act, constituted a political compromise, necessary after the Democrats lost their Senate majority with the election of Scott Brown (who replaced Ted Kennedy) in Massachusetts. Finally, the TRICARE Affirmation Act provided that the health plan of the military and the defense department would be viewed as minimal essential coverage pursuant to the Affordable Care Act. The scope of these acts has been summarized by Carolyn Heyman-Layne:

> The Affordable Care Act focused on eight main areas, covered in Title I through Title X of the Act: (1) individual insurance coverage; (2) delivery of health care; (3) prevention and public health; (4) health care workforce; (5) fraud and abuse; (6) health technology; (7) assistance for seniors and the disabled; and (8) taxes and fees. This resulted in approximately 900 pages in the consolidated version of the Act and is predicted to result in approximately 90,000 pages of regulations. The focus of most of the debate and concern is the individual insurance coverage. . . . The remaining areas contain efforts and incentives to improve the other aspects of the healthcare system, from programs to encourage health care innovation at the patient level to increased funding for methods and technologies that will increase efficiencies on an organizational or system-wide level. And of course, the taxes and fees section covers how we will pay for all of this.

Carolyn Heyman-Layne, The Affordable Care Act: Breaking it Down to the Basics, 36 AK Bar Rag 14 (2012).

b.   The Supreme Court's Response to the ACA

|| *Nat'l Fed. Indep. Bus. v. Sebelius* ||
132 S. Ct. 2566 (2012)

Opinion of ROBERTS, CJ[7]

Today we resolve constitutional challenges to two provisions of the Patient Protection and Affordable Care Act of 2010: the individual mandate, which

---

7. Chief Justice Roberts announced the Court's judgment. Justices Ginsburg, Breyer, Sotomayor, and Kagan joined Parts I, II, III-C of Justice Roberts's opinion. Justice Ginsburg wrote an opinion that concurred in part, concurred in the judgment in part, and dissented in part. Justice Sotomayor joined in that opinion and Justices Breyer and Kagan joined in parts of it. Justices Scalia, Kennedy, Thomas, and Alito wrote a dissenting opinion, as did Justice Thomas.–EDS.

requires individuals to purchase a health insurance policy providing a minimum level of coverage; and the Medicaid expansion, which gives funds to the States on the condition that they provide specified health care to all citizens whose income falls below a certain threshold. We do not consider whether the Act embodies sound policies. That judgment is entrusted to the Nation's elected leaders. We ask only whether Congress has the power under the Constitution to enact the challenged provisions.

. . . .

I

In 2010, Congress enacted the Patient Protection and Affordable Care Act, 124 Stat. 119. The Act aims to increase the number of Americans covered by health insurance and decrease the cost of health care. The Act's 10 titles stretch over 900 pages and contain hundreds of provisions. This case concerns constitutional challenges to two key provisions, commonly referred to as the individual mandate and the Medicaid expansion. The individual mandate requires most Americans to maintain "minimum essential" health insurance coverage. 26 U.S.C. §5000A. The mandate does not apply to some individuals, such as prisoners and undocumented aliens. §5000A(d). Many individuals will receive the required coverage through their employer, or from a government program such as Medicaid or Medicare. *See* §5000A(f). But for individuals who are not exempt and do not receive health insurance through a third party, the means of satisfying the requirement is to purchase insurance from a private company. Beginning in 2014, those who do not comply with the mandate must make a "[s]hared responsibility payment" to the Federal Government. §5000A(b)(1). That payment, which the Act describes as a "penalty," is calculated as a percentage of household income, subject to a floor based on a specified dollar amount and a ceiling based on the average annual premium the individual would have to pay for qualifying private health insurance. §5000A(c). In 2016, for example, the penalty will be 2.5 percent of an individual's household income, but no less than $695 and no more than the average yearly premium for insurance that covers 60 percent of the cost of 10 specified services (e.g., prescription drugs and hospitalization). *Ibid.*; 42 U.S.C. §18022. The Act provides that the penalty will be paid to the Internal Revenue Service with an individual's taxes, and "shall be assessed and collected in the same manner" as tax penalties, such as the penalty for claiming too large an income tax refund. 26 U.S.C. §5000A(g)(1). The Act, however, bars the IRS from using several of its normal enforcement tools, such as criminal prosecutions and levies. §5000A(g)(2). And some individuals who are subject to the mandate are nonetheless exempt from the penalty—for example, those with income below a certain threshold and members of Indian tribes. §5000A(e).

On the day the President signed the Act into law, Florida and 12 other States filed a complaint in the Federal District Court for the Northern District of Florida. Those plaintiffs—who are both respondents and petitioners here, depending on the issue—were subsequently joined by 13 more States, several individuals, and the National Federation of Independent Business. The plaintiffs alleged, among other things, that the individual mandate provisions of the Act exceeded Congress's powers under Article I of the Constitution. The District

Court agreed, holding that Congress lacked constitutional power to enact the individual mandate. 780 F. Supp. 2d 1256 (ND Fla. 2011). The District Court determined that the individual mandate could not be severed from the remainder of the Act, and therefore struck down the Act in its entirety. *Id.*, at 1305.

The Court of Appeals for the Eleventh Circuit affirmed in part and reversed in part. The court affirmed the District Court's holding that the individual mandate exceeds Congress's power. . . .

Having held the individual mandate to be unconstitutional, the majority examined whether that provision could be severed from the remainder of the Act. The majority determined that, contrary to the District Court's view, it could. . . .

The second provision of the Affordable Care Act directly challenged here is the Medicaid expansion. Enacted in 1965, Medicaid offers federal funding to States to assist pregnant women, children, needy families, the blind, the elderly, and the disabled in obtaining medical care. See 42 U.S.C. §1396a(a)(10). In order to receive that funding, States must comply with federal criteria governing matters such as who receives care and what services are provided at what cost. By 1982 every State had chosen to participate in Medicaid. Federal funds received through the Medicaid program have become a substantial part of state budgets, now constituting over 10 percent of most States' total revenue.

The Affordable Care Act expands the scope of the Medicaid program and increases the number of individuals the States must cover. For example, the Act requires state programs to provide Medicaid coverage to adults with incomes up to 133 percent of the federal poverty level, whereas many States now cover adults with children only if their income is considerably lower, and do not cover childless adults at all. The Act increases federal funding to cover the States' costs in expanding Medicaid coverage, although States will bear a portion of the costs on their own. If a State does not comply with the Act's new coverage requirements, it may lose not only the federal funding for those requirements, but all of its federal Medicaid funds.

. . . .

III

The Government advances two theories for the proposition that Congress had constitutional authority to enact the individual mandate. First, the Government argues that Congress had the power to enact the mandate under the Commerce Clause. Under that theory, Congress may order individuals to buy health insurance because the failure to do so affects interstate commerce, and could undercut the Affordable Care Act's other reforms. Second, the Government argues that if the commerce power does not support the mandate, we should nonetheless uphold it as an exercise of Congress's power to tax. According to the Government, even if Congress lacks the power to direct individuals to buy insurance, the only effect of the individual mandate is to raise taxes on those who do not do so, and thus the law may be upheld as a tax.

[In Part II A Justice Roberts concludes that the individual mandate cannot be validated under the Commerce Clause nor can it be validated under the Necessary and Proper Clause of the Constitution. The dissenting opinion of

Justices Scalia, Kennedy, Alito, and Thomas concluded that no constitutional power can give Congress the authority to provide for the individual mandate.]

C.

The exaction the Affordable Care Act imposes on those without health insurance looks like a tax in many respects. The "[s]hared responsibility payment," as the statute entitles it, is paid into the Treasury by "tax-payer[s]" when they file their tax returns. It does not apply to individuals who do not pay federal income taxes because their household income is less than the filing threshold in the Internal Revenue Code. For taxpayers who do owe the payment, its amount is determined by such familiar factors as taxable income, number of dependents, and joint filing status. The requirement is found in the Internal Revenue Code and enforced by the IRS, which—as we previously explained—must assess and collect it "in the same manner as taxes." This process yields the essential feature of any tax: it produces at least some revenue for the Government. Indeed, the payment is expected to raise about $4 billion per year by 2017.

It is of course true that the Act describes the payment as a "penalty," not a "tax." But . . . that label . . . does not determine whether the payment may be viewed as an exercise of Congress's taxing power. . . .

. . . .

[The Court's 1922 analysis in Bailey v. Drexel Furniture, 259 U.S. 20] suggests that the shared responsibility payment may for constitutional purposes be considered a tax, not a penalty: First, for most Americans the amount due will be far less than the price of insurance, and, by statute, it can never be more.[8] It may often be a reasonable financial decision to make the payment rather than purchase insurance. . . . Second, the individual mandate contains no scienter requirement. Third, the payment is collected solely by the IRS through the normal means of taxation—except that the Service is not allowed to use those means most suggestive of a punitive sanction, such as criminal prosecution. . . .

. . . .

Indeed, it is estimated that four million people each year will choose to pay the IRS rather than buy insurance. We would expect Congress to be troubled by that prospect if such conduct were unlawful. That Congress apparently regards such extensive failure to comply with the mandate as tolerable suggests that Congress did not think it was creating four million outlaws. It suggests instead that the shared responsibility payment merely imposes a tax citizens may lawfully choose to pay in lieu of buying health insurance.

. . . .

. . . Congress's authority under the taxing power is limited to requiring an individual to pay money into the Federal Treasury, no more. If a tax is properly paid, the Government has no power to compel or punish individuals subject to it. We do not make light of the severe burden that taxation—especially taxation

---

8. In 2016, for example, individuals making $35,000 a year are expected to owe the IRS about $60 for any month in which they do not have health insurance. Someone with an annual income of $100,000 a year would likely owe about $200. The price of a qualifying insurance policy is projected to be around $400 per month–EDS.

motivated by a regulatory purpose—can impose. But imposition of a tax nonetheless leaves an individual with a lawful choice to do or not do a certain act, so
long as he is willing to pay a tax levied on that choice.

The Affordable Care Act's requirement that certain individuals pay a financial penalty for not obtaining health insurance may reasonably be characterized
as a tax. Because the Constitution permits such a tax, it is not our role to forbid it,
or to pass upon its wisdom or fairness.

. . . .

IV.[9]

The States also contend that the Medicaid expansion exceeds Congress's
authority under the Spending Clause. They claim that Congress is coercing the
States to adopt the changes it wants by threatening to withhold all of a State's
Medicaid grants, unless the State accepts the new expanded funding and com-
plies with the conditions that come with it. This, they argue, violates the basic
principle that the "Federal Government may not compel the States to enact or
administer a federal regulatory program."

There is no doubt that the Act dramatically increases state obligations
under Medicaid. The current Medicaid program requires States to cover only
certain discrete categories of needy individuals—pregnant women, children,
needy families, the blind, the elderly, and the disabled. There is no mandatory
coverage for most childless adults, and the States typically do not offer any such
coverage. The States also enjoy considerable flexibility with respect to the coverage levels for parents of needy families. On average States cover only those
unemployed parents who make less than 37 percent of the federal poverty level,
and only those employed parents who make less than 63 percent of the poverty
line.

The Medicaid provisions of the Affordable Care Act, in contrast, require
States to expand their Medicaid programs by 2014 to cover all individuals under
the age of 65with incomes below 133 percent of the federal poverty line. The Act
also establishes a new "[e]ssential health benefits" package, which States must
provide to all new Medicaid recipients—a level sufficient to satisfy a recipient's
obligations under the individual mandate. The Affordable Care Act provides
that the Federal Government will pay 100 percent of the costs of covering these
newly eligible individuals through 2016. In the following years, the federal payment level gradually decreases, to a minimum of 90 percent. In light of the
expansion in coverage mandated by the Act, the Federal Government estimates
that its Medicaid spending will increase by approximately $100 billion per year,
nearly 40 percent above current levels.

The Spending Clause grants Congress the power "to pay the Debts and
provide for the . . . general Welfare of the United States." U.S. Const., Art. I, §8,
cl. 1. We have long recognized that Congress may use this power to grant federal
funds to the States, and may condition such a grant upon the States' "taking
certain actions that Congress could not require them to take." Such measures
"encourage a State to regulate in a particular way, [and] influenc[e] a State's

---

9. Justices Breyer and Kagan joined Part IV. The four dissenting justices agreed
that the expansion of Medicaid provided for in the Act was unconstitutional.–EDS.

policy choices." The conditions imposed by Congress ensure that the funds are used by the States to "provide for the . . . general Welfare" in the manner Congress intended.

At the same time, our cases have recognized limits on Congress's power under the Spending Clause to secure state compliance with federal objectives.

. . . .

Permitting the Federal Government to force the States to implement a federal program would threaten the political accountability key to our federal system. "[W]here the Federal Government directs the States to regulate, it maybe state officials who will bear the brunt of public disapproval, while the federal officials who devised the regulatory program may remain insulated from the electoral ramifications of their decision." Spending Clause programs do not pose this danger when a State has a legitimate choice whether to accept the federal conditions in exchange for federal funds. In such a situation, state officials can fairly be held politically accountable for choosing to accept or refuse the federal offer. But when the State has no choice, the Federal Government can achieve its objectives without accountability. . . . Indeed, this danger is heightened when Congress acts under the Spending Clause, because Congress can use that power to implement federal policy it could not impose directly under its enumerated powers.

. . . .

In this case, the financial "inducement" Congress has chosen is much more than "relatively mild encouragement"—it is a gun to the head. Section 1396c of the Medicaid Act provides that if a State's Medicaid plan does not comply with the Act's requirements, the Secretary of Health and Human Services may declare that "further payments will not be made to the State." A State that opts out of the Affordable Care Act's expansion in health care coverage thus stands to lose not merely "a relatively small percentage" of its existing Medicaid funding, but all of it. Medicaid spending accounts for over 20 percent of the average State's total budget, with federal funds covering 50 to 83 percent of those costs.

. . . .

The Medicaid expansion . . . accomplishes a shift in kind, not merely degree. The original program was designed to cover medical services for four particular categories of the needy: the disabled, the blind, the elderly, and needy families with dependent children. Previous amendments to Medicaid eligibility merely altered and expanded the boundaries of these categories. Under the Affordable Care Act, Medicaid is transformed into a program to meet the health care needs of the entire nonelderly population with income below 133 percent of the poverty level. It is no longer a program to care for the neediest among us, but rather an element of a comprehensive national plan to provide universal health insurance coverage.

Indeed, the manner in which the expansion is structured indicates that while Congress may have styled the expansion a mere alteration of existing Medicaid, it recognized it was enlisting the States in a new health care program. Congress created a separate funding provision to cover the costs of providing services to any person made newly eligible by the expansion. While Congress pays 50 to 83 percent of the costs of covering individuals currently enrolled in Medicaid once the expansion is fully implemented Congress will pay 90 percent of the costs for newly eligible persons. The conditions on use of the different funds are also distinct. Congress mandated that newly eligible persons receive a level of coverage that is less comprehensive than the traditional Medicaid benefit package.

. . . .

B

Nothing in our opinion precludes Congress from offering funds under the Affordable Care Act to expand the availability of health care, and requiring that States accepting such funds comply with the conditions on their use. What Congress is not free to do is to penalize States that choose not to participate in that new program by taking away their existing Medicaid funding.

. . . .

The Court today limits the financial pressure the Secretary may apply to induce States to accept the terms of the Medicaid expansion. As a practical matter, that means States may now choose to reject the expansion; that is the whole point. But that does not mean all or even any will. Some States may indeed decline to participate, either because they are unsure they will be able to afford their share of the new funding obligations, or because they are unwilling to commit the administrative resources necessary to support the expansion. Other States, however, may voluntarily sign up, finding the idea of expanding Medicaid coverage attractive, particularly given the level of federal funding the Act offers at the outset.

We have no way of knowing how many States will accept the terms of the expansion, but we do not believe Congress would have wanted the whole Act to fall, simply because some may choose not to participate. The other reforms Congress enacted, after all, will remain "fully operative as a law," and will still function in a way "consistent with Congress' basic objectives in enacting the statute." Confident that Congress would not have intended anything different, we conclude that the rest of the Act need not fall in light of our constitutional holding.

GINSBURG, J. [10]

. . . .

V.

Through Medicaid, Congress has offered the States an opportunity to furnish health care to the poor with the aid of federal financing. To receive federal Medicaid funds, States must provide health benefits to specified categories of needy persons, including pregnant women, children, parents, and adults with disabilities. Guaranteed eligibility varies by category: for some it is tied to the federal poverty level (incomes up to 100% or 133%); for others it depends on criteria such as eligibility for designated state or federal assistance programs. The ACA enlarges the population of needy people States must cover to include adults under age 65 with incomes up to 133% of the federal poverty level. The

---

10. Justice Ginsburg concurred in part, concurred in the judgment, and dissented in part. Only Justice Sotomayor joined the part of the opinion reprinted above–EDS.

spending power conferred by the Constitution, the Court has never doubted, permits Congress to define the contours of programs financed with federal funds. And to expand coverage, Congress could have recalled the existing legislation, and replaced it with a new law making Medicaid as embracive of the poor as Congress chose. The question posed by the 2010 Medicaid expansion, then, is essentially this: To cover a notably larger population, must Congress take the repeal/reenact route, or may it achieve the same result by amending existing law? The answer should be that Congress may expand by amendment the classes of needy persons entitled to Medicaid benefits. A ritualistic requirement that Congress repeal and reenact spending legislation in order to enlarge the population served by a federally funded program would advance no constitutional principle and would scarcely serve the interests of federalism. To the contrary, such a requirement would rigidify Congress' efforts to empower States by partnering with them in the implementation of federal programs.

Medicaid is a prototypical example of federal–state cooperation in serving the Nation's general welfare. Rather than authorizing a federal agency to administer a uniform national health-care system for the poor, Congress offered States the opportunity to tailor Medicaid grants to their particular needs, so long as they remain within bounds set by federal law. In shaping Medicaid, Congress did not endeavor to fix permanently the terms participating states must meet; instead, Congress reserved the "right to alter, amend, or repeal" any provision of the Medicaid Act. States, for their part, agreed to amend their own Medicaid plans consistent with changes from time to time made in the federal law. And from 1965 to the present, States have regularly conformed to Congress' alterations of the Medicaid Act.

The Chief Justice acknowledges that Congress may "condition the receipt of [federal] funds on the States' complying with restrictions on the use of those funds," but nevertheless concludes that the 2010 expansion is unduly coercive. His conclusion rests on three premises, each of them essential to his theory. First, the Medicaid expansion is, in The Chief Justice's view, a new grant program, not an addition to the Medicaid program existing before the ACA's enactment. Congress, The Chief Justice maintains, has threatened States with the loss of funds from an old program in an effort to get them to adopt a new one. Second, the expansion was unforeseeable by the States when they first signed on to Medicaid. Third, the threatened loss of funding is so large that the States have no real choice but to participate in the Medicaid expansion. The Chief Justice therefore—for the first time ever—finds an exercise of Congress' spending power unconstitutionally coercive.

Medicaid, as amended by the ACA, however, is not two spending programs; it is a single program with a constant aim—to enable poor persons to receive basic health care when they need it. Given past expansions, plus express statutory warning that Congress may change the requirements participating States must meet, there can be no tenable claim that the ACA fails for lack of notice.

. . .

A.

Compared to past alterations, the ACA is notable for the extent to which the Federal Government will pick up the tab. Medicaid's 2010 expansion is financed largely by federal outlays. In 2014, federal funds will cover 100% of the costs for newly eligible beneficiaries; that rate will gradually decrease before settling at 90% in 2020. By comparison, federal contributions toward the care of beneficiaries eligible pre-ACA range from 50% to 83%, and averaged 57% between 2005 and 2008.

Nor will the expansion exorbitantly increase state Medicaid spending. The Congressional Budget Office (CBO) projects that States will spend 0.8% more than they would have, absent the ACA. . . .

Finally, any fair appraisal of Medicaid would require acknowledgment of the considerable autonomy States enjoy under the Act. Far from "conscript[ing] state agencies into the national bureaucratic army," Medicaid "is designed to advance cooperative federalism." Subject to its basic requirements, the Medicaid Act empowers States to "select dramatically different levels of funding and coverage, alter and experiment with different financing and delivery modes, and opt to cover (or not to cover) a range of particular procedures and therapies. States have leveraged this policy discretion to generate a myriad of dramatically different Medicaid programs over the past several decades." The ACA does not jettison this approach. States, as first-line administrators, will continue to guide the distribution of substantial resources among their needy populations.

The alternative to conditional federal spending, it bears emphasis, is not state autonomy but state marginalization. In 1965, Congress elected to nationalize health coverage for seniors through Medicare. It could similarly have established Medicaid as an exclusively federal program. Instead, Congress gave the States the opportunity to partner in the program's administration and development. Absent from the nationalized model, of course, is the state-level policy discretion and experimentation that is Medicaid's hallmark; undoubtedly the interests of federalism are better served when States retain a meaningful role in the implementation of a program of such importance.

. . . .

D

Congress has delegated to the Secretary of Health and Human Services the authority to withhold, in whole or in part, federal Medicaid funds from States that fail to comply with the Medicaid Act as originally composed and as subsequently amended. The Chief Justice, however, holds that the Constitution precludes the Secretary from withholding "existing" Medicaid funds based on States' refusal to comply with the expanded Medicaid program. . . . I disagree that any such withholding would violate the Spending Clause. Accordingly, I would affirm the decision of the Court of Appeals for the Eleventh Circuit in this regard. But in view of THE CHIEF JUSTICE's disposition, I agree with him that the Medicaid Act's severability clause determines the appropriate remedy. That clause provides that "[i]f any provision of [the Medicaid Act], or the application thereof to any person or circumstance, is held invalid, the remainder of the chapter, and the application of such provision to other persons or circumstances shall not be affected thereby."

The Court does not strike down any provision of the ACA. It prohibits only the "application" of the Secretary's authority to withhold Medicaid funds from States that decline to conform their Medicaid plans to the ACA's requirements.

Thus the ACA's authorization of funds to finance the expansion remains intact, and the Secretary's authority to withhold funds for reasons other than noncompliance with the expansion remains unaffected.

[A dissenting opinion by Justices Scalia, Kennedy, Thomas, and Alito (none of whom took primary responsibility for authorship) would have invalidated both the individual mandate and the Medicaid expansion. They further concluded that with the invalidation of these central provisions, the ACA as a whole could not survive. They would thus have invalidated the Act as a whole.]

NOTES AND QUESTIONS

1. *Consequences of the decision for Medicaid's expansion.* Justice Roberts's opinion notes the impossibility of predicting how many, if any, states might, in fact, refuse to participate in the expanded Medicaid program envisioned by the ACA as a result of the Court's decision in Nat'l Fed. Indep. Bus. v. Sebelius, 132 S. Ct. 2566 (2012) (NFIB v. Sebelius). In fact, in the week following the Court's decision, at least five state governors (in Florida, Iowa, Louisiana, South Carolina, and Wisconsin—all states that joined the lawsuit against the ACA) announced that they did not intend to have their states participate in an expanded Medicaid program. In mid-July 2012, Texas Governor Rick Perry opted out of the Medicaid expansion and declined to participate in the development of state exchanges. In a letter to HHS Secretary Sebelius, Perry wrote:

> In the ObamaCare plan, the federal government sought to force the states to expand their Medicaid programs by—in the words of the Supreme Court—putting a gun to their heads.[11] Now that the "gun to the head" has been removed, please relay this message to the President: I oppose both the expansion of Medicaid as provided in the Patient Protection and Affordable Care Act and the creation of a so-called "state" insurance exchange, because both represent brazen intrusions into the sovereignty of our state.

Letter from Gov. Rick Perry to Sec. Sebelius, July 9, 2012, available at http://governor.state.tx.us/files/press-office/O-SebeliusKathleen201207090024.pdf. A number of other state officials (in Nebraska, Nevada, and New Jersey) suggested their states also might opt out, even though much of the expense for the Medicaid expansion would fall on the federal government.

2. *Consequences of states' opting out of Medicaid expansion for those who would have been covered.* States' opting out of the expansion may have dismal consequences for a very large number of poor people for whom the ACA was expected to provide health care coverage. Moreover, a provision in the ACA lifts a bar (erected with the 2009 federal stimulus law) against states making it more difficult for adults to become Medicaid participants. As a result, states could opt out of an expanded Medicaid program, *and* they could limit the number of adults covered by Medicaid as compared with pre-ACA Medicaid programs. N. C. Aizenman & Sandhya Somashekhar, More State Leaders Considering Opting Out of Medicaid Expansion, Wash. Post, Jul. 3, 2012, available at www.whasingtonpost.com; Phil Galewitz, States Could Cut Medicaid Rolls in 2014 as a Result of Court

---

11. Justice Roberts used this metaphor in Part IV(A) of his opinion. This part reflected only Roberts's opinion.–Eds.

Ruling, Kaiser Health News, July 3, 2012, http://www.kaiserhealthnews.org/
Stories/2012/July/03/states-could-cut-medicaid-rolls-after-ruling.aspx; AHLAlerts:
American Health Line's Blog, Medicaid: Where Each State Stands on the Medicaid
Expansion (July 6, 2012), http://ahlalerts.com/2012/07/03/medicaid-where-
each-state-stands-on-the-medicaid-expansion/ (last visited July 6, 2012).

An Urban Institute Report, issued soon after the Court's decision in NFIB
v. Sebelius estimated that about 15.1 million adults (not eligible for Medicaid
coverage under the pre-ACA structure) would become eligible if every state were
to accept the Medicaid expansion. Even more, at the time, 11.5 million people in
this group were living below the federal poverty level and would not qualify for other
forms of subsidized health care coverage. Genevieve M. Kenney et al., Opting Out of
the Medicaid Expansion Under the ACA: How Many Uninsured Adults Would Not
Be Eligible for Medicaid?, Urban Institute Health Policy Center, Research of
Record, July 5, 2012, http://www.urban.org/publications/412607.html.

Federal subsidies and tax credits are available under the Act to people
earning between 100 and 400 percent of the federal poverty level. It was assumed
by those who drafted the ACA that people below the poverty level would all be
covered by states' expanded Medicaid programs. Thus, the consequences of the
Supreme Court's decision may be terribly harsh for precisely the people most in
need of assistance.

3. *Revising notion of the "worthy" and undeserving poor.*   In concluding an
article about the expansion of Medicaid under the ACA written before the
Court's decision in NFIB v. Sebelius, Renee Landers and Patrick Leeman distinguished the social parameters of the original Medicaid program from that
envisioned by the ACA:

> In defining categories of presumptively deserving individuals, such as children,
> pregnant women, and individuals with disabilities, the original Medicaid
> program while bringing the impact of federal law to the problem of medical
> poverty, was an outgrowth of [a] "sad" approach [that "separate[s] the
> deserving poor from the deliberately idle"]. The ACA eliminates reliance on
> [such an approach] and seeks to use the Medicaid program to provide access to
> health insurance and access to health care for all low-income people regardless
> of status.

Renee M. Landers & Patrick A. Leeman, Medicaid Expansion Under the 2010
Health Care Reform Legislation: The Continuing Evolution of Medicaid's
Central Role in American Health Care, 7 NAELA J. 142, 164 (2011).

4. *Implementation of state exchanges.*   As the December 2012 deadline for
states to declare their intention to set up state-run exchanges (in effect, insurance
marketplaces) approached, a surprisingly large number of states had declined to do
so. Margot Sanger-Katz, Health Excahnges a Tough Sell with Many States, National
Journal, Dec. 14, 2012, http://nationaljournal.com/healthcare/health-exchanges-
a-tough-sell-with-many-states-20121214; David Morgan, U.S. Faces Task of Running
Dozens of Health Exchanges, Reuters, Dec. 13, 2012, http://www.reuters.com/
article/2012/12/13/us-usa-healthcare-exchanges-idUSBRE8BC0XB20121213.
Some of these states may agree to share responsibilities for their exchanges with
the federal government, Others (as of December 2012, over 20 states) seemed to
favor exchanges run exclusively by the federal government. Id. A political
dimension to the decision has been apparent in many states. The majority of

states declining to establish their own exchanges have Republic governors while the majority of states declaring an intention to implement their own exchanges have Democratic governors. Sanger-Katz, supra; Sean Lengell, State Steer Clear of Health Exchange, Wash. Times, Dec. 13, 2012, http://www.washingtontimes. com/news/2012/dec/13/states-steer-clear-of-health-exchange/.

5. *Additional court challenges to the ACA.*   The Court's decision in NFIB v. Sebelius did not end challenges to the ACA. Several legal challenges to various parts of the legislation remained active in late 2012. In addition, within weeks of the Court's decision, Republicans in the House released legislation aimed at repealing the ACA. Repeal of Obamacare Act, H.R. 6079 (112th Cong. July 9, 2012), available at http://thomas.loc.gov/cgi-bin/query/z?c112:H.R.6079. The legislation was passed by a vote of 244–185 with five Democrats voting with Republicans for repeal. House Approves Legislation to Repeal Health Care Reform Law, BNA, July 11, 2012, http://healthlawrc.bna.com/hlrc/4225/split_ display.adp?fedfid=27294450&vname=hcenotallissues&jd=a0d3m6v0h0&split=0. In 2012, President Obama announced his intention to veto repeal legislation if it should reach his desk.

6. *Bibliographic note.*   Timothy Stoltzfus Jost & Sara Rosenbaum, The Supreme Court and the Future of Medicaid, New Eng. J. Med., July 25, 2012, www.nejm.org; Neil Siegel, Free Riding on Benevolence: Collective Action Federalism and the Minimum Coverage Provision, 75 L. & Contemp. Probs. (2012); Mark A. Hall, Commerce Clause Challenges to Health Care Reform, 159 U. Penn. L. Rev. (2011); Ruth Mason, Federalism and the Taxing Power, 99 Calif. L. Rev. 975 (2011); Randy E. Barnett, Commandeering the People: Why the Individual Health Insurance Mandate is Unconstitutional, 5 NYU J.L. & Liberty 581 (2010).

CHALLENGING ISSUES: NFIB v. SEBELIUS AND MEDICAID

You sit on a committee, formed by a not-for-profit committed to improving health care in the United States. The committee has been asked to consider the implications of and possible responses to that part of NFIB v. Sebelius that found the ACA's Medicaid expansion to be unconstitutional. Your committee has been given the report of a recent study showing that any expansion in states' Medicaid programs after 2000 resulted in better health care and decreased mortality.

Your committee is concerned about coercing states. It is also concerned about those people who would have been covered by the Medicaid expansion but now will not be covered (in states that opt out of the expanded program). How do you think Congress should respond, if at all, to the Court's finding the Medicaid expansion unconstitutional?

Table of Cases

Index